Criminal Procedure

A Contemporary Perspective

James R. Acker, JD, PhD
Associate Professor
School of Criminal Justice
Nelson A. Rockefeller College of Public Affairs and Policy
University at Albany
State University of New York
Albany, New York

David C. Brody, JD, PhD
Assistant Professor
Criminal Justice Program
Washington State University-Spokane
Spokane, Washington

AN ASPEN PUBLICATION®
Aspen Publishers, Inc.
Gaithersburg, Maryland
1999

Library of Congress Cataloging-in-Publication Data

Acker, James R., 1951–
Criminal procedure : a contemporary perspective / James R. Acker, David C. Brody.
p. cm.
ISBN 0-8342-1061-4
1. Criminal procedure—United States.   I. Brody, David C.   II. Title.
KF9619.A72165   1999   98-26479
345.73'05—dc21   CIP

Orders: (800) 638-8437
Customer Service: (800) 234-1660

About Aspen Publishers • For more than 35 years, Aspen has been a leading professional publisher in a variety of disciplines. Aspen's vast information resources are available in both print and electronic formats. We are committed to providing the highest quality information available in the most appropriate format for our customers. Visit Aspen's Internet site for more information resources, directories, articles, and a searchable version of Aspen's full catalog, including the most recent publications: **http://www.aspenpublishers.com**

Aspen Publishers, Inc. • The hallmark of quality in publishing
Member of the worldwide Wolters Kluwer group.

Editorial Services: Ruth Bloom
Library of Congress Catalog Card Number: 98-26479
ISBN: 0-8342-1061-4

Printed in the United States of America

1 2 3 4 5

To **Jenny, Elizabeth,** and **Anna,** who helped bring these pages into being, literally and transcendentally; and to brother **Steve,** who somehow eluded the lure of law but turned out all right anyway.

J.R.A.

To **Wendy** and **Seth** for always being there.

D.C.B.

Table of Contents

Preface

Criminal procedure is an especially captivating area of the law. In broad terms, the rules and legal principles that form the corpus of criminal procedure law define the respective powers and rights of government and citizens as they relate to law enforcement officials' investigation of crimes, the prosecution of suspected offenders, and pretrial and trial proceedings in the courts. Although many rules of criminal procedure are statutory, the foundational principles, which are the primary focus of this book, generally spring from the federal Constitution and analogous state constitutional provisions.

The court decisions that give substance to criminal procedure law often embody the classical qualities of drama. Good is pitted against evil. The protagonists, whose imperfections are a testament to their humanity, are confronted with momentous and tormenting ethical dilemmas. The judges give voice to poignant sub-themes, and their decisive narrative works an uneasy and often unsettling resolution of the crises that sustain the plot. Yet, case law is decidedly nonfiction. Harsh realities and important principles of government underlie criminal procedure judicial decisions.

On the one hand are persons suspected of committing heinous crimes: murder, rape, burglary, robbery, assaults, serious drug offenses, and others. These are crimes that cause untold suffering, and undermine the value system that binds organized society. On the other hand are the fundamental liberties and procedural safeguards that protect citizens—both innocent and guilty—against governmental overreaching. A society dedicated exclusively to uncovering evidence of crimes and punishing law violators would be intolerably oppressive to a people who cherish individual freedoms.

This book provides an introduction to the conceptually intriguing and practically important rules and principles of criminal procedure law. It has three main objectives. First, it makes use of the case method of study as a tool to help students develop and sharpen the analytical skills necessary to understand the origins, content, and continuing evolution of the law. The study of law involves much more than acquiring familiarity with black-letter rules or summaries of case holdings. Although the substantive rules and doctrines of the law are important, of equal importance is gaining an appreciation for the *methods* of law, to understand the legal process as a principled way of analyzing questions, building on precedent, and drawing distinctions and analogies between changing fact patterns to resolve novel issues. There is no substitute for carefully studying judicial decisions to become adept at legal analysis, and to understand the genesis of the values and principles that motivate the law's development over time and its application to different case circumstances.

The book's second objective is to concentrate on United States Supreme Court decisions interpreting the federal Constitution, which form the backbone of criminal procedure law, but concurrently to make students aware that state constitutions represent an additional and increasingly important source of judicial authority. U.S. Supreme Court rulings establish the minimum constitutional obligations that the federal government and the states must observe. State courts may confer additional rights to persons within their jurisdiction through the interpretation of state constitutional provisions. State constitutions frequently are worded differently from the U.S. Constitution, and the rights they afford may reflect the unique traditions or history of a state. Where appropriate, state courts have not been reluctant to recognize state constitutional rights that exceed those conferred by the U.S. Constitution. Consequently, state constitutional decisions are sprinkled throughout this book to illustrate this important dimension of criminal procedure law, and to heighten students' awareness about this aspect of American federalism.

The book's third objective is to introduce students to the reference materials and strategies used for basic legal research. The law, and even a subpart of it such as criminal procedure, is vast and constantly changing. Students who are familiar with only the cases and legal principles gleaned from this book will find that their knowledge of criminal procedure is limited and risks becoming outdated. Legal research skills enable students—as well as professors, lawyers, judges, and practitioners—to investigate an unlimited array of issues and to keep pace with developments in the law. Legal research skills can be acquired with a bit of discipline and practice, and they pay handsome dividends. Pointers explaining how to conduct legal research appear throughout this book, and Appendix A provides a summary, with examples, of the reference materials and techniques that will permit students to find the law through their own initiative.

This book's design reflects a few basic assumptions that we readily make about undergraduate students and their aptitude for studying legal materials. It is our unwavering belief, based on several years of experience with these and other assigned readings, that undergraduates can and will rise to the challenge of analyzing case decisions. We are convinced that college students, properly motivated, are fully capable of participating in a dialogue exploring the reasoning and implications of judicial decisions, and that their individual and collective learning experiences are immeasurably richer as a result of this process. We do not subscribe to the view that case analysis should be the exclusive province of lawyers and law students, and that others must be satisfied reading narrative accounts "about" the law. To the contrary, we have found that students readily adapt to case analysis and that class hours typically are filled with lively debate and informed discussion. We hope, and believe, that the case method of study offers students practice using analytical skills that will serve them far beyond the classroom experience. In short, we unflinchingly support using the case method to teach law in undergraduate classrooms, and we could neither justify nor enjoy doing otherwise.

Instructors should find enough in these pages to give students a comprehensive introduction to criminal procedure law. Although we had to make some difficult choices about subject and case coverage, we have tried not to short-change important topics at the expense of others. Instructors teaching semester-long classes may not be able to assign all materials in this book. We deemed it preferable to be overinclusive, in order to give faculty choices about what areas to cover in detail and what to skim or skip, rather than to err on the side of underinclusion. We would appreciate hearing from instructors who adopt this book, to let us know if we have neglected to include issues or cases that they would like to have had addressed. We will try to be responsive in future editions.

James R. Acker
University at Albany
School of Criminal Justice
Albany, New York

David C. Brody
Washington State University-Spokane
Department of Political Science/
Criminal Justice Program
Spokane, Washington

Acknowledgments

This book evolved over several years of classroom experimentation. We owe a debt to generations of students who coped with photocopies of edited case decisions, cobbled together by a few rough transitional passages. We gained much from their feedback, and we hope they gained a bit, as well.

Jo Anne DeSilva went several rounds with the text of this book on her word processor. We thank her for her efforts and fine work product.

We also owe a debt to the editors of Aspen Publishers, Inc.—*Susan Beauchamp, Ruth Bloom, Kathleen McGuire Gilbert, Laureece Woodson, and their colleagues*—for their invaluable help and support as our ideas for a criminal procedure book were transformed into these pages. Thank you, one and all.

This book reflects the combined efforts of the Acker family. Daughters Elizabeth and Anna, who one day hopefully will be reintroduced to these materials far more civilly, good-naturedly cut and pasted case decisions, and then cut and pasted some more, in the unceasing effort to reduce prolix judicial writings to manageable proportions. Jenny helped photocopy, collate, and provided sustenance and comfort throughout this book's gestation. For all of their help, and mostly for just being there and being who they are, Jim Acker is supremely grateful.

David Brody is equally grateful to his wife Wendy Molyneux and the prominent role she played in the completion of this book. Be it her uncanny ability to turn legalese into prose and her eye for detail, or the patience, love, and encouragement she has provided, David Brody too is supremely grateful.

Table of Cases

Note: Page numbers in *italics* denote figures and exhibits.

CHAPTER 1

The Law of Criminal Procedure: Of Means and Ends

THE CHALLENGES OF CRIMINAL PROCEDURE LAW

Procedural issues dominate the daily administration of criminal justice. The legal rules and principles that regulate the administration of criminal justice make up the body of criminal procedure law. Criminal procedure law traditionally is understood as governing (1) *police work,* including the detection and investigation of crimes and arrest decisions; (2) the *pretrial decisions* of magistrates, prosecutors, grand juries, and judges, involving such matters as bail, the preliminary review and screening of charges, and filing of formal criminal charges; (3) the *adjudication* of charges through guilty pleas and trials; (4) *sentencing;* and (5) *appeals* and *postconviction review* of guilty verdicts and sentences. This book focuses on the law governing police practices, pretrial decisions, and the adjudication process. These issues form the core of criminal procedure law. Concentrating on them allows us to give them the attention that their significance and complexity demand.

Few areas of the law are as captivating as criminal procedure. Although many state and federal rules of criminal procedure are defined by statute, the principles animating these rules invariably spring from the U.S. Constitution and related state constitutional provisions. The courts, especially the U.S. Supreme Court, determine the scope and limits of these constitutional principles as they decide cases involving murder, rape, armed robbery, drug offenses, and other serious crimes. Through their case decisions, the courts put the law into action.

Individual citizens suffer profoundly at the hands of criminals. Society generally is injured when criminal acts disrupt people's lives, undermine moral values, and inspire fear and insecurity.

At the same time, individuals accused of committing crimes have much at stake. Tremendous stigma, or social disapproval, accompanies a criminal accusation and conviction. Once convicted, offenders face fines, probationary supervision, jail, prison, or even execution. Some individuals accused of committing a crime have valid defenses, in the form of excuse or justification, or they may not even have been involved in the crime they have been accused of committing. The general public, no less than those who are directly enmeshed in the criminal justice system, have an interest in ensuring that the criminal laws are administered fairly.

Each criminal case decided by the courts potentially involves issues that transcend particular parties and crimes. These cases provide a forum for resolving the perpetual tensions involved in preserving personal liberties and maintaining order under law. On the one hand, *reliable fact finding* is essential if the criminal justice system is to ensure both that the guilty are punished and that the innocent remain free. The "verdict" rendered by a judge or jury at the conclusion of a trial is an announcement that literally means "speak the truth."

However, ascertaining the truth about suspected crimes cannot be the exclusive function of the criminal justice process. Few people would condone using the rack or other forms of torture to coerce confessions from suspected criminals or would agree that citizens should be strip-searched at the whim of a police officer, or would enthusiastically entertain a search party in their homes in the dead of night. Such activities might prove highly effective in detecting criminal activity and even in discriminating between the guilty and the innocent. Yet they illustrate that limits must be placed on fact-finding initiatives, even if those limits impede an otherwise commendable search for the truth. *Safeguarding individual freedoms, checking abuses of power by law enforcement officials, and preserving basic fairness in government-citizen interactions* also are important goals of the law of criminal procedure.

The law strives to maintain a balance between truth seeking and individual liberties within a federalistic system of government. Each of the 50 states in this country has a unique set of criminal laws and operates its own court system. The federal government also enacts laws, maintains a judicial system, and has been invested with specific, enumerated powers relative to the states and individual citizens. *Federalism* is another concern of criminal procedure law. Justice Brandeis observed many years ago that "it is one of the happy incidents of the federal system that a single courageous state may, if its citizens choose, serve as a laboratory; and try novel social and economic experiments without risk to the rest of the country." *New York Ice Co. v. Liebmann*, 285 U.S. 262, 311, 52 S. Ct. 371, 386–87, 76 L. Ed. 747, 771 (1932) (Brandeis, J., dissenting).

Another goal of criminal procedure law is to promote *finality* in criminal cases. Sometimes defendants benefit by rules designed to achieve the final resolution of charges. For example, double-jeopardy principles prevent the retrial of a defendant who is acquitted of a crime, even if compelling evidence of guilt surfaces after the trial. Statutes of limitation and speedy-trial provisions may prohibit suspected offenders from ever being brought to trial when there are unjustifiable delays in filing or prosecuting criminal charges. Finality interests also may be asserted by the government or invoked by the courts to the defendant's detriment. Thus, appellate courts may refuse to consider defendants' claims of error that were not preserved by a timely objection during trial, when immediate corrective action could have been taken. Similarly, federal courts may decline to review issues in state cases that were not presented on appeal to the state courts or that were not raised at the first opportunity in the federal courts through a petition for a writ of habeas corpus.

A federal statute, 28 U.S.C. § 2254(a), authorizes the federal courts to "entertain an application for a writ of habeas corpus in behalf of a person in custody pursuant to the judgment of a state court only on the ground that he is in custody in violation of the Constitution or laws or treaties of the United States." Significant restrictions have been imposed in recent years on the availability of federal habeas corpus review by both the Supreme Court and Congress. A respect for the finality of state court judgments has been a major reason for these limitations. Curtailing repeated reviews of criminal convictions and sentences is further justified in the name of preserving scarce judicial resources and by the belief that justice is best served when an offender ultimately is required to accept the legitimacy of his or her punishment.

Criminal procedure law also is concerned with *administrative issues.* Rules that promote efficiency, that help preserve scarce resources and minimize costs and delay, and that are easily understood and applied may be favored over other rules. Of course, administrative concerns sometimes clash with principles that reflect other important values.

One of the principal challenges confronting criminal procedure law is to respect and preserve the diverse objectives of the criminal justice system, mindful of relevant operating constraints, and to reconcile potentially conflicting interests under the unique facts and circumstances of individual cases. This process requires *identifying* the rights and interests at stake in cases, *assigning appropriate weight* to the respective interests, and then *balancing* or accommodating those interests to arrive at a *decision* of the case issues. Even if not recognized formally, these ingredients are implicit in most court decisions involving issues of constitutional criminal procedure.

CRIMINAL PROCEDURE LAW IN ACTION: A CASE STUDY

Briefing a Case

The first case presented for study, *Brewer v. Williams,* demonstrates how difficult it can be to reconcile the competing ends of the law of criminal procedure. These difficulties are vividly illustrated in the often-passionate opinions of the Supreme Court justices, who divided by a vote of 5–4 about the proper resolution of the issues raised in this case. As you read *Brewer v. Williams,* it will be important for you to understand precisely what the Supreme Court ruled and what reasons supported this decision. Since not all students will have had experience reading judicial decisions, a few prefatory remarks may facilitate this assignment.

Studying case opinions helps reveal the law as a principled and dynamic process. Legal rules are in constant evolution. They are refined in response to changing social conditions and novel factual circumstances. It is important to know the origins and history of rules of law to gain a full understanding of their form and application. Carefully studying judicial opinions helps illuminate the legal principles that control case decisions. Although knowledge of legal rules is valuable, the analytical skills associated with identifying the premises of judicial decisions, extracting general principles from the rules announced in cases, and testing the application of these principles in different fact situations unquestionably are a truer measure of a student's understanding of the law.

While the payoffs from studying judicial decisions are considerable, a commensurate investment is required. Reading case law is significantly more time consuming, and challenging, than reading summaries or narrative accounts of case decisions. This is especially true of the first few encounters with judicial opinions. One tested method for helping to extract meaning from a case decision is "briefing" the case.

A *brief* is simply a structured summary of a case decision. It is prepared as a basis for improved analysis, as a reference tool for class discussion, and as an aid to review course materials in preparation for examinations. A brief can, and doubtlessly should, be individualized for your analysis, reference, and review, but some basic matters about a case decision should be addressed. A brief should begin with the case's name and complete citation. It is important to know the court deciding the case and the year of the decision. The full citation contains this information and will enable you to look up the case and read it in its entirety if you later wish to do so. We additionally recommend that you record the page in this book at which the case you are briefing begins for easy reference between your notes and the text.

The *critical components* of a case brief are:

1. facts
2. issue(s)
3. holding and rationale

The *facts* of the case, of course, must be gleaned from the opinion. The facts reported in the opinion will have been reduced significantly and sometimes transformed to bear faint resemblance to the facts that emerged at a trial. This filtering process is especially evident as a case progresses through different appellate courts and other layers of judicial review. Nevertheless, these are the only facts at your disposal, and you must rely on them as you read and prepare to brief the case. Since your job is to summarize the case, you should not mechanically report all of the facts supplied in the court's narrative but rather focus on the *relevant* facts. Facts are relevant only to the extent that they relate to the issue, and ultimately the holding in a case. Thus, you should be selective in the facts or historical events that you record.

The *judicial history* of a case is usually included as a part of the facts. This history consists of an account of where the case originated and how it arrived in the court responsible for the opinion you are briefing. For example, you might note that the defendant—often abbreviated as "D" or "Δ"(the Greek letter delta)—was convicted of murder in a specific state trial court, that his or her conviction was affirmed on appeal by the state court of appeals and by the state supreme court, and that the U.S. Supreme Court then granted certiorari (exercised its discretionary authority to review the case). We discuss the typical progression of a criminal case

through the state and federal court systems in greater detail in Chapter 2.

The *issue* is a statement of the legal question decided by the court. Cases occasionally involve more than a single legal issue. Courts sometimes state the issue that they are deciding early in an opinion, and quite clearly. At other times, courts seem unwilling or unable to pinpoint the questions they are deciding, and you will have to frame case issues as you understand them. You should take care to state the issue concisely and accurately. Be mindful of the fact that how a court defines an issue can be crucial to the resolution of a case. There may be times when you take exception with how a court states an issue, and you should make note of your disagreement.

The statement of the issue in your brief should capture the crux of the controversy confronting the court and should always be written in the form of a question. It should be sufficiently comprehensive to inform a listener about what the case involves. A question framed along the lines of "Should the confession be admissible?" or "Should the police have secured a warrant?" is not adequate.

Consider the greater understanding of a case conveyed by issues stated in the following terms: "Does the federal Constitution require the states to appoint legal counsel for a person charged with a felony who is too poor to hire a lawyer?" "Would the capital punishment of an offender who was only 16 years old at the time he committed murder amount to cruel and unusual punishment, in violation of the Eighth Amendment to the U.S. Constitution?"

Stating the issue presented in a case accurately and with the proper degree of precision— neither hopelessly general nor detailed and convoluted to the point of incomprehensibility— can be a true art form. This is perhaps the most important step in understanding the case, so you should be prepared to devote the necessary thought and effort to defining the question before the court.

The ***holding*** of a case usually can be stated in the form of a complete response to the issue you have identified. For example, "The cruel-and-unusual-punishments clause of the Eighth Amendment does not in all cases prohibit the execution of offenders who were just 16 years old when they committed a capital crime" answers the question posed in the issue stated above. The holding reveals what the court decided in the case you are briefing, and it also can serve as a statement of the general rule that can be extracted from the case decision. The rule then becomes precedent, or the basis of future decisions in like cases. The doctrine of precedent, or ***stare decisis***, plays a central role in the evolution of case law. Lawyers and judges examine the analogies and distinctions that can be made between cases to help determine whether the rule announced in a previous decision should govern the resolution of a case that later comes before a court.

The ***rationale*** is the explanation of how a court arrived at its holding. To justify their rulings, courts typically rely on precedent, the text of constitutions and statutes, history, logic, policy implications, value preferences, empirical evidence, case facts, and other sources and techniques. You may not always agree with or be persuaded by the rationale offered to support a court's holding. Indeed, the regularity with which concurring and dissenting opinions are written should convince you that there is ample room for disagreement with the prevailing rationale in case decisions. Thus, as you outline the reasons offered in support of a court's decision, you should think critically about them and make note of any questions that occur to you. Concurring and dissenting opinions can be quite helpful to suggest possible flaws or weaknesses in the majority opinion's rationale.

In the U.S. Supreme Court: *Brewer v. Williams*

You should routinely brief all of the principal decisions you read. This practice is not just for beginners but is invaluable to all students as they prepare for examinations.

Make an effort to brief *Brewer v. Williams* by identifying the facts, issues, holding, and rationale of this decision. Be particularly alert to the different interests related to the criminal justice process that are implicated in this case and how they are prioritized by the justices.

For example, how could "the truth" best be served in deciding *Brewer v. Williams*? If fact-finding accuracy emerges as the paramount consideration, are there corresponding sacrifices to individual liberties? The crime for which Williams was convicted was committed almost nine years before the case was decided by the U.S. Supreme Court. Should the likely difficulties associated with retrying Williams after such a long time be considered in deciding whether he should be given a new trial? Are issues of federalism significant, in that the case was considered by the federal courts on Williams's petition for a writ of habeas corpus after the Iowa courts had ruled against Williams on the very same claims? Will the police be able to understand, and the courts clearly administer, the rule of law resulting from the Supreme Court decision?

Note that there may be neither easy nor consistent answers to these questions. The widely divergent opinions of the Supreme Court justices attest to this fact. At this time, you should study *Brewer v. Williams* by identifying the several ends of the law of criminal procedure that come into play in this case. Pay particular attention to the values that contribute to the balancing and reconciliation of these sometimes conflicting ends.

Brewer v. Williams, 430 U.S. 387, 97 S. Ct. 1232, 51 L. Ed. 2d 424 (1977)

Mr. Justice **Stewart** delivered the opinion of the Court. . . .

I

On the afternoon of December 24, 1968, a 10-year-old girl named Pamela Powers went with her family to the YMCA in Des Moines, Iowa, to watch a wrestling tournament in which her brother was participating. When she failed to return from a trip to the washroom, a search for her began. The search was unsuccessful.

Robert Williams, who had recently escaped from a mental hospital, was a resident of the YMCA. Soon after the girl's disappearance Williams was seen in the YMCA lobby carrying some clothing and a large bundle wrapped in a blanket. He obtained help from a 14-year-old boy in opening the street door of the YMCA and the door to his automobile parked outside. When Williams placed the bundle in the front seat of his car the boy "saw two legs in it and they were skinny and white." Before anyone could see what was in the bundle Williams drove away. His abandoned car was found the following day in Davenport, Iowa, roughly 160 miles east of Des Moines. A warrant was then issued in Des Moines for his arrest on a charge of abduction.

On the morning of December 26, a Des Moines lawyer named Henry McKnight went to the Des Moines police station and informed the officers present that he had just received a long distance call from Williams, and that he had advised Williams to turn himself in to the Davenport police. Williams did surrender that morning to the police in Davenport, and they booked him on the charge specified in the arrest warrant and gave him the warnings required by Miranda v Arizona, 384 US 436, 16 L Ed 2d 694, 86 S Ct 1602.

The Davenport police then telephoned their counterparts in Des Moines to inform them that Williams had surrendered. McKnight, the lawyer, was still in the Des Moines police headquarters, and Williams conversed with McKnight on the telephone. In the presence of the Des Moines chief of police and a police detective named Leaming, McKnight advised Williams that Des Moines police officers would be driving to Davenport to pick him up, that the officers would not interrogate him or mistreat him, and that Williams was not to talk to the officers about Pamela Powers until after consulting with McKnight upon his return to Des Moines. As a result of these conversations, it was agreed between McKnight and the Des Moines police officials that Detective Leaming and a fellow officer would drive to Davenport to pick up Williams, that they would bring him directly back to Des Moines, and that they would not question him during the trip.

In the meantime Williams was arraigned before a judge in Davenport on the outstanding arrest warrant. The judge advised him of his Miranda rights and committed him to jail. Before leaving the courtroom, Williams conferred with a lawyer named Kelly, who advised him not to make any statements until consulting with Mc-Knight back in Des Moines.

Detective Leaming and his fellow officer arrived in Davenport about noon to pick up Williams and return him to Des Moines. Soon after their arrival they met with Williams and Kelly, who, they understood, was acting as Williams' lawyer. Detective Leaming repeated the Miranda warnings, and told Williams:

"[W]e both know that you're being represented here by Mr. Kelly and you're being represented by Mr. McKnight in Des Moines, and…I want you to remember this because we'll be visiting between here and Des Moines."

Williams then conferred again with Kelly alone, and after this conference Kelly reiterated to Detective Leaming that Williams was not to be questioned about the disappearance of Pamela Powers until after he had consulted with Mc-Knight back in Des Moines. When Leaming expressed some reservations, Kelly firmly stated that the agreement with McKnight was to be carried out—that there was to be no interrogation of

Williams during the automobile journey to Des Moines. Kelly was denied permission to ride in the police car back to Des Moines with Williams and the two officers.

The two detectives, with Williams in their charge, then set out on the 160-mile drive. At no time during the trip did Williams express a willingness to be interrogated in the absence of an attorney. Instead, he stated several times that "[w]hen I get to Des Moines and see Mr. Mc-Knight, I am going to tell you the whole story." Detective Leaming knew that Williams was a former mental patient, and knew also that he was deeply religious.

The detective and his prisoner soon embarked on a wide-ranging conversation covering a variety of topics, including the subject of religion. Then, not long after leaving Davenport and reaching the interstate highway, Detective Leaming delivered what has been referred to in the briefs and oral arguments as the "Christian burial speech." Addressing Williams as "Reverend," the detective said:

> "I want to give you something to think about while we're traveling down the road. . . . Number one, I want you to observe the weather conditions, it's raining, it's sleeting, it's freezing, driving is very treacherous, visibility is poor, it's going to be dark early this evening. They are predicting several inches of snow for tonight, and I feel that you yourself are the only person that knows where this little girl's body is, that you yourself have only been there once, and if you get a snow on top of it you yourself may be unable to find it. And, since we will be going right past the area on the way into Des Moines, I feel that we could stop and locate the body, that the parents of this little girl should be entitled to a Christian burial for the little girl who was snatched away from them on Christmas [E]ve and murdered. And I feel we should stop and locate it on the way in rather than waiting until morning and trying to come back out after a snow storm and possibly not being able to find it at all."

Williams asked Detective Leaming why he thought their route to Des Moines would be tak-

ing them past the girl's body, and Leaming responded that he knew the body was in the area of Mitchellville—a town they would be passing on the way to Des Moines.[1] Leaming then stated: "I do not want you to answer me. I don't want to discuss it any further. Just think about it as we're riding down the road." . . .

The car continued towards Des Moines, and as it approached Mitchellville, Williams said that he would show the officers where the body was. He then directed the police to the body of Pamela Powers.

Williams was indicted for first-degree murder. Before trial, his counsel moved to suppress all evidence relating to or resulting from any statements Williams had made during the automobile ride from Davenport to Des Moines. After an evidentiary hearing the trial judge denied the motion. He found that "an agreement was made between defense counsel and the police officials to the effect that the Defendant was not to be questioned on the return trip to Des Moines," and that the evidence in question had been elicited from Williams during "a critical stage in the proceedings requiring the presence of counsel on his request." The judge ruled, however, that Williams had "waived his right to have an attorney present during the giving of such information."

The evidence in question was introduced over counsel's continuing objection at the subsequent trial. The jury found Williams guilty of murder, and the judgment of conviction was affirmed by the Iowa Supreme Court. . . .

Williams then petitioned for a writ of habeas corpus in the United States District Court for the Southern District of Iowa. . . .

The District Court made findings of fact as summarized above, and concluded as a matter of law that the evidence in question had been wrongly admitted at Williams' trial.

* * *

The Court of Appeals for the Eighth Circuit, with one judge dissenting, affirmed this judgment, and denied a petition for rehearing en

---

1. The fact of the matter, of course, was that Detective Leaming possessed no such knowledge.

banc. We granted certiorari to consider the constitutional issues presented.

II

* * *

B

* * *

[T]here is no need to review in this case the doctrine of Miranda v Arizona, a doctrine designed to secure the constitutional privilege against compulsory self-incrimination.

It is equally unnecessary to evaluate the ruling of the District Court that Williams' self-incriminating statements were, indeed, involuntarily made. Cf. Spano v New York, 360 US 315, 79 S Ct 1202, 3 L Ed 2d 1265. For it is clear that the judgment before us must in any event be affirmed upon the ground that Williams was deprived of a different constitutional right—the right to the assistance of counsel.

This right, guaranteed by the Sixth and Fourteenth Amendments, is indispensable to the fair administration of our adversary system of criminal justice. Its vital need at the pretrial stage has perhaps nowhere been more succinctly explained than in Mr. Justice Sutherland's memorable words for the Court 44 years ago in Powell v Alabama, 287 US 45, 57, 53 S Ct 55, 77 L Ed 158 [(1932)].

"[D]uring perhaps the most critical period of the proceedings against these defendants, that is to say, from the time of their arraignment until the beginning of their trial, when consultation, thoroughgoing investigation and preparation were vitally important, the defendants did not have the aid of counsel in any real sense, although they were as much entitled to such aid during that period as at the trial itself."

There has occasionally been a difference of opinion within the Court as to the peripheral scope of this constitutional right.

But its basic contours, which are identical in state and federal contexts, are too well established to require extensive elaboration here. Whatever else it may mean, the right to counsel granted by the Sixth and Fourteenth Amendments means at least that a person is entitled to the help of a lawyer at or after the time that judicial proceedings have been initiated against him—"whether by way of formal charge, preliminary hearing, indictment, information, or arraignment." Kirby v Illinois, [406 US 682, 689, 92 S Ct 1877, 32 L Ed 2d 411 [(1972)].

There can be no doubt in the present case that judicial proceedings had been initiated against Williams before the start of the automobile ride from Davenport to Des Moines. A warrant had been issued for his arrest, he had been arraigned on that warrant before a judge in a Davenport courtroom, and he had been committed by the court to confinement in jail. The State does not contend otherwise.

There can be no serious doubt, either, that Detective Leaming deliberately and designedly set out to elicit information from Williams just as surely as—and perhaps more effectively than—if he had formally interrogated him. Detective Leaming was fully aware before departing for Des Moines that Williams was being represented in Davenport by Kelly and in Des Moines by McKnight. Yet he purposely sought during Williams' isolation from his lawyers to obtain as much incriminating information as possible. Indeed, Detective Leaming conceded as much when he testified at Williams' trial:

"Q. In fact, Captain, whether he was a mental patient or not, you were trying to get all the information you could before he got to his lawyer, weren't you?

"A. I was sure hoping to find out where that little girl was, yes, sir.

"Q. Well, I'll put it this way: You was [sic] hoping to get all the information you could before Williams got back to McKnight, weren't you?

"A. Yes, sir."[6]

---

6. Counsel for petitioner, in the course of oral argument in this Court, acknowledged that the "Christian burial speech" was tantamount to interrogation.

* * *,

The circumstances of this case are thus constitutionally indistinguishable from those presented in Massiah v United States, [377 US 201 845 S Ct 1199, 12 L Ed 2d 246 (1964)]. The petitioner in that case was indicted for violating the federal narcotics law. He retained a lawyer, pleaded not guilty, and was released on bail. While he was free on bail a federal agent succeeded by surreptitious means in listening to incriminating statements made by him. Evidence of these statements was introduced against the petitioner at his trial, and he was convicted. This Court reversed the conviction, holding "that the petitioner was denied the basic protections of that guarantee [the right to counsel] when there was used against him at his trial evidence of his own incriminating words, which federal agents had deliberately elicited from him after he had been indicted and in the absence of his counsel." 377 US, at 206, 84 S Ct 1199, 12 L Ed 2d 246.

That the incriminating statements were elicited surreptitiously in the Massiah case, and otherwise here, is constitutionally irrelevant. Rather, the clear rule of Massiah is that once adversary proceedings have commenced against an individual, he has a right to legal representation when the government interrogates him. It thus requires no wooden or technical application of the Massiah doctrine to conclude that Williams was entitled to the assistance of counsel guaranteed to him by the Sixth and Fourteenth Amendments.

III

The Iowa courts recognized that Williams had been denied the constitutional right to the assistance of counsel. They held, however, that he had waived that right during the course of the automobile trip from Davenport to Des Moines.

* * *

The District Court and the Court of Appeals were correct in the view that the question of waiver was not a question of historical fact, but one which, in the words of Mr. Justice Frankfurter, requires "application of constitutional principles to the facts as found. ..." Brown v Allen,

344 US 443, 507, 73 S Ct 397, 97 L Ed 469 [(1953)] (separate opinion).

The District Court and the Court of Appeals were also correct in their understanding of the proper standard to be applied in determining the question of waiver as a matter of federal constitutional law—that it was incumbent upon the State to prove "an intentional relinquishment or abandonment of a known right or privilege." Johnson v Zerbst, 304 US, [458,] 464, 58 S Ct 1019, 82 L Ed 1461, [1938]. That standard has been reiterated in many cases. We have said that the right to counsel does not depend upon a request by the defendant, and that courts indulge in every reasonable presumption against waiver.

This strict standard applies equally to an alleged waiver of the right to counsel whether at trial or at a critical stage of pretrial proceedings.

We conclude, finally, that the Court of Appeals was correct in holding that, judged by these standards, the record in this case falls far short of sustaining petitioner's burden. It is true that Williams had been informed of and appeared to understand his right to counsel. But waiver requires not merely comprehension but relinquishment, and Williams' consistent reliance upon the advice of counsel in dealing with the authorities refutes any suggestion that he waived that right.

* * *

Despite Williams' express and implicit assertions of his right to counsel, Detective Leaming proceeded to elicit incriminating statements from Williams. Leaming did not preface this effort by telling Williams that he had a right to the presence of a lawyer, and made no effort at all to ascertain whether Williams wished to relinquish that right. The circumstances of record in this case thus provide no reasonable basis for finding that Williams waived his right to the assistance of counsel.

The Court of Appeals did not hold, nor do we, that under the circumstances of this case Williams *could not,* without notice to counsel, have waived his rights under the Sixth and Fourteenth Amendments. It only held, as do we, that he did not.

IV

The crime of which Williams was convicted was senseless and brutal, calling for swift and energetic action by the police to apprehend the perpetrator and gather evidence with which he could be convicted. No mission of law enforcement officials is more important. Yet "[d]isinterested zeal for the public good does not assure either wisdom or right in the methods it pursues." Haley v Ohio, 332 US 596, 605, 92 L Ed 224, 68 S Ct 302 [(1948)] (Frankfurter, J., concurring in judgment). Although we do not lightly affirm the issuance of a writ of habeas corpus in this case, so clear a violation of the Sixth and Fourteenth Amendments as here occurred cannot be condoned. The pressures on state executive and judicial officers charged with the administration of the criminal law are great, especially when the crime is murder and the victim a small child. But it is precisely the predictability of those pressures that makes imperative a resolute loyalty to the guarantees that the Constitution extends to us all.

* * *

Mr. Justice **Marshall,** concurring.

* * *

The dissenters have, I believe, lost sight of the fundamental constitutional backbone of our criminal law. They seem to think that Detective Leaming's actions were perfectly proper, indeed laudable, examples of "good police work." In my view, good police work is something far different from catching the criminal at any price. It is equally important that the police, as guardians of the law, fulfill their responsibility to obey its commands scrupulously. For "in the end life and liberty can be as much endangered from illegal methods used to convict those thought to be criminals as from the actual criminals themselves." Spano v New York, 360 US 315, 320–321, 79 S Ct 1202 , 3 L Ed 2d 1265 (1959).

In this case, there can be no doubt that Detective Leaming consciously and knowingly set out to violate Williams' Sixth Amendment right to counsel and his Fifth Amendment privilege against self-incrimination.

* * *

Leaming knowingly isolated Williams from the protection of his lawyers and during that period he intentionally "persuaded" him to give incriminating evidence. It is this intentional police misconduct—not good police practice—that the Court rightly condemns. The heinous nature of the crime is no excuse, as the dissenters would have it, for condoning knowing and intentional police transgression of the constitutional rights of a defendant. If Williams is to go free—and given the ingenuity of Iowa prosecutors on retrial or in a civil commitment proceeding, I doubt very much that there is any chance a dangerous criminal will be loosed on the streets, the blood-curdling cries of the dissents notwithstanding it will hardly be because he deserves it. It will be because Detective Leaming, knowing full well that he risked reversal of Williams' conviction, intentionally denied Williams the right of *every* American under the Sixth Amendment to have the protective shield of a lawyer between himself and the awesome power of the state.

I think it appropriate here to recall not Mr. Justice Cardozo's opinion in People v Defore, 242 NY 13, 150 NE 585 (1926), see opinion of The Chief Justice, post, at 416, and n 1, but rather the closing words of Mr. Justice Brandeis' great dissent in Olmstead v United States, 277 US 438, 471, 485, 48 S Ct 564, 72 L Ed 944, (1928):

"In a government of laws, existence of the government will be imperilled if it fails to observe the law scrupulously. Our Government is the potent, the omnipresent teacher. For good or for ill, it teaches the whole people by its example. Crime is contagious. If the Government becomes a lawbreaker, it breeds contempt for law; it invites every man to become a law unto himself; it invites anarchy. To declare that in the administration of the criminal law the end justifies the means—to declare that the Government may commit crimes in order to secure the conviction of a private criminal—would bring terrible retribution. Against that pernicious doctrine this Court should resolutely set its face."

Mr. Justice **Stevens,** concurring.

* * *

Nothing that we write, no matter how well reasoned or forcefully expressed, can bring back the victim of this tragedy or undo the consequences of the official neglect which led to the respondent's escape from a state mental institution. The emotional aspects of the case make it difficult to decide dispassionately, but do not qualify our obligation to apply the law with an eye to the future as well as with concern for the result in the particular case before us.

Underlying the surface issues in this case is the question whether a fugitive from justice can rely on his lawyer's advice given in connection with a decision to surrender voluntarily. The defendant placed his trust in an experienced Iowa trial lawyer who in turn trusted the Iowa law enforcement authorities to honor a commitment made during negotiations which led to the apprehension of a potentially dangerous person. Under any analysis, this was a critical stage of the proceeding in which the participation of an independent professional was of vital importance to the accused and to society. At this stage—as in countless others in which the law profoundly affects the life of the individual—the lawyer is the essential medium through which the demands and commitments of the sovereign are communicated to the citizen. If, in the long run, we are seriously concerned about the individual's effective representation by counsel, the State cannot be permitted to dishonor its promise to this lawyer.

Mr. Chief Justice **Burger,** dissenting.

The result in this case ought to be intolerable in any society which purports to call itself an organized society. It continues the Court—by the narrowest margin—on the much-criticized course of punishing the public for the mistakes and misdeeds of law enforcement officers, instead of punishing the officer directly, if in fact he is guilty of wrongdoing. It mechanically and blindly keeps reliable evidence from juries whether the claimed constitutional violation involves gross police misconduct or honest human error.

Williams is guilty of the savage murder of a small child; no member of the Court contends he is not. While in custody, and after no fewer than *five* warnings of his rights to silence and to counsel, he led police to the concealed body of his victim. The Court concedes Williams was not threatened or coerced and that he spoke and acted voluntarily and with full awareness of his constitutional rights. In the face of all this, the Court now holds that because Williams was prompted by the detective's statement—not interrogation but a statement—the jury must not be told how the police found the body.

Today's holding fulfills Judge (later Mr. Justice) Cardozo's grim prophecy that someday some court might carry the exclusionary rule to the absurd extent that its operative effect would exclude evidence relating to the body of a murder victim because of the means by which it was found.[1] In so ruling the Court regresses to playing a grisly game of "hide and seek," once more exalting the sporting theory of criminal justice which has been experiencing a decline in our jurisprudence.

* * *

(1)
*The Court Concedes Williams'
Disclosures Were Voluntary*

Under well-settled precedents which the Court freely acknowledges, it is very clear that Williams had made a valid waiver of his Fifth Amendment right to silence and his Sixth Amendment right to counsel when he led police to the child's body. Indeed, even under the Court's analysis I do not understand how a contrary conclusion is possible.

* * *

The evidence is uncontradicted that Williams had abundant knowledge of his right to have counsel present and of his right to silence. Since the Court does not question his mental competence, it boggles the mind to suggest that Williams could not understand that leading police to

---

1. "The criminal is to go free because the constable has blundered. . . . A room is searched against the law, and the body of a murdered man is found. . . . The privacy of the home has been infringed, and the murderer goes free." People v Defore, 242 NY 13, 21, 23–24, 150 NE 585, 587, 588 (1926).

the child's body would have other than the most serious consequences. All of the elements necessary to make out a valid waiver are shown by the record and acknowledged by the Court; we thus are left to guess how the Court reached its holding.

* * *

(2)
*The Exclusionary Rule Should Not
Be Applied to Non-Egregious Police
Conduct*

Even if there was no waiver, and assuming a technical violation occurred, the Court errs gravely in mechanically applying the exclusionary rule without considering whether that Draconian judicial doctrine should be invoked in these circumstances, or indeed whether any of its conceivable goals will be furthered by its application here.

The obvious flaws of the exclusionary rule as a judicial remedy are familiar.

Today's holding interrupts what has been a more rational perception of the constitutional and social utility of excluding reliable evidence from the truth-seeking process. In its Fourth Amendment context, we have now recognized that the exclusionary rule is in no sense a *personal* constitutional right, but a judicially conceived remedial device designed to safeguard and effectuate guaranteed legal rights generally.

We have repeatedly emphasized that deterrence of unconstitutional or otherwise unlawful police conduct is the only valid justification for excluding reliable and probative evidence from the criminal factfinding process.

Accordingly, unlawfully obtained evidence is not automatically excluded from the factfinding process in all circumstances. In a variety of contexts we inquire whether application of the rule will promote its objectives sufficiently to justify the enormous cost it imposes on society.

* * *

This is, of course, the familiar balancing process applicable to cases in which important competing interests are at stake. It is a recognition, albeit belated, that "the policies behind the exclusionary rule are not absolute," Stone v

Powell, supra, at 488, 96 S Ct 3037, 49 L Ed 2d 1067. It acknowledges that so serious an infringement with the crucial truthseeking function of a criminal prosecution should be allowed only when imperative to safeguard constitutional rights. An important factor in this amalgam is whether the violation at issue may properly be classed as "egregious." The Court understandably does not try to characterize the police actions here as "egregious."

Against this background, it is striking that the Court fails even to consider whether the benefits secured by application of the exclusionary rule in this case outweighed its obvious social costs.

* * *

We can all agree on "'[t]he abhorrence of society to the use of involuntary confessions,'" and the need to preserve the integrity of the human personality and individual free will.

But use of Williams' disclosures and their fruits carries no risk whatever of unreliability, for the body was found where he said it would be found. Moreover, since the Court makes no issue of voluntariness, no dangers are posed to individual dignity or free will.

* * *

[T]he fundamental purpose of the Sixth Amendment is to safeguard the fairness of the trial and the integrity of the factfinding process. In this case, where the evidence of how the child's body was found is of unquestioned reliability, and since the Court accepts Williams' disclosures as voluntary and uncoerced, there is no issue either of fairness or evidentiary reliability to justify suppression of truth. It appears suppression is mandated here for no other reason than the Court's general impression that it may have a beneficial effect on future police conduct; indeed, the Court fails to say even that much in defense of its holding.

* * *

This case, like Stone v Powell, comes to us by way of habeas corpus after a fair trial and appeal in the state courts. Relevant factors in this case are thus indistinguishable from those in Stone, and from those in other Fourth Amendment cases suggesting a balancing approach toward utilization of the exclusionary sanction. Rather than adopting a formalistic analysis varying with the constitutional provision invoked, we should apply the exclusionary rule on the basis of its benefits and costs, at least in those cases where the police conduct at issue is far from being outrageous or egregious.

* * *

Mr. Justice **White,** with whom Mr. Justice **Blackmun** and Mr. Justice **Rehnquist** join, dissenting.

* * *

The consequence of the majority's decision is, as the majority recognizes, extremely serious. A mentally disturbed killer whose guilt is not in question may be released. Why? Apparently, the answer is that the majority believes that the law enforcement officers acted in a way which involves some risk of injury to society and that such conduct should be deterred. However, the officers' conduct did not, and was not likely to, jeopardize the fairness of respondent's trial or in any way risk the conviction of an innocent man—the risk against which the Sixth Amend-

ment guarantee of assistance of counsel is designed to protect.

The police did nothing "wrong," let alone anything "unconstitutional."

* * *

Mr. Justice **Blackmun,** with whom Mr. Justice **White** and Mr. Justice **Rehnquist** join, dissenting.

* * *

This was a brutal, tragic, and heinous crime inflicted upon a young girl on the afternoon of the day before Christmas. With the exclusionary rule operating as the Court effectuates it, the decision today probably means that, as a practical matter, no new trial will be possible at this date eight years after the crime, and that this respondent necessarily will go free. That, of course, is not the standard by which a case of this kind strictly is to be judged. But, as Judge Webster in dissent below observed, 509 F2d, at 237, placing the case in sensible and proper perspective: "The evidence of Williams' guilt was overwhelming. No challenge is made to the reliability of the fact-finding process." I am in full agreement with that observation.

Notes and Questions

1. Is there any doubt that Williams was, in the words of Chief Justice Burger, "guilty of the savage murder of a small child"? If his guilt is clear, what possible social interests can justify upsetting his conviction? In this regard, which sentiments do you find more convincing: those expressed by Judge (later, Justice) Cardozo in *People v. Defore,* 242 N.Y. 13, 150 N.E. 585 (1926), as quoted in Chief Justice Burger's dissent at n. 1, or those of Justice Brandeis in *Olmstead v. United States,* 277 U.S. 430, 48 S. Ct. 564, 72 L. Ed. 944 (1928) (dissenting), as quoted in Justice Marshall's concurring opinion?

2. What do you make of Chief Justice Burger's implicit concession that the conclusion reached by the majority opinion would be justifiable if the police misconduct were classified as being "outrageous or egregious"? Since the evidence discovered in this case undoubtedly would remain reliable, why should it matter if Williams's rights were violated by egregious misconduct? If a cost-benefit analysis should precede a decision to exclude evidence following a violation of rights, would it matter if Williams had been suspected of shoplifting rather than kidnapping and murder? Precisely how should the "costs" and "benefits" of a rule resulting in the suppression of potentially probative evidence be measured?

3. If Williams had not pointed out the location of his victim's body to the police but instead was returned to Des Moines and had the opportunity to confer with his lawyer, Mr. McKnight, what do you suppose the lawyer would have advised Williams to do? If McKnight knew that Williams in fact was guilty, or if Williams had told him the location of the body, would the lawyer have been legally or ethically obliged to disclose this information to the police? Why or why not? Would your answer change if Williams had told McKnight he had released the girl alive, scantily clad, in a wooded area near Mitchellville? What, exactly, do you perceive defense counsel's role to be in defending a client like Williams, and why does the Court place such great importance on Williams's right to the assistance of counsel? (See Chapter 8 for further discussion of these issues.)

4. The majority opinion refrains from ruling that "Williams *could not* . . . have waived his rights" but instead declares that under the circumstances of this case "he did not." If Williams repeatedly was advised that he did not have to talk to the police, and if he was not coerced into doing so, why don't the facts support a waiver? What would it take before a waiver of rights would be effective?

5. What constitutional rights are at stake in this case? Which provisions of the U.S. Constitution are involved?

6. Is the general rule derived from *Brewer v. Williams* that a suspect cannot make a confession to the police without a lawyer? Is the police conduct in this case, and in particular "the Christian burial speech," important to the result? If so, how would you *generally* describe what the police did to secure Williams's incriminating statements and cooperation? Are any facts relating to Williams or his situation important to the general rule to be extracted from this case? Does it matter that Williams may be mentally ill? That he had spoken to a lawyer? That his lawyers had instructed the police not to question him? That he was taken in front of a judge in Davenport and "arraigned" before making his incriminating statements? In this context, what does it mean for a suspect to be "arraigned"? (See Chapter 2, at pp. 52–53.)

ADDITIONAL MEANS-ENDS PROBLEMS

Carl B. Klockars, "The Dirty Harry Problem," 452 *The Annals of the American Academy of Political and Social Science* 33 (Nov. 1980)

---

* * *

The Dirty Harry problem draws its name from the 1971 Warner Brothers film *Dirty Harry* and its chief protagonist, antihero Inspector Harry "Dirty Harry" Callahan. The film features a number of events which dramatize the Dirty Harry

Source: Reprinted with permission from C.B. Klockars, The Dirty Harry Problem, *The Annals of the American Academy of Political and Social Science,* Vol. 33, pp. 33–50, © 1980.

problem in different ways, but the one which does so most explicitly and most completely places Harry in the following situation. A 14-year-old girl has been kidnapped and is being held captive by a psychopathic killer. The killer, "Scorpio," who has already struck twice, demands $200,000 ransom to release the girl, who is buried with just enough oxygen to keep her alive for a few hours. Harry gets the job of delivering the ransom and, after enormous exertion, finally meets Scorpio. At their meeting Scorpio decides to renege on his bargain, let the girl die, and kill Harry. Harry manages to stab Scorpio in the leg before he does so, but not before Scorpio seriously wounds Harry's partner, an inexperienced, idealistic, slightly ethnic, former sociology major.

Scorpio escapes, but Harry manages to track him down through the clinic where he was treated for his wounded leg. After learning that Scorpio lives on the grounds of a nearby football stadium, Harry breaks into his apartment, finds guns and other evidence of his guilt, and finally confronts Scorpio on the 50-yard line, where Harry shoots him in the leg as he is trying to escape. Standing over Scorpio, Harry demands to know where the girl is buried. Scorpio refuses to disclose her location, demanding his rights to a lawyer. As the camera draws back from the scene Harry stands on Scorpio's bullet-mangled

leg to torture a confession of the girl's location from him.

As it turns out, the girl is already dead and Scorpio must be set free. Neither the gun found in the illegal search, nor the confession Harry extorted, nor any of its fruits—including the girl's body—would be admissible in court.

* * *

The Dirty Harry problem asks when and to what extent does the morally good end warrant or justify an ethically, politically, or legally dangerous means to its achievement? In itself, this question assumes the possibility of a genuine moral dilemma and posits its existence in a means-ends arrangement which may be expressed schematically as follows:

		MEANS	
		Morally Good (+)	Morally Dirty (−)
E N D S	Morally good (+)	A + +	B − + The Dirty Harry Problem
	Morally dirty (−)	C + −	D − −

It is important to specify clearly the terms of the Dirty Harry problem not only to show that it must involve the juxtaposition of good ends and dirty means, but also to show what must be proven to demonstrate that a Dirty Harry problem exists. If one could show, for example, that box B is always empirically empty or that in any given case the terms of the situation are better read in some other means-ends arrangement, Dirty Harry problems vanish. At this first level, however, I suspect that no one could exclude the core scene of *Dirty Harry* from the class of Dirty Harry problems. There is no question that saving

the life of an innocent victim of kidnapping is a "good" thing nor that grinding the bullet-mangled leg of Scorpio to extort a confession from him is "dirty."[2]

---

2. "Dirty" here means both "repugnant" in that it offends widely shared standards of human decency and dignity and "dangerous" in that it breaks commonly shared and supported norms, rules, or laws for conduct. To "dirty" acts there must be both a deontologically based face validity of immorality and a consequentialist threat to the prevailing rules for social order.

There is, in addition, a second level of criteria of an empirical and epistemological nature that must be met before a Dirty Harry problem actually comes into being. They involve the connection between the dirty act and the good end. Principally, what must be known and, importantly, known before the dirty act is committed, is that it will result in the achievement of the good end. In any absolute sense this is, of course, impossible to know, in that no acts are ever completely certain in their consequences. Thus the question is always a matter of probabilities. But it is helpful to break those probabilities into classes which attach to various subcategories of the overall question. In the given case, this level of problem would seem to require that three questions be satisfied, though not all with the same level of certainty.

In *Dirty Harry,* the first question is, Is Scorpio able to provide the information Dirty Harry seeks? It is an epistemological question about which, in *Dirty Harry,* we are absolutely certain.

* * *

Second, we must know there are means, dirty means and nothing other than dirty means, which are likely to achieve the good end. One can, of course, never be sure that one is aware of or has considered all possible alternatives, but in *Dirty Harry* there would appear to be no reason for Scorpio in his rational self-interest to confess to the girl's location without being coerced to do so.

The third question which must be satisfied at this empirical and epistemological level concedes that dirty means are the only method which will be effective, but asks whether or not, in the end, they will be in vain. We know in *Dirty Harry* that they were, and Harry himself, at the time of the ransom demand, admits he believes that the girl is already dead. Does not this possibility or likelihood that the girl is dead destroy the justification for Harry's dirty act? Although it surely would if Harry knew for certain that the girl was dead, I do not think it does insofar as even a small probability of her being saved exists. The reason is that the good to be achieved is so unquestionably good and so passionately felt that even a small possibility of its achievement demands that it be tried. For example, were we to ask, If it were your daughter would you want Harry to do what he did? it would be this passionate sense of unquestionable good that we are trying to dramatize.

* * *

Once we have satisfied ourselves that a Dirty Harry problem is conceptually possible and that, in fact, we can specify one set of concrete circumstances in which it exists, one might think that the most difficult question of all is, What ought to be done? I do not think it is. I suspect that there are very few people who would not want Harry to do something dirty in the situation specified. I know I would want him to do what he did, and what is more, I would want anyone who policed for me to be prepared to do so as well. Put differently, I want to have as police officers men and women of moral courage and sensitivity.

But to those who would want exactly that, the Dirty Harry problem poses its most irksome conclusion. Namely, that one cannot, at least in the specific case at hand, have a policeman who is both just and innocent. The troublesome issue in the Dirty Harry problem is not whether under some utilitarian calculus a right choice can be made, but that the choice must always be between at least two wrongs. And in choosing to do either wrong, the policeman inevitably taints or tarnishes himself.

* * *

Dirty Harry problems arise quite often. For policemen, real, everyday policemen, Dirty Harry problems are part of their job and thus considerably more than rare or artificial dramatic exceptions.

* * *

Although the exclusionary rule is the manifest target of *Dirty Harry,* it more than anything else, makes Dirty Harry problems a reality in everyday policing. It is the great virtue of exclusionary rules—applying in various forms to stops, searches, seizures, and interrogations—that they hit directly upon the intolerable, though often, I think, moral desire of police to punish. These rules make the very simple point to police that the more they wish to see a felon punished, the more they are advised to be scrupulous in their treatment of him. Put differently, the best thing Harry could have done for Scorpio was to step on his leg, extort his confession, and break into his apartment.

* * *

If Dirty Harry problems can be shown to exist in their technical dimensions—as genuine means-ends problems where only dirty means will work—the question of the magnitude and urgency of the ends that the dirty means may be employed to achieve must still be confronted. Specifically, it must be shown that the ends of dirty means are so desirable that the failure to achieve them would cast the person who is in a position to do so in moral disrepute.

The two most widely acknowledged ends of policing are peace keeping and law enforcement.

* * *

An interpretation of law enforcement which is compatible with empirical studies of police behavior—as peace keeping is—and police talk in America—which peace keeping generally is not—is an understanding of the ends of law enforcement as punishment. There are, of course, many theories of punishment, but the police seem inclined toward the simplest: the belief that certain people who have committed certain acts deserve to be punished for them. What can one say of the compelling and unquestionable character of this retributive ambition as an end of policing and policemen?

* * *

The alternative the Dirty Harry problem leads us to is ensuring that the craftsman regards his dirty means as dirty by applying the same retributive principles of punishment to his wrongful acts that he is quite willing to apply to others! It is, in fact, only when his wrongful acts are punished that he will come to see them as wrongful and will appreciate the genuine moral—rather than technical or occupational—choice he makes in resorting to them.

* * *

If under such conditions our craftsman police officer is still willing to risk the employment of dirty means to achieve what he understands to be unquestionably good ends, he will not only know that he has behaved justly, but that in doing so he must run the risk of becoming genuinely guilty as well.

In urging the punishment of policemen who resort to dirty means to achieve some unquestionably good and morally compelling end, we recognize that we create a Dirty Harry problem for ourselves and for those we urge to effect such punishments. It is a fitting end, one which teaches once again that the danger in Dirty Harry problems is never in their resolution, but in thinking that one has found a resolution with which one can truly live in peace.

Notes and Questions

1. Is it possible to reconcile Professor Klockar's conclusions about Inspector Callahan's (Dirty Harry) torturing Scorpio to attempt to learn the whereabouts of the girl Scorpio had kidnapped—"I know I would want him to do what he did"—with his "urging the punishment of policemen who resort to dirty means to achieve some unquestionably good and morally compelling end"?

2. Do you think that Inspector Callahan's tactics were justified under the circumstances? Does your answer to this question dictate what should be done with evidence uncovered as a result of these tactics? That is, if Harry justifiably broke into Scorpio's apartment and stood on Scorpio's "bullet-mangled leg" in order to find the kidnapped child, does it necessarily follow that the resulting evidence should be admitted at a later trial? Conversely, even if Harry was wrong in his actions, is it inevitable that the evidence must be excluded at a later trial? What ends of criminal procedure

law are in conflict in this particular Dirty Harry problem?

3. Professor Klockars suggests that Dirty Harry problems occur often in everyday police work. The vast majority of such dilemmas doubtlessly are resolved without ever coming to the attention of the courts. Nevertheless, some

means-ends problems eventually are considered judicially, allowing judgment to be rendered dispassionately, and long after the questionable law enforcement practices took place. Consider the following cases, the first of which bears more than a passing similarity to Inspector Callahan's fictional interaction with Scorpio.

Leon v. State, 410 So. 2d 201 (Fla. App.), rev. den., 417 So. 2d 329 (Fla. 1982)

SCHWARTZ, Judge.

Leon was convicted of kidnapping Louis Gachelin and the possession of a firearm in the commission of that felony. The only point on his appeal which deserves discussion is the claim that his formal confessions should have been suppressed as the product of police threats and physical violence which had admittedly been asserted against him. We do not agree.

The issue arises from a highly unusual sequence of events. For our purposes, it began when Leon arrived at a shopping center parking lot for a prearranged meeting to collect a ransom from Gachelin's brother, Frank. At that time, the victim was being confined at gunpoint in an unknown location by Leon's co-defendant, Frantz Armand. After an inconclusive confrontation, Leon drew a gun on Frank, whereupon the defendant was at once taken into custody by a number of officers who had accompanied Frank to the scene. For the very good reason that Louis' life was in grave danger from Armand if Leon (or the officers) did not return within a short time, the police immediately demanded that the defendant tell them where he was. When he at first refused, he was set upon by several of the officers. They threatened and physically abused him by twisting his arm behind his back and choking him until he revealed where Louis was being held. The officers went to the designated apartment, rescued Louis and arrested Armand.

In the meantime, Leon was taken to the police station. There, he was questioned by detectives who had not been involved in the violence at the scene of his arrest, in the presence of none of

the officers who had. After being informed of his rights and signing a *Miranda* waiver form which stated—as confirmed by the interrogating officers, who themselves employed no improper methods—that he did so understandingly, voluntarily, and "of [his] own free will without any threats or promises,"[2] Leon gave full oral and written confessions to the crime. This process was concluded some five hours after his arrest.

Before trial, the defendant moved to suppress the police-station statements on the ground that they resulted from the allegedly improper police activity which occurred when he was arrested. (The prosecution announced that it would not seek to introduce testimony as to what he was forced to say at that time.) The court denied the motion essentially because the later confessions were given independently of the earlier events.

---

2. At the hearing on his motion to suppress, the defendant contrarily stated that he had spoken to the detectives only "because I was scared, because they [the arresting officers] told me they would kill me." While this testimony may be disregarded in the face of the contrary evidence, it is noteworthy that Leon never suggested that he was influenced by a concern that he had already irretrievably incriminated himself by the first statement that he knew where the victim was. Hence, we do not consider, and it is not argued, that the so-called "cat out of the bag" analysis of the admissibility of subsequent confessions is applicable or helpful in resolving the present case. Cf. *United States v. Bayer*, 331 U.S. 532, 67 S. Ct. 1394, 91 L. Ed. 1654 (1947).

* * *

The record amply supports this determination. It is well settled that, under appropriate circumstances, the effect of an initial impropriety, even a coercive one, in securing a confession may be removed by intervening events, with the result that a subsequent statement is rendered "free of the primary taint" and thus admissible into evidence as the expression of a free and voluntary act.

We hold that the trial judge properly found that the threats and violence which took place at the scene of the arrest did not constitutionally infect the later confessions and that this rule is therefore applicable here.

In reaching this conclusion, we have considered the effect of numerous factors. Among the most important is that the force and threats asserted upon Leon in the parking lot were understandably motivated by the immediate necessity to find the victim and save his life. Unlike the situation in every authority cited by the defendant, and while it may have had that collateral effect, the violence was *not* inflicted in order to secure a confession or provide other evidence to establish the defendant's guilt.

Several decisions—and none which hold otherwise have been cited or discovered—have determined that a confession is not invalidated merely because persons other than those who obtained it have, for their own reasons, previously inflicted even unjustified force upon the defendant.[3]

* * *

Although the rationale has not previously been spelled out, the fact that any coercion was not employed to get a confession is highly significant...in terms of the basic issue with which the "taint" decisions are all concerned: whether the ultimate confession is a product of or is caused by the force, or by an exercise of the defendant's own will. When it appears—and it is known to the defendant—that the force is unrelated to whether he confesses or not, it is impossible, on the face of it, to say that a later statement has been *caused* by the effect of that coercion or fear of its repetition. This observation applies with particular force to the present case. It must have been obvious to Leon that the arresting

officers attacked him only to learn the victim's whereabouts, and that his revelation of that location entirely satisfied their wishes. Thereafter, there was no basis to believe that any force would be used for any other reason—specifically, to secure a confession. Indeed, this is therefore the perhaps unique case in which, by its cathartic effect, the very making of the defendant's initial utterance was itself an important factor in dissipating the effect of the coercive influence which produced it. Because he had already told the police what they wanted to know, and the reason the force was asserted had therefore vanished, the effect of the violence may be deemed to have entirely passed when Leon gave the confessions now in question.

The elimination of any causative effect of the coercion is shown also by the more commonly discussed elements that a complete set of *Miranda* warnings was meticulously given, understood, and waived before the subsequent statements; that over five hours transpired between the violence and the formalization of those statements; and that the confessions were secured by entirely different officers than those who employed the coercive tactics.

* * *

For these reasons, we find no basis to disturb the trial judge's conclusion that, considering the totality of the circumstances, the challenged confessions were freely and voluntarily made.

* * *

FERGUSON, Judge (dissenting).

* * *

For the first time in history, and the majority concedes as much, there is articulated a distinction between violent police conduct, the purpose of which is to gain information which might save a life, and such conduct employed for the pur-

---

3. . . . We do not attempt to resolve the moral and philosophical problem of whether the force used on Leon in the emergency, life-threatening situation presented to the arresting officers was "justified" or "proper."

pose of obtaining evidence to be used in a court of law. The majority holds that where the illegal conduct is motivated by the first consideration no coercive taint will attach so as to render inadmissible evidence subsequently obtained for the purpose of securing a conviction. In essence, evidence of the whereabouts of a victim may be obtained using "rack and pinion" techniques if the officer on the scene determines the situation life-threatening, and after the information sought has been extracted the status is "deemed" as if the illegality had never occurred—an eerie proposition which should be rejected outright for all too obvious reasons. This rationale would dispose of the requirement imposed upon the State to show that an accused, at the time of giving a subsequent confession, was free from external pressures associated with an earlier illegality.

* * *

The circumstances here during and following the arrest were oppressive. There was no break in the stream of events following the initial physical abuse, the taking into custody, and the confession.

* * *

After this defendant was arrested he was taken from the scene to other locations and not transported to police headquarters for more than one hour. Approximately two hours after arrival at the station he had signed a written waiver of his constitutional rights. Contrary to the trial court's finding, defendant, for the entire period beginning with the violent apprehension to the confession, was continually in custody of the same authority and the same officers who were present at the scene of the apprehension, some of whom had taken an active part in it. No reweighing of the evidence is necessary to reach the conclusion that the state failed in its burden of showing by a preponderance of the evidence that defendant voluntarily and intelligently waived his constitutional rights. The confession should have been suppressed.

Notes and Questions

1. How would you characterize the police conduct that initially resulted in Leon's revealing the whereabouts of his kidnap victim? Do you suppose that this is the type of behavior that Chief Justice Burger would consider "outrageous and egregious"? That Professor Klockars would affirm that "I know I would want [them] to do what [they] did"? Consider footnote 3 in the majority opinion in *Leon.*

2. It is important to observe that Leon made two sets of statements, the first in the shopping center parking lot when the police accosted him (S1) and the second when he later was taken to the police station (S2). Which statements were admitted into evidence at his trial? Under the majority opinion's analysis, is the court confronted with a true Dirty Harry problem in *Leon*? What if Leon had not confessed at the police station and if only S1 were at issue: Should those statements be admissible in evidence?

3. After his conviction was affirmed by the Florida state courts, Leon sought a new trial by petitioning the federal courts for habeas corpus relief. The federal courts agreed that Leon's constitutional rights had not been violated. *See Leon v. Wainwright*, 734 F.2d 770 (11th Cir. 1984).

Next, consider the facts of *Brown v. Mississippi*, which was decided by the U.S. Supreme Court in 1936. These facts are quoted from a dissenting opinion written by a judge on the Mississippi Supreme Court. The state supreme court had approved admitting the defendants' confessions into evidence and had affirmed their convictions and death sentences.

Brown v. Mississippi, 297 U.S. 278, 56 S. Ct. 461, 80 L. Ed. 682 (1936)

* * *

"The crime with which these defendants, all ignorant negroes, are charged, was discovered about one o'clock p.m. on Friday, March 30,1934. On that night one Dial, a deputy sheriff, accompanied by others, came to the home of Ellington, one of the defendants, and requested him to accompany them to the house of the deceased, and there a number of white men were gathered, who began to accuse the defendant of the crime. Upon his denial they seized him, and with the participation of the deputy they hanged him by a rope to the limb of a tree, and, having let him down, they hung him again, and when he was let down the second time, and he still protested his innocence, he was tied to a tree and whipped, and, still declining to accede to the demands that he confess, he was finally released and he returned with some difficulty to his home, suffering intense pain and agony. The record of the testimony shows that the signs of the rope on his neck were plainly visible during the so-called trial. A day or two thereafter the said deputy, accompanied by another, returned to the home of the said defendant and arrested him, and departed with the prisoner towards the jail in an adjoining county, but went by a route which led into the State of Alabama; and while on the way, in that State, the deputy stopped and again severely whipped the defendant, declaring that he would continue the whipping until he confessed, and the defendant then agreed to confess to such a statement as the deputy would dictate, and he did so, after which he was delivered to jail.

"The other two defendants, Ed Brown and Henry Shields, were also arrested and taken to the same jail. On Sunday night, April 1, 1934, the same deputy, accompanied by a number of white men, one of whom was also an officer, and by the jailer, came to the jail, and the two last named defendants were made to strip and they were laid over chairs and their backs were cut to pieces with a leather strap with buckles on it, and they were likewise made by the deputy definitely to understand that the whipping would be continued unless and until they confessed, and not only confessed, but confessed in every matter of detail as demanded by those present; and in this manner the defendants confessed the crime, and, as the whippings progressed and were repeated, they changed or adjusted their confession in all particulars of detail so as to conform to the demands of their torturers. When the confessions had been obtained in the exact form and contents as desired by the mob, they left with the parting admonition and warning that, if the defendants changed their story at any time in any respect from the last stated, the perpetrators of the outrage would administer the same or equally effective treatment.

* * *

The defendants were put on the stand, and by their testimony the facts and the details thereof as to the manner by which the confessions were extorted from them were fully developed, and it is further disclosed by the record that the same deputy, Dial, under whose guiding hand and active participation the tortures to coerce the confessions were administered, was actively in the performance of the supposed duties of a court deputy in the courthouse and in the presence of the prisoners during what is denominated, in complimentary terms, the trial of these defendants. This deputy was put on the stand by the state in rebuttal, and admitted the whippings. It is interesting to note that in his testimony with reference to the whipping of the defendant Ellington, and in response to the injury as to how severely he was whipped, the deputy stated, 'Not too much for a negro; not as much as I would have done if it were left to me.'

* * *

The facts are not only undisputed, they are admitted, and admitted to have been done by officers of the state, in conjunction with other participants, and all this was definitely well known to everybody connected with the trial, and during the trial, including the state's prosecuting attorney and the trial judge presiding."

* * *

Notes and Questions

1. What action would you take if you were a federal court judge confronted with the facts in *Brown v. Mississippi?* Should it matter that a state court had already reviewed the defendants' claims and found no constitutional error?

2. What new concern arises in connection with the defendants' confessions in *Brown v. Mississippi* that was not an issue in *Brewer v. Williams, Leon v. State,* or the hypothetical Dirty Harry problem? Would your resolution of the issues presented in *Brown* be any different if, after having been subjected to the deputy sheriff's course of conduct, the defendants had led the deputy to a hidden grave in which the murder victim was buried?

3. The Supreme Court unanimously reversed the Mississippi Supreme Court's judgment in *Brown v. Mississippi.* Chief Justice Hughes explained that

the State is free to regulate the procedure of its courts in accordance with its own conceptions of policy, unless in doing so it "offends some principle of justice so rooted in the traditions and conscience of our peo-

ple as to be ranked as fundamental." *Quoting Snyder v. Massachusetts,* 291 U.S. 97, 105, 54 S. Ct. 330, 332, 78 L. Ed. 674, 677 (1934).

He concluded that "it would be difficult to conceive of methods more revolting to the sense of justice than those taken to procure the confessions of these petitioners, and the use of the confessions thus obtained as the bases for conviction and sentence was a clear denial of due process."

4. What principles of justice are "so rooted in the traditions and conscience of our people as to be ranked as fundamental"? If the police went too far in *Brown v. Mississippi,* what about the police taking a suspected seller of illegal drugs to the hospital to have his stomach pumped after observing the suspect swallow what appeared to be drugs? Should such methods be disapproved? Would it matter if the police were in a position to observe the suspect swallow the substance only after they had illegally entered his home?

Rochin v. California, 342 U.S. 165, 72 S. Ct. 205, 96 L. Ed. 183 (1952)

Mr. Justice **Frankfurter delivered the opinion of the Court.

Having "some information that [the petitioner here] was selling narcotics," three deputy sheriffs of the County of Los Angeles, on the morning of July 1, 1949, made for the two-story dwelling house in which Rochin lived with his mother, common-law wife, brothers and sisters. Finding the outside door open, they entered and then forced open the door to Rochin's room on the second floor. Inside they found petitioner sitting partly dressed on the side of the bed, upon which his wife was lying. On a "night stand" beside the bed the deputies spied two capsules. When asked "Whose stuff [sic] in this?" Rochin seized the capsules and put them in his mouth.

A struggle ensued, in the course of which the three officers "jumped upon him" and attempted to extract the capsules. The force they applied proved unavailing against Rochin's resistance. He was handcuffed and taken to a hospital. At the direction of one of the officers a doctor forced an emetic solution through a tube into Rochin's stomach against his will. This "stomach pumping" produced vomiting. In the vomited matter were found two capsules which proved to contain morphine.

Rochin was brought to trial before a California Superior Court, sitting without a jury, on the charge of possessing "a preparation of morphine" in violation of the California Health and Safety Code, 1947, § 11.500. Rochin was convicted and sentenced to sixty days' imprisonment. The chief evidence against him was the two capsules.

* * *

We are compelled to conclude that the proceedings by which this conviction was obtained do more than offend some fastidious squeamish or private sentimentalism about combatting crime too energetically. This is conduct that shocks the conscience. Illegally breaking into the privacy of the petitioner, the struggle to open his mouth and remove what was there, the forcible extraction of his stomach's contents—this course of proceeding by agents of government to obtain evidence is bound to offend even hardened sensibilities. They are methods too close to the rack and the screw to permit of constitutional differentiation.

It has long since ceased to be true that due process of law is heedless of the means by which otherwise relevant and credible evidence is obtained. This was not true even before the series of recent cases enforced the constitutional principle that the States may not base convictions upon confessions, however much verified, obtained by coercion. These decisions are not arbitrary exceptions to the comprehensive right of States to fashion their own rules of evidence for criminal trials. They are not sports in our constitutional law but applications of a general principle. They are only instances of the general requirement that States in their prosecutions respect certain decencies of civilized conduct. Due process of law, as a historic and generative principle, precludes defining, and thereby confining, these standards of conduct more precisely than to say that convictions cannot be brought about by methods that offend "a sense of justice." It would be a stultification of the responsibility which the course of constitutional history has cast upon this Court to hold that in order to convict a man the police cannot extract by force what is in his mind but can extract what is in his stomach.

To attempt in this case to distinguish what lawyers call "real evidence" from verbal evidence is to ignore the reasons for excluding coerced confessions. Use of involuntary verbal confessions in State criminal trials is constitutionally obnoxious not only because of their unreliability. They are inadmissible under the Due Process Clause even though statements contained in them may be independently established as true. Coerced confessions offend the community's sense of fair play and decency. So here, to sanction the brutal conduct which naturally enough was condemned by the court whose judgment is before us, would be to afford brutality the cloak of law. Nothing would be more calculated to discredit law and therefore by brutalize the temper of a society.

* * *

Notes and Questions

1. If clarity of rules and the related ability of the police and courts to follow and apply those rules are legitimate concerns of the law of criminal procedure, how successful is Justice Frankfurter's explanation that the police conduct in *Rochin* "shocks the conscience"? What sort of guidance does a "shock-the-conscience" test provide for future cases? Whose conscience? How far must conduct go before it becomes shocking? Because the sheriff deputies escorted Rochin to a hospital for procedures supervised by a physician, precisely what did the Court find shocking to the conscience in this case?

2. Note that the Court relied on the Fourteenth Amendment's due process clause to invalidate the convictions in both *Brown v. Mississippi* and *Rochin v. California*. "Due process of law" is an inherently imprecise standard. You may have wondered why, in *Brown,* the justices did not base their decision on the more specific prohibition against compelled self-incrimination that is found within the Fifth Amendment, or in *Rochin* why the Court did not invoke the Fourth

Amendment's protection against unreasonable searches and seizures. The answers largely lie in the dates these cases were decided (1936 and 1952, respectively) and the Court's position at those times on whether rights specified in the Fifth Amendment, the Fourth Amendment, and elsewhere in the Bill of Rights directly applied to criminal proceedings in the state courts. We elaborate on this issue in Chapter 2.

3. Justice Frankfurter acknowledged elsewhere in *Rochin* that giving meaning to a concept such as due process of law "is a function of the process of judgment, [and] the judgment is bound to fall differently at different times and differently at the same time through different judges." Nevertheless, he insisted that

> the vague contours of the Due Process Clause do not leave judges at large. We may not draw on our merely personal and private notions and disregard the limits that bind judges in their judicial function. Even though the concept of due process of law is

not final and fixed, these limits are derived from considerations that are fused in the whole nature of our judicial process. ...These are considerations deeply rooted in reason and in the compelling traditions of the legal profession.

342 U.S., at 170–71, 72 S. Ct., at 208–09, 96 L. Ed., at 189.

When standards are so imprecise, is there any doubt that, try as they might to avoid it, the general life experiences and values that inform judges' reason will influence the decision of cases? Isn't this inevitable? Is it altogether bad?

* * * * *

Value judgments undeniably play a role in constitutional adjudication and in the law generally. The following excerpt is from a classic writing that describes how different value orientations can have significant implications for how criminal justice is administered and for criminal procedure law.

Herbert L. Packer, *The Limits of the Criminal Sanction* 152–173 (Stanford University Press, 1968)

...The kind of criminal process we have depends importantly on certain value choices that are reflected, explicitly or implicitly, in its habitual functioning. The kind of model we need is one that permits us to recognize explicitly the value choices that underlie the details of the criminal process. In a word, what we need is a *normative* model or models. It will take more than one model, but it will not take more than two.

* * *

I call these two models the Due Process Model and the Crime Control Model.

* * *

Crime Control Values. The value system that underlies the Crime Control Model is based on the proposition that the repression of criminal conduct is by far the most important function to be performed by the criminal process. The failure of law enforcement to bring criminal conduct under tight control is viewed as leading to the breakdown of public order and thence to the disappearance of an important condition of human freedom. If the laws go unenforced—which is to say, if it is perceived that there is a high percentage of failure to apprehend and convict in the criminal process—a general disregard for legal controls tends to develop. The law-abiding citizen then becomes the victim of all sorts of unjustifiable invasions of his interests. His security of person and property is sharply diminished, and, therefore, so is his liberty to function as a member of society. The claim ultimately is that the criminal process is a positive guarantor of social freedom. In order to achieve this high purpose, the Crime Control Model requires that primary attention be paid to the efficiency with which the criminal process operates to screen suspects, determine guilt, and secure appropriate dispositions of persons convicted of crime.

Efficiency of operation is not, of course, a criterion that can be applied in a vacuum. By "efficiency" we mean the system's capacity to apprehend, try, convict, and dispose of a high proportion of criminal offenders whose offenses become known.

* * *

The model, in order to operate successfully, must produce a high rate of apprehension and conviction, and must do so in a context where the magnitudes being dealt with are very large and the resources for dealing with them are very limited. There must then be a premium on speed and finality. Speed, in turn, depends on informality and on uniformity; finality depends on minimizing the occasions for challenge. The process must not be cluttered up with ceremonious rituals that do not advance the progress of a case. Facts can be established more quickly through interrogation in a police station than through the formal process of examination and cross-examination in a court. It follows that extra-judicial processes should be preferred to judicial processes, informal operations to formal ones. But informality is not enough; there must also be uniformity. Routine, stereotyped procedures are essential if large numbers are being handled.

* * *

The criminal process, in this model, is seen as a screening process in which each successive stage—pre-arrest investigation, arrest, post-arrest investigation, preparation for trial, trial or entry of plea conviction, disposition—involves a series of routinized operations whose success is gauged primarily by their tendency to pass the case along to a successful conclusion.

What is a successful conclusion? One that throws off at an early stage those cases in which it appears unlikely that the person apprehended is an offender and then secures, as expeditiously as possible, the conviction of the rest, with a minimum of occasions for challenge, let alone post-audit. By the application of adminis-

trative expertness, primarily that of the police and prosecutors, an early determination of probable innocence or guilt emerges. Those who are probably innocent are screened out. Those who are probably guilty are passed quickly through the remaining stages of the process. The key to the operation of the model regarding those who are not screened out is what I shall call a presumption of guilt.

* * *

The presumption of guilt is what makes it possible for the system to deal efficiently with large numbers, as the Crime Control Model demands. The supposition is that the screening processes operated by police and prosecutors are reliable indicators of probable guilt. Once a man has been arrested and investigated without being found to be probably innocent, or, to put it differently, once a determination has been made that there is enough evidence of guilt to permit holding him for further action, then all subsequent activity directed toward him is based on the view that he is probably guilty. The precise point at which this occurs will vary from case to case; in many cases it will occur as soon as the suspect is arrested, or even before, if the evidence of probable guilt that has come to the attention of the authorities is sufficiently strong. But in any case the presumption of guilt will begin to operate well before the "suspect" becomes a "defendant."

The presumption of guilt is not, of course, a thing. Nor is it even a rule of law in the usual sense. It simply is the consequence of a complex of attitudes, a mood. If there is confidence in the reliability of informal administrative fact-finding activities that take place in the early stages of the criminal process, the remaining stages of the process can be relatively perfunctory without any loss in operating efficiency. The presumption of guilt, as it operates in the Crime Control Model, is the operational expression of that confidence.

* * *

In the presumption of guilt this model finds a factual predicate for the position that the dominant goal of repressing crime can be achieved through highly summary processes without any great loss of efficiency (as previously defined), because of the probability that, in the run of cases, the preliminary screening processes operated by the police and the prosecuting officials contain adequate guarantees of reliable fact-finding. Indeed, the model takes an even stronger position. It is that subsequent processes, particularly those of a formal adjudicatory nature, are unlikely to produce as reliable fact-finding as the expert administrative process that precedes them is capable of. The criminal process thus must put special weight on the quality of administrative fact-finding. It becomes important, then, to place as few restrictions as possible on the character of the administrative fact-finding processes and to limit restrictions to such as enhance reliability, excluding those designed for other purposes.

* * *

In this model, as I have suggested, the center of gravity for the process lies in the early, administrative fact-finding stages. The complementary proposition is that the subsequent stages are relatively unimportant and should be truncated as much as possible. This, too, produces tensions with presently dominant ideology. The pure Crime Control Model has very little use for many conspicuous features of the adjudicative process, and in real life works out a number of ingenious compromises with them. Even in the pure model, however, there have to be devices for dealing with the suspect after the preliminary screening process has resulted in a determination of probable guilt. The focal device, as we shall see, is the plea of guilty: through its use, adjudicative fact-finding is reduced to a minimum. It might be said of the Crime Control Model that, when reduced to its barest essentials and operating at its most successful pitch, it offers two possibilities: an administrative fact-finding process leading (1) to exoneration of the suspect or (2) to the entry of a plea of guilty.

Due Process Values. If the Crime Control Model resembles an assembly line, the Due Process Model looks very much like an obstacle course. Each of its successive stages is designed to present formidable impediments to carrying the accused any further along in the process. Its ideology is not the converse of that

underlying the Crime Control Model. It does not rest on the idea that it is not socially desirable to repress crime, although critics of its application have been known to claim so. Its ideology is composed of a complex of ideas, some of them based on judgments about the efficacy of crime control devices, others having to do with quite different considerations.

* * *

The Due Process Model encounters its rival on the Crime Control Model's own ground in respect to the reliability of fact-finding processes. The Crime Control Model, as we have suggested, places heavy reliance on the ability of investigative and prosecutorial officers, acting in an informal setting in which their distinctive skills are given full sway, to elicit and reconstruct a tolerably accurate account of what actually took place in an alleged criminal event. The Due Process Model rejects this premise and substitutes for it a view of informal, nonadjudicative fact-finding that stresses the possibility of error. People are notoriously poor observers of disturbing events—the more emotion-arousing the context, the greater the possibility that recollection will be incorrect: confessions and admissions by persons in police custody may be induced by physical or psychological coercion so that the police end up hearing what the suspect thinks they want to hear rather than the truth; witnesses may be animated by a bias or interest that no one would trouble to discover except one specially charged with protecting the interests of the accused (as the police are not). Considerations of this kind all lead to a rejection of informal fact-finding processes as definitive of factual guilt and to an insistence on formal, adjudicative, adversary fact-finding processes in which the factual case against the accused is publicly heard by an impartial tribunal and is evaluated only after the accused has had a full opportunity to discredit the case against him. Even then, the distrust of fact-finding processes that animates the Due Process Model is not dissipated. The possibilities of human error being what they are, further scrutiny is necessary, or at least must be available, in case facts have been overlooked or suppressed in the heat of battle. How far this subsequent scrutiny must be available is a hotly controverted issue today. In the pure Due Process Model the answer would be: at least as long as there is an allegation of factual error that has not received an adjudicative hearing in a fact-finding context. The demand for finality is thus very low in the Due Process Model.

This strand of due process ideology is not enough to sustain the model. If all that were at issue between the two models was a series of questions about the reliability of fact-finding processes, we would have but one model of the criminal process, the nature of whose constituent elements would pose questions of fact not of value.

* * *

It still remains to ask how much weight is to be given to the competing demands of reliability (a high degree of probability in each case that factual guilt has been accurately determined) and efficiency (expeditious handling of the large numbers of cases that the process ingests). The Crime Control Model is more optimistic about the improbability of error in a significant number of cases; but it is also, though only in part therefore, more tolerant about the amount of error that it will put up with. The Due Process Model insists on the prevention and elimination of mistakes to the extent possible; the Crime Control Model accepts the probability of mistakes up to the level at which they interfere with the goal of repressing crime, either because too many guilty people are escaping, or, more subtly, because general awareness of the unreliability of the process leads to a decrease in the deterrent efficacy of the criminal law. In this view, reliability and efficiency are not polar opposites but rather complementary characteristics. The system is reliable *because* efficient; reliability becomes a matter of independent concern only when it becomes so attenuated as to impair efficiency. All of this the Due Process Model rejects. If efficiency demands short-cuts around reliability, then absolute efficiency must be rejected. The aim of the process is at least as much to protect the factually innocent as it is to convict the factually guilty.

* * *

The combination of stigma and loss of liberty that is embodied in the end result of the criminal process is viewed as being the heaviest deprivation that government can inflict on the individual. Furthermore, the processes that culminate in these highly afflictive sanctions are seen as in themselves coercive, restricting, and demeaning. Power is always subject to abuse—sometimes subtle, other times, as in the criminal process, open and ugly. Precisely because of its potency in subjecting the individual to the coercive power of the state, the criminal process must, in this model, be subjected to controls that prevent it from operating with maximal efficiency. According to this ideology, maximal efficiency means maximal tyranny. And, although no one would assert that minimal efficiency means minimal tyranny, the proponents of the Due Process Model would accept with considerable equanimity a substantial diminution in the efficiency with which the criminal process operates in the interest of preventing official oppression of the individual.

The most modest-seeming but potentially far-reaching mechanism by which the Due Process Model implements these anti-authoritarian values is the doctrine of legal guilt. According to this doctrine, a person is not to be held guilty of crime merely on a showing that in all probability, based upon reliable evidence, he did factually what he is said to have done. Instead, he is to be held guilty if and only if these factual determinations are made in procedurally regular fashion and by authorities acting within competencies duly allocated to them. Furthermore, he is not to be held guilty, even though the factual determination is or might be adverse to him, if various rules designed to protect him and to safeguard the integrity of the process are not given effect; the tribunal that convicts him must have the power to deal with his kind of case ("jurisdiction") and must be geographically appropriate ("venue"); too long a time must not have elapsed since the offense was committed ("statute of limitations"); he must not have been previously convicted or acquitted of the same or a substantially similar offense ("double jeopardy"); he must not fall within a category of persons, such as children or the insane, who are legally immune to conviction ("criminal responsibility"); and so on. None of these requirements has anything to do with the factual question of whether the person did or did not engage in the conduct that is charged as the offense against him; yet favorable answers to any of them will mean that he is legally innocent. Wherever the competence to make adequate factual determinations lies, it is apparent that only a tribunal that is aware of these guilt-defeating doctrines and is willing to apply them can be viewed as competent to make determinations of legal guilt. The police and the prosecutors are ruled out by lack of competence, in the first instance, and by lack of assurance of willingness, in the second. Only an impartial tribunal can be trusted to make determinations of legal as opposed to factual guilt.

* * *

The possibility of legal innocence is expanded enormously when the criminal process is viewed as the appropriate forum for correcting its own abuses. This notion may well account for a greater amount of the distance between the two models than any other. In theory the Crime Control Model can tolerate rules that forbid illegal arrests, unreasonable searches, coercive interrogations, and the like. What it cannot tolerate is the vindication of those rules in the criminal process itself through the exclusion of evidence illegally obtained or through the reversal of convictions in cases where the criminal process has breached the rules laid down for its observance. And the Due Process Model, although it may in the first instance be addressed to the maintenance of reliable fact-finding techniques, comes eventually to incorporate prophylactic and deterrent rules that result in the release of the factually guilty even in cases in which blotting out the illegality would still leave an adjudicative fact-finder convinced of the accused person's guilt. Only by penalizing errant police and prosecutors within the criminal process itself can adequate pressure be maintained, so the argument runs, to induce conformity with the Due Process Model.

Another strand in the complex of attitudes underlying the Due Process Model is the idea—itself a shorthand statement for a complex of attitudes—of equality. This notion has only recently emerged as an explicit basis for pressing the demands of the Due Process Model, but it appears to represent, at least in its potential, a most powerful norm for influencing official con-duct. Stated most starkly, the ideal of equality holds that "there can be no equal justice where the kind of trial a man gets depends on the amount of money he has." The factual predicate underlying this assertion is that there are gross inequalities in the financial means of criminal defendants as a class, that in an adversary system of criminal justice an effective defense is largely a function of the resources that can be mustered on behalf of the accused, and that the very large proportion of criminal defendants who are, operationally speaking, "indigent" will thus be denied an effective defense.

* * *

There is a final strand of thought in the Due Process Model that is often ignored but that needs to be candidly faced if thought on the subject is not to be obscured. This is a mood of skepticism about the morality and utility of the criminal sanction, taken either as a whole or in some of its applications.

* * *

In short, doubts about the ends for which power is being exercised create pressure to limit the discretion with which that power is exercised.

* * *

There are two kinds of problems that need to be dealt with in any model of the criminal process. One is what the rules shall be. The other is how the rules shall be implemented. The second is at least as important as the first. As we shall see time and again in our detailed development of the models, the distinctive difference between the two models is not only in the rules of conduct that they lay down but also in the sanctions that are to be invoked when a claim is presented that the rules have been breached and, no less importantly, in the timing that is permitted or required for the invocation of those sanctions.

As I have already suggested, the Due Process Model locates at least some of the sanctions for breach of the operative rules in the criminal process itself. The relation between these two aspects of the process—the rules and the sanctions for their breach—is a purely formal one unless there is some mechanism for bringing them into play with each other. The hinge between them in the Due Process Model is the availability of legal counsel. This has a double aspect. Many of the rules that the model requires are couched in terms of the availability of counsel to do various things at various stages of the process—this is the conventionally recognized aspect; beyond it, there is a pervasive assumption that counsel is necessary in order to invoke sanctions for breach of any of the rules. The more freely available these sanctions are, the more important is the role of counsel in seeing to it that the sanctions are appropriately invoked. If the process is seen as a series of occasions for checking its own operation, the role of counsel is a much more nearly central one than is the case in a process that is seen as primarily concerned with expeditious determination of factual guilt. And if equality of operation is a governing norm, the availability of counsel to some is seen as requiring it for all. Of all the controverted aspects of the criminal process, the right to counsel, including the role of government in its provision, is the most dependent on what one's model of the process looks like, and the least susceptible of resolution unless one has confronted the antinomies of the two models.

* * *

What assumptions do we make about the sources of authority to shape the real-world operations of the criminal process? Recognizing that our models are only models, what agencies of government have the power to pick and choose between their competing demands? Once again, the limiting features of the American context come into play. Ours is not a system of legislative supremacy. The distinctively American institution of judicial review exercises a limiting and ultimately a shaping influence on the criminal process. Because the Crime Control Model is basically an affirmative model, emphasizing at every turn the existence and exercise of official power, its validating authority is ultimately legislative (although proximately administrative). Because the Due Process Model is basically a negative model, asserting limits on the nature of official power and on the modes of its exercise, its validating authority is judicial and requires an appeal to supra-legislative law, to the law of the Constitution. To the extent that tensions between the two models are resolved by deference to the Due Process Model, the authoritative force at work is the judicial power, working in the distinctively judicial mode of invoking the sanction of nullity. That is at once the strength and the weakness of the Due Process Model: its strength because in our system the appeal to the Constitution provides the last and the overriding word; its weakness because saying no in specific cases is an exercise in futility unless there is a general willingness on the part of the officials who operate the process to apply negative prescriptions across the board. It is no accident that statements reinforcing the Due Process Model come from the courts, while at the same time facts denying it are established by the police and prosecutors.

CONCLUSION

The issues introduced in this chapter illustrate many of the fundamental tensions that are inherent in criminal procedure law. Few other areas of law require the resolution of such dramatically opposed interests, with such compelling consequences to both individual citizens and the government. The operating rules of criminal procedure law must prioritize and often resolve conflicts between profoundly significant constitutional and policy objectives. These rules must be effective in the uncompromising context of the investigation and trial of criminal cases in which individuals and entire communities may have suffered grievous wrongs. As Justice Frankfurter once observed, "It is a fair summary of history to say that the safeguards of liberty have frequently been forged in controversies involving not very nice people." *United States v. Rabinowitz,* 336 U.S. 56, 69, 70 S. Ct. 430, 94 L. Ed. 653 (1950) (dissenting opinion).

One of the objectives of criminal procedure law is to promote reliable fact finding, or the ascertainment of the truth. This goal occasionally must be tempered in order to protect the individual liberties cherished by Americans, including rights to be free from overbearing police, prosecutorial, and judicial conduct. Respecting the sovereignty of the states within this country's federalistic governmental system and helping to resolve cases finally and efficiently are additional ends of the law of criminal procedure. Assigning those interests weight and then balancing them to choose between competing interests is largely the task of the courts through their interpretation and application of statutes and constitutional principles.

We have stressed in this chapter that the study of criminal procedure law appropriately focuses on the reasoning and analysis employed by the courts in justifying their decisions. It is far more important to understand how and why a court decided a case as it did than simply to be able to recite the case holding. We strongly urge that you "brief" cases in the course of your studies to promote your understanding of the reasoning used by the courts and your ability to apply relevant legal principles in different contexts. There is no better tool for critically analyzing judicial rationale than the briefing process.

Value judgments often influence the resolution of criminal procedure issues. Professor Packer's description of the "crime control" and "due-process" models of criminal procedure is one helpful summary of the dominant competing values in this area of law. You undoubtedly will notice the clash between the crime control and due-process schools of thought in the cases that lie ahead. Indeed, justifying preferences for the principles represented by these different models, in the context of deciding individual cases, is perhaps the principal recurring challenge in criminal procedure law.

CHAPTER 2

Building Blocks for the Study of Criminal Procedure Law

In this chapter, we cover several topics that help establish a foundation for the specific issues that will be addressed subsequently in this book. We first describe the structure of the state and federal court systems and explain how a criminal case is processed leading up to court action. Next, we discuss the case reporters in which judicial opinions are published and rules for citing those reporters. We then review the historical controversy surrounding whether the freedoms enumerated in the U.S. Constitution's Bill of Rights apply to state proceedings. The next section considers the significance of state constitutions to criminal procedure law. Finally, we offer brief comment on the importance of students' becoming familiar with legal research techniques, a topic that is addressed at greater length in Appendix A of this book.

This chapter is unusual in that we depart from the *case method* of study—which you already have encountered when we considered *Brewer v. Williams*—in favor of a narrative description of these topics. The remainder of this book relies heavily on presenting judicial decisions to convey information and, more importantly, to help sharpen analytical skills. At least some of the subjects considered in this chapter will be familiar to some students, while other topics may be new to most readers. As all of the issues will resurface in later cases, this discussion introduces rather than serves as a comprehensive account of these important subjects.

ON COURTS AND CONSTITUTIONS: STATE AND FEDERAL RELATIONSHIPS

One of the distinguishing features of American government is *federalism,* or the division of power between the states and the national government. Following much impassioned debate, the framers of the U.S. Constitution defined the proper relationship between the state and federal governments and their respective spheres of authority. The Constitution enumerates and thus limits the power of the legislative, executive, and judicial branches of the federal government.

The Tenth Amendment to the Constitution, which was ratified in 1791, three years after the Constitution was adopted, provides that powers not delegated to the federal government by that founding charter are reserved to the states. The Tenth Amendment, the last in the group of amendments known as the Bill of Rights, was adopted as part of a compromise between the Federalists, who favored a strong national government and urged that the U.S. Constitution be ratified by the original 13 states, and the Anti-federalists, who distrusted the idea of a strong national sovereign and opposed ratification of the Constitution for that reason.

State governments and the federal government have distinctive powers in some matters, and in other areas their authority overlaps. For the most part, the states have control over the criminal laws they choose to adopt and over deciding how violators of those laws should be punished. The federal government, through Congress, has defined certain conduct as crimes against the national sovereign, and these offenses are punished according to federal law. The overwhelming number of crimes committed in this country are offenses against states and are prosecuted and disposed of in the state courts and state criminal justice systems. Nevertheless, as state and local police, prosecutors, courts, and corrections officials process suspected, accused, and convicted offenders, they are obliged to comply with many commands of the U.S. Constitution.

The application of federal constitutional rights to state criminal justice systems evolved over a good part of the 20th century. This evolution included a particularly tumultuous period during the 1960s when, under the leadership of Chief Justice Earl Warren, the Supreme Court dramatically changed the legal landscape of state and federal relationships. As a prelude to this discussion, and because familiarity with this country's court systems is important to other material that we will encounter, we begin by examining the structure of the state and federal judicial systems and the relationship between them.

The State and Federal Court Systems

Refer once again to the facts of *Brewer v. Williams,* which we presented in Chapter 1. We will use the judicial history of this case to help describe the state and federal court systems and to illustrate how a criminal case might be processed through them.

The State Court Process

Pretrial Proceedings. Robert Williams was *arrested* by the Davenport police after turning himself in on December 26, 1968. An arrest warrant had previously issued, authorizing the police to take Williams into custody for the abduction of Pamela Powers. As we will see later, the police can and often do make arrests without a warrant. Williams also was suspected of committing murder, but the death of his victim had not yet been confirmed, and since he was already in custody for abduction, it was not necessary to arrest him immediately for the more serious offense. Abduction, or kidnapping, is a state crime, and Williams's case eventually would be tried in the Iowa state courts.[1]

Immediately following his arrest, Williams was *booked* on the abduction charge. When the police book a suspected offender, they record the suspect's name and address, the offense for which the suspect was arrested, and the date and time of the booking. The suspect is fingerprinted and photographed. These record-keeping procedures are usually completed at the police station or at the local jail. They are performed routinely, and they do not determine whether or with what offense a suspect later will formally be charged.

A *complaint* was filed with a magistrate, accusing Williams of abducting his victim. A complaint is a brief statement of the specific charges against the suspect. It must be supported by the sworn statement of a complainant affirming that, to the best of the complainant's knowledge, the allegations in the complaint are true. The complainant need not be the victim or a witness of the alleged crime; in fact, the arresting police officer, who may have no direct knowledge of the facts supporting the complaint, often serves as the complainant.

Since an arrest warrant had issued in this case, a judge or a magistrate had already determined that there was "probable cause" to believe that Williams had committed the crime with which he was charged in the complaint. As we will see, a defendant who is in custody on the basis of a police decision to arrest has a right to a prompt judicial determination that probable cause supports his or her continued detention. This proceeding is sometimes called a *Gerstein hearing,* after the name of the Supreme Court case mandating this procedure. *See Gerstein v. Pugh,* 420 U.S. 103, 95 S. Ct. 854, 43 L. Ed. 2d 54 (1975); *County of Riverside v. McLaughlin,* 500 U.S. 44, 111 S. Ct. 1661, 114 L. Ed. 2d 49 (1991). (See Chapter 6, pages 465–466.) Thus, had Williams been arrested without a warrant, a magistrate or judge would have reviewed the information supporting the complaint to make a probable-cause determination. Ordinarily, such review is required within 48 hours of arrest.

While still in Davenport, and before being driven to Des Moines by Detective Leaming and another police officer, "Williams was arraigned before a judge…on the outstanding arrest warrant. The judge advised him of his Miranda rights and committed him to jail." This *arraignment on the complaint*—which should not be confused with a later, postindictment or postinformation proceeding also called an arraignment—is known as the *first appearance* or the *initial appearance,* or by other names in different states. The first appearance or arraignment on the complaint is a brief, nonadversarial proceeding. Magistrates, who are court officials but are not necessarily lawyers, and are not judges, preside at first appearances in many jurisdictions. At this proceeding, Williams physically appeared before the Davenport judge. The judge was responsible for informing Williams of the charge made in the complaint and advising him of certain rights, including his right to representation by counsel, his right to appointment of counsel if indigent, and his right to remain silent. An inquiry into indigency is made so that the judge or magistrate can determine whether the accused qualifies for court-appointed counsel. Williams, of course, was already being represented by attorney McKnight in Des Moines and by attorney Kelly in Davenport. The judge was also responsible for considering *setting bail* for Williams and for fixing bail at a specific amount if Williams qualified. Defendants charged with less serious crimes sometimes are released on their own recognizance, or promise to appear, meaning that they will have to post no bail to secure their release pending further proceedings.

The next step in a typical state felony prosecution is the *preliminary hearing,* which is an adversarial hearing at which the prosecution must present evidence sufficient to convince a judge that there is probable cause to believe that the accused committed the crime alleged in the complaint. A preliminary hearing normally is held between several days and a few weeks after a first appearance. The defense rarely puts on evidence at a preliminary hearing, since the judge's job is not to decide guilt or innocence but only to determine whether credible evidence or probable cause supports the charges. This hearing allows the defense to examine some of the witnesses and evidence that the prosecution will use if and when the case is scheduled for trial. If the judge concludes that there is probable cause to believe that the defendant committed the charged crime—and seldom is this threshold showing not satisfied—the defendant is bound over for further proceedings.

In Robert Williams's case, a grand jury returned an *indictment* charging first-degree murder. The Supreme Court's opinion does not reveal at what point or why the prosecution declined to go forward on the abduction charge or when Williams was first charged with murder. A grand jury indictment is a formal charge, reflecting the judgment of at least a majority of the citizens serving on the grand jury that there is probable cause to believe that the accused committed the crime. Grand juries commonly number up to 23 people. They operate in secrecy and hear only from witnesses summoned by the prosecutor, although they have the authority to require additional witnesses to appear. The grand jury action may seem redundant to the preliminary hearing, at which probable cause also is considered. However, the grand jury historically was considered important because decisions are made by an independent panel of citizens, who presumably serve as a check against potential prosecutorial or judicial biases. Furthermore, a preliminary hearing becomes unnecessary when a grand jury returns a true bill of indictment before the preliminary hearing is scheduled to take place. Bypassing the preliminary hearing can be advantageous to the prosecution because it does not have to present witnesses or other evidence in an adversarial proceeding. We consider the grand jury process in greater detail in Chapter 6.

Many states do not make use of grand juries. Instead, a prosecutor's *information* serves as the formal charging instrument for felony trials. To provide a check on prosecutorial charging powers, a preliminary hearing and a judicial determination of probable cause usually are mandatory where prosecutors' information is the exclusive charging instrument.

The defendant then is *arraigned on the indictment or information*. The indictment or information replaces the complaint as the formal charging instrument. In this context, an arraignment is a summary proceeding at which the defendant appears in court, is advised of the charges filed, and is asked to enter a plea of guilty or not guilty to the charges. It is not uncommon for defendants to waive their right to appear at the arraignment and for their attorneys to enter a not-guilty plea on their behalf. A not-guilty plea entered at the arraignment later can be switched to a plea of guilty.

Pretrial motions must be filed not later than the arraignment in some states, or within a fixed number of days after the arraignment. Williams's counsel filed a pretrial motion "to suppress all evidence relating to or resulting from any statements Williams had made during the automobile ride from Davenport to Des Moines." Evidentiary issues that the parties know will arise during the trial frequently must be called to the trial court's attention by motion prior to trial and are resolved during a pretrial hearing. Such a procedure has several advantages. If the judge rules in the defendant's favor and, for example, orders that the contested evidence be suppressed (not admitted at the trial), the prosecution may decide that it cannot proceed to trial, and the charges may be dismissed. Alternatively, the prosecutor may decide to appeal the trial judge's ruling and ask a higher court to reverse the decision. There would be no double-jeopardy bar to such an appeal because the defendant would not previously have been exposed to a trial. Resolving motions to suppress evidence and other evidentiary issues at pretrial hearings also avoids delays during the trial and significant idle time for jurors, who are not allowed to be present while motions of this nature are litigated. After conducting a hearing, the trial judge in Williams's case denied the motion to suppress evidence and ruled that Williams's statement to Detective Leaming and the murder victim's body would be admissible at the trial. This ruling, of course, gave rise to the issue that the U.S. Supreme Court would finally address several years later.

The Trial Court. Trial courts are separated into two or more divisions in all states. In some states, traffic cases, civil disputes, and criminal cases are assigned to different courts. In many states, criminal courts are further divided. Their jurisdiction may vary according to the seriousness of a charge (e.g., misdemeanor or felony), and they may differ in whether a jury trial is available. There is little uniformity in what the different divisions of trial courts are called throughout the country. Thus, a felony trial court might be called a *district court*, as in Iowa, or a *superior court*, a *county court*, a *circuit court*, or other names, including, in New York, confusingly, a *supreme court*.

The principal job of the trial courts is to determine whether a criminal defendant is guilty as charged and, if so, to impose sentence.

As we will see, defendants have the right to be tried by a jury whenever they have been accused of committing a nonpetty crime. (See Chapter 10 pages ___.) A jury trial can be waived in most jurisdictions so that "bench trials" can be conducted by a judge sitting without a jury. In all jurisdictions, a large percentage of cases—sometimes 90% or more—are disposed of by guilty pleas. Sentencing decisions usually are made by judges, although in capital trials, juries frequently decide or recommend sentence. In a few states, juries make sentencing decisions in noncapital trials as well.

Williams's trial for first-degree murder in the Polk County District Court began approximately four months after he surrendered to the police, on April 30, 1969. The trial lasted one week. The jury returned its guilty verdict on May 6, and Williams was sentenced to life imprisonment on May 14. *State v. Williams*, 182 N.W.2d 396, 398 (Iowa 1970).

Appeals, Discretionary Review, and Postconviction Motions. In all states, a defendant has the right to *appeal* a criminal conviction. Most states have two levels of appeals courts, although several smaller and less populous states have just one appellate court. In two-tiered systems, the intermediate court usually is known as the state court of appeals. The highest court in a jurisdiction, including those states with a single appellate court, normally is called the ***state supreme court***. There are a few exceptions to this rule. For example, the highest courts in Maryland and New York are called the ***court of appeals***, and in Maine and Massachusetts, the ***supreme judicial court***. In both Oklahoma and Texas, a ***court of criminal appeals*** is the court of highest authority in criminal cases.

Robert Williams's 1969 first-degree murder conviction was appealed directly to the Iowa Supreme Court. The Iowa Court of Appeals was not created until 1977. Even if the state court of appeals had been in existence in 1969, William's appeal might have bypassed it. The most serious convictions—those involving capital offenses or, in jurisdictions without the death penalty, cases resulting in sentences of life imprisonment—often are appealed directly to the state supreme court. However, appeals normally are taken to the state court of appeals in jurisdictions that have two levels of appellate courts.

A defendant normally has a right to one and only one appeal of his or her trial conviction. Further review usually is allowed only at the discretion of a higher court. The normal method of asking a higher court to consider a case following the initial appeal is by a ***petition for a writ of certiorari***, or a petition for discretionary review. A state supreme court usually will review a court of appeals' decision in a criminal case only if it determines that the issues are novel and/or of such general importance that they merit consideration. Either the defendant or the state may petition a higher court to grant "cert." A court's denial of certiorari in no way indicates that the lower court's judgment was correct or that it is being affirmed; it simply means that the higher court chose not to consider the issues raised.

The Iowa Supreme Court affirmed Robert Williams's murder conviction on December 15, 1970. *State v. Williams*, 182 N.W.2d 396 (Iowa 1970). Following a state supreme court's adverse action on appeal or on writ of certiorari, a criminal defendant has three options to seek further judicial review of his or her conviction and sentence: (1) return to the state trial court with a motion for postconviction review to raise issues that could not have been considered on the original appeal of the conviction; (2) petition the U.S. Supreme Court to issue its writ of certiorari and consider the case; or (3) file a petition for a writ of habeas corpus in a U.S. district court, asking that court to review federal constitutional issues presented in the case.

A state postconviction motion typically raises a claim that could not have been presented on appeal. This happens when the record reviewed by the appeals court is missing information necessary for the issue's resolution. The most common claims of this nature involve allegations that defense counsel provided ineffective representation; that prosecutorial misconduct tainted the trial, such as the failure to disclose exculpatory evidence or the use of perjured testimony; and that newly discovered evidence supporting the defendant's innocence surfaced after the completion of the trial. When confronted with such claims, the trial-level court will preside over an evidentiary hearing where necessary and rule on the defendant's motion for a new trial. Then, on the basis of the record developed at this hearing, either the defendant or the state is in a position to appeal an adverse ruling to the appropriate state appeals court. Until a defendant has "exhausted state remedies" by raising challenges to a conviction or sentence in the state courts, these issues will not be considered by the federal courts. Because a defendant generally is required to join all possible issues in a single federal habeas corpus petition, state postconviction claims usually must be pursued sooner rather than later.

A state defendant's other postappeal options for challenging his or her conviction or sentence—filing a petition for a writ of certiorari in the U.S. Supreme Court and filing a petition for a writ of habeas corpus—involve the federal court system. Robert Williams chose to file a federal habeas corpus petition. We review the federal court system in the next section.

The Federal Court System

The federal courts are organized similarly to state court systems. Federal crimes are prosecuted in federal trial courts, which are the U.S. district courts. If a defendant is convicted, he or she has the right to appeal to an intermediate appellate court, the United States Court of Appeals in the appropriate federal circuit. The U.S. Supreme Court is at the top of the federal court system. Virtually all of the Supreme Court's docket is determined by the justices' discretionary decisions to hear cases on petitions for writ of certiorari. The Court will hear a case if four of the nine members of the Supreme Court vote to grant "cert." Each year, the Supreme Court receives roughly 5,000 to 7,000 certiorari petitions, yet the justices typically decide no more than 100 to 130 cases. The pretrial process in the federal system, from arrest to booking, the filing of a complaint, a magistrate's determination of probable cause to support an arrestee's detention, the suspect's first appearance before a magistrate, the preliminary hearing, indictment by grand jury (which is required in federal felony cases), arraignment, and pretrial motions, also closely resembles typical state criminal justice procedures.

Ninety-four U.S. district courts are scattered throughout the United States and U.S. territories. At least one federal district court exists in each state and the District of Columbia. Larger and more heavily populated states are served by two or more U.S. district courts. Such states are subdivided into the Northern, Southern, Eastern, Western, and/or Middle Districts, and the district courts within the state divide their business accordingly. One or more (sometimes many more) judges are assigned to each U.S. district court; the 94 courts are staffed by roughly 650 judges. Even when two or more judges have been appointed to the same court, U.S. district court judges almost always decide cases individually, rather than in teams or panels.

In addition to presiding over federal criminal trials, U.S. district court judges perform other functions, including the important job of ruling on the federal habeas corpus petitions filed by state prisoners. A federal statute, 28 U.S.C. § 2254, authorizes state prisoners to petition a federal district court for habeas corpus relief on the ground that their conviction or sentence was obtained or imposed in violation of the U.S. Constitution. A federal court's review is limited to federal constitutional issues, so questions that turn solely on the proper interpretation or application of state law cannot be considered. Nor will federal district courts entertain state prisoners' habeas corpus petitions in the absence of compliance with a number of procedural requirements imposed by statute and Supreme Court rulings. Additionally, citing the strong interest in preserving the finality of criminal convictions, the Supreme Court has insulated most claims based on alleged Fourth Amendment violations from federal habeas corpus review.

> Where the State has provided an opportunity for full and fair litigation of a Fourth Amendment claim, a state prisoner may not be granted federal habeas corpus relief on the ground that evidence sustained in an unconstitutional search or seizure was introduced at his trial.

Stone v. Powell, 428 U.S. 465, 494, 96 S. Ct. 3037, 3052, 49 L. Ed. 2d 1067, 1088 (1976) (footnotes omitted).

Following the Iowa Supreme Court's rejection of his appeal, Robert Williams filed a petition for a writ of habeas corpus in the U.S. District Court for the Southern District of Iowa. He claimed that his federal constitutional rights had been violated, including his Sixth and Fourteenth Amendment right to the assistance of counsel. Williams named Lou Brewer, the warden of the prison in which he was incarcerated, as the state official who allegedly was confining him in violation of his federal constitutional rights. This case accordingly was named *Williams v. Brewer*. The federal district court agreed that Williams's federal constitutional rights had been violated and issued an order requiring the state of Iowa either to release Williams or to provide him with a new trial free of constitutional error. The court announced this decision on March 28, 1974. *Williams v. Brewer*, 375 F. Supp. 170 (S.D. Iowa 1974).

U.S. courts of appeals decide appeals from U.S. district court rulings. The 50 states and federal territories are divided into 11 geographic regions or circuits. One U.S. court of appeals presides over each of these circuits. Another U.S. court of appeals is assigned to the District of Columbia, owing to the large amount of federal business conducted in the nation's capital. Additionally, the Federal Circuit Court of Appeals has been designated to decide appeals in patent, copyright, trademark, and other specialized cases. Figure 2–1 shows how these federal circuits are distributed across the country.

The U.S. courts of appeals decide appeals only from the U.S. district courts within their circuit. Thus, the First Circuit Court of Appeals resolves appeals from the federal district courts that sit in Maine, New Hampshire, and Massachusetts; the Second Circuit Court of Appeals hears appeals from the U.S. district courts in Vermont, New York, and Connecticut; and so on. (See Figure 2–1.) The authority of the respective U.S. courts of appeals does not extend beyond their geographic boundaries. For example, while all of the federal district courts in Maine, New Hampshire, and Massachusetts must abide by the rulings of the First Circuit Court of Appeals, no other district court in the country is required to do so. The different U.S. courts of appeals occasionally disagree about the proper interpretation of the law, and these disagreements may not be resolved until the Supreme Court announces a rule that binds all of the federal courts.

Cases appealed to the U.S. courts of appeals are initially considered by three-judge panels. Most of these courts have between 9 and 16 fully active (nonsenior) judges, although the First Circuit has fewer (about 5) and the Ninth Circuit includes significantly more (about 24) active judges. The party who loses the appeal can ask all judges on the court to sit *en banc* ("in the bench") and reconsider the decision of a three-judge panel. Such *en banc* hearings are rare and are granted only in particularly controversial cases.

Since a federal district court in Iowa granted Robert Williams's habeas corpus petition, the state, through the person of Warden Brewer, filed an appeal to the Eighth Circuit Court of Appeals. The court of appeals affirmed the district court's ruling on December 31, 1974. *Williams v. Brewer*, 509 F.2d 227 (8th Cir. 1974). It denied the state's request for a rehearing *en banc* on January 30, 1975.

The court of last resort in the federal system, and on all issues of federal law, is the U.S.

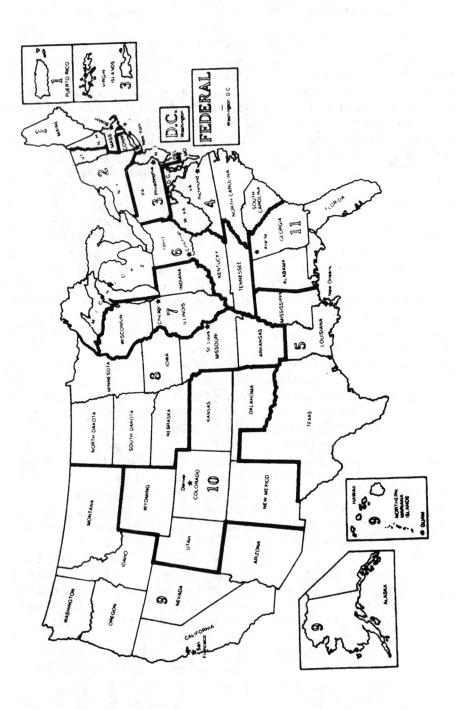

Figure 2–1 The Thirteen Federal Judicial Circuits. *Source:* Reprinted with permission from *125 West's Federal Reporter* 3rd, © 1997, West Group.

Supreme Court. Nine justices serve on the Supreme Court, one of whom is appointed by the president as the chief justice. As we have discussed, it is quite rare for the Supreme Court to hear cases on appeal; the justices almost always choose the cases they will decide by considering petitions for a writ of certiorari.

The state of Iowa, once again acting through its representative, Warden Brewer, filed a petition for a writ of certiorari asking the Supreme Court to review the Eighth Circuit Court of Appeals' decision that had granted Robert Williams a new trial. Warden Brewer thus became defined as the "petitioner." Since Williams had to file a response to the cert. petition, he was identified as the "respondent." Four or more of the justices voted to consider the case, and the Supreme Court granted certiorari on December 15, 1975. *Brewer v. Williams,* 423 U.S. 1031, 96 S. Ct. 561, 46 L. Ed. 2d 404 (1975). Lawyers for the parties thereafter were required to file briefs with the Supreme Court and to present oral arguments to the justices. In this context, a *brief* is the written argument and collection of authorities submitted to a court, which is something quite different from the study aid we described in Chapter 1.

As you have read, the Supreme Court affirmed the Eighth Circuit Court of Appeals ruling in a 5–4 decision announced on March 23, 1977. *Brewer v. Williams,* 430 U.S. 387, 97 S. Ct. 1232, 51 L. Ed. 2d 424 (1977). On May 16, 1977, the Justices rejected Iowa's last-ditch request to reconsider their decision. *Brewer v. Williams,* 431 U.S. 925, 97 S. Ct. 2200, 53 L. Ed. 2d 240 (1977). With that action, the Supreme Court's decision became final, and Iowa was required to give Williams a new trial (nearly nine years after his crime) or to release him from prison. We later return to this case's continuing journey through the courts. (See Chapter 3, pp. 119–122.)

Case Reporters and Case Citations

The judicial decisions presented in this book originally were published in volumes called *case reporters.* We have already used citations to several state and federal case reporters, and you will encounter many more in the following pages. We pause here to offer a brief description of case reporters and to explain legal citation conventions. This information will enable you to locate unedited case opinions in a library if you ever want to read a case in its entirety, and you must be familiar with case reporters and citation styles to conduct legal research.

State Cases. State trial court opinions are not published in case reporters in the overwhelming majority of the states. Most of the trial courts' business involves resolving individual factual disputes and applying established rules of law to those facts. Their work is of great significance to the administration of justice and to the involved parties, but their rulings have no precedential value in other cases. Almost all of the opinions published in state case reporters are written by appellate court judges.

Published state court opinions are included in the case reporters that make up West Publishing Company's National Reporter System. West Publishing Company is the largest publisher of law books in this country. Approximately 22 states rely exclusively on West's case reporters to publish their courts' opinions. The remaining states also make use of "official" case reporters that are published at the direction of the state government. In these states, West's case reporters publish the same opinions and serve as the "unofficial" reporter.

The official state case reporters that are not part of West's system are not widely used for legal research, and libraries outside of the home state typically do not stock these volumes. Nevertheless, you may be in a state, such as Arizona, Connecticut, Nebraska, or North Carolina, in which these reporters are used and may be cited. Illustrative citations to case opinions published in the official reporters of those states are as follows:

State v. Spears, 184 Ariz. 277 (1996)
State v. Felder, 39 Conn. App. 840 (1995)
State v. Schlund, 249 Neb. 173 (1996)

State v. Claypoole, 118 N.C. App. 714 (1995)

In each instance, these citations reflect the name of the case, followed by the volume number, an abbreviation for the name of the case reporter, the page at which the opinion starts, and the year in which the court reached its decision. For example, the opinion in *State v. Spears* is reported in volume 184 of the *Arizona Reports,* beginning at page 277, and the case was decided in 1996. The opinion in *State v. Felder* is in volume 39 of the *Connecticut Appellate Reports,* beginning at page 840, and the case was decided in 1995.

You will find West Publishing Company's case reporters to be much more widely available in libraries and, because of indexing aids that have been added, to be far more useful for conducting legal research than the official case reporters that are used in some states. West has divided the states into seven geographic regions,

as shown on the map in Figure 2–2. Different case reporters publish state court opinions from the different regions. Each case reporter originally was published many years ago, so each set now is in its second series. Thus, the West Publishing Company's regional reporters are as follows:

Atlantic Reporter, 2d Series (A.2d)
North Eastern Reporter, 2d Series (N.E.2d)
North Western Reporter, 2d Series (N.W.2d)
Pacific Reporter, 2d Series (P.2d)
South Eastern Reporter, 2d Series (S.E.2d)
South Western Reporter, 2d Series (S.W.2d)
Southern Reporter, 2d Series (So. 2d)

The geographic regions into which the states have been grouped were created by West Publishing Company solely for their publication purposes. They are not analogous to the federal judicial circuits that we considered earlier, in which each of the U.S. district courts within a

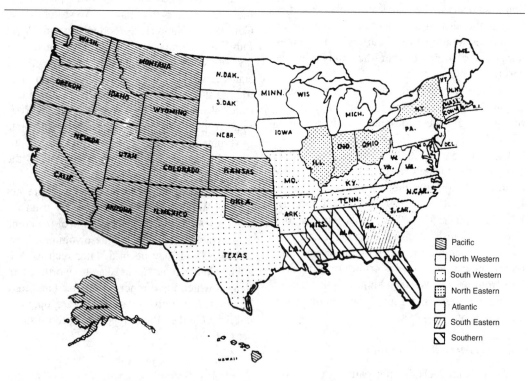

Legend:
- Pacific
- North Western
- South Western
- North Eastern
- Atlantic
- South Eastern
- Southern

Figure 2–2 Geographic Regions of the West Publishing Company's National Reporter System. *Source:* Reprinted with permission from *West's Regional Reporters* © 1997, West Group.

circuit is bound by court of appeals' rulings from that same circuit. In other words, even though state court opinions from Alabama, Florida, Louisiana, and Mississippi are published in the *Southern Reporter, 2d Series,* this does *not* mean that Alabama appellate court opinions have any special significance to the courts in the other states.

Citations to cases in West's regional reporters follow the same convention that we saw earlier: case name, volume number, abbreviation for the case reporter, page at which the opinion starts, and year of decision. When only the West reporter is cited, an abbreviation for the state court deciding the case must be included; this information is provided within the parentheses immediately preceding the year of decision. Examples of standard citation formats are as follows:

> *People v. Young,* 908 P.2d 1147 (Colo. App. 1995)
>
> *State v. Landherr,* 542 N.W.2d 687 (Minn. App. 1996)
>
> *State v. Evans,* 668 A.2d 1256 (R.I. 1996)
>
> *State v. Bland,* 457 S.E.2d 611 (S.C. 1995)

The first case, *People v. Young,* can be found in volume 908 of the *Pacific Reporter, 2d Series,* beginning at page 1147. It was decided by the Colorado Court of Appeals in 1995. *State v. Evans* is published in volume 668 of the *Atlantic Reporter, 2d Series,* beginning at page 1256. It was decided by the Rhode Island Supreme Court in 1996. The citation to West's case reporter should always be provided, because it is the one that most people will find convenient to use. Thus, a complete citation to the cases that we earlier identified only through the official state reporter citation would be as follows:

> *State v. Spears,* 184 Ariz. 277, 908 P.2d 1062 (1996)
>
> or
>
> *State v. Spears,* 908 P.2d 1062 (Ariz. 1996)
>
> *State v. Felder,* 39 Conn. App. 840, 668 A.2d 382 (1995)
>
> or

> *State v. Felder,* 668 A.2d 382 (Conn. App. 1995)
>
> *State v. Schlund,* 249 Neb. 173, 542 N.W.2d 421 (1996)
>
> or
>
> *State v. Schlund,* 542 N.W.2d 421 (Neb. 1996)
>
> *State v. Claypoole,* 118 N.C. App. 714, 457 S.E.2d 322 (1995)
>
> or
>
> *State v. Claypoole,* 457 S.E.2d 322 (N.C. App. 1995)

Generally, it is acceptable, and even appropriate, to cite only the West reporter and to identify the state court deciding the case in parentheses. An exception to this rule exists when a document is intended for use in one of those states that relies on official case reporters; then the official cites to court opinions from that state (but not other states) should be provided in addition to the citation to the West reporter. For details about the proper citation of case reporters and other legal reference materials, consult *The Bluebook: A Uniform System of Citation* (16th ed. 1996) or *The University of Chicago Manual of Legal Citation* (1989).

Federal Cases. Since 1932, the published opinions of U.S. district courts have appeared in the *Federal Supplement* (abbreviated "F. Supp.") case reporter, which is a product of West Publishing Company. Unlike state trial court judges, the judges sitting on federal district courts often do write opinions that are published in case reporters. The citation to a federal district court judge's opinion in the *Federal Supplement* should appear as follows:

> *United States v. Rhodes,* 921 F. Supp. 261 (M.D. Pa. 1996)
>
> *Barrett v. United States,* 845 F. Supp. 774 (D. Kan. 1994)

These citations conform to the style that also is used for state cases. Thus, the opinion in *United States v. Rhodes* is published in volume 921 of the *Federal Supplement,* beginning at page 261. It was written by the U.S. District Court for the Middle District of Pennsylvania, and the case was decided in 1996. The *Federal*

Supplement is the only case reporter that publishes U.S. district court opinions.

U.S. court of appeals decisions are published in West's *Federal Reporter.* The *Federal Reporter* began its third series (F.3d) in 1993. The *Federal Reporter, 2d Series* (F.2d) was published between 1924 and 1993. The *Federal Reporter* (F.) appeared between 1880 and 1924. The citation to a U.S. court of appeals decision should include the case name, volume, abbreviation of the appropriate *Federal Reporter* series, the page at which the opinion starts, identification of the particular court of appeals responsible for the opinion, and the year of the decision. For example:

> *Selsor v. Kaiser,* 81 F.3d 1492 (10th Cir. 1996)
>
> *United States v. Blackburn,* 940 F.2d 107 (4th Cir. 1991)

Since 1932, *F.2d* and *F.3d* have contained exclusively U.S. court of appeals opinions. Earlier *F.2d* reporters and the original *Federal Reporter* series included both U.S. court of appeals and U.S. district court opinions.

U.S. Supreme Court opinions are published in three different case reporters. The official reporter for U.S. Supreme Court opinions, which is published by the federal government, is the *United States Reports* ("U.S."). West Publishing Company produces the *Supreme Court Reporter* ("S. Ct."), which reports the justices' opinions *verbatim,* yet also includes the indexing and editorial aids that make West's entire system of case reporters so convenient to use. The third reporter for Supreme Court decisions is the *United States Supreme Court Reports, Lawyers' Edition* ("L. Ed."), now in its second series ("L. Ed. 2d"), which is published by Lawyers Cooperative Publishing Company. The *Lawyers' Edition* reporters also reprint Supreme Court opinions *verbatim* and contain unique indexing and reference aids.

Supreme Court opinions must be cited as they appear in the official *United States Reports* whenever available in that form. Recently decided cases may not be available in the official reporter, owing to the time lag of several months to a year or more between a case's decision and its publication in the *United States Reports.* Supreme Court opinions are published within a few weeks of case decisions in the *Supreme Court Reporter* and in *Lawyers' Edition.* It generally is permissible to cite only the *United States Reports.* The *Supreme Court Reporter* or *Lawyers' Edition* must be cited only when the official case report has not yet been published. Nevertheless, for readers' convenience, this book and many other resources cite all three reporters in which Supreme Court decisions are published. Thus, the citation of a U.S. Supreme Court decision would take the following form:

> *Harmelin v. Michigan,* 501 U.S. 957, 111 S. Ct. 2680, 115 L. Ed. 2d 836 (1991)
>
> *United States v. Calandra,* 414 U.S. 338, 94 S. Ct. 613, 38 L. Ed. 2d 561 (1974)

By now, you should be able to decipher the citations to court decisions in a case like *Brewer v. Williams.* More generally, you should be able to tell instantly whether a state or federal court decided a case and the level of the court, simply by seeing the case's citation. Check your understanding of these citation conventions, and of how cases progress through the state and federal courts, by tracing the path that Robert Williams's case took from the 1969 trial in the Polk County (Iowa) District Court to the U.S. Supreme Court decision in 1977. (See Figure 2–3.)

The Bill of Rights of the U.S. Constitution and Its Application to the States

As we have discussed, the U.S. Constitution was ratified in 1788 after extensive debate between Federalists, who favored its adoption, and Antifederalists, who objected to several features of the new Constitution. Federalists, including Alexander Hamilton, John Jay, and James Madison, who collaborated on the essays that make up the famous *Federalist Papers,* perceived the need for a strong national government. They cited numerous deficiencies in the

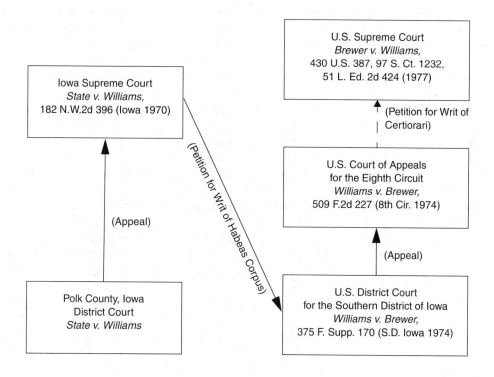

Figure 2–3 Progress of Robert Williams's Case through the Courts

Articles of Confederation, which was the nation's governing charter prior to 1788. Under the Articles of Confederation, the federal government had no authority to levy taxes, to regulate interstate commerce, or to preempt the states from coining money. Leadership in the executive branch was diffused among a series of special committees, and no federal judiciary had been created. For their part, Antifederalists such as Patrick Henry, Luther Martin, and George Mason feared that state sovereignty would suffer by the creation of a powerful central government. Although this concern was largely motivated by economic interests, the prospect of concentrating too much power in the national government also stirred memories of King George's tyrannical reign and was cited as a threat to individual liberties.

One step taken by the Federalists to mollify the Antifederalists and to bolster their case for ratification was to promise that immediately upon adoption of the Constitution, the first Congress would prepare and submit to the states a number of amendments that would specifically limit the powers of the new federal government. Such assurances were made in several state conventions in which the Constitution's ratification was debated. The crucial point for our purposes is that the proposed amendments to the Constitution would serve as limitations on the *federal* government; certainly, the Antifederalists and others contemplating this action had no desire to see the state governments subjected to additional regulation.

True to this plan, Congress approved a dozen amendments to the newly ratified Constitution in 1789 and then forwarded them to the state legislatures for their consideration. The required approval of three-fourths of the state legislatures was secured for 10 of these amendments by 1791.[2] These original amendments to the Constitution are collectively known as the Bill of Rights. Several of them limited the new government's power over individuals in ways that are directly relevant to criminal procedure law. (Select amendments to the U.S. Constitution are reprinted in Appendix B.) In light of the government's extraordinary authority to punish people by fine, imprisonment, and even execution in the enforcement of criminal laws, and the related risk that this authority would be abused, it is understandable that the Bill of Rights devoted such attention to the protection of individual liberties in this context. Nevertheless, it merits emphasis that the Bill of Rights protections originally were enacted as limitations on the power of the *federal* government and that they were not meant to apply against the states or influence the enforcement of state criminal laws. *Cf. Barron v. The Mayor and City Council of Baltimore,* 32 U.S. (7 Pet.) 243, 8 L. Ed. 672 (1833).

The adoption of the Fourteenth Amendment in 1868 represented a significant departure from the design of the first 10 amendments. The Fourteenth Amendment was specifically addressed to *state* governments. In relevant part, it provides that

> No State shall make or enforce any law which shall abridge the privileges and immunities of citizens of the United States; nor shall any State deprive any person of life, liberty, or property, without due process of law; nor deny to any person within its jurisdiction the equal protection of the laws.

Controversy brewed for several generations about the nature of the relationship between the Fourteenth Amendment and the specific rights guaranteed in the Bill of Rights. Questions particularly focused on the meaning of the due process clause in this context. When the Fourteenth Amendment promised that no "State [shall] deprive any person of life, liberty, or property, without due process of law," was this a shorthand way of saying that the states must recognize the same rights in their criminal proceedings as the ones spelled out in the Bill of Rights? In other words, must the states respect protections against unreasonable searches and seizures (as in the Fourth Amendment), against compelled self-incrimination, double jeopardy, and the right to indictment by grand jury (Fifth Amendment), of the rights to a speedy and public trial by jury, notice of the accusation, confrontation, compulsory process, and the assistance of counsel (Sixth Amendment), and of the rights to bail and freedom from cruel and unusual punishments (Eighth Amendment) or else violate an individual's rights to due process of law?

Alternatively, it was plausible that there was no necessary correspondence, and certainly not a one-to-one relationship between the specific guarantees of the Bill of Rights and the states' obligations under the Fourteenth Amendment's due-process clause. After all, had the drafters of the Fourteenth Amendment intended the due-process clause to have such scope, they could have chosen language to accomplish this result unambiguously. Moreover, to interpret the Fourteenth Amendment's due-process guarantee to include the individual rights itemized in the first 10 amendments seemed at odds with the Fifth Amendment and the inclusion of its due-process clause in the Bill of Rights. The Fifth Amendment similarly guarantees that "[n]o person shall be…deprived of life, liberty, or property, without due process of law." Wouldn't the due-process clause of the Fifth Amendment be redundant, or superfluous, if due process of law was synonymous with the rights enumerated elsewhere in the Bill of Rights? Under this interpretation, due process was not an empty formality, since the states would be constrained to recognize fundamental fairness in individual cases. Within this limitation, however, the states would have far more flexibility in processing criminal cases than if they were bound to observe the specific provisions of the Bill of Rights.

An intermediate position was that some but not necessarily all of the Bill of Rights guarantees applied to the states by operation of the Fourteenth Amendment's due-process clause. The challenge was to articulate a standard or method for separating those Bill of Rights guarantees that are essential to due process of law from those that are not. Once the essentials of due process were identified, the states presumably would be required to abide by the same specific rules and procedures associated with the right as applied to the federal government.

The Supreme Court struggled for several years during the middle part of the 20th century to choose between these competing theories. Justice Black, supported by Justice Douglas, championed the position that all Bill of Rights protections are binding on the states by operation of the Fourteenth Amendment's due-process clause. This view became known as the *total incorporation* position. As Justice Black was quick to point out, a principal virtue of this view consisted of its limiting judicial discretion. It did so by minimizing the need for judges to bring meaning to the vague concept of due process of law as fundamental fairness and by dispensing with the requirement for judicially rating some Bill of Rights guarantees as essential to due process while excluding others. However, Justice Black's forcefully argued position regarding total incorporation never persuaded a majority of the Supreme Court. *See, e.g., Adamson v. California*, 332 U.S. 46, 68–92, 67 S. Ct. 1672, 1684–96, 91 L. Ed. 1903, 1917–30 (1947) (Black, J., dissenting).

Justices Frankfurter and Harlan were among the leading proponents of the view that the Fourteenth Amendment's due-process clause did not specifically "incorporate" any of the Bill of Rights protections but instead required the states to observe *fundamental fairness* in their dealings with persons suspected, accused, or convicted of committing crimes. In construing due process as a command for fundamental fairness, they emphasized federalism and deference to the states, the desirability of allowing experimentation in matters of criminal justice, and the lack of textual or historical support for the incorporation position. The flexibility of this approach and its adaptability to individual case circumstances were touted as strengths that more than compensated for its relative vagueness and lack of predictability. Supporters of this position denied that the personal views of judges would subjectively define fundamental fairness. They frequently cited Justice Cardozo's observation in *Palko v. Connecticut*, 302 U.S. 319, 325, 58 S. Ct. 149, 152, 82 L. Ed. 288, 292 (1937), that specific protections are enforceable against the states by virtue of the Fourteenth Amendment's due-process clause if they "have been found to be implicit in the concept of ordered liberty." *See, e.g., Wolf v. Colorado*, 338 U.S. 25, 27, 69 S. Ct. 1359, 1361, 93 L. Ed. 1782, 1785 (1949) (Frankfurter, J.); *Duncan v. Louisiana*, 391 U.S. 145, 178–80, 88 S. Ct. 1444, 1464–65, 20 L. Ed. 2d 491 (1968) (Harlan, J., dissenting).

The "incorporation versus fundamental fairness" controversy came to a head in the 1960s in a series of criminal procedure cases decided during Earl Warren's tenure as Chief Justice of the Supreme Court. In what has been hailed by some as a "due-process revolution" that dramatically reshaped the federal-state landscape in criminal procedure law, the Warren Court *selectively incorporated* most of the Bill of Rights guarantees through the Fourteenth Amendment's due-process clause by ruling that they must be observed in state proceedings. Eschewing both the total incorporation and the fundamental fairness philosophies, a majority of the justices examined the specific criminal procedure rights in the first 10 amendments to determine whether each should apply to the states. If a right was incorporated, it applied in state cases according to the same rules ("jot for jot") as it did in federal cases. Justice White's opinion for the Court in *Duncan v. Louisiana*, 391 U.S. 145,

88 S. Ct. 1444, 20 L. Ed. 2d 491 (1968), held that the Sixth Amendment right to trial by jury applies to the states through the Fourteenth Amendment's due-process clause. We repro-

duce the portion of this opinion that explains the standard used by the Court when it selectively incorporates Bill of Rights protections via the Fourteenth Amendment.

Duncan v. Louisiana, 391 U.S. 145, 88 S. Ct. 1444, 20 L. Ed. 2d 491 (1968)

Mr. Justice WHITE delivered the opinion of the Court....

The Fourteenth Amendment denies the States the power to "deprive any person of life, liberty, or property, without due process of law." In resolving conflicting claims concerning the meaning of this spacious language, the Court has looked increasingly to the Bill of Rights for guidance; many of the rights guaranteed by the first eight Amendments to the Constitution have been held to be protected against state action by the Due Process Clause of the Fourteenth Amendment. That clause now protects the right to compensation for property taken by the State;[4] the rights of speech, press, and religion covered by the First Amendment;[5] the Fourth Amendment rights to be free from unreasonable searches and seizures and to have excluded from criminal trials any evidence illegally seized;[6] the right guaranteed by the Fifth Amendment to be free of compelled self-incrimination;[7] and the Sixth Amendment rights to counsel,[8] to a speedy[9] and public[10] trial, to con-

frontation of opposing witnesses,[11] and to compulsory process for obtaining witnesses.[12]

The test for determining whether a right extended by the Fifth and Sixth Amendments with respect to federal criminal proceedings is also protected against state action by the Fourteenth Amendment has been phrased in a variety of ways in the opinions of this Court. The question has been asked whether a right is among those "fundamental principles of liberty and justice which lie at the base of all our civil and political institutions,'" Powell v. State of Alabama, 287 U.S. 45, 67, 53 S. Ct. 55, 63, 77 L. Ed. 158 (1932); whether it is "basic in our system of jurisprudence," In re Oliver, 333 U.S. 257, 273, 68 S.Ct. 499, 507, 92 L.Ed. 682 (1948); and whether it is "a fundamental right, essential to a fair trial," Gideon v. Wainwright, 372 U.S. 335, 343–344, 83 S.Ct. 792, 796, 9 L.Ed.2d 799 (1963): The claim before us is that the right to trial by jury guaranteed by the Sixth Amendment meets these tests. The position of Louisiana, on the other hand, is that the Constitution imposes upon the States no duty to give a jury trial in any criminal case, regardless of the seriousness of the crime or the size of the punishment which may be imposed. Because we believe that trial by jury in criminal cases is fundamental to the American scheme of justice, we hold that the Fourteenth Amendment guarantees a right of jury trial in all criminal cases which—were they

---

4. Chicago, B. & Q. R. Co. v. City of Chicago, 166 U.S. 226, 17 S.Ct. 581, 41 L.Ed. 979 (1897).
5. See, e g., Fiske v. State of Kansas, 274 U.S. 380, 47 S.Ct. 655, 71 L.Ed. 1108 (1927).
6. See Mapp v. State of Ohio, 367 U.S. 643, 81 S.Ct. 1684, 6 L.Ed.2d 1081 (1961).
7. Malloy v. Hogan, 378 U.S. 1, 84 S.Ct. 1489, 12 L. Ed. 2d 653 (1964).
8. Gideon v. Wainwright, 372 U.S. 335, 83 S.Ct. 792, 9 L.Ed.2d 799 (1963).
9. Klopfer v. State of North Carolina, 386 U.S. 213, 87 S.Ct. 988, 18 L.Ed.2d 1 (1967).
10. In re Oliver, 333 U.S. 257, 68 S.Ct. 499, 92 L.Ed. 682 (1948).

---

11. Pointer v. State of Texas, 380 U.S. 400, 85 S.Ct. 1065, 13 L.Ed.2d 923 (1965).
12. Washington v. State of Texas, 388 U.S. 14, 87 S.Ct. 1920, 18 L.Ed.2d 1019 (1967).

to be tried in a federal court—would come within the Sixth Amendment's guarantee.[14] Since we consider the appeal before us to be such a case, we hold that the Constitution was violated when appellant's demand for jury trial was refused. ...

Notes and Questions

1. Can you imagine a system of justice that could fairly be administered without using a body of citizens (i.e., a trial jury) to listen to evidence and decide whether a defendant is guilty of criminal charges? Would such a system resemble the way criminal justice actually is administered in the United States? Which of these questions was of principal interest to the Court in *Duncan*?

---

14. In one sense recent cases applying provisions of the first eight Amendments to the States represent a new approach to the "incorporation" debate. Earlier the Court can be seen as having asked, when inquiring into whether some particular procedural safeguard was required of a State, if a civilized system could be imagined that would not accord the particular protection. For example, Palko v. State of Connecticut, 302 U.S. 319, 325, 58 S.Ct. 149, 152, 82 L.Ed. 288 (1937), stated: "The right to trial by jury and the immunity from prosecution except as the result of an indictment may have value and importance. Even so, they are not of the very essence of a scheme of ordered liberty. * * * Few would be so narrow or provincial as to maintain that a fair and enlightened system of justice would be impossible without them." The recent cases, on the other hand, have proceeded upon the valid assumption that state criminal processes are not imaginary and theoretical schemes but actual systems bearing virtually every characteristic of the common-law system that has been developing contemporaneously in England and in this country. The question thus is whether given this kind of system a particular procedure is fundamental—whether, that is, a procedure is necessary to an Anglo-American regime of ordered liberty. It is this sort of inquiry that can justify the conclusions that state courts must exclude evidence seized in violation of the Fourth Amendment, Mapp v. State of Ohio, 367 U.S. 643, 81 S.Ct. 1684, 6 L.Ed.2d 1081 (1961); that state prosecutors may not comment on a defendant's failure to testify, Griffin v. State of California, 380 U.S. 609, 85 S.Ct. 1229, 14 L.Ed.2d 106 (1965); and that criminal punishment may not be imposed for the status of narcotics addiction.

2. Justice Harlan's lengthy dissenting opinion in *Duncan* is a spirited refutation of selective incorporation and a defense of the position "that 'due process of law' requires only that criminal trials be fundamentally fair." In his view, "The Bill of Rights is not necessarily irrelevant to the search for guidance in interpreting the Fourteenth Amendment, but the reason for and nature of its relevance must be articulated." He argued that the Court's task

Robinson v. State of California, 370 U.S. 660, 82 S.Ct. 1417, 8 L.Ed.2d 758 (1962). Of immediate relevance for this case are the Court's holdings that the States must comply with certain provisions of the Sixth Amendment, specifically that the States may not refuse a speedy trial, confrontation of witnesses, and the assistance, at state expense if necessary, of counsel). See cases cited in nn. 8–12, supra. Of each of these determinations that a constitutional provision originally written to bind the Federal Government should bind the States as well it might be said that the limitation in question is not necessarily fundamental to fairness in every criminal system that might be imagined but is fundamental in the context of the criminal processes maintained by the American States.

When the inquiry is approached in this way the question whether the States can impose criminal punishment without granting a jury trial appears quite different from the way it appeared in the older cases opining that States might abolish jury trial. A criminal process which was fair and equitable but used no juries is easy to imagine. It would make use of alternative guarantees and protections which would serve the purposes that the jury serves in the English and American systems. Yet no American State has undertaken to construct such a system. Instead, every American State, including Louisiana, uses the jury extensively, and imposes very serious punishments only after a trial at which the defendant has a right to a jury's verdict. In every State, including Louisiana, the structure and style of the criminal process—the supporting framework and the subsidiary procedures—are of the sort that naturally complement jury trial, and have developed in connection with and in reliance upon jury trial.

is to start with the words "liberty" and "due process of law" and attempt to define them in a way that accords with American traditions and our system of government. This approach, involving a much more discriminating process of adjudication than does "incorporation" is, albeit difficult, the one that was followed throughout the nineteenth and most of the present century. It entails a "gradual process of judicial inclusion and exclusion," seeking, with due recognition of constitutional tolerance for state experimentation and disparity, to ascertain those "immutable principles of justice which inhere in the very idea of free government which no member of the Union may disregard."

Do standards such as these strike you as being more *subjective*—that is, determined according to the predilections of individual judges—or *objective*—that is, ascertainable by reference to external, neutral principles? Do they provide meaningful guidance to the police, prosecutors, and other courts? Is their generality and flexibility more of an asset or a liability to constitutional adjudication?

The controversy surrounding the incorporation of Bill of Rights protections through the Fourteenth Amendment to apply in state criminal proceedings marked a tremendously significant chapter in the development of constitutional criminal procedure. Through the cases cited in Justice White's opinion in *Duncan v. Louisiana*, as well as others, the Supreme Court proceeded to "federalize" state criminal procedure rules by selectively incorporating Bill of Rights guarantees. Today, with only a few exceptions, the same rights spelled out in the first 10 amendments that relate to criminal procedure must be observed in the state courts. For example, the Supreme Court has declined to require the states to use grand jury indictments to begin felony prosecutions, even though the Fifth Amendment provides for indictment by grand jury in "capital or otherwise infamous crime[s]," (i.e., felonies), and such a procedure must be followed in federal criminal prosecutions. *See Hurtado v. California*, 110 U.S. 516, 4 S. Ct. 111, 28 L. Ed. 232 (1884). Nor have the justices explicitly ruled that the Eighth Amendment's prohibition against "excessive bail" applies to state proceedings, *Stack v. Boyle*, 342 U.S. 1, 72 S. Ct. 1, 96 L. Ed. 3 (1951), although in dictum the Court has suggested that the bail clause "has been assumed to have application to the States through the Fourteenth Amendment." *Schilb v. Kuebel*, 404 U.S. 357, 365, 92 S. Ct. 479, 484, 30 L. Ed. 2d 502, 511 (1971). Additionally, nonunanimous jury verdicts are constitutionally permissible in state criminal trials but not in federal trials. *Apodaca v. Oregon*, 406 U.S. 404, 92 S. Ct. 1628, 32 L. Ed. 2d 184 (1972); *John-son v. Louisiana*, 406 U.S. 356, 92 S. Ct. 1620, 32 L. Ed. 2d 152 (1972).

In the wake of the "due-process revolution" produced by Warren Court decisions during the 1960s, state and federal rules of constitutional criminal procedure increasingly became homogenized. As the Supreme Court established rights that both federal and state criminal justice officials were constitutionally required to observe, the states generally were forced to respond by affording defendants greater protections in order to satisfy these threshold expectations. There is no question that criminal procedure law has been fundamentally transformed as a result of the Supreme Court's selective incorporation of Bill of Rights protections to the states. However, federal constitutional standards have not entirely displaced state sources of law in criminal procedure issues. We next consider the significance of state constitutions to criminal procedure law.

The New Federalism: State Constitutions and Criminal Procedure Law

Referring to himself and the other members of the Supreme Court, Justice Jackson once remarked that "we are not final because we are infallible, but we are infallible only because we are final." *Brown v. Allen*, 344 U.S. 443, 540, 72 S. Ct. 397, 427, 97 L. Ed. 469, 533 (1953) (concurring in the result). This observation accurately summarizes the Supreme Court's authority in interpreting the U.S. Constitution. Under the Constitution's "supremacy clause,"[3] the state courts are required to honor the Supreme Court's federal constitutional decisions even if they disagree with them. State judges are not at liberty either to diminish the scope of federal constitutional protections defined by the Supreme Court or to rule that the Supreme Court misinterpreted the federal Constitution by not going far enough to protect individual rights.

Supreme Court rulings that interpret the Bill of Rights, the Fourteenth Amendment, and other federal constitutional provisions merely determine whether government conduct squares with minimally acceptable constitutional standards. Even though they cannot cut back on federal constitutional safeguards, the states are perfectly free to enact statutes that give individuals a greater measure of rights. Enhanced protections for individual liberties also can be provided through another source: state constitutions. When "a state court decision indicates clearly and expressly that it" does not rest on an interpretation of federal law, but "is alternatively based on bona fide separate, adequate, and independent grounds, [the Supreme Court], of course, will not undertake to review the decision." *Michigan v. Long*, 463 U.S. 1032, 1041, 103 S. Ct. 3469, 3476, 77 L. Ed. 2d 1201, 1214 (1983). In other words, a state court can rely on a state statute or a state constitutional provision to extend (but not diminish) a criminal defendant's rights beyond what is required by the federal Constitution. When it takes such action, its state law ruling is insulated from further review by the U.S. Supreme Court.

For the most part, the notion that state constitutions could be interpreted to provide individuals with a greater measure of protection in criminal cases than the federal Constitution requires was little more than an interesting abstraction during the first two-thirds of the 20th century. Although cases like *Brown v. Mississippi* (see Chapter 1, p. 21) were not typical of the brand of justice administered by the state courts, it is fair to say that pretrial and trial procedures had a rough-and-ready quality in many state criminal cases. Federal constitutional rulings, especially during the Warren Court years, generally advanced the due process model of criminal procedure by light-years in the state courts.

Warren Burger replaced Earl Warren as Chief Justice of the U.S. Supreme Court in 1969. By 1972, President Nixon, who had campaigned under a tough "law and order" platform, had named three additional justices to the Court. The decisions of the Burger Court through the 1970s and into the mid-1980s produced much "crime control" rhetoric. Although they worked few fundamental changes in Warren Court rulings, they often chipped away at rights established under the earlier cases. By the time that Chief Justice Burger retired in 1986 and William Rehnquist was appointed to replace him as Chief Justice, there was no doubt that the Supreme Court had tilted dramatically away from the due-process orientation of the Warren Court. The justices increasingly embraced crime control values that promoted "truth" over procedural regularity, emphasized respecting the finality of convictions, and reduced the role of the federal courts in overseeing the states' administration of criminal justice.[4]

Beginning in the 1970s, and coincident with these trends in U.S. Supreme Court rulings, many state courts rediscovered state constitutions as a source of individual rights. State court judges increasingly relied on their state constitutions to confer rights exceeding those recognized under federal constitutional rulings. In

1986, Justice Brennan identified the renaissance of state constitutionalism as "probably the most important development in constitutional jurisprudence of our time."[5] This same trend has been hailed as "a new 'Constitutional Revolution'."[6] Although federal constitutional criminal procedure remains the dominant jurisprudence and justifies the bulk of our attention, state constitutional doctrine has made major inroads in criminal procedure law. Accordingly, U.S. Supreme Court cases presented in the following pages regularly will be complemented by parallel state supreme court decisions that rely on state constitutional rights.

There are many reasons that a criminal procedure issue, such as the legality of a search, the admissibility of a confession, or the right to confront witnesses, might be resolved differently on state constitutional grounds than under the federal Constitution. Unique language might be used in the separate constitutions, and such *textual differences* potentially can affect the application and scope of rights. Even where constitutions are worded identically, a unique *history* surrounding a right, or other evidence regarding the *intent of the framers* in adopting a particular provision, including preexisting state law, might produce different interpretations of state and federal constitutions. When the Supreme Court interprets the U.S. Constitution, it must be mindful that the rules that it derives will bind states throughout the nation. The states are rich with countless sources of diversity. State constitutional rulings, of course, apply no farther than the court's state boundaries. State courts are not constrained by concerns of *federalism*, and their decisions apply to a population that—relative to the entire country—is more likely to share *common values, traditions*, and a similar *lifestyle*.

Some courts have cited *structural differences* between the federal and state constitutions as justifying different interpretations of rights. As the Supreme Court of Washington explained, the U.S. Constitution

is a grant of enumerated powers to the federal government, and [a state constitution] serves to limit the sovereign power which inheres directly in the people and indirectly in their elected representatives. Hence the explicit affirmation of fundamental rights in our state constitution may be seen as a guarantee of those rights rather than as a restriction on them.

State v. Gunwall, 106 Wash. 2d 54, 720 P.2d 808, 812 (1986).

For a variety of reasons, not all state courts are as willing as others to resort to their state constitutions as independent sources of rights. Some commentators have criticized courts that appear to rely on state constitutional grounds simply as a means of departing from Supreme Court federal constitutional rulings that they dislike. They persuasively argue that state constitutional rulings should be consistent and principled rather than ad hoc and reactive to Supreme Court decisions.[7] This general concern raises a procedural issue that recurs in state constitutional adjudication: Should state courts first consider state constitutional grounds to decide cases and only thereafter consult federal constitutional law (if necessary), or should federal constitutional issues be considered first and state constitutions be consulted only as necessary? These different approaches to state constitutional analysis have been labeled the *primacy model*[8] and the *interstitial*, or *supplementary, model*,[9] respectively. State courts differ in the approaches they follow.

The many differences among state constitutions, state courts, and the analytical approaches and techniques that the courts use make it difficult to generalize about state constitutional adjudication in criminal procedure law. You will get the flavor of how state courts and the U.S. Supreme Court occasionally analyze and resolve issues very differently through the notes and case excerpts in the following chapters that highlight state constitutional rulings. Justice Jackson's observations about the Supreme Court's being the "final" and "infallible" arbiter of cases, with which we introduced this section, retain full force when applied to issues involving federal law and the U.S. Constitution. As you consider state courts' departures from Supreme Court rulings, in reliance on state constitutions, you should more fully appreciate that Justice Jackson's comments were not meant to apply to cases decided on state law grounds.

A WORD ABOUT LEGAL RESEARCH TECHNIQUES

One of this book's objectives is to prepare students to find answers to law-related questions, whether they arise from the cases presented in this text or from different sources. You occasionally will encounter words in a court's opinion that you do not understand. A court's reasoning or its conclusions in a case may be confusing. Or you may become interested in a legal issue, and want to explore it in greater depth. Studying law involves much more than becoming familiar with a body of rules and underlying principles. Such knowledge is little more than a starting point in an analytical process that tests the application of legal doctrine in novel contexts. This process puts a premium on students' abilities to ask questions and to analyze issues critically. Like other disciplines, legal studies require a methodology for researching unanswered questions. We thus provide tips about legal reference materials and techniques for using them.

Appendix A describes printed reference materials and a computerized base, WEST-LAW, through which legal research can be pursued. We periodically illustrate how legal research techniques can be used to investigate questions suggested by the cases in these materials. Law books and the computerized WEST-LAW system are very efficiently organized and, after a bit of practice, are surprisingly easy to use. The time invested to learn about legal research tools and techniques will reap invaluable dividends. We recommend that students read Appendix A at this time. A more complete description of legal research references and methods, with an emphasis on criminal justice, can be obtained by consulting James R. Acker and Richard Irving's *Basic Legal Research for Criminal Justice and the Social Sciences* (Aspen Publishers, Inc., 1998).

As we take advantage of opportunities to explain how questions raised by these materials can be investigated through applied legal research techniques, we will make use of the following symbol: 📖. At the conclusion of the case or other reading with a passage that has been marked by the 📖 symbol, we elaborate on how related additional information can be assembled through legal research. To illustrate, we reproduce very brief portions of the opinions of Justice Stewart and Justice Marshall from *Brewer v. Williams.*

Brewer v. Williams, 430 U.S. 387, 97 S. Ct. 1232, 51 L. Ed. 2d 424 (1977)

Mr. Justice **Stewart** delivered the opinion of the Court. . . .

In the meantime Williams was arraigned before a judge in Davenport on the outstanding arrest warrant. The judge advised him of his Miranda rights and committed him to jail. ...

Mr. Justice **Marshall,** concurring...

If Williams is to go free—and given the ingenuity of Iowa's prosecutors on retrial or in a civil commitment proceeding, I doubt very much that there is any chance a dangerous criminal will be loosed on the streets. ...

Legal Research Notes

📖 **1.** Shortly after his arrest and booking, Robert Williams was "arraigned before a judge in Davenport on the outstanding arrest warrant." What does it mean for a suspected offender to be "arraigned" in this context? To get help defining unfamiliar words, it often is handy to start with a *law dictionary*. (See Appendix A for additional details.) *Black's Law Dictionary* (6th ed. 1990) defines *arraignment* as the "procedure whereby the accused is brought before the court to plead to the criminal charge against him in the indictment or information." We know that it is much too early in the development of the case against Williams for an indictment or an information to have been returned. As we reread the passage from Justice Stewart's opinion, we note that Williams was "arraigned...on the outstanding arrest warrant." An arrest warrant is not at all the equivalent of an indictment or an information. We thus surmise that the general definition of *arraignment* provided in the law dictionary may not apply in this context.

Another secondary authority that could help us with the meaning of this term is *Words and Phrases*. (See Appendix A for additional details.) Volume 4 of the alphabetically arranged *Words and Phrases* provides us with definitions of *arraignment* taken from court decisions in many different jurisdictions. Most of these definitions essentially replicate the law dictionary's definition. One taken from an Iowa court's decision provides:

> Where proceeding...before Iowa magistrate...did not consist of reading indictment to defendant or stating...substance of charge and calling on defendant to plead thereto, [the] appearance [did not] constitute "arraignment" within meaning of Rules of Criminal Procedure.

4 *Words and Phrases* "Arraignment" (Supp. 1995), *citing State v. Hempton,* 310 N.W.2d 206, 207 (Iowa 1981). By consulting *State v. Hempton,* we learn that the Iowa Supreme Court rejected the defendant's assertion, made to support the argument that a state speedy trial rule had been violated, that an arraignment "refers to the accused's first appearance in court after his arrest." *Id.*

This information gives us increasing cause to be suspicious that Justice Stewart—who has no reason to be an expert in Iowa state law—was not using *arraignment* in its customary sense or in the way that the term normally is understood under Iowa law. The second edition of the legal encyclopedia *American Jurisprudence (Am. Jur. 2d)* confirms that under state procedures generally, "The purpose and necessity of an arraignment are to fix the identity of the accused, to inform him of the charge against him and to give him an opportunity to plead." 21 *Am. Jur. 2d,* "Criminal Law," § 433, pp. 716–17. (See Appendix A.) We learn from an adjacent section of *Am. Jur. 2d* that Williams's appearance before the Davenport judge almost certainly is more accurately called his "first appearance," described as follows:

> One arrested...on a warrant issued by a magistrate on the filing of a complaint or affidavit must be brought with reasonable promptness before a magistrate to be advised of his rights, including his right to a preliminary examination, and his right to have bail set if the offense is bailable. 21 *Am. Jur. 2d,* "Criminal Law," § 408, p. 677

To delve further into this issue, we can refer to Iowa law. We would expect pretrial criminal procedures to be regulated by statute. We could use the Iowa statute books, if we have access to them, or else WESTLAW (see Appendix A) to try to determine if Williams actually was "arraigned" before the Davenport judge or whether he instead was taken for his "first appearance" or some other procedure. Through the General Index to the *Iowa Code Annotated* or its equivalent in WESTLAW, it is a simple enough matter to locate the Iowa Rules of Criminal Procedure. Rule 2 governs "Proceedings before the Magistrate," and Rule 8 applies to "Arraignment and Plea."

Iowa Rule of Criminal Procedure 2

(1) Initial appearance of defendant. An officer making an arrest with or without a warrant shall take the arrested person without unnecessary delay before a committing magistrate.
…
(2) Statement by the magistrate. The magistrate shall inform a defendant who appears before the magistrate after arrest…of the complaint against the defendant, of the defendant's right to retain counsel, of the defendant's right to request the appointment of counsel if the defendant is unable by reason of indigency to obtain counsel, of the general circumstances under which the defendant may secure pretrial release…and shall provide the defendant with a copy of the complaint. The magistrate shall also inform the defendant that he or she is not required to make a statement and that any statement made by the defendant may be used against him or her.

The "initial appearance" described in this rule seems to correspond to the proceeding in which Williams participated following his arrest. In contrast, the "arraignment" described

in Iowa Rule of Criminal Procedure 8 is a significantly different procedure.

Iowa Rule of Criminal Procedure 8

(1) Conduct of arraignment. . . . Arraignment shall consist of reading the indictment to the defendant or stating to the defendant the substance of the charge and calling on the defendant to plead thereto.

The arraignment procedure described by this rule is a far more conventional use of the term than Justice Stewart's use of it in *Brewer v. Williams.* We have been able to discern that Williams almost certainly was participating in what would more accurately be called an "initial appearance," at least under the contemporary rules of criminal procedure in Iowa. In fairness to Justice Stewart, in some jurisdictions an initial appearance is known, at least informally, as an "arraignment on the complaint." Nor have we definitively resolved what this proceeding was called in Iowa in 1968, when it occurred, or in 1977, when Justice Stewart's opinion appeared. *Cf. State v. Sefchek,* 261 Iowa 1159, 1170, 157 N.W.2d 128, 135 (1968) (describing a case in which the defendant was arrested on the evening of May 23, 1966, and was "arraigned" the following afternoon). In any event, the point of this exercise is not so much to establish that Justice Stewart was correct or incorrect in describing Williams's December 26, 1968, appearance before the Davenport, Iowa, judge as an "arraignment" as to attempt to clarify how this term is conventionally used and to suggest how legal research can help shed light on an issue of this nature.

📖 **2.** Justice Marshall suggested in his concurring opinion that the reversal of Williams's 1969 murder conviction and the suppression from evidence of his statements to Detective Leaming and the "fruits" of those statements (the victim's body) would not necessarily result in Williams's going free. Is there a way of checking Justice Marshall's prophecy if we are curious about Williams's fate following his victory in the Supreme Court?

As you might expect, research aids exist that enable us to track the developments in a case following a published judicial decision. This tracking system depends on the existence of other published opinions involving the case. Thus, if the prosecution decided not to retry Williams, or if Williams were retried and acquitted, no case reports would reflect these events, and we could not detect them through routine legal research methods. However, we would be able to locate later published decisions related to *Brewer v. Williams* by **"Shepardizing"** that case. (See Appendix A for additional details.) *Shepard's* citators, and the analogous services provided by WESTLAW, were created for more compelling reasons than to allow us to satisfy our curiosity about defendants in particular cases. The law, including case law, is in constant flux. It is imperative to be able to confirm whether the rule of law announced in a case decided as long ago as *Brewer v. Williams*, or any other case, remains effective or whether it has been modified or overruled. In addition to supplying the judicial history of a case, a *Shepard's* identifies all reported cases that have cited the case being *Shepardized*, and indicates whether the case has been overruled, reversed, modified, affirmed, or cited for other purposes. This type of information is extremely useful for finding other cases related to the one being *Shepardized* and for tracing developments in the law, as well as for ascertaining the continued vitality of the case being *Shepardized*.

We have a more limited objective for *Shepardizing Brewer v. Williams*. This is the relatively straightforward task of checking for later reported decisions to see if Justice Marshall's suspicions were correct that Williams would remain confined pursuant to renewed prosecutorial and judicial action. When we examine *Shepard's United States Citations*, we find several citations denoting the "same case" or a "connected case" to the Supreme Court's 1977 decision in *Brewer v. Williams;* looking up these

citations in the case reporters would solve our mystery. Using WESTLAW's "Insta-Cite" command provides an even more direct way of answering our question. (See Appendix A.) Among other information, this command supplies us with the *direct history* of *Brewer v. Williams* (prior and subsequent decisions involving the same parties, facts, and issues) and *related references* (decisions involving the same parties and facts but different issues).

We would learn from the cases cited in these sources that Robert Williams indeed was retried and again was convicted of murder following the Supreme Court's remand in *Brewer v. Williams*. The Iowa Supreme Court affirmed the conviction, and the U.S. Supreme Court denied certiorari. *State v. Williams*, 285 N.W.2d 248 (Iowa 1979), *cert. denied*, 446 U.S. 921, 100 S. Ct. 1859, 64 L. Ed. 2d 277 (1980). The federal district court rejected Williams's subsequent petition for a writ of habeas corpus, but the Eighth Circuit Court of Appeals reversed and ruled that Williams once again was entitled to a new trial. *Williams v. Nix*, 528 F. Supp. 664 (S.D. Iowa 1981), *rev'd*, 700 F.2d 1164 (8th Cir. 1983). Williams's case then returned to the U.S. Supreme Court for a second time. *Nix v. Williams*, 467 U.S. 431, 104 S. Ct. 2501, 81 L. Ed. 2d 377 (1984). We will learn what the Supreme Court decided in *Nix v. Williams* when we consider this case in Chapter 3 (see p. 119). Judicial action involving Williams's case came to a halt the next year. *Williams v. Nix*, 751 F.2d 956 (8th Cir.), *cert. denied*, 471 U.S. 1138, 105 S. Ct. 2681, 86 L. Ed. 2d 699 (1985).

* * * * *

Legal research skills make it possible to explore and learn more about virtually any legal issues that you will confront during your studies. They are a tremendous asset for completing research papers, complementing assigned readings, and generally expanding your knowledge about the law. We again urge you to devote sufficient time to studying Appendix A in this book and practicing the techniques described to become familiar with legal research references and techniques. We are confident that you will be repaid handsomely for your efforts.

CONCLUSION

In this chapter, we have deviated from the customary format of succeeding chapters, which emphasizes the case method of study and puts a premium on analyzing judicial decisions. We have made this departure to provide background information that is importantly related to the ensuing cases and materials.

We first introduced the independent, yet interrelated structure of the state and federal court systems. We illustrated the steps through which criminal cases typically progress in the court systems, using *Brewer v. Williams* as an example. This review examined the pretrial, trial, and postconviction stages of both the state and federal judicial systems. We also described the case reporters in which judicial opinions are published and corresponding citation conventions. This information is necessary to be able to locate court decisions in legal reference materials.

Next, we discussed the origins of the Bill of Rights, or the first 10 amendments to the U.S. Constitution. We emphasized the original understanding that those constitutional amendments were designed to limit the authority of the *federal* government, and not the states. The subsequent enactment of the Fourteenth Amendment, with its stipulation that "nor shall any *State* deprive any person of life, liberty, or property, without due process of law" (emphasis added), eventually would work dramatic changes in criminal procedure law. Through a series of cases decided in the 1960s, the Warren Court "selectively incorporated" most of the criminal procedure safeguards contained in the Bill of Rights and made them applicable to the states by operation of the Fourteenth Amendment's due-process clause. As a consequence, these fundamental constitutional rights now must be observed in state criminal proceedings.

Requiring the states to observe the protections spelled out in the Bill of Rights means that suspects and defendants in state proceedings must be afforded at least those rights. The states remain free to provide safeguards that exceed this federal floor, or threshold. State and federal statutes sometimes provide rights to suspects and the accused in criminal cases that go beyond the federal constitutional minima, as do state courts' interpretations of state constitutional provisions. Developments in state constitutional law represent a dynamic and increasingly important part of the study of criminal procedure law. So that we do not neglect this "new federalism," we occasionally consider state constitutional rulings in connection with U.S. Supreme Court decisions that establish federal constitutional criminal procedure doctrine.

Finally, we have stressed the importance of being able to find answers to questions of law independently of this book and of being able to keep up with future developments in the law. Familiarity with basic legal research techniques will equip students with these skills. We provided a brief legal research exercise in this chapter, and we present others throughout this book. Appendix A provides a guide that we hope will be useful in helping to introduce students to the reference materials and techniques necessary for basic legal research.

NOTES

1. Kidnapping also can be a federal crime when the victim is transported across state lines, but there was no evidence of interstate transportation in this case.
2. In 1992, one of the two original constitutional amendments proposed by Congress in 1789 that had not been approved by the states over 200 years earlier finally secured the concurrence of three-fourths of the state legislatures. Now listed as the 27th Amendment to the Constitution, it provides: "No law, varying the compensation for the services of the Senators and Representatives, shall take effect, until an election of Representatives shall have intervened." The lone

proposed amendment of 1789 that was not ratified by the states would have required that at least one representative be sent to the House of Representatives for each 50,000 persons in a state.

3. U.S. Constitution, art. VI [2]:

    The Constitution, and the Laws of the United States, which shall be made in Pursuance thereof, and all Treaties made, or which shall be made, under the Authority of the United States, shall be the Supreme Law of the Land; and the Judges in every State shall be bound thereby, any Thing in the Constitution or Laws of any State to the Contrary notwithstanding.

4. *See* James R. Acker, "The Law of the Future," in *Crime and Justice in the Year 2010* (John Klofas & Stan Stojkovic, eds., Brooks/Cole 1995).

5. Utter & Pitler, *Presenting a State Constitutional Argument: Comment on Theory and Technique,* 20 *Ind. L. Rev.* 635, 638 (1987) (*quoting* "The Fourteenth Amendment," Address by Justice William J. Brennan, Jr., American Bar Association Section on Indi-

vidual Rights and Responsibilities, New York University Law School (Aug. 8, 1986)). *See generally* Brennan, *State Constitutions and the Protection of Individual Rights,* 90 *Harv. L. Rev.* 489 (1977).

6. Williams, *State Constitutional Law Processes,* 24 *Wm. & Mary L. Rev.* 169, 171 (1983).

7. *See, e.g.,* Shapiro, *State Constitutional Doctrine and the Criminal Process,* 16 *Seton Hall L. Rev.* 630, 647 (1986); Collins, *Reliance on State Constitutions: Some Random Thoughts,* 54 *Miss. L.J.* 371, 375–76 (1984).

8. *See, e.g.,* Utter, *Swimming in the Jaws of the Crocodile: State Court Comment on Federal Constitutional Issues When Disposing of Cases on State Constitutional Grounds,* 63 *Tex. L. Rev.* 1025, 1028 (1985); Pollock, *Adequate and Independent Grounds as a Means of Balancing the Relationship between State and Federal Courts,* 63 *Tex. L. Rev.* 977, 983 (1985).

9. *See* Utter, *supra* note 8, at 1028–29; *Developments in the Law: The Interpretation of State Constitutional Rights,* 95 *Harv. L. Rev.* 1324, 1358 (1982).

CHAPTER 3

The Law of Search and Seizure

The right of the people to be secure in their persons, houses, papers and effects, against unreasonable searches and seizures, shall not be violated, and no Warrants shall issue, but upon probable cause, supported by Oath or affirmation, and particularly describing the place to be searched, and the persons or things to be seized.

—U.S. Constitution, Fourth Amendment

The Framers of the Fourth Amendment were characteristically succinct. They used just 53 words to enshrine in the Bill of Rights the pre-cious freedoms guaranteed by this provision. Notice how the Fourth Amendment is written. Its first clause protects people's rights to "be secure—in their "persons, houses, papers and effects"—against "unreasonable searches and seizures." The amendment's second clause pro-hibits warrants from being issued unless they are based on "probable cause" and supported by the applicant's "Oath or affirmation." It addi-tionally requires that warrants "particularly" describe "the place to be searched, and the per-sons or things to be seized."

Notwithstanding its brevity, the Fourth Amendment has generated hundreds of Supreme Court decisions attempting to explain its meaning. It has produced an enormous volume of scholarly analysis examining its scope and proper interpretation. An elaborate array of detailed rules, caveats, and exceptions has been created by the courts in their struggle to apply the amendment's provisions to individual cases. What is so evocative about these 53 words? By the end of this chapter, you should appreciate the rich complexities of Fourth Amendment law, and you will be in a much better position to answer this question.

In the following pages, we will examine a host of issues related to the Fourth Amendment and the law of search and seizure. For example, we will consider the interests that the Fourth Amendment was designed to safeguard by exploring the definitions of a "search" and a "seizure" and what makes a search or a seizure "unreasonable." We will investigate the relationship between the Fourth Amendment's first clause—which prohibits unreasonable searches and seizures—and its second clause, which governs the warrant process. Should it be presumed that a search or seizure conducted without the prior authorization of a warrant *is* "unreasonable"? If so, would exceptional circumstances ever make a warrantless search or seizure reasonable? What did the Framers mean by the "probable-cause" requirement that is a part of the warrant clause? Must all searches and seizures at least be supported by "probable cause" if they are to be reasonable?

Note that the Fourth Amendment does not explain what should happen if a search or seizure is conducted unconstitutionally. What should the remedy be? Should the police be punished? Should an illegally seized person be released, or should unlawfully seized evidence or contraband—such as a murder weapon, drugs, or a confession—be ruled inadmissible at trial?

By prohibiting unreasonable searches and seizures, and through its regulation of the warrant process, the Fourth Amendment places important limits on law enforcement officers' efforts to detect and investigate crimes. Imagine a society that imposed no restrictions on the police's authority to search people's homes or their persons or to arrest them on suspicion of a crime. Permitting warrantless home searches at 3:00 a.m., allowing indiscriminate searches of people and their purses, backpacks, and other belongings, and granting the police unlimited authority to arrest and detain citizens almost certainly would help law enforcement officials uncover evidence of criminal wrongdoing and apprehend people who commit crimes. However, such benefits would come at a cost that most Americans would be unwilling to bear.

By the same token, if the Constitution absolutely forbade the investigation of individuals suspected of committing crimes, the police would be unable to carry out law enforcement functions necessary to protect society and its law-abiding citizens. The Framers of the Fourth Amendment appreciated the need for legitimate law enforcement activity. Accordingly, they did not ban all searches and seizures, only "unreasonable" ones. They specifically approved of searches and seizures conducted pursuant to warrants based on probable cause that particularly describe what or whom is to be searched or seized.

The Fourth Amendment requires a comparative assessment, or balancing, of individual citizens' freedoms and the legitimate needs of law enforcement. Working out the appropriate balancing of interests in search and seizure cases is not always easy, especially since the stakes for both individuals and the government tend to be high. As a result, search and seizure law is both intriguing and challenging. We begin by considering the particular interests protected by the Fourth Amendment.

ON "SEARCHES," "SEIZURES," AND WARRANT REQUIREMENTS

Searches and Reasonable Expectations of Privacy

Katz v. United States, 389 U.S. 347, 88 S. Ct. 507, 19 L. Ed. 2d 576 (1967)

Mr. Justice **Stewart** delivered the opinion of the Court.

The petitioner was convicted in the District Court for the Southern District of California under an eight-count indictment charging him with transmitting wagering information by telephone from Los Angeles to Miami and Boston, in violation of a federal statute. At trial the Government was permitted, over the petitioner's objection, to introduce evidence of the petitioner's end of telephone conversations, overheard by FBI agents who had attached an electronic listening and recording device to the outside of the public telephone booth from which he had placed his calls. In affirming his conviction, the Court of Appeals rejected the contention that the recordings had been obtained in violation of the Fourth Amendment, because "[t]here was no physical entrance into the area occupied by [the petitioner]." We granted certiorari in order to consider the constitutional questions thus presented.

The petitioner has phrased those questions as follows:

"A. Whether a public telephone booth is a constitutionally protected area so that evidence obtained by attaching an electronic listening recording device to the top of such a booth is obtained in violation of the right to privacy of the user of the booth.

"B. Whether physical penetration of a constitutionally protected area is necessary before a search and seizure can be said to be violative of the Fourth Amendment to the United States Constitution."

We decline to adopt this formulation of the issues. In the first place, the correct solution of Fourth Amendment problems is not necessarily promoted by incantation of the phrase "constitutionally protected area." Secondly, the Fourth Amendment cannot be translated into a general constitutional "right to privacy." That Amendment protects individual privacy against certain kinds of governmental intrusion, but its protections go further, and often have nothing to do with privacy at all. Other provisions of the Constitution protect personal privacy from other forms of governmental invasion. But the protection of a person's *general* right to privacy—his right to be let alone by other people—is, like the protection of his property and of his very life, left largely to the law of the individual States.

Because of the misleading way the issues have been formulated, the parties have attached great significance to the characterization of the telephone booth from which the petitioner placed his calls. The petitioner has strenuously argued that the booth was a "constitutionally protected area." The Government has maintained with equal vigor that it was not. But this effort to decide whether or not a given "area," viewed in the abstract, is "constitutionally protected" deflects attention from the problem presented by this case. For the Fourth Amendment protects people, not places. What a person knowingly exposes to the public, even in his own home or office, is not a subject of Fourth

Amendment protection. But what he seeks to preserve as private, even in an area accessible to the public, may be constitutionally protected.

The Government stresses the fact that the telephone booth from which the petitioner made his calls was constructed partly of glass, so that he was as visible after he entered it as he would have been if he had remained outside. But what he sought to exclude when he entered the booth was not the intruding eye—it was the uninvited ear. He did not shed his right to do so simply because he made his calls from a place where he might be seen. No less than an individual in a business office, in a friend's apartment, or in a taxicab, a person in a telephone booth may rely upon the protection of the Fourth Amendment. One who occupies it, shuts the door behind him, and pays the toll that permits him to place a call is surely entitled to assume that the words he utters into the mouthpiece will not be broadcast to the world. To read the Constitution more narrowly is to ignore the vital role that the public telephone has come to play in private communication.

The Government contends, however, that the activities of its agents in this case should not be tested by Fourth Amendment requirements, for the surveillance technique they employed involved no physical penetration of the telephone booth from which the petitioner placed his calls. . . .

[A]lthough a closely divided Court supposed in Olmstead [v United States, 277 US 438, 48 S. Ct. 564, 72 L Ed 944 (1928)] that surveillance without any trespass and without the seizure of any material object fell outside the ambit of the Constitution, we have since departed from the narrow view on which that decision rested. Indeed, we have expressly held that the Fourth Amendment governs not only the seizure of tangible items, but extends as well to the recording of oral statements, overheard without any "technical trespass under . . . local property law." Silverman v United States, 365 US 505, 511 [81 S Ct 679, 5 L Ed 2d 734 (1961)].

Once this much is acknowledged, and once it is recognized that the Fourth Amendment protects people—and not simply "areas"—against unreasonable searches and seizures, it becomes clear that the reach of that Amendment cannot turn upon the presence or absence of a physical intrusion into any given enclosure.

We conclude that the underpinnings of Olmstead and Goldman [v. United States, 316 U.S. 129, 62 S. Ct. 993, 86 L. Ed. 1322 (1942)] have been so eroded by our subsequent decisions that the "trespass" doctrine there enunciated can no longer be regarded as controlling. The Government's activities in electronically listening to and recording the petitioner's words violated the privacy upon which he justifiably relied while using the telephone booth and thus constituted a "search and seizure" within the meaning of the Fourth Amendment. The fact that the electronic device employed to achieve that end did not happen to penetrate the wall of the booth can have no constitutional significance.

The question remaining for decision, then, is whether the search and seizure conducted in this case complied with constitutional standards. In that regard, the Government's position is that its agents acted in an entirely defensible manner: They did not begin their electronic surveillance until investigation of the petitioner's activities had established a strong probability that he was using the telephone in question to transmit gambling information to persons in other States, in violation of federal law. Moreover, the surveillance was limited, both in scope and in duration, to the specific purpose of establishing the contents of the petitioner's unlawful telephonic communications. The agents confined their surveillance to the brief periods during which he used the telephone booth, and they took great care to overhear only the conversations of the petitioner himself.

Accepting this account of the Government's actions as accurate, it is clear that this surveillance was so narrowly circumscribed that a duly authorized magistrate, properly notified of the need for such investigation, specifically informed of the basis on which it was to proceed, and clearly apprised of the precise intrusion it would entail, could constitutionally have authorized, with appropriate safeguards, the very limited search and seizure that the Government asserts in fact took place. . . .

It is apparent that the agents in this case acted with restraint. Yet the inescapable fact is that this restraint was imposed by the agents themselves, not by a judicial officer. They were not required, before commencing the search, to present their estimate of probable cause for detached scrutiny by a neutral magistrate. They were not compelled, during the conduct of the search itself, to observe precise limits established in advance by a specific court order. Nor were they directed, after the search had been completed, to notify the authorizing magistrate in detail of all that had been seized. In the absence of such safeguards, this Court has never sustained a search upon the sole ground that officers reasonably expected to find evidence of a particular crime and voluntarily confined their activities to the least intrusive means consistent with that end. Searches conducted without warrants have been held unlawful "notwithstanding facts unquestionably showing probable cause," Agnello v United States, 269 US 20, 33, 46 S Ct 4, 70 L Ed 145, 149 [(1925)], for the Constitution requires "that the deliberate, impartial judgment of a judicial officer . . . be interposed between the citizen and the police. . . ." Wong Sun v United States, 371 US 471, 481–482, 83 S Ct 407, 9 L Ed 2d 441, 451 [(1963)]. "Over and again this Court has emphasized that the mandate of the [Fourth] Amendment requires adherence to judicial processes," United States v Jeffers, 342 US 48, 51, 72 S Ct 93, 96 L Ed 59, 64 [(1951)], and that searches conducted outside the judicial process, without prior approval by judge or magistrate, are per se unreasonable under the Fourth Amendment—subject only to a few specifically established and well-delineated exceptions. . . .

The Government does not question these basic principles. Rather, it urges the creation of a new exception to cover this case. It argues that surveillance of a telephone booth should be exempted from the usual requirement of advance authorization by a magistrate upon a showing of probable cause. We cannot agree. Omission of such authorization "bypasses the safeguards provided by an objective predetermination of probable cause, and substitutes instead the far less reliable procedure of an after-the-event justification for the . . . search, too likely to be subtly influenced by the familiar shortcomings of hindsight judgment." Beck v

Ohio, 379 US 89, 96, 85 S Ct 223, 13 L Ed 2d 142, 147 [(1964)].

And bypassing a neutral predetermination of the *scope* of a search leaves individuals secure from Fourth Amendment violations "only in the discretion of the police."

These considerations do not vanish when the search in question is transferred from the setting of a home, an office, or a hotel room to that of a telephone booth. Wherever a man may be, he is entitled to know that he will remain free from unreasonable searches and seizures. The government agents here ignored "the procedure of antecedent justification . . . that is central to the Fourth Amendment," a procedure that we hold to be a constitutional precondition of the kind of electronic surveillance involved in this case. Because the surveillance here failed to meet that condition, and because it led to the petitioner's conviction, the judgment must be reversed.

It is so ordered.

* * *

Mr. Justice **Harlan**, concurring.

* * *

As the Court's opinion states, "the Fourth Amendment protects people, not places." The question, however, is what protection it affords to those people. Generally, as here, the answer to that question requires reference to a "place." My understanding of the rule that has emerged from prior decisions is that there is a twofold requirement, first that a person have exhibited an actual (subjective) expectation of privacy and, second, that the expectation be one that society is prepared to recognize as "reasonable." Thus a man's home is, for most purposes, a place where he expects privacy, but objects, activities, or statements that he exposes to the "plain view" of outsiders are not "protected" because no intention to keep them to himself has been exhibited. On the other hand, conversations in the open would not be protected against being overheard, for the expectation of privacy under the circumstances would be unreasonable.

The critical fact in this case is that "[o]ne who occupies it, [a telephone booth] shuts the door behind him, and pays the toll that permits him to place a call is surely entitled to assume" that his conversation is not being intercepted. The point is not that the booth is "accessible to the public" at other times, but that it is a temporarily private place whose momentary occupants' expectations of freedom from intrusion are recognized as reasonable. . . .

Mr. Justice **Black**, dissenting. . . .

My basic objection is twofold: (1) I do not believe that the words of the Amendment will bear the meaning given them by today's decision, and (2) I do not believe that it is the proper role of this Court to rewrite the Amendment in order "to bring it into harmony with the times" and thus reach a result that many people believe to be desirable.

While I realize that an argument based on the meaning of words lacks the scope, and no doubt the appeal, of broad policy discussions and philosophical discourses on such nebulous subjects as privacy, for me the language of the Amendment is the crucial place to look in construing a written document such as our Constitution. . . .

The Fourth Amendment says that

"The right of the people to be secure in their persons, houses, papers, and effects, against unreasonable searches and seizures, shall not be violated, and no Warrants shall issue, but upon probable cause, supported by Oath or affirmation, and particularly describing the place to be searched, and the persons or things to be seized."

The first clause protects "persons, houses, papers, and effects, against unreasonable searches and seizures. . . ." These words connote the idea of tangible things with size, form, and weight, things capable of being searched, seized, or both. The second clause of the Amendment still further establishes its Framers' purpose to limit its protection to tangible things by providing that no warrants shall issue but those "particularly describing the place to be searched, and the persons or things to be seized." A conversation overheard by eavesdropping whether by plain snooping or wiretapping, is not tangible and, under the normally accepted meanings of the words, can neither be searched nor seized. . . .

Since I see no way in which the words of the Fourth Amendment can be construed to apply to eavesdropping, that closes the matter for me. In interpreting the Bill of Rights, I willingly go as far as liberal construction of the language takes me, but I simply cannot in good conscience give a meaning to words which they have never before been thought to have and which they certainly do not have in common ordinary usage. I will not distort the words of the Amendment in order to "keep the Constitution up to date" or "to bring it into harmony with the times." It was never meant that this Court have such power, which in effect would make us a continuously functioning constitutional convention. . . .

The Fourth Amendment protects privacy only to the extent that it prohibits unreasonable searches and seizures of "persons, houses, papers, and effects." No general right is created by the Amendment so as to give this Court the unlimited power to hold unconstitutional everything which affects privacy. Certainly the Framers, well acquainted as they were with the excesses of governmental power, did not intend to grant this Court such omnipotent lawmaking authority as that. The history of governments proves that it is dangerous to freedom to repose such powers in courts. . . .

Notes and Questions

1. *Katz* presents multiple issues, some of which are fundamentally important to search and seizure law. In what precise sense was Katz "searched"? Why did the parties make an issue of whether the listening device physically penetrated the telephone booth and argue so vigorously about whether the phone booth could fairly be characterized as a "constitutionally protected area"? What of the point made by Justice Black in his dissent: Does the language used in the Fourth Amendment seem to contemplate that spoken words can either be "searched" or "seized"? Exactly what did the FBI agents do wrong when they made use of the listening and

recording device attached to the outside of the phone booth? Is the Court saying that the use of such devices is flatly prohibited because individuals are entitled to assume that their telephone conversations are conducted in private?

2. What if one of the FBI agents had simply positioned himself as if waiting to make use of the phone when Katz was through with it and overheard Katz's end of the conversation through the glass booth? Should it matter whether Katz had left the door to the phone booth open or closed, or whether he was shouting or whispering? What if, while conducting a large-scale crackdown on gambling, the FBI posted in all public phone booths in the Los Angeles area conspicuous signs that read: "WARNING: INDIVIDUALS USING THIS TELEPHONE SHOULD BE ADVISED THAT THEIR CONVERSATIONS MAY BE SUBJECT TO INTERCEPTION AND RECORDING THROUGH LISTENING DEVICES INSTALLED AND MONITORED BY THE FBI"? *See* Amsterdam, "Perspectives on the Fourth Amendment," 58 *Minn. L. Rev.* 349, 384 (1974).

3. In *Smith v. Maryland*, 442 U.S. 735, 99 S. Ct. 2577, 71 L. Ed. 2d 220 (1979), a woman was robbed and later began receiving threatening and obscene phone calls from a man who identified himself as the robber. The police traced ownership of a car that had been prowling outside of the victim's house to Michael Lee Smith, the petitioner. Thereafter, the police requested the telephone company to activate a "pen register" from the company's central office to record the telephone numbers dialed from Smith's phone. The pen register did not have the capacity to monitor or intercept conversations; it merely recorded the electrical impulses triggered by dialing the telephone. No warrant or court order was obtained in this process. Smith was arrested after the pen register revealed that his telephone indeed had been used to dial the phone number of the robbery victim. This and other evidence led to Smith's conviction for robbery. The question presented to the Supreme Court was "whether the installation and use of a pen register constitutes a 'search' within the meaning of the Fourth Amendment." 442 U.S., at 736.

The Court, per Blackmun, J. (with Justice Powell not participating, and three justices dissenting), rejected Smith's claim that "he had a 'legitimate expectation of privacy' regarding the numbers he dialed on his phone." It thus concluded that the installation and use of the pen register did not constitute "a 'search.'" 442 U.S., at 742. "First, we doubt that people in general entertain any actual expectation of privacy in the numbers they dial." *Id.* Telephone users were presumed to know that telephone companies had the capacity to record the numbers that they dialed and in fact regularly did so, as when billing for long-distance calls. "Second, even if petitioner did harbor some subjective expectation that the phone numbers he dialed would remain private, this expectation is not 'one that society is prepared to recognize as "reasonable." *Katz v. United States*, 389 U.S. at 361.' *Id.* at 743. The petitioner, it was held, had "assumed the risk" that the phone company, which he knew or should have known could monitor the numbers dialed from his telephone, might reveal them to the police. *Id.* at 744. "We therefore conclude that petitioner in all probability entertained no actual expectation of privacy in the phone numbers he dialed, and that even if he did, his expectation was not 'legitimate.' The installation and use of a pen register, consequently, was not a 'search,' and no warrant was required." *Id.* at 745–46.

4. Acting on a tip that the respondent in *California v. Ciraolo*, 476 U.S. 207, 106 S. Ct. 1809, 90 L. Ed. 2d 210 (1986) was growing marijuana in his back yard, two Santa Clara police officers secured an airplane and flew at an altitude of 1,000 feet over respondent's property to investigate. Ciraolo's back yard was surrounded by two fences—one 6 feet tall and the other 10 feet tall—and thus could not be observed from ground level. The police officers did not obtain a search warrant before flying the plane over Ciraolo's property. They were able to identify several 8-foot– to 10-foot–high marijuana plants growing within the fenced area of Ciraolo's back yard and took several aerial photographs with a standard 35-mm camera. Armed with this information, the officers later obtained a search warrant. After the warrant was executed, 73 marijuana plants were seized from Ciraolo's back yard. Ciraolo moved to suppress—that is, to prohibit the evidence from being used to help prove his guilt—the marijuana plants, claiming that the police had "searched" his premises when they peered into his back yard from the vantage point of the airplane. He argued that the "search" was unlawful because it had not been authorized by a warrant. The trial court denied this motion, the marijuana plants were admitted into evidence, and Ciraolo was convicted of cultivating the illegal substance. On appeal, however, the California Court of Appeals agreed with Ciraolo's contention and reversed his conviction. The U.S. Supreme Court reversed (5–4), through an opinion written by Chief Justice Burger.

The majority opinion conceded that Ciraolo had "clearly . . . met the test of manifesting his own subjective intent and desire to maintain privacy as to his unlawful agricultural pursuits." Yet it concluded that Ciraolo's claim that his back yard had been illegally "searched" must fail because Ciraolo did not qualify under the second part of the *Katz* inquiry: "Is society willing to recognize that [subjective] expectation [of privacy] as reasonable?" The Chief Justice reasoned that

the observations by Officers Shultz and Rodriquez in this case took place within public navigable airspace in a physically nonintrusive manner; from this point they were able to observe plants readily discernible to the naked eye as marijuana. That the observation from aircraft was directed at identifying the plants and the officers were trained to recognize marijuana is irrelevant. Such observation is precisely what a judicial officer needs to provide a basis for a warrant. Any member of the public flying in this airspace who glanced down could have seen everything that these officers observed. On this record, we readily conclude that respondent's expectation that his garden was protected from such observation is unreasonable and is not an expectation that society is prepared to honor.

5. Just three years after deciding *Ciraolo*, the Court considered a similar question in *Florida v. Riley*, 488 U.S. 445, 109 S. Ct. 693, 102 L. Ed. 2d 835 (1989): "Whether surveillance of the interior of a partially covered greenhouse in a residential backyard from the vantage point of a helicopter located 400 feet above the green-

house constitutes a 'search' for which a warrant is required under the Fourth Amendment." Imagine a police helicopter hovering over a residence at an altitude of 400 feet to allow law enforcement officers to peer down and inspect the homeowner's property. Should this activity be characterized as a "search"? The answer to this question largely determines whether the police can make helicopter surveillances without first obtaining judicial authorization (i.e., a search warrant). The Supreme Court, through a plurality opinion authored by Justice White and joined by three other justices, relied on *Ciraolo* to conclude that the helicopter-assisted inspection of the property did not violate a reasonable expectation of privacy and hence did not constitute a "search." Justice O'Connor concurred in the judgment, and four justices dissented. Justice Brennan's dissent argued that *Riley* tipped the scales too far in favor of law enforcement:

The Fourth Amendment demands that we temper our efforts to apprehend criminals with a concern for the impact on our fundamental liberties of the methods we use. I hope it will be a matter of concern to my colleagues that the police surveillance methods they would sanction were among those described forty years ago in George Orwell's dread vision of life in the 1980's:

The black-mustachio'd face gazed down from every commanding corner. There was one on the house front immediately opposite. BIG BROTHER IS WATCHING YOU, the caption said. . . . In the far distance a helicopter skimmed down between the roofs, hovered for an instant like a bluebottle, and darted away again with a curving flight. It was the Police Patrol, snooping into people's windows. G. Orwell, Nineteen Eighty-Four 4 (1949).

* * * * *

The following cases consider whether other police activities amount to a "search" under the terms of the Fourth Amendment. Pay particular attention to the theme of "assumption of risk" and how that doctrine figures into the Court's conclusions about whether citizens successfully can assert that they retain a reasonable expectation of privacy under the presented facts. We start with a case that may seem unlikely to involve fundamental freedoms but that implicates principles basic to determining the proper scope of the Fourth Amendment. *California v. Greenwood* addresses whether the police's inspection of garbage deposited by the occupant of a dwelling at his curbside is a "search" within the meaning of the Fourth Amendment.

California v. Greenwood, 486 U.S. 35, 108 S. Ct. 1625, 100 L. Ed. 2d 30 (1988)

Justice **White** delivered the opinion of the Court.

The issue here is whether the Fourth Amendment prohibits the warrantless search and seizure of garbage left for collection outside the curtilage of a home. We conclude, in accordance with the vast majority of lower courts that have addressed the issue, that it does not.

I

In early 1984, Investigator Jenny Stracner of the Laguna Beach Police Department received information indicating that respondent Greenwood might be engaged in narcotics trafficking. . . .

Stracner sought to investigate this information by conducting a surveillance of Greenwood's home. She observed several vehicles make brief stops at the house during the late-night and early-morning hours, and she followed a truck from the house to a residence that had previously been under investigation as a narcotics trafficking location.

On April 6, 1984, Stracner asked the neighborhood's regular trash collector to pick up the plastic garbage bags that Greenwood had left on the curb in front of his house and to turn the bags over to her without mixing their contents with garbage from other houses. The trash collector cleaned his truck bin of other refuse, collected the garbage bags from the street in front of Greenwood's house, and turned the bags over to Stracner. The officer searched through the rubbish and found items indicative of narcotics use. She recited the information that she had gleaned from the trash search in an affidavit in support of a warrant to search Greenwood's home.

Police officers encountered both respondents at the house later that day when they arrived to execute the warrant. The police discovered quantities of cocaine and hashish during their search of the house. Respondents were arrested on felony narcotics charges. They subsequently posted bail.

The police continued to receive reports of many late-night visitors to the Greenwood house. On May 4, Investigator Robert Rahaeuser obtained Greenwood's garbage from the regular trash collector in the same manner as had Stracner. The garbage again contained evidence of narcotics use.

Rahaeuser secured another search warrant for Greenwood's home based on the information from the second trash search. The police found more narcotics and evidence of narcotics trafficking when they executed the warrant. Greenwood was again arrested.

The Superior Court dismissed the charges against respondents on the authority of People v Krivda, 5 Cal 3d 357, 486 P2d 1262 (1971), which held that warrantless trash searches violate the Fourth Amendment and the California Constitution. The court found that the police would not have had probable cause to search the Greenwood home without the evidence obtained from the trash searches.

The Court of Appeal affirmed. . . .

II

The warrantless search and seizure of the garbage bags left at the curb outside the Greenwood house would violate the Fourth Amendment only if respondents manifested a subjective expectation of privacy in their garbage that society accepts as objectively reasonable. . . . Respondents do not disagree with this standard.

They assert, however, that they had, and exhibited, an expectation of privacy with respect to the trash that was searched by the police: The trash, which was placed on the street for collection at a fixed time, was contained in opaque plastic bags, which the garbage collector was expected to pick up, mingle with the trash of others, and deposit at the garbage dump. The trash was only temporarily on the street, and there was little likelihood that it would be inspected by anyone.

It may well be that respondents did not expect that the contents of their garbage bags would become known to the police or other members of the public. An expectation of privacy does not give rise to Fourth Amendment protection, however, unless society is prepared to accept that expectation as objectively reasonable.

Here, we conclude that respondents exposed their garbage to the public sufficiently to defeat their claim to Fourth Amendment protection. It is common knowledge that plastic garbage bags left on or at the side of a public street are readily accessible to animals, children, scavengers, snoops,[4] and other members of the public. Moreover, respondents placed their refuse at the curb for the express purpose of conveying it to a third party, the trash collector, who might himself have sorted through respondents' trash or permitted others, such as the police, to do so. Accordingly, having deposited their garbage "in an area particularly suited for public inspection and, in a manner of speaking, public consumption, for the express purpose of having strangers take it," United States v Reicherter, 647 F2d 397, 399 (CA 3 1981), respondents could have

---

4. Even the refuse of prominent Americans has not been invulnerable. In 1975, for example, a reporter for a weekly tabloid seized five bags of garbage from the sidewalk outside the home of Secretary of State Henry Kissinger. Washington Post, July 9, 1975, p A1, col. 8. A newspaper editorial criticizing this journalistic "trash-picking" observed that "[e]vidently . . . 'everybody does it.'" Washington Post, July 10, 1975, p A18, col 1. We of course do not, as the dissent implies, "bas[e] [our] conclusion" that individuals have no reasonable expectation of privacy in their garbage on this "sole incident."

had no reasonable expectation of privacy in the inculpatory items that they discarded.

Furthermore, as we have held, the police cannot reasonably be expected to avert their eyes from evidence of criminal activity that could have been observed by any member of the public. Hence, "[w]hat a person knowingly exposes to the public, even in his own home or office, is not a subject of Fourth Amendment protection." Katz v United States, supra, at 351, 88 S Ct 507, 19 L Ed 2d 576 . . . .

The judgment of the California Court of Appeals is therefore reversed, and this case is remanded for further proceedings not inconsistent with this opinion.

It is so ordered.

Justice **Kennedy** took no part in the consideration or decision of this case.

Justice **Brennan**, with whom Justice **Marshall** joins, dissenting. . . .

Scrutiny of another's trash is contrary to commonly accepted notions of civilized behavior. I suspect, therefore, that members of our society will be shocked to learn that the Court, the ultimate guarantor of liberty, deems unreasonable our expectation that the aspects of our private lives that are concealed safely in a trash bag will not become public. . . .

Respondents deserve no less protection just because Greenwood used the bags to discard rather than to transport his personal effects. Their contents are not inherently any less private, and Greenwood's decision to discard them, at least in the manner in which he did, does not diminish his expectation of privacy.

A trash bag, like any of the above-mentioned containers, "is a common repository for one's personal effects" and, even more than many of them, is "therefore . . . inevitably associated with the expectation of privacy." . . . See California v Rooney, 483 US 307, 320–21, n 3, 107 S Ct 2852, 97 L Ed 2d 258 (1987) (White, J., dissenting) (renowned archaeologist Emil Haury once said, "If you want to know what is really going on in a community, look at its garbage").

A single bag of trash testifies eloquently to the eating, reading, and recreational habits of the person who produced it. A search of trash, like a search of the bedroom, can relate intimate details about sexual practices, health, and personal hygiene. Like rifling through desk drawers or intercepting phone calls, rummaging through trash can divulge the target's financial and professional status, political affiliations and inclinations, private thoughts, personal relationships, and romantic interests. It cannot be doubted that a sealed trash bag harbors telling evidence of the "intimate activity associated with the 'sanctity of a man's home and the privacies of life,'" which the Fourth Amendment is designed to protect.

* * *

In evaluating the reasonableness of Greenwood's expectation that his sealed trash bags would not be invaded, the Court has held that we must look to "understandings that are recognized and permitted by society." Most of us, I believe, would be incensed to discover a meddler—whether a neighbor, a reporter, or a detective—scrutinizing our sealed trash containers to discover some detail of our personal lives. That was, quite naturally, the reaction to the sole incident on which the Court bases its conclusion that "snoops" and the like defeat the expectation of privacy in trash. Ante, n 4. When a tabloid reporter examined then-Secretary of State Henry Kissinger's trash and published his findings, Kissinger was "really revolted" by the intrusion and his wife suffered "grave anguish." N.Y. Times, July 9, 1975, p A1, col 8. The public response roundly condemning the reporter demonstrates that society not only recognized those reactions as reasonable, but shared them as well.

* * *

That is not to deny that isolated intrusions into opaque, sealed trash containers occur. When, acting on their own, "animals, children, scavengers, snoops, [or] other members of the general public," *actually* rummage through a bag of trash and expose its contents to plain view, "police cannot reasonably be expected to avert their eyes from evidence of criminal activity that could have been observed by any member of the public." . . .

Had Greenwood flaunted his intimate activity by strewing his trash all over the curb for all to see, or had some nongovernmental intruder invaded his privacy and done the same, I could accept the Court's conclusion that an expectation of privacy would have been unreasonable. Similarly, had police searching the city dump run across incriminating evidence that, despite commingling with the trash of others, still retained its identity as Greenwood's, we would have a different case. But all that Greenwood "exposed . . . to the public," were the exteriors of several opaque, sealed containers. . . .

The mere *possibility* that unwelcome meddlers *might* open and rummage through the containers does not negate the expectation of privacy in its contents any more than the possibility of a burglary negates an expectation of privacy in the home; or the possibility of a private intrusion negates an expectation of privacy in an unopened package; or the possibility that an operator will listen in on a telephone conversation negates an expectation of privacy in the words spoken on the telephone.

* * *

Nor is it dispositive that "respondents placed their refuse at the curb for the express purpose of conveying it to a third party, . . . who might himself have sorted through respondents' trash or permitted others, such as police, to do so." In the first place, Greenwood can hardly be faulted for leaving trash on his curb when a county ordinance commanded him to do so. . . . More importantly, even the voluntary relinquishment of possession or control over an effect does not necessarily amount to a relinquishment of a privacy expectation in it. Were it otherwise, a letter or package would lose all Fourth Amendment protection when placed in a mail box or other depository with the "express purpose" of entrusting it to the postal officer or a private carrier; those bailees are just as likely as trash collectors (and certainly have greater incentive) to "sor[t] through" the personal effects entrusted to them, "or permi[t] others, such as police to do so." Yet, it has been clear for at least 110 years that the possibility of such an intrusion does not justify a warrantless search by police in the first instance. . . .

Notes and Questions

1. As the majority opinion in *Greenwood* observes, it is possible that the contents of garbage bags left outside for disposal might be strewn about by dogs or vandals, picked through by scavengers, investigated by nosy neighbors, or even itemized by reporters for news tabloids. Did Greenwood's garbage bag actually suffer any of these calamities? Is the mere possibility that such events *could* occur sufficient to justify the police in opening and examining the contents of the garbage bag? Is it possible that a sealed envelope deposited with the post office *might* be torn sometime before its delivery, exposing the letter included inside? Might the family dog rip the envelope open if it was placed through the mail slot of the addressee's home? If so, does *Greenwood* suggest that the police can make a warrantless inspection of a letter entrusted to the post office for delivery, or are garbage bags and mailing envelopes distinguishable? Cf. *United States v. Van Leeuwen*, 397 U.S. 249, 90 S. Ct. 1029, 25 L. Ed. 2d 282 (1970).

2. Is the difference between a garbage bag left at the curbside and a letter mailed at the post office that the garbage depositor well knows and expects (or reasonably should know) that his or her garbage will be picked up and taken to a public dumpsite and thereby presumably will be exposed to anyone who might stumble upon it, whereas the person mailing the letter knows (or reasonably expects) that, in the normal course of postal operations, the contents of the letter should be exposed to no one other than the addressee? By entrusting his or her garbage bag to a third party (the garbage collectors) who eventually may open it, does an individual "assume the risk" that the third party might share its contents with others, including the police? What alternatives would a homeowner such as Greenwood have who did not want to incur such a risk by leaving his garbage bags out for collec-

tion? And for what types of risks should he reasonably be held accountable? Should a person be required to assume the risk that the garbage collectors for whom he or she leaves garbage—for the purpose of delivering it to a dump—will take the exceptional action of routing the garbage to a police officer instead of to a landfill? Should he or she be required to assume *certain* risks—such as those presented by dogs or scavengers—but not be held responsible for assuming other kinds of "extraordinary" risks wholly outside of his or her (reasonable) anticipation—such as that the garbage collectors will deliver his or her garbage to the police?

3. Some state courts have rejected *Greenwood* and have interpreted their state constitutions to protect citizens from warrantless police inspections of their garbage. The New Jersey Supreme Court did so in *State v. Hempele*, which is presented below. Article I, paragraph 7 of the New Jersey Constitution is worded almost identically to the Fourth Amendment. Two defendants, Hempele and Pasanen, claimed that the warrantless inspection of garbage bags left on the curb violated their rights under the state constitution's protection against unreasonable searches and seizures. The majority opinion in *Hempele* provides our first opportunity to study a state constitutional ruling. As you read *Hempele*, try to identify the general reasons that the court offers for interpreting its state constitution differently from how the U.S. Supreme Court interprets the federal Constitution. In addition, note the specific grounds for the New Jersey Supreme Court's disagreement with Justice White's reasoning in his majority opinion in *Greenwood*. Be prepared to defend your view about which decision—*Greenwood* or *Hempele*—results in a better balancing of the state and individual interests associated with garbage "searches."

State v. Hempele, 120 N.J. 182, 576 A.2d 793 (1990)

CLIFFORD, J.

* * *

We now determine whether the New Jersey Constitution protects curbside garbage from unreasonable searches and seizures. Despite the similarity between the text of article I, paragraph 7 of the New Jersey Constitution and the text of the fourth amendment, we have found on several occasions that the former "affords our citizens greater protection against unreasonable searches and seizures than does the fourth amendment." . . .

For most of our country's history, the primary source of protection of individual rights has been state constitutions, not the federal Bill of Rights. The genius of federalism is that the fundamental rights of citizens are protected not only by the United States Constitution but also by the laws of each of the states. The system may be untidy on occasion, but that untidiness invests it with "a vibrant diversity." Pollock, "Adequate and Independent State Grounds as a Means of Balancing the Relationship Between State and Federal Courts," 63 Tex. L. Rev. 977, 979 (1985). "As tempting as it may be to harmonize results under the state and federal constitutions, federalism contemplated that state courts may grant greater protection to individual rights if they choose." Id. at 980.

When the United States Constitution affords our citizens less protection than does the New Jersey Constitution, we have not merely the authority to give full effect to the State protection, we have the duty to do so. . . .

Cognizant of the diversity of laws, customs, and mores within its jurisdiction, the United States Supreme Court is necessarily "hesitant to impose on a national level far-reaching constitutional rules binding on each and every state." That Court establishes no more than the floor of constitutional protection. The Supreme Court must be especially cautious in fourth-amendment cases. When determining whether a search warrant is necessary in a specific circum-

stance, the Court must take note of the disparity in warrant-application procedures among the several states, and must consider whether a warrant requirement in that situation might overload the procedure in any one state. In contrast, we are fortunate to have in New Jersey a procedure that allows for the speedy and reliable issuance of search warrants based on probable cause. A warrant requirement is not so great a burden in New Jersey as it might be in other states. . . .

IV

In determining whether the warrantless search of defendants' garbage violated article I, paragraph 7 of the New Jersey Constitution, we apply a slightly different test from the one used in California v. Greenwood. In that case the Supreme Court turned to the two-pronged inquiry first enunciated by Justice Harlan in Katz v. United States, 389 U.S. 347, 88 S. Ct. 507, 19 L. Ed. 2d 576 (1967). Under that analysis the determination of fourth-amendment protections rests on "a twofold requirement, first that a person have exhibited an actual (subjective) expectation of privacy and, second, that the expectation be one that society is prepared to recognize as 'reasonable.'" Id. at 361, 88 S. Ct. at 516, 19 L. Ed. 2d at 588 (Harlan, J., concurring).

We decline to follow that test because a defendant's "actual (subjective) expectation of privacy" does not determine the New Jersey Constitution's restraints on the State's power to search and seize. Justice Harlan himself apparently reached a similar conclusion when he later wrote that the analysis under Katz "must, in my view, transcend the search for subjective expectations * * * ." United States v. White, 401 U.S. 745, 786, 91 S. Ct. 1122, 1143, 28 L. Ed. 2d 453, 478 (1971) (Harlan, J., dissenting). . . .

Moreover, the two-prong analysis entails an arbitrary distinction between facts that manifest a subjective privacy expectation and those that indicate the reasonableness of the privacy expectation. We are unaware of any reasoned discourse distinguishing which evidence goes to the first prong and which evidence goes to the second. Both prongs are dependent on objective criteria, as would be apparent in a case involving the constitutionality of a warrantless search of a purse made of clear plastic. Because an expectation of privacy in the contents of a handbag can be reasonable, the question would be whether the transparency of the purse affects the constitutionality of the search. One might argue that although a privacy expectation of the contents of a purse is normally reasonable, the owner here failed to "exhibit an actual (subjective) expectation in privacy" because the purse was transparent. On the other hand, one might argue that a subjective expectation of privacy in the contents of a transparent purse is not "one that society is prepared to recognize as 'reasonable.'"

Thus the objective fact of the transparency of the purse could be evidence either of a failure to manifest a subjective privacy expectation or of the unreasonableness of that subjective privacy expectation. The decision to apply that fact to one prong rather than the other would be arbitrary. That choice, furthermore, would probably not affect the final determination of whether the contents are constitutionally protected. We conclude, therefore, that the manifestation of a subjective privacy expectation should not be a separate requirement for protection under article 1, paragraph 7. Instead, the New Jersey Constitution requires only that an expectation of privacy be reasonable. . . .

The one-step test better reflects the underlying principles of search-and-seizure law. Article 1, paragraph 7 does not "ask[ ] what we expect of government. [It] tell[s] us what we should demand of government." Amsterdam, "Perspectives On the Fourth Amendment," 58 Minn. L. Rev. 349, 384 (1974) [hereinafter Amsterdam]. "The right of the people to be secure in their persons, houses, papers, and effects, against unreasonable searches and seizures, shall not be violated" when there can be a reasonable expectation of privacy in them. N.J. Const. of 1947 art. I, para. 7.

-A-

In determining the reasonableness of an expectation of privacy in curbside garbage left for collection, we start from the premise that "[e]xpectations of privacy are established by general social norms." Robbins v California, 453 U.S. 420, 428, 101 S. Ct. 2841, 2847, 69 L. Ed. 2d 744, 751 (1981) (plurality opinion), overruled on other grounds, United States v. Ross, 456 U.S. 798, 102 S. Ct. 2157, 72 L. Ed. 2d 572 (1982).

The "ultimate question" is whether, if garbage searches are "permitted to go unregulated by constitutional restraints, the amount of privacy and freedom remaining to citizens would be diminished to a compass inconsistent with the aims of a free and open society." Amsterdam, supra, 58 Minn. L. Rev. at 403. With that question in mind, we first examine whether it is reasonable for a person to want to keep the contents of his or her garbage private.

Clues to people's most private traits and affairs can be found in their garbage. "[A]lmost every human activity ultimately manifests itself in waste products and * * * any individual may understandably wish to maintain the confidentiality of his refuse." State v. Smith, 510 P.2d 793, 798 (Alaska) (upholding warrantless search of dumpster), cert. denied, 414 U.S. 1086, 94 S. Ct. 603, 38 L. Ed. 2d 489 (1973). . . .

Most people seem to have an interest in keeping such matters private; few publicize them voluntarily. Undoubtedly many would be upset to see a neighbor or stranger sifting through their garbage, perusing their discarded mail, reading their bank statements, looking at their empty pharmaceutical bottles, and checking receipts to see what videotapes they rent. . . .

Given the secrets that refuse can disclose, it is reasonable for a person to prefer that his or her garbage remain private.

-B-

Like the fourth amendment, article I, paragraph 7 "provides protection to the owner of every container that conceals its contents from plain view." . . .

-C-

The State relies on the three reasons cited in Greenwood for excepting garbage-search cases from the "opaque container" rule: garbage left on the curb is not invulnerable to inspection by outsiders; the disposal of garbage bags is entrusted to a third party; and the police need not "avert their eyes" from evidence visible to the public. . . .

-1-

The Court held in Greenwood that an expectation of privacy in plastic garbage bags left at the side of the street is not reasonable because the bags are "readily accessible to animals, children, scavengers, snoops, and other members of the public." 486 U.S. at 40, 108 S. Ct. at 1628, 100 L. Ed. 2d at 36–37 (footnotes omitted).

The accessibility of garbage to outsiders, however, is not dispositive, because a person can maintain a privacy interest in something that is not completely vulnerable to prying eyes. Otherwise article I, paragraph 7 would protect only that which is under lock-and-key. (Even then, locksmiths, lock pickers, and people wielding sticks of dynamite could gain access.) . . .

The government could not arbitrarily search parked automobiles even though "[e]very person who parks his or her car on a side street in Greenwich Village voluntarily runs the risk that it will be burglarized." Amsterdam, supra, 58 Minn. L. Rev. at 406. . . .

Although a person may realize that an unwelcome scavenger might sort through his or her garbage, "such expectations would not necessarily include a detailed, systematized inspection of the garbage by law enforcement personnel." Smith v. State, supra, 510 P.2d at 803 (Rabinowitz, C.J., dissenting). . . .

A person's awareness that leaving garbage for disposal may entail privacy risks "hardly means that government is constitutionally unconstrained in adding to those risks." Amsterdam, supra, 58 Minn. L. Rev. at 406. There is a difference between a homeless person scavenging for food and clothes, and an officer of the State scrutinizing the contents of a garbage bag for incriminating materials. . . . A privacy expectation in garbage can be reasonable even though the contents are not invulnerable to inspection by outsiders. We expect officers of the State to be more knowledgeable and respectful of people's privacy than are dogs and curious children.

-2-

The Supreme Court also rejected a privacy expectation in garbage because the defendants had placed their garbage on the curb for removal by a third party "who might himself have sorted through respondents' trash or permitted others, such as the police, to do so." California v. Greenwood, supra, 486 U.S. at 40, 108 S. Ct. at 1629, 100 L. Ed. 2d at 37. That premise is predicated on three assumptions: first, that garbage collectors have the right to look through closed garbage bags; second, that garbage collectors have sufficient authority over the bags to consent to a police search; third, that because garbage collectors can consent to a search, the police need neither a warrant nor consent for a search. The first is debatable. The second is dubious. The third is downright disturbing. . . .

We need not pause over either of the first two propositions because the third is so plainly wrong. Even if a landlord could enter a tenant's premises and did have sufficient common authority to "permit[ ] others, such as the police, to do so," California v. Greenwood, supra 486 U.S. at 40, 108 S. Ct. at 1629, 100 L. Ed. 2d at 37, the police certainly could not conduct a warrantless search without the landlord's consent. There is no principle "to the effect that the police are free to do what some individual has been authorized to do." 1 W. LaFave, Search and Seizure § 2.6(c) at 48 (1990 Supp.) (emphasis omitted) [hereinafter LaFave]. The possibility of consent by a third party does not abolish all constitutional protections against unreasonable searches and seizures. A wife can have a reasonable expectation of privacy in her home even though her husband can consent to a search. The police could not search her house without a warrant or consent just because her husband could have consented. Thus even if a trash collector does have sufficient authority to consent to a garbage search, it does not follow that any reasonable expectation of privacy in garbage is lost and that the police can therefore search the bags without such consent.

We realize that in Greenwood a garbage collector turned the bags over to the police. However, the Court neither relied on that fact nor implied that the garbage collector had "consented" to the search. Rather, it emphasized that there can be "no reasonable expectation of privacy" in garbage deposited "'for the express purpose of having strangers take it.'" 486 U.S. at 41, 108 S. Ct. at 1629, 100 L. Ed. 2d at 37 (quoting United States v. Reicherter, 647 F.2d 397, 399 (3d Cir. 1981)). Moreover, the Court's reliance on Reicherter suggests that its position would have been the same even if the police had seized Greenwood's garbage on their own. In Reicherter the police, posing as garbage collectors, seized the trash themselves. Nor did the Court strengthen its view by saying that "'a person has no legitimate expectation of privacy in information he voluntarily turns over to third parties.'" 486 U.S. at 41, 108 S. Ct. at 1629, 100 L. Ed. 2d at 37 (quoting Smith v. Maryland, 442 U.S. [735,] 743–44, 99 S. Ct. at 2581–82, 61 L. Ed. 2d at 229 [(1970)]). That principle is not relevant here; it applies only when a person "physically expose[s] the evidence to a third party." See, e.g., United States v. Miller, 425 U.S. 435, 442, 96 S. Ct. 1619, 1623, 48 L. Ed. 2d 71, 79 (1976) (bank depositor has no "legitimate 'expectation of privacy'" in financial information "voluntarily conveyed to * * * banks and exposed to their employees").

Conveying information to another is different from conveying an opaque bag containing information. People do not compromise their privacy interest in the contents of a container when they turn that container over to a third party. . . .

Materials given to public or private carriers for delivery are constitutionally protected. United States v. Jacobsen, 466 U.S. 109, 114, 104 S. Ct. 1652, 1657, 80 L. Ed. 2d 85, 94 (1984); United States v. Van Leeuwen, 397 U.S. 249, 251, 90 S. Ct. 1029, 1031, 25 L. Ed. 2d 282, 284–85 (1970); Ex parte Jackson, 96 U.S. 727, 732, 24 L. Ed. 877, 879 (1878). That principle suggests that garbage does not lose constitutional protection merely because it is handed over to a collector. . . .

Entrusting the disposal of a trash bag to the garbage collector does not negate a reasonable expectation of privacy in the contents. It should be reasonable to expect that those who are authorized to remove trash will do so in the manner provided by ordinance or private contract.

-3-

The Court in Greenwood also cited the maxim that "the police cannot reasonably be expected to avert their eyes from evidence of criminal activity that could have been observed by any member of the public." 486 U.S. at 41, 108 S. Ct. at 1629, 100 L. Ed. 2d at 37. That assertion, although obviously true, is hardly relevant. The question here is not whether the police should "avert their eyes," but whether they can dig through garbage that is concealed from the public eye. The cases here might be different had the garbage been strewn across the front yard for all to see. Under those conditions these defendants might have forsaken any privacy expectation. That situation, however, is not now before us.

After referring to the "aversion" principle, Greenwood cited Katz for the proposition that "'[w]hat a person knowingly exposes to the public, even in his own home or office, is not a subject of Fourth Amendment protection.'" 486 U.S. at 41, 108 S. Ct. at 1629, 100 L. Ed. 2d at 37 (quoting Katz v. United States, supra, 389 U.S. at 351, 88 S. Ct. at 511, 19 L. Ed. 2d at 576). The use of that quotation is curious because immediately following that sentence in Katz is a more appropriate passage: "What a person * * * seeks to preserve as private, even in an area accessible to the public, may be constitutionally protected." Katz v. United States, supra, 389 U.S. at 351–52, 88 S. Ct. at 511, 19 L. Ed. 2d at 582. Although garbage bags are placed in areas accessible to the public, the contents are not exposed to the public.

By enclosing their trash in opaque bags, people can maintain the privacy of their garbage even though they may place them in an area accessible to the public. "Aversion" simply does not apply. . . .

-D-

The garbage searched in Pasanen was enclosed in gray plastic trash bags. In Hempele, the police seized white trash bags that had been placed in a plastic garbage can. If those were ordinary trash bags, they concealed their contents from plain view. A person has as much right to privacy in items concealed in a garbage bag as in items concealed in other opaque containers. Defendants had a reasonable expectation of privacy in the contents of their trash bags and can claim the protection of article I, paragraph 7. . . .

Article I, paragraph 7 confers "as against the government, the right to be let alone—the most comprehensive of rights and the right most valued by civilized men." Olmstead v. United States, 277 U.S. 438, 478, 48 S. Ct. 564, 572, 72 L. Ed. 944, 956 (1927) (Brandeis, J., dissenting). Permitting the police to pick and poke their way through garbage bags to peruse without cause the vestiges of a person's most private affairs would be repugnant to that ideal. A free and civilized society should comport itself with more decency. . . .

* * * * *

The New Jersey Supreme Court took pains in *Hempele* to insist that "there is no 'unique New Jersey state attitude about garbage'" and that its decision did not rest on such a premise. A few other state courts have rejected the holding in *Greenwood* on state constitutional grounds. *See, e.g., State v. Boland*, 115 Wash. 2d 571, 800 P. 2d 1112 (1990); *State v. Tanaka*, 67 Ha. 658, 701 P. 2d 1274 (1985) (pre-*Greenwood*).

* * * * *

Another important issue related to "searches" and "reasonable expectations of privacy" involves the "open-fields" doctrine. In *Hester v. United States*, 265 U.S. 57, 44 S. Ct. 445, 68 L. Ed. 898 (1924), federal revenue officers entered land owned by the petitioner's father and discovered evidence of illegal moonshine whiskey. The officers did not have either an arrest warrant or a search warrant when they set foot upon the grounds, which led to the petitioner's claim that his Fourth Amendment rights had been violated. Justice Holmes's opinion for the Court rejected this contention and summarily held that "the special protection accorded by the Fourth Amendment to the people in their 'persons, houses, papers and effects,' is not extended to the open fields." The relative age of the decision in *Hester*, and the intervening decision in *Katz*, which overruled some other Fourth Amendment cases dating back to that era, produced uncertainty about whether the "open-fields" doctrine announced in *Hester* remained good law. The Supreme Court addressed this question in *Oliver v. United States*.

Oliver v. United States, 466 U.S. 170, 104 S. Ct. 1735, 80 L. Ed. 2d 214 (1984)

Justice **Powell** delivered the opinion of the Court.

The "open fields" doctrine, first enunciated by this Court in Hester v United States, 265 US 57, 44 S Ct 445, 68 L Ed 898 (1924), permits police officers to enter and search a field without a warrant. We granted certiorari in these cases to clarify confusion that has arisen as to the continued vitality of the doctrine.

I

No. 82–15. Acting on reports that marihuana was being raised on the farm of petitioner Oliver, two narcotics agents of the Kentucky State

Police went to the farm to investigate.[1] Arriving at the farm, they drove past petitioner's house to a locked gate with a "No Trespassing" sign. A footpath led around one side of the gate. The agents walked around the gate and along the road for several hundred yards, passing a barn and a parked camper. At that point, someone standing in front of the camper shouted: "No hunting is allowed, come back up here." The officers shouted back that they were Kentucky

---

1. It is conceded that the police did not have a warrant authorizing the search, that there was no probable cause for the search, and that no exception to the warrant requirement is applicable.

State Police officers, but found no one when they returned to the camper. The officers resumed their investigation of the farm and found a field of marihuana over a mile from petitioner's home.

Petitioner was arrested and indicted for "manufactur[ing]" a "controlled substance." 21 USC § 841(a)(1). After a pretrial hearing, the District Court suppressed evidence of the discovery of the marihuana field. Applying Katz v United States, 389 US 347, 357, 88 S Ct 507, 19 L Ed 2d 576, (1967), the court found that petitioner had a reasonable expectation that the field would remain private because petitioner "had done all that could be expected of him to assert his privacy in the area of farm that was searched." He had posted "No Trespassing" signs at regular intervals and had locked the gate at the entrance to the center of the farm.

Further, the court noted that the field itself is highly secluded: it is bounded on all sides by woods, fences, and embankments and cannot be seen from any point of public access. The court concluded that this was not an "open" field that invited casual intrusion.

The Court of Appeals for the Sixth Circuit, sitting en banc, reversed the District Court. . . .

We granted certiorari.

No. 82–1273. After receiving an anonymous tip that marihuana was being grown in the woods behind respondent Thornton's residence, two police officers entered the woods by a path between this residence and a neighboring house. They followed a footpath through the woods until they reached two marihuana patches fenced with chicken wire. Later, the officers determined that the patches were on the property of respondent, obtained a warrant to search the property, and seized the marihuana. On the basis of this evidence, respondent was arrested and indicted.

The trial court granted respondent's motion to suppress the fruits of the second search. The warrant for this search was premised on information that the police had obtained during their previous warrantless search, that the court found to be unreasonable. "No Trespassing" signs and the secluded location of the marihuana patches evinced a reasonable expecta-

tion of privacy. Therefore, the court held, the open fields doctrine did not apply.

The Maine Supreme Judicial Court affirmed. . . .

We granted certiorari.

II

The rule announced in Hester v United States was founded upon the explicit language of the Fourth Amendment. That Amendment indicates with some precision the places and things encompassed by its protections. As Justice Holmes explained for the Court in his characteristically laconic style: "[T]he special protection accorded by the Fourth Amendment to the people in their 'persons, houses, papers, and effects,' is not extended to the open fields. The distinction between the latter and the house is as old as the common law." Hester v United States, 265 US, at 59, 44 S Ct 445, 68 L Ed 898.[6]

---

6. The dissent offers no basis for its suggestion that Hester rests upon some narrow, unarticulated principle rather than upon the reasoning enunciated by the Court's opinion in that case. Nor have subsequent cases discredited Hester's reasoning. This Court frequently has relied on the explicit language of the Fourth Amendment as delineating the scope of its affirmative protections. As these cases, decided after Katz, indicate, Katz' "reasonable expectation of privacy" standard did not sever Fourth Amendment doctrine from the Amendment's language. Katz itself construed the Amendment's protection of the person against unreasonable searches to encompass electronic eavesdropping of telephone conversations sought to be kept private; and Katz' fundamental recognition that "the Fourth Amendment protects people— and not simply 'areas'—against unreasonable searches and seizures," see 389 US, at 353, 88 S Ct 507, 19 L Ed 2d 576, is faithful to the Amendment's language. As Katz demonstrates, the Court fairly may respect the constraints of the Constitution's language without wedding itself to an unreasoning literalism. In contrast, the dissent's approach would ignore the language of the Constitution itself as well as overturn this Court's governing precedent.

Nor are the open fields "effects" within the meaning of the Fourth Amendment. In this respect, it is suggestive that James Madison's proposed draft of what became the Fourth Amendment preserves "[t]he rights of the people to be secured in their persons, their houses, their papers, and their other property, from all unreasonable searches and seizures. . . ."

Although Congress' revisions of Madison's proposal broadened the scope of the Amendment in some respects, the term "effects" is less inclusive than "property" and cannot be said to encompass open fields.[7] We conclude, as did the Court in deciding Hester v. United States, that the government's intrusion upon the open fields is not one of those "unreasonable searches" proscribed by the text of the Fourth Amendment.

III

This interpretation of the Fourth Amendment's language is consistent with the understanding of the right to privacy expressed in our Fourth Amendment jurisprudence. Since Katz v United States, 389 US 347, 88 S Ct 507, 19 L Ed 576 (1967), the touchstone of [Fourth] Amendment analysis has been the question whether a person has a "constitutionally protected reasonable expectation of privacy." Id., at 360, 88 S Ct 507, 19 L Ed 2d 576 (Harlan, J., concurring). The Amendment does not protect the merely subjective expectation of privacy, but only those "expectation[s] that society is prepared to recognize as 'reasonable.'"

A

No single factor determines whether an individual legitimately may claim under the Fourth Amendment that a place should be free of government intrusion not authorized by warrant. In assessing the degree to which a search infringes upon individual privacy, the Court has given weight to such factors as the intention of the Framers of the Fourth Amendment, the uses to which the individual has put a location, and our societal understanding that certain areas deserve the most scrupulous protection from government invasion. These factors are equally relevant to determining whether the government's intrusion upon open fields without a warrant or probable cause violates reasonable expectations of privacy and is therefore a search proscribed by the Amendment.

In this light, the rule of Hester v United States, supra, that we reaffirm today, may be understood as providing that an individual may not legitimately demand privacy for activities conducted out of doors in fields, except in the area immediately surrounding the home. This rule is true to the conception of the right to privacy embodied in the Fourth Amendment. The Amendment reflects the recognition of the Founders that certain enclaves should be free from arbitrary government interference. For example, the Court since the enactment of the Fourth Amendment has stressed "the overriding respect for the sanctity of the home that has been embedded in our traditions since the origins of the Republic." Payton v New York, [445 US 573,] 601, [100 S Ct 1371, 63 L Ed 2d 639 (1980)].

In contrast, open fields do not provide the setting for those intimate activities that the amendment is intended to shelter from government interference or surveillance. There is no societal interest in protecting the privacy of those activities, such as the cultivation of crops, that occur in open fields. Moreover, as a practical matter these lands usually are accessible to the public and the police in ways that a home, an office, or commercial structure would not be. It is not generally true that fences or "No Trespassing" signs effectively bar the public from viewing open fields in rural areas. And both petitioner Oliver and respondent Thornton concede that the public and police lawfully may survey lands from the air. For these reasons, the asserted expectation

---

7. The Framers would have understood the term "effects" to be limited to personal, rather than real, property.

of privacy in open fields is not an expectation that "society recognizes as reasonable."[10]

The historical underpinnings of the open fields doctrine also demonstrate that the doctrine is consistent with respect for "reasonable expectations of privacy." As Justice Holmes, writing for the Court, observed in Hester, 265 US, at 59, 44 S Ct 445, 68 L Ed 898, the common law distinguished "open fields" from the "curtilage," the land immediately surrounding and associated with the home. See 4 W. Blackstone, Commentaries. The distinction implies that only the curtilage, not the neighboring open fields, warrants the Fourth Amendment protections that attach to the home. At common law, the curtilage is the area to which extends the intimate activity associated with the "sanctity of a man's home and the privacies of life," Boyd v United States, 116 US 616, 630, 6 S Ct 524, 29 L Ed 746, (1886), and therefore has been considered part of the home itself for Fourth Amendment purposes. Thus, courts have extended Fourth Amendment protection to the curtilage; and they have defined the curtilage, as did the common law, by reference to the factors that determine whether an individual reasonably may expect that an area immediately adjacent to the home will remain private. Conversely, the common law implies, as we reaffirm today, that no expectation of privacy legitimately attaches to open fields.[11]

We conclude, from the text of the Fourth Amendment and from the historical and contemporary understanding of its purposes, that an individual has no legitimate expectation that open fields will remain free from warrantless intrusion by government officers.

B

Petitioner Oliver and respondent Thornton contend, to the contrary, that the circumstances of a search sometimes may indicate that reasonable expectations of privacy were violated; and that courts therefore should analyze these circumstances on a case-by-case basis. The language of the Fourth Amendment itself answers their contention.

Nor would a case-by-case approach provide a workable accommodation between the needs of law enforcement and the interests protected by the Fourth Amendment. Under this approach, police officers would have to guess before every search whether landowners had erected fences sufficiently high, posted a sufficient number of warning signs, or located contraband in an area sufficiently secluded to establish a right of privacy. The lawfulness of a search would turn on "'[a] highly sophisticated set of rules, qualified by all sorts of ifs, ands, and buts and requiring the drawing of subtle nuances and hairline distinctions. . . .'" New York v Belton, 453 US 454, 458, 101 S Ct 2860, 69 L Ed 2d 768 (1981).

This Court repeatedly has acknowledged the difficulties created for courts, police, and citizens by an ad hoc, case-by-case definition of Fourth

---

10. The dissent conceives of open fields as bustling with private activity as diverse as lovers' trysts and worship services. But in most instances police will disturb no one when they enter upon open fields. These fields, by their very character as open and unoccupied, are unlikely to provide the setting for activities whose privacy is sought to be protected by the Fourth Amendment. One need think only of the vast expanse of some western ranches or of the undeveloped woods of the Northwest to see the unreality of the dissent's conception. Further, the Fourth Amendment provides ample protection to activities in the open fields that might implicate an individual's privacy. An individual who enters a place defined to be "public" for Fourth Amendment analysis does not lose all claims to privacy or personal security. For example, the Fourth Amendment's protections against unreasonable arrest or unreasonable seizure of effects upon the person remain fully applicable.

11. Neither petitioner Oliver nor respondent Thornton has contended that the property searched was within the curtilage. Nor is it necessary in these cases to consider the scope of the curtilage exception to the open fields doctrine or the degree of Fourth Amendment protection afforded the curtilage, as opposed to the home itself. It is clear, however, that the term "open fields" may include any unoccupied or undeveloped area outside of the curtilage. An open field need be neither "open" nor a "field" as those terms are used in common speech. . . .

Amendment standards to be applied in differing factual circumstances. The ad hoc approach not only makes it difficult for the policeman to discern the scope of his authority, it also creates a danger that constitutional rights will be arbitrarily and inequitably enforced.[12]

IV

In any event, while the factors that petitioner Oliver and respondent Thornton urge the courts to consider may be relevant to Fourth Amendment analysis in some contexts, these factors cannot be decisive on the question whether the search of an open field is subject to the Amendment. Initially, we reject the suggestion that steps taken to protect privacy establish that expectations of privacy in an open field are legitimate. It is true, of course, that petitioner Oliver and respondent Thornton, in order to conceal their criminal activities, planted the marihuana upon secluded land and erected fences and "No Trespassing" signs around the property. And it may be that because of such precautions, few members of the public stumbled upon the marihuana crops seized by the police. Neither of these suppositions demonstrates, however, that the expectation of privacy was *legitimate* in the sense required by the Fourth Amendment. The test of legitimacy is not whether the individual chooses to conceal assertedly "private" activity.[13] Rather, the correct inquiry is whether the

government's intrusion infringes upon the personal and societal values protected by the Fourth Amendment. As we have explained, we find no basis for concluding that a police inspection of open fields accomplishes such an infringement.

Nor is the government's intrusion upon an open field a "search" in the constitutional sense because that intrusion is a trespass at common law. The existence of a property right is but one element in determining whether expectations of privacy are legitimate. "'The premise that property interests control the right of the Government to search and seize has been discredited.'" Katz, 389 US, at 353. "[E]ven a property interest in premises may not be sufficient to establish a legitimate expectation of privacy with respect to particular items located on the premises or activity conducted thereon." Rakas v. Illinois, 439 US, at 144, n 12.

The common law may guide consideration of what areas are protected by the Fourth Amendment by defining areas whose invasion by others is wrongful. The law of trespass, however, forbids intrusions upon land that the Fourth Amendment would not proscribe. For trespass law extends to instances where the exercise of the right to exclude vindicates no legitimate privacy interest. Thus, in the case of open fields, the general rights of property protected by the common law of trespass have little or no relevance to the applicability of the Fourth Amendment.

V

We conclude that the open fields doctrine, as enunciated in Hester, is consistent with the plain language of the Fourth Amendment and its historical purposes. Moreover, Justice Holmes' interpretation of the Amendment in Hester accords with the "reasonable expectation of privacy" analysis developed in subsequent decisions of this Court. We therefore affirm Oliver v United States; Maine v Thornton is reversed and remanded for further proceedings not inconsistent with this opinion.

It is so ordered.

* * *

---

12. The clarity of the open fields doctrine that we reaffirm today is not sacrificed, as the dissent suggests, by our recognition that the curtilage remains within the protections of the Fourth Amendment. Most of the many millions of acres that are "open fields" are not close to any structure and so not arguably within the curtilage. And, for most homes, the boundaries of the curtilage will be clearly marked; and the conception defining the curtilage—as the area around the home to which the activity of home life extends—is a familiar one easily understood from our daily experience. The occasional difficulties that courts might have in applying this, like other, legal concepts, do not argue for the unprecedented expansion of the Fourth Amendment advocated by the dissent.

13. Certainly, the Framers did not intend that the Fourth Amendment should shelter criminal activity wherever persons with criminal intent choose to erect barriers and post "No Trespassing" signs.

Justice **Marshall**, with whom Justice **Brennan** and Justice **Stevens** join, dissenting.

In each of these consolidated cases, police officers, ignoring clearly visible "No Trespassing" signs, entered upon private land in search of evidence of a crime. At a spot that could not be seen from any vantage point accessible to the public, the police discovered contraband, which was subsequently used to incriminate the owner of the land. In neither case did the police have a warrant authorizing their activities.

The Court holds that police conduct of this sort does not constitute an "unreasonable search" within the meaning of the Fourth Amendment.

* * *

I

The first ground on which the Court rests its decision is that the Fourth Amendment "indicates with some precision the places and things encompassed by its protections," and that real property is not included in the list of protected spaces and possessions. This line of argument has several flaws. Most obviously, it is inconsistent with the results of many of our previous decisions, none of which the Court purports to overrule. For example, neither a public telephone booth nor a conversation conducted therein can fairly be described as a person, house, paper, or effect; yet we have held that the Fourth Amendment forbids the police without a warrant to eavesdrop on such a conversation. Nor can it plausibly be argued that an office or commercial establishment is covered by the plain language of the Amendment; yet we have held that such premises are entitled to constitutional protection if they are marked in a fashion that alerts the public to the fact that they are private.

Indeed, the Court's reading of the plain language of the Fourth Amendment is incapable of explaining even its own holding in this case. The Court rules that the curtilage, a zone of real property surrounding a dwelling, is entitled to constitutional protection. We are not told, however, whether the curtilage is a "house" or an "effect"—or why, if the curtilage can be incorporated into the list of things and spaces shielded by the Amendment, a field cannot.

The Court's inability to reconcile its parsimonious reading of the phrase "persons, houses, papers, and effects" with our prior decisions or even its own holding is a symptom of a more fundamental infirmity in the Court's reasoning. The Fourth Amendment, like the other central provisions of the Bill of Rights that loom large in our modern jurisprudence, was designed, not to prescribe with "precision" permissible and impermissible activities, but to identify a fundamental human liberty that should be shielded forever from government intrusion. We do not construe constitutional provisions of this sort the way we do statutes, whose drafters can be expected to indicate with some comprehensiveness and exactitude the conduct they wish to forbid or control and to change those prescriptions when they become obsolete. Rather, we strive, when interpreting these seminal constitutional provisions, to effectuate their purposes— to lend them meanings that ensure that the liberties the Framers sought to protect are not undermined by the changing activities of government officials.

The liberty shielded by the Fourth Amendment, as we have often acknowledged, is freedom "from unreasonable government intrusions into . . . legitimate expectations of privacy." That freedom would be incompletely protected if only government conduct that impinged upon a person, house, paper, or effect were subject to constitutional scrutiny. Accordingly, we have repudiated the proposition that the Fourth Amendment applies only to a limited set of locales or kinds of property. In Katz v United States, we expressly rejected a proffered locational theory of the coverage of the Amendment, holding that it "protects people, not places." . . .

II

The second ground for the Court's decision is its contention that any interest a landowner might have in the privacy of his woods and fields is not one that "society is prepared to recognize as 'reasonable.'" . . . But the Court's conclusion cannot withstand scrutiny.

As the Court acknowledges, we have traditionally looked to a variety of factors in determining whether an expectation of privacy asserted in a physical space is "reasonable." Though those factors do not lend themselves to precise taxonomy, they may be roughly grouped into three categories. First, we consider whether the expectation at issue is rooted in entitlements defined by positive law. Second, we consider the nature of the uses to which spaces of the sort in question can be put. Third, we consider whether the person claiming a privacy interest manifested that interest to the public in a way that most people would understand and respect. When the expectations of privacy asserted by petitioner Oliver and respondent Thornton are examined through these lenses, it becomes clear that those expectations are entitled to constitutional protection.

A

We have frequently acknowledged that privacy interests are not coterminous with property rights. However, because "property rights reflect society's explicit recognition of a person's authority to act as he wishes in certain areas, [they] should be considered in determining whether an individual's expectations of privacy are reasonable." Rakas v Illinois, 439 US 128, 153 (1978) (Powell, J., concurring). . . .

It is undisputed that Oliver and Thornton each owned the land into which the police intruded. That fact alone provides considerable support for their assertion of legitimate privacy interests in their woods and fields. But even more telling is the nature of the sanctions that Oliver and Thornton could invoke, under local law, for violation of their property rights. In Kentucky, a knowing entry upon fenced or otherwise enclosed land, or upon unenclosed land conspicuously posted with signs excluding the public, constitutes criminal trespass. The law in Maine is similar.

* * *

Thus, positive law not only recognizes the legitimacy of Oliver's and Thornton's insistence that strangers keep off their land, but subjects those who refuse to respect their wishes to the most severe of penalties—criminal liability. Under these circumstances, it is hard to credit the Court's assertion that Oliver's and Thornton's expectations of privacy were not of a sort that society is prepared to recognize as reasonable.

B

The uses to which a place is put are highly relevant to the assessment of a privacy interest asserted therein. If, in light of our shared sensibilities, those activities are of a kind in which people should be able to engage without fear of intrusion by private persons or governmental officials, we extend the protection of the Fourth Amendment to the space in question, even in the absence of any entitlement derived from positive law.[13]

Privately owned woods and fields that are not exposed to public view regularly are employed in a variety of ways that society acknowledges deserve privacy. Many landowners like to take solitary walks on their property, confident that they will not be confronted in their rambles by strangers or policemen. Others conduct agricultural businesses on their property. Some landowners use their secluded spaces to meet lovers, others to gather together with fellow worshippers, still others to engage in sustained creative endeavor. Private land is sometimes used as a refuge for wildlife, where flora and fauna are protected from human intervention of any kind. Our respect for the freedom of landowners to use their posted "open fields" in ways such as these partially explains the seriousness with which the positive law regards deliberate invasions of such spaces, and substantially reinforces the landowners' contention that their expectations of privacy are "reasonable."

---

13. In most circumstances, this inquiry requires analysis of the sorts of use to which a given space is susceptible, not the manner in which the person asserting an expectation of privacy in the space was in fact employing it. . . . Thus, the majority's contention that, because the cultivation of marihuana is not an activity that society wishes to protect, Oliver and Thornton had no legitimate privacy interest in their fields, ante, at 182–183, and n 13, reflects a misunderstanding of the level of generality on which the constitutional analysis must proceed.

C

Whether a person "took normal precautions to maintain his privacy" in a given space affects whether his interest is one protected by the Fourth Amendment. Rawlings v Kentucky, 448 US 98, 105 (1980). The reason why such precautions are relevant is that we do not insist that a person who has a right to exclude others exercise that right. A claim to privacy is therefore strengthened by the fact that the claimant somehow manifested to other people his desire that they keep their distance. . . .

As indicated above, a deliberate entry by a private citizen onto private property marked with "No Trespassing" signs will expose him to criminal liability. I see no reason why a government official should not be obliged to respect such unequivocal and universally understood manifestations of a landowner's desire for privacy. . . .

III

A clear, easily administrable rule emerges from the analysis set forth above: Private land marked in a fashion sufficient to render entry thereon a criminal trespass under the law of the State in which the land lies is protected by the Fourth Amendment's proscription of unreasonable searches and seizures. One of the advantages of the foregoing rule is that it draws upon a doctrine already familiar to both citizens and government officials. In each jurisdiction, a substantial body of statutory and case law defines the precautions a landowner must take in order to avail himself of the sanctions of the criminal law. The police know that body of law, because they are entrusted with responsibility for enforcing it against the public; it therefore would not be difficult for the police to abide by it themselves.

By contrast, the doctrine announced by the Court today is incapable of determinate application. Police officers, making warrantless entries upon private land, will be obliged in the future to make on-the-spot judgments as to how far the curtilage extends, and to stay outside that zone. In addition, we may expect to see a spate of litigation over the question of how much improvement is necessary to remove private land from the category of "unoccupied or undeveloped area" to which the "open fields exception" is now deemed applicable.

The Court's holding not only ill serves the need to make constitutional doctrine "workable for application by rank-and-file, trained police officers," it withdraws the shield of the Fourth Amendment from privacy interests that clearly deserve protection. . . .

Notes and Questions

1. Recall that both Oliver and Thornton had posted "No Trespassing" signs on their property. Oliver had blocked the entry road to his farm with a locked gate. Each man's marijuana garden was on a secluded plot of land. Criminal trespass laws were in effect in each of their states. How does the Court justify its conclusion that "an individual has no legitimate expectation that open fields will remain free from warrantless intrusion by government officers?" Is it sufficient to rely on the text of the Fourth Amendment? On the apparent intent of the Framers of the amendment? On history, or the precedential effect of *Hester v. United States*? On what sources could (or do) the justices rely to gain a "contemporary understanding of [the amendment's] purposes"?

2. What, precisely, are "open fields"? In footnote 11 of the majority opinion, the Court cautions that "an open field need be neither 'open' nor a 'field' as those terms are used in common speech."

📖 **3.** *Legal research note.* The decision in *Oliver* draws a distinction between open fields and "curtilage" and recognizes that individuals do retain a reasonable expectation of privacy in the curtilage area. If you are uncertain about the meaning of a legal term, such as *curtilage*, and need a quick definition, a *law dictionary* generally can supply one. Law dictionaries are easy to use—they can be consulted just as a Webster's dictionary is—and they provide basic definitions. However, too much reliance should not be placed on law dictionaries. The meanings of many legal terms are so complex and context dependent that even the best dictionary cannot provide a completely authoritative definition. If you were to look up *curtilage* in *Black's Law Dictionary* (6th ed., 1990), you would find the following definition:

> For search and seizure purposes, [curtilage] includes those out-buildings which are directly and intimately connected with the habitation and in proximity thereto and the land or grounds surrounding the dwelling which are necessary and convenient and habitually used for family purposes and carrying on domestic employment. (*Citing* State v. Hanson, 113 N.H. 689, 313 A.2d 730, 732 (1973).)

Another way to get a better understanding of the meaning of legal terms is to consult the multivolume set of books, *Words and Phrases*. There, definitions of legal terms that have been extracted from judicial decisions are set forth, frequently at length and in different contexts. The *Words and Phrases* set is arranged alphabetically. "Curtilage" is included in volume 10A, a book that covers the terms *creditor acquiring lien* through *cystotomy*. Roughly seven pages of one-paragraph definitions of *curtilage* are provided in the hard-covered volume of *Words and Phrases*, including a section that specifically pertains to the term's meaning in the context of "searches." A cumulative paper supplement is inserted as a pocket part in the back of the bound volume. The supplement provides several more definitions of curtilage derived from case law. For example, "'Curtilage' for search and seizure purposes is usually defined as a small piece of land, not necessarily enclosed, around a dwelling house and generally includes buildings used for domestic purposes in conduct of

family affairs." (*Citing* State v. Kendor, 60 Ha. 301, 588 P.2d 447, 449 (1979).)

You should practice using a law dictionary and *Words and Phrases* by looking up other terms, such as *search*, *reasonable expectation of privacy*, and *open fields*. Remember that these sources are best used as starting points; do not consider them to be the "final authority" for the meaning of a term. Generally, case law must be consulted and analyzed to capture the full meaning of a concept such as curtilage. Appendix A provides a fuller explanation of how to use law dictionaries and *Words and Phrases* for research purposes.

4. In *United States v. Dunn*, 480 U.S. 294,107 S. Ct. 1134, 94 L. Ed. 2d 326 (1987), the Supreme Court ruled that "the area near a barn, located approximately 50 yards from a fence surrounding a ranch house [is not], for Fourth Amendment purposes, within the curtilage of the house." 480 U.S., at 296. Justice White's majority opinion explained that

> curtilage questions should be resolved with particular reference to four factors: the proximity of the area claimed to be curtilage to the home, whether the area is included within an enclosure surrounding the home, the nature of the uses to which the area is put, and the steps taken by the resident to protect the area from observation by people passing by. 480 U.S., at 301.

5. Some courts have rejected the open fields doctrine as a matter of state constitutional law. *See, e.g., State v. Dixson*, 307 Or. 195, 766 P.2d 1015 (1988); *State v. Kirchoff*, 587 A.2d 988 (Vt. 1991). New York's highest court, the New York Court of Appeals, explained why it took such action in *People v. Scott.*

People v. Scott, 79 N.Y.2d 474, 593 N.E.2d 1328, 583 N.Y.S.2d 920 (1992)

Hancock, J.

* * *

In considering whether the Oliver rule should be adopted as New York law, we note that the Oliver majority's holding that the Amendment covers persons, houses, papers and effects—but not land—seems directly contrary to the basic concept of post-Katz decisions that the Amendment protects a person's privacy, not particular places; more particularly, it protects people from unreasonable government intrusions into their legitimate expectations of privacy"; . . .

While we agree with Justice Marshall's dissent as to these evident contradictions, we find that Oliver majority's literal interpretation of the Amendment's language and its reliance on history to support it, to be of little relevance, in any event (see, e.g., the majority's reference [Oliver v. United States, supra, 466 U.S., at 176–177, 104 S. Ct., at 1740] to the rejection of James Madison's proposed draft which had included "other property" in addition to "persons", "houses", and "papers"). For we are concerned here with a provision in a different Constitution with its own unique history.

As pointed out in P.J. Video, 68 N.Y.2d [296,] 304, n. 4, 508 N.Y.S.2d 907, 501 N.E.2d 556 [(1986)], the guarantee against unreasonable searches and seizures found in article I, § 12 was originally contained in a New York statute (Civil Rights Law § 8); it was not added to the State Constitution until 1938. The available constitutional history is sparse and provides little guidance. It should be noted, moreover, that the texts of article I, § 12 and the Fourth Amendment are not the same. The New York provision contains a clause not found in the Fourth Amendment (see, NY Const., art I, § 12, 2d para [providing protection against interception of telephone and telegraph communications, contrary to the now obsolete rule of Olmstead v. United States).

Thus, the significant question before us does not pertain to the Oliver majority's first basis for its holding—i.e., its literal textual analysis of the Amendment. The question is whether we should adopt the Court's second ground for its decision and its basis for not applying the Katz test to open land: the categorical holding that an expectation of privacy in land outside the curtilage (manifested by posting or erecting fences) is not one which society is prepared to recognize as reasonable. We believe that under the law of this State the citizens are entitled to more protection. A constitutional rule which permits State agents to invade private lands for no reason at all—without permission and in outright disregard of the owner's efforts to maintain privacy by fencing or posting signs—is one that we cannot accept as adequately preserving fundamental rights of New York citizens. Such a rule is contrary to New York decisions, particularly those adopting the Katz rationale in search and seizure cases. It is also incompatible with Justice Brandeis' Olmstead dissent declaring the "right to be let alone—the most comprehensive of rights and the right most valued by civilized men" (Olmstead v. United States, 277 U.S., at 478, 48 S. Ct. at 572)—a core principle reflected in our cases vindicating a broader privacy right in areas other than search and seizure.

It is true that not every property right entails a protectible privacy interest. Nevertheless, "property rights reflect society's explicit recognition of a person's authority to act as he wishes in certain areas, and therefore should be considered in determining whether an individual's expectations of privacy are reasonable." (Rakas v. Illinois, 439 U.S. 128, 153, 99 S. Ct. 421, 435, 58 L. Ed. 2d 387 [(1978)] [Powell, J., concurring].) That a land-owner has a legal right to exclude the public is recognized in the sections of New York's Penal Law dealing with offenses involving damage to and intrusion upon property (see, Penal Law art. 140, particularly § 140.05 [trespass], and § 140.10[a] [criminal trespass in the third degree]. . . .

Our Legislature has recognized the owner's right to prohibit entry on land in the posting provisions of the Environmental Conservation Law (see, ECL 11-2111, 11-2113, 71-0925, 71-0919) and in General Obligations Law § 9-103, enacted for the purpose of dissuading landowners from posting their property and encouraging them to admit the public. Despite the People's urging, we do not dismiss so lightly the fact that the police were violating defendant's property rights and committing criminal and civil trespass by entering the land. As Justice Brandeis observed, "Our Government is the potent, the omnipresent teacher. For good or for ill, it teaches the whole people by its example. Crime is contagious. If the Government becomes a lawbreaker, it breeds contempt for law" (Olmstead v. United States, 277 U.S. at 485, 48 S. Ct. at 575 [Brandeis, J., dissenting]. . . .

But it is in the search and seizure cases decided after Katz that it becomes plain that the Oliver majority's categorical no-protection rule would be inimical to New York law. Our Court, in applying both Federal and State law, has consistently adhered to the concept introduced in Katz: that the Fourth Amendment and article I, § 12 protect the privacy rights of persons, not places. . . .

Moreover, we find troublesome, as did Justice Marshall, the Oliver Court's suggestion that the very conduct discovered by the government's illegal trespass (i.e., growing marihuana) could be considered as a relevant factor in determining whether the police had violated defendant's rights. Such after-the-fact justification for illegal police conduct would not be compatible with New York's recognition of fairness as an essential concern in criminal jurisprudence. The reasoning of the Oliver majority, seems, to be this, in effect: that law-abiding persons should have nothing to hide on their property and, thus, there can be no reasonable objection to the State's unpermitted entry on posted or fenced land to conduct a general search for contraband. But this presupposes the ideal of a conforming society, a concept which seems foreign to New York's tradition of tolerance of the unconventional and of what may appear bizarre or even offensive. So also does this reasoning ignore the truism that even law-abiding citizens may have good reasons for keeping their activities private and the general notion that the only legitimate purpose for governmental infringement on the rights of the individual is to prevent harm to others.

We do not find the Oliver Court's reasoning acceptable as a justification under article I, § 12 for a nonconsensual governmental search of properly posted or fenced land outside the curtilage. . . .

In rejecting the Oliver majority's reversion to a pre-Katz application of the Fourth Amendment based on property concepts and a literal interpretation of its text, we have done so primarily for these reasons: (1) since the Katz decision in 1967 our Court, in countless search and seizure cases, has applied the Katz expectation of privacy rationale, and to accept Oliver's return to what was thought to have been the abandoned Hester-Olmstead conception of the Fourth Amendment would be contrary to our post-Katz case law; (2) the rule that an owner can never have an expectation of privacy in open lands is repugnant to New York's acceptance of "the right

to be let alone" (Olmstead v. United States, 277 U.S., at 478, 48 S. Ct. at 575 [Brandeis, J., dissenting]) as a fundamental right deserving legal protection; (3) the unbridled license given to agents of the State to roam at will without permission on private property in search of incriminating evidence is repugnant to the most basic notions of fairness in our criminal law.

These reasons we are convinced, require us to reject Oliver and to turn instead to our State Constitution for the protection of our citizens' rights. . . .

For the dissenters, it seems, these reasons are far from enough; for it is obvious that the dissent's distress is not only with this decision but with the general concept of State constitutionalism.

What would meet the requirements of the noninterpretative method of analysis which we are accused of scuttling (dissenting opn., at 518, at 948 of 583 N.Y.S.2d, at 1356 of 593 N.E.2d) is not clear; but we decline to adopt any rigid method of analysis which would, except in unusual circumstances, require us to interpret provisions of the State Constitution in "Lockstep" with the Supreme Court's interpretations of similarly worded provisions of the Federal Constitution. Fortunately, we believe, our Court has never adopted the "Lockstep" model or any other fixed analytical formula, for determining when the proper protection of fundamental rights requires resort to the State Constitution. Our role, as we see it, is to analyze the particular case and the Federal constitutional rule at issue in order to determine whether under established New York law and traditions some greater degree of protection must be given. In this case we are convinced that it must be. For, as Justice William Brennan has emphasized, "state courts cannot rest when they have afforded their citizens the full protections of the federal Constitution" and without "the independent protective force of state law * * * the full realization of our liberties cannot be guaranteed" (Brennan, State Constitutions and the Protection of Individual Rights, 90 Harv. L. Rev. 489, 491).

We hold that where landowners fence or post "No Trespassing" signs on their private property or, by some other means, indicate unmistakably that entry is not permitted, the expectation that their privacy rights will be respected and that they will be free from unwanted intrusions is reasonable. In the case at bar, the warrantless entries . . . of the police, were illegal under N.Y. Constitution, article I, § 12. That the property was posted with "No Trespassing" signs is undisputed. The People do not contend—notwithstanding this posting—that defendant permitted others on his land or that, in some other way, he failed to manifest a subjective expectation of privacy. Nor do they claim that the area where the marihuana was allegedly being cultivated was in plain view from a place of public access. The search warrant obtained on the basis of these illegal entries was, therefore, a nullity and the seizure of the evidence discovered upon its execution should have been suppressed. . . .

* * * * *

6. In your view, does the Supreme Court opinion in *Oliver* or the New York Court of Appeals decision in *Scott* work a better balance between the liberty interests of citizens and the government's interest in effective law enforcement? To put this question another way, would you prefer to live in a jurisdiction that followed the rule of *Oliver v. United States* and allowed the police routinely to enter "open fields" without a warrant or one that did not recognize the open fields doctrine, at least "where landowners fence or post 'No Trespassing' signs on their private property or, by some other means, indicate unmistakably that entry is not permitted" (*People v. Scott*)?

Seizures: Possessory Interests

The Fourth Amendment specifically contemplates that "persons" and their "effects" or "things" can be seized. Later in this chapter, we will examine what it means for a person to be "seized" by a law enforcement officer. We now briefly consider the meaning of "seizures" as that concept applies to personal effects.

Katz and related cases have helped give meaning to the concept of a "search." You should convince yourself that it is possible for a personal item such as a purse, a backpack, or a suitcase to be confiscated by the police (i.e., seized) without its contents being exposed (i.e., no search). "Seizures" and "searches" are conceptually distinct. Justice Stevens explained how they differ in his concurring opinion in *Texas v. Brown*, 460 U.S. 730, 747–748, 103 S. Ct. 1535, 75 L. Ed. 2d 502 (1983).

Although our Fourth Amendment cases sometimes refer indiscriminately to searches and seizures, there are important differences between the two. . . . The Amendment protects two different interests of the citizen—the interest in retaining possession of property and the interest in maintaining personal privacy. A seizure threatens the former, a search the latter. As a matter of timing, a seizure is usually proceeded by a search, but when a container is involved the converse is often true. Significantly, the two protected interests are not always present to the same extent; for example, the seizure of a locked suitcase does not necessarily compromise the secrecy of its contents, and the search of a stopped vehicle does not necessarily deprive its owner of possession. . . .

The Court provided a more formal definition of a seizure of personal effects in *United States v. Jacobsen*, 466 U.S. 109, 113, 104 S. Ct. 1652, 80 L. Ed. 2d 85 (1984).

. . . The first clause of the Fourth Amendment provides that the "right of the people to be secure in their persons, houses, papers and effects, against unreasonable searches and seizures, shall not be violated. . . ." This text protects two types of expectations, one involving "searches," the other "seizures." A "search" occurs when an expectation of privacy that society is prepared to consider reasonable is infringed. A "seizure" of property occurs when there is some meaningful interference with an individual's possessory interests in that property. This Court has also consistently construed this protection as proscribing only governmental action; it is wholly inapplicable "to a search or seizure, even an unreasonable one, effected by a private individual not acting as an agent of the Government or with the participation or knowledge of any governmental official." Walter v United States, 447 US 649, 662, 100 S. Ct. 2395, 65 L. Ed. 2d 410 (1980) (Blackmun, J., dissenting). . . .

*   *   *   *   *

Consider the following case facts. The suspicions of law enforcement officers at Miami International Airport were aroused by a man who identified himself as Raymond Place. After ascertaining that Place's destination was New York's La Guardia Airport, the Miami police notified federal Drug Enforcement Administration (DEA) officers in New York that Place might be carrying narcotics. The DEA agents located Place following his arrival in New York and requested permission to search his suitcases. Place refused to give consent. Thereafter:

. . . one of the agents told him that they were going to take the luggage to a federal judge to try to obtain a search warrant and that Place was free to accompany them. Place declined, but obtained from one of the agents telephone numbers at which the agents could be reached. The agents then took the bags to Kennedy Airport, where they subjected the bags to a "sniff test" by a trained narcotics detection dog. The dog reacted positively to the smaller of the two bags but ambiguously to the larger bag. Approximately 90 minutes had elapsed since the seizure of respondent's luggage. Because it was late on a Friday afternoon,

the agents retained the luggage until Monday morning, when they secured a search warrant from a magistrate for the smaller bag. Upon opening that bag, the agents discovered 1.125 grams of cocaine. . . .

The cocaine discovered in Place's suitcase later was admitted as evidence in a federal criminal trial, and Place was convicted of violating federal drug laws. The Second Circuit Court of Appeals reversed his conviction on the ground that his suitcases had been unreasonably seized, and the Supreme Court granted certiorari. Justice O'Connor's majority opinion for the Court observed:

. . . The Fourth Amendment protects the "right of the people to be secure in their persons, houses, papers, *and effects*, against unreasonable searches and seizures." (Emphasis added.) Although in the context of personal property, and particularly containers, the Fourth Amendment challenge is typically to the subsequent search of the container rather than to its initial seizure by the authorities, our cases reveal some general principles regarding seizures. In the ordinary case, the Court has viewed a seizure of personal property as per se unreasonable within the meaning of the Fourth Amendment unless it is accomplished pursuant to a judicial warrant issued upon probable cause and particularly describing the items to be seized. Where law enforcement authorities have probable cause to believe that a container holds contraband or evidence of a crime, but have not secured a warrant, the Court has interpreted the Amendment to permit seizure of the property, pending issuance of a warrant to examine its contents, if the exigencies of the circumstances demand it or some other recognized exception to the warrant requirement is present.

For example, "objects such as weapons or contraband found in a public place may be seized by the police without a warrant,"

Payton v New York, 445 US 573, 587, 100 S Ct 1371, 63 L. Ed. 2d 639 (1980), because, under these circumstances, the risk of the item's disappearance or use for its intended purpose before a warrant may be obtained outweighs the interest in possession.

In this case, the Government asks us to recognize the reasonableness under the Fourth Amendment of warrantless seizures of personal luggage from the custody of the owner on the basis of less than probable cause, for the purpose of pursuing a limited course of investigation, short of opening the luggage, that would quickly confirm or dispel the authorities' suspicion. . . .

The Court ultimately accepted the government's invitation to allow personal effects to be seized temporarily even in the absence of "probable cause" to believe the property was connected with contraband or otherwise related to criminal activity. However, it insisted that the police at least have "reasonable suspicion" that the effects were associated with criminal wrongdoing and that a seizure based on such a showing must be brief in duration. (The Court's reasoning relied heavily on *Terry v. Ohio*, 392 U.S. 1, 88 S. Ct. 1868, 20 L. Ed. 2d 889 (1968), a case that we will consider in detail later in this chapter.) Relying on these principles, the Court ruled that the seizure of Place's luggage was constitutionally unreasonable.

There is no doubt that the agents made a "seizure" of Place's luggage for purposes of the Fourth Amendment when, following his refusal to consent to a search, the agent told Place that he was going to take the luggage to a federal judge to secure issuance of a warrant. . . .

The premise of the Government's argument is that seizures of property are generally less intrusive than seizures of the person. While true in some circumstances, that premise is faulty on the facts we address in this case. The precise type of detention we confront here is seizure of personal luggage from the immediate possession of the suspect for the purpose of arranging exposure to a narcotics detection dog. Particularly in the case of detention of luggage within the traveler's immediate possession, the police conduct intrudes on both the suspect's possessory interest in his luggage as well as his liberty interest in proceeding with his itinerary. The person whose luggage is detained is technically still free to continue his travels or carry out other personal activities pending release of the luggage. Moreover, he is not subjected to the coercive atmosphere of a custodial confinement or to the public indignity of being personally detained. Nevertheless, such a seizure can effectively restrain the person since he is subjected to the possible disruption of his travel plans in order to remain with his luggage or to arrange for its return. . . .

The length of the detention of respondent's luggage alone precludes the conclusion that the seizure was reasonable in the absence of probable cause. . . . Moreover, in assessing the effect of the length of the detention, we take into account whether the police diligently pursue their investigation. We note that here the New York agents knew the time of Place's scheduled arrival at La Guardia, had ample time to arrange for their additional investigation at that location, and thereby could have minimized the intrusion on respondent's Fourth Amendment interests. . . .

Although the 90-minute detention of respondent's luggage is sufficient to render the seizure unreasonable, the violation was exacerbated by the failure of the agents to accurately inform respondent of the place to which they were transporting his luggage, of the length of time he might be dispossessed, and of what arrangements would be made for return of the luggage if the investigation dispelled the suspicion. In short, we hold that the detention of respondent's luggage in this case went beyond the narrow authority possessed by police to

detain briefly luggage reasonably suspected to contain narcotics. . . .

Notes and Questions

1. The dog-sniff of Place's luggage did not occur until 90 minutes after the bags were seized—a delay that the Court found to be unreasonable under the circumstances. Assume that the dog's alerting to the luggage gave the agents probable cause to believe that illegal drugs were concealed within the bags. Why didn't they immediately open the luggage? Why did they hold the bags over the entire weekend and not attempt to open them until the following Monday morning?

2. Under *Katz v. United States* and *California v. Greenwood*, what issue is raised by the DEA agents arranging for their trained dog to smell Place's luggage? Should the police be allowed to arrange for a dog-sniff without securing a search warrant? Or without at least having probable cause or "reasonable suspicion"? The answer to these questions, of course, depends on whether a dog-sniff is a "search." Justice O'Connor's majority opinion in *Place* held that it is not.

The Fourth Amendment "protects people from unreasonable government intrusions into their legitimate expectations of privacy."

We have affirmed that a person possesses a privacy interest in the contents of personal luggage that is protected by the Fourth Amendment. A "canine sniff" by a well-trained narcotics detection dog, however, does not require opening the luggage. It does not expose noncontraband items that otherwise would remain hidden from public view, as does, for example, an officer's rummaging through the contents of the luggage. Thus, the manner in which information is obtained through this investigative technique is much less intrusive than a typical search. Moreover, the sniff discloses only the presence or absence of narcotics, a contraband item. Thus, despite the fact that the sniff tells the authorities something about the contents of the luggage, the information obtained is limited.

This limited disclosure also ensures that the owner of the property is not subjected to the embarrassment and inconvenience entailed in less discriminate and more intrusive investigative methods.

In these respects, the canine sniff is sui generis. We are aware of no other investigative procedure that is so limited both in the manner in which the information is obtained and in the content of the information revealed by the procedure. Therefore, we conclude that the particular course of investigation that the agents intended to pursue here—exposure of respondent's luggage, which was located in a public place, to a trained canine—did not constitute a "search" within the meaning of the Fourth Amendment. . . .

* * * * *

Justices Brennan, Marshall, and Blackmun did not join in the Court's conclusion that a dog-sniff of luggage is not a "search." In a later case, Justice Brennan disparagingly characterized trained drug-sniffing dogs as "'canine cocaine connoisseur[s],'" *United States v. Jacobsen*, 466 U.S. 109, 138, 104 S. Ct. 1652, 80 L. Ed. 2d 85 (1984) (dissenting opinion), *citing People v. Evans*, 65 Cal. App. 3d 924, 932, 134 Cal. Rptr. 436, 440 (1977). He warned that technology and increasingly sophisticated snooping devices threatened "to override the limits of law in the area of criminal investigation." 466 U.S., at 138.

Some state courts have used state constitutional grounds to reject *Place's* holding that dog-sniffs arranged by the police are not "searches," at least under certain circumstances. Citing the relatively unintrusive nature of dog-sniffs, those courts typically authorize them on "reasonable suspicion," rather than demanding the more onerous showing of "probable cause" or requiring a warrant. *See, e.g., People v. Dunn*, 77 N.Y.2d 19, 564 N.E.2d 1054, 563 N.Y.S.2d 388 (1990), *cert. denied*, 501 U.S. 1219, 111 S. Ct.

2830, 115 L. Ed. 2d 1000 (1991); *State v. Pellicci*, 133 N.H. 523, 580 A.2d 710 (1990); *Commonwealth v. Johnston*, 515 Pa. 454, 530 A.2d 74 (1987); *Commonwealth v. Martin*, 534 Pa. 136, 626 A.2d 556 (1993) (requiring probable cause for dog-sniff of a person); *People v. Unruh*, 713 P.2d 370 (Colo.), *cert. denied*, 476 U.S. 1171, 106 S. Ct. 2894, 90 L. Ed. 2d 981 (1986). *See* B. Latzer, *State Constitutional Criminal Law* § 3:5 (1995).

The General Interests Protected by the Warrant Clause

Search Warrants

The Court asserted in *Katz v. United States*, 389 U.S. 347, 357, 88 S. Ct. 507, 19 L. Ed. 2d 576 (1967), that "searches conducted outside of the judicial process, without prior approval by judge or magistrate, are per se unreasonable under the Fourth Amendment—subject only to a few specifically established and well-delineated exceptions." At least four reasons explain the presumptive requirement for search warrants.

A Neutral and Detached Magistrate. People have a right "to be secure in their . . . houses . . . against unreasonable searches and seizures." If the search of a home might be justified on probable cause to believe that illegal drugs are hidden there, who should be entrusted to determine whether probable cause exists: a police officer or a judge or a magistrate? Consider Justice Jackson's answer to this question in *Johnson v. United States*, 333 U.S. 10, 13–14, 68 S. Ct. 367, 92 L. Ed. 436 (1948).

The point of the Fourth Amendment, which often is not grasped by zealous officers, is not that it denies law enforcement the support of the usual inferences which reasonable men draw from evidence. Its protection consists in requiring that those inferences be drawn by a neutral and detached magistrate instead of being judged by the officer engaged in the often competitive enterprise of ferreting out crime. Any assumption that evidence sufficient to support a magistrate's distinterested determination to issue a search warrant will justify the officers in making a search without a warrant would reduce the Amendment to a nullity and leave the people's home secure only in the discretion of police officers. Crime, even in the privacy of one's own quarters, is, of course, of grave concern to society, and the law allows such crime to be reached on proper showing. The right of officers to thrust themselves into a home is also a grave concern, not only to the individual but to a society which chooses to dwell in reasonable security and freedom from surveillance. When the right of privacy must reasonably yield to the right of search is, as a rule, to be decided by a judicial officer, not by a policeman or Government enforcement agent.

The Court occasionally has been asked to decide whether the person issuing a search warrant qualifies as a "neutral and detached" judicial officer. For example, it has concluded that search warrants approved under the following circumstances failed the requirement for a "neutral and detached" judicial officer:

- A search warrant signed by the state attorney general, who later served as the chief prosecutor in the defendant's trial. *Coolidge v. New Hampshire*, 403 U.S. 443, 91 S. Ct. 2022, 29 L. Ed. 2d 564 (1971).

- A search warrant approved by an unsalaried justice of the peace, who was paid a $5 fee on issuing a warrant but received nothing if he denied a warrant application. *Connally v. Georgia*, 429 U.S. 245, 97 S. Ct. 546, 50 L. Ed. 2d 444 (1977).

- A search warrant issued by a magistrate authorizing the seizure of "obscene" items, when the magistrate accompanied the police to the book store in question and actively assisted in the search for incriminating materials. Under these circumstances, the magistrate had failed to maintain detached neutrality: "He was not acting as a judicial officer but as an adjunct law-enforcement officer." *Lo-Ji Sales, Inc. v. New York*, 442 U.S. 319, 327, 99 S. Ct. 2319, 60 L. Ed. 2d 920 (1979).

Particularity. The scope of a search conducted pursuant to a warrant is limited by the terms of the warrant, which must "particularly describ[e] the place to be searched, and the persons or things to be seized." A warrantless search is not so limited. In *Stanford v. Texas*, 379 U.S. 476, 85 S. Ct. 506, 13 L. Ed. 2d 431 (1965), the Court recounted the colonists' abhorrence of general searches conducted under the authority of writs of assistance and then explained the significance of this history to the warrant clause's particularity requirement.

. . . The Fourth Amendment provides that "no Warrants shall issue, but upon probable cause, supported by Oath or affirmation, and *particularly describing* the place to be searched, and the persons or *things to be seized*." (Emphasis supplied.)

These words are precise and clear. They reflect the determination of those who wrote the Bill of Rights that the people of this new Nation should forever "be secure in their persons, houses, papers, and effects" from intrusion and seizure by officers acting under the unbridled authority of a general warrant. Vivid in the memory of the newly independent Americans were those general warrants known as writs of assistance under which officers of the Crown had so bedeviled the colonists. The hated writs of assistance had given customs officials blanket authority to search where they pleased for goods imported in violation of the British tax laws. They were denounced by James Otis as "the worst instrument of arbitrary power, the most destructive of English liberty, and the fundamental principles of law, that ever was found in an English law book," because they placed "the liberty of every man in the hands of every petty officer." The historic occasion of that denunciation, in 1761 at Boston, has been characterized as "perhaps the most prominent event which inaugurated the resistance of the colonies of the oppressions of the mother country. 'Then and there,' said John Adams, 'then and there was the first scene of the first act of opposition to the arbitrary claims of Great Britain. Then and there the child Independence was born.'" Boyd v. United States, 116 US 616, 625, 6 S. Ct. 524, 29 L. Ed. 746, 749 (1886).

Antecedent Justification. It is fundamental that probable cause must exist *before* a search is conducted. What is discovered as the result of a search cannot be used, in hindsight, to justify the search. A warrant must be supported by probable cause supplied in advance of the search. One of the purposes of the warrant requirement "is to prevent hindsight from coloring the evaluation of the reasonableness of a search or seizure." *United States v. Martinez-Fuerte*, 428 U.S. 543, 565, 96 S. Ct. 3074, 49 L. Ed. 2d 1116 (1976). For example, the surest way to guarantee that probable cause existed *before* a police officer discovered marijuana during a search of an individual's home is to require the officer to recite the facts known about the suspected crime to a judge or magistrate in advance of the actual search.

Assurance to the Citizen. Having one's home or personal effects searched by a police officer can be very unsettling. It may be even more distressing if doubts exist about the officer's authority to conduct the search or the appropriate limits of it. A search warrant presented to a citizen, which has been signed by a judge or magistrate and particularly describes the scope and objects of the search, can at least help to alleviate the latter fears. The Supreme Court recognized this point in a case raising the question whether a safety and housing code inspector must obtain a search warrant if a homeowner denies the inspector's request for admission:

When [an] inspector [without a warrant] demands entry, the occupant has no way of knowing whether enforcement of the municipal code involved requires inspection of his premises, no way of knowing the lawful limits of the inspector's power to search, and no way of knowing whether the inspector himself is acting under proper authorization. *Camara v. Municipal Court of City and County of San Francisco*, 387 U.S. 523, 532, 87 S. Ct. 1727, 18 L. Ed. 2d 930 (1967).

Arrest Warrants

In light of the persuasive justifications underlying the general requirement for search warrants, does it follow that the police ordinarily must have a warrant to make an arrest? At least for arrests made outside of private premises, the Court has answered this question in the negative. *United States v. Watson*, 423 U.S. 411, 96 S. Ct. 820, 46 L. Ed. 2d 598 (1976). Are the different expectations governing search warrants and arrest warrants logically consistent? Consider Justice Powell's concurring opinion in *Watson*, 423 U.S., at 428.

There is no more basic constitutional rule in the Fourth Amendment area than that which makes a warrantless search unreasonable except in a few "jealously and carefully drawn" exceptional circumstances. . . .

Since the Fourth Amendment speaks equally to both searches and seizures, and since an arrest, the taking hold of one's person, is quintessentially a seizure, it would seem that the constitutional provision should impose the same limitations upon arrests that it does upon searches. Indeed, as an abstract matter an argument can be made that the restrictions upon arrest perhaps should be greater. A search may cause only annoyance and temporary inconvenience to the law-abiding citizen, assuming more serious dimension only when it turns up evidence of criminality. An arrest, however, is a serious personal intrusion regardless of whether the person seized is guilty or innocent. . . . Logic therefore would seem to dictate that arrests be subject to the warrant requirement at least to the same extent as searches.

But logic sometimes must defer to history and experience. The Court's opinion emphasizes the historical sanction accorded warrantless felony arrests. . . .

At common law, "A peace officer was permitted to arrest without a warrant for a misdemeanor or felony committed in his presence as well as for a felony not committed in his presence if there was reasonable grounds for making the arrest." *Watson*, 423 U.S., at 418. This rule was carried forward from colonial times and was widely recognized in the states. Indeed, Congress had granted numerous federal law enforcement authorities—including postal inspectors, who were responsible for the arrest in *Watson*—to make warrantless arrests on probable cause. One justification for the historical rule, as well as the decision in *Watson*, was the reality that "a constitutional rule permitting felony arrests only with a warrant or in exigent circumstances could severely hamper effective law enforcement." 423 U.S., at 431 (Powell, J., concurring).

In *Payton v. New York*, 445 U.S. 573, 100 S. Ct. 1371, 63 L. Ed. 2d 639 (1980), the Court addressed a question expressly left open in *Watson*: "'whether and under what circumstances an officer may enter a suspect's home to make a warrantless arrest.'" Pursuant to a New York statute authorizing them to do so, police made warrantless entries into the homes of two individuals whom they had probable cause to arrest. Each suspect was arrested, and in each case, evidence was seized from the dwellings. The evidence later was used to help convict the defendants of crimes. In a 6–3 decision authored by Justice Stevens, the Court ruled that the warrantless home entries were unreasonable under the Fourth Amendment. Justice Stevens emphasized that each case involved "routine arrests in which there was ample time to obtain a warrant." They did not involve "the sort of emergency or dangerous situation, described in our cases as 'exigent circumstances,' that would justify a warrantless entry into a home for the purpose of either arrest or search." 445 U.S., at 583. Under those circumstances, the police needed at least an arrest warrant to gain entry into an individual's home for the purpose of making an arrest.

> The critical point is that any differences in the intrusiveness of entries to search and entries to arrest are merely ones of degree rather than of kind. The two intrusions share this fundamental characteristic: the breach of the entrance to an individual's home. The Fourth Amendment protects the individual's privacy in a variety of settings. In none is the zone of privacy more clearly defined than when bounded by the unambiguous physical dimensions of an individual's home—a zone that finds its roots in clear and specific constitutional terms: "The right of the people to be secure in their . . . houses . . . shall not be violated." . . . In terms that apply equally to seizures of property and to seizures of persons, the Fourth Amendment has drawn a firm line at the entrance to the house. Absent exigent circumstances, that threshold may not reasonably be crossed without a warrant. 445 U.S., at 589–590.

Note that under *Payton*, an arrest warrant suffices to allow the police entry to a home to make an arrest. A search warrant is not required.

> It is true that an arrest warrant may afford less protection than a search warrant requirement, but it will suffice to interpose the magistrate's determination of probable cause between the zealous officer and the citizen. If there is sufficient evidence of a citizen's participation in a felony to persuade a judicial officer that his arrest is justified, it is constitutionally reasonable to require him to open his doors to the officers of the law. Thus, for Fourth Amendment purposes, an arrest warrant founded on probable cause implicitly carries with it the limited authority to enter a dwelling in which the suspect lives when there is reason to believe the suspect is within. 445 U.S., at 602–603.

If officers have an arrest warrant for X, may they search Y's home under the authority of that warrant when they have probable cause to believe that X is inside? In *Steagald v. United States*, 451 U.S. 204, 101 S. Ct. 1642, 68 L. Ed. 2d 38 (1981), the Supreme Court answered this question in the negative. Justice Marshall's majority opinion reasoned that a third party's (Y) right of privacy in his or her home is not compromised by a suspect's (X) presence in it. Accordingly, a warrant to search a third party's home for a suspect who does not live there is required for the police to gain entry, absent the third party's consent or the existence of exigent circumstances; a warrant for the suspect's arrest is not sufficient. Were the rule otherwise, the police, "armed solely with an arrest warrant for a single person, . . . could search all the homes

of that individual's friends and acquaintances."
451 U.S., at 215.

When law enforcement officers have a warrant to search a dwelling, may they detain its occupant while making the search and then arrest him or her on the basis of the results of the search? The Supreme Court upheld this practice in *Michigan v. Summers*, 452 U.S. 692, 101 S. Ct. 2587, 69 L. Ed. 2d 340 (1981). "A warrant to search for contraband founded on probable cause implicitly carries with it the limited authority to detain the occupants of the premises while a proper search is conducted." 452 U.S., at 705.

THE EXCLUSIONARY RULE

Suppose that an individual's Fourth Amendment rights have been infringed by an unreasonable search or seizure or through a violation of the warrant clause. Should an unlawful arrest prohibit the suspect's prosecution? Should evidence that has been illegally seized be banned from a criminal trial? Or should criminal proceedings be unaffected by breaches of the Fourth Amendment, leaving individuals whose rights have been violated to seek redress elsewhere, such as through a civil action for money damages or by seeing the offending law enforcement officer disciplined? As we have noted, the text of the Fourth Amendment does not address how rights violations should be remedied.

It has long been settled that an unlawful arrest does not result in the arrestee's being immune from prosecution and does not require the dismissal of a charge against that person.

There are authorities of the highest respectability which hold that . . . forcible abduction is no sufficient reason why the party should not answer when brought within the jurisdiction of the court which has the right to try him for . . . an offense, and presents no valid objection to his trial in such court.

Ker v. Illinois, 119 U.S. 436, 444, 7 S. Ct. 225, 30 L. Ed. 421 (1886).

Due process of law is satisfied when one present in court is convicted of crime after having been fairly apprized [sic] of the charges against him and after a fair trial in accordance with constitutional procedural safeguards. There is nothing in the Constitution that requires a court to permit a guilty person rightfully convicted to escape justice because he was brought to trial against his will. *Frisbie v. Collins*, 342 U.S. 519, 522, 72 S. Ct. 509, 96 L. Ed. 541 (1952).

See also United States v. Alvarez-Machain, 504 U.S. 655, 112 S. Ct. 2188, 119 L. Ed. 2d 441 (1992) (officially authorized kidnapping of foreign citizen from Mexico does not prohibit his trial in the United States for violation of U.S. criminal laws).

Although a person's unlawful seizure does not make a subsequent prosecution illegal, an unlawful arrest may still have significant *evidentiary* consequences. As we shall see, statements and tangible items of evidence that directly result from the illegal seizure of a person may be inadmissible in a criminal trial. Similarly, the exclusion or "suppression" of evidence may be ordered following an unlawful search of a person, his or her premises, or effects.

Evidence that the prosecution would like to offer against a defendant in a criminal trial might be ruled inadmissible for many different reasons. Some evidence is "privileged"—such as attorney-client communications or confidential conversations between marital partners—and thus cannot be used in trials. Other evidence is not sufficiently trustworthy to be admitted—including some forms of "hearsay," the testimony of a young child who does not understand the difference between the truth and a lie, and expert testimony based on speculative or unfounded "scientific" assumptions like the results of a lie detector test. Sometimes, the violation of an individual's rights results in the exclusion of evidence. Although Fourth Amendment violations are not unique in this regard, "the exclusionary rule" tends to be especially controversial in search and seizure cases.

It often is argued that the evidence obtained in violation of the Fourth Amendment is uniquely reliable and that barring its use consequently comes at extraordinary expense to the truth-finding function of a criminal trial. For example, the trustworthiness of a coerced confession may be suspect, justifying its exclusion from evidence. Identification procedures may be so unfairly suggestive that eyewitness testimony is properly barred. Similarly, testimony that is untested by cross-examination may be insufficiently probative to allow it to be considered by a judge or jury. However, what of a gun seized from an accused, the spent cartridges of which are matched to a murder weapon? What of a bag full of marked money found after a bank robbery during a search of the defendant's apartment, or 20 tons of marijuana stored in the hull of a ship? Although the gun, the money, or the marijuana may have been secured in violation of the involved individuals' Fourth Amendment rights, there is no doubt about their reliability. Nevertheless, in each case, "the exclusionary rule" might operate to prohibit the seized items from being used as evidence.

Debate about the exclusionary rule has been long-standing. More recently, empirical evidence that sheds light on some of the presumed benefits and costs of the exclusionary rule has been produced. As we review the evolution of the exclusionary rule, pay particular attention to the arguments advanced in support of it and against it and to how the Supreme Court's willingness to accept different arguments has changed over the years.

Origins and Evolution of the Exclusionary Rule

In 1911, federal and state law enforcement officers made a warrantless entry of the Kansas City home of Fremont Weeks. They seized numerous items, including several of Weeks's personal papers. The home was entered, and the evidence was seized without a search warrant, in violation of Weeks's Fourth Amendment rights. Nevertheless, some of the evidence was used to support Weeks's conviction in federal court for using the U.S. mails to transport illegal lottery coupons. The U.S. Supreme Court reversed. In a unanimous opinion written by Justice Day, the Court ruled that the evidence seized in violation of Weeks's Fourth Amendment rights should not have been admitted at his trial. *Weeks v. United States*, 232 U.S. 383, 34 S. Ct. 341, 58 L. Ed. 652 (1914).

* * *

The effect of the 4th Amendment is to put the courts of the United States and Federal officials, in the exercise of their power and authority, under limitations and restraints as to the exercise of such power and authority, and to forever secure the people, their persons, houses, papers, and effects, against all unreasonable searches and seizures under the guise of law. This protection reaches all alike, whether accused of crime or not, and the duty of giving to it force and effect is obligatory upon all intrusted under our Federal system with the enforcement of the laws. The tendency of those who execute the criminal laws of the country to obtain conviction by means of unlawful seizures. . . should find no sanction in the judgments of the courts, which are charged at all times with the support of the Constitution, and to which people of all conditions have a right to appeal for the maintenance of such fundamental rights.

The case in the aspect in which we are dealing with it involves the right of the court in a criminal prosecution to retain for the purposes of evidence the letters and correspondence of the accused, seized in his house in his absence and without his authority, by a United States marshal holding no warrant for his arrest and none for the search of his premises. . . . If letters and private documents can thus be seized and held and used in evidence against a citizen accused of an offense, the protection of the 4th Amendment, declaring his right to be secure against such searches and seizures, is of no value, and, so far as those thus placed are concerned, might as well be stricken from the Constitution. The efforts of the courts and their officials to bring the guilty to punishment, praiseworthy as they are, are not to be aided by the sacrifice of those great principles established by years of endeavor and suffering which have resulted in their embodiment in the fundamental law of the land. . . .

[T]he 4th Amendment was intended to secure the citizen in person and property against unlawful invasion of the sanctity of his home by officers of the law, acting under legislative or judicial sanction. This protection is equally extended to the action of the government and officers of the law acting under it. To sanction such proceedings would be to affirm by judicial decision a manifest neglect, if not an open defiance, of the prohibitions of the Constitution, intended for the protection of the people against such unauthorized action. . . .

Make special note of the fact that *Weeks* involved a Fourth Amendment violation committed by federal law enforcement officers and the use of illegally seized evidence in a *federal* trial. State police had accompanied the federal authorities on the warrantless search of Weeks's home and had apparently seized evidence that may have been of use in a state criminal prosecution. The *Weeks* opinion carefully noted that

as to the papers and property seized by the [state] policemen, it does not appear that they acted under any claim of Federal authority such as would make the amend-

ment applicable to such unauthorized seizures. . . . What remedies the defendant may have against them we need not inquire, as the 4th Amendment is not directed to individual misconduct of such officials. Its limitations reach the Federal government and its agencies. 232 U.S., at 398.

Recall from our discussion in the previous chapter that the protections of the U.S. Constitution's Bill of Rights—including the Fourth Amendment—originally applied only against *federal* authorities and not against state officials. The "incorporation" of specific Bill of Rights guarantees to the states, by operation of the Fourteenth Amendment's due-process clause, was delayed for nearly half a century after the *Weeks* decision. As a consequence, you should not find the *Weeks* Court's disclaimer against applying either the Fourth Amendment or the exclusionary rule to the actions of state officials to be surprising.

Indeed, many states in that era declined to exclude unlawfully seized evidence from state criminal trials. Consider Judge (later, U.S. Supreme Court Justice) Benjamin Cardozo's famous opinion for the New York Court of Appeals in *People v. Defore*, 242 N.Y. 13, 150 N.E. 585 (1926), which rejected the exclusionary remedy for unlawful searches and seizures.

The officer might have been resisted, or sued for damages, or even prosecuted for oppression. He was subject to removal or other discipline at the hands of his superiors. These consequences are undisputed. The defendant would add another. We must determine whether evidence of criminality, procured by an act of trespass, is to be rejected as incompetent for the misconduct of the trespasser. . . .

The criminal is to go free because the constable has blundered. . . .

Evidence is not excluded because the private litigant who offers it has gathered it by lawless force. By the same token, the state, when prosecuting an offender against the peace and order of society, incurs no heavier liability. . . .

We are confirmed in this conclusion when we reflect how far-reaching in its effect upon society the new consequences would be. The pettiest peace officer would have it in his power, through overzeal or indiscretion, to confer immunity upon an offender for crimes the most flagitious. A room is searched against the law, and the body of a murdered man is found. If the place of discovery may not be proved, the other circumstances may be insufficient to connect the defendant with the crime. The privacy of the home has been infringed, and the murderer goes free. Another search, once more against the law, discloses counterfeit money or the implements of forgery. The absence of a warrant means the freedom of the forger. Like instances can be multiplied. We may not subject society to these dangers until the Legislature has spoken with a clearer voice. In so holding, we are not unmindful of the argument that, unless the evidence is excluded, the statute becomes a form and its protection an illusion. This has a strange sound . . .

Other sanctions, penal and disciplinary, supplementing the right to damages, have already been enumerated. No doubt the protection of the statute would be greater from the point of view of the individual whose privacy had been invaded if the government were required to ignore what it had learned through the invasion. The question is whether protection for the individual would not be gained at a disproportionate loss of protection for society. On the one side is the social need that crime shall be repressed. On the other, the social need that law shall not be flouted by the insolence of office. There are dangers in any choice. . . .

People v. Defore is most famous for Judge Cardozo's rejection of the proposition that "the criminal is to go free because the constable has blundered." 150 N.E., at 587. Equally famous, and of a different sentiment, is Justice Brandeis's dissenting opinion in *Olmstead v. United States*, 277 U.S. 438, 48 S. Ct. 564, 72 L. Ed. 944 (1928). The *Olmstead* majority opinion held that federal law enforcement officers' warrantless wiretapping of an outside telephone line, accomplished without physical intrusion into the defendant's premises, did not violate the Fourth Amendment. Recall that this view subsequently was rejected in *Katz v. United States*.

Mr. Justice BRANDEIS (dissenting) . . . .

The makers of our Constitution undertook to secure conditions favorable to the pursuit of happiness. They recognized the significance of man's spiritual nature, of his feelings and of his intellect. They knew that only a part of the pain, pleasure and satisfactions of life are to be found in material things. They sought to protect Americans in their beliefs, their thoughts, their emotions and their sensations. They conferred, as against the government, the right to be let alone—the most comprehensive of rights and the right most valued by civilized men. To protect that right, every unjustifiable intrusion by the government upon the privacy of the individual, whatever the means employed, must be deemed a violation of the Fourth Amendment. And the use, as evidence in a criminal proceeding, of facts ascertained by such intrusion must be deemed a violation of the Fifth.

Applying to the Fourth and Fifth Amendments the established rule of construction, the defendants' objections to the evidence obtained by wire tapping must, in my opinion, be sustained. It is, of course, immaterial where the physical connection with the telephone wires leading into the defendants' premises was made. And it is also immaterial that the intrusion was in aid of law enforcement. Experience should teach us to be most on our guard to protect liberty when the government's purposes are beneficent. Men born to freedom are naturally alert to repel invasion of their liberty by evil-minded rulers. The greatest dangers to liberty lurk in insidious encroachment by men of zeal, well-meaning but without understanding.

Independently of the constitutional question, I am of opinion that the judgment should be reversed. By the laws of Washington, wire tapping is a crime. To prove its case, the government was obliged to lay bare the crimes committed by its officers on its behalf. A federal court should not permit such a prosecution to continue. . . .

When these unlawful acts were committed they were crimes only of the officers individually. The government was innocent, in legal contemplation; for no federal official is authorized to commit a crime on its behalf. When the government, having full knowledge, sought, through the Department of Justice, to avail itself of the fruits of these acts in order to accomplish its own ends, it assumed moral responsibility for the officers' crimes.

And if this court should permit the government, by means of its officers' crimes, to effect its purpose of punishing the defendants, there would seem to be present all the elements of a ratification. If so, the government itself would become a lawbreaker.

Will this court, by sustaining the judgment below, sanction such conduct on the part of the executive? . . .

The door of a court is not barred because the plaintiff has committed a crime. The confirmed criminal is as much entitled to redress as his most virtuous fellow citizen; no record of crime, however long, makes one an outlaw. The court's aid is denied only when he who seeks it has violated the law in connection with the very transaction as to which he seeks legal redress. Then aid is denied despite the defendant's wrong. It is denied in order to maintain respect for law; in order to promote confidence in the administration of justice; in order to pre-serve the judicial process from contamination. . . .

Decency, security, and liberty alike demand that government officials shall be subjected to the same rules of conduct that are commands to the citizen. In a government of laws, existence of the government will be imperiled if it fails to observe the law scrupulously. Our government is the potent, the omnipresent teacher. For good or for ill, it teaches the whole people by its example. Crime is contagious. If the government becomes a lawbreaker, it breeds contempt for law; it invites every man to become a law unto himself; it invites anarchy. To declare that in the administration of the criminal law the end justifies the means—to declare that the government may commit crimes in order to secure the conviction of a private criminal—would bring terrible retribution. Against that pernicious doctrine this court should resolutely set its face.

The Supreme Court first directly considered whether the Constitution requires the suppression of unlawfully seized evidence in *state* criminal trials in *Wolf v. Colorado*, 338 U.S. 25, 69 S. Ct. 1359, 93 L. Ed. 1782 (1949). In ruling that it did not, Justice Frankfurter's majority opinion drew a sharp distinction between whether the Constitution forbids state law enforcement officials from violating individuals' *rights* to be secure from unreasonable searches and seizures and what *remedy*, if any, the Constitution commands when those rights are violated. As to the former point, the Court held that:

> The security of one's privacy against arbitrary intrusion by the police—which is at the core of the Fourth Amendment—is basic to a free society. It is therefore implicit in "the concept of ordered liberty" and as such enforceable against the States through the Due Process Clause. . . .

Accordingly, we have no hesitation in saying that were a State affirmatively to sanction such police incursion into privacy it would run counter to the guaranty of the Fourteenth Amendment.

However, the Court ruled that the Constitution did not require state courts to exclude unlawfully seized evidence from criminal trials. Referring to the "core" right of privacy that the Constitution protected, the *Wolf* Court continued:

But the ways of enforcing such a basic right raise questions of a different order. How such arbitrary conduct should be checked, what remedies against it should be afforded, the means by which the right should be made effective, are all questions that are not to be so dogmatically answered as to preclude the varying solutions which spring from an allowable range of judgment on issues not susceptible of quantitative solution.

The majority opinion observed that roughly two-thirds of the states declined to follow the *Weeks* exclusionary rule in 1949, and it pointed out that those states "have not left the right to privacy without other means of protection." Three justices dissented. Justice Murphy scoffed at the notion that measures other than the exclusion of evidence could possibly be

effective to secure people's rights against unreasonable searches and seizures.

If we would attempt the enforcement of the search and seizure clause in the ordinary case today, we are limited to three devices: judicial exclusion of the illegally obtained evidence; criminal prosecution of violators; and civil action against violators in the action of trespass.

Alternatives are deceptive. Their very statement conveys the impression that one possibility is as effective as the next. In this case their statement is blinding. For there is but one alternative to the rule of exclusion. That is no sanction at all. . . .

Justice Murphy dismissed as fanciful the expectation that "a District Attorney [would] . . . prosecute himself or his associates for well-meaning violations of the search and seizure clause during a raid the District Attorney or his associates had ordered." He called a civil action for damages "an illusory remedy" because of the unlikelihood that the party whose rights had been violated would prevail or would be awarded anything more than a nominal sum of money. "The conclusion is inescapable," he said, "that but one remedy exists to deter violations of the search and seizure clause. That is the rule which excludes illegally seized evidence." Twelve years later, in *Mapp v. Ohio*, a majority of the Court would agree.

Mapp v. Ohio, 367 U.S. 643, 81 S. Ct. 1684, 6 L. Ed. 2d 1081 (1961)

Mr. Justice Clark delivered the opinion of the Court. . . .

On May 23, 1957, three Cleveland police officers arrived at appellant's residence in that city pursuant to information that "a person [was] hiding out in the home, who was wanted for questioning in connection with a recent bombing, and

that there was a large amount of policy paraphernalia being hidden in the home." Miss Mapp and her daughter by a former marriage lived on the top floor of the two-family dwelling. Upon their arrival at that house, the officers knocked on the door and demanded entrance but appellant, after telephoning her attorney, refused to admit them without a search warrant. They advised their headquarters of the situation and undertook a surveillance of the house.

The officers again sought entrance some three hours later when four or more additional officers arrived on the scene. When Miss Mapp did not come to the door immediately, at least one of the several doors to the house was forcibly opened and the policemen gained admittance. Meanwhile Miss Mapp's attorney arrived, but the officers, having secured their own entry, and continuing in their defiance of the law, would permit him neither to see Miss Mapp nor to enter the house. It appears that Miss Mapp was halfway down the stairs from the upper floor to the front door when the officers, in this highhanded manner, broke into the hall. She demanded to see the search warrant. A paper, claimed to be a warrant, was held up by one of the officers. She grabbed the "warrant" and placed it in her bosom. A struggle ensued in which the officers recovered the piece of paper and as a result of which they handcuffed appellant because she had been "belligerent" in resisting their official rescue of the "warrant" from her person. Running roughshod over appellant, a policeman "grabbed" her, "twisted [her] hand," and she "yelled [and] pleaded with him" because "it was hurting." Appellant, in handcuffs, was then forcibly taken upstairs to her bedroom where the officers searched a dresser, a chest of drawers, a closet and some suitcases. They also looked into a photo album and through personal papers belonging to the appellant. The search spread to the rest of the second floor including the child's bedroom, the living room, the kitchen and a dinette. The basement of the building and a trunk found therein were also searched. The obscene materials for possession of which she was ultimately convicted were discovered in the course of that widespread search.

At the trial no search warrant was produced by the prosecution, nor was the failure to produce one explained or accounted for. . . .

The State says that even if the search were made without authority, or otherwise unreasonably, it is not prevented from using the constitutionally seized evidence at trial, citing Wolf v Colorado, 338 US 25, 69 S. Ct. 1359, 93 L. Ed. 1782 (1949), in which this Court did indeed hold "that in a prosecution in a State court for a State crime the Fourteenth Amendment does not forbid the admission of evidence obtained by an unreasonable search and seizure." At p. 33. On this appeal, it is urged once again that we review that holding.

I.

* * *

[I]n the year 1914, in the Weeks Case, this Court "for the first time" held that "in a federal prosecution the Fourth Amendment barred the use of evidence secured through an illegal search and seizure." Wolf v Colorado (338 US at 28). This Court has ever since required of federal law officers a strict adherence to that command which this Court has held to be a clear, specific, and constitutionally required—even if judicially implied—deterrent safeguard without insistence upon which the Fourth Amendment would have been reduced to "a form of words." Holmes, J., Silverthorne Lumber Co. v United States, 251 US 385, 392, 40 S. Ct. 182, 64 L. Ed. 319, 321 (1920). . . .

There are in the cases of this Court some passing references to the Weeks rule as being one of evidence. But the plain and unequivocal language of Weeks—and its later paraphrase in Wolf—to the effect that the Weeks rule is of constitutional origin, remains entirely undisturbed.

* * *

II.

In 1949, 35 years after Weeks was announced, this Court, in Wolf v Colorado again for the first time, discussed the effect of the Fourth Amendment upon the States through the operation of the Due Process Clause of the Fourteenth Amendment. It said:

"[W]e have no hesitation in saying that were a State affirmatively to sanction such police incursion into privacy it would run counter to the guaranty of the Fourteenth Amendment."

Nevertheless, after declaring that the "security of one's privacy against arbitrary intrusion by the police" is "implicit in 'the concept of ordered liberty' and as such enforceable against the States through the Due Process Clause," and announcing that it "stoutly adhere[d]" to the Weeks decision, the Court decided that the Weeks exclusionary rule would not then be imposed upon the States as "an essential ingredient of the right."

The Court's reasons for not considering essential to the right to privacy, as a curb imposed upon the States by the Due Process Clause, that which decades before had been posited as part and parcel of the Fourth Amendment's limitation upon federal encroachment of individual privacy, were bottomed on factual considerations.

While they are not basically relevant to a decision that the exclusionary rule is an essential ingredient of the Fourth Amendment as the right it embodies is vouchsafed against the States by the Due Process Clause, we will consider the current validity of the factual grounds upon which Wolf was based.

The Court in Wolf first stated that "[t]he contrariety of views of the States" on the adoption of the exclusionary rule of Weeks was "particularly impressive" and, in this connection, that it could not "brush aside the experience of States which deem the incidence of such conduct by the police too slight to call for a deterrent remedy . . . by overriding the [States'] relevant rules of evidence." While in 1949, prior to the Wolf Case, almost two-thirds of the States were opposed to the use of the exclusionary rule, now, despite the Wolf Case, more than half of those since passing upon it, by their own legislative or judicial decision, have wholly or partly adopted or adhered to the Weeks rule. . . .

[T]he second basis elaborated in Wolf in support of its failure to enforce the exclusionary doctrine against the States was that "other means of protection" have been afforded "the right to privacy." The experience of California that such other remedies have been worthless and futile is buttressed by the experience of other States. The obvious futility of relegating the Fourth Amendment to the protection of other remedies has, moreover, been recognized by this Court since Wolf. . . .

III.

. . . Today we once again examine Wolf's constitutional documentation of the right to privacy free from unreasonable state intrusion, and,

after its dozen years on our books, are led by it to close the only courtroom door remaining open to evidence secured by official lawlessness in flagrant abuse of that basic right, reserved to all persons as a specific guarantee against that very same unlawful conduct. We hold that all evidence obtained by searches and seizures in violation of the Constitution is, by that same authority, inadmissible in a state court.

IV.

Since the Fourth Amendment's right of privacy has been declared enforceable against the States through the Due Process Clause of the Fourteenth, it is enforceable against them by the same sanction of exclusion as is used against the Federal Government. Were it otherwise, then just as without the Weeks rule the assurance against unreasonable federal searches and seizures would be "a form of words," valueless and undeserving of mention in a perpetual charter of inestimable human liberties, so too, without that rule the freedom from state invasions of privacy would be so ephemeral and so neatly severed from its conceptual nexus with the freedom from all brutish means of coercing evidence as not to merit this Court's high regard as a freedom "implicit in the concept of ordered liberty." . . .

Therefore, in extending the substantive protections of due process to all constitutionally unreasonable searches—state or federal—it was logically and constitutionally necessary that the exclusion doctrine—an essential part of the right to privacy—be also insisted upon as an essential ingredient of the right newly recognized by the Wolf Case. In short, the admission of the new constitutional right by Wolf could not consistently tolerate denial of its most important constitutional privilege, namely, the exclusion of the evidence which an accused had been forced to give by reason of the unlawful seizure. To hold otherwise is to grant the right but in reality to withhold its privilege and enjoyment. Only last year the Court itself recognized that the purpose of the exclusionary rule "is to deter—to compel respect for the constitutional guaranty in the only effectively available way—by removing the incentive to disregard it." Elkins v United States (364 US at 217). . . .

V.

Moreover, our holding that the exclusionary rule is an essential part of both the Fourth and Fourteenth Amendments is not only the logical dictate of prior cases, but it also makes very good sense. There is no war between the Constitution and common sense. Presently, a federal prosecutor may make no use of evidence illegally seized, but a State's attorney across the street may, although he supposedly is operating under the enforceable prohibitions of the same Amendment. Thus the State, by admitting evidence unlawfully seized, serves to encourage disobedience to the Federal Constitution which it is bound to uphold. . . .

There are those who say, as did Justice (then Judge) Cardozo, that under our constitutional exclusionary doctrine "[t]he criminal is to go free because the constable has blundered." People v Defore, 242 NY, at 21, 150 NE, at 587. In some cases this will undoubtedly be the result. But, as was said in Elkins, "There is another consideration—the imperative of judicial integrity." 364 US, at 222. The criminal goes free, if he must, but it is the law that sets him free. Nothing can destroy a government more quickly than its failure to observe its own laws, or worse, its disregard of the charter of its own existence. . . .

The ignoble shortcut to conviction left open to the State tends to destroy the entire system of constitutional restraints on which the liberties of the people rest. Having once recognized that the right to privacy embodied in the Fourth Amendment is enforceable against the States, and that the right to be secure against rude invasions of privacy by state officers is, therefore, constitutional in origin, we can no longer permit that right to remain an empty promise. Because it is enforceable in the same manner and to like effect as other basic rights secured by the Due Process Clause, we can no longer permit it to be revocable at the whim of any police officer who, in the name of law enforcement itself, chooses to suspend its enjoyment. Our decision, founded on reason and truth, gives to the individual no more than that which the Constitution guarantees him, to the police officer no less than that to which honest law enforcement is entitled, and, to the courts, that judicial integrity so necessary in the true administration of justice. . . .

Reserved and remanded.

* * *

Mr. Justice Harlan, whom Mr. Justice Frankfurter and Mr. Justice Whittaker join, dissenting. . . .

I would not impose upon the States this federal exclusionary remedy. The reasons given by the majority for now suddenly turning its back on Wolf seem to be notably unconvincing.

First, it is said that "the factual grounds upon which Wolf was based" have since changed, in that more States now follow the Weeks exclusionary rule than was so at the time Wolf was decided. While that is true, a recent survey indicates that at present one-half of the States still adhere to the common-law non-exclusionary rule, and one, Maryland, retains the rule as to felonies.

But in any case surely all this is beside the point, as the majority itself indeed seems to recognize. Our concern here, as it was in Wolf, is not with the desirability of that rule but only with the question whether the States are Constitutionally free to follow it or not as they may themselves determine, and the relevance of the disparity of views among the States on this point lies simply in the fact that the judgment involved is a debatable one. . . .

For us the question remains, as it has always been, one of state power, not one of passing judgment on the wisdom of one state course or another. . . .

Further, we are told that imposition of the Weeks rule on the States makes "very good sense," in that it will promote recognition by state and federal officials of their "mutual obligation to respect the same fundamental criteria" in their approach to law enforcement, and will avoid "'needless conflict between state and federal courts.'"

* * *

An approach which regards the issue as one of achieving procedural symmetry or of serving administrative convenience surely disfigures the boundaries of this Court's functions in relation to the state and federal courts. Our role in promulgating the Weeks rule and its extensions . . . was quite a different one than it is here. There, in implementing the Fourth Amendment, we occupied the position of a tribunal having the ultimate responsibility for developing the standards and procedures of judicial administration within the judicial system over which it presides. Here we review state procedures whose measure is to be taken not against the specific substantive commands of the Fourth Amendment but under the flexible contours of the Due Process Clause. I do not believe that the Fourteenth Amendment empowers this Court to mould state remedies effectuating the right to freedom from "arbitrary intrusion by the police" to suit its own notions of how things should be done. . . .

[The concurring opinions of Justices Black and Douglas, and Justice Stewart's "Memorandum" opinion have been omitted.]

Notes and Questions

1. *Mapp* was among the earliest of the Warren Court decisions marking the "due-process revolution." Indeed, the undercurrent of state-federal relations and the proper role of the federal Constitution in governing state rules of criminal procedure is fundamental to the different results reached by the Court in *Wolf* and *Mapp*. In *Ker v. California*, 374 U.S. 23, 83 S. Ct. 1623, 10 L. Ed. 2d 726 (1963), the justices expressly held that the Fourth Amendment's prohibition against unreasonable searches and seizures was enforceable against the states through the Fourteenth Amendment's due-process clause.

2. What is the apparent *source* of authority for the exclusionary rule, as identified in Justice Clark's majority opinion in *Mapp*? That is, does the exclusionary remedy appear to be part and parcel of the right to be free from unreasonable searches and seizures? Or is it a judicially designed safeguard meant to protect that right, without being part of the right itself? What are the expressed *rationales*, or justifications for the exclusionary rule?

3. Beginning in the mid-1970s, the Supreme Court decided several cases limiting the application of the exclusionary rule. For example, it held that the exclusionary rule should not be used to bar illegally seized evidence from being considered by a grand jury. *United States v. Calandra*, 444 U.S. 338, 94 S. Ct. 613, 38 L. Ed. 2d 561 (1974). Nor does the exclusionary remedy apply to unlawfully seized evidence used in a civil tax action initiated by the federal government. *United States v. Janis*, 428 U.S. 433, 96 S. Ct. 3021, 49 L. Ed. 2d 1946 (1976). The justices also expanded a rule that illegally seized evidence can be used to "impeach" the credibility of a criminal defendant's trial testimony. *United States v. Havens*, 446 U.S. 620, 100 S. Ct. 1912, 64 L. Ed. 2d 559 (1980). The Court reaffirmed and arguably gave narrower application to the principle that only persons with "standing" to object that their own Fourth Amendment rights have been violated can benefit from the exclusionary rule. *Rakas v. Illinois*, 439 U.S. 128, 99 S. Ct. 421, 58 L. Ed. 2d 387 (1978). (We will consider the issue of standing later in this chapter.) In *Stone v. Powell*, 428 U.S. 465, 96 S. Ct. 3037, 49 L. Ed. 2d 1067 (1976), the justices announced that state prisoners who had been afforded "an opportunity for full and fair litigation" of Fourth Amendment claims in the state courts could no longer present such claims to the federal courts through a petition for a writ of habeas corpus.

Several themes emerged from these and other cases: that the exclusionary rule is not a personal constitutional right but a judicially created remedy; that its purpose is to deter the police from unlawful searches and seizures and not to promote "judicial integrity"; and that the presumed deterrence benefits of the rule must be carefully assessed in different contexts to determine whether they are worth the costs to the truth-finding function of a criminal trial. Be on the lookout for these themes in *United States v. Leon*, which follows. The Court in *Leon* accepted that the defendants' Fourth Amendment rights had been infringed. The justices, however, recognized a "good-faith exception" to the exclusionary rule and authorized evidence seized in violation of those rights to be admitted at their trial. See if you can square the *Leon* Court's treatment of the exclusionary rule with the *Mapp* Court's conception of it.

The Good-Faith Exception to the Exclusionary Rule

United States v. Leon, 468 U.S. 897, 104 S. Ct. 3405, 82 L. Ed. 2d 677 (1984)

[Police in Burbank, California, secured a search warrant from a state superior court judge, authorizing them to search the residence of Leon and others for illegal drugs. The warrant application was based on a tip provided by "a confidential informant of unproven reliability" and on a subsequent investigation by the police that tended to corroborate the tip. When the police executed the warrant, they found substantial quantities of drugs at the named residences. Leon and the other respondents were indicted by a federal grand jury and charged with various drug-related offenses. They filed a motion to suppress the evidence seized pursuant to the search warrant in the U.S. district court where they were to be tried. Calling the question "a close one," the court concluded that the search warrant had been issued improperly in that it was not supported by probable cause. It granted the respondents' motion to suppress the evidence in substantial part. The Ninth Circuit Court of Appeals affirmed, and the Supreme Court granted the government's petition for a writ of certiorari.]

Justice **White** delivered the opinion of the Court.

This case presents the question whether the Fourth Amendment exclusionary rule should be modified so as not to bar the use in the prosecution's case-in-chief of evidence obtained by officers acting in reasonable reliance on a search warrant issued by a detached and neutral magistrate but ultimately found to be unsupported by probable cause. To resolve this question, we must consider once again the tension between the sometimes competing goals of, on the one hand, deterring official misconduct and removing inducements to unreasonable invasions of privacy and, on the other, establishing procedures under which criminal defendants are "acquitted or convicted on the basis of all the evidence which exposes the truth." Alderman v

United States, 394 US 165, 175, 22 L Ed 2d 176, 89 S Ct 961 (1969). . . .

II

Language in opinions of this Court and of individual Justices has sometimes implied that the exclusionary rule is a necessary corollary of the Fourth Amendment, Mapp v Ohio, 367 US 643, 651, 655–657 (1961); Olmstead v United States, 277 US 438, 462–463 (1928). . . .

These implications need not detain us long. . . . [T]he Fourth Amendment "has never been interpreted to proscribe the introduction of illegally seized evidence in all proceedings or against all persons." Stone v Powell, 428 US 465, 486, 49 L Ed 2d 1067, 96 S Ct 3037 (1976).

A

The Fourth Amendment contains no provision expressly precluding the use of evidence obtained in violation of its commands, and an examination of its origin and purposes makes clear that the use of fruits of a past unlawful search or seizure "work[s] no new Fourth Amendment wrong." United States v Calandra, 414 US 338, 354, 94 S Ct 613, 38 L Ed 2d 561 (1974). The wrong condemned by the Amendment is "fully accomplished" by the unlawful search or seizure itself, ibid., and the exclusionary rule is neither intended nor able to "cure the invasion of the defendant's rights which he has already suffered." Stone v Powell, supra, at 540, 49 L Ed 2d 1067, 96 S Ct 3037 (White, J., dissenting). The rule thus operates as "a judicially created remedy designed to safeguard Fourth Amendment rights generally through its deterrent effect, rather than a personal constitutional right of the person aggrieved." United States v Calandra, supra, at 348.

Whether the exclusionary sanction is appropriately imposed in a particular case, our decisions make clear, is "an issue separate from the question whether the Fourth Amendment rights of the party seeking to invoke the rule were violated by police conduct."

Only the former question is currently before us, and it must be resolved by weighing the costs and benefits of preventing the use in the prosecution's case-in-chief of inherently trustworthy tangible evidence obtained in reliance on a search warrant issued by a detached and neutral magistrate that ultimately is found to be defective.

The substantial social costs exacted by the exclusionary rule for the vindication of Fourth Amendment rights have long been a source of concern. "Our cases have consistently recognized that unbending application of the exclusionary sanction to enforce ideals of government rectitude would impede unacceptably the truth-finding functions of judge and jury." United States v Payner, 447 US 727, 734, 65 L Ed 2d 468, 100 S Ct 2439 (1980). An objectionable collateral consequence of this interference with the criminal justice system's truth-finding function is that some guilty defendants may go free or receive reduced sentences as a result of favorable plea bargains. Particularly when law enforcement officers have acted in objective good faith or their transgressions have been minor, the magnitude of the benefit conferred on such guilty defendants offends basic concepts of the criminal justice system. Indiscriminate application of the exclusionary rule, therefore, may well "generat[e] disrespect for the law and the administration of justice." Accordingly, "[a]s with any remedial device, the application of the rule has been restricted to those areas where its remedial objectives are thought most efficaciously served." United States v Calandra, supra, at 348.

B

Close attention to those remedial objectives has characterized our recent decisions concerning the scope of the Fourth Amendment exclusionary rule. The Court has, to be sure, not seriously questioned, "in the absence of a more efficacious sanction, the continued application of the rule to suppress evidence from the [prosecution's] case where a Fourth Amendment viola-

tion has been substantial and deliberate. . . ." Franks v Delaware, 438 US 154, 171, 57 L Ed 2d 667, 98 S Ct 2674 (1978). Nevertheless, the balancing approach that has evolved in various contexts—including criminal trials—"forcefully suggest[s] that the exclusionary rule be more generally modified to permit the introduction of evidence obtained in the reasonable good-faith belief that a search or seizure was in accord with the Fourth Amendment."

In Stone v Powell, the Court emphasized the costs of the exclusionary rule, expressed its view that limiting the circumstances under which Fourth Amendment claims could be raised in federal habeas corpus proceedings would not reduce the rule's deterrent effect, id., at 489–495, 49 L Ed 2d 1067, 96 S Ct 3037, and held that a state prisoner who has been afforded a full and fair opportunity to litigate a Fourth Amendment claim may not obtain federal habeas relief on the ground that unlawfully obtained evidence had been introduced at his trial. Proposed extensions of the exclusionary rule to proceedings other than the criminal trial itself have been evaluated and rejected under the same analytic approach. In United States v Calandra, for example, we declined to allow grand jury witnesses to refuse to answer questions based on evidence obtained from an unlawful search or seizure since "[a]ny incremental deterrent effect which might be achieved by extending the rule to grand jury proceedings is uncertain at best." Similarly, in United States v Janis, we permitted the use in federal civil proceedings of evidence illegally seized by state officials since the likelihood of deterring police misconduct through such an extension of the exclusionary rule was insufficient to outweigh its substantial social costs. . . .

As cases considering the use of unlawfully obtained evidence in criminal trials themselves make clear, it does not follow from the emphasis on the exclusionary rule's deterrent value that "anything which deters illegal searches is thereby commanded by the Fourth Amendment." . . . Standing to invoke the rule has thus been limited to cases in which the prosecution seeks to use the fruits of an illegal search or seizure against the victim of police misconduct.

Even defendants with standing to challenge the introduction in their criminal trials of unlawfully obtained evidence cannot prevent every conceivable use of such evidence. Evidence obtained in violation of the Fourth Amendment and inadmissible in the prosecution's case-in-chief may be used to impeach a defendant's . . . testimony. . . .

When considering the use of evidence obtained in violation of the Fourth Amendment in the prosecution's case-in-chief, moreover, we have declined to adopt a per se or but for rule that would render inadmissible any evidence that came to light through a chain of causation that began with an illegal arrest. Brown v Illinois, 422 US 590, 95 S Ct 2254, 45 L Ed 2d 416 (1975); Wong Sun v United States, [371 U.S. 471,] 487–488, 9 L Ed 2d 441, 83 S Ct 407 [(1963)].

* * *

Not surprisingly in view of this purpose, an assessment of the flagrancy of the police misconduct constitutes an important step in the calculus.

The same attention to the purposes underlying the exclusionary rule also has characterized decisions not involving the scope of the rule itself. We have not required suppression of the fruits of a search incident to an arrest made in good-faith reliance on a substantive criminal statute that subsequently is declared unconstitutional. Michigan v DeFillippo, 443 US 31, 99 S Ct 2627, 61 L Ed 2d 343 (1979). . . .

As yet, we have not recognized any form of good-faith exception to the Fourth Amendment exclusionary rule. But the balancing approach that has evolved during the years of experience with the rule provides strong support for the modification currently urged upon us. As we discuss below, our evaluation of the costs and benefits of suppressing reliable physical evidence seized by officers reasonably relying on a warrant issued by a detached and neutral magistrate leads to the conclusion that such evidence should be admissible in the prosecution's case-in-chief.

III

A

Because a search warrant "provides the detached scrutiny of a neutral magistrate, which is a more reliable safeguard against improper searches than the hurried judgment of a law enforcement officer 'engaged in the often competitive enterprise of ferreting out crime,'" we have expressed a strong preference for warrants and declared that "in a doubtful or marginal case a search under a warrant may be sustainable where without one it would fail."

Reasonable minds frequently may differ on the question whether a particular affidavit establishes probable cause, and we have thus concluded that the preference for warrants is most appropriately effectuated by according "great deference" to a magistrate's determination.

Deference to the magistrate, however, is not boundless. It is clear, first, that the deference accorded to a magistrate's finding of probable cause does not preclude inquiry into the knowing or reckless falsity of the affidavit on which that determination was based. Franks v Delaware, 438 US 154, 98 S Ct 2674, 57 L Ed 2d 667 (1978). Second, the courts must also insist that the magistrate purport to "perform his 'neutral and detached' function and not serve merely as a rubber stamp for the police." Aguilar v Texas, [378 U.S. 108,] 111, 84 S Ct 1509, 12 L Ed 2d 723 [(1964)]. . . .

Third, reviewing courts will not defer to a warrant based on an affidavit that does not "provide the magistrate with a substantial basis for determining the existence of probable cause." "Sufficient information must be presented to the magistrate to allow that official to determine probable cause; his action cannot be a mere ratification of the bare conclusions of others."

Even if the warrant application was supported by more than a "bare bones" affidavit, a reviewing court may properly conclude that, notwithstanding the deference that magistrates deserve, the warrant was invalid because the magistrate's probable-cause determination reflected an improper analysis of the totality of the circumstances, or because the form of the warrant was improper in some respect.

Only in the first of these three situations, however, has the Court set forth a rationale for suppressing evidence obtained pursuant to a search warrant; in the other areas, it has simply excluded such evidence without considering whether Fourth Amendment interests will be advanced. To the extent that proponents of exclusion rely on its behavioral effects on judges and magistrates in these areas, their reliance is misplaced. First, the exclusionary rule is designed to deter police misconduct rather than to punish the errors of judges and magistrates. Second, there exists no evidence suggesting that judges and magistrates are inclined to ignore or subvert the Fourth Amendment or that lawlessness among these actors requires application of the extreme sanction of exclusion.[14]

Third, and most important, we discern no basis, and are offered none, for believing that exclusion of evidence seized pursuant to a warrant will have a significant deterrent effect on the issuing judge or magistrate. . . . Judges and magistrates are not adjuncts to the law enforcement team; as neutral judicial officers, they have no stake in the outcome of particular criminal prosecutions. The threat of exclusion thus cannot be expected significantly to deter them. Imposition of the exclusionary sanction is not necessary meaningfully to inform judicial officers of their errors, and we cannot conclude that admitting evidence obtained pursuant to a warrant while at the same time declaring that the warrant was somehow defective will in any way reduce judicial officers' professional incentives to comply with the Fourth Amendment, encourage them to repeat their mistakes, or lead to the granting of all colorable warrant requests.

B

If exclusion of evidence obtained pursuant to a subsequently invalidated warrant is to have any deterrent effect, therefore, it must alter the behavior of individual law enforcement officers or the policies of their departments. One could argue that applying the exclusionary rule in cases where the police failed to demonstrate probable cause in the warrant application deters future inadequate presentations or "magistrate shopping" and thus promotes the ends of the Fourth Amendment. Suppressing evidence obtained pursuant to a technically defective warrant supported by probable cause also might encourage officers to scrutinize more closely the form of the warrant and to point out suspected judicial errors. We find such arguments speculative and conclude that suppression of evidence obtained pursuant to a warrant should be ordered only on a case-by-case basis and only in those unusual cases in which exclusion will further the purposes of the exclusionary rule.[19]

We have frequently questioned whether the exclusionary rule can have any deterrent effect when the offending officers acted in the objectively reasonable belief that their conduct did not violate the Fourth Amendment. "No empirical researcher, proponent or opponent of the rule, has yet been able to establish with any assurance whether the rule has a deterrent effect. . . ." United States v Janis, 428 US, at 452, n 22, 96 S Ct 3021, 49 L Ed 2d 1046. But even assuming that the rule effectively deters some police misconduct and provides incentives for the law enforcement profession as a whole to conduct itself in accord with the Fourth Amendment, it cannot be expected, and should not be applied,

---

14. Although there are assertions that some magistrates become rubber stamps for the police and others may be unable effectively to screen police conduct, we are not convinced that this is a problem of major proportions.

---

19. Our discussion of the deterrent effect of excluding evidence obtained in reasonable reliance on a subsequently invalidated warrant assumes, of course, that the officers properly executed the warrant and searched only those places and for those objects that it was reasonable to believe were covered by the warrant. . . .

to deter objectively reasonable law enforcement activity. . . .[20]

* * *

This is particularly true, we believe, when an officer acting with objective good faith has obtained a search warrant from a judge or magistrate and acted within its scope. In most such cases, there is no police illegality and thus nothing to deter. It is the magistrate's responsibility to determine whether the officer's allegations establish probable cause and, if so, to issue a warrant comporting in form with the requirements of the Fourth Amendment. In the ordinary case, an officer cannot be expected to question the magistrate's probable-cause determination or his judgment that the form of the warrant is technically sufficient.

* * *

Penalizing the officer for the magistrate's error, rather than his own, cannot logically contribute to the deterrence of Fourth Amendment violations.[23]

---

20. We emphasize that the standard of reasonableness we adopt is an objective one. Many objections to a good-faith exception assume that the exception will turn on the subjective good faith of individual officers. "Grounding the modification in objective reasonableness, however, retains the value of the exclusionary rule as an incentive for the law enforcement profession as a whole to conduct themselves in accord with the Fourth Amendment." The objective standard we adopt, moreover, requires officers to have a reasonable knowledge of what the law prohibits. . . .

23. . . . Our cases establish that the question whether the use of illegally obtained evidence in judicial proceedings represents judicial participation in a Fourth Amendment violation and offends the integrity of the courts "is essentially the same as the inquiry into whether exclusion would serve a deterrent purpose. . . . The analysis showing that exclusion in this case has no demonstrated deterrent effect and is unlikely to have any significant such effect shows, by the same reasoning, that the admission of the evidence is unlikely to encourage violations of the Fourth Amendment." Absent unusual circumstances, when a Fourth Amendment violation has occurred because the police have reasonably relied on a warrant issued by a detached and neutral magistrate but ultimately found to be defective, "the integrity of the courts is not implicated."

C

We conclude that the marginal or nonexistent benefits produced by suppressing evidence obtained in objectively reasonable reliance on a subsequently invalidated search warrant cannot justify the substantial costs of exclusion. We do not suggest, however, that exclusion is always inappropriate in cases where an officer has obtained a warrant and abided by its terms.

* * *

Suppression therefore remains an appropriate remedy if the magistrate or judge in issuing a warrant was misled by information in an affidavit that the affiant knew was false or would have known was false except for his reckless disregard of the truth. Franks v Delaware, 438 US 154, 98 S Ct 2674, 57 L Ed 2d 667 (1978). The exception we recognize today will also not apply in cases where the issuing magistrate wholly abandoned his judicial role in the manner condemned in Lo-Ji Sales, Inc. v New York, 442 US 319, 99 S Ct 2319, 60 L Ed 2d 920 (1979); in such circumstances, no reasonably well-trained officer should rely on the warrant. Nor would an officer manifest objective good faith in relying on a warrant based on an affidavit "so lacking in indicia of probable cause as to render official belief in its existence entirely unreasonable."

Finally, depending on the circumstances of the particular case, a warrant may be so facially deficient—i.e., in failing to particularize the place to be searched or the things to be seized—that the executing officers cannot reasonably presume it to be valid.

In so limiting the suppression remedy, we leave untouched the probable-cause standard and the various requirements for a valid warrant. . . .

Nor are we persuaded that application of a good-faith exception to searches conducted pursuant to warrants will preclude review of the constitutionality of the search or seizure, deny needed guidance from the courts, or freeze Fourth Amendment law in its present state. There is no need for courts to adopt the inflexible practice of always deciding whether the officers' conduct manifested objective good faith before turning to the question whether the Fourth Amendment has been violated. . . .

IV

When the principles we have enunciated today are applied to the facts of this case, it is apparent that the judgement of the Court of Appeals cannot stand. . . .

Justice **Brennan**, with whom Justice **Marshall** joins, dissenting. . . .

It now appears that the Court's victory over the Fourth Amendment is complete. That today's decision represents the piece de resistance of the Court's past efforts cannot be doubted, for today the Court sanctions the use in the prosecution's case-in-chief of illegally obtained evidence against the individual whose rights have been violated—a result that had previously been thought to be foreclosed.

The Court seeks to justify this result on the ground that the "costs" of adhering to the exclusionary rule in cases like those before us exceed the "benefits." But the language of deterrence and of cost/benefit analysis, if used indiscriminately, can have a narcotic effect. It creates an illusion of technical precision and ineluctability. It suggests that not only constitutional principle but also empirical data supports the majority's result. When the Court's analysis is examined carefully, however, it is clear that we have not been treated to an honest assessment of the merits of the exclusionary rule, but have instead been drawn into a curious world where the "costs" of excluding illegally obtained evidence loom to exaggerated heights and where the "benefits" of such exclusion are made to disappear with a mere wave of the hand. . . .

A proper understanding of the broad purposes sought to be served by the Fourth Amendment demonstrates that the principles embodied in the exclusionary rule rest upon a far firmer constitutional foundation than the shifting sands of the Court's deterrence rationale. But even if I were to accept the Court's chosen method of analyzing the question posed by these cases, I would still conclude that the Court's decision cannot be justified.

I

* * *

A

At bottom, the Court's decision turns on the proposition that the exclusionary rule is merely a

"'judicially created remedy designed to safeguard Fourth Amendment rights generally through its deterrent effect, rather than a personal constitutional right.'"

The germ of that idea is found in Wolf v Colorado, and although I had thought that such a narrow conception of the rule had been forever put to rest by our decision in Mapp v Ohio, it has been revived by the present Court and reaches full flower with today's decision. The essence of this view, as expressed initially in the Calandra opinion and as reiterated today, is that the sole "purpose of the Fourth Amendment is to prevent unreasonable governmental intrusions into the privacy of one's person, house, papers, or effects. The wrong condemned is the unjustified governmental invasion of these areas of an individual's life. That wrong . . . is *fully accomplished* by the original search without probable cause."

This reading of the Amendment implies that its proscriptions are directly solely at those government agents who may actually invade an individual's constitutionally protected privacy. . . .

Because the only constitutionally cognizable injury has already been "fully accomplished" by the police by the time a case comes before the courts, the Constitution is not itself violated if the judge decides to admit the tainted evidence. Indeed, the most the judge *can* do is wring his hands and hope that perhaps by excluding such evidence he can deter future transgressions by the police.

Such a reading appears plausible, because, as critics of the exclusionary rule never tire of repeating, the Fourth Amendment makes no express provision for the exclusion of evidence secured in violation of its commands. A short answer to this claim, of course, is that many of the Constitution's most vital imperatives are stated in general terms and the task of giving meaning to these precepts is therefore left to subsequent judicial decision-making in the context of concrete cases. . . .

A more direct answer may be supplied by recognizing that the Amendment, like other provisions of the Bill of Rights, restrains the power of the government as a whole; it does not specify only a particular agency and exempt all others. The judiciary is responsible, no less than the executive, for ensuring that constitutional rights are respected.

When that fact is kept in mind, the role of the courts and their possible involvement in the concerns of the Fourth Amendment comes into sharper focus. Because seizures are executed principally to secure evidence, and because such evidence generally has utility in our legal system only in the context of a trial supervised by a judge, it is apparent that the admission of illegally obtained evidence implicates the same constitutional concerns as the initial seizure of that evidence. Indeed, by admitting unlawfully seized evidence, the judiciary becomes a part of what is in fact a single governmental action prohibited by the terms of the Amendment. . . .

The Amendment therefore must be read to condemn not only the initial unconstitutional invasion of privacy—which is done, after all, for the purpose of securing evidence—but also the subsequent use of any evidence so obtained.

The Court evades this principle by drawing an artificial line between the constitutional rights and responsibilities that are engaged by actions of the police and those that are engaged when a defendant appears before the courts. According to the Court, the substantive protections of the Fourth Amendment are wholly exhausted at the moment when police unlawfully invade an individual's privacy and thus no substantive force remains to those protections at the time of trial when the government seeks to use evidence obtained by the police.

I submit that such a crabbed reading of the Fourth Amendment casts aside the teaching of those Justices who first formulated the exclusionary rule, and rests ultimately on an impoverished understanding of judicial responsibility in our constitutional scheme. For my part, "[t]he right of the people to be secure in their persons, houses, papers and effects, against unreasonable searches and seizures" comprises a personal right to exclude all evidence secured by means of unreasonable searches and seizures. The right to be free from the initial invasion of privacy and the right of exclusion are coordinate components of the central embracing right to be free from unreasonable searches and seizures. . . .

B

From the foregoing, it is clear why the question whether the exclusion of evidence would deter future police misconduct was never considered a relevant concern in the early cases from Weeks to Olmstead. In those formative decisions, the Court plainly understood that the exclusion of illegally obtained evidence was compelled not by judicially fashioned remedial purposes, but rather by a direct constitutional command.

* * *

[T]he deterrence theory is both misguided and unworkable. First, the Court has frequently bewailed the "cost" of excluding reliable evidence. In large part, this criticism rests upon a refusal to acknowledge the function of the Fourth Amendment itself. If nothing else, the Amendment plainly operates to disable the government from gathering information and securing evidence in certain ways. In practical terms, of course, this restriction of official power means that some incriminating evidence inevitably will go undetected if the government obeys these constitutional restraints. It is the loss of that evidence that is the "price" our society pays for enjoying the freedom and privacy safeguarded by the Fourth Amendment. Thus, some criminal will go free *not*, in Justice (then Judge) Cardozo's misleading epigram, "because the constable has blundered," People v Defore, 242 NY 13, 21, 140 NY 585, 587 (1926), but rather because official compliance with Fourth Amendment requirements makes it more difficult to catch criminals. Understood in this way, the Amendment directly contemplates that some reliable and incriminating evidence will be lost to the government; therefore, it is not the exclusionary rule, but the Amendment itself that has imposed this cost. . . .

III

Even if I were to accept the Court's general approach to the exclusionary rule, I could not agree with today's result. There is no question that in the hands of the present Court the deterrence rationale has proved to be a powerful tool for confining the scope of the rule. . . .

Thus, in this bit of judicial stagecraft, while the sets sometimes change, the actors always have the same lines. Given this well-rehearsed pattern, one might have predicted with some assurance how the present case would unfold. First there is the ritual incantation of the "substantial social costs" exacted by the exclusionary rule, followed by the virtually foreordained conclusion that, given the marginal benefits, application of the rule in the circumstances of these cases is not warranted. Upon analysis, however, such a result cannot be justified even on the Court's own terms.

At the outset, the Court suggests that society has been asked to pay a high price—in terms either of setting guilty persons free or of impeding the proper functioning of trials—as a result of excluding relevant physical evidence in cases where the police, in conducting searches and seizing evidence, have made only an "objectively reasonable" mistake concerning the constitutionality of their actions. But what evidence is there to support such a claim?

Significantly, the Court points to none, and, indeed, as the Court acknowledges, recent studies have demonstrated that the "costs" of the exclusionary rule—calculated in terms of dropped prosecutions and lost convictions—are quite low. Contrary to the claims of the rule's critics that exclusion leads to "the release of countless guilty criminals," these studies have demonstrated that federal and state prosecutors very rarely drop cases because of potential search and seizure problems. For example, a 1979 study prepared at the request of Congress by the General Accounting Office reported that only 0.4% of all cases actually declined for prosecution by federal prosecutors were declined primarily because of illegal search problems. Report of the Comptroller General of the United States, Impact of the Exclusionary Rule on Federal Criminal Prosecutions 14 (1979). If the GAO data are restated as a percentage of *all* arrests, the study shows that only 0.2% of all felony arrests are declined for prosecution because of potential exclusionary rule problems.[11] Of course, these data describe only the costs attributable to the exclusion of evidence in all cases; the costs due to the exclusion of evidence in the narrower category of cases where police have made objectively reasonable mistakes must necessarily be even smaller. The Court, however, ignores this distinction and mistakenly weighs the aggregated costs of exclusion in *all* cases, irrespective of the circumstances that led to exclusion, against the potential benefits associated with only those cases in which evidence is excluded because police reasonably but mistakenly believe that their conduct does not violate the Fourth Amendment. When such faulty scales are used, it is little wonder that the balance tips in favor of restricting the application of the rule.

What then supports the Court's insistence that this evidence be admitted? Apparently, the Court's only answer is that even though the costs of exclusion are not very substantial, the potential deterrent effect in these circumstances is so marginal that exclusion cannot be justified. The key to the Court's conclusion in this respect is its belief that the prospective deterrent effect

---

11. In a series of recent studies, researchers have attempted to quantify the actual costs of the rule. A recent National Institute of Justice study based on data for the four year period 1976–1979 gathered by the California Bureau of Criminal Statistics showed that 4.8% of all cases that were declined for prosecution by California prosecutors were rejected because of illegally seized evidence. National Institute of Justice, Criminal Justice Research Report—The Effects of the Exclusionary Rule: A Study in California 1 (1982). However, if these data are calculated as a percentage of all arrests that were declined for prosecution, they show that only 0.8% of all arrests were rejected for prosecution because of illegally seized evidence.

In another measure of the rule's impact—the number of prosecutions that are dismissed or result in acquittals in cases where evidence has been excluded—the available data again show that the Court's past assessment of the rule's costs has generally been exaggerated. For example, a study based on data from 9 mid-sized counties in Illinois, Michigan and Pennsylvania reveals that motions to suppress physical evidence were filed in approximately 5% of the 7,500 cases studied, but that such motions were successful in only 0.7% of all these cases. The study also shows that only 0.6% of all cases resulted in acquittals because evidence had been excluded. In the GAO study, suppression motions were filed in 10.5% of all federal criminal cases surveyed, but of the motions filed, approximately 80–90% were denied. Evidence was actually excluded in only 1.3% of the cases studied, and only 0.7% of all cases resulted in acquittals or dismissals after evidence was excluded. And in another study based on data from cases during 1978 and 1979 in San Diego and Jacksonville, it was shown that only 1% of all cases resulting in nonconviction were caused by illegal searches.

of the exclusionary rule operates only in those situations in which police officers, when deciding whether to go forward with some particular search, have reason to know that their planned conduct will violate the requirements of the Fourth Amendment. . . .

The flaw in the Court's argument, however, is that its logic captures only one comparatively minor element of the generally acknowledged deterrent purposes of the exclusionary rule. To be sure, the rule operates to some extent to deter future misconduct by individual officers who have had evidence suppressed in their own cases. But what the Court overlooks is that the deterrence rationale for the rule is not designed to be, nor should it be thought of as, a form of "punishment" of individual police officers for their failures to obey the restraints imposed by the Fourth Amendment.

Instead, the chief deterrent function of the rule is its tendency to promote institutional compliance with Fourth Amendment requirements on the part of law enforcement agencies generally. Thus, as the Court has previously recognized, "over the long term, [the] demonstration [provided by the exclusionary rule] that our society attaches serious consequences to violation of constitutional rights is thought to encourage those who formulate law enforcement policies, and the officers who implement them, to incorporate Fourth Amendment ideals into their value system." Stone v Powell, 427 US, at 492, 96 S Ct 3037, 49 L Ed 2d 1067. It is only through such an institution-wide mechanism that information concerning Fourth Amendment standards can be effectively communicated to rank and file officers.

If the overall educational effect of the exclusionary rule is considered, application of the rule to even those situations in which individual police officers have acted on the basis of a reasonable but mistaken belief that their conduct was authorized can still be expected to have a considerable long-term deterrent effect. If evidence is consistently excluded in these circumstances, police departments will surely be prompted to instruct their officers to devote greater care and attention to providing sufficient information to establish probable cause when applying for a warrant, and to review with some attention the form of the warrant that they have been issued, rather than automatically assuming that whatever document the magistrate has signed will necessarily comport with Fourth Amendment requirements.

After today's decision, however, that institutional incentive will be lost. Indeed, the Court's "reasonable mistake" exception to the exclusionary rule will tend to put a premium on police ignorance of the law. Armed with the assurance provided by today's decision that evidence will always be admissible whenever an officer has "reasonably" relied upon a warrant, police departments will be encouraged to train officers that if a warrant has simply been signed, it is reasonable, without more, to rely on it. Since in close cases there will no longer be any incentive to err on the side of constitutional behavior, police would have every reason to adopt a "let's-wait-until-its-decided" approach in situations in which there is a question about a warrant's validity or the basis for its issuance.

Although the Court brushes these concerns aside, a host of grave consequences can be expected to result from its decision to carve this new exception out of the exclusionary rule. A chief consequence of today's decision will be to convey a clear and unambiguous message to magistrates that their decisions to issue warrants are now insulated from subsequent judicial review. Creation of this new exception for good faith reliance upon a warrant implicitly tells magistrates that they need not take much care in reviewing warrant applications, since their mistakes will from now on have virtually no consequence: If their decision to issue a warrant was correct, the evidence will be admitted; if their decision was incorrect but the police relied in good faith on the warrant, the evidence will also be admitted. Inevitably, the care and attention devoted to such an inconsequential chore will dwindle. . . .

Moreover, the good faith exception will encourage police to provide only the bare minimum of information in future warrant applications. The police will now know that if they can secure a warrant, so long as the circumstances of its issuance are not "entirely unreasonable," all police conduct pursuant to that warrant will be protected from further judicial review. . . .

IV

When the public, as it quite properly has done in the past as well as in the present, demands that those in government increase their efforts to combat crime, it is all too easy for those government officials to seek expedient solutions. In contrast to such costly and difficult measures as building more prisons, improving law enforcement methods, or hiring more prosecutors and judges to relieve the overburdened court systems in the country's metropolitan areas, the relaxation of Fourth Amendment standards seems a tempting, costless means of meeting the public's demand for better law enforcement. In the long run, however, we as a society pay a heavy price for such expediency, because as Justice Jackson observed, the rights guaranteed in the Fourth Amendment "are not mere second-class rights but belong in the catalog of indispensable freedoms." Brinegar v United States, 338 US 160, 180, 69 S Ct 1302, 93 L Ed 1879 (1949) (dissenting opinion). Once lost, such rights are difficult to recover. There is hope, however, that in time this or some later Court will restore these precious freedoms to their rightful place as a primary protection for our citizens against overreaching officialdom.

I dissent.

Justice **Stevens**, . . . dissenting . . .

Today, for the first time, this Court holds that although the Constitution has been violated, no court should do anything about it at any time and in any proceeding. In my judgment, the Constitution requires more. Courts simply cannot escape their responsibility for redressing constitutional violations if they admit evidence obtained through unreasonable searches and seizures, since the entire point of police conduct that violates the Fourth Amendment is to obtain evidence for use at trial. If such evidence is admitted, then the courts become not merely the final and necessary link in an unconstitutional chain of events, but its actual motivating force. . . .

Nor should we so easily concede the existence of a constitutional violation for which there is no remedy. To do so is to convert a Bill of Rights into an unenforced honor code that the police may follow in their discretion. The Constitution requires more; it requires a *remedy*. . . .

It is of course true that the exclusionary rule exerts a high price—the loss of probative evidence of guilt. But that price is one courts have often been required to pay to serve important social goals. That price is also one the Fourth Amendment requires us to pay, assuming as we must that the Framers intended that its strictures "shall not be violated." For in all such cases, as Justice Stewart has observed, "the same extremely relevant evidence would not have been obtained had the police officer complied with the commands of the fourth amendment in the first place." . . .

We could, of course, facilitate the process of administering justice to those who violate the criminal laws by ignoring the commands of the Fourth Amendment—indeed, by ignoring the entire Bill of Rights—but it is the very purpose of a Bill of Rights to identify values that may not be sacrificed to expediency. In a just society those who govern, as well as those who are governed, must obey the law. . . .

Notes and Questions

1. The Court also applied the good-faith exception in a companion case to *Leon—Massachusetts v. Sheppard*, 468 U.S. 981, 104 S. Ct. 3424, 82 L. Ed. 2d 737 (1984). A police detective in *Sheppard* applied for a warrant to search the defendant's home for evidence of a murder. Because it was Sunday, the detective applied for the warrant at the home of a judge, and a suitable form for a homicide search warrant could not be produced. Although the judge told the detective that the warrant he signed would authorize a search for evidence of a murder, the written warrant erroneously permitted a search only for evidence of controlled substances. On executing the search warrant, the detective and other officers seized evidence of the murder. The evidence was ordered suppressed by the state court because to the extent the warrant was intended to authorize a search for evidence of a homicide, it failed to "particularly describ[e]" the items to be seized. The U.S. Supreme Court reversed. It ruled that because "there was an objectively reasonable basis for the officers' mistaken belief" that "the warrant authorized the search that they conducted," the evidence was admissible by application of the good-faith exception to the exclusionary rule. "We refuse to rule that an officer is required to disbelieve a judge who has just advised him, by word and by action, that the warrant he possesses authorizes him to conduct the search he has requested." 468 U.S., at 989–990. Justice Stevens concurred in the result, and Justices Brennan and Marshall dissented.

2. The good-faith exception to the exclusionary rule has been rejected by several states as a matter of state constitutional law. *See, e.g., State v. Guzman*, 122 Idaho 981, 842 P.2d 660 (1992); *State v. Oakes*, 157 Vt. 171, 598 A.2d 119 (1991); *Commonwealth v. Edmunds*, 526 Pa. 374, 586 A.2d 887 (1991); *State v. Marsala*, 216 Conn. 150, 579 A.2d 58 (1990); *People v. Bigelow*, 66 N.Y.2d 417, 488 N.E.2d 451, 497 N.Y.S.2d 630 (1985). Many of those decisions rely on arguments similar to the ones advanced in Justice Brennan's dissent in *Leon*. The New Jersey Supreme Court's ruling in *State v. Novembrino*, 105 N.J. 95, 519 A.2d 820 (1987), is illustrative.

State v. Novembrino, 105 N.J. 95, 519 A.2d 820 (1987)

Stein, J.

. . .

We note that one of the most frequently recurring themes in the criticism that has been directed at the Leon decision is that it will tend to undermine the motivation of law-enforcement officers to comply with the constitutional requirement of probable cause. Professor LaFave makes the argument cogently:

Under the pre-Leon version of the exclusionary rule, police had finally come to learn that it was not enough that they had gotten a piece of paper called a warrant. Because that warrant was subject to challenge at the later motion to suppress, it was important to the police that the warrant be properly issued or that the warrant request be turned down at a time when it might be possible to acquire necessary additional information without compromising the investigation. Consequently, there had developed in many localities the very sound practice of going through the warrant-issuing process with the greatest of care, often by having the affidavit reviewed by individuals other than the magistrate. * * * But under Leon there is no reason to go through such cautious procedures and every reason not to. Why take the risk that some conscientious prosecutor or police supervisor will say the application is insufficient when, if some magistrate can be induced to issue a warrant on the basis of it, the affidavit is thereafter virtually immune from challenge? There is thus no escaping the fact that, as the Leon dissenters put it, the "long-run effect" of that case "unquestionably will be to undermine the integrity of the warrant process." [1 LaFave, Search and Seizure, (1986 Pocket Part), § 1.2, at 20.]

We find this criticism of the "good-faith" exception to be persuasive. One obvious consequence of the application of the exclusionary rule in New Jersey has been the encouragement of law-enforcement officials to comply with the constitutionally-mandated probable-cause standard in order to avoid the suppression of evidence. The Leon rule avoids suppression of evidence even if the constitutional standard is violated, requiring only that the officer executing the defective warrant have an objectively reasonable basis for relying on it. Whatever else may be said for or against the Leon rule, the good-faith exception will inevitably and inexorably diminish the quality of evidence presented in search-warrant applications. By eliminating any cost for noncompliance with the constitutional requirement of probable cause, the good-faith exception assures us that the constitutional standard will be diluted. . . .

Ultimately, we focus on the inevitable tension between the proposed good-faith exception and the guarantee contained in our State Constitution that search warrants "shall not issue except upon probable cause." In the twenty-five years during which we have applied the exclusionary rule in New Jersey, we have perceived no dilution of our probable-cause standard; rather, efforts to comply with the constitutional mandate have been enhanced. Nor do we perceive that application of the exclusionary rule has in any significant way impaired the ability of law-enforcement officials to enforce the criminal laws. The statistical evidence is to the contrary . . . .

The exclusionary rule, by virtue of its consistent application over the past twenty-five years, has become an integral element of our state-constitutional guarantee that search warrants will not issue without probable cause. Its function is not merely to deter police misconduct. The rule also serves as the indispensable mechanism for vindicating the constitutional right to be free from unreasonable searches. Because we believe that the good-faith exception to the exclusionary rule adopted in Leon would tend to undermine the constitutionally-guaranteed standard of probable cause, and in the process disrupt the highly effective procedures employed by our criminal justice system to accommodate that constitutional guarantee without impairing law enforcement, we decline to recognize a good-faith exception to the exclusionary rule. . . .

3. Note that Justice White identified four "exceptions to the good-faith exception" in his opinion in *Leon*. In other words, even when the police conduct a search under the authority of a warrant, there are still circumstances under which evidence may be suppressed if the warrant is defective. Make sure that you can identify these "exceptions." Are they consistent with the Court's general justifications for the exclusionary rule?

4. In both *Leon* and *Sheppard*, the good-faith exception to the exclusionary rule was applied in cases involving defective search warrants, on which the police had reasonably relied when seizing the disputed evidence. The good-faith exception was extended beyond the context of a deficient warrant in *Arizona v. Evans*, 514 U.S. 1, 115 S. Ct. 1185, 131 L. Ed. 2d 34 (1995). A police officer pulled Evans's car over to cite him for a traffic violation. The officer then ran a computer check, which indicated that an outstanding warrant existed for Evans's arrest. The officer accordingly placed Evans under arrest, and a subsequent search of Evans and his car produced marijuana. Later, it was determined that the computer report of the outstanding arrest warrant for Evans was erroneous. A court had quashed (invalidated) the warrant over two weeks earlier. However, due to an oversight by a court clerk, the computer records were not cor-

rected. Although no valid arrest warrant actually supported Evans's arrest, the Supreme Court ruled (7–2) that the marijuana discovered by the officer was admissible pursuant to the good-faith exception. Chief Justice Rehnquist explained that "the exclusionary rule was historically designed as a means of deterring police misconduct, not mistakes by court employees." Moreover, "because court clerks are not adjuncts to the law enforcement team . . . , the threat of exclusion of evidence could not be expected to deter" them from committing mistakes of the type made in Evans's case. The arresting officer was "acting objectively reasonably when he relied upon the police computer record," making the good-faith exception to the exclusionary rule appropriate.

Would you expect a different result in *Evans* had the police—rather than a clerk of court—been responsible for the computer error? What if errors in the computer records, even if caused by court personnel, were persistent and widespread? Could a police officer continue to act "objectively reasonably" in reliance on such records?

Can you imagine other contexts to which the good-faith exception to the exclusionary rule might be extended?

📖 **5.** *Legal research note.* Let us say you are interested in finding some references that discuss the pros and cons of the good-faith exception to the exclusionary rule. The best authorities for this purpose probably are law review articles. Unlike some other types of references, law review articles typically do more than *describe* rules of law and case holdings. They usually engage in critical analysis of the law. We can easily locate law review articles that discuss *United States v. Leon*. One way to begin is to consult an *Index to Legal Periodicals* (*ILP*) that indexes law review articles published shortly after *Leon* was decided.

Thus, we could refer to volume 24 of the *ILP*, which (as is reported on its spine and cover) covers law review articles published between September 1984 and August 1985. We could look in the Table of Cases in the rear of the *ILP*, under "*Leon; United States v.*" There, we find citations to nine law review articles pertaining to this case. For example, we might want to consult one of the cited articles: "98 *Harv. L. Rev.* 108–

18 N. '84" (volume 98 of the *Harvard Law Review* at pages 108–118, which was published in November, 1984). Alternatively, we could check the "Subject and Author Index" of the *ILP*, looking under either "exclusionary rule" or "search and seizure." Under the former heading, we find several articles cited that may be of interest; for example, "The Road to Exclusion Is Paved with Bad Intentions: A Bad Faith Corollary to the Good Faith Exception," by J. Bacigal, in 87 *W. Va. L. Rev.* 747–763 (1985). We would use later volumes of the *ILP* in the same manner to find more recently published law review articles.

To avoid the inconvenience of leafing through multiple volumes of the *ILP* in search of citations, we could use *LegalTrac*, a CD-Rom database that collects law review articles published between 1980 and the present and categorizes them by subject and key words. Using the "Subject Guide" of *LegalTrac*, we can type in "good-faith exception," and press "Enter." We immediately are referred to a slew of citations to law review articles, beginning with the most recently published one, that we can jot down or print from the screen and later investigate. Similarly, by typing "United States v. Leon" into the "Key Word" search option, we are given citations to numerous promising law review articles.

Another efficient way to find relevant law review articles is through using the computerized legal research system WESTLAW. For this example, we select the "jlr" database (journals and law reviews). We might opt for the "Natural Language" search method, and simply enter "good-faith exception to exclusionary rule." WESTLAW will retrieve and display the entire text of law review articles identified through this search strategy. The computer initially provides 20 articles, ranked in terms of relevance to the search strategy. We can read the individual articles or advance to the next one by entering "r" (rank). To retrieve more than the original 20 articles, simply enter "next."

Fruit of the Poisonous Tree

As we have seen, the exclusionary rule is designed to deter the police from violating people's Fourth Amendment rights. Application of the rule normally prohibits evidence directly resulting from an illegal search or seizure from being used to prove guilt in a criminal trial. The "fruit of the poisonous tree" is the colorful metaphor describing the relationship between a constitutional violation and the related discovery of evidence. If the evidence—the "fruit"—is a direct product of the illegality—the "poisonous tree"—then it is tainted by the constitutional violation and should not be used in a trial. For example, the "fruit" of the unreasonable search conducted in *Katz v. United States* was the telephone conversation overheard by the authorities, which was ruled inadmissible as evidence.

Does it follow, however, that *no* evidence seized following the violation of a suspect's constitutional rights can ever be admitted as evidence? If it can be shown that "but for" the constitutional violation the police would not have discovered incriminating evidence, must that evidence be suppressed?

This general question is addressed in *Wong Sun v. United States*. We strongly urge you to "brief" *Wong Sun* (as you should other cases) for a better understanding of the facts. As an initial matter, note that there are two defendants in this case—James Wah Toy and Wong Sun—and that the Court makes different rulings about the admissibility of evidence against them. If you understand why the cases involving Toy and Wong Sun are treated differently, you will understand the essence of the fruit-of-the-poisonous tree rule.

Wong Sun v. United States, 371 U.S. 471, 83 S. Ct. 407, 9 L. Ed. 2d 441 (1963)

[The defendants James Wah Toy and Wong Sun were convicted of the "fraudulent and knowing transportation and concealment of illegally imported heroin" following trial in a federal district court in San Francisco.

[Federal narcotics agents had arrested one Hom Way, finding heroin in his possession. Hom Way, who had never before served as an informant, told the agents that he had purchased the heroin from the proprietor of a laundry on Leavenworth Street. He knew the proprietor only as "Blackie Toy."

[Several agents thereupon went to a laundry on Leavenworth Street at about 6:00 A.M. The defendant James Wah Toy operated the laundry, but there was no showing that he was "Blackie" Toy. Toy answered the doorbell and told the men to return at the laundry's 8:00 opening time. When the men identified themselves as narcotics agents, Toy slammed the door and ran into his bedroom. The agents broke the door down, arrested and handcuffed Toy, and searched the dwelling but found no narcotics. When confronted with the fact that Hom Way had identified him as the source of his heroin, Toy denied that he had been selling narcotics but offered that someone known to him only as "Johnny" was. Toy further volunteered that he and Johnny had smoked heroin in Johnny's house the night before. Toy described where Johnny's house was.

[The agents left Toy's dwelling and located the house described by Toy. Inside they found Johnny Yee, who surrendered less than 1 ounce of heroin to the agents.

[Within the hour, both Toy and Yee were questioned at the Office of the Bureau of Narcotics. Yee there stated that the heroin had been brought to him by Toy and another man known to him only as "Sea Dog."

[Toy was questioned about "Sea Dog's" identity and disclosed that "Sea Dog" was the defendant Wong Sun. Toy thereafter pointed out Wong Sun's residence to the agents.

[The agents went to the dwelling, entered after identifying themselves to Wong Sun's wife, and arrested Wong Sun inside.

[The defendants Toy and Wong Sun, and also Johnny Yee, were arraigned before a U.S. commissioner and were released on their own recognizance. Within a few days, each of the men was interrogated by the federal agents at the Narcotics Bureau after having been advised of his rights. Toy and Wong Sun made statements to the agents, although each refused to sign them when they were reduced to writing.

[Toy and Wong Sun were tried jointly on the charges. Johnny Yee was to be the principal witness against them, but the government excused him after he repudiated the statement that he had given the federal agents and then invoked his privilege against self-incrimination. None of Yee's damaging statements were offered against the defendants at their trial, and the original informant, Hom Way, did not testify.

[Four items of evidence used to support the convictions of Toy and Wong Sun were at issue in the Supreme Court. They were "(1) the statement made orally by petitioner Toy in his bedroom at the time of his arrest; (2) the heroin surrendered to the agents by Johnny Yee; (3) petitioner Toy's pretrial unsigned statement; and (4) petitioner Wong Sun's similar statement."

[The Supreme Court ruled that the unsigned pretrial statements of Toy and Wong Sun should not have been admitted at their trial because they were not corroborated by independent evidence. Both defendants' convictions were reversed, although the lack of corroborative evidence for the confession was the only reason supporting the reversal in Wong Sun's case.

[Of relevance here are the rulings made by the Supreme Court concerning the admissibility of the four items of evidence mentioned above, in light of the Court's determination that neither Toy's nor Wong Sun's arrest had been supported by probable cause.] Mr. Justice Brennan delivered the opinion of the Court. . . .

II.

It is conceded that Toy's declarations in his bedroom are to be excluded if they are held to be "fruits" of the agents' unlawful action.

In order to make effective the fundamental constitutional guarantees of sanctity of the home and inviolability of the person, this Court held nearly half a century ago that evidence seized during an unlawful search could not constitute proof against the victim of the search. Weeks v United States, 232 US 383 [(1914)].

The exclusionary prohibition extends as well to the indirect as the direct products of such invasions. Silverthorne Lumber Co. v United States, 251 US 385, 40 S Ct 182, 64 L Ed 319 [(1920)]. Mr. Justice Holmes, speaking for the Court in that case, in holding that the Government might not make use of information obtained during an unlawful search to subpoena from the victims the very documents illegally viewed, expressed succinctly the policy of the broad exclusionary rule:

"The essence of a provision forbidding the acquisition of evidence in a certain way is that not merely evidence so acquired shall not be used before the Court but that it shall not be used at all. Of course this does not mean that the facts thus obtained become sacred and inaccessible. If knowledge of them is gained from an independent source they may be proved like any others, but the knowledge gained by the Government's own wrong cannot be used by it in the way proposed." 251 US, at 392.

The exclusionary rule has traditionally barred from trial physical, tangible materials obtained either during or as a direct result of an unlawful invasion. . . .

[V]erbal evidence which derives so immediately from an unlawful entry and an unauthorized arrest as the officers' action in the present case is no less the "fruit" of official illegality than the more common tangible fruits of the unwarranted intrusion. . . .

The Government argues that Toy's statements to the officers in his bedroom, although closely consequent upon the invasion which we hold unlawful, were nevertheless admissible because they resulted from "an intervening independent act of a free will." This contention, however, takes insufficient account of the circumstances. Six or seven officers had broken the door and followed on Toy's heels into the bedroom where his wife and child were sleeping. He had been almost immediately handcuffed and arrested. Under such circumstances it is unreasonable to infer that Toy's response was sufficiently an act of free will to purge the primary taint of the unlawful invasion. . . .

Thus we find no substantial reason to omit Toy's declarations from the protection of the exclusionary rule.

III.

We now consider whether the exclusion of Toy's declarations requires also the exclusion of the narcotics taken from Yee, to which those declarations led the police. The prosecutor candidly told the trial court that "we wouldn't have found those drugs except that Mr. Toy helped us to." Hence this is not the case envisioned by this Court where the exclusionary rule has no application because the Government learned of the evidence "from an independent source," Silverthorne Lumber Co. v United States, 251 US 385, 392, nor is this a case in which the connection between the lawless conduct of the police and the discovery of the challenged evidence has "become so attenuated as to dissipate the taint." Nardone v United States, 308 US 338, 341, 60 S Ct 266, 84 L Ed 307, 312 [(1939)]. We need not hold that all evidence is "fruit of the poisonous tree" simply because it would not have come to light but for the illegal actions of the police. Rather, the more apt question in such a case is "whether, granting establishment of the primary illegality, the evidence to which instant objection is made has been come at by exploitation of that illegality or instead by means sufficiently distinguishable to be purged of the primary taint." Maguire, Evidence of Guilt, 221 (1959). We think it clear that the narcotics were "come at by the exploitation of that illegality" and hence that they may not be used against Toy.

IV.

It remains only to consider Toy's unsigned statement. We need not decide whether, in light of the fact that Toy was free on his own recognizance when he made the statement, that statement was a fruit of the illegal arrest. . . .

V.

We turn now to the case of the other petitioner, Wong Sun. We have no occasion to disagree with the finding of the Court of Appeals that his arrest, also, was without probable cause or reasonable grounds. At all events no evidentiary consequences turn upon that question. For Wong Sun's unsigned confession was not the fruit of that arrest, and was therefore properly admitted at trial. On the evidence that Wong Sun had been released on his own recognizance after a lawful arraignment, and had returned voluntarily several days later to make the statement, we hold that the connection between the arrest and the statement had "become so attenuated as to dissipate the taint." Nardone v United States, 308 US 338, 341, 60 S Ct 266, 84 L Ed 307, 312 [(1939)]. . . .

We must then consider the admissibility of the narcotics surrendered by Yee. Our holding, supra, that this ounce of heroin was inadmissible against Toy does not compel a like result with respect to Wong Sun. The exclusion of the narcotics as to Toy was required solely by their tainted relationship to information unlawfully obtained from Toy, and not by any official impropriety connected with their surrender by Yee. The seizure of this heroin invaded no right of privacy of person or premises which would entitle Wong Sun to object to its use at his trial.[18]

* * *

[The dissenting opinion of Justice Clark, joined by Justices Harlan, Stewart, and White, is omitted.]

---

18. This case is not like Jones v United States, 362 US 257, 4 L Ed 2d 697, 80 S Ct 725, [(1960)],where the person challenging the seizure of evidence was lawfully on the premises at the time of the search. Nor is it like Chapman v United States, 365 US 610, 81 S Ct 776, 5 L Ed 2d 828 [(1961)], where we held that a landlord could not lawfully consent to a search of his tenant's premises. See generally Edwards, Standing to Suppress Unreasonably Seized Evidence, 47 NW U L Rev 471 (1952).

Notes and Questions

1. How does the Court justify the different results in Toy's and Wong Sun's cases under the fruit-of-the-poisonous-tree rule?

2. *Wong Sun* was decided three years prior to *Miranda v. Arizona*, 384 U.S. 436, 86 S. Ct. 1602, 16 L. Ed. 2d 694 (1966), which we will consider in detail in Chapter 4. Under *Miranda*, the police must advise suspects of their constitutional rights and secure a waiver of those rights if statements obtained during custodial interrogation are to be admitted into evidence. Assume that a suspect has been unlawfully arrested, in violation of the Fourth Amendment. If the police administer *Miranda* warnings and secure a waiver, should a subsequent confession be admissible? Under the fruit-of-the-poisonous-tree doctrine, do *Miranda* warnings "purge the primary taint" of the unlawful arrest or constitute a "break in the causal chain" between the Fourth Amendment violation and its evidentiary fruit— the confession? The Court considered this issue in *Brown v. Illinois*, 422 U.S. 590, 95 S. Ct. 2254, 45 L. Ed. 2d 416 (1975) but declined to give a categorical "yes" or "no" answer to it.

* * *

If Miranda warnings, by themselves, were held to attenuate the taint of an unconstitutional arrest, regardless of how wanton and purposeful the Fourth Amendment violation, the effect of the exclusionary rule would be substantially diluted.

Arrests made without warrant or without probable cause, for questioning or "investigation," would be encouraged by the knowledge that evidence derived therefrom could well be made admissible at trial by the simple expedient of giving Miranda warnings. Any incentive to avoid Fourth Amendment violations would be eviscerated by making the warnings, in effect, a "cure-all," and the constitutional guarantee against unlawful searches and seizures could be said to be reduced to "a form of words."

It is entirely possible, of course, as the State here argues, that persons arrested illegally frequently may decide to confess, as an act of free will unaffected by the initial illegality. But the Miranda warnings, *alone* and per se, cannot always make the act sufficiently a product of free will to break, for Fourth Amendment purposes, the causal connection between the illegality and the confession. They cannot assure in every case that the Fourth Amendment violation has not been unduly exploited.

* * *

The question whether a confession is the product of a free will under Wong Sun must be answered on the facts of each case. No single fact is dispositive. The workings of the human mind are too complex, and the possibilities of misconduct too diverse, to permit protection of the Fourth Amendment to turn on such a talismanic test. The Miranda warnings are an important factor, to be sure, in determining whether the confession is obtained by exploitation of an illegal arrest. But they are not the only factor to be considered. The temporal proximity of the arrest and the confession, the presence of intervening circumstances, and, particularly, the purpose and flagrancy of the official misconduct are all relevant. The voluntariness of the statement is a threshold requirement. And the burden of showing admissibility rests, of course, on the prosecution. . . .

Citing the flagrant nature of the police misconduct and the absence of significant intervening variables between Brown's illegal arrest and his confession, the Court in *Brown* ruled that the confession was an inadmissible fruit of the Fourth Amendment.

3. Refer once again to *Leon v. State* in Chapter 1. Does the court's decision to admit Leon's second confession into evidence—after his initial statement had been coerced by physical force—seem justifiable under the fruit-of-the-poisonous-tree doctrine?

4. In *New York v. Harris*, 495 U.S. 14, 110 S. Ct. 1640, 109 L. Ed. 2d 13 (1990), police made a warrantless entry into the defendant's apartment, arrested him, and advised him of his *Miranda* rights. The defendant admitted to committing a murder. Because no exigent circumstances justified the police's entering the apartment without a warrant to make the arrest, this intrusion violated the defendant's Fourth Amendment rights under the rule of *Payton v. New York*, 445 U.S. 573, 100 S. Ct. 1371, 63 L. Ed. 2d 639 (1980). The defendant was taken to the police station, was readministered his *Miranda* rights, and made another confession. The trial court suppressed the first confession, given inside of the apartment, on the basis of the police's unlawful entry. However, it admitted the second confession, which was given in the police station. The Supreme Court agreed that the trial court's actions were appropriate. In ruling that the second confession was admissible, the Court declined even to engage in a fruit-of-the-poisonous-tree analysis. It distinguished *Brown v. Illinois, supra*, in which the police lacked probable cause to make an arrest. In *Harris*, the police had probable cause to arrest; the Fourth Amendment violation was confined to the warrantless entry of the defendant's apartment. Once the defendant was removed from his home, there was no continuing Fourth Amendment violation. Writing for a 5–4 majority of the Court, Justice White explained: "We hold that, where the police have probable cause to arrest a suspect, the exclusionary rule does not bar the State's use of a statement made by the defendant outside of his home, even though the statement is taken after an arrest made in the home in violation of Payton." 495 U.S., at 21. On remand, the New York Court of Appeals declined to follow the Supreme Court's ruling. It held that "our State Constitution requires that statements obtained from an accused following a *Payton* violation must be suppressed unless the taint resulting from the violation has been attenuated." *People v. Harris*, 77 N.Y.2d 434, 570 N.E.2d 1051, 1053, 568 N.Y.S.2d 702 (1991). *See also State v. Geisler*, 222 Conn. 672, 610 A.2d 1225 (1992) (rejecting *New York v. Harris* on state constitutional grounds).

5. In *Wong Sun*, the Supreme Court ruled that the heroin discovered in Johnny Yee's residence was inadmissible against Toy, yet admissible against Wong Sun. Do you understand why?

See footnote 18 in the Court's opinion. We will consider the concept of "standing" in later in this chapter.

📖 **6. *Legal Research Note.*** Want more information about the fruit-of-the-poisonous-tree doctrine? Try consulting an *A.L.R. (American Law Review)* "annotation." These annotations generally provide an excellent description of state, federal, or U.S. Supreme Court case law covering a variety of legal issues. *A.L.R.* through *A.L.R. 5th* cover state cases; *A.L.R. Federal* discusses federal cases; and annotations found at the back of the *United States Supreme Court Reports, Lawyers' Edition*, cover U.S. Supreme Court cases. *A.L.R.* annotations typically collect and summarize an exhaustive supply of case holdings related to the subject of the annotation. A good *A.L.R.* annotation can be an excellent starting point for researching an issue. To find annotations, consult the detailed *A.L.R. Index for*

A.L.R., A.L.R. 2d through 5th, A.L.R. Federal, and L. Ed. 2d. Start by looking for a particular topic, in this case, "search and seizure" (which refers you to "fruits of the poisonous tree doctrine, this index"), or "fruit of the poisonous tree." Under the latter heading, a number of annotations are listed that cover different aspects of the fruit-of-the-poisonous-tree rule. The first annotation indexed is "Generally, 43 ALR 3d 385." Thus, to take advantage of a general discussion of cases involving the fruit-of-the-poisonous-tree rule, we would read the annotation in volume 43 of *A.L.R. 3d*, beginning at page 385. The pocket part to the annotation covers the most recent cases relevant to this topic. This annotation also refers you to several other handy references. If you take the time to consult it, we think you will be impressed with how helpful *A.L.R.* annotations can be to your legal research efforts.

Inevitable Discovery

In Chapter 1, we introduced some of the competing values that criminal procedure law must reconcile when we considered *Brewer v. Williams*, the "Christian burial speech" case. You will recall that Robert Williams's murder conviction was overturned in this 1977 decision because Detective Leaming had deliberately elicited incriminating statements from Williams in violation of the latter's Sixth Amendment right to counsel. Those statements had been introduced into evidence and helped support

Williams's conviction. Williams had told Leaming where he had disposed of his 10-year-old victim's body. He also directed the police to the location of the body. As some of the justices had predicted, Williams was retried after the 1977 Supreme Court decision. *Nix v. Williams* involves a violation of the Sixth Amendment right to counsel rather than the Fourth Amendment. Nevertheless, we present this case here because it is the principal Supreme Court decision addressing the "inevitable-discovery" doctrine, which is an important exception to the exclusionary rule.

Nix v. Williams, 467 U.S. 431, 104 S. Ct. 2501, 81 L. Ed. 2d 377 (1984)

Chief Justice Burger delivered the opinion of the Court.

[In 1969, the respondent Williams was convicted of the first-degree murder of 10-year-old Pamela Powers. That conviction was reversed because a police detective had gained an

admission from Williams concerning the whereabouts of the victim's body in violation of Williams's right to the assistance of counsel, guaranteed under the Sixth and Fourteenth Amendments. *Brewer v. Williams*, 430 U.S. 387 (1977).

[Williams was retried for the murder in 1977.]

* * *

At Williams' second trial in 1977 in the Iowa court, the prosecution did not offer Williams' statements into evidence, nor did it seek to show that Williams had directed the police to the child's body. However, evidence of the condition of her body as it was found, articles and photographs of her clothing, and the results of post mortem medical and chemical tests on the body were admitted. The trial court concluded that the State had proved by a preponderance of the evidence that, if the search had not been suspended and Williams had not led the police to the victim, her body would have been discovered "*within a short time*" in essentially the same condition as it was actually found. . . .

The challenged evidence was admitted and the jury again found Williams guilty of first-degree murder; he was sentenced to life in prison.

On appeal, the Supreme Court of Iowa again affirmed. 285 NW2d 248 (1979). That court held that there was in fact a "hypothetical independent source" exception to the Exclusionary Rule. . . .

In 1980 Williams renewed his attack on the state-court conviction by seeking a writ of habeas corpus in the United States District Court for the Southern District of Iowa. The District Court conducted its own independent review of the evidence and concluded, as had the state courts, that the body would inevitably have been found by the searchers in essentially the same condition it was in when Williams led police to its discovery. The District Court denied Williams' petition. 528 F Supp 664 (1981).

The Court of Appeals for the Eighth Circuit reversed. 700 F2d 1164 (1983). . . .

II

A

The Iowa Supreme Court correctly stated that the "vast majority" of all courts, both state and federal, recognize an inevitable discovery exception to the Exclusionary Rule. We are now urged to adopt and apply the so-called ultimate or inevitable discovery exception to the Exclusionary Rule.

Williams contends that evidence of the body's location and condition is "fruit of the poisonous tree," i.e., the "fruit" or product of Detective Leaming's plea to help the child's parents give her "a Christian burial," which this Court had already held equated to interrogation. He contends that admitting the challenged evidence violated the Sixth Amendment whether it would have been inevitably discovered or not. Williams also contends that, if the inevitable discovery doctrine is constitutionally permissible, it must include a threshold showing of police good faith.

B

* * *

The core rationale consistently advanced by this Court for extending the Exclusionary Rule to evidence that is the fruit of unlawful police conduct has been that this admittedly drastic and socially costly course is needed to deter police from violations of constitutional and statutory protections. This Court has accepted the argument that the way to ensure such protections is to exclude evidence seized as a result of such violations notwithstanding the high social cost of letting persons obviously guilty go unpunished for their crimes. On this rationale, the prosecution is not to be put in a better position than it would have been in if no illegality had transpired.

By contrast, the derivative evidence analysis ensures that the prosecution is not put in a *worse* position simply because of some earlier police error or misconduct. The independent source doctrine allows admission of evidence that has been discovered by means wholly independent of any constitutional violation. That doctrine, although closely related to the inevitable discovery doctrine, does not apply here; Williams' statements to Leaming indeed led police to the child's body, but that is not the whole story. The independent source doctrine teaches us that the interest of society in deterring unlawful police conduct and the public interest in having juries receive all probative evidence of a crime are properly balanced by putting the police in the same, not a *worse*, position than they would have been in if no police error or misconduct had occurred.

When the challenged evidence has an independent source, exclusion of such evidence would put the police in a worse position than they would have been in absent any error or violation. There is a functional similarity between these two doctrines in that exclusion of evidence that would inevitably have been discovered would also put the government in a worse position, because the police would have obtained that evidence if no misconduct had taken place. Thus, while the independent source exception would not justify admission of evidence in this case, its rationale is wholly consistent with and justifies our adoption of the ultimate or inevitable discovery exception to the Exclusionary Rule.

It is clear that the cases implementing the Exclusionary Rule "begin with the premise that the challenged evidence is *in some sense* the product of illegal governmental activity." United States v Crews, 445 US 463, 471, 100 S Ct 1244, 63 L Ed 2d 537 (1980) (emphasis added). Of course, this does not end the inquiry. If the prosecution can establish by a preponderance of the evidence that the information ultimately or inevitably would have been discovered by lawful means—here the volunteers' search—then the deterrence rationale has so little basis that the evidence should be received. Anything less would reject logic, experience, and common sense.

The requirement that the prosecution must prove the absence of bad faith, imposed here by the Court of Appeals, would place courts in the position of withholding from juries relevant and undoubted truth that would have been available to police absent any unlawful police activity. Of course, that view would put the police in a *worse* position than they would have been in if no unlawful conduct had transpired. And, of equal importance, it wholly fails to take into account the enormous societal cost of excluding truth in the search for truth in the administration of justice. Nothing in this Court's prior holdings supports any such formalistic, pointless, and punitive approach. . . .

Significant disincentives to obtaining evidence illegally—including the possibility of departmental discipline and civil liability—also lessen the likelihood that the ultimate or inevitable discovery exception will promote police misconduct. In these circumstances, the societal costs of the Exclusionary Rule far outweigh any possible benefits to deterrence that a good-faith requirement might produce. . . .

C

The Court of Appeals did not find it necessary to consider whether the record fairly supported the finding that the volunteer search party would ultimately or inevitably have discovered the victim's body. However, three courts independently reviewing the evidence have found that the body of the child inevitably would have been found by the searchers. Williams challenges these findings, asserting that the record contains only the "post hoc rationalization" that the search efforts would have proceeded two and one-half miles into Polk County where Williams had led police to the body.

When that challenge was made at the suppression hearing preceding Williams' second trial, the prosecution offered the testimony of Agent Ruxlow of the Iowa Bureau of Criminal Investigation. Ruxlow had organized and directed some 200 volunteers who were searching for the child's body.

The searchers were instructed "to check all the roads, the ditches, any culverts. . . . If they came upon any abandoned farm buildings, they were instructed to go onto the property and search those abandoned farm buildings or any other places where a small child could be secreted." Ruxlow testified that he marked off highway maps of Poweshiek and Jasper Counties in grid fashion, divided the volunteers into teams of four to six persons, and assigned each team to search specific grid areas. Ruxlow also testified that, if the search had not been suspended because of Williams' promised cooperation, it would have continued into Polk County, using the same grid system. Although he had previously marked off into grids only the highway maps of Poweshiek and Jasper Counties, Ruxlow had obtained a map of Polk County, which he said he would have marked off in the same manner had it been necessary for the search to continue.

The search had commenced at approximately 10 a.m. and moved westward through Poweshiek County into Jasper County. At approximately 3 p.m., after Williams had volunteered to cooperate with the police, Officer Leaming, who was in the police car with Williams, sent word to Ruxlow and the other Special Agent directing the search to meet him at the Grinnell truck stop and the search was suspended at that time. Ruxlow also stated that he was "under the impression that there was a possibility" that Williams would lead them to the child's body at that time. The search was not resumed once it was learned that Williams had led the police to the body, which was found two and one-half miles from where the search had stopped in what would have been the easternmost grid to be searched in Polk County. There was testimony that it would have taken an additional three to five hours to discover the body if the search had continued; the body was found near a culvert, one of the kinds of places the teams had been specifically directed to search.

On this record it is clear that the search parties were approaching the actual location of the body and we are satisfied, along with three courts earlier, that the volunteer search teams would have resumed the search had Williams not earlier led the police to the body and the body inevitably would have been found.

* * *

The judgment of the Court of Appeals is reversed, and the case is remanded for further proceedings consistent with this opinion.

It is so ordered.

* * *

Justice **Brennan**, with whom Justice **Marshall** joins, dissenting.

* * *

To the extent that today's decision adopts this "inevitable discovery" exception to the exclusionary rule, it simply acknowledges a doctrine that is akin to the "independent source" exception first recognized by the Court in Silverthorne Lumber Co. v United States, 251 US 385, 392, 40 S Ct 182, 64 L Ed 319 (1920).

In particular, the Court concludes that unconstitutionally obtained evidence may be admitted at trial if it inevitably would have been discovered in the same condition by an independent line of investigation that was already being pursued when the constitutional violation occurred. . . . I agree that in these circumstances the "inevitable discovery" exception to the exclusionary rule is consistent with the requirements of the Constitution.

In its zealous efforts to emasculate the exclusionary rule, however, the Court loses sight of the crucial difference between the "inevitable discovery" doctrine and the "independent source" exception from which it is derived. When properly applied, the "independent source" exception allows the prosecution to use evidence only if it was, in fact, obtained by fully lawful means. It therefore does no violence to the constitutional protections that the exclusionary rule is meant to enforce. The "inevitable discovery" exception is likewise compatible with the Constitution, though it differs in one key respect from its next of kin: specifically, the evidence sought to be introduced at trial has not actually been obtained from an independent source, but rather would have been discovered as a matter of course if independent investigations were allowed to proceed.

In my view, this distinction should require that the government satisfy a heightened burden of proof before it is allowed to use such evidence. The inevitable discovery exception necessarily implicates a hypothetical finding that differs in kind from the factual finding that precedes application of the independent source rule. To ensure that this hypothetical finding is narrowly confined to circumstances that are functionally equivalent to an independent source, and to protect fully the fundamental rights served by the exclusionary rule, I would require clear and convincing evidence before concluding that the government had met its burden of proof on this issue. Increasing the burden of proof serves to impress the factfinder with the importance of the decision and thereby reduces the risk that illegally obtained evidence will be admitted.

Because the lower courts did not impose such a requirement, I would remand this case for application of this heightened burden of proof by the lower courts in the first instance. I am therefore unable to join either the Court's opinion or its judgment.

Notes and Questions

1. What if the search party in *Nix v. Williams* had not been 200-strong and had not approached to within 2 1/2 miles of where the body was discovered when the search was called off? If only a dozen people had been looking for the body and had been over 10 miles from it but headed in its general direction when the search was terminated, what would the result be? What is the significance of the disagreement between the majority and dissenting opinions regarding the burden of proof required to show that the body inevitably would have been discovered?

2. The Court of Appeals had decided that the state must prove that the original constitutional violation was not committed in bad faith in order to benefit from the inevitable-discovery rule. How does such a requirement relate to the purposes of the exclusionary rule? Why does Chief Justice Burger's opinion for the Supreme Court reject this requirement?

3. What if no search party had actively been searching for the body but if testimony had been offered that the next day a search party would have been formed and that the search would have proceeded county by county pursuant to the gridded-map system described in the majority opinion? Under those circumstances, would application of the inevitable-discovery rule be justified?

STANDING

As a general principle, a party requesting relief from a court must allege that he or she has personally suffered an injury that the court can redress. The "injury in fact" requirement means that the party must "'show that he personally suffered some actual or threatened injury as a result of the putatively illegal conduct' of the [other party]." *Valley Forge Christian College v. Americans United for Separation of Church and State*, 454 U.S. 464, 472, 102 S. Ct. 752, 70 L. Ed. 2d 700 (1982). This concept is known as "standing." The standing requirement helps to ensure that the courts are resolving actual controversies between parties, as opposed to rendering abstract policy or advisory decisions.

For example, an environmentalist living in New Hampshire might be dismayed about a plan to bury toxic radioactive waste under Utah's salt flats. He or she almost certainly would be barred by the "standing" requirement from bringing a lawsuit to challenge the plan because he or she could not demonstrate how he or she personally would suffer a concrete, tangible injury if the plan went ahead. On the other hand, a Utah resident whose back yard abutted the property where the wastes were scheduled to be buried would have a much more convincing claim to standing if he or she wanted to bring suit.

The standing requirement also applies in criminal cases. Generally, a criminal defendant can hope to prevail on a claim involving a denial of constitutional rights only if his or her personal rights are at issue. In other words, if police violated Tom's constitutional rights and thereby obtained evidence that incriminated Sue, Sue would not have standing to object to the introduction of that evidence against her (unless, of course, she could show that her rights also were directly infringed by the police action). Only Tom would have standing to protest against the use of the evidence in his own case.

The standing doctrine has obvious significance to search and seizure issues. For example, a bank robber might hide his mask and gun in a friend's house. The police, in turn, might unlawfully search the friend's house and discover those items. Would the bank robber have standing to complain about the unlawful search when he tried to have the mask and gun suppressed from evidence? Would it matter if the robber was physically present in his friend's house when the search occurred? What if the robber was an overnight guest at his friend's house; would that make a difference? What if the robber was a passenger in his friend's car, and evidence was found during a search of the vehicle: Would the robber have standing to argue that the search was illegal?

Rakas v. Illinois, 439 U.S. 128, 99 S. Ct. 421, 58 L. Ed. 2d 387 (1978)

Mr. Justice **Rehnquist** delivered the opinion of the Court.

Petitioners were convicted of armed robbery in the Circuit Court of Kankakee County, Ill., and their convictions were affirmed on appeal. At their trial, the prosecution offered into evidence a sawed-off rifle and rifle shells that had been seized by police during a search of an automobile in which petitioners had been passengers. Neither petitioner is the owner of the automobile and neither has ever asserted that he owned the rifle or shells seized. The Illinois Appellate Court held that petitioners lacked standing to object to the allegedly unlawful search and seizure and denied their motion to suppress the evidence. We granted certiorari in light of the obvious importance of the issues raised to the administration of criminal justice, and now affirm.

I

Because we are not here concerned with the issue of probable cause, a brief description of the events leading to the search of the automobile will suffice. A police officer on a routine patrol received a radio call notifying him of a robbery of a clothing store in Bourbonnais, Illinois, and describing the getaway car. Shortly thereafter, the officer spotted an automobile which he thought might be the getaway car. After following the car for some time and after the arrival of assistance, he and several other officers stopped the vehicle. The occupants of the automobile, petitioners and two female companions, were ordered out of the car and, after the occupants had left the car, two officers searched the interior of the vehicle. They discovered a box of rifle shells in the glove compartment, which had been locked, and a sawed-off rifle under the front passenger seat. After discovering the rifle and the shells, the officers took petitioners to the station and placed them under arrest.

Before trial petitioners moved to suppress the rifle and shells seized from the car on the ground that the search violated the Fourth and Fourteenth Amendments. They conceded that they did not own the automobile and were simply passengers; the owner of the car had been the driver of the vehicle at the time of the search. Nor did they assert that they owned the rifle or the shells seized. The prosecutor challenged petitioners' standing to object to the lawfulness of the search of the car because neither the car, the shells nor the rifle belonged to them. The trial court agreed that petitioners lacked standing and denied the motion to suppress the evidence. In view of this holding, the court did not determine whether there was probable cause for the search and seizure. . . .

II

Petitioners first urge us to relax or broaden the rule of standing enunciated in Jones v United States, 362 US 257, 80 S Ct 725, 4 L Ed 2d 697 (1960), so that any criminal defendant at whom a search was "directed" would have standing to contest the legality of that search and object to the admission at trial of evidence obtained as a result of the search. Alternatively, petitioners argue that they have standing to object to the search under Jones because they were "legitimately on [the] premises" at the time of the search.

The concept of standing discussed in Jones focuses on whether the person seeking to challenge the legality of a search as a basis for suppressing evidence was himself the "victim" of the search or seizure. Adoption of the so-called "target" theory advanced by petitioners would in effect permit a defendant to assert that a violation of the Fourth Amendment rights of a third party entitled him to have evidence suppressed at his trial. If we reject petitioners' request for a broadened rule of standing such as this, and reaffirm the holding of Jones and other cases that Fourth Amendment rights are personal rights that may not be asserted vicariously, we will have occasion to re-examine the "standing" terminology emphasized in Jones. For we are not at all sure that the determination of a motion to suppress is materially aided by labeling the inquiry identified in Jones as one of standing, rather than simply recognizing it as one involving the substantive question of whether or not the proponent of the motion to suppress has had his own Fourth Amendment rights infringed by the search and seizure which he seeks to challenge . . .

A

We decline to extend the rule of standing in Fourth Amendment cases in the manner suggested by petitioners. As we stated in Alderman v United States, 394 US 165, 174, 89 S Ct 961, 22 L Ed 2d 176 (1969); "Fourth Amendment rights are personal rights which, like some other constitutional rights, may not be vicariously asserted." A person who is aggrieved by an illegal search and seizure only through the introduction of damaging evidence secured by a search of a third person's premises or property has not had any of his Fourth Amendment rights infringed. . . .

In Jones, the Court set forth two alternative holdings: It established a rule of "automatic" standing to contest an allegedly illegal search where the same possession needed to establish standing is an essential element of the offense charged; and second, it stated that "anyone legitimately on premises where a search occurs may challenge its legality by way of a motion to suppress." 362 US, at 264, 267. Had the Court intended to adopt the target theory now put forth by petitioners, neither of the above two holdings would have been necessary since Jones was the "target" of the police search in that case. . . .

Conferring standing to raise vicarious Fourth Amendment claims would necessarily mean a more widespread invocation of the exclusionary rule during criminal trials. . . . Each time the exclusionary rule is applied it exacts a substantial social cost for the vindication of Fourth Amendment rights. Relevant and reliable evidence is kept from the trier of fact and the search for truth at trial is deflected. Since our cases generally have held that one whose Fourth Amendment rights are violated may successfully suppress evidence obtained in the course of an illegal search and seizure, misgivings as to the benefit of enlarging the class of persons who may invoke that rule are properly considered when deciding whether to expand standing to assert Fourth Amendment violations.

B

* * *

[H]aving rejected petitioners' target theory and reaffirmed the principle that the "rights assured by the Fourth Amendment are personal rights, [which] . . . may be enforced by exclusion of evidence only at the instance of one whose own protection was infringed by the search and seizure," Simmons v United States, 390 US, at 389, the question necessarily arises whether it serves any useful analytical purpose to consider this principle a matter of standing, distinct from the merits of a defendant's Fourth Amendment claim. We can think of no decided cases of this Court that would have come out differently had we concluded, as we do now, that the type of standing requirement discussed in Jones and reaffirmed today is more properly subsumed under substantive Fourth Amendment doctrine. Rigorous application of the principle that the rights secured by this Amendment are personal, in place of a notion of "standing," will produce no additional situations in which evidence must be excluded. The inquiry under either approach is the same. But we think the better analysis forthrightly focuses on the extent of a particular defendant's rights under the Fourth Amendment, rather than on any theoretically separate, but invariably intertwined concept of standing. . . .

It should be emphasized that nothing we say here casts the least doubt on cases which recognize that, as a general proposition, the issue of standing involves two inquiries: first, whether the proponent of a particular legal right has alleged "injury in fact," and, second, whether the proponent is asserting his own legal rights and interests rather than basing his claim for relief upon the rights of third parties. But this Court's long history of insistence that Fourth Amendment rights are personal in nature has already answered many of these traditional standing inquiries, and we think that definition of those rights is more properly placed within the purview of substantive Fourth Amendment law than within that of standing.

Analyzed in these terms, the question is whether the challenged search or seizure violated the Fourth Amendment rights of a criminal defendant who seeks to exclude the evidence obtained during it. That inquiry in turn requires a determination of whether the disputed search and seizure has infringed an interest of the defendant which the Fourth Amendment was designed to protect. We are under no illusion that by dispensing with the rubric of standing used in Jones we have rendered any simpler the determination of whether the proponent of a motion to suppress is entitled to contest the legality of a search and seizure. But by frankly recognizing that this aspect of the analysis belongs more properly under the heading of substantive Fourth Amendment doctrine than under the heading of standing, we think the decision of this issue will rest on sounder logical footing.

C

Here petitioners, who were passengers occupying a car which they neither owned nor leased, seek to analogize their position to that of the defendant in Jones v United States. In Jones, petitioner was present at the time of the search of an apartment which was owned by a friend. The friend had given Jones permission to use the apartment and a key to it, with which Jones had admitted himself on the day of the search. He had a suit and shirt at the apartment and had slept there "maybe a night," but his home was elsewhere. At the time of the search, Jones was the only occupant of the apartment because the lessee was away for a period of several days. Under these circumstances, this Court stated that while one wrongfully on the premises could not move to suppress evidence obtained as a result of searching them, "anyone legitimately on premises where a search occurs may challenge its legality." Petitioners argue that their occupancy of the automobile in question was comparable to that of Jones in the apart-

ment and that they therefore have standing to contest the legality of the search—or as we have rephrased the inquiry, that they, like Jones, had their Fourth Amendment rights violated by the search.

We do not question the conclusion in Jones that the defendant in that case suffered a violation of his personal Fourth Amendment rights if the search in question was unlawful. Nonetheless, we believe that the phrase "legitimately on premises" coined in Jones creates too broad a gauge for measurement of Fourth Amendment rights. For example, applied literally, this statement would permit a casual visitor who has never seen, or been permitted to visit the basement of another's house to object to a search of the basement if the visitor happened to be in the kitchen of the house at the time of the search. Likewise, a casual visitor who walks into a house one minute before a search of the house commences and leaves one minute after the search ends would be able to contest the legality of the search. The first visitor would have absolutely no interest or legitimate expectation of privacy in the basement, the second would have none in the house, and it advances no purpose served by the Fourth Amendment to permit either of them to object to the lawfulness of the search.[11]

We think that Jones on its facts merely stands for the unremarkable proposition that a person can have a legally sufficient interest in a place other than his own home so that the Fourth Amendment protects him from unreasonable governmental intrusion into that place. In defining the scope of that interest, we adhere to the view expressed in Jones and echoed in later cases that arcane distinctions developed in property and tort law between guests, licensees, invitees, and the like, ought not to control. But the Jones statement that a person need only be "legitimately on premises" in order to challenge the validity of the search of a dwelling place cannot be taken in its full sweep beyond the facts of that case. . . .

[T]he holding in Jones can best be explained by the fact that Jones had a legitimate expectation of privacy in the premises he was using and

---

11. This is not to say that such visitors could not contest the lawfulness of the seizure of evidence or the search if their own property were seized during the search.

therefore could claim the protection of the Fourth Amendment with respect to a governmental invasion of those premises, even though his "interest" in those premises might not have been a recognized property interest at common law.[12]

Our Brother White in dissent expresses the view that by rejecting the phrase "legitimately on [the] premises" as the appropriate measure of Fourth Amendment rights, we are abandoning a thoroughly workable, "bright line" test in favor of a less certain analysis of whether the facts of a particular case give rise to a legitimate expectation of privacy. If "legitimately on premises" were the successful litmus test of Fourth Amendment

___

12. Obviously, however, a "legitimate" expectation of privacy by definition means more than a subjective expectation of not being discovered. A burglar plying his trade in a summer cabin during the off season may have a thoroughly justified subjective expectation of privacy, but it is not one which the law recognizes as "legitimate." His presence, in the words of Jones, is "wrongful"; his expectation is not "one that society is prepared to recognize as 'reasonable.'" Katz v United States, 389 US, at 361, 19 L Ed 2d 576, 88 S Ct 507 (1967) (Harlan, J., concurring). And it would, of course, be merely tautological to fall back on the notion that those expectations of privacy which are legitimate depend primarily on cases deciding exclusionary-rule issues in criminal cases. Legitimation of expectations of privacy by law must have a source outside of the Fourth Amendment, either by reference to concepts of real or personal property law or to understandings that are recognized and permitted by society. One of the main rights attaching to property is the right to exclude others, and one who owns or lawfully possesses or controls property will in all likelihood have a legitimate expectation of privacy by virtue of this right to exclude. Expectations of privacy protected by the Fourth Amendment, of course, need not be based on a common-law interest in real or personal property, or on the invasion of such an interest. These ideas were rejected both in Jones, supra, and Katz, supra. But by focusing on legitimate expectations of privacy in Fourth Amendment jurisprudence, the Court has not altogether abandoned use of property concepts in determining the presence or absence of the privacy interests protected by the Amendment. . . .

On the other hand, even a property interest in premises may not be sufficient to establish a legitimate expectation of privacy with respect to particular items located on the premises or activity conducted thereon.

rights that he assumes it is, his approach would have at least the merit of easy application, whatever it lacked in fidelity to the history and purposes of the Fourth Amendment. . . .

The dissent itself shows that the facile consistency it is striving for is illusory. The dissenters concede that "there comes a point when use of an area is shared with so many that one simply cannot reasonably expect seclusion." But surely the "point" referred to is not one demarcating a line which is black on one side and white on another; it is inevitably a point which separates one shade of gray from another. We are likewise told by the dissent that a person "legitimately on *private* premises . . . , though his privacy is *not absolute*, is entitled to expect that he is sharing it only with those persons [allowed there] and that governmental officials will intrude only with *consent* or by complying with the Fourth Amendment." (emphasis added). This single sentence describing the contours of the supposedly easily applied rule virtually abounds with unanswered questions: What are "private" premises? Indeed, what are the "premises?" It may be easy to describe the "premises" when one is confronted with a 1-room apartment, but what of the case of a 10-room house, or a house with an attached garage that is searched? Also, if one's privacy is not absolute, how is it bounded? If he risks governmental intrusion "with consent," who may give that consent? . . .

Our disagreement with the dissent is not that it leaves these questions unanswered, or that the questions are necessarily irrelevant in the context of the analysis contained in this opinion. Our disagreement is rather with the dissent's bland and self-refuting assumption that there will not be fine lines to be drawn in Fourth Amendment cases as in other areas of the law, and that its rubric, rather than a meaningful exegesis of Fourth Amendment doctrine, is more desirable or more easily resolves Fourth Amendment cases. In abandoning "legitimately on premises" for the doctrine that we announce today, we are not forsaking a time-tested and workable rule, which has produced consistent results when applied, solely for the sake of fidelity to the values underlying the Fourth Amendment. Rather, we are rejecting blind adherence to a phrase which at most has superficial clarity and which conceals underneath that thin veneer all of the problems of line drawing which must be faced in any conscientious effort to apply the Fourth Amendment. . . . We would not wish to be understood as saying that legitimate presence on the premises is irrelevant to one's expectation of privacy, but it cannot be deemed controlling.

D

Judged by the foregoing analysis, petitioners' claims must fail. They asserted neither a property nor a possessory interest in the automobile, nor an interest in the property seized. And as we have previously indicated, the fact that they were "legitimately on [the] premises" in the sense that they were in the car with the permission of its owner is not determinative of whether they had a legitimate expectation of privacy in the particular areas of the automobile searched. It is unnecessary for us to decide here whether the same expectations of privacy are warranted in a car as would be justified in a dwelling place in analogous circumstances. We have on numerous occasions pointed out that cars are not to be treated identically with houses or apartments for Fourth Amendment purposes. But here petitioners' claim is one which would fail even in an analogous situation in a dwelling place, since they made no showing that they had any legitimate expectation of privacy in the glove compartment or area under the seat of the car in which they were merely passengers. Like the trunk of [an] automobile, these are areas in which a passenger qua passenger simply would not normally have a legitimate expectation of privacy.

Jones v United States, 362 US 257, 4 L Ed 2d 697, 80 S Ct 725 (1960) and Katz v United States, 389 US 347, 88 S Ct 507, 19 L Ed 2d 576 (1967), involved significantly different factual circumstances. Jones not only had permission to use the apartment of his friend, but had a key to the apartment with which he admitted himself on the day of the search and kept possessions in the apartment. Except with respect to his friend, Jones had complete dominion and control over the apartment and could exclude others from it. Likewise in Katz, the defendant occupied the telephone booth, shut the door behind him to exclude all others and paid the toll, which "entitled [him] to assume that the words he utter[ed]

into the mouthpiece [would] not be broadcast to the world." Id., at 352, 19 L Ed 2d 576, 88 S Ct 507. Katz and Jones could legitimately expect privacy in the areas which were the subject of the search and seizure each sought to contest. No such showing was made by these petitioners with respect to those portions of the automobile which were searched and from which incriminating evidence was seized. . . .

Mr. Justice **White**, with whom Mr. Justice **Brennan**, Mr. Justice **Marshall**, and Mr. Justice **Stevens** join, dissenting.

The Court today holds that the Fourth Amendment protects property, not people, and specifically that a legitimate occupant of an automobile may not invoke the exclusionary rule and challenge a search of that vehicle unless he happens to own or have a possessory interest in it. Though professing to acknowledge that the primary purpose of the Fourth Amendment's prohibition of unreasonable searches is the protection of privacy—not property—the Court nonetheless effectively ties the application of the Fourth Amendment and the exclusionary rule in this situation to property law concepts. Insofar as passengers are concerned, the Court's opinion today declares an "open season" on automobiles. However unlawful stopping and searching a car may be, absent a possessory or ownership interest, no "mere" passenger may object, regardless of his relationship to the owner. . . .

[O]ne consistent theme in our decisions under the Fourth Amendment has been, until now, that "the Amendment does not shield only those who have title to the searched premises." Mancusi v DeForte, 392 US, [364,] 367, 88 S Ct 2120, 20 L Ed 2d 1154 [(1968)]. Though there comes a point when use of an area is shared with so many that one simply cannot reasonably expect seclusion, short of that limit a person legitimately on private premises knows the others allowed there and, though his privacy is not absolute, is entitled to expect that he is sharing it only with those persons and that governmental officials will intrude only with consent or by complying with the Fourth Amendment.

It is true that the Court asserts that it is not limiting the Fourth Amendment bar against unreasonable searches to the protection of property rights, but in reality it is doing exactly that.[14] Petitioners were in a private place with the permission of the owner, but the Court states that that is not sufficient to establish entitlement to a legitimate expectation of privacy. But if that is not sufficient, what would be? We are not told, and it is hard to imagine anything short of a property interest that would satisfy the majority. Insofar as the Court's rationale is concerned, no passenger in an automobile, without an ownership or possessory interest and regardless of his relationship to the owner, may claim Fourth Amendment protection against illegal stops and searches of the automobile in which he is rightfully present. The Court approves the result in Jones, but it fails to give any explanation why the facts in Jones differ, in a fashion material to the Fourth Amendment, from the facts here.[15] More importantly, how is the Court able to avoid answering the question why presence in a pri-

_____

14. The Court's reliance on property law concepts is additionally shown by its suggestion that visitors could "contest the lawfulness of the seizure of evidence or the search if their own property were seized during the search." What difference should that property interest make to constitutional protection against unreasonable searches, which is concerned with privacy? Contrary to the Court's suggestion, a legitimate passenger in a car expects to enjoy the privacy of the vehicle whether or not he happens to carry some item along for the ride. We have never before limited our concern for a person's privacy to those situations in which he is in possession of personal property. Even a person living in a barren room without possessions is entitled to expect that the police will not intrude without cause.

15. Jones had permission to use the apartment, had slept in it one night, had a key, had left a suit and a shirt there, and was the only occupant at the time of the search. Petitioners here had permission to be in the car and were occupying it at the time of the search. Thus the only distinguishing fact is that Jones could exclude others from the apartment by using his friend's key. But petitioners and their friend the owner had excluded others by entering the automobile and shutting the doors. Petitioners did not need a key because the owner was present. Similarly, the Court attempts to distinguish Katz on the theory that Katz had "shut the door behind him to exclude all others," but petitioners here did exactly the same. The car doors remained closed until the police ordered them opened at gunpoint.

vate place with the owner's permission is sufficient? . . .

As a control on governmental power, the Fourth Amendment assures that some expectations of privacy are justified and will be protected from official intrusion. That should be true in this instance, for if protected zones of privacy can only be purchased or obtained by possession of property, then much of our daily lives will be unshielded from unreasonable governmental prying, and the reach of the Fourth Amendment will have been narrowed to protect chiefly those with possessory interests in real or personal property. . . .

The Jones rule is relatively easily applied by police and courts; the rule announced today will not provide law enforcement officials with a bright line between the protected and the unprotected. Only rarely will police know whether one private party has or has not been granted a sufficient possessory or other interest by another private party. Surely in this case the officers had no such knowledge. The Court's rule will ensnare defendants and police in needless litigation over factors that should not be determinative of Fourth Amendment rights.

More importantly, the ruling today undercuts the force of the exclusionary rule in the one area in which its use is most certainly justified—the deterrence of bad-faith violations of the Fourth Amendment. This decision invites police to engage in patently unreasonable searches every time an automobile contains more than one occupant. Should something be found, only the owner of the vehicle, or of the item, will have standing to seek suppression, and the evidence will presumably be usable against the other occupants.

* * *

After this decision, police will have little to lose by unreasonably searching vehicles occupied by more than one person.

Of course, most police officers will decline the Court's invitation and will continue to do their jobs as best they can in accord with the Fourth Amendment. But the very purpose of the Bill of Rights was to answer the justified fear that governmental agents cannot be left totally to their own devices, and the Bill of Rights is enforceable in the courts because human experience teaches that not all such officials will otherwise adhere to the stated precepts. Some policemen simply do act in bad faith, even if for understandable ends, and some deterrent is needed. . . .

Notes and Questions

1. Justice Rehnquist's opinion emphasizes that Rakas never asserted a property interest in the items taken from the car. If he had claimed ownership of the seized items, would he have standing to challenge the legality of the search? Note that an admission of ownership can be made out of the presence of the jury to support a motion to suppress evidence and that such an admission cannot be used to incriminate the defendant. See Simmons v. United States, 390 U.S. 377, 88 S. Ct. 967, 19 L. Ed. 2d 1247 (1968). Two years after Rakas discarded the "legitimately on the premises" aspect of the automatic standing rule of Jones v. United States, 362 U.S. 257, 80 S. Ct. 725, 4 L. Ed. 2d 697 (1960), the Court in United States v. Salvucci, 448 U.S. 83, 100 S. Ct. 2547, 65 L. Ed. 2d 619 (1980) abandoned the other part of the automatic standing rule and expressly overruled Jones. In Salvucci, the justices ruled that "defendants charged with crimes of possession may only claim the benefits of the exclusionary rule if their own Fourth Amendment rights have in fact been violated." 448 U.S., at 85. A similar ruling was central to the Court's decision in Rawlings v. Kentucky, 448 U.S. 98, 100 S. Ct. 2556, 65 L. Ed. 2d 633 (1980).

In Rawlings, the defendant had placed his illegal drugs in a friend's purse. Police searched the purse in the defendant's presence, and he admitted ownership of them. After he was charged with illegal possession of the drugs, he moved to suppress the evidence obtained from the purse. The state court ruled that he lacked standing to object to the search of his friend's purse, and the U.S. Supreme Court agreed.

At the time petitioner dumped thousands of dollars worth of illegal drugs into Cox's purse, he had known her for only a few days. According to Cox's uncontested testimony, petitioner had never sought or received access to her purse prior to that sudden bailment. Contrast Jones v. United States, 362 U.S. 257, 259, 80 S. Ct. 725, 4 L. Ed. 2d 697 (1960). Nor did petitioner have any right to exclude other persons from access to Cox's purse. See Rakas v. Illinois, 439 U.S., at 149. In fact, Cox testified that Bob Stallons, a longtime acquaintance and frequent companion of Cox's, had free access to her purse and on the very morning of the arrest had rummaged through its contents in search of a hairbrush. Moreover, even assuming that petitioner's version of the bailment is correct and that Cox did consent to the transfer of possession, the precipitous nature of the transaction hardly supports a reasonable inference that petitioner took normal precautions to maintain his privacy. In addition to all the foregoing facts, the record also contains a frank admission by petitioner that he had no subjective expectation that Cox's purpose would remain free from governmental intrusion, an admission credited by both the trial court and the Supreme Court of Kentucky.

Petitioner contends nevertheless that, because he claimed ownership of the drugs in Cox's purse, he should be entitled to challenge the search regardless of his expectation of privacy. We disagree. While petitioner's ownership of the drugs is undoubtedly one fact to be considered in this case, Rakas emphatically rejected the notion that "arcane" concepts of property law ought to control the ability to claim the protections of the Fourth Amendment.

Had petitioner placed his drugs in plain view, he would still have owned them, but he could not claim any legitimate expectation of privacy. Prior to Rakas, petitioner might have been given "standing" in such a case to challenge a "search" that netted those drugs but probably would have lost his claim on the merits. After Rakas, the two inquiries merge into one: whether governmental officials violated any legitimate expectation of privacy held by petitioner.

In sum, we find no reason to overturn the lower court's conclusion that petitioner had no legitimate expectation of privacy in Cox's purse at the time of the search.

2. After *Rakas* and *Rawlings*, under what circumstances does a passenger have standing to contest the legality of a search of a car? When can a visitor to another's home challenge the lawfulness of a search of the home? Recall that although the Court in *Rakas* rejected the proposition that being "legitimately on the premises" conferred automatic standing to challenge a search, it nevertheless did "not question the conclusion in Jones [v. United States, *supra*] that the defendant in that case suffered a violation of his personal Fourth Amendment rights if the search in question was unlawful." Review the facts of *Jones*, as described in *Rakas*, if you have doubts about why the justices were willing to recognize Jones's standing.

3. The defendant in *Minnesota v. Olson*, 495 U.S. 91, 110 S. Ct. 1684, 109 L. Ed. 2d 85 (1990), was a suspect in a robbery-murder. He had spent the night as a visitor in the home of two women and had a change of clothes with him. The police made a warrantless, nonconsensual entry into the home to arrest Olson, who subsequently made incriminating statements. Olson thereafter moved to suppress his statements. He claimed that under *Payton v. New York*, 445 U.S. 573, 100 S. Ct. 1371, 63 L. Ed. 2d 639 (1980) (see p. 91), the police's warrantless entry into the home to arrest him was unlawful and that his statement was a fruit of the illegal arrest. In light of Olson's status as a visitor in the home, did he have standing to challenge the police's allegedly unlawful entry of the home? The Court, in an opinion authored by Justice White, ruled (7–2) that Olson's status as an overnight guest gave him a legitimate expectation of privacy in the home. He thus had standing to challenge the police's warrantless entry. In arriving at this conclusion, the Court first responded to the state's argument that Olson's status differed from that of the defendant in *Jones v. United States* and that under *Rakas* those differences deprived Olson of standing to raise the alleged *Payton* violation.

. . . The distinctions relied on by the State between this case and Jones are not legally determinative. The State emphasizes that in this case Olson was never left alone in the duplex or given a key, whereas in Jones the owner of the apartment was away and Jones had a key with which he could come and go and admit and exclude others. These differences are crucial, it is argued, because in not disturbing the holding in Jones, the Court pointed out that while his host was away, Jones had complete dominion and control over the apartment and could exclude others from it. Rakas, 439 US, at 149. We do not understand Rakas, however, to hold that an overnight guest can never have a legitimate expectation of privacy except when his host is away and he has a key, or that only when those facts are present may an overnight guest assert the "unremarkable proposition," id., at 142, that a person may have a sufficient interest in a place other than his home to enable him to be free in that place from unreasonable searches and seizures.

To hold that an overnight guest has a legitimate expectation of privacy in his host's home merely recognizes the everyday expectations of privacy that we all share. Staying overnight in another's home is a longstanding social custom that serves functions recognized as valuable by society. We stay in others' homes when we travel to a strange city for business or pleasure, when we visit our parents, children, or more distant relatives out of town, when we are in between jobs or homes, or when we house-sit for a friend. We will all be hosts and we will all be guests many times in our lives. From either perspective, we think that society recognizes that a houseguest has a legitimate expectation of privacy in his host's home.

From the overnight guest's perspective, he seeks shelter in another's home precisely because it provides him with privacy, a place where he and his possessions will not be disturbed by anyone but his host and those his host allows inside. We are at our most vulnerable when we are asleep because we cannot monitor our own safety or the security of our belongings. It is for this reason that, although we may spend all day in public places, when we cannot sleep in our own home we seek out another private place to sleep, whether it be a hotel room, or the home of a friend. Society expects at least as much privacy in these places as in a telephone booth—"a temporarily private place whose momentary occupants' expectations of freedom from intrusion are recognized as reasonable," Katz, 389 US, at 361 (Harlan, J., concurring).

That the guest has a host who has ultimate control of the house is not inconsistent with the guest having a legitimate expectation of privacy. The houseguest is there with the permission of his host, who is willing to share his house and his privacy with his guest. It is unlikely that the guest will be confined to a restricted area of the house; and when the host is away or asleep, the guest will have a measure of control over the premises. The host may admit or exclude from the house as he prefers, but it is unlikely that he will admit someone who wants to see or meet with the guest over the objection of the guest. On the other hand, few houseguests will invite others to visit them while they are guests without consulting their hosts; but the latter, who have the authority to exclude despite the wishes of the guest, will often be accommodating. The point is that hosts will more likely than not respect the privacy interests of their guests, who are entitled to a legitimate expectation of privacy despite the fact that they have no legal interest in the premises and do not have the legal authority to determine who may or may not enter the household. If the untrammeled power to admit and exclude were essential to Fourth Amendment protection, an adult daughter temporarily living in the home of her parents would have no legitimate expectation of privacy because her right to admit or exclude would be subject to her parents' veto.

Because respondent's expectation of privacy in the Bergstrom home was rooted in "understandings that are recognized and permitted by society," Rakas, supra, at 144, n. 12, it was legitimate, and respondent can claim the protection of the Fourth Amendment.

* * *

*   *   *   *   *

Olson's incriminating statements were made "less than an hour after his arrest, . . . at police headquarters." 495 U.S., at 94. Assuming that there were no exigent circumstances justifying the police's warrantless entry of the home, should the statements be suppressed as unlawful fruits of the poisonous tree? Before you answer, consider *where* the confession was made. *See New York v. Harris*, 495 U.S. 14, 110 S. Ct. 1640, 109 L. Ed. 2d 13 (1990), discussed *supra* at p. 118. In *Olson*, the Court noted that "the State had not argued that, if the arrest was illegal, [Olson's] statement was nevertheless not tainted by the illegality. . . . We will therefore not raise sua sponte the applicability of New York v. Harris." 495 U.S., at 95 n. 2. (By referring to *Black's* or another law dictionary, you can verify that *sua sponte* means "of . . . its own will or motion; without prompting or suggestion.")

4. The approach to standing adopted by the U.S. Supreme Court in *Rakas v. Illinois* and *United States v. Salvucci* is not followed as a matter of state constitutional law in several jurisdictions. The states that reject the *Rakas-Salvucci* approach typically allow third parties greater latitude in asserting search and seizure rights. *See, e.g., Commonwealth v. Amendola*, 406 Mass. 592, 550 N.E.2d 121 (1990); *State v. Sidebotham*, 124 N.H. 682, 474 A.2d 1377 (1984); *State v. Alston*, 88 N.J. 211, 440 A.2d 1311 (1981); *Commonwealth v. Sell*, 504 Pa. 46, 470 A.2d 457 (1983); *State v. Wright*, 157 Vt. 653, 596 A.2d 925 (1991). *See* B. Latzer, *State Constitutional Criminal Law* § 2:17 (1995).

📖 **5. Legal Research Note.** If you find the case law about the standing doctrine to be unclear and if you think you would benefit from a straightforward description of this topic, you could consult either a treatise on the Fourth Amendment or a legal encyclopedia article.

The most comprehensive treatise you will find is Wayne LaFave's *Search and Seizure: A Treatise on the Fourth Amendment* (3d ed. 1996,

West Publishing Co.), which is updated annually with pocket-part supplements. The index to this five-volume treatise is in the back of volume 5. Simply look up "standing," and you will be referred to numerous subissues under this heading that are discussed at section 11.3 of the treatise. This section (which also happens to appear in volume 5) covers 10 different subissues related to "standing" and extends well over 100 pages. Professor LaFave, who is one of the country's leading authorities on Fourth Amendment issues, provides an extremely helpful discussion and analysis of court cases.

Legal encyclopedia articles present a general discussion of subjects, along with citations to relevant cases. The two legal encyclopedias of national scope are *Corpus Juris Secundum*

(C.J.S.), published by West, and *American Jurisprudence, 2d (Am. Jur. 2d)*, published by *Lawyers Cooperative Publishing*. Both sets of encyclopedias make use of subject-index volumes. We will choose *C.J.S.* for this example. Look under "Searches and Seizures" in the General Index to *C.J.S.* One of the subtopics indexed is "Standing to object in general," which refers us to "Searches and S § 19." Topics are arranged alphabetically in *C.J.S.*, and we can locate "searches and seizures" in volume 79. Section 19 of the article on "searches and seizures" provides a general discussion of the standing rule and explains that subsequent sections give specific coverage of different aspects of this topic. A pocket part supplement updates the discussion, including citations to recent case decisions.

ARREST AND "STOP AND FRISK"

As we have seen, the Fourth Amendment regulates "seizures" of "persons." In this section, we will learn about two categories of seizures of the person: arrests and what commonly are known as "stops." The Fourth Amendment governs both types of seizures. However, they differ in important respects, including (1) the standard or test used to determine whether an arrest or stop is justified; (2) the factual showing required to satisfy the respective legal standards; and (3) what the police lawfully can (and cannot) do after making an arrest or stop, including (a) how long they can detain a suspect and (b) whether and how thoroughly the suspect can be searched. We begin by considering these issues in the more traditional context of arrests.

Arrests

Probable Cause: The Legal Standard and Supporting Facts

Draper v. United States, 358 U.S. 307, 79 S. Ct. 329, 3 L. Ed. 2d 327 (1959)

Mr. Justice **Whittaker** delivered the opinion of the Court.

Petitioner was convicted of knowingly concealing and transporting narcotic drugs in Denver, Colorado, in violation of 35 Stat 614, as amended, 21 USC § 174. His conviction was based in part on the use in evidence against him of two "envelopes containing [865 grains of] heroin" and a hypodermic syringe that had been taken from his person, following his arrest, by the arresting officer. Before the trial, he moved to suppress that evidence as having been secured through an unlawful search and seizure. After hearing, the District Court found that the arresting officer had probable cause to arrest petitioner without a warrant and that the subsequent search and seizure were therefore incident to a lawful arrest, and overruled the motion to suppress. . . .

The evidence offered at the hearing on the motion to suppress was not substantially disputed. It established that one Marsh, a federal narcotic agent with 29 years' experience, was stationed at Denver; that one Hereford had been engaged as a "special employee" of the Bureau of Narcotics at Denver for about six months, and from time to time gave information to Marsh regarding violations of the narcotics laws, for which Hereford was paid small sums of money, and that Marsh had always found the information given by Hereford to be accurate and reliable. On September 3, 1956, Hereford told Marsh that James Draper (petitioner) recently had taken up abode at a stated address in Denver and "was peddling narcotics to several addicts" in that city. Four days later, on September 7, Hereford told Marsh "that Draper had gone to Chicago the day before [September 6] by train [and] that he was going to bring back three ounces of heroin [and] that he would return to Denver either on the morning of the 8th of September or the morning of the 9th of September also by train." Hereford also gave Marsh a detailed physical description of Draper and of the clothing he was wearing,[2] and said that he would be carrying "a tan zipper bag," and that he habitually "walked real fast."

On the morning of September 8, Marsh and a Denver police officer went to the Denver Union Station and kept watch over all incoming trains from Chicago, but they did not see anyone fitting the description that Hereford had given. Repeating the process on the morning of September 9, they saw a person, having the exact physical attributes and wearing the precise clothing described by Hereford, alight from an incoming Chicago train and start walking "fast" toward the exit. He was carrying a tan zipper bag in his right hand and the left was thrust in his raincoat pocket. Marsh, accompanied by the police officer, overtook, stopped and arrested him.

_____

2. Hereford told Marsh that Draper was a Negro of light brown complexion, 27 years of age, 5 feet 8 inches tall, weighed about 160 pounds, and that he was wearing a light colored raincoat, brown slacks and black shoes.

They then searched him and found the two "envelopes containing heroin" clutched in his left hand in his raincoat pocket, and found the syringe in the tan zipper bag. Marsh then took him (petitioner) into custody. Hereford died four days after the arrest and therefore did not testify at the hearing on the motion. . . .

The crucial question for us then is whether knowledge of the related facts and circumstances gave Marsh "probable cause" within the meaning of the Fourth Amendment . . . to believe that petitioner had committed or was committing a violation of the narcotic laws. If it did, the arrest, though without a warrant, was lawful and the subsequent search of petitioner's person and the seizure of the found heroin were validly made incident to a lawful arrest, and therefore the motion to suppress was properly overruled and the heroin was competently received in evidence at the trial.

Petitioner . . . contends (1) that the information given by Hereford to Marsh was "hearsay" and, because hearsay is not legally competent evidence in a criminal trial, could not legally have been considered, but should have been put out of mind, by Marsh in assessing whether he had "probable cause" . . . to arrest petitioner without a warrant, and (2) that, even if hearsay could lawfully have been considered, Marsh's information should be held insufficient to show "probable cause" . . . to believe that petitioner had violated or was violating the narcotic laws and to justify his arrest without a warrant.

Considering the first contention, we find petitioner entirely in error. Brinegar v United States, 338 US 160, 172, 173, [69 S Ct 1302, 93 L Ed 1879 (1949)] has settled the question the other way. There, in a similar situation, the convict contended "that the factors relating to inadmissibility of the evidence [for] *purposes of proving guilt at the trial*, deprive[d] the evidence as a whole of sufficiency to show probable cause for the search. . . ." Id. 338 US at 172. (Emphasis added.) But this Court, rejecting that contention, said: "[T]he so-called distinction places a wholly unwarranted emphasis upon the criterion of admissibility in evidence, to prove the accused's guilt, of the facts relied upon to show probable cause. That emphasis, we think, goes much too far in confusing and disregarding the difference between what is required to prove guilt in a criminal case and what is required to show probable cause for arrest or search. It approaches requiring (if it does not in practical effect require) proof sufficient to establish guilt in order to substantiate the existence of probable cause. There is a large difference between the two things to be proved [guilt and probable cause], as well as between the tribunals which determine them, and therefore a like difference in the quanta and modes of proof required to establish them." 338 US, at 172, 173.

Nor can we agree with petitioner's second contention that Marsh's information was insufficient to show probable cause . . . to believe that petitioner had violated or was violating the narcotic laws and to justify his arrest without a warrant. The information given to narcotic agent Marsh by "special employee" Hereford may have been hearsay to Marsh, but coming from one employed for that purpose and whose information had always been found accurate and reliable, it is clear that Marsh would have been derelict in his duties had he not pursued it. And when, in pursuing that information, he saw a man, having the exact physical attributes and wearing the precise clothing and carrying the tan zipper bag that Hereford had described, alight from one of the very trains from the very place stated by Hereford and start to walk at a "fast" pace toward the station exit, Marsh had personally verified every facet of the information given him by Hereford except whether petitioner had accomplished his mission and had the three ounces of heroin on his person or in his bag. And surely, with every other bit of Hereford's information being thus personally verified, Marsh had "reasonable grounds" to believe that the remaining unverified bit of Hereford's information—that Draper would have the heroin with him—was likewise true.

"In dealing with probable cause . . . as the very name implies, we deal with probabilities. These are not technical; they are the factual and practical considerations of everyday life on which reasonable and prudent men, not legal technicians, act." Brinegar v United States, supra (338 US at 175). Probable cause exists where "the facts and circumstances within [the arresting officers'] knowledge and of which they had reasonably trustworthy information [are] sufficient in themselves to warrant a man of reasonable caution in the belief that" an offense has been or is being committed. Carroll v United States, 267 US 132, 162 [, 45 S Ct 280, 69 L Ed 543 (1925)].

We believe that, under the facts and circumstances here, Marsh had probable cause . . . to believe that petitioner was committing a violation of the laws of the United States relating to narcotic drugs at the time he arrested him. The arrest was therefore lawful, and the subsequent search and seizure, having been made incident to that lawful arrest, were likewise valid. It follows that petitioner's motion to suppress was properly denied and that the seized heroin was competent evidence lawfully received at the trial.

Affirmed.

The Chief Justice and Mr. Justice Frankfurter took no part in the consideration or decision of this case.

Mr. Justice Douglas, dissenting.

* * *

Notes and Questions

1. The Court in *Draper* offers a definition of "probable cause," which is the constitutional standard against which the legality of arrests is measured. Does the definition help clarify the meaning of *probable cause*? Does *Draper* at least make clear that both the *type* and the *amount* of evidence necessary to establish probable cause differ from the proof expected in trials?

2. If the law requires "probable cause" to believe that an offense has been or is being committed and that a particular suspect is the perpetrator, what *facts* are capable of supporting the conclusion that probable cause exists?

Specifically, can you identify any facts in *Draper* that help give us confidence that the informant (Hereford) was a reliable or trustworthy source of information?

Did Officer Marsh rely exclusively on Hereford's tip to make the arrest? What portions of the tip was Marsh able to confirm before he arrested Draper? Do you think it is important that most or all of the details that Hereford supplied the officer checked out as being accurate before the arrest was made?

Do we have any way of knowing how Hereford got his information about Draper's involvement with drugs? That is, are we told what Hereford saw or heard to support his tip that Draper was peddling narcotics or how he purported to know that Draper would be returning from Chicago with heroin in his possession?

Why was Officer Marsh waiting at the Denver train station on September 8 and 9? Why should we care?

3. We will examine probable cause in greater detail later in this chapter when we consider search warrants. Note that in all cases, probable cause is measured against an objective standard. Although a police officer initially might decide to make an arrest without a warrant, a court later will review the basis for the officer's decision and ultimately will determine whether probable cause existed. In some cases, probable cause can be based on the officer's direct observation of criminal activity. In other cases, an informant's report or tip might provide the exclusive basis for probable cause. In still other situations, probable cause may be based on some combination of an informant's tip and a police investigation. *Draper* falls into this last category of cases.

4. Probable cause operates as a threshold for arrest decisions. Once this standard is satisfied, the police have the authority to make an arrest, but they normally have discretion to decline to do so as well. Of course, it is not unusual for the police to refrain from making arrests, even when they have probable cause to believe that an individual has committed an offense.

* * * * *

If the police have probable cause to believe an offense has been committed, is the suspect's arrest always lawful? For example, suppose that the police observe a suspect commit a minor offense—one that gives them the authority to make an arrest but that they usually would decline to make. If they have a hunch that the suspect may be involved in more serious criminal activity and are "really" interested in investigating their hunch, would making the arrest for the minor offense be an illegitimate "pretext" for exploring the suspected serious activity, for which they lack probable cause? The Court considered this issue in *Whren v. United States*.

Whren v. United States, 517 U.S. 806, 116 S. Ct. 1769, 135 L. Ed. 2d 89 (1996)

Justice **Scalia** delivered the opinion of the Court.

In this case we decide whether the temporary detention of a motorist who the police have probable cause to believe has committed a civil traffic violation is inconsistent with the Fourth Amendment's prohibition against unreasonable seizures unless a reasonable officer would have been motivated to stop the car by a desire to enforce the traffic laws.

I

On the evening of June 10, 1993, plainclothes vice-squad officers of the District of Columbia Metropolitan Police Department were patrolling a "high drug area" of the city in an unmarked car. Their suspicions were aroused when they passed a dark Pathfinder truck with temporary license plates and youthful occupants waiting at a stop sign, the driver looking down into the lap of the passenger at his right. The truck remained stopped at the intersection for what seemed an unusually long time—more than 20 seconds. When the police car executed a U-turn in order to head back toward the truck, the Pathfinder turned suddenly to its right, without signalling, and sped off at an "unreasonable" speed. The policemen followed, and in a short while overtook the Pathfinder when it stopped behind other traffic at a red light. They pulled up alongside, and Officer Ephraim Soto stepped out and approached the driver's door, identifying himself as a police officer and directing the driver, petitioner Brown, to put the vehicle in park. When Soto drew up to the driver's window, he immediately observed two large plastic bags of what appeared to be crack cocaine in petitioner Whren's hands. Petitioners were arrested, and quantities of several types of illegal drugs were retrieved from the vehicle.

Petitioners were charged in a four-count indictment with violating various federal drug laws. . . .

At a pretrial suppression hearing, they challenged the legality of the stop and the resulting seizure of the drugs. They argued that the stop had not been justified by probable cause to believe, or even reasonable suspicion, that petitioners were engaged in illegal drug-dealing activity; and that Officer Soto's asserted ground for approaching the vehicle—to give the driver a warning concerning traffic violations—was pretextual. The District Court denied the suppression motion. . . .

Petitioners were convicted of the counts at issue here. The Court of Appeals affirmed the convictions, holding with respect to the suppression issue that, "regardless of whether a police officer subjectively believes that the occupants of an automobile may be engaging in some other illegal behavior, a traffic stop is permissible as long as a reasonable officer in the same circumstances *could have* stopped the car for the suspected traffic violation." 53 F. 3d 371, 374–375 (CADC 1995). We granted certiorari.

II

. . .

Petitioners accept that Officer Soto had probable cause to believe that various provisions of the District of Columbia traffic code had been violated. . . . They argue, however, that "in the unique context of civil traffic regulations" probable cause is not enough. Since, they contend, the use of automobiles is so heavily and minutely regulated that total compliance with traffic and safety rules is nearly impossible, a police officer will almost invariably be able to catch any given motorist in a technical violation. This creates the temptation to use traffic stops as a means of investigating other law violations, as to which no probable cause or even articulable suspicion exists. Petitioners, who are both black, further contend that police officers might decide which motorists to stop based on decidedly impermissible factors, such as the race of the car's occupants. To avoid this danger, they say, the Fourth Amendment test for traffic stops should be, not the normal one (applied by the Court of Appeals) of whether probable cause existed to justify the stop; but rather, whether a police officer, acting reasonably, would have made the stop for the reason given.

A

Petitioners contend that the standard they propose is consistent with our past cases' disapproval of police attempts to use valid bases of action against citizens as pretexts for pursuing other investigatory agendas. . . . But only an undiscerning reader would regard these cases as endorsing the principle that ulterior motives can invalidate police conduct that is justifiable on the basis of probable cause to believe that a violation of law has occurred. In each case we were addressing the validity of a search conducted in the *absence* of probable cause. Our quoted statements simply explain that the exemption from the need for probable cause (and warrant), which is accorded to searches made for the purpose of inventory or administrative regulation, is not accorded to searches that are *not* made for those purposes. . . .

Not only have we never held, outside the context of inventory search or administrative inspection (discussed above), that an officer's motive invalidates objectively justifiable behavior under the Fourth Amendment; but we have repeatedly held and asserted the contrary. . . .

We think these cases foreclose any argument that the constitutional reasonableness of traffic stops depends on the actual motivations of the individual officers involved. We of course agree with petitioners that the Constitution prohibits selective enforcement of the law based on considerations such as race. But the constitutional basis for objecting to intentionally discriminatory application of laws is the Equal Protection

Clause, not the Fourth Amendment. Subjective intentions play no role in ordinary, probable-cause Fourth Amendment analysis.

B

Recognizing that we have been unwilling to entertain Fourth Amendment challenges based on the actual motivations of individual officers, petitioners disavow any intention to make the individual officer's subjective good faith the touchstone of "reasonableness." They insist that the standard they have put forward—whether the officer's conduct deviated materially from usual police practices, so that a reasonable officer in the same circumstances would not have made the stop for the reasons given—is an "objective" one.

But although framed in empirical terms, this approach is plainly and indisputably driven by subjective considerations. Its whole purpose is to prevent the police from doing under the guise of enforcing the traffic code what they would like to do for different reasons. Petitioners' proposed standard may not use the word "pretext," but it is designed to combat nothing other than the per-ceived "danger" of the pretextual stop, albeit only indirectly and over the run of cases. Instead of asking whether the individual officer had the proper state of mind, the petitioners would have us ask, in effect, whether (based on general police practices) it is plausible to believe that the officer had the proper state of mind.

Why one would frame a test designed to com-bat pretext in such fashion that the court cannot take into account *actual* and *admitted pretext* is a curiosity that can only be explained by the fact that our cases have foreclosed the more sensi-ble option. If those cases were based only upon the evidentiary difficulty of establishing subjec-tive intent, petitioners' attempt to root out subjec-tive vices through objective means might make sense. But they were not based only upon that, or indeed even principally upon that. Their prin-cipal basis—which applies equally to attempts to reach subjective intent through ostensibly objec-tive means—is simply that the Fourth Amend-ment's concern with "reasonableness" allows certain actions to be taken in certain circum-stances, *whatever* the subjective intent. . . .

But even if our concern had been only an evi-dentiary one, petitioners' proposal would by no means assuage it. Indeed, it seems to us some-what easier to figure out the intent of an individ-ual officer than to plumb the collective con-sciousness of law enforcement in order to deter-mine whether a "reasonable officer" would have been moved to act upon the traffic violation. While police manuals and standard procedures may sometimes provide objective assistance, ordinarily one would be reduced to speculating about the hypothetical reaction of a hypothetical constable—an exercise that might be called vir-tual subjectivity.

Moreover, police enforcement practices, even if they could be practicably assessed by a judge, vary from place to place and from time to time. We cannot accept that the search and seizure protections of the Fourth Amendment are so variable, and can be made to turn upon such trivialities. The difficulty is illustrated by petition-ers' arguments in this case. Their claim that a reasonable officer would not have made this stop is based largely on District of Columbia police regulations which permit plainclothes officers in unmarked vehicles to enforce traffic laws "only in the case of a violation that is so grave as to pose an *immediate threat* to the safety of others." This basis of invalidation would not apply in jurisdictions that had a different practice. And it would not have applied even in the District of Columbia, if Officer Soto had been wearing a uniform or patrolling in a marked police cruiser.

. . .

III

In what would appear to be an elaboration on the "reasonable officer" test, petitioners argue that the balancing inherent in any Fourth Amendment inquiry requires us to weigh the governmental and individual interests implicated in a traffic stop such as we have here. That bal-ancing, petitioners claim, does not support investigation of minor traffic infractions by plain-clothes police in unmarked vehicles; such inves-tigation only minimally advances the govern-ment's interest in traffic safety, and may indeed retard it by producing motorist confusion and alarm—a view said to be supported by the Metropolitan Police Department's own regulations generally prohibiting this practice. And as for the Fourth Amendment interests of the individuals concerned, petitioners point out that our cases acknowledge that even ordinary traffic stops entail "a possibly unsettling show of authority"; that they at best "interfere with freedom of movement, are inconvenient, and consume time" and at worst "may create substantial anxiety," *Prouse*, 440 US, at 657, 59 L Ed 2d 660, 99 S Ct 1391. That anxiety is likely to be even more pronounced when the stop is conducted by plainclothes officers in unmarked cars.

It is of course true that in principle every Fourth Amendment case, since it turns upon a "reasonableness" determination, involves a balancing of all relevant factors. With rare exceptions not applicable here, however, the result of that balancing is not in doubt where the search or seizure is based upon probable cause. . . .

Where probable cause has existed, the only cases in which we have found it necessary actually to perform the "balancing" analysis involved searches or seizures conducted in an extraordinary manner, unusually harmful to an individual's privacy or even physical interests—such as, for example, seizure by means of deadly force, see *Tennessee v Garner*, 471 US 1, 105 S Ct 1694, 85 L Ed 2d 1 (1985), unannounced entry into a home, see *Wilson v Arkansas*, 514 US 927, 131 L Ed 2d 976, 115 S Ct 1914 (1995), entry into a home without a warrant, see *Welsh v Wisconsin*, 466 US 740, 104 S Ct 2091, 80 L Ed 2d 732 (1984), or physical penetration of the body, see *Winston v Lee*, 470 US 753, 105 S Ct 1611, 84 L Ed 2d 662 (1985). The making of a traffic stop out-of-uniform does not remotely qualify as such an extreme practice, and so is governed by the usual rule that probable cause to believe the law has been broken "outbalances" private interest in avoiding police contact.

Petitioners urge as an extraordinary factor in this case that the "multitude of applicable traffic and equipment regulations" is so large and so difficult to obey perfectly that virtually everyone is guilty of violation, permitting the police to single out almost whomever they wish for a stop. But we are aware of no principle that would allow us to decide at what point a code of law becomes so expansive and so commonly violated that infraction itself can no longer be the ordinary measure of the lawfulness of enforcement. And even if we could identify such exorbitant codes, we do not know by what standard (or what right) we would decide, as petitioners would have us do, which particular provisions are sufficiently important to merit enforcement.

For the run-of-the-mine case, which this surely is, we think there is no realistic alternative to the traditional common-law rule that probable cause justifies a search and seizure.

* * *

Here the District Court found that the officers had probable cause to believe that petitioners had violated the traffic code. That rendered the stop reasonable under the Fourth Amendment, the evidence thereby discovered admissible, and the upholding of the convictions by the Court of Appeals for the District of Columbia Circuit correct.

Judgment affirmed.

Notes and Questions

1. Why should police officers' "subjective intentions play no role in ordinary, probable-cause Fourth Amendment analysis"? The defendants in *Whren* were young African Americans who were driving in a "high-drug area" of Washington, D.C. Do you think the police (especially plainclothes officers in an unmarked car) would have stopped a middle-aged couple in a suburban area of the city for making a turn without signaling or for traveling at an "unreasonable" speed? What dangers are associated with "pretextual" stops? Did the defendants in *Whren* offer workable ground rules for identifying when a stop is "pretextual"? Does the Court offer a workable solution to the risk that African Americans or other discrete groups may be singled out and arrested for traffic violations so that the police can investigate other possible wrongdoing?

2. Note that the Court distinguished seizures based on probable cause, such as occurred in *Whren*, from other Fourth Amendment activity not based on probable cause, such as "inventory" searches and "administrative" searches. Justice Scalia explained that

An inventory search is the search of property lawfully seized and detained, in order to ensure that it is harmless, to secure valuable items (such as might be kept in a towed car), and to protect against false claims of loss or damage. See *South Dakota v. Opperman*, 428 U.S. 364, 369, 96 S. Ct. 3092, 49 L. Ed. 2d 1000 (1976). 135 L. Ed. 2d, at 96 n. 1.

An administrative inspection is the inspection of business premises conducted by authorities responsible for enforcing a pervasive regulatory scheme—for example, unannounced inspection of a mine for compliance with health and safety standards. See *Donovan v. Dewey*, 452 U.S. 594, 599–605, 101 S. Ct. 2534, 69 L. Ed. 2d 262 (1981). 135 L. Ed. 2d, at 96 n. 2.

The Court also exempted a small class of cases based on probable cause—those involving "search or seizures conducted in an extraordinary manner, unusually harmful to an individual's privacy or even physical interests"—from the normal rule that it will not engage in a balancing of interests when probable cause exists.

Search Incident to a Lawful Arrest

We already have noted the presumption that warrantless searches "are *per se* unreasonable under the Fourth Amendment—subject only to a few specifically established and well-delineated exceptions." *Katz v. United States*, 389 U.S. 347, 357, 88 S. Ct. 507, 19 L. Ed. 2d 576 (1967). Later in this chapter, we will consider the several exceptions to the search warrant "requirement." We pause here to introduce one of those exceptions: the police's authority to make a warrantless search of a person incident to a lawful arrest. Although we give more detailed coverage to this exception later, it is helpful to consider it now in anticipation of our study of the police's "stop and frisk" powers. We will want to be able to distinguish an "arrest" from a "stop," and also a full-blown search incident to an arrest from the more limited "frisk" that may accompany a stop.

As we begin to consider the police's authority to search a person incident to an arrest, it is important to keep in mind the necessary sequence of these events. "It is axiomatic that an incident search may not precede an arrest and serve as part of its justification." *Sibron v. New York*, 392 U.S. 40, 62–63, 88 S. Ct. 1889, 20 L. Ed. 2d 917 (1968). In other words, a law enforcement officer must have probable cause to make an arrest *before* the search is conducted. "An arrest is not justified by what the subsequent search discloses." *United States v. Henry*, 361 U.S. 98, 103, 80 S. Ct. 168, 4 L. Ed. 2d 134 (1959).

We now examine the justifications for allowing the warrantless search of a person incident to a lawful arrest.

United States v. Robinson, 414 U.S. 218, 94 S. Ct. 467, 38 L. Ed. 2d 427 (1973)

[Officer Jenks, a 15-year veteran of the District of Columbia police force, observed the defendant, Robinson, driving a 1965 Cadillac in Washington, D.C. Four days earlier, the officer had run a check on Robinson's driver's license and determined that it had been revoked. He thus ordered Robinson to stop the car and placed him under arrest for "operating after revocation and obtaining a permit by misrepresentation," an offense punishable by jail, fine, or both. It was not contested that probable cause existed to make the arrest. Pursuant to police department procedures, Officer Jenks began a patdown of Robinson, who had emerged from his car. The officer felt an object in the breast pocket of the heavy coat that Robinson was wearing but "couldn't tell what it was" nor the size of it. Jenks then reached into Robinson's pocket. He removed a crumpled cigarette package. Inside of the package were several capsules of heroin, which eventually were introduced against Robinson in support of his conviction for possession and "facilitation of concealment" of that substance. Robinson challenged the admission of the heroin on the ground that it resulted from an unlawful search of his person.]

Mr. Justice **Rehnquist** delivered the opinion of the Court. . . .

I

It is well settled that a search incident to a lawful arrest is a traditional exception to the warrant requirement of the Fourth Amendment. This general exception has historically been formulated into two distinct propositions. The first is that a search may be made of the *person* of the arrestee by virtue of the lawful arrest. The second is that a search may be made of the area within the control of the arrestee.

Examination of this Court's decisions show that these two propositions have been treated quite differently. The validity of the search of a person incident to a lawful arrest has been regarded as settled from its first enunciation, and has remained virtually unchallenged until the present case. The validity of the second proposition, while likewise conceded in principle, has been subject to differing interpretations as to the extent of the area which may be searched.

Because the rule requiring exclusion of evidence obtained in violation of the Fourth Amendment was first enunciated in Weeks v United States, 232 US 383, 34 S Ct 341, 58 L Ed 652 (1914), it is understandable that virtually all of this Court's search-and-seizure law has been

developed since that time. In Weeks, the Court made clear its recognition of the validity of a search incident to a lawful arrest:

"What then is the present case? Before answering that inquiry specifically, it may be well by a process of exclusion to state what it is not. It is not an assertion of the right on the part of the Government, always recognized under English and American law, to search the person of the accused when legally arrested to discover and seize the fruits or evidences of crime. This right has been uniformly maintained by many cases." 232 US, at 392.

Agnello v United States, 269 US 20, 46 S Ct 4, 70 L Ed 145 (1925), decided 11 years after Weeks, repeats the categorical recognition of the validity of a search incident to lawful arrest:

"The right without a search warrant contemporaneously to search persons lawfully arrested while committing crime and to search the place where the arrest is made in order to find and seize things connected with the crime as the fruits or as the means by which it was committed, as well as weapons and other things to effect an escape from custody, is not to be doubted." Id., at 30. . . .

II

In its decision of this case, the Court of Appeals decided that even after a police officer lawfully places a suspect under arrest for the purpose of taking him into custody, he may not ordinarily proceed to fully search the prisoner. He must instead conduct a limited frisk of the outer clothing and remove such weapons that he may, as a result of that limited frisk, reasonably believe and ascertain that the suspect has in his possession. While recognizing that Terry v Ohio, 392 US 1, 88 S Ct 1868, 20 L Ed 2d 889 (1968), dealt with a permissible "frisk" incident to an investigative stop based on less than probable cause to arrest, the Court of Appeals felt that the principles of that case should be carried over to this probable-cause arrest for driving while one's license is revoked. Since there would be no further evidence of such a crime to be obtained in a search of the arrestee, the court held that only a search for weapons could be justified.

* * *

The Court of Appeals in effect determined that the *only* reason supporting the authority for a *full* search incident to lawful arrest was the possibility of discovery of evidence or fruits. Concluding that there could be no evidence or fruits in the case of an offense such as that with which respondent was charged, it held that any protective search would have to be limited by the conditions laid down in Terry for a search upon less than probable cause to arrest. Quite apart from the fact that Terry clearly recognized the distinction between the two types of searches, and that a different rule governed one than governed the other, we find additional reason to disagree with the Court of Appeals.

The justification or reason for the authority to search incident to a lawful arrest rests quite as much on the need to disarm the suspect in order to take him into custody as it does on the need to preserve evidence on his person for later use at trial. The standards traditionally governing a search incident to lawful arrest are not, therefore, commuted to the stricter Terry standards by the absence of probable fruits or further evidence of the particular crime for which the arrest is made.

Nor are we inclined, on the basis of what seems to us to be a rather speculative judgment, to qualify the breadth of the general authority to search incident to a lawful custodial arrest on an assumption that persons arrested for the offense of driving while their licenses have been revoked are less likely to possess dangerous weapons than are those arrested for other crimes.[5] It is

---

5. Such an assumption appears at least questionable in light of the available statistical data concerning assaults on police officers who are in the course of making arrests. The danger to the police officer flows from the fact of the arrest, and its attendant proximity, stress and uncertainty, and not from the grounds for arrest. One study concludes that approximately 30% of the shootings of police officers occur when an officer stops a person in an automobile. Bristow, Police Officer Shootings—A Tactical Evaluation, 54 J Crim L C & P S 93 (1963). The Government in its brief notes that the Uniform Crime Reports, prepared by the Federal Bureau of Investigation, indicate that a significant percentage of murdered police officers occurs when the officers are making traffic stops. Those reports indicate that during January–March, 1973, 35 police officers were murdered; 11 of those officers were killed while engaged in traffic stops.

scarcely open to doubt that the danger to an officer is far greater in the case of the extended exposure which follows the taking of a suspect into custody and transporting him to the police station than in the case of the relatively fleeting contact resulting from the typical Terry-type stop. This is an adequate basis for treating all custodial arrests alike for purposes of search justification.

But quite apart from these distinctions, our more fundamental disagreement with the Court of Appeals arises from its suggestion that there must be litigated in each case the issue of whether or not there was present one of the reasons supporting the authority for a search of the person incident to a lawful arrest. We do not think the long line of authorities of this Court dating back to Weeks, or what we can glean from the history of practice in this country and in England, requires such a case-by-case adjudication. A police officer's determination as to how and where to search the person of a suspect whom he has arrested is necessarily a quick ad hoc judgment which the Fourth Amendment does not require to be broken down in each instance into an analysis of each step in the search. The authority to search the person incident to a lawful custodial arrest, while based upon the need to disarm and to discover evidence, does not depend on what a court may later decide was the probability in a particular arrest situation that weapons or evidence would in fact be found upon the person of the suspect. A custodial arrest of a suspect based on probable cause is a reasonable intrusion under the Fourth Amendment: that intrusion being lawful, a search incident to the arrest requires no additional justification. It is the fact of the lawful arrest which establishes the authority to search, and we hold that in the case of a lawful custodial arrest a full search of the person is not only an exception to the warrant requirement of the Fourth Amendment, but is also a "reasonable" search under that Amendment. . . .

Mr. Justice Powell, concurring. . . .

The Fourth Amendment safeguards the right of "the people to be secure in their persons, houses, papers, and effects, against unreasonable searches and seizures. . . ." These are areas of an individual's life about which he entertains legitimate expectations of privacy. I believe that an individual lawfully subjected to a custodial arrest retains no significant Fourth Amendment interest in the privacy of his person. Under this view the custodial arrest is the significant intrusion of state power into the privacy of one's person. If the arrest is lawful, the privacy interest guarded by the Fourth Amendment is subordinated to a legitimate and overriding governmental concern. No reason then exists to frustrate law enforcement by requiring some independent justification for a search incident to a lawful custodial arrest. This seems to me the reason that a valid arrest justifies a full search of the person, even if that search is not narrowly limited by the twin rationales of seizing evidence and disarming the arrestee. The search incident to arrest is reasonable under the Fourth Amendment because the privacy interest protected by that constitutional guarantee is legitimately abated by the fact of arrest.

Mr. Justice **Marshall**, with whom Mr. Justice **Douglas** and Mr. Justice **Brennan** join, dissenting.

Certain fundamental principles have characterized this Court's Fourth Amendment jurisprudence over the years. Perhaps the most basic of these was expressed by Mr. Justice Butler, speaking for a unanimous Court in Go-Bart Co. v. United States, 282 US 344, 51 S Ct 153, 75 L Ed 374 (1931): "There is no formula for the determination of reasonableness. Each case is to be decided on its own facts and circumstances." Id., at 357. . . .

In the present case, however, the majority turns its back on these principles, holding that "the fact of the lawful arrest" always establishes the authority to conduct a full search of the arrestee's person, regardless of whether in a particular case "there was present one of the reasons supporting the authority for a search of the person incident to a lawful arrest."

The majority's approach represents a clear and marked departure from our long tradition of case-by-case adjudication of the reasonableness of searches and seizures under the Fourth Amendment. I continue to believe that "[t]he scheme of the Fourth Amendment becomes meaningful only when it is assured that at some point the conduct of those charged with enforcing the laws can be subjected to the more detached, neutral scrutiny of a judge who must evaluate search or seizure in light of the particular circumstances." Terry v Ohio, 392 US 1, 21, 88 S Ct 1868, 20 L Ed 2d 889 (1968). Because I find the majority's reasoning to be at odds with these fundamental principles, I must respectfully dissent. . . .

Notes and Questions

1. In *Gustafson v. Florida*, 414 U.S. 260, 94 S. Ct. 488, 38 L. Ed. 2d 456 (1973), a companion case to *Robinson*, the Court made it clear that the officer's reliance on police department procedures in patting down and searching the arrestee in *Robinson* was not essential to the conclusion that his actions were "reasonable." *Gustafson* involved facts remarkably similar to *Robinson*: a motor vehicle arrest, a search of the driver's person, and finding a controlled substance within a cigarette pack. However, no departmental policy governed the involved police officer's discretion to make full custodial arrests and searches. The Court, per Rehnquist, J., over the dissents of Justices Marshall, Douglas, and Brennan, did "not find these differences determinative of the constitutional issue," 414 U.S., at 265, and upheld the search incident to the arrest.

2. For what crime was Robinson initially arrested? Would it be reasonable to justify a search of his person because the police might discover evidence related to this offense?

3. How likely is it that a motorist arrested for a traffic offense will be armed and present a danger to the officer? Are you persuaded by the Court's assertion that motor vehicle stops inherently present a danger to the police? Justice Rehnquist cites a social science study in support of this proposition. For a critique of Justice Rehnquist's reliance on this study, see *Pennsylvania v. Mimms*, 434 U.S. 106, 98 S. Ct. 330, 54 L. Ed. 2d 331 (1977) (Stevens, J., dissenting).

4. What are the virtues of a *per se*, or across-the-board, rule allowing the police to conduct a search incident to a lawful arrest in all cases? What are the virtues of the alternative approach, which would require specific, individualized justification for a search on a case-by-case basis?

5. Do you agree with Justice Powell's essential point: "that an individual lawfully subjected to a custodial arrest retains no significant Fourth Amendment interest in the privacy of his person"?

6. We will consider the permissible *scope* of a search incident to an arrest later in this chapter. This issue involves how wide-ranging a search may be after a suspect is arrested.

7. Relying on state constitutional grounds, some state courts have rejected *Robinson's per se* rule regarding the police's authority to search a person incident to an arrest. Those courts generally restrict the right to search for evidence to cases involving crimes where evidence could be concealed. Some state courts require articulable, reasonable suspicion to believe than an arrestee is armed to justify a search for weapons following an arrest for a minor crime. *See Zehrung v. State*, 569 P.2d 189 (Alaska, 1977); *State v. Kaluna*, 55 Ha. 361, 520 P.2d 51 (1974); *State v. Caraher*, 293 Or. 741, 653 P.2d 942 (1982). *See* B. Latzer, *State Constitutional Criminal Law* § 3:21 (1995).

Stop and Frisk

We now consider seizures of the person that fall short of a traditional arrest. We also explore the related issue involving searches that are less intrusive than a full-scale search incident to an arrest. In common parlance, these are the subjects of "stop" and "frisk." Consistent with our study of arrests, we will want to be able to identify the legal standard (analogous to probable cause) required to justify a "stop" and also to gain a feel for the factual showing necessary to satisfy that standard. You should be especially attentive to the differences between an arrest and a stop, and a full search of the person versus a frisk, and be able to explain why it is important to keep these concepts distinct. We begin with the landmark case of *Terry v. Ohio*.

Terry v. Ohio, 392 U.S. 1, 88 S. Ct. 1868, 20 L. Ed. 2d 889 (1968)

Mr. Chief Justice **Warren** delivered the opinion of the Court.

This case presents serious questions concerning the role of the Fourth Amendment in the confrontation on the street between the citizen and the policeman investigating suspicious circumstances.

Petitioner Terry was convicted of carrying a concealed weapon and sentenced to the statutorily prescribed term of one to three years in the penitentiary. Following the denial of a pretrial motion to suppress, the prosecution introduced in evidence two revolvers and a number of bullets seized from Terry and a codefendant, Rich-

ard Chilton, by Cleveland Police Detective Martin McFadden. At the hearing on the motion to suppress this evidence, Officer McFadden testified that while he was patrolling in plain clothes in downtown Cleveland at approximately 2:30 in the afternoon of October 31, 1963, his attention was attracted by two men, Chilton and Terry, standing on the corner of Huron Road and Euclid Avenue. He had never seen the two men before, and he was unable to say precisely what first drew his eye to them. However, he testified that he had been a policeman for 39 years and a detective for 35 and that he had been assigned to patrol this vicinity of downtown Cleveland for shoplifters and pickpockets for 30 years. He explained that he had developed routine habits of observation over the years and that he would "stand and watch people or walk and watch people at many intervals of the day." He added: "Now, in this case when I looked over they didn't look right to me at the time."

His interest aroused, Officer McFadden took up a post of observation in the entrance to a store 300 to 400 feet away from the two men. "I get more purpose to watch them when I seen their movements," he testified. He saw one of the men leave the other one and walk southwest on Huron Road, past some stores. The man paused for a moment and looked in a store window, then walked on a short distance, turned around and walked back toward the corner, pausing once again to look in the same store window. He rejoined his companion at the corner, and the two conferred briefly. Then the second man went through the same series of motions, strolling down Huron Road, looking in the same window, walking on a short distance, turning back, peering in the store window again, and returning to confer with the first man at the corner. The two men repeated this ritual alternately between five and six times apiece—in all roughly a dozen trips. At one point, while the two were standing together on the corner, a third man approached them and engaged them briefly in conversation. This man then left the two others and walked west on Euclid Avenue. Chilton and Terry resumed their measured pacing, peering, and conferring. After this had gone on for 10 to 12 minutes, the two men walked off together, heading west on Euclid Avenue, following the path taken earlier by the third man.

By this time Officer McFadden had become thoroughly suspicious. He testified that after observing their elaborately casual and oft-repeated reconnaissance of the store window on Huron Road, he suspected the two men of "casing a job, a stick-up," and that he considered it his duty as a police officer to investigate further. He added that he feared "they may have a gun." Thus, Officer McFadden followed Chilton and Terry and saw them stop in front of Zucker's store to talk to the same man who had conferred with them earlier on the street corner. Deciding that the situation was ripe for direct action, Officer McFadden approached the three men,

identified himself as a police officer and asked for their names. At this point his knowledge was confined to what he had observed. He was not acquainted with any of the three men by name or by sight, and he had received no information concerning them from any other source. When the men "mumbled something" in response to his inquiries, Officer McFadden grabbed petitioner Terry, spun him around so that they were facing the other two, with Terry between McFadden and the others, and patted down the outside of his clothing. In the left breast pocket of Terry's overcoat Officer McFadden felt a pistol. He reached inside the overcoat pocket, but was unable to remove the gun. At this point, keeping Terry between himself and the others, the officer ordered all three men to enter Zucker's store. As they went in, he removed Terry's overcoat completely, removed a .38-caliber revolver from the pocket and ordered all three men to face the wall with their hands raised. Officer McFadden proceeded to pat down the outer clothing of Chilton and the third man, Katz. He discovered another revolver in the outer pocket of Chilton's overcoat, but no weapons were found on Katz. The officer testified that he only patted the men down to see whether they had weapons, and that he did not put his hands beneath the outer garments of either Terry or Chilton until he felt their guns. So far as appears from the record, he never placed his hands beneath Katz' outer garments. Officer McFadden seized Chilton's gun, asked the proprietor of the store to call a police wagon, and took all three men to the station, where Chilton and Terry were formally charged with carrying concealed weapons. . . .

I.

* * *

Unquestionably petitioner was entitled to the protection of the Fourth Amendment as he walked down the street in Cleveland. The question is whether in all the circumstances of this on-the-street encounter, his right to personal security was violated by an unreasonable search and seizure.

We would be less than candid if we did not acknowledge that this question thrusts to the fore difficult and troublesome issues regarding a sensitive area of police activity—issues which have never before been squarely presented to this Court. Reflective of the tensions involved are the practical and constitutional arguments pressed with great vigor on both sides of the public debate over the power of the police to "stop and frisk"—as it is sometimes euphemistically termed—suspicious persons.

On the one hand, it is frequently argued that in dealing with the rapidly unfolding and often dangerous situations on city streets the police are in need of an escalating set of flexible responses, graduated in relation to the amount of information they possess. For this purpose it is urged that distinctions should be made between a "stop" and an "arrest" (or a "seizure" of a person), and between a "frisk" and a "search." . . .

On the other side the argument is made that the authority of the police must be strictly circumscribed by the law of arrest and search as it has developed to date in the traditional jurisprudence of the Fourth Amendment. . . .

The heart of the Fourth Amendment, the argument runs, is a severe requirement of specific justification for any intrusion upon protected personal security, coupled with a highly developed system of judicial controls to enforce upon the agents of the State the commands of the Constitution. . . .

In this context we approach the issues in this case mindful of the limitations of the judicial function in controlling the myriad daily situations in which policemen and citizens confront each other on the street. . . .

Proper adjudication of cases in which the exclusionary rule is invoked demands a constant awareness of these limitations. The wholesale harassment by certain elements of the police community, of which minority groups, particularly Negroes, frequently complain, will not be stopped by the exclusion of any evidence from any criminal trial. Yet a rigid and unthinking application of the exclusionary rule, in futile protest against practices which it can never be used effectively to control, may exact a high toll in human injury and frustration of efforts to prevent crime. No judicial opinion can comprehend the protean variety of the street encounter, and we can only judge the facts of the case before us. . . .

Having thus roughly sketched the perimeters of the constitutional debate over the limits on police investigative conduct in general and the background against which this case presents itself, we turn our attention to the quite narrow question posed by the facts before us: whether it is always unreasonable for a policeman to seize a person and subject him to a limited search for weapons unless there is probable cause for an arrest. . . .

II.

Our first task is to establish at what point in this encounter the Fourth Amendment becomes relevant. That is, we must decide whether and when Officer McFadden "seized" Terry and whether and when he conducted a "search." There is some suggestion in the use of such terms as "stop" and "frisk" that such police conduct is outside the purview of the Fourth Amendment because neither action rises to the level of a "search" or "seizure" within the meaning of the Constitution. We emphatically reject this notion. It is quite plain that the Fourth Amendment governs "seizures" of the person which do not eventuate in a trip to the station house and prosecution for crime—"arrests" in traditional terminology. It must be recognized that whenever a police officer accosts an individual and restrains his freedom to walk away, he has "seized" that person. And it is nothing less than sheer torture of the English language to suggest that a careful exploration of the outer surfaces of a person's clothing all over his or her body in an attempt to find weapons is not a "search." Moreover, it is simply fantastic to urge that such a procedure performed in public by a policeman while the citizen stands helpless, perhaps facing a wall with his hands raised, is a "petty indignity."[13] It is a serious intrusion upon the sanctity of the person, which may inflict great indignity and arouse strong resentment, and it is not to be undertaken lightly. . . .

---

13. Consider the following apt description: "[T]he officer must feel with sensitive fingers every portion of the prisoner's body. A thorough search must be made of the prisoner's arms and armpits, waistline and back, the groin and area around the testicles, and entire surface of the legs down to the feet." Priar & Martin, Searching and Disarming Criminals, 45 J Crim L.C. & P.S. 481 (1954).

The distinctions of classical "stop-and-frisk" theory thus serve to divert attention from the central inquiry under the Fourth Amendment— the reasonableness in all the circumstances of the particular governmental invasion of a citizen's personal security. "Search" and "seizure" are not talismans. We therefore reject the notions that the Fourth Amendment does not come into play at all as a limitation upon police conduct if the officers stop short of something called a "technical arrest" or a "full-blown search."

In this case there can be no question, then, that Officer McFadden "seized" petitioner and subjected him to a "search" when he took hold of him and patted down the outer surfaces of his clothing. We must decide whether at that point it was reasonable for Officer McFadden to have interfered with petitioner's personal security as he did.[16] And in determining whether the seizure and search were "unreasonable" our inquiry is a dual one—whether the officer's action was justified at its inception, and whether it was reasonably related in scope to the circumstances which justified the interference in the first place.

III.

. . . In order to assess the reasonableness of Officer McFadden's conduct as a general proposition, it is necessary "first to focus upon the governmental interest which allegedly justifies official intrusion upon the constitutionally protected interests of the private citizen," for there is "no ready test for determining reasonableness

other than by balancing the need to search [or seize] against the invasion which the search [or seizure] entails." Camara v. Municipal Court, 387 US 523, 534–535, 536–537 (1967). And in justifying the particular intrusion the police officer must be able to point to specific and articulable facts which, taken together with rational inferences from those facts, reasonably warrant that intrusion. The scheme of the Fourth Amendment becomes meaningful only when it is assured that at some point the conduct of those charged with enforcing the laws can be subjected to the more detached, neutral scrutiny of a judge who must evaluate the reasonableness of a particular search or seizure in light of the particular circumstances. And in making that assessment it is imperative that the facts be judged against an objective standard: would the facts available to the officer at the moment of the seizure or the search "warrant a man of reasonable caution in the belief" that the action taken was appropriate?

Anything less would invite intrusions upon constitutionally guaranteed rights based on nothing more substantial than inarticulate hunches, a result this Court has consistently refused to sanction. And simple "'good faith on the part of the arresting officer is not enough.' . . . If subjective good faith alone were the test, the protections of the Fourth Amendment would evaporate, and the people would be 'secure in their persons, houses, papers, and effects,' only in the discretion of the police."

Applying these principles to this case, we consider first the nature and extent of the governmental interests involved. One general interest is of course that of effective crime prevention and detection; it is this interest which underlies the recognition that a police officer may in appropriate circumstances and in an appropriate manner approach a person for purposes of investigating possibly criminal behavior even though there is no probable cause to make an arrest. It was this legitimate investigation function Officer McFadden was discharging when he decided to approach petitioner and his companions. He had observed Terry, Chilton, and Katz go through a series of acts, each of them perhaps innocent in itself, but which taken together warranted further investigation. There is nothing unusual in two men standing together on a

---

16. We thus decide nothing today concerning the constitutional propriety of an investigative "seizure" upon less than probable cause for purposes of "detention" and/or interrogation. Obviously, not all personal intercourse between policemen and citizens involve "seizures" of persons. Only when the officer, by means of physical force or show of authority, has in some way restrained the liberty of a citizen may we conclude that a "seizure" has occurred. We cannot tell with any certainty upon this record whether any such "seizure" took place here prior to Officer McFadden's initiation of physical contact for purposes of searching Terry for weapons, and we thus may assume that up to that point no intrusion upon constitutionally protected rights had occurred.

street corner, perhaps waiting for someone. Nor is there anything suspicious about people in such circumstances strolling up and down the street, singly or in pairs. Store windows, moreover, are made to be looked in. But the story is quite different where, as here, two men hover about a street corner for an extended period of time, at the end of which it becomes apparent that they are not waiting for anyone or anything; where these men pace alternately along an identical route, pausing to stare in the same store window roughly 24 times; where each completion of this route is followed immediately by a conference between the two men on the corner; where they are joined in one of these conferences by a third man who leaves swiftly; and where the two men finally follow the third and rejoin him a couple of blocks away. It would have been poor police work indeed for an officer of 30 years' experience in the detection of thievery from stores in this same neighborhood to have failed to investigate this behavior further.

The crux of this case, however, is not the propriety of Officer McFadden's taking steps to investigate petitioner's suspicious behavior, but rather, whether there was justification for McFadden's invasion of Terry's personal security by searching him for weapons in the course of that investigation. We are now concerned with more than the governmental interest in investigating crime; in addition, there is the more immediate interest of the police officer in taking steps to assure himself that the person with whom he is dealing is not armed with a weapon that could unexpectedly and fatally be used against him. Certainly it would be unreasonable to require that police officers take unnecessary risks in the performance of their duties. American criminals have a long tradition in armed violence, and every year in this country many law enforcement officers are killed in the line of duty, and thousands more are wounded. Virtually all of these deaths and a substantial portion of the injuries are inflicted with guns and knives.

In view of these facts, we cannot blind ourselves to the need for law enforcement officers to protect themselves and other prospective victims of violence in situations where they may lack probable cause for an arrest. When an officer is justified in believing that the individual whose suspicious behavior he is investigating at close range is armed and presently dangerous to the officers or to others, it would appear to be clearly unreasonable to deny the officer the power to take necessary measures to determine whether the person is in fact carrying a weapon and to neutralize the threat of physical harm.

We must still consider, however, the nature and quality of the intrusion on individual rights which must be accepted if police officers are to be conceded the right to search for weapons in situations where probable cause to arrest for crime is lacking. Even a limited search of the outer clothing for weapons constitutes a severe, though brief, intrusion upon cherished personal security, and it must surely be an annoying, frightening, and perhaps humiliating experience.

* * *

Petitioner does not argue that a police officer should refrain from making any investigation of suspicious circumstances until such time as he has probable cause to make an arrest; nor does he deny that police officers in properly discharging their investigative function may find themselves confronting persons who might well be armed and dangerous. Moreover, he does not say that an officer is always unjustified in searching a suspect to discover weapons. Rather, he says it is unreasonable for the policeman to take that step until such time as the situation evolves to a point where there is probable cause to make an arrest. When that point has been reached, petitioner would concede the officer's right to conduct a search of the suspect for weapons, fruits or instrumentalities of the crime, or "mere" evidence, incident to the arrest.

There are two weaknesses in this line of reasoning, however. First, it fails to take account of traditional limitations upon the scope of searches, and thus recognizes no distinction in purpose, character, and extent between a search incident to an arrest and a limited search for weapons. The former, although justified in part by the acknowledged necessity to protect the arresting officer from assault with a concealed weapon, is also justified on other grounds, and can therefore involve a relatively extensive exploration of the person. A search for weapons in the absence of probable cause to arrest, however, must, like any other search, be strictly circumscribed by the exigencies which justify its initiation. Thus it must be limited to that which is necessary for the discovery of weapons which might be used to harm the officer or others nearby, and may realistically be characterized as something less than a "full" search, even though it remains a serious intrusion.

A second, and related, objection to petitioner's argument is that it assumes that the law of arrest has already worked out the balance between the particular interests involved here—the neutralization of danger to the policeman in the investigative circumstance and the sanctity of the individual. But this is not so. An arrest is a wholly different kind of intrusion upon individual freedom from a limited search for weapons, and the interests each is designed to serve are likewise quite different. An arrest is the initial stage of a criminal prosecution. It is intended to vindicate society's interest in having its laws obeyed, and it is inevitably accompanied by future interference with the individual's freedom of movement, whether or not trial or conviction ultimately follows. The protective search for weapons, on the other hand, constitutes a brief, though far from inconsiderable, intrusion upon the sanctity of the person. It does not follow that because an officer may lawfully arrest a person only when he is apprised of facts sufficient to warrant a belief that the person has committed or is committing a crime, the officer is equally unjustified, absent that kind of evidence, in making any intrusions short of an arrest. Moreover, a perfectly reasonable apprehension of danger may arise long before the officer is possessed of adequate information to justify taking a person into custody for the purpose of prosecuting him for a crime. Petitioner's reliance on cases which have worked out standards of reasonableness with regard to "seizures" constituting arrests and searches incident therefore is thus misplaced. It assumes that the interests sought to be vindicated and the invasions of personal security may be equated in the two cases, and thereby ignores a vital aspect of the analysis of the reasonableness of particular types of conduct under the Fourth Amendment.

Our evaluation of the proper balance that has to be struck in this type of case leads us to conclude that there must be a narrowly drawn authority to permit a reasonable search for weapons for the protection of the police officer, where he has reason to believe that he is dealing with an armed and dangerous individual, regardless of whether he has probable cause to arrest the individual for a crime. The officer need not be absolutely certain that the individual is armed; the issue is whether a reasonably prudent man in the circumstances would be warranted in the belief that his safety or that of others was in danger.

And in determining whether the officer acted reasonably in such circumstances, due weight must be given, not to his inchoate and unparticularized suspicion or "hunch," but to the specific reasonable inferences which he is entitled to draw from the facts in light of his experience.

IV.

We must now examine the conduct of Officer McFadden in this case to determine whether his search and seizure of petitioner were reasonable, both at their inception and as conducted. . . . We think on the facts and circumstances Officer McFadden detailed before the trial judge a reasonably prudent man would have been warranted in believing petitioner was armed and thus presented a threat to the officer's safety while he was investigating his suspicious behavior. . . .

The manner in which the seizure and search were conducted is, of course, as vital a part of the inquiry as whether they were warranted at all. The Fourth Amendment proceeds as much by limitations upon the scope of governmental action as by imposing preconditions upon its initiation. . . . Thus, evidence may not be introduced if it was discovered by means of a seizure and search which were not reasonably related in scope to the justification for their initiation.

We need not develop at length in this case, however, the limitations which the Fourth Amendment places upon a protective seizure and search for weapons. These limitations will have to be developed in the concrete factual circumstances of individual cases. Suffice it to note that such a search, unlike a search without a warrant incident to a lawful arrest, is not justified by any need to prevent the disappearance or destruction of evidence of crime. The sole justification of the search in the present situation is the protection of the police officer and others nearby, and it must therefore be confined in scope to an intrusion reasonably designed to discover guns, knives, clubs, or other hidden instruments for the assault of the police officer.

The scope of the search in this case presents no serious problem in light of these standards. Officer McFadden patted down the outer clothing of petitioner and his two companions. He did not place his hands in their pockets or under the outer surface of their garments until he had felt weapons, and then he merely reached for and removed the guns. . . . Officer McFadden confined his search strictly to what was minimally necessary to learn whether the men were armed and to disarm them once he discovered the weapons. He did not conduct a general exploratory search for whatever evidence of criminal activity he might find.

V.

We conclude that the revolver seized from Terry was properly admitted in evidence against him. At the time he seized petitioner and searched him for weapons, Officer McFadden had reasonable grounds to believe that petitioner was armed and dangerous, and it was necessary for the protection of himself and others to take swift measures to discover the true facts and neutralize the threat of harm if it materialized. The policeman carefully restricted his search to what was appropriate to the discovery of the particular items which he sought. Each case of this sort will, of course, have to be decided on its own facts. We merely hold today that where a police officer observes unusual conduct which leads him reasonably to conclude in light of his experience that criminal activity may be afoot and that the persons with whom he is dealing may be armed and presently dangerous, where in the course of investigating this behavior he identifies himself as a policeman and makes reasonable inquiries, and where nothing in the initial stages of the encounter serves to dispel his reasonable fear for his own or others' safety, he is entitled for the protection of himself and others in the area to conduct a carefully limited search of the outer clothing of such persons in an attempt to discover weapons which might be used to assault him. Such a search is a reasonable search under the Fourth Amendment, and any weapons seized may properly be introduced in evidence against the person from whom they were taken.

Affirmed. . . .

Mr. Justice HARLAN, concurring. . . .

A police officer's right to make an on-the-street 'stop' and an accompanying 'frisk' for weapons is of course bounded by the protections afforded by the Fourth and Fourteenth Amendments. The Court holds, and I agree, that while the right does not depend upon possession by the officer of a valid warrant, nor upon the existence of probable cause, such activities must be reasonable under the circumstances as the officer credibly relates them in court. Since the question in this and most cases is whether evidence produced by a frisk is admissible, the problem is to determine what makes a frisk reasonable. . . .

The state courts held . . . that when an officer is lawfully confronting a possibly hostile person in the line of duty he has a right, springing only from the necessity of the situation and not from any broader right to disarm, to frisk for his own protection. This holding, with which I agree and with which I think the Court agrees, offers the only satisfactory basis I can think of for affirming this conviction. The holding has, however, two logical corollaries that I do not think the Court has fully expressed.

In the first place, if the frisk is justified in order to protect the officer during an encounter with a citizen, the officer must first have constitutional grounds to insist on an encounter, to make a forcible stop. Any person, including a policeman, is at liberty to avoid a person he considers dangerous. If and when a policeman has a right instead to disarm such a person for his own protection, he must first have a right not to avoid him but to be in his presence. That right must be more than the liberty (again, possessed by every citizen) to address questions to other persons, for ordinarily the person addressed has an equal right to ignore his interrogator and walk away; he certainly need not submit to a frisk for the questioner's protection. I would make it perfectly clear that the right to frisk in this case depends upon the reasonableness of a forcible stop to investigate a suspected crime.

Where such a stop is reasonable, however, the right to frisk must be immediate and automatic if the reason for the stop is, as here, an articulable suspicion of a crime of violence. Just as a full search incident to a lawful arrest requires no additional justification, a limited frisk incident to a lawful stop must often be rapid and routine. There is no reason why an officer, rightfully but forcibly confronting a person suspected of a serious crime, should have to ask one question and take the risk that the answer might be a bullet. . . .

Mr. Justice White, concurring.

* * *

I think an additional word is in order concerning the matter of interrogation during an investigative stop. There is nothing in the Constitution which prevents a policeman from addressing questions to anyone on the streets. Absent special circumstances, the person approached may not be detained or frisked but may refuse to cooperate and go on his way. However, given the proper circumstances, such as those in this case, it seems to me the person may be briefly detained against his will while pertinent questions are directed to him. Of course, the person stopped is not obliged to answer, answers may not be compelled, and refusal to answer furnishes no basis for an arrest, although it may alert the officer to the need for continued observation. In my view, it is temporary detention, warranted by the circumstances which chiefly justifies the protective frisk for weapons. Perhaps the frisk itself, where proper, will have beneficial results whether questions are asked or not. If weapons are found, an arrest will follow. If none are found, the frisk may nevertheless serve preventive ends because of its unmistakable message that suspicion has been aroused. But if the investigative stop is sustainable at all, constitutional rights are not necessarily violated if pertinent questions are asked and the person is restrained briefly in the process.

Mr. Justice **Douglas,** dissenting.

I agree that petitioner was "seized" within the meaning of the Fourth Amendment. I also agree that frisking petitioner and his companions for guns was a "search." But it is a mystery how that "search" and that "seizure" can be constitutional by Fourth Amendment standards, unless there was "probable cause" to believe that (1) a crime had been committed or (2) a crime was in the process of being committed or (3) a crime was about to be committed.

The opinion of the Court disclaims the existence of "probable cause." If loitering were in issue and that was the offense charged, there would be "probable cause" shown. But the crime here is carrying concealed weapons, and there is no basis for concluding that the officer had "probable cause" for believing that the crime was being committed. Had a warrant been sought, a magistrate would, therefore, have been unauthorized to issue one, for he can act only if there is a showing of "probable cause." We hold today that the police have greater authority to make a "seizure" and conduct a "search" than a judge has to authorize such action. We have said precisely the opposite over and over again. . . .

To give the police greater power than a magistrate is to take a long step down the totalitarian path.

* * *

There have been powerful hydraulic pressures throughout our history that bear heavily on the Court to water down constitutional guarantees and give the police the upper hand. That hydraulic pressure has probably never been greater than it is today.

Yet if the individual is no longer to be sovereign, if the police can pick him up whenever they do not like the cut of his jib, if they can "seize" and "search" him in their discretion, we enter a new regime. The decision to enter it should be made only after a full debate by the people of this country.

Notes and Questions

1. *Terry* is an important case because, among other things, it unlinked the two principal clauses of the Fourth Amendment—the prohibition against unreasonable searches and seizures and the provision that no warrants shall issue but upon probable cause. Before *Terry*, it generally was understood that because probable cause is necessary to justify a search or seizure under the Fourth Amendment's warrants clause, a warrantless search or seizure conducted without probable cause must certainly be "unreasonable" under the first clause of the Amendment. *Terry*, however, dispensed with the need for probable cause for some searches and seizures. The opinion instead approves of a balancing test that weighs law enforcement's interests against the degree of intrusion on the individual to determine whether a search or seizure is unreasonable. You must be cautious, however, about applying *Terry's* balancing test for unreasonableness beyond the context of "stops" and "frisks."

2. Is a "stop" a "seizure" within the meaning of the Fourth Amendment? How does a "stop" differ from an arrest? When, precisely, did the "stop" occur in *Terry*? Was Officer McFadden justified in stopping Terry and his companions because "they didn't look right to me at the time"? What standard does the *Terry* Court apply to assess the legality of the stop? (*Terry's* murky standard is described in later cases as "reasonable suspicion"—which remains murky but at least is more simply stated than the test used in *Terry*.)

3. Comparatively little discussion is given to the "stop" in *Terry*. Chief Justice Warren's opinion asserts that

> the crux of this case . . . is not the propriety of Officer McFadden's taking steps to investigate petitioner's suspicious behavior, but rather, whether there was justification for McFadden's invasion of Terry's personal security by searching him for weapons in the course of that investigation.

Is a "frisk" a "search" within the meaning of the Fourth Amendment? How does a "frisk" differ from a search incident to an arrest? What, precisely, was Officer McFadden's reason for frisking Terry, and how did he conduct the frisk? At what point did McFadden's search of Terry proceed beyond a "frisk"? What justified this more intrusive search? Does it appear from *Terry* that a police officer may routinely frisk a suspect who has been stopped, or is something more required?

4. Note that when Officer McFadden approached Terry, Chilton, and Katz and asked for their names, they "'mumbled something' in response." Of what significance was McFadden's request that they account for themselves? Of what significance was the mumbled response? Was Terry legally obligated to respond to the officer's inquiry? See Justice White's opinion in this regard. If he was not, why was the officer justified in grabbing Terry, spinning him around, and patting down his overcoat because he did not receive a satisfactory response to his question?

5. Two companion cases were decided with *Terry*: *Sibron v. New York* and *Peters v. New York*, 392 U.S. 40, 88 S. Ct. 1889, 20 L. Ed. 2d 917 (1968). Those cases helped explain and define the proper limits of *Terry*. In *Sibron* the facts, in brief, were as follows:

> . . . Officer Martin testified that while he was patrolling his beat in uniform on March 9, 1965, he observed Sibron "continually from the hours of 4:00 P.M. to 12:00, midnight . . . in the vicinity of 742 Broadway." He stated that during this period of time he saw Sibron in conversation with six or eight persons whom he (Patrolman Martin) knew from past experience to be narcotics addicts. The officer testified that he did not overhear any of these conversations, and that he did not see anything pass between Sibron and any of the others. Late in the evening Sibron entered a restaurant. Patrolman Martin saw Sibron speak with three more known addicts inside the restaurant. Once again, nothing was overheard and nothing was seen to pass between Sibron and the addicts. Sibron sat down and ordered pie and coffee, and, as he was eating, Patrolman Martin approached him and told him to come outside. Once outside, the officer said to Sibron, "You know what I am after." According to the officer, Sibron "mumbled something and reached into his pocket." Simultaneously, Patrolman Martin thrust his hand into the same pocket, discovering several glassine envelopes, which, it turned out, contained heroin. . . .

Peters involved the following facts:

. . . Officer Samuel Lasky of the New York City Police Department was at home in his apartment in Mount Vernon, New York, at about 1 p.m. on July 10, 1964. He had just finished taking a shower and was drying himself when he heard a noise at his door. His attempt to investigate was interrupted by a telephone call, but when he returned and looked through the peephole into the hall, Officer Lasky saw "two men tiptoeing out of the alcove toward the stairway." He immediately called the police, put on some civilian clothes and armed himself with his service revolver. Returning to the peephole, he saw "a tall man tiptoeing away from the alcove and followed by his shorter man, Mr. Peters, toward the stairway." Officer Lasky testified that he had lived in the 120-unit building for 12 years and that he did not recognize either of the men as tenants. Believing that he had happened upon the two men in the course of an attempted burglary, Officer Lasky opened his door, entered the hallway and slammed the door loudly behind him. This precipitated a flight down the stairs on the part of the two men, and Officer Lasky gave chase. His apartment was located on the sixth floor, and he apprehended Peters between the fourth and fifth floors. Grabbing Peters by the collar, he continued down another flight in unsuccessful pursuit of the other man. Peters explained his presence in the building to Officer Lasky by saying that he was visiting a girl friend. However, he declined to reveal the girl friend's name, on the ground that she was a married woman. Officer Lasky patted Peters down for weapons, and discovered a hard object in his pocket. He stated at the hearing that the object did not feel like a gun, but that it might have been a knife. He removed the object from Peters' pocket. It was an opaque plastic envelope, containing burglar's tools. . . .

How would you rule concerning the reasonableness of the seizures and searches in these cases? In *Sibron*, Chief Justice Warren's opinion for the Court concluded that Officer Martin's actions did not measure up to the *Terry* requirements.

Turning to the facts of Sibron's case, it is clear that the heroin was inadmissible in evidence against him. The prosecution has quite properly abandoned the notion that there was probable cause to arrest Sibron for any crime at the time Patrolman Martin accosted him in the restaurant, took him outside and searched him. The officer was not acquainted with Sibron and had no information concerning him. He merely saw Sibron talking to a number of known narcotics addicts over a period of eight hours. It must be emphasized that Patrolman Martin was completely ignorant regarding the content of these conversations, and that he saw nothing pass between Sibron and the addicts. So far as he knew, they might indeed "have been talking about the World Series." The inference that persons who talk to narcotics addicts are engaged in the criminal traffic in narcotics is simply not the sort of reasonable inference required to support an intrusion by the police upon an individual's personal security. . . .

If Patrolman Martin lacked probable cause for an arrest, however, his seizure and search of Sibron might still have been justified at the outset if he had reasonable grounds to believe that Sibron was armed and dangerous. Terry v Ohio. . . .

The police officer is not entitled to seize and search every person whom he sees on the street or of whom he makes inquiries. Before he places a hand on the person of a citizen in search of anything, he must have constitutionally adequate, reasonable grounds for doing so. In the case of the self-protective search for weapons, he must be able to point to particular facts from which he reasonably inferred that the individual was armed and dangerous. Terry v. Ohio, supra. Patrolman Martin's testimony reveals no such facts. The suspect's mere act of talking with a number of known narcotics addicts over an eight-hour period no more gives rise to reasonable fear of life or limb on the part of the police officer than it justifies an arrest for committing a crime.

Nor did Patrolman Martin urge that when Sibron put his hand in his pocket, he feared that he was going for a weapon and acted in self-defense. His opening statement to Sibron—"You know what I am after"—made it abundantly clear that he sought narcotics, and his testimony at the hearing left no doubt that he thought there were narcotics in Sibron's pocket. . . .

The Court continued that even if adequate grounds had existed to justify Officer Martin's "seizure" of Sibron, the scope of the search was not sufficiently limited to comply with *Terry*.

In this case, with no attempt at an initial limited exploration for arms, Patrolman Martin thrust his hand into Sibron's pocket and took from him envelopes of heroin. His testimony shows that he was looking for narcotics, and he found them. The search was not reasonably limited in scope to the accomplishment of the only goal which might conceivably have justified its inception—the protection of the officer by disarming a potentially dangerous man. . . .

Sibron thus served as a reminder that *Terry* had not declared an "open season" for the police to seize and search people whom they considered to be "suspicious." In *Peters*, on the other hand, the Court seemed to be signaling that *Terry's* "stop and frisk" analysis would be reserved for exceptional cases and that the more traditional rationale based on probable cause, arrests, and searches incident to arrest would remain the norm. The Court ruled that "the search in Peters' case was wholly reasonable" because it "was properly incident to a lawful arrest."

. . . By the time Officer Lasky caught up with Peters on the stairway between the fourth and fifth floors of the apartment building, he had probable cause to arrest him for attempted burglary. The officer heard strange noises at his door which apparently led him to believe that someone sought to force entry. When he investigated these noises he saw two men, whom he had never seen before in his 12 years in the building, tiptoeing furtively about the hallway. They were still engaged in these maneuvers after he called the police and dressed hurriedly. And when Officer Lasky entered the hallway, the men fled down the stairs. It is difficult to conceive of stronger grounds for an arrest, short of actual eyewitness observation of criminal activity. . . .

When the policeman grabbed Peters by the collar, he abruptly 'seized' him and curtailed his freedom of movement on the basis of probable cause to believe that he was engaged in criminal activity. At that point he had the authority to search Peters, and the incident search was obviously justified 'by the need to seize weapons and other things which might be used to assault an officer or effect an escape, as well as by the need to prevent destruction of evidence of the crime.' Preston v. United States, 376 U.S. 364, 367, 84 S. Ct. 881, 883, 11 L. Ed. 2d 777 (1964). . . .

*   *   *   *   *

Terry quickly spawned a succession of follow-up cases confronting issues that had not been resolved in the Court's 1968 decision. We now consider *Terry's* progeny.

Reasonable Suspicion

Adams v. Williams, 407 U.S. 143, 92 S. Ct. 1921, 32 L. Ed. 2d 612 (1972)

Mr. Justice **Rehnquist** delivered the opinion of the Court. . . .

Police Sgt. John Connolly was alone early in the morning on car patrol duty in a high-crime area of Bridgeport, Connecticut. At approximately 2:15 a.m., a person known to Sgt. Connolly approached his cruiser and informed him that an individual seated in a nearby vehicle was carrying narcotics and had a gun at his waist.

After calling for assistance on his car radio, Sgt. Connolly approached the vehicle to investigate the informant's report. Connolly tapped on the car window and asked the occupant, Robert Williams, to open the door. When Williams rolled down the window instead, the sergeant reached into the car and removed a fully loaded revolver from Williams' waistband. The gun had not been visible to Connolly from outside the car, but it was in precisely the place indicated by the informant. Williams was then arrested by Connolly for unlawful possession of the pistol. A search incident to that arrest was conducted after other officers arrived. They found substantial quantities of heroin on Williams' person and in the car, and they found a machete and a second revolver hidden in the automobile. . . .

The Court recognized in Terry that the policeman making a reasonable investigatory stop should not be denied the opportunity to protect himself from attack by a hostile suspect. "When an officer is justified in believing that the individual whose suspicious behavior he is investigating at close range is armed and presently dangerous to the officer or to others," he may conduct a limited protective search for concealed weapons. The purpose of this limited search is not to discover evidence of crime, but to allow the officer to pursue his investigation without fear of violence, and thus the frisk for weapons might be equally necessary and reasonable, whether or not carrying a concealed weapon violated any applicable state law. So long as the officer is entitled to make a forcible

stop,[1] and has reason to believe that the suspect is armed and dangerous, he may conduct a weapons search limited in scope to this protective purpose.

Applying these principles to the present case, we believe that Sgt. Connolly acted justifiably in responding to his informant's tip. The informant was known to him personally and had provided him with information in the past. This is a stronger case than obtains in the case of an anonymous telephone tip. The informant here came forward personally to give information that was immediately verifiable at the scene. Indeed, under Connecticut law, the informant might have been subject to immediate arrest for making a false complaint had Sgt. Connolly's investigation proved the tip incorrect. Thus, while the Court's decisions indicate that this informant's unverified tip may have been insufficient for a narcotics arrest or search warrant, the information carried enough indicia of reliability to justify the officer's forcible stop of Williams.

In reaching this conclusion, we reject respondent's argument that reasonable cause for a stop and frisk can only be based on the officer's personal observation, rather than on information supplied by another person. Informants' tips, like all other clues and evidence coming to a policeman on the scene, may vary greatly in their value and reliability. One simple rule will not cover every situation. Some tips, completely lacking in indicia of reliability, would either warrant no police response or require further investigation before a forcible stop of a suspect would be authorized. But in some situations—for example, when the victim of a street crime seeks immediate police aid and gives a description of his assailant, or when a credible informant warns of a specific impending crime—the sub-

---

1. Petitioner does not contend that Williams acted voluntarily in rolling down the window of his car.

tleties of the hearsay rule should not thwart an appropriate police response.

While properly investigating the activity of a person who was reported to be carrying narcotics and a concealed weapon and who was sitting alone in a car in a high-crime area at 2:15 in the morning, Sgt. Connolly had ample reason to fear for his safety. When Williams rolled down his window, rather than complying with the policeman's request to step out of the car so that his movements could more easily be seen, the revolver allegedly at Williams' waist became an even greater threat. Under these circumstances the policeman's action in reaching to the spot where the gun was thought to be hidden constituted a limited intrusion designed to insure his safety, and we conclude that it was reasonable. The loaded gun seized as a result of this intrusion was therefore admissible at Williams' trial.

Once Sgt. Connolly had found the gun precisely where the informant had predicted, probable cause existed to arrest Williams for unlawful possession of the weapon.

* * *

In the present case the policeman found Williams in possession of a gun in precisely the place predicted by the informant. This tended to corroborate the reliability of the informant's further report of narcotics and, together with the surrounding circumstances, certainly suggested no lawful explanation for possession of the gun. Probable cause does not require the same type of specific evidence of each element of the offense as would be needed to support a conviction.

Under the circumstances surrounding Williams' possession of the gun seized by Sgt. Connolly, the arrest on the weapons charge was supported by probable cause, and the search of his person and of the car incident to that arrest was lawful. The fruits of the search were therefore properly admitted at Williams' trial. . . .

Mr. Justice **Brennan**, dissenting.

The crucial question on which this case turns, as the Court concedes, is whether, there being no contention that Williams acted voluntarily in rolling down the window of his car, the State had shown sufficient cause to justify Sgt. Connolly's "forcible" stop. I would affirm, believing, for the following reasons stated by Judge, now Chief

Judge, Friendly, dissenting, 436 F2d, at 38–39, that the State did not make that showing:

"To begin, I have the gravest hesitancy in extending [Terry v Ohio, 392 US 1, [88 S Ct 1868], 20 L Ed 2d 889 (1968)] to crimes like the possession of narcotics. . . . There is too much danger that, instead of the stop being the object and the protective frisk an incident thereto, the reverse will be true. Against that we have here the added fact of the report that Williams had a gun on his person. . . . [But] Connecticut allows its citizens to carry weapons, concealed or otherwise, at will, provided only they have a permit, Conn. Gen State §§ 29–35 and 29–38, and gives its police officers no special authority to stop for the purpose of determining whether the citizen has one. . . .

"If I am wrong in thinking that Terry should not be applied at all to mere possessory offense, . . . I would not find the combination of Officer Connolly's almost meaningless observation and the tip in this case to be sufficient justification for the intrusion. The tip suffered from a threefold defect, with each fold compounding the others. The informer was unnamed, he was not shown to have been reliable with respect to guns or narcotics, and he gave no information which demonstrated personal knowledge or—what is worse—could not readily have been manufactured by the officer after the event. To my mind, it has not been sufficiently recognized that the difference between this sort of tip and the accurate prediction of an unusual event is as important on the latter score as on the former. [In Draper v United States, 358 US 307, [79 S Ct 329, 3 L Ed 2d 327] (1959),] Narcotics Agent Marsh would hardly have been at the Denver Station at the exact moment of the arrival of the train Draper had taken from Chicago unless *someone* had told him *something* important, although the agent might later have embroidered the details to fit the observed facts. . . . There is no such guarantee of a patrolling officer's veracity when he testifies to a 'tip' from an unnamed informer saying no more than that the officer will find a gun and narcotics on a man across the street, as he later does. If the state wishes to rely on a tip of that nature to validate a stop and frisk, revelation of the name of the informer or demonstration that his name is unknown and could not reasonably have been ascertained should be the price.

"Terry v Ohio was intended to free a police officer from the rigidity of a rule that would prevent his doing anything to a man reasonably suspected of being about to commit or having just committed a crime of violence, no matter how grave the problem or impelling the need for swift action, unless the officer had what a court would later determine to be probable cause for arrest. It was meant for the serious cases of imminent danger or of harm recently perpetrated to persons or property, not the conventional ones of possessory offenses. If it is to be extended to the latter at all, this should be only where observation by the officer himself or well authenticated information shows 'that criminal activity may be afoot.' . . . I greatly fear that if the [contrary view] should be followed, Terry will have opened the sluicegates for serious and unintended erosion of the protection of the Fourth Amendment."

Mr. Justice **Marshall**, with whom Mr. Justice **Douglas** joins, dissenting. . . .

As I read Terry, an officer may act on the basis of *reliable* information short of probable cause to make a stop, and ultimately a frisk, if necessary; but, the officer may not use unreliable, unsubstantiated, conclusory hearsay to justify an invasion of liberty. Terry never meant to approve the kind of knee-jerk police reaction that we have before us in this case.

Even assuming that the officer had some legitimate reason for relying on the informant, Terry requires, before any stop and frisk is made, that the reliable information in the officer's possession demonstrate that the suspect is both armed and *dangerous*. The fact remains Connecticut specifically authorizes persons to carry guns so long as they have a permit. Thus, there was no reason for the officer to infer from anything that the informant said that the respondent was dangerous. His frisk was, therefore, illegal under Terry.

Even if I could agree with the Court that the stop and frisk in this case was proper, I could not go further and sustain the arrest, and the subsequent searches. It takes probable cause to justify an arrest and search and seizure incident thereto.

* * *

Once the officer seized the gun from respondent, it is uncontradicted that he did not ask whether respondent had a license to carry it, or whether respondent carried it for any other legal reason under Connecticut law. Rather, the officer placed him under arrest immediately and hastened to search his person. Since Connecticut has not ma[d]e it illegal for private citizens to carry guns, there is nothing in the facts of this case to warrant a man "of prudence and caution" to believe that any offense had been committed merely because respondent had a gun on his person. Any implication that respondent's silence was some sort of a tacit admission of guilt would be utterly absurd. . . .

Notes and Questions

1. *Adams v. Williams* differs from *Terry* in several respects. One of these differences involves how the police officer became suspicious of the suspect. Officer McFadden had personally observed Terry and his companions apparently casing a store for a robbery. In contrast, Officer Connolly placed substantial reliance on an informant's tip about Williams. What do we know about the informant? Is there any basis for concluding that the informant is reliable? Of what significance is it that Officer Connolly could have made an "immediate arrest for making a false complaint" had the informant led him astray?

2. Are we told how the informant acquired the information that he relayed to the officer? The lower court opinion quoted in Justice Brennan's dissent suggests that the tips supplied in *Adams v. Williams* and *Draper v. United States* are critically different. How so?

3. Since Williams already was seated and stationary when the officer approached him, when did the "stop" occur? (See footnote 1 in the Court's opinion.)

4. Did Officer Connolly conduct a pat-down of Williams's outer garments before retrieving the gun? Was the search nevertheless reasonable under *Terry*? Why?

5. Since Connecticut law at the time did not make it unlawful for a properly licensed individual to carry a concealed firearm, why was Williams's arrest lawful in the absence of some evidence that he lacked a license?

6. *Adams v. Williams*, like *Terry*, does not use the "reasonable suspicion" label to describe the standard of proof necessary to support an investigative stop. Nevertheless, "reasonable suspicion" now is commonly accepted as being required to satisfy *Terry*. This term is explicitly used in the next case.

Alabama v. White, 496 U.S. 325, 110 S. Ct. 2412, 110 L. Ed. 2d 301 (1990)

Justice **White** delivered the opinion of the Court. . . .

On April 22, 1987, at approximately 3 p.m., Corporal B. H. Davis of the Montgomery Police Department received a telephone call from an anonymous person, stating that Vanessa White would be leaving 235-C Lynwood Terrace Apartments at a particular time in a brown Plymouth station wagon with the right taillight lens broken, that she would be going to Dobey's Motel, and that she would be in possession of about an ounce of cocaine inside a brown attaché case. Corporal Davis and his partner, Corporal P. A. Reynolds, proceeded to the Lynwood Terrace Apartments. The officers saw a brown Plymouth station wagon with a broken right taillight in the parking lot in front of the 235 building. The officers observed respondent leave the 235 building, carrying nothing in her hands, and enter the station wagon. They followed the vehicle as it drove the most direct route to Dobey's Motel. When the vehicle reached the Mobile Highway, on which Dobey's Motel is located, Corporal Reynolds requested a patrol unit to stop the vehicle. The vehicle was stopped at approximately 4:18 p.m., just short of Dobey's Motel. Corporal Davis asked respondent to step to the rear of her car, where he informed her that she had been stopped because she was suspected of carrying cocaine in the vehicle. He asked if they could look for cocaine and respondent said they could look. The officers found a locked brown attaché case in the car and, upon request, respondent provided the combination to the lock. The officers found marijuana in the attaché case and

placed respondent under arrest. During processing at the station, the officers found three milligrams of cocaine in respondent's purse.

Respondent was charged in Montgomery County court with possession of marijuana and possession of cocaine. The trial court denied respondent's motion to suppress and she pleaded guilty to the charges, reserving the right to appeal the denial of her suppression motion. The Court of Criminal Appeals of Alabama held that the officers did not have the reasonable suspicion necessary under Terry v Ohio, 392 US 1, 88 S Ct 1868, 20 L Ed 2d 889 (1968), to justify the investigatory stop of respondent's car, and that the marijuana and cocaine were fruits of respondent's unconstitutional detention. . . .

Adams v. Williams, 407 US 143, 92 S Ct 1921, 32 L Ed 2d 612 (1972), sustained a Terry stop and frisk undertaken on the basis of a tip given in person by a known informant who had provided information in the past. We concluded that, while the unverified tip may have been insufficient to support an arrest or search warrant, the information carried sufficient "indicia of reliability" to justify a forcible stop. 407 US, at 147, 92 S Ct 1921, 32 L Ed 2d 612. We did not address the issue of anonymous tips in Adams, except to say that "[t]his is a stronger case than obtains in the case of an anonymous telephone tip," id., at 146, 32 L Ed 2d 612, 92 S Ct 1921.

Illinois v Gates, 462 US 213, 76 L Ed 2d 527, 103 S Ct 2317 (1983), dealt with an anonymous tip in the probable cause context. The Court there abandoned the "two-pronged test" of Aguilar v Texas, 378 US 108, 84 S Ct 1509, 12 L Ed

2d 723 (1964), and Spinelli v United States, 393 US 410, 89 S Ct 584, 21 L Ed 2d 637 (1969), in favor of a "totality of the circumstances" approach to determining whether an informant's tip establishes probable cause. Gates made clear, however, that those factors that had been considered critical under Aguilar and Spinelli— an informant's "veracity," "reliability," and "basis of knowledge"—remain "highly relevant in determining the value of his report." These factors are also relevant in the reasonable suspicion context, although allowance must be made in applying them for the lesser showing required to meet that standard.

The opinion in Gates recognized that an anonymous tip alone seldom demonstrates the informant's basis of knowledge or veracity. . . . Simply put, a tip such as this one, standing alone, would not "'warrant a man of reasonable caution in the belief' that [a stop] was appropriate." Terry, supra, at 22.

As there was in Gates, however, in this case there is more than the tip itself. The tip was not as detailed, and the corroboration was not as complete, as in Gates, but the required degree of suspicion was likewise not as high. . . .

Reasonable suspicion is a less demanding standard than probable cause not only in the sense that reasonable suspicion can be established with information that is different in quantity or content than that required to establish probable cause, but also in the sense that reasonable suspicion can arise from information that is less reliable than that required to show probable cause. . . . Reasonable suspicion, like probable cause, is dependent upon both the content of information possessed by police and its degree of reliability. Both factors—quantity and quality— are considered in the "totality of the circumstances—the whole picture," United States v Cortez, 449 US 411, 417, 101 S Ct 690, 66 L Ed 2d 621 (1981), that must be taken into account when evaluating whether there is reasonable suspicion. Thus, if a tip has a relatively low degree of reliability, more information will be required to establish the requisite quantum of suspicion than would be required if the tip were more reliable. . . .

Contrary to the court below, we conclude that when the officers stopped respondent, the anonymous tip had been sufficiently corroborated to furnish reasonable suspicion that respondent was engaged in criminal activity and that the investigative stop therefore did not violate the Fourth Amendment.

It is true that not every detail mentioned by the tipster was verified, such as the name of the woman leaving the building or the precise apartment from which she left; but the officers did corroborate that a woman left the 235 building and got into the particular vehicle that was described by the caller. With respect to the time of departure predicted by the informant, Corporal Davis testified that the caller gave a particular time when the woman would be leaving, but he did not state what that time was. He did testify that, after the call, he and his partner proceeded to the Lynwood Terrace Apartments to put the 235 building under surveillance. Given the fact that the officers proceeded to the indicated address immediately after the call and that respondent emerged not too long thereafter, it appears from the record before us that respondent's departure from the building was within the time frame predicted by the caller. As for the caller's prediction of respondent's destination it is true that the officers stopped her just short of Dobey's Motel and did not know whether she would have pulled in or continued on past it. But given that the four-mile route driven by respondent was the most direct route possible to Dobey's Motel, 550 So 2d, at 1075, but nevertheless involved several turns, we think respondent's destination was significantly corroborated.

The Court's opinion in Gates gave credit to the proposition that because an informant is shown to be right about some things, he is probably right about other facts that he has alleged, including the claim that the object of the tip is engaged in criminal activity. Thus, it is not unreasonable to conclude in this case that the independent corroboration by the police of significant aspects of the informer's predictions imparted some degree of reliability to the other allegations made by the caller.

We think it also important that, as in Gates, "the anonymous [tip] contained a range of details relating not just to easily obtained facts and conditions existing at the time of the tip, but to future actions of third parties ordinarily not easily predicted." The fact that the officers found a car precisely matching the caller's description in front of the 235 building is an example of the former. Anyone could have "predicted" that fact because it was a condition presumably existing at the time of the call. What was important was the caller's ability to predict respondent's *future behavior*, because it demonstrated inside information—a special familiarity with respondent's affairs. The general public would have had no way of knowing that respondent would shortly leave the building, get in the described car, and drive the most direct route to Dobey's Motel. Because only a small number of people are generally privy to an individual's itinerary, it is reasonable for police to believe that a person with access to such information is likely to also have access to reliable information about that individual's illegal activities. When significant aspects of the caller's predictions were verified, there was reason to believe not only that the caller was honest but also that he was well informed, at least well enough to justify the stop.

Although it is a close case, we conclude that under the totality of the circumstances the anonymous tip, as corroborated, exhibited sufficient indicia of reliability to justify the investigatory stop of respondent's car. . . .

Justice **Stevens**, with whom Justice **Brennan** and Justice **Marshall** join, dissenting.

Millions of people leave their apartments at about the same time every day carrying an attaché case and heading for a destination known to their neighbors. Usually, however, the neighbors do not know what the briefcase contains. An anonymous neighbor's prediction about somebody's time of departure and probable destination is anything but a reliable basis for assuming that the commuter is in possession of an illegal substance—particularly when the person is not even carrying the attaché case described by the tipster.

* * *

Anybody with enough knowledge about a given person to make her the target of a prank, or to harbor a grudge against her, will certainly be able to formulate a tip about her like the one predicting Vanessa White's excursion. In addition, under the Court's holding, every citizen is subject to being seized and questioned by an officer who is prepared to testify that the warrantless stop was based on an anonymous tip predicting whatever conduct the officer just observed. Fortunately, the vast majority of those in our law enforcement community would not adopt such a practice. But the Fourth Amendment was intended to protect the citizen from the overzealous and unscrupulous officer as well as from those who are conscientious and truthful. This decision makes a mockery of that protection.

I respectfully dissent.

Notes and Questions

1. In your view, does the anonymous tip in *Alabama v. White*, coupled with the police follow-up investigation, give you confidence that White was not just "the target of a prank" or was not simply being set up by someone with "a grudge against her"? Most people follow routines. Perhaps you routinely leave your residence at approximately the same time on particular days of the week to make it to one of your classes. You may even carry the same backpack or "attaché case" with you each time you go. Could an anonymous tip to the police that you were carrying contraband and that you would leave your residence with your backpack, headed toward class, at a specific time, in combination with the police's confirmation of the latter details, give the police "reasonable suspicion" to stop you?

2. Once White was stopped, under what authority did the police search her attaché case? You should be clear that the search was *not* justified as a *Terry*-type "frisk." We will consider consent searches later in this chapter.

In *United States v. Sokolow*, 490 U.S. 1, 109 S. Ct. 1581, 104 L. Ed. 2d 1 (1989), Chief Justice Rehnquist's opinion for the Court elaborated on the meaning of "reasonable suspicion."

Respondent Andrew Sokolow was stopped by Drug Enforcement Administration (DEA) agents upon his arrival at Honolulu International Airport. The agents found 1,063 grams of cocaine in his carry-on luggage. When respondent was stopped, the agents knew, inter alia, that (1) he paid $2,100 for two airplane tickets from a roll of $20 bills; (2) he traveled under a name that did not match the name under which his telephone number was listed; (3) his original destination was Miami, a source city for illicit drugs; (4) he stayed in Miami for only 48 hours, even though a round-trip flight from Honolulu to Miami takes 20 hours; (5) he appeared nervous during his trip; and (6) he checked none of his luggage. . . .

Our decision, . . . turns on whether the agents had a reasonable suspicion that respondent was engaged in wrongdoing when they encountered him on the sidewalk. In Terry v Ohio, we held that the police can stop and briefly detain a person for investigative purposes if the officer has a reasonable suspicion supported by articulable facts that criminal activity "may be afoot," even if the officer lacks probable cause.

The officer, of course, must be able to articulate something more than an "inchoate and unparticularized suspicion or 'hunch.'" The Fourth Amendment requires "some minimal level of objective justification" for making the stop. That level of suspicion is considerably less than proof of wrongdoing by a preponderance of the evidence. We have held that probable cause means "a fair probability that contraband or evidence of a crime will be found," Illinois v. Gates, 462 US 213, 238, 103 S Ct 2317, 76 L Ed 2d 527 (1983), and the level of suspicion required for a Terry stop is obviously less demanding than that for probable cause.

The concept of reasonable suspicion, like probable cause, is not "readily, or even usefully, reduced to a neat set of legal rules." . . .

In evaluating the validity of a stop such as this, we must consider "the totality of the circumstances—the whole picture." United States v Cortez, 449 US 411, 417, 101 S Ct 690, 66 L Ed 2d 621 (1981). As we said in Cortez:

"The process does not deal with hard certainties, but with probabilities. Long before the law of probabilities was articulated as such, practical people formulated certain common-sense conclusions about human behavior; jurors or fact-finders are permitted to do the same—and so are law enforcement officers." Id., at 418. . . .

Paying $2,100 in cash for two airplane tickets is out of the ordinary, and it is even more out of the ordinary to pay that sum from a roll of $20 bills containing nearly twice that amount of cash. Most business travelers, we feel confident, purchase airline tickets by credit card or check so as to have a record for tax or business purposes, and few vacationers carry with them thousands of dollars in $20 bills. We also think the agents had a reasonable ground to believe that respondent was traveling under an alias; the evidence was by no means conclusive, but it was sufficient to warrant consideration. While a trip from Honolulu to Miami, standing alone, is not a cause for any sort of suspicion, here there was more: surely few residents of Honolulu travel from that city for 20 hours to spend 48 hours in Miami during the month of July.

Any one of these factors is not by itself proof of any illegal conduct and is quite consistent with innocent travel. But we think taken together they amount to reasonable suspicion. . . .

The majority opinion observed that the DEA agents had matched Sokolow's characteristics to a "drug courier profile" but disavowed that the profile was significant to the conclusion that reasonable suspicion justified the stop. 490 U.S., at 10. Justice Marshall's dissent in *Sokolow* questioned the reliability of such profiles and criticized the police's reliance on them.

The Stop

Two key questions, in addition to whether reasonable suspicion exists, surround the definition of *Terry* stops: (1) Has the suspect been "seized" (at all), and (2) if so, does the seizure qualify as a limited "stop" or as a more intrusive "arrest?" We begin by considering the meaning of a "seizure."

California v. Hodari D., 499 U.S. 621, 111 S. Ct. 1547, 113 L. Ed. 2d 690 (1991)

Justice **Scalia** delivered the opinion of the Court.

Late one evening in April 1988, Officers Brian McColgin and Jerry Pertoso were on patrol in a high-crime area of Oakland, California. They were dressed in street clothes but wearing jackets with "Police" embossed on both front and back. Their unmarked car proceeded west on Foothill Boulevard, and turned south onto 63rd Avenue. As they rounded the corner, they saw four or five youths huddled around a small red car parked at the curb. When the youths saw the officers' car approaching they apparently panicked, and took flight. The respondent here, Hodari D., and one companion ran west through an alley; the others fled south. The red car also headed south, at a high rate of speed.

The officers were suspicious and gave chase. McColgin remained in the car and continued south on 63rd Avenue; Pertoso left the car, ran back north along 63rd, then west on Foothill Boulevard, and turned south on 62nd Avenue. Hodari, meanwhile, emerged from the alley onto 62nd and ran north. Looking behind as he ran, he did not turn and see Pertoso until the officer was almost upon him, whereupon he tossed away what appeared to be a small rock. A moment later, Pertoso tackled Hodari, handcuffed him, and radioed for assistance. Hodari was found to be carrying $130 in cash and a pager; and the rock he had discarded was found to be crack cocaine.

In the juvenile proceeding brought against him, Hodari moved to suppress the evidence relating to the cocaine. The court denied the motion without opinion. The California Court of Appeal reversed, holding that Hodari had been "seized" when he saw Officer Pertoso running towards him, that this seizure was unreasonable under the Fourth Amendment, and that the evidence of cocaine had to be suppressed as the fruit of that illegal seizure. . . .

As this case comes to us, the only issue presented is whether, at the time he dropped the drugs, Hodari had been "seized" within the meaning of the Fourth Amendment.[1] If so, respondent argues, the drugs were the fruit of that seizure and the evidence concerning them was

---

1. California conceded below that Officer Pertoso did not have the "reasonable suspicion" required to justify stopping Hodari. That it would be unreasonable to stop, for brief inquiry, young men who scatter in panic upon the mere sighting of the police is not self-evident, and arguably contradicts proverbial common sense. See Proverbs 28:1 ("The wicked flee when no man pursueth"). We do not decide that point here, but rely entirely upon the State's concession.

properly excluded. If not, the drugs were abandoned by Hodari and lawfully recovered by the police, and the evidence should have been admitted. . . .

We have long understood that the Fourth Amendment's protection against "unreasonable . . . seizures" includes seizure of the person. From the time of the founding to the present, the word "seizure" has meant a "taking possession," 2 N. Webster, An American Dictionary of the English Language 67 (1828). For most purposes at common law, the word connoted not merely grasping, or applying physical force to, the animate or inanimate object in question, but actually bringing it within physical control. . . . To constitute an arrest, however—the quintessential "seizure of the person" under our Fourth Amendment jurisprudence—the mere grasping or application of physical force with lawful authority, whether or not it succeeded in subduing the arrestee, was sufficient. . . .

To say that an arrest is effected by the slightest application of physical force, despite the arrestee's escape, is not to say that for Fourth Amendment purposes there is a *continuing* arrest during the period of fugitivity. If, for example, Pertoso had laid his hands upon Hodari to arrest him, but Hodari had broken away and had *then* cast away the cocaine, it would hardly be realistic to say that that disclosure had been made during the course of an arrest. The present case, however, is even one step further removed. It does not involve the application of any physical force; Hodari was untouched by Officer Pertoso at the time he discarded the cocaine. His defense relies instead upon the proposition that a seizure occurs "when the officer, by means of physical force *or show of authority,* has in some way restrained the liberty of a citizen." Terry v Ohio, 392 US 1, 19, n 16, 88 S Ct 1868, 20 L Ed 2d 889 (1968) (emphasis added). Hodari contends (and we accept as true for purposes of this decision) that Pertoso's pursuit qualified as a "show of authority" calling upon Hodari to halt. The narrow question before us is whether, with respect to a show of authority as with respect to application of physical force, a seizure occurs even though the subject does not yield. We hold that it does not.

The language of the Fourth Amendment, of course, cannot sustain respondent's contention. The word "seizure" readily bears the meaning of a laying on of hands or application of physical force to restrain movement, even when it is ultimately unsuccessful. . . . It does not remotely apply, however, to the prospect of a policeman yelling "Stop, in the name of the law!" at a fleeing form that continues to flee. That is no seizure.

. . . An arrest requires *either* physical force (as described above) *or,* where that is absent, *submission* to the assertion of authority.

. . . We do not think it desirable, even as a policy matter, to stretch the Fourth Amendment beyond its words and beyond the meaning of arrest, as respondent urges. Street pursuits always place the public at some risk, and compliance with police orders to stop should therefore be encouraged. Only a few of those orders, we must presume, will be without adequate basis, and since the addressee has no ready means of identifying the deficient ones it almost invariably is the responsible course to comply. Unlawful orders will not be deterred, moreover, by sanctioning through the exclusionary rule those of them that are *not* obeyed. Since policemen do not command "Stop!" expecting to be ignored, or give chase hoping to be outrun, it fully suffices to apply the deterrent to their genuine, successful seizures.

Respondent contends that his position is sustained by the so-called Mendenhall test, formulated by Justice Stewart's opinion in United States v. Mendenhall, 446 US 544, 544, 64 L Ed 2d 497, 100 S Ct 1870 (1980), and adopted by the Court in later cases, "A person has been 'seized' within the meaning of the Fourth Amendment only if, in view of all the circumstances surrounding the incident, a reasonable person would have believed that he was not free to leave." In seeking to rely upon that test here, respondent fails to read it carefully. It says that a person has been seized "only if," not that he has been seized "whenever"; it states a *necessary,* but not a *sufficient* condition for seizure—or, more precisely, for seizure effected through a "show of authority." Mendenhall established that the test for existence of a "show of authority" is an objective one: not whether the citizen perceived that he was being ordered to restrict his movement, but whether the officer's words and actions would have conveyed that to a reasonable person.

* * *

In sum, assuming that Pertoso's pursuit in the present case constituted a "show of authority" enjoining Hodari to halt, since Hodari did not comply with that injunction he was not seized until he was tackled. The cocaine abandoned while he was running was in this case not the fruit of the seizure, and his motion to exclude evidence of it was properly denied. . . .

Justice **Stevens**, with whom Justice **Marshall** joins, dissenting. . . .

For the purposes of decision, the following propositions are not in dispute. First, when Officer Pertoso began his pursuit of respondent,[4] the officer did not have a lawful basis for either stopping or arresting respondent. Second, the officer's chase amounted to a "show of force" as soon as respondent saw the officer nearly upon him. Third, the act of discarding the rock of cocaine was the direct consequence of the show of force. Fourth, as the Court correctly demonstrates, no common-law arrest occurred until the officer tackled respondent. Thus, the Court is quite right in concluding that the abandonment of the rock was not the fruit of a common-law arrest.

* * *

The decisions in Katz and Terry unequivocally reject the notion that the common law of arrest defines the limits of the term "seizure" in the Fourth Amendment. In Katz, the Court abandoned the narrow view that would have limited a seizure to a material object, and instead, held that the Fourth Amendment extended to the recording of oral statements. And in Terry, the Court abandoned its traditional view that a seizure under the Fourth Amendment required probable cause, and instead, expanded the definition of a seizure to include an investigative stop made on less than probable cause. Thus, the major premise underpinning the majority's entire analysis today—that the common law of arrest should define the term "seizure" for Fourth Amendment purposes—is seriously flawed. . . .

The Court fares no better when it tries to explain why the proper definition of the term "seizure" has been an open question until today. In Terry, in addition to stating that a seizure occurs "whenever a police officer accosts an individual and restrains his freedom to walk away," 392 US, at 16, 88 S Ct 1868, 20 L Ed 2d 889, the Court noted that a seizure occurs "when the officer, by means of physical force or show of authority, has in some way restrained the liberty of a citizen. . . ." Id., at 19, n 16. The touchstone of a seizure is the restraint of an individual's personal liberty "*in some way.*" Ibid. (emphasis added.) Today the Court's reaction to respondent's reliance on Terry is to demonstrate that in "show of force" cases no common-law arrest occurs unless the arrestee *submits.* . . .

Even though momentary, a seizure occurs whenever an objective evaluation of a police officer's show of force conveys the message that the citizen is not entirely free to leave—in other words, that his or her liberty is being restrained in a significant way.

* * *

"The 'free to leave' concept, in other words, has nothing to do with a particular suspect's choice to flee rather than submit or with his assessment of the probability of successful flight. Were it otherwise, police would be encouraged to utilize a very threatening but sufficiently slow chase as an evidence-gathering technique whenever they lack even the reasonable suspicion needed for a Terry stop." 3 W. LaFave, Search and Seizure § 9.2, p 61 (2d ed 1987, Supp 1991).

* * *

Because the facts of this case are somewhat unusual, it is appropriate to note that the same

---

4. The Court's gratuitous quotation from Proverbs 28:1, see ante, at n 1, mistakenly assumes that innocent residents have no reason to fear the sudden approach of strangers. We have previously considered, and rejected, this ivory-towered analysis of the real world for it fails to describe the experience of many residents, particularly if they are members of a minority. It has long been "a matter of common knowledge that men who are entirely innocent do sometimes fly from the scene of a crime through fear of being apprehended as the guilty parties, or from an unwillingness to appear as witnesses. Nor is it true as an accepted axiom of criminal law that 'the wicked flee when no man pursueth, but the righteous are as bold as a lion.'" Alberty v. United States, 162 US 499, 511, 16 S Ct 864, 40 L Ed 1051 (1896).

issue would arise if the show of force took the form of a command to "freeze," a warning shot, or the sound of sirens accompanied by a patrol car's flashing lights. In any of these situations, there may be a significant time interval between the initiation of the officer's show of force and the complete submission by the citizen. At least on the facts of this case, the Court concludes that the timing of the seizure is governed by the citizen's reaction, rather than by the officer's conduct. One consequence of this conclusion is that the point at which the interaction between citizen and police officer becomes a seizure occurs, not when a reasonable citizen believes he or she is no longer free to go, but rather, only after the officer exercises control over the citizen.

In my view, our interests in effective law enforcement and in personal liberty would be better served by adhering to a standard that "allows the police to determine in advance whether the conduct contemplated will implicate the Fourth Amendment." Chesternut, 486 US, at 574. The range of possible responses to a police show of force, and the multitude of problems that may arise in determining whether, and at which moment, there has been "submission," can only create uncertainty and generate litigation. . . .

It seems equally clear to me that the constitutionality of a police officer's show of force should be measured by the conditions that exist at the time of the officer's action. A search must be justified on the basis of the facts available at the time it is initiated; the subsequent discovery of evidence does not retroactively validate an unconstitutional search. The same approach should apply to seizures; the character of the citizen's response should not govern the constitutionality of the officer's conduct. . . .

In an airport setting, may a drug enforcement agent now approach a group of passengers with his gun drawn, announce a "baggage search," and rely on the passengers' reactions to justify his investigative stops? The holding of today's majority fails to recognize the coercive and intimidating nature of such behavior and creates a rule that may allow such behavior to go unchecked.

The deterrent purposes of the exclusionary rule focus on the conduct of law enforcement officers, and on discouraging improper behavior on their part, and not on the reaction of the citizen to the show of force. In the present case, if Officer Pertoso had succeeded in tackling respondent before he dropped the rock of cocaine, the rock unquestionably would have been excluded as the fruit of the officer's unlawful seizure. Instead, under the Court's logic-chopping analysis, the exclusionary rule has no application because an attempt to make an unconstitutional seizure is beyond the coverage of the Fourth Amendment, no matter how outrageous or unreasonable the officer's conduct may be. . . .

Notes and Questions

1. *United States v. Mendenhall*, 446 U.S. 544, 100 S. Ct. 1870, 64 L. Ed. 2d 497 (1980), which is discussed in *Hodari D.*, involved the following facts. Drug Enforcement Administration agents at the Detroit Airport observed Mendenhall deplane from a flight from Los Angeles. Suspicious that she was a drug courier, the agents approached Mendenhall, identified themselves, and asked to see her identification and airline ticket. The name on her ticket did not match the name on her driver's license. Mendenhall became visibly nervous. The agents returned her ticket to her and asked her to accompany them to a small office to answer some questions.

Mendenhall accompanied the agents and in the office consented to a search of her person and handbag. Drugs were found during the search. Justice Stewart's opinion, which was joined only by Justice Rehnquist and which provides the definition of "seizure" quoted in *Hodari D.*, concluded that

no "seizure" of the respondent occurred [when the DEA agents initially approached her]. The events took place in the public concourse. The agents wore no uniforms and displayed no weapons. They did not summon the respondent to their presence, but instead approached her and identified themselves as federal agents. They requested, but did not demand to see the respondent's identification and ticket. Such conduct, without more, did not amount to an intrusion upon any constitutionally protected interest. 446 U.S., at 555.

2. Assume that you are on a bus trip from Miami to Atlanta, with the bus making numerous stops at cities in between to pick up and discharge passengers. At one of those intermediary stops, two police officers board the bus and walk down its narrow aisle. The officers approach where you are seated, eye you, and then ask to inspect your ticket and see some identification. You comply, and your ticket and ID are returned to you. The officers then "explain their presence as narcotics agents on the lookout for illegal drugs" and ask permission to search your luggage. What would you do? At this point, have you been "seized" by the officers? Would you (as a reasonable person) feel "free to leave" the officer's presence? In light of the fact that you are miles away from both your starting point and your destination, where would you go? Could you even get past the officers in the bus's aisle?

These were the essential facts and issue in *Florida v. Bostick*, 501 U.S. 429, 111 S. Ct. 2382, 115 L. Ed. 2d 389 (1991). Bostick had consented to the search of his luggage, and the police had found cocaine inside of it. He subsequently argued that the consent was the product of his unlawful "seizure" by the police on the bus. The Florida Supreme Court agreed, ruling that "bus sweeps" conducted by the police in all cases constitute seizures within the meaning of the Fourth Amendment. The U.S. Supreme Court reversed, in an opinion written by Justice O'Connor.

. . . Our cases make it clear that a seizure does not occur simply because a police officer approaches an individual and asks a few questions. So long as a reasonable person would feel free "to disregard the

police and go about his business," California v Hodari D., 499 US 621, 628, 111 S Ct 1547, 113 L Ed 2d 690 (1991), the encounter is consensual and no reasonable suspicion is required. The encounter will not trigger Fourth Amendment scrutiny unless it loses its consensual nature. . . .

Here, . . . the mere fact that Bostick did not feel free to leave the bus does not mean that the police seized him. Bostick was a passenger on a bus that was scheduled to depart. He would not have felt free to leave the bus even if the police had not been present. Bostick's movements were "confined" in a sense, but this was the natural result of his decision to take the bus; it says nothing about whether or not the police conduct at issue was coercive. . . .

Accordingly, the "free to leave" analysis on which Bostick relies is inapplicable. In such a situation, the appropriate inquiry is whether a reasonable person would feel free to decline the officers' requests or otherwise terminate the encounter. . . .

The majority opinion expressed doubt that Bostick had been "seized" under this definition but remanded the case so that the Florida Supreme Court could consider the issue, applying the appropriate test. Justices Marshall, Blackmun, and Stevens dissented.

3. Some state courts have declined to adopt *Hodari D.'s* definition of a "seizure" on state constitutional grounds. Those courts generally have expressed a preference for the *Mendenhall* formulation: whether "a reasonable person would have believed that he was not free to leave." Departing from *Hodari D.*, they apply this test even when a citizen who has not been physically apprehended declines to submit to a police officer's show of authority. *See, e.g., State v. Quino*, 74 Ha. 161, 840 P.2d 358 (1992); *State v. Oquendo*, 233 Conn. 635, 613 A.2d 1300 (1992); *In re Welfare of E.D.J.*, 502 N.W.2d 779 (Minn. 1993). *See* B. Latzer, *State Constitutional Criminal Law* § 3:23 (1995).

Assuming, now, that a citizen has been "seized" within the meaning of the Fourth Amendment, when is that seizure a "stop," and when is it an "arrest"? Discriminating between a stop and an arrest can be critically important for two reasons. First, whereas a stop can be justified on reasonable suspicion, an arrest must meet the more demanding probable-cause standard. Second, as we shall consider directly, and as *Terry* makes clear, the permissible scope of a frisk falls far short of a search incident to an arrest. The issue of how and whether a brief investigative stop might be transformed into a *de facto* arrest arises in the next case.

United States v. Sharpe, 470 U.S. 675, 105 S. Ct. 1568, 84 L. Ed. 2d 605 (1985)

[While on patrol in a coastal area near the border of North Carolina and South Carolina, Agent Cooke of the Drug Enforcement Administration (DEA) spotted a blue pickup truck with an attached camper shell driving down the highway in tandem with a Pontiac. Sharpe was driving the Pontiac, and Savage was driving the pickup truck. A quilted material covered the windows of the truck, which appeared to be heavily loaded. After Agent Cooke followed the two vehicles for approximately 20 miles, he decided to make an "investigative stop" and radioed the South Carolina State Highway Patrol for assistance. Officer Thrasher, driving a marked patrol car, responded and joined the procession. Almost immediately, the Pontiac and the pickup turned off of the highway onto a campground road, maintaining a speed of 55 to 60 miles an hour, although the speed limit was 35 mph. When the vehicles eventually rejoined the highway, Officer Thrasher turned on his squad car's flashing light and motioned for Sharpe, the lead driver, to bring the Pontiac to a stop. "As Sharpe moved the Pontiac into the right lane, the pickup truck cut between the Pontiac and Thrasher's patrol car, nearly hitting the patrol car, and continued down the highway." Officer Thrasher pursued the pickup and succeeded in stopping it about one-half mile from where the Pontiac had pulled over. Agent Cooke had remained behind with the Pontiac. Cooke radioed for additional assistance, which arrived approximately 10 minutes later. Cooke thereupon joined Officer Thrasher, who had secured Savage's driver's license and the truck's vehicle registration. Savage earlier had requested permission to leave, but Officer Thrasher informed him that he was not free to do so. The remaining essential facts are reported in Chief Justice Burger's opinion for the Court.]

Agent Cooke arrived at the scene approximately 15 minutes after the truck had been stopped. Thrasher handed Cooke Savage's license and the bill of sale for the truck; Cooke noted that the bill of sale bore the same name as Sharpe's license. Cooke identified himself to Savage as a DEA agent and said that he thought the truck was loaded with marihuana. Cooke twice sought permission to search the camper, but Savage declined to give it, explaining that he was not the owner of the truck. Cooke then stepped on the rear of the truck and, observing that it did not sink any lower, confirmed his suspicion that it was probably overloaded. He put his nose against the rear window, which was covered from the inside, and reported that he could smell marihuana. Without seeking Savage's permission, Cooke removed the keys from the ignition, opened the rear of the camper, and observed a large number of burlap-wrapped bales resembling bales of marihuana that Cooke had seen in previous investigations. Agent Cooke then placed Savage under arrest and left him with Thrasher.

Cooke returned to the Pontiac and arrested Sharpe. . . . That evening, DEA agents took the truck to the Federal Building in Charleston, South Carolina. Several days later, Cooke supervised the unloading of the truck, which contained 43 bales weighing a total of 2,629 pounds. Acting without a search warrant, Cooke had eight randomly selected bales opened and sampled. Chemical tests showed that the samples were marihuana.

Sharpe and Savage were charged with possession of a controlled substance with intent to distribute it. . . . The United States District Court for the District of South Carolina denied respondents' motion to suppress the contraband, and respondents were convicted.

A divided panel of the Court of Appeals for the Fourth Circuit reversed the convictions. . . .

The Fourth Amendment is not, of course, a guarantee against *all* searches and seizures, but only against *unreasonable* searches and seizures. . . . In Terry v Ohio, we adopted a dual inquiry for evaluating the reasonableness of an investigative stop. Under this approach, we examine

"whether the officer's action was justified at its inception, and whether it was reasonably related in scope to the circumstances which justified the interference in the first place." Id., at 20.

As to the first part of this inquiry, the Court of Appeals assumed that the police had an articulable and reasonable suspicion that Sharpe and Savage were engaged in marihuana trafficking, given the setting and all the circumstances when the police attempted to stop the Pontiac and the pickup. That assumption is abundantly supported by the record.[3] As to the second part of the inquiry, however, the court concluded that the 30- to 40-minute detention of Sharpe and the 20-minute detention of Savage "failed to

meet the [Fourth Amendment's] requirement of brevity." Ibid. . . .

The Court of Appeals did not question the reasonableness of Officer Thrasher's or Agent Cooke's conduct during their detention of Savage. Rather, the court concluded that the length of the detention alone transformed it from a Terry stop into a de facto arrest. . . .

Obviously, if an investigative stop continues indefinitely, at some point it can no longer be justified as an investigative stop. But our cases impose no rigid time limitation on Terry stops. While it is clear that "the brevity of the invasion of the individual's Fourth Amendment interests is an important factor in determining whether the seizure is so minimally intrusive as to be justifiable on reasonable suspicion," United States v Place, supra, at 709, we have emphasized the need to consider the law enforcement purposes to be served by the stop as well as the time reasonably needed to effectuate those purposes. Much as a "bright line" rule would be desirable, in evaluating whether an investigative detention is unreasonable, common sense and ordinary human experience must govern over rigid criteria.

* * *

The Court of Appeals' decision would effectively establish a per se rule that a 20-minute detention is too long to be justified under the Terry doctrine. Such a result is clearly and fundamentally at odds with our approach in this area.

In assessing whether a detention is too long in duration to be justified as an investigative stop, we consider it appropriate to examine whether the police diligently pursued a means of investigation that was likely to confirm or dispel their suspicions quickly, during which time it was necessary to detain the defendant. A court making this assessment should take care to consider whether the police are acting in a swiftly developing situation, and in such cases the court should not indulge in unrealistic second-guessing. . . . A creative judge engaged in post hoc evaluation of police conduct can almost always imagine some alternative means by which the objectives of the police might have been accomplished. But "[t]he fact that the protection of the public might, in the abstract, have been accom-

---

3. Agent Cooke had observed the vehicles traveling in tandem for 20 miles in an area near the coast known to be frequented by drug traffickers. Cooke testified that pickup trucks with camper shells were often used to transport large quantities of marihuana. App. 10. Savage's pickup truck appeared to be heavily loaded, and the windows of the camper were covered with a quilted bed-sheet material rather than curtains. Finally, both vehicles took evasive actions and started speeding as soon as Officer Thrasher began following them in his marked car. See n 1, supra. Perhaps none of these facts, standing alone, would give rise to a reasonable suspicion; but taken together as appraised by an experienced law enforcement officer, they provided clear justification to stop the vehicle and pursue a limited investigation.

plished by 'less intrusive' means does not, in itself, render the search unreasonable." Cady v Dombrowski, 413 US 433, 337, 93 S Ct 2523, 37 L Ed 2d 706 (1973). The question is not simply whether some other alternative was available, but whether the police acted unreasonably in failing to recognize or to pursue it.

We readily conclude that, given the circumstances facing him, Agent Cooke pursued his investigation in a diligent and reasonable manner. During most of Savage's 20-minute detention, Cooke was attempting to contact Thrasher and enlisting the help of the local police who remained with Sharpe while Cooke left to pursue Officer Thrasher and the pickup. Once Cooke reached Officer Thrasher and Savage, he proceeded expeditiously: within the space of a few minutes, he examined Savage's driver's license and the truck's bill of sale, requested (and was denied) permission to search the truck, stepped on the rear bumper and noted that the truck did not move, confirming his suspicion that it was probably overloaded. He then detected the odor of marihuana.

Clearly this case does not involve any delay unnecessary to the legitimate investigation of the law enforcement officers. Respondents presented no evidence that the officers were dilatory in their investigation. The delay in this case was attributable almost entirely to the evasive actions of Savage, who sought to elude the police as Sharpe moved his Pontiac to the side of the road. Except for Savage's maneuvers, only a short and certainly permissible pre-arrest detention would likely have taken place. The somewhat longer detention was simply the result of a "graduate[d] . . . respons(e) to the demands of [the] particular situation," Place, supra, at 709, n 10.

We reject the contention that a 20-minute stop is unreasonable when the police have acted diligently and a suspect's actions contribute to the added delay about which he complains. The judgment of the Court of Appeals is reversed, and the case is remanded for further proceedings consistent with this opinion. . . .

Justice **Marshall**, concurring in the judgment.

I join the result in this case because only the evasive actions of the defendants here turned what otherwise would have been a permissibly brief Terry stop into the prolonged encounter now at issue. I write separately, however, because in my view the Court understates the importance of Terry's brevity requirement to the constitutionality of Terry stops.

Terry v Ohio recognized a "narrowly drawn" exception to the probable cause requirement of the Fourth Amendment for certain seizures of the person that do not rise to the level of full arrests. Two justifications supported this "major development in Fourth Amendment jurisprudence." Pennsylvania v Mimms, 434 US 115, 98 S Ct 330, 54 L Ed 2d 331 (1977) (Stevens, J., dissenting). First, a legitimate Terry stop—brief and narrowly circumscribed—was said to involve a "wholly different kind of intrusion upon individual freedom" than a traditional arrest. Terry, 392 US, at 26, 88 S Ct 1868, 20 L Ed 2d 889, 44 Ohio Ops 2d 383. Second, under some circumstances, the government's interest in preventing imminent criminal activity could be substantial enough to outweigh the still-serious privacy interests implicated by a limited Terry stop. Id., at 27. Thus, when the intrusion on the individual is minimal, and when law enforcement interests outweigh the privacy interests infringed in a Terry encounter, a stop based on objectively reasonable and articulable suspicions, rather than upon probable cause, is consistent with the Fourth Amendment.

To those who rank zealous law enforcement above all other values, it may be tempting to divorce Terry from its rationales and merge the two prongs of Terry into the single requirement that the police act reasonably under all the circumstances when they stop and investigate on less than probable cause. As long as the police are acting diligently to complete their investigation, it is difficult to maintain that law enforcement goals would better be served by releasing an individual after a brief stop than by continuing to detain him for as long as necessary to discover whether probable cause can be established. But while the preservation of order is important to any society, the "needs of law enforcement stand in constant tension with the Constitution's protections of the individual against certain exercises of official power. It is precisely the predictability of these pressures that counsels a resolute loyalty to constitutional safeguards." Almeida-Sanchez v United States, 413 US 266, 273, 93 S Ct 2535, 37 L Ed 2d 596

(1973). Terry must be justified, not because it makes law enforcement easier, but because a Terry stop does not constitute the sort of arrest that the Constitution requires be made only upon probable cause.

For this reason, in reviewing any Terry stop, the "critical threshold issue is the intrusiveness of the seizure." Regardless how efficient it may be for law enforcement officials to engage in prolonged questioning to investigate a crime, or how reasonable in light of law enforcement objectives it may be to detain a suspect until various inquiries can be made and answered, a seizure that in duration, scope, or means goes beyond the bounds of Terry cannot be reconciled with the Fourth Amendment in the absence of probable cause. Legitimate law enforcement interests that do not rise to the level of probable cause simply cannot turn an overly intrusive seizure into a constitutionally permissible one.

In my view, the length of the stop in and of itself may make the stop sufficiently intrusive to be unjustifiable in the absence of probable cause to arrest.

* * *

The Court has "declined to adopt any outside time limitation for a permissible Terry stop." While a Terry stop must be brief no matter what the needs of the authorities, I agree that Terry's brevity requirement is not to be judged by a stopwatch but rather by the facts of particular stops. At the same time, the time it takes to "briefly stop [the] person, ask questions, or check identification," and, if warranted, to conduct a brief pat-down for weapons, is typically

just a few minutes. In my view, anything beyond this short period is presumptively a de facto arrest. That presumption can be overcome by showing that a lengthier detention was not unduly *intrusive* for some reason; as in this case, for example, the suspects, rather than the police, may have prolonged the stop. It cannot, however, be overcome simply by showing that police needs required a more intrusive stop. . . .

The very least that ought to be true of Terry's brevity requirement is that, if the initial encounter provides no greater grounds for suspicion than existed before the stop, the individual must be free to leave after the few minutes permitted for the initial encounter. Such a clear rule would provide officials with necessary and desirable certainty and would adequately protects the important liberty and privacy interests upon which Terry stops infringe.

In light of these principles, I cannot join the Court's opinion. The Court offers a hodgepodge of reasons to explain why the 20 minute stop at issue here was permissible. At points we are told that the stop was no longer than "necessary" and that the police acted "diligently" in pursuing their investigation, all of which seems to suggest that, as long a stop is no longer than necessary to the "legitimate investigation of the law enforcement officers," the stop is perfectly lawful. As I have just argued, such reasoning puts the horse before the cart by failing to focus on the critical threshold question of the intrusiveness of the stop, particularly its length. . . .

[The dissenting opinions of Justices Brennan and Stevens are omitted.]

Notes and Questions

1. Could a 16-hour detention ever be considered reasonable without probable cause? In a unique context—that involving an international traveler seeking entry to this country at the border—the Supreme Court ruled that a detention of this duration was justifiable on reasonable suspicion. In *United States v. Montoya de Hernandez*, 473 U.S. 531, 105 S. Ct. 3304, 87 L. Ed. 2d 381 (1985), U.S. Customs agents detained Montoya de Hernandez on her arrival

at the Los Angeles Airport on a flight from Colombia. She possessed a large amount of cash and gave a dubious account of her presence in the country. The agents suspected that she was "a 'balloon swallower,' one who attempts to smuggle narcotics into this country hidden in her alimentary canal." Her distended abdomen lent credence to this supposition. Montoya de Hernandez was given the choice of submitting to an x-ray inspection or waiting in a room with a wastebasket and no toilet facilities until "nature took its course." The resulting 16-hour wait ended with a court-ordered physician's examination during which a balloon containing a foreign substance was removed from Montoya de Hernandez's rectum. Over the next several days, "She passed 88 balloons containing a total of 528 grams of 80% pure cocaine hydrochloride." In upholding the legality of the 16-hour detention based on reasonable suspicion, Justice Rehnquist's opinion for the Court first noted that

here the seizure of respondent took place at the international border. Since the founding of our Republic, Congress has granted the Executive plenary authority to conduct routine searches and seizures at the border, without probable cause or a warrant, in order to regulate the collection of duties and to prevent the introduction of contraband into this country. . . .

Consistently, therefore, with Congress' power to protect the Nation by stopping and examining persons entering this country, the Fourth Amendment's balance of reasonableness is qualitatively different at the international border than in the interior. Routine searches of the persons and effects of entrants are not subject to any requirement of reasonable suspicion, probable cause, or warrant. . . .

The Court recognized that neither the duration nor the degree of intrusiveness of Montoya de Hernandez's detention was "routine" but concluded that they were justified under the "reasonable suspicion" standard under the circumstances.

Here, respondent was detained incommunicado for almost 16 hours before inspectors sought a warrant; the warrant then took a number of hours to procure, through no apparent fault of the inspectors. This length of time undoubtedly exceeds any other detention we have approved under reasonable suspicion. But we have also consistently rejected hard-and-fast time limits. Sharpe, supra; Place, supra, at 709, n 10, 103 S Ct 2637, 77 L Ed 2d 110.

Instead, "common sense and ordinary human experience must govern over rigid criteria." Sharpe, supra, at 685.

The rudimentary knowledge of the human body which judges possess in common with the rest of humankind tells us that alimentary canal smuggling cannot be detected in the amount of time in which other illegal activity may be investigated through brief Terry-type stops. It presents few, if any external signs; a quick frisk will not do, nor will even a strip search. In the case of respondent the inspectors had available, as an alternative to simply awaiting her bowel movement, an x ray. They offered her the alternative of submitting herself to that procedure. But when she refused that alternative, the customs inspectors were left with only two practical alternatives: detain her for such time as necessary to confirm their suspicions, a detention which would last much longer than the typical Terry stop, or turn her loose into the interior carrying the reasonably suspected contraband drugs.

The inspectors in this case followed this former procedure. They no doubt expected that respondent, having recently disembarked from a 10-hour direct flight with a full and stiff abdomen, would produce a bowel movement without extended delay. But her visible efforts to resist the call of nature, which the court below labeled "heroic," disappointed this expectation and in turn caused her humiliation and discomfort. Our prior cases have refused to charge police with delays in investigatory detention attributable to the suspect's evasive actions, see Sharpe, supra at 687–688, and that principle applies here as well. Respondent alone was responsible for much of the duration and discomfort of the seizure.

Under these circumstances, we conclude that the detention in this case was not unreasonably long.

* * *

[Justices Brennan and Marshall dissented.]

2. The Court has given additional consideration to the permissible limits of a seizure based on reasonable suspicion in *Florida v. Royer*, 460 U.S. 491, 103 S. Ct. 1319, 75 L. Ed. 2d 229 (1983) (finding seizure unreasonable), and *United States v. Place*, 462 U.S. 696, 103 S. Ct. 2637, 77 L. Ed. 2d 110 (1983) (finding seizure of luggage unreasonable).

The Frisk

In *Terry* and *Sibron v. New York*, the Court explained that the *object* of a protective frisk must be to detect weapons and that the *scope* of a frisk initially is limited to a pat-down of the suspect's outer garments and person. However, what should an officer do if, while conducting a frisk for weapons, his or her hands detect, not a knife or a gun, but an object that feels like drugs or some other form of contraband? Furthermore, what if a frisk of the suspect's person produces no evidence of a weapon but if another area—say, the interior of a car, or a bag or a purse—is immediately accessible to the suspect and might contain a weapon? Is the officer strictly limited to frisking the suspect's person, or may the "frisk" extend as well to adjoining areas and accessible containers? The first question is addressed in *Minnesota v. Dickerson*.

Minnesota v. Dickerson, 508 U.S. 366, 113 S. Ct. 2130, 124 L. Ed. 2d 334 (1993)

Justice **White** delivered the opinion of the Court.

In this case, we consider whether the Fourth Amendment permits the seizure of contraband detected through a police officer's sense of touch during a protective patdown search.

I

On the evening of November 9, 1989, two Minneapolis police officers were patrolling an area on the city's north side in a marked squad car. At about 8:15 p.m., one of the officers observed respondent leaving a 12-unit apartment building on Morgan Avenue North. The officer, having previously responded to complaints of drug sales in the building's hallways and having executed several search warrants on the premises, considered the building to be a notorious "crack house." According to testimony credited by the trial court, respondent began walking toward the police but, upon spotting the squad car and making eye contact with one of the officers, abruptly halted and began walking in the opposite direction. His suspicion aroused, this officer watched as respondent turned and entered an alley on the other side of the apartment building. Based upon respondent's seemingly evasive actions and the fact that he had just left a building known for cocaine traffic, the officers decided to stop respondent and investigate further.

The officers pulled their squad car into the alley and ordered respondent to stop and submit to a patdown search. The search revealed no weapons, but the officer conducting the search did take an interest in a small lump in respondent's nylon jacket. The officer later testified:

> "[A]s I pat-searched the front of his body, I felt a lump, a small lump, in the front pocket. I examined it with my fingers and it slid and it felt to be a lump of crack cocaine in cellophane." Tr 9 (Feb. 20, 1990).

The officer then reached into respondent's pocket and retrieved a small plastic bag containing one fifth of one gram of crack cocaine.

Respondent was arrested and charged in Hennepin County District Court with possession of a controlled substance.

Before trial, respondent moved to suppress the cocaine. The trial court first concluded that the officers were justified under Terry v Ohio, 392 US 1, 88 S Ct 1868, 20 L Ed 2d 889 (1968), in stopping respondent to investigate whether he might be engaged in criminal activity. The court further found that the officers were justified in frisking respondent to ensure that he was not carrying a weapon. Finally, analogizing to the "plain-view" doctrine, under which officers may make a warrantless seizure of contraband found in plain view during a lawful search for other items, the trial court ruled that the officers' seizure of the cocaine did not violate the Fourth Amendment. . . .

His suppression motion having failed, respondent proceeded to trial and was found guilty.

On appeal, the Minnesota Court of Appeals reversed. . . .

The Minnesota Supreme Court affirmed. . . .

The court . . . appeared to adopt a categorical rule barring the seizure of any contraband detected by an officer through the sense of touch during a patdown search for weapons. The court further noted that "[e]ven if we recognized a 'plain feel' exception, the search in this case would not qualify" because "[t]he pat search of the defendant went far beyond what is permissible under Terry." Id., at 843 and 844, n 1. As the State Supreme Court read the record, the officer conducting the search ascertained that the lump in respondent's jacket was contraband only after probing and investigating what he certainly knew was not a weapon.

We granted certiorari, to resolve a conflict among the state and federal courts over whether contraband detected through the sense of touch during a patdown search may be admitted into evidence. We now affirm. . . .

Terry . . . held that "[w]hen an officer is justified in believing that the individual whose suspicious behavior he is investigating at close range is armed and presently dangerous to the officer or to others," the officer may conduct a patdown search "to determine whether the person is in fact carrying a weapon." 392 US, at 24. "The purpose of this limited search is not to discover evidence of crime, but to allow the officer to pur-

sue his investigation without fear of violence. . . ." Adams, supra, at 146. Rather, a protective search—permitted without a warrant and on the basis of reasonable suspicion less than probable cause—must be strictly "limited to that which is necessary for the discovery of weapons which might be used to harm the officer or others nearby." Terry, supra, at 26.

If the protective search goes beyond what is necessary to determine if the suspect is armed, it is no longer valid under Terry and its fruits will be suppressed. Sibron v New York, 392 US 40, 65–66, 20 L Ed 2d 917, 88 S Ct 1889 (1968).

These principles were settled 25 years ago when, on the same day, the Court announced its decisions in Terry and Sibron. The question presented today is whether police officers may seize nonthreatening contraband detected during a protective patdown search of the sort permitted by Terry. We think the answer is clearly that they may, so long as the officer's search stays within the bounds marked by Terry.

B

We have already held that police officers, at least under certain circumstances, may seize contraband detected during the lawful execution of a Terry search. Michigan v Long, supra. . . .

The Court in Long justified this latter holding by reference to our cases under the "plain-view" doctrine. Under that doctrine, if police are lawfully in a position from which they view an object, if its incriminating character is immediately apparent, and if the officers have a lawful right of access to the object, they may seize it without a warrant. See Horton v California, 496 US 128, 136–137, 110 S Ct 2301, 110 L Ed 2d 112 (1990).

If, however, the police lack probable cause to believe that an object in plain view is contraband without conducting some further search of the object—i.e., if "its incriminating character [is not] 'immediately apparent,'" Horton, supra, at 136, 110 S Ct 2301, 110 L Ed 2d 112—the plain-view doctrine cannot justify its seizure.

We think that this doctrine has an obvious application by analogy to cases in which an officer discovers contraband through the sense of touch during an otherwise lawful search. The rationale of the plain view doctrine is that if contraband is left in open view and is observed by a police officer from a lawful vantage point, there has been no invasion of a legitimate expectation of privacy and thus no "search" within the meaning of the Fourth Amendment—or at least no search independent of the initial intrusion that gave the officers their vantage point. The warrantless seizure of contraband that presents itself in this manner is deemed justified by the realization that resort to a neutral magistrate under such circumstances would often be impracticable and would do little to promote the objectives of the Fourth Amendment. The same can be said of tactile discoveries of contraband. If a police officer lawfully pats down a suspect's outer clothing and feels an object whose contour or mass makes its identity immediately apparent, there has been no invasion of the suspect's privacy beyond that already authorized by the officer's search for weapons; if the object is contraband, its warrantless seizure would be justified by the same practical considerations that inhere in the plain view context.

The Minnesota Supreme Court rejected an analogy to the plain-view doctrine on two grounds: first, its belief that "the sense of touch is inherently less immediate and less reliable than the sense of sight," and second, that "the sense of touch is far more intrusive into the personal privacy that is at the core of the [F]ourth [A]mendment." 481 NW2d, at 845. We have a someone different view. First, Terry itself demonstrates that the sense of touch is capable of revealing the nature of an object with sufficient reliability to support a seizure. The very premise of Terry, after all, is that officers will be able to detect the presence of weapons through the sense of touch and Terry upheld precisely such a seizure. Even if it were true that the sense of touch is generally less reliable than the sense of sight, that only suggests that officers will less often be able to justify seizures of unseen contraband. Regardless of whether the officer detects the contraband by sight or by touch, however, the Fourth Amendment's requirement that the officer have probable cause to believe that the item is contraband before seizing it ensures against excessively speculative seizures. The Court's second concern—that touch is more intrusive into privacy than is sight—is inapposite in light of the fact that the intrusion

the court fears has already been authorized by the lawful search for weapons. The seizure of an item whose identity is already known occasions no further invasion of privacy. Accordingly, the suspect's privacy interests are not advanced by a categorical rule barring the seizure of contraband plainly detected through the sense of touch.

III

It remains to apply these principles to the facts of this case. Respondent has not challenged the finding made by the trial court and affirmed by both the Court of Appeals and the State Supreme Court that the police were justified under Terry in stopping him and frisking him for weapons. Thus, the dispositive question before this Court is whether the officer who conducted the search was acting within the lawful bounds marked by Terry at the time he gained probable cause to believe that the lump in respondent's jacket was contraband. The State District Court did not make precise findings on this point, instead finding simply that the officer, after feeling "a small, hard object wrapped in plastic" in respondent's pocket, "formed the opinion that the object . . . was crack . . . cocaine." The District Court also noted that the officer made "no claim that he suspected this object to be a weapon." . . . The Minnesota Supreme Court, after "a close examination of the record," held that the officer's own testimony "belies any notion that he 'immediately'" recognized the lump as crack cocaine. See 481 NW2d, at 844. Rather, the court concluded, the officer determined that the lump was contraband only after "squeezing, sliding and otherwise manipulating the contents of the defendant's pocket"—a pocket which the officer already knew contained no weapon. Ibid.

Under the State Supreme Court's interpretation of the record before it, it is clear that the court was correct in holding that the police officer in this case overstepped the bounds of the "strictly circumscribed" search for weapons allowed under Terry. Where, as here, "an officer who is executing a valid search for one item seizes a different item," this Court rightly "has been sensitive to the danger . . . that officers will enlarge a specific authorization, furnished by a warrant or an exigency, into the equivalent of a general warrant to rummage and seize at will." Texas v Brown, 460 US, at 748 (Stevens, J., concurring in judgment). Here, the officer's continued exploration of respondent's pocket after having concluded that it contained no weapon was unrelated to "[t]he sole justification of the search [under Terry:] . . . the protection of the police officer and others nearby." 392 US, at 29. It therefore amounted to the sort of evidentiary search that Terry expressly refused to authorize, and that we have condemned in subsequent cases.

* * *

Although the officer was lawfully in a position to feel the lump in respondent's pocket, because Terry entitled him to place his hands upon

respondent's jacket, the court below determined that the incriminating character of the object was not immediately apparent to him. Rather, the officer determined that the item was contraband only after conducting a further search, one not authorized by Terry or by any other exception to the warrant requirement. Because this further search of respondent's pocket was constitutionally invalid, the seizure of the cocaine that followed is likewise unconstitutional.

For these reasons, the judgment of the Minnesota Supreme Court is affirmed.

[Chief Justice Rehnquist, joined by Justices Blackmun and Thomas, concurred in part and dissented in part, arguing that the case should be remanded for more precise findings regarding the police officer's manipulation of the lump detected in Dickerson's jacket pocket.]

Notes and Questions

1. We will consider the "plain-view" exception to the search warrant requirement, on which the "plain-touch" or "plain-feel" argument advanced in *Dickerson* was based, later in this chapter.

2. In a decision rendered just prior to *Dickerson*, the New York Court of Appeals rejected the

"plain-touch" doctrine accepted in principle by the Supreme Court in *Dickerson*. The New York Court based its decision in *People v. Diaz* on both federal and state constitutional grounds.

People v. Diaz, 81 N.Y.2d 106, 612 N.E.2d 298, 595 N.Y.S.2d 940 (1993)

Hancock, J. . . .

. . . [T]he very concept of "plain touch" is a contradiction in terms: the idea of plainness cannot logically be associated with information concerning a concealed item which is available only through the sensory perceptions of someone who touches it.

Our determination to reject the People's proposed extension of the plain view exception is compelled by practical considerations as well as logic. The identity and criminal nature of a concealed object are not likely to be discernible upon a mere touch or pat within the scope of the intrusion authorized by Terry. While in most instances seeing an object will instantly reveal

its identity and nature, touching is inherently less reliable and cannot conclusively establish an object's identity or criminal nature. Moreover, knowledge concerning an object merely from feeling it through an exterior covering is necessarily based on the police officer's expert opinion—a type of knowledge which cannot be equated with information obtained by seeing it.

Finally, an opinion of a police officer that the object touched is evidence of criminality will predictably, at least in some circumstances, require a degree of pinching, squeezing or probing beyond the limited intrusion allowed under Terry. The proposed "plain touch" exception could thus invite a blurring of the limits to Terry searches and the sanctioning of warrantless searches on information obtained from an initial intrusion which, itself, amounts to an unauthorized warrantless search (see, State v. Collins, 139 Ariz. 434, 438, 679 P.2d 80, 84 [1983] [a "plain touch" exception would "invite the use of weapons' searches as a pretext for unwarranted searches, and thus to severely erode the protection of the Fourth Amendment"]). We do not believe that such a "bootstrapping" justification for warrantless searches can be countenanced under the State or Federal Constitution. . . .

Do you think that the Supreme Court in *Dickerson* or the New York Court of Appeals in *Diaz* has the better argument about the "plain-touch" doctrine on "logical" grounds? That is, do you agree with the New York Court (and the Minnesota Supreme Court's opinion in *Dickerson*) that the sense of touch is inherently less reliable than the sense of sight? Even if it is, is it sufficiently less reliable that touching an object that does not appear to be a weapon should *never* give a law enforcement officer the right to seize it?

Are the "practical considerations" cited by the *Diaz* Court in rejecting the "plain-touch" rule more persuasive? Are the courts likely to have trouble limiting application of this rule to appropriate cases? What, precisely, did the police officer do wrong in *Dickerson*?

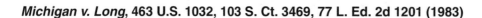

We now consider a second question relating to the proper scope of a *Terry* frisk. Assuming that a police officer reasonably may frisk the person of a suspect for weapons, must the frisk stop there, or can it ever extend to an area within the suspect's reach where a weapon could be stored, or to a purse, bag, or other container in the suspect's possession or control?

Michigan v. Long, 463 U.S. 1032, 103 S. Ct. 3469, 77 L. Ed. 2d 1201 (1983)

Justice O'CONNOR delivered the opinion of the Court. . . .

Deputies Howell and Lewis were on patrol in a rural area one evening when, shortly after midnight, they observed a car traveling erratically, and at excessive speed.[1] The officers observed the car turning down a side road, where it swerved off into a shallow ditch. The officers

---

1. It is clear, and the respondent concedes, that if the officers had arrested Long for speeding or for driving while intoxicated, they could have searched the passenger compartment under *New York v. Belton*, 453 U.S. 454, 101 S. Ct. 2860, 69 L. Ed. 2d 768 (1961), and the trunk under *United States v. Ross*, 456 U.S. 796, 102 S. Ct. 2157, 72 L. Ed. 2d 572 (1982), if they had probable cause to believe that the trunk contained contraband.

However, at oral argument, the State informed us that while Long could have been arrested for a speeding violation under Michigan law, he was not arrested because "[a]s a matter of practice," police in Michigan do not arrest for speeding violations unless "more" is involved. The officers did issue Long an appearance ticket. The petitioner also confirmed that the officers could have arrested Long for driving while intoxicated but they "would have to go through a process to make a determination as to whether the party is intoxicated and then go from that point."

The court below treated this case as involving a protective search, and not a search justified by probable cause to arrest for speeding, driving while intoxicated, or any other offense. Further, the petitioner does not argue that if probable cause to arrest exists, but the officers do not actually effect the arrest, that the police may nevertheless conduct a search as broad as those authorized by *Belton* and *Ross*. Accordingly, we do not address that issue.

stopped to investigate. Long, the only occupant of the automobile, met the deputies at the rear of the car, which was protruding from the ditch onto the road. The door on the driver's side of the vehicle was left open.

Deputy Howell requested Long to produce his operator's license, but he did not respond. After the request was repeated, Long produced his license. Long again failed to respond when Howell requested him to produce the vehicle registration. After another repeated request, Long, whom Howell thought "appeared to be under the influence of something," 413 Mich. 461, 469, 320 N.W.2d 866, 868 (1982), turned from the officers and began walking toward the open door of the vehicle. The officers followed Long and both observed a large hunting knife on the floorboard of the driver's side of the car. The officers then stopped Long's progress and subjected him to a *Terry* protective pat-down, which revealed no weapons.

Long and Deputy Lewis then stood by the rear of the vehicle while Deputy Howell shined his flashlight into the interior of the vehicle, but did not actually enter it. The purpose of Howell's action was "to search for other weapons." *Id.*, 413 Mich. at 469, 320 N.W.2d, at 868. The officer noticed that something was protruding from under the armrest on the front seat. He knelt in the vehicle and lifted the armrest. He saw an open pouch on the front seat, and upon flashing his light on the pouch, determined that it contained what appeared to be marijuana. After Deputy Howell showed the pouch and its contents to Deputy Lewis, Long was arrested for possession of marijuana. A further search of the interior of the vehicle, including the glovebox, revealed neither more contraband nor the vehicle registration. The officers decided to impound the vehicle. Deputy Howell opened the trunk, which did not have a lock, and discovered inside it approximately 75 pounds of marijuana.

The Barry County Circuit Court denied Long's motion to suppress the marijuana taken from both the interior of the car and its trunk. He was subsequently convicted of possession of marijuana. . . . The Michigan Supreme Court reversed. . . .

We granted certiorari in this case to consider the important question of the authority of a police officer to protect himself by conducting a *Terry*-type search of the passenger compartment of a motor vehicle during the lawful investigatory stop of the occupant of the vehicle. . . .

The court below held, and respondent Long contends, that Deputy Howell's entry into the vehicle cannot be justified under the principles set forth in *Terry* because "*Terry* authorized only a limited pat-down search of a *person* suspected of criminal activity" rather than a search of an area. Although *Terry* did involve the protective frisk of a person, we believe that the police action in this case is justified by the principles that we have already established in Terry and other cases.

* * *

Our past cases indicate that protection of police and others can justify protective searches when police have a reasonable belief that the suspect poses a danger, that roadside encounters between police and suspects are especially hazardous, and that danger may arise from the possible presence of weapons in the area surrounding a suspect. These principles compel our conclusion that the search of the passenger compartment of an automobile, limited to those areas in which a weapon may be placed or hidden, is permissible if the police officer possesses a reasonable belief based on "specific and articulable facts which, taken together with the rational inferences from those facts, reasonably warrant" the officers in believing that the suspect is dangerous and the suspect may gain immediate control of weapons.[14] See *Terry*, 392

---

14. We stress that our decision does not mean that the police may conduct automobile searches *whenever* they conduct an investigative stop, although the "bright line" that we drew in *Belton* clearly authorizes such a search whenever officers effect a custodial arrest. An additional interest exists in the arrest context, i.e., preservation of evidence, and this justifies an "automatic" search. However, that additional interest does not exist in the *Terry* context. A *Terry* search, "unlike a search without a warrant incident to a lawful arrest, is not justified by any need to prevent the disappearance or destruction of evidence of crime. . . . The sole justification of the search . . . is the protection of police officers and others nearby. . . ." 392 U.S., at 29, 88 S. Ct., at 1884. What we borrow now from *Chimel v. California*, 395 U.S. 752, 89 S. Ct. 2034, 23 L. Ed. 2d 685 (1969) and *Belton* is merely the recognition that part of the reason to allow area

U.S., at 21, 88 S.Ct., at 1880. "[T]he issue is whether a reasonably prudent man in the circumstances would be warranted in the belief that his safety or that of others was in danger." *Id.*, at 27, 88 S.Ct., at 1883. If a suspect is "dangerous," he is no less dangerous simply because he is not arrested. If, while conducting a legitimate *Terry* search of the interior of the automobile, the officer should, as here, discover contraband other than weapons, he clearly cannot be required to ignore the contraband, and the Fourth Amendment does not require its suppression in such circumstances.

The circumstances of this case clearly justified Deputies Howell and Lewis in their reasonable believe that Long posed a danger if he were permitted to reenter his vehicle. The hour was late and the area rural. Long was driving his automobile at excessive speed, and his car swerved into a ditch. The officers had to repeat their questions to Long, who appeared to be "under the influence" of some intoxicant. Long was not frisked until the officers observed that there was a large knife in the interior of the car into which Long was about to reenter. The subsequent search of the car was restricted to those areas to which Long would generally have immediate control, and that could contain a weapon. The trial court determined that the leather pouch containing marijuana could have contained a weapon. It is clear that the intrusion was "strictly circumscribed by the exigencies which justifi[ed] its initiation." *Terry, supra*, 392 U.S., at 26, 88 S. Ct., at 1882.

In evaluating the validity of an officer's investigative or protective conduct under *Terry*, the "[t]ouchstone of our analysis is always 'the reasonableness of all circumstances of the particular governmental intrusion of a citizen's personal security.'" *Pennsylvania v. Mimms, supra*, 434 U.S., at 108–109, 98 S. Ct., at 332–333 (quoting *Terry, supra*, 392 U.S., at 19, 88 S. Ct., at 1879). In this case, the officers did not act unreasonably in taking preventive measures to ensure that there were no other weapons within Long's immediate grasp before permitting him to reenter his automobile. Therefore, the balancing required by *Terry* clearly weighs in favor of allowing the police to conduct an area search of the passenger compartment to uncover weapons, as long as they possess an articulable and objectively reasonable belief that the suspect is potentially dangerous.

The Michigan Supreme Court appeared to believe that it was not reasonable for the officers to fear that Long could injure them, because he was effectively under their control during the investigative stop and could not get access to any weapons that might have been located in the automobile. This reasoning is mistaken in several respects. During any investigative detention, the suspect is "in the control" of the officers in the sense that he "may be briefly detained against his will. . . ." *Terry, supra*, 392 U.S., at 34, 88 S. Ct., at 1886 (WHITE, J., concurring). Just as a *Terry* suspect on the street may, despite being under the brief control of a police officer, reach into his clothing and retrieve a weapon, so might a *Terry* suspect in Long's position break away from police control and retrieve a weapon from his automobile. In addition, if the suspect is not placed under arrest, he will be permitted to reenter his automobile, and he will then have access to any weapons inside. Or, as here, the suspect may be permitted to reenter the vehicle before the *Terry* investigation is over, and again, may have access to weapons. In any event, we stress that a *Terry* investigation such as the one that occurred here, involves a police investigation "at close range," *Terry, supra*, 392 U.S., at 24, 88 S. Ct., at 1881, when the officer remains particularly vulnerable in part *because* a full custodial arrest has not been effected, and the officer must make a "quick decision as to how to protect himself and others from possible danger. . . ." *Id.*, at 28, 88 S. Ct., at 1883. In such circumstances, we have not required that officers adopt alternative means to ensure their safety in order

---

searches incident to an arrest is that the arrestee, who may not himself be armed, may be able to gain access to weapons to injure officers or others nearby, or otherwise to hinder legitimate police activity. This recognition applies as well in the *Terry* context. However, because the interest in collecting and preserving evidence is not present in the *Terry* context, we require that officers who conduct area searches during investigative detentions must do so only when they have the level of suspicion identified in *Terry*.

to avoid the intrusion involved in a *Terry* encounter.[16] . . .

Justice BRENNAN, with whom Justice MARSHALL joins, dissenting . . .

[T]he scope of a search is determined not only by reference to its purpose, but also by reference to its intrusiveness. Yet the Court today holds that a search of a car (and the containers within it) that is not even occupied by the suspect is only as intrusive as, or perhaps less intrusive than, thrusting a hand into a pocket after an initial patdown has suggested the presence of concealed objects that might be used as weapons.

The Court suggests no limit on the "area search" it now authorizes. The Court states that a "search of the passenger compartment of an automobile, limited to those areas in which a weapon may be placed or hidden, is permissible if the police officer possesses a reasonable belief based on 'specific and articulable facts which, taken together with the rational inferences from those facts, reasonably warrant' the officers to believe that the suspect is dangerous and the suspect may gain immediate control of weapons." Presumably a weapon "may be placed or hidden" anywhere in a car. A weapon also might be hidden in a container in the car. In this case, the Court upholds the officer's search of a leather pouch because it "could have contained a weapon." In addition, the Court's requirement that an officer have a reasonable suspicion that a suspect is armed and dangerous does little to check the initiation of an area search. In this case, the officers saw a hunting knife in the car, but the Court does not base its holding that the subsequent search was permissible on the ground that possession of the knife may have been illegal under state law. See *ante*, at n. 16. An individual can lawfully possess many things that can be used as weapons. A hammer, or a baseball bat, can be used as a very effective weapon. Finally, the Court relies on the following facts to conclude that the officers had a reasonable suspicion that respondent was presently dangerous: the hour was late; the area was rural; respondent had been driving at an excessive speed; he had been involved in an accident; he was not immediately responsive to the officers' questions; and he appeared to be under the influence of some intoxicant. Based on these facts, one might reasonably conclude that respondent was drunk. A drunk driver is indeed dangerous while driving, but not while stopped on the roadside by the police. Even when an intoxicated person lawfully has in his car an object that could be used as a weapon, it requires imagination to conclude that he is presently dangerous. Even assuming that the facts in this case justified the officers' initial "frisk" of respondent, they hardly provide adequate justification for a search of a suspect's car and the containers within it. This represents an intrusion not just different in degree, but in kind, from the intrusion sanctioned by *Terry*. In short, the implications of the Court's decision are frightening.

The Court also rejects the Michigan Supreme Court's view that it "was not reasonable for the officers to fear that [respondent] could injure them, because he was effectively under their control during the investigative stop and could

---

16. Long makes a number of arguments concerning the invalidity of the search of the passenger compartment. The thrust of these arguments is that *Terry* searches are limited in scope and that an area search is fundamentally inconsistent with this limited scope. We have recognized that *Terry* searches are limited insofar as they may not be conducted in the absence of an articulable suspicion that the intrusion is justified, and that they are protective in nature and limited to weapons. However, neither of these concerns is violated by our decision. To engage in an area search, which is limited to seeking weapons, the officer must have an articulable suspicion that the suspect is potentially dangerous. Long also argues that there cannot be a legitimate *Terry* search based on the discovery of the hunting knife because Long possessed that weapon legally. Assuming *arguendo* that Long possessed the knife lawfully, we have expressly rejected the view that the validity of a *Terry* search depends on whether the weapon is possessed in accordance with state law. See *Adams v. Williams, supra*, 407 U.S., at 146, . . . Justice BRENNAN suggests that we are expanding the scope of a *Terry*-type search to include a search incident to a valid arrest. However, our opinion clearly indicates that the area search that we approve is limited to a search for weapons in circumstances where the officers have a reasonable belief that the suspect is potentially dangerous to them.

not get access to any weapons that might have been located in the automobile." In this regard, the Court states: "[W]e stress that a *Terry* investigation, such as the one that occurred here, involves a police investigation at close range, . . . when the officer remains particularly vulnerable in part *because* a full custodial arrest has not been effected, and the officer must make a 'quick decision as to how to protect himself and others from possible danger.' In such circumstances, we have not required that officers adopt alternative means to ensure their safety in order to avoid the intrusion involved in a *Terry* encounter." Putting aside the fact that the search at issue here involved a far more serious intrusion than that "involved in a *Terry* encounter," and as such might suggest the need for resort to "alternative means," the Court's reasoning is perverse. The Court's argument in essence is that the *absence* of probable cause to arrest compels the conclusion that a broad search, traditionally associated in scope with a search incident to arrest, must be permitted based on reasonable suspicion. . . .

Of course, police should not be exposed to unnecessary danger in the performance of their duties. But a search of a car and the containers within it based on nothing more than reasonable suspicion, even under the circumstances present here, cannot be sustained without doing violence to the requirements of the Fourth Amendment. There is no reason in this case why the officers could not have pursued less intrusive, but equally effective, means of insuring their safety.[7]

The Court takes a long step toward "balancing" into oblivion the protections the Fourth Amendment affords. . . .

7. The police, for example, could have continued to detain respondent outside the car and asked him to tell them where his registration was. The police then could have retrieved the registration themselves. This would have resulted in an intrusion substantially less severe than the one at issue here.

Notes and Questions

1. Is there any indication that *Long's* "area-frisk" rule is limited to protective searches of automobiles? Several lower court cases have allowed the police to conduct protective frisks of personal items such as purses, knapsacks, briefcases, and other possessions within a suspect's immediate control that reasonably could contain a weapon *See, e.g., State v. Ortiz*, 67 Ha. 181, 683 P.2d 822 (1984); *Servis v. Commonwealth*, 6 Va. App. 507, 371 S.E.2d 156 (1988); *United States v. McClinnhan*, 660 F.2d 500 (D.C. Cir. 1981).

2. Note that the officers who encountered Long after he drove his car into a ditch did not initially place him under arrest. Had they done so, the search of the car's passenger compartment could have been justified on grounds other than a protective frisk for weapons. See footnote 1 of Justice O'Connor's opinion. We will consider those alternative grounds when we study *New York v. Belton*, 453 U.S. 454, 101 S. Ct. 2860, 69 L. Ed. 2d 768 (1981), later in this chapter. You should also make note that special rules apply to automobile searches; we will consider these rules in *California v. Acevedo*, 500 U.S. 565, 111 S. Ct. 1982, 114 L. Ed. 2d 619 (1991), and related cases.

3. What gave the officers in *Long* a reasonable basis for believing that he posed a danger? Would the hunting knife spotted in the car, by itself, justify the protective frisk? Is it important that "the hour was late and the area rural"? That "Long was driving his automobile at excessive speed and his car swerved into a ditch"? That Long "appeared to be 'under the influence' of some intoxicant"?

THE SEARCH WARRANT "REQUIREMENT"

We already have considered the reasons, including a portion of the history, explaining why a search warrant—issued by a neutral judicial officer, and particularly describing the place to be searched and the items to be seized—normally must issue in advance of a search to make the search legal. Although we soon will consider several exceptions to this rule, in this section we explore three important issues related to search warrants. First, we give more detailed consideration to the meaning of "probable cause." Second, we examine the warrant clause's "particularity" requirement. Finally, we consider whether the manner in which the police conduct, or "execute," a search pursuant to a warrant can render the search unreasonable.

Probable Cause To Search

Probable cause to search should be analyzed separately from probable cause to arrest. In the first place, the question "Probable cause to believe what?" has a different answer in the search and arrest contexts. As we have seen, if the question relates to an arrest, we are interested in whether probable cause exists to believe that a crime has been or is being committed and that a particular individual is responsible. In the context of searches, we want to know whether there is probable cause to believe that a seizable object is in the place to be searched.

In addition, it is possible to have probable cause to search without having probable cause to arrest. This could occur, for example, if good reason existed to believe that an individual or an organization (such as a student newspaper) had evidence of criminal activity (e.g., photographs of a campus demonstration that included criminal conduct) but was not believed to be a participant in the suspected crime. *See Zurcher v. Stanford Daily*, 436 U.S. 547, 98 S. Ct. 1970, 56 L. Ed. 2d 525 (1978).

Nevertheless, similarities also exist, particularly in how probable cause is substantiated for making an arrest or search. These principles also apply to how reasonable suspicion is determined in the context of *Terry* stops. Thus, cases like *Draper v. United States* (p. 133), *Adams v. Williams* (p. 155), and *Alabama v. White* (p. 158) already have introduced us to concepts that will be useful as we examine probable cause to search.

In the search warrant context, it is imperative that the magistrate (or judge) arrive at an *independent* judgment that there is probable cause to believe that a seizable item is located in the place to be searched. The magistrate cannot blindly rely on conclusions or inferences drawn by police officers. Accordingly, the officers who apply for a warrant *must detail the underlying facts* so that the magistrate him- or herself can determine whether probable cause exists.

A classic set of facts in which the information supplied by the police was ruled insufficient for the magistrate to reach an independent determination about probable cause was presented in *Aguilar v. Texas*, 373 U.S. 108, 84 S. Ct. 1509, 12 L. Ed. 2d 723 (1964). There, a justice of the peace had issued a search warrant on the basis of an application submitted by police officers which read, in relevant part, "Affiants have received reliable information from a credible person and do believe that heroin, marijuana, barbiturates and other narcotics and narcotic paraphernalia are being kept at the above described premises for the purpose of sale and use contrary to the provisions of the law."

For just a moment, put yourself in the shoes of the justice of the peace who has been asked to approve the search warrant in *Aguilar*. Assume that the police who filled out the sworn affidavit (the *affiants*) gave you no more information than is reported above. Remember the cardinal rule in this area: you, as the judicial officer, must be provided with sufficient underlying facts so that you personally can arrive at an independent judgment about whether probable cause exists. Does the affidavit permit you to make this decision on the basis of your own evaluation of the facts, or do you find yourself dependent on conclusions or inferences drawn by the police? For example, precisely what "information" did the police receive, and what supports the judgment that it is "reliable"? You may recall from *Draper v. United States* that probable cause may be based on hearsay. Accordingly, the police can report what they heard their informant say, and the informant need not appear before the magistrate during the warrant application process. Nevertheless, what did the police offer in *Aguilar* to substantiate their claim that a "credible" person supplied their information?

The Supreme Court ruled that the search warrant in *Aguilar* had been issued improperly. Rather than making an independent assessment of the facts necessary to supply probable cause, the justice of the peace had served "merely as a rubber stamp for the police." The justices concluded that

> although an affidavit [in support of an application for a search warrant] may be based on hearsay information and need not reflect the direct personal observation of the affiant . . . the magistrate must be informed of some of the underlying circumstances from which the informant concluded that the narcotics were where he claimed they were, and some of the underlying circumstances from which the officer concluded that the informant . . . was "credible" or his information "reliable." 378 U.S., at 114–115 (cites omitted).

This latter passage identifies two crucial components of probable-cause decisions that depend on informants' tips. The first relates to the informant's *basis of knowledge* ("the underlying circumstances from which the informant concluded that the narcotics were where he claimed they were"). The second concerns the informant's *veracity* (credibility) or *reliability* ("the underlying circumstances from which the officer concluded that the informant was 'credible' or his information 'reliable'").

Five years after deciding *Aguilar*, the Court elaborated on the probable-cause requirements for a search warrant in *Spinelli v. United States*, 393 U.S. 410, 89 S. Ct. 584, 21 L. Ed. 2d 637 (1969). The justices ruled in *Spinelli* that information supplied by an informant, even though inadequate by itself to justify issuing a search warrant, might help establish probable cause when the police independently gather information corroborating all or part of the informant's tip.

In *Spinelli*, the FBI had been "informed by a confidential reliable informant that William Spinelli is operating a handbook and accepting wagers . . . by means of the telephones which have been assigned" specified phone numbers. FBI agents then sought to verify facts supplied by the informant, since the tip was clearly inadequate under *Aguilar* to supply probable cause for a search warrant for Spinelli's apartment. They did so by confirming that Spinelli indeed operated telephones with the identified phone numbers and by tracking Spinelli's movements over a five-day period. They communicated this additional information to the magistrate when they applied for the search warrant. The Court confirmed that independent corroboration of an informant's tip by law enforcement agents is properly considered by a magistrate for determining whether probable cause exists to issue a search warrant but ruled that under the facts of Spinelli's case, the corroborative information remained insufficient to provide probable cause.

How might the corroboration of an informant's tip by the police help provide probable cause for a search warrant under *Aguilar* and *Spinelli*? Might the magistrate get a better indication that the informant was a credible source if some of the information that he or she had supplied to police panned out as being accurate? Might the magistrate reasonably conclude that, if details supplied by the informant in some respects checked out as being accurate, it would be more likely that the informant was privy to knowledge important for the issuance of a warrant?

Aguilar and *Spinelli* reigned for the next several years as the principal cases governing probable cause in the search warrant context. The "two-pronged *Aguilar-Spinelli* test" for probable cause widely was understood as requiring that the informant's basis of knowledge and veracity or reliability must *independently* meet a threshold of sufficiency before an informant's tip could be used to help establish probable cause. The following article, written by Judge Charles E. Moylan, Jr., offers a helpful explanation of the *Aguilar-Spinelli* test.

Charles E. Moylan, Jr., "*Illinois v. Gates*: What It Did and What It Did Not Do," 20 *Criminal Law Bulletin* 93, 96–98, 100–101 (1984)

---

* * *

What *Aguilar* Does

A judge in his chambers or in his kitchen deciding whether probable cause exists to justify the crossing of a threshold faces the same decisional problem that he faces in his courtroom deciding whether adequate evidence of guilt exists. In any forum and on any issue, he relies on information coming to him from the outside world. The source of information in the courtroom is generally called a witness; the source of information in the chambers or the kitchen is generally the policeman who is applying for the warrant. With respect to either type of source, the judge asks himself two fundamental questions: (1) Why should I believe him? and (2) Does he know what he is talking about? With respect to primary sources who are standing right in front of the judge in either forum, the judge assures himself as to the source's veracity by placing the source under oath, with its sanctions of perjury and possible perdition. The judge furthermore requires that those sources furnish him with firsthand facts, the raw data of their sense perception, and not pass on their bare conclusions—either as to probable cause or as to guilt or innocence. In the probable-cause setting specifically, the oath or affirmation is required by the very words of the Fourth Amendment; the prohibition against the "bare conclusion" comes from the 1933 Supreme Court decision of *Nathanson v. United States*, [290 U.S. 41, 545 S. Ct. 11, 78 L.Ed 159].

Sometimes, however, the applicant for the warrant is a mere conduit for information coming in from a secondary source: to wit, an informant. All *Aguilar* requires is that the same rules that govern the reception of information from the primary source apply also to the reception of information from this secondary source. The judge must still require satisfactory answers to those two very fundamental, and conceptually different, questions: (1) Why should I believe him? and (2) Does he know what he is talking about?

Since the secondary source (frequently, an informant) is not present before the judge, there obviously can be no administration of an oath. What is required, therefore, is simply some reasonable substitute for the oath, such as, but not limited to, a demonstrated good "track record" by the informant. This is what the so-called veracity prong is all about—the data furnished by the policeman which enable the judge to conclude that the informant is worthy of belief.

The other, "basis of knowledge," prong of *Aguilar* simply requires that the secondary source (the informant) pass on firsthand knowledge just as it has always been required that the primary source pass on firsthand knowledge. *Aguilar's* house is just as protected from the "bare conclusion" of the secondary source as *Nathanson's* house has always been protected from the "bare conclusion" of the primary source.

Shorn of its technical language, this is the simple function of the so-called two-pronged test of *Aguilar*. On the issue of probable cause, the judge is assessing information from a nonpresent, secondary source. To credit and to evaluate that information, he needs the answers to two questions.

The "Two-Pronged" Test	
Veracity	*Basis of Knowledge*
Why should I believe him?	Does he know what he is talking about?
"[T]he magistrate must be informed of . . . some of the underlying circumstances from which the officer concluded that the informant . . . was 'credible' or his information 'reliable.'"	"[T]he magistrate must be informed of some of the underlying circumstances from which the informant concluded that . . . narcotics were where he claimed they were."

Before we get to the extrinsic or supplemental satisfactions of this two-pronged test, all of which come from *Spinelli*, the simple, straightforward *Aguilar*ean analysis only requires the judge to evaluate (1) what the policeman recites *about* the informant in order to determine the informant's "veracity" and (2) the observations that come ultimately *from* the informant in order to determine the informant's "basis of knowledge.". . .

The Essential Function of *Spinelli*

In 1969, *Spinelli* not only "explicated" *Aguilar* and coined the phrase "the two-pronged test" but also supplemented *Aguilar*. It provided two buttressing devices by which the judge might repair a structural flaw in either of *Aguilar*'s prongs.

If the police officer has not told the judge enough directly about the informant to persuade the judge that the informant is worthy of belief (the veracity prong), the police may nonetheless demonstrate the informant's veracity by the technique of "independent police verification." They make their own firsthand observations, which may in some significant measure corroborate, authenticate, or verify the story told by the informant. If the police observations are sufficient in and of themselves to establish probable cause, then the informant's story is redundant and can simply be factored out. Sometimes, however, the independent observations are not enough standing alone to establish probable cause but nonetheless demonstrate that the informant's story is checking out to be the truth. To the extent to which some of the story is shown to be true, this enhances the likelihood that the remaining unverified part of the story is also

true. "Independent police verification" is simply the present-tense equivalent of a good past track record. In the latter case, the informant was shown to be truthful in the past; in the former case, the informant is being shown to be truthful in the present.

The problem with the "basis of knowledge" prong is very different. What is being guarded against is the "bare conclusion" of the informant, just as *Nathanson v. United States* guarded against the "bare conclusion" of the police affiant himself. The fundamental principle is that if either the primary source (the policeman) or the secondary source (the informant) is permitted to offer a "bare conclusion," then it is the source who is deciding that probable cause exists and not the judge. The judge would be serving simply as the rubber stamp of the source's conclusion. This delegation of authority is not permitted by the Fourth Amendment. What is required from either a primary source or a secondary source is the raw data of sense perception so that the judge can take the observations and add them up for himself. It is the judge who must decide whether the building blocks of raw data add up to probable cause.

Spinelli pointed out the further danger that an informant, if not pinned down to his own firsthand observations, might be passing on a merely underworld rumor or bit of barroom gossip. The direct way to satisfy *Aguilar* is for the story from the informant to state explicitly that the informant saw the following with his own eyes and heard the following with his own ears. This is the "basis of knowledge" prong. If those reassuring words as to firsthand observation are missing, however, *Spinelli* provided the buttressing technique of "self-verifying detail." From the very richness and fullness of the story told by the informant, the judge may sometimes infer firsthand knowledge even if he has not been given an explicit assurance in that regard. Rumors tend to be skeletal; richness of detail suggests probable firsthand knowledge. "Self-verifying detail" is simply the indirect avenue to concluding a sound "basis of knowledge" on the informant's part. . . .

* * * * *

As you read *Illinois v. Gates*, presented below, be prepared to explain how the Supreme Court modified the *Aguilar-Spinelli* test for probable cause. Also consider whether you think that this modification was necessary in light of the facts and whether it was well advised as a matter of law.

Illinois v. Gates, 462 U.S. 213, 103 S. Ct. 2317, 76 L. Ed. 2d 527 (1983)

Mr. Justice **Rehnquist** delivered the opinion of the Court. . . .

Bloomingdale, Ill., is a suburb of Chicago located in DuPage County. On May 3, 1978, the Bloomingdale Police Department received by mail an anonymous handwritten letter which read as follows:

"This letter is to inform you that you have a couple in your town who strictly make their living on selling drugs. They are Sue and Lance Gates, they live on Greenway, off Bloomingdale Rd. in the condominiums. Most of their buys are done in Florida. Sue his wife drives their car to Florida, where she leaves it to be loaded up with drugs, then Lance flys down and drives it back. Sue flys back after she drops the car off in Florida. May 3 she is driving down there again and Lance will be flying down in a few days to drive it back. At the time Lance drives the car back he has the trunk loaded with over $100,000.00 in drugs. Presently they have over $100,000.00 worth of drugs in their basement.

They brag about the fact they never have to work, and make their entire living on pushers.

I guarantee if you watch them carefully you will make a big catch. They are friends with some big drug dealers, who visit their house often.

Lance & Susan Gates
Greenway
in Condominiums

The letter was referred by the Chief of Police of the Bloomingdale Police Department to Detective Mader, who decided to pursue the tip. Mader learned, from the office of the Illinois Secretary of State, that an Illinois driver's license had been issued to one Lance Gates, residing at a stated address in Bloomingdale. He contacted a confidential informant, whose examination of certain financial records revealed a more recent address for the Gates, and he also learned from a police officer assigned to O'Hare Airport that "L. Gates" had made a reservation on Eastern Airlines flight 245 to West Palm Beach, Fla., scheduled to depart from Chicago on May 5 at 4:15 p.m.

Mader then made arrangements with an agent of the Drug Enforcement Administration for surveillance of the May 5 Eastern Airlines flight. The agent later reported to Mader that Gates had boarded the flight, and that federal agents in Florida had observed him arrive in West Palm Beach and take a taxi to the nearby Holiday Inn. They also reported that Gates went to a room registered to one Susan Gates and that, at 7:00 a.m. the next morning, Gates and an unidentified woman left the motel in a Mercury bearing Illinois license plates and drove northbound on an interstate frequently used by travelers to the Chicago area. In addition, the DEA agent informed Mader that the license plate number on the Mercury registered to a Hornet station wagon owned by Gates. The agent also advised Mader that the driving time between West Palm Beach and Bloomingdale was approximately 22 to 24 hours.

Mader signed an affidavit setting forth the foregoing facts, and submitted it to a judge of the Circuit Court of DuPage County, together with a copy of the anonymous letter. The judge of that court thereupon issued a search warrant for the Gates' residence and for their automobile. . . .

At 5:15 a.m. on March 7th, only 36 hours after he had flown out of Chicago, Lance Gates, and his wife, returned to their home in Bloomingdale, driving the car in which they had left West Palm Beach some 22 hours earlier. The Bloomingdale police were awaiting them, searched the trunk of the Mercury, and uncovered approximately 350 pounds of marijuana. A search of the Gates' home revealed marijuana, weapons, and other contraband. The Illinois Circuit Court ordered suppression of all these items, on the ground that the affidavit submitted to the Circuit Judge failed to support the necessary determination of probable cause to believe that the Gates' automobile and home contained the contraband in question. This decision was affirmed in turn by the Illinois Appellate Court and by a divided vote of the Supreme Court of Illinois.

The Illinois Supreme Court concluded—and we are inclined to agree—that, standing alone, the anonymous letter sent to the Bloomingdale Police Department would not provide the basis for a magistrate's determination that there was probable cause to believe contraband would be found in the Gates' car and home. The letter provides virtually nothing from which one might conclude that its author is either honest or his information reliable; likewise, the letter gives absolutely no indication of the basis for the writer's predictions regarding the Gates' criminal activities. Something more was required, then, before a magistrate could conclude that there was probable cause to believe that contraband would be found in the Gates' home and car.

The Illinois Supreme Court also properly recognized that Detective Mader's affidavit might be capable of supplementing the anonymous letter with information sufficient to permit a determination of probable cause. In holding that the affidavit in fact did not contain sufficient additional information to sustain a determination of probable cause, the Illinois court applied a "two-pronged test," derived from our decision in Spinelli v United States, 393 US 410, 89 S Ct

584, 21 L Ed 2d 637 (1969). The Illinois Supreme Court, like some others, apparently understood Spinelli as requiring that the anonymous letter satisfy each of two independent requirements before it could be relied on. According to this view, the letter, as supplemented by Mader's affidavit, first had to adequately reveal the "basis of knowledge" of the letter writer—the particular means by which he came by the information given in his report. Second, it had to provide facts sufficiently establishing either the "veracity" of the affiant's informant, or, alternatively, the "reliability" of the informant's report in this particular case. . . .

We agree with the Illinois Supreme Court that an informant's "veracity," "reliability" and "basis of knowledge" are all highly relevant in determining the value of his report. We do not agree, however, that these elements should be understood as entirely separate and independent requirements to be rigidly exacted in every case, which the opinion of the Supreme Court of Illinois would imply. Rather, as detailed below, they should be understood simply as closely intertwined issues that may usefully illuminate the commonsense, practical question whether there is "probable cause" to believe that contraband or evidence is located in a particular place.

This totality of the circumstances approach is far more consistent with our prior treatment of probable cause than is any rigid demand that specific "tests" be satisfied by every informant's tip. Perhaps the central teaching of our decisions bearing on the probable cause standard is that it is a "practical, nontechnical conception." Brinegar v United States, 338 US 160, 176, 69 S Ct 1302, 93 L Ed 1879 (1949). . . .

As these comments illustrate, probable cause is a fluid concept—turning on the assessment of probabilities in particular factual contexts—not readily, or even usefully, reduced to a neat set of legal rules. Informants' tips doubtless come in many shapes and sizes from many different types of persons. . . . Rigid legal rules are ill-suited to an area of such diversity. "One simple rule will not cover every situation."

Moreover, the "two-pronged test" directs analysis into two largely independent channels—the informant's "veracity" or "reliability" and his "basis of knowledge." There are persuasive arguments against according these two elements such independent status. Instead, they are better understood as relevant considerations in the totality of circumstances analysis that traditionally has guided probable cause determinations: a deficiency in one may be compensated for, in determining the overall reliability of a tip, by a strong showing as to the other, or by some other indicia of reliability.

If, for example, a particular informant is known for the unusual reliability of his predictions of certain types of criminal activities in a locality, his failure, in a particular case, to thoroughly set forth the basis of his knowledge surely should not serve as an absolute bar to a finding of probable cause based on his tip. Likewise, if an unquestionably honest citizen comes forward with a report of criminal activity—which if fabricated would subject him to criminal liability—we have found rigorous scrutiny of the basis of his knowledge unnecessary. Conversely, even if we entertain some doubt as to an informant's motives, his explicit and detailed description of alleged wrongdoing, along with a statement that the event was observed first-hand, entitles his tip to greater weight than might otherwise be the case. Unlike a totality of circumstances analysis, which permits a balanced assessment of the relative weights of all the various indicia of reliability (and unreliability) attending an informant's tip, the "two-pronged test" has encouraged an excessively technical dissection of informants' tips, with undue attention being focused on issues that cannot sensibly be divorced from the other facts presented to the magistrate. . . .

We also have recognized that affidavits "are normally drafted by nonlawyers in the midst and haste of a criminal investigation. Technical requirements of elaborate specificity once exacted under common law pleading have no proper place in this area." Ventresca, supra, 380 US, at 108, 85 S Ct 741, 13 L Ed 2d 684. Likewise, search and arrest warrants long have been issued by persons who are neither lawyers nor judges, and who certainly do not remain abreast of each judicial refinement of the nature of "probable cause." The rigorous inquiry into the Spinelli prongs and the complex superstructure of evidentiary and analytical rules that some have seen implicit in our Spinelli decision, cannot be reconciled with the fact that many warrants are—quite properly, —issued on the basis of nontechnical, common-sense judgments of laymen applying a standard less demanding than those used in more formal legal proceedings. Likewise, given the informal, often hurried context in which it must be applied, the "built-in subtleties," of the "two-pronged test" are particularly unlikely to assist magistrates in determining probable cause.

Similarly, we have repeatedly said that after-the-fact scrutiny by courts of the sufficiency of an affidavit should not take the form of de novo review. A magistrate's "determination of probable cause should be paid great deference by reviewing courts." Spinelli, supra, 393 US, at 419, 89 S Ct 584, 21 L Ed 2d 637. "A grudging or negative attitude by reviewing courts toward warrants" is inconsistent with the Fourth Amendment's strong preference for searches conducted pursuant to a warrant. . . .

If the affidavits submitted by police officers are subjected to the type of scrutiny some courts have deemed appropriate, police might well resort to warrantless searches, with the hope of relying on consent or some other exception to the warrant clause that might develop at the time of the search. In addition, the possession of a warrant by officers conducting an arrest or search greatly reduces the perception of unlawful or intrusive police conduct, by assuring "the individual whose property is searched or seized of the lawful authority of the executing officer, his need to search, and the limits of his power to search." Reflecting this preference for the warrant process, the traditional standard for review of an issuing magistrate's probable cause determination has been that so long as the magistrate had a "substantial basis for . . . conclud[ing]" that a search would uncover evidence of wrongdoing, the Fourth Amendment requires no more. We think reaffirmation of this standard better serves the purpose of encouraging recourse to the warrant procedure and is more consistent with our traditional deference to the probable cause determinations of magistrates than is the "two-pronged test."

Finally, the direction taken by decisions following Spinelli poorly serves "the most basic function of any government": "to provide for the security of the individual and of his property." Miranda v Arizona, 384 US 436, 539 (1966) (White, J., dissenting). The strictures that inevitably accompany the "two-pronged test" cannot avoid seriously impeding the task of law enforcement. If, as the Illinois Supreme Court apparently thought, that test must be rigorously applied in every case, anonymous tips would be of greatly diminished value in police work. . . .

For all these reasons, we conclude that it is wiser to abandon the "two-pronged test" established by our decisions in Aguilar and Spinelli. In its place we reaffirm the totality of the circumstances analysis that traditionally has informed probable cause determinations. The task of the issuing magistrate is simply to make a practical, common-sense decision whether, given all the circumstances set forth in the affidavit before him, including the "veracity" and "basis of knowledge" of persons supplying hearsay information, there is a fair probability that contraband or evidence of a crime will be found in a particular place. And the duty of a reviewing court is simply to ensure that the magistrate had a "substantial basis for . . . conclud[ing]" that probable cause existed. We are convinced that this flexible, easily applied standard will better achieve the accommodation of public and private interests that the Fourth Amendment requires than does the approach that has developed from Aguilar and Spinelli.

Our earlier cases illustrate the limits beyond which a magistrate may not venture in issuing a warrant. . . . Sufficient information must be presented to the magistrate to allow that official to determine probable cause; his action cannot be a mere ratification of the bare conclusions of others. In order to ensure that such an abdication of the magistrate's duty does not occur, courts must continue to conscientiously review the sufficiency of affidavits on which warrants are issued. But when we move beyond the "bare bones" affidavits present in cases such as . . . Aguilar, this area simply does not lend itself to a prescribed set of rules, like that which had developed from Spinelli. Instead, the flexible, common-sense standard . . . better serves the purpose of the Fourth Amendment's probable cause requirement. . . .

Our decisions applying the totality of circumstances analysis outlined above have consistently recognized the value of corroboration of details of an informant's tip by independent police work. . . .

Our decision in Draper v United States, 358 US 307, 79 S Ct 329, 3 L Ed 2d 327 (1959) is the classic case on the value of corroborative efforts of police officials. . . .

The showing of probable cause in the present case was fully as compelling as that in Draper. Even standing alone, the facts obtained through the independent investigation of Mader and the DEA at least suggested that the Gates were involved in drug trafficking. In addition to being a popular vacation site, Florida is well-known as a source of narcotics and other illegal drugs. Lance Gates' flight to Palm Beach, his brief, overnight stay in a motel, and apparent immediate return north to Chicago in the family car, conveniently awaiting him in West Palm Beach, is as suggestive of a pre-arranged drug run, as it is of an ordinary vacation trip.

In addition, the magistrate could rely on the anonymous letter, which had been corroborated in major part by Mader's efforts—just as had occurred in Draper. The Supreme Court of Illinois reasoned that Draper involved an informant who had given reliable information on previous occasions, while the honesty and reliability of the anonymous informant in this case were unknown to the Bloomingdale police. While this distinction might be an apt one at the time the police department received the anonymous letter, it became far less significant after Mader's independent investigative work occurred. The corroboration of the letter's predictions that the Gates' car would be in Florida, that Lance Gates would fly to Florida in the next day or so, and that he would drive the car north toward Bloomingdale all indicated, albeit not with certainty, that the informant's other assertions also were true. "Because an informant is right about some things, he is more probably right about other facts," Spinelli, supra, 393 US, at 427, 89 S Ct 584, 21 L Ed 2d 637 (White, J., concurring)—including the claim regarding the Gates' illegal activity. This may well not be the type of "reliability" or "veracity" necessary to satisfy some views of the "veracity prong" of Spinelli, but we think it suffices for the practical, common-sense judgment called for in making a probable cause determination. It is enough, for purposes of assessing probable cause, that "corroboration through other sources of information reduced the chances of a reckless or prevaricating tale," thus providing "a substantial basis for crediting the hearsay." Jones v United States, 362 US, at 269, 271.

Finally, the anonymous letter contained a range of details relating not just to easily obtained facts and conditions existing at the time of the tip, but to future actions of third parties ordinarily not easily predicted. The letter writer's accurate information as to the travel plans of each of the Gates was of a character likely obtained only from the Gates themselves, or from someone familiar with their not entirely ordinary travel plans. If the informant had access to accurate information of this type a magistrate could properly conclude that it was not unlikely that he also had access to reliable information of the Gates' alleged illegal activities.[14] Of course, the Gates' travel plans might have been learned from a talkative neighbor or travel agent; under the "two-pronged test" developed from Spinelli, the character of the details in the anonymous letter might well not permit a sufficiently clear inference regarding the letter writer's "basis of knowledge." But, as discussed previously, probable cause does not demand the certainty we associate with formal trials. It is enough that there was a fair probability that the writer of the anonymous letter had obtained his entire story either from the Gates or someone they trusted. And corroboration of major portions of the letter's predictions provides just this probability. It is apparent, therefore, that the judge issuing the warrant had a "substantial basis for . . . conclud[ing]" that probable cause to search the Gates' home and car existed. The judgment of

the Supreme Court of Illinois therefore must be reversed.

Justice **White**, concurring in the judgment.

* * *

Abandoning the "two-pronged test" of Aguilar v Texas, 378 US 108, 84 S Ct 1509, 12 L Ed 2d 723 (1964), and Spinelli v United States, 393 US 410, 89 S Ct 584, 21 L Ed 2d 637 (1969), the Court upholds the validity of the warrant under a new "totality of the circumstances" approach. Although I agree that the warrant should be upheld, I reach this conclusion in accordance with the Aguilar-Spinelli framework.

For present purposes, the Aguilar-Spinelli rules can be summed up as follows. First, an affidavit based on an informant's tip, standing alone, cannot provide probable cause for issuance of a warrant unless the tip includes information that apprises the magistrate of the informant's basis for concluding that the contraband is where he claims it is (the "basis of knowledge" prong), *and* the affiant informs the magistrate of his basis for believing that the informant is credible (the "veracity" prong).[20] Second, if a tip fails under either or both of the two prongs, probable cause may yet be established by independent police investigatory work that corroborates the tip to such an extent that it supports "both the inference that the informer

---

14. The dissent seizes on one inaccuracy in the anonymous informant's letter—its statement that Sue Gates would fly from Florida to Illinois, when in fact she drove—and argues that the probative value of the entire tip was undermined by this allegedly "material mistake." We have never required that informants used by the police be infallible, and can see no reason to impose such a requirement in this case. Probable cause, particularly when police have obtained a warrant, simply does not require the perfection the dissent finds necessary. . . .

---

20. The "veracity" prong is satisfied by a recitation in the affidavit that the informant previously supplied accurate information to the police, see McCray v Illinois, 386 US 300, 303–304, 87 S Ct 1056, 18 L Ed 2d 62 (1967), or by proof that the informant gave his information against his penal interest, see United States v Harris, 403 US 573, 583–583, 91 S Ct 2075, 29 L Ed 2d 723 (1971) (plurality opinion). The "basis of knowledge" prong is satisfied by a statement from the informant that he personally observed the criminal activity, or, if he came by the information indirectly, by a satisfactory explanation of why his sources were reliable, or, in the absence of a statement detailing the manner in which the information was gathered, by a description of the accused's criminal activity in sufficient detail that the magistrate may infer that the informant is relying on something more substantial than casual rumor or an individual's general reputation. Spinelli v United States, 393 US 410, 416, 89 S Ct 584, 21 L Ed 2d 637 (1969).

was generally trustworthy and that he made his charge on the basis of information obtained in a reliable way." Spinelli, supra, at 417. In instances where the officers rely on corroboration, the ultimate question is whether the corroborated tip "is as trustworthy as a tip which would pass Aguilar's tests without independent corroboration." Id., at 415.

In the present case, it is undisputed that the anonymous tip, by itself, did not furnish probable cause. The question is whether those portions of the affidavit describing the results of the police investigation of the respondents, when considered in light of the tip, "would permit the suspicions engendered by the informant's report to ripen into a judgment that a crime was probably being committed." Spinelli, supra, at 418. . . .

The critical issue is not whether the activities observed by the police are innocent or suspicious. Instead, the proper focus should be on whether the actions of the suspects, whatever their nature, give rise to an inference that the informant is credible and that he obtained his information in a reliable manner. . . .

As in Draper, the police investigation in the present case satisfactorily demonstrated that the informant's tip was as trustworthy as one that would alone satisfy the Aguilar tests. . . .

The Court agrees that the warrant was valid, but, in the process of reaching this conclusion, it overrules the Aguilar-Spinelli tests and replaces them with a "totality of the circumstances" standard. As shown above, it is not at all necessary to overrule Aguilar-Spinelli in order to reverse the judgment below. Therefore, because I am inclined to believe that, when applied properly, the Aguilar-Spinelli rules play an appropriate role in probable cause determinations, and because the Court's holding may foretell an evisceration of the probable cause standard, I do not join the Court's holding. . . .

I am reluctant to approve any standard that does not expressly require, as a prerequisite to issuance of a warrant, some showing of facts from which an inference may be drawn that the informant was credible and that his information was obtained in a reliable way. . . .

Justice **Brennan**, with whom Justice **Marshall** joins, dissenting. . . .

In recognition of the judiciary's role as the only effective guardian of Fourth Amendment rights, this Court has developed over the last half century a set of coherent rules governing a magistrate's consideration of a warrant application and the showings that are necessary to support a finding of probable cause. We start with the proposition that a neutral and detached magistrate, and not the police, should determine whether there is probable cause to support the issuance of a warrant.

* * *

In order to emphasize the magistrate's role as an independent arbiter of probable cause and to insure that searches or seizures are not effected on less than probable cause, the Court has insisted that police officers provide magistrates with the underlying facts and circumstances that support the officers' conclusions. . . .

The use of hearsay to support the issuance of a warrant presents special problems because informants, unlike police officers, are not regarded as presumptively reliable or honest. Moreover, the basis for an informant's conclusions is not always clear from an affidavit that merely reports those conclusions. If the conclusory allegations of a police officer are insufficient to support a finding of probable cause, surely the conclusory allegations of an informant should a fortiori be insufficient. . . .

Findings of probable cause, and attendant intrusions, should not be authorized unless there is some assurance that the information on which they are based has been obtained in a reliable way by an honest or credible person. As applied to police officers, the rules focus on the way in which the information was acquired. As applied to informants, the rules focus both on the honesty or credibility of the informant and on the reliability of the way in which the information was acquired. Insofar as it is more complicated, an evaluation of affidavits based on hearsay involves a more difficult inquiry. . . .

Aguilar and Spinelli require the police to provide magistrates with certain crucial information. They also provide structure for magistrates' probable cause inquiries. In so doing, Aguilar and Spinelli preserve the role of magistrates as independent arbiters of probable cause, insure greater accuracy in probable cause determinations, and advance the substantive value of precluding findings of probable cause, and attendant intrusions, based on anything less than information from an honest or credible person who has acquired his information in a reliable way. Neither the standards nor their effects are inconsistent with a "practical, nontechnical" conception of probable cause. Once a magistrate has determined that he has information before him that he can reasonably say has been obtained in a reliable way by a credible person, he has ample room to use his common sense and to apply a practical, nontechnical conception of probable cause. . . .

The Court also insists that the Aguilar-Spinelli standards must be abandoned because they are inconsistent with the fact that non-lawyers frequently serve as magistrates. To the contrary, the standards help to structure probable cause inquiries and, properly interpreted, may actually help a non-lawyer magistrate in making a probable cause determination. . . .

The Court's complete failure to provide any persuasive reason for rejecting Aguilar and Spinelli doubtlessly reflects impatience with what it perceives to be "overly technical" rules governing searches and seizures under the Fourth Amendment. Words such as "practical," "nontechnical," and "commonsense," as used in the Court's opinion, are but code words for an overly permissive attitude towards police practices in derogation of the rights secured by the Fourth Amendment. Everyone shares the Court's concern over the horrors of drug trafficking, but under our Constitution only measures consistent with the Fourth Amendment may be employed by government to cure this evil. . . .

* * *

Notes and Questions

1. Justices White and Brennan both seem concerned that the "practical, common-sense decision" that the Court in *Gates* encourages magistrates to make regarding whether "there is a fair probability that contraband or evidence of a crime will be found in a particular place" provides insufficient guidance to police and magistrates alike and thus undermines the interests protected by the Fourth Amendment's probable-cause requirement. Do you agree? Or do you agree with the majority that the *Aguilar-Spinelli* test was too rigid and excessively technical, and perhaps inimical to government's ability "to provide for the security of the individual and of his property"? Do these differing views suggest a clash of the "due-process" and "crime control" models of criminal procedure described in Packer in Chapter 1?

2. Several state courts essentially have agreed with the views of Justices White and Brennan and have declined on state constitutional grounds to abandon the *Aguilar-Spinelli* rule in favor of *Gates*'s test for probable cause.

See, e.g., People v. Griminger, 71 N.Y.2d 635, 524 N.E.2d 409, 529 N.Y.S.2d 55 (1988); *State v. Jacumin*, 778 S.W.2d 430 (Tenn. 1989); *Commonwealth v. Upton*, 394 Mass. 363, 476 N.E.2d 548 (1985); *State v. Jackson*, 102 Wash. 2d 432, 688 P.2d 136 (1984); *State v. Jones*, 706 P.2d 317 (Alaska 1985). *See* B. Latzer, *State Constitutional Criminal Law* § 3:13 (1995).

3. At this point, you should consider *United States v. Leon* and the good-faith exception to the exclusionary rule. *Gates* was decided one year before *Leon*. In fact, at the Court's request, the parties briefed and presented argument about whether the Court should recognize a good-faith exception to the exclusionary rule in *Gates*. Because the search warrant in *Gates* was ruled to have been properly issued, the Court declined to reach the good-faith exception issue. Now, as a practical matter, how likely is it that the *Gates* convictions would have been disturbed even if the Supreme Court had concluded that the search warrant was not supported by probable cause?

The process of applying for a search warrant is informal, frequently relies on hearsay, and requires no "hearing" at which the person whose premises or effects are the subject of the warrant has a chance to be represented and to challenge the reliability of the evidence presented or to offer any other input. Does the individual whose rights have been adversely affected by a search pursuant to a warrant ever have the opportunity to dispute the evidence on which the warrant issued—that is, to suggest that the police misrepresented the evidence, that an informant lied, or that the magistrate should not have believed the evidence supporting the warrant? In *Franks v. Delaware*, 438 U.S. 154, 98 S. Ct. 2674, 57 L. Ed. 2d 667 (1978), the Court ruled that the facts presented in an affidavit filed in connection with a search warrant application can be challenged only in exceptional circumstances. To merit a hearing to challenge the sworn information used by the police to secure a search warrant, the defendant must make "a substantial preliminary showing that a false statement knowingly and intentionally, or with reckless disregard for the truth, was included by the affiant in the warrant affidavit, and . . . [that] the allegedly false statement is necessary to the finding of probable cause." 438 U.S., at 155–156. Justice Blackmun's opinion for the Court summarized the requirements as follows:

> There is, of course, a presumption of validity with respect to the affidavit supporting the search warrant. To mandate an evidentiary hearing, the challenger's attack must be more than conclusory and must be supported by more than a mere desire to cross examine. There must be allegations of deliberate falsehood or of reckless disregard for the truth, and those allegations must be accompanied by an offer of proof.

> They should point out specifically the portion of the warrant affidavit that is claimed to be false; and they should be accompanied by a statement of supporting reasons. Affidavits or sworn or otherwise reliable statements of witnesses should be furnished, or their absence satisfactorily explained. Allegations of negligence or innocent mistake are insufficient. The deliberate falsity or reckless disregard whose impeachment is permitted today is only that of the affiant, not of any nongovernmental informant. Finally, if these requirements are met, and if, when material that is the subject of the alleged falsity or reckless disregard is set to one side, there remains sufficient content in the warrant affidavit to support a finding of probable cause, no hearing is required. On the other hand, if the remaining content is insufficient, the defendant is entitled, under the Fourth and Fourteenth Amendments, to his hearing. Whether he will prevail at that hearing is, of course, another issue. . . .

The Particularity Requirement

The Fourth Amendment states that warrants must "particularly describ[e] the place to be searched, and the persons or things to be seized." We first considered the particularity requirement in *Stanford v. Texas* (p. 89), which described the colonists' extreme distaste for general warrant and writs of assistance. Those papers essentially gave customs agents and other of the crown's executive officers *carte blanche* to search the colonists' homes and establishments. The Fourth Amendment prohibits searches from turning into unregulated fishing expeditions conducted at the whim of the executing officers by requiring that magistrates detail in warrants the things to be seized.

In *Andresen v. Maryland,* 427 U.S. 463, 96 S. Ct. 2737, 49 L. Ed. 2d 627 (1976), a judge issued a warrant authorizing the police to search the defendant's law office for a long list of itemized documents. However, the warrant concluded that the officers were directed to seize the enumerated documents, "together with other fruits, instrumentalities and evidence of crime at this [time] unknown." The defendant contended that the latter clause converted the search warrant into a general warrant, in violation of the Fourth Amendment's particularity requirement. Justice Blackmun's opinion for the Court (7–2) rejected this argument.

. . . [W]e agree with the determination of the Court of Special Appeals of Maryland that the challenged phrase must be read as authorizing only the search for and seizure of evidence relating to "the crime of false pretenses with respect to Lot 13T." The challenged phrase is not a separate sentence. Instead, it appears in each warrant at the end of a sentence containing a lengthy list of specified and particular items to be seized, all pertaining to Lot 13T. We think it is clear from the context that the term "crime" in the warrant refers only to the crime of false pretenses with respect to the sale of Lot 13T. The "other fruits" clause is one of a series that follows the colon after the word "Maryland." All clauses in the series are limited by what precedes that colon, namely, "items pertaining to . . . lot 13, block T." The warrants, accordingly, did not authorize the executing officers to conduct a search for evidence of other crimes but only to search for and seize evidence relevant to the crime of false pretenses and Lot 13T. . . .

In addition to describing with particularity the "things to be seized," a warrant also must particularly describe "the place to be searched."

Questions about this provision sometimes arise when a warrant authorizes the police to search the "premises" at a specific address, and those premises actually consist of two or more apartments or other individual dwelling units. For example, in *Maryland v. Garrison,* 480 U.S. 79, 107 S. Ct. 1013, 94 L. Ed. 2d 72 (1987), Baltimore police officers obtained a warrant to search one Lawrence McWebb and "the premises known as 2036 Park Avenue third floor apartment" for marijuana and related paraphernalia. When they applied for the warrant, the police

reasonably believed that there was only one apartment on the premises described in the warrant. In fact, the third floor was divided into two apartments, one occupied by McWebb and one by respondent. Before the officers executing the warrant became aware that they were in a separate apartment occupied by respondent, they had discovered

drugs that eventually were used to convict Garrison of a crime. Through an opinion written by Justice Stevens, the Supreme Court (6–3) upheld the warrant and the ensuing search.

In this case there is no claim that the "person or things to be seized" were inadequately described or that there was no probable cause to believe that those things might be found in "the place to be searched" as it was described in the warrant. With the benefit of hindsight, however, we now know that the description of that place was broader than appropriate because it was based on the mistaken belief that there was only one apartment on the third floor of the building at 2036 Park Avenue. The question is whether that factual mistake invalidated a warrant that undoubtedly would have been valid if it had reflected a completely accurate understanding of the building's floor plan.

Plainly, if the officers had known, or even if they should have known, that there were two separate dwelling units on the third floor of 2036 Park Avenue, they would have been obligated to exclude respondent's apartment from the scope of the requested warrant. But we must judge the constitutionality of their conduct in light of the information available to them at the time they acted. Those items of evidence that emerge after the warrant is issued have no bearing on whether or not a warrant was validly issued. Just as the discovery of contraband cannot validate a warrant invalid when issued, so is it equally clear that the discovery of facts demonstrating that a valid warrant was unnecessarily broad does not retroactively invalidate the warrant. The validity of the warrant must be assessed on the basis of the information that the officers disclosed, or had a duty to discover and to disclose, to the issuing magistrate.[10] On the basis of that information, we agree with the conclusion of all three Maryland courts that the warrant, insofar as it authorized a

search that turned out to be ambiguous in scope, was valid when it issued.

The question whether the execution of the warrant violated respondent's constitutional right to be secure in his home is somewhat less clear. We have no difficulty concluding that the officers' entry into the third-floor common area was legal; they carried a warrant for those premises, and they were accompanied by McWebb, who provided the key that they used to open the door giving access to the third-floor common area. If the officers had known, or should have known, that the third floor contained two apartments before they entered the living quarters on the third floor, and thus had been aware of the error in the warrant, they would have been obligated to limit their search to McWebb's apartment. Moreover, as the officers recognized, they were required to discontinue the search of respondent's apartment as soon as they discovered that there were two separate units on the third floor and therefore were put on notice of the risk that they might be in a unit erroneously included within the terms of the warrant. The officers' conduct and the limits of the search were based on the information available as the search proceeded. While the purposes justifying a police search strictly limit the permissible extent of the search, the Court has also recognized the need to allow some latitude for honest mistakes that are made by officers in the dangerous and difficult process of making arrests and executing search warrants. . . .

. . . [T]he validity of the search of respondent's apartment pursuant to a warrant authorizing the search of the entire third floor depends on whether the officers' failure to realize the overbreadth of the warrant was objectively understandable and reasonable. Here it unquestionably was. The objective facts available to the officers at the time suggested no distinction between McWebb's apartment and the third-floor premises.

---

10. Arguments can certainly be made that the police in this case should have been able to ascertain that there was more than one apartment on the third floor of this building. It contained seven separate dwelling units and it was surely possible that two of them might be on the third floor. But the record also establishes that Officer Marcus made specific inquiries to determine the identity of the occupants of the third floor premises. The officer went to 2036 Park Avenue and found that it matched the description given by the informant: a three-story brick dwelling with the numerals 2-0-3-6 affixed to the front of the premises. App 7. The officer "made a check with the Baltimore Gas and Electric Company and discovered that the premises of 2036 Park Ave. third floor was in the name of Lawrence McWebb." Ibid. Officer Marcus testified at the suppression hearing that he inquired of the Baltimore Gas and Electric Company in whose name the third floor apartment was listed: "I asked if there is a front or rear or middle room. They told me, one third floor was only listed to Lawrence McWebb." Id., at 36–38. The officer also discovered from a check with the Baltimore Police Department that the police records of Lawrence McWebb matched the address and physical description given by the informant. . . .

For that reason, the officers properly responded to the command contained in a valid warrant even if the warrant is interpreted as authorizing a search limited to McWebb's apartment rather than the entire third floor. Prior to the officers' discovery of the factual mistake, they perceived McWebb's apartment and the third-floor premises as one and the same; therefore their execution of the warrant reasonably included the entire third floor.[13] Under either interpretation of the warrant, the officers' conduct was consistent with a reasonable effort to ascertain and identify the place intended to be searched within the meaning of the Fourth Amendment. . . .

The general rule regarding the requirement for a particular description of the place to be searched is that it "is enough if the description is such that the officer with a search warrant can, with reasonable effort, ascertain and identify the place intended." *Steele v. United States*, 267 U.S. 498, 503, 45 S. Ct. 414, 69 L. Ed. 757 (1925).

Execution of a Search Warrant

Even if a search warrant is supported by probable cause and particularly describes the place to be searched and things to be seized, the manner in which the search is conducted can present nettlesome issues. For example, what if a properly issued warrant authorizes the seizure of a named item (e.g., drugs), but if, while searching for that item, the police discover a different one (e.g., an explosive device) that is not named in the warrant? May the police seize the unnamed item, or must they ignore it because its seizure is not authorized by the search warrant? We will confront this issue when we discuss the "plain-view" exception to the warrant requirement in the next section.

Sometimes, search warrants become "stale." For example, a warrant signed in January authorizing the search of a dwelling for illegal drugs may be hopelessly outdated if the police delay until April to conduct the search. Even if probable cause existed to believe that illegal drugs were in the named residence when the warrant issued, there may be no basis to assume that the drugs remain there several months later. Although the Fourth Amendment imposes no inflexible time limit defining when a delay between the issuance and execution of a search warrant is "unreasonable," statutes in many jurisdictions dictate that search warrants remain valid no longer than a fixed period after they are signed. *See, e.g.*, Federal Rule of Criminal Procedure 41(c)(1) (search warrant shall command the officer to search "within a specified period of time not to exceed 10 days").

📖 *Legal Research Note.* How would you find whether a statute in your state fixes a time within which a search warrant must be executed? This should be a relatively simple process. First, locate the statute books for your state. Use the "General Index" accompanying the statutes to look up "warrants," "search warrants," "search and seizure," or perhaps some broader subject, such as "criminal procedure," with a subtopic "warrant" or "search warrant." Then look for a specific appropriate subtopic, such as "execution" or "time limitations." You should be referred to the sections of the statutes or rules of criminal procedure that deal generally with search warrants. With a bit of luck, you may be directed to the specific section governing the maximum time that can transpire between issuance and execution of the warrant. After you read the applicable statute or rule, check the pocket part to see if the section has

---

13. We expressly distinguish the facts of this case from a situation in which the police know there are two apartments on a certain floor of a building, and have probable cause to believe that drugs are being sold out of that floor, but do not know in which of the two apartments the illegal transactions are taking place. A search pursuant to a warrant authorizing a search of the entire floor under those circumstances could present quite different issues from the ones before us in this case.

been changed or repealed. You also can read the accompanying "annotations," which provide brief descriptions of and citations to cases that have interpreted or applied the statute or rule.

Let's try to find out if there is a statutory time limit in Illinois for the execution of a search warrant. We begin by consulting the *General Index* for *West's Smith-Hurd Illinois Compiled Statutes Annotated.* This index is arranged alphabetically by subject. When we look under "search warrant," the index directs us to "searches and seizures, this index." One of the many subtopics under "searches and seizures" is "warrants." "Warrants" also has scores of subtopics, one of which is "execution." We are referred to two statutory sections in connection with this subtopic—725 ILCS 5/108-5 and 725 ILCS 5/108-6.

Although Illinois's numbering system is a bit more complicated than some other states, it is not difficult to locate the named sections of the Illinois Compiled Statutes Annotated. The spines of the statute book are numbered, and it is easy to find the volume with "Chapter 725 1/1 to 5/108." We want to locate Chapter 725, section 5/108-5 and section 5/108-6, and read those two provisions. The latter one states, in part, that "the [search] warrant shall be executed within 96 hours from the time of issuance." The pocket part reveals no changes in the legislation. Accompanying commentary and case annotations are available, if you wish to find out more about this statute. Note that the 96-hour (four-day) time limit is significantly shorter than the 10-day period fixed by the federal rule.

*   *   *   *   *

Many statutes also require that search warrants be executed during daytime hours (e.g., 6:00 a.m. through 10:00 p.m.) unless the issuing judge or magistrate specifically approved of a nighttime search. *See, e.g.,* Federal Rule of Criminal Procedure 41(c)(1), (h). In *Gooding v. United States,* 416 U.S. 430, 94 S. Ct. 1780, 40 L. Ed. 2d 250 (1974), the Supreme Court ruled that a federal statute governing searches for controlled substances "requires no special showing for a nighttime search, other than a showing that the contraband is likely to be on the property or person to be searched at that time." 416 U.S., at 458. Justice Marshall's dissenting opinion protested that "the intrusion upon privacy engendered by a search of a residence at night is of an order of magnitude greater than that produced by an ordinary search." 416 U.S., at 463. He suggested that the Constitution might even require "a showing of additional justification for a search [of a private home during nighttime] over and above the ordinary showing of probable cause." 416 U.S., at 465. He noted that "this constitutional question is not presented in this case and need not be resolved here." *Id.*

*   *   *   *   *

Assume that the police have reason to believe that an individual has illegal drugs in the form of pills in his or her home and that they secure a warrant authorizing a search of the home for the pills. How should they go about executing the warrant? What might happen to the drugs if they knock on the door, identify themselves as police officers, and announce that they have a search warrant for the premises? On the other hand, what might happen if they simply burst through the door unannounced in an attempt to surprise the resident? What if the police have reason to believe that the resident might be armed? Would that possibility make a "no-knock" entry more advisable or less advisable? Does the way in which the police gain entry to a dwelling under the authority of a search warrant affect the "reasonableness" of the search? The Court confronted this general question in *Wilson v. Arkansas.*

Wilson v. Arkansas, 514 U.S. 927, 115 S. Ct. 1914, 131 L. Ed. 2d 976 (1995)

Justice **Thomas** delivered the opinion of the Court.

At the time of the framing, the common law of search and seizure recognized a law enforcement officer's authority to break open the doors of a dwelling, but generally indicated that he first ought to announce his presence and authority. In this case, we hold that this common-law "knock and announce" principle forms a part of the reasonableness inquiry under the Fourth Amendment.

I

During November and December 1992, petitioner Sharlene Wilson made a series of narcotics sales to an informant acting at the direction of the Arkansas State Police. In late November, the informant purchased marijuana and methamphetamine at the home that petitioner shared with Bryson Jacobs. On December 30, the informant telephoned petitioner at her home and arranged to meet her at a local store to buy some marijuana. According to testimony presented below, petitioner produced a semiautomatic pistol at this meeting and waved it in the informant's face, threatening to kill her if she turned out to be working for the police. Petitioner then sold the informant a bag of marijuana.

The next day, police officers applied for and obtained warrants to search petitioner's home and to arrest both petitioner and Jacobs. Affidavits filed in support of the warrants set forth the details of the narcotics transactions and stated that Jacobs had previously been convicted of arson and firebombing. The search was conducted later that afternoon. Police officers found the main door to petitioner's home open. While opening an unlocked screen door and entering the residence, they identified themselves as police officers and stated that they had a warrant. Once inside the home, the officers seized marijuana, methamphetamine, valium, narcotics paraphernalia, a gun, and ammunition. They also found petitioner in the bathroom, flushing marijuana down the toilet. Petitioner and Jacobs

were arrested and charged with the delivery of marijuana, delivery of methamphetamine, possession of drug paraphernalia, and possession of marijuana.

Before trial, petitioner filed a motion to suppress the evidence seized during the search. Petitioner asserted that the search was invalid on various grounds, including that the officers had failed to "knock and announce" before entering her home. The trial court summarily denied the suppression motion. After a jury trial, petitioner was convicted of all charges and sentenced to 32 years in prison.

The Arkansas Supreme Court affirmed petitioner's conviction on appeal. 317 Ark. 548, 878 SW2d 755 (1994). The court noted that "the officers entered the home *while they were identifying themselves*," but it rejected petitioner's argument that "the Fourth Amendment requires officers to knock and announce prior to entering the residence." *Id.*, at 553, 878 SW2d, at 758 (emphasis added). Finding "no authority for [petitioner's] theory that the knock and announce principle is required by the Fourth Amendment," the court concluded that neither Arkansas law nor the Fourth Amendment required suppression of the evidence. *Ibid.*

We granted certiorari to resolve the conflict among the lower courts as to whether the common-law knock-and-announce principle forms a part of the Fourth Amendment reasonableness inquiry. We hold that it does, and accordingly reverse and remand.

II

The Fourth Amendment to the Constitution protects "[t]he right of the people to be secure in their persons, houses, papers, and effects, against unreasonable searches and seizures." In evaluating the scope of this right, we have looked to the traditional protections against unreasonable searches and seizures afforded by the common law at the time of the framing. "Although the underlying command of the Fourth Amendment is always that searches and seizures be reasonable," *New Jersey v T.L.O.*, 469 US 325, 337, 105 S Ct 733, 83 L Ed 2d 720 (1985), our effort to give content to this term may be guided by the meaning ascribed to it by the Framers of the Amendment. An examination of the common law of search and seizure leaves no doubt that the reasonableness of a search of a dwelling may depend in part on whether law enforcement officers announced their presence and authority prior to entering.

Although the common law generally protected a man's house as "his castle of defence and asylym," 3 W Blackstone, Commentaries (hereinafter Blackstone), common-law courts long have held that "when the King is party, the sheriff (if the doors be not open) may break the party's house, either to arrest him, or to do other execution of the K[ing]'s process, if otherwise he cannot enter." *Semayne's Case*, 5 Co Rep 91a, 91b, 77 Eng Rep 194, 195 (KB 1603). To this rule, however, common-law courts appended an important qualification:

"But before he breaks it, he ought to signify the cause of his coming, and to make request to open doors. . . , for the law without a default in the owner abhors the destruction or breaking of any house (which is for the habitation and safety of man) by which great damage and inconvenience might ensue to the party, when no default is in him; for perhaps he did not know of the process, of which, if he had notice, it is to be presumed that he would obey it. . . ." *Ibid.*, 77 Eng Rep, at 195–196. . . .

Several prominent founding-era commentators agreed on this basic principle. According to Sir Matthew Hale, the "constant practice" at common law was that "the officer may break open the door, if he be sure the offender is there, if after acquainting them of the business, and demanding the prisoner, he refuses to open the door." See 1 M. Hale, Pleas of the Crown *582. . . .

The common-law knock-and-announce principle was woven quickly into the fabric of early American law. Most of the States that ratified the Fourth Amendment had enacted constitutional provisions or statutes generally incorporating English common law, . . . and a few States had enacted statutes specifically embracing the common-law view that the breaking of the door of a dwelling was permitted once admittance was refused. . . . Early American courts similarly embraced the common-law knock-and-announce principle.

Our own cases have acknowledged that the common-law principle of announcement is "embedded in Anglo-American law," *Miller v United States*, 357 US 301, 313, 78 S Ct 1190, 2 L Ed 2d 1332 (1958), but we have never squarely held that this principle is an element of the reasonableness inquiry under the Fourth Amendment. We now so hold. Given the long-standing common-law endorsement of the practice of announcement, we have little doubt that the Framers of the Fourth Amendment thought that the method of an officer's entry into a dwelling was among the factors to be considered in assessing the reasonableness of a search or seizure. Contrary to the decision below, we hold that in some circumstances an officer's unannounced entry into a home might be unreasonable under the Fourth Amendment.

This is not to say, of course, that every entry must be preceded by an announcement. The Fourth Amendment's flexible requirement of reasonableness should not be read to mandate a rigid rule of announcement that ignores countervailing law enforcement interests. As even petitioner concedes, the common-law principle of announcement was never stated as an inflexible rule requiring announcement under all circumstances. . . .

Indeed, at the time of the framing, the common-law admonition that an officer "ought to signify the cause of his coming," *Semayne's Case*, 5 Co Rep, at 91b, 77 Eng Rep, at 195, had not been extended conclusively to the context of felony arrests. . . .

The common-law principle gradually was applied to cases involving felonies, but at the same time the courts continued to recognize that under certain circumstances the presumption in favor of announcement necessarily would give way to contrary considerations.

Thus, because the common-law rule was justified in part by the belief that announcement generally would avoid "the destruction or breaking of any house . . . by which great damage and inconvenience might ensue," *Semayne's Case, supra*, at 91b, 77 Eng Rep, at 196, courts acknowledged that the presumption in favor of announcement would yield under circumstances presenting a threat of physical violence. . . .

Similarly, courts held that an officer may dispense with announcement in cases where a prisoner escapes from him and retreats to his dwelling. Proof of "demand and refusal" was deemed unnecessary in such cases because it would be a "senseless ceremony" to require an officer in pursuit of a recently escaped arrestee to make an announcement prior to breaking the door to retake him. Finally, courts have indicated that unannounced entry may be justified where police officers have reason to believe that evidence would likely be destroyed if advance notice were given.

We need not attempt a comprehensive catalog of the relevant countervailing factors here. For now, we leave to the lower courts the task of determining the circumstances under which an unannounced entry is reasonable under the Fourth Amendment. We simply hold that although a search or seizure of a dwelling might be constitutionally defective if police officers enter without prior announcement, law enforcement interests may also establish the reasonableness of an unannounced entry.

III

Respondent contends that the judgment below should be affirmed because the unannounced entry in this case was justified for two reasons. First, respondent argues that police officers reasonably believed that a prior announcement would have placed them in peril, given their knowledge that petitioner had threatened a government informant with a semiautomatic weapon and that Mr. Jacobs had previously been convicted of arson and firebombing. Second, respondent suggests that prior announcement would have produced an unreasonable risk that petitioner would destroy easily disposable narcotics evidence.

These considerations may well provide the necessary justification for the unannounced entry in this case. Because the Arkansas Supreme Court did not address their sufficiency, however, we remand to allow the state courts to make any necessary findings of fact and to make the determination of reasonableness in the first instance. . . .

Notes and Questions

1. What do you think is the most likely resolution of this case on its remand to the state courts? On the basis of the facts presented in the opinion, would you be inclined to conclude that the officers' unannounced entry was reasonable or unreasonable?

2. *Legal Research Note.* We can try to find out how the Arkansas state courts actually ruled following the Supreme Court's decision in *Wilson* by "*Shepardizing*" the opinion. *Shepard's* case citators provide much valuable information. They report each time that another judicial decision has cited the case you are *Shepardizing*. A *Shepard's* provides the citation to the specific page within a decision where the case you are *Shepardizing* was cited. Finding later cases that have cited the decision you are *Shepardizing* can be useful for several reasons. For example, you might expect that cases citing *Wilson* have something to do with the "knock and announce" principle. Since the Supreme Court decided *Wilson* in 1995, newer lower court decisions may

involve interesting applications of the rule. The Supreme Court might have modified the rule or even overruled *Wilson*. *Shepard's* will report whether a case is "good law" by noting if a course has reversed or overruled an earlier decision. The *Shepard's* also gives the "judicial history" of cases, meaning that it gives citations to a case as it worked its way up from the lower courts to a higher court and also after a higher court remanded a case for further action in a lower court. This latter function allows us to use a *Shepard's* to determine if the Arkansas state courts have reported a decision following the Supreme Court's remand of *Wilson*.

To begin the process of *Shepardizing*, we first go to the appropriate collection of *Shepard's*. A separate set of *Shepard's* exists for the U.S. Supreme Court, for the federal circuit courts (e.g., F.2d and F.3d), for the federal district courts (F. Supp.), for West regional state reporters (e.g., A.2d, N.E.2d, S.W.2d), and for most state reporters. For this example, we could

Shepardize either the U.S. Supreme Court's decision in *Wilson* or the Arkansas Supreme Court decision that was reviewed by the U.S. Supreme Court in 1995. Let us use the latter decision. Justice Thomas's opinion tells us that the state case being reviewed by the U.S. Supreme Court was reported at 317 Ark. 548, 878 S.W.2d 755 (1994). We will *Shepardize* the state case by using the *Shepard's* for the *Southwestern Reporter, 2d.*

We first find the *oldest* volume of *Shepard's Southwestern Reporter Citations* that includes our case (848 S.W.2d 755). The spines of the bound *Shepard's* volumes reveal that one volume includes citations analyzing 709 S.W.2d through 920 S.W.2d. Accordingly, we start with this book. Then, we collect all *more recently* published *Shepard's* volumes. Unlike many other legal reference materials, *Shepard's* have no pocket supplements, so we must locate all later bound and paper issues. For each volume of the *Shepard's*, starting with the oldest, we simply flip through the pages looking for the citation to our case. We stop when we see "vol. 878" at the top of the page, and "-755-" within the page.

The *Shepard's* volumes confirm that the U.S. Supreme Court reversed (indicated by an "r") the decision. They also provide us with the citation to the Supreme Court's opinion and to several other cases that have cited the state court decision. However, as of June 1997 (when this was written), there was no indication that the Arkansas courts had issued a decision following the remand. It may be too early to expect a published decision. On the other hand, the case may have been decided by the state courts in a brief order that was not published. You should check the most recent (post–June 1997) *Shepard's Southwestern Reporter Citations* for later developments.

3. Do cases involving felony drug investigations present such an inherently great risk that evidence will be destroyed or violence will ensue if the police knock and announce their identity and purpose prior to executing a search warrant, that "no-knock" entries always are reasonable? The Wisconsin Supreme Court thought so, but the United States Supreme Court, through Justice Stevens, unanimously disagreed, in *Rich-*

ards v. Wisconsin, 520 U.S. 385, 117 S. Ct. 1416, 137 L. Ed. 2d 615 (1997). The Court rejected the "considerable overgeneralization" that all felony drug cases require "no-knock" entries.

For example, while drug investigation frequently does pose special risks to officer safety and the preservation of evidence, not every drug investigation will pose these risks to a substantial degree. For example, a search could be conducted at a time when the only individuals present in a residence have no connection with the drug activity and thus will be unlikely to threaten officers or destroy evidence. Or the police could know that the drugs being searched for were of a type or in a location that made them impossible to destroy quickly. In those situations, the asserted governmental interests in preserving evidence and maintaining safety may not outweigh the individual privacy interests intruded upon by a no-knock entry. Wisconsin's blanket rule impermissibly insulates these cases from judicial review.

A second difficulty with permitting a criminal-category exception to the knock-and-announce requirement is that the reasons for creating an exception in one category can, relatively easily, be applied to others. Armed bank robbers, for example, are, by definition, likely to have weapons, and the fruits of their crime may be destroyed without too much difficulty. If a per se exception were allowed for each category of criminal investigation that included a considerable—albeit hypothetical—risk of danger to officers or destruction of evidence, the knock-and-announce element of the Fourth Amendment's reasonableness requirement would be meaningless.

Thus, the fact that felony drug investigations may frequently present circumstances warranting a no-knock entry cannot remove from the neutral scrutiny of a reviewing court the reasonableness of the police decision not to knock and announce in a particular case. Instead, in each case, it is the duty of a court confronted with the question to determine whether the facts and circumstances of the particular entry justified dispensing with the knock-and-announce requirement.

In order to justify a "no-knock" entry, the police must have a reasonable suspicion that knocking and announcing their presence, under the particular circumstances, would be dangerous or futile, or that it would inhibit the effective investigation of the crime by, for example, allowing the destruction of evidence. This standard—as opposed to a probable cause require-ment—strikes the appropriate balance between the legitimate law enforcement concerns at issue in the execution of search warrants and the individual privacy interests affected by no-knock entries. . . .

Although the Court rejected "the Wisconsin court's blanket exception to the knock-and-announce requirement," it concluded that "the officers' no-knock entry into Richards' hotel room did not violate the Fourth Amendment" because "the circumstances in this case show that the officers had a reasonable suspicion that Richards might destroy evidence if given further opportunity to do so."

EXCEPTIONS TO THE WARRANT "REQUIREMENT"

We have repeatedly encountered the Supreme Court's pronouncement that warrantless searches "are *per se* unreasonable under the Fourth Amendment—subject only to a few specifically established and well-delineated exceptions." *Katz v. United States*, 389 U.S. 347, 357, 88 S. Ct. 507, 19 L. Ed. 2d 576 (1967). We now consider the exceptions to the search warrant requirement. At the end of this section, you may wish to evaluate whether you agree with the Court's assessment that these exceptions are "few[,] specifically established and well-delin-eated."

Search Incident to Lawful Arrest

As we have seen, the police are authorized to search individuals whom they have lawfully arrested without first securing a search warrant. A warrantless search incident to an arrest is justified by the need for the police to secure potential weapons and evidence. The suspect's privacy rights also have been significantly diminished by the arrest. *United States v. Robinson*, 414 U.S. 218, 94 S. Ct. 467, 38 L. Ed. 2d 427 (1973). However, we have yet to consider the permissible *scope* of the search that an officer is authorized to make incident to an arrest. Is such a search strictly confined to the arrestee's person, and is a warrant required if the search extends to effects or the surrounding area or premises? Can a warrantless search be made of the arrestee's car if, as in *Robinson*, the arrest occurs following a motor vehicle violation? Can packages and other containers within the arrestee's possession be searched without a warrant? Issues like these are important aspects of the "search incident to a lawful arrest" exception to the warrant requirement.

Chimel v. California, 395 U.S. 752, 89 S. Ct. 2034, 23 L. Ed. 2d 685 (1969)

Mr. Justice **Stewart** delivered the opinion of the Court.

This case raises basic questions concerning the permissible scope under the Fourth Amendment of a search incident to a lawful arrest.

The relevant facts are essentially undisputed. Late in the afternoon of September 13, 1965, three police officers arrived at the Santa Ana, California, home of the petitioner with a warrant authorizing his arrest for the burglary of a coin shop. The officers knocked on the door, identified themselves to the petitioner's wife, and asked if they might come inside. She ushered them into the house, where they waited 10 or 15 minutes until the petitioner returned home from work. When the petitioner entered the house, one of the officers handed him the arrest warrant and asked for permission to "look around." The petitioner objected, but was advised that "on the basis of the lawful arrest," the officers would nonetheless conduct a search. No search warrant had been issued.

Accompanied by the petitioner's wife, the officers then looked through the entire three-bedroom house, including the attic, the garage, and a small workshop. In some rooms the search was relatively cursory. In the master bedroom and sewing room, however, the officers directed the petitioner's wife to open drawers and "to physically move contents of the drawers from side to side so that [they] might view any items that would have come from [the] burglary." After completing the search, they seized numerous items—primarily coins, but also several medals, tokens, and a few other objects. The entire search took between 45 minutes and an hour.

At the petitioner's subsequent state trial on two charges of burglary, the items taken from his house were admitted into evidence against him, over his objection that they had been unconstitutionally seized. He was convicted, and the judgments of conviction were affirmed by both the California Court of Appeal, 61 Cal Rptr 714, and the California Supreme Court, 68 Cal 2d 436, 439 P2d 333. . . .

Without deciding the question, we proceed on the hypothesis that the California courts were correct in holding that the arrest of the petitioner was valid under the Constitution. This brings us directly to the question whether the warrantless search of the petitioner's entire house can be constitutionally justified as incident to that arrest. The decisions of this Court bearing upon that question have been far from consistent, as even the most cursory review makes evident. . . .

Only last Term in Terry v Ohio, 392 US 1, 88 S Ct 1868, 20 L Ed 2d 889, we emphasized that "the police must, whenever practicable, obtain advance judicial approval of searches and seizures through the warrant procedure," id., at 20, and that "[t]he scope of [a] search must be 'strictly tied to and justified by' the circumstances which rendered its initiation permissible." Id., at 19. The search undertaken by the officer in that "stop and frisk" case was sustained under that test, because it was no more than a "protective . . . search for weapons." Id., at 29. . . .

A similar analysis underlies the "search incident to arrest" principle, and marks its proper extent. When an arrest is made, it is reasonable for the arresting officer to search the person arrested in order to remove any weapons that the latter might seek to use in order to resist arrest or effect his escape. Otherwise, the officer's safety might well be endangered, and the arrest itself frustrated. In addition, it is entirely reasonable for the arresting officer to search for and seize any evidence on the arrestee's person in order to prevent its concealment or destruction. And the area into which an arrestee might reach in order to grab a weapon or evidentiary items must, of course, be governed by a like rule. A gun on a table or in a drawer in front of one who is arrested can be as dangerous to the arresting officer as one concealed in the clothing of the person arrested. There is ample justification, therefore, for a search of the arrestee's person and the area "within his immediate control"—construing that phrase to mean the area from within which he might gain possession of a weapon or destructible evidence.

There is no comparable justification, however, for routinely searching any room other than that in which an arrest occurs—or, for that matter, for searching through all the desk drawers or other closed or concealed areas in that room itself. Such searches, in the absence of well-recognized exceptions, may be made only under the authority of a search warrant. The "adherence to judicial processes" mandated by the Fourth Amendment requires no less. . . .

It is argued in the present case that it is "reasonable" to search a man's house when he is arrested in it. But that argument is founded on little more than a subjective view regarding the acceptability of certain sorts of police conduct, and not on considerations relevant to Fourth Amendment interests. Under such an unconfined analysis, Fourth Amendment protection in this area would approach the evaporation point. It is not easy to explain why, for instance, it is less subjectively "reasonable" to search a man's house when he is arrested on his front lawn—or just down the street—than it is when he happens to be in the house at the time of arrest. . . .

No consideration relevant to the Fourth Amendment suggests any point of rational limitation, once the search is allowed to go beyond the area from which the person arrested might obtain weapons or evidentiary items. The only reasoned distinction is one between a search of the person arrested and the area within his reach on the one hand, and more extensive searches on the other.[12] . . .

[T]he general point so forcefully made by Judge Learned Hand in United States v Kirschenblatt, 16 F2d 202, remains:

"After arresting a man in his house, to rummage at will among his papers in search of whatever will convict him, appears to us to be indistinguishable from what might be done under a general warrant; indeed, the warrant would give more protection, for presumably it must be issued by a magistrate. True, by hypothesis the power would not exist, if the supposed offender were not found on the premises; but it is small consolation to know that one's papers are safe only so long as one is not at home." Id., at 203. . .

Application of sound Fourth Amendment principles to the facts of this case produces a clear result. The search here went far beyond the petitioner's person and the area from within which he might have obtained either a weapon or something that could have been used against him. There was no constitutional justification, in the absence of a search warrant, for extending the search beyond that area. The scope of the search was, therefore, "unreasonable" under the Fourth and Fourteenth Amendments, and the petitioner's conviction cannot stand.

Reversed.

Mr. Justice **White**, with whom Mr. Justice **Black** joins, dissenting.

---

12. It is argued in dissent that so long as there is probable cause to search the place where an arrest occurs, a search of that place should be permitted even though no search warrant has been obtained. This position seems to be based principally on two premises: first, that once an arrest has been made, the additional invasion of privacy stemming from the accompanying search is "relatively minor"; and second, that the victim of the search may "shortly thereafter" obtain a judicial determination of whether the search was justified by probable cause. With respect to the second premise, one may initially question whether all of the States in fact provide the speedy suppression procedures the dissent assumes. More

fundamentally, however, we cannot accept the view that Fourth Amendment interests are vindicated so long as "the rights of the criminal" are "protect[ed] . . . against introduction of evidence seized without probable cause." The Amendment is designed to prevent, not simply to redress, unlawful police action. In any event, we cannot join in characterizing the invasion of privacy that results from a top-to-bottom search of a man's house as "minor." And we can see no reason why, simply because some interferences with an individual's privacy and freedom of movement has lawfully taken place, further intrusions should automatically be allowed despite the absence of a warrant that the Fourth Amendment would otherwise require.

Few areas of the law have been as subject to shifting constitutional standards over the last 50 years as that of the search "incident to an arrest." There has been a remarkable instability in this whole area, which has seen at least four major shifts in emphasis. Today's opinion makes an untimely fifth. In my view, the Court should not now abandon the old rule. . . .

The rule which has prevailed, but for very brief or doubtful periods of aberration, is that a search incident to an arrest may extend to those areas under the control of the defendant and where items subject to constitutional seizure may be found. The justification for this rule must, under the language of the Fourth Amendment, lie in the reasonableness of the rule. . . .

Applying this reasonableness test to the area of searches incident to arrests, one thing is clear at the outset. Search of an arrested man and of the items within his immediate reach must in almost every case be reasonable. There is always a danger that the suspect will try to escape, seizing concealed weapons with which to overpower and injure the arresting officers, and there is a danger that he may destroy evidence vital to the prosecution. Circumstances in which these justifications would not apply are sufficiently rare that inquiry is not made into searches of this scope, which have been considered reasonable throughout.

The justifications which make such a search reasonable obviously do not apply to the search of areas to which the accused does not have ready physical access. This is not enough, however, to prove such searches unconstitutional. The Court has always held, and does not today deny, that when there is probable cause to search and it is "impracticable" for one reason or another to get a search warrant, then a warrantless search may be reasonable. . . .

This is not to say that a search can be reasonable without regard to the probable cause to believe that seizable items are on the premises.

But when there are exigent circumstances, and probable cause, then the search may be made without a warrant, reasonably. An arrest itself may often create an emergency situation making it impracticable to obtain a warrant before embarking on a related search. Again assuming that there is probable cause to search premises at the spot where a suspect is arrested, it seems to me unreasonable to require the police to leave the scene in order to obtain a search warranty when they are already legally there to make a valid arrest, and when there must almost always be a strong possibility that confederates of the arrested man will in the meanwhile remove the items for which the police have probable cause to search. This must so often be the case that it seems to me as unreasonable to require a warrant for a search of the premises as to require a warrant for search of the person and his very immediate surroundings. . . .

If circumstances so often require the warrantless arrest that the law generally permits it, the typical situation will find the arresting officers lawfully on the premises without arrest or search warrant. Like the majority, I would permit the police to search the person of a suspect and the area under his immediate control either to assure the safety of the officers or to prevent the destruction of evidence. And like the majority, I see nothing in the arrest alone furnishing probable cause for a search of any broader scope. However, where as here the existence of probable cause is independently established and would justify a warrant for a broader search for evidence, I would follow past cases and permit such a search to be carried out without a warrant, since the fact of arrest supplies an exigent circumstance justifying police action before the evidence can be removed, and also alerts the suspect to the fact of the search so that he can immediately seek judicial determination of probable cause in an adversary proceeding, and appropriate redress. . . .

Notes and Questions

1. As discussed in *Chimel*, the Supreme Court had vacillated for years about the permissible scope of a search incident to a lawful arrest. *Chimel's* limitation of a search incident to arrest to the arrestee's "grabbing area" has prevailed, although proper application of this rule is not always easy.

2. For example, what if an officer makes a custodial arrest of the driver of a car? Can all or parts of the car be searched incident to the arrest? Should the permissible scope of the search be determined on a case-by-case basis, or should a general rule that can be applied in all cases govern?

In *New York v. Belton*, 453 U.S. 454, 101 S. Ct. 2860, 69 L. Ed. 2d 768 (1981), a police officer stopped a car for speeding. When the officer approached the car, he smelled burnt marijuana and saw other evidence of marijuana use. The officer ordered the four men who occupied the vehicle out of the car and placed them under arrest. He patted down each of the men and separated them so that they would not be in physical contact with each other. "He then searched the passenger compartment of the car. On the back seat, he found a black leather jacket belonging to Belton. He unzipped one of the pockets of the jacket and discovered cocaine." A court subsequently denied Belton's motion to suppress the cocaine, and Belton pleaded guilty to a related offense, preserving his right to appeal. "The New York Court of Appeals reversed, holding that 'a warrantless search of the zippered pockets of an inaccessible jacket may not be upheld as a search incident to a lawful arrest where there is no longer any danger that the arrestee or a confederate might gain access to the article.'"

The Supreme Court granted certiorari and, in a 5–1–3 decision, with Justice Stevens concurring in the judgment, reversed. Justice Stewart's majority opinion emphasized the need for a "bright line" rule that would give the police guidance in the recurring situation involving "the proper scope of a search of the interior of an automobile incident to a lawful custodial arrest of its occupants."

When a person cannot know how a court will apply a settled principle to a recurring factual situation, that person cannot know the scope of his constitutional protection, nor can a policeman know the scope of his authority. While the Chimel case established that a search incident to an arrest may not stray beyond the area within the immediate control of the arrestee, courts have found no workable definition of "the area within the immediate control of the arrestee" when that area arguably includes the interior of an automobile and the arrestee is its recent occupant. Our reading of the cases suggests the generalization that articles inside the relatively narrow compass of the passenger compartment of an automobile are in fact generally, even if not inevitably, within "the area into which an arrestee might reach in order to grab a weapon or evidentiary item." Chimel, *supra*, at 763. In order to establish the workable rule this category of cases requires, we read Chimel's definition of the limits of the area that may be searched in light of that generalization. Accordingly, we hold that when a policeman has made a lawful custodial arrest of the occupant of an automobile, he may, as a contemporaneous incident of that arrest, search the passenger compartment of that automobile.[3]

It follows from this conclusion that the police may also examine the contents of any containers found within the passenger compartment, for if the passenger compartment is within the reach of the arrestee, so also will containers in it be within his reach.[4]

Such a container may, of course, be searched whether it is open or closed,

---

3. Our holding today does no more than determine the meaning of Chimel's principles in this particular and problematic content. It in no way alters the fundamental principles established in the Chimel case regarding the basic scope of searches incident to lawful custodial arrests.

4. "Container" here denotes any object capable of holding another object. It thus includes closed or open glove compartments, consoles, or other receptacles located anywhere within the passenger compartment, as well as luggage, boxes, bags, clothing, and the like. Our holding encompasses only the interior of the passenger compartment of an automobile and does not encompass the trunk.

since the justification for the search is not that the arrestee has no privacy interest in the container, but that the lawful custodial arrest justifies the infringement of any privacy interest the arrestee may have.

* * *

It is not questioned that the respondent was the subject of a lawful custodial arrest on a charge of possessing marijuana. The search of the respondent's jacket followed immediately upon that arrest. The jacket was located inside the passenger compartment of the car in which the respondent had been a passenger just before he was arrested. The jacket was thus within the area which we have concluded was "within the arrestee's immediate control" within the meaning of the Chimel case. The search of the jacket, therefore, was a search incident to a lawful custodial arrest, and it did not violate the Fourth and Fourteenth Amendments. Accordingly, the judgment is reversed.

Justice Brennan's dissent warned that "the Court today substantially expands the permissible scope of searches incident to arrest by permitting police officers to search areas and containers the arrestee could not possibly reach at the time of the arrest." He also took issue with the majority's contention that its "bright line" rule would provide the desired guidance to the police and the courts.

Thus, although the Court concludes that a warrantless search of a car may take place even though the suspect was arrested outside the car, it does not indicate how long after the suspect's arrest that search may validly be conducted. Would a warrantless search incident to arrest be valid if conducted five minutes after the suspect left his car? Thirty minutes? Three hours? Does it matter whether the suspect is standing in close proximity to the car when the search is conducted? Does it matter whether the police formed probable cause to arrest before or after the suspect left his car? And *why* is the rule announced today necessarily limited to searches of cars? What if a suspect is seen walking out of a house where the police, peering in from outside, had formed probable cause to believe a crime was being committed? Could the police then arrest that suspect and enter the house to conduct a search incident to arrest? Even assuming today's rule is limited to searches of the "interior" of cars—an assumption not demanded by logic—what is meant by "interior"? Does it include locked glove compartments, the interior of door panels, or the area under the floorboards? Are special rules necessary for station wagons and hatchbacks, where the luggage compartment may be reached through the interior, or taxicabs, where a glass panel might separate the driver's compartment from the rest of the car? Are the only containers that may be searched those that are large enough to be "capable of holding another object"? Or does the new rule apply to any container, even if it "could hold neither a weapon nor evidence of the criminal conduct for which the suspect was arrested"? . . .

Remember that *Belton* involves the search incident to arrest exception to the search warrant requirement. The Court did *not* apply the "automobile exception," *see* 453 U.S., at 462 n. 6, which we will consider later in this section.

The *Belton* rule has been criticized by some state courts, and a few have rejected it on state constitutional grounds. *See People v. Blasich*, 73 N.Y.2d 673, 541 N.E.2d 40, 543 N.Y.S.2d 40 (1989); *State v. Hernandez*, 410 So. 2d 1381 (La. 1982); *State v. Brown*, 63 Ohio St. 3d 349, 588 N.E.2d 113, *cert. denied*, 506 U.S. 862, 113 S. Ct. 182, 121 L. Ed. 2d 127 (1992); *State v. Pierce*, 136 N.J. 184, 642 A.2d 947 (1994); *State v. Stroud*, 106 Wash. 2d 144, 720 P. 2d 436 (1986) (rejecting *Belton* as applied to locked containers or a locked glove compartment). *See* B. Latzer, *State Constitutional Criminal Law* § 3:27 (1995).

Belton holds that containers within the passenger compartment of a car may be searched incident to the arrest of the car's occupant. Should purses, briefcases, boxes, and other containers in an arrestee's possession generally be subject to a warrantless search incident to an arrest? Should it matter how accessible the insides of the container are to the arrestee? What if the police have secured the package and removed it from the arrestee's control? In *Belton*, the Supreme Court criticized

arrest, because Trooper Nicot, by the very act of searching the respondent's jacket and seizing the contents of its pocket, had gained "exclusive control" of them. But under this fallacious theory no search or seizure incident to a lawful custodial arrest would ever be valid; by seizing an article even on the arrestee's person, an officer may be said to have reduced that article to his "exclusive control." 453 U.S., at 461–462 n. 5.

> the theory of the Court of Appeals that the search and seizure in the present case could not have been incident to the respondent's

In light of this reasoning about container searches, what went wrong in the following case?

United States v. Chadwick, 433 U.S. 1, 97 S. Ct. 2476, 53 L. Ed. 2d 538 (1977)

Mr. Chief Justice **Burger** delivered the opinion of the Court.

We granted certiorari in this case to decide whether a search warrant is required before federal agents may open a locked footlocker which they have lawfully seized at the time of the arrest of its owners, when there is probable cause to believe the footlocker contains contraband.

On May 8, 1973, Amtrak railroad officials in San Diego observed respondents Gregory Machado and Bridget Leary load a brown footlocker onto a train bound for Boston. Their suspicions were aroused when they noticed that the trunk was unusually heavy for its size, and that it was leaking talcum powder, a substance often used to mask the odor of marihuana or hashish. Because Machado matched a profile used to spot drug traffickers, the railroad officials reported these circumstances to federal agents in San Diego, who in turn relayed the information, together with detailed descriptions of Machado and the footlocker, to their counterparts in Boston.

When the train arrived in Boston two days later, federal narcotics agents were on hand. Though the officers had not obtained an arrest or search warrant, they had with them a police dog trained to detect marihuana. The agents identified Machado and Leary and kept them under surveillance as they claimed their suit-cases and the footlocker, which had been transported by baggage cart from the train to the departure area. Machado and Leavy lifted the footlocker from the baggage cart, placed it on the floor and sat down on it.

The agents then released the dog near the footlocker. Without alerting respondents, the dog signaled the presence of a controlled substance inside. Respondent Chadwick then joined Machado and Leary, and they engaged an attendant to move the footlocker outside to Chadwick's waiting automobile. Machado, Chadwick, and the attendant together lifted the 200-pound footlocker into the trunk of the car, while Leary waited in the front seat. At that point, while the trunk of the car was still open and before the car engine had been started, the officers arrested all three. A search disclosed no weapons, but the keys to the footlocker were apparently taken from Machado.

Respondents were taken to the Federal Building in Boston; the agents followed with Chadwick's car and the footlocker. As the Government concedes, from the moment of respondents' arrests at about 9 p.m., the footlocker remained under the exclusive control of law enforcement officers at all times. The footlocker and luggage were placed in the Federal Building, where, as one of the agents later testified, "there was no risk that whatever was contained in the footlocker trunk would be removed by the defendants or their associates." App 44. The agents had no reason to believe that the footlocker contained explosives or other inherently dangerous items, or that it contained evidence which would lose its value unless the footlocker were opened at once. Facilities were readily available in which the footlocker could have been stored securely; it is not contended that there was any exigency calling for an immediate search.

At the Federal Building an hour and a half after the arrests, the agents opened the footlocker and luggage. They did not obtain respondents' consent; they did not secure a search warrant. The footlocker was locked with a padlock and a regular trunk lock. It is unclear whether it was opened with the keys taken from respondent Machado, or by other means. Large amounts of marihuana were found in the footlocker.

* * *

Our fundamental inquiry in considering Fourth Amendment issues is whether or not a search or seizure is reasonable under all the circumstances. The judicial warrant has a significant role to play in that it provides the detached scrutiny of a neutral magistrate, which is a more reliable safeguard against improper searches than the hurried judgment of a law enforcement officer "engaged in the often competitive enterprise of ferreting out crime." Johnson v United States, 333 US 10, 68 S Ct 367, 14, 92 L Ed 436 (1948). Once a lawful search has begun, it is also far more likely that it will not exceed proper bounds when it is done pursuant to a judicial authorization "particularly describing the place to be searched and the persons or things to be seized." Further, a warrant assures the individual whose property is searched or seized of the lawful authority of the executing officer, his need to search, and the limits of his power to search.

Just as the Fourth Amendment "protects people, not places," the protections a judicial warrant offers against erroneous governmental intrusions are effective whether applied in or out of the home. . . .

In this case, important Fourth Amendment privacy interests were at stake. By placing personal effects inside a double-locked footlocker, res-pondents manifested an expectation that the contents would remain free from public examination. No less than one who locks the doors of his home against intruders, one who safeguards his personal possessions in this manner is due the protection of the Fourth Amendment Warrant Clause. There being no exigency, it was unreasonable for the Government to conduct this search without the safeguards a judicial warrant provides.

The Government does not contend that the footlocker's brief contact with Chadwick's car makes this an automobile search, but it is argued that the rationale of our automobile search cases demonstrates the reasonableness of permitting warrantless searches of luggage; the Government views such luggage as analogous to motor vehicles for Fourth Amendment purposes. It is true that, like the footlocker in issue here, automobiles are "effects" under the Fourth Amendment, and searches and seizures of automobiles are therefore subject to the constitutional standard of reasonableness. But this Court has recognized significant differences between motor vehicles and other property which permit warrantless searches of automobiles in circumstances in which warrantless searches would not be reasonable in other contexts. . . .

The factors which diminish the privacy aspects of an automobile do not apply to respondents' footlocker. Luggage contents are not open to a public view, except as a condition to a border entry or common carrier travel; nor is luggage subject to regular inspections and official scrutiny on a continuing basis. Unlike an automobile, whose primary function is transportation, luggage is intended as a repository of personal effects. In sum, a person's expectations of privacy in personal luggage are substantially greater than in an automobile.

Nor does the footlocker's mobility justify dispensing with the added protections of the Warrant Clause. Once the federal agents had seized it at the railroad station and had safely transferred it to the Boston Federal Building under their exclusive control, there was not the slightest danger that the footlocker or its contents could have been removed before a valid search warrant could be obtained. The initial seizure and detention of the footlocker, the validity of which respondents do not contest, were sufficient to guard against any risk that evidence might be lost. With the footlocker safely immobilized, it was unreasonable to undertake the additional and greater intrusion of a search without a warrant.

Finally, the Government urges that the Constitution permits the warrantless search of any property in the possession of a person arrested in public, so long as there is probable cause to believe that the property contains contraband or evidence of crime. Although recognizing that the footlocker was not within respondents' immediate control, the Government insists that the search was reasonable because the footlocker was seized contemporaneously with respondents' arrests and was searched as soon thereafter as was practicable. The reasons justifying search in a custodial arrest are quite different. When a custodial arrest is made, there is always some danger that the person arrested may seek to use a weapon, or that evidence may be concealed or destroyed. To safeguard himself and others, and to prevent the loss of evidence, it has been held reasonable for the arresting officer to conduct a prompt, warrantless "search of the arrestee's person and the area 'within his immediate control'—construing that phrase to mean the area from within which he might gain possession of a weapon or destructible evidence." Chimel v California, 395 US, at 763.

Such searches may be conducted without a warrant, and they may also be made whether or not there is probable cause to believe that the person arrested may have a weapon or is about to destroy evidence. The potential dangers lurking in all custodial arrests make warrantless searches of items within the "immediate control" area reasonable without requiring the arresting officer to calculate the probability that weapons or destructible evidence may be involved. However, warrantless searches of luggage or other property seized at the time of an arrest cannot be justified as incident to that arrest either if the "search is remote in time or place from the arrest," Preston v United States, 376 US, at 367, 84 S Ct 881, 11 L Ed 2d 777, or no exigency exists. Once law enforcement officers have reduced luggage or other personal property not immediately associated with the person of the arrestee to their exclusive control, and there is no longer any danger that the arrestee might

gain access to the property to seize a weapon or destroy evidence, a search of that property is no longer an incident of the arrest.

Here the search was conducted more than an hour after federal agents had gained exclusive control of the footlocker and long after respondents were securely in custody; the search therefore cannot be viewed as incidental to the arrest or as justified by any other exigency. Even though on this record the issuance of a warrant by a judicial officer was reasonably predictable, a line must be drawn. In our view, when no exigency is shown to support the need for an immediate search, the Warrant Clause places the line at the point where the property to be searched comes under the exclusive dominion of police authority. Respondents were therefore entitled to the protection of the Warrant Clause with the evaluation of a neutral magistrate, before their privacy interests in the contents of the footlocker were invaded.[10] . . .

Mr. Justice **Blackmun**, with whom Mr. Justice **Rehnquist** joins, dissenting. . . .

A person arrested in a public place is likely to have various kinds of property with him: items inside his clothing, a briefcase or suitcase, packages, or a vehicle. In such instances the police cannot very well leave the property on the sidewalk or street while they go to get a warrant. The items may be stolen by a passer-by or removed by the suspect's confederates. Rather than requiring the police to "post a guard" over such property, I think it is surely reasonable for the police to take the items along to the station with the arrested person. . . .

As the Court in Robinson recognized, custodial arrest is such a serious deprivation that various lesser invasions of privacy may be fairly regarded as incidental. An arrested person, of course, has an additional privacy interest in the objects in his possession at the time of arrest. To

---

10. Unlike searches of the person, United States v Robinson, 414 US 218, 94 S Ct 467, 38 L Ed 2d 427 (1973); United States v Edwards, 415 US 800, 94 S Ct 1234, 39 L Ed 2d 771 (1974), searches of possessions within an arrestee's immediate control cannot be justified by any reduced expectations of privacy caused by the arrest. Respondents' privacy interest in the contents of the footlocker was not eliminated simply because they were under arrest.

be sure, allowing impoundment of those objects pursuant to arrest, but requiring a warrant for examination of their contents, would protect that incremental privacy interest in cases where the police assessment of probable cause is subsequently rejected by a magistrate. But a countervailing consideration is that a warrant would be routinely forthcoming in the vast majority of situations where the property has been seized in conjunction with the valid arrest of a person in a public place. I therefore doubt that requiring the authorities to go through the formality of obtaining a warrant in this situation would have much practical effect in protecting Fourth Amendment values.

I believe this sort of practical evaluation underlies the Court's decisions permitting clothing, personal effects, and automobiles to be searched without a warrant as an incident of arrest, even though it would be possible simply to impound these items until a warrant could be obtained. The Court's opinion does not explain why a wallet carried in the arrested person's clothing, but not the footlocker in the present case, is subject to "reduced expectations of privacy caused by the arrest."

Nor does the Court explain how such items as purses or briefcases fit into the dichotomy.[2] Perhaps the holding in the present case will be limited in the future to objects that are relatively immobile by virtue of their size or absence of a means of propulsion. . . .

The approach taken by the Court has the perverse result of allowing fortuitous circumstances to control the outcome of the present case.

*   *   *

[I]f the agents had postponed the arrest just a few minutes longer until the respondents started to drive away, then the car could have been seized, taken to the agents' office, and all its contents—including the footlocker—searched without a warrant.

_____

2. The Courts of Appeals generally have held that it is proper for the police to seize a briefcase or package in the possession of a person at the time of arrest, and subsequently to search the property without a warrant after the arrested person has been taken into custody. . . .

Alternatively, the agents could have made a search of the footlocker at the time and place of the arrests. Machado and Leary were standing next to an open automobile trunk containing the footlocker, and thus it was within the area of their "immediate control." And certainly the footlocker would have been properly subject to search at the time if the arrest had occurred a few minutes earlier while Machado and Leary were seated on it.[5] . . .

*   *   *   *   *

On the basis of your reading of the majority and dissenting opinions in *Chadwick,* how do you think the Court would respond to warrantless searches of "effects" subsequent to an individual's arrest under the following circumstances?

1. A footlocker is confiscated under the same conditions as in *Chadwick,* but the arrestees are suspected terrorists, believed to be responsible for numerous railroad station bombings.
2. The arrest is made when the suspects are seated on the trunk, and the officers immediately unlock and open the trunk.

_____

5. Chimel v California, 395 US 752, 763, 23 L Ed 2d 685, 89 S Ct 2034 (1969), authorizes an on-the-spot search of the area within the "immediate control" of an arrested person. It is well established that an immediate search of packages or luggage carried by an arrested person is proper. See Draper v United States, 358 US 307, 310–311, 79 S Ct 329, 3 L Ed 2d 327 (1959). Such searches have been sustained by the Courts of Appeals even if they occurred after the arrested person had been handcuffed and thus could no longer gain access to the property in question. Searches under the Chimel rationale have also been approved when the suitcase or briefcase was close by, but not touching, the arrested person. United States v French, 545 F2d 1021 (CA5 1977) (suitcase "within an arm's length" of arrested person); United States v Frick, 490 F2d 666 (CA5 1973), cert denied sub nom Peterson v United States, 419 US 831, 95 S Ct 55, 42 L Ed 2d 57 (1974) (briefcase lying on seat of automobile next to which person was arrested).

3. The suspects have opened the lid of the trunk and appear to be inventorying its contents at the time of the arrest.
4. The container searched is not a trunk but a briefcase within the arrestee's possession.
5. The container searched is a briefcase that the suspect placed on a bench some 10 feet away just prior to his arrest.
6. The container is a briefcase, but it is not searched until after the suspect has been handcuffed and placed in a patrol car.

* * * * *

In *Maryland v. Buie*, 494 U.S. 325, 110 S. Ct. 1093, 108 L. Ed. 2d 276 (1990), the Court was confronted with the following facts. Two men, one of whom was wearing a red running suit, committed an armed robbery of a pizza establishment. The police secured arrest warrants for the two suspects, Jeremy Buie and Lloyd Allen. Two days after the robbery, after it was confirmed that Buie was in his home, six or seven police officers were dispatched to place him under arrest. The police entered the home under the authority of the arrest warrant, *see Payton v. New York*, 445 U.S. 573, 100 S. Ct. 1371, 63 L. Ed. 2d 639 (1980), and arrested, searched, and handcuffed Buie after he surfaced from the basement. Thereafter, a detective "entered the basement 'in case there was someone else' down there. He noticed a red running suit lying in plain view on a stack of clothing and seized it. The trial court denied Buie's motion to suppress the running suit." The Maryland Court of Appeals reversed.

The Supreme Court framed the issue in *Buie* as follows:

A "protective sweep" is a quick and limited search of a premises, incident to an arrest and conducted to protect the safety of police officers or others. It is narrowly confined to a cursory visual inspection of those places in which a person might be hiding. In this case we must decide what level of justification is required by the Fourth and Fourteenth Amendments before police officers, while effecting the arrest of a suspect in his home pursuant to an arrest warrant, may conduct a warrantless protective sweep of all or part of the premises. . . .

The state had urged that the police in all cases be allowed to make a protective sweep as a part of an in-home arrest, without any "level of objective justification." 494 U.S., at 334 n. 2. Conversely, Buie argued that the police needed a search warrant or at least probable cause to believe that another person was in the house and posed a potential threat to them before they were allowed to enter his basement pursuant to the protective sweep. The Court (7–2), in an opinion written by Justice White, rejected both parties' arguments and adopted the following rule:

We conclude that the Fourth Amendment would permit the protective sweep undertaken here if the searching officer "possesse[d] a reasonable belief based on 'specific and articulable facts which, taken together with the rational inferences from those facts, reasonably warrant[ed]' the officer in believing," Michigan v Long, 463 US 1032, 1049–1050, 103 S Ct 3469, 77 L Ed 2d 1201 (1983) (quoting Terry v Ohio, 392 US 1, 21, 88 S Ct 1868, 20 L Ed 2d 889 (1968)), that the area swept harbored an individual posing a danger to the officer or others. . . .

The Court supported its rule, in part, by relying on *Terry v. Ohio*, 392 U.S. 1, 88 S. Ct. 1868, 20 L. Ed. 2d 889 (1968) and *Michigan v. Long*, 463 U.S. 1032, 103 S. Ct. 3469, 77 L. Ed. 2d 1201 (1983).

. . . Possessing an arrest warrant and probable cause to believe Buie was in his home, the officers were entitled to enter and to search anywhere in the house in which Buie might be found. Once he was found, however, the search for him was over, and there was no longer that particular justification for entering any rooms that had not yet been searched.

That Buie had an expectation of privacy in those remaining areas of his house, however, does not mean such rooms were immune from entry. In Terry and Long we were concerned with the immediate interest of the police officers in taking steps to assure themselves that the persons with whom they were dealing were not armed with or able to gain immediate control of a weapon that could unexpectedly and fatally be used against them. In the instant case, there is an analogous interest of the officers in taking steps to assure themselves that the house in which a suspect is being or has just been arrested is not harboring other persons who are dangerous and who could unexpectedly launch an attack. The risk of danger in the context of an arrest in the home is as great as, if not greater than, it is in an on-the-street or roadside investigatory encounter. A Terry or Long frisk occurs before a police-citizen confrontation has escalated to the point of arrest. A protective sweep, in contrast, occurs as an adjunct to the serious step of taking a person into custody for the purpose of prosecuting him for a crime. Moreover, unlike an encounter on the street or along a highway, an in-home arrest puts the officer at the disadvantage of being on his adversary's "turf." An ambush in a confined setting of unknown configuration is more to be feared than it is in open, more familiar surroundings. . . .

Nor do we here suggest, as the State does, that entering rooms not examined prior to the arrest is a de minimis intrusion that may be disregarded. We are quite sure, however, that the arresting officers are permitted in such circumstances to take reasonable steps to ensure their safety after, and while making, the arrest. That interest is sufficient to outweigh the intrusion such procedures may entail.

We agree with the State, as did the court below, that a warrant was not required. We also hold that as an incident to the arrest the officers could, as a precautionary matter and without probable cause or reasonable suspicion, look in closets and other spaces immediately adjoining the place of arrest from which an attack could be imme-

diately launched. Beyond that, however, we hold that there must be articulable facts which, taken together with the rational inferences from those facts, would warrant a reasonably prudent officer in believing that the area to be swept harbors an individual posing a danger to those on the arrest scene. This is no more and no less than was required in Terry and Long, and as in those cases, we think this balance is the proper one.

We should emphasize that such a protective sweep, aimed at protecting the arresting officers, if justified by the circumstances, is nevertheless not a full search of the premises, but may extend only to a cursory inspection of those spaces where a person may be found. The sweep lasts no longer than is necessary to dispel the reasonable suspicion of danger and in any event no longer than it takes to complete the arrest and depart the premises.

Affirmance is not required by Chimel v California, 395 US 752, 23 L Ed 2d 685, 89 S Ct 2034 (1969), where it was held that in the absence of a search warrant, the justifiable search incident to an in-home arrest could not extend beyond the arrestee's person and the area from within which the arrestee might have obtained a weapon. . . . The type of search we authorize today is far removed from the "top-to-bottom" search involved in Chimel; moreover, it is decidedly not "automati[c]," but may be conducted only when justified by a reasonable, articulable suspicion that the house is harboring a person posing a danger to those on the arrest scene. . . .

The Court thus vacated the Maryland Court of Appeals' ruling that the running suit discovered during the protective sweep was inadmissible and remanded the case "for further proceedings not inconsistent with this opinion."

Notes and Questions

1. How should the state court rule on the remand? Under the facts of Buie, was there reasonable suspicion to believe that the basement, where the running suit was found, "harbored an individual posing a danger to the officers or others"?

2. In addition to authorizing protective sweeps following in-home arrests under the reasonable-suspicion standard, note that *Buie* also held that "as an incident to the arrest the officers could, as a precautionary matter and without probable cause or reasonable suspicion, look in closets and other spaces immediately adjoining the place of arrest from which an attack could be immediately launched." Is this holding simply an application of *Chimel v. California's* rule defining the permissible area of a search incident to an arrest? Justice Brennan thought it went beyond *Chimel*, as he explained in his dissenting opinion, 494 U.S., at 342–343 n. 6.

6. The Court's decision also to expand the "search incident to arrest" exception previously recognized in Chimel v California, allowing police officers without *any* requisite level of suspicion to look into "closets and other spaces immediately adjoining the place of arrest from which an attack could be immediately launched," is equally disquieting. Chimel established that police officers may presume as a matter of law, without need for factual support in a particular case, that arrestees might take advantage of weapons or destroy evidence in the area "within [their] immediate control"; therefore, a protective search of that area is per se reasonable under the Fourth Amendment. Chimel, supra, at 763. I find much less plausible the Court's implicit assumption today that arrestees are likely to sprinkle hidden allies throughout the rooms in which they might be arrested. Hence there is no comparable justification for permitting arresting officers to presume as a matter of law that they are threatened by ambush from "immediately adjoining" spaces.

Consent Searches

The protections in the Bill of Rights generally are designed to safeguard individual liberties. Accordingly, an individual who does not feel the need for a particular safeguard may choose to relinquish it. In subsequent chapters, we will study how people can effectively waive their "*Miranda* rights" in the context of self-incrimination issues, their right to counsel, and other constitutional protections. We now take up the topic of consent searches. If an individual gives valid consent to the search of his or her person, effects, or premises, the ensuing search is not "unreasonable" even in the absence of a warrant or exigent circumstances.

Two major issues surround consent searches. The first involves the prerequisites for valid or effective consent. For example, should we take at face value a person's affirmative response to a police officer's request to search her purse? Or his or her home? Does it matter if the person does not understand that he or she need not agree to the request? Does it matter if the person (reasonably) believes that withholding consent would be futile because the police will go ahead and search anyway?

The second issue concerns who is authorized to give consent for a search. Assume, for example, that you share an apartment or dormitory room with a roommate. Can your roommate give legally valid consent for the police to search your common living area? To search your bedroom? Can parents consent to the search of their child's room or belongings? Conversely, can the child consent to the search of his or her parents' home or possessions? Does it matter whether the person giving permission for the search actually lacks the authority to consent? If the police (reasonably) believe that the person granting permission is authorized to consent, is the search lawful?

The Requirements for Effective "Consent": Voluntariness

Before a citizen's agreement to a police officer's request to conduct a search is recognized as being effective, it should at a minimum be given voluntarily. For example, "consent" to a request to search given only because a person's arm is being twisted, or a gun pointed at him or her, certainly should not be recognized as legally binding. "When a prosecutor seeks to rely upon consent to justify the lawfulness of a search, he has the burden of proving that the consent was, in fact, freely and voluntarily given." *Bumper v North Carolina*, 391 U.S. 543, 548, 88 S. Ct. 1788, 20 L. Ed. 2d 797 (1968).

In *Bumper*, "a 66-year-old Negro widow, in a house located in a rural area at the end of an isolated mile-long dirt road," told four white police officers to "go ahead" and search her house after they informed her that they had a search warrant authorizing them to do so. No search warrant, in fact, was ever produced. The lawfulness of the search and the seizure of a gun that was offered at the trial of the widow's grandson, thus turned on whether the search could be justified on the theory that the police had obtained valid consent. The Court in *Bumper* showed no hesitation in concluding that "consent" given under the claimed authority of a search warrant, where the individual has no apparent right to resist the search, amounted to coercion. "Where there is coercion there cannot be consent." 391 U.S., at 550.

In *Schneckloth v. Bustamonte*, 412 U.S. 218, 93 S. Ct. 2041, 36 L. Ed. 2d 854 (1973), the Court, per Stewart, J., reaffirmed *Bumper* but probed more deeply into the meaning of "voluntariness." Specifically, the *Schneckloth* Court ruled that the subject of a search did not have to be advised of his right to be free from a warrantless search in order to make the consent to search "voluntary." The standard announced was based on the "totality of the circumstances."

When the subject of a search is not in custody and the State attempts to justify a search on the basis of his consent, the Fourth and Fourteenth Amendments require that it demonstrate that the consent was in fact voluntarily given, and not the result of duress or coercion, express or implied. Voluntariness is a question of fact to be determined from all the circumstances, and while the subject's knowledge of a right to refuse is a factor to be taken into account, the prosecution is not required to demonstrate such knowledge as a prerequisite to establishing a voluntary consent. 412 U.S., at 248–249.

Schneckloth thus made the critically important distinction between "voluntary" decisions and decisions that are both voluntary and "knowing." It ruled that "knowing" that one has a right to refuse to consent to an officer's request to search is *not* an indispensable requirement for the consent to be effective. In the process, the court held that the police are under no affirmative obligation to tell people that they are entitled to withhold their consent to a search. We will encounter different rules—specifically, that the decision to give up a constitutional right must be "knowing, intelligent and voluntary" for it to be valid—when we study rights protected by the Fifth and Sixth Amendments, including the protection against compelled self-incrimination and the right to counsel.

It should be clear that a decision can be made "voluntarily," even though it may be ill informed or ill advised because the person making it lacks important knowledge and information. For example, you might "voluntarily" decide to get a flu shot. You make a doctor's appointment, roll up your sleeve, endure the needle and injection, and then go on your way. You later find out (hypothetically) that this particular shot is only effective against 20% of the flu viruses in circulation and that it also causes lingering, adverse side effects for about 25% of the people who get it. If you had possessed this knowledge earlier, you never would have chosen to have the shot. In retrospect, you made a bad decision—one you would not have made had you possessed greater knowledge. Nevertheless, your decision was voluntary because nobody "made" you get the shot.

In the Fourth Amendment context, *Schneckloth* means that it is quite possible for a person to give effective consent to search—because the assent is voluntary—even though he or she did not know that he or she could decline the officer's request to search. Indeed, do you think that an individual who had something to hide—for example, cocaine in a handbag—ever would consent to a search if she knew that her secret were safe if she just said "no"? People with something to hide occasionally may be motivated by guilt to "come clean," and others may (correctly) surmise that if they withhold consent the police will detain them and perhaps be able to secure a search warrant. Nevertheless, it is a safe assumption that some people honestly do not know that they have the right to tell the police that they cannot search their car, backpack, apartment, or home when they are asked to consent to a search. The Court in *Schneckloth* explained why "voluntary" consent to search is all that is required.

> While knowledge of the right to refuse consent is one factor to be taken into account, the government need not establish such knowledge as the *sine qua non* of an effective consent. As with police questioning, two competing concerns must be accommodated in determining the meaning of a "voluntary" consent—the legitimate need for such searches and the equally important requirement of assuring the absence of coercion.
>
> In situations where the police have some evidence of illicit activity, but lack probable cause to arrest or search, a search authorized by a valid consent may be the only

means of obtaining important and reliable evidence. . . . And in those cases where there is probable cause to arrest or search, but where the police lack a warrant, a consent search may still be valuable. If the search is conducted and proves fruitless, that in itself may convince the police that an arrest with its possible stigma and embarrassment is unnecessary, or that a far more extensive search pursuant to a warrant is not justified. In short, a search pursuant to consent may result in considerably less inconvenience for the subject of the search, and, properly conducted, is a constitutionally permissible and wholly legitimate aspect of effective police activity.

> But the Fourth and Fourteenth Amendments require that a consent not be coerced, by explicit or implicit means, by implied threat or covert force. . . .
>
> In examining all the surrounding circumstances to determine if in fact the consent to search was coerced, account must be taken of subtly coercive police questions, as well as the possibly vulnerable subjective state of the person who consents. . . .
>
> The approach of the Court of Appeals for the Ninth Circuit finds no support in any of our decisions that have attempted to define the meaning of "voluntariness." Its ruling, that the State must affirmatively prove that the subject of the search knew that he had a right to refuse consent, would, in practice, create serious doubt whether consent searches could continue to be conducted. . . .
>
> Any defendant who was the subject of a search authorized solely by his consent could effectively frustrate the introduction into evidence of the fruits of that search by simply failing to testify that he in fact knew he could refuse to consent. And the near impossibility of meeting this prosecutorial burden suggests why this Court has never accepted any such litmus-paper test of voluntariness. . . .
>
> One alternative that would go far toward proving that the subject of a search did

know he had a right to refuse consent would be to advise him of that right before eliciting his consent. That, however, is a suggestion that has been almost universally repudiated by both federal and state courts, and, we think, rightly so. For it would be thoroughly impractical to impose on the normal consent search the detailed requirements of an effective warning. Consent searches are part of the standard investigatory techniques of law enforcement agencies. They normally occur on the highway, or in a person's home or office, and under informal and unstructured conditions. The circumstances that prompt the initial request to search may develop quickly or be a logical extension of investigative police questioning. The police may seek to investigate further suspicious circumstances or to follow up leads developed in questioning persons at the scene of a crime. These situations are a far cry from the structured atmosphere of a trial where, assisted by counsel if he chooses, a defendant is informed of his trial rights. And, while surely a closer question, these situations are still immeasurably far removed from "custodial interrogation" where, in Miranda v Arizona, supra, we found that the Constitution required certain now familiar warnings as a prerequisite to police interrogation. . . .

Consequently, we cannot accept the position of the Court of Appeals in this case that proof of knowledge of the right to refuse consent is a necessary prerequisite to demonstrating a "voluntary" consent. Rather, it is only by analyzing all the circumstances of an individual consent that it can be ascertained whether in fact it was voluntary or coerced. . . .

It is said, however, that a "consent" is a "waiver" of a person's rights under the Fourth and Fourteenth Amendments. The argument is that by allowing the police to conduct a search, a person "waives" whatever right he had to prevent the police from searching. It is argued that under the doctrine of Johnson v Zerbst, 304 US 458, 464, 58 S Ct 1019, 82 L Ed 1461, to establish such a "waiver" the State must demonstrate "an intentional relinquishment or abandonment of a known right or privilege."

But these standards were enunciated in Johnson in the context of the safeguards of a fair criminal trial. Our cases do not reflect an uncritical demand for a knowing and intelligent waiver in every situation where a person has failed to invoke a constitutional protection. . . .

The requirement of a "knowing" and "intelligent" waiver was articulated in a case involving the validity of a defendant's decision to forgo a right constitutionally guaranteed to protect a fair trial and the reliability of the truth-determining process. Johnson v Zerbst, supra, dealt with the denial of counsel in a federal criminal trial. . . .

Almost without exception, the requirement of a knowing and intelligent waiver has been applied only to those rights which the Constitution guarantees to a criminal defendant in order to preserve a fair trial. . . .

The guarantees afforded a criminal defendant at trial also protect him at certain stages before the actual trial, and any alleged waiver must meet the strict standard of an intentional relinquishment of a "known" right. But the "trial" guarantees that have been applied to the "pre-trial" stage of the criminal process are similarly designed to protect the fairness of the trial itself. . . .

There is a vast difference between those rights that protect a fair criminal trial and the rights guaranteed under the Fourth Amendment. Nothing, either in the purposes behind requiring a "knowing" and "intelligent" waiver of trial rights, or in the practical application of such a requirement suggests that it ought to be extended to the constitutional guarantee against unreasonable searches and seizures.

A strict standard of waiver has been applied to those rights guaranteed to a criminal defendant to insure that he will be accorded the greatest possible opportunity to utilize every facet of the constitutional model of a fair criminal trial. Any trial conducted in derogation of that model leaves open the possibility that the trial reached an unfair result precisely because all the protections specified in the Constitution were not provided. A prime example is the right to counsel. For without that right, a wholly innocent accused faces the real and substantial danger that simply because of his lack of legal expertise he may be convicted. . . . The Constitution requires that every effort be made to see to it that a defendant in a criminal case has not unknowingly relinquished the basic protections that the Framers thought indispensable to a fair trial.

The protections of the Fourth Amendment are of a wholly different order, and have nothing whatever to do with promoting the fair ascertainment of truth at a criminal trial. . . .

Nor can it even be said that a search, as opposed to an eventual trial, is somehow "unfair" if a person consents to a search. While the Fourth and Fourteenth Amendments limit the circumstances under which the police can conduct a search, there is nothing constitutionally suspect in a person's voluntarily allowing a search. . . . And, unlike those constitutional guaran-

tees that protect a defendant at trial, it cannot be said every reasonable presumption ought to be indulged against voluntary relinquishment. . . . Rather, the community has a real interest in encouraging consent, for the resulting search may yield necessary evidence for the solution and prosecution of crime, evidence that may insure that a wholly innocent person is not wrongly charged with a criminal offense. . . .

It would be unrealistic to expect that in the informal, unstructured context of a consent search, a policeman, upon pain of tainting the evidence obtained, could make the detailed type of examination demanded by Johnson. . . .

It is also argued that the failure to require the Government to establish knowledge as a prerequisite to a valid consent, will relegate the Fourth Amendment to the special province of "the sophisticated, the knowledgeable and the privileged." We cannot agree. The traditional definition of voluntariness we accept today has always taken into account evidence of minimal schooling, low intelligence, and the lack of any effective warnings to a person of his rights; and the voluntariness of any statement taken under those conditions has been carefully scrutinized to determine whether it was in fact voluntarily given. . . .

Notes and Questions

1. Under *Schneckloth's* rule, is a person's knowledge of his or her right to withhold consent to search irrelevant to the voluntariness issue? Who has the burden of proving whether consent was given voluntarily?

2. Despite the majority opinion's statement contrary, does the *Schneckloth* rule effectively "relegate the Fourth Amendment to the special province of 'the sophisticated, the knowledgeable and the privileged'"? That is, are only people who have come into contact with the criminal justice system, or who have studied it, likely to

understand that they do not have to consent to a search when a police officer makes such a request?

3. In *Ohio v. Robinette*, 519 U.S. 33, 117 S. Ct. 417, 136 L. Ed. 2d 347 (1996), a police officer stopped Robinette for speeding on an interstate highway north of Dayton. After the officer ran a computer check on Robinette, returned his driver's license to him, and issued him a verbal warning, he asked Robinette whether he was carrying anything illegal in his car. Robinette replied that he was not. The officer then asked if he could search the car. Robinette consented to the search, which produced a small amount of marijuana and another illegal substance. The Ohio Supreme Court ruled that the illegal drugs were inadmissible as evidence, stating that

> citizens stopped for traffic offenses [must] be clearly informed by the detaining officer when they are free to go after a valid detention, before an officer attempts to engage in a consensual interrogation. Any attempt at consensual interrogation must be preceded by the phrase "At this time you are legally free to go" or by words of similar import.

The U.S. Supreme Court reversed. Chief Justice Rehnquist's majority opinion chastised the Ohio Supreme Court for adopting an inflexible, blanket rule that "a lawfully seized defendant must be advised that he is 'free to go' before his consent to search will be recognized as voluntary." In rejecting that approach, the Chief Justice explained that "the Fourth Amendment test for a valid consent to search is that the consent be voluntary, and 'voluntariness is a question of fact to be determined from all the circumstances,' [quoting Schneckloth v. Bustamonte, 412 U.S. 218, 248–249 (1973)]. The Supreme Court of Ohio having held otherwise, its judgment is reversed."

Justice Ginsburg concurred in the judgment, and Justice Stevens dissented.

4. The New Jersey Supreme Court has rejected Schneckloth on state constitutional grounds, holding that knowledge of the right to refuse consent is necessary for a consent to search to be voluntary and thus legally effective. State v. Johnson, 68 N.J. 349, 346 A.2d 66 (1975).

Who Has the Authority To Give Consent?

Let us now assume that a person "voluntarily" consents to a police search of premises or effects but that someone else's interests are affected by the search. For example, can the proprietor of a hotel consent to the authorities' search of a room rented by a patron? In answering this question in the negative, the Supreme Court observed:

> It is important to bear in mind that it was the petitioner's constitutional right which was at stake here, and not the night clerk's nor the hotel's. It was a right, therefore, which only the petitioner could waive by word or deed, either directly or through an agent. Stoner v. California, 376 U.S. 483, 489, 84 S. Ct. 889, 11 L. Ed. 2d 856 (1964).

This principle received elaboration in United States v. Matlock, 415 U.S. 164, 94 S. Ct. 988, 39 L. Ed. 2d 242 (1974). In Matlock, the woman with whom the defendant shared living arrangements consented to authorities' search of a bedroom that she and the defendant jointly occupied. In a diaper bag stored in a closet in this room, law enforcement officers found money that linked the defendant to the robbery of a bank. The Court, per White, J., concluded that the consent to search the room given by the woman was valid and binding against the defendant.

> The voluntary consent of any joint occupant of a residence to search the premises jointly occupied is valid against the co-occupant, permitting evidence discovered in the search to be admitted against him at a criminal trial. . . . When the prosecution seeks to justify a warrantless search by proof of voluntary consent, it is not limited to proof that consent was given by the

defendant, but may show that permission to search was obtained from a third party who possessed common authority over or other sufficient relation to the premises or effects sought to be inspected. 415 U.S., at 169, 171.

The majority explained that "common authority"

is, of course, not to be implied from the mere property interest a third party has in the property. The authority which justifies the third-party consent does not rest upon the law of property with its attendant historical and legal refinements . . . but rests rather on mutual use of the property by persons generally having joint access or control for most purposes, so that it is reasonable to recognize that any of the co-

inhabitants has the right to permit the inspection in his own right and that the others have assumed the risk that one of their number might permit the common area to be searched. *Id.* at 171 n. 7.

Justices Douglas, Brennan, and Marshall dissented.

In *Matlock*, the party consenting to the search had the *actual* authority to do so, based on her joint occupancy and use of the premises and its effects. However, what of the situation involving a person who has the *apparent* authority to consent but lacks the actual authority to do so? If the police (reasonably) rely on the apparent authority, conduct a search, and seize incriminating evidence, may that evidence be admitted against the person who actually retained the right to exclude the police and did not consent to their entry and search?

Illinois v. Rodriguez, 497 U.S. 177, 110 S. Ct. 2793, 111 L. Ed. 2d 148 (1990)

Justice SCALIA delivered the opinion of the Court.

In *United States v. Matlock*, 415 US 164, 94 S. Ct. 988, 39 L. Ed. 2d 242 (1974), this Court reaffirmed that a warrantless entry and search by law enforcement officials does not violate the Fourth Amendment's proscription of "unreasonable searches and seizures" if the officers have obtained the consent of a third party who possesses common authority over the premises. The present case presents an issue we expressly reserved in *Matlock*, see *id.*, at 177, n. 14, 94 S. Ct. at 996: whether a warrantless entry is valid when based upon the consent of a third party whom the police, at the time of the entry, reasonably believe to possess common authority over the premises, but who in fact does not do so.

I

Respondent Edward Rodriguez was arrested at his apartment by law enforcement officers and

charged with possession of illegal drugs. The police gained entry to the apartment with the consent and assistance of Gail Fischer, who had lived there with respondent for several months. The relevant facts leading to the arrest are as follows.

On July 26, 1985, police were summoned to the residence of Dorothy Jackson on South Wolcott in Chicago. They were met by Ms. Jackson's daughter, Gail Fischer, who showed signs of a severe beating. She told the officers that she had been assaulted by respondent Edward Rodriguez earlier that day in an apartment on South California. Fischer stated that Rodriguez was then asleep in the apartment, and she consented to travel there with the police in order to unlock the door with her key so that the officers could enter and arrest him. During this conversation, Fischer several times referred to the apartment on South California as "our" apartment, and said that she had clothes and furniture there. It is unclear whether she indicated that she currently lived at the apartment, or only that she used to live there.

The police officers drove to the apartment on South California, accompanied by Fischer. They did not obtain an arrest warrant for Rodriguez, nor did they seek a search warrant for the apartment. At the apartment, Fischer unlocked the door with her key and gave the officers permission to enter. They moved through the door into the living room, where they observed in plain view drug paraphernalia and containers filled with white powder that they believed (correctly, as later analysis showed) to be cocaine. They proceeded to the bedroom, where they found Rodriguez asleep and discovered additional containers of white powder in two open attaché cases. The officers arrested Rodriguez and seized the drugs and related paraphernalia.

Rodriguez was charged with possession of a controlled substance with intent to deliver. He moved to suppress all evidence seized at the time of his arrest, claiming that Fischer had vacated the apartment several weeks earlier and had no authority to consent to the entry. The Cook County Circuit Court granted the motion, holding that at the time she consented to the entry Fischer did not have common authority over the apartment. . . . The Circuit Court also rejected the State's contention that, even if Fischer did not possess common authority over the premises, there was no Fourth Amendment violation if the police *reasonably believed* at the time of their entry that Fischer possessed the authority to consent.

The Appellate Court of Illinois affirmed the Circuit Court in all respects. . . .

II

The Fourth Amendment generally prohibits the warrantless entry of a person's home, whether to make an arrest or to search for specific objects. The prohibition does not apply, however, to situations in which voluntary consent has been obtained, either from the individual whose property is searched, see *Schneckloth v. Bustamonte*, 412 U.S. 218, 93 S. Ct. 2041, 36 L. Ed. 2d 854 (1973), or from a third party who possesses common authority over the premises, see *United States v. Matlock, supra*, 415 U.S., at 171, 94 S. Ct., at 993. The State of

Illinois contends that that exception applies in the present case.

As we stated in *Matlock*, 415 U.S., at 171, n. 7, 94 S. Ct., at 993, n. 7, "[c]ommon authority" rests "on mutual use of the property by persons generally having joint access or control for most purposes. . . ." The burden of establishing that common authority rests upon the State. On the basis of this record, it is clear that burden was not sustained. The evidence showed that although Fischer, with her two small children, had lived with Rodriguez beginning in December 1984, she had moved out on July 1, 1985, almost a month before the search at issue here, and had gone to live with her mother. She took her and her children's clothing with her, though leaving behind some furniture and household effects. During the period after July 1 she sometimes spent the night at Rodriguez's apartment, but never invited her friends there, and never went there herself when he was not home. Her name was not on the lease nor did she contribute to the rent. She had a key to the apartment, which she said at trial she had taken without Rodriguez's knowledge (though she testified at the preliminary hearing that Rodriguez had given her the key). On these facts the State has not established that, with respect to the South California apartment, Fischer had "joint access or control for most purposes." To the contrary, the Appellate Court's determination of no common authority over the apartment was obviously correct.

III

* * *

On the merits of the issue, respondent asserts that permitting a reasonable belief of common authority to validate an entry would cause a defendant's Fourth Amendment rights to be "vicariously waived." Brief for Respondent 32. We disagree.

We have been unyielding in our insistence that a defendant's waiver of his trial rights cannot be given effect unless it is "knowing" and "intelligent." . . .

What Rodriguez is assured by the trial right of the exclusionary rule, where it applies, is that no evidence seized in violation of the Fourth

Amendment will be introduced at his trial unless he consents. What he is assured by the Fourth Amendment itself, however, is not that no government search of his house will occur unless he consents; but that no such search will occur that is "unreasonable." U.S. Const., Amdt. 4. There are various elements, of course, that can make a search of a person's house "reasonable"—one of which is the consent of the person or his cotenant. The essence of respondent's argument is that we should impose upon this element a requirement that we have not imposed upon other elements that regularly compel government officers to exercise judgment regarding the facts: namely, the requirement that their judgment be not only responsible but correct. . . .

It is apparent that in order to satisfy the "reasonableness" requirement of the Fourth Amendment, what is generally demanded of the many factual determinations that must regularly be made by agents of the government—whether the magistrate issuing a warrant, the police officer executing a warrant, or the police officer conducting a search or seizure under one of the exceptions to the warrant requirement—is not that they always be correct, but that they always be reasonable. As we put it in *Brinegar v. United States*, 338 U.S. 160, 176, 69 S. Ct. 1302, 1311, 93 L. Ed. 1879 (1949):

> "Because many situations which confront officers in the course of executing their duties are more or less ambiguous, room must be allowed for some mistakes on their part. But the mistakes must be those of reasonable men, acting on facts leading sensibly to their conclusions of probability."

We see no reason to depart from this general rule with respect to facts bearing upon the authority to consent to a search. Whether the basis for such authority exists is the sort of recurring factual question to which law enforcement officials must be expected to apply their judgment; and all the Fourth Amendment requires is that they answer it reasonably.

* * *

[W]hat we hold today does not suggest that law enforcement officers may always accept a person's invitation to enter premises. Even when the invitation is accompanied by an explicit assertion that the person lives there, the surrounding circumstances could conceivably be such that a reasonable person would doubt its truth and not act upon it without further inquiry. As with other factual determinations bearing upon search and seizure, determination of consent to enter must "be judged against an objective standard: would the facts available to the officer at the moment . . . 'warrant a man of reasonable caution in the belief'" that the consenting party had authority over the premises? *Terry v. Ohio*, 392 U.S. 1, 21–22, 88 S. Ct. 1868, 1880, 20 L. Ed. 2d 889 (1968). If not, then warrantless entry without further inquiry is unlawful unless authority actually exists. But if so, the search is valid.

In the present case, the Appellate Court found it unnecessary to determine whether the officers reasonably believed that Fischer had the authority to consent, because it ruled as a matter of law that a reasonable belief could not validate the entry. Since we find that ruling to be in error, we remand for consideration of that question.

* * *

Justice MARSHALL, with whom Justice BRENNAN and Justice STEVENS join, dissenting.

* * *

The majority agrees with the Illinois appellate court's determination that Fischer did not have authority to consent to the officers' entry of Rodriguez's apartment. The Court holds that the warrantless entry into Rodriguez's home was nonetheless valid if the officers reasonably believed that Fischer had authority to consent. The majority's defense of this position rests on a misconception of the basis for third-party consent searches. That such searches do not give rise to claims of constitutional violations rests not on the premise that they are "reasonable" under the Fourth Amendment, but on the premise that a person may voluntarily limit his expectation of privacy by allowing others to exercise authority over his possessions. Cf. *Katz v. United States*, 389 U.S. 347, 351, 88 S. Ct. 507, 511, 19 L. Ed. 2d 576 (1967) ("What a person knowingly exposes to the public, even in his home or office, is not a subject of Fourth Amendment protection"). Thus, an individual's decision to permit another "joint access [to] or control [over the property] for most purposes," *United States v. Matlock*, 415 U.S. 164, 171, n. 7, 94 S. Ct. 988, 993, n. 7, 39 L. Ed. 2d 242 (1974), limits that individual's reasonable expectation of privacy and to that extent limits his Fourth Amendment protections. . . . If an individual has not so limited his expectation of privacy, the police may not dispense with the safeguards established by the Fourth Amendment.

The baseline for the reasonableness of a search or seizure in the home is the presence of a warrant. . . . Because the sole law enforcement purpose underlying the third-party consent searches is avoiding the inconvenience of securing a warrant, a departure from the warrant requirement is not justified simply because an officer reasonably believes a third party has consented to a search of the defendant's home.

* * *

Unlike searches conducted pursuant to the recognized exceptions to the warrant requirement, third-party consent searches are not based on an exigency and therefore serve no compelling social goal. Police officers, when faced with the choice of relying on consent by a third party or securing a warrant, should secure a warrant, and must therefore accept the risk of error should they instead choose to rely on consent.

Our prior cases discussing searches based on third-party consent have never suggested that such searches are "reasonable." In *United States v. Matlock*, this Court upheld a warrantless search conducted pursuant to the consent of a third party who was living with the defendant. The Court rejected the defendant's challenge to the search, stating that a person who permits others to have "joint access or control for most purposes . . . assume[s] the risk that [such persons] might permit the common area to be searched." . . . As the Court's assumption-of-risk analysis makes clear, third-party consent limits a person's ability to challenge the reasonableness of the search only because that person voluntarily has relinquished some of his expectation of privacy by sharing access or control over his property with another person. . . .

Even if the officers reasonably believed that Fischer had authority to consent, she did not, and Rodriguez's expectation of privacy was therefore undiminished. Rodriguez accordingly can challenge the warrantless intrusion into his home as a violation of the Fourth Amendment. . . .

Notes and Questions

1. What should be required before the police's reliance on the apparent authority of a third person to consent to a search is considered "reasonable"? Was the officers' reliance on Gail Fischer's apparent authority in *Rodriguez* reasonable? Should the police be expected to collect information similar to that cited by Justice Scalia to demonstrate that Fischer lacked the actual authority to consent to the search—for example, to determine whether her name was on the lease to the apartment or whether she contributed to the rent?

2. The courts generally recognize consent given by parents to search a child's room in their dwelling, at least when the child is not an adult or when a part of the dwelling has not exclusively been reserved for the child. *See United States v. Peterson*, 524 F.2d 167 (4th Cir. 1975). Children normally are not able to give effective consent to a search of their parents' home, although exceptions sometimes are made. *See United States v. Clutter*, 914 F.2d 775 (6th Cir. 1990).

Hot Pursuit and Other Exigencies

We have observed that "the Fourth Amendment . . . prohibits the police from making a warrantless and non-consensual entry into a suspect's home in order to make a routine felony arrest." *Payton v. New York*, 445 U.S. 573, 576, 100 S. Ct. 1371, 63 L. Ed. 2d 639 (1980). However, the *Payton* Court emphasized that "we have no occasion to consider the sort of emergency or dangerous situation, described in our cases as 'exigent circumstances,' that would justify a warrantless entry into a home for the purpose of either arrest or search." 445 U.S., at 583. We now examine "nonroutine" cases that arguably present "exigent circumstances" justifying a warrantless search. We begin with circumstances considered under the "hot pursuit" exception to the warrant requirement.

Hot Pursuit

Imagine a high-speed chase, with the police hot on the heels of a suspected criminal. If the suspect sprints into his house and slams the door in the faces of the fast-approaching officers, has he thereby reached a safe haven, where he can avoid being arrested at least until the police return with a warrant?

In *Warden v. Hayden*, 387 U.S. 294, 87 S. Ct. 1642, 18 L. Ed. 2d 782 (1967), police arrived at the home of an armed robbery suspect less than five minutes after he reportedly had dashed into the premises after fleeing the scene of the holdup. Several officers made a warrantless entry into the home after the suspect's wife answered their knock on the door. The officers fanned throughout the house in search of the robber. The defendant was found feigning sleep in an upstairs bedroom. One officer, attracted by the sound of running water in the bathroom, discovered a shotgun and a pistol in the flush tank of the commode. Ammunition for the guns was found under the bed's mattress and in a bureau drawer. Meanwhile, another officer, searching the basement for "a man or the money," found a jacket and pair of pants in a washing machine

that fit the description of those worn by the robber. The Supreme Court upheld both the warrantless entry into the home and the subsequent search.

The police were informed that an armed robbery had taken place, and that the suspect had entered 2111 Cocoa Lane less than five minutes before they reached it. They acted reasonably when they entered the house and began to search for a man of the description they had been given and for weapons which he had used in the robbery or might use against them. The Fourth Amendment does not require police officers to delay in the course of an investigation if to do so would gravely endanger their lives or the lives of others. Speed here was essential, and only a thorough search of the house for persons and weapons could have insured that Hayden was the only man present and that the police had control of all weapons which could be used against them or to effect an escape.

We do not rely upon Harris v United States, in sustaining the validity of the search. The principal issue in Harris was whether the search there could properly be regarded as incident to the lawful arrest, since Harris was in custody before the search was made and the evidence seized. Here, the seizures occurred prior to or immediately contemporaneous with Hayden's arrest, as part of an effort to find a suspected felon, armed, within the house into which he had run only minutes before the police arrived. The permissible scope of search must, therefore, at the least, be as broad as may reasonably be necessary to prevent the dangers that the suspect at large in the house may resist or escape.

It is argued that, while the weapons, ammunition, and cap may have been seized in the course of a search for weapons, the officer who seized the clothing was searching neither for the suspect nor for weapons when he looked into the washing machine in which he found the clothing. But even if we assume, although we do not decide, that the exigent circumstances in this case made lawful a search without warrant only for the suspect or his weapons, it cannot be said on this record that the officer who found the clothes in the washing machine was not searching for weapons. He testified that he was searching for the man or the money, but his failure to state explicitly that he was searching for weapons, in the absence of a specific question to that effect, can hardly be accorded controlling weight. He knew that the robber was armed and he did not know that some weapons had been found at the time he opened the machine. In these circumstances the inference that he was in fact also looking for weapons is fully justified. . . .

The Court also discarded the "mere evidence" rule in *Warden v. Hayden*. This rule had been to the effect that only instrumentalities, fruits, and contraband of an offense, and not merely evidence used to show that the suspect had committed the crime, could be seized and admitted into evidence by the government following a lawfully conducted search.

The *Hayden* Court did not use the specific term *hot pursuit* in sustaining the warrantless entry and search of the suspect's home. The principle, as well as the term, was applied in *United States v. Santana*, 427 U.S. 38, 96 S. Ct. 2406, 49 L. Ed. 2d 300 (1976). In *Santana*, the defendant retreated from her doorway to within her house after the police pulled up to within 15 feet of her, emerged from their vehicle and shouted, "Police!" An officer followed the defendant into her home and seized her in the vestibule area. Two packets of heroin fell from the defendant's person to the floor during this action. The Court held the officer's warrantless entry into the home to be reasonable under the circumstances.

The only remaining question is whether her act of retreating into her house could thwart an otherwise proper arrest. We hold that it could not. In Warden v. Hayden, 387 U.S. 294, 87 S. Ct. 1642, 18 L. Ed. 2d 782 (1967), we recognized the right of police, who had probable cause to believe that an armed robber had entered a house a few minutes before, to make a warrantless entry to arrest the robber and to search for weapons. This case, involving a true "hot pursuit,"[3] is clearly governed by Warden; the need to act quickly here is even greater than in that case while the intrusion is much less. The District Court was correct in concluding that "hot pursuit" means some sort of a chase, but it need not be an extended hue and cry "in and about (the) public streets." The fact that the pursuit here ended almost as soon as it began did not render it any the less a "hot pursuit" sufficient to justify the warrantless entry into Santana's house. Once Santana saw the police, there was likewise a realistic expectation that any delay would result in destruction of evidence. See Vale v. Louisiana, 399 U.S. 30, 35, 90 S. Ct. 1969, 1972, 26 L. Ed. 2d 409 (1970). Once she had been arrested the search, incident to that arrest, which produced the drugs and money was clearly justified. . . .

*   *   *   *   *

In *Welsh v. Wisconsin*, 466 U.S. 740, 104 S. Ct. 2091, 80 L. Ed. 2d 732 (1984), the Supreme Court granted certiorari to decide "whether, and if so under what circumstances, the Fourth Amendment prohibits the police from making a

---

3. Warden was based upon the "exigencies of the situation," 387 U.S., at 298, and did not use the term "hot pursuit" or even involve a "hot pursuit" in the sense that that term would normally be understood. That phrase first appears in Johnson v. United States, 333 U.S. 10, 16 n. 7, 68 S. Ct. 367, 370, 92 L. Ed. 436 (1948), where it was recognized that some element of a chase will usually be involved in a "hot pursuit" case.

warrantless night entry of a person's home in order to arrest him for violation of a nonjailable traffic offense." A passerby notified the police after observing a car veer erratically and then swerve off the road into an open field. The driver, who appeared to be "either very inebriated or very sick," walked away from the car before the police responded. After the police arrived and questioned the witness, an officer determined that the car was registered to Welsh, who lived within easy walking distance of where the car had been abandoned. The officer thus proceeded to Welsh's residence. The time was about 9:00 p.m., and it was late April. The officer had no warrant.

Welsh's stepdaughter admitted the officer to the home. The state courts failed to rule whether consent was given for the entry, and the Supreme Court assumed, "for purposes of this decision, . . . that there was no valid consent to enter the petitioner's home." 466 U.S., at 743 n. 1. The police officer found Welsh in bed in an upstairs bedroom, and arrested him for driving while intoxicated (DWI). A first offense of DWI was a noncriminal violation in Wisconsin, subject only to a $200 fine and a civil forfeiture proceeding. A DWI second offense was a misdemeanor punishable by one year in jail and a $500 fine. Although Welsh actually had a prior DWI violation on his record, making him eligible for the misdemeanor conviction and harsher punishment,

> the police conducting the warrantless entry of his home did not know that the petitioner had ever been . . . convicted of a prior violation for driving while intoxicated. It must be assumed, therefore, that at the time of the arrest the police were acting as if they were investigating and actually arresting for a nonjailable traffic offense that constituted only a civil violation. . . . 466 U.S., at 746 n. 6.

The Wisconsin Supreme Court approved of the police officer's warrantless entry into Welsh's home, "relying on the existence of three factors that it believed constituted exigent circumstances: the need for 'hot pursuit' of a suspect, the need to prevent physical harm to the offender and the public, and the need to prevent destruction of evidence." 466 U.S., at 747–748. The Supreme Court reversed (6–2, with Chief Justice Burger voting to dismiss the writ of certiorari as improvidently granted). Justice Brennan's majority opinion relied heavily on the fact that Wisconsin treated DWI as a nonjailable, civil violation.

> Our hesitation in finding exigent circumstances, particularly when warrantless arrests in the home are at issue, is especially appropriate when the underlying offense for which there is probable cause to arrest is relatively minor. Before agents of the government may invade the sanctity of the home, the burden is on the government to demonstrate exigent circumstances that overcome the presumption of unreasonableness that attaches to all warrantless home entries. When the government's interest is only to arrest for a minor offense, that presumption of unreasonableness is difficult to rebut, and the government usually should be allowed to make such arrests only with a warrant issued upon probable cause by a neutral and detached magistrate. . . .

> We therefore conclude that the common-sense approach utilized by most lower courts is required by the Fourth Amendment prohibition on "unreasonable searches and seizures," and hold that an important factor to be considered when determining whether any exigency exists is the gravity of the underlying offense for which the arrest is being made. Moreover, although no exigency is created simply because there is probable cause to believe that a serious crime has been committed, see Payton, application of the exigent-circumstances exception in the context of a home entry should rarely be sanctioned when there is probable cause to believe that

only a minor offense, such as the kind at issue in this case, has been committed.

Application of this principle to the facts of the present case is relatively straightforward. The petitioner was arrested in the privacy of his own bedroom for a noncriminal, traffic offense. The State attempts to justify the arrest by relying on the hot-pursuit doctrine, on the threat to public safety, and on the need to preserve evidence of the petitioner's blood-alcohol level. On the facts of this case, however, the claim of hot pursuit is unconvincing because there was no immediate or continuous pursuit of the petitioner from the scene of a crime. Moreover, because the petitioner had already arrived home, and had abandoned his car at the scene of the accident, there was little remaining threat to the public safety. Hence, the only potential emergency claimed by the State was the need to ascertain the petitioner's blood-alcohol level.

Even assuming, however, that the underlying facts would support a finding of this exigent circumstance, mere similarity to other cases involving the imminent destruction of evidence is not sufficient. The State of Wisconsin has chosen to classify the first offense for driving while intoxicated as a noncriminal, civil forfeiture offense for which no imprisonment is possible. This is the best indication of the State's interest in precipitating an arrest, and is one that can be easily identified both by the courts and by officers faced with a decision to arrest. Given this expression of the State's interest, a warrantless home arrest cannot be upheld simply because evidence of the petitioner's blood-alcohol level might have dissipated while the police obtained a warrant. To allow a warrantless home entry on these facts would be to approve unreasonable police behavior that the principles of the Fourth Amendment will not sanction.

* * *

* * * * *

If Welsh had been suspected of a hit and run and not just first-offense DWI, would the officer's warrantless home entry have been reasonable? Would it matter if the hit and run involved only property damage, or also personal injury? Do you need to know how severely the different kinds of hit and run can be punished to answer this question? Does it make sense to allow the maximum punishment for an offense to weigh so heavily in a decision about the legality of a warrantless entry into a home?

The Court dismissed hot pursuit as a justification for the warrantless entry of Welsh's home "because there was no immediate or continuous pursuit of the petitioner from the scene of a crime." Since there was no continuing threat to safety, and since the need to preserve evidence for a civil violation was insufficiently weighty to justify the warrantless intrusion, the police officer should have procured a warrant for Welsh's arrest or for a search of his premises. An alternative justification for the home entry—that the police had validly obtained consent to enter Welsh's home—was explicitly left open for the state courts to consider on remand. 466 U.S., at 755, n. 15.

Related Exigencies

An exigency somewhat analogous to "hot pursuit" was presented in *Michigan v. Tyler*, 436 U.S. 499, 98 S. Ct. 1942, 56 L. Ed. 2d 486 (1978). Firefighters entered a furniture store in response to a fire call. They extinguished the flames and made an initial, unsuccessful search to attempt to determine the cause of the fire. Inspectors left the scene and returned, without a warrant, to reenter the burned premises about four hours later. They continued their investigation. Several days later, another warrantless entry was made, and another search was conducted. Evidence obtained pursuant to the searches led to the defendants' conviction for conspiracy to burn real property.

The Court held that the initial search, conducted just after the fire was extinguished, and the reentry and search four hours later to investigate further the origins of the blaze, were constitutionally permissible. However, the entry made several days later could not be sustained without a warrant. Because the first reentry was "no more than an actual confirmation" of the entry made to fight the fire, which was clearly justified by exigent circumstances, and because "visibility was severely hindered by darkness, steam and smoke" immediately after the fire, that initial reentry required no warrant. 436 U.S., at 511. The subsequent entries, "however, were clearly detached from the initial exigency and warrantless entry." Since "these searches were conducted without valid warrants and without consent, they were invalid under the Fourth and Fourteenth Amendments." *Id.*

In *Mincey v. Arizona*, 437 U.S. 385, 98 S. Ct. 2408, 57 L. Ed. 2d 290 (1978), the Supreme Court declined to recognize a "murder scene exception" that would permit the warrantless search of a homicide scene without regard to whether "hot pursuit" was a factor in the investigation. Police officers secured an apartment where a murder had occurred, apprehended the suspect, and made an initial search for victims. Thereafter, homicide detectives arrived on the scene. The detectives began a search of the premises, which extended over four days and reached nearly every crevice of the apartment. No search warrant ever was obtained. The state offered several justifications for the search, all of which the Court rejected. One of the reasons offered in support of the warrantless search involved the inherent exigencies in a homicide situation.

The State's second argument in support of its categorical exception to the warrant requirement is that a possible homicide presents an emergency situation demanding immediate action. We do not question the right of the police to respond to emergency situations. Numerous state and federal cases have recognized that the Fourth Amendment does not bar police officers from making warrantless entries and searches when they reasonably believe that a person within is in need of immediate aid. Similarly, when the police come upon the scene of a homicide they may make a prompt warrantless search of the area to see if there are other victims or if a killer is still on the premises. Cf. Michigan v Tyler, supra, at 509–510, 98 S Ct 1942, 56 L Ed 2d 486. "The need to protect or preserve life or avoid serious injury is justification for what would be otherwise illegal absent an exigency or emergency." Wayne v United States, 115 US App DC 234, 241, 318 F2d 205, 212 (opinion of Burger, J.). And the police may seize any evidence that is in plain view during the course of their legitimate emergency activities.

But a warrantless search must be "strictly circumscribed by the exigencies which justify its initiation," Terry v Ohio, 392 US, at 25–26, 20 L Ed 2d 889, 88 S Ct 1868, and it simply cannot be contended that this search was justified by any emergency threatening life or limb. All the persons in Mincey's apartment had been located before the investigating homicide officers arrived there and began their search. And a four-day search that included opening dresser drawers and ripping up carpets can hardly be rationalized in terms of the legitimate concerns that justify an emergency search.

Third, the State points to the vital public interest in the prompt investigation of the extremely serious crime of murder. No one can doubt the importance of this goal. But the public interest in the investigation of other serious crimes is comparable. If the warrantless search of a homicide scene is reasonable, why not the warrantless search of the scene of a rape, a robbery, or a burglary? "No consideration relevant to the Fourth Amendment suggests any point of rational limitation" of such a doctrine.

Chimel v California, supra, at 766, 89 S Ct 2034, 23 L Ed 2d 685 . . . .

Except for the fact that the offense under investigation was a homicide, there were no exigent circumstances in this case. . . .

There was no indication that evidence would be lost, destroyed, or removed during the time required to obtain a search warrant. Indeed, the police guard at the apartment minimized that possibility. And there is no suggestion that a search warrant could not easily and conveniently have been obtained. We decline to hold that the seriousness of the offense under investigation itself creates exigent circumstances of the kind that under the Fourth Amendment justify a warrantless search. . . .

Plain View

An item in "plain view" technically cannot be "searched" within the meaning of the Fourth Amendment because what is exposed for others to see cannot support a legitimate expectation of privacy. In this sense, the plain-view doctrine does not really qualify as an exception to the search warrant requirement. Rather, it allows the police to make a warrantless *seizure* of items exposed to their view. Nevertheless, the plain-view doctrine is intimately related to the search warrant requirement. Because virtually everything seized by the police at some point is visible to them—that is, it is in their "plain view"—limitations must be placed on their authority to be in a position to come across contraband or other incriminating evidence in the first place. As we shall see, application of the plain-view doctrine in large part is designed to ensure that the police do not engage in general, exploratory searches prior to seizing an item that they see.

The plain-view doctrine has several important applications, many of which we already have encountered. For example, the Court approved a "protective sweep" of a house in *Buie v. Maryland* (p. 211), on reasonable suspicion, to allow the police to look for other persons who might pose a danger to them. Yet the officer in *Buie* spotted, not a dangerous confederate, but a red running suit. Why could the running suit be seized? Similarly, in *Warden v. Hayden* (p. 223), an officer found incriminating items of clothing while in hot pursuit of a fleeing felon and in search of the felon's gun. Why could the clothing be seized? Relying by analogy on the plain-view doctrine, the state in *Minnesota v. Dickerson* argued that crack cocaine lawfully could be seized even though the officer's pat-down search was justified solely to detect the presence of weapons. Conceptually, is that argument sound?

The plain-view doctrine received lengthy treatment in Justice Stewart's plurality opinion in *Coolidge v. New Hampshire*, 403 U.S. 443, 464–473, 91 S. Ct. 2022, 20 L. Ed. 2d 564 (1971). This portion of *Coolidge* is discussed at length in *Horton v. California*, which is reproduced below. *Horton* instructs that two conditions must be satisfied under the plain-view doctrine to justify a warrantless seizure. These conditions help to keep "plain view" from being abused to circumvent the Fourth Amendment's search warrant requirement. First, the police must lawfully be on the premises or in a position to observe items that are discovered in plain view. Second, it must be "immediately apparent" to the police that the items in plain view properly can be seized. *Horton* addresses whether a third requirement also must be met: that the evidence was discovered "inadvertently."

Horton v. California, 496 U.S. 128, 110 S. Ct. 2301, 110 L. Ed. 2d 112 (1990)

Justice **Stevens** delivered the opinion of the Court.

In this case we revisit an issue that was considered, but not conclusively resolved, in Coolidge v New Hampshire, 403 US 443, 91 S Ct 2022, 29 L Ed 2d 564 (1971): Whether the warrantless seizure of evidence of crime in plain view is prohibited by the Fourth Amendment if the discovery of the evidence was not inadvertent. We conclude that even though inadvertence is a characteristic of most legitimate "plain view" seizures, it is not a necessary condition.

Petitioner was convicted of the armed robbery of Erwin Wallaker, the treasurer of the San Jose Coin Club. . . .

Sergeant LaRault, an experienced police officer, investigated the crime and determined that there was probable cause to search petitioner's home for the proceeds of the robbery and for the weapons used by the robbers. His affidavit for a search warrant referred to police reports that described the weapons as well as the proceeds, but the warrant issued by the Magistrate only authorized a search for the proceeds, including three specifically described rings.

Pursuant to the warrant, LaRault searched petitioner's residence, but he did not find the stolen property. During the course of the search, however, he discovered the weapons in plain view and seized them. Specifically, he seized an Uzi machine gun, a .38 caliber revolver, two stun guns, a handcuff key, a San Jose Coin Club advertising brochure, and a few items of clothing identified by the victim. LaRault testified that while he was searching for the rings, he also was interested in finding other evidence connecting petitioner to the robbery. Thus, the seized evidence was not discovered "inadvertently."

The trial [court] refused to suppress the evidence found in petitioner's home and, after a jury trial, petitioner was found guilty and sentenced to prison. The California Court of Appeal affirmed. App. 43. It rejected petitioner's argument that our decision in Coolidge required suppression of the seized evidence that had not been listed in the warrant because its discovery was not inadvertent. . . .

The right to security in person and property protected by the Fourth Amendment may be invaded in quite different ways by searches and seizures. A search compromises the individual interest in privacy; a seizure deprives the individual of dominion over his or her person or property. United States v Jacobson, 466 US 109, 113, 105 S Ct 1622, 80 L Ed 2d 85 (1984). The "plain view" doctrine is often considered an exception to the general rule that warrantless searches are presumptively unreasonable, but this characterization overlooks the important difference between searches and seizures. If an article is already in plain view, neither its observation nor its seizure would involve any invasion of privacy. A seizure of the article, however, would obviously invade the owner's possessory interest. If "plain view" justifies an exception from an otherwise applicable warrant requirement, therefore, it must be an exception that is addressed to the concerns that are implicated by seizures rather than by searches.

The criteria that generally guide "plain view" seizures were set forth in Coolidge v New Hampshire. . . .

"It is well established that under certain circumstances the police may seize evidence in plain view without a warrant. But it is important to keep in mind that, in the vast majority of cases, *any* evidence seized by the police will be in plain view, at least at the moment of seizure. The problem with the 'plain view' doctrine has been to identify the circumstances in which plain view has legal significance rather than being simply the normal concomitant of any search, legal or illegal.

"An example of the applicability of the 'plain view' doctrine is the situation in which the police have a warrant to search a given area for specified objects, and in the course of the search come across some other article of incriminating character. Where the initial intrusion that brings the police within plain view of such an article is supported, not by a warrant, but by one of the recognized exceptions to the warrant requirement, the seizure is also legitimate. Thus the police may inadvertently come across evidence while in 'hot pursuit' of a fleeing suspect. And an object that comes into view during a search incident to arrest that is appropriately limited in scope under existing law may be seized without a warrant. Finally, the 'plain view' doctrine has been applied where a police officer is not searching for evidence against the accused, but nonetheless inadvertently comes across an incriminating object.

"What the 'plain view' cases have in common is that the police officer in each of them had a prior justification for an intrusion in the course of which he came inadvertently across a piece of evidence incriminating the accused. The doctrine serves to supplement the prior justification—whether it be a warrant for another object, hot pursuit, search incident to lawful arrest, or some other legitimate reason for being present unconnected with a search directed against the accused—and permits the warrantless seizure. Of course, the extension of the original justification is legitimate only where it is immediately apparent to the police that they have evidence before them; the 'plain view' doctrine may not be used to extend a general exploratory search from one object to another until something incriminating at last emerges." Id., at 465–466 (footnote omitted).

Justice Stewart then described the two limitations on the doctrine that he found implicit in its rationale: First, "that plain view *alone* is never enough to justify the warrantless seizure of evidence," id., at 478, and second, "that the discovery of evidence in plain view must be inadvertent." Id., at 469.

Justice Stewart's analysis of the "plain view" doctrine did not command a majority and a plurality of the Court has since made clear that the discussion is "not a binding precedent." Texas v Brown, 460 US, at 737. . . .

It is, of course, an essential predicate to any valid warrantless seizure of incriminating evidence that the officer did not violate the Fourth Amendment in arriving at the place from which the evidence could be plainly viewed. There are, moreover, two additional conditions that must be satisfied to justify the warrantless seizure. First,

not only must the item be in plain view, its incriminating character must also be "immediately apparent." . . . Second, not only must the officer be lawfully located in a place from which the object can be plainly seen, but he or she must also have a lawful right of access to the object itself. . . .

Justice Stewart concluded that the inadvertence requirement was necessary to avoid a violation of the express constitutional requirement that a valid warrant must particularly describe the things to be seized. He explained:

"The rationale of the exception to the warrant requirement, as just stated, is that a plain-view seizure will not turn an initially valid (and therefore limited) search into a 'general' one, while the inconvenience of procuring a warrant to cover an inadvertent discovery is great. But where the discovery is anticipated, where the police know in advance the location of the evidence and intend to seize it, the situation is altogether different. The requirement of a warrant to seize imposes no inconvenience whatever, or at least none which is constitutionally cognizable in a legal system that regards warrantless searches as 'per se unreasonable' in the absence of 'exigent circumstances.'

"If the initial intrusion is bottomed upon a warrant that fails to mention a particular object, though the police know its location and intend to seize it, then there is a violation of the express constitutional requirement of 'Warrants . . . particularly describing . . . [the] things to be seized.'" 403 US, at 469–471.

We find two flaws in this reasoning. First, evenhanded law enforcement is best achieved by the application of objective standards of conduct, rather than standards that depend upon the subjective state of mind of the officer. The fact that an officer is interested in an item of evidence and fully expects to find it in the course of a search should not invalidate its seizure if the search is confined in area and duration by the terms of a warrant or a valid exception to the warrant requirement. If the officer has knowledge approaching certainty that the item will be found, we see no reason why he or she would deliberately omit a particular description of the item to be seized from the application for a search warrant. Specification of the additional item could only permit the officer to expand the scope of the search. On the other hand, if he or she has a valid warrant to search for one item and merely a suspicion concerning the second, whether or not it amounts to probable cause, we fail to see why that suspicion should immunize the second item from seizure if it is found during a lawful search for the first. The hypothetical case put by Justice White in his dissenting opin-ion in Coolidge is instructive:

"Let us suppose officers secure a warrant to search a house for a rifle. While staying well within the range of a rifle search, they discover two photographs of the murder victim, both in plain sight in the bedroom. Assume also that the discovery of the one photograph was inadvert-ent but finding the other was anticipated. The Court would permit the seizure of only one of the photographs. But in terms of the 'minor' peril to Fourth Amendment values there is surely no dif-ference between these two photographs: the interference with possession is the same in each case and the officers' appraisal of the photo-graph they expected to see is no less reliable than their judgment about the other. And in both situations the actual inconvenience and danger to evidence remain identical if the officers must depart and secure a warrant." Id., at 516.

Second, the suggestion that the inadvertence requirement is necessary to prevent the police from conducting general searches, or from con-verting specific warrants into general warrants, is not persuasive because that interest is already served by the requirements that no war-rant issue unless it "particularly describ[es] the place to be searched and the persons or things to be seized," and that a warrantless search be circumscribed by the exigencies which justify its initiation. Scrupulous adherence to these requirements serves the interests in limiting the area and duration of the search that the inad-vertence requirement inadequately protects. Once those commands have been satisfied and the officer haw a lawful right of access, however, no additional Fourth Amendment interest is fur-thered by requiring that the discovery of evi-dence be inadvertent. If the scope of the search exceeds that permitted by the terms of a validly issued warrant or the character of the relevant exception from the warrant requirement, the subsequent seizure is unconstitutional without more.

In this case, the scope of the search was not enlarged in the slightest by the omission of any reference to the weapons in the warrant. Indeed, if the three rings and other items named in the warrant had been found at the outset—or if peti-tioner had them in his possession and had responded to the warrant by producing them immediately—no search for weapons could have taken place. Again, Justice White's dissenting opinion in Coolidge is instructive:

"Police with a warrant for a rifle may search only places where rifles might be and must ter-minate the search once the rifle is found; the inadvertence rule will in no way reduce the num-ber of places into which they may lawfully look." 403 US, at 517, 91 S Ct 2022, 29 L Ed 2d 564.

As we have already suggested, by hypothesis the seizure of an object in plain view does not involve an intrusion of privacy. If the interest in privacy has been invaded, the violation must have occurred before the object came into plain view and there is no need for an inadvertence limitation on seizures to condemn it. The prohibi-tion against general searches and general war-rants serves primarily as a protection against unjustified intrusions on privacy. But reliance on privacy concerns that support that prohibition is misplaced when the inquiry concerns the scope of an exception that merely authorizes an officer with a lawful right of access to an item to seize it without a warrant.

In this case the items seized from petitioner's home were discovered during a lawful search authorized by a valid warrant. When they were discovered, it was immediately apparent to the officer that they constituted incriminating evi-dence. He had probable cause, not only to obtain a warrant to search for the stolen prop-erty, but also to believe that the weapons and handguns had been used in the crime he was investigating. The search was authorized by the warrant, the seizure was authorized by the "plain view" doctrine. The judgment is affirmed. . . .

Justice **Brennan**, with whom Justice **Marshall** joins, dissenting.

* * *

In eschewing the inadvertent discovery requirement, the majority ignores the Fourth Amendment's express command that warrants particularly describe not only the *places* to be searched, but also the *things* to be seized. I respectfully dissent from this rewriting of the Fourth Amendment. . . .

The Amendment protects two distinct interests. The prohibition against unreasonable searches and the requirement that a warrant "particularly describ[e] the place to be searched" protect an interest in privacy. The prohibition against unreasonable seizures and the requirement that a warrant "particularly describ[e] . . . the . . . things to be seized" protect a possessory interest in property. . . . The Fourth Amendment, by its terms, declares privacy and possessory interests to be equally important. . . .

The Amendment protects these equally important interests in precisely the same manner: by requiring a neutral and detached magistrate to evaluate, before the search or seizure, the government's showing of probable cause and its particular description of the place to be searched and the items to be seized. Accordingly, just as a warrantless search is per se unreasonable absent exigent circumstances, so too a seizure of personal property is "per se unreasonable within the meaning of the Fourth Amendment unless it is accomplished pursuant to a judicial warrant issued upon probable cause and particularly describing the items to be seized." United States v Place, 462 US 696, 701, 103 S Ct 2637, 77 L Ed 2d 110 (1983).

A decision to invade a possessory interest in property is too important to be left to the discretion of zealous officers "engaged in the often competitive enterprise of ferreting out crime."

Johnson v United States, 333 US 10, 68 S Ct 367, 14, 92 L Ed 436 (1948). . . .

The plain view doctrine is an exception to the general rule that a seizure of personal property must be authorized by a warrant. As Justice Stewart explained in Coolidge, 403 US, at 470, 91 S Ct 2022, 29 L Ed 2d 564 we accept a warrantless seizure when an officer is lawfully in a location and inadvertently sees evidence of a crime because of "the inconvenience of procuring a warrant" to seize this newly discovered piece of evidence. But "where the discovery is anticipated, where the police know in advance the location of the evidence and intend to seize it," the argument that procuring a warrant would be "inconvenient" loses much, if not all, of its force. Ibid. Barring an exigency, there is no reason why the police officers could not have obtained a warrant to seize this evidence before entering the premises. The rationale behind the inadvertent discovery requirement is simply that we will not excuse officers from the general requirement of a warrant to seize if the officers know the location of evidence, have probable cause to seize it, intend to seize it, and yet do not bother to obtain a warrant particularly describing that evidence. . . .

It is true that the inadvertent discovery requirement furthers no privacy interests. The requirement in no way reduces the scope of a search or the number of places into which officers may look. But it does protect possessory interests. . . . The inadvertent discovery requirement is essential if we are to take seriously the Fourth Amendment's protection of possessory interests as well as privacy interests. . . .

Horton rejected the Coolidge plurality's suggestion that evidence must be discovered "inadvertently" to be admissible under the plain-view doctrine. The following case, *Arizona v. Hicks*, focuses on the meaning of the requirement that it must be "immediately apparent" to the police that evidence if seizable if it is to be admissible under the plain-view rationale.

Arizona v. Hicks, 480 U.S. 321, 107 S. Ct. 1144, 94 L. Ed. 2d 347 (1987)

Justice **Scalia** delivered the opinion of the Court.

. . . [I]n the present case to decide whether this "plain view" doctrine may be invoked when the police have less than probable cause to believe that the item in question is evidence of a crime or is contraband.

I

On April 18, 1984, a bullet was fired through the door of respondent's apartment, striking and injuring a man in the apartment below. Police officers arrived and entered respondent's apartment to search for the shooter, for other victims, and for weapons. They found and seized three weapons, including a sawed-off rifle, and in the course of their search also discovered a stocking-cap mask.

One of the policemen, Officer Nelson, noticed two sets of expensive stereo components, which seemed out of place in the squalid and otherwise ill-appointed four-room apartment. Suspecting that they were stolen, he read and recorded their serial numbers—moving some of the components, including a Bang and Olufsen turntable, in order to do so—which he then reported by phone to his headquarters. On being advised that the turntable had been taken in an armed robbery, he seized it immediately. It was later determined that some of the other serial numbers matched those on other stereo equipment taken in the same armed robbery, and a warrant was obtained and executed to seize that equipment as well. Respondent was subsequently indicted for the robbery.

The state trial court granted respondent's motion to suppress the evidence that had been seized. The Court of Appeals of Arizona affirmed. . . . Both courts—the trial court explicitly and the Court of Appeals by necessary implication—rejected the State's contention that Officer Nelson's actions were justified under the "plain view" doctrine of Coolidge v New Hampshire. . . .

II

As an initial matter, the State argues that Officer Nelson's actions constituted neither a "search" nor a "seizure" within the meaning of the Fourth Amendment. We agree that the mere recording of the serial numbers did not constitute a seizure. To be sure, that was the first step in a process by which respondent was eventually deprived of the stereo equipment. In and of itself, however, it did not "meaningfully interfere" with respondent's possessory interest in either the serial numbers or the equipment, and therefore did not amount to a seizure.

Officer Nelson's moving of the equipment, however, did constitute a "search" separate and apart from the search for the shooter, victims, and weapons that was the lawful objective of his entry into the apartment. Merely inspecting those parts of the turntable that came into view during the latter search would not have constituted an independent search, because it would have produced no additional invasion of respondent's privacy interest. But taking action, unrelated to the objectives of the authorized intrusion, which exposed to view concealed portions of the apartment or its contents, did produce a new invasion of respondent's privacy unjustified by the exigent circumstance that validated the entry. This is why, contrary to Justice Powell's suggestion, the "distinction between 'looking' at the suspicious object in plain view and 'moving' it even a few inches" is much more than trivial for purposes of the Fourth Amendment. It matters not that the search uncovered nothing of any great personal value to the respondent—serial numbers rather than (what might conceivably have been hidden behind or under the equipment) letters or photographs. A search is a search, even if it happens to disclose nothing but the bottom of a turntable.

III

The remaining question is whether the search was "reasonable" under the Fourth Amendment.

On this aspect of the case we reject, at the outset, the apparent position of the Arizona Court of Appeals that because the officers' action directed to the stereo equipment was unrelated to the justification for their entry into respondent's apartment, it was ipso facto unreasonable. That lack of relationship *always* exists with regard to action validated under the "plain view" doctrine; where action is taken for the purpose justifying the entry, invocation of the doctrine is superfluous.

We turn, then, to application of the doctrine to the facts of this case. "It is well established that under certain circumstances the police may seize evidence in plain view without a warrant," Coolidge v New Hampshire, 403 US, at 465, 91 S Ct 2022, 29 L Ed 2d 564 (plurality) (emphasis added). Those circumstances include situations "[w]here the initial intrusion that brings the police within plain view of such [evidence] is supported . . . by one of the recognized exceptions to the warrant requirement," ibid., such as the exigent-circumstances intrusion here. It would be absurd to say that an object could lawfully be seized and taken from the premises, but could not be moved for closer examination. It is clear, therefore, that the search here was valid if the "plain view" doctrine would have sustained a seizure of the equipment.

There is no doubt it would have done so if Officer Nelson had probable cause to believe that the equipment was stolen. The State has conceded, however, that he had only a "reasonable suspicion," by which it means something less than probable cause. We have not ruled on the question whether probable cause is required in order to invoke the "plain view" doctrine. . . .

We now hold that probable cause is required. To say otherwise would be to cut the "plain view" doctrine loose from its theoretical and practical moorings. The theory of that doctrine consists of extending to nonpublic places such as the home, where searches and seizures without a warrant are presumptively unreasonable, the police's longstanding authority to make warrantless seizures in public places of such objects as weapons and contraband. And the practical justification for that extension is the desirability of sparing police, whose viewing of the object in the course of a lawful search is as legitimate as it would have been in a public place, the incon-

venience and the risk—to themselves or to preservation of the evidence—of going to obtain a warrant. Dispensing with the need for a warrant is worlds apart from permitting a lesser standard of *cause* for the seizure than a warrant would require, i.e., the standard of probable cause. No reason is apparent why an object should routinely be seizable on lesser grounds, during an unrelated search and seizure, than would have been needed to obtain a warrant for the same object if it had been known to be on the premises. . . .

The same considerations preclude us from holding that, even though probable cause would have been necessary for a *seizure*, the *search* of objects in plain view that occurred here could be sustained on lesser grounds. A dwelling-place search, no less than a dwelling-place seizure, requires probable cause, and there is no reason in theory or practicality why application of the plain-view doctrine would supplant that requirement. Although the interest protected by the Fourth Amendment injunction against unreasonable searches is quite different from that protected by its injunction against unreasonable seizures, neither the one nor the other is of inferior worth or necessarily requires only lesser protection. We have not elsewhere drawn a categorical distinction between the two insofar as concerns the degree of justification needed to establish the reasonableness of police action, and we see no reason for a distinction in the particular circumstances before us here. Indeed, to treat searches more liberally would especially erode the plurality's warning in Coolidge that "the 'plain view' doctrine may not be used to extend a general exploratory search from one object to another until something incriminating at last emerges." 403 US, at 466. In short, whether legal authority to move the equipment could be found only as an inevitable concomitant of the authority to seize it, or also as a consequence of some independent power to search certain objects in plain view, probable cause to believe the equipment was stolen was required.

Justice O'Connor's dissent suggests that we uphold the action here on the ground that it was a "cursory inspection" rather than a "full-blown search," and could therefore be justified by reasonable suspicion instead of probable cause. As already noted, a truly cursory inspection—one that involves merely looking at what is already exposed to view, without disturbing it—is not a "search" for Fourth Amendment purposes, and therefore does not even require reasonable suspicion. We are unwilling to send police and judges into a new thicket of Fourth Amendment law, to seek a creature of uncertain description that is neither a plain-view inspection nor yet a "full-blown search." . . .

Justice Powell's dissent reasonably asks what it is we would have had Officer Nelson do in these circumstances. The answer depends, of course, upon whether he had probable cause to conduct a search, a question that was not preserved in this case. If he had, then he should have done precisely what he did.

If not, then he should have followed up his suspicions, if possible, by means other than a search—just as he would have had to do if, while walking along the street, he had noticed the same suspicious stereo equipment sitting inside a house a few feet away from him, beneath an open window. It may well be that, in such circumstances, no effective means short of a search exist. But there is nothing new in the realization that the Constitution sometimes insulates the criminality of a few in order to protect the privacy of us all. Our disagreement with the dissenters pertains to where the proper balance should be struck; we choose to adhere to the textual and traditional standard of probable cause. . . .

Justice Powell, with whom The **Chief Justice** and Justice **O'Connor** join, dissenting.

* * *

The officers' suspicion that the stereo components at issue were stolen was both reasonable and based on specific, articulable facts. Indeed, the State was unwise to concede the absence of probable cause. . . .

It is fair to ask what Officer Nelson should have done in these circumstances. Accepting the State's concession that he lacked probable cause, he could not have obtained a warrant to seize the stereo components. Neither could he have remained on the premises and forcibly prevented their removal. Officer Nelson's testimony indicates that he was able to read some of the serial numbers without moving the components. To read the serial number on a Bang and

Olufsen turntable, however, he had to "turn it around or turn it upside down." . . .

The Court holds that there was an unlawful search of the turntable. It agrees that the "mere recording of the serial numbers did not constitute a seizure." . . . But the Court further holds that "Officer Nelson's moving of the equipment . . . did constitute a 'search' . . . ." It perceives a constitutional distinction between reading a serial number on an object and moving or picking up an identical object to see its serial number. . . . With all respect, this distinction between "looking" at a suspicious object in plain view and "moving" it even a few inches trivializes the Fourth Amendment.[4] The Court's new rule will cause uncertainty, and could deter conscientious police officers from lawfully obtaining evidence necessary to convict guilty persons. Apart from the importance of rationality in the interpretation of the Fourth Amendment, today's decision may handicap law enforcement without enhancing privacy interests. Accordingly, I dissent.

Justice **O'Connor**, with whom The **Chief Justice** and Justice **Powell** join, dissenting.

* * *

I agree with the Court that even under the plain view doctrine, probable cause is required before the police seize an item, or conduct a full-block search of evidence in plain view. Such a requirement of probable cause will prevent the plain view doctrine from authorizing general

---

4. Numerous articles that frequently are stolen have identifying numbers, including expensive watches and cameras, and also credit cards. Assume for example that an officer reasonably suspects that two identical watches, both in plain view, have been stolen. Under the Court's decision, if one watch is lying face up and the other lying face down, reading the serial number on one of the watches would not be a search. But turning over the other watch to read its serial number would be a search. Moreover, the officer's ability to read a serial number may depend on its location in a room and light conditions at a particular time. Would there be a constitutional difference if an officer, on the basis of a reasonable suspicion, used a pocket flashlight or turned on a light to read a number rather than moving the object to a point where a serial number was clearly visible?

searches. This is not to say, however, that even a mere inspection of a suspicious item must be supported by probable cause. When a police officer makes a cursory inspection of a suspicious item in plain view in order to determine whether it is indeed evidence of a crime, there is no "exploratory rummaging." Only those items that the police officer "reasonably suspects" as evidence of a crime may be inspected, and perhaps more importantly, the scope of such an inspection is quite limited. In short, if police officers have a reasonable, articulable suspicion that an object they come across during the course of a lawful search is evidence of a crime, in my view they may make a cursory examination of the object to verify their suspicion. If the officers wish to go beyond such a cursory examination of the object, however, they must have probable cause.

* * *

In my view, the balance of the governmental and privacy interests strongly supports a reasonable suspicion standard for the cursory examination of items in plain view. The additional intrusion caused by an inspection of an item in plain view for its serial number is minuscule. . . .

Weighted against this minimal additional invasion of privacy are rather major gains in law enforcement. The use of identification numbers in tracing stolen property is a powerful law enforcement tool. . . . Given the prevalence of mass produced goods in our national economy, a serial number is often the only sure method of detecting stolen property. The balance of governmental and private interests strongly supports the view accepted by a majority of courts that a standard of reasonable suspicion meets the requirements of the Fourth Amendment.

* * *

Notes and Questions

1. Why does moving a piece of stereo equipment constitute a "search"? Did the information produced—the unit's serial number—in any way implicate Hicks's privacy interests? Is Justice O'Connor's point well taken, that the intrusion on individual privacy is so slight that a lower standard of justification—reasonable suspicion—should allow the police to take such action?

2. If it must be "immediately apparent" that an object in plain view is contraband, evidence of a crime, or otherwise properly subject to seizure, what if Officer Nelson had probable cause to believe the stereo was stolen: Would he then have been justified in moving parts of the stereo to see the serial numbers?

3. If "probable cause" is the equivalent of "immediately apparent," think back to *Chimel v. California* (p. 202). Assume that the police had probable cause to believe that the proceeds of the coin store robbery were hidden in Chimel's dresser in his bedroom. Would a warrantless seizure of them be permissible under *Hicks*?

4. In *Texas v. Brown*, 460 U.S. 730, 103 S. Ct. 1535, 75 L. Ed. 2d 502 (1983), a police officer stopped the car that Clifford Brown was driving at a routine driver's license checkpoint shortly before midnight. The officer stood outside by the driver's window and requested Brown to produce his driver's license. In the process, the officer shone his flashlight into the interior of the car and saw that Brown was holding between two of his fingers "an opaque, green party balloon, knotted about one half inch from the tip." The officer testified that, on the basis of his prior experience, "he was aware that narcotics frequently were packaged in balloons like the one in Brown's hand." When Brown was unable to produce a driver's license, he was instructed to get out of the car. As Brown complied with this order the officer reached into the car, picked up the balloon and felt what apparently was a powdery substance inside of it. Brown then was advised that he was under arrest. The substance in the balloon later was tested and proved to be heroin.

Should the warrantless seizure of the balloon in *Brown* be upheld under the plain-view doctrine?

Justice Rehnquist's plurality opinion concluded that the plain-view requirements were satisfied. The opinion first noted that "the police officer must lawfully make an 'initial intrusion' or otherwise properly be in a position from which he can view a particular area." There was no dispute in *Brown* that the officer had lawfully stopped the car, and no serious argument that his shining the light into the interior and peering into it were improper.

The opinion then discussed the "immediately apparent" requirement. "It must be 'immediately apparent' to the police that the items they observe may be evidence of a crime, contraband, or otherwise subject to seizure." Here, Justice Rehnquist took exception with the lower court's demanding that the officer must have "known" that the balloon contained illicit narcotics to justify its seizure. The officer needed only "probable cause" for the seizure to satisfy the "immediately apparent" requirement. In *Brown*,

"The fact that [the officer] could not see through the opaque fabric of the balloon is all but irrelevant: the distinctive character of the balloon itself spoke volumes as to its contents—particularly to the trained eye of the officer."

Justices Powell and Blackmun concurred in the judgment in *Brown*, as did Justices Stevens, Brennan, and Marshall in a separate opinion.

5. In *State v. Murray*, 134 N.H. 613, 598 A.2d 206 (1991), the New Hampshire Supreme Court announced that "inadvertent discovery" remained a part of the state constitutional requirements for application of the plain-view exception to the warrant requirement. It thus rejected the U.S. Supreme Court's position in *Horton v. California*. *See also State v. Ball*, 124 N.H. 226, 471 A.2d 347 (1983); B. Latzer, *State Constitutional Criminal Law* § 3:18 (1995).

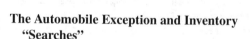

The Automobile Exception and Inventory "Searches"

The Automobile Exception

Almost from the time they first hit the roadways, automobiles have occupied a special place in the jurisprudence of the Fourth Amendment. *E.g., Carroll v. United States*, 267 U.S. 132, 45 S. Ct. 280, 69 L. Ed. 543 (1925). The warrant requirement has been relaxed for car searches for two principal reasons. First, the *inherent mobility* of a car is said to create an exigency that obviates the need for a warrant. If a car is left unguarded while the police leave to acquire a search warrant, there is a danger that the vehicle and its contents will not be anywhere to be found by the time the officers return. The second reason justifying less rigorous Fourth Amendment protections is the

diminished expectation of privacy that people presumably have in autos and their contents. Motor vehicles are subject to comprehensive governmental regulation and licensing requirements and may be stopped and inspected for a variety of reasons. Additionally, because of the general "public nature" of travel by auto, most people presumably have a diminished expectation of privacy in their cars.

Each of these justifications has gradually been extended. We shall see that an auto, even if reduced to the exclusive custody and control of the police, may still be searched under the gloss of the "inherent mobility" rationale. We further will observe that regardless of the efforts a person makes to conceal his or her possessions within a car, a warrantless search of containers, packages, and other items within the car may be upheld solely on the basis of a police officer's determination that probable cause exists to search the auto for contraband.

Chambers v. Maroney, 399 U.S. 42, 90 S. Ct. 1975, 26 L. Ed. 2d 419 (1970)

[Two men robbed a Pennsylvania gas station at gunpoint, taking the currency from the cash register and ordering the attendant to place the coins from the register in one of his gloves and then turn the glove over to them. Witnesses reported seeing a blue station wagon circling the block and later speeding away from a parking lot close to the gas station. Four men, one of whom was wearing a green sweater, reportedly were in the car. The gas station attendant said that one of the robbers was wearing a green sweater and the other a trench coat. Within an hour of the robbery, police stopped a blue station wagon approximately two miles from the gas station. Four men were in the car. One of them wore a green sweater, and there was a trench coat in the car. The occupants of the car were arrested. The car was not immediately searched; instead, it was driven by a police officer to the police station. At the station house the auto was thoroughly searched. Concealed within it were two revolvers, a glove with change in it, and cards bearing the name of the attendant at a gas station that had been robbed a week earlier. The defendant, Chambers, was convicted of both gas station robberies. Evidence seized from the car was introduced at his trial.]

Mr. Justice **White** delivered the opinion of the Court.

The principal question in this case concerns the admissibility of evidence seized from an automobile, in which petitioner was riding at the time of his arrest, after the automobile was taken to a police station and was there thoroughly searched without a warrant.

* * *

We pass quickly the claim that the search of the automobile was the fruit of an unlawful arrest. Both the courts below thought the arresting officers had probable cause to make the arrest. We agree.

* * *

Even so, the search that produced the incriminating evidence was made at the police station some time after the arrest and cannot be justified as a search incident to an arrest: "Once an accused is under arrest and in custody, then a search made at another place, without a warrant, is simply not incident to the arrest." Preston v United States, 376 US 364, 367, 84 S Ct 881, 11 L Ed 2d 777, 780 (1964). . . . [T]he reasons that have been thought sufficient to justify warrantless searches carried out in connection with an arrest no longer obtain when the accused is safely in custody at the station house.

There are, however, alternative grounds arguably justifying the search of the car in this case. . . . [T]he police had probable cause to believe that the robbers, carrying guns and the fruits of the crime, had fled the scene in a light blue compact station wagon which would be carrying four men, one wearing a green sweater and another wearing a trench coat. As the state courts correctly held, there was probable cause to arrest the occupants of the station wagon that the officers stopped; just as obviously was there probable cause to search the car for guns and stolen money.

In terms of the circumstances justifying a warrantless search, the Court has long distinguished between an automobile and a home or office. In Carroll v United States, 267 US 132, 45 S Ct 280, 69 L Ed 543 (1925), the issue was the admissibility in evidence of contraband liquor seized in a warrantless search of a car on the highway. After surveying the law from the time of the adoption of the Fourth Amendment onward, the Court held that automobiles and other conveyances may be searched without a warrant in circumstances that would not justify the search without a warrant of a house or an office, provided that there is probable cause to believe that the car contains articles that the officers are entitled to seize. The Court expressed its holding as follows:

"We have made a somewhat extended reference to these statutes to show that the guaranty of freedom from unreasonable searches and seizures by the Fourth Amendment has been construed, practically since the beginning of the Government, as recognizing a necessary difference between a search of a store, dwelling house or other structure in respect of which a proper official warrant readily may be obtained, and a search of a ship, motor boat, wagon or automobile, for contraband goods, where it is not practicable to secure a warrant because the vehicle can be quickly moved out of the locality or jurisdiction in which the warrant must be sought.

"Having thus established that contraband goods concealed and illegally transported in an automobile or other vehicle may be searched for without a warrant, we come now to consider under what circumstances such search may be made. . . . [T]hose lawfully within the country, entitled to use the public highways, have a right to free passage without interruption or search unless there is known to a competent official authorized to search, probable cause for believing that their vehicles are carrying contraband or illegal merchandise. . . .

"The measure of legality of such a seizure is, therefore, that the seizing officer shall have reasonable or probable cause for believing that the automobile which he stops and seizes has contraband liquor therein which is being illegally transported." 267 US, at 153–154, 155–156.

The Court also noted that the search of an auto on probable cause proceeds on a theory wholly different from that justifying the search incident to an arrest:

"The right to search and the validity of the seizure are not dependent on the right to arrest. They are dependent on the reasonable cause the seizing officer has for belief that the contents of the automobile offend against the law." 267 US, at 158–159.

Finding that there was probable cause for the search and seizure at issue before it, the Court affirmed the convictions. . . .

Neither Carroll, supra, nor other cases in this Court require or suggest that in every conceivable circumstance the search of an auto even with probable cause may be made without the extra protection for privacy that a warrant affords. But the circumstances that furnish probable cause to search a particular auto for particular articles are most often unforeseeable;

moreover, the opportunity to search is fleeting since a car is readily movable. Where this is true, as in Carroll and the case before us now, if an effective search is to be made at any time, either the search must be made immediately without a warrant or the car itself must be seized and held without a warrant for whatever period is necessary to obtain a warrant for the search.[9]

In enforcing the Fourth Amendment's prohibition against unreasonable searches and seizures, the Court has insisted upon probable cause as a minimum requirement for a reasonable search permitted by the Constitution. As a general rule, it has also required the judgment of a magistrate on the probable-cause issue and the issuance of a warrant before a search is made. Only in exigent circumstances will the judgment of the police as to probable cause serve as a sufficient authorization for a search. Carroll holds a search warrant unnecessary where there is probable cause to search an automobile stopped on the highway; the car is movable, the occupants are alerted, and the car's contents may never be found again if a warrant must be obtained. Hence an immediate search is constitutionally permissible.

Arguably, because of the preference for a magistrate's judgment, only the immobilization of the car should be permitted until a search warrant is obtained; arguably, only the "lesser" intrusion is permissible until the magistrate authorizes the "greater." But which is the "greater" and which the "lesser" intrusion is itself a debatable question and the answer may depend on a variety of circumstances. For constitutional purposes, we see no difference between on the one hand seizing and holding a car before presenting the probable cause issue to a magistrate and on the other hand carrying out an immediate search without a warrant. Given probable cause to search, either course is reasonable under the Fourth Amendment.

---

9. Following the car until a warrant can be obtained seems an impractical alternative since, among other things, the car may be taken out of the jurisdiction. Tracing the car and searching it hours or days later would of course permit instruments or fruits of crime to be removed from the car before the search.

On the facts before us, the blue station wagon could have been searched on the spot when it was stopped since there was probable cause to search and it was a fleeting target for a search. The probable-cause factor still obtained at the station house and so did the mobility of the car unless the Fourth Amendment permits a warrantless seizure of the car and the denial of its use to anyone until a warrant is secured. In that event there is little to choose in terms of practical consequences between an immediate search without a warrant and the car's immobilization until a warrant is obtained.[10] The same consequences may not follow where there is unforeseeable cause to search a house. But as Carroll held, for the purposes of the Fourth Amendment there is a constitutional difference between houses and cars. . . .

Mr. Justice **Blackmun** took no part in the consideration or decision of this case.

Mr. Justice **Harlan**, concurring in part and dissenting in part.

* * *

Where officers have probable cause to search a vehicle on a public way, a further limited exception to the warrant requirement is reasonable because "the vehicle can be quickly moved out of the locality or jurisdiction in which the warrant must be sought." Carroll v United States, 267 US 132, 153. Because the officers might be deprived of valuable evidence if required to obtain a warrant before effecting any search or seizure, I agree with the Court that they should be permitted to take the steps necessary to preserve evidence and to make a search possible.

The Court holds that those steps include making a warrantless search of the entire vehicle on the highway—a conclusion reached by the Court in Carroll without discussion—and indeed appears to go further and to condone the removal of the car to the police station for a warrantless search there at the convenience of the police. I cannot agree that this result is consistent with our insistence in other areas that departures from the warrant requirement strictly conform to the exigency presented.

The Court concedes that the police could prevent removal of the evidence by temporarily seizing the car for the time necessary to obtain a warrant. It does not dispute that such a course would fully protect the interests of effective law enforcement; rather it states that whether temporary seizure is a "lesser" intrusion than warrantless search "is itself a debatable question and the answer may depend on a variety of circumstances."[8] I believe it clear that a warrantless search involves the greater sacrifice of Fourth Amendment values.

The Fourth Amendment proscribes, to be sure, unreasonable "seizures" as well as "searches." However, in the circumstances in which this problem is likely to occur, the lesser intrusion will almost always be the simple seizure of the car for the period—perhaps a day—necessary to enable the officers to obtain a search warrant. In the first place, as this case shows, the very facts establishing probable cause to search will often also justify arrest of the occupants of the vehicle. Since the occupants themselves are to be taken into custody, they will suffer minimal further inconvenience from the temporary immobilization of their vehicle. Even where no arrests are made, persons who wish to avoid a search—either to protect their privacy or to conceal incriminating evidence—will almost certainly prefer a brief loss of the use of the vehicle in exchange for the oppor-

---

10. It was not unreasonable in this case to take the car to the station house. All occupants in the car were arrested in a dark parking lot in the middle of the night. A careful search at this point was impractical and perhaps not safe for the officers, and it would serve the owner's convenience and safety of his car to have the vehicle and the keys together at the station house.

8. The Court, unable to decide whether search or temporary seizure is the "lesser" intrusion, in this case authorizes both. The Court concludes that it was reasonable for the police to take the car to the station, where they searched it once to no avail. The searching officers then entered the station, interrogated petitioner and the car's owner, and returned later for another search of the car—this one successful. At all times the car and its contents were secure against removal or destruction. Nevertheless, the Court approves the searches without even an inquiry into the officers' ability promptly to take their case before a magistrate.

tunity to have a magistrate pass upon the justification for the search. To be sure, one can conceive of instances in which the occupant, having nothing to hide and lacking concern for the privacy of the automobile, would be more deeply offended by a temporary immobilization of his vehicle than by a prompt search of it. However, such a person always remains free to consent to an immediate search, thus avoiding any delay. Where consent is not forthcoming, the occupants of the car have an interest in privacy that is protected by the Fourth Amendment even where the circumstances justify a temporary seizure. The Court's endorsement of a warrantless invasion of that privacy where another course would suffice is simply inconsistent with our repeated stress on the Fourth Amendment's mandate of "'adherence to judicial processes.'" E.g., Katz v United States, 389 US, at 357, 88 S Ct 507, 19 L Ed 2d at 585.[9]

Notes and Questions

1. Once the car in *Chambers* had been driven to the police station, did it retain its "inherent mobility"? After the police seized the car and reduced it to their control, why were they not required to get a search warrant before searching it? Would such a requirement be unduly burdensome? With whom do you agree—Justice White or Justice Harlan—regarding whether the seizure of the car or its search represents the greater intrusion? Why not follow Justice Harlan's suggestion and just ask the driver whether he would prefer to consent to a search or have the police seize the vehicle and hold it pending their application for a search warrant?

2. In *Coolidge v. New Hampshire*, 403 U.S. 443, 91 S. Ct. 2022, 29 L. Ed. 2d 564 (1971), Justice Stewart's plurality opinion appeared to limit *Chambers* to its holding that both probable cause and exigent circumstances must exist to justify the warrantless search of a car. The defendant in *Coolidge* was arrested while his auto was parked in the driveway of his home, and he could not conceivably gain access to it. The car was towed to the police station, placed under guard, and later searched without a warrant. The Court disapproved of the warrantless search and seizure of incriminating items from the car.

"Chambers . . . is of no help to the State, since that case held only that, where the police may stop and search an automobile under *Carroll*, they may also seize it and search it at the police station. . . . Here, there was probable cause, but no exigent circumstances justified the police in proceeding without a warrant." 403 U.S., at 463–64 (plurality opinion).

Justice Stewart conceded that

it is true that the actual search of the automobile in Chambers was made at the police station many more hours after the car had been stopped on the highway, when the car was no longer movable, any "exigent circumstances" had passed, and, for all the record shows, there was a magistrate easily available. Nonetheless, the analogy to this case is misleading. The rationale of Chambers is that given a justified initial intrusion, there is little difference between a search on the open highway and a later search at the station. Here we deal with the prior question of *whether* the initial intrusion is justified. For this purpose it seems abundantly clear that there is a significant constitutional difference between

---

9. Circumstances might arise in which it would be impracticable to immobilize the car for the time required to obtain a warrant—for example, where a single police officer must take arrested suspects to the station, and has no way of protecting the suspects' car during his absence. In such situations it might be wholly reasonable to perform an on-the-spot search based on probable cause. However, where nothing in the situation makes impracticable the obtaining of a warrant, I cannot join the Court in shunting aside that vital Fourth Amendment safeguard.

stopping, seizing and searching a car on the open highway, and entering private property to seize and search an unoccupied, parked vehicle not then being used for any illegal purposes. 403 U.S., at 463 n. 20.

In ringing terms, the *Coolidge* plurality opinion admonished that "the word 'automobile' is not a talisman in whose presence the Fourth Amendment fades away and disappears." 403 U.S., at 461.

Keep in mind that *Coolidge* is of limited precedential value because Justice Stewart's opinion did not command a majority of the Court. Later cases have liberalized the Court's car search rules rather than limiting them.

*   *   *   *   *

Can the warrantless search of an auto, based on probable cause, extend not only to loose items, readily visible in the car, but also to closed packages and containers inside of the car?

Be sure to distinguish this issue from *New York v. Belton*, where the Court ruled that containers found within the passenger area of a car may be searched incident to the arrest of the car's occupant. *Belton* (1) presumes a lawful arrest, (2) applies only to those containers found in the auto's passenger area and not the trunk, and (3) does not require probable cause to search the car. The search is automatically permitted as an incident to the arrest.

The question we now raise is different. For example, what if the police have probable cause to believe that drugs are located somewhere within a suspect's car? On searching the car's trunk, they find a closed box, bag, suitcase, or other container that could possibly contain the drugs. May they open the container without a warrant? Does an individual's "expectation of privacy" in a sealed container carried inside of a car survive the "automobile exception" to the search warrant requirement? What does *United States v. Chadwick* (p. 207) suggest the rule would be if the police came across the container outside of the car? Could they search it on probable cause alone, without a warrant? Must they

seize the container and then apply for a warrant? If a container outside of a car normally cannot be searched without a warrant (absent an exigent circumstance), does the act of placing it inside of the car somehow cause the package to lose its individual identity so that it essentially merges with "the car" and thus can be searched without a warrant? Should it matter if the police have probable cause to search a specific container, as opposed to the whole car?

The question of what rule to apply to the search of closed containers found within cars bedeviled the Supreme Court for several years. The relevant decisions are discussed in *United States v. Ross*, 456 U.S. 798, 102 S. Ct. 2157, 72 L. Ed. 2d 572 (1982). Washington, D.C., police officers who encountered Ross driving his car had probable cause to believe that drugs were located somewhere in the car. They arrested Ross, took his car keys, and opened the car's trunk. They had no search warrant. Inside of the trunk, they found a closed brown paper bag and a zippered red leather pouch. They opened the paper bag at the scene of the arrest and discovered that it contained heroin. They unzipped the pouch after the car was removed to the police station and found $3,200 in cash. The D.C. Circuit Court of Appeals (en banc) ruled that the police should have secured a search warrant before opening the paper bag and the leather pouch. It ordered the heroin and the money suppressed from evidence.

The Supreme Court reversed. Justice Stevens's majority opinion first reviewed *Carroll v. United States* and the general justification for permitting warrantless searches of automobiles on probable cause to believe that they contain contraband. It then discussed cases squarely addressing the warrantless search of containers, including containers found within cars. Finally, it explained why the police could search a container found in a car—so long as (1) the search was supported by probable cause to believe that contraband was located somewhere within the car (as opposed to being located specifically within the container) and (2) the container reasonably could hold the object of the search.

United States v. Ross, 456 U.S. 798, 102 S. Ct. 2157, 72 L. Ed. 2d 572 (1982)

Justice **Stevens** delivered the opinion of the Court.

* * *

III

The rationale justifying a warrantless search of an automobile that is believed to be transporting contraband arguably applies with equal force to any movable container that is believed to be carrying an illicit substance. That argument, however, was squarely rejected in United States v Chadwick, 433 US 1, 97 S Ct 2476, 53 L Ed 2d 538.

The Court in Chadwick specifically rejected the argument that the warrantless search was "reasonable" because a footlocker has some of the mobile characteristics that support warrantless searches of automobiles. The Court recognized that "a person's expectations of privacy in personal luggage are substantially greater than in an automobile," and noted that the practical problems associated with the temporary detention of a piece of luggage during the period of time necessary to obtain a warrant are significantly less than those associated with the detention of an automobile. In ruling that the warrantless search of the footlocker was unjustified, the Court reaffirmed the general principle that closed packages and containers may not be searched without a warrant. . . .

The facts in Arkansas v Sanders, 442 US 753, 99 S Ct 2586, 61 L Ed 2d 235, were similar to those in Chadwick. In Sanders, a Little Rock police officer received information from a reliable informant that Sanders would arrive at the local airport on a specified flight that afternoon carrying a green suitcase containing marijuana. The officer went to the airport. Sanders arrived on schedule and retrieved a green suitcase from the airline baggage service. Sanders gave the suitcase to a waiting companion who placed it in the trunk of a taxi. Sanders and his companion drove off in the cab; police officers followed and stopped the taxi several blocks from the airport.

The officers opened the trunk, seized the suitcase, and searched it on the scene without a warrant. As predicted, the suitcase contained marijuana.

The Arkansas Supreme Court ruled that the warrantless search of the suitcase was impermissible under the Fourth Amendment, and this Court affirmed. As in Chadwick, the mere fact that the suitcase had been placed in the trunk of the vehicle did not render the automobile exception of Carroll applicable; the police had probable cause to seize the suitcase before it was placed in the trunk of the cab and did not have probable cause to search the taxi itself. Since the suitcase had been placed in the trunk, no danger existed that its contents could have been secreted elsewhere in the vehicle. . . .

Robbins v California, 453 US 420, 101 S Ct 2841, 69 L Ed 2d 714, however, was a case in which suspicion was not directed at a specific container. In that case the Court for the first time was forced to consider whether police officers who were entitled to conduct a warrantless search of an automobile stopped on a public roadway may open a container found within the vehicle. In the early morning of January 5, 1975, police officers stopped Robbins' station wagon because he was driving erratically. Robbins got out of the car, but later returned to obtain the vehicle's registration papers. When he opened the car door, the officers smelled marijuana smoke. One of the officers searched Robbins and discovered a vial of liquid; in a search of the interior of the car the officer found marijuana. The police officers then opened the tailgate of the station wagon and raised the cover of a recessed luggage compartment. In the compartment they found two packages wrapped in green opaque plastic. The police unwrapped the packages and discovered a large amount of marijuana in each.

* * *

Writing for a plurality, Justice Stewart rejected the argument that the outward appearance of the packages precluded Robbins from having a reasonable expectation of privacy in their contents. He also squarely rejected the argument that there is a constitutional distinction between searches of luggage and searches of "less worthy" containers. Justice Stewart reasoned that all containers are equally protected by the Fourth Amendment unless their contents are in plain view. The plurality concluded that the warrantless search was impermissible because Chadwick and Sanders had established that "a closed piece of luggage found in a lawfully searched car is constitutionally protected to the same extent as are closed pieces of luggage found anywhere else." 453 US, at 425, 101 S Ct 2841, 69 L Ed 2d 744. . . .

Unlike Chadwick and Sanders, in this case police officers had probable cause to search respondent's entire vehicle. Unlike Robbins, in this case the parties have squarely addressed the question whether, in the course of a legitimate warrantless search of an automobile, police are entitled to open containers found within the vehicle. We now address that question. Its answer is determined by the scope of the search that is authorized by the exception to the warrant requirement set forth in Carroll.

IV

In Carroll itself, the whiskey that the prohibition agents seized was not in plain view. It was discovered only after an officer opened the rumble seat and tore open the upholstery of the lazyback. The Court did not find the scope of the search unreasonable. Having stopped Carroll and Kiro on a public road and subjected them to the indignity of a vehicle search—which the Court found to be a reasonable intrusion on their privacy because it was based on probable cause that their vehicle was transporting contraband—prohibition agents were entitled to tear open a portion of the roadster itself. The scope of the search was no greater than a magistrate could have authorized by issuing a warrant based on the probable cause that justified the search. Since such a warrant could have authorized the agents to open the rear portion of the roadster and to rip the upholstery in their search for concealed whiskey, the search was constitutionally permissible.

In Chambers v Maroney the police found weapons and stolen property "concealed in a compartment under the dashboard." 399 US, at 44, 90 S Ct 1975, 26 L Ed 2d 419. No suggestion was made that the scope of the search was impermissible. It would be illogical to assume that the outcome of Chambers—or the outcome of Carroll itself—would have been different if the police had found the secreted contraband enclosed within a secondary container and had opened that container without a warrant. If it was reasonable for prohibition agents to rip open the upholstery in Carroll, it certainly would have been reasonable for them to look into a burlap sack stashed inside; if it was reasonable to open the concealed compartment in Chambers, it would have been equally reasonable to open a paper bag crumpled within it. A contrary rule could produce absurd results inconsistent with the decision in Carroll itself. . . .

As we have stated, the decision in Carroll was based on the Court's appraisal of practical considerations viewed in the perspective of history. It is therefore significant that the practical consequences of the Carroll decision would be largely nullified if the permissible scope of a warrantless search of an automobile did not include containers and packages found inside the vehicle. Contraband goods rarely are strewn across the trunk or floor of a car; since by their very nature such goods must be withheld from public view, they rarely can be placed in an automobile unless they are enclosed within some form of container. . . .

A lawful search of fixed premises generally extends to the entire area in which the object of the search may be found and is not limited by the possibility that separate acts of entry or opening may be required to complete the search. Thus, a warrant that authorizes an officer to search a home for illegal weapons also provides authority to open closets, chests, drawers, and containers in which the weapon might be found. A warrant to open a footlocker to search for marijuana would also authorize the opening of packages found inside. A warrant to search a vehicle would support a search of every part of the vehicle that might contain the object of the search. When a legitimate search is under way, and when its purpose and its limits have been precisely defined, nice distinctions between closets, drawers, and containers, in the case of a home, or between glove compartments, upholstered seats, trunks, and wrapped packages, in the case of a vehicle, must give way to the interest in the prompt and efficient completion of the task at hand.[28]

This rule applies equally to all containers, as indeed we believe it must. One point on which the Court was in virtually unanimous agreement in Robbins was that a constitutional distinction between "worthy" and "unworthy" containers could be improper. Even though such a distinction perhaps could evolve in a series of cases in which paper bags, locked trunks, lunch buckets, and orange crates were placed on one side of the line or the other, the central purpose of the Fourth Amendment forecloses such a distinction. . . .

[T]he protection afforded by the Amendment varies in different settings. The luggage carried by a traveler entering the country may be searched at random by a customs officer; the luggage may be searched no matter how great the traveler's desire to conceal the contents may be. A container carried at the time of arrest often may be searched without a warrant and even without any specific suspicion concerning its contents. A container that may conceal the object of a search authorized by a warrant may be opened immediately; the individual's interest in privacy must give way to the magistrate's official determination of probable cause.

In the same manner, an individual's expectation of privacy in a vehicle and its contents may not survive if probable cause is given to believe that the vehicle is transporting contraband. Certainly the privacy interests in a car's trunk or glove compartment may be no less than those in a movable container. An individual undoubtedly has a significant interest that the upholstery of his automobile will not be ripped or a hidden compartment within it opened. These interests must yield to the authority of a search, however, which—in light of Carroll—does not itself require the prior approval of a magistrate. The scope of a warrantless search based on probable cause is no narrower—and no broader—than the scope of a search authorized by a warrant supported by probable cause. Only the prior approval of the magistrate is waived; the search otherwise is as the magistrate could authorize.

The scope of a warrantless search of an automobile thus is not defined by the nature of the container in which the contraband is secreted. Rather, it is defined by the object of the search and the places in which there is probable cause to believe that it may be found. Just as probable cause to believe that a stolen lawnmower may be found in a garage will not support a warrant to search an upstairs bedroom, probable cause to believe that undocumented aliens are being transported in a van will not justify a warrantless search of a suitcase. Probable cause to believe that a container placed in the trunk of a taxi contains contraband or evidence does not justify a search of the entire cab.

V

Our decision today is inconsistent with the disposition in Robbins v California and with the portion of the opinion in Arkansas v Sanders on which the plurality in Robbins relied. . . .

We hold that the scope of the warrantless search authorized . . . is no broader and no narrower than a magistrate could legitimately authorize by warrant. If probable cause justifies the search of a lawfully stopped vehicle, it justifies the search of every part of the vehicle and its contents that may conceal the object of the search.

---

28. The practical considerations that justify a warrantless search of an automobile continue to apply until the entire search of the automobile and its contents has been completed. Arguably, the entire vehicle itself (including its upholstery) could be searched without a warrant, with all wrapped articles and containers found during that search then taken to a magistrate. But prohibiting police from opening immediately a container in which the object of the search is most likely to be found and instead forcing them first to comb the entire vehicle would actually exacerbate the intrusion on privacy interests. Moreover, until the container itself was opened the police could never be certain that the contraband was not secreted in a yet undiscovered portion of the vehicle; thus in every case in which a container was found, the vehicle would need to be secured while a warrant was obtained. Such a requirement would be directly inconsistent with the rationale supporting the decisions in Carroll and Chambers.

The judgment of the Court of Appeals is reversed.

* * *

Justice **Marshall**, with whom Justice **Brennan** joins, dissenting.

The majority today not only repeals all realistic limits on warrantless automobile searches, it repeals the Fourth Amendment warrant requirement itself. By equating a police officer's estimation of probable cause with a magistrate's, the Court utterly disregards the value of a neutral and detached magistrate.

* * *

The safeguards embodied in the warrant requirement apply as forcefully to automobile searches as to any others.

Our cases do recognize a narrow exception to the warrant requirement for certain automobile searches. Throughout our decisions, two major considerations have been advanced to justify the automobile exception to the warrant requirement. . . .

First, these searches have been justified on the basis of the exigency of the mobility of the automobile.

* * *

In many cases, however, the police will, prior to searching the car, have cause to arrest the occupants and bring them to the station for booking. In this situation, the police can ordinarily seize the automobile and bring it to the station. Because the vehicle is now in the exclusive control of the authorities, any subsequent search cannot be justified by the mobility of the car. Rather, an immediate warrantless search of the vehicle is permitted because of the second major justification for the automobile exception: the diminished expectation of privacy in an automobile. . . .

The majority's rule is flatly inconsistent with these established Fourth Amendment principles concerning the scope of the automobile exception and the importance of the warrant requirement. . . .

The practical mobility problem—deciding what to do with both the car and the occupants if an immediate search is not conducted—is simply not present in the case of movable containers, which can easily be seized and brought to the magistrate. The lesser expectation of privacy rationale also has little force. A container, as opposed to the car itself, does not reflect diminished privacy interests. Moreover, the practical corollary that this Court has recognized—that depriving occupants of the use of a car may be a greater intrusion than an immediate search—is of doubtful relevance here, since the owner of a container will rarely suffer significant inconvenience by being deprived of its use while a warrant is being obtained. . . .

The only convincing explanation I discern for the majority's broad rule is expediency: it assists police in conducting automobile searches, ensuring that the private containers into which criminal suspects often place goods will no longer be a Fourth Amendment shield. "When a legitimate search is under way," the Court instructs us, "nice distinctions between . . . glove compartments, upholstered seats, trunks, and wrapped packages . . . must give way to the interest in the prompt and efficient completion of the task at hand." No "nice distinctions" are necessary, however, to comprehend the well-recognized differences between movable containers (which, even after today's decision, would be subject to the warrant requirement if located outside an automobile), and the automobile itself, together with its integral parts. Nor can I pass by the majority's glib assertion that the "prompt and efficient completion of the task at hand" is paramount to the Fourth Amendment interests of our citizens. I had thought it well established that "the mere fact that law enforcement may be made more efficient can never by itself justify disregard of the Fourth Amendment." Mincey v Arizona, 437 US 385, 393, 98 S Ct 2408, 57 L Ed 2d 290, (1978). . . .

* * * * *

In Ross, the police had probable cause to believe that drugs were located somewhere within Ross's car. The facts thus differed from *Arkansas v. Sanders*, discussed in *Ross*, where there was probable cause to believe that the defendant had drugs in a suitcase, which he then placed in his car. The *Sanders* court disapproved of the warrantless search of the suitcase.

It concluded that since probable cause was specific to the suitcase, the contact between the suitcase and the car did not transform the search into an "automobile" search for which no warrant was needed.

California v. Acevedo, reprinted below, involved facts that were virtually indistinguishable from the facts in *Sanders.* Law enforcement officers saw Charles Acevedo enter the apartment of an individual suspected of selling drugs. Acevedo left the apartment 10 minutes later, carrying a brown paper bag. He placed the bag in the trunk of his car and began to drive away. Police officers stopped the vehicle, opened the trunk and the paper bag inside of it, and found marijuana. After Acevedo's motion to suppress the marijuana was denied, he was convicted, and he appealed.

California v. Acevedo, 500 U.S. 565, 111 S. Ct. 1982, 114 L. Ed. 2d 619 (1991)

Justice **Blackmun** delivered the opinion of the Court.

* * *

The California Court of Appeal, Fourth District, concluded that the marijuana found in the paper bag in the car's trunk should have been suppressed. People v Acevedo, 216 Cal App 3d 586, 265 Cal Rptr 23 (1990). The court concluded that the officers had probable cause to believe that the paper bag contained drugs but lacked probable cause to suspect that Acevedo's car, itself, otherwise contained contraband. Because the officers' probable cause was directed specifically at the bag, the court held that the case was controlled by United States v Chadwick, 433 US 1, 97 S Ct 2476, 53 L Ed 2d 538, (1977), rather than by United States v Ross, 456 US 798, 102 S Ct 2157, 72 L Ed 2d 572 (1982). Although the court agreed that the officers could seize the paper bag, it held that, under Chadwick, they could not open the bag without first obtaining a warrant for that purpose. The court then recognized "the anomalous nature" of the dichotomy between the rule in Chadwick and the rule in Ross. That dichotomy dictates that if there is probable cause to search a car, then the entire car—including any closed container found therein—may be searched without a warrant, but if there is probable cause only as to a container in the car, the container may be held but not searched until a warrant is obtained. . . .

We now must decide the question deferred in Ross: whether the Fourth Amendment requires the police to obtain a warrant to open the sack in a movable vehicle simply because they lack probable cause to search the entire car. We conclude that it does not.

Dissenters in Ross asked why the suitcase in Sanders was "more private, less difficult for police to seize and store, or in any other relevant respect more properly subject to the warrant requirement, than a container that police discover in a probable-cause search of an entire automobile?" We now agree that a container found after a general search of the automobile and a container found in a car after a limited search for the container are equally easy for the police to store and for the suspect to hide or destroy. In fact, we see no principled distinction in terms of either the privacy expectation or the exigent circumstances between the paper bag found by the police in Ross and the paper bag found by the police here. Furthermore, by attempting to distinguish between a container for which the police are specifically searching and a container which they come across in a car, we have provided only minimal protection for privacy and have impeded effective law enforcement. . . . .

At the moment when officers stop an automobile, it may be less than clear whether they suspect with a high degree of certainty that the vehicle contains drugs in a bag or simply contains drugs. If the police know that they may open a bag only if they are actually searching the entire car, they may search more extensively than they otherwise would in order to establish the general probable cause required by Ross. . . .

To the extent that the Chadwick-Sanders rule protects privacy, its protection is minimal. Law enforcement officers may seize a container and hold it until they obtain a search warrant. Chadwick, 433 US, at 13, 97 S Ct 2476, 53 L Ed 2d 538. "Since the police, by hypothesis, have probable cause to seize the property, we can assume that a warrant will be routinely forthcoming in the overwhelming majority of cases." Sanders, 442 US, at 770, 99 S Ct 2586, 61 L Ed 2d 235 (dissenting opinion). And the police often will be able to search containers without a warrant, despite the Chadwick-Sanders rule, as a search incident to a lawful arrest. . . .

Under Belton, the same probable cause to believe that a container holds drugs will allow the police to arrest the person transporting the container and search it.

Finally, the search of a paper bag intrudes far less on individual privacy than does the incursion sanctioned long ago in Carroll. In that case, prohibition agents slashed the upholstery of the automobile. This Court nonetheless found their search to be reasonable under the Fourth Amendment. If destroying the interior of an automobile is not unreasonable, we cannot conclude that looking inside a closed container is. In light of the minimal protection to privacy afforded by the Chadwick-Sanders rule, and our serious doubt whether that rule substantially serves privacy interests, we now hold that the Fourth Amendment does not compel separate treatment for an automobile search that extends only to a container within the vehicle.

The Chadwick-Sanders rule not only has failed to protect privacy but it has also confused courts and police officers and impeded effective law enforcement. . . .

The Chadwick rule, as applied in Sanders, has devolved into an anomaly such that the more likely the police are to discover drugs in a container, the less authority they have to search it. We have noted the virtue of providing '"clear and unequivocal" guidelines to the law enforcement profession.'" The Chadwick-Sanders rule is the antithesis of a '"clear and unequivocal' guideline."'. . .

Although we have recognized firmly that the doctrine of stare decisis serves profoundly important purposes in our legal system, this Court has overruled a prior case on the comparatively rare occasion when it had bred confusion or been a derelict or led to anomalous results.

Sanders was explicitly undermined in Ross, and the existence of the dual regimes for automobile searches that uncover containers has proved as confusing as the Chadwick and Sanders dissenters predicted. We conclude that it is better to adopt one clear-cut rule to govern automobile searches and eliminate the warrant requirement for closed containers set forth in Sanders.

The interpretation of the Carroll doctrine set forth in Ross now applies to all searches of containers found in an automobile. In other words, the police may search without a warrant if their search is supported by probable cause. The Court in Ross put it this way:

"The scope of a warrantless search of an automobile . . . is not defined by the nature of the container in which the contraband is secreted. Rather, it is defined by the object of the search and the places in which there is probable cause to believe that it may be found." 456 US, at 824, 102 S Ct 2157, 72 L Ed 2d 572.

It went on to note: "Probable cause to believe that a container placed in the trunk of a taxi contains contraband or evidence does not justify a search of the entire cab." We reaffirm that principle. In the case before us, the police had probable cause to believe that the paper bag in the automobile's trunk contained marijuana. That probable cause now allows a warrantless search of the paper bag. The facts in the record reveal that the police did not have probable cause to believe that contraband was hidden in any other part of the automobile and a search of the entire vehicle would have been without probable cause and unreasonable under the Fourth Amendment. . . .

Justice **Stevens**, with whom Justice **Marshall** joins, dissenting.

* * *

Our decisions have always acknowledged that the warrant requirement imposes a burden on law enforcement. And our cases have not questioned that trained professionals normally make reliable assessments of the existence of probable cause to conduct a search. We have repeatedly held, however, that these factors are outweighed by the individual interest in privacy that is protected by advance judicial approval. The Fourth Amendment dictates that the privacy interest is paramount, no matter how marginal the risk of error might be if the legality of warrantless searches were judged only after the fact. . . .

The Court does not attempt to identify any exigent circumstances that would justify its refusal to apply the general rule against warrantless searches. Instead, it advances these three arguments: First, the rules identified in the foregoing cases are confusing and anomalous. Second, the rules do not protect any significant interest in privacy. And third, the rules impede effective law enforcement. None of these arguments withstands scrutiny.

The "Confusion"

In the nine years since Ross was decided, the Court has considered three cases in which the police had probable cause to search a particular container and one in which they had probable cause to search two vehicles. The decisions in all four of those cases were perfectly straightforward and provide no evidence of confusion in the state or lower federal courts. . . .

To the extent there was any "anomaly" in our prior jurisprudence, the Court has "cured" it at the expense of creating a more serious paradox. For, surely it is anomalous to prohibit a search of a briefcase while the owner is carrying it exposed on a public street yet to permit a search once the owner has placed the briefcase in the locked trunk of his car. One's privacy interest in one's luggage can certainly not be diminished by one's removing it from a public thoroughfare and placing it—out of sight—in a privately owned vehicle. Nor is the danger that evidence will escape increased if the luggage is in a car rather than on the street. In either location, if the police have probable cause, they are authorized to seize the luggage and to detain it until they obtain judicial approval for a search. Any line demarking an exception to the warrant requirement will appear blurred at the edges, but the Court has certainly erred if it believes that, by erasing one line and drawing another, it has drawn a clearer boundary. . . .

The Privacy Argument

The Court's statement that Chadwick and Sanders provide only "minimal protection to privacy," is also unpersuasive. Every citizen clearly has an interest in the privacy of the contents of his or her luggage, briefcase, handbag or any other container that conceals private papers and effects from public scrutiny. . . .

Under the Court's holding today, the privacy interest that protects the contents of a suitcase or a briefcase from a warrantless search when it is in public view simply vanishes when its owner climbs into a taxicab. Unquestionably the rejection of the Sanders line of cases by today's decision will result in a significant loss of individual privacy. . . .

The Burden on Law Enforcement

The Court's suggestion that Chadwick and Sanders have created a significant burden on effective law enforcement is unsupported, inaccurate, and, in any event, an insufficient reason for creating a new exception to the warrant requirement.

Despite repeated claims that Chadwick and Sanders have "impeded effective law enforcement," the Court cites no authority for its contentions. Moreover, all evidence that does exist points to the contrary conclusion. In the years since Ross was decided, the Court has heard argument in 30 Fourth Amendment cases involving narcotics. In all but one, the government was the petitioner. All save two involved a search or seizure without a warrant or with a defective warrant. And, in all except three, the Court upheld the constitutionality of the search or seizure.

In the meantime, the flow of narcotics cases through the courts has steadily and dramatically increased. No impartial observer could criticize this Court for hindering the progress of the war on drugs. On the contrary, decisions like the one the Court makes today will support the conclusion that this Court has become a loyal foot soldier in the Executive's fight against crime.

Even if the warrant requirement does inconvenience the police to some extent, the fact does not distinguish this constitutional requirement from any other procedural protection secured by the Bill of Rights. It is merely a part of the price that our society must pay in order to preserve its freedom. . . .

Notes and Questions

1. Would the police in *Acevedo* have been justified in searching the entire car?

2. If the police in *Ross* had probable cause to believe that Ross was transporting stolen television sets instead of illegal drugs, could they have searched the paper bag and the leather pouch?

3. The "automobile exception," of course, applies to other types of vehicles, such as motorcycles, boats, and airplanes. Sometimes, vehicles serve multiple purposes. Mobile homes are a good example. Is a mobile home more like an "automobile" or more like a home for purposes of the Fourth Amendment?

In *California v. Carney*, 471 U.S. 386, 105 S. Ct. 2066, 85 L. Ed. 2d 406 (1985), law enforcement agents questioned a youth shortly after he emerged from Carney's Dodge Mini Motor Home, which was parked in a San Diego parking lot.

The youth told the agents that he had received marihuana in return for allowing Carney sexual contacts.

At the officers' request, the youth returned to the motor home and knocked on its door; Carney stepped out. The agents identified themselves as law enforcement officers. Without a warrant or consent, one agent entered the motor home and observed marihuana, plastic bags, and a scale of the kind used in weighing drugs on a table.

Carney subsequently was convicted of possession of marijuana for sale. The conviction was based in part on the marijuana and related items seized during the police officers' warrantless entry of the mobile home. Although accepting that the officers had probable cause to believe that the mobile home contained evidence of a crime, the California Supreme Court rejected the state's argument that the warrantless entry was justified under the "automobile exception." It ruled that "the expectations of privacy in a motor home are more like those in a dwelling than in an automobile because the primary function of motor homes is not to provide transportation but to 'provide the occupant with living quarters.'" The U.S. Supreme Court reversed (6–3), through an opinion written by Chief Justice Burger.

When a vehicle is being used on the highways, or if it is readily capable of such use and is found stationary in a place not regularly used for residential purposes—temporary or otherwise—the two justifications for the vehicle exception come into play. First, the vehicle is obviously readily mobile by the turn of an ignition key, if not actually moving. Second, there is a reduced expectation of privacy stemming from its use as a licensed motor vehicle subject to a range of police regulation inapplicable to a fixed dwelling. At least in these circumstances, the overriding societal interests in effective law enforcement justify an immediate search before the vehicle and its occupants become unavailable.

While it is true that respondent's vehicle possessed some, if not many of the attributes of a home, it is equally clear that the vehicle falls clearly within the scope of the exception laid down in Carroll and applied in succeeding cases. Like the automobile in Carroll, respondent's motor home was readily mobile. Absent the prompt search and seizure, it could readily have been moved beyond the reach of the police. Furthermore, the vehicle was licensed to "operate on public streets; [was] serviced in public places; . . . and [was] subject to extensive regulation and inspection." Rakas v Illinois, 439 US 128, 154, n 2, 99 S Ct 421, 58 L Ed 2d 387 (1978) (Powell, J., concurring). And the vehicle was so situated that an objective observer would conclude that it was being used not as a residence, but as a vehicle. . . . Our application of the vehicle exception has never turned on the other uses to which a vehicle might be put. The exception has historically turned on the ready mobility of the vehicle, and on the presence of the vehicle in a setting that objectively indicates that the vehicle is being used for transportation.[3] These two requirements for application of the exception ensure that law enforcement officials are not unnecessarily hamstrung in their efforts to detect and prosecute criminal activity, and that the legitimate privacy interests of the public are protected. Applying the vehicle exception in these circumstances allows the essential purposes served by the exception to be fulfilled, while assuring that the exception will acknowledge legitimate privacy interests. . . .

Inventory "Searches"

Even though the automobile exception allows the police to search a car without a warrant, they still need probable cause to believe the car or a container in the car secretes contraband or another seizable item. Of course, under *New York v. Belton* (p. 205), the police may search the passenger compartment of a car, including containers, without probable cause incident to the arrest of the car's occupant. *See also Michigan v. Long* (p. 176; permitting protective search of a car when *Terry v. Ohio's* reasonable suspicion test is met). Are there additional circumstances under which a car can be searched without probable cause? Consider *South Dakota v. Opperman*, below, and the "inventory" rationale.

South Dakota v. Opperman, 428 U.S. 364, 96 S. Ct. 3092, 49 L. Ed. 2d 1000 (1976)

Mr. Chief Justice **Burger** delivered the opinion of the Court.

We review the judgment of the Supreme Court of South Dakota, holding that local police violated the Fourth Amendment to the Federal Constitution, as applicable to the States under the Fourteenth Amendment, when they conducted a routine inventory search of an automobile lawfully impounded by police for violations of municipal parking ordinances.

---

3. We need not pass on the application of the vehicle exception to a motor home that is situated in a way or place that objectively indicates that it is being used as a residence. Among the factors that might be relevant in determining whether a warrant would be required in such a circumstance is its location, whether the vehicle is readily mobile or instead, for instance, elevated on blocks, whether the vehicle is licensed, whether it is connected to utilities, and whether it has convenient access to a public road.

(1)

Local ordinances prohibit parking in certain areas of downtown Vermillion, S.D., between the hours of 2 a.m. and 6 a.m. During the early morning hours of December 10, 1973, a Vermillion police officer observed respondent's unoccupied vehicle illegally parked in the restricted zone. At approximately 3 a.m., the officer issued an overtime parking ticket and placed it on the car's windshield. The citation warned:

"Vehicles in violation of any parking ordinance may be towed from the area."

At approximately 10 o'clock on the same morning, another officer issued a second ticket for an overtime parking violation. These circumstances were routinely reported to police headquarters, and after the vehicle was inspected, the car was towed to the city impound lot.

From outside the car at the impound lot, a police officer observed a watch on the dashboard and other items of personal property located on the back seat and back floorboard. At the officer's direction, the car door was then unlocked and, using a standard inventory form pursuant to standard police procedures, the officer inventoried the contents of the car, including the contents of the glove compartment, which was unlocked. There he found marihuana contained in a plastic bag. All items, including the contraband, were removed to the police department for safekeeping.[1] During the late afternoon of December 10, respondent appeared at the police department to claim his property. The marihuana was retained by police.

Respondent was subsequently arrested on charges of possession of marihuana. His motion to suppress the evidence yielded by the inventory search was denied; he was convicted after a jury trial and sentenced to a fine of $100 and 14 days' incarceration in the county jail. . . .

(2)

This Court has traditionally drawn a distinction between automobiles and homes or offices in relation to the Fourth Amendment. Although automobiles are "effects" and thus within the reach of the Fourth Amendment, warrantless examinations of automobiles have been upheld in circumstances in which a search of a home or office would not.

The reason for this well-settled distinction is twofold. First, the inherent mobility of automobiles creates circumstances of such exigency that, as a practical necessity, rigorous enforcement of the warrant requirement is impossible. But the Court has also upheld warrantless searches where no immediate danger was presented that the car would be removed from the jurisdiction. Besides the element of mobility, less rigorous warrant requirements govern because the expectation of privacy with respect to one's automobile is significantly less than that relating to one's home or office. In discharging their varied responsibilities for ensuring the public safety, law enforcement officials are necessarily brought into frequent contact with automobiles. Most of this contact is distinctly noncriminal in nature. Automobiles, unlike homes, are subjected to pervasive and continuing governmental regulation and controls, including periodic inspection and licensing requirements. As an everyday occurrence, police stop and examine vehicles when license plates or inspection stickers have expired, or if other violations, such as exhaust fumes or excessive noise, are noted, or if headlights or other safety equipment are not in proper working order.

The expectation of privacy as to automobiles is further diminished by the obviously public nature of automobile travel. . . .

In the interests of public safety and as part of what the Court has called "community caretaking functions," automobiles are frequently taken into police custody. Vehicle accidents present one such occasion. To permit the uninterrupted flow of traffic and in some circumstances to preserve evidence, disabled or damaged vehicles will often be removed from the highways or streets at the behest of police engaged solely in caretaking and traffic-control activities. Police will also frequently remove and impound automobiles which violate parking ordinances and which thereby jeopardize both the public safety and the efficient movement of vehicular traffic. The authority of police to seize and remove from the streets vehicles impeding traffic or threatening public safety and convenience is beyond challenge.

When vehicles are impounded, local police departments generally follow a routine practice of securing and inventorying the automobiles'

---

1. At respondent's trial, the officer who conducted the inventory testified as follows:

"Q: Any why did you inventory this car?

"A: Mainly for safekeeping, because we have had a lot of trouble in the past of people getting into the impound lot and breaking into cars and stealing stuff out of them.

"Q: Do you know whether the vehicles that were broken into . . . were locked or unlocked?

A: Both of them were locked, they would be locked." Record 74.

In describing the impound lot, the officer stated:

"A. It's the old county highway yard. It has a wooden fence partially around part of it, and kind of a dilapidated wire fence, a make-shift fence." Id., at 73.

contents. These procedures developed in response to three distinct needs: the protection of the owner's property while it remains in police custody, the protection of the police against claims or disputes over lost or stolen property, and the protection of the police from potential danger. The practice has been viewed as essential to respond to incidents of theft or vandalism. In addition, police frequently attempt to determine whether a vehicle has been stolen and thereafter abandoned.

These caretaking procedures have almost uniformly been upheld by the state courts, which by virtue of the localized nature of traffic regulation have had considerable occasion to deal with the issue. Applying the Fourth Amendment standard of "reasonableness,"[5] the state courts have overwhelmingly concluded that, even if an inventory is characterized as a "search,"[6] the intrusion is constitutionally permissible.

The majority of the Federal Courts of Appeals have likewise sustained inventory procedures as reasonable police intrusions. . . .

(3)

The decisions of this Court point unmistakably to the conclusion reached by both federal and state courts that inventories pursuant to standard police procedures are reasonable. . . .

[I]n Cady v. Dombrowski, the Court upheld a warrantless search of an automobile towed to a private garage even though no probable cause existed to believe that the vehicle contained fruits of a crime. The sole justification for the warrantless incursion was that it was incident to the caretaking function of the local police to protect the community's safety. Indeed, the protective search was instituted solely because local police "were under the impression" that the incapacitated driver, a Chicago police officer, was required to carry his service revolver at all times; the police had reasonable grounds to believe a weapon might be in the car, and thus available to vandals. 413 US, at 436. The Court carefully noted that the protective search was carried out in accordance with *standard procedures* in the local police department, a factor tending to ensure that the intrusion would be limited in scope to the extent necessary to carry out the caretaking function. . . .

The Vermillion police were indisputably engaged in a caretaking search of a lawfully impounded automobile. The inventory was conducted only after the car had been impounded for multiple parking violations. The owner, having left his car illegally parked for an extended period, and thus subject to impoundment, was not present to make other arrangements for the safekeeping of his belongings. The inventory itself was prompted by the presence in plain view of a number of valuables inside the car. As in Cady, there is no suggestion whatever that this standard procedure, essentially like that fol-

---

5. In analyzing the issue of reasonableness *vel non*, the courts have not sought to determine whether a protective inventory was justified by "probable cause." The standard of probable cause is peculiarly related to criminal investigations, not routine, noncriminal procedures. The probable-cause approach is unhelpful when analysis centers upon the reasonableness of routine administrative caretaking functions, particularly when no claim is made that the protective procedures are a subterfuge for criminal investigations.

In view of the noncriminal context of inventory searches, and the inapplicability in such a setting of the requirement of probable cause, courts have held—and quite correctly—that search warrants are not required, linked as the warrant requirement textu-

ally is to the probable-cause concept. We have frequently observed that the warrant requirement assures that legal inferences and conclusions as to probable cause will be drawn by a neutral magistrate unrelated to the criminal investigative-enforcement process. With respect to noninvestigative police inventories of automobiles lawfully within governmental custody, however, the policies underlying the warrant requirement, . . . are inapplicable.

6. Given the benign noncriminal context of the intrusion, some courts have concluded that an inventory does not constitute a search for Fourth Amendment purposes. Other courts have expressed doubts as to whether the intrusion is classifiable as a search. Petitioner, however, has expressly abandoned the contention that the inventory in this case is exempt from the Fourth Amendment standard of reasonableness.

lowed throughout the country, was a pretext concealing an investigatory police motive.[10]

On this record we conclude that in following standard police procedures, prevailing throughout the country and approved by the overwhelming majority of courts, the conduct of the police was not "unreasonable" under the Fourth Amendment.

* * *

Mr. Justice **Marshall**, with whom Mr. Justice **Brennan** and Mr. Justice **Stewart** join, dissenting.

The Court today holds that the Fourth Amendment permits a routine police inventory search of the closed glove compartment of a locked automobile impounded for ordinary traffic violations. Under the Court's holding, such a search may be made without attempting to secure the consent of the owner and without any particular reason to believe the impounded automobile contains contraband, evidence, or valuables or presents any danger to its custodians or the public. Because I believe this holding to be contrary to sound elaboration of established Fourth Amendment principles, I dissent. . . .

To begin with, the Court appears to suggest by reference to a "diminished" expectation of privacy, that a person's constitutional interest in protecting the integrity of closed compartments of his locked automobile may routinely be sacrificed to governmental interests requiring interference with that privacy that are less compelling than would be necessary to justify a search of similar scope of the person's home or office. This has never been the law. . . .

Second, the Court suggests that the search for valuables in the closed glove compartment might be justified as a measure to protect the police against lost property claims. Again, this suggestion is belied by the record, since— although the Court declines to discuss it—the South Dakota Supreme Court's interpretation of state law explicitly absolves the police, as "gratuitous depositors," from any obligation beyond inventorying objects in plain view and locking the car. Moreover, . . . it may well be doubted that an inventory procedure would in an event work significantly to minimize the frustrations of false claims.

Finally, the Court suggests that the public interest in protecting valuables that may be found inside a closed compartment of an impounded car may justify the inventory procedure. I recognize the genuineness of this governmental interest in protecting property from pilferage. But even if I assume that the posting of a guard would be fiscally impossible as an alternative means to the same protective end, I cannot agree with the Court's conclusion. The Court's result authorizes—indeed it appears to require—the routine search of nearly every car impounded. In my view, the Constitution does not permit such searches as a matter of routine; absent specific consent, such a search is permissible only in exceptional circumstances of particular necessity. . . .

The Court's result in this case elevates the conservation of property interests—indeed mere possibilities of property interests—above the privacy and security interests protected by the Fourth Amendment. For this reason I dissent.

---

10. The inventory was not unreasonable in scope. Respondent's motion to suppress in state court challenged the inventory only as to items inside the car not in plain view. But once the policeman was lawfully inside the car to secure the personal property in plain view, it was not unreasonable to open the unlocked glove compartment, to which vandals would have had ready and unobstructed access once inside the car.

The "consent" theory advanced by the dissent rests on the assumption that the inventory is exclusively for the protection of the car owner. It is not. The protection of the municipality and public officers from claims of lost or stolen property and the protection of the public from vandals who might find a firearm, Cady v. Dombrowski, or as here, contraband drugs, are also crucial.

* * *

Statement of Justice **White**.

Although I do not subscribe to all of my Brother Marshall's dissenting opinion, . . . I agree with most of his analysis and conclusions and consequently dissent from the judgment of the Court.

Notes and Questions

1. On remand, the South Dakota Supreme Court held that the inventory search of Opperman's car violated the defendant's search and seizure protections under the South Dakota Constitution. *State v. Opperman*, 247 N.W.2d 673 (S.D. 1976). This holding later was modified in *State v. Flittie*, 425 N.W.2d 1 (S.D. 1988).

Other state courts have relied on state constitutional provisions to limit inventory searches. Some decisions hold that the police may not routinely open closed containers to inventory their contents. *E.g., State v. Daniel*, 589 P.2d 408 (Alaska 1979); *State v. Sawyer*, 174 Mont. 512, 571 P.2d 1131 (1977) (limiting inventory to items in plain view from outside the vehicle). Other state court decisions specify that inventory searches are unlawful if the car's owner is denied the opportunity to make alternative arrangements for safekeeping the vehicle so that it does not have to be towed and impounded. *See, e.g., State v. Mangold*, 82 N.J. 575, 414 A.2d 1312 (1980); *State v. Lunsford*, 655 S.W.2d 921 (Tenn. 1983). *See generally* B. Latzer, *State Constitutional Criminal Law* § 3:26 (1995).

2. In *Opperman*, the Supreme Court emphasized that adherence to "standard police procedures" was an important check against an inventory search being used as "a pretext concealing an investigatory police motive." In *Colorado v. Bertine*, 479 U.S. 367, 107 S. Ct. 738, 93 L. Ed. 2d 739 (1987), the Court upheld the legality of an inventory search over the defendant's objection that "departmental regulations gave the police officers discretion to choose between impounding his van and parking and locking it in a public parking place." Chief Justice Rehnquist's opinion for the Court (7–2) rejected that argument.

> Nothing in Opperman . . . prohibits the exercise of police discretion so long as that discretion is exercised according to standard criteria and on the basis of something other than suspicion of evidence of criminal activity. Here, the discretion afforded the Boulder police was exercised in light of standardized criteria, related to the feasibility and appropriateness of parking and locking a vehicle rather than impounding it. There was no showing that the police chose to impound Bertine's van in order to investigate suspected criminal activity.

However, in *Florida v. Wells*, 495 U.S. 1, 110 S. Ct. 1632, 109 L. Ed. 2d 1 (1990), the Court ruled that an inventory search was unconstitutional because "the Florida Highway Patrol had no policy whatever with respect to the opening of closed containers encountered during an inventory search."

3. In *Colorado v. Bertine, supra*, the Court permitted the scope of an inventory search to extend to closed containers within a vehicle. When police officers opened the backpack that the defendant had left in his impounded van pursuant to an inventory search, they found illegal drugs and a large amount of cash. The *Opperman* rationale was considered controlling.

> In the present case, . . . there was no showing that the police, who were following standardized procedures, acted in bad faith or for the sole purpose of investigation. . . .
>
> By securing the property, the police protected the property from unauthorized interference. Knowledge of the precise nature of the property helped guard against claims of theft, vandalism, or negligence. Such knowledge also helped to avert any danger to police or others that may have been posed by the property. . . .

4. In *Colorado v. Bertine, supra*, the Court also rejected the argument that Bertine, who had been arrested for drunk driving and who thus was present when the police made the decision to tow and impound his van, should "have been offered the opportunity to make other arrangements for the safekeeping of his property."

> [W]hile giving Bertine an opportunity to make alternate arrangements would un-

doubtedly have been possible, we said in [Illinois v.] Lafayette:

"[t]he real question is not what 'could have been achieved,' but whether the Fourth Amendment *requires* such steps . . . The reasonableness of any particular governmental activity does not necessarily or invariably turn on the existence of alternative 'less intrusive' means." Lafayette, 462 US, at 647 (emphasis in original).

5. Inventory searches do not invariably involve motor vehicles. For example, in *Illinois v. Lafayette*, 462 U.S. 640, 103 S. Ct. 2605, 77 L. Ed. 2d 65 (1983), the defendant was arrested for disturbing the peace. He was taken to a police station. As he was being booked, a police officer opened the shoulder bag the arrestee had in his possession and found 10 amphetamine pills inside the plastic wrap of a cigarette package. The state court

held that the search was not a valid inventory of respondent's belongings. It purported to distinguish South Dakota v. Opperman, on the basis that there is a greater privacy interest in a purse-type shoulder bag than in an automobile, and that the State's legitimate interests could have been met in a less intrusive manner, by "sealing [the shoulder bag] within a plastic bag or box and placing it in a secured locker." 462 U.S., at 642–643.

The U.S. Supreme Court reversed, upholding the search of the shoulder bag as a valid inventory procedure. Chief Justice Burger wrote the opinion; Justices Marshall and Brennan concurred only in the judgment.

The question here is whether, consistent with the Fourth Amendment, it is reasonable for police to search the personal effects of a person under lawful arrest as part of the routine administrative procedure at a police station house incident to booking and jailing the suspect. The justification for such searches does not rest on probable cause, and hence the absence of a warrant is immaterial to the reasonableness of the search. Indeed, we have previously

established that the inventory search constitutes a well-defined exception to the warrant requirement. See South Dakota v. Opperman. . . .

At the station house, it is entirely proper for police to remove and list or inventory property found on the person or in the possession of an arrested person who is to be jailed. A range of governmental interests supports an inventory process. It is not unheard of for persons employed in police activities to steal property taken from arrested persons; similarly, arrested persons have been known to make false claims regarding what was taken from their possession at the station house. A standardized procedure for making a list or inventory as soon as reasonable after reaching the stationhouse not only deters false claims but also inhibits theft or careless handling of articles taken from the arrested person. Arrested persons have also been known to injure themselves—or others—with belts, knives, drugs, or other items on their person while being detained. Dangerous instrumentalities—such as razor blades, bombs, or weapons—can be concealed in innocent-looking articles taken from the arrestee's possession. The bare recital of these mundane realities justifies reasonable measures by police to limit these risks—either while the items are in police possession or at the time they are returned to the arrestee upon his release. Examining all the items removed from the arrestee's person or possession and listing or inventorying them is an entirely reasonable administrative procedure. It is immaterial whether the police actually fear any particular package or container; the need to protect against such risks arises independently of a particular officer's subjective concerns. Finally, inspection of an arrestee's personal property may assist the police in ascertaining or verifying his identity. In short, every consideration of orderly police administration benefiting both police and the public points toward the appropriateness of the examination of respondent's shoulder bag prior to his incarceration.

CONCLUSION

Although we have given lengthy consideration to the Fourth Amendment in this chapter, several interesting issues remain that we have not been able to cover. Some of these topics have been hinted at in cases addressing other issues. For example, references have been sprinkled throughout the chapter to searches that occur at international borders (*see, e.g., Almeida-Sanchez v. United States*, 413 U.S. 266, 93 S. Ct. 2535, 37 L. Ed. 2d 596 (1973); *United States v. Montoya de Hernandez*, 473 U.S. 531, 105 S. Ct. 3304, 87 L. Ed. 2d 381 (1985)); to regulatory and administrative searches (*see, e.g. Camara v. Municipal Court of City and County of San Francisco*, 387 U.S. 523, 87 S. Ct. 1727, 18 L. Ed. 2d 930 (1967); *Marshall v. Barlow's Inc.*, 436 U.S. 307, 98 S. Ct. 1816, 56 L. Ed. 2d 305 (1978); *New York v. Burger*, 482 U.S. 691, 107 S. Ct. 2636, 96 L. Ed. 2d 601 (1987)); and to other Fourth Amendment issues.

We have not had the opportunity to present Supreme Court decisions involving such interesting issues as mandatory drug testing conducted without probable cause or reasonable suspicion (*see, e.g., Skinner v. Railway Labor Executives Association*, 489 U.S. 602, 109 S. Ct. 1402, 103 L. Ed. 2d 639 (1989); *Vernonia School District 47J v. Acton*, 515 U.S. 646, 115 S. Ct. 2386, 132 L. Ed. 2d 564 (1995)); suspicionless stops of motorists at sobriety checkpoints (*Michigan Department of State Police v. Sitz*, 496 U.S. 444, 110 S. Ct. 2481, 110 L. Ed. 2d 412 (1990)) or by police officers on roving patrols (*Delaware v. Prouse*, 440 U.S. 648, 99 S. Ct. 1391, 59 L. Ed. 2d 660 (1979)); or searches of secondary school students (*New Jersey v. T.L.O.*, 469 U.S. 325, 105 S. Ct. 733, 73 L. Ed. 2d 720 (1985)).

Nevertheless, you have been introduced to a great number of issues important to the Fourth Amendment and the law of search and seizure. By now, you should have a good working understanding of the interests protected by the Fourth Amendment. You should be able to define a "search" and a "seizure" and to explain why it is so important to give meaning to those concepts. You should be familiar with the justifications for the exclusionary rule and the circumstances resulting in its application. You should understand the notion of "standing" and its importance to Fourth Amendment law. We devoted significant attention to arrests and *Terry v. Ohio's* "stop and frisk" rules and to the concepts of probable cause and reasonable suspicion. We finished the chapter by examining the search warrant "requirement" and the many exceptions to it. If you are comfortable with the topics discussed in this chapter, you will have acquired a firm understanding of the constitutional law governing searches and seizures.

CHAPTER 4

Interrogation, Confessions, and Self-Incrimination

In this chapter, we examine police interrogation practices, confessions, and the use of incriminating statements in criminal trials. These issues implicate different constitutional safeguards, including the Fourteenth Amendment's due-process clause, the Fifth Amendment's right against compelled self-incrimination, and the Sixth Amendment's right to counsel.

Self-incrimination issues address a complex mix of values. The law strives to further those values and, when necessary, to achieve a balance between law enforcement's and individuals' conflicting interests. Justice Goldberg summarized "the policies of the privilege" against compelled self-incrimination in an oft-quoted passage from *Murphy v. Waterfront Commission*, 378 U.S. 52, 55, 84 S. Ct. 1594, 12 L. Ed. 2d 678 (1964).

The privilege against self-incrimination "registers an important advance in the development of our liberty—'one of the great landmarks in man's struggle to make himself civilized.'" Ullmann v. United States, 350 U.S. 422, 426, 76 S.Ct. 497, 500, 100 L.Ed. 511 [(1956)]. It reflects many of our fundamental values and most noble aspirations: our unwillingness to subject those suspected of crime to the cruel trilemma of self-accusation, perjury or contempt; our preference for an accusatorial rather than an inquisitorial system of criminal justice; our fear that self-incriminating statements will be elicited by inhumane treatment and abuses; our sense of fair play which dictates "a fair state-individual balance by requiring the government to leave the individual alone until good cause is shown for disturbing him and by requiring the government in its contest with the individual to shoulder the entire load," 8 Wigmore, Evidence (McNaughton rev., 1961), 317; our respect for the inviolability of the human personality and of the right of each individual "to a private enclave where he may lead a private life," United States v. Grunewald, 233 F.2d 556, 581–582 (2d Cir. 1956) (Frank J., dissenting), rev'd 353 U.S. 391, 77 S.Ct. 963, 1 L.Ed.2d 931 [(1957)]; our distrust of self-deprecatory statements; and our realization that the privilege, while sometimes "a shelter to the guilty," is often "a protection to the innocent." Quinn v. United States, 349 U.S. 155, 162, 75 S.Ct. 668, 673, 99 L.Ed. 964 [(1955)].

Justice Goldberg's statement is conspicuously silent about the legitimate law enforcement objectives associated with securing confessions. Suspects' statements obviously assist the police in their investigation of crimes. Confessions are powerful evidence of guilt and facilitate the arrest, prosecution, conviction, and punishment of wrongdoers. They also can help ensure that innocent people will not be wrongly accused or convicted of crimes. Some scholars (and judges) take the view that "the law governing police interrogation in the United States is overly restrictive and formalistic." J. Grano, *Confessions, Truth, and the Law* 3 (1993). They believe that "the goal of discovering the truth should play a dominant role in designing the rules that govern criminal procedure." *Id.* at 6. Justice White, while dissenting from the Supreme Court's famous decision in *Miranda v. Arizona*, 384 U.S. 436, 537, 539, 86 S. Ct. 1602, 16 L. Ed. 2d 694 (1966), which regulated police interrogation of criminal suspects, argued that

the Court's duty to assess the consequences of its action is not satisfied by the utterance of the truth that a value of our system of criminal justice is "to respect the inviolability of the human personality" and to require

government to produce the evidence against the accused by its own independent labors. More than the human dignity of the accused is involved; the human personality of others in the society must also be preserved. Thus the values reflected by the privilege are not the sole desideratum; society's interest in the general security is of equal weight. . . .

The most basic function of any government is to provide for the security of the individual and of his property. These ends of society are served by the criminal laws which for the most part are aimed at the prevention of crime. Without the reasonably effective performance of the task of preventing private violence and retaliation, it is idle to talk about human dignity and civilized values. . . .

It should not be difficult to categorize Justice Goldberg's and Justice White's respective views about the law governing self-incrimination as conforming most closely to the "due-process" and "crime control" models of criminal procedure. What should the law's role be in promoting different values and policy objectives in the context of confessions? If someone is suspected of committing a crime, what more direct and justifiable way could there be of resolving the matter than simply asking the person about his or her involvement? Should it not be presumed that the innocent will make a convincing denial and that the guilty will falter and thus justly face punishment? What harm *can* there be in asking—and expecting an answer from—an individual about suspected criminal activity?

As Justice Frankfurter observed, "The privilege against self-incrimination is a specific provision of which it is peculiarly true that a page of history is worth a volume of logic." *Ullmann v. United States*, 350 U.S. 422, 438, 76 S. Ct. 497, 100 L. Ed. 511 (1956), *quoting New York Trust Co. v. Eisner*, 256 U.S. 345, 349, 41 S. Ct. 506, 65 L. Ed. 963 (1921). This fascinating history cannot be recounted in full here. It has been very ably described elsewhere (see L. Levy,

Origins of the Fifth Amendment: The Right Against Self-Incrimination (1968)), and bits and pieces of it are presented in the judicial decisions reproduced in this chapter.

The right against compelled self-incrimination has roots that date at least as far back as thirteenth-century England. The Catholic Church, which exerted tremendous influence over the Crown and matters of government, then adopted the *inquisitio* proceeding to discover and sanction misconduct among the clergy. From this practice sprang the more widespread Inquisition, the mission of which was to identify heretics who were untrue to the Church's religious teachings. The inquisitional method of proof had several characteristic features. It relied heavily on an oath that suspected heretics were required to swear, known as the oath *de veritate*, or the oath *ex officio*, obligating them to respond truthfully to all questions asked.

> Confession of guilt was central to the whole inquisitional process, and the oath, which was administered at the very outset of the proceedings, was reckoned as indispensable to the confession. The accused, knowing neither the charges against him, nor his accusers, nor the evidence, was immediately placed between hammer and anvil: he must take the oath or be condemned as guilty, yet if he took the oath he exposed himself to the nearly certain risk of punishment for perjury—and his lies were evidence of his guilt—or condemned himself by admissions which his judge regarded as damaging, perhaps as a confession to the unnamed crime. L. Levy, *Origins of the Fifth Amendment*, 23–24 (1968).

Suspects unwilling to confess their infidelity were frequently tortured. Inquisitional procedures were not used in the common-law courts that dispensed the king's justice throughout England, but they were adopted by the King's Council, composed of prominent nobility, bishops, and jurists, which sometimes acted as a court. The judicial branch of the council came

to be known as the infamous Court of Star Chamber, where torture, the oath, and other cruel techniques commonly were used to coerce confessions. The methods of the Inquisition eventually came to be recognized as a gross abuse of official authority. The memory of those abuses was largely responsible for the right against compelled self-incrimination that is embedded in the Fifth Amendment.

The protections of the Fifth Amendment, in common with other Bill of Rights safeguards, did not originally extend to the states. In fact, not until 1964, in *Malloy v. Hogan*, 378 U.S. 1, 84 S. Ct. 1489, 12 L. Ed. 2d 653, was the Fifth Amendment right against compelled self-incrimination made applicable to the states by operation of the Fourteenth Amendment's due-process clause. Nevertheless, the Supreme Court made repeated efforts to use the federal Constitution to regulate police interrogation practices in both state and federal criminal proceedings well before the "due-process revolution" of the Warren Court era. We now consider those efforts.

We begin with the Court's reliance on due-process grounds to condemn involuntary confessions. This rationale was applied most commonly to state cases that arose between the 1930s and the early 1960s, but, as we shall see, involuntariness remains a viable means for challenging incriminating statements even today. Then, tracing the historical evolution of case law, we consider the justices' use of their non-constitutional, supervisory powers over the federal courts to regulate police interrogation methods in federal cases. We next examine the Court's experimentation with the Sixth Amendment right to counsel to oversee the questioning of criminal suspects. More extensive consideration is given to the continuing significance of the Sixth Amendment in this context in the section "Miranda and Its Progeny" later in this chapter. We devote most of our attention to the Fifth Amendment's right against compelled self-incrimination, to the Court's 1966 decision of *Miranda v. Arizona*, and to the post-*Miranda* cases that have dominated the law of police interrogation and confessions for the past several decades.

THE ROAD TO MIRANDA v. ARIZONA

Involuntary Confessions

Toward the end of the nineteenth century, the Supreme Court reviewed several federal criminal convictions involving challenged confessions. For example, in *Hopt v. Utah*, 110 U.S. 574, 4 S. Ct. 202, 28 L. Ed. 262 (1884), the justices relied on common-law evidentiary principles to express disapproval of confessions obtained by "inducements, threats, or promises," citing the dubious trustworthiness of such statements. 110 U.S., at 584–585. In *Bram v. United States*, 168 U.S. 532, 18 S. Ct. 183, 42 L. Ed. 568 (1897), the Court specifically invoked the Fifth Amendment's protection against compelled self-incrimination to bar the admission of an involuntary confession in a federal criminal trial. 168 U.S., at 542–548. However, the justices shortly thereafter expressly refused to apply the Fifth Amendment's self-incrimination clause to state trials. *Twining v. New Jersey*, 211 U.S. 78, 29 S. Ct. 14, 53 L. Ed. 97 (1908). Even with regard to federal proceedings, the Court failed to develop or build on the Fifth Amendment groundwork laid in *Bram* for many years to come. *See* O. Stephens, *The Supreme Court and Confessions of Guilt,* 24–28 (1973).

The Court first invalidated a state court's use of a confession in *Brown v. Mississippi*, 297 U.S. 278, 56 S. Ct. 461, 80 L. Ed. 682 (1936). We earlier considered *Brown* in Chapter 1 (p. 21). You will recall that in this case a Mississippi deputy sheriff unabashedly admitted whipping the (African American) suspects in a murder, hanging them from a tree, and otherwise using physical coercion to produce confessions that led to convictions and death sentences. The Supreme Court ruled that the use of the coerced confessions as evidence was unconstitutional. However, Chief Justice Hughes's decision did not rest on the Fifth Amendment's guarantee against compelled self-incrimination.

The question in this case is whether convictions, which rest solely upon confessions shown to have been extorted by officers of the state by brutality and violence, are consistent with the due process of law required by the Fourteenth Amendment of the Constitution of the United States. . . .

The state stresses the statement in Twining v. New Jersey, 211 U.S. 78, 114, 29 S. Ct. 14, 26, 53 L.Ed. 97 [(1908)], that "exemption from compulsory self-incrimination in the courts of the states is not secured by any part of the Federal Constitution," . . . But the question of the right of the state to withdraw the privilege against self-incrimination is not here involved. . . .

The state is free to regulate the procedure of its courts in accordance with its own conceptions of policy, unless in so doing it "offends some principle of justice so rooted in the traditions and conscience of our people as to be ranked as fundamental."

The state may abolish trial by jury. It may dispense with indictment by a grand jury and substitute complaint or information. But the freedom of the state in establishing its policy is the freedom of constitutional government and is limited by the requirement of due process of law. Because a state may dispense with a jury trial, it does not follow that it may substitute trial by ordeal. The rack and torture chamber may not be substituted for the witness stand. . . .

The due process clause requires "that state action, whether through one agency or another, shall be consistent with the fundamental principles of liberty and justice which lie at the base of all our civil and political institutions." It would be difficult to conceive of methods more revolting to the sense of justice than those taken to procure the confessions of these petitioners, and the use of the confessions thus obtained as the basis for conviction and sentence was a clear denial of due process. . . .

What, precisely, explains the conclusion in *Brown* that the use of the confessions violated the defendants' due-process rights? Is it the implicit assumption that incriminating statements produced by such methods may be unreliable? Could interrogation methods short of physical coercion offend due process? Would the statements be admissible if corroborated and proven to be trustworthy?

Brown stood for the principle that due process prohibits the use of "involuntary" confessions to prove guilt. The Court struggled over the next three decades to give meaning to the concept of involuntariness. Rules providing general guidance proved to be elusive because only careful consideration of the "totality of the circumstances" of each individual case could resolve whether a confession was involuntary. Relevant factors included both *police interrogation tactics* and the *characteristics of the individual* being questioned.

In addition to the outright brutality that was evident in *Brown*, other interrogation methods used by the police inspired the Court's disapproval. For example, the interrogation tactics used in *Ashcraft v. Tennessee*, 322 U.S. 143, 64 S. Ct. 921, 88 L. Ed. 1192 (1944), were considered to be "so inherently coercive" as to render a confession "involuntary" and hence inadmissible under due process of law: "For thirty-six hours after [the defendant's] seizure during which period he was held incommunicado, without sleep or rest, relays of officers, experienced investigators, and highly trained lawyers questioned him without respite." 322 U.S., at 153. Other physical deprivations, such as prolonged denial of food, *Payne v. Arkansas*, 356 U.S. 560, 78 S. Ct. 844, 2 L. Ed. 2d 975 (1958), or of clothing, *Malinski v. New York*, 324 U.S. 401, 65 S. Ct. 781, 89 L. Ed. 1029 (1945), and seclusion from counsel, family, and friends, *Haynes v. Washington*, 373 U.S. 503, 83 S. Ct. 1336, 10 L. Ed. 2d 513 (1963), *Ward v. Texas*, 316 U.S. 547, 62 S. Ct. 1139, 86 L. Ed. 1663

(1942), could help support the conclusion that a confession was involuntary. Yet the Court also made clear that psychological pressures, no less than physical ones, could undermine the voluntariness of a statement.

> If [the confession] is the product of sustained pressure by the police it does not issue from a free choice. When a suspect speaks because he is overborne, it is immaterial whether he has been subjected to a physical or mental ordeal. Eventual yielding to questioning under such circumstances is plainly the product of the suction process of interrogation and therefore the reverse of voluntary. *Watts v. Indiana*, 338 U.S. 49, 53, 69 S. Ct. 1347, 93 L. Ed. 1801 (1949).

The characteristics of the suspect being interrogated also helped determine whether a confession was considered to be involuntary. Statements were less likely to be found involuntary if the suspect was relatively well educated, *Crooker v. California*, 357 U.S. 433, 78 S. Ct. 1287, 2 L. Ed. 2d 1448 (1958) (suspect had completed one year of law school), or was an experienced criminal, *Stein v. New York*, 346 U.S. 156, 185, 73 S. Ct. 1077, 97 L. Ed. 1522 (1953). On the other hand, the voluntariness of a confession was closely scrutinized if a suspect was youthful, *Gallegos v. Colorado*, 370 U.S. 49, 82 S. Ct. 1209, 8 L. Ed. 2d 325 (1962) (14 years old), *Haley v. Ohio*, 332 U.S. 596, 68 S. Ct. 302, 92 L. Ed. 224 (1948) (15 years old); had little education or was of low intelligence, *Culombe v. Connecticut*, 367 U.S. 568, 81 S. Ct. 1860, 6 L. Ed. 2d 1037 (1961); was ill, *Jackson v. Denno*, 378 U.S. 368, 84 S. Ct. 1744, 12 L. Ed. 2d 908 (1964); or was mentally disturbed, *Blackburn v. Alabama*, 361 U.S. 199, 80 S. Ct. 274, 4 L. Ed. 2d 242 (1960).

The Court thus considered both police interrogation tactics and the characteristics of the accused in the totality of the circumstances contributing to its assessment of the voluntariness of a statement. The justices eventually clarified whether their central concern involved the *reliability* of confessions or the *methods* used to obtain them. In *Spano v. New York*, 360 U.S. 315, 320–321, 79 S. Ct. 1202, 3 L. Ed. 2d 1265 (1959), Chief Justice Warren explained that

> the abhorrence of society to the use of involuntary confessions does not turn alone on their inherent untrustworthiness. It also turns on the deep-rooted feeling that the police must obey the law while enforcing the law; that in the end life and liberty can be as much endangered from illegal methods used to convict those thought to be criminals as from the actual criminals themselves.

See also Rogers v. Richmond, 365 U.S. 534, 81 S. Ct. 735, 5 L. Ed. 2d 760 (1961); *Blackburn v. Alabama, supra.*

The voluntariness test had many drawbacks. The biggest problem was its unclarity and its consequent inability to give meaningful guidance to law enforcement officials and the lower courts about the ground rules for the police's questioning of suspected criminals. This lack of clarity was virtually unavoidable, since the test depended on such abstract concepts as whether a suspect's will had been overborne or whether a statement was the product of free choice.

Even if those concepts could be defined adequately, application of the voluntariness standard depended on the idiosyncratic facts—the totality of the circumstances—of each case in which a confession was challenged. What actually happened over the course of an interrogation procedure often was vigorously disputed and impossible to reconstruct. "Swearing contests" between the police and suspects almost always were resolved in favor of the police. The fact-bound nature of the voluntariness inquiry made it especially difficult for appellate courts, including the Supreme Court, to regulate the behavior of the police. Trial courts, which first ruled on the admissibility of confessions, suffered from the doctrinal unclarity and could not

always be trusted to promote the due-process norms underlying the High Court's decisions.

Acutely aware of these problems, the Supreme Court tentatively began to explore alternative rules to bring order to the self-incrimination area.

The McNabb-Mallory Rule

In *McNabb v. United States*, 318 U.S. 332, 63 S. Ct. 608, 87 L. Ed. 819 (1943), Benjamin, Freeman, and Raymond McNabb were convicted of murdering a federal revenue agent who was investigating the illegal whiskey operation being run on the McNabbs' Tennessee mountain land. The convictions rested largely on incriminating statements that the three men had made. Freeman and Raymond McNabb were arrested at their home during the night and taken to jail, where they were questioned over a 14-hour period by numerous officers. Benjamin McNabb voluntarily surrendered to federal authorities after his cousins' arrest. He also was placed in jail and questioned continuously for five or six hours. Only after securing incriminating statements from the men did the federal law enforcement officers take them to appear before a judicial officer for a determination of the legality of their arrests. Several federal statutes required that arrestees promptly be presented before a judicial officer for this purpose.

The McNabbs challenged the admissibility of their confessions at their trials and on appeal. Justice Frankfurter's opinion for the Supreme Court ruled that the confessions had been obtained unlawfully but specifically declined to rest this conclusion on a constitutional violation. Instead, it relied on the Supreme Court's inherent authority to supervise "the administration of criminal justice in the federal courts." 318 U.S., at 340.

> The principles governing the admissibility of evidence in federal criminal trials have not been restricted . . . to those derived solely from the Constitution. In the exercise

of its supervisory authority over the administration of criminal justice in the federal courts, this Court has, from the very beginning of its history, formulated rules of evidence to be applied in federal criminal prosecutions. . . .

Quite apart from the Constitution, therefore, we are constrained to hold that the evidence elicited from the petitioners in the circumstances disclosed here must be excluded. For in their treatment of the petitioners the arresting officers assumed functions which Congress has explicitly denied them. They subjected the accused to the pressures of a procedure which is wholly incompatible with the vital but very restricted duties of the investigating and arresting officers of the Government and which tends to undermine the integrity of the criminal proceeding. Congress has explicitly commanded that "It shall be the duty of the marshal, his deputy, or other officer, who may arrest a person charged with any crime or offense, to take the defendant before the nearest United States commissioner or the nearest judicial officer having jurisdiction under existing laws for a hearing, commitment, or taking bail for trial. . . ." 18 U.S.C. § 595. . .

Legislation such as this, requiring that the police must with reasonable promptness show legal cause for detaining arrested persons, constitutes an important safeguard— not only in assuring protection for the innocent but also in securing conviction of the guilty by methods that commend themselves to a progressive and self-confident society. For this procedural requirement checks resort to those reprehensible practices known as the "third degree" which, though universally rejected as indefensible, still find their way into use. It aims to avoid all the evil implications of secret interrogation of persons accused of crime. It reflects not a sentimental but a sturdy view of law enforcement. It outlaws easy but self-defeating ways in which brutality is substi-

tuted for brains as an instrument of crime detection. A statute carrying such purposes is expressive of a general legislative policy to which courts should not be heedless when appropriate situations call for its application. . . .

The circumstances in which the statements admitted in evidence against the petitioners were secured reveal a plain disregard of the duty enjoined by Congress upon federal law officers. Freeman and Raymond McNabb were arrested in the middle of the night at their home. Instead of being brought before a United States Commissioner or a judicial officer, as the law requires, in order to determine the sufficiency of the justification for their detention, they were put in a barren cell and kept there for fourteen hours. For two days they were subjected to unremitting questioning by numerous officers. Benjamin's confession was secured by detaining him unlawfully and questioning him continuously for five or six hours. The McNabbs had to submit to all this without the aid of friends or the benefit of counsel. The record leaves no room for doubt that the questioning of the petitioners took place while they were in the custody of the arresting officers and before any order of commitment was made. Plainly, a conviction resting on evidence secured through such a flagrant disregard of the procedure which Congress has commanded cannot be allowed to stand without making the courts themselves accomplices in wilful disobedience of law. Congress has not explicitly forbidden the use of evidence so procured. But to permit such evidence to be made the basis of a conviction in the federal courts would stultify the policy which Congress has enacted into law. . . .

In holding that the petitioners' admissions were improperly received in evidence against them, and that having been based on this evidence their convictions cannot stand, we confine ourselves to our limited function as the court of ultimate review of the standards, formulated and applied by federal courts in the trial of criminal cases. We are not concerned with law enforcement practices except in so far as courts themselves become instruments of law enforcement. We hold only that a decent regard for the duty of courts as agencies of justice and custodians of liberty forbids that men should be convicted upon evidence secured under the circumstances revealed here. . . . The history of liberty has largely been the history of observance of procedural safeguards. And the effective administration of criminal justice hardly requires disregard of fair procedures imposed by law. . . .

Three years after the *McNabb* decision, Rule 5(a) of the Federal Rules of Criminal Procedure was adopted. This rule provided, in relevant part, that "an officer making an arrest . . . shall take the arrested person without unnecessary delay before the nearest available commissioner or before any other nearby officer empowered to commit persons charged with offenses against the laws of the United States." This rule of procedure, which was binding only in the federal courts, figured significantly in the Court's decision of *Mallory v. United States*, 354 U.S. 449, 77 S. Ct. 1356, 1 L. Ed. 2d 1479 (1957).

Mallory was convicted of rape in the U.S. District Court for the District of Columbia and was sentenced to death. He was arrested for the crime and taken to police headquarters at about 2:30 one afternoon. Following repeated questioning, he made an initial incriminating statement approximately seven hours after his arrest. Not until after Mallory repeated his confession, at about 10:00 p.m., did the police attempt to arraign him before a U.S. commissioner, as required by Federal Rule of Criminal Procedure 5(a). Relying heavily on the policies espoused in *McNabb*, the Court, once again through Justice Frankfurter, ruled that Mallory's confession had been secured and introduced into evidence improperly.

The duty enjoined upon arresting officers to arraign "without unnecessary delay" indicates that the command does not call for mechanical or automatic obedience. Circumstances may justify a brief delay between arrest and arraignment. . . . But the delay must not be of a nature to give opportunity for the extraction of a confession.

The circumstances of this case preclude a holding that arraignment was "without unnecessary delay." Petitioner was arrested in the early afternoon and was detained at headquarters within the vicinity of numerous committing magistrates. Even though the police had ample evidence from other sources than the petitioner for regarding the petitioner as the chief suspect, they first questioned him for approximately a half hour. When this inquiry of a nineteen-year-old lad of limited intelligence produced no confession, the police asked him to submit to a "lie-detector" test. He was not told of his rights to counsel or to a preliminary examination before a magistrate, nor was he warned that he might keep silent and "that any statement made by him may be used against him." After four hours of further detention at headquarters, during which arraignment could easily have been made in the same building in which the police headquarters were housed, petitioner was examined by the lie-detector operator for another hour and a half before his story began to waver. Not until he had confessed, when any judicial caution had lost its purpose, did the police arraign him.

We cannot sanction this extended delay, resulting in confession, without subordinating the general rule of prompt arraignment to the discretion of arresting officers in finding exceptional circumstances for its disregard. . . .

It is not the function of the police to arrest, as it were, at large and to use an interrogating process at police headquarters in order to determine whom they should charge before a committing magistrate on "probable cause." . . .

Although the requirement that an arrestee be taken before a judicial officer for arraignment "without unnecessary delay" unavoidably had somewhat variable definition from case to case, the *McNabb-Mallory* rule spared the federal courts from making many of the painstaking case-by-case determinations required to assess the voluntariness of confessions. Under this rule, the focus was on the length of delay between arrest and an initial appearance before a judicial officer and on the reasons for any substantial delay rather than on police questioning tactics or the characteristics of individual suspects. A confession produced during a period of unnecessary delay between arrest and arraignment was presumed to be tainted and therefore was inadmissible.

The *McNabb-Mallory* rule thus simplified the work of the federal courts in reviewing confessions and provided for somewhat greater clarity, but it did not resolve all problems in this area of law. The rule was not a constitutional requirement and had no application to state criminal procedures. Nor could it in all cases displace inquiry into the voluntariness of a confession. The Court thus continued to pursue other avenues for overseeing police interrogation practices.

The Right to Counsel: Massiah and Escobedo

The justices broke new ground in two cases decided during 1964, *Massiah v. United States*, 377 U.S. 201, 84 S. Ct. 1199, 12 L. Ed. 2d 246 (1964), and *Escobedo v. Illinois*, 378 U.S. 478, 84 S. Ct. 1758, 12 L. Ed. 2d 977 (1964). Each decision evaluated the admissibility of incriminating statements under the Sixth Amendment's right-to-counsel guarantee.

In *Massiah*, the defendant and a man named Colson had been indicted on federal narcotics charges. Massiah retained an attorney, pleaded

not guilty, posted bail, and was released pending trial. Colson also was released but, unbeknownst to Massiah, decided to cooperate with the government in its investigation of the alleged narcotics trafficking. Federal agents installed a radio transmitter under the seat of Colson's car, and an agent monitored the receiving end. By prearrangement, a law enforcement officer thus was able to listen in on a lengthy conversation that took place between Massiah and Colson in Colson's car. Massiah made several incriminating statements during the course of this conversation. The agent monitoring the conversation testified about it at Massiah's trial, and Massiah was convicted of various narcotics offenses.

Massiah challenged the admissibility of the incriminating statements under various theories, including alleged violation of his rights under the Fourth, Fifth, and Sixth Amendments. The Court seized on the latter ground in ruling that the statements had been obtained and admitted into evidence unlawfully. Justice Stewart's opinion emphasized that Massiah had been indicted and had retained the services of counsel and that the agents had acted deliberately in attempting to secure incriminating statements from him.

Here we deal not with a state court conviction, but with a federal case, where the specific guarantee of the Sixth Amendment [right to counsel] directly applies. . . . We hold that the petitioner was denied the basic protections of that guarantee when there was used against him at his trial evidence of his own incriminating words, which federal agents had deliberately elicited from him after he had been indicted and in the absence of his counsel. 377 U.S., at 205–206.

Massiah already had been indicted when the agents "deliberately elicited" his incriminating statements. For the most part, police interrogation of suspected criminals occurs significantly earlier in the criminal justice process, when a crime still is being investigated and far in advance of the time that formal criminal charges have been made. We will revisit the *Massiah* rule and the circumstances under which the Sixth Amendment becomes relevant to the interrogation process later in this chapter. Also notice that *Massiah* involved a federal criminal prosecution. As the Court noted, "[T]he specific guarantee of the Sixth Amendment directly applies."

Escobedo v. Illinois differed from *Massiah* in each of these respects. The defendant's incriminating statements were obtained during the police investigation of a killing, before an indictment or other formal charges had been filed. *Escobedo* also was a state case rather than a federal criminal prosecution. Nevertheless, during the previous year, the Court had decided *Gideon v. Wainwright*, 372 U.S. 335, 83 S. Ct. 792, 9 L. Ed. 2d 799 (1963), in which it had ruled that the Sixth Amendment right to counsel applied to the states by operation of the Fourteenth Amendment's due-process clause. (We consider *Gideon* in Chapter 8, *infra*.) Of far greater significance was that, unlike *Massiah, Escobedo* did "not involve the deliberate interrogation of a defendant after the initiation of judicial proceedings against him." In the view of the dissenters, "It is 'that fact' . . . which makes all the difference." *Escobedo v. Illinois*, 378 U.S., at 493 (Stewart, J., dissenting). A majority of the Court, however, disagreed.

Danny Escobedo had been arrested and interrogated by Chicago police for the fatal shooting of his brother-in-law. He was ordered released from custody pursuant to a state court writ of habeas corpus secured by his retained lawyer. Several days later, the police returned to Escobedo's house, handcuffed him, and removed him to the police station. They told Escobedo that Benedict DiGerlando had accused him of having fired the fatal shots. DiGerlando was in custody and later would be indicted with Escobedo for the murder.

At the police station, officers began interrogating Escobedo, notwithstanding his repeated requests to see his lawyer. Meanwhile, Escobedo's retained attorney arrived at the police station and demanded that he be allowed to speak with his client. The police refused to allow the attorney to meet with Escobedo, who was still undergoing interrogation. The investigators questioning Escobedo again asserted that DiGerlando had pinned the shooting on him. After Escobedo replied that DiGerlando was lying, the officers asked him if he would tell DiGerlando that to his face. Escobedo agreed, and he was allowed to confront DiGerlando. He then made the first of several statements implicating himself in the murder by telling DiGerlando, "I didn't shoot Manuel, you did." At no time was Escobedo advised of any of his rights. Escobedo's statements were admitted at his trial, and he was convicted of murder.

As previously noted, *Escobedo* differed from *Massiah* because Escobedo's incriminating statements were the product of a preindictment interrogation. Emphasizing that Escobedo functionally had been "accused" of the crime, instead of simply being a suspect in a general investigation, and that he had made repeated requests for his lawyer, Justice Goldberg's majority opinion refused to give significance to the absence of an indictment at the time of the questioning in ruling that Escobedo's Sixth and Fourteenth Amendment rights had been violated.

> We hold, therefore, that where, as here, the investigation is no longer a general inquiry into an unsolved crime but has begun to focus on a particular suspect, the suspect has been taken into police custody, the police carry out a process of interrogations that lends itself to eliciting incriminating statements, the suspect has requested and been denied an opportunity to consult with his lawyer, and the police have not effectively warned him of his absolute constitutional right to remain silent, the accused has been denied "the Assistance of Counsel" in violation of the Sixth Amendment to the Constitution as "made obligatory upon the States by the Fourteenth Amendment," *Gideon v. Wainwright*, 372

U.S. at 342 . . . , and that no statement elicited by the police during the interrogation may be used against him at a criminal trial. 378 U.S., at 490–491.

The *Escobedo* holding obviously was tailored very narrowly to fit the circumstances of that case. The qualifications placed on the recognized "right to counsel" all but swallowed the rule in its entirety. Not surprisingly, *Escobedo* caused massive confusion in the lower courts charged with its implementation.

The confused and confusing state of the law governing police interrogation practices and confessions still desperately required clarification. The same year that *Massiah* and *Escobedo* were decided, the Supreme Court ruled that the Fifth Amendment right against compelled self-incrimination applied to the states through the Fourteenth Amendment's due-process clause. *Malloy v. Hogan*, 378 U.S. 1, 84 S. Ct. 1489, 12 L. Ed. 2d 653 (1964). The stage thus was set for the Court's seminal ruling in *Miranda v. Arizona*.

MIRANDA AND ITS PROGENY

Miranda v. Arizona

The following cases were decided by state or federal appellate courts in 1965. Each involves self-incrimination issues. Consider the facts of these cases in light of the law that was then in effect. Imagine that you are a Supreme Court justice who must decide whether the confessions should have been admissible at the defendants' trials.

Case No. 1

On March 3, 1963, a man forced a young woman into his car, tied her hands and ankles, drove several miles to a desert area outside of town, and raped her. He then drove her back to an area near her home and let her out of the car. She ran into her house, and a member of her family called the police. Ten days later, police officers investigating the rape went to the home of a 23-year-old man of Mexican descent who had an eighth-grade education. This man previously had been "committed to the custody of juvenile authorities on various charges, including burglary, attempted rape and assault." He also had a prior criminal record. The man was taken to the police station, was placed in a lineup with "four other Mexican males," and there was identified by the complaining witness as her rapist.

He then was removed to an interrogation room where, during a two-hour session with police investigators, he made an oral confession and signed a written statement. At no time was the man, who was indigent, told that he had the right to consult with an attorney before being questioned. His signed statement included the admission that "I make this statement voluntarily and of my own free will, with no threats, coercion, or promises of immunity, and with full knowledge of my legal rights, understanding any statement I make may be used against me." His confession, which paralleled the version of the offense described by the complaining witness, ended with the fact that after he had released his victim he had "asked her to say a prayer for me."

The man was indicted for the crimes of kidnapping and rape. His oral and written confessions were introduced as evidence at his trial. He offered no evidence in his own defense. He was convicted of both charges and sentenced to two concurrent terms of 20 to 30 years in prison. Those sentences were imposed consecutively with a 20- to 25-year prison term for an unrelated robbery.

The state supreme court affirmed the convictions on appeal. The court noted that the voluntariness of the confessions was not in question and indeed could not be questioned.

The officers testified that there were no threats or use of any force or coercion, and no promise of immunity; that defendant was advised of his rights, and that any statement he made might be used against him . . . [and] that defendant was identified, interrogated and signed confessions in . . . approximately two hours.

It rejected the defendant's contention that the confessions should not have been admissible because no attorney was present and because he had not been advised of his right to have an attorney before giving his statements.

The state court concluded that the defendant had no right to counsel because, under *Escobedo v. Illinois*, 378 U.S. 478, 84 S. Ct. 1758, 12 L. Ed. 2d 977 (1964), that right became effective only under limited circumstances:

(1) The general inquiry into an unsolved crime must have begun to focus on a particular suspect; (2) The suspect must have been taken into police custody; (3) The police in its interrogation must have elicited an incriminating statement; (4) *The suspect must have requested and been denied an opportunity to consult with his lawyer*; (5) The police must not have effectively warned the suspect of his constitutional rights to remain silent. (Emphasis added.)

At no time prior to making his statements had the defendant requested counsel.

Case No. 2

A Brooklyn dress shop was robbed on October 11, 1960. Three days later, the police picked up a man and took him to detective headquarters for questioning. The man orally admitted the robbery, and while at the station he was identified by the store owner and a salesperson as the robber. The suspect then was formally arrested and detained at another police station for approximately eight hours. At 11:00 p.m. that same day, an assistant district attorney questioned the man in the presence of a stenographer, who transcribed the man's admissions.

The man also signed a statement of confession. There was no record that the man had been advised of a right to counsel when he was initially questioned by police, and the transcript of his questioning at the hands of the assistant district attorney revealed that he had not been advised of any rights to counsel or against self-incrimination.

A detective testified about the initial oral confession at the man's trial for first-degree robbery. A transcript of the statement that the man had given to the assistant district attorney also was admitted into evidence. The trial judge charged the jury, in part, that "the law doesn't say that the confession is void or invalidated because the police officer didn't advise the defendant as to his rights. Did you hear what I said? I am telling you what the law of the State of New York is." The man was convicted of the robbery charge and sentenced to 30 to 60 years' imprisonment. The conviction was affirmed by the state's intermediate and highest appellate courts without opinion.

Case No. 3

On March 20, 1963, at 9:45 p.m., a man suspected of committing two local robberies was arrested by Kansas City police. An FBI report also indicated that he was wanted on felony charges in California. The man was placed in a lineup and was identified by observers as the perpetrator of the local robberies. Under questioning by the Kansas City police, he denied involvement in the offenses. He was formally "booked" on the charges at 11:45 p.m. The next morning, the man was interrogated again by the police on the local charges. It did not appear that the Kansas City police had at any time advised the man about any of his "rights" prior to questioning him.

At about 11:45 a.m., immediately after local police finished interrogating the man, FBI agents began questioning him about robberies of a bank and a federally insured savings and loan institution in Sacramento, California. Those robberies had been committed in February and early March of that year. Some two or two and one-half hours later, the man signed detailed statements confessing to the two California robberies.

The man's statement was admitted into evidence against him at his federal trial on the two California robbery charges. An FBI agent testified, and the signed statement contained a paragraph to the effect that the man had been advised "that he didn't have to make a statement; that any statement that he made could be used against him in a court of law; that he had the right to consult an attorney." There was no clear indication when this advice had been given. The trial judge found that "the agents made no threats or promises" to the man. Also introduced as evidence at the trial was "marked money" from the bank robbery that was in the man's possession when he was arrested in Kansas City, as well as identification testimony offered by several witnesses to the robbery. The man was convicted of each robbery and was sentenced to two consecutive terms of 15 years' imprisonment.

Case No. 4

A series of purse snatchings and beatings took place in Los Angeles in December 1962 and January 1963. One of those offenses resulted in the death of a victim. Police investigating the robberies and murder were led to the home of a man who had cashed a check taken during one of the robberies. The man was at home with his wife and three other persons when the police arrived on the evening of January 31, 1963. The police placed him under arrest. In response to their request, the man told the police to "go ahead" and search his house. The search uncovered numerous items taken from the robbery victims, including belongings owned by the deceased victim. The other four persons in the man's home were thereupon arrested as well.

Beginning on the evening of January 31 and continuing over the next five days, the police questioned the man on nine separate occasions.

He initially denied knowledge of the robberies. He later stated that he had found a check that had been taken in one of the robberies and then speculated that another occupant of the house must have brought the robbery items into his house. Finally, on February 5, he admitted robbing the victim who had died from a blow to the head during the robbery. He denied hitting this person but conceded that he might have kicked her in the head while escaping the scene. Then, for the first time, he was taken before a magistrate. The other four people who had been arrested were released.

The man's confession was admitted into evidence at his trial for murder and robbery. There was no indication that he had been "informed prior to his confession of his rights to counsel and to remain silent or whether he otherwise knowingly and intelligently waived those rights." He was convicted of the charges and sentenced to death. On appeal, the state supreme court reversed the convictions. It interpreted *Escobedo v. Illinois* as requiring the state to show that the man had been advised of his right to remain silent and his right to counsel and that he had chosen to forgo those rights. Absent those showings, the confession was improperly admitted at the man's trial.

* * * * *

What do these four cases appear to have in common? Each case involves a serious crime: rape-kidnapping, robbery, bank robbery, and robbery-murder. Each involves an admission of guilt by a suspect who was (a) taken into custody by the police, (b) questioned, and (c) not specifically advised of his "rights" to remain silent and/or to legal counsel. The suspects' confessions were used at their trials to establish guilt. In two of the appellate court decisions, *Escobedo v. Illinois* figured prominently, but in each it was interpreted quite differently. In three of the four cases, the confessions were upheld as having been obtained lawfully, whereas in the fourth case the confession was ruled inadmissible.

Given the facts of these cases, how would you have ruled on the confession issues? Were the confessions "involuntary" or, in the federal case, obtained in violation of the *McNabb-Mallory* rule, or was the suspects' right to counsel violated under *Massiah* or *Escobedo*?

The four cases presenting these issues are

- Case No. 1—*State v. Miranda*, 98 Ariz. 18, 401 P.2d 721 (1965)
- Case No. 2—*People v. Vignera*, 21 A.D.2d 752, 252 N.Y.S.2d 19 (1964) (no opinion), *aff'd without opinion*, 15 N.Y.2d 970, 259 N.Y.S.2d 857 (1965)
- Case No. 3—*Westover v.United States*, 342 F.2d 684 (9th Cir. 1965)
- Case No. 4—*People v. Stewart*, 43 Cal. 201, 400 P.2d 97 (1965)

When these cases wound their way up to the U.S. Supreme Court, they were consolidated for decision in the case now universally known as *Miranda v. Arizona*, 384 U.S. 436, 86 S. Ct. 1602, 16 L. Ed. 2d 694 (1966).

Miranda sprawls over 109 pages in the *United States Reports*. It was decided by a 5–4 vote. As you read the opinions in *Miranda*, be sure to keep in mind the pre-1966 law relating to confessions. Approach *Miranda* not simply as "the answer" to the general issues raised by police interrogation practices and confessions in criminal cases but with a critical eye, attuned to the several questions of law and fact suggested by this revolutionary decision.

Miranda v. Arizona, 384 U.S. 436, 86 S. Ct. 1602, 16 L. Ed. 2d 694 (1966)

Mr. Chief Justice Warren delivered the opinion of the Court.

The cases before us raise questions which go to the roots of our concepts of American criminal jurisprudence: the restraints society must observe consistent with the Federal Constitution in prosecuting individuals for crime. More specifically, we deal with the admissibility of statements obtained from an individual who is subjected to custodial police interrogation and the necessity for procedures which assure that the individual is accorded his privilege under the Fifth Amendment to the Constitution not to be compelled to incriminate himself.

We dealt with certain phases of this problem recently in Escobedo v. Illinois, 378 US 478, 84 S Ct 1758, 12 L ed 2d 977, (1964). . . .

This case has been the subject of judicial interpretation and spirited legal debate since it was decided two years ago. . . .

We granted certiorari in these cases, in order further to explore some facets of the problems, thus exposed, of applying the privilege against self-incrimination to in-custody interrogation, and to give concrete constitutional guidelines for law enforcement agencies and courts to follow.

Our holding will be spelled out with some specificity in the pages which follow but briefly stated it is this: the prosecution may not use statements, whether exculpatory or inculpatory, stemming from custodial interrogation of the defendant unless it demonstrates the use of procedural safeguards effective to secure the privilege against self-incrimination. By custodial interrogation, we mean questioning initiated by law enforcement officers after a person has been taken into custody or otherwise deprived of his freedom of action in any significant way.[4] As for the procedural safeguards to be employed, unless other fully effective means are devised to inform accused persons of their right of silence and to assure a continuous opportunity to exercise it, the following measures are required. Prior to any questioning, the person must be warned that he has a right to remain silent, that any statement he does make may be used as evidence against him, and that he has a right to the presence of an attorney, either retained or

---

4. This is what we meant in Escobedo when we spoke of an investigation which had focused on an accused.

appointed. The defendant may waive effectuation of these rights, provided the waiver is made voluntarily, knowingly and intelligently. If, however, he indicates in any manner and at any stage of the process that he wishes to consult with an attorney before speaking there can be no questioning. Likewise, if the individual is alone and indicates in any manner that he does not wish to be interrogated, the police may not question him. The mere fact that he may have answered some questions or volunteered some statements on his own does not deprive him of the right to refrain from answering any further inquiries until he has consulted with an attorney and thereafter consents to be questioned.

The constitutional issue we decide in each of these cases is the admissibility of statements obtained from a defendant questioned while in custody or otherwise deprived of his freedom of action in any significant way. In each, the defendant was questioned by police officers, detectives, or a prosecuting attorney in a room in which he was cut off from the outside world. In none of these cases was the defendant given a full and effective warning of his rights at the outset of the interrogation process. In all the cases, the questioning elicited oral admissions, and in three of them, signed statements as well which were admitted at their trials. They all thus share salient features—incommunicado interrogation of individuals in a police-dominated atmosphere, resulting in self-incriminating statements without full warnings of constitutional rights.

An understanding of the nature and setting of this in-custody interrogation is essential to our decisions today. The difficulty in depicting what transpires at such interrogations stems from the fact that in this country they have largely taken place incommunicado. From extensive factual studies undertaken in the early 1930's, including the famous Wickersham Report to Congress by a Presidential Commission, it is clear that police violence and the "third degree" flourished at that time. In a series of cases decided by this Court long after these studies, the police resorted to physical brutality—beating, hanging, whipping—and to sustained and protracted questioning incommunicado in order to extort confessions. The Commission on Civil Rights in 1961 found much evidence to indicate that "some policemen still resort to physical force to obtain confes-

sions," 1961 Comm'n on Civil Rights Rep, Justice, pt 5, 17. The use of physical brutality and violence is not, unfortunately, relegated to the past or to any part of the country. . . . Again we stress that the modern practice of in-custody interrogation is psychologically rather than physically oriented. . . . Interrogation still takes place in privacy. Privacy results in secrecy and this in turn results in a gap in our knowledge as to what in fact goes on in the interrogation rooms. A valuable source of information about present police practices, however, may be found in various police manuals and texts which document procedures employed with success in the past, and which recommend various other effective tactics. These texts are used by law enforcement agencies themselves as guides.[9] It should be noted that these texts professedly present the most enlightened and effective means presently used to obtain statements through custodial interrogation. By considering these texts and other data, it is possible to describe procedures observed and noted around the country.

The officers are told by the manuals that the "principal psychological factor contributing to a successful interrogation is *privacy*— being alone with the person under interrogation." . . . To highlight the isolation and unfamiliar surroundings, the manuals instruct the police to display an air of confidence in the suspect's guilt and from out-

---

9. The methods described in Inbau & Reid, Criminal Interrogation and Confessions (1962), are a revision and enlargement of material presented in three prior editions of a predecessor text, Lie Detection and Criminal Interrogation (3d ed. 1953). The authors and their associates are officers of the Chicago Police Scientific Crime Detection Laboratory and have had extensive experience in writing, lecturing and speaking to law enforcement authorities over a 20-year period. They say that the techniques portrayed in their manuals reflect their experiences and are the most effective psychological stratagems to employ during interrogations. Similarly, the techniques described in O'Hara, Fundamentals of Criminal Investigation (1956), were gleaned from long service as observer, lecturer in police science, and work as a federal criminal investigator. All these texts have had rather extensive use among law enforcement agencies and among students of police science, with total sales and circulation of over 44,000.

ward appearance to maintain only an interest in confirming certain details. The guilt of the subject is to be posited as a fact. The interrogator should direct his comments toward the reasons why the subject committed the act, rather than court failure by asking the subject whether he did it. Like other men, perhaps the subject has had a bad family life, had an unhappy childhood, had too much to drink, had an unrequited desire for women. The officers are instructed to minimize the moral seriousness of the offense, to cast blame on the victim or on society. These tactics are designed to put the subject in a psychological state where his story is but an elaboration of what the police purport to know already—that he is guilty. Explanations to the contrary are dismissed and discouraged. . . .

The manuals suggest that the suspect be offered legal excuses for his actions in order to obtain an initial admission of guilt. Where there is a suspected revenge-killing, for example, the interrogator may say:

"Joe, you probably didn't go out looking for this fellow with the purpose of shooting him. My guess is, however, that you expected something from him and that's why you carried a gun—for your own protection. You knew him for what he was, no good. Then when you met him he probably started using foul, abusive language and he gave some indication that he was about to pull a gun on you, and that's when you had to act to save your own life. That's about it, isn't it, Joe?"

Having then obtained the admission of shooting, the interrogator is advised to refer to circumstantial evidence which negates the self-defense explanation. This should enable him to secure the entire story. . . .

When the techniques described above prove unavailing, the texts recommend they be alternated with a show of some hostility. One ploy often used has been termed the "friendly-unfriendly" or the "Mutt and Jeff" act:

". . . In this technique, two agents are employed. Mutt, the relentless investigator, who knows the subject is guilty and is not going to waste any time. He's sent a dozen men away for this crime and he's going to send the subject away for the full term. Jeff, on the other hand, is obviously a kindhearted man. He has a family himself. He has a brother who was involved in a little scrape like this. He disapproves of Mutt and

his tactics and will arrange to get him off the case if the subject will cooperate. He can't hold Mutt off for very long. The subject would be wise to make a quick decision. The technique is applied by having both investigators present while Mutt acts out his role. Jeff may stand by quietly and demur at some of Mutt's tactics. When Jeff makes his plea for cooperation, Mutt is not present in the room."

The interrogators sometimes are instructed to induce a confession out of trickery. The technique here is quite effective in crimes which require identification or which run in series. In the identification situation, the interrogator may take a break in his questioning to place the subject among a group of men in a line-up. "The witness or complainant (previously coached, if necessary) studies the line-up and confidently points out the subject as the guilty party." Then the questioning resumes "as though there were now no doubt about the guilt of the subject." A variation on this technique is called the "reverse line-up":

"The accused is placed in a line-up, but this time he is identified by several fictitious witnesses or victims who associated him with different offenses. It is expected that the subject will become desperate and confess to the offense under investigation in order to escape from the false accusations."

The manuals also contain instructions for police on how to handle the individual who refuses to discuss the matter entirely, or who asks for an attorney or relatives. The examiner is to concede him the right to remain silent. "This usually has a very undermining effect. First of all, he is disappointed in his expectation of an unfavorable reaction on the part of the interrogator. Secondly, a concession of this right to remain silent impresses the subject with the apparent fairness of his interrogator." After this psychological conditioning, however, the officer is told to point out the incriminating significance of the suspect's refusal to talk:

"Joe, you have a right to remain silent. That's your privilege and I'm the last person in the world who'll try to take it away from you. If that's the way you want to leave this, O.K. But let me ask you this. Suppose you were in my shoes and I were in yours and you called me in to ask me about this and I told you, 'I don't want to answer any of your questions.' You'd think I had something to hide, and you'd probably be right in thinking that. That's exactly what I'll have to think about you, and so will everybody else. So let's sit here and talk this whole thing over."

Few will persist in their initial refusal to talk, it is said, if this monologue is employed correctly. In the event that the subject wishes to speak to a relative or an attorney, the following advice is tendered:

"[T]he interrogator should respond by suggesting that the subject first tell the truth to the interrogator himself rather than get anyone else involved in the matter. If the request is for an attorney, the interrogator may suggest that the subject save himself or his family the expense of any such professional service, particularly if he is innocent of the offense under investigation. The interrogator may also add, 'Joe, I'm only looking for the truth, and if you're telling the truth, that's it. You can handle this by yourself.'"

From these representative samples of interrogation techniques, the setting prescribed by the manuals and observed in practice becomes clear. In essence, it is this: To be alone with the subject is essential to prevent distraction and to deprive him of any outside support. The aura of confidence in his guilt undermines his will to resist. He merely confirms the preconceived story the police seek to have him describe. Patience and persistence, at times relentless questioning, are employed. To obtain a confession, the interrogator must "patiently maneuver himself or his quarry into a position from which the desired objective may be attained." When normal procedures fail to produce the needed result, the police may resort to deceptive stratagems such as giving false legal advice. It is important to keep the subject off balance, for example, by trading on his insecurity about himself or his surroundings. The police then persuade, trick, or cajole him out of exercising his constitutional rights.

Even without employing brutality, the "third degree" or the specific stratagems described above, the very fact of custodial interrogation exacts a heavy toll on individual liberty and trades on the weakness of individuals. . . .

In the cases before us today, given this background, we concern ourselves primarily with this interrogation atmosphere and the evils it can bring. . . .

In these cases, we might not find the defendants' statements to have been involuntary in traditional terms. Our concern for adequate safeguards to protect precious Fifth Amendment rights is, of course, not lessened in the slightest. In each of the cases, the defendant was thrust into an unfamiliar atmosphere and run through menacing police interrogation procedures. The potentiality for compulsion is forcefully apparent, for example, in Miranda, where the indigent Mexican defendant was a seriously disturbed individual with pronounced sexual fantasies, and in Stewart, in which the defendant was an indigent Los Angeles Negro who had dropped out of school in the sixth grade. To be sure, the records do not evince overt physical coercion or patent psychological ploys. The fact remains that in none of these cases did the officers undertake to afford appropriate safeguards at the outset of the interrogation to insure that the statements were truly the product of free choice.

It is obvious that such an interrogation environment is created for no purpose other than to subjugate the individual to the will of his examiner. This atmosphere carries its own badge of intimidation. To be sure, this is not physical intimidation, but it is equally destructive of human dignity. The current practice of incommunicado interrogation is at odds with one of our Nation's most cherished principles—that the individual may not be compelled to incriminate himself. Unless adequate protective devices are employed to dispel the compulsion inherent in custodial surroundings, no statement obtained from the defendant can truly be the product of his free choice.

From the foregoing, we can readily perceive an intimate connection between the privilege against self-incrimination and police custodial questioning. It is fitting to turn to history and precedent underlying the Self-Incrimination Clause to determine its applicability in this situation. . . .

[W]e may view the historical development of the privilege as one which groped for the proper scope of governmental power over the citizen. . . . We have recently noted that the privilege against self-incrimination—the essential mainstay of our adversary system—is founded on a complex of values. All these policies point to one overriding thought: the constitutional foundation underlying the privilege is the respect a government—state or federal—must accord to the dignity and integrity of its citizens. To maintain a "fair state-individual balance," to require the government "to shoulder the entire load," 8 Wigmore, Evidence 317 (McNaughton rev. 1961), to respect the inviolability of the human personality, our accusatory system of criminal justice demands that the government seeking to punish an individual produce the evidence against him by its own independent labors, rather than by the cruel, simple expedient of compelling it from his own mouth. In sum, the privilege is fulfilled only when the person is guaranteed the right "to remain silent unless he chooses to speak in the unfettered exercise of his own will." Malloy v. Hogan, 378 US 1, 8, 12 L ed 2d 653, 659, 84 S Ct 1489 (1964).

The question in these cases is whether the privilege is fully applicable during a period of custodial interrogation. In this Court, the privilege has consistently been accorded a liberal construction. We are satisfied that all the principles embodied in the privilege apply to informal compulsion exerted by law-enforcement officers during in-custody questioning. An individual swept from familiar surroundings into police custody, surrounded by antagonistic forces, and subjected to the techniques of persuasion described above cannot be otherwise than under compulsion to speak. . . .

In addition to the expansive historical development of the privilege and the sound policies which have nurtured its evolution, judicial precedent thus clearly establishes its application to incommunicado interrogation. The presence of counsel, in all the cases before us today, would be the adequate protective device necessary to make the process of police interrogation conform to the dictates of the privilege. His presence would insure that statements made in the government-established atmosphere are not the product of compulsion. It was in this manner that Escobedo explicated another facet of the pretrial privilege, noted in many of the Court's prior decisions: the protection of rights at trial. That counsel is present when statements are taken from an individual during interrogation obviously enhances the integrity of the fact-finding processes in court. The presence of an attorney, and the warnings delivered to the individual, enable the defendant under otherwise compelling circumstances to tell his story without fear, effectively, and in a way that eliminates the evils in the interrogation process.

Today, then, there can be no doubt that the Fifth Amendment privilege is available outside of criminal court proceedings and serves to protect persons in all settings in which their freedom of action is curtailed in any significant way from being compelled to incriminate themselves. We have concluded that without proper safeguards the process of in-custody interrogation of persons suspected or accused of crime contains inherently compelling pressures which work to undermine the individual's will to resist and to compel him to speak where he would not otherwise do so freely. In order to combat these pressures and to permit a full opportunity to exercise the privilege against self-incrimination, the accused must be adequately and effectively apprised of his rights and the exercise of those rights must be fully honored.

It is impossible for us to foresee the potential alternatives for protecting the privilege which might be devised by Congress or the States in the exercise of their creative rulemaking capacities. Therefore we cannot say that the Constitution necessarily requires adherence to any particular solution for the inherent compulsions of the interrogation process as it is presently conducted. Our decision in no way creates a constitutional straitjacket which will handicap sound efforts at reform, nor is it intended to have this effect. We encourage Congress and the States to continue their laudable search for increasingly effective ways of protecting the rights of the individual while promoting efficient enforcement of our criminal laws. However, unless we are shown other procedures which are at least as effective in apprising accused persons of their right of silence and in assuring a continuous opportunity to exercise it, the following safeguards must be observed.

At the outset, if a person in custody is to be subjected to interrogation, he must first be informed in clear and unequivocal terms that he has the right to remain silent. For those unaware of the privilege, the warning is needed simply to make them aware of it—the threshold requirement for an intelligent decision as to its exercise.

More important, such a warning is an absolute prerequisite in overcoming the inherent pressures of the interrogation atmosphere. It is not just the subnormal or woefully ignorant who succumb to an interrogator's imprecations, whether implied or expressly stated, that the interrogation will continue until a confession is obtained or that silence in the face of accusation is itself damning and will bode ill when presented to a jury. Further, the warning will show the individual that his interrogators are prepared to recognize his privilege should he choose to exercise it.

The Fifth Amendment privilege is so fundamental to our system of constitutional rule and the expedient of giving an adequate warning as to the availability of the privilege so simple, we will not pause to inquire in individual cases whether the defendant was aware of his rights without a warning being given. Assessments of the knowledge the defendant possessed, based on information as to his age, education, intelligence, or prior contact with authorities, can never be more than speculation; a warning is a clear cut fact. More important, whatever the background of the person interrogated, a warning at the time of the interrogation is indispensable to overcome its pressures and to insure that the individual knows he is free to exercise the privilege at that point in time.

The warning of the right to remain silent must be accompanied by the explanation that anything said can and will be used against the individual in court. This warning is needed in order to make him aware not only of the privilege, but also of the consequences of forgoing it. It is only through an awareness of these consequences that there can be any assurance of real understanding and intelligent exercise of the privilege. Moreover, this warning may serve to make the individual more acutely aware that he is faced with a phase of the adversary system—that he is not in the presence of persons acting solely in his interest. The circumstances surrounding in-custody interrogation can operate very quickly to overbear the will of one merely made aware of his privilege by his interrogators. Therefore, the right to have counsel present at the interrogation is indispensable to the protection of the Fifth Amendment privilege under the system we delineate today. Our aim is to assure that the individual's right to choose between silence and speech remains unfettered throughout the interrogation process. A once-stated warning, delivered by those who will conduct the interrogation, cannot itself suffice to that end among those who most require knowledge of their rights. A mere warning given by the interrogators is not alone sufficient to accomplish that end. Thus, the need for counsel to protect the Fifth Amendment privilege comprehends not merely a right to consult with counsel prior to questioning, but also to have counsel present during any questioning if the defendant so desires.

The presence of counsel at the interrogation may serve several significant subsidiary functions as well. If the accused decides to talk to his interrogators, the assistance of counsel can mitigate the dangers of untrustworthiness. With a lawyer present the likelihood that the police will practice coercion is reduced, and if coercion is nevertheless exercised the lawyer can testify to it in court. The presence of a lawyer can also help to guarantee that the accused gives a fully accurate statement to the police and that the statement is rightly reported by the prosecution at trial.

An individual need not make a pre-interrogation request for a lawyer. While such request affirmatively secures his right to have one, his failure to ask for a lawyer does not constitute a waiver. No effective waiver of the right to counsel during interrogation can be recognized unless specifically made after the warnings we here delineate have been given. The accused who does not know his rights and therefore does not make a request may be the person who most needs counsel. . . .

Accordingly we hold that an individual held for interrogation must be clearly informed that he has the right to consult with a lawyer and to have the lawyer with him during interrogation under the system for protecting the privilege we delineate today. As with the warnings of the right to remain silent and that anything stated can be used in evidence against him, this warning is an absolute prerequisite to interrogation. No amount of circumstantial evidence that the person may have been aware of this right will suffice to stand in its stead. Only through such a warning is there ascertainable assurance that the accused was aware of this right.

If an individual indicates that he wishes the assistance of counsel before any interrogation occurs, the authorities cannot rationally ignore or deny his request on the basis that the individual does not have or cannot afford a retained attorney. The financial ability of the individual has no relationship to the scope of the rights involved here. The privilege against self-incrimination secured by the Constitution applies to all individuals. The need for counsel in order to protect the privilege exists for the indigent as well as the affluent. In fact, were we to limit these constitutional rights to those who can retain an attorney, our decisions today would be of little significance. The cases before us as well as the vast majority of confession cases with which we have dealt in the past involve those unable to retain counsel. While authorities are not required to relieve the accused of his poverty, they have the obligation not to take advantage of indigence in the administration of justice.

In order fully to apprise a person interrogated of the extent of his rights under this system then, it is necessary to warn him not only that he has the right to consult with an attorney, but also that if he is indigent a lawyer will be appointed to represent him. Without this additional warning, the admonition of the right to consult with counsel would often be understood as meaning only that he can consult with a lawyer if he has one or has the funds to obtain one. As with the warnings of the right to remain silent and of the general right to counsel, only by effective and express explanation to the indigent of this right can there be assurance that he was truly in a position to exercise it.

Once warnings have been given, the subsequent procedure is clear. If the individual indicates in any manner, at any time prior to or during questioning, that he wishes to remain silent, the interrogation must cease. At this point he has shown that he intends to exercise his Fifth Amendment privilege; any statement taken after the person invokes his privilege cannot be other than the product of compulsion, subtle or otherwise. Without the right to cut off questioning, the setting of in-custody interrogation operates on the individual to overcome free choice in producing a statement after the privilege has been once invoked. If the individual states that he wants an attorney, the interrogation must

cease until an attorney is present. At that time, the individual must have an opportunity to confer with the attorney and to have him present during any subsequent questioning. If the individual cannot obtain an attorney and he indicates that he wants one before speaking to police, they must respect his decision to remain silent.

This does not mean, as some have suggested, that each police station must have a "station house lawyer" present at all times to advise prisoners. It does mean, however, that if police propose to interrogate a person they must make known to him that he is entitled to a lawyer and that if he cannot afford one, a lawyer will be provided for him prior to any interrogation. If authorities conclude that they will not provide counsel during a reasonable period of time in which investigation in the field is carried out, they may refrain from doing so without violating the person's Fifth Amendment privilege so long as they do not question him during that time.

If the interrogation continues without the presence of an attorney and a statement is taken, a heavy burden rests on the government to demonstrate that the defendant knowingly and intelligently waived his privilege against self-incrimination and his right to retained or appointed counsel. This Court has always set high standards of proof for the waiver of constitutional rights, Johnson v. Zerbst, 304 US 458, 58 S Ct 1019, 82 L ed 1461 (1938), and we reassert these standards as applied to in-custody interrogation. Since the State is responsible for establishing the isolated circumstances under which the interrogation takes place and has the only means of making available corroborated evidence of warnings given during incommunicado interrogation, the burden is rightly on its shoulders. An express statement that the individual is willing to make a statement and does not want an attorney followed closely by a statement could constitute a waiver. But a valid waiver will not be presumed simply from the silence of the accused after warnings are given or simply from the fact that a confession was in fact eventually obtained. . . .

Whatever the testimony of the authorities as to waiver of rights by an accused, the fact of lengthy interrogation or incommunicado incarceration before a statement is made is strong evidence that the accused did not validly waive his rights. In these circumstances the fact that the individual eventually made a statement is consistent with the conclusion that the compelling influence of the interrogation finally forced him to do so. It is inconsistent with any notion of a voluntary relinquishment of the privilege. Moreover, any evidence that the accused was threatened, tricked, or cajoled into a waiver will, of course, show that the defendant did not voluntarily waive his privilege. The requirement of warnings and waiver of rights is a fundamental with respect to the Fifth Amendment privilege and not simply a preliminary ritual to existing methods of interrogation.

The warnings required and the waiver necessary in accordance with our opinion today are, in the absence of a fully effective equivalent, prerequisites to the admissibility of any statement made by a defendant. No distinction can be drawn between statements which are direct confessions and statements which amount to "admissions" of part or all of an offense. The privilege against self-incrimination protects the individual from being compelled to incriminate himself in any manner; it does not distinguish degrees of incrimination. Similarly, for precisely the same reason, no distinction may be drawn between inculpatory statements and statements alleged to be merely "exculpatory." . . .

The principles announced today deal with the protection which must be given to the privilege against self-incrimination when the individual is first subjected to police interrogation while in custody at the station or otherwise deprived of his freedom of action in any significant way. It is at this point that our adversary system of criminal proceedings commences, distinguishing itself at the outset from the inquisitorial system recognized in some countries. Under the system of warnings we delineate today or under any other system which may be devised and found effective, the safeguards to be erected about the privilege must come into play at this point.

Our decision is not intended to hamper the traditional function of police officers in investigating crime. When an individual is in custody on probable cause, the police may, of course, seek out evidence in the field to be used at trial against him. . . .

In dealing with statements obtained through interrogation, we do not purport to find all confessions inadmissible. Confessions remain a proper element in law enforcement. Any statement given freely and voluntarily without any compelling influences is, of course, admissible in evidence. The fundamental import of the privilege while an individual is in custody is not whether he is allowed to talk to the police without the benefit of warnings and counsel, but whether he can be interrogated. There is no requirement that police stop a person who enters a police station and states that he wishes to confess to a crime or a person who calls the police to offer a confession or any other statement he desires to make. Volunteered statements of any kind are not barred by the Fifth Amendment and their admissibility is not affected by our holding today.

To summarize, we hold that when an individual is taken into custody or otherwise deprived of his freedom by the authorities in any significant way and is subjected to questioning, the privilege against self-incrimination is jeopardized. Procedural safeguards must be employed to protect the privilege, and unless other fully effective means are adopted to notify the person of his right of silence and to assure that the exercise of the right will be scrupulously honored, the following measures are required. He must be warned prior to any questioning that he has the right to remain silent, that anything he says can be used against him in a court of law, that he has the right to the presence of an attorney, and that if he cannot afford an attorney one will be appointed for him prior to any questioning if he so desires. Opportunity to exercise these rights must be afforded to him throughout the interrogation. After such warnings have been given, and such opportunity afforded him, the individual may knowingly and intelligently waive these rights and agree to answer questions or make a statement. But unless and until such warnings and waiver are demonstrated by the prosecution at trial, no evidence obtained as a result of interrogation can be used against him.

A recurrent argument made in these cases is that society's need for interrogation outweighs the privilege. This argument is not unfamiliar to this Court. . . .

In announcing these principles, we are not unmindful of the burdens which law enforcement officials must bear, often under trying circumstances. We also fully recognize the obligation of all citizens to aid in enforcing the criminal laws. This Court, while protecting individual rights, has always given ample latitude to law enforcement agencies in the legitimate exercise of their duties. The limits we have placed on the interrogation process should not constitute an undue interference with a proper system of law enforcement. As we have noted, our decision does not in any way preclude police from carrying out their traditional investigatory functions. Although confessions may play an important role in some convictions, the cases before us present graphic examples of the overstatement of the "need" for confessions. In each case authorities conducted interrogations ranging up to five days in duration despite the presence, through standard investigating practices, of considerable evidence against each defendant.

Over the years the Federal Bureau of Investigation has compiled an exemplary record of effective law enforcement while advising any suspect or arrested person, at the outset of an interview, that he is not required to make a statement, that any statement may be used against him in court, that the individual may obtain the services of an attorney of his own choice and, more recently, that he has a right to free counsel if he is unable to pay. . . .

The practice of the FBI can readily be emulated by state and local enforcement agencies. The experience in some other countries also suggests that the danger to law enforcement in curbs on interrogation is overplayed. There appears to have been no marked detrimental effect on criminal law enforcement in these jurisdictions as a result of these rules. Conditions of law enforcement in our country are sufficiently similar to permit reference to this experience as assurance that lawlessness will not result from warning an individual of his rights or allowing him to exercise them. . . .

Because of the nature of the problem and because of its recurrent significance in numerous cases, we have to this point discussed the relationship of the Fifth Amendment privilege to police interrogation without specific concentration on the facts of the cases before us. We turn now to these facts to consider the application to these cases of the constitutional principles discussed above. In each instance, we have concluded that statements were obtained from the defendant under circumstances that did not meet constitutional standards for protection of the privilege. . . .

Mr. Justice Clark, dissenting in Nos. 759, 760, and 761, and concurring in the result in No. 584. . . .

I would continue to follow . . . the "totality of circumstances" rule. . . . I would consider in each case whether the police officer prior to custodial interrogation added the warning that the suspect might have counsel present at the interrogation and, further, that a court would appoint one at his request if he was too poor to employ counsel. In the absence of warnings, the burden would be on the State to prove that counsel was knowingly and intelligently waived or that in the totality of the circumstances, including the failure to give the necessary warnings, the confession was clearly voluntary.

Rather than employing the arbitrary Fifth Amendment rule which the Court lays down I would follow the more pliable dictates of the Due Process Clauses of the Fifth and Fourteenth Amendments which we are accustomed to administering and which we know from our cases are effective instruments in protecting persons in police custody. In this way we would not be acting in the dark nor in one full sweep changing the traditional rules of custodial interrogation which this Court has for so long recognized as a justifiable and proper tool in balancing individual rights against the rights of society. It will be soon enough to go further when we are able to appraise with somewhat better accuracy the effect of such a holding. . . .

Mr. Justice Harlan, whom Mr. Justice Stewart and Mr. Justice White join, dissenting.

I believe the decision of the Court represents poor constitutional law and entails harmful consequences for the country at large. How serious these consequences may prove to be only time can tell. . . .

The new rules are not designed to guard against police brutality or other unmistakably banned forms of coercion. Those who use third-degree tactics and deny them in court are equally able and destined to lie as skillfully about warnings and waivers. Rather, the thrust of the new rules is to negate all pressures, to reinforce the nervous or ignorant suspect, and ultimately to discourage any confession at all. The Court's opinion in my view reveals no adequate basis for extending the Fifth Amendment's privilege against self-incrimination to the police station. Far more important, it fails to show that the Court's new rules are well supported, let alone compelled, by Fifth Amendment precedents.

Examined as an expression of public policy, the Court's new regime proves so dubious that there can be no due compensation for its weakness in constitutional law. . . .

Without at all subscribing to the generally black picture of police conduct painted by the Court, I think it must be frankly recognized at the outset that police questioning allowable under due process precedents may inherently entail some pressure on the suspect and may seek advantage in his ignorance or weaknesses. . . . Until today, the role of the Constitution has been only to sift out *undue* pressure, not to assure spontaneous confessions.

The Court's new rules aim to offset these minor pressures and disadvantages intrinsic to any kind of police interrogation. The rules do not serve due process interests in preventing blatant coercion since, as I noted earlier, they do nothing to contain the policeman who is prepared to lie from the start. The rules work for reliability in confessions almost only in the Pickwickian sense that they can prevent some from being given at all.[12]

What the Court largely ignores is that its rules impair, if they will not eventually serve wholly to frustrate, an instrument of law enforcement that has long and quite reasonably been thought worth the price paid for it. There can be little doubt that the Court's new code would markedly decrease the number of confessions. To warn the suspect that he may remain silent and remind him that his confession may be used in court are minor obstructions. To require also an

express waiver by the suspect and an end to questioning whenever he demurs must heavily handicap questioning. And to suggest or provide counsel for the suspect simply invites the end of the interrogation.

How much harm this decision will inflict on law enforcement cannot fairly be predicted with accuracy. Evidence on the role of confessions is notoriously incomplete. . . .

We do know that some crimes cannot be solved without confessions, that ample expert testimony attests to their importance in crime control, and that the Court is taking a real risk with society's welfare in imposing its new regime on the country. The social costs of crime are too great to call the new rules anything but a hazardous experimentation. . . .

It is no secret that concern has been expressed lest long-range and lasting reforms be frustrated by this Court's too rapid departure from existing constitutional standards. Despite the Court's disclaimer, the practical effect of the decision made today must inevitably be to handicap seriously sound efforts at reform, not least by removing options necessary to a just compromise of competing interests. Of course legislative reform is rarely speedy or unanimous, though this Court has been more patient in the past. But the legislative reforms when they come would have the vast advantage of empirical data and comprehensive study, they would allow experimentation and use of solutions not open to the courts, and they would restore the initiative in criminal law reform to those forums where it truly belongs. . . .

Mr. Justice White, with whom Mr. Justice Harlan and Mr. Justice Stewart join, dissenting. . . .

That the Court's holding today is neither compelled nor even strongly suggested by the language of the Fifth Amendment, is at odds with American and English legal history, and involves a departure from a long line of precedent does not prove either that the Court has exceeded its powers or that the Court is wrong or unwise in its present reinterpretation of the Fifth Amendment. It does, however, underscore the obvious—that the Court has not discovered or found the law in making today's decision, nor has it derived it from some irrefutable sources; what it has done is to make new law and new public policy in much the same way that it has in the course of

---

12. The Court's vision of a lawyer "mitigat[ing] the dangers of untrustworthiness" by witnessing coercion and assisting accuracy in the confession is largely a fancy; for if counsel arrives, there is rarely going to be a police station confession. Watts v. Indiana, 338 US 49, 59, 69 S Ct 1347, 93 L Ed 1801 [(1949)] (separate opinion of Jackson, J.): "[A]ny lawyer worth his salt will tell the suspect in no uncertain terms to make no statement to police under any circumstances."

interpreting other great clauses of the Constitution. This is what the Court historically has done. Indeed, it is what it must do and will continue to do until and unless there is some fundamental change in the constitutional distribution of governmental powers.

But if the Court is here and now to announce new and fundamental policy to govern certain aspects of our affairs, it is wholly legitimate to examine the mode of this or any other constitutional decision in this Court and to inquire into the advisability of its end product in terms of the long-range interest of the country. At the very least the Court's text and reasoning should withstand analysis and be a fair exposition of the constitutional provision which its opinion interprets.

First, we may inquire what are the textual and factual bases of this new fundamental rule. To reach the result announced on the grounds it does, the Court must stay within the confines of the Fifth Amendment, which forbids self-incrimination only if *compelled*. Hence the core of the Court's opinion is that because of the "compulsion inherent in custodial surroundings, no statement obtained from [a] defendant [in custody] can truly be the product of his free choice," absent the use of adequate protective devices as described by the Court. However, the Court does not point to any sudden inrush of new knowledge requiring the rejection of 70 years' experience. Rather than asserting new knowledge, the Court concedes that it cannot truly know what occurs during custodial questioning, because of the innate secrecy of such proceedings. It extrapolates a picture of what it conceives to be the norm from police investigatorial manuals, published in 1959 and 1962 or earlier, without any attempt to allow for adjustments in police practices that may have occurred in the wake of more recent decisions of state appellate tribunals or this Court. But even if the relentless application of the described procedures could lead to involuntary confessions, it most assuredly does not follow that each and every case will disclose this kind of interrogation or this kind of consequence. Insofar as appears from the Court's opinion, it has not examined a single transcript of any police interrogation, let alone the interrogation that took place in any one of these cases which it decides today. Judged by

any of the standards for empirical investigation utilized in the social sciences the factual basis for the Court's premise is patently inadequate. . . .

[E]ven if one assumed that there was an adequate factual basis for the conclusion that all confessions obtained during in custody interrogation are the product of compulsion, the rule propounded by the Court would still be irrational, for, apparently, it is only if the accused is also warned of his right to counsel and waives both that right and the right against self-incrimination that the inherent compulsiveness of interrogation disappears. But if the defendant may not answer without a warning a question such as "Where were you last night?" without having his answer be a compelled one, how can the Court ever accept his negative answer to the question of whether he wants to consult his retained counsel or counsel whom the court will appoint?

. . .

Criticism of the Court's opinion, however, cannot stop with a demonstration that the factual and textual bases for the rule it propounds are, at best, less than compelling. Equally relevant is an assessment of the rule's consequences measured against community values. The Court's duty to assess the consequences of its action is not satisfied by the utterance of the truth that a value of our system of criminal justice is "to respect the inviolability of the human personality" and to require government to produce the evidence against the accused by its own independent labors. More than the human dignity of the accused is involved; the human personality of others in the society must also be preserved. Thus the values reflected by the privilege are not the sole desideratum; society's interest in the general security is of equal weight. . . .

The most basic function of any government is to provide for the security of the individual and of his property. Lanzetta v. New Jersey, 306 US 451, 455, 59 S Ct 618, 83 L Ed 888 [(1939)]. These ends of society are served by the criminal laws which for the most part are aimed at the prevention of crime. Without the reasonably effective performance of the task of preventing private violence and retaliation, it is idle to talk about human dignity and civilized values. . . .

The rule announced today will measurably weaken the ability of the criminal law to perform these tasks. It is a deliberate calculus to prevent interrogations, to reduce the incidence of confessions and pleas of guilty and to increase the number of trials.

I have no desire whatsoever to share the responsibility for any such impact on the present criminal process. . . .

Notes and Questions

1. The problem. On what sources or authorities does Chief Justice Warren's majority opinion in *Miranda* rely to make the case that police interrogation tactics threaten the Fifth Amendment prohibition against compelled self-incrimination? Does the opinion rely on testimony about those practices? Does it depend on the facts of the four cases before the Court? What difficulties does the Chief Justice note in obtaining reliable evidence about the methods that police officers use to question suspects? To what does the Court resort to "fill the gap in our knowledge as to what in fact goes on in interrogation rooms"? What assurance is given that these sources describe representative interrogation procedures?

How, precisely, should "the problem" to which the Court attempts to respond in *Miranda* be described? Does the problem involve confessions in general or some smaller subset of confessions? Does it involve all confessions produced by police questioning, or is it limited to the products of a specific type of questioning? Does it extend to all types of statements or only to statements that are directly incriminating?

How does the Court's definition of "the problem" relate to the constitutional right against *compelled* self-incrimination? Does the concern seem to be with physical compulsion or a different kind of compulsion? What conditions identified by the Court combine to produce that compulsion?

2. The solution. After defining how the police interrogation practices at issue threaten the right against compelled self-incrimination, the majority opinion in *Miranda* details its solution to the problem. You undoubtedly were familiar with the *Miranda* "warnings" long before reading this decision. The Court's desire "to give concrete constitutional guidelines for law enforcement agencies and courts to follow" clearly motivated the use of the specific warnings as a partial response to a problem that had existed for many years and had defied resolution through the other approaches we have considered: the voluntariness standard, the *McNabb-Mallory* rule, and the right-to-counsel theory. But is the *Miranda* Court's solution really so straightforward?

The administration of the *Miranda* rights is an important part of but not the entire remedy that the Court fashions. Another facet of the solution involves the *waiver* of those rights. To be effective, how must a suspect's waiver, or willingness to relinquish the specified rights, be made? What are the prerequisites of an effective decision to forgo those rights? Who has the burden of establishing whether a valid waiver of the *Miranda* rights occurred, and how can such proof be made?

3. There is considerable dispute over how effective *Miranda* has been either in bringing clarity to the rules governing police interrogation of suspected criminals or in providing meaningful protections for individuals' rights against compelled self-incrimination. Another aspect of *Miranda* also concerned the Court, as well as the general public, when the decision was announced. The dissenting opinions of Justices Harlan and White darkly warned about the adverse impact that *Miranda* would have on law enforcement. Nevertheless, research studies published shortly after the decision suggested that *Miranda* had had a negligible effect in reducing the number of confessions, guilty pleas, or trial convictions. *See* Project, "Interrogations in New Haven: The Impact of *Miranda*," 76 *Yale L. J.* 1519 (1967); Medalie, Zeitz, & Alexander, "Custodial Police Interrogation in Our Nation's Capital: The Attempt to Implement *Miranda*," 66 *Mich. L. Rev.* 1347 (1968); Wettick, "*Miranda* in Pittsburgh: A Statistical Study," 29 *U. Pitt. L. Rev.* 1 (1967). Recent evaluations have reported more mixed conclusions about *Miranda*'s impact. *See* Cassell, "*Miranda*'s Social Costs: An Empirical Reassessment," 90

Nw. U. L. Rev. 387 (1996); Schulhofer, "Miranda's Practical Effect: Substantial Benefits and Vanishingly Small Social Costs," 90 Nw. U. L. Rev. 500 (1996); Leo, "The Impact of Miranda Revisited," 86 J. Crim. Law & Criminol. 621 (1996); Cassell & Hayman, "Police Interrogation in the 1990s: An Empirical Study of the Effects of Miranda," 43 U.C.L.A. L. Rev. 839 (1996).

The Court attempted in *Miranda* to bring clarity to the troubled law of self-incrimination and thus to give much-needed guidance to the police and lower courts about the governing rules. Even if advances were made, the decision raised a host of vexing questions about those rules and their application. We now consider these second-generation issues.

"In Custody"

The *Miranda* requirements apply only to *"custodial"* interrogation. "By custodial interrogation, we mean questioning initiated by law enforcement officers *after a person has been taken into custody or otherwise deprived of his freedom of action in any significant way.*" 384 U.S., at 444 (emphasis added). The Court elaborated:

> Our decision is not intended to hamper the traditional function of police officers in investigating crime. . . . When an individual is in custody on probable cause, the police may, of course, seek out evidence in the field to be used at trial against him. Such investigation may include inquiry of persons not under restraint. General on-the-scene questioning as to facts surrounding a crime or other general questioning of citizens in the fact-finding process is not affected by our holding. It is an act of responsible citizenship for individuals to give whatever information they may have to aid in law enforcement. In such situations the compelling atmosphere inherent in the process of in-custody interrogation is not necessarily present. 384 U.S., at 477–478.

When a police officer approaches an individual on the street and asks, "What's going on here?" (obviously an interrogation), *Miranda* warnings do not necessarily have to be administered for the answer to be admissible in a criminal trial. This is true even if the response is highly incriminating. If you have ever been in a situation like this, with a police officer posing questions to you at arm's length, you might feel considerable pressure to respond. Even if, as the *Miranda* Court suggested, such an atmosphere is not as "compelling" as a custodial interrogation, might it still produce such pressure that most people would have great difficulty in not responding? Whatever the answer is to this question, which we leave to your introspection, a crucial legal distinction remains between custodial and noncustodial interrogation. *Miranda* warnings are required only in the former context.

As a starting point, it is clear that *custodial* is not a synonym for "at the police station." Consider the facts from the following case, which was decided just three years after *Miranda*.

Orozco v. Texas, 394 U.S. 324, 89 S. Ct. 1095, 22 L. Ed. 2d 311 (1969)

Mr. Justice Black delivered the opinion of the Court.
. . . At about 4 a.m. four police officers arrived at petitioner's boardinghouse, were admitted by an unidentified woman, and were told that petitioner was asleep in the bedroom. All four officers entered the bedroom and began to question

petitioner. From the moment he gave his name, according to the testimony of one of the officers, petitioner was not free to go where he pleased but was "under arrest." . . .

The trial testimony clearly shows that the officers questioned petitioner about incriminating facts without first informing him of his right to remain silent, his right to have the advice of a lawyer before making any statement, and his right to have a lawyer appointed to assist him if he could not afford to hire one. . . .

The State has argued here that since petitioner was interrogated on his own bed, in familiar surroundings, our Miranda holding should not apply. It is true that the Court did say in Miranda that "compulsion to speak in the isolated setting of the police station may well be greater than in courts or other official investigations, where there are often impartial observers to guard against intimidation or trickery." 384 U.S., at 461. But the opinion iterated and reiterated the absolute necessity for officers interrogating people "in custody" to give the described warnings.

According to the officer's testimony, petitioner was under arrest and not free to leave when he was questioned in his bedroom in the early hours of the morning. The Miranda opinion declared that the warnings were required when the person being interrogated was "in custody at the station or otherwise deprived of his freedom of action in any significant way." 384 U.S., at 477. (Emphasis supplied.) The decision of this Court in Miranda was reached after careful consideration and lengthy opinions were announced by both the majority and dissenting Justices. There is no need to canvass those arguments again. We do not, as the dissent implies, expand or extend to the slightest extent our Miranda decision. We do adhere to our well-considered holding in that case and therefore reverse the conviction below. . . .

Mr. Justice Fortas took no part in the consideration or decision of this case. . . .

Mr. Justice White, with whom Mr. Justice Stewart joins, dissenting. . . .

Just as *Orozco* confirms that questioning need not be conducted within the confines of a police station to be considered "custodial," the next case confirms the converse: merely because questioning does occur at a police station, it is not necessarily "custodial" within the meaning of *Miranda*.

Oregon v. Mathiason, 429 U.S. 492, 97 S. Ct. 711, 50 L. Ed. 2d 714 (1977)

Per Curiam.

. . .

The Supreme Court of Oregon described the factual situation surrounding the confession as follows:

"An officer of the State Police investigated a theft at a residence near Pendleton. He asked the lady of the house which had been burglarized if she suspected anyone. She replied that the defendant was the only one she could think of. The defendant was a parolee and a 'close associate' of her son. The officer tried to contact defendant on three or four occasions with no success. Finally, about 25 days after the burglary, the officer left his card at defendant's apartment with a note asking him to call

because 'I'd like to discuss something with you.' The next afternoon the defendant did call. The officer asked where it would be convenient to meet. The defendant had no preference; so the officer asked if the defendant could meet him at the state patrol office in about an hour and a half, about 5:00 p.m. The patrol office was about two blocks from defendant's apartment. The building housed several state agencies.

"The officer met defendant in the hallway, shook hands and took him into an office. The defendant was told he was not under arrest. The door was closed. The two sat across a desk. The police radio in another room could be heard. The officer told defendant he wanted to talk to him about a burglary and that his truthfulness would possibly be considered by the district attorney or judge. The officer further advised that the police believed defendant was involved in the burglary and [falsely stated that] defendant's fingerprints were found at the scene. The defendant sat for a few minutes and then said he had taken the property. This occurred within five minutes after defendant had come to the office. The officer then advised defendant of his Miranda rights and took a taped confession.

"At the end of the taped conversation the officer told defendant he was not arresting him at this time; he was released to go about his job and return to his family. The officer said he was referring the case to the district attorney for him to determine whether criminal charges would be brought. It was 5:30 p.m. when the defendant left the office. . . .

The Supreme Court of Oregon reasoned from these facts that:

"We hold the interrogation took place in a 'coercive environment.' The parties were in the offices of the State Police; they were alone behind closed doors; the officer informed the defendant he was a suspect in a theft and the authorities had evidence incriminating him in the crime; and the defendant was a parolee under supervision. We are of the opinion that this evidence is not overcome by the evidence that the defendant came to the office in response to a request and was told he was not under arrest."

Our decision in Miranda set forth rules of police procedure applicable to "custodial interrogation." "By custodial interrogation, we mean questioning initiated by law enforcement officers after a person has been taken into custody or otherwise deprived of his freedom of action in any significant way." 384 U.S., at 444. . . .

In the present case, however, there is no indication that the questioning took place in a context where respondent's freedom to depart was restricted in any way. He came voluntarily to the police station, where he was immediately informed that he was not under arrest. At the close of a ½ hour interview respondent did in fact leave the police station without hindrance. It is clear from these facts that Mathiason was not in custody "or otherwise deprived of his freedom of action in any significant way." . . .

Any interview of one suspected of a crime by a police officer will have coercive aspects to it, simply by virtue of the fact that the police officer is part of a law enforcement system which may ultimately cause the suspect to be charged with a crime. But police officers are not required to administer Miranda warnings to everyone whom they question. Nor is the requirement of warnings to be imposed simply because the questioning takes place in the station house, or because the questioned person is one whom the police suspect. Miranda warnings are required only where there has been such a restriction on a person's freedom as to render him "in custody." It was *that* sort of coercive environment to which Miranda by its terms was made applicable, and to which it is limited.

The officer's false statement about having discovered Mathiason's fingerprints at the scene was found by the Supreme Court of Oregon to be another circumstance contributing to the coercive environment which makes the Miranda rationale applicable. Whatever relevance this fact may have to other issues in the case, it has nothing to do with whether respondent was in custody for purposes of the Miranda rule.

Mr. Justice Brennan would grant the writ but dissents from the summary disposition and would set the case for oral argument.

Mr. Justice Marshall, dissenting.

The respondent in this case was interrogated behind closed doors at police headquarters in connection with a burglary investigation. He had been named by the victim of the burglary as a suspect, and was told by the police that they believe he was involved. He was falsely informed that his fingerprints had been found at the scene, and in effect was advised that by cooperating with the police he could help himself. Not until after he had confessed was he given the warnings set forth in Miranda v. Arizona. . . .

It is true that respondent was not formally placed under arrest, but surely formalities alone cannot control. At the very least, if respondent entertained an objectively reasonable belief that he was not free to leave during the questioning, then he was "deprived of his freedom of action in a significant way."[1] . . .

More fundamentally, however, I cannot agree with the Court's conclusion that if respondent were not in custody no warnings were required. . . .

In my view, even if respondent were not in custody, the coercive elements in the instant case were so pervasive as to require Miranda-type warnings. Respondent was interrogated in "privacy" and in "unfamiliar surroundings," fac-tors on which Miranda places great stress. The investigation had focused on respondent. And respondent was subjected to some of the "deceptive stratagems," Miranda v. Arizona, supra, at 455, which called forth the Miranda decision. I therefore agree with the Oregon Supreme Court that to excuse the absence of warnings given these facts is "contrary to the rationale expressed in Miranda." . . .

Mr. Justice Stevens, dissenting. . . .

Notes and Questions

1. As a parolee, Mathiason faced almost cer-tain return to prison on a showing that he had committed another crime. The police officer questioning him led Mathiason to believe that his fingerprints had been found at the scene of the crime and suggested that his truthfulness might receive favorable consideration by the prosecu-tor or judge. Is it reasonable to assume that Mathiason would have experienced significant psychological pressure when the officer asked about his involvement in the burglary?

2. Does Mathiason's likely state of mind make a difference to the Court? Should it? Is the "in-custody" aspect of *Miranda* best characterized as a physical condition? As a psychological con-dition? As some combination of objective physi-cal circumstances and subjective psychological experiences?

* * * * *

In our study of the Fourth Amendment in the preceding chapter, we devoted considerable attention to the concept of a seizure of a person. Is it fair to assume that an individual who has been "seized" under the terms of the Fourth Amendment also is "in custody" for purposes of *Miranda*? This issue is considered in the next case, which provides further definition of the "in-custody" component of *Miranda*.

Berkemer v. McCarty, 468 U.S. 420, 104 S. Ct. 3138, 82 L. Ed. 2d 317 (1984)

Justice Marshall delivered the opinion of the Court. . . .

On the evening of March 31, 1980, Trooper Williams of the Ohio State Highway Patrol observed respondent's car weaving in and out of a lane on Interstate Highway 270. After following the car for two miles, Williams forced respondent to stop and asked him to get out of the vehicle.

When respondent complied, Williams noticed that he was having difficulty standing. At that point, "Williams concluded that [respondent] would be charged with a traffic offense and, therefore, his freedom to leave the scene was terminated." However, respondent was not told that he would be taken into custody. Williams then asked respondent to perform a field sobri-ety test, commonly known as a "balancing test." Respondent could not do so without falling.

While still at the scene of the traffic stop, Will-iams asked respondent whether he had been using intoxicants. Respondent replied that "he had consumed two beers and had smoked sev-

---

1. . . . It has been noted that as a logical matter, a person who honestly but unreasonably believes he is in custody is subject to the same coercive pressures as one whose belief is reasonable; this suggests that such persons also are entitled to warnings.

eral joints of marijuana a short time before." Respondent's speech was slurred, and Williams had difficulty understanding him. Williams thereupon formally placed respondent under arrest and transported him in the patrol car to the Franklin County Jail.

At the jail, respondent was given an intoxilyzer test to determine the concentration of alcohol in his blood. The test did not detect any alcohol whatsoever in respondent's system. Williams then resumed questioning respondent in order to obtain information for inclusion in the State Highway Patrol Alcohol Influence Report. Respondent answered affirmatively a question whether he had been drinking. When then asked if he was under the influence of alcohol, he said, "I guess, barely." Williams next asked respondent to indicate on the form whether the marijuana he had smoked had been treated with any chemicals. In the section of the report headed "Remarks," respondent wrote, "No ang[el] dust or PCP in the pot. Rick McCarty."

At no point in this sequence of events did Williams or anyone else tell respondent that he had a right to remain silent, to consult with an attorney, and to have an attorney appointed for him if he could not afford one.

Respondent was charged with operating a motor vehicle while under the influence of alcohol and/or drugs in violation of Ohio Rev Code Ann § 4511.19 (Supp 1983). Under Ohio law, that offense is a first-degree misdemeanor and is punishable by fine or imprisonment for up to 6 months. . . .

Respondent moved to exclude the various incriminating statements he had made to Patrolman Williams on the ground that introduction into evidence of those statements would violate the Fifth Amendment insofar as he had not been informed of his constitutional rights prior to his interrogation. . . .

[The trial court denied the motion, and McCarty was convicted, sentenced to 90 days in jail, 80 of which were suspended, and fined. The Ohio Supreme Court affirmed his conviction, and a federal district court denied his petition for a writ of habeas corpus. The Sixth Circuit Court of Appeals reversed, ruling that McCarty's postarrest statements were obtained in violation of

Miranda. The court "was less clear" regarding the admissibility of the statements McCarty made before he was formally placed under arrest.]

[Justice Marshall's opinion first rejected the state's contention that *Miranda* warnings need not be administered in cases that involve only a misdemeanor traffic offense. It then affirmed that McCarty's unwarned, postarrest statements made in response to the questions associated with the Alcohol Influence Report were taken in violation of *Miranda*. It then turned to the admissibility of the prearrest statements.]

To assess the admissibility of the self-incriminating statements made by respondent prior to his formal arrest, we are obliged to address a second issue concerning the scope of our decision in Miranda: whether the roadside questioning of a motorist detained pursuant to a routine traffic stop should be considered "custodial interrogation." Respondent urges that it should, on the ground that Miranda by its terms applies whenever "a person has been taken into custody *or otherwise deprived of his freedom of action in any significant way,*" 384 US, at 444.

It must be acknowledged at the outset that a traffic stop significantly curtails the "freedom of action" of the driver and the passengers, if any, of the detained vehicle. Under the law of most States, it is a crime either to ignore a policeman's signal to stop one's car or, once having stopped, to drive away without permission. Certainly few motorists would feel free either to disobey a directive to pull over or to leave the scene of a traffic stop without being told they might do so. Partly for these reasons, we have long acknowledged that "stopping an automobile and detaining its occupants constitute a 'seizure' within the meaning of [the Fourth] Amendmen[t], even though the purpose of the stop is limited and the resulting detention quite brief." Delaware v. Prouse, 440 US 648, 653, 99 S Ct 1391, 59 L Ed 2d 660 (1979) (citations omitted).

However, we decline to accord talismanic power to the phrase in the Miranda opinion emphasized by respondent. Fidelity to the doctrine announced in Miranda requires that it be enforced strictly, but only in those types of situations in which the concerns that powered the decision are implicated. Thus, we must decide whether a traffic stop exerts upon a detained person pressures that sufficiently impair his free exercise of his privilege against self-incrimination to require that he be warned of his constitutional rights.

Two features of an ordinary traffic stop mitigate the danger that a person questioned will be induced "to speak where he would not otherwise do so freely," Miranda v. Arizona, 384 US, at 467. First, detention of a motorist pursuant to a traffic stop is presumptively temporary and brief. The vast majority of roadside detentions last only a few minutes. A motorist's expectations, when he sees a policeman's light flashing behind him, are that he will be obliged to spend a short period of time answering questions and waiting while the officer checks his license and registration, that he may then be given a citation, but that in the end he most likely will be allowed to continue on his way. In this respect, questioning incident to an ordinary traffic stop is quite different from stationhouse interrogation, which frequently is prolonged, and in which the detainee often is aware that questioning will continue until he provides his interrogators the answers they seek. See id., at 451.[27]

Second, circumstances associated with the typical traffic stop are not such that the motorist feels completely at the mercy of the police. To be sure, the aura of authority surrounding an armed, uniformed officer and the knowledge that the officer has some discretion in deciding whether to issue a citation, in combination, exert some pressure on the detainee to respond to questions. But other aspects of the situation substantially offset these forces. Perhaps most importantly, the typical traffic stop is public, at least to some degree. Passersby, on foot or in other cars, witness the interaction of officer and motorist. This exposure to public view both

reduces the ability of an unscrupulous policeman to use illegitimate means to elicit self-incriminating statements and diminishes the motorist's fear that, if he does not cooperate, he will be subjected to abuse. The fact that the detained motorist typically is confronted by only one or at most two policemen further mutes his sense of vulnerability. In short, the atmosphere surrounding an ordinary traffic stop is substantially less "police dominated" than that surrounding the kinds of interrogation at issue in Miranda itself, and in the subsequent cases in which we have applied Miranda.

In both of these respects, the usual traffic stop is more analogous to a so-called "Terry stop," see Terry v. Ohio, 392 US 1, 88 S Ct 1868, 20 L Ed 2d 889 (1968), than to a formal arrest. Under the Fourth Amendment, we have held, a policeman who lacks probable cause but whose "observations lead him reasonably to suspect" that a particular person has committed, is committing, or is about to commit a crime, may detain that person briefly in order to "investigate the circumstances that provoke suspicion." Typically, this means that the officer may ask the detainee a moderate number of questions to determine his identity and to try to obtain information confirming or dispelling the officer's suspicions. But the detainee is not obliged to respond. And, unless the detainee's answers provide the officer with probable cause to arrest him, he must then be released. The comparatively nonthreatening character of detentions of this sort explains the absence of any suggestion in our opinions that Terry stops are subject to the dictates of Miranda. The similarly noncoercive aspect of ordinary traffic stops prompts us to hold that persons temporarily detained pursuant to such stops are not "in custody" for the purposes of Miranda.

Respondent contends that to "exempt" traffic stops from the coverage of Miranda will open the way to widespread abuse. Policemen will simply delay formally arresting detained motorists, and will subject them to sustained and intimidating interrogation at the scene of their initial detention. . . .

We are confident that the state of affairs projected by respondent will not come to pass. It is settled that the safeguards prescribed by Miranda become applicable as soon as a sus-

---

27. The brevity and spontaneity of an ordinary traffic stop also reduces the danger that the driver through subterfuge will be made to incriminate himself. One of the investigative techniques that Miranda was designed to guard against was the use by police of various kinds of trickery—such as "Mutt and Jeff" routines—to elicit confessions from suspects. A police officer who stops a suspect on the highway has little chance to develop or implement a plan of this sort.

pect's freedom of action is curtailed to a "degree associated with formal arrest." California v. Beheler, 463 US 1121, 1125, 77 103 S Ct 3517, L Ed 2d 1275 (1983) (per curiam). If a motorist who has been detained pursuant to a traffic stop thereafter is subjected to treatment that renders him "in custody" for practical purposes, he will be entitled to the full panoply of protections prescribed by Miranda.

Admittedly, our adherence to the doctrine just recounted will mean that the police and lower courts will continue occasionally to have difficulty deciding exactly when a suspect has been taken into custody.

Turning to the case before us, we find nothing in the record that indicates that respondent should have been given Miranda warnings at any point prior to the time Trooper Williams placed him under arrest. For the reasons indicated above, we reject the contention that the initial stop of respondent's car, by itself, rendered him "in custody." And respondent has failed to demonstrate that, at any time between the initial stop and the arrest, he was subjected to restraints comparable to those associated with a formal arrest. Only a short period of time elapsed between the stop and the arrest. At no point during that interval was respondent informed that his detention would not be temporary. Although Trooper Williams apparently decided as soon as respondent stepped out of his car that respondent would be taken into custody and charged with a traffic offense, Williams never communicated his intention to respondent. A policeman's unarticulated plan has no bearing on the question whether a suspect was "in custody" at a particular time; the only relevant inquiry is how a reasonable man in the suspect's position would have understood his situation. Nor do other aspects of the interaction of Williams and respondent support the contention that respondent was exposed to "custodial interrogation" at the scene of the stop. From aught that appears in the stipulation of facts, a single police officer asked respondent a modest number of questions and requested him to perform a simple balancing test at a location visible to passing motorists. Treatment of this sort cannot fairly be characterized as the functional equivalent of formal arrest.

We conclude, in short, that respondent was not taken into custody for the purposes of Miranda until Williams arrested him. Consequently, the statements respondent made prior to that point were admissible against him. . . .

Notes and Questions

1. How persuasive do you find Justice Marshall's argument that a traffic stop such as occurred in *McCarty* is not sufficiently "police dominated" to merit *Miranda's* protections? In particular, of what relevance is the fact that "the typical traffic stop is public"? Is the interaction between officer and citizen during a traffic stop truly "public" in nature when motorists presumably view it while driving by at a speed of 55 m.p.h.? What about the fact that "only one or at most two" police officers are involved in typical traffic stops? Why should the number of officers matter?

2. If the Court is not adopting a per se rule that a traffic stop can never represent "custody" for purposes of *Miranda*, under what circumstances would such a stop require the warnings and a waiver before a suspect can be questioned?

3. Trooper Williams concluded that he would charge McCarty and thus not allow him to leave the scene of the stop well before McCarty was formally arrested and before the prearrest statements were obtained in response to questioning. Once the officer had decided that McCarty would not be allowed to leave, why wasn't McCarty "in custody"?

After the Court affirmed in *Berkemer v. McCarty* that *Miranda* applies in misdemeanor cases, just as it does in felonies, there was no serious dispute that McCarty's postarrest statements in response to police questioning were inadmissible. When he made the incriminating statements, he was in jail, a condition that cer-tainly seems to epitomize being "in custody." Or does it? Consider *Illinois v. Perkins*.

Illinois v. Perkins, 496 U.S. 292, 110 S. Ct. 2394, 110 L. Ed. 2d 243 (1990)

Justice Kennedy delivered the opinion of the Court.

An undercover government agent was placed in the cell of respondent Perkins, who was incarcerated on charges unrelated to the subject of the agent's investigation. Respondent made statements that implicated him in the crime that the agent sought to solve. Respondent claims that the statements should be inadmissible because he had not been given Miranda warnings by the agent. We hold that the statements are admissible. Miranda warnings are not required when the suspect is unaware that he is speaking to a law enforcement officer and gives a voluntary statement.

I

In November 1984, Richard Stephenson was murdered in a suburb of East St. Louis, Illinois. The murder remained unsolved until March 1986, when one Donald Charlton told police that he had learned about a homicide from a fellow inmate at the Graham Correctional Facility, where Charlton had been serving a sentence for burglary. The fellow inmate was Lloyd Perkins, who is the respondent here. . . .

By the time the police heard Charlton's account, respondent had been released from Graham, but police traced him to a jail in Mont-gomery County, Illinois, where he was being held pending trial on a charge of aggravated bat-tery, unrelated to the Stephenson murder. The police wanted to investigate further respondent's connection to the Stephenson murder, but feared that the use of an eavesdropping device would prove impracticable and unsafe. They decided instead to place an undercover agent in the cellblock with respondent and Charlton. The plan was for Charlton and undercover agent John Parisi to pose as escapees from a work release program who had been arrested in the course of a burglary. Parisi and Charlton were instructed to engage respondent in casual con-versation and report anything he said about the Stephenson murder.

Parisi, using the alias "Vito Bianco," and Charl-ton, both clothed in jail garb, were placed in the cellblock with respondent at the Montgomery County Jail. Respondent greeted Charlton who, after a brief conversation with respondent, intro-duced Parisi by his alias. Parisi told respondent that he "wasn't going to do any more time," and suggested that the three of them escape. Respondent replied that the Montgomery County jail was "rinky-dink" and that they could "break out." The trio met in respondent's cell later that evening, after the other inmates were asleep, to refine their plan. Respondent said that his girlfriend could smuggle in a pistol. Charlton said "Hey, I'm not a murderer, I'm a burglar. That's your guys' profession." After telling Charl-ton that he would be responsible for any murder that occurred, Parisi asked respondent if he had ever "done" anybody. Respondent said that he had, and proceeded to describe at length the events of the Stephenson murder. Parisi and respondent then engaged in some casual con-versation before respondent went to sleep. Parisi did not give respondent Miranda warnings before the conversations.

Respondent was charged with the Stephen-son murder. Before trial, he moved to suppress the statements made to Parisi in the jail. The trial court granted the motion to suppress, and the State appealed. The Appellate Court of Illinois affirmed, holding that Miranda v. Arizona, 384 US 436, 86 S Ct 1602, 16 L Ed 2d 694 (1966), prohibits all undercover contacts with incarcer-ated suspects which are reasonably likely to elicit an incriminating response.

We granted certiorari, to decide whether an undercover law enforcement officer must give

Miranda warnings to an incarcerated suspect before asking him questions that may elicit an incriminating response. We now reverse. . . .

The warning mandated by Miranda was meant to preserve the privilege during "incommunicado interrogation of individuals in a police-dominated atmosphere." That atmosphere is said to generate "inherently compelling pressures which work to undermine the individual's will to resist and to compel him to speak where he would not otherwise do so freely." "Fidelity to the doctrine announced in Miranda requires that it be enforced strictly, but only in those types of situations in which the concerns that powered the decision are implicated." Berkemer v. McCarty, 468 US 420, 437, 104 S Ct 3138, 82 L Ed 2d 317 (1984).

Conversations between suspects and undercover agents do not implicate the concerns underlying Miranda. The essential ingredients of a "police-dominated atmosphere" and compulsion are not present when an incarcerated person speaks freely to someone that he believes to be a fellow inmate. Coercion is determined from the perspective of the suspect. When a suspect considers himself in the company of cellmates and not officers, the coercive atmosphere is lacking. There is no empirical basis for the assumption that a suspect speaking to those whom he assumes are not officers will feel compelled to speak by the fear of reprisal for remaining silent or in the hope of more lenient treatment should he confess.

It is the premise of Miranda that the danger of coercion results from the interaction of custody and official interrogation. We reject the argument that Miranda warnings are required whenever a suspect is in custody in a technical sense and converses with someone who happens to be a government agent. Questioning by captors, who appear to control the suspect's fate, may create mutually reinforcing pressures that the Court has assumed will weaken the suspect's will, but where a suspect does not know that he is conversing with a government agent, these pressures do not exist. Miranda forbids coercion, not mere strategic deception by taking advantage of a suspect's misplaced trust in one he supposes to be a fellow prisoner. As we recognized in Miranda, "[c]onfessions remain a proper element in law enforcement. Any statement given freely and voluntarily without any compelling influences is, of course, admissible in evidence." Ploys to mislead a suspect or lull him into a false sense of security that do not rise to the level of compulsion or coercion to speak are not within Miranda's concerns. Cf. Oregon v. Mathiason, 429 US 492, 495–496, 97 S Ct 711, 50 L Ed 2d 714 (1977) (per curiam); Moran v. Burbine, 475 US 412, 106 S Ct 1135, 89 L Ed 2d 410 (1986). . . .

The tactic employed here to elicit a voluntary confession from a suspect does not violate the Self-Incrimination Clause. We held in Hoffa v. United States, 385 US 293, 87 S Ct 408, 17 L Ed 2d 374 (1966), that placing an undercover agent near a suspect in order to gather incriminating information was permissible under the Fifth Amendment. . . . The only difference between this case and Hoffa is that the suspect here was incarcerated, but detention, whether or not for the crime in question, does not warrant a presumption that the use of an undercover agent to speak with an incarcerated suspect makes any confession thus obtained involuntary. . . . Where the suspect does not know that he is speaking to a government agent there is no reason to assume the possibility that the suspect might feel coerced. (The bare fact of custody may not in every instance require a warning even when the suspect is aware that he is speaking to an official, but we do not have occasion to explore that issue here.)

This Court's Sixth Amendment decisions . . . also do not avail respondent. . . .

In the instant case no charges had been filed on the subject of the interrogation, and our Sixth Amendment precedents are not applicable.

We hold that an undercover law enforcement officer posing as a fellow inmate need not give Miranda warnings to an incarcerated suspect before asking questions that may elicit an incriminating response. The statements at issue in this case were voluntary, and there is no federal obstacle to their admissibility at trial. . . .

Justice Brennan, concurring in the judgment. . . .

Although I do not subscribe to the majority's characterization of Miranda in its entirety, I do agree that when a suspect does not know that his questioner is a police agent, such questioning does not amount to "interrogation" in an "inherently coercive" environment so as to require application of Miranda. Since the only issue raised at this stage of the litigation is the applicability of Miranda,* I concur in the judgment of the Court.

This is not to say that I believe the Constitution condones the method by which the police extracted the confession in this case. To the contrary, the deception and manipulation practiced on respondent raise a substantial claim that the confession was obtained in violation of the Due Process Clause. . . .

Justice Marshall, dissenting.

Because Perkins was interrogated by police while he was in custody, Miranda required that the officer inform him of his rights. In rejecting that conclusion, the Court finds that "conversations" between undercover agents and suspects are devoid of the coercion inherent in stationhouse interrogations conducted by law enforcement officials who openly represent the State. Miranda was not, however, concerned solely with police *coercion*. It dealt with *any* police tactics that may operate to compel a suspect in custody to make incriminating statements without full awareness of his constitutional rights. . . .

The compulsion proscribed by Miranda includes deception by the police. See Miranda, supra, at 453 (indicting police tactics "to induce a confession out of trickery," such as using fictitious witnesses or false accusations); . . . Although the Court did not find trickery by itself sufficient to constitute compulsion in Hoffa v. United States, 385 US 293, 87 S Ct 408, 17 L Ed 2d 374 (1966), the defendant in that case was not in custody. Perkins, however, was interrogated while incarcerated. . . .

Custody works to the State's advantage in obtaining incriminating information. The psychological pressures inherent in confinement increase the suspect's anxiety, making him likely to seek relief by talking with others. The inmate is thus more susceptible to efforts by undercover agents to elicit information from him. Similarly, where the suspect is incarcerated, the constant threat of physical danger peculiar to the prison environment may make him demonstrate his toughness to other inmates by recounting or inventing past violent acts. "Because the suspect's ability to select people with whom he can confide is completely within their control, the police have a unique opportunity to exploit the suspect's vulnerability. In short, the police can insure that if the pressures of confinement lead the suspect to confide in anyone, it will be a police agent." White, Police Trickery in Inducing Confessions, 127 U Pa L Rev 581, 605 (1979). . . .

Thus, the pressures unique to custody allow the police to use deceptive interrogation tactics to compel a suspect to make incriminating statement[s]. The compulsion is not eliminated by the suspect's ignorance of his interrogator's true identity. The exception carved out of the Miranda doctrine today may well result in a proliferation of departmental policies to encourage police officers to conduct interrogations of confined suspects through undercover agents, thereby circumventing the need to administer Miranda warnings. Indeed, if Miranda now requires a police officer to issue warnings only in those situations in which the suspect might feel compelled "to speak by the fear of reprisal for remaining silent or in the hope of more lenient treatment should he confess," presumably it

---

*As the case comes to us, it involves only the question whether Miranda applies to the questioning of an incarcerated suspect by an undercover agent. Nothing in the Court's opinion suggests that, had respondent previously invoked his Fifth Amendment right to counsel or right to silence, his statements would be admissible. If respondent had invoked either right, the inquiry would focus on whether he subsequently waived the particular right. See Edwards v. Arizona, 451 US 477, 101 S Ct 1880, 68 L Ed 2d 378 (1981); Michigan v. Mosley, 423 US 96, 104, 96 S Ct 321, 46 L Ed 2d 313 (1975). As the Court made clear in Moran v. Burbine, 475 US 412, 421, 106 S Ct 1135, 89 L Ed 2d 410 (1986), the waiver of Miranda rights "must [be] voluntary in the sense that it [must be] the product of a free and deliberate choice rather than *intimidation, coercion or deception*." (Emphasis added). Since respondent was in custody on an unrelated charge when he was questioned, he may be able to challenge the admission of these statements if he previously had invoked his Miranda rights with respect to that charge. See Arizona v. Roberson, 486 US 675, 108 S Ct 2093, 100 L Ed 2d 704 (1988); Mosley, supra, at 104, 46 L Ed 2d 313, 96 S Ct 321. Similarly, if respondent had been formally charged on the unrelated charge and had invoked his Sixth Amendment right to counsel, he may have a Sixth Amendment challenge to the admissibility of these statements.

allows custodial interrogation by an undercover officer posing as a member of the clergy or a suspect's defense attorney. . . . The Court's adoption of the "undercover agent" exception to the Miranda rule thus is necessarily also the adoption of a substantial loophole in our jurisprudence protecting suspects' Fifth Amendment rights. . . .

Notes and Questions

1. In *Oregon v. Mathiason*, the Court appeared to be uninterested in the suspect's subjective experiences when it rejected the contention that he was "in custody" for purposes of *Miranda*. In *Perkins*, the suspect's (subjective) lack of appreciation that he was being questioned by a police officer in the jail cell block appears to be determinative that he was not "in custody" within the meaning of *Miranda*. Is the Court being consistent in its conceptualization of "in custody"?

2. How clear-cut is the line between "coercion" and "strategic deception"? Is it fair to allow the police to use deception to deny a suspect knowledge of a fact that almost certainly would cause the suspect to refrain from making incriminating statements?

3. At the time that Perkins made his incriminating statements, he had not yet been formally charged with committing the murder. His case thus is distinguishable from *Massiah v. United States*, which we considered earlier, at p. 267. *Massiah* relied on the Sixth Amendment right to counsel to rule that incriminating statements were inadmissible in evidence. We return to Sixth Amendment issues later in this chapter

4. State constitutional rulings defining *in custody* in the *Miranda* context generally conform to the federal rulings. *See* B. Latzer, *State Constitutional Criminal Law* § 4.4 (1995).

Interrogation

Much as the "custodial" limitation on *Miranda* is important, so is the requirement for "interrogation." Recall *Miranda's* caveat concerning "volunteered" statements—those offered not in response to questioning.

In dealing with statements obtained through interrogation, we do not purport to find all confessions inadmissible. Confessions remain a proper element in law enforcement. Any statement given freely and voluntarily without any compelling influences is, of course, admissible in evidence. The fundamental import of the privilege while an individual is in custody is not whether he is allowed to talk to the police without the benefit of warnings and counsel, but whether he can be interrogated. There is no requirement that police stop a person who enters a police station and states that he wishes to confess to a crime, or a person who calls the police to offer a confession or any other statement he desires to make. Volunteered statements of any kind are not barred by the Fifth Amendment and their admissibility is not affected by our holding today. 383 U.S., at 478.

It is the *interplay* or combination of "custody" and "interrogation" that creates the police-dominated, psychologically coercive environment that was of concern to the *Miranda* court. *See* Y. Kamisar, "*Brewer v. Williams*, *Massiah*, and *Miranda*: What Is 'Interrogation'? When Does It Matter?" in Y. Kamisar (ed.), *Police Interrogation and Confessions: Essays in Law and Policy* 139, 195–197 (1980). Cases such as *Oregon v. Mathiason, Berkemer v.*

McCarty, and *Illinois v. Perkins* clearly establish that the police may interrogate a criminal suspect without first giving *Miranda* warnings as long as the suspect is not "in custody." The converse also is true. The incriminating statements made by a person in police custody are admissible without the prior administration of *Miranda* warnings as long as those statements are not the product of "interrogation."

We still must distinguish between a "volunteered" statement and a statement made in response to "interrogation." *Rhode Island v. Innis*, presented below, provides a definition of "interrogation."

Rhode Island v. Innis, 446 U.S. 291, 100 S. Ct. 1682, 64 L. Ed. 2d 297 (1980)

Mr. Justice Stewart delivered the opinion of the Court.

[A Rhode Island taxicab driver disappeared after being dispatched to pick up a customer. Four days later, his body was discovered in a shallow grave. He had been killed by a shotgun blast to the back of his head. The following day, another taxicab driver reported to the police that he had been robbed by a man brandishing a sawed-off shotgun. He identified a photograph of the respondent Innis as the robber.

[Just hours after Innis's photo had been identified, a police officer on patrol spotted Innis standing on the side of a street. The officer placed Innis under arrest and advised him of his *Miranda* rights. The officer did not attempt to converse with Innis. He simply placed a call for assistance and awaited the arrival of backup units.]

* * *

Within minutes, Sergeant Sears arrived at the scene of the arrest, and he also gave the respondent the Miranda warnings. Immediately thereafter, Captain Leyden and other police officers arrived. Captain Leyden advised the respondent of his Miranda rights. The respondent stated that he understood those rights and wanted to speak with a lawyer. Captain Leyden then directed that the respondent be placed in a "caged wagon," a four-door police car with a wire screen mesh between the front and rear seats, and be driven to the central police station. Three officers, Patrolmen Gleckman, Williams, and McKenna, were assigned to accompany the respondent to the central station. They placed

the respondent in the vehicle and shut the doors. Captain Leyden then instructed the officers not to question the respondent or intimidate or coerce him in any way. The three officers then entered the vehicle, and it departed.

While en route to the central station, Patrolman Gleckman initiated a conversation with Patrolman McKenna concerning the missing shotgun. As Patrolman Gleckman later testified:

"A. At this point, I was talking back and forth with Patrolman McKenna stating that I frequent this area while on patrol and [that because a school for handicapped children is located nearby,] there's a lot of handicapped children running around in this area, and God forbid one of them might find a weapon with shells and they might hurt themselves."

Patrolman McKenna apparently shared his fellow officer's concern:

"A. I more or less concurred with him [Gleckman] that it was a safety factor and that we should, you know, continue to search for the weapon and try to find it."

While Patrolman Williams said nothing, he overheard the conversation between the two officers:

"A. He [Gleckman] said it would be too bad if the little—I believe he said a girl—would pick up the gun, maybe kill herself."

The respondent then interrupted the conversation, stating that the officers should turn the car around so he could show them where the gun was located. At this point, Patrolman McKenna radioed back to Captain Leyden that they were returning to the scene of the arrest, and that the respondent would inform them of the location of the gun. At the time the respondent indicated that the officers should turn back, they had traveled no more than a mile, a trip encompassing only a few minutes.

The police vehicle then returned to the scene of the arrest where a search for the shotgun was in progress. There, Captain Leyden again advised the respondent of his Miranda rights. The respondent replied that he understood those rights but that he "wanted to get the gun out of the way because of the kids in the area in the school." The respondent then led the police to a nearby field, where he pointed out the shotgun under some rocks by the side of the road.

[Innis subsequently was convicted of the robbery, kidnapping, and murder of the first taxi driver. The trial court admitted the shotgun and testimony about Innis's statements into evidence. By vote of 3–2, the Rhode Island Supreme Court reversed, concluding that Innis had invoked his *Miranda* rights and that the police had violated those rights by "interrogating" him in the absence of counsel. The U.S. Supreme Court granted certiorari "to address for the first time the meaning of 'interrogation' under Miranda v. Arizona."]

* * *

In the present case, the parties are in agreement that the respondent was fully informed of his Miranda rights and that he invoked his Miranda right to counsel when he told Captain Leyden that he wished to consult with a lawyer. It is also uncontested that the respondent was "in custody" while being transported to the police station. The issue, therefore, is whether the respondent was "interrogated" by the police officers in violation of the respondent's undisputed right under Miranda to remain silent until he had consulted with a lawyer.[2] In resolving this

_____

2. Since we conclude that the respondent was not "interrogated" for Miranda purposes, we do not reach the question whether the respondent waived his right under Miranda to be free from interrogation until counsel was present.

issue, we first define the term "interrogation" under Miranda before turning to a consideration of the facts of this case.

A

The starting point for defining "interrogation" in this context is, of course, the Court's Miranda opinion. There the Court observed that "[b]y custodial interrogation, we mean *questioning* initiated by law enforcement officers after a person has been taken into custody or otherwise deprived of his freedom of action in any significant way." [3836.5.] at 444 (emphasis added). This passage and other references throughout the opinion to "questioning" might suggest that the Miranda rules were to apply only to those police interrogation practices that involve express questioning of a defendant while in custody.

We do not, however, construe the Miranda opinion so narrowly. The concern of the Court in Miranda was that the "interrogation environment" created by the interplay of interrogation and custody would "subjugate the individual to the will of his examiner" and thereby undermine the privilege against compulsory self-incrimination. Id., at 457–458.

The police practices that evoked this concern included several that did not involve express questioning. For example, one of the practices discussed in Miranda was the use of line-ups in which a coached witness would pick the defendant as the perpetrator. This was designed to establish that the defendant was in fact guilty as a predicate for further interrogation. Id., at 453. A variation on this theme discussed in Miranda was the so-called "reverse line-up" in which a defendant would be identified by coached witnesses as the perpetrator of a fictitious crime, with the object of inducing him to confess to the actual crime of which he was suspected in order to escape the false prosecution. Ibid. The Court in Miranda also included in its survey of interrogation practices the use of psychological ploys, such as to "posi[t]" "the guilt of the subject," to "minimize the moral seriousness of the offense," and "to cast blame on the victim or on society." Id., at 450. It is clear that these techniques of persuasion, no less than express questioning, were thought, in a custodial setting, to amount to interrogation.

This is not to say, however, that all statements obtained by the police after a person has been taken into custody are to be considered the product of interrogation. As the Court in Miranda noted:

"Confessions remain a proper element in law enforcement. Any statement given freely and voluntarily without any compelling influences is, of course, admissible in evidence.

The fundamental import of the privilege while an individual is in custody is not whether he is allowed to talk to the police without the benefit of warnings and counsel, but whether he can be interrogated. . . . Volunteered statements of any kind are not barred by the Fifth Amendment and their admissibility is not affected by our holding today." Id., at 478 (emphasis added).

It is clear therefore that the special procedural safeguards outlined in Miranda are required not where a suspect is simply taken into custody, but rather where a suspect in custody is subjected to interrogation. "Interrogation," as conceptualized in the Miranda opinion, must reflect a measure of compulsion above and beyond that inherent in custody itself.

We conclude that the Miranda safeguards come into play whenever a person in custody is subjected to either express questioning or its functional equivalent. That is to say, the term "interrogation" under Miranda refers not only to express questioning, but also to any words or actions on the part of the police (other than those normally attendant to arrest and custody) that the police should know are reasonably likely to elicit an incriminating response from the suspect. The latter portion of this definition focuses primarily upon the perceptions of the suspect, rather than the intent of the police. This focus reflects the fact that the Miranda safeguards were designed to vest a suspect in custody with an added measure of protection against coercive police practices, without regard to objective proof of the underlying intent of the police. A practice that the police should know is reasonably likely to evoke an incriminating response

from a suspect thus amounts to interrogation.[7] But, since the police surely cannot be held accountable for the unforeseeable results of their words or actions, the definition of interrogation can extend only to words or actions on the part of police officers that they *should have known* were reasonably likely to elicit an incriminating response.[8]

B

Turning to the facts of the present case, we conclude that the respondent was not "interrogated" within the meaning of Miranda. It is undisputed that the first prong of the definition of "interrogation" was not satisfied, for the conversation between Patrolmen Gleckman and McKenna included no express questioning of the respondent. Rather, that conversation was, at least in form, nothing more than a dialogue between the two officers to which no response from the respondent was invited.

Moreover, it cannot be fairly concluded that the respondent was subjected to the "functional equivalent" of questioning. It cannot be said, in short, that Patrolmen Gleckman and McKenna should have known that their conversation was reasonably likely to elicit an incriminating response from the respondent. There is nothing in the record to suggest that the officers were aware that the respondent was peculiarly susceptible to an appeal to his conscience concerning the safety of handicapped children. Nor is there anything in the record to suggest that the police knew that the respondent was unusually disoriented or upset at the time of his arrest.

---

7. This is not to say that the intent of the police is irrelevant, for it may well have a bearing on whether the police should have known that their words or actions were reasonably likely to evoke an incriminating response. In particular, where a police practice is designed to elicit an incriminating response from the accused, it is unlikely that the practice will not also be one which the police should have known was reasonably likely to have that effect.

8. Any knowledge the police may have had concerning the unusual susceptibility of a defendant to a particular form of persuasion might be an important factor in determining whether the police should have known that their words or actions were reasonably likely to elicit an incriminating response from the suspect.

The case thus boils down to whether, in the context of a brief conversation, the officers should have known that the respondent would suddenly be moved to make a self-incriminating response. Given the fact that the entire conversation appears to have consisted of no more than a few offhand remarks, we cannot say that the officers should have known that it was reasonably likely that Innis would so respond. This is not a case where the police carried on a lengthy harangue in the presence of the suspect. Nor does the record support the respondent's contention that, under the circumstances, the officers' comments were particularly "evocative." It is our view, therefore, that the respondent was not subjected by the police to words or actions that the police should have known were reasonably likely to elicit an incriminating response from him. . . .

Mr. Justice Marshall, with whom Mr. Justice Brennan joins, dissenting.

I am substantially in agreement with the Court's definition of "interrogation" within the meaning of Miranda v. Arizona . . . [T]he Court requires an objective inquiry into the likely effect of police conduct on a typical individual, taking into account any special susceptibility of the suspect to certain kinds of pressure of which the police know or have reason to know.

I am utterly at a loss, however, to understand how this objective standard as applied to the facts before us can rationally lead to the conclusion that there was no interrogation. . . .

One can scarcely imagine a stronger appeal to the conscience of a suspect—*any* suspect—than the assertion that if the weapon is not found an innocent person will be hurt or killed. And not just any innocent person, but an innocent child—a little girl—a helpless, handicapped little girl on her way to school. The notion that such an appeal could not be expected to have any effect unless the suspect were known to have some special interest in handicapped children verges on the ludicrous. As a matter of fact, the appeal to a suspect to confess for the sake of others, to "display some evidence of decency and honor," is a classic interrogation technique. See, e.g., F. Inbau & J. Reid, Criminal Interrogation and Confessions 60–62 (2d ed. 1967).

Gleckman's remarks would obviously have constituted interrogation if they had been explicitly directed to respondent, and the result should not be different because they were nominally addressed to McKenna. This is not a case where police officers speaking among themselves are accidentally overheard by a suspect. These officers were "talking back and forth" in close quarters with the handcuffed suspect, traveling past the very place where they believed the weapon was located. They knew respondent would hear and attend to their conversation, and they are chargeable with knowledge of and responsibility for the pressures to speak which they created. . . .

Mr. Justice Stevens, dissenting.

* * *

Notes and Questions

1. Is *Innis's* definition of "interrogation" an objective test, a subjective test (relying on the intent of the involved officers and/or the impact of the police's words or actions on a particular suspect), or some combination thereof? In this regard, especially note footnotes 7 and 8 in Justice Stewart's majority opinion.

2. Extracting the test for "interrogation" from *Innis* is much less difficult than applying that test to the facts of the case. Who has the more convincing argument concerning whether Innis was "interrogated": Justice Stewart, in his majority opinion, or Justice Marshall, in his dissent?

3. What if there really were no school for handicapped children in the area, and Officers Gleckman and McKenna had just made up this story? Would (should) that change the majority's decision about whether their exchange was the functional equivalent of express questioning?

4. Refer once again to *Brewer v. Williams*, reproduced in Chapter 1 at p. 6. Recall that the Court decided that case on Sixth Amendment grounds and did not consider whether Williams's *Miranda* rights had been violated. If the case had been analyzed under *Miranda*, should Detective Leaming's "Christian burial speech" have been characterized as a form of "interrogation"? Are Leaming's remarks in *Brewer v. Williams* distinguishable from the police offic-

ers' remarks in *Innis* about the possibility of a handicapped child finding the shotgun? If so, how?

5. "The *Innis* test for 'interrogation' has been approved [under] state [constitutional] provisions apparently without exception." B. Latzer, *State Constitutional Criminal Law* § 4:5 (1995).

William Mauro "freely admitted" to the police that he had killed his son. After leading officers to his son's body, he was arrested and advised of his *Miranda* rights. He then was taken to the police station, where he asked to speak with a lawyer before making additional statements. Mauro's wife, who had been talking with a detective in another room, insisted to be allowed to speak with her husband. The police were "reluctant" to permit the meeting but did so after telling both Mr. and Mrs. Mauro that a police officer would have to be "present in the room to observe and hear what was going on." An officer thus stationed himself in the room and, using a clearly visible tape recorder, recorded their conversation. The recording of the conversation later was played at Mauro's murder trial to help negate his plea of not guilty by reason of insanity. Mauro was convicted of murder and sentenced to death. The Arizona Supreme Court reversed, finding that

by allowing Mauro to speak with his wife in the presence of a police officer, the detectives interrogated Mauro within the meaning of Miranda. This interrogation was impermissible, the court said, because Mauro previously had invoked the right to have counsel present before being questioned further. The court noted that both detectives had acknowledged in pretrial hearings that they knew it was "possible" that Mauro might make incriminating statements if he saw his wife. . . .

The Supreme Court reversed, through a 5–4 decision authored by Justice Powell.

The Arizona Supreme Court was correct to note that there was a "possibility" that Mauro would incriminate himself while talking to his wife. It also emphasized that the officers were aware of that possibility when they agreed to allow the Mauros to talk to each other. But the actions in this case were far less questionable than the "subtle compulsion" that we held *not* to be interrogation in Innis. Officers do not interrogate a suspect simply by hoping that he will incriminate himself. . . . Mauro was not subjected to compelling influences, psychological ploys, or direct questioning. Thus, his volunteered statements cannot properly be considered the result of police interrogation.

In deciding whether particular police conduct is interrogation, we must remember the purpose behind our decisions in Miranda . . .: preventing government officials from using the coercive nature of confinement to extract confessions that would not be given in an unrestrained environment. The government actions in this case do not implicate this purpose in any way. Police departments need not adopt inflexible rules barring suspects from speaking with their spouses, nor must they ignore legitimate security concerns by allowing spouses to meet in private. In short, the officers in this case acted reasonably and lawfully by allowing Mrs. Mauro to speak with her husband. In this situation, the Federal Constitution does not forbid use of Mauro's subsequent statements at his criminal trial. . . .

Justice Stevens, Brennan, Marshall, and Blackmun dissented.

The Miranda Warnings

Duckworth v. Eagan, 492 U.S. 195, 109 S. Ct. 2875, 106 L. Ed. 2d 166 (1989)

Chief Justice REHNQUIST delivered the opinion of the Court.

[The respondent Eagan was convicted of attempted murder in an Indiana state court. Among the evidence supporting his conviction was his own confession to stabbing the victim and the knife and several items of clothing associated with the stabbing. He was sentenced to 35 years in prison. The state courts and the U.S. district court upheld Eagan's conviction, but the U.S. Court of Appeals for the Seventh Circuit reversed, concluding that the warnings given Eagan prior to his confession were inadequate under *Miranda v. Arizona*. The warnings appeared on a waiver form used by the Hammond, Indiana, police. The form provided:

[Before we ask you any questions, you must understand your rights. You have the right to remain silent. Anything you say can be used against you in court. *You have the right to talk to a lawyer for advice before we ask you any questions, and to have him with you during questioning.* You have this right to the advice and presence of a lawyer even if you cannot afford to hire one. *We have no way of giving you a lawyer, but one will be appointed for you, if you wish, if and when you go to court.* If you wish to answer questions now without a lawyer present, you have the right to stop answering questions at any time. You also have the right to stop answering at any time until you've talked to a lawyer. (Emphasis added by court.)

[Although additional warnings were given Eagan prior to his confession, the court of appeals ruled that the later warnings did not cure the deficiencies that it perceived in the administration of rights quoted above. Those perceived deficiencies are described in the Chief Justice's and Justice Marshall's opinions, which follow.]

* * *

In *Miranda v. Arizona*, 384 U.S. 436, 86 S.Ct. 1602, 16 L.Ed.2d 694 (1966), the Court established certain procedural safeguards that require police to advise criminal suspects of their rights under the Fifth and Fourteenth Amendments before commencing custodial interrogation. In now-familiar words, the Court said that the suspect must be told that "he has the right to remain silent, that anything he says can be used against him in a court of law, that he has the right to the presence of an attorney, and that if he cannot afford an attorney one will be appointed for him prior to any questioning if he so desires." *Id.*, at 479. . . .

We have never insisted that *Miranda* warnings be given in the exact form described in that decision. In *Miranda* itself, the Court said that "[t]he warnings required and the waiver necessary in accordance with our opinion today are, *in the absence of a fully effective equivalent*, prerequisites to the admissibility of any statement made by a defendant." 384 U.S., at 476 (emphasis added). In *California v. Prysock*, 453 U.S. 355, 101 S.Ct. 2806, 69 L.E.2d 696 (1981), we stated that "the 'rigidity' of *Miranda* [does not] exten[d] to the precise formulation of the warnings given a criminal defendant," and that "no talismanic incantation [is] required to satisfy its strictures." *Id*, at 359.

Miranda has not been limited to stationhouse questioning, see *Rhode Island v. Innis,* [446 U.S. 291, 100 S.Ct. 1682, 64 L.Ed.2d 297 (1980)] (police car), and the officer in the field may not always have access to printed *Miranda* warnings, or he may inadvertently depart from routine practice, particularly if a suspect requests an elaboration of the warnings. The prophylactic *Miranda* warnings are "not themselves rights protected by the Constitution but [are] instead measures to insure that the right against compulsory self-incrimination [is] protected." *Michigan v. Tucker*, 417 U.S. 433, 444, 94 S.Ct. 2357, 41 L.Ed.2d 182 (1974). Reviewing courts therefore need not examine *Miranda* warnings as if construing a will or defining the terms of an easement. The inquiry is simply whether the warnings reasonably "convey[y] to [a suspect] his rights as required by *Miranda*." *Prysock, supra*, 453 U.S., at 361.

We think the initial warnings given to respondent touched all of the bases required by *Miranda*. The police told respondent that he had the right to remain silent, that anything he said could be used against him in court, that he had the right to speak to an attorney before and during questioning, that he had "this right to the advice and presence of a lawyer even if [he could] not afford to hire one," and that he had the "right to stop answering at any time until [he] talked to a lawyer." As noted, the police also added that they could not provide respondent with a lawyer, but that one would be appointed "if and when you go to court." The Court of Appeals thought this "if and when you go to court" language suggested that "only those accused who can afford an attorney have the right to have one present before answering any questions," and "implie[d] that if the accused does not 'go to court,' *i.e.*[,] the government does not file charges, the accused is not entitled to [counsel] at all."

In our view, the Court of Appeals misapprehended the effect of the inclusion of "if and when you go to court" language in *Miranda* warnings. First, this instruction accurately described the procedure for the appointment of counsel in Indiana. Under Indiana law, counsel is appointed at the defendant's initial appearance in court, Ind. Code § 35-33-7-6 (1988), and formal charges must be filed at or before that hearing. § 35-33-7-3(a). We think it must be relatively commonplace for a suspect, after receiving *Miranda* warnings, to ask *when* he will obtain counsel. The "if and when you go to court" advice simply anticipates that question. Second, *Miranda* does not require that attorneys be producible on call, but only that the suspect be informed, as here, that he has the right to an attorney before and during questioning, and that an attorney would

be appointed for him if he could not afford one. The Court in *Miranda* emphasized that it was not suggesting that "each police station must have a 'station house lawyer' present at all times to advise prisoners." 384 U.S., at 474. If the police cannot provide appointed counsel, *Miranda* requires only that the police not question a suspect unless he waives his right to counsel. *Ibid.* Here, respondent did just that.

Respondent relies on language in *California v. Prysock*, where we suggested that *Miranda* warnings would not be sufficient "if the reference to the right to appointed counsel was linked [to a] future point in time *after* the police interrogation." 453 U.S., at 360 (emphasis added). . . . But the vice referred to in *Prysock* was that such warnings would not apprise the accused of his right to have an attorney present if he chose to answer questions. The warnings in this case did not suffer from that defect. Of the eight sentences in the initial warnings, one described respondent's right to counsel "before [the police] ask[ed] [him] questions," while another stated his right to "stop answering at any time until [he] talk[ed] to a lawyer." We hold that the initial warnings given to respondent, in their totality, satisfied *Miranda*, and therefore that his statement as well as the knife and the clothing were all properly admitted into evidence.

Justice MARSHALL, with whom Justice BRENNAN joins, and with whom Justice BLACKMUN and Justice STEVENS join as to Part I, dissenting.

* * *

I

In *Miranda*, the Court held that law enforcement officers who take a suspect into custody must inform the suspect of, among other things, his right to have counsel appointed to represent him before and during interrogation. . . .

Miranda mandated no specific verbal formulation that police must use, but the Court, speaking through Chief Justice Warren, emphasized repeatedly that the offer of appointed counsel must be "effective and express." . . . A clear and unequivocal offer to provide appointed counsel prior to questioning is, in short, an "absolute pre-requisite to interrogation." *Id.*, at 471. . . .

Eagan was initially advised that he had the right to the presence of counsel before and during questioning. But in the very next breath, the police informed Eagan that, if he could not afford a lawyer, one would be appointed to represent him only "if and when" he went to court. As the Court of Appeals found, Eagan could easily have concluded from the "if and when" caveat that only "those accused who can afford an attorney have the right to have one present before answering any questions; those who are not so fortunate must wait." Eagan was, after all, never told that questioning would be *delayed* until a lawyer was appointed "if and when" Egan did, in fact, go to court. Thus, the "if and when" caveat may well have had the effect of negating the initial promise that counsel could be present. . . .

In lawyer-like fashion, THE CHIEF JUSTICE parses the initial warnings given Eagan and finds that the most plausible interpretation is that Eagan would not be questioned until a lawyer was appointed when he later appeared in court. What goes wholly overlooked in THE CHIEF JUSTICE's analysis is that the recipients of police warnings are often frightened suspects unlettered in the law, not lawyers or judges or others schooled in interpreting legal or semantic nuance. . . .

Even if the typical suspect could draw the inference the majority does—that questioning will not commence until a lawyer is provided at a later court appearance—a warning qualified by an "if and when" caveat still fails to give a sus-pect any indication of *when* he will be taken to court. Upon hearing the warnings given in this case, a suspect would likely conclude that no lawyer would be provided until trial. . . . Furthermore, the negative implication of the caveat is that, if the suspect is never taken to court, he "is not entitled to an attorney at all." An unwitting suspect harboring uncertainty on this score is precisely the sort of person who may feel compelled to talk "voluntarily" to the police, without the presence of counsel, in an effort to extricate himself from his predicament. . . . The threat of an indefinite deferral of interrogations, in a system like Indiana's, thus constitutes an effective means by which the police can pressure a suspect to speak without the presence of counsel. Sanctioning such police practices simply because the warnings given do not misrepresent state law does nothing more than let the state-law tail wag the federal constitutional dog. . . .

It poses no great burden on law enforcement officers to eradicate the confusion stemming from the "if and when" caveat. Deleting the sentence containing the offending language is all that needs to be done. Purged of this language, the warning tells the suspect in a straightforward fashion that he has the right to the presence of a lawyer before and during questioning, and that a lawyer will be appointed if he cannot afford one. The suspect is given no reason to believe that the appointment of an attorney may come after interrogation.

* * *

Notes and Questions

1. Is the ruling in *Duckworth v. Eagan* more likely to promote or to detract from *Miranda's* goal of providing clear, consistent, and easily followed rules to regulate police interrogation procedures?

2. Chief Justice Rehnquist's opinion suggests that deviations from the *Miranda* court's formulation of the warnings will be tolerated as long as the rights given a suspect "reasonably 'convey]'" the required information, and as long as the changes do not impart inaccurate or mis-leading information. Using this reasoning, would the following variation in the *Miranda* warnings be likely to pass constitutional scrutiny: "Anything you say can be used *for or against you* in a court of law"? See *Commonwealth v. Singleton*, 439 Pa. 185, 266 A.2d 753, 755–756 (1970), which found such a "warning" constitutionally infirm because

the word "for" . . . acts as a subtle inducement to speak, helps neutralize the suspect's awareness of the hostile environment, and vitiates the intended impact of the warning. . . . Since the deviation here involved is hardly likely to give suspects a heightened understanding of their constitutional rights, and is in fact likely to undercut the effect of the warning by offering an inducement to speak, we find it impermissible.

Invocation of the Miranda Rights

The *Miranda* Court explained that if a suspect "indicates in any manner and at any stage of the process that he wishes to consult with an attorney before speaking there can be no questioning. Likewise, if the individual is alone and indicates in any manner that he does not wish to be interrogated, the police may not question him." 384 U.S., at 444–445. *See also id.* at 473–474.

We already have encountered difficult definitional questions raised by *Miranda*, including the meaning of such basic concepts as "custodial" and "interrogation." We now consider two issues related to the *invocation* of Miranda rights. First, we ask what an individual must say or do to assert the right to remain silent or to the assistance of counsel. This is an important question because if a suspect does invoke either of those rights, the police are expected immediately to honor their expression by ceasing or refraining from interrogation. Second, we consider whether it ever is permissible for the police to resume their interrogation of a suspect after the suspect has invoked *Miranda's* protections. Can a suspect effectively waive his or her *Miranda* rights, once having invoked those safeguards? If so, under what circumstances? We begin by considering how suspects can indicate that they are invoking their *Miranda* rights.

Invoking Miranda's Protections

In *Fare v. Michael C.*, 442 U.S. 707, 99 S. Ct. 2560, 61 L. Ed. 2d 197 (1979), the Supreme Court confronted whether a suspect had invoked his right either to consult with an attorney or to remain silent prior to confessing to a murder in response to police questioning. Sixteen-year-old Michael C. was on probation to the juvenile court in his home state of California. Michael C. had a record of committing several juvenile offenses, including the burglary of guns and purse snatching, and he had served time in a juvenile corrections facility. He was taken into custody by the police for questioning about a robbery and murder. Michael C.'s probation officer previously had told him that he should contact that officer if he ever got into trouble with the police. Juvenile court probation officers had a statutory duty to "advise and care for" the youths whom they supervised, but they also investigated alleged offenses, initiated delinquency petitions against, and sometimes testified against probationers in court. Michael C. was fully advised of his *Miranda* rights, and the following dialogue then took place between the police and him:

"Q. . . . Do you understand all of these rights as I have explained them to you?

"A. Yeah.

"Q. Okay, do you wish to give up your right to remain silent and talk to us about this murder?

"A. What murder? I don't know about no murder.

"Q. I'll explain to you which one it is if you want to talk to us about it.

"A. Yeah, I might talk to you.

"Q. Do you want to give up your right to have an attorney present here while we talk about it?

"A. Can I have my probation officer here?

"Q. Well I can't get a hold of your proba-tion officer right now. You have the right to an attorney.

"A. How I know you guys won't pull no police officer in and tell me he's an attor-ney?

"Q. Huh?

"A. [How I know you guys won't pull no police officer in and tell me he's an attor-ney?]

"Q. Your probation officer is Mr. Chris-tiansen.

"A. Yeah.

"Q. Well I'm not going to call Mr. Chris-tiansen tonight. There's a good chance we can talk to him later, but I'm not going to call him right now. If you want to talk to us without an attorney present, you can. If you don't want to, you don't have to. But if you want to say something, you can, and if you don't want to say something you don't have to. That's your right. You understand that right?

"A. Yeah.

"Q. Okay, will you talk to us without an attorney present?

"A. Yeah I want to talk to you."

After this exchange, Michael C. made incriminating statements and drew sketches in response to questions about the murder. This evidence was admitted against Michael C. in a juvenile court proceeding. He was adjudicated delinquent and ordered committed to a juvenile corrections facility.

If Michael C.'s request to have his probation officer present amounted to an invocation of his right to counsel or to remain silent, further questioning should have ceased and the incrimi-nating statements and sketches would have been obtained in violation of *Miranda*. In a 5–4 deci-sion, per Blackmun, J., the Supreme Court ruled that this request did not invoke the protections of *Miranda*.

The rule in Miranda . . . was based on this Court's perception that the lawyer occupies a critical position in our legal sys-tem because of his unique ability to protect the Fifth Amendment rights of a client undergoing custodial interrogation. Because of this special ability of the lawyer to help the client preserve his Fifth Amendment rights once the client becomes enmeshed in the adversary process, the Court found that "the right to have counsel present at the interrogation is indispensable to the protec-tion of the Fifth Amendment privilege under the system" established by the Court. Moreover, the lawyer's presence helps guard against overreaching by the police and ensures that any statements actually obtained are accurately transcribed for pre-sentation into evidence.

The per se aspect of Miranda was thus based on the unique role the lawyer plays in the adversary system of criminal justice in this country. Whether it is a minor or an adult who stands accused, the lawyer is the one person to whom society as a whole looks as the protector of the legal rights of that person in his dealings with the police and the courts. For this reason, the Court fashioned in Miranda the rigid rule that an accused's request for an attorney is per se an invocation of his Fifth Amendment rights, requiring that all interrogation cease.

A probation officer is not in the same posture with regard to either the accused or the system of justice as a whole. Often he is not trained in the law, and so is not in a position to advise the accused as to his legal rights. Neither is he a trained advo-cate, skilled in the representation of the interests of his client before both police and courts. He does not assume the power to act on behalf of his client by virtue of his status as adviser, nor are the communications of the accused to the probation officer shielded by the lawyer-client privilege.

Moreover, the probation officer is the employee of the State which seeks to prosecute the alleged offender. He is a peace officer, and as such is allied, to a greater or lesser extent, with his fellow peace officers. He owes an obligation to the State, notwithstanding the obligation he may also owe the juvenile under his supervision. In most cases, the probation officer is duty bound to report wrongdoing by the juvenile when it comes to his attention, even if by communication from the juvenile himself. Indeed, when this case arose, the probation officer had the responsibility for filing the petition alleging wrongdoing by the juvenile and seeking to have him taken into the custody of the Juvenile Court. It was respondent's probation officer who filed the petition against him, and it is the acting chief of probation for the State of California, a probation officer, who is petitioner in this Court today. . . .

We thus believe it clear that the probation officer is not in a position to offer the type of legal assistance necessary to protect the Fifth Amendment rights of an accused undergoing custodial interrogation that a lawyer can offer. The Court in Miranda recognized that "the attorney plays a vital role in the administration of criminal justice under our Constitution." 384 US, at 481. It is this pivotal role of legal counsel that justifies the per se rule established in Miranda, and that distinguishes the request for counsel from the request for a probation officer, a clergyman, or a close friend. A probation officer simply is not necessary, in the way an attorney is, for the protection of the legal rights of the accused, juvenile or adult. He is significantly handicapped by the position he occupies in the juvenile system from serving as an effective protector of the rights of a juvenile suspected of a crime. . . .

Nor do we believe that a request by a juvenile to speak with his probation officer constitutes a per se request to remain silent. As indicated, since a probation officer does not fulfill the important role in protecting the rights of the accused juvenile that an attorney plays, we decline to find that the request for the probation officer is tantamount to the request for an attorney. And there is nothing inherent in the request for a probation officer that requires us to find that a juvenile's request to see one necessarily constitutes an expression of the juvenile's right to remain silent. [C]ourts may take into account such a request in evaluating whether a juvenile in fact had waived his Fifth Amendment rights before confessing. But in other circumstances such a request might well be consistent with a desire to speak with the police. In the absence of further evidence that the minor intended in the circumstances to invoke his Fifth Amendment rights by such a request, we decline to attach such overwhelming significance to this request. . . .

Mr. Justice Marshall, with whom Mr. Justice Brennan and Mr. Justice Stevens join, dissenting. . . .

As this Court has consistently recognized, the coerciveness of the custodial setting is of heightened concern where, as here, a juvenile is under investigation. . . . It is therefore critical in the present context that we construe Miranda's prophylactic requirements broadly to accomplish their intended purpose—"dispel[ling] the compulsion inherent in custodial surroundings." 384 US, at 458. To effectuate this purpose the Court must ensure that the "protective device" of legal counsel be readily available, and that any intimation of a desire to preclude questioning be scrupulously honored. Thus, I believe Miranda requires that interrogation cease whenever a juvenile requests an adult who is obligated to represent his interests. Such a request, in my judgment, constitutes both an attempt to obtain advice and a general invocation of the right to silence. For, as the California Supreme Court recognized, "'[i]t is fatuous to assume that a minor in custody will be in a position to call an attorney for assistance,'" or that he will trust the police to obtain a lawyer for him.[1] A juvenile in these circumstances will likely turn to his parents, or another adult responsible for his welfare, as the only means of securing legal counsel. Moreover, a request for such adult assistance is surely inconsistent with a present desire to speak freely. Requiring a strict verbal formula to invoke the protections of Miranda would "protect the knowledgeable accused from stationhouse coercion while abandoning the young person who knows no more than to ask for the . . . person he trusts." Chaney v. Wainwright, 561 F2d 1129, 1134 (5th Cir 1977) (Goldberg, J., dissenting).

On my reading of Miranda, a California juvenile's request for his probation officer should be treated as a per se assertion of Fifth Amendment rights. The California Supreme Court determined that probation officers have a statutory duty to represent minors' interests and, indeed, are "trusted guardian figure[s]" to whom a juvenile would likely turn. Hence, a juvenile's request for a probation officer may frequently be an attempt to secure pro-

tection from the coercive aspects of custodial questioning.[2] . . .

Thus, given the role of probation officers under California law, a juvenile's request to see his officer may reflect a desire for precisely the kind of assistance Miranda guarantees an accused before he waives his Fifth Amendment rights. At the very least, such a request signals a desire to remain silent until contact with the officer is made. Because the Court's contrary determination withdraws the safeguards of Miranda from those most in need of protection, I respectfully dissent.

Mr. Justice Powell, dissenting.

* * *

---

1. The facts of the instant case are illustrative. When the police offered to obtain an attorney for respondent, he replied: "How I know you guys won't pull no police officer in and tell me he's an attorney?" Significantly, the police made no attempt to allay that concern.

---

2. The Court intimates that construing a request for a probation officer as an invocation of the Fifth Amendment privilege would undermine the specificity of Miranda's prophylactic rules. Yet the Court concedes that the statutory duty to "advise and care for the juvenile defendant," distinguishes probation officers from other adults, such as coaches and clergymen. Since law-enforcement officials should be on notice of such legal relationships, they would presumably have no difficulty determining whether a suspect has asserted his Fifth Amendment rights.

Although I agree with my Brother Powell that, on the facts here, respondent was not "subjected to a fair interrogation free from inherently coercive circumstances," post, I do not believe a case-by-case approach provides police sufficient guidance, or affords juveniles adequate protection.

Notes and Questions

1. Would you expect a different result in *Fare v. Michael C.* if Michael C. had asked to see his father or mother? In what respects is a parent unlike a probation officer? Unlike an attorney? Would Michael C. at least have a stronger argument that he had invoked his right to silence if he had requested to see one of his parents? Through legislation, many states provide that a juvenile cannot waive his or her self-incrimination rights without having first consulted with a parent or guardian.

2. What if the police had complied with Michael C.'s request and if, after meeting with Michael C., his probation officer persuaded him to make a full confession to the police? Do you suppose the dissenters in *Michael C.* would be comfortable with such a result?

3. Is *Fare v. Michael C.* consistent with *Miranda's* mandate that if the suspect "indicates in any manner" his desire for counsel or to remain silent, questioning by the police should stop? How clear must the suspect's indication be to be effective? Consider the following case.

* * * * *

The petitioner in *Davis v. United States*, 512 U.S. 452, 114 S. Ct. 2350, 129 L. Ed. 2d 362 (1994), was convicted of murder pursuant to a military court-martial proceeding and was sentenced to life imprisonment. Incriminating statements that he made during an interview with Naval Investigative Service (NIS) officers were used as evidence in support of his conviction. Davis had been advised of his *Miranda* rights and had waived those rights, "both orally and in writing." The following then transpired.

About an hour and a half into the interview, petitioner said, "Maybe I should talk to a lawyer." According to the uncontradicted testimony of one of the interviewing agents, the interview then proceeded as follows:

"[We m]ade it very clear that we're not here to violate his rights, that if he wants a lawyer, then we will stop any kind of questioning with him, that we weren't going to pursue the matter unless we have it clarified is he asking for a lawyer or is he just making a comment about a lawyer, and he said, [']No, I'm not asking for a lawyer,' and then he continued on, and said, 'No, I don't want a lawyer.'"

After a short break, the agents reminded petitioner of his rights to remain silent and to counsel. The interview then continued for another hour, until petitioner said, "I think I want a lawyer before I say anything else." At that point, questioning ceased. . . .

The Court, through an opinion written by Justice O'Connor, phrased the issue in *Davis* as follows:

In *Edwards v. Arizona*, 451 U.S. 477, 101 S Ct 1880, 68 L. Ed. 2d 378 (1981), we held that law enforcement officers must immediately cease questioning a suspect who has clearly asserted his right to have counsel present during custodial interrogation. In this case we decide how law enforcement officers should respond when a suspect makes a reference to counsel that is insufficiently clear to invoke the *Edwards* prohibition on further questioning. . . .

We will consider *Edwards v. Arizona* in the next section of this chapter. Justice O'Connor observed that to apply the *Edwards* rule, the courts must

"determine whether the accused *actually invoked* his right to counsel." To avoid difficulties of proof and to provide guidance to officers conducting interrogations, this is an objective inquiry. Invocation of the *Miranda* right to counsel "requires, at a minimum, some statement that can reasonably be construed to be an expression of a desire for the assistance of an attorney." *McNeil v. Wisconsin*, [501 U.S. 171, 178, 111 S. Ct. 2204, 115 L.Ed. 158 [(1991)]. But if a suspect makes a reference to an attorney that is ambiguous or equivocal in that a reasonable officer in light of the circumstances would have understood only that the suspect *might* be invoking the right to counsel, our precedents do not require the cessation of questioning. . . .

Rather, the suspect must unambiguously request counsel. . . . Although a suspect need not "speak with the discrimination of an Oxford don," *post*, (Souter, J., concurring in judgment), he must articulate his desire to have counsel present sufficiently clearly that a reasonable police officer in the circumstances would understand the statement to be a request for an attorney. If the statement fails to meet the requisite level of clarity, *Edwards* does not require that the officers stop questioning the suspect.

We decline petitioner's invitation to extend *Edwards* and require law enforcement officers to cease questioning immediately upon the making of an ambiguous or equivocal reference to an attorney. The rationale underlying *Edwards* is that the police must respect a suspect's wishes regarding his right to have an attorney present during custodial interrogation. But when the officers conducting the questioning reasonably do not know whether or not the suspect wants a lawyer, a rule requiring the immediate cessation of questioning "would transform the *Miranda* safeguards into wholly irrational obstacles to legitimate police investigative activity," *Michigan v. Mosley*, 423 U.S. 96, 102, 96 S. Ct. 321, 46 L. Ed. 2d 313 (1975), because it would needlessly prevent the police from questioning a suspect in the absence of counsel even if the suspect did not wish to have a lawyer present. . . .

We recognize that requiring a clear assertion of the right to counsel might disadvantage some suspects who—because of fear, intimidation, lack of linguistic skills, or a variety of other reasons—will not clearly articulate their right to counsel although they actually want to have a lawyer present. But the primary protection afforded suspects subject to custodial interrogation is the *Miranda* warnings themselves. . . . A suspect who knowingly and voluntarily waives his right to counsel after having that right explained to him has indicated his willingness to deal with the police unassisted. Although *Edwards* provides an additional protection—if a suspect subsequently requests an attorney, questioning must cease—it is one that must be affirmatively invoked by the suspect.

In considering how a suspect must invoke the right to counsel, we must consider the other side of the *Miranda* equation: the need for effective law enforcement. . . . The *Edwards* rule—questioning must cease if the suspect asks for a lawyer—provides a bright line that can be applied by officers in the real world of investigation and interrogation without unduly hampering the gathering of information. But if we were to require questioning to cease if a suspect makes a statement that *might* be a request for an attorney, this clarity and ease of application would be lost. Police officers would be forced to make difficult judgment calls about whether the suspect in fact wants a lawyer even though he hasn't said so, with the threat of suppression if they guess wrong. We therefore hold that, after a knowing and voluntary waiver of the *Miranda* rights, law enforcement officers may continue questioning until and unless the suspect clearly requests an attorney. Of course, when a suspect makes an ambiguous or equivocal statement it will often be good police practice for the interviewing officers to clarify whether or not he actually wants an attorney. That was the procedure followed by the NIS agents in this case. Clarifying questions help protect the rights of the suspect by ensuring that he gets an attorney if he wants one, and will minimize the chance of a confession being suppressed due to subsequent judicial second-guessing as to the meaning of the suspect's statement regarding counsel. But we decline to adopt a rule requiring officers to ask clarifying questions. If the suspect's statement is not an unambiguous or unequivocal request for counsel, the officers have no obligation to stop questioning him.

To recapitulate: We held in *Miranda* that a suspect is entitled to the assistance of counsel during custodial interrogation even though the Constitution does not provide for such assistance. We held in *Edwards* that if the suspect invokes the right to counsel at any time, the police must immediately cease questioning him until an attorney is present. But we are unwilling to create a third layer of prophylaxis to prevent police questioning when the suspect *might* want a lawyer. Unless the suspect actually requests an attorney, questioning may continue.

The courts below found that petitioner's remark to the NIS agents—"Maybe I should talk to a lawyer"—was not a request for counsel, and we see no reason to disturb that conclusion. The NIS agents therefore were not required to stop questioning petitioner, though it was entirely proper for them to clarify whether petitioner in fact wanted a lawyer. . . .

Justice Souter, joined by Justices Blackmun, Stevens, and Ginsburg, concurred only in the judgment in *Davis*. In his view, interrogators faced with "an ambiguous statement that might reasonably be understood as expressing that a lawyer be summoned (and questioning cease)" would have an affirmative duty to ask clarifying questions designed to verify "whether the individual meant to ask for a lawyer." In Justice Souter's judgment, the questioners in *Davis* complied with this duty. Differing from the majority opinion, Justice Souter would not have found it acceptable if the questioners had simply ignored Davis's ambiguous statement and, without seeking to clarify it, had persisted in their interrogation.

Resumption of Questioning Following the Invocation of Miranda Rights

As *Davis v. United States, supra,* suggests, a suspect initially may decide to waive his or her *Miranda* rights, respond to questioning, and then later invoke his or her right to counsel or silence. The original waiver is not irrevocable. "The mere fact that [the suspect] may have answered some questions or volunteered some statements on his own does not deprive him of the right to refrain from answering any further inquiries until he has consulted with an attorney and thereafter consents to be questioned." *Miranda v. Arizona*, 384 U.S., at 445.

In this section, we consider the reverse situation. What of the suspect who initially requests an attorney or invokes his or her right to silence? Do the police forever lose the opportunity to question the suspect? May the police resume questioning if they administer a fresh set of warnings and the suspect then agrees to waive his or her rights? Should it matter whether it is the police or the suspect who takes the initiative in the resumption of questioning?

We first consider the case of suspects who are questioned after they invoke the right to remain silent.

The respondent in *Michigan v. Mosley*, 423 U.S. 96, 96 S. Ct. 321, 46 L. Ed. 2d 313 (1975), was arrested for two robberies. He was given *Miranda* warnings and stated that he did not want to talk about the robberies. The police immediately terminated their attempt to question him, and he was locked in a jail cell. About two hours later, a homicide detective, who had not been involved in the prior events, had Mosley brought from his cell to an office in the homicide bureau. The detective's purpose was to question Mosley about "an unrelated holdup murder." The detective readministered the *Miranda* warnings, and Mosley signed a "*Miranda* rights" waiver form. He subsequently made statements implicating himself in the murder. Those statements helped support his conviction for first-degree murder.

The Michigan Court of Appeals reversed, holding that the homicide detective's interrogation of Mosley was improper because Mosley had invoked his right to silence in response to the prior attempts to question him about the robbery charges. The Supreme Court reversed (7–2) through an opinion authored by Justice Stewart.

A reasonable and faithful interpretation of the Miranda opinion must rest on the intention of the Court in that case to adopt "fully effective means . . . to notify the person of his right of silence and to assure that the exercise of the right will be scrupulously honored. . . ." 384 U.S., at 479. The critical safeguard identified in the passage at issue is a person's "right to cut off questioning." Id., at 474. Through the exercise of his option to terminate questioning he can control the time at which questioning occurs, the subjects discussed, and the duration of the interrogation. The requirement that law enforcement authorities must respect a person's exercise of that option counteracts the coercive pressures of the custodial setting. We therefore conclude that the admissibility of statements obtained after the person in custody has decided to remain silent depends under Miranda on whether his "right to cut off questioning" was "scrupulously honored."

A review of the circumstances leading to Mosley's confession reveals that his "right to cut off questioning" was fully respected in this case. Before his initial interrogation, Mosley was carefully advised that he was under no obligation to answer any questions and could remain silent if he wished. He orally acknowledged that he understood the Miranda warnings and then signed a printed notification-of-rights form. When Mosley stated that he did not want to discuss the robberies, Detective Cowie immediately ceased the interrogation and did not try either to resume the questioning or in any way to persuade Mosley to reconsider his position. After an interval of more than two hours, Mosley was questioned by another police officer at another location about an unrelated holdup murder. He was given full and complete Miranda warnings at the outset of the second interrogation. He was thus reminded again that he could remain silent and could consult with a lawyer, and was carefully given a full and fair opportunity to exercise these options. The subsequent questioning did not undercut Mosley's previous decision not to answer Detective Cowie's inquiries. . . .

This is not a case, therefore, where the police failed to honor a decision of a person in custody to cut off questioning, either by refusing to discontinue the interrogation upon request or by persisting in repeated efforts to wear down his resistance and make him change his mind. In contrast to such practices, the police here immediately ceased the interrogation, resumed questioning only after the passage of a significant period of time and the provision of a fresh set of warnings, and restricted the second interrogation to a crime that had not been a subject of the earlier interrogation. . . .

* * * * *

How important was it in *Mosley* that the second interrogation pertained "to a crime that had not been a subject of the earlier interrogation" attempt? That more than two hours passed between Mosley's invocation of his right to silence and the second round of questioning? That "another police officer" conducted the new questioning, "at another location"? Which of these factors seems to be essential to the Court's conclusion that Mosley's "right to cut off questioning" had been "scrupulously honored"? What other factors could be important: That the police officer who originally attempted to question Mosley about the robbery promptly respected Mosley's expression that he did not want to talk? That Mosley waived his rights after a new set of *Miranda* warnings was given?

* * * * *

Does it matter that Mosley invoked his right to *silence* instead of requesting the assistance of an *attorney*? Consider the line of cases originating with *Edwards v. Arizona*, 451 U.S. 477, 101 S. Ct. 1880, 68 L. Ed. 2d 378 (1981).

The petitioner in *Edwards* was arrested for a series of offenses and given his *Miranda* warnings. He said that he understood his rights and agreed to respond to questioning. After being told that another suspect had implicated him in the crimes, Edwards attempted to "make a deal" with the authorities. He stated, however, that "I want an attorney before making a deal." Questioning then ceased, and Edwards was removed to the county jail. The next morning, a jail guard called upon Edwards at his cell and told him that detectives wanted to speak with him. Edwards replied that he did not want to talk with anyone, but the guard responded that he "had to" and took Edwards to where the detectives were waiting. Edwards had not had the chance to confer with an attorney. The detectives readvised Edwards of his *Miranda* rights, and Edwards agreed to speak with them, eventually confessing to the crimes. The state courts upheld the admissibility of the confession at Edwards's trial. The Supreme Court, through White, J. (with Chief Justice Burger and Justices Powell and Rehnquist concurring in the result), reversed.

[A]lthough we have held that after initially being advised of his Miranda rights, the accused may himself validly waive his rights and respond to interrogation, see North Carolina v. Butler, [441 U.S. 369, 99 S. Ct. 1755, 60 L. Ed. 2d 286 (1979)] the Court has strongly indicated that additional safeguards are necessary when the accused asks for counsel; and we now hold that when an accused has invoked his right to have counsel present during custodial interrogation, a valid waiver of that right cannot be established by showing only that he responded to further police-initiated custodial interrogation even if he has been advised of his rights. We further hold that an accused, such as Edwards, having expressed his desire to deal with the police only through counsel, is not subject to further interrogation by the authorities until counsel has been made available to him, unless the accused himself initiates further communication, exchanges, or conversations with the police. . . .

* * * * *

We learn more about the policies underlying the *Edwards* rule, and what it means for a suspect to "initiate[ ] further communication, exchanges, or conversations with the police," in the following cases.

Oregon v. Bradshaw, 462 U.S. 1039, 103 S. Ct. 2830, 77 L. Ed. 2d 405 (1983)

Justice Rehnquist announced the judgment of the Court and delivered an opinion, in which The Chief Justice, Justice White, and Justice O'Connor joined. . . .

In September 1980, Oregon police were investigating the death of one Lowell Reynolds in Tillamook County. Reynolds' body had been found in his wrecked pickup truck, in which he appeared to have been a passenger at the time the vehicle left the roadway, struck a tree and an embankment, and finally came to rest on its side in a shallow creek. . . . During the investigation of Reynolds' death, respondent was asked to accompany a police officer to the Rockaway Police Station for questioning.

Once at the station, respondent was advised of his rights as required by Miranda v. Arizona, 384 US 436 [(1966)]. Respondent then repeated to the police his earlier account of the events of the evening of Reynolds' death, admitting that he had provided Reynolds and others with liquor for a party at Reynolds' house, but denying involvement in the traffic accident that apparently killed Reynolds.

At this point, respondent was placed under arrest for furnishing liquor to Reynolds, a minor, and again advised of his Miranda rights. A police officer then told respondent the officer's theory of how the traffic accident that killed Reynolds occurred; a theory which placed respondent behind the wheel of the vehicle. Respondent again denied his involvement, and said "I do want an attorney before it goes very much further." The officer immediately terminated the conversation.

Sometime later respondent was transferred from the Rockaway Police Station to the Tillamook County Jail, a distance of some 10 to 15 miles. Either just before, or during, his trip from Rockaway to Tillamook, respondent inquired of a police officer, "Well, what is going to happen to me now?" The officer answered by saying: "You do not have to talk to me. You have requested an attorney and I don't want you talking to me unless you so desire because anything you say—because—since you have requested an attorney, you know, it has to be at your own free will." Respondent said he understood. There followed a discussion between respondent and the officer concerning where respondent was being taken and the offense with which he would be charged. The officer suggested that respondent might help himself by taking a polygraph examination. Respondent agreed to take such an examination, saying that he was willing to do whatever he could to clear up the matter.

The next day, following another reading to respondent of his Miranda rights, and respondent's signing a written waiver of those rights, the polygraph was administered. At its conclusion, the examiner told respondent that he did not believe respondent was telling the truth. Respondent then recanted his earlier story, admitting that he had been at the wheel of the vehicle in which Reynolds was killed, that he had consumed a considerable amount of alcohol, and that he had passed out at the wheel before the vehicle left the roadway and came to rest in the creek.

Respondent was charged with first-degree manslaughter, driving while under the influence of intoxicants, and driving while his license was revoked. His motion to suppress the statements described above was denied, and he was found guilty after a bench trial. The Oregon Court of Appeals, relying on our decision in Edwards v. Arizona, reversed, concluding that the statements had been obtained in violation of respondent's Fifth Amendment rights. We now conclude that the Oregon Court of Appeals misapplied our decision in Edwards. Respondent's question in the present case, "Well, what is going to happen to me now?", admittedly was asked prior to respondent's being "subject[ed] to further interrogation by the authorities." . . .

We think the Oregon Court of Appeals misapprehended the test laid down in Edwards. We did not there hold that the "initiation" of a conversation by a defendant such as respondent would amount to a waiver of a previously invoked right to counsel; we held that after the right to counsel had been asserted by an accused, further interrogation of the accused should not take place "unless the accused himself initiates further communication, exchanges, or conversations with the police." This was in effect a prophylactic rule, designed to protect an accused in police custody from being badgered by police officers in the manner in which the defendant in Edwards was. . . .

But even if a conversation taking place after the accused has "expressed his desire to deal with the police only through counsel," is initiated by the accused, where reinterrogation follows, the burden remains upon the prosecution to show that subsequent events indicated a waiver of the Fifth Amendment right to have counsel present during the interrogation.

Thus, the Oregon Court of Appeals was wrong in thinking that an "initiation" of a conversation or discussion by an accused not only satisfied the Edwards rule, but ex proprio vigore sufficed to show a waiver of the previously asserted right to counsel. The inquiries are separate, and clarity of application is not gained by melding them together.

There can be no doubt in this case that in asking, "Well, what is going to happen to me now?", respondent "initiated" further conversation in the ordinary dictionary sense of that word. While we doubt that it would be desirable to build a superstructure of legal refinements around the word "initiate" in this context, there are undoubtedly situations where a bare inquiry by either a defendant or by a police officer should not be held to "initiate" any conversation or dialogue. There are some inquiries, such as a request for a drink of water or a request to use a telephone, that are so routine that they cannot be fairly said to represent a desire on the part of an accused to open up a more generalized discussion relating directly or indirectly to the investigation. Such inquiries or statements, by either an accused or a police officer, relating to routine incidents of the custodial relationship, will not generally "initiate" a conversation in the sense in which that word was used in Edwards. Although ambiguous, the respondent's question in this case as to what was going to happen to him evinced a willingness and a desire for a generalized discussion about the investigation; it was not merely a necessary inquiry arising out of the incidents of the custodial relationship. It could reasonably have been interpreted by the officer as relating generally to the investigation. . . . On these facts we believe that there was not a violation of the Edwards rule.

Since there was no violation of the Edwards rule in this case, the next inquiry was "whether a valid waiver of the right to counsel and the right to silence had occurred, that is, whether the purported waiver was knowing and intelligent and found to be so under the totality of the circumstances, including the necessary fact that the accused, not the police, reopened the dialogue with the authorities." Edwards v. Arizona, 451 US, at 486, n 9. As we have said many times before, this determination depends upon "'the particular facts and circumstances surrounding [the] case, including the background, experience, and conduct of the accused.'"

The state trial court made this inquiry and, in the words of the Oregon Court of Appeals, "found that the police made no threats, promises or inducements to talk, that defendant was properly advised of his rights and understood them and that within a short time after requesting an attorney he changed his mind without any impropriety on the part of the police. The court held that the statements made to the polygraph examiner were voluntary and the result of a knowing waiver of his right to remain silent."

We have no reason to dispute these conclusions, based as they are upon the trial court's firsthand observation of the witnesses to the events involved. The judgment of the Oregon Court of Appeals is therefore reversed, and the cause is remanded for further proceedings.

It is so ordered.

Justice Powell, concurring in the judgment. . . .

Justice Marshall, with whom Justice Brennan, Justice Blackmun, and Justice Stevens join, dissenting.

The significance of the invocation of the right to counsel is premised in part on a lawyer's "unique ability to protect the Fifth Amendment rights of a client undergoing custodial interrogation." The Oregon Court of Appeals properly applied Edwards. When this Court in Edwards spoke of "initiat[ing] further communication" with the police and "reopen[ing] the dialogue with the authorities," it obviously had in mind communication or dialogue *about the subject matter of the criminal investigation*. The rule announced in Edwards was designed to ensure that any interrogation subsequent to an invocation of the right to counsel be at the instance of the accused, not the authorities. Thus, a question or statement which does not invite further interrogation before an attorney is present cannot qualify as "initiation" under Edwards. To hold otherwise would drastically undermine the safeguards that Miranda and Edwards carefully erected around the right to counsel in the custodial setting. . . .

I agree with the plurality that, in order to constitute "initiation" under Edwards, an accused's inquiry must demonstrate a desire to discuss the subject matter of the criminal investigation. I am baffled, however, at the plurality's application of that standard to the facts of this case. The plurality asserts that respondent's question, "[W]hat is going to happen to me now?", evinced both "a willingness and a desire for a generalized discussion about the investigation."

If respondent's question had been posed by Jean-Paul Sartre before a class of philosophy students, it might well have evinced a desire for a "generalized" discussion. But under the circumstances of this case, it is plain that respondent's only "desire" was to find out where the police were going to take him. As the Oregon Court of Appeals stated, respondent's query came only minutes after his invocation of the right to counsel and was simply "a normal reaction to being taken from the police station and placed in a police car, obviously for transport to some destination." On these facts, I fail to see how respondent's question can be considered "initiation of a conversation about the subject matter of the criminal investigation."

* * *

Notes and Questions

1. The Court's 4–1–4 division in *Bradshaw* shows that reasonable people can disagree about whether the inquiry "Well, what is going to happen to me now?" demonstrates (in the words of Justice Rehnquist) "a willingness and a desire for a generalized discussion about the investigation" or whether (in Justice Marshall's words), "It is plain that [Bradshaw's] only 'desire' was to find out where the police were going to take him." The interpretation of facts requires the exercise of judgment. Do the different conclusions reached in *Bradshaw* arguably reflect the crime control and due-process orientations of the respective justices, or do logical grounds seem to support the divergent interpretations of Bradshaw's question?

2. *Legal research note.* Need help with the meaning of *ex proprio vigore*? *Black's Law Dictionary* or another law dictionary can provide that help. *Black's* (6th ed. 1990) gives the following definition: "By their or its own force" (p. 582). In the context in which this phrase is used in *Bradshaw*, it means that the Oregon Court of Appeals believed that a suspect's "initiation" of a further conversation with the police about the crime sufficed "by its own force" simultaneously to waive the suspect's *Miranda* rights. The Supreme Court, of course, repudiated that supposition in *Bradshaw*, explaining that the "initiation" and "waiver" issues involve separate determinations.

In *Michigan v. Mosley, supra,* we noted the potential significance of the fact that after Mosley invoked his right to *silence,* the police readministered *Miranda* warnings and interrogated him about a *different crime* than was the subject of the initial interrogation attempt. The Court mentioned this fact in support of its conclusion that Mosley's right to cut off questioning had been "scrupulously honored." Should interrogating a suspect about a different offense be significant in the context of the *Edwards* rule, where the suspect has invoked his or her right to *counsel*?

In *Arizona v. Roberson,* 486 U.S. 675, 108 S. Ct. 2093, 100 L. Ed. 2d 704 (1988), a burglary suspect was arrested, was given his *Miranda* rights, and stated that he "wanted a lawyer before answering questions." Three days later, while the suspect was still in custody, a different police officer, who was unaware that Roberson had invoked his right to counsel, questioned Roberson about an unrelated burglary after advising him of his *Miranda* rights and securing a waiver. Roberson made incriminating statements, which the state sought to use at his trial for the unrelated burglary. The trial court suppressed the statements, ruling that they were obtained in violation of *Edwards.* The state appellate courts affirmed, as did the U.S. Supreme Court (6–2) through an opinion written by Justice Stevens.

The *Roberson* Court first distinguished *Mosley*: "As Mosley made clear, a suspect's decision to cut off questioning, unlike his request for counsel, does not raise the presumption that he is unable to proceed without a lawyer's advice. See [423 U.S.,] at 101, n. 7." The majority opinion then responded to the state's argument that the policies advanced by *Edwards* permitted the prosecution's use of Roberson's incriminating statements.

Petitioner reasons that "the chances that an accused will be questioned so repeatedly and in such quick succession that it will 'undermine the will' of the person questioned, or will constitute 'badger[ing],'" are so minute as not to warrant consideration, if the officers are truly pursuing separate investigations." It is by no means clear, though, that police engaged in separate investigations will be any less eager than police involved in only one inquiry to question a suspect in custody. Further, to a suspect who has indicated his inability to cope with the pressures of custodial interrogation by requesting counsel, any further interrogation without counsel having been provided will surely exacerbate whatever compulsion to speak the suspect may be feeling. Thus, we also disagree with petitioner's contention that fresh sets of Miranda warnings will "reassure" a suspect who has been denied the counsel he has clearly requested that his rights have remained untrammeled. . . .

* * * * *

To what, precisely, is the suspect entitled who invokes his or her right to counsel in the *Edwards* context? What if the police terminate their interrogation attempts when the suspect asks for a lawyer, and the suspect thereafter is allowed to confer with counsel? After the lawyer leaves, may the police approach the suspect, readminister *Miranda* warnings, and attempt to secure a waiver and elicit incriminating statements? Or must the suspect still "initiate" subsequent conversations with the police, even after the suspect has consulted his or her lawyer?

This issue arose in *Minnick v. Mississippi*, 498 U.S. 146, 111 S. Ct. 486, 112 L. Ed. 2d 489 (1990). Minnick escaped from a Mississippi jail with a fellow inmate. The two men were burglarizing a home when they were surprised by the return of the homeowner and a companion, whom they shot and killed. Four months later, Minnick was arrested in California and held in a San Diego jail. The arrest was made on Friday, August 22, 1986. FBI agents administered Minnick his *Miranda* rights on Saturday, August 23. Minnick acknowledged that he understood his rights but stated that he would not answer "very many" questions. During the questioning, he told the agents: "'Come back Monday when I have a lawyer,' and stated that he would make a

more complete statement then with his lawyer present." The FBI agents then terminated their interview.

After the FBI interview, an appointed attorney met with petitioner. Petitioner spoke with the lawyer on two or three occasions, though it is not clear from the record whether all of these conferences were in person.

On Monday, August 25, Deputy Sheriff J. C. Denham of Clarke County, Mississippi, came to the San Diego jail to question Minnick. Minnick testified that his jailers again told him he would "have to talk" to Denham and that he "could not refuse." Denham advised petitioner of his rights, and petitioner again declined to sign a rights waiver form. Petitioner told Denham about the escape and then proceeded to describe the events [surrounding the killings]. . . .

Minnick's statements were admitted at his Mississippi trial, and he was convicted of murder and sentenced to death. The Mississippi Supreme Court ruled that the statements had properly been admitted into evidence and affirmed the conviction and sentence. The Supreme Court granted certiorari and reversed, ruling that Minnick's statements were admitted into evidence in violation of *Edwards v. Arizona*. Justice Kennedy authored the majority opinion in this 6–2 decision.

Edwards is "designed to prevent police from badgering a defendant into waiving his previously asserted Miranda rights." . . . The rule ensures that any statement made in subsequent interrogation is not the result of coercive pressures. Edwards conserves judicial resources which would otherwise be expended in making difficult determinations of voluntariness, and implements the protections of Miranda in practical and straight-forward terms.

The merit of the Edwards decision lies in the clarity of its command and the certainty of its application.

The Mississippi Supreme Court relied on our statement in Edwards that an accused who invokes his right to counsel "is not subject to further interrogation by the authorities until counsel has been made available to him. . . ." 451 US, at 484–485. We do not interpret this language to mean, as the Mississippi court thought, that the protection of Edwards terminates once counsel has consulted with the suspect. In context, the requirement that counsel be "made available" to the accused refers to more than an opportunity to consult with an attorney outside the interrogation room.

In Edwards, we focused on Miranda's instruction that when the accused invokes his right to counsel, "the interrogation must cease until an attorney is *present*," 384 US, at 474 (emphasis added), agreeing with Edwards' contention that he had not waived his right "to have counsel *present* during custodial interrogation." 451 US, at 482 (emphasis added). . . .

Our emphasis on counsel's *presence* at interrogation is not unique to Edwards. It derives from Miranda, where we said that in the cases before us "[t]he presence of counsel . . . would be the adequate protective device necessary to make the process of police interrogation conform to the dictates of the [Fifth Amendment] privilege. His presence would insure that statements made in the government-established atmosphere are not the product of compulsion." 384 US, at 466. . . . In our view, a fair reading of Edwards and subsequent cases demonstrates that we have interpreted the rule to bar police-initiated interrogation unless the accused has counsel with him at the time of questioning. Whatever the ambiguities of our earlier cases on this point, we now hold that when counsel is requested, interrogation must cease, and officials may not reinitiate interrogation without counsel present, whether or not the accused has consulted with his attorney.

We consider our ruling to be an appropriate and necessary application of the Edwards rule. A single consultation with an attorney does not remove the suspect from persistent attempts by officials to persuade him to waive his rights, or from the coercive pressures that accompany custody and that may increase as custody is prolonged. The case before us well illustrates the pressures, and abuses, that may be concomitants of custody. Petitioner testified that though he resisted, he was required to submit to both the FBI and the Denham interviews. In the latter instance, the compulsion to submit to interrogation followed petitioner's unequivocal request during the FBI interview that questioning cease until counsel was present. The case illustrates also that consultation is not always effective in instructing the suspect of his rights. One plausible interpretation of the record is that petitioner thought he could keep his admissions out of evidence by refusing to sign a formal waiver of rights. If the authorities had complied with Minnick's request to have counsel present during interrogation, the attorney could have corrected Minnick's misunderstanding, or indeed counseled him that he need not make a statement at all. We decline to remove protection from police-initiated questioning based on isolated consultations with counsel who is absent when the interrogation resumes.

The exception to Edwards here proposed is inconsistent with Edwards' purpose to protect the suspect's right to have counsel present at custodial interrogation.

The exception proposed, furthermore, would undermine the advantages flowing from Edwards' "clear and unequivocal" character. . . .

In addition, adopting the rule proposed would leave far from certain the sort of consultation required to displace Edwards. Consultation is not a precise concept, for it may encompass variations from a telephone call to say that the attorney is in route, to a hurried interchange between the attorney and client in a detention facility corridor, to a lengthy in-person conference in which the attorney gives full and adequate advice respecting all matters that might be covered in further interrogations. And even with the necessary scope of consultation settled, the officials in charge of the case would have to confirm the occurrence and, possibly, the extent of consultation to determine whether further interrogation is permissible. The necessary inquiries could interfere with the attorney-client privilege.

Added to these difficulties in definition and application of the proposed rule is our concern over its consequence that the suspect whose counsel is prompt would lose the protection of Edwards, while the one whose counsel is dilatory would not. There is more than irony to this result. There is a strong possibility that it would distort the proper conception of the attorney's duty to the client and set us on a course at odds with what ought to be effective representation.

Both waiver of rights and admission of guilt are consistent with the affirmation of individual responsibility that is a principle of the criminal justice system. It does not detract from this principle, however, to insist that neither admissions nor waivers are effective unless there are both particular and systemic assurances that the coercive pressures of custody were not the inducing cause. . . .

Edwards does not foreclose finding a waiver of Fifth Amendment protections after counsel has been requested, provided the accused has initiated the conversation or discussions with the authorities; but that is not the case before us. There can be no doubt that the interrogation in question was initiated by the police; it was a formal interview which petitioner was compelled to attend. Since petitioner made a specific request for counsel before the interview, the police-initiated interrogation was impermissible. Petitioner's statement to Denham was not admissible at trial. . . .

Justice Souter took no part in the consideration or decision of this case.

Justice Scalia, with whom The Chief Justice joins, dissenting.

The Court today establishes an irrebuttable presumption that a criminal suspect, after invoking his Miranda right to counsel, can *never* validly waive that right during any police-initiated encounter, even after the suspect has been provided multiple Miranda warnings and has actually consulted his attorney. . . . Because I see no justification for applying the Edwards irrebuttable presumption when a criminal suspect has actually consulted with his attorney, I respectfully dissent. . . .

The Zerbst [Johnson v. Zerbst, 304 U.S. 458, 58 S. Ct. 1019, 82 L. Ed. 1461 (1938)] waiver standard, and the means of applying it, are familiar: Waiver is "an intentional relinquishment or abandonment of a known right or privilege;" and whether such a relinquishment or abandonment has occurred depends "in each case, upon the particular facts and circumstances surrounding that case, including the background, experience, and conduct of the accused." . . .

Edwards, however, broke with this approach, holding that a defendant's waiver of his Miranda right to counsel, made in the course of a police-initiated encounter after he had requested counsel but before counsel had been provided, was per se involuntary. The case stands as a solitary exception to our waiver jurisprudence. . . .

The existence and the importance of the Miranda-created right "to have counsel *present*" are unquestioned here. What is questioned is why a State should not be given the opportunity to prove (under Zerbst) that the right was *voluntarily waived* by a suspect who, after having been read his Miranda rights twice and having consulted with counsel at least twice, chose to speak to a police officer (and to admit his involvement in two murders) without counsel present.

Edwards did not assert the principle that no waiver of the Miranda right "to have counsel *present*" is possible. It simply adopted the presumption that no waiver is *voluntary* in certain circumstances, and the issue before us today is how broadly those circumstances are to be defined. They should not, in my view, extend beyond the circumstances present in Edwards itself—where the suspect in custody asked to consult an attorney, and was interrogated before that attorney had ever been provided. In those circumstances, the Edwards rule rests upon an assumption similar to that of Miranda itself: that when a suspect in police custody is first questioned he is likely to be ignorant of his rights and to feel isolated in a hostile environment. This likelihood is thought to justify special protection against unknowing or coerced waiver of rights. After a suspect has seen his request for an attorney honored, however, and has actually spoken with that attorney, the probabilities change. The suspect then knows that he has an advocate on his side, and that the police will permit him to consult that advocate. He almost certainly also has a heightened awareness (above what the Miranda warning itself will provide) of his right to remain silent—since at the earliest opportunity "any lawyer worth his salt will tell the suspect in no uncertain terms to make no statement to the police under any circumstances." Watts v. Indiana, 338 US 49, 59, 69 S Ct 1347, 93 L Ed 1801 (1949) (Opinion of Jackson, J.).

Under these circumstances, an irrebuttable presumption that any police-prompted confession is the result of ignorance of rights, or of coercion, has no genuine basis in fact. . . .

If and when post-consultation police inquiry becomes so protracted or threatening as to constitute coercion, the Zerbst standard will afford the needed protection.

One should not underestimate the extent to which the Court's expansion of Edwards constricts law enforcement. Today's ruling, that the invocation of a right to counsel permanently prevents a police-initiated waiver, makes it largely impossible for the police to urge a prisoner who has initially declined to confess to change his mind—or indeed, even to ask whether he has changed his mind. Many persons in custody will invoke the Miranda right to counsel during the first interrogation, so that the permanent prohibition will attach at once. . . .

It seems obvious to me that, even in Edwards itself but surely in today's decision, we have gone far beyond any genuine concern about suspects who do not *know* their right to remain silent, or who have been *coerced* to abandon it. Both holdings are explicable, in my view, only as an effort to protect suspects against what is regarded as their own folly.

* * * * *

Do you suppose that Minnick followed his lawyer's advice when he finally relented and spoke with the police? How could you know what the lawyer advised? Would compromising the attorney-client confidentiality privilege present a problem if Justice Scalia's views in *Minnick* had prevailed?

Miranda allows suspects who have neither asked for nor seen an attorney to waive their *Miranda* rights. In light of this fact, why should a suspect like Minnick, who had the benefit of conferring with a lawyer, *not* be allowed to waive his *Miranda* rights? Who should be in a better position to make a "knowing, intelligent, and voluntary" waiver—the suspect who has or has not had the prior chance to talk with an attorney?

The Waiver of *Miranda* Rights

The *Miranda* Court went on at some length about the subject of waiving, or forgoing, the self-incrimination protections guaranteed by that decision.

If the interrogation continues without the presence of an attorney and a statement is taken, a heavy burden rests on the government to demonstrate that the defendant knowingly and intelligently waived his privilege against self-incrimination and his right to retained or appointed counsel. . . .
An express statement that the individual is willing to make a statement and does not want an attorney followed closely by a statement could constitute a waiver. But a valid waiver will not be presumed simply from the silence of the accused after warnings are given or simply from the fact that a confession was in fact eventually obtained. 384 U.S., at 475.

The Court additionally made it clear that the

failure [of the accused] to ask for a lawyer does not constitute a waiver. No effective waiver of the right to counsel during interrogation can be recognized unless specifically made after the warnings we here delineated have been given. 384 U.S., at 470.

How literal is the suggestion that "no effective waiver . . . can be recognized unless specifically made"? The respondent in *North Carolina v. Butler*, 441 U.S. 369, 99 S. Ct. 1755, 60 L. Ed. 2d 286 (1979), was arrested for the armed robbery of a gas station and shooting its attendant. He was apprised of his *Miranda* rights and stated that he understood them. He refused to sign a written waiver-of-rights form. "He was told that he need neither speak nor sign the form, but that the agents would like him to talk to them. The respondent replied: 'I will talk with you but I am not signing any form.' He

then made inculpatory statements." 441 U.S., at 371. The respondent was described as being literate and having an 11th-grade education.

Finding that Butler had effectively waived his *Miranda* rights, the trial court admitted the incriminating statements into evidence. The North Carolina Supreme Court reversed. It reasoned that *Miranda* required that a waiver of rights must be "specifically made" to be effective, and it failed to find evidence of Butler's "*specific* oral waiver." 441 U.S., at 372 (emphasis in original). The Supreme Court reversed through a 5–3 decision authored by Justice Stewart. Referring to the *Miranda* Court's discussion of the requirements for an effective waiver of rights, Justice Stewart's opinion explained that

the Court held that an express statement can constitute a waiver, and that silence alone after such warnings cannot do so. But the Court did not hold that such an express statement is indispensable to a finding of waiver.
An express written or oral statement of waiver of the right to remain silent or of the right to counsel is usually strong proof of the validity of that waiver, but is not inevitably either necessary or sufficient to establish waiver. The question is not one of form, but rather whether the defendant in fact knowingly and voluntarily waived the rights delineated in the Miranda case. As was unequivocally said in Miranda, mere silence is not enough. That does not mean that the defendant's silence, coupled with an understanding of his rights and a course of conduct indicating waiver, may never support a conclusion that a defendant has waived his rights. The courts must presume that a defendant did not waive his rights; the prosecution's burden is great; but in at least some cases waiver can be clearly inferred from the actions and words of the person interrogated. . . .
There is no doubt that this respondent was adequately and effectively apprised of

his rights. The only question is whether he waived the exercise of one of those rights, the right to the presence of a lawyer. Neither the state court nor the respondent has offered any reason why there must be a negative answer to that question in the absence of an *express* waiver. . . . Even when a right so fundamental as that to counsel at trial is involved, the question of waiver must be determined on "the particular facts and circumstances surrounding that case, including the background, experience, and conduct of the accused." Johnson v. Zerbst, 304 U.S. 458, 464, 58 S. Ct. 1019, 82 L. Ed. 1461 [(1938)]. . . .

By creating an inflexible rule that no implicit waiver can ever suffice, the North Carolina Supreme Court has gone beyond the requirements of federal organic law. . . .

Although an explicit waiver is not essential for an effective relinquishment of *Miranda* rights, the Court in *Butler* did reaffirm that "mere silence" will not allow the prosecution to sustain its "great" burden of demonstrating a knowing and intelligent waiver. *See also Tague v. Louisiana*, 444 U.S. 469, 100 S. Ct. 652, 62 L. Ed. 2d 622 (1980) (per curiam). Evidence supporting the sufficiency of a waiver of *Miranda* rights normally lies somewhere between the extremes of an express statement that "I understand and desire to waive my rights" and cases where "no evidence at all [is] introduced to prove that [a suspect] knowingly and intelligently waived his rights." *Tague v. Louisiana, supra,* 444 U.S., at 471. Determining the validity of a *Miranda* rights waiver is not always straightforward, as the Court's opinion in *Fare v. Michael C.*, 442 U.S. 707, 99 S. Ct. 2560, 61 L. Ed. 2d 197 (1979), illustrates. Refer to our earlier consideration of *Fare v. Michael C.* (p. 303) for a refresher about the facts of this case.

We noted in North Carolina v. Butler, 441 U.S., at 373, that the question whether the accused waived his rights "is not one of form, but rather whether the defendant in fact knowingly and voluntarily waived the rights delineated in the Miranda case." Thus, the determination whether statements obtained during custodial interrogation are admissible against the accused is to be made upon an inquiry into the totality of the circumstances surrounding the interrogation, to ascertain whether the accused in fact knowingly and voluntarily decided to forgo his rights to remain silent and to have the assistance of counsel. Miranda v. Arizona, 384 U.S., at 475–477. . . . The totality approach permits—indeed, it mandates—inquiry into all the circumstances surrounding the interrogation. This includes evaluation of the juvenile's age, experience, education, background, and intelligence, and into whether he has the capacity to understand the warnings given him, the nature of his Fifth Amendment rights, and the consequences of waiving those rights.

Courts repeatedly must deal with these issues of waiver with regard to a broad variety of constitutional rights. There is no reason to assume that such courts—especially juvenile courts, with their special expertise in this area—will be unable to apply the totality-of-the-circumstances analysis so as to take into account those special concerns that are present when young persons, often with limited experience and education and with immature judgment, are involved. Where the age and experience of a juvenile indicate that his request for his probation officer or his parents is, in fact, an invocation of his right to remain silent, the totality approach will allow the court the necessary flexibility to take this into account in making a waiver determination. At the same time, that approach refrains from imposing rigid restraints on police and courts in dealing with an experienced older juvenile with an extensive prior record who knowingly and intelligently waives his Fifth Amendment rights and voluntarily consents to interrogation. . . .

The Juvenile Court found that under this approach, respondent in fact had waived his Fifth Amendment rights and consented to interrogation by the police after his request to see his probation officer was denied. . . .

We feel that the conclusion of the Juvenile Court was correct. The transcript of the interrogation reveals that the police officers conducting the interrogation took care to ensure that respondent understood his rights. They fully explained to respondent that he was being questioned in connection with a murder. They then informed him of all the rights delineated in Miranda, and ascertained that respondent understood those rights. There is no indication in the record that respondent failed to understand what the officers told him. Moreover, after his request to see his probation officer had been denied, and after the police officer once more had explained his rights to him, respondent clearly expressed his willingness to waive his rights and continue the interrogation.

Further, no special factors indicate that respondent was unable to understand the nature of his actions. He was a 16½-year-old juvenile with considerable experience with the police. He had a record of several arrests. He had served time in a youth camp, and he had been on probation for several years. He was under the full-time supervision of probation authorities. There is no indication that he was of insufficient intelligence to understand the rights he was waiving, or what the consequences of that waiver would be. He was not worn down by improper interrogation tactics or lengthy questioning or by trickery or deceit.

On these facts, we think it clear that respondent voluntarily and knowingly waived his Fifth Amendment rights. . . .

* * * * *

Of what, precisely, must the suspect be aware and/or informed before a waiver of *Miranda* rights is "knowing and voluntary"? May the police withhold from the suspect that his or her lawyer wants to consult with him or her prior to any police interrogation? Or assume that the police get a suspect to incriminate him- or herself in violation of *Miranda* and thereafter administer proper warnings and obtain a second confession. If the suspect is unaware that his or her initial confession was secured unlawfully and would be inadmissible as evidence, does the suspect "knowingly" waive his or her rights prior to making the second confession? Finally, must the police apprise the suspect of the full scope of the anticipated interrogation before the suspect's waiver of *Miranda* rights is effective? We confront these issues in the following cases.

Moran v. Burbine, 475 U.S. 412, 106 S. Ct. 1135, 89 L. Ed. 2d 410 (1986)

Justice O'Connor delivered the opinion of the Court.

* * *

I

On the morning of March 3, 1977, Mary Jo Hickey was found unconscious in a factory parking lot in Providence, Rhode Island. Suffering from injuries to her skull apparently inflicted by a metal pipe found at the scene, she was rushed to a nearby hospital. Three weeks later she died from her wounds.

Several months after her death, the Cranston, Rhode Island police arrested respondent and two others in connection with a local burglary. Detective Ferranti informed respondent of his Miranda rights. When respondent refused to execute a written waiver, Detective Ferranti spoke separately with the two other suspects arrested on the breaking and entering charge and obtained statements . . . implicating respondent in Ms. Hickey's murder. At approximately 6:00 p.m., Detective Ferranti telephoned the police in Providence to convey the information he had uncovered. An hour later, three officers from that department arrived at the Cranston headquarters for the purpose of questioning respondent about the murder.

That same evening, at about 7:45 p.m., respondent's sister telephoned the Public Defender's Office to obtain legal assistance for her brother. Her sole concern was the breaking and entering charge, as she was unaware that respondent was then under suspicion for murder. She asked for Richard Casparian who had been scheduled to meet with respondent earlier that afternoon to discuss another charge unrelated to either the break-in or the murder. As soon as the conversation ended, the attorney who took the call attempted to reach Mr. Casparian. When those efforts were unsuccessful, she telephoned Allegra Munson, another Assistant Public Defender, and told her about respondent's arrest and his sister's subsequent request that the office represent him.

At 8:15 p.m., Ms. Munson telephoned the Cranston police station and asked that her call be transferred to the detective division. In the words of the Supreme Court of Rhode Island, whose factual findings we treat as presumptively correct, the conversation proceeded as follows:

"A male voice responded with the word 'Detectives.' Ms. Munson identified herself and asked if Brian Burbine was being held; the person responded affirmatively. Ms. Munson explained to the person that Burbine was represented by attorney Casparian who was not available; she further stated that she would act as Burbine's legal counsel in the event that the police intended to place him in a lineup or question him. The unidentified person told Ms. Munson that the police would not be questioning Burbine or putting him in a lineup and that they were through with him for the night. Ms. Munson was not informed that the Providence Police were at the Cranston police station or that Burbine was a suspect in Mary's murder."

At all relevant times, respondent was unaware of his sister's efforts to retain counsel and of the fact and contents of Ms. Munson's telephone conversation.

Less than an hour later, the police brought respondent to an interrogation room and conducted the first of a series of interviews concerning the murder. Prior to each session, respondent was informed of his Miranda rights, and on three separate occasions he signed a written form acknowledging that he understood his right to the presence of an attorney and explicitly indicating that he "[did] not want an attorney called or appointed for [him]" before he gave a statement. . . . Eventually, respondent signed three written statements fully admitting to the murder.

Prior to trial, respondent moved to suppress the statements. The court denied the motion, finding that respondent had received the Miranda warnings and had "knowingly, intelligently, and voluntarily waived his privilege against self-incrimination [and] his right to counsel." . . .

The jury found respondent guilty of murder in the first degree, and he appealed to the Supreme Court of Rhode Island. A divided court rejected his contention that the Fifth and Fourteenth Amendments to the Constitution required the suppression of the inculpatory statements and affirmed the conviction. . . .

After unsuccessfully petitioning the United States District Court for the District of Rhode Island for a writ of habeas corpus, 589 F Supp 1245 (1984), respondent appealed to the Court of Appeals for the First Circuit. That court reversed. 753 F2d 178 (1985). . . .

We granted certiorari to decide whether a pre-arraignment confession preceded by an otherwise valid waiver must be suppressed either because the police misinformed an inquiring attorney about their plans concerning the suspect or because they failed to inform the suspect of the attorney's efforts to reach him. We now reverse.

II

In Miranda v. Arizona, the Court recognized that custodial interrogations, by their very nature, generate "compelling pressures which work to undermine the individual's will to resist and to compel him to speak where he would not otherwise do so freely." 384 US, at 467. To combat this inherent compulsion, and thereby protect the Fifth Amendment privilege against self incrimination, Miranda imposed on the police an obligation to follow certain procedures in their dealings with the accused. . . .

Respondent does not dispute that the Providence police followed these procedures with precision. The record amply supports the state-court findings that the police administered the required warnings, sought to assure that respondent understood his rights, and obtained an express written waiver prior to eliciting each of the three statements. Nor does respondent contest the Rhode Island courts' determination that he at no point requested the presence of a lawyer. He contends instead that the confessions must be suppressed because the police's failure to inform him of the attorney's telephone call deprived him of information essential to his ability to knowingly waive his Fifth Amendment rights. In the alternative, he suggests that to fully protect the Fifth Amendment values served by Miranda, we should extend that decision to condemn the conduct of the Providence police. We address each contention in turn.

A

Echoing the standard first articulated in Johnson v. Zerbst, 304 US 458, 464, 58 S Ct 1019, 82 L Ed 1461 (1938), Miranda holds that "[t]he defendant may waive effectuation" of the rights conveyed in the warnings "provided the waiver is made voluntarily, knowingly and intelligently." 384 US, at 444, 475. The inquiry has two distinct dimensions.

First the relinquishment of the right must have been voluntary in the sense that it was the product of a free and deliberate choice rather than intimidation, coercion or deception. Second, the waiver must have been made with a full awareness both of the nature of the right being abandoned and the consequences of the decision to abandon it. Only if the "totality of the circumstances surrounding the interrogation" reveal both an uncoerced choice and the requisite level of comprehension may a court properly conclude that the Miranda rights have been waived.

Under this standard, we have no doubt that respondent validly waived his right to remain silent and to the presence of counsel. The voluntariness of the waiver is not at issue. As the Court of Appeals correctly acknowledged, the record is devoid of any suggestion that police resorted to physical or psychological pressure to elicit the statements. Nor is there any question about respondent's comprehension of the full panoply of rights set out in the Miranda warnings and of the potential consequences of a decision to relinquish them. Nonetheless, the Court of Appeals believed that the "[d]eliberate or reckless" conduct of the police, in particular their failure to inform respondent of the telephone call, fatally undermined the validity of the otherwise proper waiver. We find this conclusion untenable as a matter of both logic and precedent.

Events occurring outside of the presence of the suspect and entirely unknown to him surely can have no bearing on the capacity to comprehend and knowingly relinquish a constitutional right. Under the analysis of the Court of Appeals, the same defendant, armed with the same information and confronted with precisely the same police conduct, would have knowingly waived his Miranda rights had a lawyer not telephoned the police station to inquire about his status. Nothing in any of our waiver decisions or in our understanding of the essential components of a valid waiver requires so incongruous a result. No doubt the additional information would have been useful to respondent; perhaps even it might have affected his decision to confess. But we have never read the Constitution to require that the police supply a suspect with a flow of information to help him calibrate his self interest in deciding whether to speak or stand by his rights. Once it is determined that a suspect's decision not to rely on his rights was uncoerced, that he at all times knew he could stand mute and request a lawyer, and that he was aware of the state's intention to use his statements to secure a conviction, the analysis is complete and the waiver is valid as a matter of law.[1] The

---

1. The dissent incorrectly reads our analysis of the components of a valid waiver to be inconsistent with the Court's holding in Edwards v. Arizona. When a suspect *has* requested counsel, the interrogation must cease, regardless of any question of waiver, unless the suspect himself initiates the conversation.

Court of Appeals' conclusion to the contrary was in error.

Nor do we believe that the level of the police's culpability in failing to inform respondent of the telephone call has any bearing on the validity of the waiver. . . . But whether intentional or inadvertent, the state of mind of the police is irrelevant to the question of the intelligence and voluntariness of respondent's election to abandon his rights. Although highly inappropriate, even deliberate deception of an attorney could not possibly affect a suspect's decision to waive his Miranda rights unless he were at least aware of the incident. . . .

Nor was the failure to inform respondent of the telephone call the kind of "trick[ery]" that can vitiate the validity of a waiver. Miranda, 384 US, at 476. Granting that the "deliberate or reckless" withholding of information is objectionable as a matter or ethics, such conduct is only relevant to the constitutional validity of a waiver if it deprives a defendant of knowledge essential to his ability to understand the nature of his rights and the consequences of abandoning them. Because respondent's voluntary decision to speak was made with full awareness and comprehension of all the information Miranda requires the police to convey, the waivers were valid.

B

At oral argument respondent acknowledged that a constitutional rule requiring the police to inform a suspect of an attorney's efforts to reach him would represent a significant extension of

---

In the course of its lengthy exposition, however, the dissent never comes to grips with the crucial distinguishing feature of this case—that Burbine at no point requested the presence of counsel, as was his right under Miranda to do. We do not quarrel with the dissent's characterization of police interrogation as a "privilege terminable at the will of the suspect." We reject, however, the dissent's entirely undefended suggestion that the Fifth Amendment "right to cousel" requires anything more than that the police inform the suspect of his right to representation and honor his request that the interrogation cease until his attorney is present. See, e.g., Michigan v. Mosley, 423 US 96, 104, n 10, 96 S Ct 321, 46 L Ed 2d 313 (1975).

our precedents. He contends, however, that the conduct of the Providence police was so inimical to the Fifth Amendment values Miranda seeks to protect that we should read that decision to condemn their behavior.

At the outset, while we share respondent's distaste for the deliberate misleading of an officer of the court, reading Miranda to forbid police deception of an *attorney* "would cut [the decision] completely loose from its own explicitly stated rationale." Beckwith v. United States, 425 US 341, 345, 96 S Ct 1612, 48 L Ed 2d 1, (1976). As is now well established, "[t]he . . . Miranda warnings are not themselves rights protected by the Constitution but [are] instead measures to insure that the [suspect's] right against compulsory self-incrimination [is] protected." New York v. Quarles, 467 US 649, 654, 104 S Ct 2626, 81 L Ed 2d 550 (1984), quoting Michigan v. Tucker, 417 US 433, 94 S Ct 2357, 444, 41 L Ed 2d 182 (1974). Their objective is not to mold police conduct for its own sake. Nothing in the Constitution vests in us the authority to mandate a code of behavior for state officials wholly unconnected to any federal right or privilege. The purpose of the Miranda warnings instead is to dissipate the compulsion inherent in custodial interrogation and, in so doing, guard against abridgement of the suspect's Fifth Amendment rights. Clearly, a rule that focuses on how the police treat an attorney—conduct that has no relevance at all to the degree of compulsion experienced by the defendant during interrogation—would ignore both Miranda's mission and its only source of legitimacy.

Nor are we prepared to adopt a rule requiring that the police inform a suspect of an attorney's efforts to reach him. While such a rule might add marginally to Miranda's goal of dispelling the compulsion inherent in custodial interrogation, overriding practical considerations counsel against its adoption. As we have stressed on numerous occasions, "[o]ne of the principal advantages" of Miranda is the ease and clarity of its application. Berkemer v. McCarty, 468 US 420, 430, 104 S Ct 3138, 82 L Ed 2d 317 (1984).

We have little doubt that the approach urged by respondent and endorsed by the Court of Appeals would have the inevitable consequence of muddying Miranda's otherwise relatively clear waters. The legal questions it would spawn are legion: To what extent should the police be held accountable for knowing that the accused has counsel? Is it enough that someone in the station house knows, or must the interrogating officer himself know of counsel's efforts to contact the suspect? Do counsel's efforts to talk to the suspect concerning one criminal investigation trigger the obligation to inform the defendant before interrogation may proceed on a wholly separate matter? We are unwilling to modify Miranda in a manner that would so clearly undermine the decision's central "virtue of informing police and prosecutors with specificity . . . what they may do in conducting [a] custodial interrogation, and of informing courts under what circumstances statements obtained during such interrogation are not admissible." Fare v. Michael C., supra, at 718.

Moreover, problems of clarity to one side, reading Miranda to require the police in each instance to inform a suspect of an attorney's efforts to reach him would work a substantial and, we think, inappropriate shift in the subtle balance struck in that decision. Custodial interrogations implicate two competing concerns. On the one hand, "the need for police questioning as a tool for effective enforcement of criminal laws" cannot be doubted. Admissions of guilt are more than merely "desirable," they are essential to society's compelling interest in finding, convicting and punishing those who violate the law. On the other hand, the Court has recognized that the interrogation process is "inherently coercive" and that, as a consequence, there exists a substantial risk that the police will inadvertently traverse the fine line between legitimate efforts to elicit admissions and constitutionally impermissible compulsion. Miranda attempted to reconcile these opposing concerns by giving the *defendant* the power to exert some control over the course of the interrogation. Declining to adopt the more extreme position that the actual presence of a lawyer was necessary to dispel the coercion inherent in custodial interrogation, the Court found that the suspect's Fifth Amendment rights could be adequately protected by less intrusive means. Police questioning, often an essential part of the investigatory process, could continue in its traditional form, the Court held, but only if the suspect clearly understood that, at any time, he could bring the proceeding to a halt or, short

of that, call in an attorney to give advice and monitor the conduct of his interrogators.

The position urged by respondent would upset this carefully drawn approach in a manner that is both unnecessary for the protection of the Fifth Amendment privilege and injurious to legitimate law enforcement. . . .

We acknowledge that a number of state courts have reached a contrary conclusion. . . .

Nothing we say today disables the States from adopting different requirements for the conduct of its employees and officials as a matter of state law. We hold only that the Court of Appeals erred in construing the Fifth Amendment to the Federal Constitution to require the exclusion of respondent's three confessions. . . .

IV

Finally, respondent contends that the conduct of the police was so offensive as to deprive him of the fundamental fairness guaranteed by the Due Process Clause of the Fourteenth Amendment. Focusing primarily on the impropriety of conveying false information to an attorney, he invites us to declare that such behavior should be condemned as violative of canons fundamental to the "'traditions and conscience of our people.'" Rochin v. California, 342 US 165, 169, 72 S Ct 205, 96 L Ed 183 (1952), quoting Snyder v. Massachusetts, 291 US 97, 105, 54 S Ct 330, 78 L Ed 674 (1934). We do not question that on facts more egregious than those presented here police deception might rise to a level of a due process violation. We hold only that, on these facts, the challenged conduct falls short of the kind of misbehavior that so shocks the sensibilities of civilized society as to warrant a federal intrusion into the criminal processes of the States. . . .

Justice Stevens, with whom Justice Brennan and Justice Marshall join, dissenting.

This case poses fundamental questions about our system of justice. As this Court has long recognized, and reaffirmed only weeks ago, "ours is an accusatorial and not an inquisitorial system." Miller v. Fenton, 474 US 104, 110, 106 S Ct 445, 88 L Ed 2d 405 (1985).[1] The Court's opinion today represents a startling departure from that basic insight. . . .

---

1. Justice Frankfurter succinctly explained the character of that distinction in his opinion in Watts v. Indiana, 338 US 49, 54, 69 S Ct 1347, 93 L Ed 1801 (1949):

The murder of Mary Jo Hickey was a vicious crime, fully meriting a sense of outrage and a desire to find and prosecute the perpetrator swiftly and effectively. . . .

The recognition that ours is an accusatorial, and not an inquisitorial system nevertheless requires that the government's actions, even in responding to this brutal crime, respect those liberties and rights that distinguish this society from most others.

Police interference with communications between an attorney and his client is a recurrent problem. The factual variations in the many state court opinions condemning this interference as a violation of the federal Constitution suggest the variety of contexts in which the problem emerges. In Oklahoma, police led a lawyer to several different locations while they interrogated the suspect;[16] in Oregon, police moved a suspect to a new location when they learned that his lawyer was on his way;[17] in Illinois,

---

"Ours is the accusatorial as opposed to the inquisitorial system. Such has been the characteristic of Anglo-American criminal justice since it freed itself from practices borrowed by the Star Chamber from the Continent whereby an accused was interrogated in secret for hours on end. Under our system society carries the burden of proving its charge against the accused not out of his own mouth. It must establish its case, not by interrogation of the accused even under judicial safeguards, but by evidence independently secured through skillful investigation. The law will not suffer a prisoner to be made the deluded instrument of his own conviction.' 2 Hawkins, Pleas of the Crown, c 46, § 34 (8th ed 1824). The requirement of specific charges, their proof beyond a reasonable doubt, the protection of the accused from confessions extorted through whatever form of police pressures, the right to a prompt hearing before a magistrate, the right to assistance of counsel, to be supplied by government when circumstances make it necessary, the duty to advise an accused of his constitutional rights—these are all characteristics of the accusatorial system and manifestations of its demands. Protracted, systematic and uncontrolled subjection of an accused to interrogation by the police for the purpose of eliciting disclosures or confession is subversive of the accusatorial system." . . .

16. Lewis v. State, 695 P2d 528 (Okla Crim 1984).

17. State v. Haynes, 288 Ore 59, 602 P2d 272 (1979).

authorities failed to tell a suspect that his lawyer had arrived at the jail and asked to see him;[18] in Massachusetts, police did not tell suspects that their lawyers were at or near the police station.[19] In all these cases, the police not only failed to inform the suspect, but also misled the attorneys. The scenarios vary, but the core problem of police interference remains. . . .

Although there are a number of ambiguities in the record, the state court findings established (1) that Attorney Munson made her call at about 8:15 p.m.; (2) that she was given false information; (3) that Burbine was not told of her call; and (4) that he was thereafter given the Miranda warnings, waived his rights, and signed three incriminating statements without receiving any advice from an attorney. The remainder of the record underscores two points. The first is the context of the call—a context in which two police departments were on the verge of resolving a highly publicized, hauntingly brutal homicide and in which, as Lieutenant Gannon testified, the police were aware that counsel's advice to remain silent might be an obstacle to obtaining a confession. The second is the extent of the uncertainty about the events that motivated Burbine's decision to waive his rights. The lawyer-free privacy of the interrogation room, so exalted by the majority, provides great difficulties in determining what actually transpired. It is not simply the ambiguity that is troublesome; if so, the problem would be not unlike other difficult evidentiary problems. Rather, the particularly troublesome aspect is that the ambiguity arises in the very situation—incommunicado interrogation—for which this Court has developed strict presumptions and for which this Court has, in the past, imposed the heaviest burden of justification on the government. It is in this context, and the larger context of our accusatorial system, that the deceptive conduct of the police must be evaluated.

---

18. People v. Smith, 93 Ill 2d 179, 442 NE2d 1325 (1982).

19. Commonwealth v. McKenna, 355 Mass 313, 244 NE2d 560 (1969).

II

Well-settled principles of law lead inexorably to the conclusion that the failure to inform Burbine of the call from his attorney makes the subsequent waiver of his constitutional rights invalid. Analysis should begin with an acknowledgment that the burden of proving the validity of a waiver of constitutional rights is always on the *government*. When such a waiver occurs in a custodial setting, that burden is an especially heavy one because custodial interrogation is inherently coercive, because disinterested witnesses are seldom available to describe what actually happened, and because history has taught us that the danger of overreaching during incommunicado interrogation is so real.

In applying this heavy presumption against the validity of waivers, this Court has sometimes relied on a case-by-case totality of the circumstances analysis. We have found, however, that some custodial interrogation situations require strict presumptions against the validity of a waiver. Miranda established that a waiver is not valid in the absence of certain warnings. Edwards v. Arizona, 451 US 477, 101 S Ct 1880, 68 L Ed 2d 378 (1981), similarly established that a waiver is not valid if police initiate questioning after the defendant has invoked his right to counsel. In these circumstances, the waiver is invalid as a matter of law even if the evidence overwhelmingly establishes, as a matter of fact, that "a suspect's decision not to rely on his rights was uncoerced, that he at all times knew that he could stand mute and request a lawyer, and that he was aware of the state's intention to use his statement to secure a conviction." In light of our decision in Edwards, the Court is simply wrong in stating that "the analysis is complete and the waiver is valid as a matter of law" when these facts have been established. Like the failure to give warnings and like police initiation of interrogation after a request for counsel, police deception of a suspect through omission of information regarding attorney communications greatly exacerbates the inherent problems of incommunicado interrogation and requires a clear principle to safeguard the presumption against the waiver of constitutional rights. As in those situa-

tions, the police deception should render a subsequent waiver invalid. . . .

As the Court notes, the question is whether the deceptive police conduct "deprives a defendant of knowledge essential to his ability to understand the nature of his rights and the consequences of abandoning them." . . .

[S]ettled principles about construing waivers of constitutional rights and about the need for strict presumptions in custodial interrogations, as well as a plain reading of the Miranda opinion itself, overwhelmingly support the conclusion reached by almost every state court that has considered the matter—a suspect's waiver of his right to counsel is invalid if police refuse to inform the suspect of his counsel's communications.

III

The Court makes the alternative argument that requiring police to inform a suspect of his attorney's communications to and about him is not required because it would upset the careful "balance" of Miranda. . . .

[A] rule requiring the police to inform a suspect of an attorney's call would have two predictable effects. It would serve "Miranda's goal of dispelling the compulsion inherent in custodial interrogation" and it would disserve the goal of custodial interrogation because it would result in fewer confessions. By a process of balancing these two concerns, the Court finds the benefit to the individual outweighed by the "substantial cost to society's legitimate and substantial interest in securing admissions of guilt."

The "cost" that concerns the Court amounts to nothing more than an acknowledgment that the law enforcement interest in obtaining convictions suffers whenever a suspect exercises the rights that are afforded by our system of criminal justice. In other words, it is the fear that an individual may exercise his rights that tips the scales of justice for the Court today. The principle that ours is an accusatorial, not an inquisitorial, system, however, has repeatedly led the Court to reject that fear as a valid reason for inhibiting the invocation of rights.

IV

The Court also argues that a rule requiring the police to inform a suspect of an attorney's efforts to reach him would have an additional cost: it would undermine the "clarity" of the rule of the Miranda case. This argument is not supported by any reference to the experience in the States that have adopted such a rule. The Court merely professes concern about its ability to answer three quite simple questions.[46]

Moreover, the Court's evaluation of the interest in "clarity" is rather one-sided. For a police officer with a printed card containing the exact text he is supposed to recite, perhaps the rule is clear. But the interest in clarity that the Miranda decision was intended to serve is not merely for the benefit of the police. Rather, the decision was also, and primarily, intended to provide adequate guidance to the person in custody who is being asked to waive the protections afforded by the Constitution. . . .

V

At the time Attorney Munson made her call to the Cranston Police Station, she was acting as Burbine's attorney. Under ordinary principles of agency law the deliberate deception of Munson was tantamount to deliberate deception of her client. . . .

---

46. Thus, the Court asks itself:

(1) "To what extent should the police be held accountable for knowing that the accused has counsel?" The simple answer is that police should be held accountable to the extent that the attorney or the suspect informs the police of the representation.

(2) "Is it enough that someone in the station house knows, or must the interrogating officer himself know of counsel's efforts to contact the suspect?" Obviously, police should be held responsible for getting a message of this importance from one officer to another.

(3) "Do counsel's efforts to talk to the suspect concerning one criminal investigation trigger the obligation to inform the defendant before interrogation may proceed on a wholly separate matter?" As the facts of this case forcefully demonstrate, the answer is "yes."

* * *

In my view, as a matter of law, the police deception of Munson was tantamount to deception of Burbine himself. It constituted a violation of Burbine's right to have an attorney present during the questioning that began shortly thereafter.

The possible reach of the Court's opinion is stunning. For the majority seems to suggest that police may deny counsel all access to a client who is being held. At least since Escobedo v. Illinois, it has been widely accepted that police may not simply deny attorneys access to their clients who are in custody. . . .

In sharp contrast to the majority, I firmly believe that the right to counsel at custodial interrogation is infringed by police treatment of an attorney that prevents or impedes the attorney's representation of the suspect at that interrogation.

VI

The Court devotes precisely five sentences to its conclusion that the police interference in the attorney's representation of Burbine did not violate the Due Process Clause. In the majority's view, the due process analysis is a simple "shock the conscience" test. Finding its conscience troubled, but not shocked, the majority rejects the due process challenge.

In a variety of circumstances, however, the Court has given a more thoughtful consideration to the requirements of due process. . . .

What emerges from these cases is, not the majority's simple "shock the conscience" test, but the principle that due process requires fairness, integrity, and honor in the operation of the criminal justice system, and in its treatment of the citizen's cardinal constitutional protections. . . .

Police interference with communications between an attorney and his client violates the due process requirement of fundamental fairness. Burbine's attorney was given completely false information about the lack of questioning; moreover, she was not told that her client would be questioned regarding a murder charge about which she was unaware. Burbine, in turn, was not told that his attorney had phoned and that she had been informed that he would not be questioned. Quite simply, the Rhode Island police effectively drove a wedge between an attorney and a suspect through misinformation and omissions. . . .

VII

This case turns on a proper appraisal of the role of the lawyer in our society. If a lawyer is seen as a nettlesome obstacle to the pursuit of wrongdoers—as in an inquisitorial society—then the Court's decision today makes a good deal of sense. If a lawyer is seen as an aid to the understanding and protection of constitutional rights—as in an accusatorial society—then today's decision makes no sense at all.

Notes and Questions

1. The majority opinion in *Moran v. Burbine* rejects three separate arguments that the police conduct in this case violated Burbine's constitutional rights. First, it rejects the proposition that when the police deprive a suspect of the information that his or her attorney has attempted to reach him or her prior to any questioning, the suspect's waiver of his or her *Miranda* rights is not made "knowingly." Second, it declines to "extend" *Miranda* to forbid the police from depriving a suspect of such information. Finally, it rejects a due-process challenge to the admissibility of Burbine's incriminating statements.

2. Regarding the first of these arguments, what does the Court hold that a suspect must "know" before his or her waiver of *Miranda* rights is effective? Is the Court's rejection of Burbine's contention that he was entitled to know that his lawyer was trying to contact him consistent with its acknowledgment that "no doubt the additional information would have been useful to respondent; perhaps even it might have affected his decision to confess"?

3. Burbine's second argument was that the underlying policies promoted by *Miranda* require the suppression of his confessions even if he "knew" that he had the right to a lawyer and that anything he said could be used against him. Can you cite any cases that support his general argument? Justice Stevens relies on *Edwards v. Arizona* in support of this point. Is this reliance on *Edwards* convincing? Note that Edwards "knew" that he had a right to a lawyer and to remain silent, yet that the Court still refused to recognize his waiver of *Miranda* rights. It did so to promote a policy objective related to this *Miranda* decision: to discourage the police from "badgering" suspects who had invoked their right to counsel. Nevertheless, is *Edwards* distinguishable (in a meaningful way) from *Burbine*?

4. Burbine's due-process–based challenge to the admissibility of his confessions is dispatched summarily by the Court's conclusion that the police conduct—though perhaps ethically inappropriate—did not "so shock the sensibilities of civilized society as to warrant" suppression of the statements. If the police's behavior in giving "Burbine's attorney . . . completely false information," withholding from the lawyer that "her client would be questioned regarding a murder charge about which she was unaware," and denying Burbine knowledge of the fact that "his attorney had phoned and that she had been informed that he would not be questioned" (see Justice Stevens' dissent) is permissible, then what do you suppose is required before the Court's conscience is shocked?

5. Several states have accepted Justice O'Connor's implicit invitation in *Burbine* to adopt "different requirements for the conduct of [their] employees and officials as a matter of state law." The Connecticut Supreme Court rejected the *Burbine* rule in *State v. Stoddard*, 206 Conn. 157, 537 A.2d 446 (1988), relying on Article I, § 8 of the Connecticut Constitution, which provides: "No person shall be compelled to give evidence against himself, nor be deprived of life, liberty or property without due process of law." It first noted that the U.S. Supreme Court in *Burbine* relied on "principles of federalism . . . [and] was also prompted by a reluctance to intrude into the administration of state criminal processes." It then continued:

The appropriate task for this court, then, is to ascertain the independent meaning of the due process clause of article first, § 8, of the Connecticut constitution. This state has had a long history of recognizing the significance of the right to counsel, even before that right attained federal constitutional importance. . . .

While this history specifically illuminates the right to counsel that attaches after the initiation of adversary judicial proceedings, it also informs the due process concerns raised by police interference with counsel's access to a custodial suspect. In recently reiterating that Miranda warnings are "independently required" under the due process clause of article first, § 8, of the Connecticut constitution; we recognized, once again, the "'unique ability'" of counsel to protect the rights of a client undergoing, or confronting the imminent possibility of, interrogation.

This recognition is in service of the traditional belief that an accused may be convicted only if "exacting measures have been taken to assure that the accused has been treated with the most scrupulous fairness" by law enforcement officials.

In light of both the historical record and our due process tradition, we conclude that a suspect must be informed promptly of timely efforts by counsel to render pertinent legal assistance. Armed with that information, the suspect must be permitted to choose whether he wishes to speak with counsel, in which event interrogation must cease, or whether he will forego assistance of counsel, in which event counsel need not be afforded access to the suspect. The police may not preclude the suspect from exercising the choice to which he is constitutionally entitled by responding in less than forthright fashion to the efforts by counsel to contact the suspect. The police, because they are responsible for the suspect's isolation, have a duty to act reasonably, diligently and promptly to provide counsel with accurate information and to apprise the suspect of the efforts by counsel. . . .

We are unwilling, . . . to dismiss counsel's effort to communicate as constitutionally insignificant to the capacity of the suspect to make a knowing and intelligent choice whether he or she will invoke the right to counsel. Miranda warnings refer only to an abstract right to counsel. . . . Faced with a concrete offer of assistance, however, a suspect may well decide to reclaim his or her continuing right to legal assistance. "To pass up an abstract offer to call some unknown lawyer is very different from refusing to talk with an identified attorney actually available to provide at least initial assistance and advice, whatever might be arranged in the long run. A suspect indifferent to the first offer may well react quite differently to the second." State v. Haynes, 288 Or. 59, 72, 602 P.2d 272 (1979), cert. denied, 446 U.S. 945, 100 S.Ct. 2175, 64 L.Ed.2d 802 (1980). We cannot therefore conclude that a decision to forego the abstract offer contained in Miranda embodies an implied rejection of a specific opportunity to confer with a known lawyer. Accordingly, the lack of authority of counsel to invoke the personal right of the suspect is no bar to the imposition of a duty to inform a suspect of counsel's efforts. . . .

Although we agree with the defendant that the police have a duty to inform a custodial suspect of counsel's efforts to provide legal advice, our inquiry is not at an end. We must next consider in what circumstances statements obtained in violation of this duty must be suppressed. . . .

The question before us is how to interpolate into the calculus of waiver the failure of the police to inform a suspect of inquiries by counsel. Courts in other jurisdictions have taken two views of this issue. Some have adopted a per se rule of exclusion in order to enforce the duty to inform. Others have taken a more open ended examination of the totality of the circumstances.

In the majority of reported cases, the rule has been that a lack of knowledge always fatally undermines the suspect's continuing right to claim the presence of counsel. . . .

We do not agree with the majority rule. The decision to speak or to stand mute is a personal right of the suspect. That decision, made on the basis of full knowledge of all relevant circumstances, belongs exclusively to him. Had the police officials in this case properly responded with the communication, the defendant might conceivably have taken the advice of counsel to remain silent. By the same token, the suspect might have chosen to cooperate with the police and waive the presence of counsel. We therefore decline to impose, by judicial fiat, a blanket rule of exclusion or admissibility. Reliance on the totality of the circumstances is consistent with existing rules for the evaluation of the validity of a waiver. The critical question is whether the information not conveyed by the police would likely have changed the defendant's appraisal and understanding of the circumstances. Of particular, but not exclusive, relevance are such facts and circumstances as the relationship of the suspect to the attorney, the nature of counsel's request, the extent to which the police had reasonable notice of counsel's request and the conduct of the suspect. . . .

The record in this case, taken as a whole, reveals at least a reasonable likelihood that the defendant would have invoked his right to counsel had the police fulfilled their duty to inform. First, the content of counsel's aborted communications over a period of two days was pertinent to the exercise of the right to counsel. Because counsel's requests to speak with the defendant were phrased generally, and not specifically limited to a topic, such as bail, that has no bearing on the right to counsel, we can fairly infer that counsel would have advised the defendant to remain silent. Watts v. Indiana, 338 U.S. 49, 59, 69 S.Ct. 1347, 93 L.Ed. 1801 (1949) (Jackson, J., concurring). Second, because counsel was a member of a firm that had previously represented the defendant, the defendant could reasonably have been expected to respond to counsel's offer of assistance.

Under the totality of the circumstances, the state has not met its burden of proving by a preponderance of the evidence that the efforts of counsel, if properly communicated, would not have altered the defendant's appraisal and understanding of the circumstances. Accordingly, the trial court erred in denying the defendant's motion to suppress. . . .

Other state courts have declined to follow *Moran v. Burbine* on state law grounds, including *Haliburton v. State*, 514 So. 2d 1088 (Fla. 1987); *State v. Hattaway*, 621 So. 2d 796, 811 (La. 1993), *citing State v. Matthews*, 408 So. 2d 1274 (La. 1982); *People v. Wright*, 441 Mich. 140, 490 N.W.2d 351 (1932); *State v. Reed*, 133 N.J. 237, 627 A.2d 630 (1993). *See* B. Latzer, *State Constitutional Criminal Law* § 4:11 (1995).

* * * * *

Assume that the police obtain an initial confession (C1) from a suspect in violation of his or her *Miranda* rights. After securing that confession, they administer the *Miranda* warnings, secure the suspect's waiver, and obtain a second confession (C2). Further assume that the suspect has no idea that C1 would be inadmissible in evidence because of the *Miranda* violation and, in fact, reasons that he or she may as well provide C2 since "the cat already is out of the bag." Has the suspect made a "knowing" waiver of his or her *Miranda* rights prior to the second confession? Consider *Oregon v. Elstad*, which follows.

Oregon v. Elstad, 470 U.S. 298, 105 S. Ct. 1285, 84 L. Ed. 2d 222 (1985)

Justice O'Connor delivered the opinion of the Court. . . .

I

In December, 1981, the home of Mr. and Mrs. Gilbert Gross, in the town of Salem, Polk County, Ore., was burglarized. Missing were art objects and furnishings valued at $150,000. A witness to the burglary contacted the Polk County Sheriff's Office, implicating respondent Michael Elstad, an 18-year-old neighbor and friend of the Grosses' teenage son. Thereupon, Officers Burke and McAllister went to the home of respondent Elstad, with a warrant for his arrest. Elstad's mother answered the door. She led the officers to her son's room where he lay on his bed, clad in shorts and listening to his stereo. The officers asked him to get dressed and to accompany them into the living room. Officer McAllister asked respondent's mother to step into the kitchen, where he explained that they had a warrant for her son's arrest for the burglary of a neighbor's residence. Officer Burke remained with Elstad in the living room. He later testified:

"I sat down with Mr. Elstad and I asked him if he was aware of why Detective McAllister and myself were there to talk with him. He stated no, he had no idea why we were there. I then asked him if he knew a person by the name of Gross, and he said yes, he did, and also added that he heard that there was a robbery at the Gross house. And at that point I told Mr. Elstad that I felt he was involved in that, and he looked at me and stated, 'Yes, I was there.'" App 19–20.

The officers then escorted Elstad to the back of the patrol car. . . .

Elstad was transported to the Sheriff's headquarters and approximately one hour later, Officers Burke and McAllister joined him in McAllister's office. McAllister then advised respondent for the first time of his Miranda rights, reading from a standard card. Respondent indicated he understood his rights, and, having these rights in mind, wished to speak with the officers. Elstad gave a full statement. The statement was typed, reviewed by respondent, read back to him for correction, initialed and signed by Elstad and both officers. . . . Respondent concedes that the officers made no threats or promises either at his residence or at the Sheriff's office.

Respondent was charged with first-degree burglary. . . . Respondent moved at once to suppress his oral statement and signed confession. He contended that the statement he made in response to questioning at his house "let the cat out of the bag," citing United States v. Bayer, 331 US 532, 67 S Ct 1394, 91 L Ed 1654 (1947), and tainted the subsequent confession as "fruit of the poisonous tree," citing Wong Sun v. United States, 371 US 471, 9 L Ed 2d 441, 83 S Ct 407 (1963). The judge ruled that the statement, "I was there," had to be excluded because the defendant had not been advised of his Miranda rights. The written confession taken after Elstad's arrival at the Sheriff's office, however, was admitted in evidence. The court found:

"[H]is written statement was given freely, voluntarily and knowingly by the defendant after he had waived his right to remain silent and have counsel present which waiver was evidenced by the card which the defendant had signed. [It] was not tainted in any way by the previous brief statement between the defendant and the Sheriff's Deputies that had arrested him."

Elstad was found guilty of burglary in the first degree. He received a 5-year sentence and was ordered to pay $18,000 in restitution.

Following his conviction, respondent appealed to the Oregon Court of Appeals, relying on Wong Sun and Bayer. The State conceded that Elstad had been in custody when he made his statement, "I was there," and accordingly agreed that this statement was inadmissible as having been given without the prescribed Miranda warning. But the State maintained that any conceivable "taint" had been dissipated prior to the respondent's written confession by McAllister's careful administration of the requisite warnings. The Court of Appeals reversed respondent's conviction, identifying the crucial constitutional inquiry as "whether there was a sufficient break in the stream of events between [the] inadmissible statement and the written confession to insulate the latter statement from the effect of what went before." The Oregon court concluded:

"Regardless of the absence of actual compulsion, the coercive impact of the unconstitutionally obtained statement remains, because in a defendant's mind it has sealed his fate. It is this impact that must be dissipated in order to make a subsequent confession admissible. In determining whether it has been dissipated, lapse of time, and change of place from the original surroundings are the most important considerations."

Because of the brief period separating the two incidents, the "cat was sufficiently out of the bag to exert a coercive impact on [respondent's] later admissions."

This Court granted certiorari to consider the question whether the Self-Incrimination Clause of the Fifth Amendment requires the suppression of a confession, made after proper Miranda warnings and a valid waiver of rights, solely because the police had obtained an earlier voluntary but unwarned admission from the defendant.

II

The arguments advanced in favor of suppression of respondent's written confession rely heavily on metaphor. One metaphor, familiar from the Fourth Amendment context, would require that respondent's confession, regardless of its integrity, voluntariness, and probative value, be suppressed as the "tainted fruit of the poisonous tree" of the Miranda violation. A second metaphor questions whether a confession can be truly voluntary once the "cat is out of the bag." Taken out of context, each of these metaphors can be misleading. They should not be used to obscure fundamental differences between the role of the Fourth Amendment exclusionary rule and the function of Miranda in guarding against the prosecutorial use of compelled statements as prohibited by the Fifth Amendment. The Oregon court assumed and respondent here contends that a failure to administer Miranda warnings necessarily breeds the same consequences as police infringement of a constitutional right, so that evidence uncovered following an unwarned statement must be suppressed as "fruit of the poisonous tree." We believe this view misconstrues the nature of the protections afforded by Miranda warnings and therefore misreads the consequences of police failure to supply them.

A

* * *

Respondent's contention that his confession was tainted by the earlier failure of the police to provide Miranda warnings and must be excluded as "fruit of the poisonous tree" assumes the existence of a constitutional violation. This figure of speech is drawn from Wong Sun v. United States, 371 US 471, 83 S Ct 407, 9 L Ed 2d 441 (1963), in which the Court held that evidence and witnesses discovered as a result of a search in violation of the Fourth Amendment must be excluded from evidence.

But as we explained in Quarles and Tucker, a procedural Miranda violation differs in significant respects from violations of the Fourth Amendment, which have traditionally mandated a broad application of the "fruits" doctrine. The purpose of the Fourth Amendment exclusionary rule is to deter unreasonable searches, no matter how probative their fruits. . . .

The Miranda exclusionary rule, however, serves the Fifth Amendment and sweeps more broadly than the Fifth Amendment itself. It may be triggered even in the absence of a Fifth Amendment violation.[1] The Fifth Amendment prohibits use by the prosecution in its case in chief only of *compelled* testimony. Failure to administer Miranda warnings creates a presumption of compulsion. Consequently, unwarned statements that are otherwise voluntary within the meaning of the Fifth Amendment must nevertheless be excluded from evidence under Miranda. Thus, in the individual case, Miranda's preventive medicine provides a remedy even to the defendant who has suffered no identifiable constitutional harm. See New York v. Quarles, 467 US 649. 104 S Ct 2626, 81 L Ed 2d 550; Michigan v. Tucker, 417 US 433, 444, 94 S Ct 2357, 41 L Ed 2d 182 (1974).

But the Miranda presumption, though irrebuttable for purposes of the prosecution's case in chief, does not require that the statements and

---

1. Justice Stevens expresses puzzlement at our statement that a simple failure to administer Miranda warnings is not in itself a violation of the Fifth Amendment. Yet the Court so held in New York v. Quarles, 467 US 649, 104 S Ct 2626, 81 L Ed 2d 550 (1983), and Michigan v. Tucker, 417 US 433, 444, 94 S Ct 2357, 41 L Ed 2d 182 (1974). The Miranda Court itself recognized this point when it disclaimed any intent to create a "constitutional straight-jacket" and invited Congress and the States to suggest "potential alternatives for protecting the privilege." Miranda v. Arizona, 384 US 436, 467, 86 S Ct 1602, 16 L Ed 2d 694 (1966). A Miranda violation does not *constitute* coercion but rather affords a bright-line, legal presumption of coercion, requiring suppression of all unwarned statements. It has never been remotely suggested that any statement taken from Mr. Elstad without benefit of Miranda warnings would be admissible.

their fruits be discarded as inherently tainted. Despite the fact that patently *voluntary* statements taken in violation of Miranda must be excluded from the prosecution's case, the presumption of coercion does not bar their use for impeachment purposes on cross-examination. Harris v. New York, 401 US 222, 91 S Ct 643, 28 L Ed 2d 1 (1971). . . . Where an unwarned statement is preserved for use in situations that fall outside the sweep of the Miranda presumption, "the primary criterion of admissibility [remains] the 'old' due process voluntariness test." Schulhofer, Confessions and the Court, 79 Mich L Rev 865, 877 (1981).

In Michigan v. Tucker, the Court was asked to extend the Wong Sun fruits doctrine to suppress the testimony of a witness for the prosecution whose identity was discovered as the result of a statement taken from the accused without benefit of full Miranda warnings. As in respondent's case, the breach of the Miranda procedures in Tucker involved no actual compulsion. The Court concluded that the unwarned questioning "did not abridge respondent's constitutional privilege . . . but departed only from the prophylactic standards later laid down by this Court in Miranda to safeguard that privilege." Since there was no actual infringement of the suspect's constitutional rights, the case was not controlled by the doctrine expressed in Wong Sun that fruits of a constitutional violation must be suppressed. In deciding "how sweeping the judicially imposed consequences" of a failure to administer Miranda warnings should be, the Tucker Court noted that neither the general goal of deterring improper police conduct nor the Fifth Amendment goal of assuring trustworthy evidence would be served by suppression of the witness' testimony. The unwarned confession must, of course, be suppressed, but the Court ruled that introduction of the third-party witness' testimony did not violate Tucker's Fifth Amendment rights.

We believe that this reasoning applies with equal force when the alleged "fruit" of a noncoercive Miranda violation is neither a witness nor an article of evidence but the accused's own voluntary testimony. As in Tucker, the absence of any coercion or improper tactics undercuts the twin rationales—trustworthiness and deterrence—for a broader rule. Once warned, the suspect is free to exercise his own volition in deciding whether or not to make a statement to the authorities. . . .

Because Miranda warnings may inhibit persons from giving information, this Court has determined that they need be administered only after the person is taken into "custody" or his freedom has otherwise been significantly restrained. Unfortunately, the task of defining "custody" is a slippery one, and "policemen investigating serious crimes [cannot realistically be expected to] make no errors whatsoever." If errors are made by law enforcement officers in administering the prophylactic Miranda procedures, they should not breed the same irremediable consequences as police infringement of the Fifth Amendment itself. It is an unwarranted extension of Miranda to hold that a simple failure to administer the warnings, unaccompanied by any actual coercion or other circumstances calculated to undermine the suspect's ability to exercise his free will so taints the investigatory process that a subsequent voluntary and informed waiver is ineffective for some indeterminate period. Though Miranda requires that the unwarned admission must be suppressed, the admissibility of any subsequent statement should turn in these circumstances solely on whether it is knowingly and voluntarily made.

B

The Oregon court, however, believed that the unwarned remark compromised the voluntariness of respondent's later confession. It was the court's view that the prior *answer* and not the unwarned questioning impaired respondent's ability to give a valid waiver and that only lapse of time and change of place could dissipate what it termed the "coercive impact" of the inadmissible statement. When a prior statement is actually coerced, the time that passes between confessions, the change in place of interrogations, and the change in identity of the interrogators all bear on whether that coercion has carried over into the second confession. See Westover v. United States, decided together with Miranda v. Arizona, 384 US, at 494, 86 S Ct 1602, 16 L Ed 2d 694.

The failure of police to administer Miranda warnings does not mean that the statements received have actually been coerced, but only that courts will presume the privilege against compulsory self-incrimination has not been intelligently exercised. Of the courts that have considered whether a properly warned confession must be suppressed because it was preceded by an unwarned but clearly voluntary admission, the majority have explicitly or implicitly recognized that Westover's requirement of a break in the stream of events is inapposite. In these circumstances, a careful and thorough administration of Miranda warnings serves to cure the condition that rendered the unwarned statement inadmissible. The warning conveys the relevant information and thereafter the suspect's choice whether to exercise his privilege to remain silent should ordinarily be viewed as an "act of free will."

* * *

This Court has never held that the psychological impact of voluntary disclosure of a guilty secret qualifies as state compulsion or compromises the voluntariness of a subsequent informed waiver. The Oregon court, by adopting this expansive view of Fifth Amendment compulsion, effectively immunizes a suspect who responds to pre-Miranda warning questions from the consequences of his subsequent informed waiver of the privilege of remaining silent. This immunity comes at a high cost to legitimate law enforcement activity, while adding little desirable protection to the individual's interest in not being *compelled* to testify against himself. When neither the initial nor the subsequent admission is coerced, little justification exists for permitting the highly probative evidence of a voluntary confession to be irretrievably lost to the factfinder.

There is a vast difference between the direct consequences flowing from coercion of a confession by physical violence or other deliberate means calculated to break the suspect's will and the uncertain consequences of disclosure of a "guilty secret" freely given in response to an unwarned but noncoercive question, as in this case. . . . Certainly, in respondent's case, the causal connection between any psychological disadvantage created by his admission and his ultimate decision to cooperate is speculative and attenuated at best. It is difficult to tell with cer-

tainty what motivates a suspect to speak. . . . We must conclude that, absent deliberately coercive or improper tactics in obtaining the initial statement, the mere fact that a suspect has made an unwarned admission does not warrant a presumption of compulsion. A subsequent administration of Miranda warnings to a suspect who has given a voluntary but unwarned statement ordinarily should suffice to remove the conditions that precluded admission of the earlier statement. In such circumstances, the finder of fact may reasonably conclude that the suspect made a rational and intelligent choice whether to waive or invoke his rights.

III

Though belated, the reading of respondent's rights was undeniably complete. McAllister testified that he read the Miranda warnings aloud from a printed card and recorded Elstad's responses. There is no question that respondent knowingly and voluntarily waived his right to remain silent before he described his participation in the burglary. It is also beyond dispute that respondent's earlier remark was voluntary, within the meaning of the Fifth Amendment. Neither the environment nor the manner of either "interrogation" was coercive. . . .

The state has conceded the issue of custody and thus we must assume that Burke breached Miranda procedures in failing to administer Miranda warnings before initiating the discussion in the living room. This breach may have been the result of confusion as to whether the brief exchange qualified as "custodial interrogation" or it may simply have reflected Burke's reluctance to initiate an alarming police procedure before McAllister had spoken with respondent's mother. Whatever the reason for Burke's oversight, the incident had none of the earmarks of coercion. Nor did the officers exploit the unwarned admission to pressure respondent into waiving his right to remain silent.

Respondent, however, has argued that he was unable to give a fully *informed* waiver of his rights because he was unaware that his prior statement could not be used against him. Respondent suggests that Deputy McAllister, to cure this deficiency, should have added an additional warning to those given him at the Sheriff's office. Such a requirement is neither practicable nor constitutionally necessary. In many cases, a breach of Miranda procedures may not be identified as such until long after full Miranda warnings are administered and a valid confession obtained. The standard Miranda warnings explicitly inform the suspect of his right to consult a lawyer before speaking. Police officers are ill equipped to pinch-hit for counsel, construing the murky and difficult questions of when "custody" begins or whether a given unwarned statement will ultimately be held admissible.

This Court has never embraced the theory that a defendant's ignorance of the full consequences of his decisions vitiates their voluntariness. . . . The Court has refused to find that a defendant who confesses, after being falsely told that his codefendant has turned state's evidence, does so involuntarily. Frazier v. Cupp, 394 US 731, 739, 89 S Ct 1420, 22 L Ed 2d 684 (1969). The Court has also rejected the argument that a defendant's ignorance that a prior coerced confession could not be admitted in evidence compromised the voluntariness of his guilty plea.

Thus we have not held that the sine qua non for a knowing and voluntary waiver of the right to remain silent is a full and complete appreciation of all of the consequences flowing from the nature and the quality of the evidence in the case.

IV

The Court today in no way retreats from the bright line rule of Miranda. We do not imply that good faith excuses a failure to administer Miranda warnings; nor do we condone inherently coercive police tactics or methods offensive to due process that render the initial admission involuntary and undermine the suspect's will to invoke his rights once they are read to him. We find that the dictates of Miranda and the goals of the Fifth Amendment proscription against use of compelled testimony are fully satisfied in the circumstances of this case by barring use of the unwarned statement in the case in chief. No further purpose is served by imputing "taint" to subsequent statements obtained pursuant to a voluntary and knowing waiver. We hold today that a suspect who has once

responded to unwarned yet uncoercive questioning is not thereby disabled from waiving his rights and confessing after he has been given the requisite Miranda warnings. . . .

Justice Brennan, with whom Justice Marshall joins, dissenting.

* * *

I

The threshold question is this: What effect should an admission or confession of guilt obtained in violation of an accused's Miranda rights be presumed to have upon the voluntariness of subsequent confessions that are preceded by Miranda warnings? Relying on the "cat out of the bag" analysis of United States v. Bayer, 331 US 532, 540–541, 67 S Ct 1394, 91 L Ed 1654 (1947), the Oregon Court of Appeals held that the first confession presumptively taints subsequent confessions in such circumstances. On the specific facts of this case, the court below found that the prosecution had not rebutted this presumption. Rather, given the temporal proximity of Elstad's second confession to his first and the absence of any significant intervening circumstances, the court correctly concluded that there had not been "a sufficient break in the stream of events between [the] inadmissible statement and the written confession to insulate the latter statement from the effect of what went before."

If this Court's reversal of the judgment below reflected mere disagreement with the Oregon court's application of the "cat out of the bag" presumption to the particular facts of this case, the outcome, while clearly erroneous, would be of little lasting consequence. But the Court rejects the "cat out of the bag" presumption *entirely* and instead adopts a new rule presuming that "ordinarily" there is *no* causal connection between a confession extracted in violation of Miranda and a subsequent confession preceded by the usual Miranda warnings. . . .

The Court today sweeps aside this commonsense approach as "speculative" reasoning, adopting instead a rule that "the psychological impact of *voluntary* disclosure of a guilty secret" neither "qualifies as state compulsion" nor "compromises the voluntariness" of subsequent confessions. So long as a suspect receives the usual Miranda warnings before further interrogation, the Court reasons, the fact that he "is free to exercise his own volition in deciding whether or not to make" further confessions "ordinarily" is a sufficient "cure" and serves to break any causal connection between the illegal confession and subsequent statements.

The Court's marble-palace psychoanalysis is tidy, but it flies in the face of our own precedents, demonstrates a startling unawareness of the realities of police interrogation, and is completely out of tune with the experience of state and federal courts over the last 20 years. Perhaps the Court has grasped some psychological truth that has eluded persons far more experienced in these matters; if so, the Court owes an explanation of how so many could have been so wrong for so many years.

A

(1)

This Court has had long experience with the problem of confessions obtained after an earlier confession has been illegally secured. Subsequent confessions in these circumstances are not per se inadmissible, but the prosecution must demonstrate facts "sufficient to insulate the [subsequent] statement from the effect of all that went before." Clewis v. Texas, 386 US 707, 710, 87 S Ct 1338, 18 L Ed 2d 423 (1967). . . .

The question in each case is whether the accused's will was "overborne at the time he confessed," and the prosecution must demonstrate that the second confession "was an act independent of the [earlier] confession." Reck v. Pate, 367 US 433, 440, 444, 81 S Ct 1541, 6 L Ed 2d 948 (1961).

One of the factors that can vitiate the voluntariness of a subsequent confession is the hopeless feeling of an accused that he has nothing to lose by repeating his confession, even where the circumstances that rendered his first confession illegal have been removed. As the Court observed in United States v. Bayer, 331 US, at 540, 67 S Ct 1394, 91 L Ed 1654:

"[A]fter an accused has once let the cat out of the bag by confessing, no matter what the inducement, he is never thereafter free of the psychological and practical disadvantages of having confessed. He can never get the cat back in the bag. The secret is out for good. In such a sense, a later confession always may be looked upon as a fruit of the first."

The Court today decries the "irremediable consequences" of this reasoning, but it has always been clear that even after "let[ting] the cat out of the bag" the accused is not "perpetually disable[d]" from giving an admissible subsequent confession. Rather, we have held that subsequent confessions in such circumstances may be admitted if the prosecution demonstrates that, "[c]onsidering the 'totality of the circumstances,'" there was a "'break in the stream of events . . . sufficient to insulate'" the subsequent confession from the damning impact of the first. Darwin v. Connecticut, 391 US 346, 349, 88 S Ct 1488, 20 L Ed 2d 630 (1968). Although we have thus rejected a per se rule forbidding the introduction of subsequent statements in these circumstances, we have emphasized that the psychological impact of admissions and confessions of criminal guilt nevertheless can have a decisive impact in undermining the voluntariness of a suspect's responses to continued police interrogation and must be accounted for in determining their admissibility. . . .

(2)

Our precedents did not develop in a vacuum. They reflect an understanding of the realities of police interrogation and the everyday experience of lower courts. Expert interrogators, far from dismissing a first admission or confession as creating merely a "speculative and attenuated" disadvantage for a suspect, understand that such revelations frequently lead directly to a full confession. Standard interrogation manuals advise that "[t]he securing of the first admission is the biggest stumbling block. . . ." A. Aubry & R. Caputo, Criminal Interrogation 290 (3d ed 1980).

Interrogators describe the point of the first admission as the "break-through" and the "beachhead," R. Royal & S. Schutt, The Gentle Art of Interviewing and Interrogation: A Professional Manual and Guide 143 (1976), which once obtained will give them enormous "tactical advantages," F. Inbau & J. Reid, Criminal Interrogation and Confessions 82 (2d ed 1967). . . .

One police practice that courts have frequently encountered involves the withholding of Miranda warnings until the end of an interrogation session. Specifically, the police escort a suspect into a room, sit him down and, without explaining his Fifth Amendment rights or obtaining a knowing and voluntary waiver of those rights, interrogate him about his suspected criminal activity. If the police obtain a confession, it is then typed up, the police hand the suspect a pen for his signature, and—just before he signs—the police advise him of his Miranda rights and ask him to proceed. . . .

The variations of this practice are numerous, but the underlying problem is always the same: after hearing the witness testimony and considering the practical realities, courts have confirmed the time-honored wisdom of presuming that a first illegal confession "taints" subsequent confessions, and permitting such subsequent confessions to be admitted at trial *only* if the prosecution convincingly rebuts the presumption. . . .

Expert interrogators and experienced lower-court judges will be startled, to say the least, to learn that the connection between multiple confessions is "speculative" and that a subsequent rendition of Miranda warnings "ordinarily" enables the accused in these circumstances to exercise his "free will" and to make "a rational and intelligent choice whether to waive or invoke his rights." . . .

B

The correct approach, administered for almost 20 years by most courts with no untoward results, is to presume that an admission or confession obtained in violation of Miranda taints a subsequent confession unless the prosecution can show that the taint is so attenuated as to justify admission of the subsequent confession. . . .

Until today the Court has recognized that the dissipation inquiry requires the prosecution to demonstrate that the official illegality did not taint the challenged confession, and we have rejected the simplistic view that abstract notions

of "free will" are alone sufficient to dissipate the challenged taint. . . . Instead, we have instructed courts to consider carefully such factors as the strength of the causal connection between the illegal action and the challenged evidence, their proximity in time and place, the presence of intervening factors, and the "purpose and flagrancy of the official misconduct." . . .

Thus we have *always* rejected, until today, the notion that "individual will" alone presumptively serves to insulate a person's actions from the taint of earlier official illegality. . . .

Nor have we ever allowed Miranda warnings alone to serve talismanically to purge the taint of prior illegalities. . . .

Where an accused believes that it is futile to resist because the authorities already have elicited an admission of guilt, the mere rendition of Miranda warnings does not convey the information most critical at that point to ensuring his informed and voluntary decision to speak again: that the earlier confession may not be admissible and thus that he need not speak out of any feeling that he already has sealed his fate. The Court therefore is flatly wrong in arguing, as it does repeatedly, that the mere provision of Miranda warnings prior to subsequent interrogation supplies the accused with "the relevant information" and ensures that a subsequent confession "ordinarily" will be the product of "a rational and intelligent choice" and "an act of free will.'"

C

Perhaps because the Court is discomfited by the radical implications of its failure to apply the settled derivative-evidence presumption to violations of Miranda, it grudgingly qualifies its sweeping pronouncements with the acknowledgment that its new presumption about so-called "ordinary" Miranda violations can be overcome by the accused.

Explicitly eschewing "a per se rule," the Court suggests that its approach should not be followed where the police have employed "improper tactics" or "inherently coercive methods" that are "calculated to undermine the suspect's ability to exercise his free will." The Court thus concedes that lower courts must continue to be free to "examine the surrounding circumstances and the entire course of police conduct with respect to the suspect in evaluating the voluntariness of his statements."

The Court's concessions are potentially significant, but its analysis is wholly at odds with established dissipation analysis.

II

Not content merely to ignore the practical realities of police interrogation and the likely effects of its abolition of the derivative-evidence presumption, the Court goes on to assert that nothing in the Fifth Amendment or the general judicial policy of deterring illegal police conduct "ordinarily" requires the suppression of evidence derived proximately from a confession obtained in violation of Miranda. . . .

The Court clearly errs in suggesting that suppression of the "unwarned admission" alone will provide meaningful deterrence. The experience of lower courts demonstrates that the police frequently have refused to comply with Miranda precisely in order to obtain incriminating statements that will undermine the voluntariness of the accused's decision to speak again once he has received the usual warnings; in such circumstances, subsequent confessions often follow on a "silver platter." . . .

If a subsequent confession is truly independent of earlier, illegally obtained confessions, nothing prevents its full use to secure the accused's conviction. If the subsequent confession *did* result from the earlier illegalities, however, there is nothing "voluntary" about it. And even if a tainted subsequent confession is "highly probative," we have never until today permitted probity to override the fact that the confession was "the product of constitutionally impermissible methods in [its] inducement." In such circumstances, the Fifth Amendment makes clear that the prosecutor has no entitlement to use the confession in attempting to obtain the accused's conviction. . . .

Justice Stevens, dissenting. . . .

The desire to achieve a just result in this particular case has produced an opinion that is somewhat opaque and internally inconsistent. If I read it correctly, its conclusion rests on two untenable premises: (1) that the respondent's first confession was not the product of coercion, and (2) that no constitutional right was violated when respondent was questioned in a tranquil, domestic setting.

Even before the decision in Miranda v. Arizona, it had been recognized that police interrogation of a suspect who has been taken into custody is presumptively coercive. . . .

In my opinion, the Court's attempt to fashion a distinction between actual coercion "by physical violence or other deliberate means calculated to break the suspect's will," and irrebuttably presumed coercion cannot succeed. . . . Indeed, a major purpose of treating the presumption of coercion as irrebuttable is to avoid the kind of fact-bound inquiry that today's decision will surely engender.

As I read the Court's opinion, it expressly accepts the proposition that routine Miranda warnings will not be sufficient to overcome the presumption of coercion and thereby make a second confession admissible when an earlier confession is contained by coercion "by physical violence or other deliberate means calculated to break the suspect's will." . . . But surely the fact that an earlier confession was obtained by unlawful methods should add force to the presumption of coercion that attaches to subsequent custodial interrogation and should require the prosecutor to shoulder a heavier burden of rebuttal than in a routine case. Simple logic, as well as the interest in not providing an affirmative incentive to police misconduct, requires that result. I see no reason why the violation of a rule that is as well recognized and easily administered as the duty to give Miranda warnings should not also impose an additional burden on the prosecutor. If we are faithful to the holding in Miranda itself, when we are considering the admissibility of evidence in the prosecutor's case-in-chief, we should not try to fashion a distinction between police misconduct that warrants a finding of actual coercion and police misconduct that establishes an irrebuttable presumption of coercion.

For me, the most disturbing aspect of the Court's opinion is its somewhat opaque characterization of the police misconduct in this case. The Court appears ambivalent on the question whether there was any constitutional violation. This ambivalence is either disingenuous or completely lawless. This Court's power to require state courts to exclude probative self-incriminatory statements rests entirely on the premise that the use of such evidence violates the Federal Constitution. The same constitutional analysis applies whether the custodial interrogation is actually coercive or irrebuttably presumed to be coercive. If the Court does not accept that premise, it must regard the holding in the Miranda case itself, as well as all of the Federal jurisprudence that has evolved from that decision, as nothing more than an illegitimate exercise of raw judicial power. If the Court accepts the proposition that respondent's self-incriminatory statement was inadmissible, it must also acknowledge that the Federal Constitution protected him from custodial police interrogation without first being advised of his right to remain silent.

The source of respondent's constitutional protection is the Fifth Amendment's privilege against compelled self-incrimination that is secured against state invasion by the Due Process Clause of the Fourteenth Amendment. . . .

Notes and Questions

1. Recall our consideration of *Leon v. State* in Chapter 1, at p. 18. Would the admissibility of the accused's second confession (C2) in that case be analyzed differently from the second confession given in *Elstad*? Specifically, is the "fruit of the poisonous tree" analysis used by the Oregon Court of Appeals in *Elstad* appropriate in *Leon*? What is the crucial difference between the initial confession (C1) obtained in *Leon* and the first confession secured in *Elstad*?

2. The *Elstad* Court instructs us that "the failure of police to administer Miranda warnings does not mean that the statements received have actually been coerced, but only that courts will presume the privilege against compulsory self-incrimination has not been intelligently exercised." Citing *Michigan v. Tucker*, 417 U.S. 433, 94 S. Ct. 2357, 41 L. Ed. 2d 182 (1974), *Elstad* concludes that simple "unwarned questioning" causes "no actual infringement of the suspect's constitutional rights." Instead, *Miranda* only lays down "'prophylactic standards . . . to safeguard [the constitutional] privilege'" against compelled self-incrimination. We will consider this important point again in *New York v. Quarles*, 467 U.S. 649, 104 S. Ct. 2626, 81 L. Ed. 2d 550 (1984), *infra* at p. 365.

3. Even if the proposition is accepted that a "simple" *Miranda* violation does not result in a confession that is "coerced," in the constitutional sense, is the Court's contention accurate that "a careful and thorough administration of Miranda warnings serves to cure the condition that rendered the unwarned statement inadmissible"? For the suspect's waiver of rights to be effective prior to C2, why should not an additional "warning" be required that the prior unwarned confession (C1) will be inadmissible as evidence?

4. An important part of the holding in *Elstad* appears to be equivocal:

We must conclude that, *absent deliberately coercive or improper tactics* in obtaining the initial statement, the mere fact that a suspect has made an unwarned admission does not warrant a presumption of compulsion. A subsequent administration of Miranda warnings to a suspect who has given a voluntary but unwarned statement *ordinarily* should suffice to remove the conditions that precluded admission of the earlier statement. (Emphasis added.)

Why do you suppose the Court has attached these caveats to its ruling?

5. Consider Elstad's initial, unwarned statement. Do you agree that he was "in custody"? Was he "interrogated"? Justify your conclusions.

6. Several state courts have rejected *Elstad* on state constitutional grounds. The Tennessee Supreme Court did so in *State v. Smith*, 834 S.W.2d 915 (Tenn. 1992), and also elaborated on the considerations relevant to the "attenuation" analysis used to determine whether an unlawfully obtained initial confession taints a second confession.

Following Miranda, a Supreme Court majority has held that the prophylactic Miranda warnings are not themselves rights protected by the Constitution, but are instead measures designed to ensure that the right against compulsory self-incrimination is protected and intelligently exercised. See, e.g., Oregon v. Elstad, 470 U.S. 298, 105 S.Ct. 1285, 84 L.Ed.2d 222 (1985); New York v. Quarles, 467 U.S. 649, 104 S.Ct. 2626, 81 L.Ed.2d 550 (1984); Michigan v. Tucker, 417 U.S. 433, 94 S.Ct. 2357, 41 L.Ed.2d 182 (1974). . . .

In Elstad, a majority of the United States Supreme Court decided that, in a situation similar to that faced by the defendant in this case, a trial court must conclude that an initial confession obtained without prior warnings regarding the right against self-incrimination is inadmissible. . . .

This holding by the United States Supreme Court represented a clear break with past precedent embracing the "cat out of the bag" theory espoused in United States v. Bayer, 331 U.S. 532, 67 S.Ct. 1394, 91 L.Ed. 1654 (1947). In Bayer, the court recognized:

> Of course, after an accused has once let the cat out of the bag by confessing, no matter what the inducement, he is never thereafter free of the psychological and practical disadvantages of having confessed. He can never get the cat back in the bag. The secret is out for good. In such a sense, a later confession always may be looked upon as fruit of the first.

Even in Bayer, however, the United States Supreme Court refused to hold that an illegally-obtained confession would forever foreclose the possibility that a subsequent admissible confession could be elicited from the defendant. In fact, in that case, the court determined that the subsequent confession given six months after the defendant's first statement would not be held invalid when the "only restraint under which [the defendant] labored was that he could not leave the . . . limits [of the military base on which he lived] without permission."

We believe that adherence to the spirit and principles of Article I, § 9 of the Tennessee Constitution requires us to recognize, as a matter of Tennessee constitutional law, the inherent reasonableness of the underlying premise expressed in Bayer. Consequently, we dispute the rationale of the Elstad decision that, absent coercion in eliciting an initial confession, psychological pressures and other pressures flowing from that confession can never lead a defendant to give subsequent, involuntary, incriminating statements. As noted in Justice Brennan's dissent in Elstad, even standard interrogation manuals used by law enforcement agencies recognize that "[i]f the first admission can be obtained, 'there is every reason to expect that the first admission will lead to others, and eventually to the full confession.'" Elstad, supra, 470 U.S. at 328 (Brennan, J., dissenting).

Like the court in Bayer, however, we also refuse to hold that an initial, illegally-obtained confession forever bars the prosecution from obtaining a subsequent, admissible confession from the defendant. Rather, we hold that the provisions of Article I, § 9 of the Tennessee Constitution necessitate that we recognize that extraction of an illegal, unwarned confession from a defendant raises a rebuttable presumption that a subsequent confession, even if preceded by proper Miranda warnings, is tainted by the initial illegality. That presumption may be overcome by the prosecution, however, if the State can establish "that the taint is so attenuated as to justify admission of the subsequent confession." Elstad, supra, 470 U.S. at 335, 105 S.Ct. at 1306–07 (Brennan, J., dissenting).

In each such case, the crucial inquiry for the courts becomes whether the events and circumstances surrounding and following the initial, illegal conduct of the law enforcement officers prevented the accused from subsequently (1) making a free and informed choice to waive the State constitutional right not to provide evidence against one's self, and (2) voluntarily confessing his involvement in the crime. In addressing these questions, courts should examine the following factors:

1. The use of coercive tactics to obtain the initial, illegal confession and the causal connection between the illegal conduct and the challenged, subsequent confession;

2. The temporal proximity of the prior and subsequent confessions;

3. The reading and explanation of Miranda rights to the defendant before the subsequent confession;

4. The circumstances occurring after the arrest and continuing up until the making of the subsequent confession including, but not limited to, the length of the detention and the deprivation of food, rest, and bathroom facilities;

5. The coerciveness of the atmosphere in which any questioning took place including, but not limited to, the place where the questioning occurred, the identity of the interrogators, the form of the questions, and the repeated or prolonged nature of the questioning;

6. The presence of intervening factors including, but not limited to, consultations with counsel or family members, or the opportunity to consult with counsel, if desired;

7. The psychological effect of having already confessed, and whether the defendant was advised that the prior confession may not be admissible at trial;

8. Whether the defendant initiated the conversation that led to the subsequent confession; and

9. The defendant's sobriety, education, intelligence level, and experience with the law, as such factors relate to the defendant's ability to understand the administered Miranda rights.

In ruling upon the admissibility of a subsequent confession following the determination that an initial, unwarned confession may not be introduced in the State's case-in-chief, no single factor listed above is determinative. Rather, a court must examine the totality of the circumstances surrounding the two confessions to determine whether the subsequent confession by the defendant can truly be termed a knowing and voluntary statement.

The facts of this case demonstrate that Smith's subsequent confession was given knowingly and voluntarily. No coercive tactics were employed by the law enforcement officials to elicit either the first or the second incriminating statement given by the defendant. More than three hours elapsed between the time Smith was arrested and first given his Miranda warnings and the time when he gave his second confession to the authorities. There is no evidence in the record that Smith was in any way mistreated during that time period or that he was prevented from contacting friends, family or legal counsel. Additionally, Smith had been advised of his Miranda rights twice before his second statement was given (once at the time of his arrest and again immediately before the second statement), both the interrogators and the place of interrogation changed from the first illegally-obtained confession, and there is no indication that Smith did not fully understand the rights explained to him.

In fact, Smith acknowledged that he understood his rights and signed a written waiver of them. In response to questioning,

Smith proceeded to give Officer Hood a statement of his involvement in the crime. There is no evidence that the interrogation producing the statement was unduly prolonged so that it could be characterized as an effort to wear down Smith's resistance and overcome his free will.

The only coercive influence apparent in this record is the fact that Smith was in police custody at the time of his statement and at all relevant times after his arrest. Although police custody is inherently coercive and compelling, if we were to hold this single factor sufficient to vitiate the voluntariness of a subsequent confession, an accused could never give a voluntary confession after arrest. We are unwilling to condone such a result because of our belief that "[c]onfessions remain a proper element in law enforcement." Miranda, supra, 384 U.S. at 478, 86 S. Ct. at 1630. In short, our examination of the totality of the circumstances surrounding Smith's initial statement, his arrest and detention, and his subsequent confession leads us to the inescapable conclusion that Smith knowingly and voluntarily waived his right against self-incrimination prior to giving the written confession introduced at trial in this matter. . . .

Our ruling today that an illegally-obtained, initial confession is presumed, subject to rebuttal, to have tainted any subsequent confession, even if the later statement is preceded by proper Miranda warnings, expressly rejects the United States Supreme Court majority holding in Oregon v. Elstad. We believe, however, that the provisions of Article I, § 9 of the Tennessee Constitution mandate that the State, after illegally obtaining an incriminating statement from a defendant, must establish that the subsequent confession was given freely and voluntarily and that the constitutional right to be free from self-incrimination was not waived due solely to the psychological pressures resulting from giv-ing the previous statement. Only then can we be assured that criminal defendants are not being unconstitutionally compelled "to give evidence against [themselves]." . . .

Other state court decisions rejecting *Elstad* on state law grounds include *People v. Bethea*, 67 N.Y.2d 364, 493 N.E.2d 937, 502 N.Y.S.2d 713 (1986); and *Commonwealth v. Smith*, 412 Mass. 823, 593 N.E.2d 1288 (1992) (relying on state common law). *See* B. Latzer, *State Constitutional Criminal Law* § 4.12 (1995).

* * * * *

Another issue concerning the prerequisites of a "knowing and intelligent" waiver of *Miranda* rights arose in *Colorado v. Spring*, 479 U.S. 564, 107 S. Ct. 851, 93 L. Ed. 2d 954 (1987). John Spring was arrested by federal agents from the Bureau of Alcohol, Tobacco, and Firearms (ATF) while making an illegal sale of firearms to an undercover agent. He was advised of his *Miranda* rights and made a written waiver of them. ATF agents first questioned him about the firearms sale that resulted in his arrest. Then, because they had received a tip that Spring had shot and killed a man in Colorado, they asked Spring if he had ever shot anyone. Spring admitted that he had "shot another guy once," although he denied shooting Donald Walker, the man who had been killed in Colorado. During subsequent questioning, which was preceded by fresh *Miranda* warnings and a new waiver, Spring confessed to killing Donald Walker. His confession was admitted into evidence at his state court trial, and he was convicted of first-degree murder.

For purposes of its decision, the Supreme Court assumed that Spring's ultimate confession was a product of the initial interrogation, at which Spring admitted that he had once "shot another guy." (The Court noted that the state had not preserved the issue of whether Spring's full confession was admissible under *Oregon v. Elstad, supra*, and that it thus would not consider that theory. 479 U.S., at 572 n. 4). Spring challenged the admissibility of his confession on the ground that "his waiver of Miranda rights [during the initial interrogation] was invalid because he was not informed that he would be questioned about the Colorado murder." The Colorado Supreme Court accepted Spring's argument, reasoning that

> "the validity of Spring's waiver of constitutional rights must be determined upon an examination of the totality of the circumstances surrounding the making of the statement to determine if the waiver was voluntary, knowing and intelligent. No one factor is always determinative in that analysis. Whether, and to what extent, a suspect has been informed or is aware of the subject matter of the interrogation prior to its commencement is simply one factor in the court's evaluation of the total circumstances, although it may be a major or even a determinative factor in some situations." [713 P. 2d] at 872–873 (citations omitted).

The court concluded:

> "Here, the absence of an advisement to Spring that he would be questioned about the Colorado homicide, and the lack of any basis to conclude that at the time of the execution of the waiver, he reasonably could have expected that the interrogation would extend to that subject, are determinative factors in undermining the validity of the waiver." Id., at 874 (emphasis in original).

The U.S. Supreme Court reversed (7–2), through a decision written by Justice Powell.

There is no doubt that Spring's decision to waive his Fifth Amendment privilege was voluntary. He alleges no "coercion of a confession by physical violence or other deliberate means calculated to break [his] will," and the trial court found none. . . .

There also is no doubt that Spring's waiver of his Fifth Amendment privilege was knowingly and intelligently made: that is, that Spring understood that he had the right to remain silent and that anything he said could be used as evidence against him. The Constitution does not require that a criminal suspect know and understand every possible consequence of a waiver of the Fifth Amendment privilege. The Fifth Amendment's guarantee is both simpler and more fundamental: A defendant may not be compelled to be a witness against himself in any respect. The Miranda warnings protect this privilege by ensuring that a suspect knows that he may choose not to talk to law enforcement officers, to talk only with counsel present, or to discontinue talking at any time. The Miranda warnings ensure that a waiver of these rights is knowing and intelligent by requiring that the suspect be fully advised of this constitutional privilege, including the critical advice that whatever he chooses to say may be used as evidence against him.

In this case there is no allegation that Spring failed to understand the basic privilege guaranteed by the Fifth Amendment. Nor is there any allegation that he misunderstood the consequences of speaking freely to the law enforcement officials. In sum, we think that the trial court was indisputably correct in finding that Spring's waiver was made knowingly and intelligently within the meaning of Miranda.

Spring relies on this Court's statement in Miranda that "any evidence that the accused was threatened, tricked, or cajoled into a waiver will . . . show that the defendant did not voluntarily waive his privilege." 384 US, at 476. He contends that the failure to inform him of the potential subjects of interrogation constitutes the police trickery and deception condemned in Miranda, thus rendering his waiver of

Miranda rights invalid. Spring, however, reads this statement in Miranda out of context and without due regard to the constitutional privilege the Miranda warnings were designed to protect. . . .

This Court has never held that mere silence by law enforcement officials as to the subject matter of an interrogation is "trickery" sufficient to invalidate a suspect's waiver of Miranda rights, and we expressly decline so to hold today.[8]

Once Miranda warnings are given, it is difficult to see how official silence could cause a suspect to misunderstand the nature of his constitutional right—"his right to refuse to answer any question which might incriminate him." . . . We have held that a valid waiver does not require that an individual be informed of all information "useful" in making his decision or all information that "might . . . affec[t] his decision to confess." Moran v. Burbine. "[W]e have never read the Constitution to require that the police supply a suspect with a flow of information to help him calibrate his self-interest in deciding whether to speak or stand by his rights." Here, the additional information could affect only the

wisdom of a Miranda waiver, not its essentially voluntary and knowing nature. Accordingly, the failure of the law enforcement officials to inform Spring of the subject matter of the interrogation could not affect Spring's decision to waive his Fifth Amendment privilege in a constitutionally significant manner.

This Court's holding in Miranda specifically required that the police inform a criminal suspect that he has the right to remain silent and that *anything* he says may be used against him. There is no qualification of this broad and explicit warning. The warning, as formulated in Miranda, conveys to a suspect the nature of his constitutional privilege and the consequences of abandoning it. Accordingly, we hold that a suspect's awareness of all the possible subjects of questioning in advance of interrogation is not relevant to determining whether the suspect voluntarily, knowingly, and intelligently waived his Fifth Amendment privilege. . . .

Justice Marshall, with whom Justice Brennan joins, dissenting. . . .

Consistent with our prior decisions, the Court acknowledges that a suspect's waiver of fundamental constitutional rights, such as Miranda's protections against self-incrimination during a custodial interrogation, must be examined in light of the "'totality of the circumstances.'" Nonetheless, the Court proceeds to hold that the specific crimes and topics of investigation known to the interrogating officers before questioning begins are "not relevant" to, and in this case "could not affect," the validity of the suspect's decision to waive his Fifth Amendment privilege. It seems to me self-evident that a suspect's decision to waive this privilege will necessarily be influenced by his awareness of the scope and seriousness of the matters under investigation. . . .

---

8. In certain circumstances, the Court has found affirmative misrepresentations by the police sufficient to invalidate a suspect's waiver of the Fifth Amendment privilege. See, e.g., Lynumn v. Illinois, 372 US 528, 83 S Ct 917, 9 L Ed 2d 922 (1963) (misrepresentation by police officers that a suspect would be deprived of state financial aid for her dependent child if she failed to cooperate with authorities rendered the subsequent confession involuntary); Spano v. New York, 360 US 315, 79 S Ct 1202, 3 L Ed 2d 1265 (1959) (misrepresentation by the suspect's friend that the friend would lose his job as a police officer if the suspect failed to cooperate rendered his statement involuntary). In this case, we are not confronted with an affirmative misrepresentation by law enforcement officials as to the scope of the interrogation and do not reach the question whether a waiver of Miranda rights would be valid in such circumstances.

I would include among the relevant factors for consideration whether before waiving his Fifth Amendment rights the suspect was aware, either through the circumstances surrounding his arrest or through a specific advisement from the arresting or interrogating officers, of the crime or crimes he was suspected of committing and about which they intended to ask questions. . . .

The interrogation tactics utilized in this case demonstrate the relevance of the information Spring did not receive. The agents evidently hoped to obtain from Spring a valid confession to the federal firearms charge for which he was arrested and then parlay this admission into an additional confession of first degree murder. Spring could not have expected questions about the latter, separate offense when he agreed to waive his rights, as it occurred in a different state and was a violation of state law outside the normal investigative focus of federal Alcohol, Tobacco and Firearms agents.

"Interrogators describe the point of the first admission as the 'breakthrough' and the 'beachhead,' R. Royal & S. Schutt, The Gentle Art of Interviewing and Interrogation: A Professional Manual and Guide 143 (1976), which once obtained will give them enormous 'tactical advantages,' F. Inbau & J. Reid, Criminal Interrogation and Confessions 82 (2d ed 1967)." Oregon v. Elstad, 470 US 298, 328, 105 S Ct 1285, 84 L Ed 2d 222 (1985) (Brennan, J., dissenting). The coercive aspects of the psychological ploy intended in this case, when combined with an element of surprise which may far too easily rise to a level of deception, cannot be justified in light of Miranda's strict requirements that the suspect's waiver and confession be voluntary, knowing, and intelligent. . . . Additional questioning about entirely separate and more serious suspicions of criminal activity can take unfair advantage of the suspect's psychological state, as the unexpected questions cause the compulsive pressures suddenly to reappear. Given this technique of interrogation, a suspect's understanding of the topics planned for questioning is, therefore, at the very least "relevant" to assessing whether his decision to talk to the officers was voluntarily, knowingly, and intelligently made.

Not only is the suspect's awareness of the suspected criminal conduct relevant, its absence may be determinative in a given case. The State's burden of proving that a suspect's waiver was voluntary, knowing, and intelligent is a "heavy" one. Miranda, 334 US, at 475. We are to "'indulge every reasonable presumption against waiver' of fundamental constitutional rights." . . .

It is reasonable to conclude that, had Spring known of the federal agents' intent to ask questions about a murder unrelated to the offense for which he was arrested, he would not have consented to interrogation without first consulting his attorney. . . .

Notes and Questions

1. What if Justice Marshall is correct that Spring might not have waived his *Miranda* rights if he had "known of the federal agents' intent to ask questions about a murder unrelated to the offense for which he was arrested"? In light of *Moran v. Burbine* and *Oregon v. Elstad*, is such reasoning persuasive?

2. On the other hand, does the majority in *Spring* go too far by concluding that "a suspect's awareness of all the possible subjects of questioning in advance of interrogation is not [at all] relevant to determining whether the suspect voluntarily, knowingly, and intelligently waived his Fifth Amendment privilege"? Should such lack of awareness at least be one consideration in the "totality of the circumstances" about the validity of the waiver?

How demanding is the "heavy burden [that] rests on the government to demonstrate that the defendant knowingly and intelligently waived" his *Miranda* rights? Should proof be required beyond a reasonable doubt? By clear and convincing evidence? Simply by a preponderance of the evidence? The Court identified the burden that the prosecution must satisfy to establish an effective waiver of *Miranda* rights in *Colorado v. Connelly*, 479 U.S. 157, 107 S. Ct. 515, 93 L. Ed. 2d 473 (1986). We will consider a separate issue raised in *Connelly infra*, at p. 361. Here, we reprint only that portion of the case dealing with the burden-of-proof issue. Chief Justice Rehnquist wrote the opinion for the Court.

The Supreme Court of Colorado . . . held that the State must bear its burden of proving waiver of these Miranda rights by "clear and convincing evidence." Although we have stated in passing that the State bears a "heavy" burden in proving waiver, we have never held that the "clear and convincing evidence" standard is the appropriate one.

In Lego v. Twomey, this Court upheld a procedure in which the State established the voluntariness of a confession by no more than a preponderance of the evidence. We upheld it for two reasons. First, the voluntariness determination has nothing to do with the reliability of jury verdicts; rather, it is designed to determine the presence of police coercion. Thus, voluntariness is irrelevant to the presence or absence of the elements of a crime, which must be proved beyond a reasonable doubt. See In re Winship, 397 US 358, 90 S Ct 1068, 25 L Ed 2d 368, 51 Ohio Ops 2d 323 (1970). Second, we rejected Lego's assertion that "the importance of the values served by exclusionary rules is itself sufficient demonstration that the Constitution also requires admissibility to be proved beyond a reasonable doubt." Indeed, the Court found that "no substantial evidence has accumulated that federal rights have suffered from determining admissibility by a preponderance of the evidence."

We now reaffirm our holding in Lego: Whenever the State bears the burden of proof in a motion to suppress a statement that the defendant claims was obtained in violation of our Miranda doctrine, the State need prove waiver only by a preponderance of the evidence. . . .

Justice Blackmun declined to join the Court's opinion on the burden-of-proof issue because "that issue was neither raised nor briefed by the parties, and . . . it is not necessary to the decision." 479 U.S., at 171. Justice Stevens concurred only in a portion of the Court's judgment. Justices Brennan and Marshall dissented.

Impeachment

Use of Statements Obtained in Violation of Miranda To Impeach Credibility

Any witness who testifies at a trial must abide by his or her oath to tell the truth. This rule applies to defendants who choose to testify, no less than other witnesses. Defendants in criminal cases cannot be required to testify, but once they decide to relinquish their right to silence, they are subject to cross-examination and in most other respects are treated like other witnesses.

In all trials, it is common for the lawyer cross-examining a witness to try to "impeach" the witness's credibility or to raise doubts about the truthful nature of the witness or her testimony. Efforts to impeach testimony take many different forms. Thus, witnesses may be asked to reveal prior criminal convictions, on the theory that the jury or judge may doubt the truth-fulness of one who has been convicted of a crime. Attempts often are made to expose witnesses' potential interest in the outcome of a trial or their biases against a party or to show that they are testifying with the expectation of getting some benefit or reward in return.

One of the most common methods of attempting to impeach witnesses' credibility is by demonstrating that their testimony is inconsistent with prior statements that they have made. Witnesses whose courtroom testimony is diametrically in conflict with statements they have made on prior occasions may not be very believable. Attorneys who succeed in getting a witness to admit that she has made prior statements that are contrary to her trial testimony frequently "go for the jugular" by demanding to know (with great flourish and an appropriate tone of indignation), "So, were you lying then, or are you lying now?"

We have learned that if a defendant's statements have been obtained in violation of *Miranda*, they usually (we will consider an exception when we study *New York v. Quarles, infra* at p. 365) must be suppressed from evidence: that is, the prosecution may not use those statements to prove the defendant's guilt. But does it follow that statements produced in violation of *Miranda* cannot be used for any purpose at all? Even if they are inadmissible to prove guilt, might they be used to impeach the defendant's credibility?

Assume, for example, that a defendant confesses to possessing a large quantity of heroin but that the confession is ruled inadmissible because of a *Miranda* violation. The defendant, knowing that the confession has been suppressed, testifies at her trial that she has "never seen heroin in my life." Can the prosecutor cross-examine her about her prior admission about possessing a large quantity of heroin in an effort to impeach the credibility of her trial testimony, or is the prior statement entirely "off limits" to the prosecutor because it was obtained in violation of *Miranda*?

Note the dilemma if the statement is admissible to impeach her credibility but cannot be considered to prove guilt. The jury must be instructed that it is allowed to consider the defendant's earlier admission that she possessed heroin only for the purpose of evaluating her credibility. The jurors must further be instructed that they cannot consider her admission to prove guilt—that is, to establish that she in fact possessed the heroin. Whether jurors actually can perform such mental gymnastics and follow instructions of this nature, try as they might to comply, is another question. *See generally* D. Shafer, "The Defendant's Testimony," in S. Kassin & L. Wrightsman (eds.), *The Psychology of Evidence and Trial Procedure* 124 (1985).

We consider the use of statements obtained in violation of *Miranda* to impeach a defendant's credibility in the following two cases.

Harris v. New York, 401 U.S. 222, 91 S. Ct. 643, 28 L. Ed. 2d 1 (1971)

Mr. Chief Justice Burger delivered the opinion of the Court.

* * *

The State of New York charged petitioner in a two-count indictment with twice selling heroin to an undercover police officer. At a subsequent jury trial the officer was the State's chief witness, and he testified as to details of the two sales. A second officer verified collateral details of the sales, and a third offered testimony about the chemical analysis of the heroin.

Petitioner took the stand in his own defense. He admitted knowing the undercover police officer but denied a sale on January 4, 1966. He admitted making a sale of contents of a glassine bag to the officer on January 6 but claimed it was baking powder and part of a scheme to defraud the purchaser.

On cross-examination petitioner was asked seriatim whether he had made specified statements to the police immediately following his arrest on January 7—statements that partially contradicted petitioner's direct testimony at trial. In response to the cross-examination, petitioner testified that he could not remember virtually any of the questions or answers recited by the prosecutor. At the request of petitioner's counsel the written statement from which the prosecutor had read questions and answers in his impeaching process was placed in the record for possible use on appeal; the statement was not shown to the jury.

The trial judge instructed the jury that the statements attributed to petitioner by the prosecution could be considered only in passing on petitioner's credibility and not as evidence of guilt. In closing summations both counsel argued the substance of the impeaching statements. The jury then found petitioner guilty on the second count of the indictment. The New York Court of Appeals affirmed in a per curiam opinion, 25 NY2d 175, 250 NE2d 349 (1969).

At trial the prosecution made no effort in its case in chief to use the statements allegedly made by petitioner, conceding that they were inadmissible under Miranda v. Arizona. The transcript of the interrogation used in the impeachment, but not given to the jury, shows that no warning of a right to appointed counsel was given before questions were put to petitioner when he was taken into custody. Petitioner makes no claim that the statements made to the police were coerced or involuntary.

Some comments in the Miranda opinion can indeed be read as indicating a bar to use of an uncounseled statement for any purpose, but discussion of that issue was not at all necessary to the Court's holding and cannot be regarded as controlling. Miranda barred the prosecution from making its case with statements of an accused made while in custody prior to having or effectively waiving counsel. It does not follow from Miranda that evidence inadmissible against an accused in the prosecution's case in chief is barred for all purposes, provided of course that

the trustworthiness of the evidence satisfies legal standards.

In Walder v. United States, 347 US 62, 74 S Ct 354, 98 L Ed 503 (1954), the Court permitted physical evidence, inadmissible in the case in chief, to be used for impeachment purposes.

"It is one thing to say that the Government cannot make an affirmative use of evidence unlawfully obtained. It is quite another to say that the defendant can turn the illegal method by which evidence in the Government's possession was obtained to his own advantage, and provide himself with a shield against contradiction of his untruths. Such an extension of the Weeks doctrine would be a perversion of the Fourth Amendment.

"[T]here is hardly justification for letting the defendant affirmatively resort to perjurious testimony in reliance on the Government's disability to challenge his credibility." 347 US, at 65.

It is true that Walder was impeached as to collateral matters included in his direct examination, whereas petitioner here was impeached as to testimony bearing more directly on the crimes charged. We are not persuaded that there is a difference in principle that warrants a result different from that reached by the Court in Walder. Petitioner's testimony in his own behalf concerning the events of January 7 contrasted sharply with what he told the police shortly after his arrest. The impeachment process here undoubtedly provided valuable aid to the jury in assessing petitioner's credibility, and the benefits of this process should not be lost, in our view, because of the speculative possibility that impermissible police conduct will be encouraged thereby. Assuming that the exclusionary rule has a deterrent effect on proscribed police conduct, sufficient deterrence flows when the evidence in question is made unavailable to the prosecution in its case in chief.

Every criminal defendant is privileged to testify in his own defense, or to refuse to do so. But that privilege cannot be construed to include the right to commit perjury. Having voluntarily taken the stand, petitioner was under an obligation to speak truthfully and accurately, and the prosecution here did no more than utilize the traditional truth-testing devices of the adversary process. . . .

The shield provided by Miranda cannot be perverted into a license to use perjury by way of a defense, free from the risk of confrontation with prior inconsistent utterances. We hold, therefore, that petitioner's credibility was appropriately impeached by use of his earlier conflicting statements.

Affirmed.

Mr. Justice Black dissents.

Mr. Justice Brennan, with whom Mr. Justice Douglas and Mr. Justice Marshall join, dissenting.

* * *

Walder v. United States was not a case where tainted evidence was used to impeach an accused's direct testimony on matters directly related to the case against him. In Walder the evidence was used to impeach the accused's testimony on matters *collateral* to the crime charged. . . . The Court was careful, . . . to distinguish the situation of an accused whose testimony, as in the instant case, was a "denial of complicity in the crimes of which he was charged," that is, where illegally obtained evidence was used to impeach the accused's direct testimony on matters directly related to the case against him. As to that situation, the Court said:

"Of course, the Constitution guarantees a defendant the fullest opportunity to meet the accusation against him. He must be free to deny all the elements of the case against him without thereby giving leave to the Government to introduce by way of rebuttal evidence illegally secured by it, and therefore not available for its case in chief." 347 US, at 65.

* * *

While Walder did not identify the constitutional specifics that guarantee "a defendant the fullest opportunity to meet the accusation against him . . . [and permit him to] be free to deny all the elements of the case against him," in my view Miranda v. Arizona, identified the Fifth Amendment's privilege against self-incrimination as one of those specifics. . . . It is fulfilled only when an accused is guaranteed the right "to remain silent unless he chooses to speak in the *unfettered* exercise of his own will." The choice of whether to testify in one's own defense must therefore be "unfettered," since that choice is an exercise of the constitutional privilege. . . . The prosecution's use of the tainted statement "cuts down on

the privilege by making its assertion costly." Thus, the accused is denied an "unfettered" choice when the decision whether to take the stand is burdened by the risk that an illegally obtained prior statement may be introduced to impeach his direct testimony denying complicity in the crime charged against him. We settled this proposition in Miranda where we said:

"The privilege against self-incrimination protects the individual from being compelled to incriminate himself in *any* manner . . . . [S]tatements merely intended to be exculpatory by the defendant are often *used to impeach his testimony at trial. . . . These statements are incriminating in any meaningful sense of the word and may not be used without the full warnings and effective waiver required for any other statement."* 384 US, at 476–477 (emphasis added).

This language completely disposes of any distinction between statements used on direct as opposed to cross-examination. . . .

The objective of deterring improper police conduct is only part of the larger objective of safeguarding the integrity of our adversary system. The "essential mainstay" of that system, Miranda v. Arizona, 384 US, at 460, is the privilege against self-incrimination, which for that reason has occupied a central place in our jurisprudence since before the Nation's birth. Moreover, "we may view the historical development of the privilege as one which groped for the proper scope of governmental power over the citizen. . . . All these policies point to one overriding thought: the constitutional foundation underlying the privilege is the respect a government . . . must accord to the dignity and integrity of its citizens." Ibid. These values are plainly jeopardized if an exception against admission of tainted statements is made for those used for impeachment purposes. Moreover, it is monstrous that courts should aid or abet the lawbreaking police officer. It is abiding truth that "[n]othing can destroy a government more quickly than its failure to observe its own laws, or worse, its disregard of the charter of its own existence." Mapp v. Ohio, 367 US 648, 659 (1961). Thus, even to the extent that Miranda was aimed at deterring police practices in disregard of the Constitution, I fear that today's holding will seriously undermine the achievement of that objective. The Court today tells the police that they may freely interrogate an accused incommunicado and without counsel and know that although any statement they obtain in violation of Miranda cannot be used on the State's direct case, it may be introduced if the defendant has the temerity to testify in his own defense. This goes far toward undoing much of the progress made in conforming police methods to the Constitution. I dissent.

Oregon v. Hass, 420 U.S. 714, 95 S. Ct. 1215, 43 L. Ed. 2d 570 (1975)

Mr. Justice **Blackmun** delivered the opinion of the Court.

This case presents a variation of the fact situation encountered by the Court in Harris v. New York, 401 US 222, 91 S Ct 643, 28 L Ed 2d 1 (1971): When a suspect, who is in the custody of a state police officer, has been given full Miranda warnings and accepts them, and then later states that he would like to telephone a lawyer but is told that this cannot be done until the officer and the suspect reach the station, and the suspect then provides inculpatory information, is that information admissible in evidence solely for impeachment purposes after the suspect has taken the stand and testified contrarily to the inculpatory information, or is it inadmissible under the Fifth and Fourteenth Amendments?

* * *

We see no valid distinction to be made in the application of the principles of Harris to that case and to Hass' case. Hass' statements were made after the defendant knew [the police officer's] opposing testimony had been ruled inadmissible for the prosecution's case in chief.

As in Harris, it does not follow from Miranda that evidence inadmissible against Hass in the prosecution's case in chief is barred for all purposes, always provided that "the trustworthiness of the evidence satisfies legal standards." 401 US, at 224. Again, the impeaching material would provide valuable aid to the jury in assessing the defendant's credibility; again, "the benefits of this process should not be lost'" id., at 225, and, again, making the deterrent-effect assumption, there is sufficient deterrence when the evidence in question is made unavailable to the prosecution in its case in chief. If all this sufficed for the result in Harris, it supports and demands a like result in Hass' case. Here, too, the shield provided by Miranda is not to be perverted to a license to testify inconsistently, or even perjuriously, free from the risk of confrontation with prior inconsistent utterances.

We are, after all, always engaged in a search for truth in a criminal case so long as the search is surrounded with the safeguards provided by our Constitution.

* * *

Mr. Justice **Douglas** took no part in the consideration or decision of this case.

Mr. Justice **Brennan,** with whom Mr. Justice **Marshall** joins, dissenting.

* * *

The Court's decision today goes beyond Harris in undermining Miranda. Even after Harris, police had some incentive for following Miranda by warning an accused of his right to remain silent and his right to counsel. If the warnings were given, the accused might still make a statement which could be used in the prosecution's case in chief. Under today's holding, however, once the warnings are given, police have almost no incentive for following Miranda's requirement that "[i]f the individual states that he wants an attorney, the interrogation must cease until an attorney is present." If the requirement is followed there will almost surely be no statement since the attorney will advise the accused to remain silent. If, however, the requirement is disobeyed, the police may obtain a statement which can be used for impeachment if the accused has the temerity to testify in his own defense. Thus, after today's decision, if an individual states that he wants an attorney, police interrogation will doubtless be vigorously pressed to obtain state-

ments before the attorney arrives. I am unwilling to join this fundamental erosion of Fifth and Sixth Amendment rights and therefore dissent.

* * *

Notes and Questions

1. In light of the seemingly unequivocal language from *Miranda* quoted in Justice Brennan's dissent in *Harris v. New York*, how does the majority justify the conclusion that allowing the use of the improperly obtained statement for impeachment purposes is consistent with *Miranda*?

2. The *Miranda* violation in *Harris* involved the failure to administer adequate warnings. In *Ore-*

gon v. Hass, the violation involved the police's failure to respect the suspect's invocation of his right to counsel. What is the significance, if any, of the different nature of these violations?

3. To help understand the significance of the different types of *Miranda* violations in *Harris* and *Hass*, consider the following case, in which the Oregon Supreme Court rejects the federal rule announced in *Hass* on state constitutional grounds.

State v. Isom, 306 Or. 587, 761 P.2d 524 (Or. 1988)

LENT, Justice.

* * *

The dispositive issue is whether Article I, section 12, of the Oregon Constitution precludes the state from impeaching defendant's trial testimony with prior inconsistent statements elicited by police officers after defendant has told the officers that he did not wish to talk to them and that he wanted a lawyer. We hold that use of the statements is precluded and that the trial court erred in admitting them for impeachment purposes. . . .

Article I, section 12, of the Oregon Constitution provides, in part: "No person shall be compelled in any criminal prosecution to testify against himself." . . .

In the case before us, the interrogating officers blithely ignored defendant's request for a lawyer in the hope of obtaining statements from him to be used for impeachment purposes in the event he testified. This was not a case of a technical Miranda violation as set forth and interpreted by the federal courts.

The acts of the police officers were a violation of our earlier holdings. . . . The fact that the officers admittedly were following the federal interpretation of the utility and admissibility of such statements under federal law as set forth in Oregon v. Hass, 420 U.S. 714, 95 S.Ct. 1215, 43 L.Ed.2d 570 (1975) (reversing sub nom State v. Hass, 267 Or. 489, 517 P.2d 671 (1973)), is of no consequence. We are concerned with interpreting the Oregon Constitution on this issue and are not dependent on or restricted by federal law. We are not confronted here with a situation like that in either Harris v. New York, 401 U.S. 222, 91 S.Ct. 643, 28 L.Ed.2d 1 (1971), or State v. Brewton, 247 Or. 241, 422 P.2d 581 (1967). In those cases, no warnings were given and no request for a lawyer was ever made. We do not now decide the admissibility of such uncounseled out-of-court statements offered for impeachment purposes under Oregon law. That issue remains an open question.

The case before us could not present a better argument for the exclusion of defendant's statements for impeachment purposes. In the circumstances present in Harris and Brewton, namely, a mere failure to provide the defendants with information required by Miranda . . . the argument that exclusion of evidence from the state's case-in-chief provides sufficient incentive for police officers to give the required information is at least plausible. There is no incentive at all, however, coming from a rule that permits the admission for impeachment of statements obtained through interrogation after a suspect has refused to talk or has asked for a lawyer. Once a suspect invokes the right to remain silent or the right to consult a lawyer, the police are unlikely to get anything further without counsel present unless they continue to interrogate the suspect. Under such a rule, any statements made before the invocation of rights would still be fully admissible, and any statements made thereafter would be admissible for impeachment. Indeed, the detectives who interrogated defendant were well aware of the advantages to the state of continued interrogation; at one point in their interrogation, they even went so far as to inform defendant that his statements would be admissible only if he testified at trial. Thus, far from discouraging the police, the federal rule they were following actually encourages unconstitutional interrogation where the suspect has taken the police at their word and declined to talk.

No one, including a criminal defendant, has the "right" to give false testimony. Nor does anyone have the "right" to commit murder or robbery. But all citizens, including criminal defendants, have constitutional rights, and the state may not prove, over objection, any crime with unconstitutionally obtained evidence. The

defendant was entitled under the Oregon Constitution to have a lawyer present at the time of his out-of-court interrogation by the police. He unequivocally exercised that right by telling the police that he did not want to make any statement without his lawyer present. The police purposely disregarded that request and thereby intentionally violated defendant's constitutional right to counsel. The notion that police can continue to interrogate a person in violation of his state constitutional right to counsel and his rights against self-incrimination is pure fiction. Police officers have a duty to uphold the constitution of this state and may not intentionally violate a person's constitutional rights without serious sanctions. They have an absolute obligation to cease all questioning once the request for counsel has been made. Because defendant's statements were made after a request for counsel and were induced by continued questioning by the police, they were obtained in violation of Article I, section 12, of the Oregon Constitution and should have been suppressed by the trial court. . . .

* * * * *

4. The Hawaii Supreme Court has rejected *New York v. Harris*, in reliance on its state constitution. *State v. Santiago*, 53 Ha. 254, 492 P.2d 657 (1971).

5. *Mincey v. Arizona* (*infra*, p. 358), raises the question of whether "involuntary" confessions—as opposed to statements that involve only *Miranda* violations—may be used for impeachment purposes.

Impeachment by the Use of Silence

We have just considered whether a defendant's statements, obtained in violation of *Miranda*, can be used to impeach his credibility when his trial testimony is inconsistent with those prior statements. We now ask whether a testifying defendant's credibility can be impeached based on what he has *not* said: that is, by his prior silence under circumstances when

that silence might be construed as a tacit admission of guilt, or at least as being inconsistent with a story later told from the witness stand. The classic example of silence supporting an inference of guilt is when the only response that seven-year-old Johnny can muster to his mother's accusatory question "Did you break the cookie jar?" is to hang his head, stare miserably at his feet, and not say a word. His silence is not as conclusive as an admission of guilt and in fact may have a perfectly innocent explanation. Nevertheless, if, in response to that same question two hours later he volunteered for the first time that "the dog jumped up and knocked the cookie jar off the counter," we might reasonably wonder why he did not offer that explanation from the outset. His prior silence would, in effect, be used to impeach the credibility of his statement placing blame on the dog.

When considering the use of silence (as in "You didn't offer that explanation before, did you?") to impeach a defendant's testimony at a criminal trial, it may be important to distinguish between three time periods when the accused remained silent: (1) after he received his *Miranda* warnings, (2) before he was taken into custody or received his *Miranda* rights, and (3) after he was taken into custody but before he received his *Miranda* warnings.

Post-Warning Silence. The defendant in *Doyle v. Ohio*, 426 U.S. 610, 96 S. Ct. 2240, 49 L. Ed. 2d 91 (1976), was convicted of the felonious sale of marijuana after narcotics agents witnessed the alleged sale and found over $1,300 in marked money in his car. He was arrested and given his *Miranda* warnings minutes after the alleged sale. He testified at his trial that he never sold marijuana during the alleged transaction. He instead maintained that the alleged buyer (who was cooperating with the police) had had the drug in his possession all along and that for some unknown reason the buyer had simply thrust the marked money into the defendant's vehicle. On cross-examination, the prosecutor repeatedly asked the defendant whether he had given this same story to the arresting officers, and he repeatedly admitted that he had not.

The Supreme Court held (6–3) "that the use for impeachment purposes of petitioner's silence, at the time of arrest and after receiving *Miranda* warnings, violated the Due Process Clause of the Fourteenth Amendment." Justice Powell's majority opinion explained that the *Miranda* warnings

require that a person taken into custody be advised immediately that he has the right to remain silent, that anything he says may be used against him, and that he has a right to retained or appointed counsel before submitting to interrogation. Silence in the wake of these warnings may be nothing more than the arrestee's exercise of these *Miranda* rights. Thus, every post-arrest silence is insolubly ambiguous because of what the State is required to advise the person arrested. Moreover, while it is true that the *Miranda* warnings contain no express assurance that silence will carry no penalty, such assurance is implicit to any person who receives the warnings. In such circumstances, it would be fundamentally unfair and a deprivation of due process to allow the arrested person's silence to be used to impeach an explanation subsequently offered at trial. . . .

Prearrest/Prewarning Silence. In *Jenkins v. Anderson*, 447 U.S. 231, 100 S. Ct. 2124, 65 L. Ed. 2d 86 (1980), the defendant, Jenkins, was convicted of manslaughter for the stabbing death of Doyle Redding. He was not arrested until he turned himself in to the police two weeks after the killing. He testified at his trial, where he admitted stabbing Redding to death, but he claimed that he acted in self-defense. On cross-examination, the prosecutor asked questions that established that Jenkins had not "waited for the police to tell them what happened" and that he "had 'waited . . . at least two weeks before he did anything about surrendering himself or reporting [the stabbing] to anybody.'" 447 U.S., at 233.

The Supreme Court granted certiorari to decide "whether the use of prearrest silence to impeach a defendant's credibility violates either the Fifth or the Fourteenth Amendment." 447 U.S., at 232. Justice Powell's opinion for the Court concluded that Jenkins's constitutional rights had not been violated.

This Court's decision in Raffel v. United States, 271 US 494, 46 S Ct 566, 40 L Ed 1054 (1926), recognized that the Fifth Amendment is not violated when a defendant who testifies in his own defense is impeached with his prior silence. . . .

It can be argued that a person facing arrest will not remain silent if his failure to speak later can be used to impeach him. But the Constitution does not forbid "every government-imposed choice in the criminal process that has the effect of discouraging the exercise of constitutional rights." The "'threshold question is whether compelling the election impairs to an appreciable extent any of the policies behind the rights involved.'" The Raffel Court explicitly rejected the contention that the possibility of impeachment by prior silence is an impermissible burden upon the exercise of Fifth Amendment rights. "We are unable to see that the rule that [an accused who] testifies . . . must testify fully, adds in any substantial manner to the inescapable embarrassment which the accused must experience in determining whether he shall testify or not." 271 US, at 499. . . .

In determining whether a constitutional right has been burdened impermissibly, it also is appropriate to consider the legitimacy of the challenged governmental practice. Attempted impeachment on cross-examination of a defendant, the practice at issue here, may enhance the reliability of the criminal process. Use of such impeachment on cross-examination allows prosecutors to test the credibility of witnesses by asking them to explain prior inconsistent statements and acts. A defendant may decide not to take the witness stand because of the risk of cross-examination. But this is a choice of litigation tactics. Once a defendant decides to testify, "[t]he interests of the other party and regard for the function of courts of justice to ascertain the truth become relevant, and prevail in the balance of considerations determining the scope

and limits of the privilege against self-incrimination." Brown v. United States, 356 US 148, 156, 78 S Ct 622, 72, 2 L Ed 2d 589 (1958).

Thus, impeachment follows the defendant's own decision to cast aside his cloak of silence and advances the truth-finding function of the criminal trial. We conclude that the Fifth Amendment is not violated by the use of prearrest silence to impeach a criminal defendant's credibility.

The petitioner also contends that use of prearrest silence to impeach his credibility denied him the fundamental fairness guaranteed by the Fourteenth Amendment. We do not agree. Common law traditionally has allowed witnesses to be impeached by their previous failure to state a fact in circumstances in which that fact naturally would have been asserted. 3A J. Wigmore, Evidence § 1042, p 1056 (Chadbourn rev, 1970). Each jurisdiction may formulate its own rules of evidence to determine when prior silence is so inconsistent with present statements that impeachment by reference to such silence is probative. . . .

In this case, no governmental action induced petitioner to remain silent before arrest. The failure to speak occurred before the petitioner was taken into custody and given Miranda warnings. Consequently, the fundamental unfairness present in Doyle is not present in this case. We hold that impeachment by use of prearrest silence does not violate the Fourteenth Amendment. . . .

Justices Stewart and Stevens concurred in the judgment, and Justices Marshall and Brennan dissented.

Postarrest, Prewarning Silence. The facts in *Fletcher v. Weir*, 455 U.S. 603, 102 S. Ct. 1309, 71 L. Ed. 2d 490 (1982) (per curiam), in many respects resemble those of *Jenkins v. Anderson, supra.* Weir stabbed and killed a man during a fight, left the scene, and did not report the stabbing to the police. He was arrested some time later. "It did not appear from the record that the arresting officers had immediately read respondent his Miranda warnings." 455 U.S., at 604. Weir testified at his trial that he had stabbed his victim in self-defense. "The prosecutor cross-examined him as to why he had, *when arrested*, failed either to advance his exculpatory explanation to the arresting officers or to disclose the location of the knife he had used" in the stabbing. *Id.*, at 603–604 (emphasis added). Weir was convicted of manslaughter at his state trial but was granted federal habeas corpus relief on the ground that he "was denied due process of law . . . when the prosecutor used his post-arrest silence for impeachment purposes." *Id.*, at 604. The Supreme Court's per curiam opinion reversed (with Justice Brennan indicating that he would set the case for oral argument and Justice Marshall dissenting).

The significant difference between the present case and Doyle is that the record does not indicate that respondent Weir received any Miranda warnings during the period in which he remained silent immediately after his arrest. The majority of the Court of Appeals recognized the difference, but sought to extend Doyle to cover Weir's situation by stating that "[w]e think an arrest, by itself, is governmental action which implicitly induces a defendant to remain silent." 658 F2d, at 1131. We think that this broadening of Doyle is unsupported by the reasoning of that case and contrary to our post-Doyle decisions. . . .

In Jenkins, as in other post-Doyle cases, we have consistently explained Doyle as a case where the government had induced silence by implicitly assuring the defendant that his silence would not be used against him. . . .

In the absence of the sort of affirmative assurances embodied in the Miranda warnings, we do not believe that it violates due process of law for a State to permit cross-examination as to postarrest silence when a defendant chooses to take the stand. A State is entitled, in such situations, to leave to the judge and jury under its own rules of evidence the resolution of the extent to which postarrest silence may be deemed to impeach a criminal defendant's own testimony. . . .

* * * * *

Several state courts have declined to follow the rule of *Fletcher v. Weir*, in reliance on state constitutional provisions. *See, e.g., State v. Fisher*, 179 W. Va. 516, 370 S.E.2d 480 (1988); *State v. Sanchez*, 707 S.W.2d 575 (Tex. Crim. App. 1986); *Westmark v. State*, 693 P.2d 220 (Wyo. 1984); *Commonwealth v. Turner*, 499 Pa. 579, 454 A.2d 537 (1982). *See* B. Latzer, *State Constitutional Criminal Law* § 4:3 (1995).

* * * * *

📖 **Legal Research Note**. If you would like to find out more about the impeachment of a defendant's testimony in the context of *Miranda*, one option would be to consult the *A.L.R.* (*American Law Reports*) series for annotations on point. *A.L.R.* annotations provide a comprehensive discussion of judicial decisions that address different legal issues. To check for annotations, first refer to the *A.L.R. Index* covering *A.L.R.2d* through *A.L.R.5th*, *A.L.R. Federal*, and the *United States Supreme Court Reports, Lawyers Edition 2d*. A single index collects annotations from these different sets of *A.L.R.*, which respectively focus on state court, federal court, and U.S. Supreme Court decisions.

The logical starting point in the *Index* is "Impeachment." When we look for that topic we find a major heading, "Impeachment of Witnesses," with scores of subheadings and annotation titles. Two annotations listed in the *Index* look especially promising: "Miranda rule, propriety of using otherwise inadmissible statement, taken in violation of Miranda rule to impeach criminal defendant's credibility—state cases, 14 A.L.R.4th 676" and "Silence—pre-arrest silence, impeachment of defendant in criminal case by showing defendant's pre-arrest silence—state cases, 35 A.L.R.4th 731." Our next step would be to find the annotations identified in volumes 14 and 35 of *A.L.R.4th* and then to peruse their contents.

"Voluntariness" Revisited

As we have discussed (p. 262–264), prior to *Miranda's* arrival on the scene, confessions were admitted into evidence at state trials if they were considered to be "voluntary" under due process standards. *Miranda's* comparatively specific and clear-cut rules in large measure were implemented to replace the uncertainties of the voluntariness test. Nevertheless, a confession's voluntariness sometimes remains an issue even in this post-*Miranda* era.

We have encountered *Fare v. Michael C.*, 442 U.S. 707, 99 S. Ct. 2560, 61 L. Ed. 2d 197 (1979), twice before: once to consider whether Michael C. invoked his *Miranda* rights (p. 303) and once to examine whether he effectively waived those rights (p. 320). The facts of the case (which you should review) additionally raised the question of his confession's voluntariness. The majority opinion concluded that Michael C. had not been coerced into giving his statement. Justice Powell, in dissent, disagreed.

Mr. Justice Powell, dissenting.

This Court repeatedly has recognized that "the greatest care" must be taken to assure that an alleged confession of a juvenile was voluntary. Respondent was a young person, 16 years old at the time of his arrest and the subsequent prolonged interrogation at the stationhouse. Although respondent had had prior brushes with the law, and was under supervision by a probation officer, the taped transcript of his interrogation—as well as his testimony at the suppression hearing—demonstrates that he was immature, emotional,[2] and uneducated, and therefore was likely to be vulnerable to the skillful, two-on-one, repetitive style of interrogation to which he was subjected.

When given Miranda warnings and asked whether he desired an attorney, respondent requested permission to "have my probation officer here," a request that was refused. That officer testified later that he had communicated frequently with respondent, that respondent had serious and "extensive" family problems, and that the officer had instructed respondent to call him immediately "at any time he has a police contact, even if they stop him and talk to him on the street." The reasons given by the probation officer for having so instructed his charge were substantially the same reasons that prompt this Court to examine with special care the circumstances under which a minor's alleged confession was obtained. After stating that respondent had been "going through problems," the officer observed that "many times the kids don't understand what is going on, and what they are supposed to do relative to police. . . ." This view of the limited understanding of the average 16-year-old was borne out by respondent's question when, during interrogation, he was advised of his right to an attorney: "How I know you guys won't pull no police officer in and tell me he's an attorney?" It was during this part of the interrogation that the police had denied respondent's request to "have my probation officer here."

The police then proceeded, despite respondent's repeated denial of any connection to the murder under investigation, persistently to press interrogation until they

---

2. The Juvenile Court Judge observed that he had "heard the tapes" of the interrogation, and was "aware of the fact that Michael [respondent] was crying at the time he talked to the police officers."

extracted a confession. In In re Gault, in addressing police interrogation of detained juveniles, the Court stated:

> "If counsel was not present for some permissible reason when an admission was obtained [from a child], the greatest care must be taken to assure that the admission was voluntary, in the sense not only that it was not coerced or suggested, but also that it was not the product of ignorance of rights or of adolescent fantasy, fright or despair." 387 US, at 55.

It is clear that the interrogating police did not exercise "the greatest care" to assure that respondent's "admission was voluntary."[4] In the absence of counsel, and having refused to call the probation officer,

they nevertheless engaged in protracted interrogation.

Although I view the case as close, I am not satisfied that this particular 16-year-old boy, in this particular situation, was subjected to a fair interrogation free from inherently coercive circumstances. . . .

* * * * *

A classic example of an involuntary confession arose in *Mincey v. Arizona*, in which the Court considered whether a coerced statement—as opposed to one resulting simply from a *Miranda* violation—can be used for impeachment purposes.

Mincey v. Arizona, 437 U.S. 385, 98 S. Ct. 2408, 57 L. Ed. 2d 290 (1978)

Mr. Justice Stewart delivered the opinion of the Court.

* * *

Mincey was brought to the hospital after the shooting and taken immediately to the emergency room where he was examined and treated. He had sustained a wound in his hip, resulting in damage to the sciatic nerve and partial paralysis of his right leg. Tubes were inserted into his throat to help him breathe, and through his nose into his stomach to keep him from vom-

---

4. Minors who become embroiled with the law range from the very young up to those on the brink of majority. Some of the older minors become fully "street-wise," hardened criminals, deserving no greater consideration than that properly accorded all persons suspected of crime. Other minors are more of a child than an adult. As the Court indicated in In re Gault, 387 US 1, the facts relevant to the care to be exercised in a particular case vary widely. They include the minor's age, actual maturity, family environment, education, emotional and mental stability, and, of course, any prior record he might have.

iting; a catheter was inserted into his bladder. He received various drugs, and a device was attached to his arm so that he could be fed intravenously. He was then taken to the intensive care unit.

At about eight o'clock that evening, Detective Hust of the Tucson Police Department came to the intensive care unit to interrogate him. Mincey was unable to talk because of the tube in his mouth, and so he responded to Detective Hust's questions by writing answers on pieces of paper provided by the Hospital.

Hust told Mincey he was under arrest for the murder of a police officer, gave him the warnings required by Miranda v. Arizona, and began to ask questions about the events that had taken place in Mincey's apartment a few hours earlier. Although Mincey asked repeatedly that the interrogation stop until he could get a lawyer, Hust continued to question him until almost midnight.

After a pretrial hearing, the trial court found that Mincey had responded to this interrogation voluntarily. When Mincey took the witness stand at his trial his statements in response to Detective Hust's questions were used in an effort to impeach his testimony in several respects.

* * *

Statements made by a defendant in circumstances violating the strictures of Miranda v. Arizona, supra, are admissible for impeachment if their "trustworthiness . . . satisfies legal standards." Harris v. New York, 401 U.S. 222, 224. But *any* criminal trial use against a defendant of his *involuntary* statement is a denial of due process of law "even though there is ample evidence aside from the confession to support the conviction." If therefore, Mincey's statements to Detective Hust were not "'the product of a rational intellect and a free will,'" his conviction cannot stand. . . .

It is hard to imagine a situation less conducive to the exercise of "a rational intellect and a free will" than Mincey's. He had been seriously wounded just a few hours earlier, and had arrived at the hospital "depressed almost to the point of coma," according to his attending physician. Although he had received some treatment, his condition at the time of Hust's interrogation was still sufficiently serious that he was in the intensive care unit. He complained to Hust that the pain in his leg was "unbearable." He was evidently confused and unable to think clearly about either the events of that afternoon or the circumstances of his interrogation, since some of his written answers were on their face not entirely coherent. Finally, while Mincey was being questioned he was lying on his back on a hospital bed, encumbered by tubes, needles, and breathing apparatus. He was, in short, "at the complete mercy" of Detective Hust, unable to escape or resist the thrust of Hust's interrogation.

* * *

[D]espite Mincey's entreaties to be let alone, Hust ceased the interrogation only during intervals when Mincey lost consciousness or received medical treatment, and after each such interruption returned relentlessly to his task. The statements at issue were thus the result of virtually continuous questioning of a seriously and painfully wounded man on the edge of consciousness.

There were not present in this case some of the gross abuses that have led the Court in other cases to find confessions involuntary, such as beatings, see Brown v. Mississippi, 297 US 278, 56 S Ct 461, 80 L Ed 682, or "truth serums," see Townsend v. Sain, 372 US 293, 83 S Ct 745, 9 L Ed 2d 770. But "the blood of the accused is not the only hallmark of an unconstitutional inquisition." Determination of whether a statement is involuntary "requires more than a mere color-matching of cases." It requires careful evaluation of all the circumstances of the interrogation.

It is apparent from the record in this case that Mincey's statements were not "the product of his free and rational choice." To the contrary, the undisputed evidence makes clear that Mincey wanted *not* to answer Detective Hust. But Mincey was weakened by pain and shock, isolated from family, friends, and legal counsel, and barely conscious, and his will was simply overborne. Due process of law requires that statements obtained as these were cannot be used in any way against a defendant at his trial.

* * *

In *Harris v. New York* (p. 348) and *Oregon v. Hass* (p. 351), the justices were careful to qualify their holdings by insisting that "the trustworthiness of the [impeaching] evidence [must] satisf[y] legal standards." Is the questionable trustworthiness of coerced statements, such as those obtained from Mincey, the sole reason to bar their use?

In *New Jersey v. Portash*, 440 U.S. 450, 99 S. Ct. 1292, 59 L. Ed. 2d 501 (1979), a type of

coercion that was unlikely to affect the trustworthiness of a defendant's statement was at issue. Portash, a public official, testified before a grand jury pursuant to an immunity agreement. Portash was promised that "neither his statements nor any evidence derived from them could, under New Jersey law, be used in subsequent criminal proceedings (except in prosecutions for perjury or false swearing)." 440 U.S., at 451–452. He later was tried for misconduct in office and extortion. He sought a pretrial ruling that the testimony he had provided under the immunity agreement could not be used to impeach his testimony if he elected to testify at his trial. The trial judge denied the motion, and Portash thereafter declined to testify at his trial. He was convicted and filed an appeal.

The Supreme Court (per Stewart, J., with Justice Blackmun and Chief Justice Burger dissenting) ruled that the trial court had erred by not guaranteeing Portash immunity from impeachment.

In Harris and Hass the Court expressly noted that the defendant made "no claim that the statements made to the police were coerced or involuntary," Harris v. New York, supra, at 224, Oregon v. Hass, supra, at 722–23. That recognition was central to the decisions in those cases.

The Fifth and the Fourteenth Amendments provide that no person "shall be *compelled* in any criminal case to be a witness against himself." As we reaffirmed last Term, a defendant's compelled statements, as opposed to statements taken in violation of Miranda, may not be put to any testimonial use whatever against him in a criminal trial. "But *any* criminal trial use against a defendant of his *involuntary* statement is a denial of due process of law." (Emphasis in original.) Mincey v. Arizona, 437 US 385, 398.

Testimony given in response to a grant of legislative immunity is the essence of coerced testimony. In such cases there is no question whether physical or psychological pressures overrode the defendant's will; the witness is told to talk or face the government's coercive sanctions, notably, a conviction for contempt. The information given in response to a grant of immunity may well be more reliable than information beaten from a helpless defendant, but it is no less compelled. The Fifth and Fourteenth Amendments provide a privilege against *compelled* self-incrimination, not merely against unreliable self-incrimination. Balancing of interests was thought to be necessary in Harris and Hass when the attempt to deter unlawful police conduct collided with the need to prevent perjury. Here, by contrast, we deal with the constitutional privilege against compulsory self-incrimination in its most pristine form. Balancing, therefore, is not simply unnecessary. It is impermissible. . . .

Does *Portash* give license to the defendant to use his or her self-incrimination rights "not merely as a shield but as a sword," or does the reservation of prosecutions for perjury and false swearing from the scope of the immunity agreement adequately guard against this danger?

* * * * *

The Court said in *Mincey* that "*any* criminal trial use against a defendant of his *involuntary* statement is a denial of due process" (emphasis in original). If a defendant's involuntary confession erroneously is admitted into evidence at her trial, must her conviction automatically be reversed, or can the conviction stand if a reviewing court determines that the error was "harmless"—that is, if it is clear "beyond a reasonable doubt that the error complained of did not contribute to the verdict obtained"? *Chapman v. California*, 386 U.S. 18, 24, 87 S. Ct. 824, 17 L. Ed. 2d 705 (1967). In *Arizona v. Fulminante*, 499 U.S. 279, 111 S. Ct. 1246, 113 L. Ed. 2d 302 (1991), the Court rejected a rule of automatic reversal in favor of the "harmless error" analysis. However, concluding that admission of the defendant's involuntary confession was not harmless beyond a reasonable doubt, the Court refused to reinstate the defendant's conviction in that case.

* * * * *

If a confession is involuntary, in the sense that it is not the "product of a rational intellect and free will," does the *source* of or *reason* for the involuntariness matter? For example, in *Brown v. Mississippi* (p. 21), state law enforcement officers were the source of the coercion that overbore the defendants' free will. The same was true for the initial confession in

Leon v. State (p. 18). But what if a private party instead of an agent of the state is responsible for the coercion? Or what if the defendant's irrationality is attributable to mental illness instead of state-sanctioned coercion? Does the Constitution—which protects individuals against *governmental* overreaching—forbid the admission of such confessions into evidence? Consider the next case.

Colorado v. Connelly, 479 U.S. 157, 107 S. Ct. 515, 93 L. Ed. 2d 473 (1986)

Chief Justice Rehnquist delivered the opinion of the Court.

* * *

On August 18, 1983, Officer Patrick Anderson of the Denver Police Department was in uniform, working in an off-duty capacity in downtown Denver. Respondent Francis Connelly approached Officer Anderson and, without any prompting, stated that he had murdered someone and wanted to talk about it. Anderson immediately advised respondent that he had the right to remain silent, that anything he said could be used against him in court, and that he had the right to an attorney prior to any police questioning. Respondent stated that he understood these rights but he still wanted to talk about the murder. Understandably bewildered by this confession, Officer Anderson asked respondent several questions. Connelly denied that he had been drinking, denied that he had been taking any drugs, and stated that, in the past, he had been a patient in several mental hospitals. Officer Anderson again told Connelly that he was under no obligation to say anything. Connelly replied that it was "all right," and that he would talk to Officer Anderson because his conscience had been bothering him. To Officer Anderson, respondent appeared to understand fully the nature of his acts.

Shortly thereafter, Homicide Detective Stephen Antuna arrived. Respondent was again advised of his rights, and Detective Antuna asked him "what he had on his mind." Respondent answered that he had come all the way from Boston to confess to the murder of Mary Ann Junta, a young girl whom he had killed in Denver sometime during November 1982. Respondent was taken to police headquarters, and a search of police records revealed that the body of an unidentified female had been found in April 1983. Respondent openly detailed his story to Detective Antuna and Sergeant Thomas Haney, and readily agreed to take the officers to the scene of the killing. Under Connelly's sole direction, the two officers and respondent proceeded in a police vehicle to the location of the crime. Respondent pointed out the exact location of the murder. Throughout this episode, Detective Antuna perceived no indication whatsoever that respondent was suffering from any kind of mental illness.

Respondent was held overnight. During an interview with the public defender's office the following morning, he became visibly disoriented. He began giving confused answers to questions, and for the first time, stated that "voices" had told him to come to Denver and that he had followed the directions of these voices in confessing. Respondent was sent to a state hospital for evaluation. He was initially found incompetent to assist in his own defense. By March 1984, however, the doctors evaluating respondent determined that he was competent to proceed to trial.

At a preliminary hearing, respondent moved to suppress all of his statements. Doctor Jeffrey Metzner, a psychiatrist employed by the state hospital, testified that respondent was suffering from chronic schizophrenia and was in a psychotic state at least as of August 17, 1983, the day before he confessed. Metzner's interviews with respondent revealed that respondent was following the "voice of God." This voice instructed respondent to withdraw money from the bank, to buy an airplane ticket, and to fly from Boston to Denver. When respondent arrived from Boston, God's voice became stronger and told respondent either to confess to the killing or to commit suicide. Reluctantly following the command of the voices, respondent approached Officer Anderson and confessed.

Dr. Metzner testified that, in his expert opinion, respondent was experiencing "command hallucinations." This condition interfered with respondent's "volitional abilities; that is, his ability to make free and rational choices." Dr. Metzner further testified that Connelly's illness did not significantly impair his cognitive abilities. Thus, respondent understood the rights he had when Officer Anderson and Detective Antuna advised him that he need not speak. . . .

On the basis of this evidence the Colorado trial court decided that respondent's statements must be suppressed because they were "involuntary." Relying on our decisions in Townsend v. Sain, 372 US 293, 83 S Ct 745, 9 L Ed 2d 770 (1963), and Culombe v. Connecticut, 367 US 568, 81 S Ct 1860, 6 L Ed 2d 1037 (1961), the court ruled that a confession is admissible only if it is a product of the defendant's rational intellect and "free will." Although the court found that the police had done nothing wrong or coercive in securing respondent's confession, Connelly's illness destroyed his volition and compelled him to confess. The trial court also found that Connelly's mental state vitiated his attempted waiver of the right to counsel and the privilege against compulsory self-incrimination. Accordingly, respondent's initial statements and his custodial confession were suppressed.

The Colorado Supreme Court affirmed. 702 P2d 722 (1985). . . .

The Due Process Clause of the Fourteenth Amendment provides that no State shall "deprive any person of life, liberty, or property, without due process of law." Just last Term, in Miller v. Fenton, 474 US 104, 106 S Ct 445, 88 L Ed 2d 405 (1985), we held that by virtue of the Due Process clause "certain interrogation techniques, either in isolation or as applied to the unique characteristics of a particular suspect, are so offensive to a civilized system of justice that they must be condemned." . . .

Indeed, coercive government misconduct was the catalyst for this Court's seminal confession case, Brown v. Mississippi, 297 US 278, 56 S Ct 461, 80 L Ed 682 (1936). In that case, police officers extracted confessions from the accused through brutal torture. The Court had little difficulty concluding that even though the Fifth Amendment did not at that time apply to the States, the actions of the police were "revolting to the sense of justice." Id., at 286. . . .

Thus the cases considered by this Court over the 50 years since Brown v. Mississippi have focused upon the crucial element of police overreaching.[1] While each confession case has turned on its own set of factors justifying the conclusion that police conduct was oppressive, all have contained a substantial element of coercive police conduct. Absent police conduct causally related to the confession, there is simply no

---

1. E.g., Mincey v. Arizona, 437 US 385, 98 S Ct 2408, 57 L Ed 2d 290 (1978) (defendant subjected to four-hour interrogation while incapacitated and sedated in intensive-care unit); Greenwald v. Wisconsin, 390 US 519, 88 S Ct 1152, 20 L Ed 2d 77 (1968) (defendant, on medication, interrogated for over eighteen hours without food or sleep); Beecher v. Alabama, 389 US 35, 88 S Ct 189, 19 L Ed 2d 35 (1967) (police officers held gun to the head of wounded confessant to extract confession); Davis v. North Carolina, 384 US 737, 86 S Ct 1761, 16 L Ed 2d 895 (1966) (sixteen days of incommunicado interrogation in closed cell without windows, limited food, and coercive tactics); Reck v. Pate, 367 US 433, 81 S Ct 1541, 6 L Ed 2d 948 (1961) (defendant held for four days with inadequate food and medical attention until confession obtained); Culombe v. Connecticut, 367 US 568, 81 S Ct 1860, 6 L Ed 2d 1037 (1961) (defendant held for five days of repeated questioning during which police employed coercive tactics); Payne v. Arkansas, 356 US 560, 78 S Ct 844, 2 L Ed 2d 975 (1958) (defendant held incommunicado for three days with little food; confession obtained when officers informed defendant that Chief of Police was preparing to admit lynch mob into jail); Ashcraft v. Tennessee, 322 US 143, 64 S Ct 921, 88 L Ed 1192 (1944) (defendant questioned by relays of officers for thirty-six hours without an opportunity for sleep).

basis for concluding that any state actor has deprived a criminal defendant of due process of law. . . .

Our "involuntary confession" jurisprudence is entirely consistent with the settled law requiring some sort of "state action" to support a claim of violation of the Due Process Clause of the Fourteenth Amendment. The Colorado trial court, of course, found that the police committed no wrongful acts, and that finding has been neither challenged by the respondent nor disturbed by the Supreme Court of Colorado. The latter court, however, concluded that sufficient state action was present by virtue of the admission of the confession into evidence in a court of the State.

The difficulty with the approach of the Supreme Court of Colorado is that it fails to recognize the essential link between coercive activity of the State, on the one hand, and a resulting confession by a defendant, on the other. The flaw in respondent's constitutional argument is that it would expand our previous line of "voluntariness" cases into a far-ranging requirement that courts must divine a defendant's motivation for speaking or acting as he did even though there be no claim that governmental conduct coerced his decision.

* * *

Moreover, suppressing respondent's statements would serve absolutely no purpose in enforcing constitutional guarantees. The purpose of excluding evidence seized in violation of the Constitution is to substantially deter future violations of the Constitution. See United States v. Leon, 468 US 897, 906-913, 104 S Ct 3405, 82 L Ed 2d 677 (1984). Only if we were to establish a brand new constitution right—the right of a criminal defendant to confess to his crime only when totally rational and properly motivated—could respondent's present claim be sustained.

* * *

A statement rendered by one in the condition of respondent might be proved to be quite unreliable, but this is a matter to be governed by the evidentiary laws of the forum, and not by the Due Process Clause of the Fourteenth Amendment.

We hold that coercive police activity is a necessary predicate to the finding that a confession is not "voluntary" within the meaning of the Due Process Clause of the Fourteenth Amendment. We also conclude that the taking of respondent's statements, and their admission into evidence, constitute no violation of that Clause.

* * *

We also think that the Supreme Court of Colorado was mistaken in its analysis of the question of whether respondent had waived his Miranda rights in this case.[3] Of course, a waiver must at a minimum be "voluntary" to be effective against an accused. The Supreme Court of Colorado in addressing this question relied on the testimony of the court-appointed psychiatrist to the effect that respondent was not capable of making a "free decision with respect to his constitutional right of silence . . . and his constitutional right to confer with a lawyer before talking to the police."

We think that the Supreme Court of Colorado erred in importing into this area of constitutional law notions of "free will" that have no place there. There is obviously no reason to require more in the way of a "voluntariness" inquiry in the Miranda waiver context than in the Fourteenth Amendment confession context. The sole concern of the Fifth Amendment, on which Miranda was based, is governmental coercion. . . . The voluntariness of a waiver of this privilege has always depended on the absence of police overreaching, not on "free choice" in any broader sense of the word. . . .

Respondent urges this Court to adopt his "free will" rationale, and to find an attempted waiver invalid whenever the defendant feels compelled to waive his rights by reason of any compulsion, even if the compulsion does not flow from the police. But such a treatment of the waiver issue would "cut this Court's holding in [Miranda] completely loose from its own explicitly stated rationale." Miranda protects defendants against

---

3. Petitioner conceded at oral argument that when Officer Anderson handcuffed respondent, the custody requirement of Miranda was satisfied. For purposes of our decision we accept that concession, and we similarly assume that the police officers "interrogated" respondent within the meaning of Miranda.

government coercion leading them to surrender rights protected by the Fifth Amendment; it goes no further than that. Respondent's perception of coercion flowing from the "voice of God," however important or significant such a perception may be in other disciplines, is a matter to which the United States Constitution does not speak.

The judgment of the Supreme Court of Colorado is accordingly reversed, and the cause remanded for further proceedings not inconsistent with this opinion.

* * *

Justice **Brennan,** with whom Justice **Marshall** joins, dissenting.

* * *

The respondent's seriously impaired mental condition is clear on the record of this case. At the time of his confession, Mr. Connelly suffered from a "longstanding severe mental disorder," diagnosed as chronic paranoid schizophrenia. He had been hospitalized for psychiatric reasons five times prior to his confession; his longest hospitalization lasted for seven months. Mr. Connelly heard imaginary voices and saw nonexistent objects. He believed that his father was God, and that he was a reincarnation of Jesus.

* * *

Today's decision restricts the application of the term "involuntary" to those confessions obtained by police coercion. Confessions by mentally ill individuals or by persons coerced by parties other than police officers are now considered "voluntary." The Court's failure to recognize all forms of involuntariness or coercion as antithetical to due process reflects a refusal to acknowledge free will as a value of constitutional consequence. But due process derives much of its meaning from a conception of fundamental fairness that emphasizes the right to make vital choices voluntarily: "The Fourteenth Amendment secures against state invasion . . . the right of a person to remain silent unless he chooses to speak in the unfettered exercise of his own will. . . ." Malloy v. Hogan, 378 US 1, 8, 84 S Ct 1489, 12 L Ed 2d 653 (1964). This right requires vigilant protection if we are to safeguard the values of private conscience and human dignity.

Since the Court redefines voluntary confessions to include confessions by mentally ill individuals, the reliability of these confessions becomes a central concern. A concern for reliability is inherent in our criminal justice system, which relies upon accusatorial rather than inquisitorial practices. While an inquisitorial system prefers obtaining confessions from criminal defendants, an accusatorial system must place its faith in determinations of "guilt by evidence independently and freely secured."

* * *

Because the admission of a confession so strongly tips the balance against the defendant in the adversarial process, we must be especially careful about a confession's reliability.

* * *

Notes and Questions

1. Did the Colorado Supreme Court disagree that some sort of "state action" is required before the Fourteenth Amendment's due-process clause becomes operative? Where did the Colorado court find "state action" when it ruled that Connelly's statements should have been excluded from evidence because they were "involuntary"?

2. Chief Justice Rehnquist's majority opinion and Justice Brennan's dissent identify different policy objectives that are promoted by the suppression of involuntary statements. Do those differences help explain the divergent conclusions reached in their opinions?

3. If a police officer had threatened to kill Connelly if he did not confess, it would be clear that the confession would not be the product of Connelly's free will and that it should be suppressed as involuntary. What would result if the murder victim's father put a gun to Connelly's head and produced a confession by threatening to kill him? Would the confession be a product of Connelly's "free will"? Should it be considered "involuntary" in the psychological meaning of that term? Should it be considered "involuntary" in the legal sense of that term?

4. Does the Court analyze the voluntariness of Connelly's waiver of *Miranda* any differently than it analyzes the voluntariness of his confession? Should it?

The Public Safety Exception

We have established that statements secured in violation of *Miranda* can be used to impeach the credibility of a defendant whose trial testimony is inconsistent with those earlier state-

ments. However, we were careful to distinguish between using the unlawful confession for impeachment purposes and using it as part of the prosecution's "case-in-chief" to prove guilt, which generally is forbidden. Are there any circumstances under which an accused's incriminating statements should be admissible to prove guilt, even though the police violated his or her *Miranda* rights during custodial interrogation? In the following case, *New York v. Quarles*, a *Miranda* violation is conceded. The Court considers—and recognizes—a "public safety exception" to the normal rule that a confession produced in violation of *Miranda* cannot be used as evidence of guilt.

New York v. Quarles, **467 U.S. 649, 104 S. Ct. 2626, 81 L. Ed. 2d 550 (1984)**

Justice Rehnquist delivered the opinion of the Court.

* * *

On September 11, 1980, at approximately 12:30 am, Officer Frank Kraft and Officer Sal Scarring were on road patrol in Queens, New York, when a young woman approached their car. She told them that she had just been raped by a black male, approximately six feet tall, who was wearing a black jacket with the name "Big Ben" printed in yellow letters on the back. She told the officers that the man had just entered an A & P supermarket located nearby and that the man was carrying a gun.

The officers drove the woman to the supermarket, and Officer Kraft entered the store while Officer Scarring radioed for assistance. Officer Kraft quickly spotted respondent, who matched the description given by the woman, approaching a checkout counter. Apparently upon seeing the officer, respondent turned and ran toward the rear of the store, and Officer Kraft pursued him with a drawn gun. When respondent turned the corner at the end of an aisle, Officer Kraft lost sight of him for several seconds, and upon

regaining sight of respondent, ordered him to stop and put his hands over his head.

Although more than three other officers had arrived on the scene by that time, Officer Kraft was the first to reach respondent. He frisked him and discovered that he was wearing a shoulder holster which was then empty. After handcuffing him, Officer Kraft asked him where the gun was. Respondent nodded in the direction of some empty cartons and responded, "the gun is over there." Officer Kraft thereafter retrieved a loaded .38 caliber revolver from one of the cartons, formally placed respondent under arrest, and read him his Miranda rights from a printed card. Respondent indicated that he would be willing to answer questions without an attorney present. Officer Kraft then asked respondent if he owned the gun and where he had purchased it. Respondent answered that he did own it and that he had purchased it in Miami, Florida.

In the subsequent prosecution of respondent for criminal possession of a weapon, the judge excluded the statement, "the gun is over there," and the gun because the officer had not given respondent the warnings required by our decision in Miranda v. Arizona, before asking him where the gun was located. The judge excluded the other statements about respondent's ownership of the gun and the place of purchase, as evidence tainted by the prior Miranda violation. The Appellate Division of the Supreme Court of New York affirmed without opinion. 447 NYS2d 84 (1981).

The Court of Appeals granted leave to appeal and affirmed by a 4-3 vote. 58 NY2d 664, 444 NE2d 984 (1982).

* * *

The New York Court of Appeals was undoubtedly correct in deciding that the facts of this case come within the ambit of the Miranda decision as we have subsequently interpreted it. We agree that respondent was in police custody. Here Quarles was surrounded by at least four police officers and was handcuffed when the questioning at issue took place. As the New York Court of Appeals observed, there was nothing to suggest that any of the officers were any longer concerned for their own physical safety. The New York Court of Appeals' majority declined to express an opinion as to whether there might be an exception to the Miranda rule if the police had been acting to protect the public, because the lower courts in New York had made no factual determination that the police had acted with that motive.

We hold that on these facts there is a "public safety" exception to the requirement that Miranda warnings be given before a suspect's answers may be admitted into evidence, and that the availability of that exception does not depend upon the motivation of the individual officers involved. In a kaleidoscopic situation such as the one confronting these officers, where spontaneity rather than adherence to a police manual is necessarily the order of the day, the application of the exception which we recognize today should not be made to depend on post hoc findings at a suppression hearing concerning the subjective motivation of the arresting officer. Undoubtedly most police officers, if placed in Officer Kraft's position, would act out of a host of different, instinctive, and largely unverifiable motives—their own safety, the safety of others, and perhaps as well the desire to obtain incriminating evidence from the suspect.

Whatever the motivation of individual officers in such a situation, we do not believe that the doctrinal underpinnings of Miranda require that it be applied in all its rigor to a situation in which police officers ask questions reasonably prompted by a concern for the public safety. The Miranda decision was based in large part on this Court's view that the warnings which it required police to give to suspects in custody would reduce the likelihood that the suspects would fall victim to constitutionally impermissible practices of police interrogation in the presumptively coercive environment of the station house. The dissenters warned that the requirement of Miranda warnings would have the effect of decreasing the number of suspects who respond to police questioning. The Miranda majority, however, apparently felt that whatever the cost to society in terms of fewer convictions of guilty suspects, that cost would simply have to be borne in the interest of enlarged protection for the Fifth Amendment privilege.

The police in this case, in the very act of apprehending a suspect, were confronted with the immediate necessity of ascertaining the whereabouts of a gun which they had every reason to believe the suspect had just removed from his empty holster and discarded in the supermarket. So long as the gun was concealed somewhere in the supermarket, with its actual whereabouts unknown, it obviously posed more than one danger to the public safety: an accomplice might make use of it, a customer or employee might later come upon it.

In such a situation, if the police are required to recite the familiar Miranda warnings before asking the whereabouts of the gun, suspects in Quarles' position might well be deterred from responding. Procedural safeguards which deter a suspect from responding were deemed acceptable in Miranda in order to protect the Fifth Amendment privilege; when the primary social cost of those added protections is the possibility of fewer convictions, the Miranda majority was willing to bear that cost. Here, had Miranda warnings deterred Quarles from responding to Officer Kraft's question about the whereabouts of the gun, the cost would have been something more than merely the failure to obtain evidence useful in convicting Quarles. Officer Kraft needed an answer to his question not simply to make his case against Quarles but to insure that further danger to the public did not result from the concealment of the gun in a public area.

We conclude that the need for answers to questions in a situation posing a threat to the public safety outweighs the need for the prophylactic rule protecting the Fifth Amendment's privilege against self-incrimination. We decline to place officers such as Officer Kraft in the untenable position of having to consider, often in a matter of seconds, whether it best serves society for them to ask the necessary questions without the Miranda warnings and render whatever probative evidence they uncover inadmissible, or for them to give the warnings in order to preserve the admissibility of evidence they might uncover but possibly damage or destroy their ability to obtain that evidence and neutralize the volatile situation confronting them.[7]

In recognizing a narrow exception to the Miranda rule in this case, we acknowledge that to some degree we lessen the desirable clarity of that rule. As we have in other contexts, we recognize here the importance of a workable rule "to guide police officers, who have only limited time and expertise to reflect on and balance the social and individual interests involved in the specific circumstances they confront." But as we have pointed out, we believe that the exception which we recognize today lessens the necessity of that on-the-scene balancing process. The exception will not be difficult for police officers to apply because in each case it will be circumscribed by the exigency which justifies it. We think police officers can and will distinguish almost instinctively between questions necessary to secure their own safety or the safety of

the public and questions designed solely to elicit testimonial evidence from a suspect.

The facts of this case clearly demonstrate that distinction and an officer's ability to recognize it. Officer Kraft asked only the question necessary to locate the missing gun before advising respondent of his rights. It was only after securing the loaded revolver and giving the warnings that he continued with investigatory questions about the ownership and place of purchase of the gun. The exception which we recognize today, far from complicating the thought processes and the on-the-scene judgments of police officers, will simply free them to follow their legitimate instincts when confronting situations presenting a danger to the public safety.

We hold that the Court of Appeals in this case erred in excluding the statement, "the gun is over there," and the gun because of the officer's failure to read respondent his Miranda rights before attempting to locate the weapon. Accordingly we hold that it also erred in excluding the subsequent statements as illegal fruits of a Miranda violation.

Justice **Marshall,** with whom Justice **Brennan** and Justice **Stevens** join, dissenting.

* * *

I

The majority's entire analysis rests on the factual assumption that the public was at risk during Quarles' interrogation. This assumption is completely in conflict with the facts as found by New York's highest court. Before the interrogation began, Quarles had been "reduced to a condition of physical powerlessness." Contrary to the majority's speculations, Quarles was not believed to have, nor did he in fact have, an accomplice to come to his rescue. When the questioning began, the arresting officers were sufficiently confident of their safety to put away their guns. As Officer Kraft acknowledged at the suppression hearing, "the situation was under control." Based on Officer Kraft's own testimony, the New York Court of Appeals found: "Nothing suggests that any of the officers was by that time concerned for his own physical safety." The Court of Appeals also determined that there was no evidence that the interrogation was prompted

---

7. The dissent argues that a public safety exception to Miranda is unnecessary because in every case an officer can simply ask the necessary questions to protect himself or the public, and then the prosecution can decline to introduce any incriminating responses at a subsequent trial. But absent actual coercion by the officer, there is no constitutional imperative requiring the exclusion of the evidence that results from police inquiry of this kind; and we do not believe that the doctrinal underpinnings of Miranda require us to exclude the evidence, thus penalizing officers for asking the very questions which are the most crucial to their efforts to protect themselves and the public.

by the arresting officers' concern for the public's safety.

The majority attempts to slip away from these unambiguous findings of New York's highest court by proposing that danger be measured by objective facts rather than the subjective intentions of arresting officers. Though clever, this ploy was anticipated by the New York Court of Appeals: "[T]here is no evidence in the record before us that there were exigent circumstances posing a risk to the public safety. . . ."

The New York court's conclusion that neither Quarles nor his missing gun posed a threat to the public's safety is amply supported by the evidence presented at the suppression hearing. Again contrary to the majority's intimations, no customers or employees were wandering about the store in danger of coming across Quarles' discarded weapon. Although the supermarket was open to the public, Quarles' arrest took place during the middle of the night when the store was apparently deserted except for the clerks at the checkout counter. The police could easily have cordoned off the store and searched for the missing gun. Had they done so, they would have found the gun forthwith. In this case, there was convincing, indeed almost overwhelming, evidence to support the New York court's conclusion that Quarles' hidden weapon did not pose a risk either to the arresting officers or to the public. The majority ignores this evidence and sets aside the factual findings of the New York Court of Appeals. More cynical observers might well conclude that a state court's findings of fact "deserve a 'high measure of deference,'" only when deference works against the interests of a criminal defendant.

II

The majority's treatment of the legal issues presented in this case is no less troubling than its abuse of the facts. . . .

Before today's opinion, the procedures established in Miranda v. Arizona had "the virtue of informing police and prosecutors with specificity as to what they may do in conducting custodial interrogation, and of informing courts under what circumstances statements obtained during such interrogations are not admissible." In a chimerical quest for public safety, the majority has

abandoned the rule that brought eighteen years of doctrinal tranquility to the field of custodial interrogations. As the majority candidly concedes, a public-safety exception destroys forever the clarity of Miranda for both law enforcement officers and members of the judiciary. The Court's candor cannot mask what a serious loss the administration of justice has incurred.

This case is illustrative of the chaos the "public-safety" exception will unleash. . . .

If after plenary review two appellate courts so fundamentally differ over the threat to public safety presented by the simple and uncontested facts of this case, one must seriously question how law enforcement officers will respond to the majority's new rule in the confusion and haste of the real world. Not only will police officers have to decide whether the objective facts of an arrest justify an unconsented custodial interrogation; they will also have to remember to interrupt the interrogation and read the suspect his Miranda warnings once the focus of the inquiry shifts from protecting the public's safety to ascertaining the suspect's guilt. Disagreements of the scope of the "public-safety" exception and mistakes in its application are inevitable.[4]

* * *

III

Though unfortunate, the difficulty of administering the "public-safety" exception is not the most profound flaw in the majority's decision. The majority has lost sight of the fact that Miranda v. Arizona and our earlier custodial-interrogation cases all implemented a constitutional privilege against self-incrimination. The rules established in these cases were designed to protect criminal defendants against prosecu-

---

4. One of the peculiarities of the majority's decision is its suggestion that police officers can "distinguish almost instinctively" questions tied to public safety and questions designed to elicit testimonial evidence. Obviously, these distinctions are extraordinarily difficult to draw. In many cases—like this one—custodial questioning may serve both purposes. It is therefore wishful thinking for the majority to suggest that the intuitions of police officers will render its decision self-executing.

tions based on coerced self-incriminating statements. The majority today turns its back on these constitutional considerations, and invites the government to prosecute through the use of what necessarily are coerced statements.

The majority's error stems from a serious misunderstanding of Miranda v. Arizona and of the Fifth Amendment upon which that decision was based. The majority implies that Miranda consisted of no more than a judicial balancing act in which the benefits of "enlarged protection for the Fifth Amendment privilege" were weighed against "the cost to society in terms of fewer convictions of guilty suspects." Supposedly because the scales tipped in favor of the privilege against self-incrimination, the Miranda Court erected a prophylactic barrier around statements made during custodial interrogations. The majority now proposes to return to the scales of social utility to calculate whether Miranda's prophylactic rule remains cost-effective when threats to public's safety are added to the balance.

* * *

Whether society would be better off if the police warned suspects of their rights before beginning an interrogation or whether the advantages of giving such warnings would outweigh their costs did not inform the Miranda decision. On the contrary, the Miranda Court was concerned with the proscriptions of the Fifth Amendment, and, in particular, whether the Self-Incrimination Clause permits the government to prosecute individuals based on statements made in the course of custodial interrogations.

* * *

In fashioning its "public-safety" exception to Miranda, the majority makes no attempt to deal with the constitutional presumption established by that case. The majority does not argue that police questioning about issues of public safety is any less coercive than custodial interrogations into other matters. The majority's only contention is that police officers could more easily protect the public if Miranda did not apply to custodial interrogations concerning the public's safety. But Miranda was not a decision about public safety; it was a decision about coerced confessions.

The majority's ratio decidendi is that interrogating suspects about matters of public safety *will* be coercive. In its cost-benefit analysis, the Court's strongest argument in favor of a public-safety exception to Miranda is that the police would be better able to protect the public's safety if they were not always required to give suspects their Miranda warnings. The crux of this argument is that, by deliberately withholding Miranda warnings, the police can get information out of suspects who would refuse to respond to police questioning were they advised of their constitutional rights. The "public-safety" exception is efficacious precisely because it permits police officers to coerce criminal defendants into making involuntary statements.

* * *

The irony of the majority's decision is that the public's safety can be perfectly well protected without abridging the Fifth Amendment. If a bomb is about to explode or the public is otherwise imminently imperiled, the police are free to interrogate suspects without advising them of their constitutional rights. Such unconsented questioning may take place not only when police officers act on instinct but also when higher faculties lead them to believe that advising a suspect of his constitutional rights might decrease the likelihood that the suspect would reveal lifesaving information. If trickery is necessary to protect the public, then the police may trick a suspect into confessing. While the Fourteenth Amendment sets limits on such behavior, nothing in the Fifth Amendment or our decision in Miranda v. Arizona proscribes this sort of emergency questioning. All the Fifth Amendment forbids is the introduction of coerced statements at trial.

To a limited degree, the majority is correct that there is a cost associated with the Fifth Amendment's ban on introducing coerced self-incriminating statements at trial. Without a "public-safety" exception, there would be occasions when a defendant incriminated himself by revealing a threat to the public, and the State was unable to prosecute because the defendant retracted his statement after consulting with counsel and the police cannot find independent proof of guilt. Such occasions would not, however, be common. The prosecution does not always lose the use of incriminating information revealed in these situations. After consulting with counsel, a suspect may well volunteer to repeat his statement in hopes of gaining a favorable plea bargain or more lenient sentence. The

majority thus overstates its case when it suggests that a police officer must necessarily choose between public safety and admissibility.

* * *

Notes and Questions

1. Does the public safety exception apply to coerced confessions or just to cases involving confessions obtained in violation of *Miranda*? (See footnote 7 of the majority opinion.) Are you comfortable with the distinction between a "coerced" confession and one produced by a *Miranda* violation? Is Justice Marshall?

2. What if, before administering Quarles his *Miranda* rights, Officer Kraft had asked Quarles where he had purchased the gun? Would Quarles's response that he had bought the gun in Miami be admissible under the public safety exception? What if the officer, after retrieving the gun, had showed it to Quarles and had asked, "Is this your gun?" Would Quarles's affirmative reply be admissible if this exchange occurred prior to his receiving *Miranda* warnings? How confident are you that "police officers can and will distinguish almost instinctively between questions necessary to secure their own safety or the safety of the public and questions designed solely to elicit testimonial evidence from a suspect"? Into which category of questioning would the inquiry "Is this your gun?" fall?

3. Under the benefit-cost analysis used by the *Quarles* majority, why not allow the police to ask questions motivated by a concern for their own or the public safety without administering *Miranda* warnings—to reduce the risk that a suspect will withhold information—but then prohibit the use of the evidence in court, after the safety-related crisis has disappeared? Would this practice allow the police to realize the benefits of dispensing with *Miranda* without imposing a cost on suspects' rights? What drawbacks, if any, would there be to such an approach?

4. When is a question "reasonably prompted by a concern for the public safety"? What if

Quarles were suspected of having discarded, not a gun, but a knife? What if he had not been accused of rape but had been suspected of being a heroin user and if it was feared that he might have discarded a syringe and needle? What if his alleged weapon had been a metal pipe or a set of brass knuckles? Would police questioning to discover the whereabouts of those different items without complying with *Miranda* have been permissible under the public safety exception? Would it matter if Quarles had been cornered in a deserted store at midnight or in one teeming with business at noon? Do the facts in *Quarles* present a convincing case for applying the public safety exception to *Miranda*?

5. Legal Research Note. How could you find additional cases involving the public safety exception to *Miranda*? You would have many options. You could check secondary authorities such as *American Law Reports* (*A.L.R.*) annotations and law review articles. *Words and Phrases* probably would provide definitions of *public safety* in this context, with accompanying case citations. A treatise or case book might be of assistance, or a legal encyclopedia. You could also *Shepardize New York v. Quarles*; later cases citing *Quarles* probably relate in some way to the public safety exception.

However, we now take the opportunity to introduce the West Publishing Company's "key number system" and how this system is used to help find judicial decisions. We describe the key number system at greater length in Appendix B. It is an extremely powerful tool for legal research because it includes and connects all decisions published in West's comprehensive case reporters. The West case reporters include the regional reporters for state court cases (A.2d, N.E.2d, N.W.2d, P.2d, S.E.2d, S.W.2d, So. 2d), the federal reporters for U.S. District Court (F. Supp.) and U.S. Court of Appeals (F., F.2d, F.3d) decisions, and West's reporter for U.S. Supreme Court cases (S. Ct.).

As the editors at West read the cases published in their reporters, they identify the various principles of law discussed in majority opinions. Each principle of law is categorized under one or more logical topic heading, such as "Criminal Law," "Search and Seizure," "Homicide," "Witnesses," or one of hundreds of others. Then, the legal principle is assigned a unique "key number," which is associated with a very specific subissue of the topic. In this way, all decisions published in West case reporters that address the same issues of law are collected under the same topic and key number. Related cases share the same topic and key number no matter what court decided the case or when the case was decided.

The researcher's job, then, is to identify the topic and key number associated with the principle of law in which he or she is interested. Once the researcher accomplishes this, it is a relatively straightforward process to locate all cases that address a specific issue.

Two major strategies exist for identifying the relevant topic and key number. The first is to start with a case known to involve the legal principle that is of interest and then simply to extract the topic and key number from the case's "headnotes." We will illustrate this process in a moment. The second way is to use one of West's *Descriptive Word Indexes*, which link principles of law to specific topics and key numbers. We also demonstrate this technique.

We are interested in using the West key number system to find cases that address the public safety exception to *Miranda*. We know that *New York v. Quarles* recognized the public safety exception, so we can safely assume that the editors at West have identified the topic and key number(s) associated with this principle of law in the headnotes of the *Quarles* decision. Those headnotes are created and written by West; they are not a part of the Court's opinion, and they were not written by a judge. As the name implies, they are "notes" that appear at the "head," or start, of an opinion. The separately numbered notes summarize the principles of law discussed in a court's majority opinion. One or

more topics and key numbers are assigned to each headnote.

To illustrate this process, let us look up *New York v. Quarles* in West's *Supreme Court Reporter*. We have the citation to the case—104 S. Ct. 2626—so we can easily locate the decision at that volume (104) and beginning at that page number (2626). We reproduce the initial pages of *New York v. Quarles* as the case appears in the *Supreme Court Reporter* in Exhibit 4–1 so that you can see how the headnotes are arranged. Headnote 6 is directly associated with the public safety exception principle, as are some others. Note the topic "Criminal Law," the key symbol, and the number 412.2(3) assigned to headnote 6. We now can assume that other published cases addressing the public safety exception to *Miranda* also should be associated with "Criminal Law ⚷ 412.2(3)." We next turn to the section of the majority opinion in *Quarles* to which headnote 6 corresponds. This section is easy to locate because the West editors have inserted a bracketed 6 ([6]) into the opinion at the appropriate location. (See Exhibit 4–2.)

Now that we have a specific topic and key number associated with the public safety exception to *Miranda,* our next step is to consult West's *Case Digests*. Those digests collect and reprint headnotes from cases, with accompanying case citations. Different digests are used for different sets of case reporters. We might begin our search for other cases by using *West's Federal Practice Digest 4th*, which is the most recently published digest collecting federal cases. We first find the volume in the digest that includes "Criminal Law ⚷ 412.2(3)." That is a simple task because topics are arranged alphabetically and are printed on the books' spines and covers. We will be using volume 29 of the *Federal Practice Digest 4th*, which covers "Criminal Law ⚷ 398" through "Criminal Law ⚷ 572."

We can check the detailed outline at the beginning of the "Criminal Law" topic to identify the principle of law associated with ⚷ 412.2(3)." We see that it is described by a combination of subtopics: "Evidence—Admissions, Declarations, and Hearsay—Right to counsel, caution—Informing accused as to his rights." (See Exhibit 4–3.) Then we turn through the pages of the *Federal Practice Digest 4th* until we come to the case descriptions and citations associated with "Criminal Law ⚷ 412.2(3)." (See Exhibit 4–4.) Note, for example, the Fourth Circuit case decided in 1994, *U.S. v. Mobley*, 40 F.3d 688, certiorari denied, 115 S. Ct. 2005, 131 L. Ed. 2d 1005, which appears to include a rather extensive discussion of the public safety exception. We would discover many more federal case "squibs" or "blurbs," as these notes sometimes are called, by consulting other pages under this same topic and key number. However, you must remember that you should never rely on or directly cite what you find in a digest. You must look up the case and read it to confirm that it stands for the principles reported in the digest. Then you must *Shepardize* the case to make sure it remains good law.

The *Federal Practice Digest 4th* includes only squibs from *federal* cases. West's *Decennial Digests* and *General Digests*, on the other hand, include both state and federal cases. *Decennial Digests* come in two parts, and each part covers a five-year period. As this is being written, the most recent fully completed *Decennial Digest* is the *Tenth Decennial Digest, Part I*, which includes descriptions of cases decided between 1986 and 1991. The *Tenth Decennial Digest, Part 2*, which covers cases decided between 1991 and 1996, is still in the process of being compiled. We use volume 11 of the *Tenth Decennial Digest, Part 1* to find relevant federal and state case squibs collected under "Criminal Law ⚷ 412.2(3)." We reprint a portion of the results in Exhibit 4–5.

To find cases decided after the *Decennial Digest* was published, we must consult the *General Digests* that update the *Decennial Digest* series. We reproduce a portion of the relevant section ("Criminal Law ⚷ 412.2(3)") from volume 5 of West's *General Digest, 9th Series* (1997). (See Exhibit 4–6.)

We now briefly describe how to find the topic and key number associated with a principle of law when you do not have the good fortune of being able to start with a case on point. Recall that we located "Criminal Law ⚷ 412.2(3)" by referring to the headnotes of *New York v. Quarles*, a case that we already knew. If you have to start "from scratch," you can begin with the *Descriptive Word Index* associated with the particular case digest you are using. We will use the *Descriptive Word Index* for *West's Federal Practice Digest 4th*.

To make use of a descriptive word index, first describe the issue you are researching by listing as many words, phrases, and concepts as you can that are associated with the research issue. For example, we might list *Miranda, public safety exception, confessions, self-incrimination, criminal law, criminal procedure, interrogation*, and other words for this particular research problem. After you have made this list, look for those words, alone or in combination, in the *Descriptive Word Index*.

We were very fortunate when we performed this exercise for our issue. In the 1996 supplement to *West's Federal Practice Digest's Descriptive Word Index* (volume 98; "F–O"), we hit pay dirt when we looked under "Miranda Rule" and "Miranda Warnings." Each of these general topics lists the subtopic "Public safety exception." (See Exhibit 4–7.) "Criminal Law ⚷ 412.2(3)" is associated with those subtopics, which tells us that we will be interested in checking the *Digest* under "Criminal Law ⚷ 412.2(3)." This topic and key number, of course, are the same ones we located by starting with the headnotes and *Quarles*.

The only way you will begin to feel comfortable doing legal research is by going to the library, using the books, and practicing. We urge you to do so. Using case digests and *Descriptive Word Indexes* can be challenging at first, but you will quickly catch on to how to use them to investigate legal research issues.

Exhibit 4–1

467 U.S. 649   **NEW YORK v. QUARLES**   2626

Cite as 104 S.Ct. 2626 (1984)

S.Ct. 1076, 1083–1084, n. 15, 51 L.Ed.2d 326 (1977), where we rejected the *per se* rule and the administrative convenience that attended our former holding in *Spector Motor Service, Inc. v. O'Connor,* 340 U.S. 602, 71 S.Ct. 508, 95 L.Ed. 573 (1951). I would apply a similarly realistic approach to this case and uphold West Virginia's wholesale tax scheme.

467 U.S. 649, 81 L.Ed.2d 550

└ 649**NEW YORK**

v.

Benjamin QUARLES.

No. 82-1213.

Argued Jan. 18, 1984.

Decided June 12, 1984.

The Supreme Court, Queens County, New York, Nicholas Ferraro, J., excluded from evidence in prosecution for criminal possession of a weapon defendant's initial statement indicating whereabouts of gun and gun itself because defendant had not yet been given *Miranda* warnings at time he was asked where the gun was. Defendant's subsequent statements were also excluded as illegal fruits of a *Miranda* violation. Both the Appellate Division of the Supreme Court of New York, 85 A.D.2d 936, 447 N.Y.S.2d 84, and the New York Court of Appeals, 58 N.Y.2d 664, 458 N.Y. S.2d 520, 444 N.E.2d 984, affirmed. Certiorari was granted. The Supreme Court, Justice Rehnquist, held that defendant's initial statement indicating whereabouts of gun in supermarket where defendant was apprehended and gun itself were admissible despite officer's failure to read defendant his *Miranda* rights before attempting to locate weapon in view of existence of a "public safety" exception to requirement that *Miranda* warnings be given before a suspect's answers may be admitted into evidence and its applicability on these facts.

Reversed and remanded.

Justice O'Connor concurred in part, dissented in part, and filed an opinion.

Justice Marshall dissented and filed an opinion in which Justices Brennan and Stevens joined.

Opinion on remand, 63 N.Y.2d 923, 483 N.Y.S.2d 678, 473 N.E.2d 30.

1. Federal Courts ⚷ 503

Suppression ruling of New York Court of Appeals was a "final judgment" for purpose of extension of Supreme Court's jurisdiction over case, even though defendant had yet to be tried in state court, in view of fact that federal claim had been finally decided and later review of federal issue could not be had, whatever ultimate outcome of case, since, should New York convict defendant at trial, its claim that certain evidence was wrongfully suppressed would be moot, and should defendant be acquitted at trial, New York would be precluded from pressing its federal claim again on appeal. 28 U.S.C.A. §§ 1257, 1257(3).

2. Criminal Law ⚷ 412.2(3)

Although Fifth Amendment's strictures, unlike the Fourth's, are not removed by showing reasonableness, there are limited circumstances where judicially imposed strictures of *Miranda* are inapplicable. U.S.C.A. Const.Amends. 4, 5.

3. Criminal Law ⚷ 406(1, 3)

The Fifth Amendment itself does not prohibit all incriminating admissions; absent some officially coerced self-accusation, Fifth Amendment privilege is not violated by even the most damning admissions. U.S.C.A. Const.Amend. 5.

4. Criminal Law ⚷ 412.2(3)

Requiring *Miranda* warnings before custodial interrogation provides practical reinforcement for Fifth Amendment rights against compulsory self-incrimination. U.S.C.A. Const.Amend. 5.

5. Criminal Law ⚷ 412.2(2)

Suspect who was surrounded by at least four police officers and handcuffed when questioned was in police custody at time of questioning for purpose of determining whether case came within ambit of *Miranda*, even though he was not yet arrested.

continues

Exhibit 4–1 continued

6. Criminal Law ☜ 412.2(3)

A "public safety" exception exists to requirement that *Miranda* warnings be given before a suspect's answers may be admitted into evidence, and availability of such exception does not depend upon motivation of individual officers involved.

7. Criminal Law ☜ 412.2(3)

Doctrinal underpinnings of *Miranda* do not require that it be applied in all its rigor to a situation in which police officers ask questions reasonably prompted by a concern for the public safety.

8. Criminal Law ☜ 412.2(3)

Where suspect, when detained and frisked by police officer in supermarket, was discovered to be wearing an empty shoulder holster, thus confronting officer, who had been informed suspect was carrying a gun, with immediate necessity of ascertaining whereabouts of gun which he had every reason to believe suspect had just removed from his holster and discarded in supermarket, where an accomplice might make use of it or a customer or employee come upon it, question as to whereabouts of gun and suspect's incriminating response fell within "public safety" exception to requirement that *Miranda* warnings be given before a suspect's answers may be admitted into evidence, since officer needed answer to question not simply to make case against suspect but to insure that danger to public did not result from concealment of gun in public area.

9. Criminal Law ☜ 412.2(3)

Absent actual coercion by police officer in acting to protect himself or public by questioning a suspect before *Miranda* warnings have been given, there is no constitutional imperative requiring exclusion of evidence that results from inquiry of this kind; nei-ther do doctrinal underpinnings of *Miranda* require that such evidence be excluded, thus penalizing officers for asking the very questions which are the most crucial to their efforts to protect themselves and the public.

10. Criminal Law ☜ 412.2(3)

In view of fact that police officer's question to suspect with respect to location of gun that officer had been told suspect was carrying fell within "public safety" exception to requirement that *Miranda* warnings be given before a suspect's answers may be admitted into evidence, suspect's answer, "the gun is over there," and the gun itself were admissible in prosecution for criminal possession of a weapon despite officer's failure to read suspect his *Miranda* rights before attempting to locate weapon, as were statements by suspect subsequent to *Miranda* warnings.

Syllabus*

Respondent was charged in a New York state court with criminal possession of a weapon. The record showed that a woman approached two police officers who were on road patrol, told them that she had just been raped, described her assailant, and told them that the man had just entered a nearby supermarket and was carrying a gun. While one of the officers radioed for assistance, the other (Officer Kraft) entered the store and spotted respondent, who matched the description given by the woman. Respondent ran toward the rear of the store, and Officer Kraft pursued him with a drawn gun but lost sight of him for several seconds. Upon regaining sight of respondent, Officer Kraft ordered him to stop and put his hands over his head; frisked him and discovered that he was wearing an empty shoulder holster; and. . . .

---

*The syllabus constitutes no part of the opinion of the Court but has been prepared by the Reporter of Decisions for the convenience of the reader. See *United States v. Detroit Lumber Co.*, 200 U.S. 321, 337, 26 S.Ct. 282, 287, 50 L.Ed. 499.

Source: Reprinted with permission from *West's Supreme Court Reporter*, Vol. 104, pp. 2627–2628 © 1985, West Group.

Exhibit 4–2

467 U.S. 656   NEW YORK v. QUARLES   2631

Cite as 104 S.Ct. 2626 (1984)

compelled by police conduct which overcame his will to resist. See *Beckwith v. United States*, 425 U.S. 341, 347–348, 96 S.Ct. 1612, 1616–1617, 48 L.Ed.2d 1 (1976); *Davis v. North Carolina*, 384 U.S. 737, 738, 86 S.Ct. 1761, 1763, 16 L.Ed.2d 895 (1966). Thus the only issue before us is whether ⊥ 655 Officer Kraft was justified in failing to make available to respondent the procedural safeguards associated with the privilege against compulsory self-incrimination since *Miranda*.[5]

[5] The New York Court of Appeals was undoubtedly correct in deciding that the facts of this case come within the ambit of the *Miranda* decision as we have subsequently interpreted it. We agree that respondent was in police custody because we have noted that "the ultimate inquiry is simply whether there is a 'formal arrest or restraint on freedom of movement' of the degree associated with a formal arrest," *California v. Beheler*, 463 U.S. 1121, 1125, 103 S.Ct. 3517, 3519, 77 L.Ed.2d 1275 (1983) (*per curiam*), quoting *Oregon v. Mathiason*, 429 U.S. 492, 495, 97 S.Ct. 711, 714, 50 L.Ed.2d 714 (1977) (*per curiam*). Here Quarles was surrounded by at least four police officers and was handcuffed when the questioning at issue took place. As the New York Court of Appeals observed, there was nothing to suggest that any of the officers were any longer concerned for their own physical safety. 58 N.Y.2d at 666, 458 N.Y.S.2d, at 521, 444 N.E.2d

at 985. The New York Court of Appeals' majority declined to express an opinion as to whether there might be an exception to the *Miranda* rule if the police had been acting to protect the public, because the lower courts in New York had made no factual determination that the police had acted with that motive. *Ibid.*

[6] We hold that on these facts there is a "public safety" exception to the requirement that *Miranda* warnings be given before a suspect's answers may be admitted into evidence, ⊥ 656 and that the availability of that exception does not depend upon the motivation of the individual officers involved. In a kaleidoscopic situation such as the one confronting these officers, where spontaneity rather than adherence to a police manual is necessarily the order of the day, the application of the exception which we recognize today should not be made to depend on *post hoc* findings at a suppression hearing concerning the subjective motivation of the arresting officer.[6] Undoubtedly most police officers, if placed in Officer Kraft's position, would act out of a host of different, instinctive, and largely unverifiable motives—their own safety, the safety of others, and perhaps as well the desire to obtain incriminating evidence from the suspect.

[7] Whatever the motivation of individual officers in such a situation we do not believe that the doctrinal underpinnings of

---

5. The dissent curiously takes us to task for "endors[ing] the introduction of coerced self-incriminating statements in criminal prosecutions" *post*, at 2642, and for "sanction[ing] *sub silentio* criminal prosecutions based on compelled self-incriminating statements." *Id.*, at 2648. Of course our decision today does nothing of the kind. As the *Miranda* Court itself recognized, the failure to provide *Miranda* warnings in and of itself does not render a confession involuntary, *Miranda v. Arizona*, 384 U.S., at 457, 86 S.Ct., at 1618, and respondent is certainly free on remand to argue that his statement was coerced under traditional due process standards. Today we merely reject the only argument that respondent has raised to support the exclusion of his statement, that the statement must be *presumed* compelled because of Officer Kraft's failure to read him his *Miranda* warnings.

6. Similar approaches have been rejected in other contexts. See *Rhode Island v. Innis, supra*, 446 U.S., at 301, 100 S.Ct., at 1689 (officer's subjective intent to incriminate not determinative of whether "interrogation" occurred); *United States v. Mendenhall*, 446 U.S. 544, 554, and n. 6,100 S.Ct. 1870, 1877, and n. 6, 64 L.Ed.2d 497 (1980) (opinion of Stewart, J.) (officer's subjective intent to detain not determinative of whether a "seizure" occurred within the meaning of the Fourth Amendment); *United States v. Robinson*, 414 U.S. 218, 236, and n. 7, 94 S.Ct. 467, 477, and n. 7, 38 L.Ed.2d 427 (1973) (officer's subjective fear not determinative of necessity for "search incident to arrest" exception to the Fourth Amendment warrant requirement).

Source: Reprinted with permission from *West's Supreme Court Reporter*, Vol. 104, p. 2631 © 1985, West Group.

Exhibit 4–3

CRIMINAL LAW

X. EVIDENCE.—Continued.

(G) ADMISSIONS, DECLARATIONS, AND HEARSAY.—Continued.

    412.1. —— Voluntary character of statement.
        (1). In general.
        (2). Statements while in custody; persons to whom made.
        (3). Illegality of detention.
        (4). Interrogation and investigatory questioning.
    412.2. —— Right to counsel; caution.
        (1). In general.
        (2). Accusatory stage of proceedings.
        (3). Informing accused as to his rights.
        (4). Absence or denial of counsel.
        (5). Failure to request counsel; waiver.
    413. —— Self-serving declarations.
        (1). Admissibility in general.
        (2). Explaining, contradicting, or accompanying matters in evidence.
    414. —— Proof and effect.
    415. Declarations by person injured.
        (1). Admissibility in general.
        (2). Declarations not admissible as dying declarations.
        (3). Statements as to physical or mental condition.
        (4). Identity of accused.
        (5). Intent of person injured.
        (6). Statements exculpating accused.
        (7). Admissibility as affected by presence or nonpresence of accused.
    416. Declarations by third persons.
    417. —— In general.
        (1). Admissibility in general.
        (2). Declarations not made in presence or within hearing of accused.
        (3). Statements at preliminary examination or before grand jury.
        (5). Expressions of opinion.
        (6). Declarations as to pedigree, birth, and relationship.
        (7). Statements to arresting officers.
        (8). Declarations by persons engaged in investigating offense or arresting or prosecuting guilty party.
        (9). Declarations inculpating accused.
        (10). Declarations exculpating accused.
        (11). Statements uncommunicated to or unauthorized by accused.
        (12). Transactions with accused relative to subject-matter of offense.
        (13). Admissibility of declarations as dependent on connection of declarant or declaration with offense.
        (14). Statements corroborating or impeaching testimony of witness.
        (15). Self-incriminating or exculpating declarations.
        (16). Letters and other written communications.
    418. —— In presence of accused.
        (1). Admissibility in general.
        (2). Declarations implicating, accusing, or incriminating accused.
    418.10. Declarations while under hypnosis or influence of drugs.
    419. Hearsay in general.
        (1). Nature of hearsay evidence and admissibility in general.
        (1.5). Particular determinations, hearsay inadmissible.

Source: Reprinted with permission from *West's Federal Digest 4th*, Vol. 29, p. 24, © 1997, West Group.

Exhibit 4–4
29 *West's Federal Practice Digest 4th* at 109, "Criminal Law" (Supp. 1996)

stay denied, certiorari denied 116 S.Ct. 688, 133 L.Ed.2d 593.

C.A.4 (Va.) 1994. Part of the procedural shield, established by *Miranda,* to support every citizen's Fifth Amendment right against compelled self-incrimination is the requirement that, prior to any custodial interrogation, police advise the individual that he has the right to remain silent and the right to the presence of an attorney. U.S.C.A. Const. Amend. 5.—U.S. v. Mobley, 40 F.3d 688, certiorari denied 115 S.Ct. 2005, 131 L.Ed.2d 1005.

"Public safety exception" to requirement that *Miranda* warnings be given before suspect's answers may be admitted into evidence, which allows police officers to question suspect about location of possible weapons, applies not only to protect the public safety but also police safety, and exception is not to be analyzed in light of the subjective motive of the questioner but rather from the objective perspective of the presence of a public danger. U.S.C.A. Const.Amend. 5.—Id.

"Public safety exception" to requirement that *Miranda* warnings be given before suspect's answers may be admitted into evidence, which allows police officers to question suspect about location of possible weapons, applies both before administration of *Miranda* warnings, and after the warnings are given and right to counsel is claimed. U.S.C.A. Const.Amend. 5.—Id.

"Public safety exception" to requirement that *Miranda* warnings be given before suspect's answers may be admitted into evidence, which allows police officers to question suspect about location of possible weapons, applies only where there is an objectively reasonable need to protect the police or the public from any immediate danger associated with a weapon, and absent such circumstances posing an objective danger to the public or police, the need for the exception is not apparent, and the suspicion that the questioner is on a fishing expedition outweighs the belief that public safety motivated the questioning that is otherwise improper. U.S.C.A. Const.Amend. 5.—Id.

There was no objectively reasonable concern for immediate danger to police or public justify-

ing "public safety exception" to requirement that *Miranda* warnings be given before suspect's answers may be admitted into evidence, which allows police officers to question suspect about location of possible weapons, where defendant answered door to his apartment naked, where, by the time defendant was arrested, FBI had already made a security sweep of his premises and found that defendant was only person present, and where, as defendant was being led away, FBI agent asked him whether there were any weapons present. U.S.C.A. Const.Amend. 5.—Id.

Under the exclusionary rule, defendant's answer to FBI agent's questioning regarding presence of a weapon should not have been admitted at trial since questioning came after *Miranda* warnings had been given, after defendant had claimed right to counsel, and did not fall under the "public safety exception" to *Miranda.* U.S.C.A. Const.Amend. 5.—Id.

C.A.4 (Va.) 1990. U.S. v. Gordon, 895 F.2d 932, rehearing denied, certiorari denied 111 S.Ct. 131, 498 U.S. 846, 112 L.Ed.2d 98.

C.A.9 (Wash.) 1995. Defendant's statement to probation officer that his brother stole shotgun and put it under defendant's bed was voluntary, even though defendant was not given a second *Miranda* warning in interval between initial police interrogation and interrogation by probation officer, and thus, statement was admissible in firearms prosecution, where defendant was questioned on day he was arrested, defendant knew he was charged with offenses relating to shotgun, interrogation by probation officer began less than ten minutes after questioning by police, and probation officer was present during police officer's interrogation. 18 U.S.C.A. § 3501(b).—U.S. v. Andaverde, 64 F.3d 1305, certiorari denied 116 S.Ct. 1055, 134 L.Ed.2d 199.

When suspect is subject to custodial interrogation without first being advised of his rights, *Miranda* dictates that answers received be presumed compelled and that they be excluded from evidence at trial in prosecution's case in chief.—Id.

Defendant's statement to probation officer that he was person who put stolen shotgun under his

continues

Exhibit 4–4 continued

bed was voluntary, even though defendant had not been given *Miranda* warning since his arrest on preceding day, and thus, statement was admissible in firearms prosecution; since statement was made only one day after arrest, it was not elicited by pressures of lengthy confinement, and defendant knew that he was being charged in connection with shotgun when he made statement. 18 U.S.C.A. § 3501(b).—Id.

C.A.4 (W.Va.) 1985. Murphy v. Holland, 776 F.2d 470, certiorari granted, vacated 106 S.Ct. 1787, 475 U.S. 1138, 90 L.Ed.2d 334, on remand 845 F.2d 83, certiorari denied 109 S.Ct. 258, 488 U.S. 908, 102 L.Ed.2d 246.

C.A.7 (Wis.) 1996. Underlying purpose of *Miranda* rule is to protect individuals from compelled self-incrimination. U.S.C.A. Const.Amend. 5.—Sprosty v. Buchler, 79 F.3d 635.

C.A.7 (Wis.) 1989. U.S. v. Edwards, 885 F.2d 377, on subsequent appeal 940 F.2d 1061.

C.A.10 (Wyo.) 1996. Miranda warnings protect suspects from violation of their constitutional rights by establishing safeguard to ensure that any information elicited by police from custodial interrogation cannot be introduced against defendant unless suspect has been advised of and waived certain basic constitutional rights. U.S.C.A. Const.Amend. 5.—U.S. v. Snow, 82 F.3d 935.

C.A.10 (Wyo.) 1996. Under *Miranda,* defendant must be aware of his right to remain silent and of consequences of abandoning that right.— Harvey v. Shillinger, 76 F.3d 1528.

M.D.Ala. 1990. Record demonstrated that officers who obtained defendant's statement ade-

quately advised him of his *Miranda* rights before questioning and that defendant did not appear to have difficulty communicating with them at that time. U.S.C.A. Const.Amends. 5, 6.—Daniel v. Thigpen, 742 F.Supp. 1535.

N.D.Ala. 1994. *Miranda* warnings are not themselves constitutional rights protected by Fifth Amendment; rather, they are prophylactic measures established by Supreme Court to ensure that Fifth Amendment right against self-incrimination is protected. U.S.C.A. Const.Amend. 5.—Waldrop v. Thigpen, 857 F.Supp. 872, affirmed 77 F.3d 1308, rehearing and suggestion for rehearing denied 85 F.3d 645.

There is no talismanic incantation required to satisfy structures of *Miranda;* as long as warnings reasonably convey requirements of *Miranda,* reviewing court need not concern itself with precise formulation of warnings. U.S.C.A. Const.Amend. 5.—Id.

D.Alaska 1992. Manner in which defendant was presented with her *Miranda* rights did not prevent an effective waiver by the defendant, even though officers read defendant her rights but asked that she not respond immediately until they had played some tapes and discussed evidence with her, and defendant subsequently admitted that she did feel sorry; *Miranda* warnings were given, and defendant clearly understood them and expressly waived them. U.S.C.A. Const.Amend. 5.—U.S. v. Barnett, 814 F.Supp. 1449.

D.Ariz. 1994. Readvisement of detainees *Miranda* rights prior to each meeting with detective was necessary to remind detainee that he was in an adversarial situation and not in the presence of

Source: Reprinted with permission from *West's Federal Digest 4th*, Vol. 29, p. 109, © 1997, West Group.

Exhibit 4–5

Tenth Decennial Digest, Part 1 at 849, 855 "Criminal Law" ☞ 412.2(3) (1992)

into a false sense of security that do not rise to the level of compulsion or coercion to speak are not within concerns of *Miranda.* U.S.C.A. Const. Amend 4. 5.—Id.

U.S.Conn. 1987. *Miranda* gives defendant right to choose between speech and silence.

U.S.C.A. Const.Amend. 5.—Connecticut v. Barrett, 107 S.Ct. 828, 479 U.S. 523, 93 L.Ed.2d 920, on remand 534 A.2d 219, 205 Conn. 437.

U.S.Ill. 1988. *Miranda* warnings given to defendant were sufficient to make defendant

continues

Exhibit 4–5 continued

aware of his Sixth Amendment right to counsel during postindictment questioning; accused, who was administered *Miranda* warnings, was sufficiently apprised of nature of his Sixth Amendment rights and consequences of abandoning those rights, so that his waiver could be considered knowing and intelligent. U.S.C.A. Const. Amends. 5, 6.—Patterson v. Illinois, 108 S.Ct. 2309, 487 U.S. 285, 101 L.Ed.2d 261.

U.S.Ind. 1989. Waiver form read to suspect prior to police interrogation, which advised suspect of right to attorney and that attorney would be appointed "if and when he went to court," was not constitutionally defective, as falsely suggesting that indigents have no right to attorney unless they go to court. U.S.C.A. Const.Amend. 6.—Duckworth v. Eagan, 109 S.Ct. 2875, 492 U.S. 195, 106 L.Ed.2d 166.

Miranda advisement need not be given in exact form described in *Miranda* decision; it is enough that advisement reasonably conveys to expect his rights as required by *Miranda*.—Id.

U.S.N.Y. 1990. Attenuation analysis did not apply in deciding admissibility of statement made by suspect after he received *Miranda* warnings at station house, even though suspect's arrest violated *Payton* rule that prohibits warrantless and nonconsensual entry into suspect's home; station house statement was not product or exploitation of illegal entry into home. U.S.C.A. Const.Amend. 4.—New York v. Harris, 110 S.Ct. 1640, 495 U.S. 14, 109 L.Ed.2d 13, on remand People v. Harris, 568 N.Y.S.2d 702, 77 N.Y.2d 434, 570 N.E.2d 1051.

Not every statement taken by police while suspect is in legal custody is admissible; statements taken during legal custody would be inadmissible if they were product of coercion, if *Miranda* warnings were not given, or if there was *Edwards* violation.—Id.

Suppressing statement made by suspect after he received *Miranda* warnings at station house would not serve purpose of *Payton* rule that prohibits warrantless and nonconsensual entry into suspect's home to make felony arrest; purpose of rule is to protect the home by requiring exclusion of anything incriminating gathered by police from home. U.S.C.A. Const.Amend. 4.—Id.

U.S.Pa. 1990. Answers to questions given by suspect in driving under the influence case, prior to his receiving *Miranda* warnings, were not rendered inadmissible because slurred nature of his speech was incriminating; slurred speech was a physical characteristic of defendant and not "testimonrial," and thus not subject to Fifth Amendment protection. U.S.C.A. Const. Amends. 5, 14.—Pennsylvania v. Muniz, 110 S.Ct. 2638, 496 U.S. 582, 110 L.Ed. 2d 528.

State trial court violated drunk driving suspect's constitutional right to avoid self-incrimination by admitting his statement, made in response to police question prior to receiving *Miranda* warning, that he did not know date of his sixth birthday, despite claim that question was designed to elicit physical evidence regarding physiological functioning of defendant's brain; response was testimonial in nature because he was required to communicate an express or implied assertion of fact and belief, and suspect was thus confronted with impermissible "trilemma" of either remaining silent in coercive environment, telling truth that he did not know date and thus incriminating himself by showing impaired mental capacity, or giving a false statement which would also be ultimately incriminatory. U.S.C.A. Const. Amends. 5, 14.—Id.

Responses of suspect in driving under influence case to police questions regarding his name, address, height, weight, eye color, date of birth, and current age, were not required to be suppressed because suspect had not been given *Miranda* warning; even though questions were asked while suspect was in custody, they were of a routine booking nature and were not intended to elicit information for investigatory purposes. U.S.C.A. Const.Amends. 5, 14. (Per opinion of Justice Brennan, with three Justices concurring and the Chief Justice and three Justices concurring in result.)—Id.

Drunk driving suspect's counting at officer's request during field sobriety tests qualified as a response to "custodial interrogation" within meaning of *Miranda*. U.S.C.A. Const.Amend. 5.—Id.

Audible remarks made by suspect in driving under influence case while attempting to perform

continues

Exhibit 4–5 continued

sobriety tests and in dialogue leading up to his refusal to take breathalyzer test were admissible even though he had not been given his *Miranda* warnings; police officers' statements to suspect consisted of carefully scripted instructions as to how tests were to be performed and were not likely to be perceived as calling for any verbal response, and remarks made by suspect were consequently "voluntary." U.S.C.A. Const.Amends. 5, 14.—Id.

C.A.D.C. 1988. Statements made by defendant after he had been given *Miranda* warnings were not admissible in prosecution for making false statements where prosecutors had told him in one breath that he could remain silent but in next had said that they remained interested in putting him in front of a grand jury, where he would be compelled to testify with immunity.—U.S. v. Friedrick, 842 F.2d 382, 268 U.S. App. D.C. 386.

C.A.11 (Ala.) 1987. Defendant was not required to be readvised of his *Miranda* rights prior to interrogation, where defendant had been given complete *Miranda* warnings on same day, and only break in his questioning came during his transportation from police station to sheriff's department.—Ballard v. Johnson, 821 F.2d 568.

C.A.9 (Alaska) 1988. Under *Miranda*, person in custody must be informed prior to interrogation that he has right to remain silent and to have lawyer present; if he requests counsel, questioning must stop and cannot be resumed without lawyer unless suspect himself initiates further communication. U.S.C.A. Const.Amends. 5, 6.—Smith v. Endell, 860 F.2d 1528, certiorari denied 111 S.Ct. 510, 112 L.Ed.2d 522.

C.A.9 (Ariz.) 1991. *Miranda* warnings and rights are not themselves constitutionally mandated, but are rather procedural safeguards, or prophylactic measures, to ensure that Fifth Amendment right against compulsory incrimination is not violated. U.S.C.A. Const.Amend. 5.—Cooper v. Dupnik, 924 F.2d 1520, rehearing ordered 933 F.2d 798.

C.A.8 (Ark.) 1989. Statement signed by defendant adequately presented warning required by *Miranda*, notwithstanding that statement did not mention that attorney would be appointed if defendant could not afford to hire one; *Miranda*

did not require that warnings be given precisely as expressed in case. U.S.C.A. Const.Amend. 5.—Chambers v. Lockhart, 872 F.2d 274, rehearing denied, certiorari denied 110 S.Ct. 335, 493 U.S. 938, 107 L.Ed.2d 324.

C.A.8 (Ark.) 1989. Custodial statements made by defendant charged with aggravated robbery were voluntarily given, and thus properly used in cross-examination to impeach him; defendant was 24 years old at time of arrest and had ninth or tenth grade education, had been read his *Miranda* rights prior to taking of statement as evidenced by signature on rights waiver form, and acknowledged that he had previous experience with criminal justice system in that he had previously been arrested and convicted, and district court's conclusion that statements were voluntary was based on decision to credit testimony of police officers who denied allegations made by defendant that they had used coercion in attempt to obtain statements from defendant. U.S.C.A. Const.Amend. 5.—Houston v. Lockhart, 866 F.2d 264, rehearing denied.

C.A.9 (Cal.) 1990. *Miranda* warning given to defendant was inadequate where defendant was not informed that he had a right to have an attorney during questioning.—U.S. v. Bland, 908 F.2d 471.

C.A.9 (Cal.) 1989. "Public safety" exception to *Miranda* requirements does not allow police to obtain voluntary or coerced statements in exigent circumstances; rather, exception deals with "knowing and intelligent" aspects of requirements for waiver of constitutional rights, so that, in exigent circumstances, prudential policy of requiring warnings to insure that any waiver of rights will be informed or intelligent is outweighed by need of police to act decisively and promptly, and exception also eliminates presumption of coercion that normally results from failure to provide warnings. U.S.C.A. Const.Amends. 5, 6.—U.S. v. DeSantis, 870 F.2d 536.

"Public safety" exception to requirement that *Miranda* warnings be given also applies to permit police in public safety situation to dispense with prophylactic safeguard under *Edwards* forbidding initiation of further questioning of defendant who requests counsel; in such situation, focus should be on whether, under circumstances, state-

continues

Exhibit 4–5 continued

ments were obtained coercively, disregarding *Edwards'* prophylactic rule. U.S.C.A. Const. Amends. 5, 6.—Id.

Even if defendant asserted right to counsel when inspectors arrived at his residence to execute arrest warrant issued upon revocation of appellate bond based on finding that defendant was flight risk, "public safety" exception permitted inspector to question defendant about possibility of weapons in adjoining bedroom when defendant requested to enter adjoining bedroom to change clothes, and defendant's response that there was gun on shelf was not obtained in violation of his constitutional rights. U.S.C.A. Const.Amends. 5, 6.—Id.

C.A.9 (Cal.) 1987. Defendant's statements to police officer at time he was undergoing custodial interrogation were admissible in trial for possession of controlled substance with intent to distribute, even though defendant was not given *Miranda* warning, where police officer's question as to whether defendant had gun was asked for purpose of controlling dangerous situation involving large crowd gathering on public street in rough neighborhood, where defendant's car stood with its door open and keys in ignition.—U.S. v. Brady, 819 F.2d 884, certiorari denied 108 S.Ct. 1032, 484 U.S. 1068, 98 L.Ed.2d 996.

C.A.9 (Cal.) 1986. Narcotics task force agents were not required to administer new *Miranda* warnings before interrogating defendant who had already been interrogated by local police concerning other crimes, where no appreciable time had elapsed between end of police interrogation and beginning of narcotics investigation and defendant had been properly apprised of scope of narcotics inquiry and had done nothing initially to reserve rights to silence or counsel, but defendant had adequately asserted right to counsel during interrogation by narcotics had no right to counsel at any predisciplinary hearing investigation or disciplinary proceeding and he did not have to be so advised; warnings were given and inmate asserted a *Miranda* right. U.S.C.A. Const.Amend. 5.—Id.

Ala.Cr.App. 1990. *Miranda* does not apply to traditional investigatory functions such as general on-the-scene questioning. U.S.C.A. Const. Amends. 5, 6.—Robinson v. State, 574 So.2d 910.

Ala.Cr.App. 1990. Mere fact that defendant was suspect in case at time of police interview did not require that he be read *Miranda* rights.— Banks v. State, 570 So.2d 1282.

Ala.Cr.App. 1990. Two-part analysis must be applied when determining admissibility of statement given by accused while in custody; court must first look to see if proper *Miranda* warnings were given, and then must determine if statement was given voluntarily.—Cleckler v. State, 570 So.2d 796.

Failure of police to readvise defendant of his *Miranda* rights before reinterviewing defendant 90 minutes after defendant's assertion of his right to remain silent precluded State from proving that defendant knowingly and intelligently waived his privilege against self-incrimination, and thus statements made by defendant should have been suppressed, and admission of such statements required new trial. U.S.C.A. Const.Amend. 5.—Id.

Ala.Cr.App. 1989. For extrajudicial statement to be admissible, trial court must determine that law enforcement officers complied with *Miranda* requirements and that the statement was voluntarily given.—Callahan v. State, 557 So.2d 1292, affirmed Ex parte Callahan, 557 So.2d 1311, certiorari denied 111 S.Ct. 216, 112 L.Ed.2d 176.

Ala.Cr.App. 1989. Version of *Miranda* warnings given to juvenile arrestees is not coercive. Juvenile Procedure Rule 11(A).—Cleveland v. State, 555 So.2d 302.

Ala.Cr.App. 1989. Attempted murder defendant was not entitled to be informed of his *Miranda* rights before he made postarrest statement to victim's ex-wife, who was acting as police agent; statement was not made as result of custodial interrogation.—Bates v. State, 549 So.2d 601.

Ala.Cr.App. 1989. Once trooper smelled odor of marijuana on person of driver stopped for traffic violation and detained while trooper completed traffic ticket, trooper was justified in asking driver if he had been smoking marijuana without having advised driver of his *Miranda* rights.— Pittman v. State, 541 So.2d 583.

Ala.Cr.App. 1989. Even though investigator failed to inform defendant of his right to appointed counsel when he advised defendant of

continues

Exhibit 4–5 continued

his constitutional rights for the second time, defendant's statement made immediately thereafter was admissible where he had previously been informed of his right to appointed counsel, orally waived his rights, and never exhibited any reluctance to talk with the investigator.—Ingram v. State, 541 So.2d 78.

Ala.Cr.App. 1988. Inquiry by officer at scene of murder of defendant's three children, whereby he asked defendant about his children, was in the nature of general on-the-scene investigation and did not constitute interrogation or violate *Miranda* rule.—Bui v. State, 551 So.2d 1094, affirmed Ex parte Quang Ngoc Bui, 551 So.2d 1125, certiorari granted and vacated 111 S.Ct. 1613, 113 L.Ed.2d 712.

Ala.Cr.App. 1988. Officers were under no obligation to advise defendant prior to questioning him of the elements of the crime for which he had been arrested.—Strickland v. State, 550 So.2d 1042, affirmed Ex parte Strickland, 550 So.2d 1054.

Ala.Cr.App. 1988. *Miranda* does not apply when inculpatory statement is made to private citizen, but applies only to custodial interrogation of suspect by police.—Rankin v. State, 541 So.2d 577, writ quashed Ex parte Rankin, 541 So.2d 582.

Ala.Cr.App. 1988. Defendant, having been informed that everything that transpired in docket room was being recorded, was not entitled to *Miranda* warning before making telephone call, as defendant was not being "interrogated;" defendant was not subjected to direct questioning, psychological ploys, or compelling influences. U.S.C.A. Const.Amend. 5.—Molina v. State, 533 So.2d 701, certiorari denied 109 S.Ct. 1547, 489 U.S. 1086, 103 L.Ed.2d 851.

Ala.Cr.App. 1987. *Miranda* warnings which failed to advise defendant of right to remain silent were clearly defective.—Whittle v. State, 518 So.2d 793.

Ala.Cr.App. 1987. Murder defendant's *Miranda* rights were not violated by admission of transcript of recorded postarrest statement, despite defendant's allegations that tape recording demonstrated that defendant had not unequivocally waived his rights, where totality of circumstances indicated that defendant understood his rights and

voluntarily wished to make a statement.—Hill v. State, 516 So.2d 876.

Ala.Cr.App. 1987. Incriminating statement defendant made to officer while defendant was in custody and blood sample was being drawn from defendant was admissible in rape trial, even though statement was made before defendant was advised of his *Miranda* rights, where officer was not questioning defendant and had no intention of doing so when defendant made statement. U.S.C.A. Const.Amends. 5, 6.—West v. State, 511 So.2d 258.

Ala.Cr.App. 1986. Questioning concerning location of gun and seizure of gun along with other items on defendant's person prior to reading defendant his *Miranda* rights fell within public safety exception to *Miranda* rule allowing police officer to frisk defendant and seize gun to protect himself and others from harm.—Hubbard v. State, 500 So.2d 1204, affirmed Ex parte Hubbard, 500 So.2d 1231, post-conviction relief denied 584 So.2d 895, certiorari denied 112 S.Ct. 896, 116 L.Ed.2d 798, certiorari denied 107 S.Ct. 1591, 480 U.S. 940, 94 L.Ed.2d 780.

Ala.Cr.App. 1986. Defendant's incriminating statements made to police officer while defendant was in jail were not excludable as resulting from interrogation absent giving of *Miranda* rights, as defendant approached police officer, asking whether police officer thought defendant would be let go, and defendant responded, to police officer's answer that it would depend on what defendant had done, that defendant was the one who shot police officer.—Watkins v. State, 495 So.2d 92.

Ala.Cr.App. 1986. Criteria for courts to use in determining whether *Miranda* warnings are necessary include: probable cause to arrest, subjective intent of the police, subjective belief of the accused, and focus of the investigation.—Pate v. State, 492 So.2d 1026.

Fact that police initiated and arranged for conversation with defendant is not determinative of whether *Miranda* warnings are required.—Id.

Ala.Cr.App. 1985. Police officer was not required to advise defendant of his *Miranda* rights before questioning defendant, where officer was aware that defendant previously had been advised of his *Miranda* rights, even though officer had not been present when another officer had advised

continues

Exhibit 4–5 continued

defendant of his rights. U.S.C.A. Const.Amend. 5.—Magwood v. State, 494 So.2d 124, affirmed Ex parte Magwood, 494 So.2d 154, certiorari denied 107 S.Ct. 599, 479 U.S. 995, 93 L.Ed.2d 599.

There is no requirement that suspect be informed of his constitutional rights before each separate interrogation. U.S.C.A. Const.Amend. 5.—Id.

Determination of whether *Miranda* warnings must be repeated is one that should be made on a case-by-case basis. U.S.C.A. Const.Amend. 5.—Id.

Alaska App. 1991. *Berkemer,* which held that on scene questioning which occurs during traffic stop constitutes exception to *Miranda* warning requirements, does not apply exclusively to traffic stop for motor vehicle violations, and could apply to stop to investigate complaint that defendant damaged shopping carts with his car where circumstances surrounding stop were not substantially more coercive than a traffic stop. AS 28.35.045; U.S.C.A. Const.Amend. 4.—McCollum v. State, 808 P.2d 268.

Alaska App. 1988. Police officer must give a person *Miranda* warnings whenever the officer questions a person who is in custody.—LeMense v. State, 754 P.2d 268.

Ariz. 1990. Rule prohibiting admission of child's statement to peace officer unless certain warnings are given applies to determine admissibility of statement made by juvenile later charged as adult after transfer hearing. 17B A.R.S. Juv.Ct.Rules of Proc., Rule 18.—State v. Jimenez, 799 P.2d 785, 165 Ariz. 444.

Ariz. 1988. Voluntariness and *Miranda* violations are two separate inquiries; necessity of giving *Miranda* warnings relates to admissibility of confession based on defendant's being apprised of his right to counsel and waiving that right, not to voluntariness of confession.—State v. Tapia, 767 P.2d 5, 159 Ariz. 284.

To satisfy *Miranda,* State must show that appellant understood his rights and intelligently and

knowingly relinquished those rights before custodial interrogation began.—Id.

Ariz. 1988. Statements defendant made to psychiatrist employed by county jail were volunteered and not prompted by interrogation; therefore, psychiatrist was not required to give defendant *Miranda* warnings.—State v. Beaty, 762 P.2d 519, 158 Ariz. 232, certiorari denied 109 S.Ct. 3200, 491 U.S. 910, 105 L.Ed.2d 708, rehearing denied 110 S.Ct. 25, 492 U.S. 938, 106 L.Ed.2d 637.

Where statements are entirely spontaneous, and are not solicited by questions or acts reasonably likely to elicit confession, *Miranda* warnings are not a prerequisite for admissibility.—Id.

Ariz. 1988. Before results of any custodial interrogation may be directly used by state, authorities must tell defendant that he has right to remain silent and right to assistance of counsel. U.S.C.A. Const.Amends. 5, 6; A.R.S. Const. Art. 2, § 10.—State v. Carrillo, 750 P.2d 883, 156 Ariz. 125.

Ariz. 1987. Police are not required to use precise language contained in *Miranda* opinion.—State v. Moorman, 744 P.2d 679, 154 Ariz. 578.

Warning must inform defendant that right to counsel exists before and during interrogation; warning must not convey message that appointed counsel cannot be made available until some future time. U.S.C.A. Const.Amend. 6.—Id.

Warning informing defendant that he had right to talk to lawyer and have lawyer present during questioning adequately conveyed message to defendant that he had right to attorney before he answered any questions. U.S.C.A. Const.Amend. 6.—Id.

Ariz. App. 1990. Defendant's statements to police were admissible, where defendant's initial statements were made before he was under arrest, and defendant's subsequent statements were made after he was given *Miranda* warnings. . . .

Source: Reprinted with permission from *Tenth Decennial Digest, Part 1,* Vol. 11, p. 849, 855, © 1991, West Group.

Exhibit 4–6

5 *General Digest, 9th Series* at 373, "Criminal Law ☞ 412.2(3)" (1997)

jective views harbored by either interrogating officers or person being questioned. U.S.C.A. Const.Amend. 5.—Id.

Defendant's interview with Department of Social Services (DSS) case manager who was investigating allegations of sexual abuse was not custodial interrogation triggering *Miranda* requirements; defendant voluntarily met with manager in DSS parking lot based on victim's mother's statement that defendant would need to talk to manager sooner or later, manager was not law enforcement officer and did not wear uniform or carry gun, and at no time did manager tell defendant that he was under arrest. U.S.C.A. Const.Amend. 5.—Id.

S.D. 1996. Proper test in determining whether person need be given *Miranda* warning is not whether investigation has focused on any particular suspect, but rather, whether person being questioned is in custody or deprived of his or her freedom to leave. U.S.C.A. Const.Amend. 5.— State v. Darby, 556 N.W.2d 311.

Defendant was not in custody for *Miranda* purposes during police questioning at his home or at police station; defendant was informed that he was not under arrest and would not be arrested that day, defendant voluntarily agreed to continue questioning at police station, door to room in which defendant was questioned was unlocked, no restraints were placed on defendant, and defendant was free to move about room and free to leave. U.S.C.A. Const.Amend. 5.— Id.

Tex.App.–Corpus Christi 1996. Defendant may waive his *Miranda* rights, provided waiver is made voluntarily, knowingly, and intelligently.— Ashcraft v. State, 934 S.W.2d 727, rehearing overruled.

Court may properly conclude that *Miranda* rights have been waived only if totality of circumstances surrounding interrogation reveal both uncoerced choice and requisite level of comprehension.—Id.

W.Va. 1996. If defendant is not in custody at time of interrogation, he is not able to claim violation of his *Miranda* rights; *Miranda* rights must be given and honored only when there has been restriction on person's freedom as to render him in custody.—State v. Potter, 478 S.E.2d 742.

Whether defendant is in custody for purposes of *Miranda* requirements is determined by objective test, viewing totality of circumstances, would reasonable person in defendant's position have considered his freedom of action restricted to degree associated with formal arrest.—Id.

When determining whether defendant was in custody at time of interrogation for purposes of *Miranda* requirements, fact that questioning took place in police station is relevant consideration, but is not controlling.—Id.

Subjective undisclosed beliefs of defendant and questioning officer regarding custody are irrelevant for purposes of determining whether defendant was in custody for purposes or *Miranda* requirements.—Id.

☞ 412.2(3) Informing accused as to his rights.

C.A.8 (Minn.) 1996. Routine biographical data is exempted from *Miranda's* coverage.—U.S. v. Brown, 101 F.3d 1272.

Where police had probable cause to arrest defendant due to observation of participation in drug-related crime, police inquiry into defendant's name, and his response, were not covered by *Miranda* as question was not investigative in nature and it fell within routine booking question exception; defendant's name was not directly relevant to the substantive offense charged but was necessary to the booking process.—Id.

D.Puerto Rico 1996. *Miranda* warnings are required prior to custodial interrogation of suspect.—U.S. v. Alvelo-Ramos, 945 F.Supp. 19.

Statement by suspect in response to arresting officer's question concerning purchase price of cellular phone found in suspect's car during execution of search warrant was inadmissible; situation in which questioning occurred was custodial, officer should have been aware that question was likely to elicit incriminating answer, and question was asked prior to administration of *Miranda* warning to suspect. U.S.C.A. Const.Amend. 5.— Id.

Cal. 1997. "Public safety" exception to *Miranda* applies during police negotiations to obtain release of hostage held at gunpoint. U.S.C.A. Const.Amend. 5.—People v. Mayfield, 928 P.2d 485, 60 Cal.Rptr.2d 1, 14 C. 4th 668.

continues

Exhibit 4–6 continued

Cal.App. 2 Dist. 1996. Rescue doctrine exception to *Miranda* requirements applied to arrested suspect's admission, upon repeated questioning of officer and emergency room physician, that he swallowed six to eight pieces of rock cocaine; arresting officer had reasonable belief that suspect had consumed cocaine based upon seeing him place his hand to his mouth, subsequent recovery of cocaine dropped by suspect, and presence of white residue in suspect's mouth, officer knew cardiac arrest could result from cocaine overdose, and suspect was anxious and had elevated heart rate when received at hospital, putting him at risk for acute myocardial infarction and hemorrhagic stroke. U.S.C.A. Const.Amend. 5.—People v. Stevenson, 59 Cal.Rptr.2d 878, 51 C.A.4th 1234.

When it is arrestee's life that is in jeopardy, rather than life of victim, officer, or member of public at large, police are nevertheless justified in asking questions directed toward providing lifesaving medical treatment to arrestee without first administering *Miranda* warnings. U.S.C.A. Const.Amend. 5.—Id.

Hawaii 1996. Prior to any custodial questioning, defendant must be warned that he has right to remain silent, that any statement he does make may be used as evidence against him, and that he has right to the presence of attorney, either retained or appointed.—State v. Luton, 927 P.2d 844.

Defendant was fully apprised of his Fifth Amendment rights for purposes of determining whether he was afforded the full range of constitutional protection to which he was entitled; defendant was read his *Miranda* rights and provided with a form which explained in detail these rights, defendant was required to initial each statement of the form as an officer explained them, defendant was aware of police interrogation procedures as well as his right to counsel during custodial interrogations, and defendant specifically stated that he did not want to have attorney present. U.S.C.A. Const.Amend. 5.—Id.

La.App. 5 Cir. 1996. Before confession or inculpatory statement can be admitted into evidence, it must be established that accused who makes statement during custodial interrogation was first advised of his Miranda right to counsel

and right to remain silent and that statement was made freely and voluntarily and not under influence of fear, duress, intimidation, menaces, threats, inducements, or promises.—State v. Pittman, 683 So.2d 748 95-382 (La.App. 5 Cir. 10/1/96).

N.Y.A.D. 3 Dept. 1996. There was no violation of defendant's *Miranda* rights in connection with his written statements; defendant was fully advised of his *Miranda* rights, signed written acknowledgment and waiver of those rights, never asked for attorney or asserted his right to remain silent, and read over, corrected and signed statements.—People v. Culkin, 650 N.Y.S.2d 813.

Okl.Cr. 1996. Under certain circumstances, state is required to give defendant *Miranda* warnings prior to examination by state psychiatrist, U.S.C.A. Const.Amend. 5.—Traywicks v. State, 927 P.2d 1062.

Wis. 1996. When state seeks to admit accused's custodial statement, both federal and state constitutional protections against compelled self-incrimination require that state show that accused was adequately informed of *Miranda* rights, understood them, and knowingly and intelligently waived them, and that accused's statement was given voluntarily. U.S.C.A. Const.Amend. 5; W.S.A. Const.Art. 1, § 8.—State v. Santiago, 556 N.W.2d 687, 206 Wis.2d 3.

Although *Miranda* warnings need not be conveyed by "talismanic incantation," they must convey substantive message that suspect has right to remain silent, that anything suspect says can be used against him or her in court of law, that suspect has right to have lawyer and to have lawyer present if he or she gives statement, and that, if suspect cannot afford attorney, one will be appointed for him or her both before and during questioning. U.S.C.A. Const.Amend. 5; W.S.A. Const. Art. 1, § 8.—Id.

☞ 412.2(4). Absence or denial of counsel.

Ark. 1996. Custodial interrogation of defendant without presence of attorney of defendant's own choosing did not deprive defendant of right to counsel as contemplated by *Miranda,* where defendant was fully advised of his *Miranda* rights and invoked right to counsel, defendant consulted with public defender before giving statement, pub-

continues

Exhibit 4–6 continued

lic defender advised him not to give statement, and public defender was present when defendant went ahead and gave statement anyway. U.S.C.A. Const.Amends. 5, 6.—State v. Johnson, 934 S.W.2d 499, 326 Ark. 660.

Fla.App. 5 Dist. 1996. When suspect, after being Mirandized and agreeing to talk to police without lawyer present, indicates that he or she does not want to be interrogated further, questioning must stop. U.S.C.A. Const.Amends. 5, 14; West's F.S.A. Const. Art. 1 § 9.—State v. Moya, 684 So.2d 279.

Officer faced with equivocal assertion of suspect's right to remain silent violated neither *Miranda* nor State Constitution by stopping substantive questions but continuing to try to get suspect to make decision about whether to continue talking. U.S.C.A. Const.Amends. 5, 14; West's F.A.S.A. Const. Art. 1 § 9.—Id.

Hawaii 1996. At judicial determination of probable cause (JDPC), defendant did not enjoy the constitutional protection of the Sixth Amendment's right to counsel because JDPC was not a "critical stage" in criminal proceedings and therefore, defendant's subsequent statements to the police were not obtained in violation of the Sixth Amendment and trial court erroneously suppressed them. U.S.C.A. Const.Amend. 6.—State v. Luton, 927 P.2d 844.

Defendant invokes constitutional protection against self-incrimination when he either remains silent or expresses his desire to deal with police interrogators only through his counsel and thereafter, he cannot be further questioned until counsel has been made available to him unless defendant initiates further communication, exchanges, or conversations with police. U.S.C.A. Const.Amend. 5.—Id.

Defendant who admitted that police officers informed him of his rights and yet did not ask to see an attorney did not express or invoke his desire for counsel or his right to remain silent. U.S.C.A. Const.Amend. 5.—Id.

Defendant's representation by counsel at judicial determination of probable cause (JDPC) which was not a critical stage in the criminal proceedings such that right to counsel

Source: Reprinted with permission from *General Digest, Ninth Series*, Vol. 5, p. 373, © 1997, West Group.

Exhibit 4–7
98 *West's Federal Practice Digest's* Descriptive *Word Index* 16 (Supp. 1996)

MINES   **98 F P D 4th—16**

References are to Digest Topics and Key Numbers

MINES AND MINERALS—Cont'd
QUIETING title to claims. Mines 38

MIRANDA RULE
PUBLIC safety exception. Crim Law 412.2(3)

MIRANDA WARNINGS
PUBLIC safety exception. Crim Law 412.2(3)

MISAPPROPRIATION

TRADE secrets—
Damages. Damag 114

MISSILES
PRODUCTS liability. Prod Liab 62

MISTRIAL
CHANGING plea during trial. Crim Law 867
DOUBLE jeopardy, effect on. Double J 95–99
Acquittal, mistrial as. Double J 104

continues

Exhibit 4–7 continued

MITIGATION OF DAMAGES
CIVIL rights—
  Alternative employment. Civil R 272
RESOLUTION Trust Corporation. B & L Assoc 42(6)

MOBILE COMMUNICATIONS
  Generally. Tel 461.5

MODIFICATION
JUDGMENT, see this index Judgment

MODUS OPERANDI
EXPERT testimony. Crim Law 474.5

MONEY
RECEIVED, see this index Money Received

MONEY LAUNDERING
  Generally. U S 34
ELEMENTS. U S 34

MONOPOLIES
BAR review courses—
  Combination prohibited. Monop 12(2)
CIVIL rights, color of state or local law. Civil R 198(6)
ORGAN transplants. Monop 12(11)
SANCTIONS—
  Frivolous complaints, counterclaims and petitions.
    Fed Civ Proc 2771(4)
TRUCKING. Monop 12(16)
UNITED States magistrates, jurisdiction and proceed-
  ings. U S Mag 19

MOOT QUESTIONS
ENVIRONMENTAL protection regulations—
  Judicial review or intervention. Health & E 25.15(5.2)
HABEAS CORPUS, see this index Habeas Corpus
REVIEW of—
  Bankruptcy courts. Bankr 3781

MORAL TURPITUDE
BANKRUPTCY, discharge of liability created through.
  Bankr 3353(3)

MORTGAGES
ACCELERATION generally. Mtg 401, 403
  Curing default, individual repayment plans. Bankr
    3711(4)
BANKRUPTCY—
  Application of proceeds of sale of estate property.
    Bankr 3078(3)
  Automatic stay. Bankr 2397(1–3)
    Relief from, adequate protection. Bankr 2430.5(2)
    Relief from stay. Bankr 2422.5(5)
  Avoidability. Bankr 2784(5)
  Curing defects, individual repayment plans. Bankr
    3711(2–6)
  Estate property. Bankr 2538
  Individual repayment plans, plan provisions. Bankr
    3708 (7, 9)

Principal residence, security interest in. Bankr
  3708(9)
DEEDS in lieu of foreclosure—
  Extinguishing right of redemption. Mtg 296
FEDERAL insurance. U S 59(9)
FEDERAL loans and guaranties, see this index Housing
FIRST refusal—
  Farm credit. Banks 408
FORECLOSURE—
  Sale—
    Automatic stay. Bankr 2397(2)
INDIVIDUAL repayment plans, see Bankruptcy, ante
INSURANCE—
  Third party beneficiaries—
    Right to enforce conditions. Insurance 156(1)
REDEMPTION—
  Automatic stay. Bankr 2397(3)
  Stay of redemption period. Bankr 2362
REVERSE annuity mortgages—
  Nature of. Mtg 1
SUBORDINATION—
  Shipping. Ship 32

MOTIONS
IN LIMINE—
  Courts-martial. Mil Jus 920
LIMINE, motions in—
  Criminal cases. Crim Law 632(4)
  Federal court procedure. Fed Civ Proc 2011

MOTIVE
BANKRUPTCY—
  Reorganization cases. Bankr 3502, 3503
  Voluntary cases. Bankr 2252–2254
CIVIL rights, acts or conduct causing deprivation—
  Employment discrimination. Civil R 153
  Governmental agencies, privilege or immunity. Civil
    R 214(2)
DISCRIMINATION—
  Employment. Civil R 153

MOTORCYCLES
BANNING use of—
  Parks. Autos 5(1)

MOVING PICTURES
SEX and nudity—
  Freedom of speech and press. Const Law 90.4(4)

MULTIPLICITY OF SUITS
CRIMINAL prosecutions, restrictions on. Double J 5, 6,
  26

MUNICIPAL CORPORATIONS
CONTRACTS and contractors—
  Injunctions—
    Preliminary injunctions—
      Grounds and objections. Inj 138.63
      Proceedings. Inj 139–159.5
ELECTIONS—
  Apportionment, see this index Election Districts or
    Precincts

Nontestimonial Evidence

The Fifth Amendment right against compelled self-incrimination, which *Miranda* is designed to safeguard, clearly applies to confessions and other verbal expressions. We now consider whether the Fifth Amendment extends to other types of evidence that might be used to incriminate suspects, such as their fingerprints, a handwriting sample, a recording of their voice, a dental impression, a DNA sample, or their blood. Should the Fifth Amendment protect an individual from being "compelled" to supply such potentially incriminating evidence from his or her own person? This important question has relevance beyond the *Miranda* context, but it can figure importantly in cases raising *Miranda* issues.

The principal case in this area, *Schmerber v. California*, was decided just one week after *Miranda*. Schmerber was convicted for driving while intoxicated, a conviction based in part on a hospital physician at the direction of the police. He contended that this evidence was obtained in violation of "due process of law under the Fourteenth Amendment, as well as . . . his privilege against self-incrimination under the Fifth Amendment; his right to counsel under the Sixth Amendment; and his right not to be subjected to unreasonable searches and seizures in violation of the Fourth Amendment." We focus on the Fifth Amendment claim.

Schmerber v. California, 384 U.S. 757, 86 S. Ct. 1826, 16 L. Ed. 2d 908 (1966)

Mr. Justice **Brennan** delivered the opinion of the Court.

Petitioner was convicted in Los Angeles Municipal Court of the criminal offense of driving an automobile while under the influence of intoxicating liquor. He had been arrested at a hospital while receiving treatment for injuries suffered in an accident involving the automobile that he had apparently been driving. At the direction of a police officer, a blood sample was then withdrawn from petitioner's body by a physician at the hospital. The chemical analysis of this sample revealed a percent by weight of alcohol in his blood at the time of the offense which indicated intoxication, and the report of this analysis was admitted in evidence at the trial. Petitioner objected to receipt of this evidence of the analysis on the ground that the blood had been withdrawn despite his refusal, on the advice of his counsel, to consent to the test.

[In] Malloy v. Hogan, 378 US 1, 8, 84 S Ct 1489, 12 L Ed 2d 653 [(1964)] [w]e held that "[t]he Fourteenth Amendment secures against state invasion the same privilege that the Fifth Amendment guarantees against federal infringement—the right of a person to remain silent unless he chooses to speak in the unfettered exercise of his own will, and to suffer no penalty . . .

for such silence." We therefore must now decide whether the withdrawal of the blood and admission in evidence of the analysis involved in this case violated petitioner's privilege.

We hold that the privilege protects an accused only from being compelled to testify against himself, or otherwise provide the State with evidence of a testimonial or communicative nature,[5] and that the withdrawal of blood and use of the analysis in question in this case did not involve compulsion to these ends.

---

5. A dissent suggests that the report of the blood test was "testimonial" or "communicative," because the test was performed in order to obtain the testimony of others, communicating to the jury facts about petitioner's condition. Of course, all evidence received in court is "testimonial" or "communicative" if these words are thus used. But the Fifth Amendment relates only to acts on the part of the person to whom the privilege applies, and we use these words subject to the same limitations. A nod or head-shake is as much a "testimonial" or "communicative" act in this sense as are spoken words. But the terms as we use them do not apply to evidence of acts noncommunicative in nature as to the person asserting the privilege, even though, as here, such acts are compelled to obtain the testimony of others.

It could not be denied that in requiring petitioner to submit to the withdrawal and chemical analysis of his blood the State compelled him to submit to an attempt to discover evidence that might be used to prosecute him for a criminal offense. He submitted only after the police officer rejected his objection and directed the physician to proceed. The officer's direction to the physician to administer the test over petitioner's objection constituted compulsion for the purposes of the privilege. The critical question, then, is whether petitioner was thus compelled "to be a witness against himself."

If the scope of the privilege coincided with the complex of values it helps to protect, we might be obliged to conclude that the privilege was violated. In Miranda v. Arizona, 384 US 436, 86 S Ct 1602, 16 L Ed 694, 715 [(1966)] the Court said of the interests protected by the privilege: "All these policies point to one overriding thought: the constitutional foundation underlying the privilege is the respect a government—state or federal—must accord to the dignity and integrity of its citizens. To maintain a 'fair state-individual balance,' to require the government 'to shoulder the entire load' . . . to respect the inviolability of the human personality, our accusatory system of criminal justice demands that the government seeking to punish an individual produce the evidence against him by its own independent labors, rather than by the cruel, simple expedient of compelling it from his own mouth." The withdrawal of blood necessarily involves puncturing the skin for extraction, and the percent by weight of alcohol in the blood, as established by chemical analysis, is evidence of criminal guilt. Compelled submission fails on one view to respect the "inviolability of the human personality." Moreover, since it enables the State to rely on evidence forced from the accused, the compulsion violates at least one meaning of the requirement that the State procure the evidence against an accused "by its own independent labors."

As the passage in Miranda implicitly recognizes, however, the privilege has never been given the full scope which the values it helps to protect suggest. History and a long line of authorities in lower courts have consistently limited its protection to situations in which the State seeks to submerge those values by obtaining the evidence against an accused through "the cruel, simple expedient of compelling it from his own mouth. . . . In sum, the privilege is fulfilled only when the person is guaranteed the right 'to remain silent unless he chooses to speak in the unfettered exercise of his own will.'" Id. The leading case in this Court is Holt v. United States, 218 US 245, 31 S Ct 2, 54 L Ed 1021 [(1910)]. There the question was whether evidence was admissible that the accused, prior to trial and over his protest, put on a blouse that fitted him. It was contended that compelling the accused to submit to the demand that he model the blouse violated the privilege. Mr. Justice Holmes, speaking for the Court, rejected the argument as "based upon an extravagant extension of the Fifth Amendment," and went on to say: "[T]he prohibition of compelling a man in a criminal court to be witness against himself is a prohibition of the use of physical or moral compulsion to extort communications from him, not an exclusion of his body as evidence when it may be material. The objection in principle would forbid a jury to look at a prisoner and compare his features with a photograph in proof." 218 US, at 252–253, 54 L Ed at 1030.[7]

It is clear that the protection of the privilege reaches an accused's communications, whatever form they might take, and the compulsion of responses which are also communications, for example, compliance with a subpoena to produce one's papers. On the other hand, both federal and state courts have usually held that it offers no protection against compulsion to submit to fingerprinting, photographing, or measurements, to write or speak for identification, to appear in court, to stand, to assume a stance, to walk, or to make a particular gesture. The distinction which has emerged, often expressed in different ways, is that the privilege is a bar against compelling "communications" or "testi-

---

7. Compare Wigmore's view, "that the privilege is limited to testimonial disclosures. It was directed at the employment of legal process to *extract from the person's own lips* an admission of guilt, which would thus take the place of other evidence." 8 Wigmore, Evidence § 2263 (McNaughton rev. 1961). . . . Our holding today, however, is not to be understood as adopting the Wigmore formulation.

mony," but that compulsion which makes a suspect or accused the source of "real or physical evidence" does not violate it.

Although we agree that this distinction is a helpful framework for analysis, we are not to be understood to agree with past applications in all instances. There will be many cases in which such a distinction is not readily drawn. Some tests seemingly directed to obtain "physical evidence," for example, lie detector tests measuring changes in body function during interrogation, may actually be directed to eliciting responses which are essentially testimonial. To compel a person to submit to testing in which an effort will be made to determine his guilt or innocence on the basis of physiological responses, whether willed or not, is to evoke the spirit and history of the Fifth Amendment. Such situations call to mind the principle that the protection of the privilege "is as broad as the mischief against which it seeks to guard," Counselman v. Hitchcock, 142 US 547, 562. In the present case, however, no such problem of application is presented. Not even a shadow of testimonial compulsion upon or enforced communication by the accused was involved either in the extraction or in the chemical analysis. Petitioner's testimonial capacities were in no way implicated; indeed, his participation, except as a donor, was irrelevant to the results of the test, which depend on chemical analysis and on that alone.[9] Since the blood test evidence, although an incriminating product of compulsion, was neither petitioner's testimony nor evidence relating to some communicative act or writing by the petitioner, it was not inadmissible on privilege grounds.

* * *

Mr. Justice Black, with whom Mr. Justice Douglas joins, dissenting.

* * *

In the first place it seems to me that the compulsory extraction of petitioner's blood for analysis so that the person who analyzed it could give evidence to convict him had both a "testimonial" and a "communicative nature." The sole purpose of this project which proved to be successful was to obtain "testimony" from some persons to prove that petitioner had alcohol in his blood at the time he was arrested. And the purpose of the project was certainly "communicative" in that the analysis of the blood was to supply information to enable a witness to communicate to the court and jury that petitioner was more or less drunk.

I think it unfortunate that the Court rests so heavily for its very restrictive reading of the Fifth Amendment's privilege against self-incrimination on the words "testimonial" and "communicative." These words are not models of clarity and precision as the Court's rather labored explication shows. Nor can the Court, so far as I know, find precedent in the former opinions of this Court for using these particular words to limit the scope of the Fifth Amendment's protection.

---

9. This conclusion would not necessarily govern had the State tried to show that the accused had incriminated himself when told that he would have to be tested. Such incriminating evidence may be an unavoidable by-product of the compulsion to take the test, especially for an individual who fears the extraction or opposes it on religious grounds. If it wishes to compel persons to submit to such attempts to discover evidence, the State may have to forgo the advantage of any *testimonial* products of administering the test—products which would fall within the privilege. Indeed, there may be circumstances in which the pain, danger, or severity of an operation would almost inevitably cause a person to prefer confession to undergoing the "search," and nothing we say today should be taken as establishing the permissibility of compulsion in that case. But no such situation is presented in this case.

Petitioner has raised a similar issue in this case, in connection with a police request that he submit to a "breathalyzer" test of air expelled from his lungs for alcohol content. He refused the request, and evidence of his refusal was admitted in evidence without objection. He argues that the introduction of this evidence and a comment by the prosecutor in closing argument upon his refusal is ground for reversal under Griffin v. California, 330 US 609, 85 S Ct 1229, 14 L Ed 2d 106 [(1965)]. We think general Fifth Amendment principles, rather than the particular holding of Griffin, would be applicable in these circumstances. Since trial here was conducted after our decision in Malloy v. Hogan, supra, making those principles applicable to the States, we think petitioner's contention is foreclosed by his failure to object on this ground to the prosecutor's questions and statements.

* * *

It concedes, as it must so long as Boyd v. United States, 116 US 616, 6 S Ct 524, 29 L Ed 746, stands, that the Fifth Amendment bars a State from compelling a person to produce papers he has that might tend to incriminate him. It is a strange hierarchy of values that allows the State to extract a human being's blood to convict him of a crime because of the blood's content but proscribes compelled production of his lifeless papers. Certainly there could be few papers that would have any more "testimonial" value to convict a man of drunken driving than would an analysis of the alcoholic content of a human being's blood introduced in evidence at a trial for driving while under the influence of alcohol. In such a situation blood, of course, is not oral testimony given by an accused but it can certainly "communicate" to a court and jury the fact of guilt.

* * *

Mr. Justice Fortas, dissenting.

* * *

Notes and Questions

I. As the Court noted in *Schmerber*, several situations in which an accused has been compelled to produce self-incriminating evidence have been held to concern "nontestimonial," or "physical" or "real," evidence and thus not to constitute violations of rights protected by the Fifth Amendment. The Supreme Court has considered the following types of evidence to be "nontestimonial": the physical display of suspects in lineups, *United States v. Wade*, 388 U.S. 218, 87 S. Ct. 1926, 18 L. Ed. 2d 1149 (1967); the compelled production of handwriting exemplars, *Gilbert v. California*, 388 U.S. 263, 87 S. Ct. 1951, 18 L. Ed. 2d 1178 (1967); *United States v. Mara*, 410 U.S. 19, 93 S. Ct. 774, 35 L. Ed. 2d 99 (1973); and the compelled production of voice exemplars, *United States v. Dionisio*, 410 U.S. 1, 93 S. Ct. 764, 35 L. Ed. 2d 67 (1973). *See also, Holt v. United States*, 218 U.S. 245, 31 S. Ct. 2, 54 L. Ed. 1021 (1910) (putting on a blouse to determine whether it fit the defendant) (cited in *Schmerber*).

2. Consider the issue reserved in footnote 9 of the majority opinion. Assume that a motorist suspected of driving while intoxicated refuses a police officer's request to take a breathalyzer test. Can evidence of his or her refusal be used at his or her trial consistent with his or her Fifth Amendment right against compelled self-incrimination?

In *South Dakota v. Neville*, 459 U.S. 553, 103 S. Ct. 916, 74 L. Ed. 2d 748 (1983), the Court ruled that South Dakota's practice of admitting into evidence a motorist's refusal to submit to a blood alcohol test is permissible under the Fifth Amendment. Justice O'Connor's majority opinion, however, declined to rely on the distinction between nontestimonial and testimonial evidence. Instead, it was based on a theory of "implied consent." Under *Schmerber*, a state has the authority "to authorize police officers to administer a blood-alcohol test against the suspect's will." But "to avoid violent confrontations, the South Dakota statute permits a suspect to refuse the test, and indeed requires police officers to inform the suspect of his right to refuse." 459 U.S., at 559–560. "This permission is not without a price, however." Not only was a motorist's driver's license subject to revocation for one year, but his failure to take the blood alcohol test was admissible as evidence at his trial for driving while intoxicated. The motorist in *Neville* faced a difficult choice in deciding whether to take the blood alcohol test, but his ultimate refusal to take the test was not a "compelled" statement in violation of the Fifth Amendment.

* * * * *

[T]he values behind the Fifth Amendment are not hindered when the State offers a suspect the choice of submitting to the blood-alcohol test or having his refusal used against him. The simple blood-alcohol test is so safe, painless, and commonplace, see Schmerber, 384 US, at 771, that respondent concedes, as he must, that the State could legitimately compel the suspect, against his will, to accede to the test. Given, then, that the offer of taking a blood-alcohol test is clearly legitimate, the action becomes no *less* legitimate when the State offers a second option of refusing the test, with the attendant penalties for making that choice. Nor is this a case where the State has subtly coerced respondent into choosing the option it had no right to compel, rather than offering a true choice. To the contrary, the State wants respondent to choose to take the test, for the inference of intoxication arising from a positive blood-alcohol test is far stronger than that arising from a refusal to take the test.

In arriving at this decision, the *Neville* Court did note that

> many courts have reasoned that refusal to submit [to a blood alcohol test] is a physical act rather than a communication and for this reason is not protected by the [Fifth Amendment] privilege. . . . [Those courts suggest that] evidence of refusal to take a potentially incriminating test is similar to other circumstantial evidence of consciousness of guilt, such as escape from custody and suppression of evidence." 459 U.S., at 560–561.

Although Justice O'Connor found "considerable force in the analogies to flight and suppression of evidence," she indicated for the Court that "we decline to rest our decision on this ground." 459 U.S., at 561.

3. In *Pennsylvania v. Muniz*, 496 U.S. 582, 110 S. Ct. 2638, 110 L. Ed. 2d 528 (1990), a police officer arrested Muniz for driving while intoxicated. The officer transported Muniz to a booking center, where Muniz was asked a series of questions routinely used in drunk-driving cases. This process was both videotaped and audiotaped. Muniz had not been administered his *Miranda* rights prior to being asked those questions, which were as follows:

> Officer Hosterman first asked Muniz his name, address, height, weight, eye color, date of birth, and current age. He responded to each of these questions, stumbling over his address and age. The officer then asked Muniz, "Do you know what the date was of your sixth birthday?" After Muniz offered an inaudible reply, the officer

repeated, "When you turned six years old, do you remember what the date was?" Muniz responded, "No, I don't."

Justice Brennan's plurality opinion in *Muniz* concluded that the first seven questions constituted custodial interrogation within the meaning of *Miranda* but ruled that Muniz's answers "are nonetheless admissible because the questions fall within a 'routine booking question' exception which exempts from Miranda's coverage questions to secure the 'biographical data necessary to complete booking or pretrial services.'" 496 U.S., at 601. Then, writing for a majority of the Court, he explained why Muniz's response to the officer's question "Do you know what the date was of your sixth birthday?" was testimonial in nature and should have been excluded from evidence.

* * * * *

Under Schmerber and its progeny, we agree with the Commonwealth that any slurring of speech and other evidence of lack of muscular coordination revealed by Muniz's responses to Officer Hosterman's direct questions constitute nontestimonial components of those responses. Requiring a suspect to reveal the physical manner in which he articulates words, like requiring him to reveal the physical properties of the sound produced by his voice, does not, without more, compel him to provide a "testimonial" response for purposes of the privilege.

This does not end our inquiry, for Muniz's answer to the sixth birthday question was incriminating, not just because of his delivery, but also because of his answer's *content;* the trier of fact could infer from Muniz's answer (that he did not *know* the proper date) that his mental state was confused.

The Commonwealth and the United States as amicus curiae argue that this incriminating inference does not trigger the protections of the Fifth Amendment privilege because the inference concerns "the physiological functioning of [Muniz's] brain," which is asserted to be every bit as "real or physical" as the physiological makeup of his blood and the timbre of his voice.

But his characterization addresses the wrong question; that the "fact" to be inferred might be said to concern the physical status of Muniz's brain merely describes the way in which the inference is incriminating. The correct question for present purposes is whether the incriminating inference of mental confusion is drawn from a testimonial act or from physical evidence. . . . In this case, the question is not whether a suspect's "impaired mental faculties" can fairly be characterized as an aspect of his physiology, but rather whether Muniz's response to the sixth birthday question that gave rise to the inference of such an impairment was testimonial in nature.

We recently explained in Doe v. United States, 487 US 201, 108 S Ct 2341, 101 L Ed 2d 184 (1988), that "in order to be testimonial, an accused's communication must itself, explicitly or implicitly, relate a factual assertion or disclose information." Id., at 210. We reached this conclusion after addressing our reasoning in Schmerber, supra, and its progeny:

"The Court accordingly held that the privilege was not implicated in [the line of cases beginning with Schmerber], because the suspect was not required 'to disclose any knowledge he might have,' or 'to speak his guilt.' It is the 'extortion of information from the accused,' the attempt to force him 'to disclose the contents of his own mind,' that implicates the Self-Incrimination Clause. . . . 'Unless some attempt is made to secure a communication—written, oral or otherwise—upon which reliance is to be placed as involving [the accused's] consciousness of the facts and the operations of his mind in expressing it, the demand made upon him is not a testimonial one.' 8 Wigmore § 2265, p 386." 487 US, at 210–211.

After canvassing the purposes of the privilege recognized in prior cases, we concluded that "[t]hese policies are served when the privilege is asserted to spare the accused from having to reveal, directly or indirectly, his knowledge of facts relating him to the offense or from having to share his thoughts and beliefs with the Government." Id., at 213.

This definition of testimonial evidence reflects an awareness of the historical abuses against which the privilege against self-incrimination was aimed. "Historically, the privilege was intended to prevent the use of legal compulsion to extract from the accused a sworn communication of facts which would incriminate him. Such was the process of the ecclesiastical courts and the Star Chamber—the inquisitorial method of putting the accused upon his oath and compel-

ling him to answer questions designed to uncover uncharged offenses, without evidence from another source. The major thrust of the policies undergirding the privilege is to prevent such compulsion." Id., at 212. At its core, the privilege reflects our fierce "'unwillingness to subject those suspected of crime to the cruel trilemma of self-accusation, perjury or contempt,'" Doe, supra, at 212, that defined the operation of the Star Chamber, wherein suspects were forced to choose between revealing incriminating private thoughts and forsaking their oath by committing perjury. . . .

Whatever else it may include, therefore, the definition of "testimonial" evidence articulated in Doe must encompass all responses to questions that, if asked of a sworn suspect during a criminal trial, could place the suspect in the "cruel trilemma." . . .

Whenever a suspect is asked for a response requiring him to communicate an express or implied assertion of fact or belief, the suspect confronts the "trilemma" of truth, falsity, or silence, and hence the response (whether based on truth or falsity) contains a testimonial component.

This approach accords with each of our post-Schmerber cases finding that a particular oral or written response to express or implied questioning was nontestimonial; the questions presented in these cases did not confront the suspects with this trilemma. . . .

In contrast, the sixth birthday question in this case required a testimonial response. When Officer Hosterman asked Muniz if he knew the date of his sixth birthday and Muniz, for whatever reason, could not remember or calculate that date, he was confronted with the trilemma. By hypothesis, the inherently coercive environment created by the custodial interrogation precluded the option of remaining silent. Muniz was left with the choice of incriminating himself by admitting that he did not then know the date of his sixth birthday, or answering untruthfully by reporting a date that he did not then believe to be accurate (an incorrect guess would be incriminating as well as untruthful). The content of his truthful answer supported an inference that his mental faculties were impaired, because his assertion (he did not know the date of his sixth birthday) was different from the assertion (he knew the date was [correct date]) that the trier of fact might reasonably have expected a lucid person to provide. Hence, the incriminating inference of impaired mental faculties stemmed, not just from the fact that Muniz slurred his response, but also from a testimonial aspect of that response.

* * *

Chief Justice Rehnquist, joined by Justices White, Blackmun, and Stevens, dissented.

* * *

The Court holds that the sixth birthday question Muniz was asked required a testimonial response, and that its admission at trial therefore violated Muniz's privilege against compulsory self-incrimination. The Court says that

> "[w]hen Officer Hosterman asked Muniz if he knew the date of his sixth birthday and Muniz, for whatever reason, could not remember or calculate that date, he was confronted with the trilemma [i.e., the "'trilemma" of truth, falsity, or silence,'] . . . . Muniz was left with the choice of incriminating himself by admitting that he did not then know the date of his sixth birthday, or answering untruthfully by reporting a date that he did not then believe to be accurate (an incorrect guess would be incriminating as well as untruthful)."

As an assumption about human behavior, this statement is wrong. Muniz would no more have felt compelled to fabricate a false date than one who cannot read the letters on an eye chart feels compelled to fabricate false letters; nor does a wrong guess call into question a speaker's veracity. The Court's statement is also a flawed predicate on which to base its conclusion that Muniz's answer to this question was "testimonial" for purposes of the Fifth Amendment.

The need for the use of the human voice does not automatically make an answer testimonial, any more than does the fact that a question calls for the exhibition of one's handwriting in written characters. . . .

The sixth birthday question here was an effort on the part of the police to check how well Muniz was able to do a simple mathematical exercise. . . .

If the police may require Muniz to use his body in order to demonstrate the level of his physical coordination, there is no reason why they should not be able to require him to speak or write in order to determine his mental coordination. That was all that was sought here. Since it was permissible for the police to extract and examine a sample of Schmerber's blood to determine how much that part of his system had been affected by alcohol, I see no reason why they may not examine the functioning of Muniz's mental processes for the same purpose.

Surely if it were relevant, a suspect might be asked to take an eye examination in the course of which he might have to admit that he could not read the letters on the third line of the chart. At worst, he might utter a mistaken guess. Muniz likewise might have attempted to guess the correct response to the sixth birthday question instead of attempting to calculate the date or answer "I don't know." But the potential for giving a bad guess does not subject the suspect to the truth-falsity-silence predicament that renders a response testimonial and, therefore, within the scope of the Fifth Amendment privilege.

* * *

📖 **4. Legal research note.** One way to find more federal and state cases dealing with nontestimonial evidence is to look up the Fifth Amendment in an annotated version of the U.S. Constitution. The two leading references you can consult are the "Constitution" volumes within the *United States Code Annotated* (West Publishing Co.), and the *United States Code Service* (Lawyers Cooperative Publishing Co.). The Fifth Amendment, like other provisions of the Constitution, is reprinted in these volumes, and it is indexed with hundreds of topics and subtopics. Each individual subtopic is assigned a separate number. Connected to each number, you will find immensely helpful "annotations," or brief summaries of relevant judicial decisions, with accompanying citations.

For example, the major topic headings corresponding to the Fifth Amendment's self-incrimination clause in West's *United States Code Annotated* include "Testimonial Nature of Evidence—Generally," and "Testimonial Nature of Evidence—Physical and Mental Examination." Scores of subtopics are provided under each heading, and hundreds of case annotations corresponding to those issues are provided. Be sure to check the most recent supplementary pamphlet, as well as the bound volume of the annotated Consti-tution. By using an annotated volume of the U.S. Constitution, or of a state constitution, you can quickly and efficiently produce a large number of judicial decisions addressing spe-cific constitutional issues.

THE SIXTH AMENDMENT RIGHT TO COUNSEL AND ITS APPLICATION TO CONFESSIONS

The *Miranda* rights are designed to protect the Fifth Amendment's privilege against com-pelled self-incrimination. Although they include the right to counsel, and to a court-appointed lawyer if the suspect cannot afford to hire an attorney, *Miranda's* protections are importantly different from the Sixth Amendment's counsel provision. The Sixth Amendment guarantees that "in all criminal prosecutions, the accused shall enjoy the right . . . to have the Assistance of Counsel for his defense."

We know that *Miranda's* Fifth Amendment concerns are triggered by custodial interroga-tion. The Sixth Amendment counsel provision has no such limitation. Recall our prior consid-eration of *Massiah v. United States* (p. 267). Massiah, who had been indicted for a federal drug offense and had been released from cus-tody on bail while awaiting trial, was duped into conversing with a man named Colson, who was a codefendant and an indicted coconspirator. Their conversation was monitored by federal agents who, with Colson's cooperation, had installed a hidden transmitting device in Col-son's car. Note that the notion of custodial inter-rogation is inapposite in this context, since Massiah was not in custody and indeed was not even aware that law enforcement officers were listening to his conversation with Colson. The Court ruled, however, that *Massiah's* Sixth Amendment right to counsel had been violated by the agents' conduct.

A second crucial distinction between *Miranda* and the Sixth Amendment right to counsel also is illustrated by *Massiah*. At the time that the federal agents enlisted Colson's help in eliciting incriminating statements from Massiah, Massiah already had been indicted— that is, formally charged by a grand jury with committing the drug offense. When we return to study the Sixth Amendment counsel provision in other contexts, including the placement of suspects in lineups (see pp. 415–427), we will learn more about why the postindictment time frame is so important. For now, make note of how the Sixth Amendment, by its very lan-guage, applies to "criminal *prosecutions*" (emphasis added). The Court has ruled that the right to counsel guaranteed by the Sixth Amendment applies only after the government has taken formal steps to commence prosecu-tion of a crime, "'whether by way of formal charge, preliminary hearing, indictment, infor-mation, or arraignment.'" *Brewer v. Williams*, 430 U.S. 387, 398, 97 S. Ct. 1232, 51 L. Ed. 2d 424 (1977), *quoting Kirby v. Illinois*, 406 U.S. 682, 689, 92 S. Ct. 1877, 32 L. Ed. 2d 411 (1972). *Miranda*, of course, can apply much earlier in the criminal justice process—and typically becomes relevant during the police's investiga-tion of crimes, well before a suspect has been formally charged with committing an offense.

Just prior to deciding *Miranda* the justices briefly experimented in *Escobedo v. Illinois* (p. 268) with using the Sixth Amendment to con-trol the questioning of suspects before formal adversarial proceedings had been initiated. *Escobedo* is best understood as a temporary way station to the Court's ultimate "solution" in *Miranda* of how to regulate police interrogation practices. In *Moran v. Burbine*, 475 U.S. 412, 429, 106 S. Ct. 1135, 89 L. Ed. 2d 410 (1986), the

Court stated that "subsequent decisions foreclose any reliance on *Escobedo* . . . for the proposition that the Sixth Amendment right, in any of its manifestations, applies prior to the initiation of adversary judicial proceedings." *See also* Marcus, "A Return to the 'Bright Line Rule' of *Miranda*," 35 *William and Mary Law Review* 93, 104–105 (1993).

In addition to *Massiah* and *Escobedo*, we have considered the Sixth Amendment right to counsel in *Brewer v. Williams* (p. 6). The Supreme Court held in that case that the statements Robert Williams made in response to Detective Leaming's "Christian burial speech" had been deliberately elicited in violation of Williams's Sixth Amendment right to counsel and that Williams had not knowingly, intelligently, and voluntarily waived that right. We now focus on additional cases involving Sixth Amendment issues and confessions. We first present a portion of Justice Brennan's opinion for the Court in *Maine v. Moulton*, 474 U.S. 159, 106 S. Ct. 477, 88 L. Ed. 2d 481 (1985), which describes the significance of the Sixth Amendment right to counsel to the administration of criminal justice.

* * * * *

The right to the assistance of counsel guaranteed by the Sixth and Fourteenth Amendments is indispensable to the fair administration of our adversarial system of criminal justice. Embodying "a realistic recognition of the obvious truth that the average defendant does not have the professional legal skill to protect himself," Johnson v. Zerbst, 304 US 458, 462–463, 58 S Ct 1019, 82 L Ed 1461 (1938), the right to counsel safeguards the other rights deemed essential for the fair prosecution of a criminal proceeding. Justice Sutherland's oft-quoted explanation in Powell v. Alabama, 287 US 45, 53 S Ct 55, 77 L Ed 158 (1932), bears repetition here:

"The right to be heard would be, in many cases, of little avail if it did not comprehend the right to be heard by counsel. Even the intelligent and educated layman has small and sometimes no skill in the science of law. If charged with crime, he is incapable, generally, of determining for himself whether the indictment is good or bad. He is unfamiliar with the rules of evidence. Left without the aid of counsel he may be put on trial without a proper charge, and convicted upon incompetent evidence, or evidence irrelevant to the issue or otherwise inadmissible. He lacks both the skill and knowledge adequately to prepare his defense, even though he have a perfect one. He requires the guiding hand of counsel at every stage of the proceedings against him." Id.

As indicated in the last sentence of this paragraph, the Court has also recognized that the assistance of counsel cannot be limited to participation in a trial; to deprive a person of counsel during the period prior to trial may be more damaging than denial of counsel during the trial itself. Recognizing that the right to the assistance of counsel is shaped by the need for the assistance of counsel, we have found that the right attaches at earlier, "critical" stages in the criminal justice process "where the results might well settle the accused's fate and reduce the trial itself to a mere formality." And, "[w]hatever else it may mean, the right to counsel granted by the Sixth and Fourteenth Amendments means at least that a person is entitled to the help of a lawyer at or after the time that judicial proceedings have been initiated against him. . . ." Brewer v. Williams, 430 US 387, 398, 97 S Ct 1232, 51 L Ed 2d 424 (1977). This is because, after the initiation of adversary criminal proceedings, "'the government has committed itself to prosecute, and . . . the adverse positions of government and defendant have solidified. It is then that a defendant finds himself faced with the prosecutorial forces of organized society, and immersed in the intricacies of substantive and procedural criminal law.'"

* * * * *

The Meaning of "Deliberately Elicit"

A suspect in police custody who volunteers an incriminating statement, without being "interrogated," does not benefit from *Miranda*. See *Rhode Island v. Innis*, p. 295. In the Sixth Amendment context, an individual who makes an incriminating statement suffers no violation of his or her right to counsel unless law enforcement officials "deliberately elicit" the statement. The meaning of *deliberately elicit* is discussed in the next two cases.

United States v. Henry, 447 U.S. 264, 100 S. Ct. 2183, 65 L. Ed. 2d 115 (1980)

Mr. Chief Justice Burger delivered the opinion of the Court.

* * *

[The Janaf Branch of a federally insured bank was robbed in Norfolk, Virginia in August 1972. Henry was arrested in November 1972 and was indicted for the bank robbery two weeks later. He was held pending trial in the Norfolk city jail. A lawyer was appointed to represent him on November 27.]

On November 21, 1972, shortly after Henry was incarcerated, Government agents working on the Janaf robbery contacted one Nichols, an inmate at the Norfolk city jail, who for some time prior to this meeting had been engaged to provide confidential information to the Federal Bureau of Investigation as a paid informant. Nichols was then serving a sentence on local forgery charges. The record does not disclose whether the agent contacted Nichols specifically to acquire information about Henry or the Janaf robbery.

Nichols informed the agent that he was housed in the same cellblock with several federal prisoners awaiting trial, including Henry. The agent told him to be alert to any statements made by the federal prisoners, but not to initiate any conversation with or question Henry regarding the bank robbery. In early December, after Nichols had been released from jail, the agent again contacted Nichols, who reported that he and Henry had engaged in conversation and that Henry had told him about the robbery of the Janaf bank. Nichols was paid for furnishing the information.

* * *

Nichols testified at trial that he had "an opportunity to have some conversations with Mr. Henry while he was in the jail," and that Henry told him that on several occasions he had gone to the Janaf Branch to see which employees opened the vault. Nichols also testified that Henry described to him the details of the robbery and stated that the only evidence connecting him to the robbery was the rental receipt. The jury was not informed that Nichols was a paid Government informant.

On the basis of this testimony, Henry was convicted of bank robbery and sentenced to a term of imprisonment of 25 years. . . .

On August 28, 1975, Henry moved to vacate his sentence pursuant to 28 USC §2255. At this stage, he stated that he had just learned that Nichols was a paid Government informant and alleged that he had been intentionally placed in the same cell with Nichols so that Nichols could secure information about the robbery. Thus, Henry contended that the introduction of Nichols' testimony violated his Sixth Amendment right to the assistance of counsel.

* * *

The present case involves incriminating statements made by the accused to an undisclosed and undercover Government informant while in custody and after indictment. The Government characterizes Henry's incriminating statements as voluntary and not the result of any affirmative conduct on the part of Government agents to elicit evidence. From this, the Government argues that Henry's rights were not violated, even assuming the Sixth Amendment applies to such surreptitious confrontations; in short, it is contended that the Government has not interfered with Henry's right to counsel.

This Court first applied the Sixth Amendment to postindictment communications between the accused and agents of the Government in Massiah v. United States. . . . The Massiah holding rests squarely on interference with his right to counsel.

The question here is whether under the facts of this case, a Government agent "deliberately elicited" incriminating statements from Henry within the meaning of Massiah. Three factors are important. First, Nichols was acting under instructions as a paid informant for the Government; second, Nichols was ostensibly no more than a fellow inmate of Henry; and third, Henry was in custody and under indictment at the time he was engaged in conversation by Nichols.

The Court of Appeals viewed the record as showing that Nichols deliberately used his position to secure incriminating information from Henry when counsel was not present and held that conduct attributable to the Government. Nichols had been a paid Government informant for more than a year; moreover, the FBI agent was aware that Nichols had access to Henry and would be able to engage him in conversations without arousing Henry's suspicion. The arrangement between Nichols and the agent was on a contingent-fee basis; Nichols was to be paid only if he produced useful information.

This combination of circumstances is sufficient to support the Court of Appeals' determination. Even if the agent's statement that he did not intend that Nichols would take affirmative steps to secure incriminating information is accepted; he must have known that such propinquity likely would lead to that result.

The Government argues that the federal agents instructed Nichols not to question Henry about the robbery. Yet according to his own testimony, Nichols was not a passive listener; rather, he had "some conversations with Mr. Henry" while he was in jail and Henry's incriminatory statements were "the product of this conversa-

tion." While affirmative interrogation, absent waiver, would certainly satisfy Massiah, we are not persuaded, as the Government contends, that Brewer v. Williams, 430 US 387, 97 S Ct 1232, 51 L Ed 2d 424 (1977), modified Massiah's "deliberately elicited" test. See Rhode Island v. Innis, 446 US 291, 300, n 4, 100 S Ct 1682, 64 L Ed 2d 297 (1980).[9] In Massiah, no inquiry was made as to whether Massiah or his codefendant first raised the subject of the crime under investigation.

It is quite a different matter when the Government uses undercover agents to obtain incriminating statements from persons not in custody but suspected of criminal activity prior to the time charges are filed. In Hoffa v. United States, 385 US 293, 302, 87 S Ct 408, 17 L Ed 2d 374 (1966), for example, this Court held that "no interest legitimately protected by the Fourth Amendment is involved" because "the Fourth Amendment [does not protect] a wrongdoer's misplaced belief that a person to whom he voluntarily confides his wrongdoing will not reveal it." See also United States v. White, 401 US 745, 91 S Ct 1122, 28 L Ed 2d 453 (1971). Similarly, the Fifth Amendment has been held not to be implicated by the use of undercover Government agents before charges are filed because of the absence of the potential for compulsion. See Hoffa v. United States, supra, at 303–304, 87 S Ct 408, 17 L Ed 2d 374. But the Fourth and Fifth Amendment claims made in those cases are not relevant to the inquiry under the Sixth Amendment here—whether the Government has interfered with the right to counsel of the accused by "deliberately eliciting" incriminating statements. Our holding today does not modify White or Hoffa.

---

9. The situation where the "listening post" is an inanimate electronic device differs; such a device has no capability of leading the conversation into any particular subject or prompting any particular replies. However, that situation is not presented in this case, and there is no occasion to treat it; nor are we called upon to pass on the situation where an informant is placed in close proximity but makes no effort to stimulate conversations about the crime charged.

It is undisputed that Henry was unaware of Nichols' role as a Government informant. The Government argues that this Court should apply a less rigorous standard under the Sixth Amendment where the accused is prompted by an undisclosed undercover informant than where the accused is speaking in the hearing of persons he knows to be Government officers. That line of argument, however, seeks to infuse Fifth Amendment concerns against compelled self-incrimination into the Sixth Amendment protection of the right to the assistance of counsel. An accused speaking to a known Government agent is typically aware that his statements may be used against him. The adversary positions at that stage are well established; the parties are then "arm's-length" adversaries.

When the accused is in the company of a fellow inmate who is acting by prearrangement as a Government agent, the same cannot be said. Conversation stimulated in such circumstances may elicit information that an accused would not intentionally reveal to persons known to be Government agents. . . .

Moreover, the concept of a knowing and voluntary waiver of Sixth Amendment rights does not apply in the context of communications with an undisclosed undercover informant acting for the Government. In that setting, Henry, being unaware that Nichols was a Government agent expressly commissioned to secure evidence, cannot be held to have waived his right to the assistance of counsel.

Finally, Henry's incarceration at the time he was engaged in conversation by Nichols is also a relevant factor.[11] As a ground for imposing the prophylactic requirements in Miranda v. Arizona, 384 US 436, 467, 86 S Ct 1602, 16 L Ed 2d 694 (1966), this Court noted the powerful psychological inducements to reach for aid when a person is in confinement. While the concern in Miranda was limited to custodial police interrogation, the mere fact of custody imposes pressures on the accused; confinement may bring into play subtle influences that will make him particularly susceptible to the ploys of undercover Government agents. The Court of Appeals determined that on this record the incriminating conversations between Henry and Nichols were facilitated by Nichols' conduct and apparent status as a person sharing a common plight. . . .

By intentionally creating a situation likely to induce Henry to make incriminating statements without the assistance of counsel, the Government violated Henry's Sixth Amendment right to counsel. This is not a case where, in Justice Cardozo's words, "the constable . . . blundered," People v. DeFore, 242 NY 13, 21, 150 NE 585, 587 (1926); rather, it is one where the "constable" planned an impermissible interference with the right to the assistance of counsel.

* * *

Mr. Justice **Powell**, concurring.

* * *

The rule of Massiah serves the salutary purpose of preventing police interference with the relationship between a suspect and his counsel once formal proceedings have been initiated. But Massiah does not prohibit the introduction of spontaneous statements that are not elicited by governmental action. Thus, the Sixth Amendment is not violated when a passive listening device collects, but does not induce, incriminating comments. Similarly, the mere presence of a jailhouse informant who had been instructed to overhear conversations and to engage a criminal defendant in some conversations would not necessarily be unconstitutional. In such a case, the question would be whether the informant's actions constituted deliberate and "surreptitious interrogatio[n]" of the defendant. If they did not, then there would be no interference with the relationship between client and counsel.

* * *

I could not join the Court's opinion if it held that the mere presence or incidental conversation of an informant in a jail cell would violate

---

11. This is not to read a "custody" requirement, which is a prerequisite to the attachment of Miranda rights, into this branch of the Sixth Amendment. Massiah was in no sense in custody at the time of his conversation with his codefendant. Rather, we believe the fact of custody bears on whether the Government "deliberately elicited" the incriminating statements from Henry.

Massiah. To demonstrate an infringement of the Sixth Amendment, a defendant must show that the government engaged in conduct that, considering all of the circumstances, is the functional equivalent of interrogation. See Brewer v. Williams, 430 US, at 399, id., at 411, 412 (Powell, J., concurring). See also Rhode Island v. Innis, 446 US 291, 100 S Ct 1682, 64 L Ed 2d 297 (1980).

* * *

Mr. Justice **Blackmun,** with whom Mr. Justice **White** joins, dissenting.

* * *

Massiah mandates exclusion only if a federal agent "deliberately elicited" statements from the accused in the absence of counsel.

The word "deliberately" denotes intent. Massiah ties this intent to the act of elicitation, that is, to conduct that draws forth a response. Thus Massiah, by its own terms, covers only action undertaken with the specific intent to evoke an inculpatory disclosure.

Faced with agent Coughlin's unequivocal expression of an intent not to elicit statements from respondent Henry, but merely passively to receive them, the Court, in its decision to affirm the judgment of the Court of Appeals, has no choice but to depart from the natural meaning of the Massiah formulation. The Court deems it critical that informant Nichols had been a paid informant; that Agent Coughlin was aware that Nichols "had access" to Henry and "would be able to engage him in conversations without arousing Henry's suspicion"; and that payment to Nichols was on a contingent-fee basis. Thus, it is said, even if Coughlin's "statement is accepted . . . he must have known that such propinquity likely would lead to that result" (that is, that Nichols would take "affirmative steps to secure incriminating information"). Later, the Court goes even further, characterizing this as a case of "intentionally creating a situation *likely to induce* Henry to make incriminating statements." (Emphasis added.) This determination, coupled with the statement that Nichols "prompted" respondent Henry's remarks, leads the Court to find a Massiah violation.

Thus, while claiming to retain the "deliberately elicited" test, the Court really forges a new test that saps the word "deliberately" of all significance. The Court's extension of Massiah would cover even a "negligent" triggering of events resulting in reception of disclosures. This approach, in my view, is unsupported and unwise.

* * *

In my view, the Court not only missteps in forging a new Massiah test; it proceeds to misapply the very test it has created. . . .

A. *"Likely to Induce."* In holding that Coughlin's actions were likely to induce Henry's statements, the Court relies on three facts: a contingent-fee arrangement; Henry's assumption that Nichols was just a cellmate; and Henry's incarceration.

* * *

The Court does more than rely on dubious factors in finding that Coughlin's actions were "likely to induce" Nichols' successful prompting of Henry; it fails to focus on facts that cut strongly against that conclusion. The Court ignores Coughlin's specific instruction to Nichols that he was not to question Henry or to initiate conversation with him about the robbery. Nor does it note Nichols' likely assumption that he would not be remunerated, but reprimanded and possibly penalized, if he violated Coughlin's orders. On these facts, I cannot agree that Coughlin "must have known that [it was] likely" that Nichols would seek elicit information from Henry.

* * *

B. *"Prompting."* All Members of the Court agree that Henry's statements were properly admitted if Nichols did not "prompt" him. The record, however, gives no indication that Nichols "stimulated" Henry's remarks, with "affirmative steps to secure incriminating information." I cannot believe that Massiah requires exclusion when a cellmate previously unknown to the defendant and asked only to keep his ears open says: "It's a nice day," and the defendant responds: "It would be nicer if I hadn't robbed that bank."

* * *

Kuhlmann v. Wilson, 477 U.S. 436, 106 S. Ct. 2616, 91 L. Ed. 2d 364 (1986)

Justice Powell . . . delivered the opinion of the Court. . . .

In the early morning of July 4, 1970, respondent and two confederates robbed the Star Taxicab Garage in the Bronx, New York, and fatally shot the night dispatcher. Shortly before, employees of the garage had observed respondent, a former employee there, on the premises conversing with two other men. They also witnessed respondent fleeing after the robbery, carrying loose money in his arms. After eluding the police for four days, respondent turned himself in. Respondent admitted that he had been present when the crimes took place, claimed that he had witnessed the robbery, gave the police a description of the robbers, but denied knowing them. Respondent also denied any involvement in the robbery or murder, claiming that he had fled because he was afraid of being blamed for the crimes.

After his arraignment, respondent was confined in the Bronx House of Detention, where he was placed in a cell with a prisoner named Benny Lee. Unknown to respondent, Lee had agreed to act as a police informant. Respondent made incriminating statements that Lee reported to the police. Prior to trial, respondent moved to suppress the statements on the ground that they were obtained in violation of his right to counsel. The trial court held an evidentiary hearing on the suppression motion, which revealed that the statements were made under the following circumstances.

Before respondent arrived in the jail, Lee had entered into an arrangement with Detective Cullen, according to which Lee agreed to listen to respondent's conversations and report his remarks to Cullen. Since the police had positive evidence of respondent's participation, the purpose of placing Lee in the cell was to determine the identities of respondent's confederates. Cullen instructed Lee not to ask respondent any questions, but simply to "keep his ears open" for the names of the other perpetrators. Respondent first spoke to Lee about the crimes after he looked out the cellblock window at the Star Taxicab Garage, where the crimes had occurred. Respondent said "someone's messing with me," and began talking to Lee about the robbery, narrating the same story that he had given the police at the time of his arrest. Lee advised respondent that this explanation "didn't sound too good," but respondent did not alter his story. Over the next few days, however, respondent changed details of his original account. Respondent then received a visit from his brother, who mentioned that members of his family were upset because they believed that respondent had murdered the dispatcher. After the visit, respondent again described the crimes to Lee. Respondent now admitted that he and two other men, whom he never identified, had planned and carried out the robbery, and had murdered the dispatcher. Lee informed Cullen of respondent's statements and furnished Cullen with notes that he had written surreptitiously while sharing the cell with respondent.

After hearing the testimony of Cullen and Lee, the trial court found that Cullen had instructed Lee "to ask no questions of [respondent] about the crime but merely to listen as to what [respondent] might say in his presence." The court determined that Lee obeyed these instructions, that he "at no time asked any questions with respect to the crime," and that he "only listened to [respondent] and made notes regarding what [respondent] had to say." The trial court also found that respondent's statements to Lee were "spontaneous" and "unsolicited." Under state precedent, a defendant's volunteered statements to a police agent were admissible in evidence because the police were not required to prevent talkative defendants from making incriminating statements.

The jury convicted respondent of common-law murder and felonious possession of a weapon. . . .

[After the state courts affirmed Wilson's conviction and the U.S. District Court denied his habeas corpus petition, the Second Circuit Court of Appeals reversed.]

. . . [W]e conclude that [the Court of Appeals] erred in holding that respondent was entitled to relief under United States v. Henry, 447 US 264, 100 S Ct 2183, 65 L Ed 2d 115 (1980). As the District Court observed, Henry left open the question whether the Sixth Amendment forbids admission in evidence of an accused's statements to a jailhouse informant who was "placed in close proximity but [made] no effort to stimulate conversations about the crime charged."

* * *

[T]he primary concern of the Massiah line of decisions is secret interrogation by investigatory techniques that are the equivalent of direct police interrogation. Since "the Sixth Amendment is not violated whenever—by luck or happenstance—the State obtains incriminating statements from the accused after the right to counsel has attached," [Maine v. Moulton, 474 U.S. 159, 176, 106 S. Ct. 477, 88 L. Ed. 2d 481 (1985)] a defendant does not make out a violation of that right simply by showing that an informant, either through prior arrangement or voluntarily, reported his incriminating statements to the police. Rather, the defendant must demonstrate that the police and their informant took some action, beyond merely listening, that was designed deliberately to elicit incriminating remarks.

It is thus apparent that the Court of Appeals erred in concluding that respondent's right to counsel was violated under the circumstances of this case. . . .

The state court found that Officer Cullen had instructed Lee only to listen to respondent for the purpose of determining the identities of the other participants in the robbery and murder. The police already had solid evidence of respondent's participation. The court further found that Lee followed those instructions, that he "at no time asked any questions" of respondent concerning the pending charges, and that he "only listened" to respondent's "spontaneous" and "unsolicited" statements. The only remark made by Lee that has any support in this record was

his comment that respondent's initial version of his participation in the crimes "didn't sound too good." Without holding that any of the state court's findings were not entitled to the presumption of correctness under § 2254(d), the Court of Appeals focused on that one remark and gave a description of Lee's interaction with respondent that is completely at odds with the facts found by the trial court. In the Court of Appeals' view, "[s]ubtly and slowly, but surely, Lee's ongoing verbal intercourse with [respondent] served to exacerbate [respondent's] already troubled state of mind." After thus revising some of the trial court's findings, and ignoring other more relevant findings, the Court of Appeals concluded that the police "deliberately elicited" respondent's incriminating statements. This conclusion conflicts with the decision of every other state and federal judge who reviewed this record, and is clear error in light of the provisions and intent of § 2254(d).

* * *

Chief Justice **Burger,** concurring.

I agree fully with the Court's opinion and judgment. This case is clearly distinguishable from United States v. Henry, 447 US 264, 100 S Ct 2183, 65 L Ed 2d 115 (1980). There is a vast difference between placing an "ear" in the suspect's cell and placing a voice in the cell to encourage conversation for the "ear" to record.

* * *

Justice **Brennan,** with whom Justice **Marshall** joins, dissenting.

* * *

I disagree with the Court that the instant case presents the "listening post" question.

The state trial court simply found that Lee did not ask respondent any direct questions about the crime for which respondent was incarcerated. . . .

The Court of Appeals did not disregard the state court's finding that Lee asked respondent no direct questions regarding the crime. Rather, the Court of Appeals *expressly accepted* that finding, . . . but concluded that, as a matter of law, the deliberate elicitation standard of Henry, and Massiah, encompasses other, more subtle forms of stimulating incriminating admissions than overt questioning. The court suggested that the police deliberately placed respondent in a cell that overlooked the scene of the crime, hoping that the view would trigger an inculpatory comment to respondent's cellmate. The court also observed that, while Lee asked respondent no questions, Lee nonetheless stimulated conversation concerning respondents' role in the Star Taxicab Garage robbery and murder by remarking that respondent's exculpatory story did not "'sound too good'" and that he had better come up with a better one. Thus, the Court of Appeals concluded that the respondent's case did not present the situation reserved in Henry, where an accused makes an incriminating remark within the hearing of a jailhouse informant, who "makes no effort to stimulate conversations about the crime charged." Instead, the court determined this case to be virtually indistinguishable from Henry.

The Sixth Amendment guarantees an accused, at least after the initiation of formal charges, the right to rely on counsel as the "medium" between himself and the State. Accordingly, the Sixth Amendment "imposes on the State an affirmative obligation to respect and reserve the accused's choice to seek [the assistance of counsel]," and therefore "[t]he determination whether particular action by state agents violates the accused's right to . . . counsel must be made in light of this obligation." To be sure, the Sixth Amendment is not violated whenever, "by luck or happenstance," the State obtains incriminating statements from the accused after the right to counsel has attached. It is violated, however, when "the State obtains incriminating statements by knowingly circumventing the accused's right to have counsel present in a confrontation between the accused and a state agent." As we explained in Henry, where the accused has not waived his right to counsel, the government knowingly circumvents the defendant's right to counsel where it "deliberately elicit[s]" inculpatory admissions, that is, "intentionally create[es] a situation likely to induce [the accused] to make incriminating statements without the assistance of counsel."

* * *

In the instant case, as in Henry, the accused was incarcerated and therefore was "susceptible to the ploys of undercover Government agents." Like Nichols, Lee was a secret informant, usually received consideration for the services he rendered the police, and therefore had an incentive to produce the information which he knew the police hoped to obtain. Just as Nichols had done, Lee obeyed instructions not to question respondent and to report to the police any statements made by the respondent in Lee's presence about the crime in question. And, like Nichols, Lee encouraged respondent to talk about his crime by conversing with him on the subject over the course of several days and by telling respondent that his exculpatory story would not convince anyone without more work. However, unlike the situation in Henry, a disturbing visit from respondent's brother, rather than a conversation with the informant, seems to have been the immediate catalyst for respondent's confession to Lee. While it might appear from this sequence of events that Lee's comment regarding respondent's story and his general willingness to converse with respondent about the crime were not the *immediate* causes of respondent's admission, I think that the deliberate-elicitation standard requires consideration of the entire course of government behavior.

The State intentionally created a situation in which it was foreseeable that respondent would make incriminating statements without the assistance of counsel—it assigned respondent to a cell overlooking the scene of the crime and designated a secret informant to be respondent's cellmate. The informant, while avoiding direct questions, nonetheless developed a relationship of cellmate camaraderie with respondent and encouraged him to talk about his crime. While the coup de grace was delivered by respondent's brother, the groundwork for respondent's confession was laid by the State. Clearly the State's actions had a sufficient nexus with respondent's admission of guilt to constitute deliberate elicitation within the meaning of Henry.

* * *

Notes and Questions

l. Chief Justice Burger, who authored the majority opinion in *United States v. Henry* and concluded that Henry's Sixth Amendment rights had been violated, found *Henry* to be "clearly distinguishable" from *Kuhlmann v. Wilson*: "There is a vast difference between placing an 'ear' in the suspect's cell and placing a voice in the cell to encourage conversation for the 'ear' to record." How different are *Henry* and *Wilson*? Specifically:

a. Didn't the federal agent in *Henry* instruct the informant, Nichols, "not to initiate any conversation with or question Henry regarding the bank robbery," while the law enforcement officer in *Wilson* told the informant, Lee, "not to ask [Wilson] any questions, but simply to 'keep his ears open' for the names of the other perpetrators"?

b. The informant in *Henry* "was not a passive listener; rather, he had 'some conversations with Mr. Henry' while he was in jail and Henry's incriminating statements were 'the product of this conversation.'" At the same time, the informant in *Wilson* conversed with Wilson and "advised [him] that this explanation [which he previously had offered the police] 'didn't sound too good.'" Wilson, however, "did not alter his story" until after receiving a visit from his brother.

c. Henry and Wilson were both incarcerated.

d. Law enforcement agents in both cases knew and hoped that the respective informants might overhear valuable information.

e. The informant in *Henry* was paid. The informant in *Wilson* "usually received consideration for the services he rendered the police and therefore had an incentive to produce the information which he knew the police hoped to obtain."

f. Additionally, the authorities in *Wilson* placed the defendant in a cell block with a window overlooking "the Star Taxicab Garage, where the crimes had occurred."

In light of all of these similarities, what differences between the cases justify the different outcomes in *Henry* and *Wilson*?

2. The Court concludes in *Henry* that "by intentionally creating a situation likely to induce Henry to make incriminating statements without the assistance of counsel, the Government violated Henry's Sixth Amendment right to counsel." Does this "test" seem to survive *Kuhlmann v. Wilson*? If it does, what result would be produced by a faithful application of the test to the facts in *Wilson*?

3. Why wasn't *Miranda* an issue in either *Henry* or *Wilson*? (See *Illinois v. Perkins*, p. 291.)

4. In *Maine v. Moulton*, 474 U.S. 159, 106 S. Ct. 477, 88 L. Ed. 2d 481 (1985), the Court held that state law enforcement agents "deliberately elicited" incriminating statements from an indicted defendant, even though the defendant, rather than the government, was responsible for initiating a telephone call and requesting a meeting during which the statements were made. Justice Brennan's majority opinion first noted that "the identity of the party who instigated the meeting at which the Government obtained incriminating statements was not decisive or even important to our decisions in Massiah and Henry." 474 U.S., at 174. The police in *Moulton* had suggested that Moulton's confidante—an indicted codefendant who coincidentally (as in *Massiah*) was named Colson—should tape-record the telephone conversation and wear a body wire transmitter so that the police could tape-record their meeting. Justice Brennan explained why the police conduct violated Moulton's Sixth Amendment right to counsel.

The Sixth Amendment guarantees the accused, at least after the initiation of formal charges, the right to rely on counsel as a "medium" between him and the State. . . .

[T]his guarantee includes the State's affirmative obligation not to act in a manner that circumvents the protections accorded the accused by invoking this right. The determination whether particular action by state agents violates the accused's right to the assistance of counsel must be made in light of this obligation. Thus, the Sixth Amendment is not violated whenever—by luck or happenstance—the State obtains incriminating statements from the accused after the right to counsel has attached. However, knowing exploitation by the State of an opportunity to confront the accused without counsel being present is as much a breach of the State's obligation not to circumvent the right to the assistance of counsel as is the intentional creation of such an opportunity. Accordingly, the Sixth Amendment is violated when the State obtains incriminating statements by knowingly circumventing the accused's right to have counsel present in a confrontation between the accused and a state agent. . . .

Invocation and Waiver of the Sixth Amendment Right to Counsel

In the *Miranda* context, *Edwards v. Arizona* (p. 310) holds that once a suspect invokes his or her right to counsel, the police may not resume questioning unless the suspect "initiates" further offense-related communications and then waives his or her rights. *Arizona v. Roberson* (p. 314) held that the *Edwards* rule also prohibits police-initiated questioning about different crimes than were the subject of the original interrogation attempt. We now consider analogous issues involving the invocation and waiver of the Sixth Amendment right to counsel.

The defendants in *Michigan v. Jackson*, 475 U.S. 625, 106 S. Ct. 1404, 89 L. Ed. 2d 631 (1986), were arrested for crimes and taken before a judge or magistrate for a first appearance, or arraignment. At that proceeding, each defendant requested that a lawyer be appointed to represent him. Before either had an opportunity to consult with counsel, the police advised them of their *Miranda* rights, and each consented to be interrogated and then made incriminating statements. The Supreme Court, through a 5–1–3 opinion written by Justice Stevens, concluded that the *Edwards* rule was fully applicable and that the defendants' purported "waivers" of their Sixth Amendment right to counsel were invalid.

Edwards is grounded in the understanding that "the assertion of the right to counsel [is] a significant event," and that "additional safeguards are necessary when the accused asks for counsel." We conclude that the assertion is no less significant, and the need for additional safeguards no less clear, when the request for counsel is made at an arraignment and when the basis for the claim is the Sixth Amendment. We thus hold that, if police initiate interrogation after a defendant's assertion, at an arraignment or similar proceeding, of his right to counsel, any waiver of the defendant's right to counsel for that police-initiated interrogation is invalid. 475 U.S., at 636.

Michigan v. Jackson thus holds that the *Edwards* rule applies when an accused invokes his Sixth Amendment right to counsel. However, the Court also has ruled that Sixth Amendment rights are offense specific. Receiving the benefit of Sixth Amendment rights for one offense does not protect the suspect from police-initiated interrogation about a different crime. Furthermore, in contrast to *Arizona v. Roberson*, *supra*, "an accused's invocation of his Sixth Amendment right to counsel during a judicial proceeding [does not] constitute[] an invocation of his Miranda right to counsel" that prohibits police-initiated questioning about an unrelated offense. *McNeil v. Wisconsin*, 501 U.S. 171, 173, 111 S. Ct. 2204, 115 L. Ed. 2d 158 (1991).

The defendant in *McNeil* was arrested and was taken for an initial appearance before a judicial officer, where he was represented by a public defender. The initial appearance related to an *armed robbery* charge arising in the town of West Allis. Police officers subsequently approached McNeil, administered *Miranda* warnings, and secured his agreement to answer questions about a murder and other offenses that occurred in the town of Caledonia. He incriminated himself with respect to the Caledonia crimes. Justice Scalia's opinion for the Court first considered whether McNeil's Sixth Amendment right to counsel—which had attached for the West Allis armed robbery charge—was violated when the police questioned him about the murder and other crimes committed in Caledonia.

* * * * *

The Sixth Amendment provides that "[i]n all criminal prosecutions, the accused shall enjoy the right . . . to have the Assistance of Counsel for his defence." In Michigan v. Jackson, 475 US 625, 106 S Ct 1404, 89 L Ed 2d 631 (1986), we held that once this right to counsel has attached and has been invoked, any subsequent waiver during a police-initiated custodial interview is ineffective. It is undisputed, and we accept for purposes of the present case, that at the time petitioner provided the incriminating statements at issue, his Sixth Amendment right had attached and had been invoked with respect to the *West Allis armed robbery,* for which he had been formally charged.

The Sixth Amendment right, however, is offense specific. It cannot be invoked once for all future prosecutions, for it does not attach until a prosecution is commenced, that is, "'at or after the initiation of adversary judicial criminal proceedings—whether by way of formal charge, preliminary hearing, indictment, information, or arraignment.'" United States v. Gouveia, 467 US 180, 188, 104 S Ct 2292, 81 L Ed 2d 146 (1984). And just as the right is

offense specific, so also its Michigan v. Jackson effect of invalidating subsequent waivers in police-initiated interviews is offense specific.

"The police have an interest . . . in investigating new or additional crimes [after an individual is formally charged with one crime.] . . . [T]o exclude evidence pertaining to charges as to which the Sixth Amendment right to counsel had not attached at the time the evidence was obtained, simply because other charges were pending at that time, would unnecessarily frustrate the public's interest in the investigation of criminal activities. . . ." Maine v. Moulton, 474 US 159, 179–180, 106 S Ct 477, 88 L Ed 2d 481 (1985).

* * *

Because petitioner provided the statements at issue here before his Sixth Amendment right to counsel with respect to the *Caledonia offenses* had been (or even could have been) invoked, that right poses no bar to the admission of the statements in this case. . . .

After rejecting the Sixth Amendment as a basis for relief, the Court then considered whether the Sixth Amendment right to counsel in combination with *Miranda* and *Edwards v. Arizona* barred the use of McNeil's statements about the Caledonia offenses following his initial appearance.

* * * * *

Having described the nature and effects of both the Sixth Amendment right to counsel and the Miranda-Edwards "Fifth Amendment" right to counsel, we come at last to the issue here: Petitioner seeks to prevail by combining the two of them. He contends that, although he expressly waived his Miranda right to counsel on every occasion he was interrogated, those waivers were the invalid product of impermissible approaches, because his prior invocation of the offense-specific Sixth Amendment right with regard to the West Allis burglary was also an invocation of the nonoffense-specific Miranda-Edwards right. We think that is false as a matter of fact and inadvisable (if even permissible) as a contrary-to-fact presumption of policy.

As to the former: The purpose of the Sixth Amendment counsel guarantee—and hence the purpose of invoking it—is to "protec[t] the unaided layman at critical confrontations" with his "expert adversary," the government, *after* "the adverse positions of government and defendant have solidified" with respect to a particular alleged crime. The purpose of the Miranda-Edwards guarantee, on the other hand—and hence the purpose of invoking it—is to protect a quite different interest: the suspect's "desire to deal with the police only through counsel," Edwards, supra, at 484. This is in one respect narrower than the interest protected by the Sixth Amendment guarantee (because it relates only to custodial interrogation) and in another respect broader (because it relates to interrogation regarding *any* suspected crime and attaches whether or not the "adversarial relationship" produced by a pending prosecution has yet arisen). To invoke the Sixth Amendment interest is, as a matter of *fact, not* to invoke the Miranda-Edwards interest. One might be quite willing to speak to the police without counsel present concerning many matters, but not the matter under prosecution. It can be said, perhaps, that it is *likely* that one who has asked for counsel's assistance in defending against a prosecution would want counsel present for all custodial interrogation, even interrogation unrelated to the charge. That is not necessarily true, since suspects often believe that they can avoid the laying of charges by demonstrating an assurance of innocence through frank and unassisted answers to questions. But even if it were true, the *like-*

lihood that a suspect would wish counsel to be present is not the test for applicability of Edwards. The rule of that case applies only when the suspect "ha[s] *expressed*" his wish for the particular sort of lawyerly assistance that is the subject of Miranda. It requires, at a minimum, some statement that can reasonably be construed to be an expression of a desire for the assistance of an attorney *in dealing with custodial interrogation by the police.* Requesting the assistance of an attorney at a bail hearing does not bear that construction.

* * *

Our holding in Michigan v. Jackson, 475 US 625, 106 S Ct 1404, 89 L Ed 2d 631 (1986), does not, as petitioner asserts, contradict the foregoing distinction; to the contrary, it *rests* upon it. That case, it will be recalled, held that after the Sixth Amendment right to counsel attaches and is invoked, any statements obtained from the accused during subsequent police-initiated custodial questioning regarding the charge at issue (even if the accused purports to waive his rights) are inadmissible. The State in Jackson opposed that outcome on the ground that assertion of the Sixth Amendment right to counsel did not realistically constitute the *expression* (as Edwards required) of a wish to have counsel present during custodial interrogation. Our response to that contention was not that it *did* constitute such an expression, but that it *did not have to,* since the relevant question was not whether the Miranda "Fifth Amendment" right had been *asserted,* but whether the Sixth Amendment right to counsel had been *waived.* We said that since our "settled approach to questions of waiver requires us to give a broad, rather than a narrow, interpretation to a defendant's request for counsel, . . . we *presume* that the defendant requests the lawyer's services at every critical stage of the prosecution." 475 US, at 633 (emphasis added). The holding of Jackson implicitly rejects any equivalence in fact between invocation of the Sixth Amendment right to counsel and the expression necessary to trigger Edwards. If such invocation constituted a real (as opposed to merely a legally presumed) request for the assistance of counsel in custodial interrogation, it would have been quite unnecessary for Jackson to go on to establish, as it did, a new Sixth Amendment rule of no police-initiated interrogation; we could simply have cited and relied upon Edwards.

There remains to be considered the possibility that, even though the assertion of the Sixth Amendment right to counsel does not *in fact* imply an assertion of the Miranda "Fifth Amendment" right, we should declare it to be such as a matter of sound policy. . . . If a suspect does not wish to communicate with the police except through an attorney, he can simply tell them that when they give him the Miranda warnings. There is not the remotest chance that he will feel "badgered" by their asking to talk to him without counsel present, since the subject will not be the charge on which he has already requested counsel's assistance (for in that event Jackson would preclude initiation of the interview) and he will not have rejected uncounseled interrogation on *any* subject before (for in that event Edwards would preclude initiation of the interview). The proposed rule would, however, seriously impede effective law enforcement. The Sixth Amendment right to counsel attaches at the first formal proceeding against an accused, and in most States, at least with respect to serious offenses, free counsel is made available at that time and ordinarily requested. Thus, if we were to adopt petitioner's rule, most persons in pretrial custody for serious offenses would be *unapproachable* by police officers suspecting them of involvement in other crimes, *even though they have never expressed any unwillingness to be questioned.* Since the ready ability to obtain uncoerced confessions is not an evil but an unmitigated good, society would be the loser.

* * * * *

The Court also has considered the requirements for an effective waiver of the Sixth Amendment right to counsel in the context of incriminating statements. You may recall that in *Brewer v. Williams* (p. 6), the Court ruled (5–4) that Williams had not made a valid waiver of his right to counsel when he divulged the whereabouts of his victim's body following Detective Leaming's "Christian burial speech."

The defendant in *Patterson v. Illinois,* 487 U.S. 285, 108 S. Ct. 2389, 101 L. Ed. 2d 261 (1988), was indicted for the murder of a member of a rival street gang. A police officer transporting Patterson from a holding cell to the Cook County jail explained to him that the transfer was being made because he had been indicted. Patterson inquired which other gang members had been charged with the killing and expressed surprise on learning that one particular individual had not been indicted. When he began to explain how a witness would support his story that this unindicted individual had been centrally involved in the murder, the officer interrupted him, administered *Miranda* warnings, and secured Patterson's waiver. Patterson then gave a lengthy, incriminating statement. Later that day, after receiving a new set of *Miranda* rights and again waiving them, he repeated his confession to an assistant state's attorney.

Patterson's confessions were admitted at his trial, over objection, and he was convicted of murder. On appeal, the state courts rejected his claim "that he had not 'knowingly and intelligently' waived his Sixth Amendment right to counsel before he gave his uncounseled postindictment confessions." Patterson had argued "that the warnings he received, while adequate for the purposes of protecting his Fifth Amendment rights as guaranteed by Miranda, did not adequately inform him of his Sixth Amendment right to counsel." 487 U.S., at 289. The Supreme Court, in a 5–4 decision authored by Justice White, rejected Patterson's claim.

* * * * *

Petitioner's principal . . . claim is that questioning him without counsel present violated the Sixth Amendment because he did not validly waive his right to have counsel present during the interviews. Since it is clear that after the Miranda warnings were given to petitioner, he not only voluntarily answered questions without claiming his right to silence or his right to have a lawyer present to advise him but also executed a written waiver of his right to counsel during questioning, the specific issue posed here is whether this waiver was a "knowing and intelligent" waiver of his Sixth Amendment right.[4] See Brewer v. Williams, supra, at 401, 404, 97 S Ct 1232, 51 L Ed 2d 424; Johnson v. Zerbst, 304 US 458, 464–465, 58 S Ct 1019, 82 L Ed 1461 (1938).

In the past, this Court has held that a waiver of the Sixth Amendment right to counsel is valid only when it reflects "an intentional relinquishment or abandonment of a known right or privilege." Johnson v. Zerbst, supra, at 464. In other words, the accused must "kno[w] what he is doing" so that "his choice is made with eyes open." Adams v. United States ex rel. McCann, 317 US 269, 279, 63 S Ct 236, 87 L Ed 268

(1942). In a case arising under the Fifth Amendment, we described this requirement as "a full awareness of both the nature of the right being abandoned and the consequences of the decision to abandon it." Moran v. Burbine, 475 US 412, 421, 106 S Ct 1135, 89 L Ed 2d 410 (1986). Whichever of these formulations is used, the key inquiry in a case such as this one must be: Was the accused, who waived his Sixth Amendment rights during postindictment questioning, made sufficiently aware of his right to have counsel present during the questioning, and of the possible consequences of a decision to forgo the aid of counsel? In this case, we are convinced that by admonishing petitioner with the Miranda warnings, respondent has met this burden and that petitioner's waiver of his right to counsel at the questioning was valid.[5]

First, the Miranda warnings given petitioner made him aware of his right to have counsel present during the questioning. By telling petitioner that he had a right to consult with an attorney, to have a lawyer present while he was questioned, and even to have a lawyer appointed for him if he could not afford to retain one on his own, Officer Gresham and ASA Smith conveyed to petitioner the sum and substances of the rights that the Sixth Amendment provided him. . . . There is little more petitioner

---

4. Of course, we also require that any such waiver must be voluntary. Petitioner contested the voluntariness of his confession in the trial court and in the intermediate appellate courts, which rejected petitioner's claim that his confessions were coerced.

Petitioner does not appear to have maintained this contention before the Illinois Supreme Court, and in any event, he does not press this argument here. Thus, the "voluntariness" of petitioner's confessions is not before us.

---

5. We emphasize the significance of the fact that petitioner's waiver of counsel was only for this limited aspect of the criminal proceedings against him—only for postindictment questioning. Our decision on the validity of petitioner's waiver extends only so far.

Moreover, even within this limited context, we note that petitioner's waiver was binding on him *only* so long as he wished it to be. Under this Court's precedents, at any time during the questioning petitioner could have changed his mind, elected to have the assistance of counsel, and immediately dissolve the effectiveness of his waiver with respect to any subsequent statements. See, e.g., Michigan v. Jackson, 475 US, at 631–635, 106 S Ct 1404, 89 L Ed 2d 631 [(1986)]. Our decision today does nothing to change this rule.

could have possibly been told in an effort to satisfy this portion of the waiver injury.

Second, the Miranda warnings also served to make petitioner aware of the consequences of a decision by him to waive his Sixth Amendment rights during postindictment questioning. Petitioner knew that any statement that he made could be used against him in subsequent criminal proceedings. This is the ultimate adverse consequence petitioner could have suffered by virtue of his choice to make uncounseled admissions to the authorities. This warning also sufficed—contrary to petitioner's claim here—to let petitioner know what a lawyer could "do for him" during the postindictment questioning: namely, advise petitioner to refrain from making any such statements. By knowing what could be done with any statements he might make, and therefore, what benefit could be obtained by having the aid of counsel while making such statements, petitioner was essentially informed of the possible consequences of going without counsel during questioning. . . .

Our conclusion is supported by petitioner' inability, in the proceedings before this Court, to articulate with precision what additional information should have been provided to him before he would have been competent to waive his right to counsel. All that petitioner's brief and reply brief suggest is petitioner should have been made aware of his "right under the Sixth Amendment to the broad protection of counsel"— a rather nebulous suggestion—and the "gravity of [his] situation." But surely this latter "requirement" (if it is one) was met when Officer Gresham informed petitioner that he had been formally charged with the murder of James Jackson. . . .

As a general matter, then, an accused who is admonished with the warnings prescribed by this Court in Miranda, has been sufficiently apprised of the nature of his Sixth Amendment rights, and of the conse-

quences of abandoning those rights, so that his waiver on this basis will be considered a knowing and intelligent one.[9] . . .

We consequently reject petitioner's argument, which has some acceptance from courts and commentators, that since "the sixth amendment right [to counsel] is far superior to that of the fifth amendment right" and since "[t]he greater the right the greater the loss from a waiver of that right," waiver of an accused's Sixth Amendment right to counsel should be "more difficult" to effectuate than waiver of a suspect's Fifth Amendment rights. While our cases have recognized a "difference" between the Fifth Amendment and Sixth Amendment rights to counsel, and the "policies" behind these constitutional guarantees, we have never suggested that one right is "superior" or "greater" than the other, nor is there any support in our cases for the notion that because a Sixth Amendment right may be involved, it is more difficult to waive than the Fifth Amendment counterpart. . . .

---

9. This does not mean, of course, that all Sixth Amendment challenges to the conduct of postindictment questioning will fail whenever the challenged practice would pass constitutional muster under Miranda. For example, we have permitted a Miranda waiver to stand where a suspect was not told that his lawyer was trying to reach him during questioning; in the Sixth Amendment context, this waiver would not be valid. See Moran v. Burbine, 475 US, at 424, 428, 106 S Ct 1135, 89 L Ed 2d 410. Likewise a surreptitious conversation between an undercover police officer and an unindicted suspect would not give rise to any Miranda violation as long as the "interrogation" was not in a custodial setting; however, once the accused is indicted, such questioning would be prohibited. See United States v. Henry, 447 US 264, 273, 274–275, 100 S Ct 2183, 65 L Ed 2d 115 (1980).

Thus, because the Sixth Amendment's protection of the attorney-client relationship—"the right to rely on counsel as a 'medium' between [the accused] and the State"—extends beyond Miranda's protection of the Fifth Amendment right to counsel, see Maine v. Moulton, 474 US, at 176, 106 S Ct 477, 88 L Ed 2d 481, there will be cases where a waiver which would be valid under Miranda will not suffice for Sixth Amendment purposes. See also Michigan v. Jackson, 475 US, at 632, 106 S Ct 1404, 89 L Ed 2d 631.

Applying this approach, it is our view that whatever warnings suffice for Miranda's purposes will also be sufficient in the context of postindictment questioning. The State's decision to make an additional step and commence formal adversarial proceedings against the accused does not substantially increase the value of counsel to the accused at questioning, or expand the limited purpose that an attorney serves when the accused is questioned by authorities. With respect to this inquiry, we do not discern a substantial difference between the usefulness of a lawyer to a suspect during custodial interrogation, and his value to an accused at postindictment questioning.

Thus, we require a more searching or formal inquiry before permitting an accused to waive his right to counsel at trial than we require for a Sixth Amendment waiver during post-indictment questioning—*not* because postindictment questioning is "less important" than a trial (the analysis that petitioner's "hierarchical" approach would suggest)—but because the full "dangers and disadvantages of self-representation," during questioning are less substantial and more obvious to an accused than they are at trial. Because the role of counsel at questioning is relatively simple and limited, we see no problem in having a waiver procedure at that stage which is likewise simple and limited. So long as the accused is made aware of the "dangers and disadvantages of self-representation" during postindictment questioning, by use of the Miranda warnings, his waiver of his Sixth Amendment right to counsel at such questioning is "knowing and intelligent."

* * *

Justice **Stevens,** with whom Justice **Brennan** and Justice **Marshall** join, dissenting.

* * *

The majority premises its conclusion that Miranda warnings lay a sufficient basis for accepting a waiver of the right to counsel on the assumption that those warnings make clear to an accused "what a lawyer could 'do for him' during the postindictment questioning: namely, advise [him] to refrain from making any [incriminating] statements." Yet, this is surely a gross understatement of the disadvantage of proceeding without a lawyer and an understatement of what a defendant must understand to make a knowing waiver. The Miranda warnings do not, for example, inform the accused that a lawyer might examine the indictment for legal sufficiency before submitting his or her client to interrogation or that a lawyer is likely to be considerably more skillful at negotiating a plea bargain and that such negotiations may be most fruitful if initiated prior to any interrogation. Rather, the warnings do not even go so far as to explain to the accused the nature of the charges pending against him—advice that a court would insist upon before allowing a defendant to enter a guilty plea with or without the presence of an attorney.

Without defining precisely the nature of the inquiry required to establish a valid waiver of the Sixth Amendment right to counsel, it must be conceded that at least minimal advice is necessary—the accused must be told of the "dangers and disadvantages of self-representation."

Yet, once it is conceded that certain advice is required and that after indictment the adversary relationship between the state and the accused has solidified, it inescapably follows that a prosecutor may not conduct private interviews with a charged defendant. . .

In sum, without a careful discussion of the pitfalls of proceeding without counsel, the Sixth Amendment right cannot properly be waived. An adversary party, moreover, cannot adequately provide such advice. As a result, once the right to counsel attaches and the adversary relationship between the state and the accused solidifies, a prosecutor cannot conduct a private interview with an accused party without "dilut[ing] the protection afforded by the right to counsel," Maine v. Moulton, 474 US 159, 171, 106 S Ct 477, 88 L Ed 2d 481 (1985). . . .

It is true, of course, that the interest in effective law enforcement would benefit from an opportunity to engage in incommunicado questioning of defendants who, for reasons beyond their control, have not been able to receive the legal advice from counsel to which they are constitutionally entitled. But the Court's single-minded concentration on that interest might also lead to the toleration of similar practices at any stage of the trial. I think it clear that such private communications are intolerable not simply during trial, but at any point after adversary proceedings have commenced.

I therefore respectfully dissent.

Be certain to note that Patterson at no time requested the assistance of counsel. *See Michigan v. Jackson, supra*; *see* footnote 5 of the Court's opinion in *Patterson*. Even if he had, however, his expression of surprise to the police officer (who had advised him that he was being relocated because he had been indicted for murder) that another gang member had not been indicted arguably would have sufficed to "initiate" a crime-related conversation and thus to make further questioning permissible.

Also note that the *Patterson* Court refused to equate *Miranda* waivers and Sixth Amendment waivers for all purposes. See footnote 9 of the majority opinion.

Do you agree with Justice Stevens that an indicted defendant, such as Patterson, may be deprived of information he or she needs to make a "knowing and intelligent" waiver if the only advice he or she receives comes in the form of *Miranda* rights? Specifically, might a lawyer be necessary to advise the defendant about the possibility of trading his or her cooperation in making a statement for some concessions to be used in the plea-bargaining process? Must the accused be advised more specifically about "the 'dangers and disadvantages of self-representation'"? If so, precisely what additional information must be conveyed to make a waiver of Sixth Amendment rights "knowing and intelligent"?

CONCLUSION

In this chapter, we have reviewed several different legal concepts, rights, and rules relating to the topic of self-incrimination. We have given principal consideration to *Miranda v. Arizona* and the protection of Fifth Amendment rights, but we also have studied the condemnation of involuntary confessions by the Fourteenth Amendment's due-process clause, we have briefly noted the *McNabb-Mallory* rule and its application in the federal courts, and we have examined how the Sixth Amendment right to counsel may help regulate the confessions process after formal adversarial proceedings have been initiated against an accused. The *Miranda* doctrine, appropriately, merited the bulk of our attention.

When the four cases that were consolidated for decision in *Miranda v. Arizona* reached the Supreme Court, Chief Justice Warren's majority opinion explained that

we granted certiorari in these cases . . . in order further to explore some facets of the problems, thus exposed, of applying the privilege against self-incrimination to in-custody interrogation, *and to give concrete constitutional guidelines for law enforcement agencies and courts to follow.* 384 U.S., at 441–442 (emphasis added).

There is little doubt that *Miranda* did represent an advance, in terms of clarity of understanding and application, over the "voluntariness" test for confessions under due process of law standards. Nevertheless, we may be justifiably skeptical about the assertion that the *Miranda* rules in fact constitute "concrete . . . guidelines for law enforcement agencies and courts to follow."

The content of the warnings that must be given under *Miranda* is relatively straightforward, although after *Duckworth v. Eagan* (p.300), even those requirements are not clearcut. In addition to this facet of *Miranda*, a host of issues, some of which are quite complex, remain controversial. Giving meaning to concepts such as "in custody," "interrogation," "invocation" of the protections, and "waiver" of rights has been a far from easy task for the courts. Additionally, impeachment issues and even voluntariness questions still surface with some regularity in the confessions-interrogation area. A "public safety exception" has been created to *Miranda*, which has its own ambiguities, and the courts must sometimes make difficult distinctions between "testimonial" and "nontestimonial" evidence before *Miranda* issues are even reached.

If the waters around *Miranda* remain a bit murky and the "rigidity and precision" of its rules slightly tainted, how effective has the decision been in enabling criminal suspects to exercise their rights against compelled self-incrimination when undergoing custodial interrogation? Many observers have speculated that *Miranda* has not lived up to its expectations. A number of conditions must precede an accused's "knowingly, intelligently, and voluntarily" waiving his or her Fifth Amendment rights. The *Miranda* warnings must be communicated meaningfully by the police. They must be understood by the suspect. They must suffice to surmount the "inherent coerciveness" of the custodial interrogation setting. Both social science and anecdotal evidence casts doubt on the premises underlying the *Miranda* decision.

Must we conclude that *Miranda* is a failure? Writing in a different context, Justice Blackmun once observed that "'failure is most striking when hopes are highest.'" *McKeiver v. Pennsylvania*, 403 U.S. 528, 545, 91 S. Ct. 1976, 29 L. Ed. 2d 647 (1971) (plurality opinion) (*quoting* President's Commission on Law Enforcement and Administration of Justice, Task Force Report: Juvenile Delinquency and Youth Crime 7 (1967)). It is only fair to evaluate the *Miranda* decision in this same light. With *Miranda* in effect, the law governing custodial interrogations and waivers of the right against compelled self-incrimination may not be crystal clear. We can only speculate, or remember, what practices and principles might reign in the absence of *Miranda* as the courts attempt their difficult yet important task of regulating police interrogation of criminal suspects and achieving the proper balance between individual rights and legitimate law enforcement objectives.

Eyewitness Identification

The existence of an eyewitness to a crime is often a key component of a criminal investigation and prosecution. Not only does such a witness provide law enforcement and prosecutorial agencies with information upon which to base an arrest and indictment, but the witness's testimony at trial also can be quite important. Studies have shown that juries give great weight to the testimony of an eyewitness. E. Loftus, "Reconstructing Memory: The Incredible Eyewitness," 8 *Psychology Today* 116 (Dec. 1974).

Unfortunately, "[T]he vagaries of eyewitness identification are well known; the annals of criminal law are rife with instances of mistaken identification." *United States v. Wade*, 388 U.S. 218, 228, 87 S. Ct. 1926, 1933, 18 L. Ed. 2d 1149 (1967). Faced with this reality, the Supreme Court has taken the opportunity to indirectly regulate aspects of several procedures (primarily lineups) used by police and prosecutors to have witnesses identify suspects. While not requiring the police to use a specific set of identification procedures, the Court has taken steps to help ensure the reliability of eyewitness identification testimony presented at criminal trials.

The Court has focused on two constitutional approaches in this effort: the Sixth Amendment's right to counsel and the due-process guarantees of the Fifth and Fourteenth Amendments. In this chapter, we will examine these constitutional protections as they apply to identification procedures and eyewitness testimony at criminal trials. We also consider how state courts have interpreted their own constitutions in these areas. The first section of the chapter examines a suspect's right to counsel during different eyewitness identification procedures. The second section covers due-process protections given to a defendant when eyewitness testimony is offered in a court. The last section considers the use of expert testimony in the field of eyewitness identification.

THE RIGHT TO COUNSEL AT PRETRIAL IDENTIFICATION PROCEDURES

A defendant's Sixth Amendment right to counsel applies during critical stages of a criminal prosecution. Does a crime suspect therefore have the right to counsel at a lineup? What purpose would counsel serve at a lineup? Does the right to counsel at a lineup attach once a suspected criminal is taken to the police station for questioning? After he or she is arrested? Following an indictment? The Supreme Court addressed these issues in 1967 in three cases known as the "*Wade* trilogy."

United States v. Wade, 388 U.S. 218, 87 S. Ct. 1926, 18 L. Ed. 2d 1149 (1967)

Mr. Justice Brennan delivered the opinion of the Court.

The question here is whether courtroom identifications of an accused at trial are to be excluded from evidence because the accused was exhibited to the witnesses before trial at a post-indictment lineup conducted for identification purposes without notice to and in the absence of the accused's appointed counsel.

The federally insured bank in Eustace, Texas, was robbed on September 21, 1964. A man with a small strip of tape on each side of his face entered the bank, pointed a pistol at the female cashier and the vice president, the only persons in the bank at the time, and forced them to fill a pillowcase with the bank's money. The man then drove away with an accomplice who had been waiting in a stolen car outside the bank. On March 23, 1965, an indictment was returned against respondent, Wade, and two others for conspiring to rob the bank, and against Wade and the accomplice for the robbery itself. Wade was arrested on April 2, and counsel was appointed to represent him on April 26. Fifteen days later an FBI agent, without notice to Wade's lawyer, arranged to have the two bank employees observe a lineup made up of Wade and five or six other prisoners and conducted in a courtroom of the local county courthouse. Each person in the line wore strips of tape such as allegedly worn by the robber and upon direction each said something like "put the money in the bag," the words allegedly uttered by the robber. Both bank employees identified Wade in the lineup as the bank robber.

At trial, the two employees, when asked on direct examination if the robber was in the courtroom, pointed to Wade. The prior lineup identification was then elicited from both employees on cross-examination. At the close of testimony, Wade's counsel moved for a judgment of acquittal or, alternatively, to strike the bank officials' courtroom identifications on the ground that conduct of the lineup, without notice to and in the absence of his appointed counsel, violated his Fifth Amendment privilege against self-incrimination and his Sixth Amendment right to the assistance of counsel. The motion was denied, and Wade was convicted. . . .

* * *

I.

Neither the lineup itself nor anything shown by this record that Wade was required to do in the lineup violated his privilege against self-incrimination. We have only recently reaffirmed that the privilege "protects an accused only from being compelled to testify against himself, or otherwise provide the State with evidence of a testimonial or communicative nature. . . ."

We have no doubt that compelling the accused merely to exhibit his person for observation by a prosecution witness prior to trial involves no compulsion of the accused to give evidence having testimonial significance. It is compulsion of the accused to exhibit his physical characteristics, not compulsion to disclose any knowledge he might have. . . .

* * *

II.

The fact that the lineup involved no violation of Wade's privilege against self-incrimination does not, however, dispose of his contention that the courtroom identifications should have been excluded because the lineup was conducted without notice to and in the absence of his counsel. . . .

In this case it is urged that the assistance of counsel at the lineup was indispensable to protect Wade's most basic right as a criminal defendant—his right to a fair trial at which the witnesses against him might be meaningfully cross-examined.

The Framers of the Bill of Rights envisaged a broader role for counsel than under the practice then prevailing in England of merely advising his client in "matters of law," and eschewing any responsibility for "matters of fact." . . .

When the Bill of Rights was adopted, there were no organized police forces as we know them today. The accused confronted the prosecutor and the witnesses against him, and the evidence was marshalled, largely at the trial itself. In contrast, today's law enforcement machinery involves critical confrontations of the accused by the prosecution at pretrial proceedings where the results might well settle the accused's fate and reduce the trial itself to a mere formality. In recognition of these realities of modern criminal prosecution, our cases have construed the Sixth Amendment guarantee to apply to "critical" stages of the proceedings. The guarantee reads: "In all criminal prosecutions, the accused shall enjoy the right . . . to have the Assistance of Counsel *for his defence*." (Emphasis supplied.) The plain wording of this guarantee thus encompasses counsel's assistance whenever necessary to assure a meaningful "defence."

As early as Powell v. Alabama, we recognized that the period from arraignment to trial was "perhaps the most critical period of the proceedings . . . ," during which the accused "requires the guiding hand of counsel . . . ," if the guarantee is not to prove an empty right. That principle has since been applied to require the assistance of counsel at the type of arraignment—for example, that provided by Alabama—where certain rights might be sacrificed or lost: "What happens there may affect the whole trial. Available defenses may be irretrievably lost, if not then and there asserted. . . ." Hamilton v. Alabama, 368 US 52, 54, 82 S Ct 157, 7 L Ed 2d 114, 116. . . .

It is central to that principle that in addition to counsel's presence at trial, the accused is guaranteed that he need not stand alone against the State at any stage of the prosecution, formal or informal, in court or out, where counsel's absence might derogate from the accused's right to a fair trial. The security of that right is as much the aim of the right to counsel as it is of the other guarantees of the Sixth Amendment— the right of the accused to a speedy and public trial by an impartial jury, his right to be informed of the nature and cause of the accusation, and his right to be confronted with the witnesses

against him and to have compulsory process for obtaining witnesses in his favor. The presence of counsel at such critical confrontations, as at the trial itself, operates to assure that the accused's interests will be protected consistently with our adversary theory of criminal prosecution.

In sum, the principle of Powell v. Alabama and succeeding cases requires that we scrutinize any pretrial confrontation of the accused to determine whether the presence of his counsel is necessary to preserve the defendant's basic right to a fair trial as affected by his right meaningfully to cross-examine the witnesses against him and to have effective assistance of counsel at the trial itself. It calls upon us to analyze whether potential substantial prejudice to defendant's rights inheres in the particular confrontation and the ability of counsel to help avoid that prejudice.

III.

The Government characterizes the lineup as a mere preparatory step in the gathering of the prosecution's evidence, not different—for Sixth Amendment purposes—from various other preparatory steps, such as systematized or scientific analyzing of the accused's fingerprints, blood sample, clothing, hair, and the like. We think there are differences which preclude such stages being characterized as critical stages at which the accused has the right to the presence of his counsel. Knowledge of the techniques of science and technology is sufficiently available, and the variables in techniques few enough, that the accused has the opportunity for a meaningful confrontation of the Government's case at trial through the ordinary processes of cross-examination of the Government's expert witnesses and the presentation of the evidence of his own experts. The denial of a right to have his counsel present at such analyses does not therefore violate the Sixth Amendment; they are not critical stages since there is minimal risk that his counsel's absence at such stages might derogate from his right to a fair trial.

But the confrontation compelled by the State between the accused and the victim or witnesses to a crime to elicit identification evidence is peculiarly riddled with innumerable dangers and variable factors which might seriously, even crucially, derogate from a fair trial. The vagaries of eyewitness identification are well-known; the annals of criminal law are rife with instances of mistaken identification. Mr. Justice Frankfurter once said: "What is the worth of identification testimony even when uncontradicted? The identification of strangers is proverbially untrustworthy. The hazards of such testimony are established by a formidable number of instances in the records of English and American trials. These instances are recent—not due to the brutalities of ancient criminal procedure." A major factor contributing to the high incidence of miscarriage of justice from mistaken identification has been the degree of suggestion inherent in the manner in which the prosecution presents the suspect to witnesses for pretrial identification. A commentator has observed that "[t]he influence of improper suggestion upon identifying witnesses probably accounts for more miscarriages of justice than any other single factor—perhaps it is responsible for more such errors than all other factors combined." Wall, Eye-Witness Identification in Criminal Cases 26. Suggestion can be created intentionally or unintentionally in many subtle ways. And the dangers for the suspect are particularly grave when the witness' opportunity for observation was insubstantial, and thus his susceptibility to suggestion the greatest.

Moreover, "[i]t is a matter of common experience that, once a witness has picked out the accused at the line-up, he is not likely to go back on his word later on, so that in practice the issue of identity may (in the absence of other relevant evidence) for all practical purposes be determined there and then, before the trial."

The pretrial confrontation for purpose of identification may take the form of a lineup, also known as an "identification parade" or "showup," as in the present case, or presentation of the suspect alone to the witness, as in Stovall v. Denno, 388 US 293, 87 S Ct 1967, 18 L Ed 2d 1199. It is obvious that risks of suggestion attend either form of confrontation and increase the dangers inhering in eyewitness identification. But as is the case with secret interrogations, there is serious difficulty in depicting what transpires at lineups and other forms of identification confrontations: "Privacy results in secrecy and this is turn results in a gap in our knowledge as

to what in fact goes on. . . ." For the same reasons, the defense can seldom reconstruct the manner and mode of lineup identification for judge or jury at trial. Those participating in a lineup with the accused may often be police officers; in any event, the participants' names are rarely recorded or divulged at trial. The impediments to an objective observation are increased when the victim is the witness. Lineups are prevalent in rape and robbery prosecutions and present a particular hazard that a victim's understandable outrage may excite vengeful or spiteful motives. In any event, neither witnesses nor lineup participants are apt to be alert for conditions prejudicial to the suspect. And if they were, it would likely be of scant benefit to the suspect since neither witnesses nor lineup participants are likely to be schooled in the detection of suggestive influences. Improper influences may go undetected by a suspect, guilty or not, who experiences the emotional tension which we might expect in one being confronted with potential accusers. Even when he does observe abuse, if he has a criminal record he may be reluctant to take the stand and open up the admission of prior convictions. Moreover, any protestations by the suspect of the fairness of the lineup made at trial are likely to be in vain; the jury's choice is between the accused's unsupported version and that of the police officers present. In short, the accused's inability effectively to reconstruct at trial any unfairness that occurred at the lineup may deprive him of his only opportunity meaningfully to attack the credibility of the witness' courtroom identification.

What facts have been disclosed in specific cases about the conduct of pretrial confrontations for identification illustrate both the potential for substantial prejudice to the accused at that stage and the need for its revelation at trial. A commentator provides some striking examples:

"In a Canadian case . . . the defendant had been picked out of a line-up of six men, of which he was the only Oriental. In other cases, a black-haired suspect was placed among a group of light-haired persons, tall suspects have been made to stand with short non-suspects, and, in a case where the perpetrator of the crime was known to be a youth, a suspect under twenty was placed in a line-up with five other persons, all of whom were forty or over."

Similarly state reports, in the course of describing prior identifications admitted as evidence of guilt, reveal numerous instances of suggestive procedures, for example, that all in the lineup but the suspect were known to the identifying witness, that the other participants in a lineup were grossly dissimilar in appearance to the suspect, that only the suspect was required to wear distinctive clothing which the culprit allegedly wore, that the witness is told by the police that they have caught the culprit after which the defendant is brought before the witness alone or is viewed in jail, that the suspect is pointed out before or during a lineup, and that the participants in the lineup are asked to try on an article of clothing which fits only the suspect.

The potential for improper influence is illustrated by the circumstances, insofar as they appear, surrounding the prior identifications in the three cases we decide today. In the present case, the testimony of the identifying witnesses elicited on cross-examination revealed that those witnesses were taken to the courthouse and seated in the courtroom to await assembly of the lineup. The courtroom faced on a hallway observable to the witnesses through an open door. The cashier testified that she saw Wade "standing in the hall" within sight of an FBI agent. Five or six other prisoners later appeared in the hall. The vice president testified that he saw a person in the hall in the custody of the agent who "resembled the person that we identified as the one that had entered the bank.". . .

The few cases that have surfaced therefore reveal the existence of a process attended with hazards of serious unfairness to the criminal accused and strongly suggest the plight of the more numerous defendants who are unable to ferret out suggestive influences in the secrecy of the confrontation. We do not assume that these risks are the result of police procedures intentionally designed to prejudice an accused. Rather we assume they derive from the dangers inherent in eyewitness identification and the suggestibility inherent in the context of the pretrial identification. Williams & Hammelmann in one of the most comprehensive studies of such forms

of identification, said, "[T]he fact that the police themselves have, in a given case, little or no doubt that the man put up for identification has committed the offense, and that their chief preoccupation is with the problem of getting sufficient proof, because he has not 'come clean,' involves a danger that this persuasion may communicate itself even in a doubtful case to the witness in some way. . . ." Identification Parades, Part I, [1963] Crim L Rev 479, 483.

Insofar as the accused's conviction may rest on a courtroom identification in fact the fruit of a suspect pretrial identification which the accused is helpless to subject to effective scrutiny at trial, the accused is deprived of that right of cross-examination which is an essential safeguard to his right to confront the witnesses against him. Pointer v Texas, 380 US 400, 85 S Ct 1065, 13 L Ed 2d 923. And even though cross-examination is a precious safeguard to a fair trial, it cannot be viewed as an absolute assurance of accuracy and reliability. Thus in the present context, where so many variables and pitfalls exist, the first line of defense must be the prevention of unfairness and the lessening of the hazards of eyewitness identification at the lineup itself. The trial which might determine the accused's fate may well not be that in the courtroom but that at the pretrial confrontation, with the State aligned against the accused, the witness the sole jury, and the accused unprotected against the overreaching, intentional or unintentional, and with little or no effective appeal from the judgment there rendered by the witness—"that's the man."

Since it appears that there is grave potential for prejudice, intentional or not, in the pretrial lineup, which may not be capable of reconstruction at trial, and since presence of counsel itself can often avert prejudice and assure a meaningful confrontation at trial, there can be little doubt that for Wade the post-indictment lineup was a critical stage of the prosecution at which he was "as much entitled to such aid [of counsel] . . . as at the trial itself." Thus both Wade and his counsel should have been notified of the impending lineup, and counsel's presence should have been a requisite to conduct of the lineup, absent an "intelligent waiver." No substantial countervailing policy considerations have been advanced against the requirement of the presence of counsel. . . .

In our view counsel can hardly impede legitimate law enforcement; on the contrary, for the reasons expressed, law enforcement may be assisted by preventing the infiltration of taint in the prosecution's identification evidence. That result cannot help the guilty avoid conviction but can only help assure that the right man has been brought to justice.

Legislative or other regulations, such as those of local police departments, which eliminate the risks of abuse and unintentional suggestion at lineup proceedings and the impediments to meaningful confrontation at trial may also remove the basis for regarding the stage as "critical." But neither Congress nor the federal authorities have seen fit to provide a solution. What we hold today "in no way creates a constitutional straitjacket which will handicap sound efforts at reform, nor is it intended to have this effect."

V.

We come now to the question whether the denial of Wade's motion to strike the courtroom identification by the bank witnesses at trial because of the absence of his counsel at the lineup required, as the Court of Appeals held, the grant of a new trial at which such evidence is to be excluded. We do not think this disposition can be justified without first giving the Government the opportunity to establish by clear and convincing evidence that the in-court identifications were based upon observations of the suspect other than the lineup identification. See Murphy v Waterfront Commission, 378 US 52, 79, note 18, 84 S Ct 1594, 12 L Ed 2d 678, 695. Where, as here, the admissibility of evidence of the lineup identification itself is not involved, a per se rule of exclusion of courtroom identification would be unjustified. A rule limited solely to the exclusion of testimony concerning identification at the lineup itself, without regard to admissibility of the courtroom identification, would render the right to counsel an empty one. The lineup is most often used, as in the present case, to crystallize the witnesses' identification of the defendant for future reference. We have already noted that the lineup identification will have that effect. The State may then rest upon the witnesses' unequivocal courtroom identification, and not mention the pretrial identification as

part of the State's case at trial. Counsel is then in the predicament in which Wade's counsel found himself—realizing that possible unfairness at the lineup may be the sole means of attack upon the unequivocal courtroom identification, and having to probe in the dark in an attempt to discover and reveal unfairness, while bolstering the government witness' courtroom identification by bringing out and dwelling upon his prior identification. Since counsel's presence at the lineup would equip him to attack not only the lineup identification but the courtroom identification as well, limiting the impact of violation of the right to counsel to exclusion of evidence only of identification at the lineup itself disregards a critical element of that right.

We think it follows that the proper test to be applied in these situations is that quoted in Wong Sun v United States, 371 US 471, 488, 455, 83 S Ct 407, 9 L Ed 2d 441, "'[W]hether, granting establishment of the primary illegality, the evidence to which instant objection is made has been come at by exploitation of that illegality or instead by means sufficiently distinguishable to be purged of the primary taint.' Application of this test in the present context requires consideration of various factors; for example, the prior opportunity to observe the alleged criminal act, the existence of any discrepancy between any pre-lineup description and the defendant's actual description, any identification prior to lineup of another person, the identification by picture of the defendant prior to the lineup, failure to identify the defendant on a prior occasion, and the lapse of time between the alleged act and the lineup identification. It is also relevant to consider those facts which, despite the absence of counsel, are disclosed concerning the conduct of the lineup. . . .

On the record now before us we cannot make the determination whether the in-court identifications had an independent origin. This was not an issue at trial, although there is some evidence relevant to a determination. That inquiry is most properly made in the District Court. We therefore think the appropriate procedure to be followed is to vacate the conviction pending a hearing to determine whether the in-court identifications had an independent source, or whether, in any event, the introduction of the evidence was harmless error, and for the District Court to reinstate the conviction or order a new trial, as may be proper.

Mr. Justice White, whom Mr. Justice Harlan and Mr. Justice Stewart join, dissenting in part and concurring in part.

The Court has again propounded a broad constitutional rule barring use of a wide spectrum of relevant and probative evidence, solely because a step in its ascertainment or discovery occurs outside the presence of defense counsel. This was the approach of the Court in Miranda v. Arizona, 384 US 436, 86 S Ct 1602, 16 L Ed 2d 694, 10 ALR3d 974. I objected then to what I thought was an uncritical and doctrinaire approach without satisfactory factual foundation. I have much the same view of the present ruling and therefore dissent from the judgment and from Parts II, IV, and V of the Court's opinion.

The Court's opinion is far-reaching. It proceeds first by creating a new per se rule of constitutional law: a criminal suspect cannot be subjected to a pretrial identification process in the absence of his counsel without violating the Sixth Amendment. If he is, the State may not buttress a later courtroom identification of the witness by any reference to the previous identification. Furthermore, the courtroom identification is not admissible at all unless the State can establish by clear and convincing proof that the testimony is not the fruit of the earlier identification made in the absence of defendant's counsel—admittedly a heavy burden for the State and probably an impossible one. To all intents and purposes, courtroom identifications are barred if pretrial identifications have occurred without counsel being present.

The rule applies to any lineup, to any other techniques employed to produce an identification and a fortiori to a face-to-face encounter between the witness and the suspect alone, regardless of when the identification occurs, in time or place, and whether before or after indictment or information. It matters not how well the witness knows the suspect, whether the witness is the suspect's mother, brother, or long-time associate, and no matter how long or well the witness observed the perpetrator at the scene of the crime. The kidnap victim who has lived for days with his abductor is in the same category as the witness who has had only a fleeting glimpse of the criminal. Neither may identify the suspect without defendant's counsel being present. The same strictures apply regardless of the number of other witnesses who positively identify the defendant and regardless of the corroborative evidence showing that it was the defendant who had committed the crime.

The premise for the Court's rule is not the general unreliability of eyewitness identifications nor the difficulties inherent in observation, recall, and recognition. The Court assumes a narrower evil as the basis for its rule—improper police suggestion which contributes to erroneous identifications. The Court apparently believes that improper police procedures are so widespread that a broad prophylactic rule must be laid down, requiring the presence of counsel at all pretrial identifications, in order to detect recurring instances of police misconduct. I do not share this pervasive distrust of all official investigations. None of the materials the Court relies upon supports it. Certainly, I would bow to solid fact, but the Court quite obviously does not have before it any reliable, comprehensive survey of current police practices on which to base its new rule. Until it does, the Court should avoid excluding relevant evidence from state criminal trials. Cf. Washington v. Texas, 388 US 14, 18 L Ed 2d 1019, 87 S Ct 1920. . . .

Notes and Questions

1. Notice how limited the actual holding in *Wade* is and how many questions are left unanswered in the majority opinion. What are these unanswered questions, and how do you suppose the Court would (should) decide them?

2. In the companion case of *Gilbert v. California*, 388 U.S. 263, 87 S. Ct. 1951, 18 L. Ed. 2d 1178 (1967), several witnesses who identified Gilbert in the courtroom testified that they had identified him previously at an uncounseled, postindictment lineup. The court established a *per se* exclusionary rule for testimony regarding out-of-court identifications made in violation of a defendant's right to counsel. The Court reasoned that "only a *per se* exclusionary rule as to such testimony can be an effective sanction to assure that law enforcement authorities will respect the accused's constitutional right to the presence of counsel at the critical lineup." *Id* at 273, 87 S. Ct. at 1957.

3. What should the role of counsel be in the lineup procedure? Is counsel merely a passive observer to ensure fairness, or does he have a right, or even a duty, to take a proactive role in the process? Should this role involve making suggestions about the procedures, including making verbal objections at the time counsel feels an impropriety has occurred? Most courts have held that counsel is present for the sole purpose of observing the procedure and to ensure that the lineup is conducted fairly.

4. What is the precise remedy if a lineup is conducted in violation of *Wade*? In considering this question, keep in mind the two different types of identification that are usually involved: (1) the identification at the lineup and (2) an in-court identification at trial.

5. Should a suspect have a right to a lineup if the suspect believes it will help exonerate him or her? The vast majority of appellate courts have held that the granting of such a request is within the trial court's discretion. Although it may seem fair to allow a defendant to have a lineup conducted upon request, trial courts are hesitant to order them. The refusal to make such an order is rarely found to be reversible error. For example, in *Evans v. Superior Court*, 11 Cal. 3d 617, 522 P.2d 68, 114 Cal. Rptr. 121 (1974), the California Supreme Court held that a defendant has a right to a pretrial lineup "only when eyewitness identification is shown to be in material issue and there exists a reasonable likelihood of a mistaken identification which a lineup would tend to resolve." *Id.*, 522 P.2d at 686. Does this seem like a reasonable position?

6. In the third case in the *Wade* trilogy, *Stovall v. Denno*, 388 U.S. 293, 87 S. Ct. 1967, 18 L. Ed. 2d 1199 (1967), the Supreme Court held that *Wade* would not be applied retroactively. In other words, defendants whose cases had been resolved prior to the decision in *Wade* would not benefit from the rule announced in the case.

At what stage of the criminal justice process does the right exist to have counsel present at a lineup? This question was not specifically addressed by the Court in *Wade*. Five years after *Wade* was decided, the Supreme Court answered this question. As you read *Kirby v. Illinois*, ponder which of the Justices' opinions most closely follows the spirit of *Wade*. Note that *Wade* was decided during the era of the Warren Court, whereas *Kirby* was decided during the reign of the Burger Court.

Kirby v. Illinois, 406 U.S. 682, 92 S. Ct. 1877, 32 L. Ed. 2d 411 (1972)

Mr. Justice Stewart announced the judgment of the Court and an opinion in which The Chief Justice, Mr. Justice Blackmun, and Mr. Justice Rehnquist join.

In United States v. Wade, 388 US 218, 87 S Ct 1926, 18 L Ed 2d 1149, and Gilbert v. California, 388 US 263, 87 S Ct 1951, 18 L Ed 2d 1178, this Court held "that a post-indictment pretrial lineup at which the accused is exhibited to identifying witnesses is a critical stage of the criminal prosecution; that police conduct of such a lineup without notice to and in the absence of his counsel denies the accused his Sixth [and Fourteenth] Amendment right to counsel and calls in question the admissibility at trial of the in-court identifications of the accused by witnesses who attended the lineup." Those cases further held that no "in-court identifications" are admissible in evidence if their "source" is a lineup conducted in violation of this constitutional standard. "Only a per se exclusionary rule as to such testimony can be an effective sanction," the Court said, "to assure that law enforcement authorities will respect the accused's constitutional right to the presence of his counsel at the critical lineup." Id., at 273, 18 L Ed 2d at 1186. In the present case we are asked to extend the Wade-Gilbert per se exclusionary rule to identification testimony based upon a police station showup that took place *before* the defendant had been indicted or otherwise formally charged with any criminal offense.

On February 21, 1968, a man named Willie Shard reported to the Chicago police that the previous day two men had robbed him on a Chicago street of a wallet containing, among other things, traveler's checks and a Social Security card. On February 22, two police officers stopped the petitioner and a companion, Ralph Bean, on West Madison Street in Chicago. When asked for identification, the petitioner produced a wallet that contained three traveler's checks and a Social Security card, all bearing the name of Willie Shard. Papers with Shard's name on them were also found in Bean's possession. When asked to explain his possession of Shard's property, the petitioner first said that the traveler's checks were "play money," and then told the officers that he had won them in a crap game. The officers then arrested the petitioner and Bean and took them to a police station.

Only after arriving at the police station, and checking the records there, did the arresting officers learn of the Shard robbery. A police car was then dispatched to Shard's place of employment, where it picked up Shard and brought him to the police station. Immediately upon entering the room in the police station where the petitioner and Bean were seated at a table, Shard positively identified them as the men who had robbed him two days earlier. No lawyer was present in the room, and neither the petitioner nor Bean had asked for legal assistance, or been advised of any right to the presence of counsel.

More than six weeks later, the petitioner and Bean were indicted for the robbery of Willie Shard. Upon arraignment, counsel was appointed to represent them, and they pleaded not guilty. A pretrial motion to suppress Shard's identification testimony was denied, and at the trial Shard testified as a witness for the prosecution. In his testimony he described his identification of the two men at the police station on February 22, and identified them again in the courtroom as the men who had robbed him on February 20. He was cross-examined at length regarding the circumstances of his identification of the two defendants. The jury found both defendants guilty, and the petitioner's conviction was affirmed on appeal. . . .

In a line of constitutional cases in this Court stemming back to the Court's landmark opinion in Powell v Alabama, 287 US 45, 53 S Ct 55, 77 L Ed 158, 84 ALR 527, it has been firmly established that a person's Sixth and Fourteenth Amendment right to counsel attaches only at or after the time that adversary judicial proceedings have been initiated against him.

This is not to say that a defendant in a criminal case has a constitutional right to counsel only at the trial itself. The Powell case makes clear that the right attaches at the time of arraignment, and the Court has recently held that it exists also at the time of a preliminary hearing. But the point is that, while members of the Court have differed as to existence of the right to counsel in the contexts of some of the above cases, *all* of those cases have involved points of time at or after the initiation of adversary judicial criminal proceedings—whether by way of formal charge, preliminary hearing, indictment, information, or arraignment. . . .

The initiation of judicial criminal proceedings is far from a mere formalism. It is the starting point of our whole system of adversary criminal justice. For it is only then that the government has committed itself to prosecute, and only then that the adverse positions of government and defendant have solidified. It is then that a defendant finds himself faced with the prosecutorial forces of organized society, and immersed in the intricacies of substantive and procedural criminal law. It is this point, therefore, that marks the commencement of the "criminal prosecutions" to which alone the explicit guarantees of the Sixth Amendment are applicable.

In this case we are asked to import into a routine police investigation an absolute constitutional guarantee historically and rationally applicable only after the onset of formal prosecutorial proceedings. We decline to do so. Less than a year after Wade and Gilbert were decided, the Court explained the rule of those decisions as follows: "The rationale of those cases was that an accused is entitled to counsel at any 'critical stage of the *prosecution*,' and that a post-indictment lineup is such a 'critical stage.'" (Emphasis supplied.) Simmons v United States, 390 US 377, 382–383, 19 L Ed 2d 1247, 1252, 88 S Ct 967. We decline to depart from that rationale today by imposing a per se exclusionary rule upon testimony concerning an identification that took place long before the commencement of any prosecution whatever.

II

What has been said is not to suggest that there may not be occasions during the course of a criminal investigation when the police do abuse identification procedures. Such abuses are not beyond the reach of the Constitution. . . .

The Due Process Clause of the Fifth and Fourteenth Amendments forbids a lineup that is unnecessarily suggestive and conducive to irreparable mistaken identification. Stovall v Denno, 388 US 293, 87 S Ct 1967, 18 L Ed 2d 1199; Foster v California, 394 US 440, 89 S Ct 1127, 22 L Ed 2d 402. When a person has not been formally charged with a criminal offense, Stovall strikes the appropriate constitutional balance between the right of a suspect to be protected from prejudicial procedures and the interest of society in the prompt and purposeful investigation of an unsolved crime.

The judgment is affirmed. . . .

Mr. Justice Brennan, with whom Mr. Justice Douglas and Mr. Justice Marshall join, dissenting.

After petitioner and Ralph Bean were arrested, police officers brought Willie Shard, the robbery victim, to a room in a police station where petitioner and Bean were seated at a table with two other police officers. Shard testified at trial that the officers who brought him to the room asked him if petitioner and Bean were the robbers and that he indicated they were. The prosecutor asked him, "And you positively identified them at the police station, is that correct?" Shard answered, "Yes." Consequently, the question in this case is whether, under Gilbert v California, 388 US 263, 87 S Ct 1951, 18 L Ed 2d 1178 (1967), it was constitutional error to admit Shard's testimony that he identified petitioner at the pretrial stationhouse showup when that showup was conducted by the police without advising petitioner that he might have counsel present. Gilbert held, in the context of a post-indictment lineup, that "[o]nly a per se exclusionary rule as to such testimony can be an effective sanction to assure that law enforcement authorities will respect the accused's constitutional right to the presence of his counsel at the critical lineup." I would apply Gilbert and the principles of its companion case, United States v. Wade, 388 US 218, 87 S Ct 1926, 18 L Ed 2d 1149 (1967), and reverse. . . .

While it should go without saying, it appears necessary, in view of the plurality opinion today, to re-emphasize that Wade did not require the presence of counsel at pretrial confrontations for identification purposes simply on the basis of an abstract consideration of the words "criminal prosecutions" in the Sixth Amendment. Counsel is required at those confrontations because "the dangers inherent in eyewitness identification and the suggestibility inherent in the context of the pretrial identification," mean that protection must be afforded to the "most basic right [of] a criminal defendant—his right to a fair trial at which the witnesses against him might be meaningfully cross-examined," id., at 224, 18 L Ed 2d at 1166. . . . Hence, "the initiation of adversary judicial criminal proceedings," is completely irrelevant to whether counsel is necessary at a pretrial confrontation for identification in order to safeguard the accused's constitutional rights to confrontation and the effective assistance of counsel at his trial.

In view of Wade, it is plain, and the plurality today does not attempt to dispute it, that there inhere in a confrontation for identification conducted after arrest the identical hazards to a fair trial that inhere in such a confrontation conducted "after the onset of formal prosecutorial proceedings." Id., at 690, 32 L Ed 2d 418. The plurality apparently considers an arrest, which for present purposes we must assume to be based upon probable cause, to be nothing more than part of "a routine police investigation," and thus not "the starting point of our whole system of adversary criminal justice," id., at 689, 32 L Ed 2d at 418. An arrest, according to the plurality, does not face the accused "with the prosecutorial forces of organized society," nor immerse him "in the intricacies of substantive and procedural criminal law." Those consequences ensue, says the plurality, only with "[t]he initiation of judicial criminal proceedings," "[f]or it is only then that the government has committed itself to prosecute, and only then that the adverse positions of government and defendant have solidified." If these propositions do not amount to "mere formalism," it is difficult to know how to characterize them. An arrest evidences the belief of the police that the perpetrator of a crime has been caught. A post-arrest confrontation for identification is not "a mere preparatory step in the gathering of the prosecution's evidence." Wade, supra, at 227, 18 L Ed 2d at 1157. A primary, and frequently sole, purpose of the confrontation for identification at the stage is to accumulate proof to buttress the conclusion of the police that they have the offender in hand. The plurality offers no reason, and I can think of none, for concluding that a post-arrest confrontation for identification, unlike a post-charge confrontation, is not among those "critical confrontations of the accused by the prosecution at pretrial proceedings where the results might well settle the accused's fate and reduce the trial itself to a mere formality."

The highly suggestive form of confrontation employed in this case underscores the point. This showup was particularly fraught with the peril of mistaken identification. In the setting of a police station squad room where all present except petitioner and Bean were police officers, the danger was quite real that Shard's understandable resentment might lead him too readily to agree with the police that the pair under arrest, and the only persons exhibited to him, were indeed the robbers. "It is hard to imagine a situation more clearly conveying the suggestion to the witness that the one presented is believed guilty by the police." The State had no case without Shard's identification testimony, and safeguards against that consequence were therefore of critical importance. Shard's testimony itself demonstrates the necessity for such safeguards. On direct examination, Shard identified petitioner and Bean not as the alleged robbers on trial in the courtroom, but as the pair he saw at the police station. His testimony thus lends strong support to the observation, quoted by the Court in Wade, 388 US, at 229, 18 L Ed 2d at 1159, that "[i]t is a matter of common experience that, once a witness has picked out the accused at the line-up, he is not likely to go back on his word later on, so that in practice the issue of identity may (in the absence of other relevant evidence) for all practical purposes be determined there and then, before the trial." Williams & Hammelman, Identification Parades, Part I, [1963] Crim L Rev 479, 482. . . .

Wade and Gilbert, of course, happened to involve post-indictment confrontations. Yet even a cursory perusal of the opinions in those cases reveals that nothing at all turned upon that particular circumstance. In short, it is fair to conclude that rather than "declin[ing] to depart from [the] rationale" of Wade and Gilbert, the plurality today, albeit purporting to be engaged in "principled constitutional adjudication," refuses even to recognize that "rationale." For my part, I do not agree that we "extend" Wade and Gilbert, by holding that the principles of those cases apply to confrontations for identification conducted after arrest. Because Shard testified at trial about his identification of petitioner at the police station showup, the exclusionary rule of Gilbert requires reversal.

Notes and Questions

1. On what constitutional grounds was *Kirby* decided? Can the opinion be harmonized with the Court's opinion in *Miranda*?

2. A vast majority of lineups are conducted prior to the institution of formal proceedings against a defendant. Does this surprise you?

3. While a defendant is not entitled to an attorney at a preindictment lineup under the Federal Constitution, several states have extended such a right to defendants under their state constitution. The approach taken by the California Supreme Court in *People v. Busta-monte*, 30 Cal. 3d 88, 634 P.2d 927, 177 Cal. Rptr. 576 (1981), is illustrative.

> Judicial recognition of the right to counsel at a lineup originated as a response to the recognized unreliability of eyewitness identification. As a leading scholar then stated, "The identification of strangers is proverbially untrustworthy." Frankfurter, *The Case of Sacco and Vanzetti* (1927) p. 30. Another commentator, Judge Jerome Frank, concluded that "Perhaps erroneous identification of the accused constitutes the major cause of the known wrongful convictions." Frank & Frank, *Not Guilty* (1957) p. 61.

> In light of these dangers, a properly conducted lineup, staged as soon as feasible after the crime, and containing a number of persons whose general appearance resembles the defendant, becomes an invaluable police technique to enhance the reliability of identification. That procedure, however, clearly makes the lineup a "critical stage of the prosecution" within the language of United States v. Wade, 388 U.S. 218, 237, 87 S.Ct. 1926, 1937, 18 L.Ed.2d 1149, for when a witness has made a positive identification at a lineup, he is unlikely to change his mind. "[O]nce any identification decision is made it may well be 'irreparable.'" People v. Anderson, 205 N.W.2d 461, 485, italics omitted. Identification testimony at trial, when defendant has counsel who may cross-examine the witness, may be unshakable if an earlier lineup identification has removed the witness's doubts and committed him to the proposition that defendant is the criminal in question.

> As Justice Brennan stated in Wade, "A major factor contributing to the high incidence of miscarriage of justice from mistaken identification has been the degree of suggestion inherent in the manner in which the prosecution presents the suspect to witnesses for pretrial identification. A commen-

> tator has observed that '[t]he influence of improper suggestion upon identifying witnesses probably accounts for more miscarriages of justice than any other single factor; perhaps it is responsible for more such errors than all other factors combined.' Wall, Eye-Witness Identification in Criminal Cases 26." Pp. 228–229; see Sobel, Eyewitness Identification (1972) § 3.01. Moreover, as Wade and other cases pointed out, it is extremely difficult to reproduce the identification procedure at trial with sufficient precision to detect improper suggestion.

> We therefore conclude that a pretrial lineup is a critical stage in the prosecution of a criminal case, and that ensuring the fairness of that lineup is crucial to the protection of innocent persons accused of crime. . . .

> We turn [next] to the question whether defendant's right to counsel should be limited, as in Kirby, to postindictment lineups. As we noted earlier, the plurality opinion in Kirby did not deny that a preindictment lineup may be critical to the defense of a criminal case and may result in intractable misidentification of an innocent accused; it held, instead, that defendant has no right to counsel until the "prosecution" commences with the filing of formal charges.

> We think this a wholly unrealistic view, and note that the commentators have generally condemned Kirby's limitation of the right to counsel. . . . Indeed, to limit the right to counsel at a lineup to postindictment lineups would as a practical matter nullify that right. "The defendant who most needs protection from erroneous identification is one who is implicated primarily or solely by eyewitness testimony. Yet, because of this lack of non-eyewitness evidence, an identification of the defendant in a lineup or showup would be necessary to justify formal charges or arraignment. Consequently, the crucial confrontation necessarily will be held before the initiation of formal judicial proceedings when the defendant can be deprived of counsel. Thus Kirby removes the protective effects of counsel's presence precisely when the danger of convicting an innocent defendant upon a mistaken identi-

fication is greatest. Furthermore, after Kirby, the policy may defeat the aims of Wade and Gilbert in any case simply by delaying formal charges and holding the lineup in the absence of defense counsel." Note (1977) 29 Stan.L.Rev. 969, 996, fns. omitted. . . .

Although extending the right to counsel to preindictment lineups will thus impose an additional burden upon the police, and may delay the staging of the lineup, these consequences do not appear substantial enough to justify denying defendant this protective right. The burden of securing counsel is exactly the same as that which police departments must assume if they wish to question a defendant who invokes his right to counsel under Miranda v. Arizona, 384 U.S. 436, 86 S.Ct. 1602, 16 L.Ed.2d 694; it

is a requirement which governed all California lineups during the five years between Wade and Kirby without, so far as we are aware, significantly impeding police investigation. The delay involved in securing counsel will generally be a matter of hours at most. If conditions require immediate identification without even minimal delay, or if counsel cannot be present within a reasonable time, such exigent circumstances will justify proceeding without counsel. . . .

4. In 1995, California amended its constitution to provide that "relevant evidence shall not be excluded in any criminal proceeding." Cal. Const. Art. 1 § 28 (d). How do you think the rule developed in *Bustamonte* is affected by this provision?

After *Wade* and *Kirby*, it is clear that a defendant has a right to counsel at a postindictment lineup. Is this right limited to a live lineup (often referred to as a *corporeal lineup*), or does it apply to photographic displays as well? The Supreme Court answered this question in *United States v. Ash*.

United States v. Ash, 413 U.S. 300, 93 S. Ct. 2568, 37 L. Ed. 2d 619 (1973)

Mr. Justice BLACKMUN delivered the opinion of the Court.

In this case the Court is called upon to decide whether the Sixth Amendment grants an accused the right to have counsel present whenever the Government conducts a post-indictment photographic display, containing a picture of the accused, for the purpose of allowing a witness to attempt an identification of the offender. The United States Court of Appeals for the District of Columbia Circuit, sitting en banc, held, by a 5-to-4 vote, that the accused possesses this right to counsel. 149 U.S.App.D.C. 1, 461 F.2d 92 (1972). . . .

[Two men wearing ski masks robbed a bar in Washington, D.C., at gunpoint. Law enforcement officials received a tip from an informant that Ash was one of the robbers. On the basis of this information, police showed four people who witnessed the robbery black-and-white mug shots of five individuals, one of whom was Ash. All four witnesses identified Ash and his codefendant John Bailey as being the robbers. Both were subsequently indicted.]

In preparing for trial, the prosecutor decided to use a photographic display to determine whether the witnesses he planned to call would be able to make in-court identifications. Shortly before the trial, an FBI agent and the prosecutor showed five color photographs to the four witnesses who previously had tentatively identified the black-and-white photograph of Ash. Three of the witnesses selected the picture of Ash, but one was unable to make any selection. None of the witnesses selected the picture of Bailey which was in the group. This post-indictment[3]

---

3. Respondent Ash does not assert a right to counsel at the black-and-white photographic display in February 1966 because he recognizes that Kirby v. Illinois, 406 U.S. 682, 92 S.Ct. 1877, 32 L.Ed.2d 411 (1972), forecloses application of the Sixth Amendment to events before the initiation of adversary criminal proceedings.

identification provides the basis for respondent Ash's claim that he was denied the right to counsel at a "critical stage" of the prosecution. . . .

At trial, the three witnesses who had been inside the bank identified Ash as the gunman, but they were unwilling to state that they were certain of their identifications. None of these made an in-court identification of Bailey. The fourth witness, who had been in a car outside the bank and who had seen the fleeing robbers after they had removed their masks made positive in-court identifications of both Ash and Bailey. . . .

The jury convicted Ash on all counts. . . .

The five-member majority of the Court of Appeals held that Ash's right to counsel, guaranteed by the Sixth Amendment, was violated when his attorney was not given the opportunity to be present at the photographic displays conducted in May 1968 before the trial. The majority relied on this Court's lineup cases, United States v. Wade, 388 U.S. 218, 87 S.Ct. 1926, 18 L.Ed.2d 1149 (1967), and Gilbert v. California, 388 U.S. 263, 87 S.Ct. 1951, 18 L.Ed.2d 1178 (1967), and on Stovall v. Denno, 388 U.S. 293, 87 S.Ct. 1967, 18 L.Ed.2d 1199 (1967). . . .

II

The Court of Appeals relied exclusively on that portion of the Sixth Amendment providing, "In all criminal prosecutions, the accused shall enjoy the right . . . to have the Assistance of Counsel for his defence." The right to counsel in Anglo-American law has a rich historical heritage, and this Court has regularly drawn on that history in construing the counsel guarantee of the Sixth Amendment. . . .

The Court frequently has interpreted the Sixth Amendment to assure that the "guiding hand of counsel" is available to those in need of its assistance. See, for example, Gideon v. Wainwright, 372 U.S. 335, 344–345, 83 S.Ct. 792, 796–797, 9 L.Ed.2d 799 (1963), and Argersinger v. Hamlin, 407 U.S. 25, 31, 92 S.Ct. 2006, 2009, 32 L.Ed.2d 530 (1972).

Another factor contributing to the colonial recognition of the accused's right to counsel was the adoption of the institution of the public prosecutor from the Continental inquisitorial system.

One commentator has explained the effect of this development:

"[E]arly in the eighteenth century the American system of judicial administration adopted an institution which was (and to some extent still is) unknown in England: while rejecting the fundamental juristic concepts upon which continental Europe's inquisitorial system of criminal procedure is predicated, the colonies borrowed one of its institutions, the public prosecutor, and grafted it upon the body of English (accusatorial) procedure embodied in the common law. Presumably, this innovation was brought about by the lack of lawyers, particularly in the newly settled regions, and by the increasing distances between the colonial capitals on the eastern seaboard and the ever-receding western frontier. Its result was that, at a time when virtually all but treason trials in England were still in the nature of suits between private parties, the accused in the colonies faced a government official whose specific function it was to prosecute, and who was incomparably more familiar than the accused with the problems of procedure, the idiosyncrasies of juries, and, last but not least, the personnel of the court." F. Heller, The Sixth Amendment 20–21 (1951) (footnote omitted).

Thus, an additional motivation for the American rule was a desire to minimize the imbalance in the adversary system that otherwise resulted with the creation of a professional prosecuting official. Mr. Justice Black, writing for the Court in Johnson v. Zerbst, 304 U.S. 458, 462–463, 58 S.Ct. 1019, 1022, 82 L.Ed. 1461 (1938), spoke of this equalizing effect of the Sixth Amendment's counsel guarantee:

"It embodies a realistic recognition of the obvious truth that the average defendant does not have the professional legal skill to protect himself when brought before a tribunal with power to take his life or liberty, wherein the prosecution is presented by experienced and learned counsel."

This historical background suggests that the core purpose of the counsel guarantee was to assure "Assistance" at trial, when the accused was confronted with both the intricacies of the law and the advocacy of the public prosecutor. Later developments have led this Court to recognize that "Assistance" would be less than meaningful if it were limited to the formal trial itself.

This extension of the right to counsel to events before trial has resulted from changing patterns of criminal procedure and investigation that have tended to generate pretrial events that might appropriately be considered to be parts of the trial itself. At these newly emerging and significant events, the accused was confronted, just as at trial, by the procedural system, or by his expert adversary, or by both. In *Wade*, the Court explained the process of expanding the counsel guarantee to these confrontations:

> "When the Bill of Rights was adopted, there were no organized police forces as we know them today. The accused confronted the prosecutor and the witnesses against him, and the evidence was marshalled, largely at the trial itself. In contrast, today's law enforcement machinery involves critical confrontations of the accused by the prosecution at pretrial proceedings where the results might well settle the accused's fate and reduce the trial itself to a mere formality. In recognition of these realities of modern criminal prosecution, our cases have construed the Sixth Amendment guarantee to apply to 'critical' stages of the proceedings." 388 U.S., at 224, 87 S.Ct., at 1931 (footnote omitted).

The Court consistently has applied a historical interpretation of the guarantee, and has expanded the constitutional right to counsel only when new contexts appear presenting the same dangers that gave birth initially to the right itself. . . .

The function of counsel in rendering "Assistance" at the lineup [was] under consideration in *Wade* and its companion cases. Although the accused was not confronted there with legal questions, the lineup offered opportunities for prosecuting authorities to take advantage of the

accused. Counsel was seen by the Court as being more sensitive to, and aware of, suggestive influences than the accused himself, and as better able to reconstruct the events at trial. Counsel present at lineup would be able to remove disabilities of the accused in precisely the same fashion that counsel compensated for the disabilities of the layman at trial. Thus, the Court mentioned that the accused's memory might be dimmed by "emotional tension," that the accused's credibility at trial would be diminished by his status as defendant, and that the accused might be unable to present his version effectively without giving up his privilege against compulsory self-incrimination. United States v. Wade, 388 U.S., at 230–231, 87 S.Ct., at 1933, 1934. It was in order to compensate for these deficiencies that the Court found the need for the assistance of counsel. . . .

III

Although the Court of Appeals' majority recognized the argument that "a major purpose behind the right to counsel is to protect the defendant from errors that he himself might make if he appeared in court alone," the court concluded that "other forms of prejudice," mentioned and recognized in *Wade*, could also give rise to a right to counsel. These forms of prejudice were felt by the court to flow from the possibilities for mistaken identification inherent in the photographic display.[8]

We conclude that the dangers of mistaken identification, mentioned in *Wade*, were removed from context by the Court of Appeals and were incorrectly utilized as a sufficient basis for requiring counsel. Although *Wade* did dis-

---

8. "[T]he dangers of mistaken identification from uncounseled lineup identifications set forth in *Wade* are applicable in large measure to photographic as well as corporeal identifications. These include, notably, the possibilities of suggestive influence or mistake—particularly where witnesses had little or no opportunity for detailed observation during the crime; the difficulty of reconstructing suggestivity—even greater when the defendant is not even present; the tendency of a witness's identification, once given under these circumstances, to be frozen. While these difficulties may be somewhat mitigated by preserving the photograph

cuss possibilities for suggestion and the difficulty for reconstructing suggestivity, this discussion occurred only after the Court had concluded that the lineup constituted a trial-like confrontation, requiring the "Assistance of Counsel" to preserve the adversary process by compensating for advantages of the prosecuting authorities. . . .

After the Court in *Wade* held that a lineup constituted a trial-like confrontation requiring counsel, a more difficult issue remained in the case for consideration. The same changes in law enforcement that led to lineups and pretrial hearings also generated other events at which the accused was confronted by the prosecution. The Government had argued in *Wade* that if counsel was required at a lineup, the same forceful considerations would mandate counsel at other preparatory steps in the "gathering of the prosecution's evidence," such as, for particular example, the taking of fingerprints or blood samples. 388 U.S., at 227, 87 S.Ct., at 1932.

The Court concluded that there were differences. Rather than distinguishing these situations from the lineup in terms of the need for counsel to assure an equal confrontation at the time, the Court recognized that there were times when the subsequent trial would cure a one-sided confrontation between prosecuting authorities and the uncounseled defendant. In other words, such stages were not "critical." Referring to fingerprints, hair, clothing, and other blood samples, the Court explained:

"Knowledge of the techniques of science and technology is sufficiently available, and the variables in techniques few enough, that the accused has the opportunity for a meaningful confrontation of the Govern-

ment's case at trial through the ordinary processes of cross-examination of the Government's expert witnesses and the presentation of the evidence of his own experts." 388 U.S., at 227–228, 87 S.Ct., at 1932.

The structure of *Wade*, viewed in light of the careful limitation of the Court's language to "confrontations," makes it clear that lack of scientific precision and inability to reconstruct an event are not the tests for requiring counsel in the first instance. These are, instead, the tests to determine whether confrontation with counsel at trial can serve as a substitute for counsel at the pretrial confrontation. If accurate reconstruction is possible, the risks inherent in any confrontation still remain, but the opportunity to cure defects at trial causes the confrontation to cease to be "critical." The opinion of the Court even indicated that changes in procedure might cause a lineup to cease to be a "critical" confrontation.

"Legislative or other regulations, such as those of local police departments, which eliminate the risks of abuse and unintentional suggestion at lineup proceedings and the impediments to meaningful confrontation at trial may also remove the basis for regarding the stage as 'critical.'" 388 U.S., at 239, 87 S.Ct., at 1938 (footnote omitted).

See, however, *id.*, at 262 n., 87 S.Ct., at 1950 (opinion of Fortas, J.).

The Court of Appeals considered its analysis complete after it decided that a photographic display lacks scientific precision and ease of accurate reconstruction at trial. That analysis, under *Wade*, however, merely carries one to the point where one must establish that the trial itself can provide no substitute for counsel if a pretrial confrontation is conducted in the absence of counsel. Judge Friendly, writing for the Second Circuit in United States v. Bennett, 409 F.2d 888 (1969), recognized that the "criticality" test of *Wade*, if applied outside the confrontation context, would result in drastic expansion of the right to counsel:

"None of the classical analyses of the assistance to be given by counsel, Justice Sutherland's in Powell v. Alabama . . . and Justice Black's in Johnson v. Zerbst . . . and Gideon v. Wainwright . . . suggests that

---

shown, it may also be said that a photograph can preserve the record of a lineup; yet this does not justify a lineup without counsel. The same may be said of the opportunity to examine the participants as to what went on in the course of the identification, whether at lineup or on photograph. Sometimes this may suffice to bring out all pertinent facts, even at a lineup, but this would not suffice under *Wade* to offset the constitutional infringement wrought by proceeding without counsel. The presence of counsel avoids possibilities of suggestiveness in the manner of presentation that are otherwise eradicable." 149 U.S.App.D.C., at 9–10, 461 F.2d, at 100–101.

counsel must be present when the prosecution is interrogating witnesses in the defendant's absence even when, as here, the defendant is under arrest; counsel is rather to be provided to prevent the defendant himself from falling into traps devised by a lawyer on the other side and to see to it that all available defenses are proffered. Many other aspects of the prosecution's interviews with a victim or a witness to a crime afford just as much opportunity for undue suggestion as the display of photographs; so, too, do the defense's interviews, notably with alibi witnesses." *Id.*, at 899–900.

We now undertake the threshold analysis that must be addressed.

A substantial departure from the historical test would be necessary if the Sixth Amendment were interpreted to give Ash a right to counsel at the photographic identification in this case. Since the accused himself is not present at the time of the photographic display, and asserts no right to be present, no possibility arises that the accused might be misled by his lack of familiarity with the law or overpowered by his professional adversary. Similarly, the counsel guarantee would not be used to produce equality in a trial-like adversary confrontation. . . .

Even if we were willing to view the counsel guarantee in broad terms as a generalized protection of the adversary process, we would be unwilling to go so far as to extend the right to a portion of the prosecutor's trial-preparation interviews with witnesses. Although photography is relatively new, the interviewing of witnesses before trial is a procedure that predates the Sixth Amendment. . . .

That adversary mechanism remains as effective for a photographic display as for other parts of pretrial interviews. No greater limitations are placed on defense counsel in constructing displays, seeking witnesses, and conducting photographic identifications than those applicable to the prosecution. Selection of the picture of a person other than the accused, or the inability of a witness to make any selection, will be useful to the defense in precisely the same manner that the selection of a picture of the defendant would be useful to the prosecution. . . .

The argument has been advanced that requiring counsel might compel the police to observe more scientific procedures or might encourage them to utilize corporeal rather than photographic displays. This Court has recognized that improved procedures can minimize the dangers of suggestion. Simmons v. United States, 390 U.S. 377, 386 n. 6, 88 S.Ct. 967, 972, 19 L.Ed.2d 1247 (1968). Commentators have also proposed more accurate techniques.

Pretrial photographic identifications, however, are hardly unique in offering possibilities for the actions of the prosecutor unfairly to prejudice the accused. Evidence favorable to the accused may be withheld: testimony of witnesses may be manipulated; the results of laboratory tests may be contrived. In many ways the prosecutor, by accident or by design, may improperly subvert the trial. The primary safeguard against abuses of this kind is the ethical responsibility of the prosecutor, who, as so often has been said, may "strike hard blows" but not "foul ones." If that safeguard fails, review remains available under due process standards. These same safeguards apply to misuse of photographs. See Simmons v. United States, 390 U.S., at 384, 88 S.Ct., at 971.

We are not persuaded that the risks inherent in the use of photographic displays are so pernicious that an extraordinary system of safeguards is required.

We hold, then, that the Sixth Amendment does not grant the right to counsel at photographic displays conducted by the Government for the purpose of allowing a witness to attempt an identification of the offender. This holding requires reversal of the judgment of the Court of Appeals. Although respondent Ash has urged us to examine this photographic display under the due process standard enunciated in Simmons v. United States, 390 U.S., at 384, 88 S.Ct., at 971, the Court of Appeals, expressing the view that additional findings would be necessary, refused to decide the issue. 149 U.S.App.D.C., at 7, 461 F.2d, at 98. We decline to consider this question on this record in the first instance. It remains open, of course, on the Court of Appeals' remand to the District Court.

Reversed and remanded.

Mr. Justice STEWART, concurring in the judgment. . . .

A photographic identification is quite different from a lineup, for there are substantially fewer possibilities of impermissible suggestion when photographs are used, and those unfair influences can be readily reconstructed at trial. It is true that the defendant's photograph may be markedly different from the others displayed, but this unfairness can be demonstrated at trial from an actual comparison of the photographs used or from the witness' description of the display. Similarly, it is possible that the photographs could be arranged in a suggestive manner, or that by comment or gesture the prosecuting authorities might single out the defendant's picture. But these are the kinds of overt influence that a witness can easily recount and that would serve to impeach the identification testimony. In short, there are few possibilities for unfair suggestiveness—and those rather blatant and easily reconstructed. Accordingly, an accused would not be foreclosed from an effective cross-examination of an identification witness simply because his counsel was not present at the photographic display. For this reason, a photographic display cannot fairly be considered a "critical stage" of the prosecution. As the Court of Appeals for the Third Circuit aptly concluded:

> "If . . . the identification is not in a live lineup at which defendant may be forced to act, speak or dress in a suggestive way, where the possibilities for suggestion are multiplied, where the ability to reconstruct the events is minimized, and where the effect of a positive identification is likely to be permanent, but at a viewing of immobile photographs easily reconstructible, far less subject to subtle suggestion, and far less indelible in its effect when the witness is later brought face to face with the accused, there is even less reason to denominate the procedure a critical stage at which counsel must be present." United States ex rel. Reed v. Anderson, 461 F.2d 739, 745.

Preparing witnesses for trial by checking their identification testimony against a photographic display is little different, in my view, from the prosecutor's other interviews with the victim or other witnesses before trial. While these procedures can be improperly conducted, the possibility of irretrievable prejudice is remote, since any unfairness that does occur can usually be flushed out at trial through cross-examination of the prosecution witnesses. The presence of defense counsel at such pretrial preparatory sessions is neither appropriate nor necessary under our adversary system of justice "to preserve the defendant's basic right to a fair trial as affected by his right meaningfully to cross-examine the witnesses against him and to have effective assistance of counsel at the trial itself." United States v. Wade, *supra*, 388 U.S. at 227, 87 S.Ct., at 1932.

Mr. Justice BRENNAN, with whom Mr. Justice DOUGLAS and Mr. Justice MARSHALL join, dissenting.

The Court holds today that a pretrial display of photographs to the witnesses of a crime for the purpose of identifying the accused, unlike a lineup, does not constitute a "critical stage" of the prosecution at which the accused is constitutionally entitled to the presence of counsel. In my view, today's decision is wholly unsupportable in terms of such considerations as logic, consistency, and, indeed, fairness. As a result, I must reluctantly conclude that today's decision marks simply another step towards the complete evisceration of the fundamental constitutional principles established by this Court, only six years ago, in United States v. Wade, 388 U.S. 218, 87 S.Ct. 1926, 18 L.Ed.2d 1149 (1967); Gilbert v. California, 388 U.S. 263, 87 S.Ct. 1951, 18 L.Ed.2d 1178 (1967); and Stovall v. Denno, 388 U.S. 293, 87 S.Ct. 1967, 18 L.Ed.2d 1199 (1967). I dissent. . . .

III

As the Court of Appeals recognized, "the dangers of mistaken identification . . . set forth in *Wade* are applicable in large measure to photographic as well as corporeal identifications." 149 U.S.App.D.C., at 9, 461 F.2d, at 100. To the extent that misidentification may be attributable to a witness' faulty memory or perception, or inadequate opportunity for detailed observation during the crime, the risks are obviously as great at a photographic display as at a lineup. But "[b]ecause of the inherent limitations of photography, which presents its subject in two dimensions rather than the three dimensions of reality,

. . . a photographic identification, even when properly obtained, is clearly inferior to a properly obtained corporeal identification." P. Wall, Eye-Witness Identification in Criminal Cases 70 (1965). Indeed, noting "the hazards of initial identification by photograph," we have expressly recognized that "a corporeal identification . . . is normally more accurate" than a photographic identification. Simmons v. United States, 390 U.S. 377, 384, 386 n. 6, 88 S.Ct. 967, 971, 972, 19 L.Ed.2d 1247 (1968). Thus, in this sense at least, the dangers of misidentification are even greater at a photographic display than at a lineup.

Moreover, as in the lineup situation, the possibilities for impermissible suggestion in the context of a photographic display are manifold. Such suggestion, intentional or unintentional, may derive from three possible sources. First, the photographs themselves might tend to suggest which of the pictures is that of the suspect. For example, differences in age, pose, or other physical characteristics of the persons represented, and variations in the mounting, background, lighting, or markings of the photographs all might have the effect of singling out the accused.

Second, impermissible suggestion may inhere in the manner in which the photographs are displayed to the witness. The danger of misidentification is, of course, "increased if the police display to the witness . . . the pictures of several persons among which the photograph of a single such individual recurs or is in some way emphasized." And, if the photographs are arranged in an asymmetrical pattern, or if they are displayed in a time sequence that tends to emphasize a particular photograph, "any identification of the photograph which stands out from the rest is no more reliable than an identification of a single photograph, exhibited alone." P. Wall, *supra*, at 81.

Third, gestures or comments of the prosecutor at the time of the display may lead an otherwise uncertain witness to select the "correct" photograph. For example, the prosecutor might "indicate to the witness that [he has] other evidence that one of the persons pictured committed the crime," and might even point to a particular photograph and ask whether the person pictured "looks familiar." More subtly, the prosecutor's inflection, facial expressions, physical motions, and myriad other almost imperceptible means of communication might tend, intentionally or unintentionally, to compromise the witness' objectivity. Thus, as is the case with lineups, "[i]mproper photographic identification procedures, . . . by exerting a suggestive influence upon the witnesses, can often lead to an erroneous identification. . . ." P. Wall, *supra*, at 89. And "[r]egardless of how the initial misidentification comes about, the witness thereafter is apt to retain in his memory the image of the photograph rather than of the person actually seen . . . ." Simmons v. United States, *supra*, 390 U.S., at 383–384, 88 S.Ct., at 971. As a result, "'the issue of identity may (in the absence of other relevant evidence) for all practical purposes be determined there and then, before the trial.'" United States v. Wade, *supra*, 388 U.S., at 229, 87 S.Ct., at 1933, quoting Williams & Hammelmann, *supra*, at 482.

Moreover, as with lineups, the defense can "seldom reconstruct" at trial the mode and manner of photographic identification. It is true, of course, that the photographs used at the pretrial display might be preserved for examination at trial. But "it may also be said that a photograph can preserve the record of a lineup; yet this does not justify a lineup without counsel." Indeed, in reality, preservation of the photographs affords little protection to the unrepresented accused. For, although retention of the photographs may mitigate the dangers of misidentification due to the suggestiveness of the photographs themselves, it cannot in any sense reveal to defense counsel the more subtle, and therefore more dangerous, suggestiveness that might derive from the manner in which the photographs were displayed or any accompanying comments or gestures. Moreover, the accused cannot rely upon the witnesses themselves to expose these latter sources of suggestion, for the witnesses are not "apt to be alert for conditions prejudicial to the suspect. And if they were, it would likely be of scant benefit to the suspect" since the witnesses are hardly "likely to be schooled in the detection of suggestive influences."

Finally, and *unlike* the lineup situation, the accused himself is not even present at the photographic identification, thereby reducing the likelihood that irregularities in the procedures will ever come to light. Indeed, in *Wade*, the Government itself observed:

> "When the defendant is present—as he is during a lineup—he may personally observe the circumstances, report them to his attorney, and (if he chooses to take the stand) testify about them at trial. . . . [I]n the absence of an accused, on the other hand, there is no one present to verify the fairness of the interview or to report any irregularities. If the prosecution were tempted to engage in 'sloppy or biased or fraudulent' conduct . . ., it would be far more likely to do so when the accused is absent than when he is himself being 'used.'"

Thus, the difficulties of reconstructing at trial an uncounseled photographic display are at least equal to, and possibly greater than, those involved in reconstructing an uncounseled lineup. And, as the Government argued in *Wade*, in terms of the need for counsel, "[t]here is no meaningful difference between a witness' pretrial identification from photographs and a similar identification made at a lineup." For in both situations, "the accused's inability effectively to reconstruct at trial any unfairness that occurred at the [pretrial identification] may deprive him of his only opportunity meaningfully to attack the credibility of the witness' courtroom identification." United States v. Wade, *supra*, 388 U.S. at 231–232, 87 S.Ct., at 1935. As a result, both photographic and corporeal identifications create grave dangers that an innocent defendant might be convicted simply because of his inability to expose a tainted identification. This being so, considerations of logic, consistency, and, indeed, fairness compel the conclusion that a pretrial photographic identification, like a pretrial corporeal identification, is a "critical stage of the prosecution at which [the accused is] 'as much entitled to such aid [of counsel] . . . as at the trial itself.'" *Id.*, at 237, 87 S.Ct., at 1937, quoting Powell v. Alabama, 287 U.S., at 57, 53 S.Ct., at 60.

IV

Ironically, the Court does not seriously challenge the proposition that presence of counsel at a pretrial photographic display is essential to preserve the accused's right to a fair trial on the issue of identification. Rather, in what I can only characterize a triumph of form over substance, the Court seeks to justify its result by engrafting a wholly unprecedented—and wholly unsupportable—limitation on the Sixth Amendment right of "the accused . . . to have the Assistance of Counsel for his defence." Although apparently conceding that the right to counsel attaches, not only at the trial itself, but at all "critical stages" of the prosecution, the Court holds today that, in order to be deemed "critical," the particular "stage of the prosecution" under consideration must, at the very least, involve the physical "presence of the accused," at a "trial-like confrontation" with the Government, at which the accused requires the "guiding hand of counsel." According to the Court a pretrial photographic identification does not, of course, meet these criteria.

In support of this rather crabbed view of the Sixth Amendment, the Court cites our decisions in Coleman v. Alabama, 399 U.S. 1, 90 S.Ct. 1999, 26 L.Ed.2d 387 (1970), Massiah v. United States, 377 U.S. 201, 84 S.Ct. 1199, 12 L.Ed.2d 246 (1964), White v. Maryland, 373 U.S. 59, 83 S.Ct. 1050, 10 L.Ed.2d 193 (1963), and Hamilton v. Alabama, 368 U.S. 52, 82 S.Ct. 157, 7 L.Ed.2d 114 (1961). Admittedly, each of these decisions guaranteed the assistance of counsel in pretrial proceedings at least arguably involving the physical "presence of the accused," at a "trial-like confrontation" with the Government, at which the accused required the "guiding hand of counsel." Moreover, as the Court points out, these decisions are consistent with the view that the Sixth Amendment "embodies a realistic recognition of the obvious truth that the average defendant does not have the professional legal skill to protect himself when brought before a tribunal with power to take his life or liberty, wherein the prosecution is presented by experienced and learned counsel." Johnson v. Zerbst, 304 U.S. 458, 462–463, 58 S.Ct. 1019, 1022, 82 L.Ed. 1461 (1938). But, contrary to the Court's assumption, this is merely one *facet* of the Sixth Amendment guarantee, and the decisions relied upon by the Court represent, not the boundaries of the right to counsel, but mere applications of a far broader and more reasoned understanding of the Sixth Amendment than that espoused today.

The fundamental premise underlying *all* of this Court's decisions holding the right to counsel applicable at "critical" pretrial proceedings, is that a "stage" of the prosecution must be deemed "critical" for the purposes of the Sixth Amendment if it is one at which the presence of counsel is necessary "to protect the fairness of *the trial itself.*" Schneckloth v. Bustamonte, 412 U.S. 218, 239, 93 S.Ct. 2041, 2054, 36 L.Ed.2d 854 (1973) (emphasis added). Thus, in Hamilton v. Alabama, for example, we made clear that an arraignment under Alabama law is a "critical stage" of the prosecution, not only because the accused at such an arraignment requires "the guiding hand of counsel," but, more broadly, because "[w]hat happens there may affect the whole trial." Indeed, to exclude counsel from a pretrial proceeding at which his presence might be necessary to assure the fairness of the subsequent trial would, in practical effect, render the Sixth Amendment guarantee virtually meaningless, for it would "deny a defendant 'effective representation by counsel at the only stage when legal aid and advice would help him.'"

This established conception of the Sixth Amendment guarantee is, of course, in no sense dependent upon the physical "presence of the accused," at a "trial-like confrontation" with the Government, at which the accused requires the "guiding hand of counsel." On the contrary, in Powell v. Alabama, 287 U.S. 45, 53 S.Ct. 55, 77 L.Ed. 158 (1932), the seminal decision in this area, we explicitly held the right to counsel applicable at a stage of the pretrial proceedings involving *none* of the three criteria set forth by the Court today. In *Powell*, the defen-

dants in a state felony prosecution were not appointed counsel until the very eve of trial. This Court held, in no uncertain terms, that such an appointment could not satisfy the demands of the Sixth Amendment, for "'[i]t is vain . . . to guarantee [the accused] counsel without giving the latter any opportunity to acquaint himself with the facts or law of the case.'" *Id.*, at 59, 53 S.Ct., at 60. In other words, *Powell* made clear that, in order to preserve the accused's right to a fair trial and to "effective and substantial" assistance of counsel at that trial, the Sixth Amendment guarantee necessarily encompasses a reasonable period of time before trial during which counsel might prepare the defense. Yet it can hardly be said that this preparatory period of research and investigation involves the physical "presence of the accused," at a "trial-like confrontation" with the Government, at which the accused requires the "guiding hand of counsel." . . .

There is something ironic about the Court's conclusion today that a pretrial lineup identification is a "critical stage" of the prosecution because counsel's presence can help to compensate for the accused's deficiencies as an observer, but that a pretrial photographic identification is not a "critical stage" of the prosecution because the accused is not able to observe at all. In my view, there simply is no meaningful difference, in terms of the need for attendance of counsel, between corporeal and photographic identifications. And applying established and well-reasoned Sixth Amendment principles, I can only conclude that a pretrial photographic display, like a pretrial lineup, is a "critical stage" of the prosecution at which the accused is constitutionally entitled to the presence of counsel.

Notes and Questions

1. Which identification procedure do you feel is more reliable: a corporeal lineup or a photographic array? Why?

2. Why did the Court find that there should be counsel present at a postindictment corporeal lineup (*Wade*) but that counsel was unnecessary at a photographic lineup (*Ash*)?

3. If counsel must be present at a postindictment lineup but does not need to be present at a photographic array presented to witnesses, is there a built-in incentive for police to use the latter practice rather than the former? This possibility, coupled with doubts about the reliability of photographic identifications, has led several states to grant more protections to suspects under their state constitution than are afforded under *Ash*. In *People v. Anderson*, 389 Mich. 155, 186–187, 205 N.W.2d 461, 476 (1973), the Michigan Supreme Court held that the Michigan state constitution requires the following limitations on the use of photographic lineups:

[a.] Subject to certain exceptions, identification by photograph should not be used where the accused is in custody. . . . Some of the situations which may, in a particular case, possibly justify the use of photographs are:

[i.] It is not possible to arrange a proper lineup.

[ii.] There are insufficient number of persons available with defendant's physical characteristics.

[iii.] The nature of the case requires immediate identification.

[iv.] The witnesses are at a place far distant from the location of the in-custody accused.

[v.] The subject refuses to participate in a lineup and by his actions would seek to destroy the value of the identification.

[b.] Where there is a legitimate reason to use photographs for identification of an in-custody accused, he has the right to counsel as much as he would for corporeal identification procedures.

Does this approach seem unduly restrictive to the law enforcement process? What if counsel were required at a photographic lineup conducted prior to the suspect being arrested? Would requiring the presence of counsel at this stage unnecessarily hinder the investigatory process?

4. 📖 **Legal Research Note.** Legal periodicals, commonly referred to as *law reviews*, are an excellent source of information on virtually any topic in the law. Law reviews, which typically are run by law students, publish articles written by professors, judges, attorneys, and students. The articles in law reviews are of various quality. Many deal with legal issues in great depth.

Law reviews are excellent sources of information for a legal researcher because articles published in them tend to cite dozens, if not hundreds of cases, statutes, and other articles dealing with the subject matter of the article. Because law review articles can provide a bonanza for a person doing legal research, it is important that we know how to use them as a research tool.

Indexes of law review articles are printed in two different publications. The *Current Law Index* and the *Index to Legal Periodicals*, both of which are published several times a year, are quite similar in format and in the information they provide. Most law libraries maintain the current paperback issues of these indexes as well as the yearly bound volumes. Each volume contains only those articles published during the time period covered in that volume.

Both indexes are organized by subject, title, and author. Due to the way the indexes are arranged and bound, there are two approaches to using them. If you are looking for an item that you believe would have been published during a specific year, such as a critique of a Supreme Court opinion, you will want to start your search in the volume corresponding to the year of the opinion and then consult volumes published in the years following its announcement. If, on the other hand, you are looking for an article dealing with a specific subject, you may want to start your search with the most recent issue of an index and work your way backwards in time.

a. Provide the author's name, the article's title, and the citation for an article in the *U.C.L.A. Law Review* published in 1969 that deals with the necessity of having a lawyer present at a lineup.

b. What is the name and citation of the 1989 article written by Professor Hoffheimer and published in the *Journal of Criminal Law and Criminology* that discusses how to instruct the jury in trials involving eyewitness identification?

THE DUE-PROCESS APPROACH

Regardless of whether counsel is required or even present at an identification procedure, a defendant has a right to challenge the admissibility at trial of an identification that followed an unduly suggestive procedure. Although this notion seems logical, in the decade following the *Wade* trilogy, the lower courts struggled to determine when such an identification should be excluded from evidence. Should the fact that the police unnecessarily used suggestive identification procedures require that testimony about the out-of-court identification be excluded? Or should the reliability of the out-of-court identification remain the crucial issue, because a witness still might be able to make a dependable identification of a suspect that he or she had a good opportunity to observe or had previously known, even if the identification procedures were unnecessarily suggestive? In 1977, the Supreme Court resolved this controversy in *Manson v. Brathwaite*.

Manson v. Brathwaite, 432 U.S. 98, 97 S. Ct. 2243, 53 L. Ed. 2d 140 (1977)

Mr. Justice Blackmun delivered the opinion of the Court.

This case presents the issue as to whether the Due Process Clause of the Fourteenth Amendment compels the exclusion, in a state criminal trial, apart from any consideration of reliability, of pretrial identification evidence obtained by a police procedure that was both suggestive and unnecessary. This Court's decisions in Stovall v. Denno, 388 US 293, 87 S Ct 1967, 18 L Ed 2d 1199 (1967), and Neil v. Biggers, 409 US 188, 93 S Ct 375, 34 L Ed 2d 401 (1972), are particularly implicated.

I

Jimmy D. Glover, a full-time trooper of the Connecticut State Police, in 1970 was assigned to the Narcotics Division in an undercover capacity. On May 5 of that year, about 7:45 p.m. e.d.t., and while there was still daylight, Glover and Henry Alton Brown, an informant, went to an apartment building at 201 Westland, in Hartford, for the purpose of purchasing narcotics from "Dickie Boy" Cicero, a known narcotics dealer. Cicero, it was thought, lived on the third floor of that apartment building. Glover and Brown entered the building, observed by back up Officers D'Onofrio and Gaffey, and proceeded by stairs to the third floor. Glover knocked at the door of one of the two apartments served by the stairway. The area was illuminated by natural light from a window in the third floor hallway. The door was opened 12 to 18 inches in response to the knock. Glover observed a man standing at the door and, behind him, a woman. Brown identified himself. Glover then asked for "two things" of narcotics. The man at the door held out his hand, and Glover gave him two $10 bills. The door closed. Soon the man returned and handed Glover two glassine bags. While the door was open, Glover stood within two feet of the person from whom he made the purchase and observed his face. Five to seven minutes elapsed from the time the door first opened until it closed the second time.

Glover and Brown then left the building. This was about eight minutes after their arrival. Glover drove to headquarters where he described the seller to D'Onofrio and Gaffey. Glover at that time did not know the identity of the seller. He described him as being "a colored man, approximately five feet eleven inches tall, dark complexion, black hair, short Afro style, and having high cheekbones, and of heavy build. He was wearing at the time blue pants and a plaid shirt." D'Onofrio, suspecting from this description that respondent might be the seller, obtained a photograph of respondent from the Records Division of the Hartford Police Department. He left it at Glover's office. D'Onofrio was not acquainted with respondent personally, but did know him by sight and had seen him "[s]everal times" prior to May 5. Glover, when alone, viewed the photograph for the first time upon his return to headquarters on May 7; he identified the person shown as the one from whom he had purchased the narcotics.

The toxicological report on the contents of the glassine bags revealed the presence of heroin. The report was dated July 16, 1970.

Respondent was arrested on July 27 while visiting at the apartment of a Mrs. Ramsey on the third floor of 201 Westland. This was the apartment at which the narcotics sale had taken place on May 5.

Respondent was charged, in a two-count information, with possession and sale of heroin, in violation of Conn Gen Stat (Rev of 1958, as amended in 1969), §§ 19–481a and 19–480a (1977). At his trial in January 1971, the photograph from which Glover had identified respondent was received in evidence without objection on the part of the defense. Glover also testified that, although he had not seen respondent in the eight months that had elapsed since the sale, 'there [was] no doubt whatsoever" in his mind that the person shown on the photograph was respondent. Glover also made a positive in-court identification without objection.

No explanation was offered by the prosecution for the failure to utilize a photographic array or to conduct a lineup.

Respondent, who took the stand in his own defense, testified that on May 5, the day in question, he had been ill at his Albany Avenue apartment, and that at no time on that particular day had he been at 201 Westland. His wife testified that she recalled, after her husband had refreshed her memory, that he was home all day on May 5. . . .

The jury found respondent guilty on both counts of the information. He received a sentence of not less than six nor more than nine years. His conviction was affirmed per curiam by the Supreme Court of Connecticut. . . .

Fourteen months later, respondent filed a petition for habeas corpus in the United States District Court for the District of Connecticut. He alleged that the admission of the identification testimony at his state trial deprived him of due process of law to which he was entitled under the Fourteenth Amendment. The District Court, by an unreported written opinion based on the court's review of the state trial transcript, dismissed respondent's petition. On appeal, the United States Court of Appeals for the Second Circuit reversed. . . .

In brief summary, the court felt that evidence as to the photograph should have been excluded, regardless of reliability, because the examination of the single photograph was unnecessary and suggestive. And, in the court's view, the evidence was unreliable in any event. We granted certiorari.

II

Stovall v. Denno, supra, decided in 1967, concerned a petitioner who had been convicted in a New York court of murder. He was arrested the day following the crime and was taken by the police to a hospital where the victim's wife, also wounded in the assault, was a patient. After observing Stovall and hearing him speak, she identified him as the murderer. She later made an in-court identification. . . .

On the identification issue, the Court reviewed the practice of showing a suspect singly for purposes of identification, and the claim that this was so unnecessarily suggestive and conducive to irreparable mistaken identification that it constituted a denial of due process of law. The Court noted that the practice "has been widely condemned," but it concluded that "a claimed violation of due process of law in the conduct of a confrontation depends on the totality of the circumstances surrounding it." In that case, showing Stovall to the victim's spouse "was imperative." The Court then quoted the observations of the Court of Appeals, 355 F2d 731, 735 (CA2 1966), to the effect that the spouse was the only person who could possibly exonerate the accused; that the hospital was not far from the courthouse and jail; that no one knew how long she might live; that she was not able to visit the jail; and that taking Stovall to the hospital room was the only feasible procedure, and, under the circumstances, "'the usual police station line-up . . . was out of the question.'" 388 US, at 302, 18 L Ed 2d 1199, 87 S Ct 1967.

Neil v. Biggers, supra, decided in 1972, concerned a respondent who had been convicted in a Tennessee court of rape, on evidence consisting in part of the victim's visual and voice identification of Biggers at a station-house showup seven months after the crime. The victim had been in her assailant's presence for some time and had directly observed him indoors and under a full moon outdoors. She testified that she had "no doubt" that Biggers was her assailant. She previously had given the police a description of the assailant. She had made no identification of others presented at previous showups, lineups, or through photographs. On federal habeas, the District Court held that the confrontation was so suggestive as to violate due process. The Court of Appeals affirmed. This Court reversed on that issue, and held that the evidence properly had been allowed to go to the jury. The Court reviewed Stovall and certain later cases where it had considered the scope of due process protection against the admission of evidence derived from suggestive identification procedures. . . .

The Court concluded that general guidelines emerged from these cases "as to the relationship between suggestiveness and misidentification." The "admission of evidence of a showup without more does not violate due process." 409 US, at 198, 93 S Ct 375, 34 L Ed 2d 401. The Court expressed concern about the lapse of seven months between the crime and the confrontation and observed that this "would be a seriously negative factor in most cases." Id., at 201, 93 S Ct 375, 34 L Ed 2d 401. The "central question," however, was "whether under the 'totality of the circumstances' the identification was reliable even though the confrontation procedure was suggestive." Id., at 199. Applying that test, the Court found "no substantial likelihood of misidentification. The evidence was properly allowed to go to the jury." Id., at 201. . . .

III

In the present case the District Court observed that the "sole evidence tying Brathwaite to the possession and sale of the heroin consisted in his identifications by the police undercover agent, Jimmy Glover." On the constitutional issue, the court stated that the first inquiry was whether the police used an impermissibly suggestive procedure in obtaining the out-of-court identification. If so, the second inquiry is whether, under all the circumstances,

that suggestive procedure gave rise to a substantial likelihood of irreparable misidentification. . . .

The court concluded that there was no substantial likelihood of irreparable misidentification. It referred to the facts: Glover was within two feet of the seller. The duration of the confrontation was at least a "couple of minutes." There was natural light from a window or skylight and there was adequate light to see clearly in the hall. Glover "certainly was paying attention to identify the seller." He was a trained police officer who realized that later he would have to find and arrest the person with whom he was dealing. He gave a detailed description to D'Onofrio. The reliability of this description was supported by the fact that it enabled D'Onofrio to pick out a single photograph that was thereafter positively identified by Glover. Only two days elapsed between the crime and the photographic identification. Despite the fact that another eight months passed before the in court identification, Glover had "no doubt" that Brathwaite was the person who had sold him heroin.

The Court of Appeals confirmed that the exhibition of the single photograph to Glover was "impermissibly suggestive," 527 F2d, at 366, and felt that, in addition, "it was unnecessarily so." Id., at 367. There was no emergency and little urgency. . . .

"Evidence of an identification unnecessarily obtained by impermissibly suggestive means must be excluded under Stovall. . . . No rules less stringent than these can force police administrators and prosecutors to adopt procedures that will give fair assurance against the awful risks of misidentification." 527 F2d, at 371. Finally, the court said, even if this conclusion were wrong, the writ, nevertheless, should issue. It took judicial notice that on May 5, 1970, sunset at Hartford was at 7:53 p.m. It characterized Glover's duty as an undercover agent as one "to cause arrests to be made," and his description of the suspect as one that "could have applied to hundreds of Hartford black males." The in-court identification had "little meaning," for Brathwaite was at the counsel table. The fact that respondent was arrested in the very apartment where the sale was made was subject to a "not implausible" explanation from the respondent, "although evidently not credited by the jury." And the court was troubled by "the long and unexplained delay" in the arrest. It was too great a danger that the respondent was convicted because he was a man D'Onofrio had previously observed near the scene, was thought to be a likely offender, and was arrested when he was known to be in Mrs. Ramsey's apartment, rather than because Glover "really remembered him as the seller." Id., at 371–372.

IV

Petitioner at the outset acknowledges that "the procedure in the instant case was suggestive [because only one photograph was used] and unnecessary" [because there was no emergency or exigent circumstance]. Brief for Petitioner 10; Tr of Oral Arg 7. The respondent, in agreement with the Court of Appeals, proposes a per se rule of exclusion that he claims is dictated by the demands of the Fourteenth Amendment's guarantee of due process. He rightly observes that this is the first case in which this Court has had occasion to rule upon strictly post-Stovall out-of-court identification evidence of the challenged kind.

Since the decision in Biggers, the Courts of Appeals appear to have developed at least two approaches to such evidence. See Pulaski, Neil v. Biggers: The Supreme Court Dismantles the Wade Trilogy's Due Process Protection, 26 Stan L Rev 1097, 1111–1114 (1974). The first, or per se approach, employed by the Second Circuit in the present case, focuses on the procedures employed and requires exclusion of the out-of-court identification evidence, without regard to reliability, whenever it has been obtained through unnecessarily suggestive confrontation procedures.[10] The justifications advanced are the elimination of evidence of uncertain reliability, deterrence of the police and prosecutors,

and the stated "fair assurance against the awful risks of misidentification." 527 F2d, at 371. See Smith v. Coiner, 473 F2d 877, 882 (CA4), cert denied sub nom Wallace v. Smith, 414 US 1115, 38 L Ed 2d 743, 94 S Ct 848 (1973).

The second, or more lenient, approach is one that continues to rely on the totality of the circumstances. It permits the admission of the confrontation evidence if, despite the suggestive aspect, the out-of-court identification possesses certain features of reliability. Its adherents feel that the per se approach is not mandated by the Due Process Clause of the Fourteenth Amendment. This second approach, in contrast to the other, is ad hoc and serves to limit the societal costs imposed by a sanction that excludes relevant evidence from consideration and evaluation by the trier of fact. . . .

The respondent here stresses the . . . need for deterrence of improper identification practice, a factor he regards as preeminent. Photographic identification, it is said, continues to be needlessly employed. He notes that the legislative regulation "the Court had hoped [United States v.] Wade [388 US 218, 239, 87 S Ct 1926, 18 L Ed 2d 1149 (1967),] would engender," has not been forthcoming. He argues that a totality rule cannot be expected to have a significant deterrent impact; only a strict rule of exclusion will have direct and immediate impact on law enforcement agents. Identification evidence is so convincing to the jury that sweeping exclusionary rules are required. Fairness of the trial is threatened by suggestive confrontation evidence, and thus, it is said, an exclusionary rule has an established constitutional predicate.

There are, of course, several interests to be considered and taken into account. . . .

Usually the witness must testify about an encounter with a total stranger under circumstances of emergency or emotional stress. The witness' recollection of the stranger can be distorted easily by the circumstances or by later actions of the police. Thus, Wade and its companion cases reflect the concern that the jury not hear eyewitness testimony unless that evidence has aspects of reliability. It must be observed that both approaches before us are responsive to this concern. The per se rule, however, goes too far since its application automatically and peremptorily, and without consid-

---

10. Although the per se approach demands the exclusion of testimony concerning unnecessarily suggestive identifications, it does permit the admission of testimony concerning a subsequent identification, including an in-court identification, if the subsequent identification is determined to be reliable. 527 F2d, at 367. The totality approach, in contrast, is simpler: if the challenged identification is reliable, then testimony as to it and any identification in its wake is admissible.

eration of alleviating factors, keeps evidence from the jury that is reliable and relevant.

The second factor is deterrence. Although the per se approach has the more significant deterrent effect, the totality approach also has an influence on police behavior. The police will guard against unnecessarily suggestive procedures under the totality rule, as well as the per se one, for fear that their actions will lead to the exclusion of identifications as unreliable.

The third factor is the effect on the administration of justice. Here the per se approach suffers serious drawbacks. Since it denies the trier reliable evidence, it may result, on occasion, in the guilty going free. . . .

Certainly, inflexible rules of exclusion, that may frustrate rather than promote justice, have not been viewed recently by this Court with unlimited enthusiasm. . . .

The standard, after all, is that of fairness as required by the Due Process Clause of the Fourteenth Amendment. Stovall, with its reference to "the totality of the circumstances," and Biggers, with its continuing stress on the same totality, did not, singly or together, establish a strict exclusionary rule or new standard of due process. . . .

We therefore conclude that reliability is the linchpin in determining the admissibility of identification testimony for both pre- and post-Stovall confrontations. The factors to be considered are set out in Biggers. 409 US, at 199–200, 34 L Ed 2d 401, 93 S Ct 375. These include the opportunity of the witness to view the criminal at the time of the crime, the witness' degree of attention, the accuracy of his prior description of the criminal, the level of certainty demonstrated at the confrontation, and the time between the crime and the confrontation. Against these factors is to be weighed the corrupting effect of the suggestive identification itself.

V

We turn, then, to the facts of this case and apply the analysis:

1. The opportunity to view. Glover testified that for two to three minutes he stood at the apartment door, within two feet of the respondent. The door opened twice, and each time the man stood at the door. The moments passed, the conversation took place, and payment was made. Glover looked directly at his vendor. It was near sunset, to be sure, but the sun had not yet set, so it was not dark or even dusk or twilight. Natural light from outside entered the hallway through a window. There was natural light, as well, from inside the apartment.

2. The degree of attention. Glover was not a casual or passing observer, as is so often the case with eyewitness identification. Trooper Glover was a trained police officer on duty—and specialized and dangerous duty—when he called at the third floor of 201 Westland in Hartford on May 5, 1970. Glover himself was a Negro and unlikely to perceive only general features of "hundreds of Hartford black males," as the Court of Appeals stated, 527 F2d, at 371. It is true that Glover's duty was that of ferreting out narcotics offenders and that he would be expected in his work to produce results. But it is also true that, as a specially trained, assigned, and experienced officer, he could be expected to pay scrupulous attention to detail, for he knew that subsequently he would have to find and arrest his vendor. In addition, he knew that his claimed observations would be subject later to close scrutiny and examination at any trial.

3. The accuracy of the description. Glover's description was given to D'Onofrio within minutes after the transaction. It included the vendor's race, his height, his build, the color and style of his hair, and the high cheekbone facial feature. It also included clothing the vendor wore. No claim has been made that respondent did not possess the physical characteristics so described. D'Onofrio reacted positively at once. Two days later, when Glover was alone, he viewed the photograph D'Onofrio produced and identified its subject as the narcotics seller.

4. The witness' level of certainty. There is no dispute that the photograph in question was that of respondent. Glover, in response to a question whether the photograph was that of the person from whom he made the purchase, testified: "There is no question whatsoever." This positive assurance was repeated.

5. The time between the crime and the confrontation. Glover's description of his vendor was given to D'Onofrio within minutes of the crime. The photographic identification took place only two days later. We do not have here the passage

of weeks or months between the crime and the viewing of the photograph.

These indicators of Glover's ability to make an accurate identification are hardly outweighed by the corrupting effect of the challenged identification itself. Although identifications arising from single-photograph displays may be viewed in general with suspicion, see Simmons v. United States, 390 US, at 383, 88 S Ct 967, 19 L Ed 2d 1247, we find in the instant case little pressure on the witness to acquiesce in the suggestion that such a display entails. D'Onofrio had left the photograph at Glover's office and was not present when Glover first viewed it two days after the event. There thus was little urgency and Glover could view the photograph at his leisure. And since Glover examined the photograph alone, there was no coercive pressure to make an identification arising from the presence of another. The identification was made in circumstances allowing care and reflection.

Although it plays no part in our analysis, all this assurance as to the reliability of the identification is hardly undermined by the facts that respondent was arrested in the very apartment where the sale had taken place, and that he acknowledged his frequent visits to that apartment.

Surely, we cannot say that under all the circumstances of this case there is "a very substantial likelihood of irreparable misidentification." Short of that point, such evidence is for the jury to weigh. We are content to rely upon the good sense and judgment of American juries, for evidence with some element of untrustworthiness is customary grist for the jury mill. Juries are not so susceptible that they cannot measure intelligently the weight of identification testimony that has some questionable feature.

Of course, it would have been better had D'Onofrio presented Glover with a photographic array including "so far as practicable . . . a reasonable number of persons similar to any person then suspected whose likeness is included in the array." Model Code, § 160.2(2). The use of that procedure would have enhanced the force of the identification at trial and would have avoided the risk that the evidence would be excluded as unreliable. But we are not disposed to view D'Onofrio's failure as one of constitutional dimension to be enforced by a rigorous and unbending exclusionary rule. The defect, if there be one, goes to weight and not to substance. . . .

Mr. Justice Marshall, with whom Mr. Justice Brennan joins, dissenting.

Today's decision can come as no surprise to those who have been watching the Court dismantle the protections against mistaken eyewitness testimony erected a decade ago in United States v. Wade, 388 US 218, 87 S Ct 1926, 18 L Ed 2d 1149 (1967); Gilbert v. California, 388 US 263, 18 L Ed 2d 1178, 87 S Ct 1951 (1967); and Stovall v. Denno, 388 US 293, 87 S Ct 1967, 18 L Ed 2d 1199 (1967). But it is still distressing to see the Court virtually ignore the teaching of experience embodied in those decisions and blindly uphold the conviction of a defendant who may well be innocent.

I

The magnitude of the Court's error can be seen by analyzing the cases in the Wade trilogy and the decisions following it. The foundation of the Wade trilogy was the Court's recognition of the "high incidence of miscarriage of justice" resulting from the admission of mistaken eyewitness identification evidence at criminal trials. Relying on numerous studies made over many years by such scholars as Professor Wigmore and Mr. Justice Frankfurter, the Court concluded that "[t]he vagaries of eyewitness identification are well-known; the annals of criminal law are rife with instances of mistaken identification." It is, of course, impossible to control one source of such errors—the faulty perceptions and unreliable memories of witnesses—except through vigorously contested trials conducted by diligent counsel and judges. The Court in the Wade cases acted, however, to minimize the more preventable threat posed to accurate identification by "the degree of suggestion inherent in the manner in which the prosecution presents the suspect to witnesses for pretrial identification."

The Court did so in Wade and Gilbert v. California by prohibiting the admission at trial of evidence of pretrial confrontations at which an accused was not represented by counsel. Further protection was afforded by holding that an in-court identification following an uncounseled lineup was allowable only if the prosecution could clearly and convincingly demonstrate that it was not tainted by the constitutional violation. Only in this way, the Court held, could confrontations fraught with the danger of misidentification be made fairer, and could Sixth Amendment rights to assistance of counsel and confrontation of witnesses at trial be effectively preserved. The crux of the Wade decisions, however, was the unusual threat to the truth-seeking process posed by the frequent untrustworthiness of eyewitness identification testimony. This, combined with the fact that juries unfortunately are often unduly receptive to such evidence, is the fundamental fact of judicial experience ignored by the Court today. . . .

Stovall recognized that, regardless of Sixth Amendment principles, "the conduct of a confrontation" may be "so unnecessarily suggestive and conducive to irreparable mistaken identification" as to deny due process of law. 388 US, at 301–302, 18 L Ed 2d 1199, 87 S Ct 1967. The pretrial confrontation in Stovall was plainly suggestive,[2] and evidence of it was introduced at trial along with the witness' in-court identification. The Court ruled that there had been no violation of due process, however, because the unusual necessity for the procedure outweighed the danger of suggestion.

Stovall thus established a due process right of criminal suspects to be free from confrontations that, under all the circumstances, are unnecessarily suggestive. The right was enforceable by exclusion at trial of evidence of the constitutionally invalid identification. . . .

The development of due process protections against mistaken identification evidence, begun in Stovall, was continued in Simmons v. United States, 390 US 377, 88 S Ct 967, 19 L Ed 2d 1247 (1968). There, the Court developed a different rule to deal with the admission of in-court identification testimony that the accused claimed had been fatally tainted by a previous suggestive confrontation. In Simmons, the exclusionary effect of Stovall had already been accomplished, since the prosecution made no use of the suggestive confrontation. Simmons, therefore, did not deal with the constitutionality of the pretrial identification procedure. The only question was the impact of the Due Process Clause on an in-court identification that was not itself unnecessarily suggestive. Simmons held that due process was violated by the later identification if the pretrial procedure had been "so impermissibly suggestive as to give rise to a very substantial likelihood of irreparable misidentification." 390 US, at 384, 88 S Ct 967, 19 L Ed 2d 1247. This test focused, not on the necessity for the challenged pretrial procedure, but on the degree of suggestiveness that it entailed. In applying this test, the Court understandably considered the circumstances surrounding the witnesses' initial opportunity to view the crime. Finding that any suggestion in the pretrial confrontation had not affected the fairness of the in-court identification, Simmons rejected petitioner's due process attack on his conviction. . . .

Thus, Stovall and Simmons established two different due process tests for two very different situations. Where the prosecution sought to use evidence of a questionable pretrial identification, Stovall required its exclusion, because due process had been violated by the confrontation, unless the necessity for the unduly suggestive procedure outweighed its potential for generating an irreparably mistaken identification. The Simmons test, on the other hand, was directed to ascertaining due process violations in the introduction of in-court identification testimony that the defendant claimed was tainted by pretrial procedures. In the latter situation, a court could consider the reliability of the identification under all the circumstances. . . .

Accordingly, in determining the admissibility of the post-Stovall identification in this case, the Court considers two alternatives, a per se exclusionary rule and a totality-of-the-circumstances approach. The Court weighs three factors in deciding that the totality approach, which is essentially the test used in Biggers, should be applied. In my view, the Court wrongly evaluates the impact of these factors.

---

2. The accused, a Negro, was brought handcuffed by seven white police officers and employees of the District Attorney to the hospital room of the only witness to a murder. As the Court said of this encounter: "It is hard to imagine a situation more clearly conveying the suggestion to the witness that the one presented is believed to be guilty by the police. See Frankfurter, The Case of Sacco and Vanzetti 31–32." United States v Wade, 388 US 218, 234, 87 S Ct 1926, 18 L Ed 2d 1149 (1967).

First, the Court acknowledges that one of the factors, deterrence of police use of unnecessarily suggestive identification procedures, favors the per se rule. Indeed, it does so heavily, for such a rule would make it unquestionably clear to the police they must never use a suggestive procedure when a fairer alternative is available. I have no doubt that conduct would quickly conform to the rule.

Second, the Court gives passing consideration to the dangers of eyewitness identification recognized in the Wade trilogy. It concludes, however, that the grave risk of error does not justify adoption of the per se approach because that would too often result in exclusion of relevant evidence. In my view, this conclusion totally ignores the lessons of Wade. The dangers of mistaken identification are, as Stovall held, simply too great to permit unnecessarily suggestive identifications. Neither Biggers nor the Court's opinion today points to any contrary empirical evidence. Studies since Wade have only reinforced the validity of its assessment of the dangers of identification testimony. While the Court is "content to rely on the good sense and judgment of American juries," the impetus for Stovall and Wade was repeated miscarriages of justice resulting from juries' willingness to credit inaccurate eyewitness testimony.

Finally, the Court errs in its assessment of the relative impact of the two approaches on the administration of justice. The Court relies most heavily on this factor, finding that "reversal is a Draconian sanction" in cases where the identification is reliable despite an unnecessarily suggestive procedure used to obtain it. Relying on little more than a strong distaste for "inflexible rules of exclusion," the Court rejects the per se test. . . .

In my view, the Court's totality test will allow seriously unreliable and misleading evidence to be put before juries. Equally important, it will allow dangerous criminals to remain on the streets while citizens assume that police action has given them protection. According to my calculus, all three of the factors upon which the Court relies point to acceptance of the per se approach.

Even more disturbing than the Court's reliance on the totality test, however, is the analysis it uses, which suggests a reinterpretation of the concept of due process of law in criminal cases. The decision suggests that due process violations in identification procedures may not be measured by whether the government employed procedures violating standards of fundamental fairness. By relying on the probable accuracy of a challenged identification, instead of the necessity for its use, the Court seems to be ascertaining whether the defendant was probably guilty. Until today, I had thought that "Equal justice under law" meant that the existence of constitutional violations did not depend on the race, sex, religion, nationality, or likely guilt of the accused. The Due Process Clause requires adherence to the same high standard of fundamental fairness in dealing with every criminal defendant, whatever his personal characteristics and irrespective of the strength of the State's case against him. Strong evidence that the defendant is guilty should be relevant only to the determination whether an error of constitutional magnitude was nevertheless harmless beyond a reasonable doubt. By importing the question of guilt into the initial determination of whether there was a constitutional violation, the apparent effect of the Court's decision is to undermine the protection afforded by the Due Process Clause. "It is therefore important to note that the state courts remain free, in interpreting state constitutions, to guard against the evil clearly identified by this case."

The Court holds, as Neil v Biggers failed to, that a due process identification inquiry must take account of the suggestiveness of a confrontation and the likelihood that it led to misidentification, as recognized in Stovall and Wade. Thus, even if a witness did have an otherwise adequate opportunity to view a criminal, the later use of a highly suggestive identification procedure can render his testimony inadmissible. Indeed, it is my view that, assuming applicability of the totality test enunciated by the Court, the facts of the present case require that result.

I consider first the opportunity that Officer Glover had to view the suspect. Careful review of the record shows that he could see the heroin seller only for the time it took to speak three sentences of four or five short words, to hand over some money, and later after the door reopened, to receive the drugs in return. The entire face-to-face transaction could have taken as little as 15 or 20 seconds. But during this time, Glover's attention was not focused exclusively on the seller's face. He observed that the door was opened 12 to 18 inches, that there was a window in the room behind the door, and, most importantly, that there was a woman standing behind the man. Glover was, of course, also concentrating on the details of the transaction—he must have looked away from the seller's face to hand him the money and receive the drugs. The observation during the conversation thus may have been as brief as 5 or 10 seconds.

As the Court notes, Glover was a police officer trained in and attentive to the need for making accurate identifications. Nevertheless, both common sense and scholarly study indicate that while a trained observer such as a police officer "is somewhat less likely to make an erroneous identification than the average untrained observer, the mere fact that he has been so trained is no guarantee that he is correct in a specific case. His identification testimony should be scrutinized just as carefully as that of the normal witness." Moreover, "identifications made by policemen in highly competitive activities, such as undercover narcotic agents . . . , should be scrutinized with special care." Wall, supra, n 1. Yet it is just such a searching inquiry that the Court fails to make here.

Another factor on which the Court relies—the witness' degree of certainty in making the identification—is worthless as an indicator that he is correct. Even if Glover had been unsure initially about his identification of respondent's picture, by the time he was called at trial to present a key piece of evidence for the State that paid his salary, it is impossible to imagine his responding negatively to such questions as "is there any doubt in your mind whatsoever" that the identification was correct. As the Court noted in Wade: "'It is a matter of common experience that, once a witness has picked out the accused at the [pretrial confrontation], he is not likely to go back on his word later on.'" 388 US, at 229, 87 S Ct 1926, 18 L Ed 2d 1149, quoting Williams & Hammelmann, Identification Parades—I, Crim L Rev 479, 482 (1963).

Next, the Court finds that because the identification procedure took place two days after the crime, its reliability is enhanced. While such temporal proximity makes the identification more

reliable than one occurring months later, the fact is that the greatest memory loss occurs within hours after an event. After that, the dropoff continues much more slowly. Thus, the reliability of an identification is increased only if it was made within several hours of the crime. If the time gap is any greater, reliability necessarily decreases.

Finally, the Court makes much of the fact that Glover gave a description of the seller to D'Onofrio shortly after the incident. Despite the Court's assertion that because "Glover himself was a Negro and unlikely to perceive only general features of 'hundreds of Hartford black males,' as the Court of Appeals stated," the description given by Glover was actually no more than a general summary of the seller's appearance. We may discount entirely the seller's clothing, for that was of no significance later in the proceeding. Indeed, to the extent that Glover noticed clothes, his attention was diverted from the seller's face. Otherwise, Glover merely described vaguely the seller's height, skin color, hairstyle, and build. He did say that the seller had "high cheekbones," but there is no other mention of facial features, nor even an estimate of age. Conspicuously absent is any indication that the seller was a native of the West Indies, certainly something which a member of the black community could immediately recognize from both appearance and accent.

From all of this, I must conclude that the evidence of Glover's ability to make an accurate identification is far weaker than the Court finds it. In contrast, the procedure used to identify respondent was both extraordinarily suggestive and strongly conducive to error. In dismissing "the corrupting effect of the suggestive identification" procedure here, the Court virtually grants the police license to convict the innocent. By displaying a single photograph of respondent to the witness Glover under the circumstances in this record almost everything that could have been done wrong was done wrong.

In the first place, there was no need to use a photograph at all. Because photos are static, two-dimensional, and often outdated, they are "clearly inferior in reliability" to corporeal procedures. Wall, supra, n 1, at 70; People v Gould, 54 Cal 2d 621, 631, 354 P2d 865, 870 (1960). While the use of photographs is justifiable and often essential where the police have no knowledge of an offender's identity, the poor reliability of photos makes their use inexcusable where any other means of identification is available. Here, since Detective D'Onofrio believed that he knew the seller's identity, further investigation without resort to a photographic showup was easily possible. With little inconvenience, a corporeal lineup including Brathwaite might have been arranged. Properly conducted, such a procedure would have gone far to remove any doubt about the fairness and accuracy of the identification.

Worse still than the failure to use an easily available corporeal identification was the display to Glover of only a single picture, rather than a photo array. With good reason, such single-suspect procedures have "been widely condemned." They give no assurance that the witness can identify the criminal from among a number of persons of similar appearance, surely the strongest evidence that there was no misidentification. In Simmons v. United States, our first decision involving photographic identification, we recognized the danger that a witness seeing a suggestively displayed picture will "retain in his memory the image of the photograph rather than of the person actually seen." "Subsequent identification of the accused then shows nothing except that the picture was a good likeness." Williams & Hammelmann, supra, n 1, at 484. As Simmons warned, the danger of error is at its greatest when "the police display to the witness only the picture of a single individual . . . [and] is also heightened if the police indicate to the witness that they have other evidence that . . . the perso[n] pictured committed the crime."

The use of a single picture (or the display of a single live suspect, for that matter) is a grave error, of course, because it dramatically suggests to the witness that the person shown must be the culprit. Why else would the police choose the person? And it is deeply ingrained in human nature to agree with the expressed opinions of others—particularly others who should be more knowledgeable—when making a difficult decision. In this case, moreover, the pressure was not limited to that inherent in the display of a single photograph. Glover, the identifying witness, was a state police officer on special assignment. He knew that D'Onofrio, an experienced Hartford narcotics detective, presumably familiar with local drug operations, believed respondent to be the seller. There was at work, then, both loyalty to another police officer and deference to a better-informed colleague. Finally, of course, there was Glover's knowledge that without an identification and arrest, government funds used to buy heroin had been wasted.

The Court discounts this overwhelming evidence of suggestiveness, however. It reasons that because D'Onofrio was not present when Glover viewed the photograph, there was "little pressure on the witness to acquiesce in the suggestion." That conclusion blinks psychological reality. There is no doubt in my mind that even in D'Onofrio's absence, a clear and powerful message was telegraphed to Glover as he looked at respondent's photograph. He was emphatically told that, "*this* is the man," and he responded by identifying respondent then and at trial "whether or not he was in fact 'the man.'"

I must conclude that this record presents compelling evidence that there was "a very substantial likelihood of misidentification" of respondent Brathwaite. The suggestive display of respondent's photograph to the witness Glover likely erased any independent memory that Glover had retained of the seller from his barely adequate opportunity to observe the criminal. . . .

Notes and Questions

1. Does *Brathwaite* give the police incentive to scrupulously honor a defendant's rights at an identification procedure by avoiding even the possibility of suggestiveness? If the police act improperly, what is the likely end result? Is this result good for the criminal justice system?

2. Do *Stovall* and *Simmons* deal with two different situations? If so, in what way? Does the Court blur this distinction?

3. How is *Brathwaite* similar to and/or different from *Stovall v. Denno* and *Neil v. Biggers*?

4. What three factors were considered by the Court in reaching its opinion in *Brathwaite*? Do these factors support the Court's conclusions?

5. What is the difference between the *per se* approach used by the Second Circuit Court of Appeals in *Brathwaite* and the case-by-case approach adopted by the Supreme Court? Several state supreme courts have held that due process under their state constitution mandates the use of the *per se* approach. The Massachusetts case of Commonwealth v. Johnson, 420 Mass. 458, 650 N.E.2d 1257 (1995) portrays the contrast between the two approaches.

LIACOS, Chief Justice.

[Leopoldino Goncalves was robbed at machete point by a black male and a white female at approximately 10:50 p.m. one evening. The thieves fled in the direction of a housing project. Goncalves reported the incident to police.] He described the male assailant as a twenty-seven to thirty year old black male, six feet tall with a medium build, weighing 170 pounds, and wearing a black cap, blue jeans, and a brown sweatshirt. Goncalves was shown about six books containing photographs of suspects, but was unable to identify his assailants. . . .

The day following the incident, four police officers . . . told Goncalves that they wanted him to view two suspects. . . . When they arrived at the location where the suspects were being held, Goncalves saw a group of six to eight people. Only one adult black male, the defendant, was present and a female with a limp was the only adult white female present. The two suspects were being "detained" by police officers but they were not handcuffed. The defendant and the woman were brought forward a few steps by the officers. Goncalves then identified the pair as his assailants. Goncalves based his identification in part on the fact that the clothing worn by the suspects was the same as that worn by his assailants.

The defendant possessed several characteristics that did not match Goncalve's initial description of the male assailant. A booking photograph taken of the defendant at the time of his arrest, the day after the incident, shows that the defendant had a moustache. Yet Goncalves had never mentioned that the male assailant had a moustache. The booking sheet indicates that the

defendant is thirty-seven years old and weighs 220 pounds, whereas Goncalves had described a man of approximately twenty-seven years in age, weighing 170 pounds, with a medium build. Finally, at the time of the hearing on the motion to suppress the defendant was missing several front teeth. When describing his assailants to the police, Goncalves did not tell them that the male assailant had missing teeth.

The judge ruled that Goncalves's identification of the defendant was tainted because it was made at an unnecessarily suggestive showup. The evidence presented at the motion hearing supports this conclusion. Although one-on-one confrontations are not per se excludable, they are disfavored because of their inherently suggestive nature. Showups have been permitted when conducted in the immediate aftermath of a crime and in exigent circumstances. The showup employed by the police in this case was conducted eighteen hours after the crime. It took place in the area of the housing project where Goncalves had seen his assailants drive the previous night; the defendant was brought forward from the group before Goncalves positively identified him; and the defendant was wearing clothes similar to those worn by the male assailant. Based on these facts, the judge was warranted in concluding that the identification procedure was unnecessarily suggestive.

Although the judge found the identification procedure unnecessarily suggestive, he found that the identification was admissible because it was reliable.[3] In so doing, the judge relied on Appeals Court decisions which have adopted the "reliability test," set forth in Manson v. Brathwaite, 432 U.S. 98, 97 S.Ct. 2243, 53 L. Ed. 2d 140 (1977), regarding the admissibility of identifications obtained through unnecessarily suggestive procedures.[4]

---

3. In concluding that the identification of the defendant was reliable, the judge cited Goncalves's good opportunity to view his assailants, his certainty in identifying the defendant, and his rejection of hundreds of other photographs as well as suspects to him prior to his identification of the defendant.

4. This test, developed in Neil v. Biggers, 409 U.S. 188, 93 S.Ct. 375, 34 L.Ed.2d 401 (1972), and Manson v. Brathwaite, 432 U.S. 98, 97 S.Ct. 2243, 53 L.Ed.2d 140 (1977), is sometimes also referred to as the "totality" test or the "totality of the circumstances" test.

Although the Appeals Court has applied the due process analysis set forth in the Brathwaite case, this court has never accepted the reasoning in Brathwaite as an accurate interpretation of the due process requirements of art. 12 of the Declaration of Rights of the Massachusetts Constitution. Whether we should embrace Brathwaite, as have the majority of other States, is a question we have left open.

The rule of per se exclusion, set forth [by this court] in Commonwealth v. Botelho, states that the defendant bears the burden of demonstrating, by a preponderance of the evidence, that the "witness was subjected by the State to a confrontation that was unnecessarily suggestive and thus offensive to due process." If this is established, then the prosecution is barred from introducing that particular confrontation in evidence at trial. As for other identifications the witness may have made of the defendant, "the prosecution is limited to introducing at trial only such identifications by the witness as are shown at the suppression hearing not to be the product of the suggestive confrontation—the later identifications, to be usable, must have an independent source." The prosecution must demonstrate the existence of an independent source by "clear and convincing evidence." . . .

The case at bar presents us with the opportunity to establish our position with regard to the Brathwaite decision. We have carefully considered the matter and, for the reasons set forth, we conclude that we cannot accept Brathwaite as satisfying the requirements of art. 12. We conclude that art. 12 requires the application of the stricter per se approach described in Commonwealth v. Botelho.

Our past resistance to the so-called reliability test reflects this court's concern that the dangers present whenever eyewitness evidence is introduced against an accused require the utmost protection against mistaken identifications. There is no question that the danger of mistaken identification by a victim or a witness poses a real threat to the truth-finding process of criminal trials. Indeed, mistaken identification is believed widely to be the primary cause of erroneous convictions. Compounding this problem is the tendency of juries to be unduly receptive to eyewitness evidence. Manson v. Brathwaite, supra 432 U.S. at 120, 97 S.Ct. at 2255–2256 (Mar-

shall, J., dissenting). We have stated that "[t]he law has not taken the position that a jury can be relied on to discount the value of an identification by a proper appraisal of the unsatisfactory circumstances in which it may have been made. On the contrary, this court, like others, has read the Constitution to require that where the conditions are shown to have been highly and unnecessarily suggestive, the identification should not be brought to the attention of the jury." Commonwealth v. Marini, 375 Mass. 510, 519, 378 N.E.2d 51 (1978).

These concerns were at the heart of the Wade trilogy of cases. The Wade Court acknowledged that "the vagaries of eyewitness identification are well-known; the annals of criminal law are rife with instances of mistaken identification." United States v. Wade, 388 U.S. 218, 228, 87 S.Ct. 1926, 1932–1933, 18 L.Ed.2d 1149 (1967). In declaring that the accused has a right to counsel at a postindictment lineup, the Court recognized that the presence of counsel was necessary because

[t]he trial which might determine the accused's fate may well not be that in the courtroom but that at the pretrial confrontation, with the State aligned against the accused, the witness the sole jury, and the accused unprotected against the overreaching, intentional or unintentional, and with little or no effective appeal from the judgment there rendered by the witness—"that's the man." Id. at 235–236, 87 S.Ct. at 1936–1937.

The "reliability test" is unacceptable because it provides little or no protection from unnecessarily suggestive identification procedures, from mistaken identifications and, ultimately, from wrongful convictions. . . .

[S]tudies conducted by psychologists and legal researchers since Brathwaite have confirmed that eyewitness testimony is often hopelessly unreliable. Permitting the admission of an identification obtained through unnecessarily suggestive procedures can only serve to exacerbate this problem. Furthermore, contrary to the Brathwaite Court's unsubstantiated claim, the per se approach does not keep relevant and reliable identification evidence from the jury. Subsequent identifications shown to come from a source independent of the suggestive identification remain admissible under the per se approach. The per se approach excludes only the unnecessarily suggestive identification and subsequent tainted identifications. . . . [T]he court examines five factors in determining whether there was an independent source for subsequent identifications by the witness of the defendant. If, for example, the prosecution is able to demonstrate that the witness got a good look at his assailant and his initial description matches a description of the defendant, the court may conclude that there was an independent source and may admit evidence of any identification subsequent to the unnecessarily suggestive one.

The Brathwaite Court also discussed the public interest in deterring police from using identification procedures which are unnecessarily suggestive. The Court acknowledged that the per se rule is superior in promoting that interest because it provides greater deterrence against police misconduct. The Court nevertheless concluded: "The police will guard against unnecessarily suggestive procedures under the totality rule, as well as the per se one, for fear that their actions will lead to the exclusion of identifications as unreliable." Manson v. Brathwaite, supra 432 U.S. at 112, 97 S.Ct. at 2252.

To the contrary, it appears clear to us that the reliability test does little or nothing to discourage police from using suggestive identification procedures. One commentator has noted that "under Brathwaite, the showup has flourished, because the totality approach has failed to discourage this practice. As a deterrent to suggestive police practices, the Federal standard is quite weak. Almost any suggestive lineup will still meet reliability standards." Note, Twenty-Years of Diminishing Protection, 15 Hofstra L.Rev. 583, 606 (1987). Indeed, an example of this result is seen in the instant case: the suggestion inherent in the showup procedure that was used to identify the defendant is plain. Furthermore, the showup was unnecessarily suggestive in that it was not conducted immediately after the crime or in exigent circumstances. Yet the motion judge permitted the introduction of the identification based on his opinion that the identification was reliable. Rather than deterring

unreliable identification procedures, the effect of the Biggers-Brathwaite reliability test has been, and would be in this Commonwealth, a message to police that, absent extremely aggravating circumstances, suggestive showups will not result in suppression. Whether or not to use a more fair and accurate identification procedure is, under that test, left to the officer's discretion. . . .

[T]he Brathwaite Court [also] considered the impact of the two tests on the administration of justice. It was here that the Court found what it considered to be the most serious drawbacks of the per se approach. However, it is also here, in our view, that the Court erred most. The Court opined: "Since it denies the trier reliable evidence, [the per se approach] may result, on occasion, in the guilty going free." Manson v. Brathwaite, supra 432 U.S. at 112, 97 S.Ct. at 2252. The inverse of this is probably more accurate: the admission of unnecessarily suggestive identification procedures under the reliability test would likely result in the innocent being jailed while the guilty remain free. See Manson v. Brathwaite, supra at 127, 97 S.Ct. at 2259–2260 (Marshall, J., dissenting) ("[I]f the police and the public erroneously conclude, on the basis of an unnecessarily suggestive confrontation, that the right man has been caught and convicted, the real outlaw must still remain at large"). The Brathwaite Court disregards the wisdom of Justice Harlan when he wrote: "it is far worse to convict an innocent man than to let a guilty man go free." In re Winship, 397 U.S. 358, 372, 90 S.Ct. 1068, 1077, 25 L.Ed.2d 368 (1970) (Harlan, J., concurring). . . .

The reliability test has been widely criticized by commentators, primarily because the test eliminates the protection essential to a fair trial. The reliability test hinders, rather than aids, the fair and just administration of justice by permitting largely unreliable evidence to be admitted directly on the issue of the defendant's guilt or innocence.

This case presents an example of why we should not abandon the per se rule of exclusion and replace it with the reliability test. There is absolutely no evidence that the in-court identification of the defendant was the result of anything independent of the unnecessarily suggestive showup. For example, Goncalves's description of his assailant, given to police just after the incident, did not match the defendant's appearance, in part because the defendant possessed the unique feature of several missing teeth. Regardless of this fact, following the showup Goncalves was able to "remember" that his assailant had missing teeth.[11] Such flimsy evidence should not be permitted at trial. Only a rule of per se exclusion can ensure the continued protection against the danger of mistaken identification and wrongful convictions. Accordingly, we reject Brathwaite and affirm our confidence in the [*per se*] approach.

6. Was it necessary for the court in *Johnson* to adopt the *per se* test to reach the result that it did?

EXPERT TESTIMONY REGARDING EYEWITNESS IDENTIFICATION

The courts in each of the cases presented in this chapter have acknowledged the "vagaries of eyewitness identification" in reaching their decisions. Despite these vagaries, eyewitness testimony can be very persuasive to a jury. As a result of the combination of persuasiveness and potential for inaccuracy, over the last several decades experts increasingly have been used at trials to explain the fallibility and complexities of eyewitness identification.

As you read the leading case in this area, *State v. Chapple*, pay careful attention to the items that affect the reliability of an identification according to Dr. Loftus's testimony in *Chapple*, and their relationship to those factors listed by the Supreme Court in *Brathwaite*.

State v. Chapple, 135 Ariz. 281, 660 P.2d 1208 (1983)

FELDMAN, Justice.

Dolan Chapple was convicted on three counts of first degree murder, one count of unlawfully transporting marijuana and one count of conspiring to unlawfully transport marijuana. . . .

FACTS

The instigator of this bizarre drama was Mel Coley, a drug dealer who resided in Washington, D.C., but who was also connected with dealers in Kansas City. Coley had a history of dealing with a supplier named Bill Varnes, who lived near Phoenix. In fact, Coley, Varnes and a man named James Logan had been arrested once near Yuma, Arizona in connection with a heroin transaction. Release was accomplished fairly quickly, giving rise to a suspicion in Coley's mind that someone had "talked" to the authorities.

Coley had made a large number of drug deals through Malcolm Scott, a "middleman" who lived near Phoenix. Scott was also well acquainted with Varnes and had recently returned from Kansas City, where Scott had helped Varnes in a drug transaction involving marijuana and probably some heroin. The trip to Kansas City was not without complications, since Varnes had been "holding-out" on the Kansas City dealers who were purchasing from him. They were unhappy over this and had threatened to take whatever

---

11. As noted earlier, Goncalves' original description of the male assailant, given to police on the night of the incident, differed in several respects from the defendant's actual appearance. The defendant weighed 220 pounds, while Goncalves described his assailant as weighing 170 pounds with a medium build. The defendant was thirty-seven years of age while Goncalves described his assailant as between twenty-seven and thirty years old. Finally, the defendant was missing several teeth and had a moustache but Goncalves mentioned neither of these characteristics in his original description.

At the hearing on the motion to suppress, when asked to describe what he remembered about his assailant's appearance, Goncalves testified that he was in his late thirties, weighed about 200 pounds ("maybe more"), and had a large build. Goncalves also "remembered" while testifying that his assailant was missing some of his teeth.

action is appropriate in the drug business to collect the money they felt Varnes owed them. Coley evidently was involved in these problems and shared the feelings of his Kansas City colleagues toward Varnes.

Coley telephoned in early December 1977 and told Scott that he was interested in purchasing approximately 300 pounds of marijuana. He asked Scott to act as middleman in the transaction. Scott was to get $700 for his efforts. Scott testified that he called one or two of the Arizona suppliers with whom he was acquainted and found they could not supply the necessary quantity. He then called his sister, Pamela Buck, who was a "good friend" of Varnes and had worked with him in some drug deals. Scott asked Buck to contact her friend Varnes and see whether he could handle the sale. Buck talked to Varnes and reported to her brother that Varnes could supply the necessary amount of marijuana at an agreed upon price. . . .

On the evening of December 10 or the early morning of December 11, 1977, Coley arrived at the Phoenix airport from Washington, D.C. Scott met him at the airport and found that Coley was accompanied by two strangers who were introduced as "Dee" and "Eric." Scott drove the three men to a trailer located at his parents' farm near Higley in Pinal County, Arizona. Scott had used this trailer in the past as a meeting place to consummate drug transactions. This meeting place was part of the service which Scott provided for his "finder's fee." . . .

Later that morning the conversation between Coley, Eric and Dee indicated that it was likely there would be a "rip-off" of the marijuana and that Coley did not intend to pay for the goods. When Buck expressed to her brother the fear that Varnes would seek revenge if his goods were stolen, Scott told her not to worry because Varnes might never be seen again.

That evening, Scott and his sister met at the trailer with Coley, Eric and Dee. Varnes arrived with two companions, Eduardo Ortiz and Carlos Elsy. Ortiz and Elsy began to unload the marijuana and put it in the trailer. Buck was in the trailer with Coley, Eric and Dee at this time. Scott was some distance away, sitting on the porch of his parents' house. Buck was told by Dee or Coley that after the marijuana was unloaded she should lock herself in the bathroom.

After Ortiz and Elsy had finished unloading the marijuana and stacking it in the living room of the trailer, Dee suggested to Varnes that they go in the bedroom and "count the money." They started toward the bedroom and Buck went into the bathroom. A few moments later, Buck heard several shots, opened the bathroom door and ran out. Scott heard the shots while he was on the porch and saw a door of the trailer open. Elsy ran out, pursued by either Eric or Dee. After seeing Buck run out of the door at the other end of the trailer, Scott went back to the trailer and found Varnes dead in the bedroom of a gunshot wound to the head and Ortiz in the living room dead of a gunshot wound to the body. Subsequent ballistic tests showed they had been shot with different weapons. Elsy was outside, dead from a blow to the back of the head. . . .

Defendant does not contest any of the foregoing facts. Defendant is accused of being "Dee." He denies this. At his extradition hearing in Illinois, seven witnesses placed him in Cairo, Illinois during the entire month of December 1977, three of them testifying specifically to his presence in that town on December 11, the day of the crime. The same witnesses testified for him in the trial at which he was convicted. No direct or circumstantial evidence of any kind connects defendant to the crime, other than the testimony of Malcolm Scott and Pamela Buck, neither of whom had ever met the defendant before the crime and neither of whom saw him after the crime except at the trial. Defendant was apprehended and tried only because Malcolm Scott and Pamela Buck picked his photograph out of a lineup more than one year after the date of the crime; he was convicted because they later identified both the photographs and defendant himself at trial.

The State's position was that the identification was correct, while the defendant argued at trial that the identification was erroneous for one of two reasons. The first reason advanced by defendant is that Scott and Buck were lying to save themselves by "fingering" him. To buttress this contention, defendant established that Scott and Buck had made a "deal" with the State whereby they were granted complete immunity for their part in the crime unless the facts showed that they had knowingly participated in the killings. . . .

Defendant further argued at trial, and urges here, that even if Scott and Buck are not lying, their identification was a case of mistaken identity. The argument is that Scott and Buck picked the wrong picture out of the photographic lineup and that their subsequent photographic and in-court identifications were part of the "feedback phenomenon" and are simply continuations or repetitions of the same mistake. To support this contention of mistaken identification, defendant offered expert testimony regarding the various factors that affect the reliability of identification evidence. For the most part, that testimony was rejected by the trial court as not being within the proper sphere of expert testimony. . . .

EXPERT TESTIMONY REGARDING EYEWITNESS IDENTIFICATION

On learning of Mel Coley's participation in the crime, the sheriff's office quickly procured photographs of Coley, which were shown to Scott and Buck in a photographic lineup on December 16, 1977. Both of them identified Coley, thus providing law enforcement with the first step in its efforts to apprehend Dee and Eric. The detectives then showed Scott and Buck various photographs and lineups containing pictures of known acquaintances of Mel Coley. At this same session, Scott pointed to a picture of James Logan and stated that it resembled Dee, though he could not be sure. So far as the record shows, no follow-up was made of this tentative identification. One of the photographic lineups displayed to Scott, but not to Buck, contained a picture of the defendant, Dolan Chapple, but Scott did not identify him as Dee. At a time and in a manner not disclosed by the record, both Scott and Buck made a tentative identification of a photograph of Eric. The photograph portrayed Coley's nephew, Eric Perry.

The police continued to show the witnesses photographic lineups in an attempt to obtain an identification of Dee. Police efforts were successful on January 27, 1979, when Scott was shown a nine-picture photo lineup. For the first time, this lineup included photos of both Eric Perry, who had already been tentatively identified by Scott and Buck, and of the defendant; however, James Logan's photo was not included. Upon seeing this lineup, Scott immedi-

ately recognized Eric's picture again. About ten minutes later, Scott identified defendant's picture as Dee. Scott was then shown the picture of defendant he had failed to identify at a previous session and asked to explain why he had not previously identified it. He stated that he had no recollection of having seen it before. After Scott had identified Dee and before he could talk to his sister, the police showed Buck the same lineup. Buck identified the defendant as Dee and then re-identified Eric.

Defendant argues that the jury could have found the in-court identification unreliable for a variety of reasons. The defendant argues that the identification of Dee from photographic lineups in this case was unreliable because of the time interval which passed between the occurrence of the event and the lineup and because of the anxiety and tension inherent in the situation surrounding the entire identification process.[9] The defendant also argues that since Scott and Buck had smoked marijuana on the days of the crime, their perception would have been affected, making their identification through photographs less reliable. Further, defendant claims the January 27, 1979 identification of Dee by Scott and Buck from the photographic lineup was the product of an unconscious transfer. Defendant claims that Scott picked the picture of Dolan Chapple and identified it as Dee because he remembered that picture from the previous lineup (when he had not been able to identify defendant's picture). Defendant urges that the in-court identifications were merely reinforcements of the initial error. Defendant also argues that Eric's presence in the lineup heightened the memory transfer and increased the chance of an incorrect photographic identification. Defendant makes the further point that since the James Logan picture resembled defendant's and was not again displayed to the witnesses, the chance of mis-identification was heightened. Further, defendant claims that the identification was made on the basis of subsequently acquired information

---

9. Buck and Scott both said they were frightened for their lives during the events. Since they are the only witnesses, one might assume they were also frightened and apprehensive during the time period when Eric and Dee were both at liberty.

which affected memory. Finally, defendant argues that the confidence and certainty which Scott and Buck displayed in making their in-court identification at trial had no relation whatsoever to the accuracy of that identification and was, instead, the product of other factors.

It is against this complicated background, with identification the one issue on which the guilt or innocence of defendant hinged, that defense counsel offered the testimony of an expert on eyewitness identification in order to rebut the testimony of Malcolm Scott and his sister, Pamela Buck. The witness called by the defense was Dr. Elizabeth Loftus, a professor of psychology at the University of Washington. Dr. Loftus specializes in an area of experimental and clinical psychology dealing with perception, memory retention and recall. Her qualifications are unquestioned, and it may fairly be said that she "wrote the book" on the subject. The trial court granted the State's motion to suppress Dr. Loftus' testimony. . . . [Appellant contends] that the court erred and abused its discretion in granting the motion to suppress Dr. Loftus' testimony.

The admissibility of expert testimony is governed by Rule 702, Ariz.R. of Evid. That rule states:

> If scientific, technical, or other specialized knowledge will assist the trier of fact to understand the evidence or to determine a fact in issue, a witness qualified as an expert by knowledge, skill, experience, training, or education, may testify thereto in the form of an opinion or otherwise.

In what is probably the leading case on the subject, the Ninth Circuit affirmed the trial court's preclusion of expert evidence on eyewitness identification in *United States v. Amaral*, 488 F.2d 1148 (9th Cir. 1973). In its analysis, however, the court set out four criteria which should be applied in order to determine the admissibility of such testimony. These are: (1) qualified expert; (2) proper subject; (3) conformity to a generally accepted explanatory theory; and (4) probative value compared to prejudicial effect. *Id.* at 1153. We approve this test and find that the case at bar meets these criteria. . . .

Applying the *Amaral* test to the case at bench, we find from the record that the State has con-

ceded that the expert was qualified and that the question of conformity to generally accepted explanatory theory is not raised and appears not to be a question in this case. The two criteria which must therefore be considered are (1) determination of whether the probative value of the testimony outweighs its possible prejudicial effect and (2) determination of whether the testimony was a proper subject.

(1) PROBATIVE VALUE vs. PREJUDICE

The State argues that there would have been little probative value to the witness' testimony and great danger of unfair prejudice. . . . The contention of lack of probative value is based on the premise that the offer of proof showed that the witness would testify to general factors which were applicable to this case and affect the reliability of identification, but would not express any opinion with regard to the accuracy of the specific identification made by Scott and Buck and would not express an opinion regarding the accuracy percentage of eyewitness identification in general.

We believe that the "generality" of the testimony is a factor which favors admission. . . .

(2) PROPER SUBJECT

The remaining criterion at issue is whether the offered evidence was a proper subject for expert testimony. Ariz.R. of Evid. 702 allows expert testimony if it "will assist the trier of fact to understand the evidence or to determine a fact in issue." Put conversely, the test "is whether the subject of inquiry is one of such common knowledge that people of ordinary education could reach a conclusion as intelligently as the witness. . . ." *State v. Owens*, 112 Ariz. 223, 227, 540 P.2d 695, 699 (1975). Furthermore, the test is not whether the jury could reach some conclusion in the absence of the expert evidence, but whether the jury is qualified without such testimony "to determine intelligently and to the best possible degree the particular issue without enlightenment from those having a specialized understanding of the subject. . . ." Fed.R. Evid. 702 advisory committee note (quoting Ladd, *Expert Testimony*, 5 Vand.L.Rev. 414, 418 (1952)).

In excluding the evidence in the case at bench, the trial judge stated:

I don't find anything that's been presented in the extensive discussions that I have read in your memorandum with regard to the fact that this expert is going to testify to anything that isn't within the common experience of the people on the jury, that couldn't really be covered in cross-examination of the witnesses who made the identification, and probably will be excessively argued in closing arguments to the jury.

This basis for the view that eyewitness identification is not a proper subject for expert testimony is the same as that adopted in *United States v. Amaral, supra*, and in the great majority of cases which have routinely followed *Amaral*.

However, after a careful review of these cases and the record before us, we have concluded that although the reasons cited by the trial judge would correctly permit preclusion of such testimony in the great majority of cases, it was error to refuse the testimony in the case at bench. In reaching this conclusion, we have carefully considered the offer of proof made by the defense in light of the basic concept of "proper subject" underlying Rule 702.

We note at the outset that the law has long recognized the inherent danger in eyewitness testimony. *See United States v. Wade*, 388 U.S. 218, 87 S.Ct. 1926, 18 L.Ed.2d 1149 (1967). Of course, it is difficult to tell whether the ordinary juror shares the law's inherent caution of eyewitness identification. Experimental data indicates that many jurors "may reach intuitive conclusions about the reliability of [such] testimony that psychological research would show are misguided." Note, *Did Your Eyes Deceive You? Expert Psychological Testimony on the Unreliability of Eyewitness Identification*, 29 Stan. L.Rev. 969, 1017 (1977).

Even assuming that jurors of ordinary education need no expert testimony to enlighten them to the danger of eyewitness identification, the offer of proof indicated that Dr. Loftus' testimony would have informed the jury that there are many specific variables which affect the accuracy of identification and which apply to the facts of this case. For instance, while most jurors would no doubt realize that memory dims as time passes, Dr. Loftus presented data from experiments which showed that the "forgetting curve" is not uniform. Forgetting occurs very rapidly and then tends to level out; immediate identification is much more trustworthy than long-delayed identification. Thus, Scott's recognition of Logan's features as similar to those of Dee when Logan's picture was shown at the inception of the investigation is probably a more reliable identification than Scott's identification of Chapple's photograph in the photographic lineup thirteen months later. By the same token, Scott's failure to identify Chapple's photograph when it was first shown to him on March 26, 1978 (four months after the crime) and when Scott's ability to identify would have been far greater, is of key importance.

Another variable in the case is the effect of stress upon perception. Dr. Loftus indicated that research shows that most laymen believe that stressful events cause people to remember "better" so that what is seen in periods of stress is more accurately related later. However, experimental evidence indicates that stress causes inaccuracy of perception with subsequent distortion of recall.

Dr. Loftus would also have testified about the problems of "unconscious transfer," a phenomenon which occurs when the witness confuses a person seen in one situation with a person seen in a different situation. Dr. Loftus would have pointed out that a witness who takes part in a photo identification session without identifying any of the photographs and who then later sees a photograph of one of those persons may relate his or her familiarity with the picture to the crime rather than to the previous identification session.

Another variable involves assimilation of post-event information. Experimental evidence, shown by Dr. Loftus, confirms that witnesses frequently incorporate into their identifications inaccurate information gained subsequent to the event and confused with the event. An additional problem is the "feedback factor." We deal here with two witnesses who were related and who, according to Loftus' interview, engaged in discussions with each other about the identification of Dee. Dr. Loftus, who interviewed them, emphasized that their independent descriptions of Dee at times utilized identical language. Dr.

Loftus would have explained that through such discussions identification witnesses can reinforce their individual identifications. Such reinforcement will often tend to heighten the certainty of identification. The same may be said of the continual sessions that each witness had with the police in poring over large groups of photographs.

The last variable in this case concerns the question of confidence and its relationship to accuracy. Dr. Loftus' testimony and some experimental data indicate that there is no relationship between the confidence which a witness has in his or her identification and the actual accuracy of that identification. Again, this factor was specifically tied to the evidence in the case before us since both Scott and Buck indicated in their testimony that they were absolutely sure of their identification. Evidently their demeanor on the witness stand showed absolute confidence.

We cannot assume that the average juror would be aware of the variables concerning identification and memory about which Dr. Loftus was qualified to testify.

> Depriving [the] jurors of the benefit of scientific research on eyewitness testimony force[d] them to search for the truth without full knowledge and opportunity to evaluate the strength of the evidence. In short, this deprivation prevent[ed] [the] jurors from having "the best possible degree" of "understanding the subject" toward which the law of evidence strives. Note, *supra*, 29 Stan. L.Rev. at 1017–18.

Thus, considering the standard of Rule 702, *supra*,—whether the expert testimony will assist the jury in determining an issue before them— and the unusual facts in this case, we believe that Dr. Loftus' offered evidence was a proper subject for expert testimony and should have been admitted.

Of course, the test is not whether we believe that under these facts the evidence was admissible, but whether the trial court abused its discretion in reaching the contrary conclusion. Our review of the record leads us to the following conclusions regarding the various factors which support admission or preclusion here. Among the factors considered are the following:

1. The facts were close and one of the key factual disputes to be resolved involved the accuracy of the eyewitness identification. The preclusion ruling undercut the entire evidentiary basis for defendant's arguments on this issue.

2. The testimony offered was carefully limited to an exposition of the factors affecting reliability, with experimental data supporting the witness' testimony and no attempt was made to have the witness render opinions on the actual credibility or accuracy of the identification witnesses. Issues of ultimate fact may be the subject of expert testimony, but witnesses are not "permitted as experts on how juries should decide cases." Ariz.R. of Evid. 704 comment.

3. On the other hand, we see no significant prejudice to the State in permitting the testimony; the problem of time is not present in this case, since time spent on the crucial issue of the case can not be considered as "undue" loss of time. No other significant factor weighing against admission of the evidence seems present.

4. No question exists with regard to three of the four criteria listed in *United States v. Amaral, supra*, being fulfilled by the factual situation present in this case.

5. The key issue here pertained to the fourth criterion—the question of whether Loftus' evidence was a "proper subject" for expert testimony.

As indicated above, the key to this issue is whether the testimony might assist the jury to resolve the issues raised by the facts. In making this determination, the trial court must first consider those contentions of ultimate fact raised by the party offering the evidence and supported by evidentiary facts in the record. It must then determine whether the expert testimony will assist in resolving the issues.

In our view, the record clearly shows that Dr. Loftus' testimony would have been of considerable assistance in resolving some of the factual contentions raised by the parties in this case. Examples follow:

First, the photographs in evidence show that there is a resemblance between Logan and Chapple. Scott told the police that Logan's photograph resembled Dee. Scott then failed to identify Chapple's photograph when it was first shown to him. Considering these facts, might Scott's comments regarding the Logan photographs be considered an identification? Should it be considered more accurate than his identification of Chapple from the photographic lineup almost one year later? Loftus' testimony regarding the forgetting curve would have assisted the jury in deciding this issue.

Second, assuming the jury disregarded, as was its right, Scott's and Buck's denial of having discussed Dee's description prior to the identification of January 27, 1979, did the feedback/after-acquired information phenomena play a part in Buck's identification of defendant on the cropped-hair lineup? We cannot assume that ordinary jurors would necessarily be aware of the impact of these factors.

Third, Logan and Chapple bear some resemblance. Logan's picture had been the object of some comment between Scott and the sheriff's deputies shortly after the killing. Although he professed to have no memory of it, Scott had seen a picture of the defendant within a few months of the shooting. Was Scott's identification of defendant on the January 27, 1979 lineup therefore influenced by an unconscious transfer of memory? Since Dee evidently looked like Logan and Chapple, was this transfer phenomenon with regard to their photographs more pronounced than it was with regard to other photographs which were shown to Scott on more than one occasion?

Fourth, since a cropped-hair picture of Logan, who bore a resemblance to defendant and was tentatively identified by Scott soon after the killing, was not included in the lineup of January 1979, were Scott and Buck given a reasonable choice with respect to the photos which they examined on the occasion on which they identified Chapple?

Fifth, the opportunity for perception by the witnesses in this case was great. Most of us would assume that where the opportunity for perception has been significantly greater than the usual case, the recall of the witness and the subsequent identification must be correspondingly more accurate than in most cases. The expert testimony may well have led to the opposite conclusion, though Dr. Loftus admitted that none of her experiments had been based upon situations where the opportunity for perception had been similar to that of the case at bench. Nevertheless, it is implicit in Loftus' testimony that even in cases such as this, the other factors described by her can have a significant impact on the accuracy of later identification.

Sixth, did the witnesses' absolute confidence in the identification bear any relationship to the accuracy of that identification? Again, contrary to Dr. Loftus' opinion, most people might assume that it would.

Each of the factual issues described above is raised by evidentiary facts in the record or reasonable inferences from those facts. In effect, the trial judge ruled that all of the information necessary to resolve the conflicting factual contentions on these issues was within the common experience of the jurors and could be covered in cross-examination of the identification witnesses and argued to the jury.

It is difficult to support this conclusion. For instance, while jurors are aware that lapse of time may make identification less reliable, they are almost certainly unaware of the forgetting curve phenomenon and the resultant inference that a prompt tentative identification may be much more accurate than later positive identification. Similarly, cross-examination is unlikely to establish any evidentiary support for argument that eyewitnesses who have given similar non-factual descriptions of the criminal may have been affected by the feedback phenomenon. Again, experimental data provides evidentiary support to arguments which might otherwise be unpersuasive because they seem contrary to common "wisdom."

The phrase "within the discretion of the trial court" is often used but the reason for that phrase being applied to certain issues is seldom examined. One of the primary reasons an issue is considered discretionary is that its resolution is based on factors which vary from case to case and which involve the balance of conflicting facts and equitable considerations. *Walsh v. Centeio*, 692 F.2d 1239, 1242 (9th Cir. 1982). Thus, the phrase "within the discretion of the trial court" does not mean that the court is free to reach any conclusion it wishes. It does mean that where there are opposing equitable or factual considerations, we will not substitute our judgment for that of the trial court.

Thus, while we have no problem with the usual discretionary ruling that the trier of facts needs no assistance from expert testimony on the question of reliability of identification, the unusual facts of this case compel the contrary conclusion. The preclusion ruling here was based upon a determination that the jury would not be assisted by expert testimony because the subjects embraced by that testimony could be elicited on cross-examination and argued without the evidentiary foundation. Preclusion here was not predicated upon a balancing of conflicting factual contentions or equitable considerations; it was based upon the court's own conclusion that scientific theory regarding the working of human memory could be developed on cross-examination and effectively argued without evidentiary foundation. The examples listed above demonstrate that under the facts here this conclusion was incorrect; there were a number of substantive issues of ultimate fact on which the expert's testimony would have been of significant assistance. Accordingly, we hold that the order precluding the testimony was legally incorrect and was unsupported by the record. It was, therefore, an abuse of discretion.

In reaching this conclusion, we do not intend to "open the gates" to a flood of expert evidence on the subject. We reach the conclusion that Dr. Loftus should have been permitted to testify on the peculiar facts of this case and have no quarrel with the result reached in the vast majority of cases which we have cited above. The rule in Arizona will continue to be that in the usual case we will support the trial court's discretionary ruling on admissibility of expert testimony on eyewitness identification. Nor do we invite opinion testimony in even the most extraordinary case on the likelihood that a particular witness is correct or mistaken in identification or that eyewitness identification in general has a certain percentage of accuracy or inaccuracy. . . .

The judgment below is reversed and the case remanded for a new trial.

HAYS, Justice, concurring in part and dissenting in part:

I cannot agree with the majority's position that the trial court abused its discretion in excluding the testimony of an expert witness on eyewitness identification. With a view to preserving the integrity of the jury as finders of fact, I dissent in part.

It is the jury's task to determine the weight and credibility of a witness' testimony. What this court addresses is whether it is appropriate to have that determination put before the jury on the basis of expert witness testimony. Rule 704, Arizona Rules of Evidence, permits opinion testimony which embraces an ultimate issue if that testimony is otherwise admissible. However, Rule 704 does *not* resolve all worry about invading the province of the jury. Testimony which is of such common knowledge that persons of ordinary education and background could reach as intelligent a conclusion as the expert shall be excluded.

Courts have consistently held that expert testimony relating to eyewitness identification constitutes an invasion of the jury's province. While I recognize the problems in eyewitness testimony, I am unable to distinguish the case at bench from the wealth of cases where identification is in issue.

Identification of a criminal defendant is always crucial, notwithstanding the number of issues in a case. The fact that identification was defendant Chapple's sole defense should not compel us to carve out an exception to our rule against such testimony.

Our rules of evidence provide that a witness shall be impeached through cross-examination. "It is the responsibility of counsel during cross-examination to inquire into the witness' opportunity for observation, his capacity for observation, his attention and interest and his distraction or division of attention." *United States v. Amaral*, 488 F.2d 1148, 1153 (9th Cir. 1973). A defense attorney can properly expose through cross-examination of the witness the time interval which passed between the occurrence of the event and the line-up and, through probing questions, the effects of stress and drugs on the witness' perception. Allowing an expert to testify on the factors affecting the reliability of identification by an eyewitness is merely a guise for impeaching that witness. We cannot permit an expert to disparage the memory of a witness in order to impeach him. The ability of a person to make accurate observations is to be considered by the jury when assessing that witness' credibility.

I also disagree with the majority's conclusion that the average juror does not know that immediate identification is much more trustworthy than long-delayed identification. The average juror may not know the technical terms for this phenomenon, but that is not relevant to his ability to assess a witness' credibility.

My concern here goes beyond the borders of this case. Once we have opened the door to this sort of impeaching testimony, what is to prevent experts from attacking any real or supposed deficiency in every other mental faculty? The peculiar risk of expert testimony with its scientific aura of trustworthiness and the possibility of undue prejudice should be respected. I have great reluctance to permit academia to take over the fact-finding function of the jury. Although clothed in other guise, that will be the practical effect. With little to distinguish this case from the general rule against admitting expert testimony on eyewitness identification, we are left with no guidelines to decide the deluge of similar issues which are sure to result.

CONCLUSION

Eyewitness identification testimony is often a critical aspect of a criminal trial. Jurors tend to give more credence to the testimony of a person who has personally seen an event than to any other type of evidence presented. Thus, it is imperative that the criminal justice system do all it can to ensure the accuracy and reliability of eyewitness identifications.

As presented in this chapter, several procedural safeguards have been mandated by the U.S. Supreme Court as well as state supreme courts. A defendant has the right to have an attorney present at a lineup conducted after the commencement of formal proceedings. The right to counsel at lineups, however, is far from limitless. There is no right to counsel at a lineup conducted prior to the commencement of formal criminal proceedings. Neither is there a right to counsel at photographic lineups.

The Supreme Court has also held that all identification procedures are subject to review to ensure that they were not unnecessarily suggestive or untrustworthy. A totality-of-the-circumstances approach is used to determine if the identification was unduly suggestive *and* likely to lead to a mistaken identification. Keep in mind that even if a procedure is unduly suggestive, so long as it is reliable, it may be used at trial. In making this determination, courts consider such items as the opportunity that the witness had to observe the perpetrator, the accuracy of prior descriptions given by the witness, the witness's level of certainty, and the elapsed time between the crime and the identification procedure.

The Supreme Court has stated that reliability of eyewitness identification testimony is paramount. Thus, procedures that might be unduly suggestive but do not adversely affect the reliability of the identification should not stand in the way of the witness testifying. If the identification is not found to be unduly suggestive and unreliable, it does not violate due process and may be used at trial, subject to cross-examination by the defendant, as discussed in Chapter 10.

CHAPTER 6

The Pretrial Process

Once a person has been charged with a crime, several subtle yet important changes occur. The arrestee is no longer a suspect but is now a defendant. Additionally, the process no longer focuses on investigation but has moved to the prosecutorial phase. As we shall see in forthcoming chapters, this shift calls into play a plethora of rights afforded the defendant and simultaneously places numerous obligations on the prosecution. In this chapter, we look at the rights and burdens involved in the pretrial process—that is, the events that occur after a defendant is arrested and before he or she is brought to trial.

THE INITIAL APPEARANCE

In Chapter 3, we learned that the police normally have the authority to arrest a suspect without first obtaining a warrant. *United States v. Watson*, 423 U.S. 411, 96 S. Ct. 820, 46 L. Ed. 2d 598 (1976). Although this authority is necessary to facilitate the apprehension of suspects caught at the scene of a crime or in a situation where obtaining an arrest warrant is impractical, it does present the criminal justice system with a dilemma. Although there is a need for effective law enforcement, by permitting warrantless arrests the justice system replaces a judge's detached, neutral assessment of whether probable cause to arrest exists with the on-the-spot, heat-of-the-moment determination of a non-neutral law enforcement officer.

To limit the damage that can be caused by an erroneous warrantless arrest, courts have set various procedures to ensure that a prompt judicial determination of probable cause to arrest a person is made. Although it is not disputed that such a procedure is necessary to protect the rights of arrested persons, exactly what such a right entails has been the subject of much debate. Should a suspect have a right to a judicial determination as to whether there is probable cause to detain him at the first practicable opportunity? Within 24 hours? Within 8 hours? What if the arrest is on a weekend or holiday?

In *Gerstein v. Pugh*, 420 U.S. 103, 125, 95 S. Ct. 854, 869, 43 L. Ed. 2d 54 (1975), the U.S. Supreme Court held that "a State . . . must provide a fair and reliable determination of probable cause as a condition for any significant pretrial restraint of liberty." The Court further held that this determination must be made "promptly." Following *Gerstein*, state and lower federal courts disagreed about how "promptly" this probable-cause determination had to be made. In *County of Riverside v. McLaughlin*, the Supreme Court sought to clarify what was constitutionally required.

County of Riverside v. McLaughlin, 500 U.S. 44, 111 S. Ct. 1661, 114 L. Ed. 2d 49 (1991)

Justice O'CONNOR delivered the opinion of the Court.

In Gerstein v. Pugh, 420 U.S. 103, 95 S.Ct. 854, 43 L.Ed.2d 54 (1975), this Court held that the Fourth Amendment requires a prompt judicial determination of probable cause as a prerequisite to an extended pretrial detention following a warrantless arrest. This case requires us to define what is "prompt" under Gerstein.

I

This is a class action brought under 42 U.S.C. § 1983 challenging the manner in which the County of Riverside, California (County), provides probable cause determinations to persons arrested without a warrant. At issue is the County's policy of combining probable cause determinations with its arraignment procedures. Under County policy, which tracks closely the provisions of Cal. Penal Code Ann. § 825 (West 1985), arraignments must be conducted without unnecessary delay and, in any event, within two days of arrest. This 2-day requirement excludes from computation weekends and holidays. Thus, an individual arrested without a warrant late in the week may in some cases be held for as long as five days before receiving a probable cause determination. Over the Thanksgiving holiday, a 7-day delay is possible. . . .

III

A

In Gerstein, this Court held unconstitutional Florida procedures under which persons arrested without a warrant could remain in police custody for 30 days or more without a judicial determination of probable cause. In reaching this conclusion we attempted to reconcile important competing interests. On the one hand, States have a strong interest in protecting public safety by taking into custody those persons who

are reasonably suspected of having engaged in criminal activity, even where there has been no opportunity for a prior judicial determination of probable cause. On the other hand, prolonged detention based on incorrect or unfounded suspicion may unjustly "imperil [a] suspect's job, interrupt his source of income, and impair his family relationships." We sought to balance these competing concerns by holding that States "must provide a fair and reliable determination of probable cause as a condition for any significant pretrial restraint of liberty, and this determination must be made by a judicial officer either before or promptly after arrest."

The Court thus established a "practical compromise" between the rights of individuals and the realities of law enforcement. Under Gerstein, warrantless arrests are permitted but persons arrested without a warrant must promptly be brought before a neutral magistrate for a judicial determination of probable cause. Significantly, the Court stopped short of holding that jurisdictions were constitutionally compelled to provide a probable cause hearing immediately upon taking a suspect into custody and completing booking procedures. We acknowledged the burden that proliferation of pretrial proceedings places on the criminal justice system and recognized that the interests of everyone involved, including those persons who are arrested, might be disserved by introducing further procedural complexity into an already intricate system. Accordingly, we left it to the individual States to integrate prompt probable cause determinations into their differing systems of pretrial procedures.

In so doing, we gave proper deference to the demands of federalism. We recognized that "state systems of criminal procedure vary widely" in the nature and number of pretrial procedures they provide, and we noted that there is no single "preferred" approach. We explained further that "flexibility and experimentation by the States" with respect to integrating probable cause determinations was desirable and that each State should settle upon an approach "to accord with [the] State's pretrial procedure viewed as a whole." Our purpose in Gerstein was to make clear that the Fourth Amendment requires every State to provide prompt determinations of probable cause, but that the Constitution does not impose on the States a rigid procedural framework. Rather, individual States may choose to comply in different ways.

Inherent in Gerstein's invitation to the States to experiment and adapt was the recognition that the Fourth Amendment does not compel an immediate determination of probable cause upon completing the administrative steps incident to arrest. Plainly, if a probable cause hearing is constitutionally compelled the moment a suspect is finished being "booked," there is no room whatsoever for "flexibility and experimentation by the States." Incorporating probable cause determinations "into the procedure for setting bail or fixing other conditions of pretrial release"—which Gerstein explicitly contemplated—would be impossible. Waiting even a few hours so that a bail hearing or arraignment could take place at the same time as the probable cause determination would amount to a constitutional violation. Clearly, Gerstein is not that inflexible.

Notwithstanding Gerstein's discussion of flexibility, the Court of Appeals for the Ninth Circuit held that no flexibility was permitted. It construed Gerstein as "requir[ing] a probable cause determination to be made as soon as the administrative steps incident to arrest were completed, and that such steps should require only a brief period." 888 F.2d, at 1278 (internal quotation marks omitted). This same reading is advanced by the dissents. The foregoing discussion readily demonstrates the error of this approach. Gerstein held that probable cause determinations must be prompt—not immediate. The Court explained that "flexibility and experimentation" were "desirab[le]"; that "[t]here is no single preferred pretrial procedure"; and that "the nature of the probable cause determination usually will be shaped to accord with a State's pretrial procedure viewed as a whole." The Court of Appeals and Justice SCALIA disregard these statements, relying instead on selective quotations from the Court's opinion. As we have explained, Gerstein

struck a balance between competing interests; a proper understanding of the decision is possible only if one takes into account both sides of the equation.

Justice SCALIA claims to find support for his approach in the common law. He points to several statements from the early 1800's to the effect that an arresting officer must bring a person arrested without a warrant before a judicial officer "'as soon as he reasonably can.'" This vague admonition offers no more support for the dissent's inflexible standard than does Gerstein's statement that a hearing follow "promptly after arrest." As mentioned at the outset, the question before us today is what is "prompt" under Gerstein. We answer that question by recognizing that Gerstein struck a balance between competing interests.

B

Given that Gerstein permits jurisdictions to incorporate probable cause determinations into other pretrial procedures, some delays are inevitable. For example, where, as in Riverside County, the probable cause determination is combined with arraignment, there will be delays caused by paperwork and logistical problems. Records will have to be reviewed, charging documents drafted, appearance of counsel arranged, and appropriate bail determined. On weekends, when the number of arrests is often higher and available resources tend to be limited, arraignments may get pushed back even further. In our view, the Fourth Amendment permits a reasonable postponement of a probable cause determination while the police cope with the everyday problems of processing suspects through an overly burdened criminal justice system.

But flexibility has its limits; Gerstein is not a blank check. A State has no legitimate interest in detaining for extended periods individuals who have been arrested without probable cause. The Court recognized in Gerstein that a person arrested without a warrant is entitled to a fair and reliable determination of probable cause and that this determination must be made promptly.

Unfortunately, as lower court decisions applying Gerstein have demonstrated, it is not enough to say that probable cause determinations must be "prompt." This vague standard simply has not provided sufficient guidance. Instead, it has led to a flurry of systemic challenges to city and county practices, putting federal judges in the role of making legislative judgments and overseeing local jailhouse operations.

Our task in this case is to articulate more clearly the boundaries of what is permissible under the Fourth Amendment. Although we hesitate to announce that the Constitution compels a specific time limit, it is important to provide some degree of certainty so that States and counties may establish procedures with confidence that they fall within constitutional bounds. Taking into account the competing interests articulated in Gerstein, we believe that a jurisdiction that provides judicial determinations of probable cause within 48 hours of arrest will, as a general matter, comply with the promptness requirement of Gerstein. For this reason, such jurisdictions will be immune from systemic challenges.

This is not to say that the probable cause determination in a particular case passes constitutional muster simply because it is provided within 48 hours. Such a hearing may nonetheless violate Gerstein if the arrested individual can prove that his or her probable cause determination was delayed unreasonably. Examples of unreasonable delay are delays for the purpose of gathering additional evidence to justify the arrest, a delay motivated by ill will against the arrested individual, or delay for delay's sake. In evaluating whether the delay in a particular case is unreasonable, however, courts must allow a substantial degree of flexibility. Courts cannot ignore the often unavoidable delays in transporting arrested persons from one facility to another, handling late-night bookings where no magistrate is readily available, obtaining the presence of an arresting officer who may be busy processing other suspects or securing the premises of an arrest, and other practical realities.

Where an arrested individual does not receive a probable cause determination within 48 hours, the calculus changes. In such a case, the arrested individual does not bear the burden of proving an unreasonable delay. Rather, the burden shifts to the government to demonstrate the existence of a bona fide emergency or other extraordinary circumstance. The fact that in a particular case it may take longer than 48 hours to consolidate pretrial proceedings does not qualify as an extraordinary circumstance. Nor, for that matter, do intervening weekends. A jurisdiction that chooses to offer combined proceedings must do so as soon as is reasonably feasible, but in no event later than 48 hours after arrest.

Justice SCALIA urges that 24 hours is a more appropriate outer boundary for providing probable cause determinations. In arguing that any delay in probable cause hearings beyond completing the administrative steps incident to arrest and arranging for a magistrate is unconstitutional, Justice SCALIA, in effect, adopts the view of the Court of Appeals. Yet he ignores entirely the Court of Appeals' determination of the time required to complete those procedures. That court, better situated than this one, concluded that it takes 36 hours to process arrested persons in Riverside County. In advocating a 24-hour rule, Justice SCALIA would compel Riverside County—and countless others across the Nation—to speed up its criminal justice mechanisms substantially, presumably by allotting local tax dollars to hire additional police officers and magistrates. There may be times when the Constitution compels such direct interference with local control, but this is not one. As we have explained, Gerstein clearly contemplated a reasonable accommodation between legitimate competing concerns. We do no more than recognize that such accommodation can take place without running afoul of the Fourth Amendment.

Everyone agrees that the police should make every attempt to minimize the time a presumptively innocent individual spends in jail. One way to do so is to provide a judicial determination of probable cause immediately upon completing the administrative steps incident to arrest—i.e., as soon as the suspect has been booked, photographed, and fingerprinted. As Justice SCALIA explains, several States, laudably, have adopted this approach. The Constitution does not compel so rigid a schedule, however. Under Gerstein, jurisdictions may choose to combine probable cause determinations with other pretrial proceedings, so long as they do so promptly. This necessarily means that only certain proceedings are candidates for combination. Only those proceedings that arise very early in the pretrial process—such as bail hearings and arraignments—may be chosen. Even then, every effort must be made to expedite the combined proceedings.

IV

For the reasons we have articulated, we conclude that Riverside County is entitled to combine probable cause determinations with arraignments. The record indicates, however, that the County's current policy and practice do not comport fully with the principles we have outlined. The County's current policy is to offer combined proceedings within two days, exclusive of Saturdays, Sundays, or holidays. As a result, persons arrested on Thursdays may have to wait until the following Monday before they receive a probable cause determination. The delay is even longer if there is an intervening holiday. Thus, the County's regular practice exceeds the 48-hour period we deem constitutionally permissible, meaning that the County is not immune from systemic challenges, such as this class action.

As to arrests that occur early in the week, the County's practice is that "arraignment[s] usually tak[e] place on the last day" possible. There may well be legitimate reasons for this practice; alternatively, this may constitute delay for delay's sake. We leave it to the Court of Appeals and the District Court, on remand, to make this determination.

The judgment of the Court of Appeals is vacated, and the case is remanded for further proceedings consistent with this opinion.

Justice MARSHALL, with whom Justice BLACKMUN and Justice STEVENS join, dissenting.

In Gerstein v. Pugh, 420 U.S. 103, 95 S.Ct. 854, 43 L.Ed.2d 54 (1975), this Court held that an individual detained following a warrantless arrest is entitled to a "prompt" judicial determination of probable cause as a prerequisite to any further restraint on his liberty. I agreed with Justice SCALIA that a probable-cause hearing is sufficiently "prompt" under Gerstein only when provided immediately upon completion of the "administrative steps incident to arrest." Because the Court of Appeals correctly held that the County of Riverside must provide probable-

cause hearings as soon as it completes the administrative steps incident to arrest, I would affirm the judgment of the Court of Appeals. Accordingly, I dissent.

Justice SCALIA, dissenting. . . .

I

The Court views the task before it as one of "balanc[ing] [the] competing concerns" of "protecting public safety," on the one hand, and avoiding "prolonged detention based on incorrect or unfounded suspicion," on the other hand. It purports to reaffirm the "'practical compromise'" between these concerns struck in Gerstein v. Pugh, 420 U.S. 103, 95 S.Ct. 854, 43 L.Ed.2d 54 (1975). There is assuredly room for such an approach in resolving novel questions of search and seizure under the "reasonableness" standard that the Fourth Amendment sets forth. But not, I think, in resolving those questions on which a clear answer already existed in 1791 and has been generally adhered to by the traditions of our society ever since. As to those matters, the "balance" has already been struck, the "practical compromise" reached—and it is the function of the Bill of Rights to preserve that judgment, not only against the changing views of Presidents and Members of Congress, but also against the changing views of Justices whom Presidents appoint and Members of Congress confirm to this Court. . . .

[In Gerstein] we said that "the Fourth Amendment requires a judicial determination of probable cause as a prerequisite to extended restraint of liberty," "either before or promptly after arrest." Though how "promptly" we did not say, it was plain enough that the requirement left no room for intentional delay unrelated to the completion of "the administrative steps incident to arrest." Plain enough, at least, that all but one federal court considering the question understood Gerstein that way.

Today, however, the Court discerns something quite different in Gerstein. It finds that the plain statements set forth above (not to mention the common-law tradition of liberty upon which they were based) were trumped by the implication of a later dictum in the case which, according to the Court, manifests a "recognition that the Fourth Amendment does not compel an immediate determination of probable cause upon completing the administrative steps incident to arrest." Of course Gerstein did not say, nor do I contend, that an "immediate" determination is required. But what the Court today means by "not immediate" is that the delay can be attributable to something other than completing the administrative steps incident to arrest and arranging for the magistrate—namely, to the administrative convenience of combining the probable-cause determination with other state proceedings. The result, we learn later in the opinion, is that what Gerstein meant by "a brief period of detention to take the administrative steps incident to arrest" is two full days. I think it is clear that the case neither said nor meant any such thing. . . .

[D]etermining the outer boundary of reasonableness is a more objective and more manageable task. We were asked to undertake it in Gerstein, but declined—wisely, I think, since we had before us little data to support any figure we might choose. As the Court notes, however, Gerstein has engendered a number of cases addressing not only the scope of the procedures "incident to arrest," but also their duration. The conclusions reached by the judges in those cases, and by others who have addressed the question, are surprisingly similar. I frankly would prefer even more information, and for that purpose would have supported reargument on the single question of an outer time limit. The data available are enough to convince me, however, that certainly no more than 24 hours is needed.

With one exception, no federal court considering the question has regarded 24 hours as an inadequate amount of time to complete arrest procedures, and with the same exception every court actually setting a limit for a probable-cause determination based on those procedures has selected 24 hours. (The exception would not count Sunday within the 24-hour limit.) Federal courts have reached a similar conclusion in applying Federal Rule of Criminal Procedure 5(a), which requires presentment before a federal magistrate "without unnecessary delay." And state courts have similarly applied a 24-hour limit under state statutes requiring presentment without "unreasonable delay." New York, for example, has concluded that no more than 24 hours is necessary from arrest to arraignment. Twenty-nine States have statutes similar to New York's, which require either presentment or arraignment "without unnecessary delay" or "forthwith"; eight States explicitly require presentment or arraignment within 24 hours; and only seven States have statutes explicitly permitting a period longer than 24 hours. . . .

In my view, absent extraordinary circumstances, it is an "unreasonable seizure" within the meaning of the Fourth Amendment for the police, having arrested a suspect without a warrant, to delay a determination of probable cause for the arrest either (1) for reasons unrelated to arrangement of the probable-cause determination or completion of the steps incident to arrest, or (2) beyond 24 hours after the arrest. Like the Court, I would treat the time limit as a presumption; when the 24 hours are exceeded the burden shifts to the police to adduce unforeseeable circumstances justifying the additional delay. . . .

Notes and Questions

1. In reaching its decision in *McLaughlin*, what interests did the Court balance?

2. Was the decision reached by the Court in *McLaughlin* necessary for the effective operation of the criminal justice system? What effect do you suppose Justice Scalia's proposed rule would have on the criminal justice system? What effect would it have on a defendant?

3. In *Jenkins v. Chief Justice of the District Court*, 416 Mass. 221, 619 N.E.2d 324 (1993), the Massachusetts Supreme Judicial Court held that the Massachusetts Constitution required defendants arrested without a warrant to be presented to a magistrate no later than reasonably necessary to process the arrest and to reach the magistrate. The court ruled that under usual circumstances, the initial appearance must occur within 24 hours of arrest. How does this requirement differ from the rule announced in *McLaughlin*?

4. It is important to keep in mind that the probable-cause determination dealt with in *McLaughlin* deals with probable cause to detain a suspect. This is different from the probable-cause determination made at the preliminary hearing or grand jury, discussed below.

5. 📖 **Legal Research Note.** Federal statutes are located in the United States Code (U.S.C.). The U.S.C. is organized by titles and sections. Titles in the U.S.C. represent the general subject matter of a set of statutes, and sections are the specific statutes. For example, statutes dealing with many federal crimes are found in Title 18. Within Title 18 are hundreds of sections that represent statutes defining specific crimes.

The U.S.C. lists only the text of federal statutes. Statutes also are published in the United States Code Annotated (U.S.C.A.) (West Publishing Co.) and the United States Code Service (U.S.C.S.) (Lawyers Cooperative Publishing Co.). Both sets of these volumes also contain annotations that accompany individual statutes. Annotations consist of squibs, or brief summaries of published court opinions dealing with specific statutes. Annotations are excellent sources for discovering how courts have interpreted a statute.

Statutes for the 50 states are organized much like federal statutes. Each state has its own set of statutes. Like the U.S.C.A. and U.S.C.S., these statutes are annotated. While the numbering system and style of annotations vary from state to state, they all follow the same general concept of title and section numbers. In this chapter, we will explain how you can find both federal and state statutes and the annotations of judicial decisions that have interpreted and applied those laws.

BAIL AND PREVENTIVE DETENTION

After a person is arrested, a decision must be made whether the arrestee should be (1) released from custody on his own recognizance with no conditions other than the arrestee's promise to appear in court attached; (2) released under certain conditions, such as to avoid contact with the alleged victim or to report periodically to a pretrial release supervisor; (3) held pending the payment of bail; or (4) held without bail. A judge or magistrate normally decides what conditions of release are appropriate at the defendant's initial appearance.

While individuals arrested do not invariably have a right to be released from custody on bail, the Eighth Amendment to the United States Constitution provides that "excessive bail shall not be required." This provision gives rise to the obvious question: What is excessive bail? In *Stack v. Boyle*, the Supreme Court set forth guidelines to be used by lower courts in deciding what conditions of release or bail should be considered in a given case.

Stack v. Boyle, 342 U.S. 1, 72 S. Ct. 1, 96 L. Ed. 3 (1951)

Mr. Chief Justice VINSON delivered the opinion of the Court.

Indictments have been returned in the Southern District of California charging the twelve petitioners with conspiring to violate the Smith Act. Upon their arrest, bail was fixed for each petitioner in the widely varying amounts of $2,500, $7,500, $75,000 and $100,000. On motion of petitioner Schneiderman following arrest in the Southern District of New York, his bail was reduced to $50,000 before his removal to California. On motion of the Government to increase bail in the case of other petitioners, and after several intermediate procedural steps not material to the issues presented here, bail was fixed in the District Court for the Southern District of California in the uniform amount of $50,000 for each petitioner.

Petitioners moved to reduce bail on the ground that bail as fixed was excessive under the Eighth Amendment. In support of their motion, petitioners submitted statements as to their financial resources, family relationships, health, prior criminal records, and other information. The only evidence offered by the Government was a certified record showing that four persons previously convicted under the Smith Act in the Southern District of New York had forfeited bail. No evidence was produced relating those four persons to the petitioners in this case. At a hearing on the motion, petitioners were examined by the District Judge and cross-examined by an attorney for the Government. Petitioners' factual statements stand uncontroverted. . . .

From the passage of the Judiciary Act of 1789, to the present Federal Rules of Criminal Procedure, Rule 46(a)(1), 18 U.S.C.A., federal law has unequivocally provided that a person arrested for a non-capital offense shall be admitted to bail. This traditional right to freedom before conviction permits the unhampered preparation of a defense, and serves to prevent the infliction of punishment prior to conviction. Unless this right to bail before trial is preserved, the presumption of innocence, secured only after centuries of struggle, would lose its meaning.

The right to release before trial is conditioned upon the accused's giving adequate assurance that he will stand trial and submit to sentence if found guilty. Like the ancient practice of securing the oaths of responsible persons to stand as sureties for the accused, the modern practice of requiring a bail bond or the deposit of a sum of money subject to forfeiture serves as additional assurance of the presence of an accused. Bail set at a figure higher than an amount reasonably calculated to fulfill this purpose is "excessive" under the Eighth Amendment.

Since the function of bail is limited, the fixing of bail for any individual defendant must be based upon standards relevant to the purpose of assuring the presence of that defendant. The traditional standards as expressed in the Federal Rules of Criminal Procedure[3] are to be applied in each case to each defendant. In this case petitioners are charged with offenses under the Smith Act and, if found guilty, their convictions are subject to review with the scrupulous care demanded by our Constitution. Upon final judgment of conviction, petitioners face imprisonment of not more than five years and a fine of not more than $10,000. It is not denied that bail for each petitioner has been fixed in a sum much higher than that usually imposed for offenses with like penalties and yet there has been no factual showing to justify such action in this case. The Government asks the courts to depart from the norm by assuming, without the introduction of evidence, that each petitioner is a pawn in a conspiracy and will, in obedience to a superior, flee the jurisdiction. To infer from the fact of indictment alone a need for bail in an unusually high amount is an arbitrary act. Such conduct would inject into our own system of government the very principles of totalitarianism which Congress was seeking to guard against in passing the statute under which petitioners have been indicted.

If bail in an amount greater than that usually fixed for serious charges of crimes is required in the case of any of the petitioners, that is a matter to which evidence should be directed in a hearing so that the constitutional rights of each petitioner may be preserved. In the absence of such a showing, we are of the opinion that the fixing of bail before trial in these cases cannot be squared with the statutory and constitutional standards for admission to bail. . . .

Judgment of Court of Appeals vacated and case remanded to District Court with directions. . . .

By Mr. Justice JACKSON, whom Mr. Justice FRANKFURTER joins. . . .

---

3. Rule 46(c). "AMOUNT. If the defendant is admitted to bail, the amount thereof shall be such as in the judgment of the commissioner or court or judge or justice will insure the presence of the defendant, having regard to the nature and circumstances of the offense charged, the weight of the evidence against him, the financial ability of the defendant to give bail and the character of the defendant."

The practice of admission to bail, as it has evolved in Anglo-American law, is not a device for keeping persons in jail upon mere accusation until it is found convenient to give them a trial. On the contrary, the spirit of the procedure is to enable them to stay out of jail until a trial has found them guilty. Without this conditional privilege, even those wrongly accused are punished by a period of imprisonment while awaiting trial and are handicapped in consulting counsel, searching for evidence and witnesses, and preparing a defense. To open a way of escape from this handicap and possible injustice, Congress commands allowance of bail for one under charge of any offense not punishable by death, Fed. Rules Crim. Proc. 46(a)(1) providing: "A person arrested for an offense not punishable by death shall be admitted to bail" before conviction.

Admission to bail always involves a risk that the accused will take flight. That is a calculated risk which the law takes as the price of our system of justice. We know that Congress anticipated that bail would enable some escapes, because it provided a procedure for dealing with them. Fed.Rules Crim.Proc. 46(f).

In allowance of bail, the duty of the judge is to reduce the risk by fixing an amount reasonably calculated to hold the accused available for trial and its consequence. Fed.Rules Crim.Proc. 46(c). But the judge is not free to make the sky the limit, because the Eighth Amendment to the Constitution says: "Excessive bail shall not be required."

Congress has reduced this generality in providing more precise standards, stating that "the amount thereof shall be such as in the judgment of the commissioner or court or judge or justice will insure the presence of the defendant, having regard to the nature and circumstances of the offense charged, the weight of the evidence against him, the financial ability of the defendant to give bail and the character of the defendant." Fed.Rules Crim.Proc. 46(c). . . .

It is complained that the District Court fixed a uniform blanket bail chiefly by consideration of the nature of the accusation and did not take into account the difference in circumstances between different defendants. If this occurred, it is a clear violation of Rule 46(c). Each defendant stands before the bar of justice as an individual. Even on a conspiracy charge defendants do not lose their separateness or identity. While it might be possible that these defendants are identical in financial ability, character and relation to the charge—elements Congress has directed to be regarded in fixing bail—I think it violates the law of probabilities. Each accused is entitled to any benefits due to his good record, and misdeeds or a bad record should prejudice only those who are guilty of them. The question when application for bail is made relates to each one's trustworthiness to appear for trial and what security will supply reasonable assurance of his appearance. . . .

[T]he defect in the proceedings below appears to be, that, provoked by the flight of certain Communists after conviction, the Government demands and public opinion supports a use of the bail power to keep Communist defendants in jail before conviction. Thus, the amount is said to have been fixed not as a reasonable assurance of their presence at the trial, but also as an assurance they would remain in jail. There seems reason to believe that this may have been the spirit to which the courts below have yielded, and it is contrary to the whole policy and philosophy of bail. This is not to say that every defendant is entitled to such bail as he can provide, but he is entitled to an opportunity to make it in a reasonable amount. I think the whole matter should be reconsidered by the appropriate judges in the traditional spirit of bail procedure. . . .

Notes and Questions

1. Does it surprise you that bail is to be set at an amount to ensure the presence of the defendant at trial? Should bail serve other purposes for the good of the justice system and society?

In the years since *Stack*, the crime rate has increased. One response to this increase in crime has been legislative actions to get tougher on criminals. *United States v. Salerno* discusses the constitutionality of one such action taken by Congress: the Bail Reform Act of 1984. As you read *Salerno*, ask yourself whether its holding can be reconciled with *Stack v. Boyle*.

United States v. Salerno, 481 U.S. 739, 107 S. Ct. 2095, 95 L. Ed. 2d 697 (1987)

Chief Justice REHNQUIST delivered the opinion of the Court.

The Bail Reform Act of 1984 (Act) allows a federal court to detain an arrestee pending trial if the Government demonstrates by clear and convincing evidence after an adversary hearing that no release conditions "will reasonably assure . . . the safety of any other person and the community." The United States Court of Appeals for the Second Circuit struck down this provision of the Act as facially unconstitutional, because, in that court's words, this type of pretrial detention violates "substantive due process." We granted certiorari because of a conflict among the Courts of Appeals regarding the validity of the Act. We hold that, as against the facial attack mounted by these respondents, the Act fully comports with constitutional requirements. We therefore reverse.

I

Responding to "the alarming problem of crimes committed by persons on release," Congress formulated the Bail Reform Act of 1984, as the solution to a bail crisis in the federal courts. The Act represents the National Legislature's considered response to numerous perceived deficiencies in the federal bail process. By providing for sweeping changes in both the way federal courts consider bail applications and the circumstances under which bail is granted, Congress hoped to "give the courts adequate authority to make release decisions that give appropriate recognition to the danger a person may pose to others if released." . . . Section 3142(e) provides that "[i]f, after a hearing pursuant to the provisions of subsection (f), the judicial officer finds that no condition or combination of conditions will reasonably assure the appearance of the person as required and the safety of any other person and the community, he shall order the detention of the person prior to trial."

Section 3142(f) provides the arrestee with a number of procedural safeguards. He may request the presence of counsel at the detention hearing, he may testify and present witnesses in his behalf, as well as proffer evidence, and he may cross-examine other witnesses appearing at the hearing. If the judicial officer finds that no conditions of pretrial release can reasonably assure the safety of other persons and the community, he must state his findings of fact in writing, and support his conclusion with "clear and convincing evidence."

The judicial officer is not given unbridled discretion in making the detention determination. Congress has specified the considerations relevant to that decision. These factors include the nature and seriousness of the charges, the substantiality of the Government's evidence against the arrestee, the arrestee's background and characteristics, and the nature and seriousness of the danger posed by the suspect's release. Should a judicial officer order detention, the detainee is entitled to expedited appellate review of the detention order.

Respondents Anthony Salerno and Vincent Cafaro were arrested on March 21, 1986, after being charged in a 29-count indictment alleging various Racketeer Influenced and Corrupt Organizations Act (RICO) violations, mail and wire fraud offenses, extortion, and various criminal gambling violations. The RICO counts alleged 35 acts of racketeering activity, including fraud, extortion, gambling, and conspiracy to commit murder. At respondents' arraignment, the Government moved to have Salerno and Cafaro detained pursuant to § 3142(e), on the ground that no condition of release would assure the safety of the community or any person. The District Court held a hearing at which the Government made a detailed proffer of evidence. The Government's case showed that Salerno was the "boss" of the Genovese crime family of La

Cosa Nostra and that Cafaro was a "captain" in the Genovese family. According to the Government's proffer, based in large part on conversations intercepted by a court-ordered wiretap, the two respondents had participated in wide-ranging conspiracies to aid their illegitimate enterprises through violent means. The Government also offered the testimony of two of its trial witnesses, who would assert that Salerno personally participated in two murder conspiracies. Salerno opposed the motion for detention, challenging the credibility of the Government's witnesses. He offered the testimony of several character witnesses as well as a letter from his doctor stating that he was suffering from a serious medical condition. Cafaro presented no evidence at the hearing, but instead characterized the wiretap conversations as merely "tough talk."

The District Court granted the Government's detention motion, concluding that the Government had established by clear and convincing evidence that no condition or combination of conditions of release would ensure the safety of the community or any person. . . .

Respondents present two grounds for invalidating the Bail Reform Act's provisions permitting pretrial detention on the basis of future dangerousness. First, they rely upon the Court of Appeals' conclusion that the Act exceeds the limitations placed upon the Federal Government by the Due Process Clause of the Fifth Amendment. Second, they contend that the Act contravenes the Eighth Amendment's proscription against excessive bail. We treat these contentions in turn.

A

The Due Process Clause of the Fifth Amendment provides that "No person shall . . . be deprived of life, liberty, or property, without due process of law. . . ." This Court has held that the Due Process Clause protects individuals against two types of government action. So-called "substantive due process" prevents the government from engaging in conduct that "shocks the conscience," or interferes with rights "implicit in the concept of ordered liberty." When government action depriving a person of life, liberty, or property survives substantive due process scrutiny, it must still be implemented in a fair manner. This

requirement has traditionally been referred to as "procedural" due process.

Respondents first argue that the Act violates substantive due process because the pretrial detention it authorizes constitutes impermissible punishment before trial. The Government however, has never argued that pretrial detention could be upheld if it were "punishment." The Court of Appeals assumed that pretrial detention under the Bail Reform Act is regulatory, not penal, and we agree that it is.

As an initial matter, the mere fact that a person is detained does not inexorably lead to the conclusion that the government has imposed punishment. To determine whether a restriction on liberty constitutes impermissible punishment or permissible regulation, we first look to legislative intent. Unless Congress expressly intended to impose punitive restrictions, the punitive/regulatory distinction turns on "'whether an alternative purpose to which [the restriction] may rationally be connected is assignable for it, and whether it appears excessive in relation to the alternative purpose assigned [to it].'"

We conclude that the detention imposed by the Act falls on the regulatory side of the dichotomy. The legislative history of the Bail Reform Act clearly indicates that Congress did not formulate the pretrial detention provisions as punishment for dangerous individuals. Congress instead perceived pretrial detention as a potential solution to a pressing societal problem. There is no doubt that preventing danger to the community is a legitimate regulatory goal.

Nor are the incidents of pretrial detention excessive in relation to the regulatory goal Congress sought to achieve. The Bail Reform Act carefully limits the circumstances under which detention may be sought to the most serious of crimes. The arrestee is entitled to a prompt detention hearing and the maximum length of pretrial detention is limited by the stringent time limitations of the Speedy Trial Act. Moreover, as in Schall v. Martin, the conditions of confinement envisioned by the Act "appear to reflect the regulatory purposes relied upon by the" Government. As in Schall, the statute at issue here requires that detainees be housed in a "facility separate, to the extent practicable, from persons awaiting or serving sentences or being held in custody pending appeal." We conclude, therefore, that the pretrial detention contemplated by the Bail Reform Act is regulatory in nature, and does not constitute punishment before trial in violation of the Due Process Clause. . . .

Respondents characterize the Due Process Clause as erecting an impenetrable "wall" in this area that "no governmental interest—rational, important, compelling or otherwise—may surmount."

We do not think the Clause lays down any such categorical imperative. We have repeatedly held that the Government's regulatory interest in community safety can, in appropriate circumstances, outweigh an individual's liberty interest. For example, in times of war or insurrection, when society's interest is at its peak, the Government may detain individuals whom the government believes to be dangerous. Even outside the exigencies of war, we have found that sufficiently compelling governmental interests can justify detention of dangerous persons. Thus, we have found no absolute constitutional barrier to detention of potentially dangerous resident aliens pending deportation proceedings. We have also held that the government may detain mentally unstable individuals who present a danger to the public, Addington v. Texas, and dangerous defendants who become incompetent to stand trial, Jackson v. Indiana. . . .

Respondents characterize all of these cases as exceptions to the "general rule" of substantive due process that the government may not detain a person prior to a judgment of guilt in a criminal trial. Such a "general rule" may freely be conceded, but we think that these cases show a sufficient number of exceptions to the rule that the congressional action challenged here can hardly be characterized as totally novel. Given the well-established authority of the government, in special circumstances, to restrain individuals' liberty prior to or even without criminal trial and conviction, we think that the present statute providing for pretrial detention on the basis of dangerousness must be evaluated in precisely the same manner that we evaluated the laws in the cases discussed above.

The government's interest in preventing crime by arrestees is both legitimate and compelling. In Schall, we recognized the strength of the State's interest in preventing juvenile crime. This general concern with crime prevention is no less compelling when the suspects are adults. Indeed, "[t]he harm suffered by the victim of a crime is not dependent upon the age of the perpetrator." The Bail Reform Act of 1984 responds to an even more particularized governmental interest than the interest we sustained in Schall. The statute we upheld in Schall permitted pretrial detention of any juvenile arrested on any charge after a showing that the individual might commit some undefined further crimes. The Bail Reform Act, in contrast, narrowly focuses on a particularly acute problem in which the Government interests are overwhelming. The Act operates only on individuals who have been arrested for a specific category of extremely serious offenses. Congress specifically found that these individuals are far more likely to be responsible for dangerous acts in the community after arrest. Nor is the Act by any means a scattershot attempt to incapacitate those who are merely suspected of these serious crimes. The Government must first of all demonstrate probable cause to believe that the charged crime has been committed by the arrestee, but that is not enough. In a full-blown adversary hearing, the Government must convince a neutral decision maker by clear and convincing evidence that no conditions of release can reasonably assure the safety of the community or any person. While the Government's general interest in preventing crime is compelling, even this interest is heightened when the Government musters convincing proof that the arrestee, already indicted or held to answer for a serious crime, presents a demonstrable danger to the community. Under these narrow circumstances, society's interest in crime prevention is at its greatest.

On the other side of the scale, of course, is the individual's strong interest in liberty. We do not minimize the importance and fundamental nature of this right. But, as our cases hold, this right may, in circumstances where the government's interest is sufficiently weighty, be subordinated to the greater needs of society. We think that Congress' careful delineation of the circumstances under which detention will be permitted satisfies this standard. When the Government proves by clear and convincing evidence that an arrestee presents an identified and articulable threat to an individual or the community, we believe that, consistent with the Due Process

Clause, a court may disable the arrestee from executing that threat. . . .

B

Respondents also contend that the Bail Reform Act violates the Excessive Bail Clause of the Eighth Amendment. The Court of Appeals did not address this issue because it found that the Act violates the Due Process Clause. We think that the Act survives a challenge founded upon the Eighth Amendment. The Eighth Amendment addresses pretrial release by providing merely that "[e]xcessive bail shall not be required." This Clause, of course, says nothing about whether bail shall be available at all. Respondents nevertheless contend that this Clause grants them a right to bail calculated solely upon considerations of flight. They rely on Stack v. Boyle, in which the Court stated that "[b]ail set at a figure higher than an amount reasonably calculated [to ensure the defendant's presence at trial] is 'excessive' under the Eighth Amendment." In respondents' view, since the Bail Reform Act allows a court essentially to set bail at an infinite amount for reasons not related to the risk of flight, it violates the Excessive Bail Clause. Respondents concede that the right to bail they have discovered in the Eighth Amendment is not absolute. A court may, for example, refuse bail in capital cases. And, as the Court of Appeals noted and respondents admit, a court may refuse bail when the defendant presents a threat to the judicial process by intimidating witnesses. Respondents characterize these exceptions as consistent with what they claim to be the sole purpose of bail—to ensure the integrity of the judicial process.

While we agree that a primary function of bail is to safeguard the courts' role in adjudicating the guilt or innocence of defendants, we reject the proposition that the Eighth Amendment categorically prohibits the government from pursuing other admittedly compelling interests through regulation of pretrial release. The above-quoted dictum in Stack v. Boyle is far too slender a reed on which to rest this argument. The Court in Stack had no occasion to consider whether the Excessive Bail Clause requires courts to admit all defendants to bail, because the statute before the Court in that case in fact allowed the defen-

dants to be bailed. Thus, the Court had to determine only whether bail, admittedly available in that case, was excessive if set at a sum greater than that necessary to ensure the arrestees' presence at trial. . . .

[E]ven if we were to conclude that the Eighth Amendment imposes some substantive limitations on the National Legislature's powers in this area, we would still hold that the Bail Reform Act is valid. Nothing in the text of the Bail Clause limits permissible Government considerations solely to questions of flight. The only arguable substantive limitation of the Bail Clause is that the Government's proposed conditions of release or detention not be "excessive" in light of the perceived evil. Of course, to determine whether the Government's response is excessive, we must compare that response against the interest the Government seeks to protect by means of that response. Thus, when the Government has admitted that its only interest is in preventing flight, bail must be set by a court at a sum designed to ensure that goal, and no more. We believe that when Congress has mandated detention on the basis of a compelling interest other than prevention of flight, as it has here, the Eighth Amendment does not require release on bail.

III

In our society liberty is the norm, and detention prior to trial or without trial is the carefully limited exception. We hold that the provisions for pretrial detention in the Bail Reform Act of 1984 fall within that carefully limited exception. The Act authorizes the detention prior to trial of arrestees charged with serious felonies who are found after an adversary hearing to pose a threat to the safety of individuals or to the community which no condition of release can dispel. The numerous procedural safeguards detailed above must attend this adversary hearing. We are unwilling to say that this congressional determination, based as it is upon that primary concern of every government—a concern for the safety and indeed the lives of its citizens—on its face violates either the Due Process Clause of the Fifth Amendment or the Excessive Bail Clause of the Eighth Amendment.

The judgment of the Court of Appeals is therefore, Reversed.

Justice MARSHALL, with whom Justice BRENNAN joins, dissenting.

This case brings before the Court for the first time a statute in which Congress declares that a person innocent of any crime may be jailed indefinitely, pending the trial of allegations which are legally presumed to be untrue, if the Government shows to the satisfaction of a judge that the accused is likely to commit crimes, unrelated to the pending charges, at any time in the future. Such statutes, consistent with the usages of tyranny and the excesses of what bitter experience teaches us to call the police state, have long been thought incompatible with the fundamental human rights protected by our Constitution. Today a majority of this Court holds otherwise. Its decision disregards basic principles of justice established centuries ago and enshrined beyond the reach of governmental interference in the Bill of Rights. . . .

II

The majority approaches respondents' challenge to the Act by dividing the discussion into two sections, one concerned with the substantive guarantees implicit in the Due Process Clause, and the other concerned with the protection afforded by the Excessive Bail Clause of the Eighth Amendment. This is a sterile formalism, which divides a unitary argument into two independent parts and then professes to demonstrate that the parts are individually inadequate.

On the due process side of this false dichotomy appears an argument concerning the distinction between regulatory and punitive legislation. The majority concludes that the Act is a regulatory rather than a punitive measure. The ease with which the conclusion is reached suggests the worthlessness of the achievement. The major premise is that "[u]nless Congress expressly intended to impose punitive restrictions, the punitive/regulatory distinction turns on 'whether an alternative purpose to which [the restriction] may rationally be connected is assignable for it, and whether it appears excessive in relation to the alternative purpose assigned [to it].'" The majority finds that "Con-

gress did not formulate the pretrial detention provisions as punishment for dangerous individuals," but instead was pursuing the "legitimate regulatory goal" of "preventing danger to the community." Concluding that pretrial detention is not an excessive solution to the problem of preventing danger to the community, the majority thus finds that no substantive element of the guarantee of due process invalidates the statute.

This argument does not demonstrate the conclusion it purports to justify. Let us apply the majority's reasoning to a similar, hypothetical case. After investigation, Congress determines (not unrealistically) that a large proportion of violent crime is perpetrated by persons who are unemployed. It also determines, equally reasonably, that much violent crime is committed at night. From amongst the panoply of "potential solutions," Congress chooses a statute which permits, after judicial proceedings, the imposition of a dusk-to-dawn curfew on anyone who is unemployed. Since this is not a measure enacted for the purpose of punishing the unemployed, and since the majority finds that preventing danger to the community is a legitimate regulatory goal, the curfew statute would, according to the majority's analysis, be a mere "regulatory" detention statute, entirely compatible with the substantive components of the Due Process Clause.

The absurdity of this conclusion arises, of course, from the majority's cramped concept of substantive due process. The majority proceeds as though the only substantive right protected by the Due Process Clause is a right to be free from punishment before conviction. The majority's technique for infringing this right is simple: merely redefine any measure which is claimed to be punishment as "regulation," and, magically, the Constitution no longer prohibits its imposition. Because . . . the Due Process Clause protects other substantive rights which are infringed by this legislation, the majority's argument is merely an exercise in obfuscation.

The logic of the majority's Eighth Amendment analysis is equally unsatisfactory. The Eighth Amendment, as the majority notes, states that "[e]xcessive bail shall not be required." The majority then declares, as if it were undeniable, that: "[t]his Clause, of course, says nothing about whether bail shall be available at all." If excessive bail is imposed the defendant stays in jail. The same result is achieved if bail is denied altogether. Whether the magistrate sets bail at $1 million or refuses to set bail at all, the consequences are indistinguishable. It would be mere sophistry to suggest that the Eighth Amendment protects against the former decision, and not the latter. Indeed, such a result would lead to the conclusion that there was no need for Congress to pass a preventive detention measure of any kind; every federal magistrate and district judge could simply refuse, despite the absence of any evidence of risk of flight or danger to the community, to set bail. This would be entirely constitutional, since, according to the majority, the Eighth Amendment "says nothing about whether bail shall be available at all." . . .

The majority's attempts to deny the relevance of the Bail Clause to this case are unavailing, but the majority is nonetheless correct that the prohibition of excessive bail means that in order "to determine whether the Government's response is excessive, we must compare that response against the interest the Government seeks to protect by means of that response." The majority concedes, as it must, that "when the Government has admitted that its only interest is in preventing flight, bail must be set by a court at a sum designed to ensure that goal, and no more." But, the majority says, "when Congress has mandated detention on the basis of a compelling interest other than prevention of flight, as it has here, the Eighth Amendment does not require release on bail." This conclusion follows only if the "compelling" interest upon which Congress acted is an interest which the Constitution permits Congress to further through the denial of bail. The majority does not ask, as a result of its disingenuous division of the analysis, if there are any substantive limits contained in both the Eighth Amendment and the Due Process Clause which render this system of preventive detention unconstitutional. The majority does not ask because the answer is apparent and, to the majority, inconvenient.

III

The essence of this case may be found, ironically enough, in a provision of the Act to which the majority does not refer. [Section] 3142(j) pro-

vides that "[n]othing in this section shall be construed as modifying or limiting the presumption of innocence." But the very pith and purpose of this statute is an abhorrent limitation of the presumption of innocence. The majority's untenable conclusion that the present Act is constitutional arises from a specious denial of the role of the Bail Clause and the Due Process Clause in protecting the invaluable guarantee afforded by the presumption of innocence.

"The principle that there is a presumption of innocence in favor of the accused is the undoubted law, axiomatic and elementary, and its enforcement lies at the foundation of the administration of our criminal law." Our society's belief, reinforced over the centuries, that all are innocent until the state has proved them to be guilty, like the companion principle that guilt must be proved beyond a reasonable doubt, is "implicit in the concept of ordered liberty," and is established beyond legislative contravention in the Due Process Clause.

The statute now before us declares that persons who have been indicted may be detained if a judicial officer finds clear and convincing evidence that they pose a danger to individuals or to the community. The statute does not authorize the Government to imprison anyone it has evidence is dangerous; indictment is necessary. But let us suppose that a defendant is indicted and the Government shows by clear and convincing evidence that he is dangerous and should be detained pending a trial, at which trial the defendant is acquitted. May the Government continue to hold the defendant in detention based upon its showing that he is dangerous? The answer cannot be yes, for that would allow the Government to imprison someone for uncommitted crimes based upon "proof" not beyond a reasonable doubt. The result must therefore be that once the indictment has failed, detention cannot continue. But our fundamental principles of justice declare that the defendant is as innocent on the day before his trial as he is on the morning after his acquittal. Under this statute an untried indictment somehow acts to permit a detention, based on other charges, which after an acquittal would be unconstitutional. The conclusion is inescapable that the indictment has been turned into evidence, if not that the defendant is guilty of the crime charged, then that left to his own devices he will soon be guilty of something else. . . .

IV

There is a connection between the peculiar facts of this case and the evident constitutional defects in the statute which the Court upholds today. Respondent Cafaro was originally incarcerated for an indeterminate period at the request of the Government, which believed (or professed to believe) that his release imminently threatened the safety of the community. That threat apparently vanished, from the Government's point of view, when Cafaro agreed to act as a covert agent of the Government. There could be no more eloquent demonstration of the coercive power of authority to imprison upon prediction, or of the dangers which the almost inevitable abuses pose to the cherished liberties of a free society.

"It is a fair summary of history to say that the safeguards of liberty have frequently been forged in controversies involving not very nice people." Honoring the presumption of innocence is often difficult; sometimes we must pay substantial social costs as a result of our commitment to the values we espouse. But at the end of the day the presumption of innocence protects the innocent; the shortcuts we take with those whom we believe to be guilty injure only those wrongfully accused and, ultimately, ourselves.

Throughout the world today there are men, women, and children interned indefinitely, awaiting trials which may never come or which may be mockery of the word, because their governments believe them to be "dangerous." Our Constitution, whose construction began two centuries ago, can shelter us forever from the evils of such unchecked power. Over 200 years it has slowly, through our efforts, grown more durable, more expansive, and more just. But it cannot protect us if we lack the courage, and the self-restraint, to protect ourselves. Today a majority of the Court applies itself to an ominous exercise in demolition. Theirs is truly a decision which will go forth without authority, and come back without respect.

I dissent.

Notes and Questions

1. According to the Court, what factors should a magistrate consider in making a decision about pretrial detention? Are these factors appropriate? Do they limit the discretion given to the magistrate? How so?

2. Is preventive detention a form of punishment? Why or why not?

3. In his dissent, Justice Marshall raises the fact that defendant Cafaro was released on $1 million bail to allow him to work as a government informant. Do you agree with Justice Marshall's argument that this evidences the coercive nature of preventive detention? Do you agree with his statement that the threat posed by Cafaro to society, as previously argued by the government, vanished once he agreed to be an informant?

4. It is important to remember that the Bail Reform Act of 1984 applies only to federal prosecutions. Many state constitutions have been interpreted to prohibit the type of preventive detention approved of in *Salerno*. For example, in *State v. Sauve*, 159 Vt. 566, 570, 621 A.2d 1296, 1300 (1993), the Supreme Court of Vermont was asked to consider whether the Vermont Constitution prohibited preventive detection. As you read the following excerpt from the Court's opinion, consider how it differs from the reasoning in *Salerno*.

* * * *

We share the trial court's concern for victims of crime and public safety, but our decision today must be guided by our constitution. Its bail provision, chapter II, § 40, provides in relevant part, "Excessive bail shall not be enacted for bailable offenses. All persons, unless sentenced, or unless committed for offenses punishable by death or life imprisonment when the evidence of guilt is great, shall be bailable by sufficient sureties. Persons committed for offenses punishable by death or life imprisonment, when the evidence of guilt is great, shall not be bailable as a matter of right."

In contrast, the federal guarantee is much more limited, providing only that "[e]xcessive bail shall not be required." U.S. Const.Amend. VIII; United States v. Salerno, 481 U.S. 739, 754, 107 S.Ct. 2095, 2105, 95 L.Ed.2d 697 (1987) (Eighth Amendment does not accord a right to bail in all cases; rather its "only arguable substantive limitation" is that "conditions of release or detention not be 'excessive' in light of the perceived evil"). The extra language in our bail statute is not mere surplusage. Rather, it explicitly guarantees bail as a matter of right to defendants not charged with offenses punishable by death or life imprisonment. Charges against defendant here—unlawful mischief, burglary, trespass—are not sufficient to deny him his fundamental right to bail. . . .

We have previously recognized the constitutional necessity of protecting our citizens from pretrial detention, which undermines the presumption of innocence by "depriv[ing] a defendant of a fundamental value, the right to liberty, without an adjudication of guilt." State v. Duff, 151 Vt. 433, 440, 563 A.2d 258, 263 (1989). Our constitutional values require that liberty is and must remain the norm and "'detention prior to trial or without trial is the carefully limited exception.'"

5. 📖 **Legal Research Note.** If you know the title and section number for a statute, locating the statute is very easy. Simply go to the U.S.C., U.S.C.A., or U.S.C.S. and look for the title number on the book's spine. Once you have

the proper volume, you can either look in the book's Table of Contents or thumb through the pages to look for the correct section.

For example, the statute at issue in *Salerno* (the Bail Reform Act of 1984) can be found at 18 U.S.C.A. § 3142. Go find it. Once you have turned to it, find the annotation from the 1995 case decided by the U.S. District Court for the Northern District of New York that held that a trial court could infer that a defendant would continue to sell narcotics if released from custody due to the large amount of cocaine involved in the charges against him. What is the case name and citation?

If you do not know whether a federal statute exists for a given topic, you should consult the appropriate statutory set's index. The U.S.C., the U.S.C.A., and the U.S.C.S. have indexes arranged alphabetically based on various subjects. To find a citation for a statute, you first need to determine the topic or topics under which it might be catalogued in the index. You can then look up the word in the index. If the index does not provide the citation for the statute under the heading you initially select, the cross-referencing systems used normally will refer you to a different heading that will allow you to locate the statute you are seeking.

For example, if you did not know where to find the Bail Reform Act of 1984, you might try searching in the U.S.C.A. Index under the heading "Bail." Do this. You should notice that nothing under this heading looks promising. However, the index does say, "see also, Detention." As this does sound promising, we should look there next. When we look under "Detention" we see an entry for "Pending judicial proceedings." This sounds like the right place, and if you go to the referenced citation of 18 U.S.C.A. § 3141, you will find that the statute is the Bail Reform Act of 1984.

PRELIMINARY HEARINGS

The preliminary hearing is a formal adversarial proceeding. Although it is not guaranteed by the Constitution, it is a statutory right in the federal and many state criminal justice systems.

The primary function of a preliminary hearing is to provide a court officer (judge or magistrate) an opportunity to determine whether there is sufficient evidence to bind a defendant over for trial. If the judge finds that there is probable cause to believe that the defendant committed the crime(s) for which he or she is charged, the defendant is bound over to the trial court for further proceedings. If the judge determines that probable cause does not exist, the case is dismissed, although charges may be refiled by the prosecution at a future time.

Many procedural aspects of a preliminary hearing are similar to a trial. Both proceedings are held in open court before a judge or magistrate. The defendant has a right to be present and, as we shall see, to be represented by counsel. Witnesses are called to testify, and the defendant has the right to cross-examination. Despite these procedural similarities, there are many differences between a preliminary hearing and a criminal trial.

One difference involves the type of evidence the parties are permitted to introduce. In most jurisdictions, hearsay evidence—that is, out-of-court statements made by a nontestifying person—is permitted in preliminary hearings. Absent a legally approved exception, hearsay evidence is not permitted at a trial. Additionally, in most jurisdictions, evidence that is illegally obtained is admissible at a preliminary hearing but not at a trial.

As noted above, the formal purpose of a preliminary hearing is to provide a court officer an opportunity to determine whether there is probable cause to believe the defendant committed the crimes of which she has been accused. In reality, it is very rare that probable cause is found to be lacking at a preliminary hearing. Despite this fact, defendants seldom waive their right to a preliminary hearing because they often recognize other benefits. These benefits, as well as the ramifications of being bound over for trial, are explained in *Coleman v. Alabama.*

Coleman v. Alabama, 399 U.S. 1, 90 S. Ct. 1999, 26 L. Ed. 2d 387 (1970)

Mr. Justice BRENNAN announced the judgment of the Court and delivered the following opinion.

Petitioners were convicted in an Alabama Circuit Court of assault with intent to murder in the shooting of one Reynolds after he and his wife parked their car on an Alabama highway to change a flat tire. The Alabama Court of Appeals affirmed, 44 Ala.App. 429, 211 So.2d 917 (1968), and the Alabama Supreme Court denied review, 282 Ala. 725, 211 So.2d 927 (1968). We granted certiorari, 394 U.S. 916, 89 S.Ct. 1200, 22 L.Ed.2d 450 (1969). We vacate and remand.

Petitioners . . . argue that the preliminary hearing prior to their indictment was a "critical stage" of the prosecution and that Alabama's failure to provide them with appointed counsel at the hearing therefore unconstitutionally denied them the assistance of counsel. . . .

II

This Court has held that a person accused of crime "requires the guiding hand of counsel at every step in the proceedings against him," Pow-ell v. Alabama, 287 U.S. 45, 69, 53 S.Ct. 55, 64, 77 L.Ed. 158 (1932), and that that constitutional principle is not limited to the presence of counsel at trial. "It is central to that principle that in addition to counsel's presence at trial, the accused is guaranteed that he need not stand alone against the State at any stage of the prosecution, formal or informal, in court or out, where counsel's absence might derogate from the accused's right to a fair trial."

Accordingly,

The principle of Powell v. Alabama and succeeding cases requires that we scrutinize any pretrial confrontation of the accused to determine whether the presence of his counsel is necessary to preserve the defendant's basic right to a fair trial as affected by his right meaningfully to cross-examine the witnesses against him and to have effective assistance of counsel at the trial itself. It calls upon us to analyze whether potential substantial prejudice to defendant's rights inheres in the particular confrontation and the ability of counsel to help avoid that prejudice.

Applying this test, the Court has held that "critical stages" include the pretrial type of arraignment where certain rights may be sacrificed or lost, and the pretrial lineup. . . .

The preliminary hearing is not a required step in an Alabama prosecution. The prosecutor may seek an indictment directly from the grand jury without a preliminary hearing. Ex parte Campbell, 278 Ala. 114, 176 So.2d 242 (1965). The opinion of the Alabama Court of Appeals in this case instructs us that under Alabama law the sole purposes of a preliminary hearing are to determine whether there is sufficient evidence against the accused to warrant presenting his case to the grand jury and, if so, to fix bail if the offense is bailable. 44 Ala.App., at 433, 211 So.2d, at 920. The court continued:

> At the preliminary hearing, the accused is not required to advance any defenses, and failure to do so does not preclude him from availing himself of every defense he may have upon the trial of the case. Also Pointer v. State of Texas (380 U.S. 400, 85 S.Ct. 1065, 13 L.Ed.2d 923 (1965)) bars the admission of testimony given at a pretrial proceeding where the accused did not have the benefit of cross-examination by and through counsel. Thus, nothing occurring at the preliminary hearing in absence of counsel can substantially prejudice the rights of the accused on trial. 44 Ala.App., at 433, 211 So.2d, at 921.

This Court is of course bound by this construction of the governing Alabama law. However, from the fact that in cases where the accused has no lawyer at the hearing the Alabama courts prohibit the State's use at trial of anything that occurred at the hearing, it does not follow that the Alabama preliminary hearing is not a "critical stage" of the State's criminal process. The determination whether the hearing is a "critical stage" requiring the provision of counsel depends, as noted, upon an analysis "whether potential substantial prejudice to defendant's rights inheres in the confrontation and the ability of counsel to help avoid that prej-

udice." Plainly the guiding hand of counsel at the preliminary hearing is essential to protect the indigent accused against an erroneous or improper prosecution. First, the lawyer's skilled examination and cross-examination of witnesses may expose fatal weaknesses in the State's case that may lead the magistrate to refuse to bind the accused over. Second, in any event, the skilled interrogation of witnesses by an experienced lawyer can fashion a vital impeachment tool for use in cross-examination of the State's witnesses at the trial, or preserve testimony favorable to the accused of a witness who does not appear at the trial. Third, trained counsel can more effectively discover the case the State has against his client and make possible the preparation of a proper defense to meet that case at the trial. Fourth, counsel can also be influential at the preliminary hearing in making effective arguments for the accused on such matters as the necessity for an early psychiatric examination or bail.

The inability of the indigent accused on his own to realize these advantages of a lawyer's assistance compels the conclusion that the Alabama preliminary hearing is a "critical stage" of the State's criminal process at which the accused is "as much entitled to such aid (of counsel) as at the trial itself." Powell v. Alabama, supra, 287 U.S. at 57, 53 S.Ct. at 60.

III

There remains, then, the question of the relief to which petitioners are entitled. The trial transcript indicates that the prohibition against use by the State at trial of anything that occurred at the preliminary hearing was scrupulously observed. But on the record it cannot be said whether or not petitioners were otherwise prejudiced by the absence of counsel at the preliminary hearing. That inquiry in the first instance should more properly be made by the Alabama courts. The test to be applied is whether the denial of counsel at the preliminary hearing was harmless error under Chapman v. California, 386 U.S. 18, 87 S.Ct. 824, 17 L.Ed.2d 705 (1967).

We accordingly vacate the petitioners' convictions and remand the case to the Alabama courts for such proceedings not inconsistent with this opinion as they may deem appropriate to determine whether such denial of counsel was harmless error, and therefore whether the convictions should be reinstated or a new trial ordered.

It is so ordered. . . .

Mr. Justice WHITE, concurring.

I agree with Mr. Justice HARLAN that recent cases furnish ample ground for holding the preliminary hearing a critical event in the progress of a criminal case. I therefore join the prevailing opinion, but with some hesitation since requiring the appointment of counsel may result in fewer preliminary hearings in jurisdictions where the prosecutor is free to avoid them by taking a case directly to a grand jury. Our ruling may also invite eliminating the preliminary hearing system entirely.

I would expect the application of the harmless-error standard on remand to produce results approximating those contemplated by Mr. Justice Harlan's separately stated views. Whether denying petitioners counsel at the preliminary hearing was harmless beyond a reasonable doubt depends upon an assessment of those factors that made the denial error. But that assessment cannot ignore the fact that petitioners have been tried and found guilty by a jury. . . .

Mr. Justice HARLAN, concurring in part and dissenting in part. . . .

It would indeed be strange were this Court, having held a suspect or an accused entitled to counsel at such pretrial stages as "in-custody" police investigation, whether at the station house (Miranda) or even in the home (Orozco), now to hold that he is left to fend for himself at the first formal confrontation in the courtroom.

While, given the cases referred to, I cannot escape the conclusion that petitioners' constitutional rights must be held to have been violated by denying them appointed counsel at the preliminary hearing, I consider the scope of the Court's remand too broad and amorphous. I do not think that reversal of these convictions, for lack of counsel at the preliminary hearing, should follow unless petitioners are able to show on remand that they have been prejudiced in their defense at trial, in that favorable testimony that might otherwise have been preserved was irretrievably lost by virtue of not having counsel to help present an affirmative case at the preliminary hearing. In this regard, of course, as with any other erroneously excluded testimony, petitioners would have to show that its weight at trial would have been such as to constitute its "exclusion" reversible error, as well as demonstrate the actual likelihood that such testimony could have been presented and preserved at the preliminary hearing. In my opinion mere speculation that defense counsel might have been able to do better at trial had he been present at the preliminary hearing should not suffice to vitiate a conviction. The Court's remand under the Chapman harmless-error rule seems to me to leave the way open for that sort of speculation. . . .

Notes and Questions

1. What benefits did the court identify in having an attorney represent the accused at a preliminary hearing? Do you think the Court justifies the added burden on the criminal justice system of having attorneys represent defendants at this early stage in the adjudication process?

GRAND JURY PROCEEDINGS

In the federal system and in the criminal justice systems of more than one third of the states, formal charges against a defendant must be brought by a grand jury. A grand jury is a group of citizens (12 or more depending on the state) who review evidence of alleged wrongdoing and determine whether there is sufficient evidence to bring criminal charges against an individual. Evidence is presented to the grand jury through the testimony of witnesses in response to questions posed by a prosecutor. If the grand jury determines (usually by a majority vote) that there is probable cause to believe that a person committed a crime, it returns a true bill of indictment. An indictment is a formal charging instrument that specifies the name of the defendant, the alleged crime, the date of the crime, and the acts that constitute the crime. The specific crimes that a defendant is alleged to have committed are listed in separate counts in the indictment.

Although indictment by grand jury currently is not the predominant method of initiating state criminal charges against a defendant, this was not always the case. At the time that the Bill of Rights was adopted, all of the states required that felony prosecutions be initiated by indictment. It is not surprising that the Bill of Rights contained a similar requirement for federal prosecutions. The Fifth Amendment provides that "no person shall be held to answer for a capital, or otherwise infamous crime, unless on a presentment or indictment of a Grand Jury."

Michigan became the first state to permit felony prosecutions without a grand jury indictment in 1859. Several states thereafter followed Michigan's lead. The constitutionality of state felony prosecutions being commenced by a prosecutor's information, without grand jury indictment, was considered by the United States Supreme Court well over a century ago in *Hurtado v. California*, 110 U.S. 516, 4 S. Ct. 111, 28 L. Ed. 232 (1884). The Court held that states

are not required to present charges to a grand jury in order to prosecute an individual. The justices reasoned that the process of "examination and commitment by a magistrate, certifying to the probable guilt of the defendant, with the right on his part to the aid of counsel, and to the cross-examination of the witnesses produced for the prosecution," was a reasonable alternative to the grand jury and did not violate the Fourteenth Amendment's due-process clause. The Court also confirmed that the Fifth Amendment's grand jury provisions do not directly apply to the states. Accordingly, states are permitted to initiate prosecutions through informations or preliminary hearings.

When a grand jury is used to initiate a prosecution, the federal Constitution and state constitutions require that certain procedural safeguards and substantive requirements be observed. These requirements concern (1) the composition of the grand jury and (2) the evidence that may be presented to and considered by the grand jury.

Composition of the Grand Jury

The grand jury is made up of citizens who reside within a specific jurisdiction. One important issue concerns how closely the members of the grand jury must reflect the racial or ethnic composition of the jurisdiction from which they are selected. The Supreme Court addressed this question in *Castaneda v. Partida*.

Castaneda v. Partida, 430 U.S. 482, 97 S. Ct. 1272, 51 L. Ed. 2d 498 (1977)

Mr. Justice BLACKMUN delivered the opinion of the Court.

The sole issue presented in this case is whether the State of Texas, in the person of petitioner, the Sheriff of Hidalgo County, successfully rebutted respondent prisoner's prima facie showing of discrimination against Mexican-Americans in the state grand jury selection process. In his brief, petitioner, in claiming effective rebuttal, asserts:

"This list (of the grand jurors that indicted respondent) indicates that 50 percent of the names appearing thereon were Spanish. The record indicates that 3 of the 5 jury commissioners, 5 of the grand jurors who returned the indictment, 7 of the petit jurors, the judge presiding at the trial, and the Sheriff who served notice on the grand jurors to appear had Spanish surnames."

I

This Court on prior occasions has considered the workings of the Texas system of grand jury selection. Texas employs the "key man" system, which relies on jury commissioners to select prospective grand jurors from the community at large. The procedure begins with the state district judge's appointment of from three to five persons to serve as jury commissioners. Tex.Code Crim.Proc., Art. 19.01 (1966). The commissioners then "shall select not less than 15 nor more than 20 persons from the citizens of different portions of the county" to compose the list from which the actual grand jury will be drawn. When at least 12 of the persons on the list appear in court pursuant to summons, the district judge proceeds to "test their qualifications." The qualifications themselves are set out in Art. 19.08: A grand juror must be a citizen of Texas and of the county, be a qualified voter in the county, be "of sound mind and good moral character," be literate, have no prior felony conviction, and be under no pending indictment or other legal accusation for theft or of any felony. Interrogation under oath is the method specified for testing the prospective juror's qualifications. The precise questions to be asked are set out in Art. 19.23, which, for the most part, tracks the language of Art. 19.08. After the court finds 12 jurors who meet the statutory qualifications, they are impaneled as the grand jury.

II

Respondent, Rodrigo Partida, was indicted in March 1972 by the grand jury of the 92d District Court of Hidalgo County for the crime of burglary of a private residence at night with intent to rape. Hidalgo is one of the border counties of southern Texas. After a trial before a petit jury, respondent was convicted and sentenced to eight years in the custody of the Texas Department of Corrections. He first raised his claim of discrimination in the grand jury selection process on a motion for new trial in the State District Court. In support of his motion, respondent testified about the general existence of discrimination against Mexican-Americans in that area of Texas and introduced statistics from the 1970 census and the Hidalgo County grand jury records. The census figures show that in 1970, the population of Hidalgo County was 181,535. Persons of Spanish language or Spanish surname totaled 143,611. On the assumption that all the persons of Spanish language or Spanish surname were Mexican-Americans, these figures show that 79.1% of the county's population was Mexican-American.

Respondent's data compiled from the Hidalgo County grand jury records from 1962 to 1972 showed that over that period, the average percentage of Spanish-surnamed grand jurors was 39%. In the 2½-year period during which the District Judge who impaneled the jury that indicted respondent was in charge, the average percentage was 45.5%. On the list from which the grand jury that indicted respondent was selected, 50% were Spanish surnamed. The last set of data that respondent introduced, again from the 1970 census, illustrated a number of ways in which Mexican-Americans tend to be underprivileged, including poverty-level incomes, less desirable jobs, substandard housing, and lower levels of education. The State offered no evidence at all either attacking respondent's allegations of discrimination or demonstrating that his statistics were unreliable in any way.

The State District Court, nevertheless, denied the motion for a new trial.

On appeal, the Texas Court of Criminal Appeals affirmed the conviction. Partida v. State, 506 S.W.2d 209 (1974). Reaching the merits of the claim of grand jury discrimination, the court held that respondent had failed to make out a prima facie case. In the court's view, he should have shown how many of the females who served on the grand juries were Mexican-Americans married to men with Anglo-American surnames, how many Mexican-Americans were excused for reasons of age or health, or other legal reasons, and how many of those listed by the census would not have met the statutory qualifications of citizenship, literacy, sound mind, moral character, and lack of criminal record or accusation. Quite beyond the uncertainties in the statistics, the court found it impossible to believe that discrimination could have been directed against a Mexican-American, in light of the many elective positions held by Mexican-Americans in the county and the substantial representation of Mexican-Americans on recent grand juries.[9] In essence, the court refused to presume that Mexican-Americans would discriminate against their own kind.

After exhausting his state remedies, respondent filed his petition for habeas corpus in the Federal District Court, alleging a denial of due process and equal protection, guaranteed by the Fourteenth Amendment, because of gross under-representation of Mexican-Americans on the Hidalgo County grand juries. . . .

[T]he court concluded that respondent had made out a "bare prima facie case" of invidious discrimination with his proof of "a long continued disproportion in the composition of the grand juries in Hidalgo County." Based on an examination of the reliability of the statistics offered by respondent, however, despite the lack of evidence in the record justifying such an inquiry, the court stated that the prima facie case was weak. The court believed that the census statistics did not reflect the true situation accurately, because of recent changes in the Hidalgo County area and the court's own impression of the demographic characteristics of the Mexican-American community. . . . On balance, the court's doubts about the reliability of the statistics, coupled with its opinion that Mexican-Americans constituted a "governing majority" in the county, caused it to conclude that the prima facie case was rebutted. . . .

The United States Court of Appeals for the Fifth Circuit reversed. 524 F.2d 481 (1975). It agreed with the District Court that respondent had succeeded in making out a prima facie case. It found, however, that the State had failed to rebut that showing. . . . In light of the State's abdication of its responsibility to introduce controverting evidence, the court held that respondent was entitled to prevail.

We granted certiorari to consider whether the existence of a "governing majority" in itself can

---

9. The court noted that the foreman of the grand jury that indicted respondent was Mexican-American, and that 10 of the 20 summoned to serve had Spanish surnames. Seven of the 12 members of the petit jury that convicted him were Mexican-American. In addition, the state judge who presided over the trial was Mexican-American, as were a number of other elected officials in the county.

rebut a prima facie case of discrimination in grand jury selection, and, if not, whether the State otherwise met its burden of proof.

III

A. This Court has long recognized that "it is a denial of the equal protection of the laws to try a defendant of a particular race or color under an indictment issued by a grand jury . . . from which all persons of his race or color have, solely because of that race or color, been excluded by the State. . . ." While the earlier cases involved absolute exclusion of an identifiable group, later cases established the principle that substantial under-representation of the group constitutes a constitutional violation as well, if it results from purposeful discrimination. Recent cases have established the fact that an official act is not unconstitutional solely because it has a racially disproportionate impact. Nevertheless, as the Court [has] recognized . . . "(s)ometimes a clear pattern, unexplainable on grounds other than race, emerges from the effect of the state action even when the governing legislation appears neutral on its face." In Washington v. Davis, the application of these principles to the jury cases was considered:

> It is also clear from the cases dealing with racial discrimination in the selection of juries that the systematic exclusion of Negroes is itself such an "unequal application of the law . . . as to show intentional discrimination." . . . A prima facie case of discriminatory purpose may be proved as well by the absence of Negroes on a particular jury combined with the failure of the jury commissioners to be informed of eligible Negro jurors in a community, . . . or with racially non-neutral selection procedures. . . . With a prima facie case made out, "the burden of proof shifts to the State to rebut the presumption of unconstitutional action by showing that permissible racially neutral selection criteria and procedures have produced the monochromatic result."

Thus, in order to show that an equal protection violation has occurred in the context of grand jury selection, the defendant must show that the procedure employed resulted in substantial under-representation of his race or of the identifiable group to which he belongs. The first step is to establish that the group is one that is a recognizable, distinct class, singled out for different treatment under the laws, as written or as applied. Next, the degree of under-representation must be proved, by comparing the proportion of the group in the total population to the proportion called to serve as grand jurors, over a significant period of time. This method of proof, sometimes called the "rule of exclusion," has been held to be available as a method of proving discrimination in jury selection against a delineated class.[13] Finally, as noted above, a selection procedure that is susceptible of abuse or is not racially neutral supports the presumption of discrimination raised by the statistical showing. Once the defendant has shown substantial under-representation of his group, he has made out a prima facie case of discriminatory purpose, and the burden then shifts to the State to rebut that case.

B. In this case, it is no longer open to dispute that Mexican-Americans are a clearly identifiable class. The statistics introduced by respondent from the 1970 census illustrate disadvantages to which the group has been subject. Additionally, as in Alexander v. Louisiana, the selection procedure is not racially neutral with respect to Mexican-Americans; Spanish surnames are just as easily identifiable as race was from the questionnaires in Alexander or the notations and card colors in Whitus v. Georgia, and in Avery v. Georgia.

The disparity proved by the 1970 census statistics showed that the population of the county was 79.1% Mexican-American, but that, over an 11-year period, only 39% of the persons summoned for grand jury service were Mexican-American. This difference of 40% is greater than that found significant in Turner v. Fouche, 396 U.S. 346, 90 S.Ct. 532, 24 L.Ed.2d 567 (1970) (60% Negroes in the general population, 37% on

the grand jury lists). Since the State presented no evidence showing why the 11-year period was not reliable, we take it as the relevant base for comparison. The mathematical disparities that have been accepted by this Court as adequate for a prima facie case have all been within the range presented here. For example, in Whitus v. Georgia, 385 U.S. 545, 87 S.Ct. 643, 17 L.Ed.2d 599 (1967), the number of Negroes listed on the tax digest amounted to 27.1% of the taxpayers, but only 9.1% of those on the grand jury venire. The disparity was held to be sufficient to make out a prima facie case of discrimination. See Sims v. Georgia, 389 U.S. 404, 88 S.Ct. 523, 19 L.Ed.2d 634 (1967) (24.4% of tax lists, 4.7% of grand jury lists); Jones v. Georgia, 389 U.S. 24, 88 S.Ct. 4, 19 L.Ed.2d 25 (1967) (19.7% of tax lists, 5% of jury list). We agree with the District Court and the Court of Appeals that the proof in this case was enough to establish a prima facie case of discrimination against the Mexican-Americans in the Hidalgo County grand jury selection.

Supporting this conclusion is the fact that the Texas system of selecting grand jurors is highly subjective. The facial constitutionality of the key-man system, of course, has been accepted by this Court. Nevertheless, the Court has noted that the system is susceptible of abuse as applied.[18] Additionally, as noted, persons with Spanish surnames are readily identifiable.

The showing made by respondent therefore shifted the burden of proof to the State to dispel the inference of intentional discrimination. Inexplicably, the State introduced practically no evidence. The testimony of the State District Judge dealt principally with the selection of the jury commissioners and the instructions given to them. The commissioners themselves were not called to testify. . . . The opinion of the Texas Court of Criminal Appeals is particularly revealing as to the lack of rebuttal evidence in the record:

How many of those listed in the census figures with Mexican-American names were

---

13. The idea behind the rule of exclusion is not at all complex. If a disparity is sufficiently large, then it is unlikely that it is due solely to chance or accident, and, in the absence of evidence to the contrary, one must conclude that racial or other class-related factors entered into the section process.

18. It has been said that random selection methods similar to the federal system would probably avoid most of the potential for abuse found in the key-man system.

not citizens of the state, but were so-called "wet-backs" from the south side of the Rio Grande; how many were migrant workers and not residents of Hidalgo County; how many were illiterate and could not read and write; how many were not of sound mind and good moral character, how many had been convicted of a felony or were under indictment or legal accusation for theft or a felony; none of these facts appear in the record. 506 S.W.2d, at 211.

In fact, the census figures showed that only a small part of the population reported for Hidalgo County was not native born. Without some testimony from the grand jury commissioners about the method by which they determined the other qualifications for grand jurors prior to the statutory time for testing qualifications, it is impossible to draw any inference about literacy, sound mind and moral character, and criminal record from the statistics about the population as a whole. These are questions of disputed fact that present problems not amenable to resolution by an appellate court. We emphasize, however, that we are not saying that the statistical disparities proved here could never be explained in another case; we are simply saying that the State did not do so in this case.

C. In light of our holding that respondent proved a prima facie case of discrimination that was not rebutted by any of the evidence presently in the record, we have only to consider whether the District Court's "governing majority" theory filled the evidentiary gap. In our view, it did not dispel the presumption of purposeful discrimination in the circumstances of this case. Because of the many facets of human motivation, it would be unwise to presume as a matter of law that human beings of one definable group will not discriminate against other members of their group. . . .

IV

Rather than relying on an approach to the jury discrimination question that is as faintly defined as the "governing majority" theory is on this record, we prefer to look at all the facts that bear on the issue, such as the statistical disparities, the method of selection, and any other relevant

testimony as to the manner in which the selection process was implemented. Under this standard, the proof offered by respondent was sufficient to demonstrate a prima facie case of discrimination in grand jury selection. Since the State failed to rebut the presumption of purposeful discrimination by competent testimony, despite two opportunities to do so, we affirm the Court of Appeals' holding of a denial of equal protection of the law in the grand jury selection process in respondent's case. . . .

Mr. Justice MARSHALL, concurring.

I join fully Mr. Justice BLACKMUN's sensitive opinion for the Court. I feel compelled to write separately, however, to express my profound disagreement with the views expressed by Mr. Justice POWELL in his dissent.

As my Brother POWELL observes, there are three categories of evidence in this case that bear on the ultimate question whether respondent "demonstrated by a preponderance of the evidence that the State had deliberately and systematically den[ied] to members of [respondent's class] the right to participate as jurors in the administration of justice." First, there is the statistical evidence. That evidence reveals that for at least 10 years, Mexican-Americans have been grossly under-represented on grand juries in Hidalgo County. As Mr. Justice BLACKMUN demonstrates, it is all but impossible that this sizable disparity was produced by chance. The statistical evidence, then, at the very least supports an inference that Mexican-Americans were discriminated against in the choice of grand jurors.

Second, there is testimony concerning the grand jury selection system employed in this case. That testimony indicates that the commissioners who constructed the grand jury panels had ample opportunity to discriminate against Mexican-Americans, since the selection system is entirely discretionary and since Spanish-surnamed persons are readily identified. Indeed, for over 35 years this Court has recognized the potential for abuse inherent in the Texas grand jury selection plan. Thus the testimony concerning the selection system, by itself, only buttresses the inference of purposeful discrimination suggested by the statistics.

In every other case of which I am aware where the evidence showed both statistical disparity and discretionary selection procedures, this Court has found that a prima facie case of discrimination was established, and has required the State to explain how ostensibly neutral selection procedures had produced such nonneutral results. . . . Yet my Brother POWELL would have us conclude that the evidence here was insufficient to establish purposeful discrimination, even though no explanation has been offered for the marked under-representation of Mexican-Americans on Hidalgo County grand juries. . . .

The sole basis for Mr. Justice POWELL's conclusion lies in the third category of evidence presented: proof of "the political dominance and control by the Mexican-American majority in Hidalgo County." Like the District Court, he appears to assume without any basis in the record that all Mexican-Americans, indeed all members of all minority groups have an "inclination to assure fairness" to other members of their group. Although he concedes the possibility that minority group members will violate this "inclination," he apparently regards this possibility as more theoretical than real. Thus he would reject the inference of purposeful discrimination here absent any alternative explanation for the disparate results. I emphatically disagree.

In the first place, Mr. Justice POWELL's assumptions about human nature, plausible as they may sound, fly in the face of a great deal of social science theory and research. Social scientists agree that members of minority groups frequently respond to discrimination and prejudice by attempting to disassociate themselves from the group, even to the point of adopting the majority's negative attitudes towards the minority. Such behavior occurs with particular frequency among members of minority groups who have achieved some measure of economic or political success and thereby have gained some acceptability among the dominant group.

But even if my Brother POWELL's behavioral assumptions were more valid, I still could not agree to making them the foundation for a constitutional ruling. It seems to me that especially in reviewing claims of intentional discrimination, this Court has a solemn responsibility to avoid basing its decisions on broad generalizations concerning minority groups. If history has taught us anything, it is the danger of relying on such stereotypes. The question for decision here is not how Mexican-Americans treat other Mexican-Americans, but how the particular grand jury commissioners in Hidalgo County acted. The only reliable way to answer that question, as we have said so many times, is for the State to produce testimony concerning the manner in which the selection process operated. Because the State failed to do so after respondent established a prima facie case of discrimination, I join the Court's opinion affirming the Court of Appeals.

Mr. Chief Justice BURGER, with whom Mr. Justice POWELL and Mr. Justice REHNQUIST join, dissenting.

In addition to the views expressed in Mr. Justice POWELL's dissent, I identify one other flaw in the Court's opinion. What the majority characterizes as a prima facie case of discrimination simply will not "wash." The decisions of this Court suggest, and common sense demands, that eligible population statistics, not gross population figures, provide the relevant starting point. . . .

The failure to produce evidence relating to the eligible population in Hidalgo County undermines respondent's claim that any statistical "disparity" existed in the first instance. Particularly where, as here, substantial numbers of members of the identifiable class actually served on grand jury panels, the burden rightly rests upon the challenger to show a meaningful statistical disparity. After all, the presumption of constitutionality attaching to all state procedures has even greater force under the circumstances presented here, where exactly one-half the members of the grand jury list now challenged by respondent were members of the allegedly excluded class of Mexican-Americans.

The Court has not previously been called upon to deal at length with the sort of statistics required of persons challenging a grand jury selection system. The reason is that in our prior cases there was little doubt that members of identifiable minority groups had been excluded in large numbers. In Alexander v. Louisiana, supra, the challenger's venire included only one member of the identifiable class and the grand jury that indicted him had none. In [other cases] there was at best only token inclusion of Negroes on grand jury lists. The case before us, in contrast, involves neither tokenism nor absolute exclusion; rather, the State has used a selection system resulting in the inclusion of large numbers of Spanish-surnamed citizens on grand jury lists. In this situation, it is particularly incumbent on respondent to adduce precise statistics demonstrating a significant disparity. To do that, respondent was obligated to demonstrate that disproportionately large numbers of eligible individuals were excluded systematically from grand jury service.

Respondent offered no evidence whatever in this respect. He therefore could not have established any meaningful case of discrimination, prima facie or otherwise. In contrast to respondent's approach, which the Court's opinion accepts without analysis, the Census Bureau's statistics for 1970 demonstrate that of the adults in Hidalgo County, 72%, not 79.1% as respondent implies, are Spanish surnamed. At the onset, therefore, respondent's gross population figures are manifestly over-inclusive.

But that is only the beginning. Respondent offered no evidence whatever with respect to other basic qualifications for grand jury service. The statistics relied on in the Court's opinion suggest that 22.9% of Spanish-surnamed persons over age 25 in Hidalgo County have had no schooling at all. Since one requirement of grand jurors in Texas is literacy in the English language, approximately 20% of adult-age Mexican-Americans are very likely disqualified on that ground alone.

The Court's reliance on respondent's overbroad statistics is not the sole defect. As previously noted, one-half of the members of respondent's grand jury list bore Mexican-American surnames. Other grand jury lists at about the same time as respondent's indictment in March 1972 were predominantly Mexican-American. Thus, with respect to the September 1971 grand jury list, 70% of the prospective grand jurors were Mexican-American. In the January 1972 Term, 55% were Mexican-American. Since respondent was indicted in 1972, by what appears to have been a truly representative grand jury, the mechanical use of Hidalgo County's practices some 10 years earlier seems to me entirely indefensible. We do not know, and on this record we cannot know, whether respondent's 1970 gross population figures, which served as the basis for establishing the "disparity" complained of in this case, had any applicability at all to the period prior to 1970. Accordingly, for all we know, the 1970

figures may be totally inaccurate as to prior years; if so, the apparent disparity alleged by respondent would be increased improperly.

Therefore, I disagree both with the Court's assumption that respondent established a prima facie case and with the Court's implicit approval of respondent's method for showing an allegedly disproportionate impact of Hidalgo County's selection system upon Mexican-Americans. . . .

Mr. Justice POWELL, with whom THE CHIEF JUSTICE and Mr. Justice REHNQUIST join, dissenting.

The evidence relevant to the issue of discrimination in this case falls into three categories: First, the statistical evidence introduced by respondent in both the state and federal proceedings which shows that the 80% Mexican-American majority in Hidalgo County was not proportionately represented on the grand jury lists; second, the testimony of the state trial judge outlining the Texas grand jury selection system as it operated in this case; and third, the facts judicially noticed by the District Court with respect to the political dominance and control by the Mexican-American majority in Hidalgo County.

The Court today considers it dispositive that the lack of proportional representation of Mexican-Americans on the grand jury lists in this county would not have occurred if jurors were selected from the population wholly at random. But one may agree that the disproportion did not occur by chance without agreeing that it resulted from purposeful invidious discrimination. In my view, the circumstances of this unique case fully support the District Court's finding that the statistical disparity that is the basis of today's decision is more likely to have stemmed from neutral causes than from any intent to discriminate against Mexican-Americans.

A

The Court holds that a criminal defendant may demonstrate a violation of the Equal Protection Clause merely by showing that the procedure for selecting grand jurors "resulted in substantial under-representation of his race or of the identifiable group to which he belongs." By so holding, the Court blurs the traditional constitutional distinctions between grand and petit juries, and misapplies the equal protection analysis mandated by our most recent decisions.

The Fifth Amendment right to a grand jury does not apply to a state prosecution. Hurtado v.

California, 110 U.S. 516, 4 S.Ct. 111, 28 L.Ed. 232 (1884). A state defendant cannot complain if the State forgoes the institution of the grand jury and proceeds against him instead through prosecutorial information, as many States prefer to do. See Gerstein v. Pugh, 420 U.S. 103, 116–119, 95 S.Ct. 854, 864–865, 43 L.Ed.2d 54 (1975). Nevertheless, if a State chooses to proceed by grand jury it must proceed within the constraints imposed by the Equal Protection Clause of the Fourteenth Amendment. Thus in a line of cases beginning with Strauder v. West Virginia, 100 U.S. 303, 25 L.Ed. 664 (1880), this Court has held that a criminal defendant is denied equal protection of the law if, as a result of purposeful discrimination, members of his own race are excluded from jury service. As the Court points out, this right is applicable where purposeful discrimination results only in substantial rather than total exclusion of members of the defendant's class. But a state defendant has no right to a grand jury that reflects a fair cross-section of the community.[2] The right to a "representative" grand jury is a federal right that derives not from the requirement of equal protection but from the Fifth Amendment's explicit requirement of a grand jury. That right is similar to the right applicable to state proceedings to a representative petit jury under the Sixth Amendment. See Taylor v. Louisiana, 419 U.S. 522, 95 S.Ct. 692, 42 L.Ed.2d 690 (1975). To the extent that the Fifth and Sixth Amendments are applicable, a defendant need only show that the jury selection procedure "systematically exclude[s] distinctive groups in the community and thereby fail[s] to be reasonably representative thereof." But in a state case in which the challenge is to the grand jury, only the Fourteenth Amendment applies, and the defendant has the burden of proving a violation of the Equal Protection Clause.

Proof of discriminatory intent in such a case was explicitly mandated in our recent decisions in Washington v. Davis, 426 U.S. 229, 96 S.Ct. 2040, 48 L.Ed.2d 597 (1976), and Arlington Heights v. Metropolitan Housing Dev. Corp., 429 U.S. 252, 97 S.Ct. 555, 50 L.Ed.2d 450 (1977). In Arlington Heights we said:

> Our decision last Term in Washington v. Davis, 426 U.S. 229, 96 S.Ct. 2040, 48 L.Ed.2d 597 (1976), made it clear that official action will not be held unconstitutional solely because it results in a racially disproportionate impact. "Disproportionate impact is not irrelevant, but it is not the sole touchstone of an invidious racial discrimination." . . . Proof of a racially discriminatory intent or purpose is required to show a violation of the Equal Protection Clause. . . ."

We also identified the following standards for resolving issues of discriminatory intent or purpose:

> Determining whether invidious discriminatory purpose was a motivating factor demands a sensitive inquiry into such circumstantial and direct evidence of intent as may be available. The impact of the official action whether it "bears more heavily on one race than another,'" may provide an important starting point. Sometimes a clear pattern, unexplainable on grounds other than race, emerges from the effect of the state action even when the governing legislation appears neutral on its face. Yick Wo v. Hopkins, 118 U.S. 356, 6 S.Ct. 1064, 30 L.Ed. 220 (1886); Gomillion v. Lightfoot, 364 U.S. 339, 81 S.Ct. 125, 5 L.Ed.2d 110 (1960). The evidentiary inquiry is then relatively easy. But such cases are rare. Absent a pattern as stark as that in Gomillion or Yick Wo, impact alone is not determinative, and the Court must look to other evidence.

The analysis is essentially the same where the alleged discrimination is in the selection of a state

---

2. It may be that nondiscriminatory methods of selection will, over time, result in a representative grand jury. But the Fourteenth Amendment does not mandate that result. Nothing would prevent a State for example, from seeking to assure informed decision making by requiring that all grand jurors be lawyers familiar with the criminal law; and if that requirement should result in substantial under-representation on grand juries of some segments of the community in some areas of the State, the Fourteenth Amendment would not render the selection process unconstitutional.

grand jury. This is illustrated by the recent decision in Alexander v. Louisiana, supra, where we stated:

> This Court has never announced mathematical standards for the demonstration of "systematic" exclusion of blacks but has, rather, emphasized that a factual inquiry is necessary in each case that takes into account all possible explanatory factors. The progressive decimation of potential Negro grand jurors is indeed striking here, but we do not rest our conclusion that petitioner has demonstrated a prima facie case of invidious racial discrimination on statistical improbability alone, for the selection procedures themselves were not racially neutral. . . .

In Alexander, the evidence showed that 21% of the relevant community was Negro; the jury commission consisted of five members "all of whom were white," appointed by a white judge; the grand jury venire included 20 persons, only one of whom was a Negro (5%); and none of the 12 persons on the grand jury that indicted the defendant was Negro. This statistical array was as the Court noted "striking." Yet the statistics were not found, in isolation, to constitute a prima facie case. Only after determining that the selection system "provided a clear and easy opportunity for racial discrimination" was the Court satisfied that the burden should shift to the State.[4]

Apart from Alexander and Turner, this Court has sustained claims of grand jury discrimination in two situations. Most of the cases involve total exclusion of minorities from participation on grand juries. . . . The remainder of the cases involve severe limitation of a minority's participation by token inclusion. . . .

Considered together, Davis, Arlington Heights, and Alexander make clear that statistical evidence showing under-representation of a population group on the grand jury lists should be considered in light of "such (other) circumstantial and direct evidence of intent as may be available."

B

In this case, the following critical facts are beyond dispute: the judge who appointed the jury commissioners and later presided over respondent's trial was Mexican-American; three of the five jury commissioners were Mexican-American; 10 of the 20 members of the grand jury array were Mexican-American; 5 of the 12 grand jurors who returned the indictment, including the foreman, were Mexican-American, and 7 of the 12 petit jurors who returned the verdict of guilt were Mexican-American. In the year in which respondent was indicted, 52.5% of the persons on the grand jury list were Mexican-American. In addition, a majority of the elected officials in Hidalgo County were Mexican-American, as were a majority of the judges. That these positions of power and influence were so held is not surprising in a community where 80% of the population is Mexican-American. As was emphasized by District Judge Garza, the able Mexican-American jurist who presided over the habeas proceedings in the District Court, this case is unique. Every other jury discrimination case reaching this Court has involved a situation where the governing majority, and the resulting power over the jury selection process, was held by a white electorate and white officials.[6]

---

4. The Court's reliance on the "opportunity for discrimination" noted in Alexander is clearly misplaced. The Court has held repeatedly that the Texas system of selecting grand jurors by the use of jury commissioners is "fair on its face and capable of being utilized without discrimination." The "subjectivity" of the selection system cuts in favor of the State where, as here, those who control the selection process are members of the same class as the person claiming discrimination.

6. I do not suggest, of course, that the mere fact that Mexican-Americans constitute a majority in Hidalgo County is dispositive. There are many communities in which, by virtue of historical or other reasons, a majority of the population may not be able at a particular time to control or significantly influence political decisions or the way the system operates. But no one can contend seriously that Hidalgo County is such a community. The classic situation in which a "minority group" may suffer discrimination in a community is where it is "relegated to. . . a position of political powerlessness." Here the Mexican-Americans are not politically "powerless"; they are the majoritarian political element of the community, with demonstrated capability to elect and protect their own.

Nor do I suggest that persons in positions of power can never be shown to have discriminated against other members of the same ethnic or racial group. I would hold only that respondent's statistical evidence, without more, is insufficient to prove a claim of discrimination in this case.

The most significant fact in this case, all but ignored in the Court's opinion, is that a majority of the jury commissioners were Mexican-American. The jury commission is the body vested by Texas law with the authority to select grand jurors. . . . As Judge Garza observed: "If people in charge can choose whom they want, it is unlikely they will discriminate against themselves." 384 F.Supp. 79, 90.

That individuals are more likely to discriminate in favor of, than against, those who share their own identifiable attributes is the premise that underlies the cases recognizing that the criminal defendant has a personal right under the Fourteenth Amendment not to have members of his own class excluded from jury service. Discriminatory exclusion of members of the defendant's class has been viewed as unfairly excluding persons who may be inclined to favor the defendant. Were it not for the perceived likelihood that jurors will favor defendants of their own class, there would be no reason to suppose that a jury selection process that systematically excluded persons of a certain race would be the basis of any legitimate complaint by criminal defendants of that race. Only the individuals excluded from jury service would have a personal right to complain.

In Akins v. Texas, where apparently no Negro was on the jury commission and only 1 of 16 was on the jury panel, the Court emphasized the high threshold of proof required to brand officers of the court with discriminatory intent:

An allegation of discriminatory practices in selecting a grand jury panel challenges an essential element of proper judicial procedure; the requirement of fairness on the part of the judicial arm of government in dealing with persons charged with criminal offenses. It cannot lightly be concluded that officers of the courts disregard this accepted standard of justice.

With all respect, I am compelled to say that the Court today has "lightly" concluded that the grand jury commissioners of this county have disregarded not only their sworn duty but also their likely inclination to assure fairness to Mexican-Americans.

It matters little in this case whether such judicially noticeable facts as the composition of the grand jury commission are viewed as defeating respondent's prima facie case at the outset or as rebutting it after it was established by statistical evidence. The significance of the prima facie case is limited to its effect in shifting the burden of going forward to the State. Once the State has produced evidence either by presenting proof or by calling attention to facts subject to judicial notice the only question is whether the evidence in the record is sufficient to demonstrate deliberate and systematic discrimination in the jury selection process.

Here, respondent produced statistics showing that Mexican-Americans while substantially represented on the grand jury lists were not represented in numbers proportionate to their share of the total population. The State responded by presenting the testimony of the judge who appointed the grand jury commissioners. Other facts, such as the presence of Mexican-Americans in a majority of the elective positions of the county, entered the record through judicial notice. The testimony, together with the facts noted by the District Court, sufficed to satisfy the State's burden of production even assuming that respondent's evidence was sufficient to give rise to such a burden. Accordingly, at the close of the evidence, the question for the District Court was whether respondent had demonstrated by a preponderance of the evidence that the State had "deliberately and systematically den[ied] to members of [respondent's class] the right to participate as jurors in the administration of justice." The District Court found that the judge and jury commissioners had not intentionally discriminated against Mexican-Americans. . . .

The Court labels it "inexplicable" that the State introduced only the testimony of the state trial judge. Perhaps the State fairly may be faulted for not presenting more evidence than it did. But until today's decision one may doubt whether many lawyers, familiar with our cases, would have thought that respondent's statistics, under the circumstances of this case and prevailing in Hidalgo County, were even arguably sufficient to establish deliberate and systematic discrimination.

There is for me a sense of unreality when Justices here in Washington decide solely on the basis of inferences from statistics that the Mexican-Americans who control the levers of power in this remote border county are manipulating them to discriminate "against themselves." In contrast, the judges on the scene, the state judge who appointed the jury commissioners and presided over respondent's trial and the United States District Judge, both Mexican-Americans and familiar with the community, perceived no basis for respondent's claim of invidious discrimination.

It seems to me that the Court today, in rejecting the District Court's finding that no such discrimination took place, has erred grievously. I would reinstate the judgment of the District Court.

Notes and Questions

1. Was there any evidence that Mexican-Americans were intentionally discriminated against in the grand jury selection process? Why is this issue important to the Court's decision in *Castaneda*?

2. Do Justice Blackmun's majority opinion and Justice Powell's dissent use the same test to determine whether there was an equal-protection violation in *Castaneda*? Does it seem odd to you that the two opinions reached such different conclusions?

3. 📖 **Legal Research Note.** Let's put the legal research skills described in this chapter to work. Use the U.S.C.A. Index to find the federal statute that states the qualifications for service as a grand juror. What is the citation?

Refer to the annotations accompanying this statute. Provide the name and citation of the case that discusses whether minors should be considered in determining if an identified group was underrepresented on a grand jury. What does the blurb or squib indicate that the case held? Finally, you should *Shepardize* the case to make sure it remains good law.

Evidence Presented to the Grand Jury

Evidence is presented to the grand jury in a nonadversarial proceeding. Only the grand jurors, the prosecutor, the testifying witness, and a court stenographer are present when testimony is offered. The accused is not entitled to question witnesses or be present when they testify.

The Supreme Court has ruled that testimony that would not be admissible at trial may be presented to the grand jury. In *Costello v. United States*, the Court discussed the rationale behind this policy.

Costello v. United States, 350 U.S. 359, 76 S. Ct. 406, 100 L. Ed. 397 (1956)

Mr. Justice BLACK delivered the opinion of the Court.

We granted certiorari in this case to consider a single question: "May a defendant be required to stand trial and a conviction be sustained where only hearsay evidence was presented to the grand jury which indicted him?"

Petitioner, Frank Costello, was indicted for wilfully attempting to evade payment of income taxes due the United States for the years 1947, 1948 and 1949. The charge was that petitioner falsely and fraudulently reported less income than he and his wife actually received during the taxable years in question. . . . At . . . trial . . . the Government offered evidence designed to show increases in Costello's net worth in an attempt to prove that he had received more income during the years in question than he had reported. To establish its case the Government called and examined 144 witnesses and introduced 368 exhibits. All of the testimony and documents related to business transactions and expenditures by petitioner and his wife.

The prosecution concluded its case by calling three government agents. Their investigations had produced the evidence used against petitioner at the trial. They were allowed to summarize the vast amount of evidence already heard and to introduce computations showing, if correct, that petitioner and his wife had received far greater income than they had reported. . . .

Counsel for petitioner asked each government witness at the trial whether he had appeared before the grand jury which returned the indictment. This cross-examination developed the fact that the three investigating officers had been the only witnesses before the grand jury. After the Government concluded its case, petitioner . . . moved to dismiss the indictment on the ground that the only evidence before the grand jury was "hearsay," since the three officers had no first-hand knowledge of the transactions upon which their computations were based. Nevertheless the trial court again refused to dismiss the indictment, and petitioner was convicted. The Court of Appeals affirmed, holding that the indictment was valid even though the sole evidence before the grand jury was hearsay. Petitioner here urges: (1) that an indictment based solely on hearsay evidence violates that part of the Fifth Amendment providing that "No person shall be held to answer for a capital, or otherwise infamous crime, unless on a presentment or indictment of a Grand Jury" and (2) that if the Fifth Amendment does not invalidate an indictment based solely on hearsay we should now lay down such a rule for the guidance of federal courts.

The Fifth Amendment provides that federal prosecutions for capital or otherwise infamous crimes must be instituted by presentments or indictments of grand juries. But neither the Fifth Amendment nor any other constitutional provision prescribes the kind of evidence upon which grand juries must act. The grand jury is an English institution, brought to this country by the early colonists and incorporated in the Constitution by the Founders. There is every reason to believe that our constitutional grand jury was intended to operate substantially like its English progenitor. The basic purpose of the English grand jury was to provide a fair method for instituting criminal proceedings against persons believed to have committed crimes. Grand jurors were selected from the body of the people and their work was not hampered by rigid procedural or evidential rules. In fact, grand jurors could act on their own knowledge and were free to make their presentments or indictments on such information as they deemed satisfactory. Despite its broad power to institute criminal proceedings the grand jury grew in popular favor with the years. It acquired an independence in England free from control by the Crown or judges. Its adoption in our Constitution as the sole method for preferring charges in serious criminal cases shows the high place it held as an instrument of justice. And in this country as in England of old the grand jury has convened as a body of laymen, free from technical rules, acting in secret, pledged to indict no one because of prejudice and to free no one because of special favor. . . . [I]n 1852 Mr. Justice Nelson on circuit could say "No case has been cited, nor have we been able to find any, furnishing an authority for looking into and revising the judgment of the grand jury upon the evidence, for the purpose of determining whether or not the finding was founded upon sufficient proof." United States v. Reed, 27 Fed.Cas. 727, 738, No. 16,134.

In Holt v. United States, 218 U.S. 245, 31 S.Ct. 2, 4, 54 L.Ed. 1021, this Court had to decide whether an indictment should be quashed because supported in part by incompetent evidence. Aside from the incompetent evidence "there was very little evidence against the accused." The Court refused to hold that such an indictment should be quashed, pointing out that "The abuses of criminal practice would be enhanced if indictments could be upset on such a ground." 218 U.S. at page 248, 31 S.Ct. at page 4. The same thing is true where as here all the evidence before the grand jury was in the nature of "hearsay." If indictments were to be held open to challenge on the ground that there was inadequate or incompetent evidence before the grand jury, the resulting delay would be great indeed. The result of such a rule would be that before trial on the merits a defendant could always insist on a kind of preliminary trial to determine the competency and adequacy of the evidence before the grand jury. This is not required by the Fifth Amendment.

An indictment returned by a legally constituted and unbiased grand jury, like an information drawn by the prosecutor, if valid on its face, is enough to call for trial of the charge on the merits. The Fifth Amendment requires nothing more.

Petitioner urges that this Court should exercise its power to supervise the administration of justice in federal courts and establish a rule permitting defendants to challenge indictments on the ground that they are not supported by adequate or competent evidence. No persuasive reasons are advanced for establishing such a rule. It would run counter to the whole history of the grand jury institution, in which laymen conduct their inquiries unfettered by technical rules. Neither justice nor the concept of a fair trial requires such a change. In a trial on the merits, defendants are entitled to a strict observance of all the rules designed to bring about a fair verdict. Defendants are not entitled, however, to a rule which would result in interminable delay but add nothing to the assurance of a fair trial.

Affirmed. . . .

Notes and Questions

1. Does the decision in *Costello* seem more concerned with the threat of "interminable delay" than protecting the rights of a suspected felon? Is there anything wrong with this? Is there a better way to strike an appropriate balance between these interests?

2. Should all evidence be permitted to be presented to a grand jury? What about evidence obtained through coercion? Through an illegal search? Through an illegal lineup? In *United States v. Calandra*, 414 U.S. 338, 94 S. Ct. 613, 38 L. Ed. 2d 561 (1974), the Supreme Court considered whether it was permissible to present evidence seized in violation of a suspect's Fourth Amendment rights to a grand jury. Writing for a six-member majority, Justice Powell stated:

In deciding whether to extend the exclusionary rule to grand jury proceedings, we must weigh the potential injury to the historic role and functions of the grand jury against the potential benefits of the rule as applied in this context. It is evident that this extension of the exclusionary rule would seriously impede the grand jury. Because the grand jury does not finally adjudicate guilt or innocence, it has traditionally been allowed to pursue its investigative and accusatorial functions unimpeded by the evidentiary and procedural restrictions applicable to a criminal trial. Permitting [the invocation] of the exclusionary rule before a grand jury would precipitate adjudication of issues hitherto reserved for the trial on the merits and would delay and disrupt grand jury proceedings. . . .

[On the other hand], any incremental deterrent effect which might be achieved by extending the rule to grand jury proceedings is uncertain at best. . . . The incentive to disregard the requirement of the Fourth Amendment solely to obtain an indictment from a grand jury is substantially negated by the inadmissability of the illegally seized evidence in a subsequent criminal prosecution of the search victim.

The Court concluded that evidence seized in violation of the Fourth Amendment could be presented to a grand jury.

What if the prosecution has in its possession evidence that suggests the defendant may not have committed the crimes which the grand jury is considering? Can the prosecution keep this evidence from the grand jury? Would doing so violate the defendant's rights? The Court considered these questions in *United States v. Williams*.

United States v. Williams, 504 U.S. 36, 112 S. Ct. 1735, 118 L. Ed. 2d 352 (1992)

Justice SCALIA delivered the opinion of the Court. . . .

I

On May 4, 1988, respondent John H. Williams, Jr., a Tulsa, Oklahoma, investor, was indicted by a federal grand jury on seven counts of "knowingly mak[ing] [a] false statement or report . . . for the purpose of influencing . . . the action [of a federally insured financial institution]," in violation of 18 U.S.C. § 1014. According to the indictment, between September 1984 and November 1985 Williams supplied four Oklahoma banks with "materially false" statements that variously overstated the value of his current assets and interest income in order to influence the banks' actions on his loan requests. . . .

Williams demanded that the District Court dismiss the indictment, alleging that the Government had failed to fulfill its obligation under the Tenth Circuit's prior decision in United States v. Page, 808 F.2d 723, 728 (1987), to present "substantial exculpatory evidence" to the grand jury (emphasis omitted). His contention was that evidence which the Government had chosen not to present to the grand jury . . . belied an intent to mislead the banks, and thus directly negated an essential element of the charged offense.

The District Court initially denied Williams' motion, but upon reconsideration ordered the indictment dismissed without prejudice. It found, after a hearing, that the withheld evidence was "relevant to an essential element of the crime charged," created "'a reasonable doubt about [respondent's] guilt,'" and thus "render[ed] the grand jury's decision to indict gravely suspect." Upon the Government's appeal, the Court of Appeals affirmed the District Court's order, following its earlier decision in Page. It first sustained as not "clearly erroneous" the District Court's determination that the Government had withheld "substantial exculpatory evidence" from the grand jury. It then found that the Government's behavior "'substantially influence[d]'" the grand jury's decision to indict, or at the very least

raised a "'grave doubt that the decision to indict was free from such substantial influence.'" Under these circumstances, the Tenth Circuit concluded, it was not an abuse of discretion for the District Court to require the Government to begin anew before the grand jury. . . .

II

Respondent does not contend that the Fifth Amendment itself obliges the prosecutor to disclose substantial exculpatory evidence in his possession to the grand jury. Instead, building on our statement that the federal courts "may, within limits, formulate procedural rules not specifically required by the Constitution or the Congress," United States v. Hasting, 461 U.S. 499, 505, 103 S.Ct. 1974, 1978, 76 L.Ed.2d 96 (1983), he argues that imposition of the Tenth Circuit's disclosure rule is supported by the courts' "supervisory power." We think not. Hasting, and the cases that rely upon the principle it expresses, deal strictly with the courts' power to control their own procedures. That power has been applied not only to improve the truth-finding process of the trial, but also to prevent parties from reaping benefit or incurring harm from violations of substantive or procedural rules (imposed by the Constitution or laws) governing matters apart from the trial itself. Thus, Bank of Nova Scotia v. United States, 487 U.S. 250, 108 S.Ct. 2369, 101 L.Ed.2d 228 (1988), makes clear that the supervisory power can be used to dismiss an indictment because of misconduct before the grand jury, at least where that misconduct amounts to a violation of one of those "few, clear rules which were carefully drafted and approved by this Court and by Congress to ensure the integrity of the grand jury's functions," United States v. Mechanik, 475 U.S. 66, 74, 106 S.Ct. 938, 943, 89 L.Ed.2d 50 (1986) (O'CONNOR, J., concurring in judgment).

We did not hold in Bank of Nova Scotia, however, that the courts' supervisory power could be used, not merely as a means of enforcing or vindicating legally compelled standards of prosecutorial conduct before the grand jury, but as a means of prescribing those standards of prosecutorial conduct in the first instance—just as it may be used as a means of establishing standards of prosecutorial conduct before the courts themselves. It is this latter exercise that respondent demands. Because the grand jury is an institution separate from the courts, over whose functioning the courts do not preside, we think it clear that, as a general matter at least, no such "supervisory" judicial authority exists, and that the disclosure rule applied here exceeded the Tenth Circuit's authority.

A

"[R]ooted in long centuries of Anglo-American history," the grand jury is mentioned in the Bill of Rights, but not in the body of the Constitution. It has not been textually assigned, therefore, to any of the branches described in the first three Articles. It "'is a constitutional fixture in its own right.'" In fact the whole theory of its function is that it belongs to no branch of the institutional Government, serving as a kind of buffer or referee between the Government and the people. Although the grand jury normally operates, of course, in the courthouse and under judicial auspices, its institutional relationship with the Judicial Branch has traditionally been, so to speak, at arm's length. Judges' direct involvement in the functioning of the grand jury has generally been confined to the constitutive one of calling the grand jurors together and administering their oaths of office. . . .

No doubt in view of the grand jury proceeding's status as other than a constituent element of a "criminal prosecutio[n]," we have said that certain constitutional protections afforded defendants in criminal proceedings have no application before that body. The Double Jeopardy Clause of the Fifth Amendment does not bar a grand jury from returning an indictment when a prior grand jury has refused to do so. . . . And although "the grand jury may not force a witness to answer questions in violation of [the Fifth Amendment's] constitutional guarantee" against self-incrimination, our cases suggest that an indictment obtained through the use of evidence previously obtained in violation of the privilege against self-incrimination "is nevertheless valid."

Given the grand jury's operational separateness from its constituting court, it should come as no surprise that we have been reluctant to invoke the judicial supervisory power as a basis for prescribing modes of grand jury procedure. Over the years, we have received many requests to exercise supervision over the grand jury's evidence-taking process, but we have refused them all, including some more appealing than the one presented today. In United States v. Calandra, a grand jury witness faced questions that were allegedly based upon physical evidence the Government had obtained through a violation of the Fourth Amendment; we rejected the proposal that the exclusionary rule be extended to grand jury proceedings, because of "the potential injury to the historic role and functions of the grand jury." In Costello v. United States, 350 U.S. 359, 76 S.Ct. 406, 100 L.Ed. 397 (1956), we declined to enforce the hearsay rule in grand jury proceedings, since that "would run counter to the whole history of the grand jury institution, in which laymen conduct their inquiries unfettered by technical rules."

These authorities suggest that any power federal courts may have to fashion, on their own initiative, rules of grand jury procedure is a very limited one, not remotely comparable to the power they maintain over their own proceedings. It certainly would not permit judicial reshaping of the grand jury institution, substantially altering the traditional relationships between the prosecutor, the constituting court, and the grand jury itself. As we proceed to discuss, that would be the consequence of the proposed rule here.

B

Respondent argues that the Court of Appeals' rule can be justified as a sort of Fifth Amendment "common law," a necessary means of assuring the constitutional right to the judgment "of an independent and informed grand jury." Respondent makes a generalized appeal to functional notions: Judicial supervision of the quantity and quality of the evidence relied upon by the grand jury plainly facilitates, he says, the grand jury's performance of its twin historical responsibilities, i.e., bringing to trial those who may be justly accused and shielding the innocent from unfounded accusation and prosecution. We do not agree. The rule would neither preserve nor enhance the traditional functioning of the institution that the Fifth Amendment demands. To the contrary, requiring the prosecutor to present exculpatory as well as inculpatory evidence would alter the grand jury's historical role, transforming it from an accusatory to an adjudicatory body.

It is axiomatic that the grand jury sits not to determine guilt or innocence, but to assess whether there is adequate basis for bringing a criminal charge. That has always been so; and to make the assessment it has always been thought sufficient to hear only the prosecutor's side. . . .

Imposing upon the prosecutor a legal obligation to present exculpatory evidence in his possession would be incompatible with this system. If a "balanced" assessment of the entire matter is the objective, surely the first thing to be done—rather than requiring the prosecutor to say what he knows in defense of the target of the investigation—is to entitle the target to tender his own defense. To require the former while denying (as we do) the latter would be quite absurd. It would also be quite pointless, since it would merely invite the target to circumnavigate the system by delivering his exculpatory evidence to the prosecutor, whereupon it would have to be passed on to the grand jury—unless the prosecutor is willing to take the chance that a court will not deem the evidence important enough to qualify for mandatory disclosure.

Respondent acknowledges (as he must) that the "common law" of the grand jury is not violated if the grand jury itself chooses to hear no more evidence than that which suffices to convince it an indictment is proper. Thus, had the Government offered to familiarize the grand jury in this case with the five boxes of financial statements and deposition testimony alleged to contain exculpatory information, and had the grand jury rejected the offer as pointless, respondent would presumably agree that the resulting indictment would have been valid. Respondent insists, however, that courts must require the modern prosecutor to alert the grand jury to the nature and extent of the available exculpatory evidence, because otherwise the grand jury "merely functions as an arm of the prosecution." We reject the attempt to convert a nonexistent duty of the grand jury itself into an obligation of the prosecutor. The authority of the prosecutor to seek an indictment has long been understood to be "coterminous with the authority of the grand jury to entertain [the prosecutor's] charges." If the grand jury has no obligation to consider all "substantial exculpatory" evidence, we do not understand how the prosecutor can be said to have a binding obligation to present it.

. . .

Echoing the reasoning of the Tenth Circuit in United States v. Page, 808 F.2d, at 728, respondent argues that a rule requiring the prosecutor to disclose exculpatory evidence to the grand jury would, by removing from the docket unjustified prosecutions, save valuable judicial time. That depends, we suppose, upon what the ratio would turn out to be between unjustified prosecutions eliminated and grand jury indictments challenged—for the latter as well as the former consume "valuable judicial time." We need not pursue the matter; if there is an advantage to the proposal, Congress is free to prescribe it. For the reasons set forth above, however, we conclude that courts have no authority to prescribe such a duty pursuant to their inherent supervisory authority over their own proceedings. The judgment of the Court of Appeals is accordingly reversed, and the cause is remanded for further proceedings consistent with this opinion. . . .

Justice STEVENS, with whom Justice BLACKMUN and Justice O'CONNOR join, and with whom Justice THOMAS joins as to Parts II and III, dissenting.

The Court's opinion announces two important changes in the law. First, it justifies its special accommodation to the Solicitor General in granting certiorari to review a contention that was not advanced in either the District Court or the Court of Appeals by explaining that the fact that the issue was raised in a different case is an adequate substitute for raising it in this case. Second, it concludes that a federal court has no power to enforce the prosecutor's obligation to protect the fundamental fairness of proceedings before the grand jury. . . .

The standard for judging the consequences of prosecutorial misconduct during grand jury proceedings is essentially the same as the standard applicable to trials. In United States v. Mechanik, 475 U.S. 66, 106 S.Ct. 938, 89 L.Ed.2d 50

(1986), we held that there was "no reason not to apply [the harmless error rule] to 'errors, defects, irregularities, or variances' occurring before a grand jury just as we have applied it to such error occurring in the criminal trial itself." We repeated that holding in Bank of Nova Scotia v. United States when we rejected a defendant's argument that an indictment should be dismissed because of prosecutorial misconduct and irregularities in proceedings before the grand jury. Referring to the prosecutor's misconduct before the grand jury, we "concluded that our customary harmless-error inquiry is applicable where, as in the cases before us, a court is asked to dismiss an indictment prior to the conclusion of the trial." Moreover, in reviewing the instances of misconduct in that case, we applied precisely the same standard to the prosecutor's violations of Rule 6 of the Federal Rules of Criminal Procedure and to his violations of the general duty of fairness that applies to all judicial proceedings. This point is illustrated by the Court's comments on the prosecutor's abuse of a witness:

> The District Court found that a prosecutor was abusive to an expert defense witness during a recess and in the hearing of some grand jurors. Although the Government concedes that the treatment of the expert tax witness was improper, the witness himself testified that his testimony was unaffected by this misconduct. The prosecutors instructed the grand jury to disregard anything they may have heard in conversations between a prosecutor and a witness, and explained to the grand jury that such conversations should have no influence on its deliberations. In light of these ameliorative measures, there is nothing to indicate that the prosecutor's conduct toward this witness substantially affected the grand jury's evaluation of the testimony or its decision to indict.

Unquestionably, the plain implication of that discussion is that if the misconduct, even though not expressly forbidden by any written rule, had played a critical role in persuading the jury to return the indictment, dismissal would have been required.

In an opinion that I find difficult to comprehend, the Court today repudiates the assumptions underlying these cases and seems to suggest that the court has no authority to supervise the conduct of the prosecutor in grand jury proceedings so long as he follows the dictates of the Constitution, applicable statutes, and Rule 6 of the Federal Rules of Criminal Procedure. The Court purports to support this conclusion by invoking the doctrine of separation of powers and citing a string of cases in which we have declined to impose categorical restraints on the grand jury. Needless to say, the Court's reasoning is unpersuasive.

Although the grand jury has not been "textually assigned" to "any of the branches described in the first three Articles" of the Constitution, it is not an autonomous body completely beyond the reach of the other branches. Throughout its life, from the moment it is convened until it is discharged, the grand jury is subject to the control of the court. As Judge Learned Hand recognized over 60 years ago, "a grand jury is neither an officer nor an agent of the United States, but a part of the court." This Court has similarly characterized the grand jury:

> A grand jury is clothed with great independence in many areas, but it remains an appendage of the court, powerless to perform its investigative function without the court's aid, because powerless itself to compel the testimony of witnesses. It is the court's process which summons the witness to attend and give testimony, and it is the court which must compel a witness to testify if, after appearing, he refuses to do so. . . .

Although the Court recognizes that it may invoke its supervisory authority to fashion and enforce privilege rules applicable in grand jury proceedings, and suggests that it may also invoke its supervisory authority to fashion other limited rules of grand jury procedure, it concludes that it has no authority to prescribe "standards of prosecutorial conduct before the grand jury," because that would alter the grand jury's historic role as an independent, inquisitorial institution. I disagree.

We do not protect the integrity and independence of the grand jury by closing our eyes to the countless forms of prosecutorial misconduct that may occur inside the secrecy of the grand jury room. After all, the grand jury is not merely an investigatory body; it also serves as a "protector of citizens against arbitrary and oppressive governmental action." Explaining why the grand jury must be both "independent" and "informed," the Court wrote in Wood v. Georgia, 370 U.S. 375, 82 S.Ct. 1364, 8 L.Ed.2d 569 (1962):

> Historically, this body has been regarded as a primary security to the innocent against hasty, malicious and oppressive persecution; it serves the invaluable function in our society of standing between the accuser and the accused, whether the latter be an individual, minority group, or other, to determine whether a charge is founded upon reason or was dictated by an intimidating power or by malice and personal ill will.

It blinks reality to say that the grand jury can adequately perform this important historic role if it is intentionally misled by the prosecutor—on whose knowledge of the law and facts of the underlying criminal investigation the jurors will, of necessity, rely.

Unlike the Court, I am unwilling to hold that countless forms of prosecutorial misconduct must be tolerated—no matter how prejudicial they may be, or how seriously they may distort the legitimate function of the grand jury—simply because they are not proscribed by Rule 6 of the Federal Rules of Criminal Procedure or a statute that is applicable in grand jury proceedings. Such a sharp break with the traditional role of the federal judiciary is unprecedented, unwarranted, and unwise. Unrestrained prosecutorial misconduct in grand jury proceedings is inconsistent with the administration of justice in the federal courts and should be redressed in appropriate cases by the dismissal of indictments obtained by improper methods.

III

What, then, is the proper disposition of this case? I agree with the Government that the prosecutor is not required to place all exculpatory evidence before the grand jury. A grand jury proceeding is an ex parte investigatory proceeding to determine whether there is probable cause to believe a violation of the criminal laws has occurred, not a trial. Requiring the prosecutor to ferret out and present all evidence that could be used at trial to create a reasonable doubt as to the defendant's guilt would be inconsistent with the purpose of the grand jury proceeding and would place significant burdens on the investigation. But that does not mean that the prosecutor may mislead the grand jury into believing that there is probable cause to indict by withholding clear evidence to the contrary. I thus agree with the Department of Justice that "when a prosecutor conducting a grand jury inquiry is personally aware of substantial evidence which directly negates the guilt of a subject of the investigation, the prosecutor must present or otherwise disclose such evidence to the grand jury before seeking an indictment against such a person." U.S. Dept. of Justice, United States Attorneys' Manual P 9-11.233, p. 88 (1988).

Although I question whether the evidence withheld in this case directly negates respondent's guilt, I need not resolve my doubts because the Solicitor General did not ask the Court to review the nature of the evidence withheld. Instead, he asked us to decide the legal question whether an indictment may be dismissed because the prosecutor failed to present exculpatory evidence. Unlike the Court and Solicitor General, I believe the answer to that question is yes, if the withheld evidence would plainly preclude a finding of probable cause. I therefore cannot endorse the Court's opinion. . . .

Notes and Questions

1. Arguably, a great deal of time, money, and judicial resources would be saved if prosecutors presented exculpatory evidence to a grand jury instead of waiting until a per-

son is indicted. Why do you suppose a prosecutor would be averse to presenting all of the evidence to a grand jury in light of these considerations?

CONCLUSION

In this chapter, we have considered a number of important legal rules that govern the pretrial process, including an arrestee's right to a prompt judicial determination of probable cause and to release on bail, a suspect's rights to counsel at a preliminary hearing, the constitutional rules concerning the composition of state grand juries, and the types of evidence that grand juries are permitted or must be allowed to consider. These rules affect the interests of both parties prior to trial and also can directly affect the future course of a prosecution and trial. For example, research indicates that individuals who are incarcerated at the time of trial are more likely to be convicted and sent to jail or prison than defendants who are released from custody prior to their trial. Additionally, whether a case is presented to a grand jury or to a judge at a preliminary hearing can significantly influence the case's ultimate disposition. Decisions made during the pretrial process also can affect jail overcrowding and the size of the trial court's docket. In these and other areas, the decisions that are made following a suspect's arrest and prior to her trial can only loosely be characterized as "preliminary." They are of great potential consequence to the defendant as well as the criminal justice system.

CHAPTER 7

The Prosecutor and the Adversarial System

THE PROSECUTOR'S DUTY TO DO JUSTICE

Standard 3-1.2 The Function of the Prosecutor

* * *

(c) The duty of the prosecutor is to seek justice, not merely to convict.

—American Bar Association Standards Relating to the Administration of Criminal Justice (3d ed. 1992)

The American legal system is adversarial. In its ideal form, the adversarial system pits two equally resourceful, competent, and dedicated advocates against each other. Their job is to win the case and defeat their opponent. To this end, they make the strongest possible showing on their clients' behalf and strive to create and expose weaknesses in their counterpart's case. The advocates gather, present, and test evidence and advance all tenable arguments to promote their clients' interests. A disinterested finder of fact—a judge or jury—considers and evaluates the evidence according to rules of law. An impartial judge presides over the proceedings. Through this clash of equal and opposing advocates, in a fair and open forum, the truth presumably will emerge.

"The very premise of our adversary system of criminal justice is that partisan advocacy on both sides of a case will best promote the ultimate objective that the guilty be convicted and the innocent go free." *Herring v. New York*, 422 U.S. 853, 862, 95 S. Ct. 2550, 45 L. Ed. 2d 593 (1975). "The dual aim of our criminal justice system is 'that guilt shall not escape or innocence suffer.' . . . To this end we have placed our confidence in the adversary system, entrusting to it the primary responsibility for developing relevant facts on which a determination of guilt or innocence can be made." *United States v. Nobles*, 422 U.S. 225, 230, 95 S. Ct. 2160, 45 L. Ed. 2d 141 (1975) (cite omitted).

In this and the following chapter we study the legal functions, duties, and responsibilities of the formal advocates in the criminal justice system: the prosecutor and the defense lawyer. We know that in practice the adversarial system of justice often falls short of its lofty ideals. The vast majority of decisions affecting the administration of criminal justice are made outside of the courtroom and greatly in advance of court appearances. The low-visibility decisions made routinely by law enforcement officers and through informal discussions between prosecutors and defense counsel seem far removed from the contemplated adversarial norm. Unfortunately, it is not true that all prosecuting and defense attorneys are equally matched or equipped with comparable resources. Nor is it safe to assume that criminal defendants always receive equivalent brands of justice regardless of their socioeconomic status.

Nevertheless, it is important to scrutinize the basic premises of the adversarial system and in particular to examine the roles of the respective advocates. Do the prosecutor, in representing the government, and the defense lawyer, in representing the defendant, have equivalent obligations and responsibilities? For example, should a prosecutor seek the conviction (and maximum punishment) of all criminally accused who appear in court, irrespective of claims of innocence or mitigating circumstances? Should defense counsel advocate with equal vigor on behalf of clients whom he or she believes to be innocent and those whom he or she knows to be guilty (and quite possibly dangerous)? To what extent do rules promoting fair play or other values check each advocate from a "no-holds-barred" quest for a verdict of guilty or not guilty?

We focus in this chapter on the role of the prosecutor. Prosecuting attorneys exercise extraordinary and largely unregulated discretion in deciding who to charge, what specific charges to bring, and what form and severity of punishment to seek. The year before he was appointed to the Supreme Court, while he was still a federal prosecuting attorney, Justice Robert Jackson described the prosecutor as having "more control over life, liberty and reputation than any other person in America. His discretion is tremendous." Jackson, "The Federal Prosecutor," 24 *Journal of the American Judicature Society* 18 (1940). Many others have agreed. "[The prosecutor] has become the most powerful and important official in our criminal process." Arenella, "Reforming the Grand Jury and the State Preliminary Hearing To Prevent Conviction Without Adjudication," 78 *Michigan Law Review* 463, 498 (1980). "The discretionary power exercised by the prosecuting attorney in initiation, accusation, and discontinuance of prosecution gives him more control over an individual's liberty than any other public official." Note, "Prosecutor's Discretion," 103 *University of Pennsylvania Law Review* 1057 (1955).

As reflected by the American Bar Association (ABA) standard with which we opened this chapter, a prosecutor in the American system of criminal justice is not expected in all cases single-mindedly to pursue the goal of obtaining a conviction. "The duty of the prosecutor is to seek justice."

Berger v. United States, 295 U.S. 78, 55 S. Ct. 629, 79 L. Ed. 1314 (1935)

Mr. Justice Sutherland delivered the opinion of the court. . . .

The United States Attorney is the representative not of an ordinary party to a controversy, but of a sovereignty whose obligation to govern impartially is as compelling as its obligation to govern at all; and whose interest, therefore, in a criminal prosecution is not that it shall win a case, but that justice shall be done. As such, he is in a peculiar and very definite sense the servant of the law, the two-fold aim of which is that guilt shall not escape or innocence suffer. He may prosecute with earnestness and vigor—indeed, he should do so. But, while he may strike hard blows, he is not at liberty to strike foul ones. It is as much his duty to refrain from improper methods calculated to produce a wrongful conviction as it is to use every legitimate means to bring about a just one. . . .

In the following section, we examine the prosecutor's charging discretion. We focus on constitutional limitations on the reasons for initiating a prosecution and for filing charges of different degrees of seriousness. We next explore the prosecutor's duties regarding the use of perjured testimony and the disclosure of potentially exculpatory evidence to the defendant, even though such disclosure might weaken the prosecution's case. We conclude by considering destruction of evidence by the police and examining whether the prosecutor and the police have similar duties regarding the preservation and disclosure of evidence that could be useful to the defense.

THE PROSECUTOR'S CHARGING DISCRETION

As we discussed in the previous chapter, prosecutors are the dominant figure in the charging process. Formal charges are made in many jurisdictions through bills of indictment returned by a grand jury. Although a grand jury has the authority not to return true bills of indictment, this discretion is rarely exercised. The prosecutor largely controls the charging process by submitting bills of indictment to the grand jury and presenting supporting evidence. In other jurisdictions, prosecutors directly file criminal charges through the use of an information, which is followed by a preliminary hearing.

Although the prosecutor's charging discretion is vast, it is not without limits. We consider some of those limits in the following cases.

Selective Prosecution

Wayte v. United States, 470 U.S. 598, 105 S. Ct. 1524, 84 L. Ed. 2d 547 (1985)

Justice Powell delivered the opinion of the Court.

[A Presidential Proclamation issued in July 1980 directed males born during 1960 to register with the Selective Service System. Registrants' names and other relevant information were collected so that Selective Service would be able to identify men eligible for military duty in case a need later arose to draft them. The knowing and willful failure to register was a crime punishable by fine and imprisonment.

[The defendant, David Wayte, was a member of the class required to register, but he refused to comply. "Instead, he wrote several letters to Government officials, including the President, stating that he had not registered and did not intend to do so." Wayte's name thus was included in a Selective Service file of men who personally reported that they would not register or who were reported by others as having failed to register. Selective Service adopted a "passive enforcement" policy, under which only men in this file would be investigated or prosecuted for nonregistration. Pursuant to this policy, Selective Service mailed a letter in June 1981 to each reported violator, explaining that he was delinquent, requesting that he register, and advising him that he faced possible prosecution for noncompliance. Wayte received such a letter and ignored it.

[Thereafter, Wayte was one of approximately 285 men whose names were referred to the FBI and to U.S. Attorneys in the districts where the nonregistrants lived. Pursuant to the Justice Department's so-called "beg" policy, nonregistrants were not immediately prosecuted. Instead,

U.S. Attorneys wrote the men letters warning that prosecution would be considered unless registration was completed by a designated date, and FBI agents attempted to interview non-registrants before a prosecution was started. Finally, the President announced a "grace period" until the end of February 1982, throughout which nonregistrants could comply without penalty. Wayte still refused to register.] . . .

Over the next few months, the Department decided to begin prosecuting those young men who, despite the grace period and "beg" policy, continued to refuse to register. It recognized that under the passive enforcement system those prosecuted were "liable to be vocal proponents of nonregistration" or persons "with religious or moral objections." It also recognized that prosecutions would "undoubtedly result in allegations that the [case was] brought in retribution for the nonregistrant's exercise of his first amendment rights." The Department was advised, however, that Selective Service could not develop a more "active" enforcement system for quite some time. Because of this, the Department decided to begin seeking indictments under the passive system without further delay. On May 21, 1982, United States Attorneys were notified to begin prosecution of nonregistrants. On June 28, 1982, FBI agents interviewed petitioner, and he continued to refuse to register. Accordingly, on July 22, 1982, an indictment was returned against him for knowingly and willfully failing to register with the Selective Service.

Petitioner moved to dismiss the indictment on the ground of selective prosecution. He contended that he and the other indicted nonregistrants were "vocal" opponents of the registration program who had been impermissibly targeted (out of an estimated 674,000 nonregistrants) for prosecution on the basis of their exercise of First Amendment rights. After a hearing, the District Court for the Central District of California granted petitioner's broad request for discovery and directed the Government to produce certain documents and make certain officials available to testify. The Government produced some documents and agreed to make some Government officials available but, citing executive privilege, it withheld other documents and testimony.

On November 15, 1982, the District Court dismissed the indictment on the ground that the Government had failed to rebut petitioner's prima facie case of selective prosecution.

The Court of Appeals reversed. We granted certiorari on the question of selective prosecution.

In our criminal justice system, the Government retains "broad discretion" as to whom to prosecute. "[S]o long as the prosecutor has probable cause to believe that the accused committed an offense defined by statute, the decision whether or not to prosecute, and what charge to file or bring before a grand jury, generally rests entirely in his discretion." This broad discretion rests largely on the recognition that the decision to prosecute is particularly ill-suited to judicial review. Such factors as the strength of the case, the prosecution's general deterrence value, the Government's enforcement priorities, and the case's relationship to the Government's overall enforcement plan are not readily susceptible to the kind of analysis the courts are competent to undertake. Judicial supervision in this area, moreover, entails systemic costs of particular concern. Examining the basis of a prosecution delays the criminal proceeding, threatens to chill law enforcement by subjecting the prosecutor's motives and decisionmaking to outside inquiry, and may undermine prosecutorial effectiveness by revealing the Government's enforcement policy. All these are substantial concerns that make the courts properly hesitant to examine the decision whether to prosecute.

As we have noted in a slightly different context, however, although prosecutorial discretion is broad, it is not "'unfettered.' Selectivity in the enforcement of criminal laws is . . . subject to constitutional constraints." In particular, the decision to prosecute may not be "'deliberately based upon an unjustifiable standard such as race, religion, or other arbitrary classification,'" including the exercise of protected statutory and constitutional rights.

It is appropriate to judge selective prosecution claims according to ordinary equal protection standards. Under our prior cases, these standards require petitioner to show both that the passive enforcement system had a discriminatory effect and that it was motivated by a discriminatory purpose. All petitioner has shown here is that those eventually prosecuted, along with many not prosecuted, reported themselves as having violated the law. He has not shown that the enforcement policy selected nonregistrants for prosecution on the basis of their speech. Indeed, he could not have done so given the way the "beg" policy was carried out. The Government did not prosecute those who reported themselves but later registered. Nor did it prosecute those who protested registration but did not report themselves or were not reported by others. In fact, the Government did not even investigate those who wrote letters to Selective Service criticizing registration unless their letters stated affirmatively that they had refused to comply with the law. The Government, on the other hand, did prosecute people who reported themselves or were reported by others but who did not publicly protest. These facts demonstrate that the Government treated all reported nonregistrants similarly. It did not subject vocal nonregistrants to any special burden. Indeed, those prosecuted in effect selected themselves for prosecution by refusing to register after being reported and warned by the Government.

Even if the passive policy had a discriminatory effect, petitioner has not shown that the Government intended such a result. The evidence he presented demonstrated only that the Government was aware that the passive enforcement policy would result in prosecution of vocal objectors and that they would probably make selective prosecution claims. As we have noted, however: "'Discriminatory purpose' . . . implies more than . . . intent as awareness of consequences. It implies that the decisionmaker . . . selected or reaffirmed a particular course of action at least in part 'because of,' not merely 'in spite of,' its adverse effects upon an identifiable group."

In the present case, petitioner has not shown that the Government prosecuted him *because of* his protest activities. Absent such a showing, his claim of selective prosecution fails.

Justice **Marshall**, with whom Justice **Brennan** joins, dissenting. . . .

Notes and Questions

1. Wasn't the *effect* of the Justice Department's prosecution policy to concentrate on vocal opponents of the Selective Service registration system? If, in practice, prosecutions disproportionately were initiated against those nonregistrants who aggressively criticized the registration system, does this represent a threat to First Amendment values? Under the Court's ruling in *Wayte*, is it enough for a defendant to demonstrate an unequal pattern of prosecution to prove unlawful selective prosecution, or must something more be shown?

2. The Court holds in *Wayte* that prosecutors must be given broad latitude in making their charging decisions. What reasons are offered in support of this policy of judicial deference? Are they convincing?

3. The Justice Department seemed almost to bend over backwards not to prosecute Wayte and others like him who had failed to register with Selective Service. What if a prosecution had been commenced immediately after government officials received Wayte's initial critical letter? Would Wayte have prevailed if he could

establish that only nonregistrants like himself, who criticized the registration requirements, were subject to criminal charges? Under what circumstances can you envision a claim of illegal selective prosecution succeeding?

4. In *McCleskey v. Kemp*, 481 U.S. 279, 107 S. Ct. 1756, 95 L. Ed. 2d 262 (1987), Warren McCleskey was sentenced to death in 1978 for murdering a police officer during a robbery committed in Fulton County, Georgia. McCleskey was an African American. The murdered police officer was white. McCleskey challenged the legality of his death sentence by presenting the results of a comprehensive study of over 2,000 murders committed in Georgia during the 1970s.

"The raw numbers . . . indicate that defendants charged with killing white persons received the death penalty in 11% of the cases, but defendants charged with killing blacks received the death penalty in only 1% of the cases." 481 U.S., at 286. When the race of both defendants and victims was considered, the disparities were even more striking: "The death penalty was assessed in 22% of the cases involving black defendants and white victims; 8% of the cases involving white defendants and white victims; 1% of the cases involving black defendants and black victims; and 3% of the cases involving white defendants and black victims." *Id.* After the researchers examined the raw figures in more detail, and took into account numerous nonracial factors that could have caused the differential death sentencing rates—for example, the offender's prior criminal record, the seriousness of the crime, whether the defendant and victim were acquaintances, and many others—racial disparities still remained. Specifically, "defendants charged with killing white victims were 4.3 times as likely to receive a death sentence as defendants charged with killing blacks." *Id.*, at 287.

Prosecutors' charging decisions accounted for a substantial amount of the racial differences. The raw figures showed that "prosecutors sought the death penalty in 70% of the cases involving black defendants and white victims; 32% of the cases involving white defendants and white victims; 15% of the cases involving black defendants and black victims; and 19% of the cases involving white defendants and black victims." 481 U.S., at 287.

McCleskey argued that the racial discrepancies reflected in the charging and sentencing statistics undermined the constitutionality of Georgia's death penalty system. He maintained that the evidence of race discrimination showed that capital punishment was being administered arbitrarily, in violation of his Eighth Amendment right to be free from cruel and unusual punishment. He also argued that—as an African American offender sentenced to death for murdering a white victim—he was being denied equal protection of the law in violation of his Fourteenth Amendment rights. By a vote of 5–4, the Supreme Court rejected McCleskey's claims. Justice Powell's majority opinion found insufficient reason to question the legitimacy of prosecutors' charging decisions, even though the Court had assumed that the findings of the study McCleskey had provided were "valid statistically."

[T]he policy considerations behind a prosecutor's traditionally "wide discretion" suggest the impropriety of our requiring prosecutors to defend their decisions to seek death penalties, "often years after they were made." Moreover, absent far stronger proof, it is unnecessary to seek such a rebuttal, because a legitimate and unchallenged explanation for the decision is apparent from the record: McCleskey committed an act for which the United States Constitution and Georgia laws permit imposition of the death penalty. . . . 481 U.S., at 296–297.

* * *

[T]he capacity of prosecutorial discretion to provide individualized justice is "firmly entrenched in American law." . . . [A] prosecutor can decline to seek a death sentence in any particular case. Of course, "the power to be lenient [also] is the power to discriminate," but a capital-punishment system that did not allow for discretionary acts of leniency "would be totally alien to our notions of criminal justice." 481 U.S., at 311–312 (footnotes and references omitted).

In dissent, Justice Brennan noted that "[n]o guidelines govern prosecutorial decisions to seek the death penalty," which "provides considerable opportunity for racial considerations, however subtle and unconscious, to influence charging . . . decisions." 481 U.S., at 333–334. Justice Blackmun's dissent made a similar point. 481 U.S., at 356–358.

In light of the statistical evidence suggesting racially disproportionate charging decisions in death penalty cases, should Georgia prosecutors have been required to try to explain those disparities by pointing to racially neutral factors accounting for them?

What would a set of prosecutorial guidelines for making decisions to seek the death penalty look like? How could such charging guidelines be enforced?

5. Dissenting in *Wayte v. United States, supra,* Justice Marshall argued that the Court had answered the wrong question. The real issue, he suggested, "is whether Wayte has earned the right to discover Government documents relevant to his claim of selective prosecution." 470 U.S., at 614–615. The government had not fully complied with the district court's order that it make available to Wayte several documents related to its prosecution of men who had not registered with Selective Service.

The Court squarely addressed a defendant's right to discovery in cases of alleged selective prosecution in *United States v. Armstrong*, 517 U.S. 456, 116 S. Ct. 1480, 134 L. Ed. 2d 687 (1996). The respondents Armstrong and Hampton, both African American, were indicted in the U.S. District Court for the Central District of California on charges of conspiring to possess and distribute more than 50 grams of cocaine base, or "crack." They moved to dismiss the indictment on the ground that they had been selected for prosecution because of their race. They likewise moved for discovery from the government of statistics and information about the federal prosecutor's criteria for charging defendants in cases involving crack. In support of their motions, they offered an affidavit reciting that the defendants were African American in each of the 24 cases involving charges of conspiracy to possess and distribute crack cocaine that were closed by that prosecutor's office during 1991. The district court granted the discovery motion. When the government indicated that it would not comply with the discovery order, the district court dismissed the indictment. The Ninth Circuit Court of Appeals affirmed. The Supreme Court reversed, through an opinion written by Chief Justice Rehnquist. Justice Stevens was the lone dissenter.

A selective-prosecution claim is not a defense on the merits to the criminal charge itself, but an independent assertion that the prosecutor has brought the charge for reasons forbidden by the Constitution. Our cases delineating the necessary elements to prove a claim of selective prosecution have taken great pains to explain that the standard is a demanding one. These cases afford a "background presumption," that the showing necessary to obtain discovery should itself be a significant barrier to the litigation of insubstantial claims.

A selective-prosecution claim asks a court to exercise judicial power over a "special province" of the Executive. The Attorney General and United States Attorneys retain "'broad discretion'" to enforce the Nation's criminal laws. They have this latitude because they are designated by statute as the President's delegates to help him discharge his constitutional responsibility to "take Care that the Laws be faithfully executed." U.S. Const., Art. II, § 3.

As a result, "[t]he presumption of regularity supports" their prosecutorial decisions and "in the absence of clear evidence to the contrary, courts presume that they have properly discharged their official duties." In the ordinary case, "so long as the prosecutor has probable cause to believe that the accused committed an offense defined by statute, the decision whether or not to prosecute, and what charge to file or bring before a grand jury, generally rests entirely in his discretion." Of course, a prosecutor's discretion is "subject to constitutional constraints." One of these constraints, imposed by the equal protection component of the Due Process Clause of the Fifth Amendment, is that the decision whether to prosecute may not be based on "an unjustifiable standard such as race, religion, or other arbitrary classification." A defendant may demonstrate that the administration of a criminal law is "directed so exclusively against a particular class of persons . . . with a mind so unequal and oppressive" that the system of prosecution amounts to "a practical denial" of equal protection of the law. In order to dispel the presumption that a prosecutor has not violated equal protection, a criminal defendant must present "clear evidence to the contrary."

The requirements for a selective-prosecution claim draw on "ordinary equal protection standards." The claimant must demonstrate that the federal prosecutorial policy "had a discriminatory effect and that it was motivated by a discriminatory purpose." To establish a discriminatory effect in a race case, the claimant must show that similarly situated individuals of a different race were not prosecuted. The similarly situated requirement does not make a selective-prosecution claim impossible to prove.

Having reviewed the requirements to prove a selective-prosecution claim, we turn to the showing necessary to obtain discovery in support of such a claim. If discovery is ordered, the Government must assemble from its own files documents which might corroborate or refute the defendant's claim. Discovery thus imposes many of the costs present when the Government must respond to a prima facie case of selective prosecution. It will divert prosecutors' resources and may disclose the Government's prosecutorial strategy. The justifications for a rigorous standard for the elements of a selective-prosecution claim thus require a correspondingly rigorous standard for discovery in aid of such a claim.

In this case we consider what evidence constitutes "some evidence tending to show the existence" of the discriminatory effect element. The Court of Appeals held that a defendant may establish a colorable basis for discriminatory effect without evidence that the Government has failed to prosecute others who are similarly situated to the defendant. We think it was mistaken in this view. The vast majority of the Courts of Appeals require the defendant to produce some evidence that similarly situated defendants of other races could have been prosecuted, but were not, and this requirement is consistent with our equal protection case law.

The Court of Appeals reached its decision in part because it started "with the presumption that people of *all* races commit *all* types of crimes—not with the premise that any type of crime is the exclusive province of any particular racial or ethnic group." It cited no authority for this proposition, which seems contradicted by the most recent statistics of the United States Sentencing Commission. Those statistics show that:

More than 90% of the persons sentenced in 1994 for crack cocaine trafficking were black, 93.4% of convicted LSD dealers were white, and 91% of those convicted for pornography or prostitution were white. Presumptions at war with presumably reliable statistics have no proper place in the analysis of this issue.

The Court of Appeals also expressed concern about the "evidentiary obstacles defendants face." But all of its sister Circuits that have confronted the issue have required that defendants produce some evidence of differential treatment of similarly situated members of other races or protected classes. In the present case, if the claim of selective prosecution were well founded, it should not have been an insuperable task to prove that persons of other races were being treated differently than respondents. For instance, respondents could have investigated whether similarly situated persons of other races were prosecuted by the State of California, were known to federal law enforcement officers, but were not prosecuted in federal court. We think the required threshold—a credible showing of different treatment of similarly situated persons—adequately balances the Government's interest in vigorous prosecution and the defendant's interest in avoiding selective prosecution.

In the case before us, respondents' "study" did not constitute "some evidence tending to show the existence of the essential elements of" a selective-prosecution claim. The study failed to identify individuals who were not black, could have been prosecuted for the offenses for which respondents were charged, but were not so prosecuted. . . .

Vindictive Prosecutions

We use the term *vindictive prosecution* to refer to a prosecutor's decision to retaliate against a defendant for exercising a right conferred by law within the criminal justice system. The "selective" prosecution issues that we considered in the previous section concerned allegations that defendants were singled out for prosecution for constitutionally impermissible reasons extrinsic to the criminal justice system, such as their exercise of their First Amendment rights or their race.

Under the general subject of vindictive prosecutions, we consider, for example, whether a defendant who exercises his or her constitutional right to trial by jury can for that reason be charged with a more serious crime than a simi-

larly situated defendant who agrees to plead guilty. Similarly, assume that a defendant has his or her conviction nullified on appeal. If the defendant is given a new trial, can he or she be reprosecuted on a more serious charge? Can a harsher sentence than the one originally given be imposed if he or she is convicted at the new trial that follows the appeal?

We first examine the issue of vindictive prosecution in *Bordenkircher v. Hayes.*

Bordenkircher v. Hayes, 434 U.S. 357, 98 S. Ct. 663, 54 L. Ed. 2d 604 (1978)

Mr. Justice Stewart delivered the opinion of the Court.

The question in this case is whether the Due Process Clause of the Fourteenth Amendment is violated when a state prosecutor carries out a threat made during plea negotiations to reindict the accused on more serious charges if he does not plead guilty to the offense with which he was originally charged.

The respondent, Paul Lewis Hayes, was indicted by a Fayette County, Ky., grand jury on a charge of uttering a forged instrument in the amount of $88.30, an offense then punishable by a term of 2 to 10 years in prison. After arraignment, Hayes, his retained counsel, and the Commonwealth's Attorney met in the presence of the Clerk of the Court to discuss a possible plea agreement. During these conferences the prosecutor offered to recommend a sentence of five years in prison if Hayes would plead guilty to the indictment. He also said that if Hayes did not plead guilty and "save the court the inconvenience and necessity of a trial," he would return to the grand jury to seek an indictment under the Kentucky Habitual Criminal Act,[1]

which would subject Hayes to a mandatory sentence of life imprisonment by reason of his two prior felony convictions. Hayes chose not to plead guilty, and the prosecutor did obtain an indictment charging him under the Habitual Criminal Act. It is not disputed that the recidivist charge was fully justified by the evidence, that the prosecutor was in possession of this evidence at the time of the original indictment, and that Hayes' refusal to plead guilty to the original charge was what led to his indictment under the habitual criminal statute.

A jury found Hayes guilty on the principal charge of uttering a forged instrument and, in a separate proceeding, further found that he had twice before been convicted of felonies. As required by the habitual offender statute, he was sentenced to a life term in the penitentiary. The Kentucky Court of Appeals rejected Hayes' constitutional objections to the enhanced sentence, holding in an unpublished opinion that imprisonment for life with the possibility of parole was constitutionally permissible in light of the previous felonies of which Hayes had been convicted,[3] and that the prosecutor's decision to indict him as a habitual offender

---

1. While cross-examining Hayes during the subsequent trial proceedings the prosecutor described the plea offer in the following language: "Isn't it a fact that I told you at that time [the initial bargaining session] if you did not intend to plead guilty to five years for this charge and . . . save the court the inconvenience and necessity of a trial and taking up this time that I intended to return to the grand jury and ask them to indict you based upon these prior felony convictions?"

---

3. According to his own testimony, Hayes had pleaded guilty in 1961, when he was 17 years old, to a charge of detaining a female, a lesser included offense of rape, and as a result had served five years in the state reformatory. In 1970 he had been convicted of robbery and sentenced to five years' imprisonment, but had been released on probation immediately.

was a legitimate use of available leverage in the plea bargaining process.

On Hayes' petition for a federal writ of habeas corpus, the United States District Court for the Eastern District of Kentucky agreed that there had been no constitutional violation in the sentence or the indictment procedure, and denied the writ. The Court of Appeals for the Sixth Circuit reversed the District Court's judgment.

It may be helpful to clarify at the outset the nature of the issue in this case. While the prosecutor did not actually obtain the recidivist indictment until after the plea conferences had ended, his intention to do so was clearly expressed at the outset of the plea negotiations. Hayes was thus fully informed of the true terms of the offer when he made his decision to plead not guilty. This is not a situation, therefore, where the prosecutor without notice brought an additional and more serious charge after plea negotiations relating only to the original indictment had ended with the defendant's insistence on pleading not guilty. As a practical matter, in short, this case would be no different if the grand jury had indicted Hayes as a recidivist from the outset, and the prosecutor had offered to drop that charge as part of the plea bargain.

The Court of Appeals nonetheless drew a distinction between "concessions relating to prosecution under an existing indictment," and threats to bring more severe charges not contained in the original indictment—a line it thought necessary in order to establish a prophylactic rule to guard against the evil of prosecutorial vindictiveness. Quite apart from this chronological distinction, however, the Court of Appeals found that the prosecutor had acted vindictively in the present case since he had conceded that the indictment was influenced by his desire to induce a guilty plea. The ultimate conclusion of the Court of Appeals thus seems to have been that a prosecutor acts vindictively and in violation of due process of law whenever his charging decision is influenced by what he hopes to gain in the course of plea bargaining negotiations.

We have recently had occasion to observe that "[w]hatever might be the situation in an ideal world, the fact is that the guilty plea and the often concomitant plea bargain are important components of this country's criminal justice system. Properly administered, they can benefit all concerned." Blackledge v. Allison, 431 US 63, 71, 97 S Ct 1621, 52 L Ed 2d 135 [(1977)]. The open acknowledgment of this previously clandestine practice has led this Court to recognize the importance of counsel during plea negotiations, Brady v. United States, 397 US 742, 758, 90 S Ct 1463, 25 L Ed 2d 747 [(1970)], the need for a public record indicating that a plea was knowingly and voluntarily made, Boykin v. Alabama, 395 US 238, 242, 89 S Ct 1709, 23 L Ed 2d 274 [(1969)], and the requirement that a prosecutor's plea bargaining promise must be kept, Santobello v. New York, 404 US 257, 262, 92 S Ct 495, 30 L Ed 2d 427 [(1971)]. The decision of the Court of Appeals in the present case, however, did not deal with considerations such as these, but held that the substance of the plea offer itself violated the limitations imposed by the Due Process Clause of the Fourteenth Amendment. For the reasons that follow, we have concluded that the Court of Appeals was mistaken in so ruling.

This Court held in North Carolina v. Pearce, 395 US 711, 725, 89 S Ct 2072, 23 L Ed 2d 656 [(1969)], that the Due Process Clause of the Fourteenth Amendment "requires that vindictiveness against a defendant for having successfully attacked his first conviction must play no part in the sentence he receives after a new trial." The same principle was later applied to prohibit a prosecutor from reindicting a convicted misdemeanant on a felony charge after the defendant had invoked an appellate remedy, since in this situation there was also a "realistic likelihood of 'vindictiveness.'" Blackledge v. Perry, 417 US 21, 27, 94 S Ct 2098, 40 L Ed 2d 628 [(1974)].

In those cases the Court was dealing with the State's unilateral imposition of a penalty upon a defendant who had chosen to exercise a legal right to attack his original conviction—a situation "very different from the give-and-take negotiation common in plea bargaining between the prosecution and defense, which arguably possess relatively equal bargaining power." Parker v. North Carolina, 397 US 790, 809, 90 S Ct 1458, 25 L Ed 2d 785 [(1970)] (opinion of Brennan, J.). The Court has emphasized that the due process violation in cases such as Pearce and Perry lay not in the possibility that a defendant might be deterred from the exercise of a legal right, but rather in the danger that the State might be retaliating against the accused for lawfully attacking his conviction.

To punish a person because he has done what the law plainly allows him to do is a due process violation of the most basic sort, and for an agent of the State to pursue a course of action whose objective is to penalize a person's reliance on his legal rights is "patently unconstitutional." But in the "give-and-take" of plea bargaining, there is no such element of punishment or retaliation so long as the accused is free to accept or reject the prosecution's offer.

Plea bargaining flows from "the mutuality of advantage" to defendants and prosecutors, each with his own reasons for wanting to avoid trial. Defendants advised by competent counsel and protected by other procedural safeguards are presumptively capable of intelligent choice in response to prosecutorial persuasion, and unlikely to be driven to false self-condemnation. Indeed, acceptance of the basic legitimacy of plea bargaining necessarily implies rejection of any notion that a guilty plea is involuntary in a constitutional sense simply because it is the end result of the bargaining process. By hypothesis, the plea may have been induced by promises of a recommendation of a lenient sentence or a reduction of charges, and thus by fear of the possibility of a greater penalty upon conviction after a trial.

While confronting a defendant with the risk of more severe punishment clearly may have a "discouraging effect on the defendant's assertion of his trial rights, the imposition of these difficult choices [is] an inevitable"—and permissible—"attribute of any legitimate system which tolerates and encourages the negotiation of pleas." It follows that, by tolerating and encouraging the negotiation of pleas, this Court has necessarily accepted as constitutionally legitimate the simple reality that the prosecutor's interest at the bargaining table is to persuade the defendant to forgo his right to plead not guilty.

It is not disputed here that Hayes was properly chargeable under the recidivist statute, since he had in fact been convicted of two previous felonies. In our system, so long as the prosecutor has probable cause to believe that the accused committed an offense defined by statute, the decision whether or not to prosecute, and what charge to file or bring before a grand jury, generally rests entirely in his discretion. Within the lim-

its set by the legislature's constitutionally valid definition of chargeable offenses, 'the conscious exercise of some selectivity in enforcement is not in itself a federal constitutional violation" so long as "the selection was [not] deliberately based upon an unjustifiable standard such as race, religion, or other arbitrary classification." Oyler v. Boles, 368 US 448, 456, 82 S Ct 501, 7 L Ed 2d 446 [(1962)]. To hold that the prosecutor's desire to induce a guilty plea is an "unjustifiable standard," which, like race or religion, may play no part in his charging decision, would contradict the very premises that underlie the concept of plea bargaining itself. Moreover, a rigid constitutional rule that would prohibit a prosecutor from acting forthrightly in his dealings with the defense could only invite unhealthy subterfuge that would drive the practice of plea bargaining back into the shadows from which it has so recently emerged. There is no doubt that the breadth of discretion that our country's legal system vests in prosecuting attorneys carries with it the potential for both individual and institutional abuse. And broad though that discretion may be, there are undoubtedly constitutional limits upon its exercise. We hold only that the course of conduct engaged in by the prosecutor in this case, which no more than openly presented the defendant with the unpleasant alternatives of forgoing trial or facing charges on which he was plainly subject to prosecution, did not violate the Due Process Clause of the Fourteenth Amendment.

Mr. Justice Blackmun, with whom Mr. Justice Brennan and Mr. Justice Marshall join, dissenting.

I feel that the Court, although purporting to rule narrowly (that is, on "the course of conduct engaged in by the prosecutor in this case," is departing from, or at least restricting, the principles established in North Carolina v. Pearce, 395 US 711, 89 S Ct 2072, 23 L Ed 2d 656 (1969), and in Blackledge v. Perry, 417 US 21, 94 S Ct 2098, 40 L Ed 2d 628 (1974). . . .

In Pearce, as indeed the Court notes, it was held that "vindictiveness against a defendant for having successfully attacked his first conviction must play no part in the sentence he receives after a new trial."

The Court now says, however, that this concern with vindictiveness is of no import in the present case, despite the difference between five years in prison and a life sentence, because we are here concerned with plea bargaining where there is give-and-take negotiation, and where, it is said, "there is no such element of punishment or retaliation so long as the accused is free to accept or reject the prosecution's offer." Yet in this case vindictiveness is present to the same extent as it was thought to be in Pearce and in Perry; the prosecutor here admitted, see ante, at n 1, that the sole reason for the new indictment was to discourage the respondent from exercising his right to a trial. Even had such an admission not been made, when plea negotiations, conducted in the face of the less serious charge under the first indictment, fail, charging by a second indictment a more serious crime for the same conduct creates "a strong inference" of vindictiveness. I therefore do not understand why, as in Pearce, due process does not require that the prosecution justify its action on some basis other than discouraging respondent from the exercise of his right to a trial.

Prosecutorial vindictiveness, it seems to me, in the present narrow context, is the fact against which the Due Process Clause ought to protect. . . .

It might be argued that it really makes little difference how this case, now that it is here, is decided. The Court's holding gives plea bargaining full sway despite vindictiveness. A contrary result, however, merely would prompt the aggressive prosecutor to bring the greater charge initially in every case, and only thereafter to bargain. The consequences to the accused would still be adverse, for then he would bargain against a greater charge, face the likelihood of increased bail, and run the risk that the court would be less inclined to accept a bargained plea. Nonetheless, it is far preferable to hold the prosecution to the charge it was originally content to bring and to justify in the eyes of its public.[2]

---

2. That prosecutors, without saying so, may sometimes bring charges more serious than they think appropriate for the ultimate disposition of a case, in order to gain bargaining leverage with a defendant, does not add support to today's decision, for this Court, in its approval of the advantages to be gained from plea negotiations, has never openly sanctioned such deliberate overcharging or taken such a cynical view of the bargaining process. Normally, of course, it is impossible to show that this is what the prosecutor is doing, and the courts necessarily have deferred to the prosecutor's exercise of discretion in initial charging decisions. . . .

Mr. Justice Powell, dissenting.

* * *

Respondent was charged with the uttering of a single forged check in the amount of $88.30. Under Kentucky law, this offense was punishable by a prison term of from 2 to 10 years, apparently without regard to the amount of the forgery. During the course of plea bargaining, the prosecutor offered respondent a sentence of five years in consideration of a guilty plea. I observe, at this point, that five years in prison for the offense charged hardly could be characterized as a generous offer. Apparently respondent viewed the offer in this light and declined to accept it; he protested that he was innocent and insisted on going to trial. Respondent adhered to this position even when the prosecutor advised that he would seek a new indictment under the State's Habitual Criminal Act which would subject respondent, if convicted, to a mandatory life sentence because of two prior felony convictions.

The prosecutor's initial assessment of respondent's case led him to forgo an indictment under the habitual criminal statute. The circumstances of respondent's prior convictions are relevant to this assessment and to my view of the case. Respondent was 17 years old when he committed his first offense. He was charged with rape but pleaded guilty to the lesser included offense of "detaining a female." One of the other participants in the incident was sentenced to life imprisonment. Respondent was sent not to prison but to a reformatory where he served five years. Respondent's second offense was robbery. This time he was found guilty by a jury and was sentenced to five years in prison, but he was placed on probation and served no time. Although respondent's prior convictions brought him within the terms of the Habitual Criminal Act, the offenses themselves did not result in imprisonment; yet the addition of a conviction on a charge involving $88.30 subjected respondent to a mandatory sentence of imprisonment for life. Persons convicted of rape and murder often are not punished so severely.

No explanation appears in the record for the prosecutor's decision to escalate the charge against respondent other than respondent's

refusal to plead guilty. The prosecutor has conceded that his purpose was to discourage respondent's assertion of constitutional rights, and the
majority accepts this characterization of events.

It seems to me that the question to be asked
under the circumstances is whether the prosecutor reasonably might have charged respondent
under the Habitual Criminal Act in the first place.
The deference that courts properly accord the
exercise of a prosecutor's discretion perhaps
would foreclose judicial criticism if the prosecutor
originally had sought an indictment under that
Act, as unreasonable as it would have seemed.[2]
But here the prosecutor evidently made a reasonable, responsible judgment not to subject an individual to a mandatory life sentence when his only
new offense had societal implications as limited
as those accompanying the uttering of a single
$88 forged check and when the circumstances of
his prior convictions confirmed the inappropriate-
ness of applying the habitual criminal statute. I
think it may be inferred that the prosecutor him-

self deemed it unreasonable and not in the public
interest to put this defendant in jeopardy of a sentence of life imprisonment. Here, any inquiry into
the prosecutor's purpose is made unnecessary
by his candid acknowledgment that he threatened
to procure and in fact procured the habitual criminal indictment because of respondent's insistence on exercising his constitutional rights. We
have stated in unequivocal terms, in discussing
United States v. Jackson, 390 US 570, 88 S Ct
1209, 20 L Ed 2d 138 (1968), and North Carolina
v. Pearce, 395 US 711, 23 L Ed 2d 656, 89 S Ct
2072 (1969), that "Jackson and Pearce are clear
and subsequent cases have not dulled their force:
if the only objective of a state practice is to discourage the assertion of constitutional rights it is
'patently unconstitutional.'" Chaffin v. Stynch-
combe, 412 US 17, 32 n 20, 93 S Ct 1977, 36 L
Ed 2d 714 (1973).

* * *

Notes and Questions

1. Justice Stewart's opinion for the Court in
Bordenkircher v. Hayes distinguishes between
"the State's unilateral imposition of a penalty
upon a defendant who had chosen to exercise a
legal right" and the "very different" situation
involving "the give-and-take negotiation in plea
bargaining between the prosecution and
defense." It characterizes the circumstances in
Hayes as falling within the latter category. Is this
an apt characterization? Precisely what "give
and take" do you envision having occurred during the plea negotiations? Must more be
involved than the prosecutor instructing the
defendant that if he does not "take" what the
prosecutor offers to "give," then he must accept
the consequences? Is there roughly equal bar-

gaining leverage between the parties, or is the
prosecutor essentially in a position "unilaterally"
to stipulate the plea-bargaining conditions? We
consider plea bargaining at greater length in
Chapter 9.

2. What if the prosecutor originally had
obtained an indictment against Hayes under the
Habitual Criminal Act and had then offered to
dismiss that indictment and allow Hayes to plead
guilty to uttering a forged instrument with a recommendation for a five-year sentence? Would
his offer be perceived as a more generous
one—indeed, even as a gracious one—in con-

---

2. The majority suggests that this case cannot be
distinguished from the case where the prosecutor initially obtains an indictment under an enhancement
statute and later agrees to drop the enhancement
charge in exchange for a guilty plea. I would agree
that these two situations would be alike *only if* it were

assumed that the hypothetical prosecutor's decision
to charge under the enhancement statute was occasioned not by consideration of the public interest but
by a strategy to discourage the defendant from exercising his constitutional rights. In theory, I would condemn both practices. In practice, the hypothetical
situation is largely unreviewable. The majority's view
confuses the propriety of a particular exercise of prosecutorial discretion with its unreviewability. In the
instant case, however, we have no problem of proof.

trast to the actual circumstances of the case? Should the timing of the prosecutor's decision to pursue the indictment under the Habitual Criminal Act make a difference, either in fact or in law? What are Justice Powell's views about the timing issue?

3. *Blackledge v. Perry*, 417 U.S. 21, 94 S. Ct. 2098, 40 L. Ed. 2d 628 (1974), is described in *Bordenkircher v. Hayes* as a case involving vindictive prosecution. Perry originally was charged with misdemeanor assault with a deadly weapon. Under North Carolina law, all misdemeanors were tried before a judge sitting without a jury in a state district court. Defendants convicted in the district court had a statutory right to appeal for a trial *de novo* at the superior court level, where they were entitled to a jury trial. Perry was convicted of misdemeanor assault by the district court judge and was given a six-month jail sentence. He then exercised his right of appeal. "When an appeal is taken, the statutory scheme provides that the slate is wiped clean; the prior conviction is annulled, and the prosecution and defense begin anew in the Superior Court."

Following Perry's appeal, the prosecutor obtained an indictment charging Perry with *felonious* assault with a deadly weapon with intent to kill. This felony indictment was based on the same conduct that had served as the basis for Perry's misdemeanor assault conviction in the district court. He was convicted of the felony charge in superior court and given a five- to seven-year prison sentence.

Perry challenged his conviction and sentence on multiple grounds and was granted habeas corpus relief by the lower federal courts. The Supreme Court granted certiorari to consider whether Perry's "indictment on the felony charge constituted a penalty for his exercising his statutory right to appeal, and thus contravened the Due Process Clause of the Fourteenth Amendment." The Court ruled (7–2) that Perry's due-process rights had been violated.

Justice Stewart's majority opinion relied in part on the precedent of *North Carolina v. Pearce*, 395 U.S. 711, 89 S. Ct. 2072, 23 L. Ed. 2d 656 (1969). The defendant in *Pearce* originally was convicted of assault with intent to commit rape and was sentenced to 12 to 15 years in prison. He earned a reversal of the conviction on appeal. On retrial, he was convicted of the same crime and received a sentence that, when added to the time he had been incarcerated prior to and during the pendency of the appeal, "amounted to a longer total sentence than that originally imposed." The Court ruled that Pearce's due-process rights had been violated. It declined to place an absolute ban on a harsher sentence being imposed on a defendant following an appeal and conviction on retrial but cautioned that a more onerous sentence could be justified only under specific circumstances.

Due process of law, then, requires that vindictiveness against a defendant for having successfully attacked his first conviction must play no part in the sentence he receives after a new trial. And since the fear of such vindictiveness may unconstitutionally deter a defendant's exercise of the right to appeal or collaterally attack his first conviction, due process also requires that a defendant be freed of apprehension of such a retaliatory motivation on the part of the sentencing judge.

In order to assure the absence of such a motivation, we have concluded that whenever a judge imposes a more severe sentence upon a defendant after a new trial, the reasons for his doing so must affirmatively appear. Those reasons must be based upon objective information concerning identifiable conduct on the part of the defendant occurring after the time of the original sentencing proceeding. And the factual data upon which the increased sentence is based must be made part of the record, so that the constitutional legitimacy of the increased sentence may be fully reviewed on appeal. . . .

In *Blackledge v. Perry*, the threat or appearance of vindictiveness arose from the prosecutor's decision to obtain an indictment for a more serious offense following a defendant's appeal, instead of a judge's decision on resentencing following a successful appeal. Nevertheless, the Court considered the principles derived from *Pearce* to be controlling.

A prosecutor clearly has a considerable stake in discouraging convicted misdemeanants from appealing and thus obtaining a trial de novo in the Superior Court, since such an appeal will clearly require increased expenditures of prosecutorial resources before the defendant's conviction becomes final, and may even result in a formerly convicted defendant's going free. And, if the prosecutor has the means readily at hand to discourage such appeals—by "upping the ante" through a felony indictment whenever a convicted misdemeanant pursues his statutory appellate remedy—the State can insure that only the most hardy defendants will brave the hazards of a de novo trial.

There is, of course, no evidence that the prosecutor in this case acted in bad faith or maliciously in seeking a felony indictment against Perry. The rationale of our judgment in the Pearce case, however, was not grounded upon the proposition that actual retaliatory motivation must inevitably exist. Rather, we emphasized that "since the fear of such vindictiveness may unconstitutionally deter a defendant's exercise of the right to appeal or collaterally attack his first conviction, due process also requires that a defendant be freed of apprehension of such a retaliatory motivation on the part of the sentencing judge." We think it clear that the same considerations apply here. A person convicted of an offense is entitled to pursue his statutory right to a trial de novo, without apprehension that the State will retaliate by substituting a more serious charge for the original one, thus subjecting him to a significantly increased potential period of incarceration.

* * * * *

The *American Bar Association Standards Relating to the Administration of Criminal Justice* includes a chapter devoted to "The Prosecution Function." Is the following standard sufficiently specific to help resolve the issues that arise in cases like *United States v. Wayte, Bordenkircher v. Hayes,* and *Blackledge v. Perry*?

American Bar Association Standards Relating to the Administration of Criminal Justice (3d ed. 1992)

Standard 3-3.9 Discretion in the Charging Decision

(a) A prosecutor should not institute, or cause to be instituted, or permit the continued pendency of criminal charges when the prosecutor knows that the charges are not supported by probable cause. A prosecutor should not institute, cause to be instituted, or permit the continued pendency of criminal charges in the absence of sufficient admissible evidence to support a conviction.

(b) The prosecutor is not obliged to present all charges which the evidence might support. The prosecutor may in some circumstances and for good cause consistent with the public interest decline to prosecute, notwithstanding that sufficient evidence may exist which would support a conviction. Illustrative of the factors which the prosecutor may properly consider in exercising his or her discretion are:

(i) the prosecutor's reasonable doubt that the accused is in fact guilty;

(ii) the extent of the harm caused by the offense;

(iii) the disproportion of the authorized punishment in relation to the particular offense or the offender;

(iv) possible improper motives of a complainant;

(v) reluctance of the victim to testify;

(vi) cooperation of the accused in the apprehension or conviction of others; and

(vii) availability and likelihood of prosecution by another jurisdiction.

(c) A prosecutor should not be compelled by his or her supervisor to prosecute a case in which he or she has a reasonable doubt about the guilt of the accused.

(d) In making the decision to prosecute, the prosecutor should give no weight to the personal or political advantages or disad-vantages which might be involved or to a desire to enhance his or her record of convictions.

(e) In cases which involve a serious threat to the community, the prosecutor should not be deterred from prosecution by the fact that in the jurisdiction juries have tended to acquit persons accused of the particular kind of criminal act in question.

(f) The prosecutor should not bring or seek charges greater in number or degree than can reasonably be supported with evidence at trial or than are necessary to fairly reflect the gravity of the offense.

(g) The prosecutor should not condition a dismissal of charges, nolle prosequi, or similar action on the accused's relinquishment of the right to seek civil redress unless the accused has agreed to the action knowingly and intelligently, freely and voluntarily, and where such waiver is approved by the court.

Source: Reprinted with permission from *ABA Standards for Criminal Justice: Prosecution Function and Defense Function,* Third Edition, Standard 3-3.9, © 1993, American Bar Association.

PERJURED TESTIMONY AND EXCULPATORY EVIDENCE: THE PROSECUTOR'S DUTY

The Knowing Use of Perjured Testimony

American Bar Association Standards Relating to the Administration of Criminal Justice (3d ed. 1992)

Standard 3-5.6 Presentation of Evidence

(a) A prosecutor should not knowingly offer false evidence, whether by documents, tangible evidence, or the testimony of witnesses, or fail to seek withdrawal thereof upon discovery of its falsity.

Miller v. Pate, 386 U.S. 1, 87 S. Ct. 785, 17 L. Ed. 2d 690 (1967)

Mr. Justice Stewart delivered the opinion of the Court.

On November 26, 1955, in Canton, Illinois, an eight-year-old girl died as the result of a brutal sexual attack. The petitioner was charged with her murder.

Prior to his trial in an Illinois court, his counsel filed a motion for an order permitting a scientific inspection of the physical evidence the prosecution intended to introduce. The motion was resisted by the prosecution and denied by the court. The jury trial ended

in a verdict of guilty and a sentence of death.
. . .

There were no eyewitnesses to the brutal crime which the petitioner was charged with perpetrating. A vital component of the case against him was a pair of men's underwear shorts covered with large, dark, reddish-brown stains—People's Exhibit 3 in the trial record. These shorts had been found by a Canton policeman in a place known as the Van Buren Flats three days after the murder. The Van Buren Flats were about a mile from the scene of the crime. It was the prosecution's theory that the petitioner had been wearing these shorts when he committed the murder, and that he had afterwards removed and discarded them at the Van Buren Flats.

During the presentation of the prosecution's case, People's Exhibit 3 was variously described by witnesses in such terms as the "bloody shorts" and "a pair of jockey shorts stained with blood." Early in the trial the victim's mother testified that her daughter "had type 'A' positive blood." Evidence was later introduced to show that the petitioner's blood "was of group 'O.'"

Against this background the jury heard the testimony of a chemist for the State Bureau of Crime Identification. . . .

"I examined and tested 'People's Exhibit 3' to determine the nature of the staining material upon it. The result of the first test was that this material upon the shorts is blood. I made a second examination which disclosed that the blood is of human origin. I made a further examination which disclosed that the blood is of group 'A.'"

The petitioner, testifying in his own behalf, denied that he had ever owned or worn the shorts in evidence as People's Exhibit 3. He himself referred to the shorts as having "dried blood on them."

In argument to the jury the prosecutor made the most of People's Exhibit 3:

"Those shorts were found in the Van Buren Flats, with blood. What type blood? Not 'O' blood as the defendant has, but 'A'—type 'A.'"

And later in his argument he said to the jury:

"And, if you will recall, it has never been contradicted the blood type of Janice May was blood type 'A' positive. Blood type 'A.' Blood type 'A' on these shorts. It wasn't 'O' type as the defendant has. It is 'A' type, what the little girl had."

Such was the state of the evidence with respect to People's Exhibit 3 as the case went to the jury. And such was the state of the record as the judgment of conviction was reviewed by the Supreme Court of Illinois. The "blood stained shorts" clearly played a vital part in the case for the prosecution. They were an important link in the chain of circumstantial evidence against the petitioner, and, in the context of the revolting crime with which he was charged, their gruesomely emotional impact upon the jury was incalculable.

So matters stood with respect to People's Exhibit 3, until the present habeas corpus proceeding in the Federal District Court. In this proceeding the State was ordered to produce the stained shorts, and they were admitted in evidence. It was established that their appearance was the same as when they had been introduced at the trial as People's Exhibit 3. The petitioner was permitted to have the shorts examined by a chemical microanalyst. What the microanalyst found cast an extraordinary new light on People's Exhibit 3. The reddish-brown stains on the shorts were not blood, but paint.

The witness said that he had tested threads from each of the 10 reddish-brown stained areas on the shorts, and that he had found that all of them were encrusted with mineral pigments ". . . which one commonly uses in the preparation of paints." He found "no traces of human blood." . . .

It was further established that counsel for the prosecution had known at the time of the trial that the shorts were stained with paint. The prosecutor even admitted that the Canton police had prepared a memorandum attempting to explain "how this exhibit contains all the paint on it." . . .

The record of the petitioner's trial reflects the prosecution's consistent and repeated misrepresentation that People's Exhibit 3 was, indeed, "a garment heavily stained with blood." The prosecution's whole theory with respect to the exhibit depended upon that misrepresentation. For the theory was that the victim's assailant had discarded the shorts *because* they were stained with blood. A pair of paint-stained shorts, found in an abandoned building a mile away from the scene of the crime, was virtually valueless as evidence against the petitioner. The prosecution deliberately misrepresented the truth.

More than 30 years ago this Court held that the Fourteenth Amendment cannot tolerate a state criminal conviction obtained by the knowing use of false evidence. Mooney v. Holohan, 294 US 103, 55 S Ct 340, 79 L Ed 791 [(1935)]. There has been no deviation from that established principle. There can be no retreat from that principle here.

The judgment of the Court of Appeals is reversed, and the case is remanded for further proceedings consistent with this opinion.

It is so ordered.

Notes and Questions

1. Lloyd Eldon Miller, Jr., was released from prison in 1967, after having spent 11 years on death row. He faced numerous execution dates and once came within seven and one-half hours of being strapped into Illinois's electric chair. Charges were officially dropped against him in 1971. *See* M. L. Radelet, H. A. Bedau, & C. E. Putnam, *In Spite of Innocence: Erroneous Convictions in Capital Cases* 143 (1992). What do you suppose would motivate the police officer to testify falsely about the "blood" found on the underwear, or the prosecutor knowingly to allow that perjured testimony to be considered by the jury that convicted Miller and sentenced him to death?

2. What, precisely, is offensive to due process in *Miller v. Pate*? Is the prosecutor's knowing use of perjured testimony sufficient in and of itself to require reversal? Or must there be some legitimate risk that the perjured testimony affected the outcome of the trial? For example, if the case against Miller had not been based primarily on circumstantial evidence but had been supported by the testimony of half a dozen eye-witnesses who reported seeing Miller commit the murder, would reversal of the conviction be required? What does the Court mean when it says that "the Fourteenth Amendment cannot tolerate a state criminal conviction *obtained by* the knowing use of false evidence" (emphasis added)?

The Duty To Disclose Evidence Material to the Defense

Is a prosecutor's duty of fair play limited to refraining from using false evidence and perjured testimony, or does it have a broader scope? Consider the following cases, beginning with *Brady v. Maryland*.

Brady v. Maryland, 373 U.S. 83, 83 S. Ct. 1194, 10 L. Ed. 2d 215 (1963)

Opinion of the court by Mr. Justice Douglas, announced by Mr. Justice Brennan.

Petitioner and a companion, Boblit, were found guilty of murder in the first degree and were sentenced to death, their convictions being affirmed by the Court of Appeals of Maryland. Their trials were separate, petitioner being tried first. At his trial Brady took the stand and admitted his participation in the crime, but he claimed that Boblit did the actual killing. And, in his summation to the jury, Brady's counsel conceded that Brady was guilty of murder in the first degree, asking only that the jury return that verdict "without capital punishment." Prior to the trial petitioner's counsel had requested the prosecution to allow him to examine Boblit's extra judicial statements. Several of those statements were shown to him; but one dated July 9, 1958, in which Boblit admitted the actual homicide, was withheld by the prosecution and did not come to petitioner's notice until after he had been tried, convicted, and sentenced, and after his conviction had been affirmed.

Petitioner moved the trial court for a new trial based on the newly discovered evidence that had been suppressed by the prosecution. . . . The petition for post-conviction relief was dismissed by the trial court; and on appeal the Court of Appeals held that suppression of the evidence by the prosecution denied petitioner due process of law and remanded the case for a retrial of the question of punishment, not the question of guilt. The case is here on certiorari.

The crime in question was murder committed in the perpetration of a robbery. Punishment for that crime in Maryland is life imprisonment or death, the jury being empowered to restrict the punishment to life by addition of the words "without capital punishment." In Maryland, by reason of the state constitution, the jury in a criminal case are "the Judges of Law, as well as of fact." The question presented is whether petitioner was denied a federal right when the Court of Appeals restricted the new trial to the question of punishment.

We agree with the Court of Appeals that suppression of this confession was a violation of the Due Process Clause of the Fourteenth Amendment. . . .

This ruling is an extension of Mooney v. Holohan, 294 US 103, 112, [55 S Ct 340, 79 L Ed 791 (1935)] where the Court ruled on what nondisclosure by a prosecutor violates due process:

"It is a requirement that cannot be deemed to be satisfied by mere notice and hearing if a State has contrived a conviction through the pretense of a trial which in truth is but used as a means of depriving a defendant of liberty through a deliberate deception of court and jury by the presentation of testimony known to be perjured. Such a contrivance by a State to procure the conviction and imprisonment of a defendant is as inconsistent with the rudimentary demands of justice as is the obtaining of a like result by intimidation." . . .

In Napue v. Illinois, 360 US 264, 269, 79 S Ct 1173, 3 L Ed 2d 1217 [(1959)], we extended the test formulated in Mooney v. Holohan when we said: "The same result obtains when the State, although not soliciting false evidence, allows it to go uncorrected when it appears." . . .

We now hold that the suppression by the prosecution of evidence favorable to an accused upon request violates due process where the evidence is material either to guilt or to punishment, irrespective of the good faith or bad faith of the prosecution.

The principle of Mooney v. Holohan is not punishment of society for misdeeds of a prosecutor but avoidance of an unfair trial to the accused. Society wins not only when the guilty are convicted but when criminal trials are fair; our system of the administration of justice suffers when any accused is treated unfairly. An inscription on the walls of the Department of Justice states the proposition candidly for the federal domain: "The United States wins its point whenever justice is done its citizens in the courts." A prosecution that withholds evidence on demand of an accused which, if made available, would tend to exculpate him or reduce the penalty helps shape a trial that bears heavily on the defendant. That casts the prosecutor in the role of an architect of a proceeding that does not comport with standards of justice, even though, as in the present case, his action is not "the result of guile," to use the words of the Court of Appeals.

The question remains whether petitioner was denied a constitutional right when the Court of Appeals restricted his new trial to the question of punishment. . . .

In the present case a unanimous Court of Appeals has said that nothing in the suppressed confession "could have reduced the appellant Brady's offense below murder in the first degree." We read that statement as a ruling on the admissibility of the confession on the issue of innocence or guilt. A sporting theory of justice might assume that if the suppressed confession had been used at the first trial, the judge's ruling that it was not admissible on the issue of innocence or guilt might have been flouted by the jury just as it might have been done if the court had first admitted a confession and then stricken it from the record. But we cannot raise that trial strategy to the dignity of a constitutional right and say that the deprival of this defendant of that sporting chance through the use of a bifurcated trial denies him due process or violates the

Equal Protection Clause of the Fourteenth Amendment.

Affirmed. . . .

Mr. Justice Harlan, whom Mr. Justice Black joins, dissenting. . . .

Notes and Questions

1. Brady was granted a new sentencing hearing. He was not given a new trial regarding his murder conviction. What justifies these different results? The Court holds that due process is violated when suppressed evidence is "material" to guilt or punishment. How does the concept of materiality figure into the results reached in *Brady*?

2. Under the Court's holding, does it matter whether the prosecutor purposefully suppressed the statement in which Boblit admitted the actual killing because that statement would weaken the state's case against Brady or whether the statement was overlooked inadvertently?

3. The defense lawyer in *Brady* made a specific request to examine Boblit's out-of-court statements. If the lawyer had not made such a request, would the prosecutor have had an obligation to produce the statement in question?

* * * * *

The Court first squarely addressed the significance of a specific request being made for exculpatory evidence in *United States v. Agurs*, 427 U.S. 97, 96 S. Ct. 2392, 49 L. Ed. 2d 342 (1976). Justice Stevens's majority opinion distinguished between three types of prosecutorial breaches of duty: the knowing use of perjured testimony; the failure to disclose material evidence following the defense's specific request for such evidence; and the failure to disclose material evidence absent a defense request, or following only a nonspecific or general request. The Court applied different tests for due-process violations depending on the specific type of breach. The different tests made the *materiality*, or likely significance of the evidence to the outcome of the trial to be the determining factor.

Specifically, the *Agurs* Court ruled:

a. In the first situation, where "the prosecution's case includes perjured testimony and . . . the prosecution knew, or should have known, of the perjury," a "strict standard of materiality would be applied. . . ." A strict standard was justified "because [such cases] involve prosecutorial misconduct, but more importantly because they involve a corruption of the truth-seeking function of the trial process." The Court concluded that "a conviction obtained by the knowing use of perjury is fundamentally unfair, and must be set aside *if there is any reasonable likelihood that the false testimony could have affected the judgment of the jury*." (Emphasis added.)

b. "The second situation, illustrated by the Brady case itself, is characterized by a pretrial request for specific evidence." The Court noted that before a prosecutor's noncompliance with a request of this nature caused a due-process violation, the evidence at issue had to be "material." "A fair analysis of the holding in Brady indicates that implicit in the requirement of materiality is a concern that the suppressed evidence *might have affected the outcome of the trial*." (Emphasis added.)

c. The third situation arose in *Agurs*. Following Agurs's trial and conviction for murder, defense counsel became aware that the prosecution had evidence at its disposal that arguably was favorable to the defense. However, no pretrial request had been made of the prosecutor to disclose that evidence. The Court thus had to "consider whether the prosecutor has any constitutional duty to volunteer exculpatory matter to the defense, and if so, what standard of materiality gives rise to that duty." After concluding that the prosecutor's unique obligation to serve justice sometimes does impose a constitutional duty to disclose potentially exculpatory evidence, even absent a request from the defendant, the justices announced the proper standard of materiality. They ruled that "*if the evidence creates a reasonable doubt that did not otherwise exist*, constitutional error has been committed." (Emphasis added.) Applying this test to the facts in *Agurs*, the Court concluded that no due-process violation had occurred.

Agurs thus provided a tidy framework for analyzing alleged prosecutorial breaches of duty. The type of alleged breach—knowing use of perjury, failure to produce material evidence following a specific request, or failure to produce material evidence absent a request—first had to be identified. Then the appropriate standard for judging the materiality of the evidence at issue was selected. Finally, the relevant test was applied to the specific case facts for a decision. However, the *Agurs* analytical framework did not long endure.

* * * * *

The defendant in *United States v. Bagley*, 473 U.S. 667, 105 S. Ct. 3375, 87 L. Ed. 2d 481 (1985), was indicted on several charges of violating federal narcotics and firearms laws. The government's two principal witnesses at Bagley's trial had assisted the Bureau of Alcohol, Tobacco, and Firearms (ATF) in producing evidence against Bagley. Defense counsel had filed a pretrial discovery motion requesting, among other items, information about "any deals, promises or inducements made to witnesses in exchange for their testimony." The government disclosed no such arrangements in its response. Bagley waived a jury and was tried before a U.S. district court judge. He was convicted of the narcotics charges and acquitted of the firearms offenses. Following his trial, evidence surfaced that the two key witnesses had been paid $300 each for helping the government make its case.

Bagley argued that his due-process rights had been violated by the nondisclosure of the witnesses' arrangement with the government, which resulted in his being unable to attempt to impeach the credibility of the two witnesses by exposing the financial benefits each had reaped for testifying. The judge who had found Bagley guilty concluded "beyond a reasonable doubt . . . that had the existence of the agreements been disclosed to [him] during trial, the disclosure would have had no effect" on his verdict. He thus refused to overturn Bagley's conviction. The Ninth Circuit Court of Appeals reversed. It ruled that "the government's failure to provide requested Brady information to Bagley so that

he could effectively cross-examine two important government witnesses requires an *automatic* reversal." (Emphasis added.)

The Supreme Court reversed, rejecting the Ninth Circuit's rule of automatic reversal. In the process, Justice Blackmun's opinion—which spoke only for a plurality of the Court on this issue—dismantled the *Agurs* framework for analyzing breaches of prosecutorial duty. It focused on cases involving prosecutors' nondisclosure of potentially exculpatory evidence in response to a specific request (*Brady*) and also their nondisclosure of evidence absent a specific request (*Agurs*).

The Court has relied on and reformulated the Agurs standard for the materiality of undisclosed evidence in two subsequent cases arising outside the Brady context. In neither case did the Court's discussion of the Agurs standard distinguish among the three situations described in Agurs. In United States v. Valenzuela-Bernal, 458 US 858, 874, 102 S Ct 3440, 73 L Ed 2d 1193 (1982), the Court held that due process is violated when testimony is made unavailable to the defense by Government deportation of witnesses "only if there is a reasonable likelihood that the testimony could have affected the judgment of the trier of fact." And in Strickland v. Washington, 466 US 668, 104 S Ct 2052, 80 L Ed 2d 674 (1984), the Court held that a new trial must be granted when evidence is not introduced because of the incompetence of counsel only if "there is a reasonable probability that, but for counsel's unprofessional errors, the result of the proceeding would have been different." Id., at 694. The Strickland Court defined a "reasonable probability" as "a probability sufficient to undermine confidence in the outcome."

We find the Strickland formulation of the Agurs test for materiality sufficiently flexible to cover the "no request," "general request," and "specific request" cases of prosecutorial failure to disclose evidence favorable to the accused: The evidence is material only if there is a reasonable probability that, had the evidence been disclosed to the defense, the result of the proceeding would have been different. A "reasonable probability" is a probability sufficient to undermine confidence in the outcome.

The Government suggests that a materiality standard more favorable to the defendant reasonably might be adopted in specific request cases. The Government notes that an incomplete response to a specific request not only deprives the defense of certain evidence, but also has the effect of representing to the defense that the evidence does not exist. In reliance on this misleading representation, the defense might abandon lines of independent investigation, defenses, or trial strategies that it otherwise would have pursued.

We agree that the prosecutor's failure to respond fully to a Brady request may impair the adversary process in this manner. And the more specifically the defense requests certain evidence, thus putting the prosecutor on notice of its value, the more reasonable it is for the defense to assume from the nondisclosure that the evidence does not exist, and to make pretrial and trial decisions on the basis of this assumption. This possibility of impairment does not necessitate a different standard of materiality, however, for under the Strickland formulation the reviewing court may consider directly any adverse effect that the prosecutor's failure to respond might have had on the preparation or presentation of the defendant's case. The reviewing court should assess the possibility that such effect might have occurred in light of the totality of the circumstances and with an awareness of the difficulty of reconstructing in a post-trial proceeding the course that the defense and the trial would have taken had the defense

not been misled by the prosecutor's incomplete response.

* * *

Justice Blackmun concluded in *Bagley* "that there is a significant likelihood that the prosecutor's response to [Bagley's] discovery motion misleadingly induced defense counsel to believe that [the two witnesses] could not be impeached on the basis of bias or interest arising from inducements offered by the Government." Bagley's conviction was reversed, and the case was remanded "for a determination whether there is a reasonable probability that, had the inducement offered by the Government to [the witnesses] been disclosed to the defense, the result of the trial would have been different." Justice White, joined by Chief Justice Burger and Justice Rehnquist, concurred in the judgment. Those justices agreed that the standard of materiality announced by Justice Blackmun—that "there is a reasonable probability that, had the evidence been disclosed to the defense, the result of the proceeding would have been different"—was "'sufficiently flexible' to cover all instances of prosecutorial failure to disclose evidence favorable to the accused." Justices Marshall, Brennan, and Stevens dissented. Justice Powell did not participate.

* * * * *

In *Kyles v. Whitley,* 514 U.S. 419, 115 S. Ct. 1555, 131 L. Ed. 2d 490 (1995), a majority of the Court expressly adopted the *Bagley* Court's modification of *Agurs* and elaborated on the meaning of the *Bagley* rule. Justice Souter wrote the majority opinion in a 5-4 decision that set aside Kyles's murder conviction and death sentence.

Kyles v. Whitley, 514 U.S. 419, 115 S. Ct. 1555, 131 L. Ed. 2d 490 (1995)

Mr. Justice Souter delivered the opinion of the Court.

. . .

Bagley held that regardless of request, favorable evidence is material, and constitutional

error results from its suppression by the government, "if there is a reasonable probability that, had the evidence been disclosed to the defense, the result of the proceeding would have been different." Four aspects of materiality under *Bagley* bear emphasis. Although the constitutional duty is triggered by the potential impact of favorable but undisclosed evidence, a showing of materiality does not require demonstration by a preponderance that disclosure of the suppressed evidence would have resulted ultimately in the defendant's acquittal (whether based on the presence of reasonable doubt or acceptance of an explanation for the crime that does not inculpate the defendant). . . .

Bagley's touchstone of materiality is a "reasonable probability" of a different result, and the adjective is important. The question is not whether the defendant would more likely than not have received a different verdict with the evidence, but whether in its absence he received a fair trial, understood as a trial resulting in a verdict worthy of confidence. A "reasonable probability" of a different result is accordingly shown when the Government's evidentiary suppression "undermines confidence in the outcome of the trial." *Bagley*, 473 US, at 678.

The second aspect of *Bagley* materiality bearing emphasis here is that it is not a sufficiency of evidence test. A defendant need not demonstrate that after discounting the inculpatory evidence in light of the undisclosed evidence, there would not have been enough left to convict. The possibility of an acquittal on a criminal charge does not imply an insufficient evidentiary basis to convict. One does not show a *Brady* violation by demonstrating that some of the inculpatory evidence should have been excluded, but by showing that the favorable evidence could reasonably be taken to put the whole case in such a different light as to undermine confidence in the verdict.

Once a reviewing court applying *Bagley* has found constitutional error there is no need for further harmless-error review.

The fourth and final aspect of *Bagley* materiality to be stressed here is its definition in terms of suppressed evidence considered collectively, not item-by-item. As Justice Blackmun emphasized in the portion of his opinion written for the Court, the Constitution is not violated every time the government fails or chooses not to disclose evidence that might prove helpful to the defense. We have never held that the Constitution demands an open file policy (however such a policy might work out in practice), and the rule in

Bagley (and, hence, in *Brady*) requires less of the prosecution than the ABA Standards for Criminal Justice, which call generally for prosecutorial disclosures of any evidence tending to exculpate or mitigate. See ABA Standards for Criminal Justice, Prosecution Function and Defense Function 3-3.11(a) (3d ed 1993) ("A prosecutor should not intentionally fail to make timely disclosure to the defense, at the earliest feasible opportunity, of the existence of all evidence or information which tends to negate the guilt of the accused or mitigate the offense charged or which would tend to reduce the punishment of the accused"); ABA Model Rule of Professional Conduct 3.8(d) (1984) ("The prosecutor in a criminal case shall . . . make timely disclosure to the defense of all evidence or information known to the prosecutor that tends to negate the guilt of the accused or mitigates the offense").

While the definition of *Bagley* materiality in terms of the cumulative effect of suppression must accordingly be seen as leaving the government with a degree of discretion, it must also be understood as imposing a corresponding burden. On the one side, showing that the prosecution knew of an item of favorable evidence unknown to the defense does not amount to a *Brady* violation, without more. But the prosecution, which alone can know what is undisclosed, must be assigned the consequent responsibility to gauge the likely net effect of all such evidence and make disclosure when the point of "reasonable probability" is reached. This in turn means that the individual prosecutor has a duty to learn of any favorable evidence known to the others acting on the government's behalf in the case, including the police. But whether the prosecutor succeeds or fails in meeting this obligation (whether, that is, a failure to disclose is in good faith or bad faith, see *Brady*, 373 US, at 87), the prosecution's responsibility for failing to disclose known, favorable evidence rising to a material level of importance is inescapable.

The State of Louisiana would prefer an even more lenient rule. It pleads that some of the favorable evidence in issue here was not disclosed even to the prosecutor until after trial, and it suggested below that it should not be held accountable under *Bagley* and *Brady* for evidence known only to police investigators and not to the prosecutor. To accommodate the State in this manner would, however, amount to a serious change of course from the *Brady* line of cases. In the State's favor it may be said that no one doubts that police investigators sometimes fail to inform a prosecutor of all they know. But neither is there any serious doubt that "procedures and regulations can be established to carry [the prosecutor's] burden and to insure communication of all relevant information on each case to every lawyer who deals with it." *Giglio v. United States*, 405 US 150, 154, 92 S Ct 763, 31 L Ed 2d 104 (1972). Since, then, the prosecutor has the means to discharge the government's *Brady* responsibility if he will, any argument for excusing a prosecutor from disclosing what he does not happen to know about boils down to a plea to substitute the police for the prosecutor, and even for the courts themselves, as the final arbiters of the government's obligation to ensure fair trials.

Short of doing that, we were asked at oral argument to raise the threshold of materiality because the *Bagley* standard "makes it difficult . . . to know" from the "perspective [of the prosecutor at] trial . . . exactly what might become important later on." The State asks for "a certain amount of leeway in making a judgment call" as to the disclosure of any given piece of evidence.

Uncertainty about the degree of further "leeway" that might satisfy the State's request for a "certain amount" of it is the least of the reasons to deny the request. At bottom, what the State fails to recognize is that, with or without more leeway, the prosecution cannot be subject to any disclosure obligation without at some point having the responsibility to determine when it must act. Indeed, even if due process were thought to be

violated by every failure to disclose an item of exculpatory or impeachment evidence (leaving harmless error as the government's only fallback), the prosecutor would still be forced to make judgment calls about what would count as favorable evidence, owing to the very fact that the character of a piece of evidence as favorable will often turn on the context of the existing or potential evidentiary record. Since the prosecutor would have to exercise some judgment even if the State were subject to this most stringent disclosure obligation, it is hard to find merit in the State's complaint over the responsibility for judgment under the existing system, which does not tax the prosecutor with error for any failure to disclose, absent a further showing of materiality. Unless, indeed, the adversary system of prosecution is to descend to a gladiatorial level unmitigated by any prosecutorial obligation for the sake of truth, the government simply cannot avoid responsibility for knowing when the suppression of evidence has come to portend such an effect on a trial's outcome as to destroy confidence in its result.

This means, naturally, that a prosecutor anxious about tacking too close to the wind will disclose a favorable piece of evidence. See *Agurs*, 427 US, at 108 ("[T]he prudent prosecutor will resolve doubtful questions in favor of disclosure"). This is as it should be. Such disclosure will serve to justify trust in the prosecutor as "the representative . . . of a sovereignty . . . whose interest . . . in a criminal prosecution is not that it shall win a case, but that justice shall be done." *Berger v. United States*, 295 US 78, 88, 55 S Ct 629, 79 L Ed 1314 (1935). And it will tend to preserve the criminal trial, as distinct from the prosecutor's private deliberations, as the chosen forum for ascertaining the truth about criminal accusations. . . .

The New York Court of Appeals has rejected the *Bagley* rule on state constitutional grounds. Its opinion in *People v. Vilardi* helpfully summarizes the federal rule and explains its perceived deficiencies.

———◆———

People v. Vilardi, 76 N.Y.2d 67, 555 N.E.2d 915, 556 N.Y.S.2d 518 (1990)

KAYE, Judge.

This appeal calls upon us to determine the effect to be given to the People's failure, in an arson prosecution, to disclose a report prepared by its explosives expert that had been specifically sought by defendant in his discovery request. More particularly, we must decide whether the standard of United States v. Bagley, 473 U.S. 667, 105 S.Ct. 3375, 87 L.Ed.2d481 [(1985)] should be adopted as a matter of State law.

Defendant was convicted of arson in the first degree, attempted arson in the first degree and conspiracy, for having conspired with Ronnie and William Bernacet, Ephraim Flores and Gino Romano to plant and set off one pipe bomb below a pizzeria on Nostrand Avenue in Brooklyn, and a second below a nearby laundromat. The first bomb did not explode. It was the People's theory, however, that the bomb planted in the laundromat basement had exploded as planned, and thus the defendants were charged with arson in the first degree, as well as attempt. Damage caused by an explosion is an element of arson in the first degree.

The Bernacet brothers—who unlike defendant had made fairly extensive inculpatory statements—were tried first, on the same charges on which defendant was later tried. Among the prosecution witnesses was Officer Daniel Kiely, a member of the Bomb Squad, who had inspected the laundromat basement the day after the alleged explosion. At the Bernacets' trial, Kiely was cross-examined at length about a report he wrote the day after the incident, in which he stated that a thorough inspection of the basement revealed no evidence that there had been an explosion, but asked that the case be kept open. Although Kiely testified that he ultimately concluded (in light of reinspection of the premises a year later) that there had been an explosion, defense counsel in summation argued that there was insufficient proof of the explosion element of first degree arson, based on Kiely's first report. The Bernacet brothers were acquitted of the completed arson.

Before defendant's trial, counsel made a pretrial request for all reports "by ballistics, firearm and explosive experts" concerning the laundromat explosion. The prosecutor—not the same Assistant District Attorney who tried the Bernacets—sent him 12 reports, not including Officer Kiely's first report. At trial, no questions about that first report were asked during the brief cross-examination of Kiely, and no effort was made to argue that the People had failed to establish the explosion element of the top count.

The sole defense was that the police informant who provided much of the evidence against defendant was too unsavory to be credited. . . . Defendant was convicted on all counts.

While preparing defendant's appeal, appellate counsel reviewed the transcript of the Bernacets' trial, and realized that there was an undisclosed explosives report. Defendant made a motion to vacate the judgment of conviction, . . . arguing . . . that the undisclosed report was Brady material (and failure to disclose violated his due process rights under the State and Federal Constitutions). . . .

The Appellate Division . . . granted defendant's motion to the extent of vacating his conviction of arson in the first degree. Distinguishing this case—in which counsel had specifically sought the undisclosed report—from a case in which no specific request had been made, the Appellate Division held that the report was exculpatory, that the prosecution violated the defendant's constitutional right to be informed of exculpatory information known to the State, and that reversal was required "if there is a reasonable possibility that [the undisclosed material] contributed to the defendant's conviction." Concluding that the People had not met that standard, the Appellate Division ordered a new trial on the completed arson charge to which the exculpatory material was relevant. We now affirm.

Analysis

. . . [T]he People contend that the standard applied by the Appellate Division was erroneous. Noting that the Supreme Court has recently articulated a single standard for determination of when a prosecutor's failure to disclose evidence favorable to the defendant requires reversal (see, United States v. Bagley, supra), the People argue that . . . the Appellate Division should have applied the Bagley standard: that failure to disclose favorable evidence is "constitutional error only if the evidence [was] material in the sense that there is a reasonable probability that, had the evidence been disclosed to the defense, the result of the proceeding would have been different." The Appellate Division's assessment, according to the People, was improperly based on a "reasonable possibility" standard more favorable to defendant, as there is no longer any distinction between cases in which a specific request has been made for undisclosed Brady material and those in which it has not.

. . . [T]his court has not yet had occasion to consider, under State law, whether to adopt Bagley's broad formulation of the materiality standard in the context of a case where the prosecutor has failed to turn over particular exculpatory evidence, despite the fact that defendant has requested disclosure of that very evidence. . . . In this case . . . the withheld report is plainly exculpatory, as it suggests there was no evidence of a crucial element of the first degree arson charge; there is no dispute that the report was in the People's possession; and defendant specifically sought discovery of the very material involved here—reports of explosives experts.

. . . Federal constitutional law concerning the People's failure to disclose exculpatory evidence originated in a series of cases involving the prosecution's knowing use of perjured testimony. In Brady v. Maryland, 373 U.S. 83, 83 S.Ct. 1194, 10 L.Ed.2d 215 [(1963)], decided nearly 30 years ago, the Supreme Court established, as a matter of Federal constitutional law, that the prosecution's failure to disclose to the defense evidence in its possession both favorable and material to the defense entitles the defendant to a new trial. Brady itself involved failure to disclose evidence that had been specifically requested by the defense, and the Court noted that the nondisclosure was constitutional error if the evidence would "tend to exculpate" the defendant.

Following the Brady decision, there was considerable doubt as to whether a specific request for the exculpatory evidence might not be an indispensable element of a Brady claim. It was in response to this doubt that in United States v. Agurs, 427 U.S. 97, 96 S.Ct. 2392, 49 L.Ed.2d 342 [(1976)], the Court created a two-tiered framework for determining whether favorable evidence was "material," so that the failure to disclose it required a new trial. Evidence specifically requested by the defense was material if it "might have affected the outcome of the trial." By contrast, in cases where there had been no request, or only a general request for exculpatory material, the prosecution's duty to disclose arose entirely from the notice provided by the very nature of the evidence, and the standard for

a new trial was higher: undisclosed exculpatory evidence was material only if it "create[d] a reasonable doubt that did not otherwise exist."

In Agurs, the Court reasoned that it was appropriate to impose a lesser burden on the defendant in a "specific request" case because such a request puts the prosecutor on notice that there is particular evidence the defense does not have and believes to be important. By contrast, use of the "might have affected" standard where the prosecutor had been given no such notice might require something close to open file discovery. As the Court noted, "[w]hen the prosecutor receives a specific and relevant request, the failure to make any response is seldom, if ever, excusable," and this has been read as "reflect[ing] the view that [in the specific request cases], the prosecutor's responsibility for any resulting trial deception is clear."

This court has likewise found the prosecution's failure to turn over specifically requested evidence to be "seldom, if ever, excusable" and to verge on prosecutorial misconduct.

In Bagley, a deeply divided Supreme Court reconsidered its two-tiered approach, and replaced it with a single standard applicable in all cases. Adopting the very same test it had just formulated in Strickland v. Washington, 466 U.S. 668, 104 S.Ct. 2052, 80 L.Ed.2d 674 [(1984)] for determining ineffective assistance of counsel claims, the Court in Bagley held that undisclosed evidence is material only if there is a "reasonable probability" that it "would" have altered the outcome of the trial; a reasonable probability is "a probability sufficient to undermine confidence in the outcome." The Court opined that this standard was "sufficiently flexible" to cover both the "specific request" and "no request/general request" cases. Justice Blackmun observed that a prosecutor's failure to respond to a specific request not only deprives the defense of the exculpatory evidence (as in all Brady cases) but also may have the effect of misleading the defense to conclude that the particular evidence does not exist, and therefore to abandon its investigative and trial efforts in that direction. But he concluded that under the Strickland formulation, any such additional adverse consequences could be taken into consideration by a reviewing court in the totality of the circumstances, and no separate standard was necessary.

Thus, while continuing to give at least a theoretical preference to specific request cases, the Supreme Court's new rationale and approach are entirely different from Agurs. . . . Rather than giving more serious consideration to specific requests both because of the greater degree of notice they provide, and out of reasons of fairness and prosecutorial misconduct, in Bagley the Court jettisoned such considerations in favor of a single standard, which in some undefined measure may—or may not—include adverse consequences in the specific request context.

From a Federal standard of "seldom, if ever, excusable," it appears that the prosecution's failure to turn over specifically requested evidence, under Bagley, will now seldom, if ever, be unexcused.

Over the course of the decades since Brady was decided, the courts of this State, obviously, have had to deal on a practical level with the consequences of a prosecutor's failure to disclose evidence requested by the defense. As is the Federal rule of Brady, this court's analysis of the prosecutor's duty to disclose exculpatory evidence is rooted in cases dealing with the similar question of knowing prosecutorial use of false and misleading testimony. Notably, these cases even predate the identified Federal progenitors of Brady, and were decided entirely without reference to Federal law, based on our own view of this State's requirements for a fair trial.

Our own view of important State concerns in this matter has differed significantly from the Supreme Court's newest interpretation of the dictates of the Federal due process standard. We have long emphasized that our view of due process in this area is, in large measure, predicated both upon "elemental fairness" to the defendant, and upon concern that the prosecutor's office discharge its ethical and professional obligations. Although we have refused, in this context, to adopt a rule of automatic reversal, we have endorsed the proposition that "'the strictness of the application of the harmless error standard seems somewhat to vary, and its reciprocal, the required showing of prejudice, to vary inversely, with the degree to which the conduct of the trial has violated basic concepts of fair play.'" . . . In accordance with our long-standing

State concerns in cases involving failure to disclose material specifically requested by a defendant, we have described the standard as one premised on Agurs, and that has been understood and cited again and again as the governing standard throughout the State.

We decline to abandon these accepted principles in order to conform to the lesser protections of Bagley.

We agree with the Appellate Division that a showing of a "reasonable possibility" that the failure to disclose the exculpatory report contributed to the verdict remains the appropriate standard to measure materiality, where the prosecutor was made aware by a specific discovery request that defendant considered the material important to the defense. As we have previously noted suppression, or even negligent failure to disclose, is more serious in the face of a specific request in its potential to undermine the fairness of the trial, and ought to be given more weight than as simply one of a number of discretionary factors to be considered by a reviewing court.

Further, a backward-looking, outcome-oriented standard of review that gives dispositive weight to the strength of the People's case clearly provides diminished incentive for the prosecutor, in first responding to discovery requests, thoroughly to review files for exculpatory material, or to err on the side of disclosure where exculpatory value is debatable. Where the defense itself has provided specific notice of its interest in particular material, heightened rather than lessened prosecutorial care is appropriate.

The "reasonable possibility" standard applied by the Appellate Division—essentially a reformulation of the "seldom if ever excusable" rule—is a clear rule that properly encourages compliance with these obligations, and we therefore conclude that as a matter of State constitutional law it is preferable to Bagley. Moreover, the Strickland "reasonable probability" standard—which we have chosen not to adopt as a matter of State law despite several invitations to do so— remits the impact of the exculpatory evidence to appellate hindsight, thus significantly diminishing the vital interest this court has long recognized in a decision rendered by a jury whose ability to render that decision is unimpaired by failure to disclose important evidence.

Finally, the new Bagley standard is hardly clear. The Supreme Court itself could not muster a plurality on how the new standard was to be applied to the case before it, and the case has engendered considerable confusion.

For all of these reasons, and not because we "merely disagree[ ] with [the Supreme Court] or dislike[ ] the result reached" (concurring opn.), we choose to adhere to our existing standard as a matter of due process of law under the State Constitution.

Applying that standard in this case, we agree with the Appellate Division that defendant is entitled to a new trial on the first degree arson charge, as there was at least a reasonable possibility that defendant would not have been con-victed on that count had the exculpatory report been available to him at trial. That a contemporaneous and avowedly "thorough" inspection of the bomb site by an expert had led him to conclude that no explosion occurred well might have caused the jury to discount his contrary assertion at trial, which was based on challenged circumstantial evidence and arrived at only after the passage of a year. It is the reasonable possibility that the undisclosed evidence might have led to a trial strategy that resulted in a different outcome (as appears to have happened in the Bernacets' case) that requires reversal.

Accordingly, the order of the Appellate Division should be affirmed.

Notes and Questions

1. The New York Court of Appeals expresses concern that "the prosecutor's office discharge its ethical and professional obligations" and warns that prosecutors must not violate "basic concepts of fair play." Does the due-process standard adopted in *Vilardi* for judging the materiality of evidence that has been specifically requested seem more likely to allow courts to enforce those norms than does the *Bagley* standard? Can the *Bagley* test take account of the fact that a prosecutor has failed to comply with a defendant's specific discovery request? Should it, or should the exclusive focus be the materiality of the evidence?

2. Is the *Vilardi* test consistent with the Supreme Court's suggestion in *Brady* and other cases that "the good faith or bad faith of the prosecution" is not at issue when a prosecutor's office fails to produce potentially exculpatory evidence?

3. Should the *Vilardi* standard be applied to the police if they do not share evidence that may be favorable to the accused with the prosecutor? What does the Supreme Court suggest in *Kyles v. Whitley* about whether the prosecutor is held accountable to know what evidence the police have collected?

Is There a Duty for the Police To Preserve Potentially Exculpatory Evidence?

The police function in investigating crimes is crucial to successful prosecutions. How the police perform their jobs can affect a criminal prosecution in several different ways. For example, an unreasonable search or seizure may result in the suppression of evidence that would be useful or even essential to prove guilt. The violation of a suspect's *Miranda* rights may cause a confession to be inadmissi-ble at trial. And, as the Court made clear in *Kyles v. Whitley, supra,* the failure by the police to share potentially exculpatory evidence with a prosecutor does not insulate the prosecutor from his or her duty under *Brady* and *Bagley* to make that evidence available to the defense.

We now consider an issue that generally relates to *Brady* material and the prosecution's obligation to provide potentially exculpatory evidence to the defense. Do the police, because they serve as a vital link in the chain of a prosecution, have a duty analogous to the prosecutor's to preserve evidence that could be useful to the accused in defending against criminal charges?

Arizona v. Youngblood, 488 U.S. 51, 109 S. Ct. 333, 102 L. Ed. 2d 281 (1988)

Chief Justice Rehnquist delivered the opinion of the Court.

[On October 29, 1983 a 10-year-old boy was abducted from a church carnival by a man who drove the boy to a secluded location and repeatedly sodomized him. The man thereafter released the boy, who made his way home and was taken to a hospital and treated for rectal injuries. A physician used a "sexual assault kit" to collect evidence of the attack, including swabs of the boy's rectum and mouth and samples of the boy's saliva, blood, and hair. The police placed the kit in a secure refrigerator at the police station, and also collected the boy's T-shirt and underwear. These items of clothing were not refrigerated or frozen.

[Nine days after the attack, the boy identified Youngblood as his assailant from a photographic lineup. The following day, a police criminologist examined the sexual assault kit and determined that sexual contact had occurred but performed no other tests and did not test the boy's clothing. He returned the sexual assault kit to the refrigerator. Youngblood was located and arrested approximately four weeks later, on December 9, 1983. He subsequently was indicted on charges of child molestation, sexual assault, and kidnapping.

[An ABO blood group test later was performed on the rectal swab sample, but it failed to detect any blood group substances. The police criminologist examined the boy's clothing for the first time in January 1985. He located semen stains on both the T-shirt and the underwear, but was unsuccessful in obtaining blood group substances from the stains using the ABO technique. "He also performed a P-30 protein molecule test on the stains, which indicated that only a small quantity of semen was present on the clothing; it was inconclusive as to the assailant's identity."

[At his trial, Youngblood contended that the boy had erroneously identified him as his assailant. "[B]oth a criminologist for the State and an expert witness for respondent testified as to what might have been shown by tests performed on the samples shortly after they were gathered, or by later tests performed on the samples from the boy's clothing had the clothing been properly refrigerated. The court instructed the jury that if they found that the State had destroyed or lost evidence, they might "infer that the true fact is against the State's interest." The jury found Youngblood guilty as charged.

[The Arizona Court of Appeals reversed. It held that "when identity is an issue at trial and the police permit the destruction of evidence that could eliminate the defendant as the perpetrator, such loss is material to the defense and is a denial of due process." The Court of Appeals concluded on the basis of the expert testimony at trial that timely performance of tests with properly preserved semen samples could have produced results that might have completely exonerated respondent. The Court of Appeals reached this conclusion even though it did "not imply any bad faith on the part of the State."

[The Supreme Court granted certiorari "to consider the extent to which the Due Process Clause of the Federal Constitution requires the State to preserve evidentiary material that might be useful to a criminal defendant."]

. . .

Decision of this case requires us to again consider "what might loosely be called the area of constitutionally guaranteed access to evidence." United States v. Valenzuela-Bernal, 458 US 858, 867, 102 S Ct 3440, 73 L Ed 2d 1193 (1982). In Brady v. Maryland, we held "that the suppression by the prosecution of evidence favorable to the accused upon request violates due process where the evidence is material either to guilt or to punishment, irrespective of the good faith or bad faith of the prosecution." In United States v. Agurs, we held that the prosecution had a duty to disclose some evidence of this description even though no requests were made for it, but at the same time we rejected the notion that a "prosecutor has a constitutional duty routinely to deliver his entire file to defense counsel."

There is no question but that the State complied with Brady and Agurs here. The State disclosed relevant police reports to respondent, which contained information about the existence of the swab and the clothing, and the boy's examination at the hospital. The State provided respondent's expert with the laboratory reports and notes prepared by the police criminologist, and respondent's expert had access to the swab and to the clothing.

If respondent is to prevail on federal constitutional grounds, then, it must be because of some constitutional duty over and above that imposed by cases such as Brady and Agurs. Our most recent decision in this area of the law, California v. Trombetta, 467 US 479, 104 S Ct 2528, 81 L Ed 2d 413 (1984), arose out of a drunk driving prosecution in which the State had introduced test results indicating the concentration of alcohol in the blood of two motorists. The defendants sought to suppress the test results on the ground that the State had failed to preserve the breath samples used in the test. We rejected this argument for several reasons: first, "the officers here were acting in 'good faith and in accord with their normal practice,'" second, in the light of the procedures actually used the chances that preserved samples would have exculpated the defendants were slim, and, third, even if the samples might have shown inaccuracy in the tests, the defendants had "alternative means of demonstrating their innocence." In the present case, the likelihood that the preserved materials would have enabled the defendant to exonerate himself appears to be greater than it was in Trombetta, but here, unlike in Trombetta, the State did not attempt to make any use of the materials in its own case in chief.

Our decisions in related areas have stressed the importance for constitutional purposes of good or bad faith on the part of the Government when the claim is based on loss of evidence attributable to the Government. In United States

v. Marion, 404 US 307, 92 S Ct 455, 30 L Ed 2d 468 (1971), we said that "[n]o actual prejudice to the conduct of the defense is alleged or proved, and there is no showing that the Government intentionally delayed to gain some tactical advantage over appellees or to harass them." Similarly, in United States v. Valenzuela-Bernal, supra, we considered whether the Government's deportation of two witnesses who were illegal aliens violated due process. We held that the prompt deportation of the witnesses was justified "upon the Executive's good-faith determination that they possess no evidence favorable to the defendant in a criminal prosecution."

The Due Process Clause of the Fourteenth Amendment, as interpreted in Brady, makes the good or bad faith of the State irrelevant when the State fails to disclose to the defendant material exculpatory evidence. But we think the Due Process Clause requires a different result when we deal with the failure of the State to preserve evidentiary material of which no more can be said than that it could have been subjected to tests, the results of which might have exonerated the defendant. Part of the reason for the difference in treatment is found in the observation made by the Court in Trombetta, supra, at 486, that "[w]henever potentially exculpatory evidence is permanently lost, courts face the treacherous task of divining the import of materials whose contents are unknown and, very often, disputed." Part of it stems from our unwillingness to read the "fundamental fairness" requirement of the Due Process Clause as imposing on the police an undifferentiated and absolute duty to retain and to preserve all material that might be of conceivable evidentiary significance in a particular prosecution. We think that requiring a defendant to show bad faith on the part of the police both limits the extent of the police's obligation to preserve evidence to reasonable bounds and confines it to that class of cases where the interests of justice most clearly require it, i.e., those cases in which the police themselves by their conduct indicate that the evidence could form a basis for exonerating the defendant. We therefore hold that unless a criminal defendant can show bad faith on the part of the police, failure to preserve potentially useful evidence does not constitute a denial of due process of law.

In this case, the police collected the rectal swab and clothing on the night of the crime: respondent was not taken into custody until six weeks later. The failure of the police to refrigerate the clothing and to perform tests on the semen samples can at worst be described as negligent. None of this information was concealed from respondent at trial, and the evidence—such as it was—was made available to respondent's expert who declined to perform any tests on the samples. The Arizona Court of Appeals noted in its opinion—and we agree—that there was no suggestion of bad faith on the part of the police. It follows, therefore, from what we have said, that there was no violation of the Due Process Clause.

The Arizona Court of Appeals also referred somewhat obliquely to the State's "inability to quantitatively test" certain semen samples with the newer P-30 test. If the court means by this statement that the Due Process Clause is violated when the police fail to use a particular investigatory tool, we strongly disagree. The situation here is no different than a prosecution for drunk driving that rests on police observation alone; the defendant is free to argue to the finder of fact that a breathalizer test might have been exculpatory, but the police do not have a constitutional duty to perform any particular tests.

The judgment of the Arizona Court of Appeals is reversed, and the case is remanded for further proceedings not inconsistent with this opinion. . . .

Justice Stevens, concurring in the judgment.

Three factors are of critical importance to my evaluation of this case. First, at the time the police failed to refrigerate the victim's clothing, and thus negligently lost potentially valuable evidence, they had at least as great an interest in preserving the evidence as did the person later accused of the crime. In cases such as this, even without a prophylactic sanction such as dismissal of the indictment, the State has a strong incentive to preserve the evidence.

Second, although it is not possible to know whether the lost evidence would have revealed any relevant information, it is unlikely that the defendant was prejudiced by the State's omission. In examining witnesses and in her summation, defense counsel impressed upon the jury the fact that the State failed to preserve the evidence and that the State could have conducted tests that might well have exonerated the defendant. More significantly, the trial judge instructed the jury: "If you find that the State has . . . allowed to be destroyed or lost any evidence whose content or quality are in issue, you may infer that the true fact is against the State's interest." As a result, the uncertainty as to what the evidence might have proved was turned to the defendant's advantage.

Third, the fact that no juror chose to draw the permissive inference that proper preservation of the evidence would have demonstrated that the defendant was not the assailant suggests that the lost evidence was "immaterial." In declining defense counsel's and the court's invitations to draw the permissive inference, the jurors in effect indicated that, in their view, the other evidence at trial was so overwhelming that it was highly improbable that the lost evidence was exculpatory. Presumably, in a case involving a closer question as to guilt or innocence, the jurors would have been more ready to infer that the lost evidence was exculpatory.

With these factors in mind, I concur in the Court's judgment. I do not, however, join the Court's opinion because it announces a proposition of law that is much broader than necessary to decide this case. It states "that unless a criminal defendant can show bad faith on the part of the police, failure to preserve potentially useful evidence does not constitute a denial of due process of law." In my opinion, there may well be cases in which the defendant is unable to prove that the State acted in bad faith but in which the loss or destruction of evidence is nonetheless so critical to the defense as to make a criminal trial fundamentally unfair. This, however, is not such a case. . . .

Justice Blackmun, with whom Justice Brennan and Justice Marshall join, dissenting.

The Constitution requires that criminal defendants be provided with a fair trial, not merely a "good faith" try at a fair trial. Respondent here, by what may have been nothing more than police ineptitude, was denied the opportunity to present a full defense. That ineptitude, however, deprived respondent of his guaranteed right to due process of law.

The cases in this area clearly establish that police actions taken in bad faith are not the only species of police conduct that can result in a violation of due process. As Agurs points out, it makes no sense to overturn a conviction because a malicious prosecutor withholds information that he mistakenly believes to be material, but which actually would have been of no help to the defense. In the same way, it makes no sense to ignore the fact that a defendant has been denied a fair trial because the State allowed evidence that was material to the defense to deteriorate beyond the point of usefulness, simply because the police were inept rather than malicious.

I also doubt that the "bad faith" standard creates the bright-line rule sought by the majority. Apart from the inherent difficulty a defendant would have in obtaining evidence to show a lack of good faith, the line between "good faith" and "bad faith" is anything but bright, and the majority's formulation may well create more questions that it answers. What constitutes bad faith for these purposes? Does a defendant have to show actual malice, or would recklessness, or the deliberate failure to establish standards for maintaining and preserving evidence, be sufficient? Does "good faith police work" require a certain minimum of diligence, or will a lazy officer, who does not walk the few extra steps to the evidence refrigerator, be considered to be acting in good faith? While the majority leaves these questions for another day, its quick embrace of a bad-faith standard has not brightened the line; it only has moved the line so as to provide fewer protections for criminal defendants.

The inquiry the majority eliminates in setting up its "bad faith" rule is whether the evidence in question here was "constitutionally material," so that its destruction violates due process.

The exculpatory value of the clothing in this case cannot be determined with any certainty, precisely because the police allowed the samples to deteriorate. But we do know several important things about the evidence. First, the semen samples on the clothing undoubtedly came from the assailant. Second, the samples could have been tested, using technology available and in use at the local police department, to show either the blood type of the assailant, or that the assailant was a nonsecreter, i.e., someone who does not secrete a blood type "marker" into other body fluids, such as semen. Third, the

evidence was clearly important. A semen sample in a rape case where identity is questioned is always significant. Fourth, a reasonable police officer should have recognized that the clothing required refrigeration. Fifth, we know that an inconclusive test was done on the swab. The test suggested that the assailant was a nonsecreter, although it was equally likely that the sample on the swab was too small for accurate results to be obtained. And, sixth, we know that respondent is a secreter.

If the samples on the clothing had been tested, and the results had shown either the blood type of the assailant or that the assailant was a nonsecreter, its constitutional materiality would be clear. But the State's conduct has deprived the defendant, and the courts, of the opportunity to determine with certainty the import of this evidence: it has "interfere[d] with the accused's ability to present a defense by imposing on him a requirement which the government's own actions have rendered impossible to fulfill." Hilliard v. Spalding, 719 F2d [1443,] 1446 [(9thCir. 1983)]. Good faith or not, this is intolerable, unless the particular circumstances of the case indicate either that the evidence was not likely to prove exculpatory, or that the defendant was able to use effective alternative means to prove the point the destroyed evidence otherwise could have made.

I recognize the difficulties presented by such a situation. The societal interest in seeing criminals punished rightly requires that indictments be dismissed only when the unavailability of the evidence prevents the defendants from receiving a fair trial. In a situation where the substance of the lost evidence is known, the materiality analysis laid out in Trombetta is adequate. But in a situation like the present one, due process requires something more. Rather than allow a State's ineptitude to saddle a defendant with an impossible burden, a court should focus on the type of evidence, the possibility it might prove exculpatory, and the existence of other evidence going to the same point of contention in determining whether the failure to preserve the evidence in question violated due process. To put it succinctly, where no comparable evidence is likely to be available to the defendant, police must preserve physical evidence of a type that they reasonably should know has the potential, if tested, to reveal immutable characteristics of the criminal, and hence to exculpate a defendant charged with the crime.

Due process must also take into account the burdens that the preservation of evidence places on the police. Law enforcement officers must be provided the option, as is implicit in Trombetta, of performing the proper tests on physical evidence and then discarding it. Once a suspect has been arrested the police, after a reasonable time, may inform defense counsel of plans to discard the evidence. When the defense has been informed of the existence of the evidence,

after a reasonable time the burden of preservation may shift to the defense. There should also be flexibility to deal with evidence that is unusually dangerous or difficult to store.

Applying this standard to the facts of this case, I conclude that the Arizona Court of Appeals was correct in overturning respondent's conviction. The evidence in this case was far from conclusive, and the possibility that the evidence denied to respondent would have exonerated him was not remote. The result is that he was denied a fair trial by the actions of the State, and consequently was denied due process of law. . . .

Notes and Questions

1. If the good faith or bad faith of the prosecutor is not relevant to a claimed *Brady* violation, why is a showing of bad faith necessary for the defendant to prevail when the police fail to preserve potentially exculpatory evidence?

2. Assume that Youngblood had a codefendant, Oldblood, against whom a police officer held a personal grudge. Further assume that the officer intentionally and in bad faith destroyed physical evidence that may have been useful to Oldblood's defense. In contrast, potentially exculpatory evidence relevant to Youngblood became unavailable through no apparent bad faith on the part of the police. Would you expect different results in the resolution of Oldblood's and Youngblood's cases? Would the basic fairness of their respective trials—defined in terms of confidence that a just result had been produced based on all potentially relevant evidence—be affected by whether the police acted in bad faith? On the other hand, what inferences does Chief Justice Rehnquist suggest might be supported by the bad-faith destruction of evidence?

3. What, exactly, does *bad faith* mean in this context? Does the Court provide examples or suggest how this term should be defined?

4. In 1985, Kirk Bloodsworth was convicted of the rape and murder of a nine-year-old girl in Maryland. He was sentenced to death. His conviction was overturned on appeal, but he was again convicted on retrial and sentenced to three terms of life imprisonment. "In 1993, newly available DNA tests revealed conclusively that the semen found on the victim did not match Bloodsworth's." After spending nine years in prison, Bloodsworth was released, prosecutors dismissed the case against him, and he was officially pardoned. M. Radelet, W. Lofquist, & H. Bedau, "Prisoners Released from Death Rows Since 1970 Because of Doubts about Their Guilt," 13 *Thomas M. Cooley Law Review* 907, 926 (1996). Bloodsworth's conviction had been supported by eyewitness identification testimony. Does Kirk Bloodsworth's case have any relevance to *Youngblood*?

5. The rule in *Youngblood* has been rejected by some state courts on state constitutional grounds. *See Thorne v. Department of Public Safety*, 774 P.2d 1326 (Alaska 1989); *State v. Snagula*, 133 N.H. 600, 578 A.2d 1215 (1990); *State v. Matafeo*, 71 Ha. 183, 787 P.2d 671 (1990). *See* B. Latzer, *State Constitutional Criminal Law* § 8:7 (1995).

CONCLUSION

Prosecutors play a vitally important role in the administration of criminal justice in this country. The cases and materials in this chapter have focused on examples where something allegedly or actually has gone very wrong in a criminal prosecution: where charges may have been filed or enhanced for impermissible reasons; where perjured testimony has been used to help secure a conviction; or where important evidence material to an accused's defense has not been disclosed or preserved by the prosecutor or the police. In these different contexts, the courts have had to give meaning to the lofty imperatives that the prosecutor's duty "is to seek justice, not merely to convict" and that the accused should not be denied due process of law.

Prosecutors who are true to these ideals occupy a unique and indispensable role in the criminal justice process. Their work is important to help preserve and respect people's constitutional rights and also to help reinforce social behavioral norms and promote safety through the prosecution of criminals and enforcement of the laws. Large numbers of conscientious prosecutors appropriately balance due-process and crime control values and serve their offices well. The constitutional constraints discussed in this chapter help keep prosecutors in check who lose sight of their obligation to do justice and assist and give guidance to prosecutors who do their jobs consistent with this standard.

The Accused's Right to Counsel

Today, it is almost unthinkable that a person who is too poor to be able to hire an attorney could be forced to go to trial on a serious criminal charge without the assistance of a lawyer. A skilled legal advocate seems indispensable to advise the accused, file motions, offer evidence, cross-examine witnesses, raise objections, present arguments to a judge and jury, and provide other essentials of representation. A trial pitting a trained prosecutor against an unassisted layperson would strike most people as being manifestly unfair and unjust. Yet it was only a little over a generation ago that the Supreme Court ruled, in *Gideon v. Wainwright*, 372 U.S. 335, 83 S. Ct. 792, 9 L. Ed. 2d 799 (1963), that poor people are constitutionally entitled to court-appointed counsel to represent them at felony trials.

The English common-law rule governing the right to counsel that was effective at the American Revolution was even less forgiving than was the early law in this country. At common law, criminal defendants were flatly prohibited from being represented by a lawyer at felony trials, even if they could afford to hire one. This prohibition did not apply to misdemeanor trials or cases involving treason. It was justified on the theory that the trial judge would protect the accused's interests in felony trials. Additionally,

because public prosecutors rarely appeared on behalf of the government or the alleged victim in criminal cases, the accused normally was not matched against a trained legal adversary. F. Heller, *The Sixth Amendment to the Constitution of the United States: A Study in Constitutional Development* 109 (1951).

The Sixth Amendment to the United States Constitution, which was modeled after similar state constitutional provisions, rejected the English rule. In relevant part, the Sixth Amendment provides: "In all criminal prosecutions, the accused shall enjoy the right . . . to have the Assistance of Counsel for his defense."

This chapter focuses on the constitutional rights of people accused or convicted of crimes to be represented by counsel—during trials, appeals, and subsequent stages of the criminal justice process. We consider several issues. Does the right to the assistance of defense counsel necessarily include the right to *court-appointed* counsel for indigents who lack the financial means to hire a lawyer? If poor people do have a constitutional right to court-appointed counsel, does that right apply to the trial of all crimes, or just serious ones such as felonies? Does it apply regardless of the threatened or actual punishment, or is it a provisional right that depends on the sentence that may be or is imposed? Does the right to court-appointed counsel extend beyond the trial, so that convicted offenders are guaranteed legal representation on appeal or to pursue judicial review of their cases after the first appeal?

We explore a number of related issues as well. If a defendant has the right to an attorney, does he or she have the corollary right to forgo the services of a lawyer and represent him- or herself at a criminal trial? When defense lawyers do appear on behalf of individuals charged with a crime, are there legal and ethical limits governing how vigorously or aggressively they can represent their clients? Can (and should) defense attorneys represent clients whom they know to be guilty? Must a lawyer meet minimum standards of performance to provide the assistance of counsel guaranteed under the Constitution? If so, how should minimal performance norms be defined and enforced?

We begin by examining the existence and scope of the accused's right to court-appointed counsel in trials, appeals, and subsequent stages of the criminal justice process.

THE RIGHT TO COUNSEL: TRIAL AND BEYOND

The Road to *Gideon*

Like other provisions of the federal Constitution's Bill of Rights, the Sixth Amendment originally did not apply to the states. As we have seen, not until the 1960s did the Supreme Court begin to "incorporate" specific Bill of Rights protections through the Fourteenth Amendment to make those rights applicable to state criminal proceedings. The early, seminal case involving the right to court-appointed counsel in state criminal trials, *Powell v. Alabama*, 287 U.S. 45, 53 S. Ct. 55, 77 L. Ed. 158 (1932), ignored the Sixth Amendment's right-to-counsel provisions, and relied squarely on due process principles.

In *Powell*, seven young African Americans, who commonly were referred to as the "Scotts-boro boys," were charged with raping two young white women on a train following an altercation with several white youths. Word of the alleged assaults spread rapidly. After the defendants were arrested, an angry mob of whites awaited their arrival in Scottsboro, Alabama, where the state militia had been called to help maintain order.

The alleged rapes were committed and the seven young men were arrested on March 25, 1931. The authorized punishment for rape ranged from 10 years' imprisonment to death. The defendants were indicted and arraigned less than a week later, on March 31. "[T]hey were not asked whether they had, or were able to employ, counsel, or wished to have counsel appointed; or whether they had friends or relatives who might assist in that regard if communicated with." 287 U.S., at 52. The trial judge took the unusual move of appointing "all the members of the bar for the purpose of arraigning the defendants" and indicated that he "anticipated that the members of the bar would continue to help the defendants if no counsel appeared." 287 U.S., at 49.

The defendants' trials commenced within the week. They were split into three separate groups. On the morning that the trials began, a lawyer from out of state appeared in court at the behest of "people who are interested in these boys from Chattanooga." 287 U.S., at 55. He emphasized that he had not been hired to represent the defendants, that he was not prepared to represent them, and that he was unfamiliar with Alabama law. The judge reiterated that he had appointed all willing members of the local bar to represent the defendants. One local attorney, a Mr. Moody, volunteered "to go ahead and help" the out-of-state lawyer. "And in this casual fashion the matter of counsel in a capital case was disposed of." 287 U.S., at 56. All three trials were completed within a single day. All of the defendants were convicted and sentenced to death. The state courts affirmed the convictions, and the Supreme Court granted certiorari to consider "whether the defendants were in substance denied the right of counsel, and if so, whether such denial infringes the due process clause of the Fourteenth Amendment." 287 U.S., at 52.

Justice Sutherland's opinion for the Court first noted that "until the very morning of the trial no lawyer had been named or definitively designated to represent the defendants." 287 U.S., at 56. The appointment of "all members of the bar" amounted to "little more than an expansive gesture, imposing no substantial or definite obligation upon any one." 287 U.S., at 56. The opinion recounted the circumstances surrounding the trial.

The defendants, young, ignorant, illiterate, surrounded by hostile sentiment, haled back and forth under guard of soldiers, charged with an atrocious crime regarded with especial horror in the community where they were to be tried, were thus put in peril of their lives within a few moments after counsel for the first time charged with any degree of responsibility began to represent them.

It is not enough to assume that counsel thus precipitated into the case thought there was no defense, and exercised their best judgment in proceeding to trial without preparation. Neither they nor the court could say what a prompt and thoroughgoing investigation might disclose as to the facts. No attempt was made to investigate. No opportunity to do so was given. Defendants were immediately hurried to trial. . . .

The Court then had to determine whether the essential denial of legal representation to the defendants violated their due-process rights. This inquiry required an assessment of whether "the right involved is of such a character that it cannot be denied without violating those 'fundamental principles of liberty and justice which lie at the base of all our civil and political institutions.'" 287 U.S., at 67. Justice Sutherland's opinion made "clear that the right to the aid of counsel is of this fundamental character." 287 U.S., at 68.

It never has been doubted by this court, or any other so far as we know, that notice and hearing are preliminary steps essential to the passing of an enforceable judgment, and that they, together with a legally competent tribunal having jurisdiction of the case, constitute basic elements of the constitutional requirement of due process of law. . . .

What, then, does a hearing include? Historically and in practice, in our own country at least, it has always included the right to the aid of counsel when desired and provided by the party asserting the right. The right to be heard would be, in many cases, of little avail if it did not comprehend the right to be heard by counsel. Even the intelligent and educated layman has small and sometimes no skill in the science of law. If charged with crime, he is incapable, generally, of determining for himself whether the indictment is good or bad. He is unfamiliar with the rules of evidence. Left without the aid of counsel he may be put on trial without a proper charge, and convicted upon incompetent evidence, or evidence irrelevant to the issue or otherwise inadmissible. He lacks both the skill and knowledge adequately to prepare his defense, even though he have a perfect one. He requires the guiding hand of counsel at every step in the proceedings against him. Without it, though he be not guilty, he faces the danger of conviction because he does not know how to establish his innocence. If that be true of men of intelligence, how much more true is it of the ignorant and illiterate, or those of feeble intellect. If in any case, civil or criminal, a state or federal court were arbitrarily to refuse to hear a party by counsel, employed by and appearing for him, it reasonably may not be doubted that such a refusal would be a denial of a hearing, and, therefore, of due process in the constitutional sense. . . .

In the light of the facts outlined in the forepart of this opinion—the ignorance and illiteracy of the defendants, their youth, the circumstances of public hostility, the imprisonment and the close surveillance of the defendants by the military forces, the fact that their friends and families were all in other states and communication with them necessarily difficult, and above all that they stood in deadly peril of their lives—we think the failure of the trial court to give them reasonable time and opportunity to secure counsel was a clear denial of due process.

But passing that, and assuming their inability, even if opportunity had been given, to employ counsel, as the trial court evidently did assume, we are of opinion that, under the circumstances just stated, the necessity of counsel was so vital and imperative that the failure of the trial court to make an effective appointment of counsel was likewise a denial of due process within the meaning of the Fourteenth Amendment. Whether this would be so in other criminal prosecutions, or under other circumstances, we need not determine. All that it is necessary now to decide, as we do decide, is that in a capital case, where the defendant is unable to employ counsel, and is incapable adequately of making his own defense because of ignorance, feeblemindedness, illiteracy, or the like, it is the duty of the court, whether requested or not, to assign counsel for him as a necessary requisite of due process of law; and that duty is not discharged by an assignment at such a time or under such circumstances as to preclude the giving of effective aid in the preparation and trial of the case. To hold otherwise would be to ignore the fundamental postulate, already adverted to, "that there are certain immutable principles of justice which inhere in the very idea of free government which no member of the Union may disregard." In a case such as this, whatever may be the rule in other cases, the right to have counsel appointed, when nec-

essary, is a logical corollary from the constitutional right to be heard by counsel. . . .

Powell v. Alabama was a momentous decision. It was one of the first occasions that the Supreme Court had ruled that state criminal procedures had violated a fundamental tenet of the federal Constitution. The Court clearly perceived the need to proceed cautiously in regulating state trials. The justices pointedly refrained from establishing a general due-process right to court-appointed counsel in all state trials, or even in all state capital trials. However, the Court was less hesitant about invoking the Sixth Amendment to require the appointment of counsel for indigent defendants charged with *federal* crimes. The justices ruled in *Johnson v. Zerbst*, 304 U.S. 458, 463, 58 S. Ct. 1019, 82 L. Ed. 1461 (1938), that "the Sixth Amendment withholds from federal courts, in all criminal proceedings, the power and authority to deprive an accused of his life or liberty unless he has or waives the assistance of counsel."

The Court's comparative reluctance to "interfere" with state trials in the right-to-counsel context was apparent in *Betts v. Brady*, 316 U.S. 455, 62 S. Ct. 1252, 86 L. Ed. 1595 (1942), a case decided a decade after *Powell* and four years after *Johnson v. Zerbst*. Smith Betts was charged in a Maryland state court with robbery. Too poor to be able to hire a lawyer, he asked the trial judge to appoint him one. The judge declined Betts's request, explaining the court's practice of appointing counsel for indigent defendants only in murder and rape cases. Betts thus proceeded to trial representing himself. He cross-examined prosecution witnesses, trying to discredit testimony identifying him as the robber, and summoned and examined his own witnesses in an attempt to establish an alibi. Betts was described as "not helpless, but . . . a man forty-three years old, of ordinary intelligence and ability to take care of his own interests on that narrow issue. He had once before been in a criminal court, pleaded guilty to larceny and served a sentence and was not wholly unfamiliar with criminal procedure." 316 U.S., at 472.

He was convicted of the robbery charge and sentenced to eight years in prison. The Supreme Court heard his case on certiorari.

Justice Roberts framed the issue before the Court as being whether Betts's "conviction and sentence [constituted] a deprivation of his liberty without due process of law, in violation of the Fourteenth Amendment, because of the court's refusal to appoint counsel at his request." 316 U.S., at 461. He emphasized that due process

> formulates a concept less rigid and more fluid than those envisaged in other specific and particular provisions of the Bill of Rights. Its application is less a matter of rule. Asserted denial is to be tested by an appraisal of the totality of facts in a given case. That which may, in one setting, constitute a denial of fundamental fairness, shocking to the universal sense of justice, may, in other circumstances, and in the light of other considerations, fall short of such denial. 316 U.S., at 462.

Justice Roberts's opinion concluded that history demonstrated that "appointment of counsel is not a fundamental right, essential to a fair trial. . . . We are unable to say that the concept of due process . . . obligates the states, whatever may be their own views, to furnish counsel in every . . . case." 316 U.S., at 471. The Court thus declined to adopt a general rule requiring the appointment of counsel for indigents in all state criminal trials. Stressing the relatively straightforward nature of Betts's case, and in light of Betts's personal characteristics and experience, the majority opinion concluded that Betts's trial and conviction without the assistance of counsel did not violate fundamental fairness:

> [T]he Fourteenth Amendment prohibits the conviction and incarceration of one whose trial is offensive to the common and fundamental ideas of fairness and right, and while want of counsel in a particular case

may result in a conviction lacking in such fundamental fairness, we cannot say that the amendment embodies an inexorable command that no trial for any offense, or in any court, can be fairly conducted and justice accorded a defendant who is not represented by counsel. 316 U.S., at 473.

Justice Black dissented. Joined by Justices Douglas and Murphy, he argued that the Sixth Amendment right to counsel fully applied to the states by operation of the Fourteenth Amendment's due-process clause. He further concluded that even under the majority opinion's due-process rationale, Betts's conviction without a lawyer was inconsistent with fundamental fairness.

The holding in *Betts v. Brady* developed into a "special circumstances" rule. Although due process did not automatically require the appointment of counsel for indigents facing state criminal trials, circumstances peculiar to the case—"such as the age and education of the defendant, the conduct of the court or the prosecuting officials, and the complicated nature of the offense charged and the possible defenses thereto—[could] render criminal proceedings without counsel so apt to result in injustice as to be fundamentally unfair." *Uveges v. Pennsylvania*, 335 U.S. 437, 441, 69 S. Ct. 184, 93 L. Ed. 127 (1948).

The "special circumstances" rule derived from *Betts* prevailed, at least nominally, for the 20 years following that decision. However, it proved difficult to anticipate the precise circumstances that required the appointment of counsel. Justice Black's criticism of the rule was unrelenting, and others increasingly lent their voices to it. Journalist Anthony Lewis perceptively observed that

> [s]ometimes when a constitutional decision comes under such severe scholarly attack, the Court begins to retreat from it almost invisibly, paying it lip service but never really allowing it to stand in the way of desired results.

Something like that seemed to be happening in the 1950's to *Betts v. Brady*. Opinions still frequently cited the case. But the last time the Court actually affirmed a state criminal conviction in the face of a claimed denial of counsel was 1950. Between that decision and the grant of review in Gideon's case the Court had held in favor of every state prisoner whose counsel claim it agreed to hear. A. Lewis, *Gideon's Trumpet* 120 (1964).

Lewis's reference to "Gideon's case," of course, pertains to the landmark right-to-counsel case *Gideon v. Wainwright*. Not coincidentally, Justice Black authored the Court's opinion.

Gideon v. Wainwright, 372 U.S. 335, 83 S. Ct. 792, 9 L. Ed. 2d 799 (1963)

Mr. Justice Black delivered the opinion of the Court.

Petitioner was charged in a Florida state court with having broken and entered a poolroom with intent to commit a misdemeanor. This offense is a felony under Florida law. Appearing in court without funds and without a lawyer, petitioner asked the court to appoint counsel for him, whereupon the following colloquy took place:

"The Court: Mr. Gideon, I am sorry, but I cannot appoint Counsel to represent you in this case. Under the laws of the State of Florida, the only time the Court can appoint Counsel to represent a Defendant is when that person is charged with a capital offense. . . .

"The Defendant: The United States Supreme Court says I am entitled to be represented by Counsel."

Put to trial before a jury, Gideon conducted his defense about as well as could be expected from a layman. He made an opening statement to the jury, cross-examined the State's witnesses, presented witnesses in his own defense, declined to testify himself, and made a short argument "emphasizing his innocence to the charge contained in the Information filed in this case." The jury returned a verdict of guilty, and petitioner was sentenced to serve five years in the state prison. . . .

[Gideon's state court challenge to his conviction and sentence on the ground that the trial court had violated his federal constitutional rights by refusing to appoint counsel for him was denied.]

Since 1942, when Betts v. Brady was decided by a divided Court, the problem of a defendant's federal constitutional right to counsel in a state court has been a continuing source of controversy and litigation in both state and federal courts. To give this problem another review here, we granted certiorari. Since Gideon was proceeding in forma pauperis, we appointed counsel to represent him and requested both sides to discuss in their briefs and oral arguments the following: "Should this Court's holding in Betts v. Brady, 316 US 455, 62 S Ct 1252, 86 L Ed 1595 [(1942)], be reconsidered?" . . .

We accept Betts v. Brady's assumption, based as it was on our prior cases, that a provision of the Bill of Rights which is "fundamental and essential to a fair trial" is made obligatory upon the States by the Fourteenth Amendment. We think the Court in Betts was wrong, however, in concluding that the Sixth Amendment's guarantee of counsel is not one of these fundamental rights. Ten years before Betts v. Brady, this Court, after full consideration of all the historical data examined in Betts, had unequivocally declared that "the right to the aid of counsel is of this fundamental character." Powell v. Alabama. While the Court at the close of its Powell opinion did by its language, as this Court frequently does, limit its holding to the particular facts and circumstances of that case, its conclusions about the fundamental nature of the right to counsel are unmistakable. . . .

The fact is that in deciding as it did—that "appointment of counsel is not a fundamental right, essential to a fair trial"—the Court in Betts

v. Brady made an abrupt break with its own well-considered precedents. In returning to these old precedents, sounder we believe than the new, we but restore constitutional principles established to achieve a fair system of justice. Not only these precedents but also reason and reflection require us to recognize that in our adversary system of criminal justice, any person haled into court, who is too poor to hire a lawyer, cannot be assured a fair trial unless counsel is provided for him. This seems to us to be an obvious truth. Governments, both state and federal, quite properly spend vast sums of money to establish machinery to try defendants accused of crime. Lawyers to prosecute are everywhere deemed essential to protect the public's interest in an orderly society. Similarly, there are few defendants charged with crime, few indeed, who fail to hire the best lawyers they can get to prepare and present their defenses. That government hires lawyers to prosecute and defendants who have the money hire lawyers to defend are the strongest indications of the widespread belief that lawyers in criminal courts are necessities, not luxuries.The right of one charged with crime to counsel may not be deemed fundamental and essential to fair trials in some countries, but it is in ours. From the very beginning, our state and national constitutions and laws have laid great emphasis on procedural and substantive safeguards designed to assure fair trials before impartial tribunals in which every defendant stands equal before the law. This noble idea cannot be realized if the poor man charged with crime has to face his accusers without a lawyer to assist him. . . .

The Court in Betts v. Brady departed from the sound wisdom upon which the Court's holding in Powell v. Alabama rested. Florida, supported by two other States, has asked that Betts v. Brady be left intact. Twenty-two States, as friends of the Court, argue that Betts was "an anachronism when handed down" and that it should now be overruled. We agree. . . .

Mr. Justice Clark, concurring in the result. . . .

Mr. Justice Harlan, concurring.

I agree that Betts v. Brady should be overruled, but consider it entitled to a more respectful burial than has been accorded, at least on the part of those of us who were not on the Court when that case was decided.

I cannot subscribe to the view that Betts v. Brady represented "an abrupt break with its own well-considered precedents." In 1932, in Powell v. Alabama, a capital case, this Court declared that under the particular facts there presented— "the ignorance and illiteracy of the defendants, their youth, the circumstances of public hostility . . . and above all that they stood in deadly peril of their lives"—the state court had a duty to assign counsel for the trial as a necessary requisite of due process of law. It is evident that these limiting facts were not added to the opinion as an afterthought; they were repeatedly emphasized, and were clearly regarded as important to the result.

Thus when this Court, a decade later, decided Betts v. Brady, it did no more than to admit of the possible existence of special circumstances in noncapital as well as capital trials, while at the same time insisting that such circumstances be shown in order to establish a denial of due process. The right to appointed counsel had been recognized as being considerably broader in federal prosecutions, see Johnson v. Zerbst, but to have imposed these requirements on the States would indeed have been "an abrupt break" with the almost immediate past. The declaration that the right to appointed counsel in state prosecutions, as established in Powell v. Alabama, was not limited to capital cases was in truth not a departure from, but an extension of, existing precedent.

The principles declared in Powell and in Betts, however, have had a troubled journey throughout the years that have followed first the one case and then the other. . . .

In noncapital cases, the "special circumstances" rule has continued to exist in form while its substance has been substantially and steadily eroded. . . . The Court has come to recognize, in other words, that the mere existence of a serious criminal charge constituted in itself special circumstances requiring the services of counsel at trial. In truth the Betts v. Brady rule is no longer a reality.

This evolution, however, appears not to have been fully recognized by many state courts, in this instance charged with the front-line responsibility for the enforcement of constitutional rights. To continue a rule which is honored by this Court only with lip service is not a healthy thing and in the long run will do disservice to the federal system.

The special circumstances rule has been formally abandoned in capital cases, and the time has now come when it should be similarly abandoned in noncapital cases, at least as to offenses which, as the one involved here, carry the possibility of a substantial prison sentence. (Whether the rule should extend to *all* criminal cases need not now be decided.) This indeed does no more than to make explicit something that has long since been foreshadowed in our decisions. . . .

Notes and Questions

1. Clarence Gideon wrote the petition for writ of certiorari filed in his case in his own hand, using a pencil, and mailed it to the Supreme Court from the Florida prison in which he was incarcerated. Abe Fortas, a prominent Washington, D.C., attorney who later would be named as a Supreme Court Justice, was appointed to represent Gideon before the Supreme Court. A different court-appointed lawyer represented Gideon when his case was retried in Florida following his victory before the Supreme Court. After deliberating for a little over an hour, the jury announced its verdict: not guilty. *See* A. Lewis, *Gideon's Trumpet* (1964).

2. *Gideon* was made fully retroactive by the Supreme Court. *See Pickelsimer v. Wainwright*, 375 U.S. 2, 84 S. Ct. 80, 11 L. Ed. 2d 41 (1963) (per curiam); *Kitchens v. Smith*, 401 U.S. 847, 91 S. Ct. 1089, 28 L. Ed. 2d 519 (1971) (per curiam). Thus, indigent defendants who had been tried without counsel and convicted for serious crimes before *Gideon* was decided were entitled to challenge their uncounseled convictions and have them vacated, absent an effective waiver of counsel. Most states—approximately 35—already provided for the appointment of counsel for indigents in all felony cases prior to *Gideon*. A. Lewis, *Gideon's Trumpet* 153 (1964). This fact, in combination with the preexisting rule of *Betts v. Brady*, made *Gideon's* retroactive impact less dramatic than it otherwise would have been.

3. *Gideon* involved a felony conviction and a five-year prison sentence. It remained to be seen how comprehensive the right to court-appointed counsel would be. Specifically, did this right extend to misdemeanor trials, or to trials not resulting in a sentence of imprisonment? Later cases clarified the scope of *Gideon*.

The Right to Court-Appointed Trial Counsel: Beyond *Gideon*

Argersinger v. Hamlin, 407 U.S. 25, 92 S. Ct. 2006, 32 L. Ed. 2d 530 (1972)

Mr. Justice Douglas delivered the opinion of the Court.

Petitioner, an indigent, was charged in Florida with carrying a concealed weapon, an offense punishable by imprisonment up to six months, a $1,000 fine, or both. The trial was to a judge, and petitioner was unrepresented by counsel. He was sentenced to serve 90 days in jail, and brought this habeas corpus action in the Florida Supreme Court, alleging that, being deprived of his right to counsel, he was unable as an indigent layman properly to raise and present to the trial court good and sufficient defenses to the charges for which he stands convicted. The Florida Supreme Court by a four-to-three decision, in ruling on the right to counsel, followed the line we marked out in Duncan v. Louisiana, 391 US 145, 159, 88 S Ct 1444, 20 L Ed 2d 491 [(1968)], as respects the right to trial by jury and held that the right to court-appointed counsel extends only to trials "for non-petty offenses punishable by more than six months imprisonment."

The case is here on a petition for certiorari, which we granted. We reverse. . . .

The right to trial by jury . . . guaranteed by the Sixth Amendment by reason of the Fourteenth, was limited by Duncan v. Louisiana to trials where the potential punishment was imprisonment of six months or more. But, as the various opinions in Baldwin v. New York, 399 US 66, 90 S Ct 1886, 26 L Ed 2d 437 [(1970)], make plain, the right to trial by jury has a different genealogy and is brigaded with a system of trial to a judge alone. . . .

While there is historical support for limiting the "deep commitment" to trial by jury to "serious criminal cases," there is no such support for a similar limitation on the right to assistance of counsel. . . .

The Sixth Amendment thus extended the right to counsel beyond its common-law dimensions. But there is nothing in the language of the Amendment, its history, or in the decisions of this Court, to indicate that it was intended to embody a retraction of the right in petty offenses wherein the common law previously did require that counsel be provided.

We reject, therefore, the premise that since prosecutions for crimes punishable by imprisonment for less than six months may be tried without a jury, they may also be tried without a lawyer.

The assistance of counsel is often a requisite to the very existence of a fair trial. . . .

Both Powell and Gideon involved felonies. But their rationale has relevance to any criminal trial, where an accused is deprived of his liberty. . . .

The requirement of counsel may well be necessary for a fair trial even in a petty-offense prosecution. We are by no means convinced that legal and constitutional questions involved in a case that actually leads to imprisonment even for a brief period are any less complex than

when a person can be sent off for six months or more. . . .

Beyond the problem of trials and appeals is that of the guilty plea, a problem which looms large in misdemeanor as well as in felony cases. Counsel is needed so that the accused may know precisely what he is doing, so that he is fully aware of the prospect of going to jail or prison, and so that he is treated fairly by the prosecution.

In addition, the volume of misdemeanor cases,[4] far greater in number than felony prosecutions, may create an obsession for speedy dispositions, regardless of the fairness of the result. . . . An inevitable consequence of volume that large is the almost total preoccupation in such a court with the movement of cases. The calendar is long, speed often is substituted for care, and casually arranged out-of-court compromise too often is substituted for adjudication. Inadequate attention tends to be given to the individual defendant, whether in protecting his rights, sifting the facts at trial, deciding the social risk he presents, or determining how to deal with him after conviction. . . .

There is evidence of the prejudice which results to misdemeanor defendants from this "assembly-line justice." One study concluded that "[m]isdemeanants represented by attorneys are five times as likely to emerge from police court with all charges dismissed as are defendants who face similar charges without counsel." American Civil Liberties Union, Legal Counsel for Misdemeanants, Preliminary Report 1 (1970).

We must conclude, therefore, that the problems associated with misdemeanor and petty offenses often require the presence of counsel to insure the accused a fair trial. Mr. Justice Powell suggests that these problems are raised even in situations where there is no prospect of imprisonment. We need not consider the requirements of the Sixth Amendment as

---

4. In 1965, 314,000 defendants were charged with felonies in state courts, and 24,000 were charged with felonies in federal courts.

Exclusive of traffic offenses, however, it is estimated that there are annually between four and five million court cases involving misdemeanors. . . .

regards the right to counsel where loss of liberty is not involved, however, for here petitioner was in fact sentenced to jail. And, as we said in Baldwin v New York, 399 US, at 73, "the prospect of imprisonment for however short a time will seldom be viewed by the accused as a trivial or 'petty' matter and may well result in quite serious repercussions affecting his career and his reputation."

We hold, therefore, that absent a knowing and intelligent waiver, no person may be imprisoned for any offense, whether classified as petty, misdemeanor, or felony, unless he was represented by counsel at his trial.[7] . . .

We do not sit as an ombudsman to direct state courts how to manage their affairs but only to make clear the federal constitutional requirement. How crimes should be classified is largely a state matter. The fact that traffic charges technically fall within the category of "criminal prosecutions" does not necessarily mean that many of them will be brought into the class where imprisonment actually occurs. . . .

Under the rule we announce today, every judge will know when the trial of a misdemeanor starts that no imprisonment may be imposed, even though local law permits it, unless the accused is represented by counsel. He will have a measure of the seriousness and gravity of the offense and therefore know when to name a lawyer to represent the accused before the trial starts.

The run of misdemeanors will not be affected by today's ruling. But in those that end up in the actual deprivation of a person's liberty, the accused will receive the benefit of "the guiding hand of counsel" so necessary when one's liberty is in jeopardy.

Reversed. . . .

Mr. Chief Justice Burger, concurring in the result. . . .

Mr. Justice Powell, with whom Mr. Justice Rehnquist joins, concurring in the result. . . .

I am unable to agree with the Supreme Court of Florida that an indigent defendant, charged with a petty offense, may in every case be afforded a fair trial without the assistance of counsel. Nor can I agree with the new rule of due process, today enunciated by the Court, that "absent a knowing and intelligent waiver, no person may be imprisoned . . . unless he was represented by counsel at his trial." It seems to me that the line should not be drawn with such rigidity.

There is a middle course, between the extremes of Florida's six-month rule and the Court's rule, which comports with the requirements of the Fourteenth Amendment. I would adhere to the principle of due process that requires fundamental fairness in criminal trials, a principle which I believe encompasses the right to counsel in petty cases whenever the assistance of counsel is necessary to assure a fair trial. . . .

While counsel is often essential to a fair trial, this is by no means a universal fact. Some petty offense cases are complex; others are exceedingly simple. As a justification for furnishing counsel to indigents accused of felonies, this Court noted, "That government hires lawyers to prosecute and defendants who have the money hire lawyers to defend are the strongest indications of the widespread belief that lawyers in criminal courts are necessities, not luxuries." Yet government often does not hire lawyers to prosecute petty offenses; instead the arresting police officer presents the case. Nor does every defendant who can afford to do so hire lawyers to defend petty charges. Where the possibility of a jail sentence is remote and the probable fine seems small, or where the evidence of guilt is overwhelming, the costs of assistance of counsel may exceed the benefits. It is anomalous that the Court's opinion today will extend the right of appointed counsel to indigent defendants in cases where the right to counsel would rarely be exercised by nonindigent defendants. . . .

---

7. We do not share Mr. Justice Powell's doubt that the Nation's legal resources are insufficient to implement the rule we announce today. It has been estimated that between 1,575 and 2,300 full-time counsel would be required to represent *all* indigent misdemeanants, excluding traffic offenders.

These figures are relatively insignificant when compared to the estimated 355,200 attorneys in the United States (Statistical Abstract of the United States 153 (1971)), a number which is projected to double by the year 1985. . . .

[A]lthough the new rule is extended today only to the imprisonment category of cases, the Court's opinion foreshadows the adoption of a broad prophylactic rule applicable to all petty offenses. No one can foresee the consequences of such a drastic enlargement of the constitutional right to free counsel. But even today's decision could have a seriously adverse impact upon the day-to-day functioning of the criminal justice system. . . . The opinion is disquietingly barren of details as to how this rule will be implemented.

There are thousands of statutes and ordinances which authorize imprisonment for six months or less, usually as an alternative to a fine. These offenses include some of the most trivial of misdemeanors, ranging from spitting on the sidewalk to certain traffic offenses. They also include a variety of more serious misdemeanors. This broad spectrum of petty offense cases daily floods the lower criminal courts. The rule laid down today will confront the judges of each of these courts with an awkward dilemma. If counsel is not appointed or knowingly waived, no sentence of imprisonment for any duration may be imposed. The judge will therefore be forced to decide in advance of trial—and without hearing the evidence—whether he will forgo entirely his judicial discretion to impose some sentence of imprisonment and abandon his responsibility to consider the full range of punishments established by the legislature. His alternatives, assuming the availability of counsel, will be to appoint counsel and retain the discretion vested in him by law, or to abandon this discretion in advance and proceed without counsel.

If the latter course is followed, the first victim of the new rule is likely to be the concept that justice requires a personalized decision both as to guilt and the sentence. The notion that sentencing should be tailored to fit the crime and the individual would have to be abandoned in many categories of offenses. In resolving the dilemma as to how to administer the new rule, judges will be tempted arbitrarily to divide petty offenses into two categories—those for which sentences of imprisonment may be imposed and those in which no such sentence will be given regardless of the statutory authorization. In creating categories of offenses which by law are imprisonable but for which he would not impose jail sentences, a judge will be overruling de facto the legislative determination as to the appropriate range of punishment for the particular offense. . . .

The new rule announced today also could result in equal protection problems. There may well be an unfair and unequal treatment of individual defendants, depending on whether the individual judge has determined in advance to leave open the option of imprisonment. Thus, an accused indigent would be entitled in some courts to counsel while in other courts in the same jurisdiction an indigent accused of the same offense would have no counsel. Since the services of counsel may be essential to a fair trial even in cases in which no jail sentence is imposed, the results of this type of pretrial judgment could be arbitrary and discriminatory. . . .

To avoid these equal protection problems and to preserve a range of sentencing options as prescribed by law, most judges are likely to appoint counsel for indigents in all but the most minor offenses where jail sentences are extremely rare. It is doubtful that the States possess the necessary resources to meet this sudden expansion of the right to counsel. . . .

The majority's treatment of the consequences of the new rule . . . is not reassuring. In a footnote, it is said that there are presently 355,200 attorneys and that the number will increase rapidly, doubling by 1985. This is asserted to be sufficient to provide the number of full-time counsel, estimated by one source at between 1,575 and 2,300, to represent all indigent misdemeanants, excluding traffic offenders. It is totally unrealistic to imply that 355,200 lawyers are potentially available. Thousands of these are not in practice, and many of those who do practice work for governments, corporate legal departments, or the Armed Services and are unavailable for criminal representation. Of those in general practice, we have no indication how many are qualified to defend criminal cases or willing to accept assignments which may prove less than lucrative for most.

It is similarly unrealistic to suggest that implementation of the Court's new rule will require no more than 1,575 to 2,300 "full-time" lawyers. In few communities are there full-time public defenders available for or private lawyers specializing in petty cases. . . .

Perhaps the most serious potential impact of today's holding will be on our already overburdened local courts. The primary cause of "assembly line" justice is a volume of cases far in excess of the capacity of the system to handle efficiently and fairly. The Court's rule may well exacerbate delay and congestion in these courts. We are familiar with the common tactic of counsel of exhausting every possible legal avenue, often without due regard to its probable payoff. In some cases this may be the lawyer's duty; in other cases it will be done for purposes of delay. The absence of direct economic impact on the client, plus the omnipresent ineffective-assistance-of-counsel claim, frequently produces a decision to litigate every issue. . . .

There is an additional problem. The ability of various States and localities to furnish counsel varies widely. Even if there were adequate resources on a national basis, the uneven distribution of these resources—of lawyers, of facilities, and available funding—presents the most acute problem. . . .

The papers filed in a recent petition to this Court for a writ of certiorari serve as an example of what today's ruling will mean in some localities. In November 1971 the petition in Wright v. Town of Wood, No. 71-5722, was filed with this Court. The case, arising out of a South Dakota police magistrate court conviction for the municipal offense of public intoxication, raises the same issues before us in this case. The Court requested that the town of Wood file a response. On March 8, 1972, a lawyer occasionally employed by the town filed with the clerk an affidavit explaining why the town had not responded. He explained that Wood, South Dakota, has a population of 132, that it has no sewer or water system and is quite poor, that the office of the nearest lawyer is in a town 40 miles away, and that the town had decided that contesting this case would be an unwise allocation of its limited resources. . . .

[T]o require that counsel be furnished virtually every indigent charged with an imprisonable offense would be a practical impossibility for many small town courts. The community could simply not enforce its own laws.

Perhaps it will be said that I give undue weight both to the likelihood of short-term "chaos" and to the possibility of long-term adverse effects on the system. The answer may be given that if the Constitution requires the rule announced by the majority, the consequences are immaterial. If I were satisfied that the guarantee of due process required the assistance of counsel in every case in which a jail sentence is imposed or that the only workable method of insuring justice is to adopt the majority's rule, I would not hesitate to join the Court's opinion despite my misgivings as to its effect upon the administration of justice. . . .

I would hold that the right to counsel in petty offense cases is not absolute but is one to be determined by the trial courts exercising a judicial discretion on a case-by-case basis. . . .

It is impossible, as well as unwise, to create a precise and detailed set of guidelines for judges to follow in determining whether the appointment of counsel is necessary to assure a fair trial. Certainly three general factors should be weighed. First, the court should consider the complexity of the offense charged. For example, charges of traffic law infractions would rarely present complex legal or factual questions, but charges that contain difficult intent elements or which raise collateral legal questions, such as search-and-seizure problems, would usually be too complex for an unassisted layman. If the offense were one where the State is represented by counsel and where most defendants who can afford to do so obtain counsel, there would be a strong indication that the indigent also needs the assistance of counsel.

Second, the court should consider the probable sentence that will follow if a conviction is obtained. The more serious the likely consequences, the greater is the probability that a lawyer should be appointed. . . .

Third, the court should consider the individual factors peculiar to each case. These, of course, would be the most difficult to anticipate. One relevant factor would be the competency of the individual defendant to present his own case. The attitude of the community toward a particular defendant or particular incident would be another consideration. But there might be other reasons why a defendant would have a peculiar need for a lawyer which would compel the appointment of counsel in a case where the court would normally think this unnecessary. Obviously, the sensitivity and diligence of individual judges would be crucial to the operation of a rule of fundamental fairness requiring the

consideration of the varying factors in each case. . . .

Notes and Questions

1. Among the points made by Justice Powell in his concurring opinion is that limiting the right of court-appointed counsel only to cases resulting in actual incarceration—if, indeed, that is a correct reading of *Argersinger* (see *Scott v. Illinois*, below)—would present difficult problems of administration. He pointed out that "the judge will . . . be forced to decide in advance of trial—and without hearing the evidence—whether he will forgo entirely his judicial discretion to impose some sentence of imprisonment." Is there any apparent solution to this problem?

2. Justice Powell also observed that many state and local criminal justice systems have limited resources and could find compliance with *Argersinger* to be virtually impossible. Should resource constraints be a legitimate consider-

ation for establishing a constitutional rule defining the scope of the right to counsel?

3. Justice Douglas hints that requiring counsel to be appointed for indigent defendants who face incarceration on conviction may induce the states to reconsider the range of conduct presently defined as "criminal" and entailing jail sentences. Would such a reexamination be healthy? Is it the Supreme Court's job to instigate such changes in state criminal justice systems?

4. We consider the Sixth Amendment right to a jury trial in criminal cases in Chapter 10. Note the Court's attempt in *Argersinger* to distinguish *Duncan v. Louisiana*, where the Court refrained from ruling that the right to trial by jury necessarily applies in all state criminal cases resulting in the defendant's incarceration.

The defendant in *Argersinger* faced a maximum jail sentence of six months and actually was sentenced to 90 days in jail. What if he had been charged with the same offense but the judge

decided not to send him to jail? Would the federal Constitution still require the appointment of trial counsel if he were too poor to hire one? The Court addressed this issue in *Scott v. Illinois*.

Scott v. Illinois, 440 U.S. 367, 99 S. Ct. 1158, 59 L. Ed. 2d 383 (1979)

Mr. Justice Rehnquist delivered the opinion of the Court. . . .

Petitioner Scott was convicted of theft and fined $50 after a bench trial in the Circuit Court of Cook County, Ill. His conviction was affirmed by the state intermediate appellate court and then by the Supreme Court of Illinois, over Scott's contention that the Sixth and Fourteenth Amendments to the United States Constitution required that Illinois provide trial counsel to him at its expense.

Petitioner Scott was convicted of shoplifting merchandise valued at less than $150. The appli-

cable Illinois statute set the maximum penalty for such an offense at a $500 fine or one year in jail, or both. The petitioner argues that a line of this Court's cases culminating in Argersinger v. Hamlin requires State provision of counsel whenever imprisonment is an authorized penalty. . . .

We agree with the Supreme Court of Illinois that the Federal Constitution does not require a state trial court to appoint counsel for a criminal defendant such as petitioner, and we therefore affirm its judgment. . . .

There is considerable doubt that the Sixth Amendment itself, as originally drafted by the

Framers of the Bill of Rights, contemplated any guarantee other than the right of an accused in a criminal prosecution in a federal court to employ a lawyer to assist in his defense. . . .

The Court held in Duncan v. Louisiana, 391 US 145, 88 S Ct 1444, 20 L Ed 2d 491 (1968), that the right to jury trial in federal court guaranteed by the Sixth Amendment was applicable to the States by virtue of the Fourteenth Amendment. The Court held, however: "It is doubtless true that there is a category of petty crimes or offenses which is not subject to the Sixth Amendment jury trial provision and should not be subject to the Fourteenth Amendment jury trial requirement here applied to the States. Crimes carrying possible penalties up to six months do not require a jury trial if they otherwise qualify as petty offenses. . . ." Id., at 159 (footnote omitted). In Baldwin v. New York, 399 US 66, 69, 90 S Ct 1886, 26 L Ed 2d 437 (1970), the controlling opinion of Mr. Justice White concluded that "no offense can be deemed 'petty' for purposes of the right to trial by jury where imprisonment for more than six months is authorized." . . .

The number of separate opinions in Gideon, Duncan, Baldwin, and Argersinger, suggests that constitutional line drawing becomes more difficult as the reach of the Constitution is extended further, and as efforts are made to transpose lines from one area of Sixth Amendment jurisprudence to another. The process of incorporation creates special difficulties, for the state and federal contexts are often different and application of the same principle may have ramifications distinct in degree and kind. The range of human conduct regulated by state criminal laws is much broader than that of the federal criminal laws, particularly on the "petty" offense part of the spectrum. As a matter of constitutional adjudication, we are, therefore, less willing to extrapolate an already extended line when, although the general nature of the principle sought to be applied is clear, its precise limits and their ramifications become less so. We have now in our decided cases departed from the literal meaning of the Sixth Amendment. And we cannot fall back on the common law as it existed prior to the enactment of that Amendment, since it perversely gave less in the way of right to counsel to accused felons than to those accused of misdemeanors.

In Argersinger the Court rejected arguments that social cost or a lack of available lawyers militated against its holding, in some part because it thought these arguments were factually incorrect. But they were rejected in much larger part because of the Court's conclusion that incarceration was so severe a sanction that it should not be imposed as a result of a criminal trial unless an indigent defendant had been offered appointed counsel to assist in his defense, regardless of the cost to the States implicit in such a rule. The Court in its opinion repeatedly referred to trials "where an accused is deprived of his liberty," and to "a case that actually leads to imprisonment even for a brief period." . . .

Although the intentions of the Argersinger Court are not unmistakably clear from its opinion, we conclude today that Argersinger did indeed delimit the constitutional right to appointed counsel in state criminal proceedings. Even were the matter res nova, we believe that the central premise of Argersinger—that actual imprisonment is a penalty different in kind from fines or the mere threat of imprisonment—is eminently sound and warrants adoption of actual imprisonment as the line defining the constitutional right to appointment of counsel. Argersinger has proved reasonably workable, whereas any extension would create confusion and impose unpredictable, but necessarily substantial, costs on 50 quite diverse States. We therefore hold that the Sixth and Fourteenth Amendments to the United States Constitution require only that no indigent criminal defendant be sentenced to a term of imprisonment unless the State has afforded him the right to assistance of appointed counsel in his defense. . . .

Mr. Justice Brennan, with whom Mr. Justice Marshall and Mr. Justice Stevens join, dissenting. . . .

The Court's opinion intimates that the Court's precedents ordaining the right to appointed counsel for indigent accuseds in state criminal proceedings fail to provide a principled basis for deciding this case. That is demonstrably not so. The principles developed in the relevant precedents are clear and sound. The Court simply chooses to ignore them.

Gideon v. Wainwright held that, because representation by counsel in a criminal proceeding is "fundamental and essential to a fair trial," the Sixth Amendment right to counsel was applicable to the States through the Fourteenth Amendment. . . .

Earlier precedents had recognized that the assistance of appointed counsel was critical, not only to equalize the sides in an adversary criminal process, but also to give substance to other constitutional and procedural protections afforded criminal defendants. Gideon established the right to appointed counsel for indigent accuseds as a categorical requirement, making the Court's former case-by-case due process analysis, cf. Betts v. Brady, unnecessary in cases covered by its holding. Gideon involved a felony prosecution, but that fact was not crucial to the decision; its reasoning extended, in the words of the Sixth Amendment, to "*all* criminal prosecutions." . . .

In my view petitioner could prevail in this case without extending the right to counsel beyond what was assumed to exist in Argersinger. Neither party in that case questioned the existence of the right to counsel in trials involving "nonpetty" offenses punishable by more than six months in jail. The question the Court addressed was whether the right applied to some "petty" offenses to which the right to jury trial did not extend.

. . . Argersinger thus established a "two dimensional" test for the right to counsel: the right attaches to any "nonpetty" offense punishable by more than six months in jail and in addition to any offense where actual incarceration is likely regardless of the maximum authorized penalty. . . .

The offense of "theft" with which Scott was charged is certainly not a "petty" one. It is punishable by a sentence of up to one year in jail. Unlike many traffic or other "regulatory" offenses, it carries the moral stigma associated with common-law crimes traditionally recognized as indicative of moral depravity. The State indicated at oral argument that the services of a professional prosecutor were considered essential to the prosecution of this offense. Likewise, nonindigent defendants charged with this offense would be well advised to hire the "best lawyers they can get." Scott's right to the assistance of appointed counsel is thus plainly mandated by the logic of the Court's prior cases, including Argersinger itself.

But rather than decide consonant with the assumption in regard to nonpetty offenses that was both implicit and explicit in Argersinger, the Court today retreats to the indefensible position that the Argersinger "actual imprisonment" standard is the *only* test for determining the boundary of the Sixth Amendment right to appointed counsel in state misdemeanor cases, thus necessarily deciding that in many cases (such as this one) a defendant will have no right to appointed counsel even when he has a constitutional right to a jury trial. This is simply an intolerable result. Not only is the "actual imprisonment" standard unprecedented as the exclusive test, but the problems inherent in its application demonstrate the superiority of an "authorized imprisonment" standard that would require the appointment of counsel for indigents accused of any offense for which imprisonment for any time is authorized.

First, the "authorized imprisonment" standard more faithfully implements the principles of the Sixth Amendment identified in Gideon. The procedural rules established by state statutes are geared to the nature of the potential penalty for an offense, not to the actual penalty imposed in particular cases. The authorized penalty is also a better predictor of the stigma and other collateral consequences that attach to conviction of an offense. . . . By contrast, the "actual imprisonment" standard, as the Court's opinion in this case demonstrates, denies the right to counsel in criminal prosecutions to accuseds who suffer the severe consequences of prosecution other than imprisonment.

Second, the "authorized imprisonment" test presents no problems of administration. It avoids the necessity for time-consuming consideration of the likely sentence in each individual case before trial and the attendant problems of inaccurate predictions, unequal treatment, and apparent and actual bias. . . .

Finally, the "authorized imprisonment" test ensures that courts will not abrogate legislative judgments concerning the appropriate range of penalties to be considered for each offense. . . .

The apparent reason for the Court's adoption of the "actual imprisonment" standard for all misdemeanors is concern for the economic burden that an "authorized imprisonment" standard might place on the States. But, with all respect, that concern is both irrelevant and speculative.

This Court's role in enforcing constitutional guarantees for criminal defendants cannot be made dependent on the budgetary decisions of state governments. . . .

In any event, the extent of the alleged burden on the States is . . . speculative. Although more persons are charged with misdemeanors punishable by incarceration than are charged with felonies, a smaller percentage of persons charged with misdemeanors qualify as indigent, and misdemeanor cases as a rule require far less attorney time.

Furthermore, public defender systems have proved economically feasible, and the establishment of such systems to replace appointment of private attorneys can keep costs at acceptable levels even when the number of cases requiring appointment of counsel increases dramatically. . . .

Perhaps the strongest refutation of respondent's alarmist prophecies that an "authorized imprisonment" standard would wreak havoc on the States is that the standard has not produced that result in the substantial number of States that already provide counsel in all cases where imprisonment is authorized—States that include a large majority of the country's population and a great diversity of urban and rural environments. Moreover, of those States that do not yet provide counsel in all cases where *any* imprisonment is authorized, many provide counsel when periods of imprisonment longer than 30 days, 3 months, or 6 months are authorized. In fact, Scott would be entitled to appointed counsel under the current laws of at least 33 States.

It may well be that adoption by this Court of an "authorized imprisonment" standard would lead state and local governments to re-examine their criminal statutes. A state legislature or local government might determine that it no longer desired to authorize incarceration for certain minor offenses in light of the expense of meeting the requirements of the Constitution. In my view this re-examination is long overdue. . . .

Mr. Justice Blackmun, dissenting.

I would hold that the right to counsel secured by the Sixth and Fourteenth Amendments extends at least as far as the right to jury trial secured by those Amendments. Accordingly, I would hold that an indigent defendant in a state criminal case must be afforded appointed counsel whenever the defendant is prosecuted for a nonpetty criminal offense, that is, one punishable by more than six months' imprisonment, *or* whenever the defendant is convicted of an offense and is actually subjected to a term of imprisonment. This resolution, I feel, would provide the "bright line" that defendants, prosecutors, and trial and appellate courts all deserve and, at the same time, would reconcile on a principled basis the important considerations that led to the decisions in Duncan, Baldwin, and Argersinger. . . .

Notes and Questions

1. Is there a principled basis for denying indigents court-appointed trial counsel when a conviction does not result in incarceration?

2. What if Scott's case involved an unusually complicated search-and-seizure issue? What if he entered a plea of not guilty by reason of insanity? What if he were mentally retarded? Can you imagine any "special circumstances," akin to those considered in the aftermath of *Betts v. Brady*, where due process would require the appointment of trial counsel for an indigent who does not face incarceration, even if the Sixth Amendment does not impose such a requirement?

3. Statutes, court rules, and state constitutional provisions in several states establish a broader right to court-appointed counsel than required by *Scott*. In those states, counsel generally must be appointed for indigents whenever the law under which they are prosecuted authorizes a jail or prison sentence following conviction. *See* B. Latzer, *State Constitutional Criminal Law* § 5:4 (1995).

* * * * *

An uncounseled prior conviction obtained in violation of *Gideon* or *Argersinger* is presumptively unreliable and hence cannot be considered when sentencing an offender for a subsequent crime, *United States v. Tucker*, 404 U.S. 443, 92 S. Ct. 589, 30 L. Ed. 2d 592 (1972), to prosecute an offender as a recidivist, *Burgett v. Texas*, 389 U.S. 109, 88 S. Ct. 258, 19 L. Ed. 2d 319 (1967), or as a basis for impeaching the credibility of a witness's testimony, *Loper v. Beto*, 405 U.S. 473, 92 S. Ct. 1014, 31 L. Ed. 2d 374 (1972). Under *Scott v. Illinois,* however, an uncounseled conviction that is not coupled with a jail or prison sentence does not violate the federal Constitution. Assume that an offender has a previous misdemeanor conviction on his record. The conviction was obtained when the offender was indigent and was unrepresented by trial counsel, but he was not sentenced to jail. At a later date, the same offender is arrested for an unrelated crime. Owing to the existence of his prior conviction, he now qualifies for prosecution as a recidivist or risks an enhanced prison sentence if he is convicted of the new charge. Is it sufficient that a lawyer is appointed to represent him on this subsequent charge, when he faces a real threat of incarceration? Or, even if a lawyer represents him on the new charge, is the state unfairly being allowed to exploit his prior uncounseled conviction because he would not be risking incarceration in the absence of that uncounseled conviction?

The Supreme Court first broached this issue in *Baldasar v. Illinois*, 446 U.S. 222, 100 S. Ct. 1585, 64 L. Ed. 2d 169 (1980). Baldasar had been convicted of misdemeanor theft in May 1975. He was unrepresented by counsel and had not waived his right to counsel. His conviction resulted in a fine and probation. Six months later, he was charged with stealing a shower head worth $29 from a department store, and a lawyer was appointed to represent him at trial. He was convicted and sentenced to one to three years' imprisonment under a statute that allowed him to be treated as a felon because of his prior uncounseled theft conviction. The lawyer representing Baldasar on the second theft charge had "argued unsuccessfully that because Baldasar had not been represented by a lawyer at the first proceeding, the conviction was too unreliable to support enhancement of the second misdemeanor." 446 U.S., at 223.

The Supreme Court, with four justices dissenting, ruled that the uncounseled theft conviction could not be used to support Baldasar's prison sentence. Justice Stewart's plurality opinion concluded that *Argersinger* and *Scott* had been violated because Baldasar "was sentenced to an increased term of imprisonment *only* because he had been convicted in a previous prosecution in which he had *not* had the assistance of appointed counsel in his defense." 446 U.S., at 224 (emphasis in original). Concurring in the judgment, Justice Marshall reasoned that Baldasar's prior conviction, although constitutionally valid under *Scott*, "was not valid for all purposes. Specifically, . . . it was invalid for the purpose of depriving petitioner of his liberty." 446 U.S., at 226.

Fourteen years later, *Baldasar* was overruled. The defendant in *Nichols v. United States*, 511 U.S. 738, 114 S. Ct. 1921, 128 L. Ed. 2d 745 (1994), had been convicted without a lawyer in 1983 in a Georgia state court for misdemeanor "driving under the influence" (DUI). He was fined $250 but was not incarcerated. In 1990, Nichols pleaded guilty to a federal drug charge. His presumptive maximum sentence under the federal sentencing guidelines increased from 210 months to 235 months because of the uncounseled DUI conviction, and the judge imposed the 235-month maximum sentence. Chief Justice Rehnquist's opinion for the Court in *Nichols*, in which four other justices joined, upheld the enhanced sentence and explained why *Baldasar* no longer should be considered good law.

[Justice Powell's dissent in *Baldasar*] criticized the majority's holding as one that "undermines the rationale of *Scott* and *Argersinger* and leaves no coherent rationale in its place." The dissent opined that the majority's result misapprehended the nature of enhancement statutes which "do not alter or enlarge a prior sentence," ignored the significance of the constitutional validity of the first conviction under *Scott*, and created a "hybrid" conviction, good for the punishment actually imposed but not available for sentence enhancement in a later prosecution. Finally—and quite presciently—the dissent predicted that the Court's decision would create confusion in the lower courts. . . .

We . . . agree with the dissent in *Baldasar* that . . . an uncounseled conviction valid under *Scott* may be relied upon to enhance the sentence for a subsequent offense, even though that sentence entails imprisonment. Enhancement statutes, whether in the nature of criminal history provisions such as those contained in the Sentencing Guidelines, or recidivist statutes which are common place in state criminal laws, do not change the penalty imposed for the earlier conviction. . . . Reliance on such a conviction is also consistent with the traditional understanding of the sentencing process, which we have often recognized as less exacting than the process of establishing guilt. . . . Sentencing courts have not only taken into consideration a defendant's prior convictions, but have also considered a defendant's past criminal behavior, even if no conviction resulted from that behavior. . . .

Thus, consistently with due process, petitioner in the present case could have been sentenced more severely based simply on evidence of the underlying conduct which gave rise to the previous DUI offense. And the state need prove such conduct only by a preponderance of the evidence. Surely, then, it must be constitutionally permissible to consider a prior uncounseled misdemeanor conviction based on the same conduct where that conduct must be proven beyond a reasonable doubt. . . .

* * * * *

Justice Souter concurred in the judgment in *Nichols*, and Justices Blackmun, Stevens, and Ginsburg dissented.

In your view, is an uncounseled conviction sufficiently reliable to serve as the basis for an enhanced charge, as in *Baldasar*, or an enhanced sentence, as in *Nichols*? Is the state unfairly permitted to exploit an uncounseled prior conviction under such circumstances? Or, if the uncounseled conviction did not itself result in incarceration, is the logical implication of *Scott v. Illinois* that the conviction is constitutionally valid for all purposes?

The Court's overruling of *Baldasar* in *Nichols v. United States* should serve as a reminder that it is imperative to *Shepardize* cases to confirm their continuing validity. Although Supreme Court decisions are overturned infrequently, cases are overruled with sufficient regularity that *Shepardizing* remains obligatory. In a 1991 case, Chief Justice Rehnquist noted that in the prior 20 years the Court had "overruled in whole or in part 33 of its previous constitutional decisions." *Payne v. Tennessee*, 501 U.S. 808, 828, 111 S. Ct. 2597, 115 L. Ed. 2d 720 (1991).

Does the Right to Court-Appointed Counsel Extend beyond Trial?

To this point, we have considered cases involving the right to court-appointed counsel in criminal trials. If an indigent defendant facing incarceration cannot be forced to stand trial without the assistance of counsel, does it follow that the same defendant has a constitutional right to the assistance of counsel on appeal, in order to challenge the legality of a conviction and sentence? Does the right to counsel extend to additional proceedings, such as petitioning the Supreme Court for a writ of certiorari, or to "postconviction" proceedings in which the state courts are asked to review issues that could not be raised on appeal, such as prosecutorial misconduct, ineffective assistance of counsel, or newly discovered evidence?

The Supreme Court addressed an issue involving appellate review of an indigent's conviction in *Griffin v. Illinois*, 351 U.S. 12, 76 S. Ct. 585, 100 L. Ed. 891 (1956), a case that preceded *Gideon* by seven years. Under Illinois law, criminal defendants were not entitled to full review of their convictions on appeal unless they paid for a transcript and record of the trial proceedings and filed these documents with the appellate court. The only exception to this requirement involved indigent defendants who had been sentenced to death. Griffin and a co-defendant were convicted of armed robbery and sentenced to prison. They alleged that they were too poor to pay for the transcript and record needed for the appeal. Justice Black's plurality opinion for four members of the Court ruled that Illinois's practice denied indigent defendants due process and equal protection of the law. Justice Frankfurter concurred in the judgment, and four justices dissented.

Surely no one would contend that either a State or the Federal Government could constitutionally provide that defendants unable to pay court costs in advance should be denied the right to plead not guilty or to defend themselves in court. Such a law would make the constitutional promise of a fair trial a worthless thing. Notice, the right to be heard, and the right to counsel would under such circumstances be meaningless promises to the poor. In criminal trials a State can no more discriminate on account of poverty than on account of religion, race, or color. Plainly the ability to pay costs in advance bears no rational relationship to a defendant's guilt or innocence and could not be used as an excuse to deprive a defendant of a fair trial. . . .

There is no meaningful distinction between a rule which would deny the poor the right to defend themselves in a trial court and one which effectively denies the poor an adequate appellate review accorded to all who have money enough to pay the costs in advance. It is true that a State is not required by the Federal Constitution to provide appellate courts or a right to appellate review at all. But that is not to say that a State that does grant appellate review can do so in a way that discriminates against some convicted defendants on account of their poverty. Appellate review has now become an integral part of the Illinois trial system of finally adjudicating the guilt or innocence of a defendant. Consequently at all stages of the proceedings the Due Process and Equal Protection Clauses protect persons like petitioners from invidious discriminations.

All of the States now provide some method of appeal from criminal convictions, recognizing the importance of appellate review to a correct adjudication of guilt or innocence. Statistics show that a substantial proportion of criminal convictions are reversed by state appellate courts. Thus to deny adequate review to the poor means that many of them may lose their life, liberty or property because of unjust convictions which appellate courts would set aside. Many States have recognized this and provided aid for convicted defendants who have a right to appeal and need a transcript but are unable to pay for it. A few have not. Such a denial is a misfit in a country dedicated to affording equal justice to all and special privileges to none in the administration of its criminal law. There can be no equal justice where the kind of trial a man gets depends on the amount of money he has. Destitute defendants must be afforded as adequate appellate review as defendants who have money enough to buy transcripts. . . .

Griffin set the stage for the Supreme Court to consider whether the Constitution guarantees indigent criminal defendants the right to court-appointed counsel to assist with the appeal of their convictions. This issue was confronted in *Douglas v. California*, which was decided the same day as *Gideon*.

Douglas v. California, 372 U.S. 353, 83 S. Ct. 814, 9 L. Ed. 2d 811 (1963)

Mr. Justice Douglas delivered the opinion of the Court. . . .

The record shows that petitioners requested, and were denied, the assistance of counsel on appeal, even though it plainly appeared they were indigents. In denying petitioners' requests, the California District Court of Appeal stated that it had "gone through" the record and had come to the conclusion that "no good whatever could be served by appointment of counsel." The District Court of Appeal was acting in accordance with a California rule of criminal procedure which provides that state appellate courts, upon the request of an indigent for counsel, may make "an independent investigation of the record and determine whether it would be of advantage to the defendant or helpful to the appellate court to have counsel appointed. . . . After such investigation, appellate courts should appoint counsel if in their opinion it would be helpful to the defendant or the court, and should deny the appointment of counsel only if in their judgment such appointment would be of no value to either the defendant or the court." People v. Hyde, 51 Cal 2d 152, 154, 331 P2d 42, 43. . . .

In Griffin v. Illinois, we held that a State may not grant appellate review in such a way as to discriminate against some convicted defendants on account of their poverty. There, . . . the right to a free transcript on appeal was in issue. Here the issue is whether or not an indigent shall be denied the assistance of counsel on appeal. In either case the evil is the same: discrimination against the indigent. For there can be no equal justice where the kind of an appeal a man enjoys "depends on the amount of money he has." Griffin v. Illinois (351 US at p. 19).

In spite of California's forward treatment of indigents, under its present practice the type of an appeal a person is afforded in the District Court of Appeal hinges upon whether or not he can pay for the assistance of counsel. If he can the appellate court passes on the merits of his case only after having the full benefit of written briefs and oral argument by counsel. If he cannot the appellate court is forced to prejudge the

merits before it can even determine whether counsel should be provided. At this stage in the proceedings only the barren record speaks for the indigent, and, unless the printed pages show that an injustice has been committed, he is forced to go without a champion on appeal. Any real chance he may have had of showing that his appeal has hidden merit is deprived him when the court decides on an ex parte examination of the record that the assistance of counsel is not required.

We are not here concerned with problems that might arise from the denial of counsel for the preparation of a petition for discretionary or mandatory review beyond the stage in the appellate process at which the claims have once been presented by a lawyer and passed upon by an appellate court. We are dealing only with the *first appeal*, granted as a matter of right to rich and poor alike (Cal Penal Code §§1235, 1237), from a criminal conviction. We need not now decide whether California would have to provide counsel for an indigent seeking a discretionary hearing from the California Supreme Court after the District Court of Appeal had sustained his conviction or whether counsel must be appointed for an indigent seeking review of an appellate affirmance of his conviction in this Court by appeal as of right or by petition for a writ of certiorari which lies within the Court's discretion. But it is appropriate to observe that a State can, consistently with the Fourteenth Amendment, provide for differences so long as the result does not amount to a denial of due process or an "invidious discrimination." Absolute equality is not required; lines can be and are drawn and we often sustain them. But where the merits of *the one and only appeal* an indigent has as of right are decided without benefit of counsel, we think an unconstitutional line has been drawn between rich and poor.

When an indigent is forced to run this gantlet of a preliminary showing of merit, the right to appeal does not comport with fair procedure. . . . There is lacking that equality demanded by the Fourteenth Amendment where the rich man, who appeals as of right, enjoys the benefit of counsel's examination into the record, research of the law, and marshalling of arguments on his behalf, while the indigent, already burdened by a preliminary determination that his case is without merit, is forced to shift for himself. The indigent, where the record is unclear or the errors are hidden, has only the right to a meaningless ritual, while the rich man has a meaningful appeal. . . .

Mr. Justice Clark, dissenting. . . .

Mr. Justice Harlan, whom Mr. Justice Stewart joins, dissenting.

In holding that an indigent has an absolute right to appointed counsel on appeal of a state criminal conviction, the Court appears to rely both on the Equal Protection Clause and on the guarantees of fair procedure inherent in the Due Process Clause of the Fourteenth Amendment, with obvious emphasis on "equal protection." In my view the Equal Protection Clause is not apposite, and its application to cases like the present one can lead only to mischievous results. This case should be judged solely under the Due Process Clause, and I do not believe that the California procedure violates that provision.

EQUAL PROTECTION

To approach the present problem in terms of the Equal Protection Clause is, I submit, but to substitute resounding phrases for analysis. I dissented from this approach in Griffin v. Illinois, and I am constrained to dissent from the implicit extension of the equal protection approach here—to a case in which the State denies no one an appeal, but seeks only to keep within reasonable bounds the instances in which appellate counsel will be assigned to indigents.

The States, of course, are prohibited by the Equal Protection Clause from discriminating between "rich" and "poor" *as such* in the formulation and application of their laws. But it is a far different thing to suggest that this provision prevents the State from adopting a law of general applicability that may affect the poor more harshly than it does the rich, or, on the other hand, from making some effort to redress economic imbalances while not eliminating them entirely.

Every financial exaction which the State imposes on a uniform basis is more easily satisfied by the well-to-do than by the indigent. Yet I take it that no one would dispute the constitutional power of the State to levy a uniform sales tax, to charge tuition at a state university, to fix rates for the purchase of water from a municipal corporation, to impose a standard fine for criminal violations, or to establish minimum bail for various categories of offenses. Nor could it be contended that the State may not classify as crimes acts which the poor are more likely to commit than are the rich. And surely, there would be no basis for attacking a state law which provided benefits for the needy simply because those benefits fell short of the goods or services that others could purchase for themselves.

Laws such as these do not deny equal protection to the less fortunate for one essential reason: the Equal Protection Clause does not impose on the States "an affirmative duty to lift the handicaps flowing from differences in economic circumstances." To so construe it would be to read into the Constitution a philosophy of leveling that would be foreign to many of our basic concepts of the proper relations between government and society. The State may have a moral obligation to eliminate the evils of poverty, but it is not required by the Equal Protection Clause to give to some whatever others can afford. . . .

California does not discriminate between rich and poor in having a uniform policy permitting every one to appeal and to retain counsel, and in having a separate rule dealing *only* with the standards for the appointment of counsel for those unable to retain their own attorneys. The sole classification established by this rule is between those cases that are believed to have merit and those regarded as frivolous. And, of course, no matter how far the state rule might go in providing counsel for indigents, it could never be expected to satisfy an affirmative duty—if one existed—to place the poor on the same level as those who can afford the best legal talent available.

Parenthetically, it should be noted that if the present problem may be viewed as one of the equal protection, so may the question of the right to appointed counsel at trial, and the Court's analysis of that right in Gideon v. Wainwright. . . . is wholly unnecessary. The short way to dispose of Gideon v. Wainwright, in other words, would be simply to say that the State deprives the indigent of equal protection whenever it fails to furnish him with legal services, and perhaps with other services as well, equivalent to those that the affluent defendant can obtain.

The real question in this case, I submit, and the only one that permits of satisfactory analysis, is whether or not the state rule, as applied in this case, is consistent with the requirements of fair procedure guaranteed by the Due Process Clause. Of course, in considering this question, it must not be lost sight of that the State's responsibility under the Due Process Clause is to provide justice for all. Refusal to furnish criminal indigents with some things that others can afford may fall short of constitutional standards of fairness. The problem before us is whether this is such a case.

DUE PROCESS

It bears reiteration that California's procedure of screening its criminal appeals to determine whether or not counsel ought to be appointed denies to no one the right to appeal. . . .

We have today held that in a case such as the one before us, there is an absolute right to the services of counsel at trial. Gideon v. Wainwright. But the appellate procedures involved here stand on an entirely different constitutional footing. *First*, appellate review is in itself not required by the Fourteenth Amendment, and thus the question presented is the narrow one whether the State's rules with respect to the appointment of counsel are so arbitrary or unreasonable, *in the context of the particular appellate procedure that it has established*, as to require their invalidation. *Second*, the kinds of questions that may arise on appeal are circumscribed by the record of the proceedings that led to the conviction; they do not encompass the large variety of tactical and strategic problems that must be resolved at the trial. *Third,* as California applies its rule, the indigent appellant receives the benefit of expert and conscientious legal appraisal of the merits of his case on the basis of the trial record, and whether or not he is

assigned counsel, is guaranteed full consideration of his appeal. It would be painting with too broad a brush to conclude that under these circumstances an appeal is just like a trial.

What the Court finds constitutionally offensive in California's procedure bears a striking resemblance to the rules of this Court and many state courts of last resort on petitions for certiorari or for leave to appeal filed by indigent defendants pro se. Under the practice of this Court, only if it appears from the petition for certiorari that a case merits review is leave to proceed in forma pauperis granted, the case transferred to the Appellate Docket, and counsel appointed. Since our review is generally discretionary, and since we are often not even given the benefit of a record in the proceedings below, the disadvantages to the indigent petitioner might be regarded as more substantial than in California. But as conscientiously committed as this Court is to the great principle of "Equal Justice Under Law," it has never deemed itself constitutionally required to appoint counsel to assist in the preparation of each of the more than 1,000 pro se petitions for certiorari currently being filed each Term. We should know from our own experience that appellate courts generally go out of their way to give fair consideration to those who are unrepresented.

The Court distinguishes our review from the present case on the grounds that the California rule relates to "the *first appeal*, granted as a matter of right." But I fail to see the significance of this difference. Surely, it cannot be contended that the requirements of fair procedure are exhausted once an indigent has been given one appellate review. . . .

I cannot agree that the Constitution prohibits a State, in seeking to redress economic imbalances at its bar of justice and to provide indigents with full review, from taking reasonable steps to guard against needless expense. This is all that California has done. . . .

Notes and Questions

1. *Gideon* relied on the Sixth Amendment to hold that indigents are entitled to representation by court-appointed trial counsel in felony cases.

Douglas, conversely, relied on Fourteenth Amendment due-process and equal-protection principles. Why did the *Douglas* Court not base its decision on the Sixth Amendment? And why, do you suppose, did *Gideon* not invoke due-process and equal-protection grounds? If the Court had chosen the latter constitutional foundation for *Gideon*, would you expect a different resolution of *Scott v. Illinois*?

2. Precisely what did Justice Harlan mean when he said in his dissenting opinion in *Douglas* that "the Equal Protection Clause does not impose on the States 'an affirmative duty to lift the handicaps flowing from differences in economic circumstances.'"? If a state builds a public university system, is it obliged to waive tuition costs for those who cannot afford them? If a state builds roads, must it buy cars for poor people so that they—like more affluent citizens who are able to purchase their own vehicles—can drive on them? If, as in *Douglas*, a state provides an appeals system and guarantees indigents the right of appeal, why must it do more and also appoint counsel to assist with an appeal? What, if anything, distinguishes appeal rights from the examples involving university tuition and the provision of automobiles?

3. How far does the principle extend that "there can be no equal justice where the kind of an appeal a man enjoys 'depends on the amount of money he has'"? Should poor people be entitled to the lawyer of their choice, or simply to a lawyer? Should the right to court-appointed counsel extend beyond the first appeal and also apply when indigents petition for certiorari or seek other postappeal review of their cases?

Ross v. Moffitt, 417 U.S. 600, 94 S. Ct. 2437, 41 L. Ed. 2d 341 (1974)

[Moffitt, an indigent, was represented by court-appointed counsel in two separate state court trials in North Carolina for forgery and uttering a forged instrument. He was convicted in both cases, and again was represented by court-appointed counsel on the appeal of his convictions to the North Carolina Court of Appeals. That court affirmed both convictions. Moffitt then requested the appointment of counsel to petition the North Carolina Supreme Court for certiorari, or discretionary review, in his cases. This request was granted in one case, and an attorney was appointed to prepare a petition for a writ of certiorari to the North Carolina Supreme Court, but the request was denied in the other case. The North Carolina Supreme Court denied review in the case in which counsel had filed a petition. Moffitt's request in that case for the appointment of counsel to file a writ of certiorari on his behalf in the U.S. Supreme Court was denied. Thereafter, both the state courts and two U.S. district courts rejected his claim that he had been denied a constitutional right to the appointment of counsel for assistance in preparing certiorari petitions to the North Carolina Supreme Court and the U.S. Supreme Court. The Fourth Circuit Court of Appeals reversed, holding that Moffitt was entitled to court-appointed counsel in both circumstances.]

Mr. Justice Rehnquist delivered the opinion of the Court.

We are asked in this case to decide whether Douglas v. California, which requires appointment of counsel for indigent state defendants on their first appeal as of right, should be extended to require counsel for discretionary state appeals and for applications for review in this Court. . . .

The precise rationale for the Griffin and Douglas lines of cases has never been explicitly stated, some support being derived from the Equal Protection Clause of the Fourteenth Amendment, and some from the Due Process Clause of that Amendment. Neither clause by itself provides an entirely satisfactory basis for the result reached, each depending on a different inquiry which emphasizes different factors. "Due process" emphasizes fairness between the State and the individual dealing with the State, regardless of how other individuals in the same situation may be treated. "Equal protection," on the other hand, emphasizes disparity in treatment by a State between classes of individuals whose situations are arguably indistinguishable. . . .

We do not believe that the Due Process Clause requires North Carolina to provide respondent with counsel on his discretionary appeal to the State Supreme Court. At the trial stage of a criminal proceeding, the right of an indigent defendant to counsel is fundamental and binding upon the States by virtue of the Sixth and Fourteenth Amendments. Gideon v Wainwright. But there are significant differences between the trial and appellate stages of a criminal proceeding. The purpose of the trial stage from the State's point of view is to convert a criminal defendant from a person presumed innocent to one found guilty beyond a reasonable doubt. To accomplish this purpose, the State employs a prosecuting attorney who presents evidence to the court, challenges any witnesses offered by the defendant, argues rulings of the court, and makes direct arguments to the court and jury seeking to persuade them of the defendant's guilt. Under these circumstances "reason and reflection require us to recognize that in our adversary system of criminal justice, any person haled into court, who is too poor to hire a lawyer, cannot be assured a fair trial unless counsel is provided for him." [372 U.S. at] 344.

By contrast, it is ordinarily the defendant, rather than the State, who initiates the appellate process, seeking not to fend off the efforts of the State's prosecutor but rather to overturn a finding of guilt made by a judge or jury below. The defendant needs an attorney on appeal not as a shield to protect him against being "haled into court" by the State and stripped of his presumption of innocence, but rather as a sword to upset the prior determination of guilt. This difference is significant for, while no one would agree that the State may simply dispense with the trial stage of proceedings without a criminal defendant's consent, it is clear that the State need not provide any appeal at all. The fact that an appeal *has* been provided does not automatically mean that a State then acts unfairly by refusing to provide counsel to indigent defendants at every stage of the way. Unfairness results only if indigents are singled out by the State and denied meaningful access to the appellate system because of their poverty. That question is more profitably considered under an equal protection analysis. . . .

Despite the tendency of all rights "to declare themselves absolute to their logical extreme," there are obviously limits beyond which the equal protection analysis may not be pressed without doing violence to principles recognized in other decisions of this Court. The Fourteenth Amendment "does not require absolute equality or precisely equal advantages," nor does it require the State to "equalize economic conditions." It does require that the state appellate system be "free of unreasoned distinctions," and that indigents have an adequate opportunity to present their claims fairly within the adversary system. Griffin v. Illinois. The State cannot adopt procedures which leave an indigent defendant "entirely cut off from any appeal at all," by virtue of his indigency, Lane v Brown, 372 US [477,] 481, [83 S Ct 768, 9 L Ed 2d 892 (1963)] at 481, or extend to such indigent defendants merely a "meaningless ritual" while others in better economic circumstances have a "meaningful appeal." Douglas v. California, [372 US] at 358. The question is not one of absolutes, but one of the degrees. In this case we do not believe that the Equal Protection Clause, when interpreted in the context of these cases, requires North Carolina to provide free counsel for indigent defendants seeking to take discretionary appeals to the North Carolina Supreme Court, or to file petitions for certiorari in this Court. . . .

The facts show that respondent, in connection with his Mecklenburg County conviction, received the benefit of counsel in examining the record of his trial and in preparing an appellate brief on his behalf for the state Court of Appeals. Thus, prior to his seeking discretionary review in the State Supreme Court, his claims had "once been presented by a lawyer and passed upon by an appellate court." Douglas v. California, 372 US, at 356. We do not believe that it can be said, therefore, that a defendant in respondent's circumstances is denied meaningful access to the North Carolina Supreme Court simply because the State does not appoint counsel to aid him in seeking review in that court. At that stage he will have, at the very least, a transcript or other record of trial proceedings, a brief on his behalf in the Court of Appeals setting forth his claims of error, and in many cases an opinion by the Court of Appeals disposing of his case. These materials, supplemented by whatever submission respondent may make pro se, would appear to provide the Supreme Court of North Carolina with an adequate basis for its decision to grant or deny review.

We are fortified in this conclusion by our understanding of the function served by discretionary review in the North Carolina Supreme Court. The critical issue in that court, as we perceive it, is not whether there has been "a correct adjudication of guilt" in every individual case, but rather whether "the subject matter of the appeal has significant public interest," whether "the cause involves legal principles of major significance to the jurisprudence of the State," or whether the decision below is in probable conflict with a decision of the Supreme Court. The Supreme Court may deny certiorari even though it believes that the decision of the Court of Appeals was incorrect, since a decision which appears incorrect may nevertheless fail to satisfy any of the criteria discussed above. Once a defendant's claims of error are organized and presented in a lawyer like fashion to the Court of Appeals, the justices of the Supreme Court of North Carolina who make the decision to grant or deny discretionary review should be able to ascertain whether his case satisfies the standards established by the legislature for such review.

This is not to say, of course, that a skilled lawyer, particularly one trained in the somewhat arcane art of preparing petitions for discretionary review, would not prove helpful to any litigant able to employ him. An indigent defendant seeking review in the Supreme Court of North Carolina is therefore somewhat handicapped in comparison with a wealthy defendant who has counsel assisting him in every conceivable manner at every stage in the proceeding. But both the opportunity to have counsel prepare an initial brief in the Court of Appeals and the nature of discretionary review in the Supreme Court of North Carolina make this relative handicap far less than the handicap borne by the indigent defendant denied counsel on his initial appeal as of right in Douglas. And the fact that a particular service might be of benefit to an indigent defendant does not mean that the service is constitutionally required. The duty of the State under our cases is not to duplicate the legal arsenal that

may be privately retained by a criminal defendant in a continuing effort to reverse his conviction, but only to assure the indigent defendant an adequate opportunity to present his claims fairly in the context of the State's appellate process. We think respondent was given that opportunity under the existing North Carolina system.

Much of the discussion in the preceding section is equally relevant to the question of whether a State must provide counsel for a defendant seeking review of his conviction in this Court. North Carolina will have provided counsel for a convicted defendant's only appeal as of right, and the brief prepared by that counsel together with one and perhaps two North Carolina appellate opinions will be available to this Court in order that it may decide whether or not to grant certiorari. This Court's review, much like that of the Supreme Court of North Carolina, is discretionary and depends on numerous factors other than the perceived correctness of the judgment we are asked to review. . . .

We do not mean by this opinion to in any way discourage those States which have, as a matter of legislative choice, made counsel available to convicted defendants at all stages of judicial review. Some States which might well choose to do so as a matter of legislative policy may conceivably find that other claims for public funds within or without the criminal justice system preclude the implementation of such a policy at the present time. . . . Our reading of the Fourteenth Amendment leaves these choices to the State, and respondent was denied no right secured by the Federal Constitution when North Carolina refused to provide counsel to aid him in obtaining discretionary appellate review. . . .

Mr. Justice Douglas, with whom Mr. Justice Brennan and Mr. Justice Marshall concur, dissenting. . . .

[T]he indigent defendant proceeding without counsel is at a substantial disadvantage relative to wealthy defendants represented by counsel when he is forced to fend for himself in seeking discretionary review from the State Supreme Court or from this Court. It may well not be enough to allege error in the courts below in layman's terms; a more sophisticated approach may be demanded. . . . Furthermore, the lawyer who handled the first appeal in a case would be familiar with the facts and legal issues involved in the case. It would be a relatively easy matter for the attorney to apply his expertise in filing a petition for discretionary review to a higher court, or to advise his client that such a petition would have no chance of succeeding.

Douglas v. California was grounded on concepts of fairness and equality. The right to seek discretionary review is a substantial one, and one where a lawyer can be of significant assistance to an indigent defendant. It was correctly perceived below that the "same concepts of fairness and equality, which require counsel in a first appeal of right, require counsel in other and subsequent discretionary appeals."

Notes and Questions

1. The majority opinion concedes that a lawyer might "prove helpful to any litigant able to employ him" and that "an indigent defendant seeking [discretionary] review . . . is therefore somewhat handicapped in comparison with a wealthy defendant." Can you reconcile these concessions with the conclusion that neither due-process nor equal-protection principles require the appointment of counsel to file petitions for discretionary review on behalf of indigent defendants?

2. As Justice Rehnquist's opinion indicates, many states provide a statutory right to counsel for indigents pursuing discretionary review of their convictions. State courts occasionally have departed from the holding in *Ross v. Moffitt* on state constitutional grounds. *See People v. Valdez*, 789 P.2d 406 (Colo. 1990) (appointment of counsel required for certiorari petitions to state supreme court); *Green v. State*, 620 So. 2d 188 (Fla. 1993) (counsel must be appointed to help indigents file petitions for writs of certiorari to the U.S. Supreme Court in capital cases).

3. The rule of *Ross v. Moffitt* has been applied to postconviction collateral challenges to state court convictions and sentences. Such challenges normally involve issues that cannot be resolved on an appeal because they depend on facts that may not be fully developed in the record of trial proceedings. Allegations of ineffective assistance of counsel, prosecutorial misconduct (e.g., *Brady* violations), and claims of newly discovered evidence that undermines confidence in a guilty verdict typically are raised in postconviction proceedings. Relying heavily on the rationale of *Ross v. Moffitt*, the Supreme Court has ruled that indigents have no federal constitutional right to appointed counsel in such postconviction collateral proceedings. *See Pennsylvania v. Finley*, 481 U.S. 551, 107 S. Ct. 1990, 95 L. Ed. 2d 539 (1987); *Murray v. Giarratano*, 492 U.S. 1, 109 S. Ct. 2765, 106 L. Ed. 2d 1 (1989) (capital case). Nor is there an automatic right to court-appointed counsel in probation and parole revocation cases. However, due process requires the appointment of counsel for indigents when individual case circumstances would render such proceedings fundamentally unfair if the defendant lacks legal representation. *See Gagnon v. Scarpelli*, 411 U.S. 778, 93 S. Ct. 1756, 36 L. Ed. 2d 656 (1973) (probation revocation); *Morrissey v. Brewer*, 408 U.S. 471, 92 S. Ct. 2593, 33 L. Ed. 2d 484 (1972) (parole revocation).

A Right of Self-Representation?

If a criminal defendant has a constitutional right to be represented by a lawyer at his or her trial, can that right be transformed into an affirmative requirement to have the services of counsel? That is, must a person brought to trial for a crime be represented by an attorney, even over his or her objection, or may that person instead reject a lawyer's help and represent him- or herself? Would it matter if he or she was not likely to do nearly as good of a job as a lawyer would in defending against the charges? If there is a right of self-representation, what assurance must there be that the accused is forgoing the assistance of counsel with a full understanding that such action may not be in his or her own best interests?

Faretta v. California, 422 U.S. 806, 95 S. Ct. 2525, 45 L. Ed. 2d 562 (1975)

Mr. Justice Stewart delivered the opinion of the Court. . . .

I

Anthony Faretta was charged with grand theft in an information filed in the Superior Court of Los Angeles County, Cal. At the arraignment, the Superior Court Judge assigned to preside at the trial appointed the public defender to represent Faretta. Well before the date of trial, however, Faretta requested that he be permitted to represent himself. Questioning by the judge revealed that Faretta had once represented himself in a criminal prosecution, that he had a high school education, and that he did not want to be represented by the public defender because he believed that that office was "very loaded down with . . . a heavy case load." The judge responded that he believed Faretta was "making a mistake" and emphasized that in further proceedings Faretta would receive no special favors. Nevertheless, after establishing that Faretta wanted to represent himself and did not want a lawyer, the judge, in a "preliminary ruling," accepted Faretta's waiver of the assistance of counsel. The judge indicated, however, that he might reverse this ruling if it later appeared that Faretta was unable adequately to represent himself.

Several weeks thereafter, but still prior to trial, the judge sua sponte held a hearing to inquire into Faretta's ability to conduct his own defense, and questioned him specifically about both the hearsay rule and the state law governing the challenge of potential jurors. After consideration of Faretta's answers, and observation of his demeanor, the judge ruled that Faretta had not made an intelligent and knowing waiver of his right to the assistance of counsel, and also ruled that Faretta had no constitutional right to conduct his own defense. The judge, accordingly, reversed his earlier ruling permitting self-repre-

sentation and again appointed the public defender to represent Faretta. . . . Throughout the subsequent trial, the judge required that Faretta's defense be conducted only through the appointed lawyer from the public defender's office. At the conclusion of the trial, the jury found Faretta guilty as charged, and the judge sentenced him to prison.

The California Court of Appeal . . . affirmed the trial judge's ruling that Faretta had no federal or state constitutional right to represent himself . . . and the California Supreme Court denied review. We granted certiorari.

II

In the federal courts, the right of self-representation has been protected by statute since the beginnings of our Nation. . . .

With few exceptions, each of the several States also accords a defendant the right to represent himself in any criminal case. The Constitutions of 36 States explicitly confer that right. . .

This Court's past recognition of the right of self-representation, the federal court authority holding the right to be of constitutional dimension, and the state constitutions pointing to the right's fundamental nature form a consensus not easily ignored. "[T]he mere fact that a path is a beaten one," Mr. Justice Jackson once observed, "is a persuasive reason for following it." We confront here a nearly universal conviction, on the part of our people as well as our courts, that forcing a lawyer upon an unwilling defendant is contrary to his basic right to defend himself if he truly wants to do so.

III

This consensus is soundly premised. The right of self-representation finds support in the structure of the Sixth Amendment, as well as in the English and colonial jurisprudence from which the Amendment emerged.

. . . The Sixth Amendment does not provide merely that a defense shall be made for the accused; it grants to the accused personally the right to make his defense. It is the accused, not counsel, who must be "informed of the nature and cause of the accusation," who must be "confronted with the witnesses against him," and who must be accorded "compulsory process for obtaining witnesses in his favor." Although not stated in the Amendment in so many words, the right to self-representation—to make one's own defense personally—is thus necessarily implied by the structure of the Amendment. The right to defend is given directly to the accused; for it is he who suffers the consequences if the defense fails.

The counsel provision supplements this design. It speaks of the "assistance" of counsel, and an assistant, however expert, is still an assistant. The language and spirit of the Sixth Amendment contemplate that counsel, like the other defense tools guaranteed by the Amendment, shall be an aid to a willing defendant—not an organ of the State interposed between an unwilling defendant and his right to defend himself personally. To thrust counsel upon the accused, against his considered wish, thus violates the logic of the Amendment. In such a case, counsel is not an assistant, but a master; and the right to make a defense is stripped of the personal character upon which the Amendment insists. It is true that when a defendant chooses to have a lawyer manage and present his case, law and tradition may allocate to the counsel the power to make binding decisions of trial strategy in many areas. This allocation can only be justified, however, by the defendant's consent, at the outset, to accept counsel as his representative. . . . Unless the accused has acquiesced in such representation, the defense presented is not the defense guaranteed him by the Constitution, for, in a very real sense, it is not *his* defense.

The Sixth Amendment, when naturally read, thus implies a right of self-representation. This reading is reinforced by the Amendment's roots in English legal history. . . .

In the American Colonies the insistence upon a right of self-representation was, if anything, more fervent than in England. . . .

In sum, there is no evidence that the colonists and the Framers ever doubted the right of self-representation, or imagined that this right might be considered inferior to the right of assistance of counsel. To the contrary, the colonists and the Framers, as well as their English ancestors, always conceived of the right to counsel as an "assistance" for the accused, to be used at his option, in defending himself. The Framers selected in the Sixth Amendment a form of words that necessarily implies the right of self-representation. That conclusion is supported by centuries of consistent history.

IV

There can be no blinking the fact that the right of an accused to conduct his own defense seems to cut against the grain of this Court's decisions holding that the Constitution requires that no accused can be convicted and imprisoned unless he has been accorded the right to the assistance of counsel. See Powell v. Alabama; Johnson v. Zerbst; Gideon v. Wainwright; Argersinger v. Hamlin. For it is surely true that the basic thesis of those decisions is that the help of a lawyer is essential to assure the defendant a fair trial. And a strong argument can surely be made that the whole thrust of those decisions must inevitably lead to the conclusion that a State may constitutionally impose a lawyer upon even an unwilling defendant.

But it is one thing to hold that every defendant, rich or poor, has the right to the assistance of counsel, and quite another to say that a State may compel a defendant to accept a lawyer he does not want. . . .

It is undeniable that in most criminal prosecutions defendants could better defend with counsel's guidance than by their own unskilled efforts. But where the defendant will not voluntarily accept representation by counsel, the potential advantage of a lawyer's training and experience can be realized, if at all, only imperfectly. To force a lawyer on a defendant can only lead him to believe that the law contrives against him. Moreover, it is not inconceivable that in some rare instances, the defendant might in fact present his case more effectively by conducting his own defense. Personal liberties are not rooted in the law of averages. The right to defend is personal. The defendant, and not his lawyer or the State, will bear the personal consequences of a conviction. It is the defendant, therefore, who must be free personally to decide whether in his particular case counsel is to his advantage. And although he may conduct his own defense ultimately to his own detriment, his choice must be honored out of "that respect for the individual which is the life-blood of the law."[46]

V

When an accused manages his own defense, he relinquishes, as a purely factual matter, many of the traditional benefits associated with the right to counsel. For this reason, in order to represent himself, the accused must "knowingly and intelligently" forgo those relinquished benefits. Johnson v. Zerbst. Although a defendant need not himself have the skill and experience of a lawyer in order competently and intelligently to choose self-representation, he should be made aware of the dangers and disadvantages of self-

---

46. We are told that many criminal defendants representing themselves may use the courtroom for deliberate disruption of their trials. But the right of self-representation has been recognized from our beginnings by federal law and by most of the States, and no such result has thereby occurred. Moreover, the trial judge may terminate self-representation by a defendant who deliberately engages in serious and obstructionist misconduct. See Illinois v. Allen, 397 US 337, 90 S Ct 1057, 25 L Ed 2d 353 [(1970)]. Of course, a State may—even over objection by the accused—appoint a "standby counsel" to aid the accused if and when the accused requests help, and to be available to represent the accused in the event that termination of the defendant's self-representation is necessary.

The right of self-representation is not a license to abuse the dignity of the courtroom. Neither is it a license not to comply with relevant rules of procedural and substantive law. Thus, whatever else may or may not be open to him on appeal, a defendant who elects to represent himself cannot thereafter complain that the quality of his own defense amounted to a denial of

representation, so that the record will establish that "he knows what he is doing and his choice is made with eyes open."

Here, weeks before trial, Faretta clearly and unequivocally declared to the trial judge that he wanted to represent himself and did not want counsel. The record affirmatively shows that Faretta was literate, competent, and understanding, and that he was voluntarily exercising his informed free will. The trial judge had warned Faretta that he thought it was a mistake not to accept the assistance of counsel, and that Faretta would be required to follow all the "ground rules" of trial procedure. We need make no assessment of how well or poorly Faretta had mastered the intricacies of the hearsay rule and the California code provisions that govern challenges of potential jurors on voir dire. For his technical legal knowledge, as such, was not relevant to an assessment of his knowing exercise of the right to defend himself.

In forcing Faretta, under these circumstances, to accept against his will a state-appointed public defender, the California courts deprived him of his constitutional right to conduct his own defense. Accordingly, the judgment before us is vacated, and the case is remanded for further proceedings not inconsistent with this opinion.

It is so ordered.

Mr. Chief Justice Burger, with whom Mr. Justice Blackmun and Mr. Justice Rehnquist join, dissenting.

This case . . . is another example of the judicial tendency to constitutionalize what is thought "good." That effort fails on its own terms here, because there is nothing desirable or useful in permitting every accused person, even the most uneducated and inexperienced, to insist upon conducting his own defense to criminal charges. Moreover, there is no constitutional basis for the Court's holding, and it can only add to the problems of an already malfunctioning criminal justice system. . . .

Nor is it accurate to suggest, as the Court seems to later in its opinion, that the quality of his representation at trial is a matter with which only the accused is legitimately concerned. Although we have adopted an adversary system of criminal justice, the prosecution is more than an ordinary litigant, and the trial judge is not simply an automaton who insures that technical rules are adhered to. Both are charged with the duty of insuring that justice, in the broadest sense of that term, is achieved in every criminal trial. That goal is ill-served, and the integrity of public confidence in the system are undermined, when an easy conviction is obtained due to the defendant's ill-advised decision to waive counsel. . . .

True freedom of choice and society's interest in seeing that justice is achieved can be vindicated only if the trial court retains discretion to reject any attempted waiver of counsel and insist that the accused be tried according to the Constitution. . . .

Society has the right to expect that, when courts find new rights implied in the Constitution, their potential effect upon the resources of our criminal justice system will be considered. However, such considerations are conspicuously absent from the Court's opinion in this case.

It hardly needs repeating that courts at all levels are already handicapped by the unsupplied demand for competent advocates, with the result that it often takes far longer to complete a given case than experienced counsel would require. If we were to assume that there will be widespread exercise of the newly discovered constitutional right to self-representation, it would almost certainly follow that there will be added congestion in the courts and that the quality of justice will suffer. Moreover, . . . [i]t is totally unrealistic . . . to suggest that an accused will always be held to the consequences of a decision to conduct his own defense. Unless, as may be the case, most persons accused of crime have more wit than to insist upon the dubious benefit that the Court confers today, we can expect that many expensive and good-faith prosecutions will be nullified on appeal for reasons that trial courts are now deprived of the power to prevent.

Mr. Justice Blackmun, with whom The Chief Justice and Mr. Justice Rehnquist join, dissenting. . . .

If there is any truth to the old proverb that "[o]ne who is his own lawyer has a fool for a client," the Court by its opinion today now bestows a *constitutional* right on one to make a fool of himself.

Notes and Questions

1. Which interest seems more important: the accused's freedom of choice or society's interest in ensuring that all persons charged with a crime receive at least a minimally fair trial that is designed to produce reliable results? Are both interests served by the decision in *Faretta*? Can they be?

2. Precisely where in the Constitution does the majority opinion locate a right to self-representation?

3. What are the requirements for an effective waiver of the right to counsel? Note the majority opinion's insistence that Faretta's "technical legal knowledge, as such, was not relevant to an assessment of his knowing exercise of the right to defend himself." The Court reaffirmed this point in *Godinez v. Moran*, 509 U.S. 389, 113 S. Ct. 2680, 125 L. Ed. 2d 321 (1993), when it explained that

the competence that is required of a defendant seeking to waive his right to counsel is the competence to *waive the right*, not the competence to represent himself. In Faretta v. California we held that a defendant choosing self-representation must do so "competently and intelligently," but we made it clear that the defendant's "technical legal knowledge" is "not relevant" to the determination whether he is competent to waive his right to counsel. . . . [A] criminal defendant's ability to represent himself has no bearing upon his competence to *choose* self-representation. 509 U.S., at 399–400 (footnotes omitted) (emphasis in original).

The American Bar Association Standard for the Administration of Criminal Justice 5-8.2 (3d ed. 1992) provides as follows.

ABA Standards for Criminal Justice (3d ed. 1992)

STANDARD 5-8.2. IN-COURT WAIVER

(a) The accused's failure to request counsel or an announced intention to plead guilty should not of itself be construed to constitute a waiver of counsel in court. An accused should not be deemed to have waived the assistance of counsel until the entire process of offering counsel has been completed before a judge and a thorough inquiry into the accused's comprehension of the offer and capacity to make the choice intelligently and understandingly has been made. No waiver of counsel should occur unless the accused understands the right and knowingly and intelligently relinquishes it. No waiver should be found to have been made where it appears that the accused is unable to make an intelligent and understanding choice because of mental condition, age, education, experience, the nature or complexity of the case, or other factors. A waiver of counsel should not be accepted unless it is in writing and of record.

(b) If an accused in a proceeding involving the possibility of incarceration has not seen a lawyer and indicates an intention to waive the assistance of counsel, a lawyer should be provided before any in-court waiver is accepted. No waiver should be accepted unless the accused has at least once conferred with a lawyer. If a waiver is accepted, the offer should be renewed at each subsequent stage of the proceedings at which the accused appears without counsel.

Source: Reprinted with permission from *ABA Standards for Criminal Justice—Providing Defense Services* (Third Edition, 1992), Standard 5-8.2, © 1992, American Bar Association.

---

4. If the accused has a right to waive representation by counsel, does it also follow that when a lawyer remains on the case and serves as trial counsel, the defendant has a right to dictate how the attorney should handle the defense? Consider Standard 4-5.2 of the American Bar Association's Standards Relating to the Administration of Criminal Justice (3d ed. 1992).

Standard 4-5.2 Control and Direction of the Case

(a) Certain decisions relating to the conduct of the case are ultimately for the accused and others are ultimately for defense counsel. The decisions which are to be made by the accused after full consultation with counsel include:

(i) what pleas to enter;

(ii) whether to accept a plea agreement;

(iii) whether to waive jury trial;

(iv) whether to testify in his or her own behalf; and

(v) whether to appeal.

(b) Strategic and tactical decisions should be made by defense counsel after consultation with the client where feasible and appropriate. Such decisions include what witnesses to call, whether and how to conduct cross-examination, what jurors to accept or strike, what trial motions should be made, and what evidence should be introduced.

(c) If a disagreement on significant matters of tactics or strategy arises between defense counsel and the client, defense counsel should make a record of the circumstances, counsel's advice and reasons, and the conclusion reached. The record should be made in a manner which protects the confidentiality of the lawyer-client relationship.

———

Source: Reprinted with permission from *ABA Standards for Criminal Justice: Prosecution Function and Defense Function,* Third Edition, Standard 4-5.2, © 1993, American Bar Association.

———

5. The Supreme Court considered the role of backup or standby trial counsel appointed by a court when an accused exercises the right of self-representation in *McKaskle v. Wiggins,* 465 U.S. 168, 104 S. Ct. 944, 79 L. Ed. 2d 122 (1984). It ruled that

A defendant's Sixth Amendment rights are not violated when a trial judge appoints standby counsel—even over the defendant's objection—to relieve the judge of the need to explain and enforce basic rules of courtroom protocol or to assist the defendant in overcoming routine obstacles that stand in the way of the defendant's achievement of his own clearly indicated goals. 465 U.S., at 184.

The Court in *Wiggins* also addressed the appropriate limits of standby counsel's participation in the trial proceedings. Justice O'Connor's majority opinion first squarely rejected the proposition that standby counsel must "'be seen but not heard.'" However, the opinion simultaneously recognized that "the Faretta right must impose some limits on the extent of standby counsel's unsolicited participation."

In determining whether a defendant's Faretta rights have been respected, the primary focus must be on whether the defendant had a fair chance to present his case in his own way. . . .

First, the pro se defendant is entitled to preserve actual control over the case he chooses to present to the jury. This is the core of the Faretta right. If standby counsel's participation over the defendant's objection effectively allows counsel to make or substantially interfere with any significant tactical decisions, or to control the questioning of witnesses, or to speak instead of the defendant on any matter of importance, the Faretta right is eroded.

Second, participation by standby counsel without the defendant's consent should not be allowed to destroy the jury's perception that the defendant is representing himself. . . . From the jury's perspective, the message conveyed by the defense may depend on the messenger as on the message itself. From the defendant's own point of view, the right to appear pro se can lose much of its importance if only the lawyers in the courtroom know that the right is being exercised. Participation by standby counsel outside the presence of the jury engages only the first of these two limitations. . . .

Thus, Faretta rights are adequately vindicated in proceedings outside the presence of the jury if the pro se defendant is allowed to address the court freely on his own behalf and if disagreements between counsel and the pro se defendant are resolved in the defendant's favor whenever the matter is one that would normally be left to the discretion of counsel. . . .

Participation by standby counsel in the presence of the jury is more problematic. It is here that the defendant may legitimately claim that excessive involvement by counsel will destroy the appearance that the defendant is acting pro se. This, in turn, may erode the dignitary values that the right to self-representation is intended to promote and may undercut the defendant's presentation to the jury of his own most effective defense. Nonetheless, we believe that a categorical bar on participation by standby counsel in the presence of the jury is unnecessary. . . .

A defendant like Wiggins, who vehemently objects at the beginning of trial to standby counsel's very presence in the courtroom, may express quite different views as the trial progresses. Even when he insists that he is not waiving his Faretta rights, a pro se defendant's solicitation of or acquiescence in certain types of participation by counsel substantially undermines later protestations that counsel interfered unacceptably. . . .

Once a pro se defendant invites or agrees to any substantial participation by counsel, subsequent appearances by counsel must be presumed to be with the defendant's acquiescence, at least until the defendant expressly and unambiguously renews his request that standby counsel be silenced. Faretta rights are also not infringed when standby counsel assists the pro se defendant in overcoming routine procedural or evidentiary obstacles to the completion of some specific task, such as introducing evidence or objecting to testimony, that the defendant has clearly shown he wishes to complete. Nor are they infringed when counsel merely helps to ensure the defendant's compliance with basic rules of courtroom protocol and procedure. In neither case is there any significant interference with the defendant's actual control over the presentation of his defense. The likelihood that the defendant's appearance in the status of one defending himself will be eroded is also slight, and in any event it is tolerable. A defendant does not have a constitutional right to receive personal instruction from the trial judge on courtroom procedure. Nor does the Constitution require judges to take over chores for a pro se defendant that would normally be attended to by trained counsel as a matter of course. . . . Participation by counsel to steer a defendant through the basic procedures of trial is permissible even in the unlikely event that it somewhat undermines the pro se defendant's appearance of control over his own defense. . . .

Justices White, Brennan, and Marshall dissented in *Wiggins*, believing that standby counsel unduly interfered with the defendant's right to self-representation.

THE ROLE OF DEFENSE COUNSEL: OBLIGATIONS AND LIMITS

Zealous Advocacy

A lawyer should represent a client zealously within the bounds of the law.

> —American Bar Association
> Model Code
> of Professional
> Responsibility,
> Canon 7 (1981)

The basic duty defense counsel owes to the administration of justice and as an officer of the court is to serve as the accused's counselor and advocate with courage and devotion and to render effective, quality representation.

> —American Bar Association
> Standards
> Relating to the
> Administration of
> Criminal Justice, the
> Defense Function,
> Standard 4-1.2(b)
> (3d ed. 1992)

In 1975, Joan Little was brought to trial in North Carolina for the first-degree murder of a jail guard. The jailer's body—nude from the waist down, and with semen present—was found in the cell in which Little had been incarcerated for an unrelated offense. The guard, who was white, had suffered multiple stab wounds from an icepick. Ms. Little, a 20-year-old African American, had fled from the jail, apparently taking the guard's keys in the process. She later turned herself in to the authorities, accompanied by her lawyer, Jerry Paul.

Joan Little's trial generated "an avalanche of publicity," associated as it was with "three currently sensitive political issues—women's rights, racism, and prison reform." J. McConahay, C. Mullin, & J. Frederick, "The Uses of Social Science in Trials with Political and Racial Overtone: The Trial of Joan Little," 41 *Law & Contemporary Problems* 205, 206 (1977). Little defended against the murder charge by raising self-defense, suggesting that she had killed the jail guard while trying to ward off a sexual assault. The prosecution portrayed Little as a premeditated murderer.

In light of the several "political issues" involved, the defense considered jury selection to play an especially important role in the trial. The *voir dire*, or questioning of prospective jurors, was prolonged. It stretched over 10 working days, and defense counsel enlisted a cadre of experts to help choose the jurors. During the *voir dire* of one potential juror, Mr. Paul, lead counsel for the defense, became embroiled with the trial judge in the following exchange. The exchange resulted in Paul's citation for contempt of court, a conviction that was upheld by the state and federal courts. At the conclusion of the trial, which lasted five weeks, the jury returned a not-guilty verdict after deliberating for only 78 minutes.

Paul v. Pleasants, 551 F.2d 575 (4th Cir.), cert. denied, 434 U.S. 908, 98 S. Ct. 310, 54 L. Ed. 2d 196 (1977)

. . .

BY MR. PAUL FOR THE DEFENSE:
Q. All right, do you take any magazines?
MR. GRIFFIN [the prosecutor]: OBJECTION.
COURT: SUSTAINED. I'm going to have to get right down to—I will rule on every time you object.
Q. Do you read much?
A. Yes.
Q. All right, what do you read?
MR. GRIFFIN: OBJECTION.
COURT: OVERRULED.
A. Magazines and novels.
Q. What type of magazines?
MR. GRIFFIN: OBJECTION.
COURT: SUSTAINED.
MR. PAUL: If your Honor please, may I approach the bench.
COURT: Yes sir.
(Counsel approach bench)

COURT: I am just busting up your system right now. All right madam, will you go back in the jury room.
(NOTE: [Juror] returns to a jury room.)
COURT: All right, I'll hear you now.
MR. PAUL: If your Honor please, there is no reason that we should be bound to the traditional way of picking the jury.
COURT: Probably isn't, but that's exactly what we are going to do as from this minute on.
MR. PAUL: If your Honor please, to do that denies us due process and denies us the opportunity to effectively pick good jurors.
COURT: All right now do you want to put that in the records? I suppose you are taking that down (addressing court reporter).
MR. PAUL: We have developed a method of selecting the best jurors. For the Court to ignore the advances made in social sciences and other sciences, the aid in selecting fair jurors, is to return to a hundred years ago and makes absolutely no sense whatsoever.

COURT: I believe if it is necessary the Appellate Court has, in the last day, from you, a broad spectrum of your questions, you know, of what you're trying to do. I have my doubts—I had my doubts about it yesterday morning, but I wanted to give you full opportunity to present it, for possible appellate review. Now I want you to move to the Court, which you are now doing, that you be allowed to continue as you have started, which you are now doing.

MR. PAUL: That's what we're doing now.

COURT: All right, denied.

MR. PAUL: If your Honor please, any questions the State asks, they are allowed to ask. I think the Court has shown bias in this case in favor of the State.

COURT: All right, you can put that in the record.

MR. PAUL: And isn't giving us a fair trial.

COURT: All right, I'll let you put that in the record.

MR. PAUL: And there is no sense in the Court not allowing us to proceed in an orderly fashion when we have not disrupted the Court and we have not prolonged the examination. Our questions are only phrased in a little bit different way. Our questions take shorter time than the State's do. The only difference is our questions are not traditional.

COURT: That's right.

MR. PAUL: And that being the only difference.

COURT: No, it is not that, because I think the record will disclose the type of questions and the length it has taken. I will let the record speak for that.

MR. PAUL: The time that we have kept on it shows the State has taken longer in examining jurors than we have.

COURT: I don't agree with that.

MR. PAUL: We have evidence that i[t] has and that they have taken longer.

COURT: All right, anything else you want to say?

MR. PAUL: The only reason I can see that your Honor is now cutting us off is because we are gaining an advantage and your Honor is favoring the State and your Honor is proceeding in such a manner to insure Joan Little's conviction.

COURT: All right, you got that in the record.

MR. PAUL: And at this point we ask your Honor to recuse yourself because I don't think you are capable of giving Joan Little a fair trial and I don't intend to sit or stand here and see an innocent person go to jail for any reason and you can threaten me with contempt or anything else, but it does not worry me.

COURT: All right, you got that in the record.

MR. PAUL: And to sit there and say like the queen of hearts off with the heads because the law is the law is to take us back a hundred years.

COURT: All right.

MR. PAUL: And we intend to ask these questions. Now your Honor, they can object and you can sustain, but we intend to keep on asking the questions and in order for the appellate court to rule whether or not they were proper questions we have to ask the questions. It is apparent I'm quite disgusted with the whole matter, whole matter of ever bringing Joan Little to trial anyway. There has been one roadblock after another and one attempt after another to railroad Joan Little and I am tired of it. Now we intend to ask these questions and you can sustain the objections if you want to but the appellate court cannot make a ruling on whether or not they were proper questions unless the questions are asked.

COURT: All right, you have said that twice. I haven't said you couldn't ask the questions.

MR. PAUL: And the appellate courts cannot make a judgment on whether or not the questions would have been relevant unless they get the witness' answer into the record.

COURT: Well, I'll pass on that. Are you through?

MR. PAUL: I'm through for the moment but not through for this trial.

COURT: Yes sir. All right, let the jurors return to the courtroom.

Notes and Questions

1. Mr. Paul's reference to the "queen of hearts" is, of course, based on Lewis Carroll's *Alice's Adventures in Wonderland*. During the trial of the jack of hearts for stealing the queen's tarts, the following conversation transpired between the king and queen of hearts and Alice.

"Let the jury consider their verdict," the King said, for about the twentieth time that day.

"No, no," said the Queen. "Sentence first—verdict afterwards."

"Stuff and nonsense!" said Alice loudly. "The idea of having the sentence first!"

"Hold your tongue!" said the Queen, turning purple.

"I won't!" said Alice.

"Off with her head!" the Queen shouted at the top of her voice.

—L. Carroll, *Alice's Adventures in Wonderland* 157 (Penguin Books 1970)

2. The American Bar Association's Standards Relating to the Administration of Criminal Justice, The Defense Function (3d ed. 1992) provides in Standard 4-7.1(a) that "[a]s an officer of the court, defense counsel should support the authority of the court and the dignity of the trial courtroom by strict adherence to codes of professionalism and by manifesting a professional attitude toward the judge, opposing counsel, witnesses, jurors, and others in the courtroom."

The American Bar Association's Model Code of Professional Responsibility (1981) provides, in Disciplinary Rule 7-106(C), that "[i]n appearing in his professional capacity before a tribunal, a lawyer shall not: . . . (6) Engage in undignified or discourteous conduct which is degrading to a tribunal."

What guidance do these standards provide regarding the appropriate limits of defense counsel's zealous advocacy on behalf of a client? Did Mr. Paul's conduct run afoul of these standards?

3. Ethical Consideration 7-22 of the ABA's Model Code of Professional Responsibility declares that "respect for judicial rulings is essential to the proper administration of justice; however, a litigant or his lawyer may, in good faith and within the framework of the law, take steps to test the correctness of a ruling of a tribunal." Does this help assess the propriety of Paul's advocacy on behalf of Joan Little?

4. If you were charged with first-degree murder, would you want someone like Mr. Paul representing your interests?

In re Ryder, 263 F. Supp. 360 (E.D. Va.), affirmed, 381 F.2d 713 (4th Cir. 1967)

PER CURIAM.

This proceeding was instituted to determine whether Richard R. Ryder should be removed from the roll of attorneys qualified to practice before this court. . . .

On August 24, 1966 a man armed with a sawed-off shotgun robbed the Varina Branch of the Bank of Virginia of $7,583. Included in the currency taken were $10 bills known as "bait money," the serial numbers of which had been recorded.

On August 26, 1966 Charles Richard Cook rented safety deposit box 14 at a branch of the Richmond National Bank. Later in the day Cook was interviewed at his home by agents of the Federal Bureau of Investigation, who obtained $348 from him. Cook telephoned Ryder, who had represented him in civil litigation. Ryder came to the house and advised the agents that he represented Cook. He said that if Cook were not to be placed under arrest, he intended to take him to his office for an interview. The agents left. Cook insisted to Ryder that he had not robbed the bank. . . .

The next morning, Saturday, August 27, 1966, Ryder conferred with Cook again. He urged Cook to tell the truth, and Cook answered that a man, whose name he would not divulge, offered him $500 on the day of the robbery to put a package in a bank lockbox. Ryder did not believe this story. Ryder told Cook that if the government could trace the money in the box to him, it would be almost conclusive evidence of his guilt. He knew that Cook was under surveillance and he suspected that Cook might try to dispose of the money.

That afternoon Ryder telephoned a former officer of the Richmond Bar Association to discuss his course of action. He had known this attorney for many years and respected his judgment. The lawyer was at home and had no library available to him when Ryder telephoned. In their casual conversation Ryder told what he knew about the case, omitting names. He explained that he thought he would take the money from Cook's safety deposit box and place it in a box in his own home. This, he believed, would prevent Cook from attempting to dispose of the money. The lawyers thought that eventually F.B.I. agents would locate the money and that since it was in Ryder's possession, he could claim a privilege and thus effectively exclude it from evidence. This would prevent the government from linking Ryder's client with the bait money and would also destroy any presumption of guilt that might exist arising out of the client's exclusive possession of the evidence. . . .

On Monday morning Ryder asked Cook to come by his office. He prepared a power of attorney, which Cook signed. . . .

Ryder took the power of attorney which Cook had signed to the Richmond National Bank. He rented box 13 in his name with his office address, presented the power of attorney, entered Cook's box, took both boxes into a booth, where he found a bag of money and a sawed-off shotgun in Cook's box. The box also contained miscellaneous items which are not pertinent to this proceeding. He transferred the contents of Cook's box to his own and returned the boxes to the vault. He left the bank, and neither he nor Cook returned.

Ryder testified that he had some slight hesitation about the propriety of what he was doing. Within a half-hour after he left the bank, he talked to a retired judge and distinguished professor of law. He told this person that he wanted to discuss something in confidence. Ryder then stated that he represented a man suspected of bank robbery. . . .

Ryder testified that he told about the shotgun. The judge also testified that Ryder certainly would not have been under the impression that he—the judge—thought that he was guilty of unethical conduct.

The same day Ryder also talked with other prominent persons in Richmond—a judge of a court of record and an attorney for the Commonwealth. Again, he stated that what he intended to say was confidential. He related the circumstances and was advised that a lawyer could not receive the property and if he had received it he could not retain possession of it.

On September 7, 1966 Cook was indicted for robbing the Varina Branch of the Bank of Virginia. . . .

On September 12, 1966 F.B.I. agents procured search warrants for Cook's and Ryder's safety deposit boxes in the Richmond National Bank. They found Cook's box empty. In Ryder's box they discovered $5,920 of the $7,583 taken in the bank robbery and the sawed-off shotgun used in the robbery. . . .

On October 14, 1966 the three judges of this court removed Ryder as an attorney for Cook; suspended him from practice before the court until further order; referred the matter to the United States Attorney, who was requested to file charges within five days. . . .

The United States Attorney charged Ryder with violations of Canons 15 and 32 of the Canons of Professional Ethics of the Virginia State Bar. . . .

At the outset, we reject the suggestion that Ryder did not know the money which he transferred from Cook's box to his was stolen. We find that on August 29 when Ryder opened Cook's box and saw a bag of money and a sawed-off shotgun, he then knew Cook was involved in the bank robbery and that the money was stolen. The evidence clearly establishes this. . . .

We also find that Ryder was not motivated solely by certain expectation the government would discover the contents of his lockbox. He believed discovery was probable. In this event he intended to argue to the court that the contents of his box could not be revealed, and even if the contents were identified, his possession made the stolen money and the shotgun inadmissible against his client. He also recognized that discovery was not inevitable. His intention in this event, we find, was to assist Cook by keeping the stolen money and the shotgun concealed in his lockbox until after the trial. His conversations, and the secrecy he enjoined, immediately after he put the money and the gun in his box, show that he realized the government might not find the property.

We accept his statement that he intended eventually to return the money to its rightful owner, but we pause to say that no attorney should ever place himself in such a position. Matters involving the possible termination of an attorney-client relationship, or possible subsequent proceedings in the event of an acquittal, are too delicate to permit such a practice.

We reject the argument that Ryder's conduct was no more than the exercise of the attorney-client privilege. The fact that Cook had not been arrested or indicted at the time Ryder took possession of the gun and money is immaterial. Cook was Ryder's client and was entitled to the protection of the lawyer-client privilege.

Regardless of Cook's status, however, Ryder's conduct was not encompassed by the attorney-client privilege. A frequently quoted definition of the privilege is found in United States v. United Shoe Mach. Corp., 89 F.Supp. 357, 358 (D. Mass. 1950):

> "The privilege applies only if (1) the asserted holder of the privilege is or sought to become a client; (2) the person to whom the communication was made (a) is a member of the bar of a court, or his subordinate and (b) in connection with this communication is acting as a lawyer; (3) the communication relates to a fact of which the attorney was informed (a) by his client (b) without the presence of strangers (c) for the purpose of securing primarily either (i) an opinion on law or (ii) legal services or (iii) assistance in some legal proceeding, and not (d) for the purpose of committing a crime or tort; and (4) the privilege has been (a) claimed and (b) not waived by the client."

The essentials of the privilege have been stated in 8 Wigmore, Evidence § 2292 (McNaughton Rev. 1961):

> "(1) Where legal advice of any kind is sought (2) from a professional legal adviser in his capacity as such, (3) the communications relating to that purpose, (4) made in confidence (5) by the client, (6) are at his instance permanently protected (7) from disclosure by himself or by the legal adviser, (8) except the protection be waived."

It was Ryder, not his client, who took the initiative in transferring the incriminating possession of the stolen money and the shotgun from Cook. Ryder's conduct went far beyond the receipt and retention of a confidential communication from his client. Counsel for Ryder conceded, at the time of argument, that the acts of Ryder were not within the attorney-client privilege. . . .

Securities & Exchange Comm. v. Harrison, 80 F.Supp. 226, 230 (D.D.C. 1948), aff'd, 87 U.S.App.D.C. 232, 184 F.2d 691 (1950), judgment order vacated as moot, 340 U.S. 908, 71 S.Ct. 290, 95 L.Ed. 656 (1951), describes the privilege and its limitations:

> "That privilege has long been recognized as a very proper and necessary one to insure full and complete revelation by a person to an attorney to the end that the client may be properly advised, represented, and, in appropriate cases, defended by that attorney. To subject such revelations to exposure by the testimonial process would inevitably lead to concealments which would impair proper representation and thus interfere with proper administration of justice. While it relates to the rights of an individual, it is nonetheless recognized, as so many of our fundamental rights are, as essentially in the public interest. This privilege has, however, never been intended to be, and should not be, a cloak or shield for the perpetration of a crime or fraudulent wrong doing. One who consults an attorney to secure aid or assistance in the perpetration of a future crime or fraudulent wrong doing is not consulting that attorney for the legitimate purposes which are protected by the privilege. If, therefore, it be shown by evidence other than the disclosure of the communications between client and attorney that aid or assistance is being sought for the perpetration of crime or fraudulent wrongdoing, there is no immunity to the testimonial process respecting such communications."

In Clark v. State, 159 Tex.Cr.R. 187, 261 S.W.2d 339 (1953), cert. denied, reh. denied sub nom., Clark v. Texas, 346 U.S. 855, 905, 74 S.Ct. 69, 98 L.Ed. 369 (1953), a lawyer's advice to get rid of a gun used to commit a murder was admissible in evidence. The court observed the conversation was not within the realm of legitimate professional conduct and employment. In argument, it was generally conceded that Ryder could have been required to testify in the prosecution of Cook as to the transfer of the contents of the lockbox.

We conclude that Ryder violated Canons 15 and 32. . . .

The money in Cook's box belonged to the Bank of Virginia. The law did not authorize Cook to conceal this money or withhold it from the bank. His larceny was a continuing offense. Cook had no title or property interest in the money that he lawfully could pass to Ryder. . . .

No canon of ethics or law permitted Ryder to conceal from the Bank of Virginia its money to gain his client's acquittal.

Cook's possession of the sawed-off shotgun was illegal. 26 U.S.C. § 5851. Ryder could not lawfully receive the gun from Cook to assist Cook to avoid conviction of robbery. Cook had never mentioned the shotgun to Ryder. When Ryder discovered it in Cook's box, he took possession of it to hinder the government in the prosecution of its case, and he intended not to reveal it pending trial unless the government discovered it and a court compelled its production. No statute or canon of ethics authorized Ryder to take possession of the gun for this purpose.

Canon 15 states in part:

"* * * [T]he great trust of the lawyer is to be performed within and not without the bounds of law. The office of attorney does not permit, much less does it demand of him for any client, violation of law or any manner of fraud or chicane. He must obey his own conscience and not that of his client."

In helping Cook to conceal the shotgun and stolen money, Ryder acted without the bounds of law. He allowed the office of attorney to be used in violation of law. The scheme which he devised was a deceptive, legalistic subterfuge—rightfully denounced by the canon as chicane.

Ryder also violated Canon 32. He rendered Cook a service involving deception and disloyalty to the law. He intended that his actions should remove from Cook exclusive possession of stolen money, and thus destroy an evidentiary presumption. His service in taking possession of the shotgun and money, with the intention of retaining them until after the trial, unless discovered by the government, merits the "stern and just condemnation" the canon prescribes. . . .

We find it difficult to accept the argument that Ryder's action is excusable because if the government found Cook's box, Ryder's would easily be found, and if the government failed to find both Cook's and Ryder's boxes, no more harm would be done than if the agents failed to find only Cook's. Cook's concealment of the items in his box cannot be cited to excuse Ryder. Cook's conduct is not the measure of Ryder's ethics. The conduct of a lawyer should be above reproach. Concealment of the stolen money and the sawed-off shotgun to secure Cook's acquittal was wrong whether the property was in Cook's or Ryder's possession.

There is much to be said, however, for mitigation of the discipline to be imposed. Ryder intended to return the bank's money after his client was tried. He consulted reputable persons before and after he placed the property in his lockbox, although he did not precisely follow their advice. Were it not for these facts, we would deem proper his permanent exclusion from practice before this court. In view of the mitigating circumstances, he will be suspended from practice in this court for eighteen months effective October 14, 1966. . . .

Notes and Questions

1. Ryder consulted with several other people about the propriety of his conduct and apparently received conflicting advice. Does it appear that he intended to hide the shotgun and money indefinitely? If he presumed that the authorities eventually would locate those items, what precisely did he do that was wrong?

2. Why does the court rule that Ryder's actions were not covered by the attorney-client confidentiality privilege?

3. Assuming that Ryder knew, or strongly suspected, that Cook was responsible for the bank robbery, did he behave unethically by agreeing at the outset to represent him? Consider this question in light of the materials presented in the following section.

Guilty Clients and Hard Questions

Should a defense lawyer's zealousness in representing a client be tempered by the knowledge that his or her client is guilty? That a prosecution witness whose testimony the defense attorney may be in a position to discredit in fact is telling the truth? That the defendant whom he or she is representing is bent on committing perjury? Are there circumstances under which the communication between a defense lawyer and his or her client, which traditionally have been cloaked by a privilege of confidentiality, should be disclosed in order to achieve some greater good? These are among the "hard questions" that a defense attorney, and indeed the adversarial system in which defense counsel is expected to function, must confront and somehow resolve.

Representing Guilty Clients

Question [Monrad G. Paulsen]: *Every defense counsel hears this question at one time or another: Would you defend a guilty man?*

Answer [Harris B. Steinberg]: Of course. Putting the People to their proof is socially desirable. Furthermore, it is not the job of a lawyer to be the judge. It is his function to make the adversary system work. He has the duty to present all legitimate arguments in favor of the accused. Granted he cannot lie; he cannot suborn perjury; he cannot bribe witnesses; he cannot bribe jurors; he should not allow a defendant to get on the stand and tell a story he knows to be a lie. Everybody understands that. But the job of

the lawyer is to assist his client if he wishes to remain silent while the state makes proof beyond a reasonable doubt. After all, he is protected by this burden of proof. The defendant is protected by a presumption of innocence. Even the client who says "I did it," may not know of defenses that could be raised in regard to venue and jurisdiction. He may not understanding [sic] about the defense of mental illness. There may be some element of the crime that is missing. There are a great many things that are immoral about which men may feel a twinge of conscience and, yet, these immoral acts may contain only four out of five of the necessary and essential elements of the crime charged. There may have been violations of constitutional rights in the investigation and apprehension of the defendant, rights that have been violated but that the victim does not recognize, such as an illegal arrest, search or seizure, the illegal use of entrapment, or wiretaps. An accused person has to have a lawyer in order to avoid waiving his constitutional rights unwittingly. It is useful and proper in our adversary system for the lawyer to advance every legitimate argument that can be asserted on behalf of the defendant. I have no doubt of this principle.*

Source: Copyright 1961 by The American Law Institute. Reprinted with the permission of the American Law Institute-American Bar Association Committee on Continuing Professional Education.

Consider the observations of prominent criminal defense attorney F. Lee Bailey:

> The question that laymen put to me most frequently is "Would you defend a guilty man?" Or, "How can you defend a man you know is guilty?"
>
> The questioner is rarely satisfied with my answer. He sees no justification for defending someone who really did it. He can afford to play the moralist, it's not his neck on the guillotine. If lawyers were to shun every case in which they knew the defendant was guilty, there would be no courts. Every person who was arrested and indicted would go right to jail unless his defense counsel judged him innocent.

Guilt, like most things, is scarcely ever black or white.

F. Lee Bailey, with Harvey Aronson, *The Defense Never Rests* 57 (New American Library, 1971).

Should a criminal defense attorney defend a person whom he or she knows or believes to be guilty of a crime? What positive social value can there be in trying to secure the acquittal of a client who in fact is guilty as charged? The answers to these questions depend, in part, on the relative importance assigned to determining guilt in a factually accurate manner and to promoting other interests, such as safeguarding constitutional liberties and maintaining the appropriate balance between government and citizen in an adversarial system of law.

Monroe Freedman, "Where the Bodies Are Buried: The Adversary System and the Obligation of Confidentiality," 10 *Criminal Law Bulletin* 979, 981–984 (1974)

. . .

Role of Defense Attorney under Adversary System

Let us begin, by way of contrast, with an understanding of the role of a criminal defense attorney in a totalitarian state. As expressed by law professors at the University of Havana, "the first job of a revolutionary lawyer is not to argue that his client is innocent, but rather to determine if his client is guilty and, if so, to seek the sanction which will best rehabilitate him."

The emphasis in a free society is, of course, sharply different. Under our adversary system, the interests of the state are not absolute, or even paramount. The dignity of the individual is respected to the point that even when the citizen is known by the state to have committed a heinous offense, the individual is nevertheless accorded such rights as counsel, trial by jury, due process, and the privilege against self-incrimination.

Constitutional Rights v. Truth Seeking

A trial is, in part, a search for truth. Accordingly, those basic rights are most often characterized as procedural safeguards against error in the search for truth. Actually, however, a trial is far more than a search for truth, and the constitutional rights that are provided by our system of justice may outweigh the truth-seeking value—a fact which is manifest when we consider that those rights and others guaranteed by the Constitution may well impede the search for truth rather than further it. For example, what more effective way is there to expose a defendant's guilt than to require self-incrimination, at least to the extent of compelling the defendant to take the stand and respond to interrogation before the jury? The defendant, however, is presumed innocent, the burden is on the prosecution to prove guilt beyond a reasonable doubt, and even the guilty accused has an "absolute constitutional right" to remain silent and to put the government to its proof.

Thus, the defense lawyer's professional obligation may well be to advise the client to withhold the truth. As Justice Jackson said, "Any lawyer worth his salt will tell the suspect in no uncertain terms to make no statement to police under any circumstances." Similarly, the defense lawyer is obligated to prevent the introduction of evidence that may be wholly reliable, such as a murder weapon seized in violation of the Fourth Amendment, or a truthful but involuntary confession. Justice White has observed that although law enforcement officials must be dedicated to using only truthful evidence, "defense counsel has no comparable obligation to ascertain or present the truth. Our system assigns him a different mission. . . . We . . . insist that he defend his client whether he is innocent or guilty."

Such conduct by defense counsel does not constitute obstruction of justice. On the contrary, it is "part of the duty imposed on the most honorable defense counsel," from whom "we countenance or require conduct which in many instances has little, if any, relation to the search for truth." The same observation has been made by Justice Harlan, who noted that "in fulfilling his professional responsibilities," the lawyer "of necessity may become an obstacle to truth finding." Chief Justice Warren, too, has recognized that when the criminal defense attorney successfully obstructs efforts by the government to elicit truthful evidence in ways that violate constitutional rights, the attorney is "merely exercising . . . good professional judgment," and "carrying out what he is sworn to do under his oath—to protect to the extent of his ability the rights of his client." Chief Justice Warren concluded, "In fulfilling this responsibility the attorney plays a vital role in the administration of criminal justice under our Constitution."

Obviously, such eminent jurists would not arrive lightly at the conclusion that an officer of the court has a professional obligation to place obstacles in the path of truth. Their reasons, again, go back to the nature of our system of criminal justice and to the fundamentals of our system of government. Before we will permit the state to deprive any person of life, liberty, or property, we require that certain processes be duly followed which ensure regard for the dignity of the individual, irrespective of the impact of those processes upon the determination of truth.

By emphasizing that the adversary process has its foundations in respect for human dignity, even at the expense of the search for truth, I do not mean to deprecate the search for truth or to suggest that the adversary system is not concerned with it. On the contrary, truth is a basic value and the adversary system is one of the most efficient and the fairest method for determining it. That system proceeds on the assumption that the best way to ascertain the truth is to present to an impartial judge or jury a confrontation between the proponents of conflicting views, assigning to each the task of marshalling and presenting the evidence in as thorough and persuasive a way as possible. The truth-seeking techniques used by the advocates on each side include investigation, pretrial discovery, cross-examination of opposing witnesses, and a marshalling of the evidence in summation. Thus, the judge or jury is given the strongest possible view of each side and is put in the best possible position to make an accurate and fair judgment. Nevertheless, the point here emphasized is that in a society that honors the dignity of the individual, the high value assigned to truth seeking is not absolute and may on occasion be subordinated to even higher values.

Concept of Right to Counsel

The concept of a right to counsel is one of the most significant manifestations of our regard for the dignity of the individual. No person is required to stand alone against the awesome power of the People of New York or the Government of the United States of America. Rather, every criminal defendant is guaranteed an advocate—a "champion" against a "hostile world," the "single voice on which they must rely with confidence that his interests will be protected to the fullest extent consistent with the rules of procedure and the standards of professional conduct." In addition, the attorney serves, in significant part, to assure equality before the law. Thus, the lawyer has been referred to as "the equalizer," who "places each litigant as nearly as possible on an equal footing under the substantive and procedural law under which he is tried." . . .

Source: Copyright 1998 by West Group, 375 Hudson Street, New York, NY 10014, 1-800-328-4880, reprinted by permission of West Group, from the Criminal Law Bulletin.

Addressing Hard Questions

Even if we understand why a defense lawyer knowingly would represent and try to gain the acquittal of a guilty client, difficult questions still must be confronted regarding the lengths to which a lawyer may go in defending someone accused of a crime, whether that person is guilty or innocent. We already have considered a few of the limitations imposed on a defense lawyer's "zealous advocacy," in *Paul v. Pleasants* and *In re Ryder*. Now we address some particularly vexing ethical and legal dilemmas that defense lawyers may face when representing the criminally accused.

Monroe Freedman, "Professional Responsibility of the Criminal Defense Lawyer: The Three Hardest Questions," 64 *Michigan Law Review* 1469 (1966)

In almost any area of legal counseling and advocacy, the lawyer may be faced with the dilemma of either betraying the confidential communications of his client or participating to some extent in the purposeful deception of the court. This problem is nowhere more acute than in the practice of criminal law, particularly in the representation of the indigent accused. The purpose of this article is to analyze and attempt to resolve three of the most difficult issues in this general area:

1. Is it proper to cross-examine for the purpose of discrediting the reliability or credibility of an adverse witness whom you know to be telling the truth?

2. Is it proper to put a witness on the stand when you know he will commit perjury?

3. Is it proper to give your client legal advice when you have reason to believe that the knowledge you give him will tempt him to commit perjury?

These questions present serious difficulties with respect to a lawyer's ethical responsibilities. Moreover, if one admits the possibility of an affirmative answer, it is difficult even to discuss them without appearing to some to be unethical.[1] . . .

Source: Reprinted with permission from M. Freedman, Professional Responsibility of the Criminal Defense Lawyer: The Three Hardest Questions, *Michigan Law Review*, Vol. 64, p. 1469, © 1966.

1. The substance of this paper was recently presented to a Criminal Trial Institute attended by forty-five members of the District of Columbia Bar. As a consequence, several judges (none of whom had either heard the lecture or read it) complained to the Committee on Admissions and Grievances of the District Court for the District of Columbia, urging the author's disbarment or suspension. Only after four months of proceedings including a hearing, two meetings, and a *de novo* review by eleven federal district court judges, did the Committee announce its decision to "proceed no further in the matter."

I. THE ADVERSARY SYSTEM AND THE NECESSITY FOR CONFIDENTIALITY

At the outset, we should dispose of some common question-begging responses. The attorney is indeed an officer of the court, and he does participate in a search for truth. These two propositions, however, merely serve to state the problem in different words: As an officer of the court, participating in a search for truth, what is the attorney's special responsibility, and how does that responsibility affect his resolution of the questions posed above?

The attorney functions in an adversary system based upon the presupposition that the most effective means of determining truth is to present to a judge and jury a clash between proponents of conflicting views. . . .

The adversary system has further ramifications in a criminal case. The defendant is presumed to be innocent. The burden is on the prosecution to prove beyond a reasonable doubt that the defendant is guilty. The plea of not guilty does not necessarily mean "not guilty in fact," for the defendant may mean "not legally guilty." Even the accused who knows that he committed the crime is entitled to put the government to its proof. Indeed, the accused who knows that he is guilty has an absolute constitutional right to remain silent. The moralist might quite reasonably understand this to mean that, under these circumstances, the defendant and his lawyer are privileged to "lie" to the court in pleading not guilty. In my judgment, the moralist is right. However, our adversary system and related notions of the proper administration of criminal justice sanction the lie. . . .

There is, of course, a simple way to evade the dilemma raised by the not guilty plea. Some attorneys rationalize the problem by insisting that a lawyer never knows for sure whether his client is guilty. The client who insists upon his guilt may in fact be protecting his wife, or may know that he pulled the trigger and that the victim was killed, but not that his gun was loaded with blanks and that the fatal shot was fired from across the street. For anyone who finds this reasoning satisfactory, there is, of course, no need to think further about the issue.

It is also argued that a defense attorney can remain selectively ignorant. He can insist in his first interview with his client that, if his client is guilty, he simply does not want to know. It is inconceivable, however, that an attorney could give adequate counsel under such circumstances. How is the client to know, for example, precisely which relevant circumstance his lawyer does not want to be told? The lawyer might ask whether his client has a prior record. The client, assuming that this is the kind of knowledge that might present ethical problems for his lawyer, might respond that he has no record. The lawyer would then put the defendant on the stand and, on cross-examination, be appalled to learn that his client has two prior convictions for offenses identical to that for which he is being tried. . . .

If one recognizes that professional responsibility requires that an advocate have full knowledge of every pertinent fact, it follows that he must seek the truth from his client, not shun it. This means that he will have to dig and pry and cajole, and, even then, he will not be successful unless he can convince the client that full and confidential disclosure to his lawyer will never result in prejudice to the client by any word or action of the lawyer. . . .

II. THE SPECIFIC QUESTIONS

The first of the difficult problems posed above will now be considered: Is it proper to cross-examine for the purpose of discrediting the reliability or the credibility of a witness whom you know to be telling the truth? Assume the following situation. Your client has been falsely accused of a robbery committed at 16th and P Streets at 11:00 p.m. He tells you at first that at no time on the evening of the crime was he within six blocks of that location. However, you are able to persuade him that he must tell you the truth and that doing so will in no way prejudice him. He then reveals to you that he was at 15th and P Streets at 10:55 that evening, but that he was walking east, away from the scene of the crime, and that, by 11:00 p.m., he was six blocks away. At the trial, there are two prosecution witnesses. The first mistakenly, but with some degree of persuasion, identifies your clients as the criminal. At that point, the prosecution's case depends on this single witness, who might or might not be believed. Since your client has a prior record, you do not want to put him on the stand, but you feel that there is at least a chance for acquittal. The second prosecution witness is an elderly woman who is somewhat nervous and who wears glasses. She testifies truthfully and accurately that she saw your client at 15th and P Streets at 10:55 p.m. She has corroborated the erroneous testimony of the first witness and made conviction virtually certain. However, if you destroy her reliability through cross-examination designed to show that she is easily confused and has poor eyesight, you may not only eliminate the corroboration, but also cast doubt in the jury's mind on the prosecution's entire case. On the other hand, if you should refuse to cross-examine her because she is telling the truth, your client may well feel betrayed, since you knew of the witness's veracity only because your client confided in you, under your assurance that his truthfulness would not prejudice him.

The client would be right. Viewed strictly, the attorney's failure to cross-examine would not be violative of the client's confidence because it would not constitute a disclosure. However, the same policy that supports the obligation of confidentiality precludes the attorney from prejudicing his client's interest in any other way because of knowledge gained in his professional capacity. When a lawyer fails to cross-examine only because his client, placing confidence in the lawyer, has been candid with him, the basis for such confidence and candor collapses. Our legal system cannot tolerate such a result. . . . The client's confidences must "upon all occasions be inviolable," to avoid the "greater mischiefs" that would probably result if a client could not feel free "to repose [confidence] in the attorney to whom he resorts for legal advice and assistance." Destroy that confidence, and "a man would not venture to consult any skillful person, or would only dare to tell his counsellor half his case."

Therefore, one must conclude that the attorney is obligated to attack, if he can, the reliability or credibility of an opposing witness whom he knows to be truthful. The contrary result would inevitably impair the "perfect freedom of consultation by client with attorney," which is "essential to the administration of justice."

The second question is generally considered to be the hardest of all: Is it proper to put a witness on the stand when you know he will commit perjury? Assume, for example, that the witness in question is the accused himself, and that he has admitted to you, in response to your assurances of confidentiality, that he is guilty. However, he insists upon taking the stand to protest his innocence. There is a clear consensus among prosecutors and defense attorneys that the likelihood of conviction is increased enormously when the defendant does not take the stand. Consequently, the attorney who prevents his client from testifying only because the client has confided his guilt to him is violating that confidence by acting upon the information in a way that will seriously prejudice his client's interests.

Perhaps the most common method for avoiding the ethical problem just posed is for the lawyer to withdraw from the case, at least if there is sufficient time before trial for the client to retain another attorney. The client will then go to the nearest law office, realizing that the obligation of confidentiality is not what it has been represented to be, and withhold incriminating information or the fact of his guilt from his new attorney. On ethical grounds, the practice of withdrawing from a case under such circumstances is indefensible, since the identical perjured testimony will ultimately be presented. More important, perhaps, is the practical consideration that the new attorney will be ignorant of the perjury and therefore will be in no position to attempt to discourage the client from presenting it. Only the original attorney, who knows the truth, has that opportunity, but he loses it in the very act of evading the ethical problem. . . .

If a lawyer has discovered his client's intent to perjure himself, one possible solution to this problem is for the lawyer to approach the bench, explain his ethical difficulty to the judge, and ask to be relieved, thereby causing a mistrial. This request is certain to be denied, if only because it would empower the defendant to cause a series of mistrials in the same fashion. At this point, some feel that the lawyer has avoided the ethical problem and can put the defendant on the stand. However, one objection to this solution, apart from the violation of confidentiality, is that the lawyer's ethical problem has not been solved, but has only been transferred to the judge. Moreover, the client in such a case might well have grounds for appeal on the basis of deprivation of due process and denial of the right to counsel, since he will have been tried before, and sentenced by, a judge who has been informed of the client's guilt by his own attorney.

A solution even less satisfactory than informing the judge of the defendant's guilt would be to let the client take the stand without the attorney's participation and to omit reference to the client's testimony in closing argument. The latter solution, of course, would be as damaging as to fail entirely to argue the case to the jury, and failing to argue the case is "as improper as though the attorney had told the jury that his client had uttered a falsehood in making the statement."

Therefore, the obligation of confidentiality, in the context of our adversary system, apparently allows the attorney no alternative to putting a perjurious witness on the stand without explicit or implicit disclosure of the attorney's knowledge to either the judge or the jury. . . .

Of course, before the client testifies perjuriously, the lawyer has a duty to attempt to dissuade him on grounds of both law and morality. In addition, the client should be impressed with the fact that his untruthful alibi is tactically dangerous. There is always a strong possibility that the prosecutor will expose the perjury on cross-examination. However, for the reasons already given, the final decision must necessarily be the client's. The lawyer's best course thereafter would be to avoid any further professional relationship with a client whom he knew to have perjured himself.

The third question is whether it is proper to give your client legal advice when you have reason to believe that the knowledge you give him will tempt him to commit perjury. This may indeed be the most difficult problem of all, because giving such advice creates the appearance that the attorney is encouraging and condoning perjury.

If the lawyer is not certain what the facts are when he gives the advice, the problem is substantially minimized, if not eliminated. It is not the lawyer's function to prejudge his client as a perjurer. He cannot presume that the client will make unlawful use of his advice. Apart from this, there is a natural predisposition in most people to recollect facts, entirely honestly, in a way most favorable to their own interest. As Randolph Paul has observed, some witnesses are nervous, some are confused about their own interests, some try to be too smart for their own good, and some subconsciously do not want to understand what has happened to them. Before he begins to remember essential facts, the client is entitled to know what his own interests are. . . .

Assume that your client, on trial for his life in a first-degree murder case, has killed another man with a penknife but insists that the killing was in self-defense. You ask him, "Do you customarily carry the penknife in your pocket, do you carry it frequently or infrequently, or did you take it with you only on this occasion?" He replies, "Why do you ask me a question like that?" It is entirely appropriate to inform him that his carrying the knife only on this occasion, or infrequently, supports an inference of premeditation, while if he carried the knife constantly, or frequently, the inference of premeditation would be negated. Thus, your client's life may depend upon his recollection as to whether he carried the knife frequently or infrequently. Despite the possibility that the client or a third party might infer that the lawyer was prompting the client to lie, the lawyer must apprise the defendant of the significance of his answer. There is no conceivable ethical requirement that the lawyer trap his client into a hasty and ill-considered answer before telling him the significance of the question.

A similar problem is created if the client has given the lawyer incriminating information before being fully aware of its significance. . . .

Essentially no different from the problem discussed above, but apparently more difficult, is the so-called *Anatomy of a Murder* situation.[24] The lawyer, who has received from his client an incriminating story of murder in the first degree, says, "If the facts are as you have stated them so far, you have no defense, and you will probably be electrocuted. On the other hand, if you acted in a blind rage, there is a possibility of saving your life. Think it over, and we will talk about it tomorrow." . . . [T]he lawyer has given his client a legal opinion that might induce the client to lie. This is information which the lawyer himself would have, without advice, were he in the client's position. It is submitted that the client is entitled to have this information about the law and to make his own decision as to whether to

---

24. See Traver, *Anatomy of a Murder* (1958).

act upon it. To decide otherwise would not only penalize the less well-educated defendant, but would also prejudice the client because of his initial truthfulness in telling his story in confidence to the attorney.

III. CONCLUSION

The lawyer is an officer of the court, participating in a search for truth. Yet no lawyer would consider that he had acted unethically in pleading the statute of frauds or the statute of limitations as a bar to a just claim. Similarly, no lawyer would consider it unethical to prevent the introduction of evidence such as a murder weapon seized in violation of the fourth amendment or a truthful but involuntary confession, or to defend a guilty man on grounds of denial of a speedy trial. Such actions are permissible because there are policy considerations that at times justify frustrating the search for truth and the prosecution of a just claim. Similarly, there are policies that justify an affirmative answer to the three questions that have been posed in this article. These policies include the maintenance of an adversary system, the presumption of innocence, the prosecution's burden to prove guilt beyond a reasonable doubt, the right to counsel, and the obligation of confidentiality between lawyer and client. . . .

Notes and Questions

1. With respect to the first question posed by Professor Freedman, consider American Bar Association Standards Relating to the Administration of Criminal Justice, The Defense Function, Standard 4-7.6(b) (3d ed. 1992): "Defense counsel's belief or knowledge that the witness is telling the truth does not preclude cross-examination." Does this standard seem to vindicate Professor Freedman's position, or does it stop short of doing so? *Is* it ethical for a lawyer to use cross-examination to attempt to discredit a witness whom he or she knows to be testifying truthfully? What would be the consequences of a lawyer succeeding at that tactic? What would the consequences be if a lawyer, knowing that the witness was telling the truth, made no effort to impeach his or her credibility through cross-examination?

2. The American Bar Association's Model Code of Professional Responsibility departs sharply from Professor Freedman's views about an attorney's participation in the defendant's presentation of perjured testimony. The ABA's position is reported in *Nix v. Whiteside*, at p. 596, below.

3. Professor Freedman has partially reconsidered his response to the third, "most difficult problem of all," involving whether it is proper for a lawyer to provide legal advice when there is reason to believe that advice may inspire or result in the accused's committing perjury. When he first examined this issue in the 1966 law review article reprinted above, he concluded that an attorney should not withhold legal advice based on speculation that the client may use that information to commit perjury. He argued that the attorney's nondisclosure would disadvantage less experienced and less well-educated suspects and also would penalize suspects who initially told truthful stories to their lawyers on the understanding their communications would benefit from the privilege of confidentiality. By 1975, Professor Freedman perceived shortcomings in his prior argument.

Monroe H. Freedman, *Lawyers' Ethics in an Adversary System* 73 (Bobbs-Merrill Co. 1975)

The fallacy in that argument is that the lawyer is giving the client more than just "information about the law", but is actively participating in—indeed, initiating—a factual defense that is obviously perjurious. To suggest that the less well-educated defendant is entitled to that extent of participation by the attorney in manufacturing perjury carries the "equalizer" concept of the lawyer's role too far. Moreover, even though the client has initially been truthful in telling his story to the attorney in confidence, it does not follow that there is any breach of confidentiality if the lawyer simply declines to create a false story for the client. Accordingly, I do not believe that this is one of those situations in which the lawyer should in effect be told: "What you know to be the fact is irrelevant to your role as an advocate in an adversary system." . . .

Anatomy of a Murder was written by John Donaldson Voelker, a Michigan judge, under the pseudonym Robert Traver. The attorney's "lecture" to his client, Frederic Manion, about possible defenses to the murder with which Manion was charged makes for fascinating reading (*see* R. Traver, *Anatomy of a Murder*, 30–49 (1958)).

4. As should be apparent, Professor Freedman's own answers to "the three hardest questions" were controversial when given (see footnote 1 in Freedman's *Michigan Law Review* article, at p. 575, above; *see also* Wolfram, "Client Perjury," 50 *Southern California Law Review* 809, 824–825 n. 54 (1977)) and remain controversial today.

* * * * *

We now raise another difficult question, this one involving the scope of an attorney's duty of confidentiality regarding communications with a client. Assume that a man, Drake, has been convicted of murder and sentenced to death. Further assume that another man, Campbell, actually committed the killing for which Drake has been held responsible and that Campbell has confided his guilt to his lawyer. What should Campbell's lawyer do under these circumstances? Remain mum and allow an innocent man to be executed? Urge Campbell to confess publicly, thus risking that Campbell will be convicted and sentenced for the crime? Go directly to the authorities with this information without consulting or involving Campbell?

These questions are based on an actual case involving Henry Drake, who was convicted of murder and sentenced to die, and William "Pop" Campbell, who knew Drake was innocent and had confessed to his lawyers that he (Campbell) had committed the murder for which Drake had been convicted. *See* David A. Kaplan, "Death Row Dilemma," *The National Law Journal*, Jan. 25, 1988, at pp. 35–38. Campbell's lawyers counseled Campbell against coming forward with his story. Campbell eventually ignored that advice and admitted to the killing in a sworn statement, which the courts refused to credit. After he spent over eight years on death row, Drake's murder conviction was overturned on grounds having nothing to do with Campbell's confession. Campbell died in prison, where he also had been awaiting execution. Drake was retried and, notwithstanding the introduction into evidence of Campbell's sworn confession, again was convicted of the murder. However, this time Drake was sentenced to life imprisonment. He almost immediately became eligible for parole based on credit earned for the time served under the original conviction. He was released on parole several months after his new conviction.

Although Campbell's lawyers had advised their client against putting himself in jeopardy by making the statement designed to clear Drake, both attorneys intimated that if Drake had faced imminent execution, they would not have been able to maintain their silence. What should the lawyers have done?

David A. Kaplan, "Death Row Dilemma," *The National Law Journal*, Jan. 25, 1988, at pp. 35, 38

. . .

"It is an exquisitely difficult problem," says Prof. Geoffrey C. Hazard Jr. of the Yale Law School, referring to the ethical dilemma faced by Georgia lawyers Floyd W. Keeble Jr. and Patrick T. Beall.

Professor Hazard and other ethics commentators agree that the decision by both lawyers not to reveal Pop Campbell's recantation was within the realm of the reasonable, given the dictates of legal ethics.

"Only when a lawyer knows in advance that his client is about to take the stand and testify falsely may the lawyer stop the client—either by dissuading him or telling the judge," notes Prof. Stephen Gillers of the New York University School of Law. "So, if Keeble *knew* that Campbell was going to lie, he might have done something, though the dominant view 10 years ago was that a lawyer should do nothing."

Where Mr. Keeble and Mr. Beall said nothing of Pop Campbell's perjury *after* it was committed, Professor Gillers explains they acted "properly" under the Code of Professional Responsibility since their client had an appeal pending.

Prof. Monroe H. Freedman of the Hofstra University School of Law agrees the attorneys probably followed the letter of the American Bar Association rules, but he excoriates the pair for "moral blindness."

"If they had any . . . sense, they would have acted to save human life regardless of the rules," says Professor Freedman, though he acknowledges this wasn't a true life-and-death matter because Mr. Drake never faced imminent electrocution. He also chastises Mr. Beall for urging Mr. Campbell to keep quiet even after he expressed a desire to come forward. However, some experts suggest the two lawyers could have revealed the Campbell confidence within the confines of the rules. "Did Campbell tell the lawyers what he did for the purpose of getting legal advice?" asks Prof. Thomas D. Morgan of the Emory University School of Law. "If the 'secret' passed along wasn't for this purpose, it's not protected. I know this is a close case, but . . . maybe there was no need to keep silent."

While Professor Gillers calls that a "nice argument," he says it is "overly technical" and puts an unfair burden on a client to know what to tell a lawyer. "There has always been a tension between legal ethics and real ethics," he says. "You've got to say, 'I'm a person before I'm a lawyer.'"

Echoing that sentiment, Dean Guido Calabresi of Yale recalls a colleague's famous hypothetical: "[Prof.] Charles Black would always say that a legal system should never torture. But then he'd pose the case of the judge with a man before him who has planted a hydrogen bomb that's set to explode in half an hour in the middle of the city. The police tell the judge that they know the man *can't stand* torture. What should the judge decide?

"Confronted by the need to balance justice against the need to torture," Dean Calabresi says, "Black's answer was to permit the torture and then immediately resign from the bench."

For Dean Calabresi, there are no rules capable of governing all situations. "Any system breaks down in the extreme case," he laments, "and one never knows what one will do."

Even Professor Hazard, the principal draftsman of the ABA's newest set of ethical rules, admits as much. "Anybody who passes certain judgment on this kind of dilemma," he warns, "deserves the intellectual conundrum he finds himself in."

———

Source: Reprinted with permission from D.A. Kaplan, Death Row Dilemma, *The National Law Journal*, January 25, 1998, pp. 35–38, © 1988, New York Law Publishing.

Notes and Questions

1. For the report of another case resembling the one involving Henry Drake and "Pop" Campbell, *see State v. Macumber*, 544 P.2d 1084 (Ariz. 1976), *on appeal after remand*, 582 P.2d 162 (Ariz. 1978). This case is discussed in Hodes, "Introduction: What Ought To Be Done— What *Can* Be Done—When the Wrong Person Is in Jail or about To Be Executed? An Invitation to a Multi-Disciplined Inquiry, and a Detour about Law School Pedagogy," 29 *Loyola of Los Angeles Law Review* 1547, 1568–1582 (1996).

2. In 1996, the *Loyola of Los Angeles Law Review* provided fascinating coverage of the legal and ethical dilemmas confronting lawyers, members of the clergy, and mental health professionals who receive confidential information that another person is responsible for a murder for which an innocent person has been convicted and faces imminent execution. *See* Symposium, "The Wrong Man Is about To Be Executed for a Crime He Did Not Commit," 29 *Loyola of Los Angeles Law Review* 1543–1798 (1996).

Ineffective Assistance of Counsel

The Sixth Amendment right to the "Assistance of Counsel" requires more than simply assigning a lawyer to a criminal defendant. Implicit in this guarantee is that the lawyer fulfills the role of trained legal counsel in representing the accused. The defendant has a right, usually stated in the negative, not to be saddled with ineffective assistance of counsel. Whether an attorney's representation of an accused crosses the threshold of constitutionally ineffective assistance of counsel depends on a two-part inquiry, as the Supreme Court explained in *Strickland v. Washington*, 466 U.S. 668, 104 S. Ct. 2052, 80 L. Ed. 2d 674 (1984). This case involved an allegation that the defendant's attorney had failed to provide minimally adequate representation during a capital sentencing hearing.

Strickland v. Washington, 466 U.S. 668, 104 S. Ct. 2052, 80 L. Ed. 2d 674 (1984)

Justice O'Connor delivered the opinion of the Court. . . .

A convicted defendant's claim that counsel's assistance was so defective as to require reversal of a conviction or death sentence has two components. First, the defendant must show that counsel's performance was deficient. This requires showing that counsel made errors so serious that counsel was not functioning as the "counsel" guaranteed the defendant by the Sixth Amendment. Second, the defendant must show that the deficient performance prejudiced the defense. This requires showing that counsel's errors were so serious as to deprive the defendant of a fair trial, a trial whose result is reliable. Unless a defendant makes both showings, it cannot be said that the conviction or death sentence resulted from a breakdown in the adversary process that renders the result unreliable. . . .

[T]he proper standard for attorney performance is that of reasonably effective assistance. . . . When a convicted defendant complains of the ineffectiveness of counsel's assistance, the defendant must show that counsel's representation fell below an objective standard of reasonableness.

More specific guidelines are not appropriate. The Sixth Amendment refers simply to "counsel," not specifying particular requirements of effective assistance. It relies instead on the legal profession's maintenance of standards sufficient to justify the law's presumption that counsel will fulfill the role in the adversary process that the Amendment envisions. The proper measure of attorney performance remains simply reasonableness under prevailing professional norms.

Representation of a criminal defendant entails certain basic duties. Counsel's function is to assist the defendant, and hence counsel owes the client a duty of loyalty, a duty to avoid conflicts of interest. See Cuyler v. Sullivan [, 446 U.S. 335, 100 S. Ct. 1708, 64 L. Ed. 2d 333 (1980)]. From counsel's function as assistant to the defendant derive the overarching duty to advocate the defendant's cause and the more particular duties to consult with the defendant on important decisions and to keep the defendant informed of important developments in the course of the prosecution. Counsel also has a duty to bring to bear such skill and knowledge as will render the trial a reliable adversarial testing process.

These basic duties neither exhaustively define the obligations of counsel nor form a checklist for judicial evaluation of attorney performance. In any case presenting an ineffectiveness claim, the performance inquiry must be whether counsel's assistance was reasonable considering all the circumstances. Prevailing norms of practice as reflected in American Bar Association standards and the like, e.g., ABA Standards for Criminal Justice 4-1.1 to 4-8.6 (2d ed 1980) ("The Defense Function"), are guides to determining what is reasonable, but they are only guides. No particular set of detailed rules for counsel's conduct can satisfactorily take account of the variety of circumstances faced by defense counsel or the range of legitimate decisions regarding how best to represent a criminal defendant. Any such set of rules would interfere with the constitutionally protected independence of counsel and restrict the wide latitude counsel must have in making tactical decisions.

Indeed, the existence of detailed guidelines for representation could distract counsel from the overriding mission of vigorous advocacy of the defendant's cause. Moreover, the purpose of the effective assistance guarantee of the Sixth Amendment is not to improve the quality of legal representation, although that is a goal of considerable importance to the legal system. The purpose is simply to ensure that criminal defendants receive a fair trial.

Judicial scrutiny of counsel's performance must be highly deferential. It is all too tempting for a defendant to second guess counsel's assistance after conviction or adverse sentence, and it is all too easy for a court, examining counsel's defense after it has proved unsuccessful, to conclude that a particular act or omission of counsel was unreasonable. A fair assessment of attorney performance requires that every effort be made to eliminate the distorting effects of hindsight, to reconstruct the circumstances of counsel's challenged conduct, and to evaluate the conduct from counsel's perspective at the time. Because of the difficulties inherent in making the evaluation, a court must indulge a strong presumption that counsel's conduct falls within the wide range of reasonable professional assistance; that is, the defendant must overcome the presumption that, under the circumstances, the challenged action "might be considered sound trial strategy." . . .

The availability of intrusive post-trial inquiry into attorney performance or of detailed guidelines for its evaluation would encourage the proliferation of ineffectiveness challenges. . . . Intensive scrutiny of counsel and rigid requirements for acceptable assistance could dampen the ardor and impair the independence of defense counsel, discourage the acceptance of assigned cases, and undermine the trust between attorney and client.

Thus, a court deciding an actual ineffectiveness claim must judge the reasonableness of counsel's challenged conduct on the facts of the particular case, viewed as of the time of counsel's conduct. A convicted defendant making a claim of ineffective assistance must identify the acts or omissions of counsel that are alleged not to have been the result of reasonable professional judgment. The court must then determine whether, in light of all the circumstances, the identified acts or omissions were outside the wide range of professionally competent assistance. In making that determination, the court should keep in mind that counsel's function, as elaborated in prevailing professional norms, is to make the adversarial testing process work in the particular case. At the same time, the court should recognize that counsel is strongly presumed to have rendered adequate assistance and made all significant decisions in the exercise of reasonable professional judgment. . . .

An error by counsel, even if professionally unreasonable, does not warrant setting aside the judgment of a criminal proceeding if the error had no effect on the judgment. The purpose of the Sixth Amendment guarantee of counsel is to ensure that a defendant has the assistance necessary to justify reliance on the outcome of the proceeding. Accordingly, any deficiencies in counsel's performance must be prejudicial to the defense in order to constitute ineffective assistance under the Constitution.

In certain Sixth Amendment contexts, prejudice is presumed. Actual or constructive denial of the assistance of counsel altogether is legally presumed to result in prejudice. So are various kinds of state interference with counsel's assistance. See United States v. Cronic, [466 US 648, 104 S Ct 2039, 80 L Ed 2d 657 (1984)]. Prejudice in these circumstances is so likely that case by case inquiry into prejudice is not worth the cost. Moreover, such circumstances involve impairments of the Sixth Amendment right that are easy to identify and, for that reason and because the prosecution is directly responsible, easy for the government to prevent.

One type of actual ineffectiveness claim warrants a similar, though more limited, presumption of prejudice. In Cuyler v. Sullivan, 446 US, at 345–350 [100 S Ct 1708, 64 L Ed 2d 333 (1980)], the Court held that prejudice is presumed when counsel is burdened by an actual conflict of interest. In those circumstances counsel breaches the duty of loyalty, perhaps the most basic of counsel's duties. . . . Even so, the rule is not quite the per se rule of prejudice that exists for the Sixth Amendment claims mentioned above. Prejudice is presumed only if the defendant demonstrates that counsel "actively represented conflicting interests" and that "an actual conflict of interest adversely affected his lawyer's performance."

Conflict of interest claims aside, actual ineffectiveness claims alleging a deficiency in attorney performance are subject to a general requirement that the defendant affirmatively prove prejudice. The government is not responsible for, and hence not able to prevent, attorney errors that will result in reversal of a conviction or sentence. Attorney errors come in an infinite variety and are as likely to be utterly harmless in a particular case as they are to be prejudicial. They cannot be classified according to likelihood of causing prejudice. Nor can they be defined with sufficient precision to inform defense attorneys correctly just what conduct to avoid. Representation is an art, and an act or omission that is unprofessional in one case may be sound or even brilliant in another. Even if a defendant shows that particular errors of counsel were unreasonable, therefore, the defendant must show that they actually had an adverse effect on the defense.

It is not enough for the defendant to show that the errors had some conceivable effect on the outcome of the proceeding. Virtually every act or omission of counsel would meet that test, and not every error that conceivably could have influenced the outcome undermines the reliability of the result of the proceeding. Respondent suggests requiring a showing that the errors "impaired the presentation of the defense." That standard, however, provides no workable principle. Since any error, if it is indeed an error, "impairs" the presentation of the defense, the proposed standard is inadequate because it provides no way of deciding what impairments are sufficiently serious to warrant setting aside the outcome of the proceeding.

On the other hand, we believe that a defendant need not show that counsel's deficient conduct more likely than not altered the outcome in the case. . . . [T]he appropriate test for prejudice finds its roots in the test for materiality of exculpatory information not disclosed to the defense by the prosecution, United States v. Agurs, 427 US, [97,] 104, 112–113 [96 S Ct 2392, 49 L Ed 2d 342 (1976)]. . . . The defendant must show that there is a reasonable probability that, but for counsel's unprofessional errors, the result of the proceeding would have been different. A reasonable probability is a probability sufficient to undermine confidence in the outcome. . . .

A number of practical considerations are important for the application of the standards we have outlined. Most important, in adjudicating a claim of actual ineffectiveness of counsel, a court should keep in mind that the principles we have stated do not establish mechanical rules.

Although those principles should guide the process of decision, the ultimate focus of inquiry must be on the fundamental fairness of the proceeding whose result is being challenged. In every case the court should be concerned with whether, despite the strong presumption of reliability, the result of the particular proceeding is unreliable because of a breakdown in the adversarial process that our system counts on to produce just results. . . .

Notes and Questions

1. *Strickland's* test for ineffective assistance of counsel requires the defendant to demonstrate both that the lawyer's performance was deficient and that the trial's outcome was prejudiced, or adversely affected as a result of that performance. In other words, even if an attorney provided a woefully inadequate defense of a client, a conviction or sentence will not be disturbed unless the defendant also can show "a reasonable probability that, but for counsel's unprofessional errors, the result of the proceeding would have been different." How would a defendant make such a showing? Moreover, what constitutes constitutionally deficient performance by counsel? What does the Court mean when it requires that "in light of all the circumstances, the identified acts or omissions were outside the wide range of professionally competent assistance"? In *Strickland*, the Court concluded (7–2) that the defendant had not been afforded constitutionally ineffective assistance of counsel. *See also Burger v. Kemp*, 483 U.S. 776, 107 S. Ct. 3114, 97 L. Ed. 2d 638 (1987) (also ruling that a defendant in a capital case had not been provided ineffective assistance of counsel under the *Strickland* test).

2. The *Strickland* test for constitutionally ineffective assistance of counsel has been criticized as being excessively vague, as well as too deferential to the presumed reasonableness of trial counsel's conduct. *See, e.g.*, Bright, "Counsel for the Poor: The Death Sentence Not for the Worst Crime but for the Worst Lawyer," 103 *Yale Law Journal* 1835, 1857–1866 (1994) (providing numerous examples of arguably deficient representation of defendants in capital cases where

the courts nevertheless rejected ineffective assistance of counsel claims); Goodpaster, "The Adversary System, Advocacy, and the Effective Assistance of Counsel in Criminal Cases," 14 *New York University Review of Law and Social Change* 59 (1986). At least three state courts have declined to adopt the *Strickland* standard, in reliance on state constitutional provisions. *See State v. Aplaca*, 74 Ha. 54, 837 P.2d 1298 (1992); *Tribou v. State*, 552 A.2d 1262 (Me. 1989); *Commonwealth v. Lykus*, 406 Mass. 135, 546 N.E.2d 159, 162 (1989) (noting that the Massachusetts Constitution provides greater safeguards than the federal Constitution regarding the right to counsel, and citing *Commonwealth v. Saferian*, 366 Mass. 89, 315 N.E.2d 878 (1974), regarding the test to be applied for evaluating ineffective assistance of counsel claims). *See generally* B. Latzer, *State Constitutional Criminal Law* § 5:9 (1995).

3. As the *Strickland* Court explained, deficient performance and resulting prejudice provide the basis for one type of ineffective assistance of counsel claim. Other action also can result in a breach of the Sixth Amendment. Where a defendant has been denied the services of counsel altogether, in violation of *Gideon* or *Argersinger*, a Sixth Amendment violation "is presumed," *Strickland*, 466 U.S., at 692. "[V]arious kinds of state interference with counsel's assistance" also raise a presumption of prejudice, *id.*, and allow a defendant "to make out a claim of ineffective assistance only by pointing to specific errors made by trial counsel." *United States v. Cronic*, 466 U.S. 648, 666, 104 S. Ct. 2039, 80 L. Ed. 2d 657 (1984). Finally, "when counsel is burdened by an actual conflict of interest," prejudice is presumed "if the defendant demonstrates that counsel 'actively represented conflicting interests' and that 'an actual conflict of interest adversely affected his lawyer's performance.'" *Strickland*, 466 U.S., at 692, *quoting Cuyler v. Sullivan*, 446 U.S. 335, 350, 348, 100 S. Ct. 1708, 64 L. Ed. 2d 333 (1980). Regarding conflict of interest claims, *see also Holloway v. Arkansas*, 435 U.S. 475, 98 S. Ct. 1173, 55 L. Ed. 2d 426 (1978) (discussing a trial court's obligations in cases involving potential conflicts of interest where a single lawyer represents two or more defendants charged with the same offense).

* * * * *

We now consider a defendant's claim that he received ineffective assistance of counsel under circumstances that we already have explored in a different context: defense counsel's response to the defendant's proposal to commit perjury at his trial.

Nix v. Whiteside, 475 U.S. 157, 106 S. Ct. 988, 89 L. Ed. 2d 123 (1986)

Chief Justice Burger delivered the opinion of the Court.

We granted certiorari to decide whether the Sixth Amendment right of a criminal defendant to assistance of counsel is violated when an attorney refuses to cooperate with the defendant in presenting perjured testimony at his trial.

I

A

Whiteside was convicted of second degree murder by a jury verdict which was affirmed by the Iowa courts. The killing took place on February 8, 1977 in Cedar Rapids, Iowa. Whiteside and two others went to one Calvin Love's apartment late that night, seeking marihuana. Love was in bed when Whiteside and his companions arrived; an argument between Whiteside and Love over the marihuana ensued. At one point, Love directed his girlfriend to get his "piece," and at another point got up, then returned to his bed. According to Whiteside's testimony, Love then started to reach under his pillow and moved toward Whiteside. Whiteside stabbed Love in the chest, inflicting a fatal wound.

Whiteside was charged with murder, and when counsel was appointed he objected to the lawyer initially appointed, claiming that he felt uncomfortable with a lawyer who had formerly been a prosecutor. Gary L. Robinson was then appointed and immediately began investigation. Whiteside gave him a statement that he had stabbed Love as the latter "was pulling a pistol from underneath the pillow on the bed." Upon questioning by Robinson, however, Whiteside indicated that he had not actually seen a gun, but that he was convinced that Love had a gun. No pistol was found on the premises; shortly after the police search following the stabbing, which had revealed no weapon, the victim's family had removed all of the victim's possessions from the apartment. Robinson interviewed Whiteside's companions who were present during the stabbing and none had seen a gun during the incident. Robinson advised Whiteside that the existence of a gun was not necessary to establish the claim of self defense, and that only a reasonable belief that the victim had a gun nearby was necessary even though no gun was actually present.

Until shortly before trial, Whiteside consistently stated to Robinson that he had not actually seen a gun, but that he was convinced that Love had a gun in his hand. About a week before trial, during preparation for direct examination, Whiteside for the first time told Robinson and his associate Donna Paulsen that he had seen something "metallic" in Love's hand. When asked about this, Whiteside responded that "in Howard Cook's case there was a gun. If I don't say I saw a gun, I'm dead."

Robinson told Whiteside that such testimony would be perjury and repeated that it was not necessary to prove that a gun was available but only that Whiteside reasonably believed that he was in danger. On Whiteside's insisting that he would testify that he saw "something metallic" Robinson told him, according to Robinson's testimony,

> "we could not allow him to [testify falsely] because that would be perjury, and as officers of the court we would be suborning perjury if we allowed him to do it; . . . I advised him that if he did do that it would be my duty to advise the Court of what he was doing and that I felt he was committing perjury; also, that I probably would be allowed to attempt to impeach that particular testimony."

Robinson also indicated he would seek to withdraw from the representation if Whiteside insisted on committing perjury.

Whiteside testified in his own defense at trial and stated that he "knew" that Love had a gun and that he believed Love was reaching for a gun and he had acted swiftly in self defense. On cross examination, he admitted that he had not actually seen a gun in Love's hand. . . .

The jury returned a verdict of second-degree murder and Whiteside moved for a new trial, claiming that he had been deprived of a fair trial by Robinson's admonitions not to state that he saw a gun or "something metallic." The trial court held a hearing, heard testimony by Whiteside and Robinson, and denied the motion. The trial court made specific findings that the facts were as related by Robinson.

The Supreme Court of Iowa affirmed respondent's conviction. . . .

B

Whiteside then petitioned for a writ of habeas corpus in the United States District Court for the Southern District of Iowa. In that petition Whiteside alleged that he had been denied effective assistance of counsel and of his right to present a defense by Robinson's refusal to allow him to testify as he had proposed. The District Court denied the writ. . . .

The United States Court of Appeals for the Eighth Circuit reversed and directed that the writ of habeas corpus be granted. Whiteside v. Scurr, 744 F2d 1323 (CA8 1984). The Court of Appeals accepted the findings of the trial judge, affirmed by the Iowa Supreme Court, that trial counsel believed with good cause that Whiteside would testify falsely and acknowledged that under Harris v. New York, 401 US 222, 91 S Ct 643, 28 L Ed 2d 1 (1971), a criminal defendant's privilege to testify in his own behalf does not include a right to commit perjury. Nevertheless, the court reasoned that an intent to commit perjury, communicated to counsel, does not alter a defendant's right to effective assistance of counsel and that Robinson's admonition to Whiteside that he would inform the court of Whiteside's perjury constituted a threat to violate the attorney's duty to preserve client confidences. According to the Court of Appeals, this threatened violation of client confidences breached the standards of effective representation set down in Strickland v. Washington, 466 US 668, 104 S Ct 2052, 80 L Ed 2d 674 (1984). The court also concluded that Strickland's prejudice requirement was satisfied by an implication of prejudice from the conflict between Robinson's duty of loyalty to his client and his ethical duties. . . .

II

A

The right of an accused to testify in his defense is of relatively recent origin. Until the latter part of the preceding century, criminal defendants in this country, as at common law, were considered to be disqualified from giving sworn testimony at their own trial by reason of their interest as a party to the case. By the end of the nineteenth century, however, the disqualification was finally abolished by statute in most states and in the federal courts. Although this Court has never explicitly held that a criminal defendant has a due process right to testify in his own behalf, cases in several Circuits have so held and the right has long been assumed. We have also suggested that such a right exists as a corollary to the Fifth Amendment privilege against compelled testimony.

B

In Strickland v. Washington, we held that to obtain relief by way of federal habeas corpus on a claim of a deprivation of effective assistance of counsel under the Sixth Amendment, the movant must establish both serious attorney error and prejudice. To show such error, it must be established that the assistance rendered by counsel was constitutionally deficient in that "counsel made errors so serious that counsel was not functioning as 'counsel' guaranteed the defendant by the Sixth Amendment." To show prejudice, it must be established that the claimed lapses in counsel's performance rendered the trial unfair so as to "undermine confidence in the outcome" of the trial. . . .

[T]he Sixth Amendment inquiry is into whether the attorney's conduct was "reasonably effective." . . . When examining attorney conduct, a court must be careful not to narrow the wide range of conduct acceptable under the Sixth Amendment so restrictively as to constitutionalize particular standards of professional conduct and thereby intrude into the State's proper authority to define and apply the standards of professional conduct applicable to those it admits to practice in its courts. . . .

C

We turn next to the question presented: the definition of the range of "reasonable professional" responses to a criminal defendant client who informs counsel that he will perjure himself on the stand. We must determine whether, in this setting, Robinson's conduct fell within the wide range of professional responses to threatened client perjury acceptable under the Sixth Amendment.

In Strickland, we recognized counsel's duty of loyalty and his "overarching duty to advocate the defendant's case." Plainly, that duty is limited to legitimate, lawful conduct compatible with the very nature of a trial as a search for truth. Although counsel must take all reasonable lawful means to attain the objectives of the client, counsel is precluded from taking steps or in any

way assisting the client in presenting false evidence or otherwise violating the law. . . .

These principles have been carried through to contemporary codifications of an attorney's professional responsibility. Disciplinary Rule 7-102 of the Model Code of Professional Responsibility (1980), entitled "Representing a Client within the Bounds of the Law," provides that

"(A) In his representation of a client, a lawyer shall not:

. . .

"(4) Knowingly use perjured testimony or false evidence.

. . .

"(7) Counsel or assist his client in conduct that the lawyer knows to be illegal or fraudulent."

This provision has been adopted by Iowa, and is binding on all lawyers who appear in its courts. See Iowa Code of Professional Responsibility for Lawyers (1985). The more recent Model Rules of Professional Conduct (1983) similarly admonish attorneys to obey all laws in the course of representing a client:

"RULE 1.2 Scope of Representation

. . .

"(d) A lawyer shall not counsel a client to engage, or assist a client, in conduct that the lawyer knows is criminal or fraudulent. . . ."

Both the Model Code of Professional Conduct and the Model Rules of Professional Conduct also adopt the specific exception from the attorney-client privilege for disclosure of perjury that his client intends to commit or has committed. DR 4-101(C)(3) (intention of client to commit a crime); Rule 3.3 (lawyer has duty to disclose falsity of evidence even if disclosure compromises client confidences). Indeed, both the Model Code and the Model Rules do not merely *authorize* disclosure by counsel of client perjury; they *require* such disclosure. See Rule 3.3(a)(4); DR 7-102(B)(1).

These standards confirm that the legal profession has accepted that an attorney's ethical duty to advance the interests of his client is limited by an equally solemn duty to comply with the law and standards of professional conduct; it specifically ensures that the client may not use false evidence. This special duty of an attorney to prevent and disclose frauds upon the court derives from the recognition that perjury is as much a crime as tampering with witnesses or jurors by way of promises and threats, and undermines the administration of justice. . . . An attorney who aids false testimony by questioning a witness when perjurious responses can be anticipated, risks prosecution for subornation of perjury under Iowa Code § 720.3 (1985).

It is universally agreed that at a minimum the attorney's first duty when confronted with a proposal for perjurious testimony is to attempt to dissuade the client from the unlawful course of conduct. A statement directly in point is found in the Commentary to the Model Rules of Professional Conduct under the heading "False Evidence":

> "When false evidence is offered by the client, however, a conflict may arise between the lawyer's duty to keep the client's revelations confidential and the duty of candor to the court. Upon ascertaining that material evidence is false, the lawyer *should seek to persuade the client that the evidence should not be offered* or, if it has been offered, that its false character should immediately be disclosed." Model Rules of Professional Conduct, Rule 3.3, Comment (1983) (emphasis added).

The Commentary thus also suggests that an attorney's revelation of his client's perjury to the court is a professionally responsible and acceptable response to the conduct of a client who has actually given perjured testimony. Similarly, the Model Rules and the commentary, as well as the Code of Professional Responsibility adopted in Iowa expressly permit withdrawal from representation as an appropriate response of an attorney when the client threatens to commit perjury.

Model Rules of Professional Conduct, Rule 1.16(a)(1), Rule 1.6, Comment (1983); Code of Professional Responsibility, DR 2-110(B), (C) (1980). Withdrawal of counsel when this situation arises at trial gives rise to many difficult questions including possible mistrial and claims of double jeopardy.[6] . . .

D

Considering Robinson's representation of respondent in light of these accepted norms of professional conduct, we discern no failure to adhere to reasonable professional standards that would in any sense make out a deprivation of the Sixth Amendment right to counsel. Whether Robinson's conduct is seen as a successful attempt to dissuade his client from committing the crime of perjury, or whether seen as a "threat" to withdraw from representation and disclose the illegal scheme, Robinson's representation of Whiteside falls well within accepted standards of professional conduct and the range of reasonable professional conduct acceptable under *Strickland*. . . .

---

6. In the evolution of the contemporary standards promulgated by the American Bar Association, an early draft reflects a compromise suggesting that when the disclosure of intended perjury is made during the course of trial, when withdrawal of counsel would raise difficult questions of a mistrial holding, counsel had the option to let the defendant take the stand but decline to affirmatively assist the presentation of perjury by traditional direct examination. Instead, counsel would stand mute while the defendant undertook to present the false version in narrative form in his own words unaided by any direct examination. This conduct was thought to be a signal at least to the presiding judge that the attorney considered the testimony to be false and was seeking to disassociate himself from that course. Additionally, counsel would not be permitted to discuss the known false testimony in closing arguments. See ABA Standards for Criminal Justice, 4-7.7 (2d ed 1980). Most courts treating the subject rejected this approach and insisted on a more rigorous standard. The Eighth Circuit in this case and the Ninth Circuit have expressed approval of the "free narrative" standards.

The Rule finally promulgated in the current Model Rules of Professional Conduct rejects any participation or passive role whatever by counsel in allowing perjury to be presented without challenge.

The Court of Appeals' holding that Robinson's "action deprived [Whiteside] of due process and effective assistance of counsel" is not supported by the record since Robinson's action, at most, deprived Whiteside of his contemplated perjury. Nothing counsel did in any way undermined Whiteside's claim that he believed the victim was reaching for a gun. . . . Robinson divulged no client communications until he was compelled to do so in response to Whiteside's post-trial challenge to the quality of his performance. We see this as a case in which the attorney successfully dissuaded the client from committing the crime of perjury.

Paradoxically, even while accepting the conclusion of the Iowa trial court that Whiteside's proposed testimony would have been a criminal act, the Court of Appeals held that Robinson's efforts to persuade Whiteside not to commit that crime where improper, *first*, as forcing an impermissible choice between the right to counsel and the right to testify; and *second*, as compromising client confidences because of Robinson's threat to disclose the contemplated perjury.

Whatever the scope of a constitutional right to testify, it is elementary that such a right does not extend to testifying *falsely*. . . . The right to counsel includes no right to have a lawyer who will cooperate with planned perjury. A lawyer who would so cooperate would be at risk of prosecution for suborning perjury, and disciplinary proceedings, including suspension or disbarment.

Robinson's admonitions to his client can in no sense be said to have forced respondent into an *impermissible* choice between his right to counsel and his right to testify as he proposed for there was no *permissible* choice to testify falsely. For defense counsel to take steps to persuade a criminal defendant to testify truthfully, or to withdraw, deprives the defendant of neither his right to counsel nor the right to testify truthfully. . . . When an accused proposes to resort to perjury or to produce false evidence, one consequence is the risk of withdrawal of counsel.

On this record, the accused enjoyed continued representation within the bounds of reasonable professional conduct and did in fact exercise his right to testify; at most he was denied the right to have the assistance of counsel in the presentation of false testimony. Similarly, we can discern no breach of professional duty in Robinson's admonition to respondent that he would disclose respondent's perjury to the court. The crime of perjury in this setting is indistinguishable in substance from the crime of threatening or tampering with a witness or a juror. A defendant who informed his counsel that he was arranging to bribe or threaten witnesses or members of the jury would have no "right" to insist on counsel's assistance or silence. Counsel would not be limited to advising against that conduct. An attorney's duty of confidentiality, which totally covers the client's admission of guilt, does not extend to a client's announced plans to engage in future criminal conduct. See United States v. Clark, 289 US 1, 15, 53 S Ct 465, 77 L Ed 993 (1933). In short, the responsibility of an ethical lawyer, as an officer of the court and a key component of a system of justice, dedicated to a search for truth, is essentially the same whether the client announces an intention to bribe or threaten witnesses or jurors or to commit or procure perjury. No system of justice worthy of the name can tolerate a lesser standard. . . . Since there has been no breach of any recognized professional duty, it follows that there can be no deprivation of the right to assistance of counsel under the Strickland standard.

E

We hold that, as a matter of law, counsel's conduct complained of here cannot establish the prejudice required for relief under the second strand of the Strickland inquiry. Although a defendant need not establish that the attorney's deficient performance more likely than not altered the outcome in order to establish prejudice under Strickland, a defendant must show "that there is a reasonable probability that, but for counsel's unprofessional errors, the result of the proceeding would have been different." According to Strickland, "[a] reasonable probability is a probability sufficient to undermine confidence in the outcome." The Strickland Court noted that the "benchmark" of an ineffective assistance claim is the fairness of the adversary proceeding, and that in judging prejudice and the likelihood of a different outcome, "[a] defendant has no entitlement to the luck of a lawless decisionmaker."

Whether he was persuaded or compelled to desist from perjury, Whiteside has no valid claim that confidence in the result of his trial has been diminished by his desisting from the contemplated perjury. Even if we were to assume that the jury might have believed his perjury, it does not follow that Whiteside was prejudiced. . . . Whiteside's attorney treated Whiteside's proposed perjury in accord with professional standards, and since Whiteside's truthful testimony could not have prejudiced the result of his trial, the Court of Appeals was in error to direct the issuance of a writ of habeas corpus and must be reversed.

* * *

Justice Brennan, concurring in the judgment.

This Court has no constitutional authority to establish rules of ethical conduct for lawyers practicing in the state courts. Nor does the Court enjoy any statutory grant of jurisdiction over legal ethics. . . .

Unfortunately, the Court seems unable to resist the temptation of sharing with the legal community its vision of ethical conduct. But let there be no mistake: the Court's essay regarding what constitutes the correct response to a criminal client's suggestion that he will perjure himself is pure discourse without force of law. As Justice Blackmun observes, *that* issue is a thorny one, but it is not an issue presented by this case. Lawyers, judges, bar associations, students and others should understand that the problem has not now been "decided." . . .

Justice Blackmun, with whom Justice Brennan, Justice Marshall, and Justice Stevens join, concurring in the judgment.

How a defense attorney ought to act when faced with a client who intends to commit perjury at trial has long been a controversial issue. But I do not believe that a federal habeas corpus case challenging a state criminal conviction is an appropriate vehicle for attempting to resolve this thorny problem. When a defendant argues that he was denied effective assistance of counsel because his lawyer dissuaded him from committing perjury, the only question properly presented to this Court is whether the lawyer's actions deprived the defendant of the fair trial which the Sixth Amendment is meant to guaran-

tee. Since I believe that the respondent in this case suffered no injury justifying federal habeas relief, I concur in the Court's judgment. . . .

To the extent that Whiteside's claim rests on the assertion that he would have been acquitted had he been able to testify falsely, Whiteside claims a right the law simply does not recognize. . . . Since Whiteside was deprived of neither a fair trial nor any of the specific constitutional rights designed to guarantee a fair trial, he has suffered no prejudice. . . .

In light of respondent's failure to show any cognizable prejudice, I see no need to "grade counsel's performance." The only federal issue in this case is whether Robinson's behavior deprived Whiteside of the effective assistance of counsel; it is not whether Robinson's behavior conformed to any particular code of legal ethics.

Whether an attorney's response to what he sees as a client's plan to commit perjury violates a defendant's Sixth Amendment rights may depend on many factors: how certain the attorney is that the proposed testimony is false, the stage of the proceedings at which the attorney discovers the plan, or the ways in which the attorney may be able to dissuade his client, to name just three. The complex interaction of factors, which is likely to vary from case to case, makes inappropriate a blanket rule that defense attorneys must reveal, or threaten to reveal, a client's anticipated perjury to the court. Except in the rarest of cases, attorneys who adopt "the role of the judge or jury to determine the facts," United States ex rel Wilcox v. Johnson, 555 F2d 115, 122 (CA3 1977), pose a danger of depriving their clients of the zealous and loyal advocacy required by the Sixth Amendment.

I therefore am troubled by the Court's implicit adoption of a set of standards of professional responsibility for attorneys in state criminal proceedings. . . .

Justice Stevens, concurring in the judgment. . . .

As we view this case, it appears perfectly clear that respondent intended to commit perjury, that his lawyer knew it, and that the lawyer had a duty—both to the court and to his client, for perjured testimony can ruin an otherwise meritorious case—to take extreme measures to prevent the perjury from occurring. The lawyer was successful and, from our unanimous and remote perspective, it is now pellucidly clear that the client suffered no "legally cognizable prejudice."

Nevertheless, beneath the surface of this case there are areas of uncertainty that cannot be resolved today. A lawyer's certainty that a change in his client's recollection is a harbinger of intended perjury—as well as judicial review of such apparent certainty—should be tempered by the realization that, after reflection, the most honest witness may recall (or sincerely believe he recalls) details that he previously overlooked. Similarly, the post-trial review of a lawyer's pre-trial threat to expose perjury that had not yet been committed—and, indeed, may have been prevented by the threat—is by no means the same as review of the way in which such a threat may actually have been carried out. Thus, one can be convinced—as I am—that this lawyer's actions were a proper way to provide his client with effective representation without confronting the much more difficult questions of what a lawyer must, should, or may do after his client has given testimony that the lawyer does not believe. The answer to such questions may well be colored by the particular circumstances attending the actual event and its aftermath. . . .

Notes and Questions

1. If Whiteside had testified that he had seen a metallic object in Calvin Love's hand, would such testimony have bolstered his claim that he believed that his own life was in jeopardy and that he killed Love in self-defense? If so, why does the Court conclude that Whiteside suffered no "prejudice," under *Strickland*, when his lawyer's actions precluded him from offering such testimony?

2. In light of the Court's conclusion that Whiteside failed to demonstrate that his defense had been prejudiced by his attorney's conduct, was it necessary for Chief Justice Burger's opinion to discuss whether the lawyer's representation was deficient? Is the Chief Justice's discussion helpful regarding a defense lawyer's appropriate response to a client's threatened perjury, or, as the concurring justices suggest, would it have been preferable if this issue had not been addressed?

3. How do you think Professor Freedman, who earlier examined the range of responses an attorney can make to a defendant's threatened use of perjury (p. 575), would react to the court's opinion in *Nix v. Whiteside*? *See* Freedman, "Client Confidences and Client Perjury: Some Unanswered Questions," 136 *University of Pennsylvania Law Review* 1939 (1988).

CONCLUSION

Defense lawyers play a vital role in the adversarial system. They are expected to advocate with skill and vigor on behalf of their clients, even those who are accused and may in fact be guilty of the most serious and reprehensible crimes. At the same time, they must be ever mindful of the boundaries defining ethical and lawful conduct.

In this chapter, we have examined a number of issues related to the accused's right to counsel, including whether poor people have a constitutional entitlement to court-appointed attorneys, whether a constitutional right of self-representation exists, and the sometimes conflicting obligations of defense lawyers to their clients and the court within the adversarial system of justice. Defense attorneys are expected to champion the interests of the criminally accused and to insist that the entire constellation of rights owed criminal defendants is respected. The issues confronting defense counsel, which can be both intriguing and complex, must successfully be resolved if reliable and just results are to be achieved in criminal cases.

Guilty Pleas and Plea Bargaining

Plea bargaining is the process by which a defendant in a criminal case gives up his or her right to a trial by pleading guilty in exchange for a reduction in charge and/or sentence. Plea bargaining has become so pervasive in the criminal justice system that criminal courthouses have been referred to as "plea-bargaining courts" instead of trial courts. M. Heumann, *Plea Bargaining*, Chicago: University of Chicago Press, 1971, p. 1. There are several reasons for the pervasiveness of plea bargaining. The primary reason is that, as with all good bargains, there is something in it for all parties. The prosecutor is assured that a presumed criminal will not go scot-free. The defendant's risk of receiving the maximum or a lengthy sentence is reduced. The court is relieved from having to dedicate its scarce resources—time, money, and personnel—to a criminal trial.

In fact, it is fair to say that reliance on plea bargaining has transformed the criminal justice system.

The traditional model of the criminal process provides for an impartial trier of fact to determine guilt after a formal adversary trial and then for a judge to select a penalty appropriate for the offender from a range specified by the legislature. In practice, however, the locus of the criminal process has shifted largely from trial to plea bargaining. In the vast majority of cases, guilt and the applicable range of sentences are determined through informal negotiations between the prosecutor and the defense attorney. Note, "Plea Bargaining and the Transformation of the Criminal Process," 90 *Harv. L. Rev.* 564, 569 (1977).

While plea bargaining in some respects may be advantageous to the criminal justice system and the individuals involved in the bargain, serious questions have been raised about whether expediency wins out over justice when such bargains are struck. The plea-bargaining process also raises significant constitutional questions. In this chapter, we will examine how the Supreme Court has applied the Constitution to the practice of plea bargaining. To meet minimum constitutional requirements, a guilty plea at least must be entered into "voluntarily and intelligently." Accordingly, we must examine the characteristics that make a guilty plea intelligent and voluntary and the procedural steps that are required to ensure the presence of these characteristics. We also consider other particularly troubling aspects of the plea-bargaining process and how the Court has dealt with them.

THE GUILTY PLEA AND THE CONSTITUTION

The Supreme Court has set forth minimum procedural requirements for the acceptance of a guilty plea from a defendant. These procedures are designed to ensure that the defendant (a) understands the rights he or she is giving up by pleading guilty and (b) is giving up these rights of his or her own free will. These principles are central to *Boykin v. Alabama*, presented below.

Boykin v. Alabama, 395 U.S. 238, 89 S. Ct. 1709, 23 L. Ed. 2d 274 (1969)

Mr. Justice DOUGLAS delivered the opinion of the Court.

In the spring of 1966, within the period of a fortnight, a series of armed robberies occurred in Mobile, Alabama. The victims, in each case, were local shopkeepers open at night who were forced by a gunman to hand over money. While robbing one grocery store, the assailant fired his gun once, sending a bullet through a door into the ceiling. A few days earlier in a drugstore, the robber had allowed his gun to discharge in such a way that the bullet, on ricochet from the floor, struck a customer in the leg. Shortly thereafter, a local grand jury returned five indictments against petitioner, a 27-year-old Negro, for common-law robbery—an offense punishable in Alabama by death.

Before the matter came to trial, the court determined that petitioner was indigent and appointed counsel to represent him. Three days later, at his arraignment, petitioner pleaded guilty to all five indictments. So far as the record shows, the judge asked no questions of petitioner concerning his plea, and petitioner did not address the court.

Trial strategy may of course make a plea of guilty seem the desirable course. But the record is wholly silent on that point and throws no light on it.

Alabama provides that when a defendant pleads guilty, "the court must cause the punishment to be determined by a jury" (except where it is required to be fixed by the court) and may "cause witnesses to be examined, to ascertain the character of the offense." Ala.Code, Tit. 15, § 277 (1958). In the present case a trial of that dimension was held, the prosecution presenting its case largely through eyewitness testimony. Although counsel for petitioner engaged in cursory cross-examination, petitioner neither testified himself nor presented testimony concerning his character and background. There was nothing to indicate that he had a prior criminal record.

In instructing the jury, the judge stressed that petitioner had pleaded guilty in five cases of robbery, defined as "the felonious taking of money from another against his will by violence or by putting him in fear [carrying] from ten years minimum in the penitentiary to the supreme penalty of death by electrocution." The jury, upon deliberation, found petitioner guilty and sentenced him severally to die on each of the five indictments. . . .

A plea of guilty is more than a confession which admits that the accused did various acts; it is itself a conviction; nothing remains but to give judgment and determine punishment. Admissibility of a confession must be based on a "reliable determination on the voluntariness issue which satisfies the constitutional rights of the defendant." Jackson v. Denno, 378 U.S. 368, 387, 84 S.Ct. 1774, 1786, 12 L.Ed.2d 908 [(1964)]. The requirement that the prosecution spread on the record the prerequisites of a valid waiver is no constitutional innovation. In Carnley v. Cochran, 369 U.S. 506, 516, 82 S.Ct. 884, 890, 8 L.Ed.2d 70 [(1962)], we dealt with a problem of waiver of the right to counsel, a Sixth Amendment right. We held: "Presuming waiver from a silent record is impermissible. The record must show, or there must be an allegation and evidence which show, that an accused was offered counsel but intelligently and understandingly rejected the offer. Anything less is not waiver."

We think that the same standard must be applied to determining whether a guilty plea is voluntarily made. For, as we have said, a plea of guilty is more than an admission of conduct; it is a conviction. Ignorance, incomprehension, coercion, terror, inducements, subtle or blatant threats might be a perfect cover-up of unconstitutionality. . . .

Several federal constitutional rights are involved in a waiver that takes place when a plea of guilty is entered in a state criminal trial. First, is the privilege against compulsory self-incrimination guaranteed by the Fifth Amendment and applicable to the States by reason of the Fourteenth. Second, is the right to trial by jury. Third,

is the right to confront one's accusers. We cannot presume a waiver of these three important federal rights from a silent record.

What is at stake for an accused facing death or imprisonment demands the utmost solicitude of which courts are capable in canvassing the matter with the accused to make sure he has a full understanding of what the plea connotes and of its consequence. When the judge discharges that function, he leaves a record adequate for any review that may be later sought, and forestalls the spin-off of collateral proceedings that seek to probe murky memories. . . .

Reversed.

Notes and Questions

1. What was the precise nature of the constitutional error committed by the trial court in *Boykin*?

2. How do you suppose a plea of guilty can affirmatively be shown to be "intelligent and voluntary"? What questions would have to be posed, and what answers given?

3. In *McCarthy v. United States*, 394 U.S. 459, 89 S. Ct. 1166, 22 L. Ed. 2d 418 (1969), the Supreme Court held that the trial court erred in not personally addressing the defendant to determine that the guilty plea was made voluntarily and that the defendant knew the nature of the charge. Why would such a requirement be imposed on the trial court?

4. Putting the guilty-plea procedure in writing would help ensure that trial courts ask all of the necessary questions and would aid appellate courts in determining that such questions were asked and appropriately answered. Many courts have adopted forms or written checklists for the trial judge to follow during a guilty-plea proceeding. An example of such a form, contained in the Arizona Rules of Criminal Procedure, 17 A.R.S. (1993), is presented in Exhibit 9–1. Note that the judge, the defense attorney, and the defendant have to affirmatively indicate that each item was asked, answered, and understood. Courts regularly use forms such as this to prevent any ambiguity about whether the

defendant understood and relinquished his or her constitutional rights.

5. In *Henderson v. Morgan*, 426 U.S. 637, 96 S. Ct. 2253, 49 L. Ed. 2d 108 (1976), the Court held that a defendant's plea of guilty is not intelligently made if he or she is unaware of the specific crime he or she is admitting to having committed, as well as the critical elements of that crime.

6. Technical or formalistic errors by a court may not be attacked in collateral (habeas corpus) proceedings. In *United States v. Timmreck*, 441 U.S. 780, 99 S. Ct. 2085, 60 L. Ed. 2d 634 (1979), the trial judge, while informing the defendant of the possible punishment he could face in exchange for his plea of guilty, did not tell him that he faced a statutorily mandated period of parole following release from prison. The Supreme Court held that regardless of whether the defendant actually knew about this provision (there was some evidence that his attorney had informed him of the mandatory parole provision), Timmreck was not prejudiced by the omission. On the basis of this fact, along with the fact that Rule 11 of the Federal Rules of Criminal Procedure is a court rule and not a constitutional right, the Supreme Court held that such a technical violation of Rule 11 could not be attacked in a habeas corpus proceeding. Why do you suppose the "technical violations" were grounds for reversal in *McCarthy* but not in *Timmreck*?

Exhibit 9–1 Guilty-Plea Checklist.

GUILTY PLEA PROCEEDING

The defendant personally appearing before me, I have ascertained the following facts, noting each by initialing it.

Judge's
Initial

_____ 1. That the defendant understands the nature of the charges against him _____.

_____ 2. That the defendant understands the range of possible sentence for the offenses charged, from a suspended sentence to a maximum of _____ and that the mandatory minimum (if any) is _____.

_____ 3. That the defendant understands the following constitutional rights which he gives up by pleading guilty:

_____ (a) His right to trial by jury, if any.

_____ (b) His right to the assistance of an attorney at all stages of the proceeding, and to an appointed attorney, to be furnished free of charge, if he cannot afford one.

_____ (c) His right to confront the witnesses against him and to cross-examine them as to the truthfulness of their testimony.

_____ (d) His right to present evidence on his own behalf, and to have the state compel witnesses of his choosing to appear and testify.

_____ (e) His right to remain silent and to be presumed innocent until proven guilty beyond a reasonable doubt.

_____ 4. That the defendant wishes to give up the constitutional rights of which he has been advised.

_____ 5. That there exists a basis in fact for believing the defendant guilty of the offenses charged.

_____ 6. That the defendant and the prosecutor have entered into a plea agreement and that the defendant understands and consents to its terms.

_____ 7. That the plea is voluntary and not the result of force, threats or promises other than a plea agreement.

On the basis of these findings, I conclude that the defendant knowingly, voluntarily and intelligently pleads guilty to the above charges, and accept his plea.

_____   _____
Date   Judge

CERTIFICATION BY DEFENDANT

I certify that the judge personally advised me of the matters noted above, that I understand the constitutional rights that I am giving up by pleading guilty, and that I desire to plead guilty to the charges stated.

_____   _____
Defense Counsel, if any   Defendant

Source: Arizona Rules of Procedure, 17 A.R.S. (1993).

ALFORD PLEAS AND THE "INNOCENT" DEFENDANT

Can a defendant maintain his or her innocence and nevertheless enter into a plea bargain? Under what circumstances, if any, should such contradictory assertions be recognized? The Court confronted this issue in *North Carolina v. Alford.*

North Carolina v. Alford, 400 U.S. 25, 91 S. Ct. 160, 27 L. Ed. 2d. 162 (1970)

Mr. Justice WHITE delivered the opinion of the Court.

On December 2, 1963, Alford was indicted for first-degree murder, a capital offense under North

Carolina law. The court appointed an attorney to represent him, and this attorney questioned all but one of the various witnesses who appellee said would substantiate his claim of innocence. The witnesses, however, did not support Alford's story but gave statements that strongly indicated his guilt. Faced with strong evidence of guilt and no substantial evidentiary support for the claim of innocence, Alford's attorney recommended that he plead guilty, but left the ultimate decision to Alford himself. The prosecutor agreed to accept a plea of guilty to a charge of second-degree murder, and on December 10, 1963, Alford pleaded guilty to the reduced charge.

Before the plea was finally accepted by the trial court, the court heard the sworn testimony of a police officer who summarized the State's case. Two other witnesses besides Alford were also heard. Although there was no eyewitness to the crime, the testimony indicated that shortly before the killing Alford took his gun from his house, stated his intention to kill the victim, and returned home with the declaration that he had carried out the killing. After the summary presentation of the State's case, Alford took the stand and testified that he had not committed the murder but that he was pleading guilty because he faced the threat of the death penalty if he did not do so.[2] In response

---

2. After giving his version of the events of the night of the murder, Alford stated:

"I pleaded guilty on second degree murder because they said there is too much evidence, but I ain't shot no man, but I take the fault for the other man. We never had an argument in our life and I just pleaded guilty because they said if I didn't they would gas me for it, and that is all." In response to questions from his attorney, Alford affirmed that he had consulted several times with his attorney and with members of his family and had been informed of his rights if he chose to plead not guilty. Alford then reaffirmed his decision to plead guilty to second-degree murder:

"Q [by Alford's attorney]. And you authorized me to tender a plea of guilty to second degree murder before the court?

"A. Yes, sir.

"Q. And in doing that, that you have again affirmed your decision on that point?

"A. Well, I'm still pleading that you all got me to plead guilty. I plead the other way, circumstantial evidence; that the jury will prosecute me on—on the second. You told me to plead guilty, right. I don't—I'm not guilty but I plead guilty."

to the questions of his counsel, he acknowledged that his counsel had informed him of the difference between second- and first-degree murder and of his rights in case he chose to go to trial. The trial court then asked appellee if, in light of his denial of guilt, he still desired to plead guilty to second-degree murder and appellee answered, "Yes, sir. I plead guilty on—from the circumstances that he [Alford's attorney] told me." After eliciting information about Alford's prior criminal record, which was a long one, the trial court sentenced him to 30 years' imprisonment, the maximum penalty for second-degree murder. . . .

We held in Brady v. United States, 397 U.S. 742, 90 S.Ct. 1463, 25 L.Ed.2d 747 (1970), that a plea of guilty which would not have been entered except for the defendant's desire to avoid a possible death penalty and to limit the maximum penalty to life imprisonment or a term of years was not for that reason compelled within the meaning of the Fifth Amendment. . . . The standard was and remains whether the plea represents a voluntary and intelligent choice among the alternative courses of action open to the defendant. That he would not have pleaded except for the opportunity to limit the possible penalty does not necessarily demonstrate that the plea of guilty was not the product of a free and rational choice, especially where the defendant was represented by competent counsel whose advice was that the plea would be to the defendant's advantage. . . .

As previously recounted after Alford's plea of guilty was offered and the State's case was placed before the judge, Alford denied that he had committed the murder but reaffirmed his desire to plead guilty to avoid a possible death sentence and to limit the penalty to the 30-year maximum provided for second-degree murder. Ordinarily, a judgment of conviction resting on a plea of guilty is justified by the defendant's admission that he committed the crime charged against him and his consent that judgment be entered without a trial of any kind. The plea usually subsumes both elements, and justifiably so, even though there is no separate, express admission by the defendant that he committed the particular acts claimed to constitute the crime charged in the indictment. Here Alford entered his plea but accompanied it with the statement that he had not shot the victim.

If Alford's statements were to be credited as sincere assertions of his innocence, there obviously existed a factual and legal dispute between him and the State. Without more, it might be argued that the conviction entered on his guilty plea was invalid, since his assertion of innocence negatived any admission of guilt, which, as we observed last Term in *Brady*, is normally "[c]entral to the plea and the foundation for entering judgment against the defendant." 397 U.S., at 748, 90 S.Ct., at 1468.

In addition to Alford's statement, however, the court had heard an account of the events on the night of the murder, including information from Alford's acquaintances that he had departed from his home with his gun stating his intention to kill and that he had later declared that he had carried out his intention. Nor had Alford wavered in his desire to have trial court determine his guilt without a jury trial. Although denying the charge against him, he nevertheless preferred the dispute between him and the State to be settled by the judge in the context of a guilty plea proceeding rather than by a formal trial. Thereupon, with the State's telling evidence and Alford's denial before it, the trial court proceeded to convict and sentence Alford for second-degree murder.

State and lower federal courts are divided upon whether a guilty plea can be accepted when it is accompanied by protestations of innocence and hence contains only a waiver of trial but no admission of guilt. Some courts, giving expression to the principle that "[o]ur law only authorizes a conviction where guilt is shown," Harris v. State, 76 Tex. Cr.R. 126, 131, 172 S.W. 975, 977 (1915), require that trial judges reject such pleas. But others have concluded that they should not "force any defense on a defendant in a criminal case," particularly when advancement of the defense might "end in disaster." Tremblay v. Overholser, 199 F.Supp. 569, 570 (DC 1961). They have argued that, since "guilt, or the degree of guilt, is at times uncertain and elusive," "[a]n accused, though believing in or entertaining doubts respecting his innocence, might reasonably conclude a jury would be convinced of his guilt and that he would fare better in the sentence by pleading guilty." McCoy v. United States, 124 U.S.App.D.C. 177, 179, 363 F.2d 306, 308 (1966). As one state court observed nearly a century ago, "[r]easons other than the fact that he is guilty may induce a defendant to so plead, [and] [h]e must be permitted to judge for himself in this respect." State v. Kaufman, 51 Iowa 578, 580, 2 N.W. 275, 276 (1879) (dictum).

This Court has not confronted this precise issue, but prior decisions do yield relevant principles. In Lynch v. Overholser, 369 U.S. 705, 82 S.Ct. 1063, 8 L.Ed.2d 211 (1962), Lynch, who had been charged in the Municipal Court of the District of Columbia with drawing and negotiating bad checks, a misdemeanor punishable by a maximum of one year in jail, sought to enter a plea of guilty, but the trial judge refused to accept the plea since a psychiatric report in the judge's possession indicated that Lynch had been suffering from "a manic depressive psychosis, at the time of the crime charged," and hence might have been not guilty by reason of insanity. Although at the subsequent trial Lynch did not rely on the insanity defense, he was found not guilty by reason of insanity and committed for an indeterminate period to a mental institution. On habeas corpus, the Court ordered his release, construing the congressional legislation seemingly authorizing the commitment as not reaching a case where the accused preferred a guilty plea to a plea of insanity. The Court expressly refused to rule that Lynch had an absolute right to have his guilty plea accepted, but implied that there would have been no constitutional error had his plea been accepted even though evidence before the judge indicated that there was a valid defense.

The issue in Hudson v. United States, 272 U.S. 451, 47 S.Ct. 127, 71 L.Ed. 347 (1926), was whether a federal court has power to impose a prison sentence after accepting a plea of *nolo contendere*, a plea by which a defendant does not expressly admit his guilt, but nonetheless waives his right to a trial and authorizes the court for purposes of the case to treat him as if he were guilty.[8] The Court held that a trial court does have such power. . . . The federal courts

---

8. Courts have defined the plea of *nolo contendere* in a variety of different ways, describing it, on the one hand, as "in effect, a plea of guilty," United States v. Food & Grocery Bureau, 43 F.Supp. 974, 979 (SD Cal.1942), aff'd, 139 F.2d 973 (CA9 1943), and on the other, as a query directed to the court to determine the defendant's guilt. As a result, it is impossible to state precisely what a defendant does admit when he enters a *nolo* plea in a way that will consistently fit all the cases.

have uniformly followed this rule, even in cases involving moral turpitude. . . .

Implicit in the *nolo contendere* cases is a recognition that the Constitution does not bar imposition of a prison sentence upon an accused who is unwilling expressly to admit his guilt but who, faced with grim alternatives, is willing to waive his trial and accept the sentence.

These cases would be directly in point if Alford had simply insisted on his plea but refused to admit the crime. The fact that his plea was denominated a plea of guilty rather than a plea of *nolo contendere* is of no constitutional significance with respect to the issue now before us, for the Constitution is concerned with the practical consequences, not the formal categorizations, of state law. Thus, while most pleas of guilty consist of both a waiver of trial and an express admission of guilt, the latter element is not a constitutional requisite to the imposition of criminal penalty. An individual accused of crime may voluntarily, knowingly, and understandingly consent to the imposition of a prison sentence even if he is unwilling or unable to admit his participation in the acts constituting the crime.

Nor can we perceive any material difference between a plea that refuses to admit commission of the criminal act and a plea containing a protestation of innocence when, as in the instant case, a defendant intelligently concludes that his interests require entry of a guilty plea and the record before the judge contains strong evidence of actual guilt. Here the State had a strong case of first-degree murder against Alford. Whether he realized or disbelieved his guilt, he insisted on his plea because in his view he had absolutely nothing to gain by a trial and much to gain by pleading. Because of the overwhelming evidence against him, a trial was precisely what neither Alford nor his attorney desired. Confronted with the choice between a trial for first-degree murder, on the one hand, and a plea of guilty to second-degree murder, on the other, Alford quite reasonably chose the latter and thereby limited the maximum penalty to a 30-year term. When his plea is viewed in light of the evidence against him, which substantially negated his claim of innocence and which further provided a means by which the judge could test whether the plea was being intelligently entered, see McCarthy v. United States, 394

U.S., [459,] 466–467, 89 S.Ct., [1166,] 1170–1171, [22 L.Ed. 2d 418] (1969),[10] its validity cannot be seriously questioned. In view of the strong factual basis for the plea demonstrated by the State and Alford's clearly expressed desire to enter it despite his professed belief in his innocence, we hold that the trial judge did not commit constitutional error in accepting it.

Relying on United States v. Jackson, [390 U.S. 570, 88 S.Ct. 1209, 20 L.Ed. 2d 138 (1968)] Alford now argues in effect that the State should not have allowed him this choice but should have insisted on proving him guilty of murder in the first degree. The States in their wisdom may take this course by statute or otherwise and may prohibit the practice of accepting pleas to lesser included offenses under any circumstances. But this is not the mandate of the Fourteenth Amendment and the Bill of Rights. The prohibitions against involuntary or unintelligent pleas should not be relaxed, but neither should an exercise in arid logic render those constitutional guarantees counterproductive and put in jeopardy the very human values they were meant to preserve. . . .

Mr. Justice BRENNAN, with whom Mr. Justice DOUGLAS and Mr. Justice MARSHALL join, dissenting.

Last Term, this Court held, over my dissent, that a plea of guilty may validly be induced by an unconstitutional threat to subject the defendant to the risk of death, so long as the plea is entered in open court and the defendant is represented by competent counsel who is aware of the threat, albeit not of its unconstitutionality. Brady v. United States, 397 U.S. 742, 745–758, 90 S.Ct. 1463, 1467–1474, 25 L.Ed.2d 747 (1970); Parker v. North Carolina, 397 U.S. 790, 795, 90 S.Ct. 1458, 1461, 25 L.Ed.2d 785 (1970). Today

---

10. Because of the importance of protecting the innocent and of insuring that guilty pleas are a product of free and intelligent choice, various state and federal court decisions properly caution that pleas coupled with claims of innocence should not be accepted unless there is a factual basis for the plea, see, *e.g.,* Griffin v. United States, 132 U.S. App.D.C. 108, 110, 405 F.2d 1378, 1380 (1968); Bruce v. United States, 126 U.S.App.D.C., at 342, 379, F.2d, at 119 (1967); Commonwealth v. Cottrell, 433 Pa. 177, 249 A.2d 294 (1969); and until the judge taking the plea has inquired into and sought to resolve the conflict between the waiver of trial and the claim of innocence. . . .

the Court makes clear that its previous holding was intended to apply even when the record demonstrates that the actual effect of the unconstitutional threat was to induce a guilty plea from a defendant who was unwilling to admit his guilt.

I adhere to the view that, in any given case, the influence of such an unconstitutional threat "must necessarily be given weight in determining the voluntariness of a plea." Parker v. North Carolina, 397 U.S. at 805, 90 S.Ct., at 1458 (dissent). And, without reaching the question whether due process permits the entry of judgment upon a plea of guilty accompanied by a contemporaneous denial of acts constituting the crime, I believe that at the very least such a denial of guilt is also a relevant factor in determining whether the plea was voluntarily and intelligently made. With these factors in mind, it is sufficient in my view to state that the facts set out in the majority opinion demonstrate that Alford was "so gripped by fear of the death penalty" that his decision to plead guilty was not voluntary but was "the product of duress as much so as choice reflecting physical constraint." Haley v. Ohio, 332 U.S. 596, 606, 68 S.Ct. 302, 307, 92 L.Ed. 224 (1948) (opinion of Frankfurter, J.). Accordingly, I would affirm the judgment of the Court of Appeals.

Notes and Questions

1. Are you troubled at all by the Court's seeming indifference regarding whether Alford was actually guilty of committing the crime?

2. Consider the case of *People v. Foster*, 19 N.Y.2d 150, 225 N.E.2d 200, 278 N.Y.S.2d 200 (1967). Foster was charged with manslaughter in the first degree. Pursuant to a plea agreement, Foster pled guilty to attempted manslaughter in the second degree. On appeal, Foster argued that "he pleaded guilty to a nonexistent crime; therefore, his plea of guilty to such a charge . . . is a nullity, and . . . the judgment of conviction has no basis in law and violates due process." Id. at 152, 225 N.E. 2d at 201.

Section 1052 of the New York Penal Law provides that manslaughter in the second degree is a homicide committed "without a design to effect death": in other words, without intending to kill the victim. Section 2 of the Penal Law defines an attempt to commit a crime as "an act done with intent to commit a crime, and tending but failing to effect its commission."

"[Foster argued] that, since no intent is required in the crime of manslaughter and since an attempt to commit a crime requires an intent to commit the crime, a plea of guilty to attempted manslaughter is logically and legally impossible."

The New York Court of Appeals held that the guilty plea did not violate due process because Foster was pleading guilty to a lesser crime and because such a plea was based on a compromise for the benefit and with the consent of the defendant.

While all jurisdictions require there to be a factual basis for a plea of guilty, courts usually require only a general nexus between the original offense and the charge to which a defendant pleads guilty. Should such a nexus be required, or so long as all parties are in agreement, should they be permitted to enter into a plea agreement covering a nonexistent crime?

PLEA BARGAINING AND THE CONSTITUTION

For a guilty plea to be acceptable, it must be "voluntary." While this notion seems simple enough, it has proven to be very difficult to define in practice. Consider the voluntariness of the defendant's decision to plead guilty in *Brady v. United States*.

Brady v. United States, 397 U.S. 742, 90 S. Ct. 1463, 25 L. Ed. 2d 747 (1970)

Mr. Justice WHITE delivered the opinion of the Court.

In 1959, petitioner was charged with kidnaping in violation of 18 U.S.C. § 1201(a). Since the indictment charged that the victim of the kidnaping was not liberated unharmed, petitioner faced a maximum penalty of death if the verdict of the jury should so recommend. Petitioner, represented by competent counsel throughout, first elected to plead not guilty. Apparently because the trial judge was unwilling to try the case without a jury, petitioner made no serious attempt to reduce the possibility of a death penalty by waiving a jury trial. Upon learning that his codefendant, who had confessed to the authorities, would plead guilty and be available to testify against him, petitioner changed his plea to guilty. His plea was accepted after the trial judge twice questioned him as to the voluntariness of his plea. Petitioner was sentenced to 50 years imprisonment, later reduced to 30. . . .

II

The trial judge in 1959 found the plea voluntary before accepting it; the District Court in 1968, after an evidentiary hearing, found that the plea was voluntarily made; the Court of Appeals specifically approved the finding of voluntariness. We see no reason on this record to disturb the judgment of those courts. Petitioner, advised by competent counsel, tendered his plea after his codefendant, who had already given a confession, determined to plead guilty and became available to testify against petitioner. It was this development that the District Court found to have triggered Brady's guilty plea.

The voluntariness of Brady's plea can be determined only by considering all of the relevant circumstances surrounding it. One of these circumstances was the possibility of a heavier sentence following a guilty verdict after a trial. It may be that Brady, faced with a strong case against him and recognizing that his chances for acquittal were slight, preferred to plead guilty and thus limit the penalty to life imprisonment rather than to elect a jury trial which could result in a death penalty. But even if we assume that Brady would not have pleaded guilty except for the death penalty provision of § 1201(a), this assumption merely identifies the penalty provision as a "but for" cause of his plea. That the statute caused the plea in this sense does not necessarily prove that the plea was coerced and invalid as an involuntary act.

The State to some degree encourages pleas of guilty at every important step in the criminal process. For some people, their breach of a State's law is alone sufficient reason for surrendering themselves and accepting punishment. For others, apprehension and charge, both threatening acts by the Government, jar them into admitting their guilt. In still other cases, the post-indictment accumulation of evidence may convince the defendant and his counsel that a trial is not worth the agony and expense to the defendant and his family. All these pleas of guilty are valid in spite of the State's responsibility for some of the factors motivating the pleas; the pleas are no more improperly compelled than is the decision by a defendant at the close of State's evidence at trial that he must take the stand or face certain conviction.

Of course, the agents of the State may not produce a plea by actual or threatened physical harm or by mental coercion overbearing the will of the defendant. But nothing of the sort is claimed in this case; nor is there evidence that Brady was so gripped by fear of the death penalty or hope of leniency that he did not or could not, with the help of counsel, rationally weigh the advantages of going to trial against the advantages of pleading guilty. Brady's claim is of a different sort: that it violates the Fifth Amendment to influence or encourage a guilty plea by opportunity or promise of leniency and that a guilty plea is coerced and invalid if influenced by the fear of a possibly higher penalty for the crime charged if a conviction is obtained after the State is put to its proof.

Insofar as the voluntariness of his plea is concerned, there is little to differentiate Brady from

(1) the defendant, in a jurisdiction where the judge and jury have the same range of sentencing power, who pleads guilty because his lawyer advises him that the judge will very probably be more lenient than the jury; (2) the defendant, in a jurisdiction where the judge alone has sentencing power, who is advised by counsel that the judge is normally more lenient with defendants who plead guilty than with those who go to trial; (3) the defendant who is permitted by prosecutor and judge to plead guilty to a lesser offense included in the offense charged; and (4) the defendant who pleads guilty to certain counts with the understanding that other charges will be dropped. In each of these situations, as in Brady's case, the defendant might never plead guilty absent the possibility or certainty that the plea will result in a lesser penalty than the sentence that could be imposed after a trial and a verdict of guilty. We decline to hold, however, that a guilty plea is compelled and invalid under the Fifth Amendment whenever motivated by the defendant's desire to accept the certainty or probability of a lesser penalty rather than face a wider range of possibilities extending from acquittal to conviction and a higher penalty authorized by law for the crime charged.

The issue we deal with is inherent in the criminal law and its administration because guilty pleas are not constitutionally forbidden, because the criminal law characteristically extends to judge or jury a range of choice in setting the sentence in individual cases, and because both the State and the defendant often find it advantageous to preclude the possibility of the maximum penalty authorized by law. For a defendant who sees slight possibility of acquittal, the advantages of pleading guilty and limiting the probable penalty are obvious—his exposure is reduced, the correctional processes can begin immediately, and the practical burdens of a trial are eliminated. For the State there are also advantages—the more promptly imposed punishment after an admission of guilt may more effectively attain the objectives of punishment; and with the avoidance of trial, scarce judicial and prosecutorial resources are conserved for those cases in which there is a substantial issue of the defendant's guilt or in which there is sub-stantial doubt that the State can sustain its burden of proof. It is this mutuality of advantage that perhaps explains the fact that at present well over three-fourths of the criminal convictions in this country rest on pleas of guilty, a great many of them no doubt motivated at least in part by the hope or assurance of a lesser penalty than might be imposed if there were a guilty verdict after a trial to judge or jury.

Of course, that the prevalence of guilty pleas is explainable does not necessarily validate those pleas or the system which produces them. But we cannot hold that it is unconstitutional for the State to extend a benefit to a defendant who in turn extends a substantial benefit to the State and who demonstrates by his plea that he is ready and willing to admit his crime and to enter the correctional system in a frame of mind that affords hope for success in rehabilitation over a shorter period of time than might otherwise be necessary.

A contrary holding would require the States and Federal Government to forbid guilty pleas altogether, to provide a single invariable penalty for each crime defined by the statutes, or to place the sentencing function in a separate authority having no knowledge of the manner in which the conviction in each case was obtained. In any event, it would be necessary to forbid prosecutors and judges to accept guilty pleas to selected counts, to lesser included offenses, or to reduced charges. The Fifth Amendment does not reach so far. . . .

The standard as to the voluntariness of guilty pleas must be essentially that defined by Judge Tuttle of the Court of Appeals for the Fifth Circuit:

"'[A] plea of guilty entered by one fully aware of the direct consequences, including the actual value of any commitments made to him by the court, prosecutor, or his own counsel, must stand unless induced by threats (or promises to discontinue improper harassment), misrepresentation (including unfulfilled or unfulfillable promises), or perhaps by promises that are by their nature improper as having no proper relationship to the prosecutor's business (e.g., bribes).' 242 F.2d at page 115."

Under this standard, a plea of guilty is not invalid merely because entered to avoid the possibility of a death penalty.

III

The record before us also supports the conclusion that Brady's plea was intelligently made. He was advised by competent counsel, he was made aware of the nature of the charge against him, and there was nothing to indicate that he was incompetent or otherwise not in control of his mental faculties; once his confederate had pleaded guilty and became available to testify, he chose to plead guilty, perhaps to ensure that he would face no more than life imprisonment or a term of years. Brady was aware of precisely what he was doing when he admitted that he had kidnaped the victim and had not released her unharmed.

Often the decision to plead guilty is heavily influenced by the defendant's appraisal of the prosecution's case against him and by the apparent likelihood of securing leniency should a guilty plea be offered and accepted. Considerations like these frequently present imponderable questions for which there are no certain answers; judgments may be made that in the light of later events seem improvident, although they were perfectly sensible at the time. The rule that a plea must be intelligently made to be valid does not require that a plea be vulnerable to later attack if the defendant did not correctly assess every relevant factor entering into his decision. A defendant is not entitled to withdraw his plea merely because he discovers long after the plea has been accepted that his calculus misapprehended the quality of the State's case or the likely penalties attached to alternative courses of action. More particularly, absent misrepresentation or other impermissible conduct by state agents, a voluntary plea of guilty intelligently made in the light of the then applicable law does not become vulnerable because later judicial decisions indicate that the plea rested on a faulty premise. A plea of guilty triggered by the expectations of a competently counseled defendant that the State will have a strong case against him is not subject to later attack because the defendant's lawyer correctly advised him with respect to the then existing law as to possi-

ble penalties but later pronouncements of the courts, as in this case, hold that the maximum penalty for the crime in question was less than was reasonably assumed at the time the plea was entered.

This is not to say that guilty plea convictions hold no hazards for the innocent or that the methods of taking guilty pleas presently employed in this country are necessarily valid in all respects. This mode of conviction is no more foolproof than full trials to the court or to the jury. Accordingly, we take great precautions against unsound results, and we should continue to do so, whether conviction is by plea or by trial. We would have serious doubts about this case if the encouragement of guilty pleas by offers of leniency substantially increased the likelihood that defendants, advised by competent counsel, would falsely condemn themselves. But our view is to the contrary and is based on our expectations that courts will satisfy themselves that pleas of guilty are voluntarily and intelligently made by competent defendants with adequate advice of counsel and that there is nothing to question the accuracy and reliability of the defendants' admissions that they committed the crimes with which they are charged. In the case before us, nothing in the record impeaches Brady's plea or suggests that his admissions in open court were anything but the truth.

Although Brady's plea of guilty may well have been motivated in part by a desire to avoid a possible death penalty, we are convinced that his plea was voluntarily and intelligently made and we have no reason to doubt that his solemn admission of guilt was truthful.

Affirmed.

Mr. Justice Brennan, with whom Mr. Justice Douglas and Mr. Justice Marshall join, dissenting in Parker v. North Carolina and concurring in Brady v. United States . . .

I

The Court properly notes the grave consequences for a defendant that attach to his plea of guilty; for the plea constitutes a simultaneous surrender of numerous constitutional rights, including the privilege against compulsory self-incrimination and the right to a trial by jury, with all of its attendant safeguards. Indeed, we have pointed out that a guilty plea is more serious than a confession because it is tantamount to a conviction. Accordingly, we have insisted that a guilty plea, like any surrender of fundamental constitutional rights, reflect the unfettered choice of the defendant. In deciding whether any illicit pressures have been brought to bear on a defendant to induce a guilty plea, courts have traditionally inquired whether it was made "voluntarily" and "intelligently" with full understanding and appreciation of the consequences.

The concept of "voluntariness" contains an ambiguous element, accentuated by the Court's opinions in these cases, because the concept has been employed to analyze a variety of pressures to surrender constitutional rights, which are not all equally coercive or obvious in their coercive effect. In some cases where an "involuntary" surrender has been found, the physical or psychological tactics employed exerted so great an influence upon the accused that it could accurately be said that his will was literally overborne or completely dominated by his interrogators, who rendered him incapable of rationally weighing the legal alternatives open to him.

There is some intimation in the Court's opinions in the instant cases that, at least with respect to guilty pleas, "involuntariness" covers *only* the narrow class of cases in which the defendant's will has been literally overborne. At other points, however, the Court apparently recognizes that the term "involuntary" has traditionally been applied to situations in which an individual, while perfectly capable of rational choice, has been confronted with factors that the government may not constitutionally inject into the decision-making process. For example, in Garrity v. New Jersey, 385 U.S. 493, 87 S.Ct. 616, 17 L.Ed.2d 562 (1967), we held a surrender of the self-incrimination privilege to be involuntary when an individual was presented by the government with the possibility of discharge from his employment if he invoked the privilege. So, also, it has long been held that certain promises of leniency or threats of harsh treatment by the trial judge or the prosecutor unfairly burden or intrude upon the defendant's decision-making process. Even though the defendant is not necessarily rendered incapable of rational choice, his guilty plea nonetheless may be invalid.

Thus the legal concept of "involuntariness" has not been narrowly confined but refers to a surrender of constitutional rights influenced by considerations that the government cannot properly introduce. The critical question that divides the Court is what constitutes an impermissible factor, or, more narrowly in the context of these cases, whether the threat of the imposition of an unconstitutional death penalty is such a factor.

Even after the various meanings of "involuntary" have been identified, application of voluntariness criteria in particular circumstances remains an elusory process because it entails judicial evaluation of the effect of particular external stimuli upon the state of mind of the accused. Nevertheless, we have consistently taken great pains to insulate the accused from the more obvious and oppressive forms of physical coercion. Beyond this, in the analogous area of coerced confessions, for example, it has long been recognized that various psychological devices, some of a very subtle and sophisticated nature, may be employed to induce statements. Such influences have been condemned by this Court. Thus, a confession is not voluntary merely because it is the "product of a sentient choice," if it does not reflect a free exercise of the defendant's will. Indeed, as the Court recognizes, we held in an early case that the concept of "voluntariness" requires that a confession "not be extracted by any sort of threats or violence, nor obtained by any direct or implied promises, however slight, nor by the exertion of any improper influence." Bram v. United States, 168 U.S. 532, 542–543, 18 S.Ct. 183, 187, 42 L.Ed. 568 (1897). More recently, we held in Malloy v. Hogan, 378 U.S. 1, 84 S.Ct. 1489, 12 L.Ed.2d 653 (1964), that the Fifth and Fourteenth Amendments guarantee to every person the right "to remain silent unless he chooses to speak in the unfettered exercise of his own will, and to suffer no penalty for such silence."

The Court's answer to the stringent criterion of voluntariness imposed by *Bram* and subsequent cases is that the availability of counsel to an accused effectively offsets the illicit influence upon him that threats or promises by the government may impose. Of course, the presence of counsel is a factor to be taken into account in any overall evaluation of the voluntariness of a confession or a guilty plea. However, it hardly follows that the support provided by counsel is sufficient by itself to insulate the accused from the effect of any threat or promise by the government.

It has frequently been held, for example, that a guilty plea induced by threats or promises by the trial judge is invalid because of the risk that the trial judge's impartiality will be compromised and because of the inherently unequal bargaining power of the judge and the accused. The assistance of counsel in this situation, of course, may improve a defendant's bargaining *ability*, but it does not alter the underlying inequality of *power*. Significantly, the Court explicitly refrains from expressing its views on this issue. This is an unfortunate omission, for judicial promises of leniency in return for a guilty plea provide a useful analogy to what has occurred in the instant cases. Here, the government has promised the accused, through the legislature, that he will receive a substantially reduced sentence if he pleads guilty. In fact, the legislature has simultaneously threatened the accused with the ultimate penalty—death—if he insists upon a jury trial and has promised a penalty no greater than life imprisonment if he pleads guilty.

It was precisely this statutorily imposed dilemma that we identified in *Jackson* as having the "inevitable effect" of discouraging assertion of the right not to plead guilty and to demand a jury trial. As recognized in *Jackson*, it is inconceivable that this sort of capital penalty scheme will not have a major impact upon the decisions of many defendants to plead guilty. In any particular case, therefore, the influence of this unconstitutional factor must necessarily be given weight in determining the voluntariness of a plea. . . .

Of course, whether in a given case the penalty scheme has actually exercised its pernicious influence so as to make a guilty plea involuntary can be decided only by consideration of the factors that actually motivated the defendant to enter his plea. If a particular defendant can demonstrate that the death penalty scheme exercised a significant influence upon his decision to plead guilty, then, under *Jackson*, he is entitled to reversal of the conviction based upon his illicitly produced plea.

The Court attempts to submerge the issue of voluntariness of a plea under an unconstitutional capital punishment scheme in a general discussion of the pressures upon defendants to plead guilty which are said to arise from, *inter alia*, the venerable institution of plea bargaining. The argument appears to reduce to this: because the accused cannot be insulated from *all* inducements to plead guilty, it follows that he should be shielded from *none*.

The principal flaw in the Court's discourse on plea bargaining, however, is that it is, at best, only marginally relevant to the precise issues before us. There are critical distinctions between plea bargaining as commonly practiced and the situation presently under consideration—distinctions which, in constitutional terms, make a difference. Thus, whatever the merit, if any, of the constitutional objections to plea bargaining generally, those issues are not presently before us.

We are dealing here with the legislative imposition of a markedly more severe penalty if a defendant asserts his right to a jury trial and a concomitant legislative promise of leniency if he pleads guilty. This is very different from the give-and-take negotiation common in plea bargaining between the prosecution and defense, which arguably possess relatively equal bargaining power. No such flexibility is built into the capital penalty scheme where the government's harsh terms with respect to punishment are stated in unalterable form.

Furthermore, the legislatively ordained penalty scheme may affect any defendant, even one with respect to whom plea bargaining is wholly inappropriate because his guilt is uncertain. Thus the penalty scheme presents a clear danger that the innocent, or those not clearly guilty, or those who insist upon their innocence, will be induced nevertheless to plead guilty. This hazard necessitates particularly sensitive scrutiny of the voluntariness of guilty pleas entered under this type of death penalty scheme.

The penalty schemes involved here are also distinguishable from most plea bargaining because they involve the imposition of death—the most severe and awesome penalty known to our law. . . .

Notes and Questions

1. Is there a meaningful distinction between providing an "incentive" to forgo the rights to a trial by jury and to plead not guilty to a criminal charge and "punishing" a defendant for exercising those constitutional rights by "increasing" his or her risk of punishment if he or she insists on pleading not guilty?

2. In *Brady*, the defendant's plea was not deprived of its "intelligent" nature because defense counsel did not anticipate, at the time that the guilty plea was entered, that the law on the books would subsequently be ruled unconstitutional. What, however, of counsel's failure to advise the accused of the present availability of *existing* defenses to the charge, such as the possibility that a confession might be suppressed from evidence? Would such an oversight render the accused's plea of guilty uninformed, or make it "unintelligent" in nature? In *McMann v. Richardson*, 397 U.S. 759, 90 S. Ct. 1441, 25 L. Ed. 2d 763 (1970), the Supreme Court held that so long as counsel's advice was "within the range of competence demanded of attorneys in a criminal case," the intelligence of the guilty plea was not undermined.

3. Legal Research Note. 📖 As we have learned, a defendant's plea of guilty must be made in a "knowing, intelligent, and voluntary" fashion to be accepted as legally valid. Let's suppose that we want further understanding of what it means for conduct of this sort to be "knowing." We might start by looking up *knowing* or *knowingly* in *Black's Law Dictionary*, which should provide a definition.

Law dictionaries are easy to use. You can locate *knowingly* in *Black's Law Dictionary* in the same way that you would look the word up in *Webster's Dictionary* (see Appendix A). *Black's* defines an act as being done "knowingly" "if it is willed, is the product of conscious design, intent or plan that it be done, and is done with awareness of probable consequences."

A more useful tool for this research question is *Words and Phrases*. This collection provides a number of different definitions of legal terms, all of which are extracted from judicial decisions. Since the case decisions from which the defini-

tions are taken are cited, *Words and Phrases*, directs you to relevant judicial authority. For example, for our current research question, you could look up the word *knowing* in *Words and Phrases*. When you do this, you will note that none of the definitions appear to apply to the guilty-plea situation. You will also note, however, that *Words and Phrases* has definitions of numerous phrases that begin with *knowing* and *knowingly*. As you look through this list, you will find several definitions presented for the relevant phrase "knowing and intelligent." In looking at these definitions, we note that the phrase was defined in the context of a guilty-plea proceeding by the United States Court of Appeals for the Fifth Circuit in *United States v. Blair*, 470 F.2d 331 (5th Cir. 1972).

To be certain that the case is relevant and stands for the proposition for which it is presented in *Words and Phrases*, we should look it up. To dig deeper into what constitutes a knowing waiver, and to confirm that *Blair* is still good law, we should *Shepardize* this case. Recall that *Shepardizing* lets us see if other, more recently decided cases that may involve the term *knowing* have cited our original case. From *Shepardizing Blair*, we learn (a) that *Blair* is still good law and (b) that it has been cited in dozens of other cases. When we look up the citation 517 F.2d 592, we find that it is cited on page 592 in the 7th Circuit case of *Bachner v. United States*, 517 F.2d 589 (7th Cir. 1975), which deals with whether a plea was entered into knowingly.

Another way to find additional cases is to use the topics and key numbers from the headnotes of *Bachner*. We see that key number 273.1(1) in the topic "Criminal Law" corresponds to the definition of *knowingly*. We now are in a position to use the digests from other jurisdictions to find additional cases that involve the definition of *knowingly* in this context (see Appendix A).

You could repeat this process for the other concepts important to assessing the validity of a guilty plea. For example, let's say that you want to find the definition of *voluntary* as used in the guilty-plea context. You should test your understanding of the legal research process by using

Black's Law Dictionary to find a definition. What does the dictionary report? Can you use *Words and Phrases* to find more definitions and case citations? What is the name of the 1991 case from Mississippi that defines *voluntary*? *Shepardize* this case. Is it still good law? Provide two case citations from *Shepard's*. Finally, use the headnotes from the Mississippi case to identify the topic and key number that you can use to find other cases that define *voluntary*. What are the topic and key number? Now use the *Modern Federal Practice Digest 4th* to locate federal cases digested under that topic and key number that are of interest to your research task. Provide the citation to the 1985 case decided by the 10th Circuit Court of Appeals.

You should refer to Appendix A if you have any questions about the legal reference materials discussed in this exercise or how to use those materials.

BROKEN PROMISES

A plea agreement is somewhat like a contract. Each party gives a benefit to the other party and in return receives a benefit. In the case of plea bargaining, the defendant gives the prosecution a plea of guilty to a charge, and the prosecution gives the defendant items such as a lesser punishment, dismissal of additional charges, or a promise to make a recommendation or refrain from making a recommendation to the judge regarding the sentence to be imposed. What happens if one party performs its end of the bargain, but the other party does not? Consider *Santobello v. New York*.

Santobello v. New York, 404 U.S. 257, 92 S. Ct. 495, 30 L. Ed. 2d 427 (1971)

Mr. Chief Justice BURGER delivered the opinion of the Court. . . .

The facts are not in dispute. The State of New York indicted petitioner in 1969 on two felony counts, Promoting Gambling in the First Degree, and Possession of Gambling Records in the First Degree, N. Y. Penal Law, McKinney's Consol. Laws, c. 40, §§ 225.10, 225.20. Petitioner first entered a plea of not guilty to both counts. After negotiations, the Assistant District Attorney in charge of the case agreed to permit petitioner to plead guilty to a lesser-included offense, Possession of Gambling Records in the Second Degree, N. Y. Penal Law § 225.15, conviction of which would carry a maximum prison sentence of one year. The prosecutor agreed to make no recommendation as to the sentence.

On June 16, 1969, petitioner accordingly withdrew his plea of not guilty and entered a plea of guilty to the lesser charge. Petitioner represented to the sentencing judge that the plea was voluntary and that the facts of the case, as described by the Assistant District Attorney, were true. The court accepted the plea and set a date for sentencing. A series of delays followed, owing primarily to the absence of a pre-sentence report, so that by September 23, 1969, petitioner had still not been sentenced. By that date petitioner acquired new defense counsel. . . .

On January 9 petitioner appeared before a different judge, the judge who had presided over the case to this juncture having retired. . . . The court then turned to consideration of the sentence.

At this appearance, another prosecutor had replaced the prosecutor who had negotiated the plea. The new prosecutor recommended the maximum one-year sentence. In making this recommendation, he cited petitioner's criminal record and alleged links with organized crime. Defense counsel immediately objected on the ground that the State had promised petitioner before the plea was entered that there would be no sentence recommendation by the prosecution. He sought to adjourn the sentence hearing in order to have time to prepare proof of the first prosecutor's promise. The second prosecutor, apparently ignorant of his colleague's commitment, argued that there was nothing in the record to support petitioner's claim of a promise, but the State, in subsequent proceedings, has not contested that such a promise was made.

The sentencing judge ended discussion, with the following statement, quoting extensively from the pre-sentence report:

"Mr. Aronstein [Defense Counsel], I am not at all influenced by what the District Attorney says, so that there is no need to adjourn the sentence, and there is no need to have any testimony. It doesn't make a particle of difference what the District Attorney says he will do, or what he doesn't do.

"I have here, Mr. Aronstein, a probation report. I have here a history of a long, long serious criminal record. I have here a picture of the life history of this man. . . ."

The judge then imposed the maximum sentence of one year. . . .

This record represents another example of an unfortunate lapse in orderly prosecutorial procedures, in part, no doubt, because of the enormous increase in the workload of the often understaffed prosecutor's offices. The heavy workload may well explain these episodes, but it does not excuse them. The disposition of criminal charges by agreement between the prosecutor and the accused, sometimes loosely called "plea bargaining," is an essential component of the administration of justice. Properly administered, it is to be encouraged. If every criminal charge were subjected to a full-scale trial, the States and the Federal Government would need to multiply by many times the number of judges and court facilities.

Disposition of charges after plea discussions is not only an essential part of the process but a highly desirable part for many reasons. It leads to prompt and largely final disposition of most criminal cases; it avoids much of the corrosive impact of enforced idleness during pre-trial confinement for those who are denied release pending trial; it protects the public from those ac-cused persons who are prone to continue criminal conduct even while on pretrial release; and, by shortening the time between charge and disposition, it enhances whatever may be the rehabilitative prospects of the guilty when they are ultimately imprisoned.

However, all of these considerations presuppose fairness in securing agreement between an accused and a prosecutor. It is now clear, for example, that the accused pleading guilty must be counseled, absent a waiver. Fed.Rule Crim. Proc. 11, governing pleas in federal courts, now makes clear that the sentencing judge must develop, *on the record*, the factual basis for the plea, as, for example, by having the accused describe the conduct that gave rise to the charge. The plea must, of course, be voluntary and knowing and if it was induced by promises, the essence of those promises must in some way be made known. There is, of course, no absolute right to have a guilty plea accepted. A court may reject a plea in exercise of sound judicial discretion.

This phase of the process of criminal justice, and the adjudicative element inherent in accepting a plea of guilty, must be attended by safeguards to insure the defendant what is reasonably due in the circumstances. Those circumstances will vary, but a constant factor is that when a plea rests in any significant degree on a promise or agreement of the prosecutor, so that it can be said to be part of the inducement or consideration, such promise must be fulfilled.

On this record, petitioner "bargained" and negotiated for a particular plea in order to secure dismissal of more serious charges, but also on condition that no sentence recommendation would be made by the prosecutor. It is now conceded that the promise to abstain from a recommendation was made, and at this stage the prosecution is not in a good position to argue that its inadvertent breach of agreement is immaterial. The staff lawyers in a prosecutor's office have the burden of "letting the left hand know what the right hand is doing" or has done. That the breach of agreement was inadvertent does not lessen its impact.

We need not reach the question whether the sentencing judge would or would not have been influenced had he known all the details of the negotiations for the plea. He stated that the prosecutor's recommendation did not influence him and we have no reason to doubt that. Nevertheless, we conclude that the interests of justice and appropriate recognition of the duties of the prosecution in relation to promises made in the negotiation of pleas of guilty will be best served by remanding the case to the state courts for further consideration. The ultimate relief to which petitioner is entitled we leave to the discretion of the state court, which is in a better position to decide whether the circumstances of this case require only that there be specific performance of the agreement on the plea, in which case petitioner should be resentenced by a different judge, or whether, in the view of the state court, the circumstances require granting the relief sought by petitioner, *i.e.*, the opportunity to withdraw his plea of guilty. We emphasize that this is in no sense to question the fairness of the sentencing judge; the fault here rests on the prosecutor, not on the sentencing judge.

The judgment is vacated and the case is remanded for reconsideration not inconsistent with this opinion.

Mr. Justice DOUGLAS, concurring.

I join the opinion of the Court and add only a word. I agree both with THE CHIEF JUSTICE and with Mr. Justice MARSHALL that New York did not keep its "plea bargain" with petitioner and that it is no excuse for the default merely because a member of the prosecutor's staff who was not a party to the "plea bargain" was in charge of the case when it came before the New York court. The staff of the prosecution is a unit and each member must be presumed to know the commitments made by any other member. If responsibility could be evaded that way, the prosecution would have designed another deceptive "contrivance." . . .

However important plea bargaining may be in the administration of criminal justice, our opinions have established that a guilty plea is a serious and sobering occasion inasmuch as it constitutes a waiver of the fundamental rights to a jury trial, Duncan v. Louisiana, 391 U.S. 145, 88 S.Ct. 1444, 20 L.Ed.2d 491 [(1968)], to confront one's accusers, Pointer v. Texas, 380 U.S. 400, 85 S.Ct. 1065, 13 L.Ed.2d 923 [(1965)], to present witnesses in one's defense, Washington v. Texas, 388 U.S. 14, 87 S.Ct. 1920, 18 L.Ed.2d 1019 [(1967)], to remain silent, Malloy v. Hogan, 378 U.S. 1, 84 S.Ct. 1489, 12 L.Ed.2d 653 [(1964)], and to be convicted by proof beyond all reasonable doubt, In re Winship, 397 U.S. 358, 90 S.Ct. 1068, 25 L.Ed.2d 368 [(1970)]. Since Kercheval v. United States, 274 U.S. 220, 47 S.Ct. 582, 71 L.Ed. 1009 [(1927)], this Court has recognized that "unfairly obtained" guilty pleas in the federal courts ought to be vacated. . . .

Mr. Justice MARSHALL, with whom Mr. Justice BRENNAN and Mr. Justice STEWART join, concurring in part and dissenting in part.

I agree with much of the majority's opinion, but conclude that petitioner must be permitted to withdraw his guilty plea. This is the relief petitioner requested, and, on the facts set out by the majority, it is a form of relief to which he is entitled. . . .

Here, petitioner never claimed any automatic right to withdraw a guilty plea before sentencing. Rather, he tendered a specific reason why, in his case, the plea should be vacated. His reason was that the prosecutor had broken a promise made in return for the agreement to plead guilty. When a prosecutor breaks the bargain, he undercuts the basis for the waiver of constitutional rights implicit in the plea. This, it seems to me, provides the defendant ample justification for rescinding the plea. . . .

Notes and Questions

1. Although the Court was unanimous in agreeing that the plea bargain in *Santobello* was broken, there was disagreement about what the proper remedy should be. What possible remedies are there, and what did the Court choose? Do you think this remedy is fair?

2. What remedy should be available to the prosecution if a defendant fails to fulfill promises he or she made as part of a plea agreement? Courts have routinely held that if a defendant conceals relevant facts such as a prior felony conviction, *Hamlin v. Barrett*, 335 So. 2d 898 (Miss. 1976), or fails to perform an act that was required as part of the agreement, the prosecution is relieved of its duty to fulfill its promises. The classic example is the defendant who enters into a plea agreement but before sentencing commits another offense or performs some act specifically prohibited by the agreement. In such a case, the prosecution is free to opt out of the plea bargain.

This point was taken to an extreme by the Supreme Court in the case of *Ricketts v. Adamson*, 483 U.S. 1, 107 S. Ct. 2680, 97 L. Ed. 2d 1 (1987). Adamson was charged with first-degree murder, a crime punishable by death. In exchange for providing testimony against his accomplices, Adamson was offered the opportunity to plead guilty to second-degree murder and receive a sentence of imprisonment. The agreement expressly provided that if Adamson refused to testify, the agreement would be considered null and void, and the original charges would be reinstated. The parties entered into the plea agreement, and Adamson was sentenced to prison. He thereafter testified at the trial of his accomplices, who were subsequently convicted of first-degree murder. Those convictions, however, were reversed and the cases remanded to the Superior Court for retrial. Adamson refused to testify a second time on the ground that he had already fulfilled his obligation under the agreement. The prosecutor disagreed, claimed that Adamson violated the agreement, and reinstated the first-degree murder charge. Adamson was tried on this charge, convicted, and sentenced to death. The Supreme Court held that Adamson did in fact breach the plea agreement and that the state had a right to revoke it and reinstate the original charge. Adamson's death sentence later was vacated on other grounds.

3. Should either party be allowed to withdraw from a plea agreement up to the time the court accepts the plea and imposes sentence, or should the agreement be considered final and irrevocable once the parties enter into their agreement? Would the defendant or prosecution suffer prejudice if the agreement could be called off by either side? *See Mabry v. Johnson*, 467 U.S. 504, 104 S. Ct. 2543, 81 L. Ed. 2d 437 (1984).

THE SCOPE OF PROSECUTORIAL DISCRETION IN PLEA BARGAINING

With the advent of mandatory sentencing schemes, a repeat offender charged with committing a new crime may face substantial prison time if convicted, even if the new charge involves a relatively minor offense. For example, in *Rummel v. Estelle*, 445 U.S. 263, 100 S. Ct. 1133, 63 L. Ed. 2d 382 (1980), the defendant was sentenced to life in prison following conviction for a third nonviolent property crime under Texas's recidivist statute. Rummel's three felony convictions involved the crimes of credit card fraud, passing a forged check, and obtaining money by false pretenses; the total property value of the crimes was approximately $230. Defendants such as Rummel are often faced with the choice of receiving a life sentence if convicted under habitual offender charges at trial or a much shorter sentence if convicted via a plea agreement. Is it fair for the prosecutor to place a defendant in the position of having to risk life imprisonment if he or she refuses to enter into a plea agreement and instead exercises his or her constitutional right to a trial by a jury? This issue was addressed in *Bordenkircher v. Hayes*. (This case is reproduced in Chapter 7 at pp. 507–511.)

Notes and Questions

1. Was the prosecutor in *Bordenkircher v. Hayes* being vindictive? Does the majority opinion appear to suggest any limits on the prosecutor's "bargaining" tactics in this context?

2. Although *Bordenkircher v. Hayes* grants the prosecutor broad discretion in plea bargaining, this discretion is not limitless. In *Blackledge v. Perry*, 417 U.S. 21, 94 S. Ct. 2098, 40 L. Ed. 2d 628 (1974), cited by the dissent in *Bordenkircher v. Hayes*, the defendant was charged with and convicted of a misdemeanor following a trial before a judge in a North Carolina district court. He thereafter exercised his statutory right to a trial *de novo* before a jury in Superior Court. Prior to the new trial, the prosecutor charged the defendant with a felony, on the basis of the same operative facts. The Supreme Court held that the prosecutor's elevating the original charge from a misdemeanor to a felony violated the defendant's due-process rights. The justices ruled that the prosecutor could not get even with the defendant for exercising his right to a trial *de novo*.

3. Is *Perry* similar to *Bordenkircher v. Hayes*? Why or why not? Why does the Court reach different results in the two cases?

4. In *North Carolina v. Pearce*, 395 U.S. 711, 89 S. Ct. 2072, 23 L. Ed. 2d 656 (1969), the Supreme Court held that a defendant who successfully appeals or collaterally attacks his or her conviction and is retried and reconvicted may not be given a greater sentence than was originally imposed absent "identifiable conduct on the part of the defendant occurring after the time of the original sentencing proceeding." *Id* at 726, 89 S. Ct. at 2081. Does this ruling offer support for the dissent's position in *Bordenkircher v. Hayes*, or are the cases distinguishable?

5. Consider the hypothetical posed below by Kipnis.

Kipnis, "Plea Bargaining: A Critic's Rejoinder," 13 *Law & Society Rev.* 555 (1979)

[O]ur [legal] system can best be understood as an institutionalization of two principles. The first is that those (and only those) individuals who are clearly guilty of serious specified wrongdoing deserve an officially administered punishment proportional to their wrongdoing. Justice in punishment is realized when the guilty person receives neither more nor less punishment than is deserved. . . .

Those taking advantage of plea bargains would have these sentences discounted in some way. Obviously, either those pleading guilty have committed their crimes or they have not. If they have, they receive less than the punishment they deserve—an injustice. If they have not, they receive more than the punishment they deserve—another injustice. Under plea bargaining, it will *never* be reasonable to believe that those convicted receive the punishment they deserve. This systematic misapplication of pun-

ishment, this structural injustice, is what discredits the legitimacy of plea bargaining.

Consider another familiar context in which allocations are supposed to be made in accordance with desert: grading in an academic context. A student has turned in a term paper. The instructor, glancing at it, says that it probably deserves a C but if the student were to waive his right to a careful reading and a conscientious critique, the instructor would agree to give the student a B. The grade-point average being more important to the student than either education or "justice in grading," the student accepts the B and the instructor gets a reduced workload.

The same considerations that establish the illegitimacy of the "grade bargain" in the educational system confirm the impropriety of the plea bargain in the criminal justice system. Bargains are out of place in contexts where persons are to receive what they deserve. Our courtrooms, like our classrooms, should be such contexts. It is this objection to plea bargaining that must be central; not that it cannot be justified by any of the rationales of punishment (although I believe it cannot), but that it flies in the face of the very raison d'etre of the criminal justice system itself.

* * *

Source: Reprinted with permission from Kipnis, Plea Bargaining: A Critic's Rejoinder, *Law and Society Review,* Vol. 13, p. 555, © 1979.

You may or may not agree that the student's "grade bargaining" with the busy professor is analogous to the criminal defendant's plea bargaining with the prosecutor prior to the entry of a guilty plea in a court of law. If you can conceive of yourself in such a situation, you may want to take a further step and imagine that a right of review of this process exists. Your professor has told you, however, that if you seek such a review, your paper will receive a *very* critical reading and that he or she would not be surprised if in fact it was a D or even an F paper upon closer scrutiny. Are you now in a situation that is closer to *North Carolina v. Pearce* and *Blackledge v. Perry*, where there has been an apparent or actual threat of vindictiveness in the event that you exercise your right of review? Or would your professor's statements and anticipated actions be permissible under the principles governing *Bordenkircher v. Hayes*?

CONCLUSION

While trials receive a great deal of attention, only a very small percentage of cases are decided by trial. In fact, over 90 percent of criminal convictions are obtained through plea bargains. This is because both the prosecution and the defendant have a lot to lose by going to trial. The prosecution may lose a case entirely at trial. Additionally, trials are very expensive and time consuming. By dispensing with cases through plea bargains, the prosecution is able to allocate its resources more effectively than if every case went to trial. The defendant's incentive to enter a plea bargain is to cut his or her losses. By pleading guilty, a defendant may gain one or more of the following: (1) the dismissal of some charges, (2) an agreement as to sentence, and/or (3) a recommendation to the trial judge for a particular sentence. For these reasons, it is often quite advantageous for a defendant to enter into a plea bargain.

Before a defendant can plead guilty, however, the trial court has a duty to determine that he or she is entering into the guilty plea knowingly, voluntarily, and intelligently. If the court does not make these findings, the plea agreement may be voided by the defendant. Most courts use checklists or forms when they determine that the plea was knowingly and voluntarily entered into. While this determination takes several minutes to do, it is an important part of the plea process. Additionally, when compared to the trial process and all of its requirements, most if not all courts would agree that it is of minimal inconvenience.

CHAPTER 10

The Adjudication Process

Once an individual has been formally charged with a crime, it is still necessary to determine whether he or she in fact committed the crime. The formal charging of a defendant is merely an accusation. Unless the accusation is dismissed, the accused is entitled to a formal determination of his or her guilt or innocence[1] regarding the charges.

In examining the criminal justice system funnel (see Figure 10–1), we note that only a small percentage of individuals arrested are formally charged with a crime, that the vast majority of individuals charged with crimes have their cases resolved by plea bargaining and guilty pleas, and that only a tiny fraction of people arrested for crimes ever have their cases decided at a trial. While only a comparatively small number of cases ever result in a trial, these cases are essential to the criminal justice system goals of safeguarding the innocent from conviction and ensuring that the prosecution acts fairly whenever it attempts to prove that an accused offender is in fact guilty. With the other means of arriving at a conviction, the guilty plea, the defendant admits to committing the crime and thereby waives several important constitutional

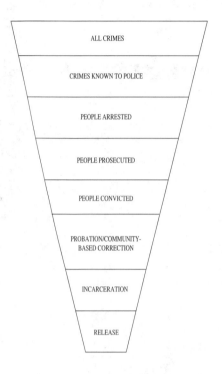

ALL CRIMES

CRIMES KNOWN TO POLICE

PEOPLE ARRESTED

PEOPLE PROSECUTED

PEOPLE CONVICTED

PROBATION/COMMUNITY-BASED CORRECTION

INCARCERATION

RELEASE

Figure 10–1 Criminal Justice Funnel

protections related to the proof of his or her guilt. A criminal trial, on the other hand, is triggered by the defendant's plea of not guilty, or denial that he or she committed the alleged crime. As a result of this plea, the government must prove, within the strictures and confines of the Constitution and Bill of Rights, that the defendant is guilty of the crime.

The trial of individuals accused of crimes dates back thousands of years. Although trials took many different forms throughout history, they served the same essential function: to resolve disputes between two or more parties. In Biblical times, it was not uncommon to appeal to divine intervention to resolve controversies through trial by ordeal. During medieval times, men would joust and duel to determine which party to a dispute was in the right. In colonial America, people suspected of being witches were weighted with rocks and thrown into water to see whether they floated, thus evidencing their innocence (of lack thereof).

The modern trial system, as we conceive it, has its roots in 13th-century England. In 1215,

the Magna Carta was signed. Article 39 of the Magna Carta stated, "No freeman shall be taken or imprisoned . . . nor will we go upon him nor will we send upon him, unless by the lawful judgement of his peers, or by the law of the land." While the judgment of one's peers guaranteed by the Magna Carta had a much different meaning in 1215 than it does now, this right evolved to become one of the cornerstones of the English justice system.

When the American colonies were settled, the colonists brought the English trial system with them. In the 17th and 18th centuries, colonial charters guaranteed individuals the right to be tried by a jury of their peers. King George's abuse of this right angered the colonists and formed one of the grievances set forth in the Declaration of Independence. At the time of the American revolution, the right to trial by jury was recognized throughout the colonies.

This practice was perpetuated under the U.S. Constitution. At the time of the Constitutional Convention in the 1780s, many Americans remained leery of the power of a centralized government reminiscent of the English monarchy from which they had recently obtained their freedom. A jury of lay citizens, to stand between the government and individuals accused of crime, was one of the bedrock protections guaranteed by the new Constitution. Article III, Section 2, of the U.S. Constitution provided, "The Trial of all Crimes . . . shall be by Jury." When the Sixth Amendment to the Constitution was ratified in 1791, an individual's right to a jury trial in criminal cases was again explicitly recognized, along with other rights considered essential to the trial process:

> In all criminal prosecutions, the accused shall enjoy the right to a speedy and public trial, by an impartial jury of the State and district wherein the crime shall have been committed, . . . to be confronted with the witnesses against him; [and] to have compulsory process for obtaining witnesses in his favor. . . .

The Fifth Amendment recognized other procedural safeguards important to the guilt determination process, including the right against double jeopardy ("nor shall any person be subject for the same offence to be twice put in jeopardy of life and limb"), the right against compelled self-incrimination ("nor shall be compelled in any criminal case to be a witness against himself"), and due-process protections ("nor be deprived of life, liberty, or property, without due process of law"). As we have seen, the Fourteenth Amendment bound the states to observe due process of law and also prohibited the states from denying "to any person within [their] jurisdiction the equal protection of the laws."

In this chapter, we examine several different aspects of the trial process. We begin by considering the right to a "speedy" trial. We next explore the requirement that an individual be "competent" to stand trial for the crime he or she has been accused of committing. The inquiry next shifts to the burden of proof required to convict a defendant of a crime.

Several issues related to trial by jury are then addressed, including whether that right literally attaches "in all criminal prosecutions" or applies only to certain charges, the meaning of the right to an "impartial" jury, the composition and selection of trial juries, and whether criminal trial verdicts must be returned by 12-member unanimous juries. We then switch to consider the accused's testimonial rights at a criminal trial. For example, may the defendant be penalized for not testifying at trial? Conversely, may the defendant be prevented from testifying? The rights of confrontation and cross-examination, including the defendant's

right to be physically present during his or her trial, then are discussed. We conclude by giving brief consideration to double-jeopardy rights.

Like the other constitutional provisions we have considered, the precise scope and meaning of the rights that we examine in this chapter cannot be gleaned from the text of the Sixth, Fifth, and Fourteenth Amendments. We thus consider how the courts have interpreted the basic constitutional protections relevant to the trial of criminal cases.

THE RIGHT TO A SPEEDY TRIAL

One basic principle of the American criminal justice system is that a person is considered innocent until proven guilty. It is therefore logical, if not essential, that a person accused of a crime should have the opportunity to have the cloud of accusation lifted promptly through a timely disposition of his or her case. Based largely on this premise, the Sixth Amendment explicitly guarantees the right to a speedy trial in all criminal prosecutions. While this general maxim is not controversial, it has been difficult if not impossible to quantify what constitutes a denial of a defendant's speedy-trial rights.

For instance, is it unconstitutional for the government to bring a person to trial three years after law enforcement officials uncover evidence of his or her illegal activity? That is the essential question faced by the Supreme Court in *United States v. Marion*. As you read *Marion*, be sure to identify the specific constitutional grounds on which the Court based its decision.

United States v. Marion, 404 U.S. 307, 92 S. Ct. 455, 30 L. Ed. 2d 468 (1971)

Mr. Justice White delivered the opinion of the Court.
[On April 21, 1970, Appellees were indicted on 19 counts of fraud, forgery, and other white-collar crimes associated with their business, Allied Enterprises, Inc. The period covered by the

indictment was March 15, 1965, to February 6, 1967. Appellees filed a motion to dismiss the indictment based on the claim that their rights to a speedy trial and due process under the Sixth and Fifth Amendments were violated by the failure to commence prosecution of the alleged offenses in a timely manner. The trial court dismissed the indictment for lack of speedy prosecution, stating that the defense was "bound to have been seriously prejudiced by the delay of some three years in bringing the prosecution that should have been brought in 1967, or at the very latest early 1968." The government appealed this decision to the United States Supreme Court.]

II

. . . [Appellees] claim that their rights to a speedy trial were violated by the period of approximately three years between the end of the criminal scheme charged and the return of the indictment; it is argued that this delay is so substantial and inherently prejudicial that the Sixth Amendment required the dismissal of the indictment. In our view, however, the Sixth Amendment speedy trial provision has no application until the putative defendant in some way becomes an "accused," an event that occurred in this case only when the appellees were indicted on April 21, 1970.

The Sixth Amendment provides that "[i]n all criminal prosecutions, the accused shall enjoy the right to a speedy and public trial. . . ." On its face, the protection of the Amendment is activated only when a criminal prosecution has begun and extends only to those persons who have been "accused" in the course of that prosecution. These provisions would seem to afford no protection to those not yet accused, nor would they seem to require the Government to discover, investigate, and accuse any person within any particular period of time. The Amendment would appear to guarantee to a criminal defendant that the Government will move with the dispatch that is appropriate to assure him an early and proper disposition of the charges against him. "[T]he essential ingredient is orderly expedition and not mere speed." Smith v. United States, 360 US 1, 10, 79 S Ct 991, 3 L Ed 2d 1041 (1959).

Our attention is called to nothing in the circumstances surrounding the adoption of the Amendment indicating that it does not mean what it appears to say, nor is there more than marginal support for the proposition that, at the time of the adoption of the Amendment, the pre-

vailing rule was that prosecutions would not be permitted if there had been long delay in presenting a charge. The framers could hardly have selected less appropriate language if they had intended the speedy trial provision to protect against pre-accusation delay. No opinions of this Court intimate support for appellees' thesis, and the courts of appeals that have considered the question in constitutional terms have never reversed a conviction or dismissed an indictment solely on the basis of the Sixth Amendment's speedy trial provision where only pre-indictment delay was involved.

Legislative efforts to implement federal and state speedy trial provisions also plainly reveal the view that these guarantees are applicable only after a person has been accused of a crime. The Court has pointed out that "[a]t the common law and in the absence of special statutes of limitations, the mere failure to find an indictment will not operate to discharge the accused from the offense nor will a nolle prosecqui entered by the Government or the failure of the grand jury to indict." United States v. Cadarr, 197 US 475, 478, 25 S Ct 487, 49 L Ed 842 (1905). Since it is "doubtless true that in some cases the power of the Government has been abused and charges have been kept hanging over the heads of citizens, and they have been committed for unreasonable periods, resulting in hardship," the Court noted that many States "[w]ith a view to preventing such wrong to the citizen . . . [and] in aid of the constitutional provisions, National and state, intended to secure to the accused a speedy trial" had passed statutes limiting the time within which such trial must occur after charge or indictment. Characteristically, these statutes to which the Court referred are triggered only when a citizen is charged or accused. The statutes vary greatly in substance, structure, and interpretation, but a common denominator is that "[i]n no event . . . [does] the right to speedy trial arise before there is some charge or arrest, even though the prosecuting authorities had knowledge of the offense long before this." Note, The Right to a Speedy Trial, 57 Col L Rev 846, 848 (1957).

No federal statute of general applicability has been enacted by Congress to enforce the speedy trial provision of the Sixth Amendment, but Federal Rule of Criminal Procedure 48(b), which has the force of law, authorizes dismissal of an indictment, information, or complaint "[i]f there is unnecessary delay in presenting the charge to a grand jury or in filing an information against a defendant who has been held to answer to the district court, or if there is unnecessary delay in bringing a defendant to trial. . . ." The rule clearly is limited to post-arrest situations.

Appellees' position is, therefore, at odds with long-standing legislative and judicial constructions of the speedy trial provisions in both national and state constitutions.

III

It is apparent also that very little support for appellees' position emerges from a consideration of the purposes of the Sixth Amendment's speedy trial provision, a guarantee that this Court has termed "an important safeguard to prevent undue and oppressive incarceration prior to trial, to minimize anxiety and concern accompanying public accusation and to limit the possibilities that long delay will impair the ability of an accused to defend himself." United States v. Ewell, 383 US 116, 120, 86 S Ct 773, 15 L Ed 2d 627 (1966); see also Klopfer v. North Carolina, 386 US 213, 221–226, 87 S Ct 988, 18 L Ed 2d 1 (1967); Dickey v. Florida, 398 US 30, 37–38, 26, 90 S Ct 1564, L Ed 2d 26 (1970). Inordinate delay between arrest, indictment, and trial may impair a defendant's ability to present an effective defense. But the major evils protected against by the speedy trial guarantee exist quite apart from actual or possible prejudice to an accused's defense. To legally arrest and detain, the Government must assert probable cause to believe the arrestee has committed a crime. Arrest is a public act that may seriously interfere with the defendant's liberty, whether he is free on bail or not, and that may disrupt his employment, drain his financial resources, curtail his associations, subject him to public obloquy, and create anxiety in him, his family and his friends. These considerations were substantial underpinnings for the decision in Klopfer v. North Carolina, supra. So viewed, it is readily understandable that it is either a formal indictment or information or else the actual restraints imposed by arrest and holding to answer a criminal charge that engage the particular protections of the speedy trial provisions of the Sixth Amendment.

Invocation of the speedy trial provision thus need not await indictment, information, or other formal charge. But we decline to extend the reach of the amendment to the period prior to arrest. Until this event occurs, a citizen suffers no restraints on his liberty and is not the subject of public accusations: his situation does not compare with that of a defendant who has been arrested and held to answer. Passage of time, whether before or after arrest, may impair memories, cause evidence to be lost, deprive the defendant of witnesses, and otherwise interfere with his ability to defend himself. But this possibility of prejudice at trial is not itself sufficient reason to wrench the Sixth Amendment from its proper context. Possible prejudice is inherent in any delay, however short; it may also weaken the Government's case.

The law has provided other mechanisms to guard against possible as distinguished from actual prejudice resulting from the passage of time between crime and arrest or charge. As we said in United States v. Ewell, [383 U.S. 116, 122, 86 S. Ct. 773, 15 L. Ed. 2d 627 (1966)] "the applicable statute of limitations . . . is . . . the primary guarantee against bringing overly stale criminal charges." Such statutes represent legislative assessments of relative interests of the State and the defendant in administering and receiving justice; they "are made for the repose of society and the protection of those who may [during the limitation] . . . have lost their means of defence." Public Schools v. Walker, 9 Wall 282, 288, 19 L Ed 576, 578 (1870). These statutes provide predictability by specifying a limit beyond which there is an irrebuttable presumption that a defendant's right to a fair trial would be prejudiced. As this Court observed in Toussie v. United States, 397 US 112, 114–115, 90 S Ct 858, 25 L Ed 2d 156 (1970): "The purpose of a statute of limitations is to limit exposure to criminal prosecution to a certain fixed period of time following the occurrence of those acts the legislature has decided to punish by criminal sanctions. Such a limitation is designed to protect individuals from having to defend themselves against charges when the basic facts may have become obscured by the passage of time and to minimize the danger of official punishment because of acts in the far-distant past. Such a time limit may also have the salutary effect of encouraging law enforcement officials promptly to investigate suspected criminal activity." There is thus no need to press the Sixth Amendment into service to guard against the mere possibility that pre-accusation delays will prejudice the defense in a criminal case since statutes of limitation already perform that function.

Since appellees rely only on potential prejudice and the passage of time between the alleged crime and the indictment, see Part IV, infra, we perhaps need go no further to dispose of this case, for the indictment was the first official act designating appellees as accused individuals and that event occurred within the statute of limitations. Nevertheless, since a criminal trial is the likely consequence of our judgment and since appellees may claim actual prejudice to their defense, it is appropriate to note here that the statute of limitations does not fully define the appellees' rights with respect to the events occurring prior to indictment. Thus, the Government concedes that the Due Process Clause of the Fifth Amendment would require dismissal of the indictment if it were shown at trial that the pre-indictment delay in this case caused substantial prejudice to appellees' rights to a fair trial and that the delay was an intentional device to gain tactical advantage over the accused. However, we need not, and could not now, determine when and in what circumstances actual prejudice resulting from preaccusation delays requires the dismissal of the prosecution. Actual prejudice to the defense of a criminal case may result from the shortest and most necessary delay; and no one suggests that every delay-caused detriment to a defendant's case should abort a criminal prosecution. To accom-

modate the sound administration of justice to the rights of the defendant to a fair trial will necessarily involve a delicate judgment based on the circumstances in each case. It would be unwise at this juncture to attempt to forecast our decision in such cases.

IV

In the case before us, neither appellee was arrested, charged, or otherwise subjected to formal restraint prior to indictment. It was this event, therefore, that transformed the appellees into "accused" defendants who are subject to the speedy trial protections of the Sixth Amendment.

The 38-month delay between the end of the scheme charged in the indictment and the date the defendants were indicted did not extend beyond the period of the applicable statute of limitations here. Appellees have not, of course, been able to claim undue delay pending trial, since the indictment was brought on April 21, 1970, and dismissed on June 8, 1970. Nor have appellees adequately demonstrated that the pre-indictment delay by the Government violated the Due Process Clause. No actual prejudice to the conduct of the defense is alleged or proved, and there is no showing that the Government intentionally delayed to gain some tactical advantage over appellees or to harass them. Appellees rely solely on the real possibility of prejudice inherent in any extended delay: that memories will dim, witnesses become inaccessible, and evidence be lost. In light of the applicable statute of limitations, however, these possibilities are not in themselves enough to demonstrate that appellees cannot receive a fair trial and to therefore justify the dismissal of the indictment. Events of the trial may demonstrate actual prejudice, but at the present time appellees' due process claims are speculative and premature.

Reversed.

Notes and Questions

1. Before a due-process violation can be established under *Marion*, a defendant must demonstrate either that the government engaged in deliberate inaction or that he or she

suffered *actual* prejudice. Does this place an unreasonable burden on a defendant? How could a defendant ever prove deliberate inaction designed to provide a tactical advantage on the part of the government?

2. Assume that in *Marion* one of the defendants signed an affidavit stating, "I wanted to testify in my trial, but I did not because I forgot the specific details of the events involved in the case due to the lengthy delay between their occurrence and the trial." Does this demonstrate actual prejudice? Why or why not? What policy implications, if any, would your decision have for prosecutors?

3. In *State v. Gray*, 917 S.W.2d 668 (Tenn. 1996), the defendant was charged with carnal knowledge of a female under the age of 12. The criminal act was alleged to have occurred 42 years before the indictment. The trial court dismissed the indictment based on the prejudice incurred by Gray resulting from the delay. The Tennessee Court of Criminal Appeal reversed the trial court and reinstated the indictment. The Court reasoned that since the preindictment delay was the result of the victim's not coming forward with her allegations until over 40 years after the incident, the delay was not caused by the government, and that the State therefore did not violate Gray's rights under the framework set forth in *Marion*.

The Tennessee Supreme Court reversed.

Having reviewed the existing law on the issue, we observe that the [*Marion*] approach to pre-accusatorial delay is, in application, extremely one-sided. It places a daunting, almost insurmountable, burden on the accused by requiring a demonstration not only that the delay has caused prejudice but also that the State orchestrated the delay in order to obtain a tactical advantage. Thus, under the facts before us, application of so stringent a standard would force a result we would consider unconstitutional, unwarranted, and unfair. To accomplish justice while preserving Gray's right to a fair trial requires, in our view, a less stringent standard.

Today we articulate a standard by which to evaluate pre-accusatorial delay and hold that an untimely prosecution may be subject to dismissal upon Fifth and Fourteenth Amendment due process grounds and under Article I, §§ 8 and 9 of the Tennessee Constitution even though in the interim the defendant was neither formally accused, restrained, nor incarcerated for the offense. In determining whether [preindictment] delay violates due process, the trial court must consider the length of the delay, the reason for the delay, and the degree of prejudice, if any, to the accused.

We now apply the standard we have articulated to the facts and circumstances here present to determine whether the prosecution of Gray shall proceed. We hold that it shall not. We find that the length of the delay was profoundly excessive, and no reasonable justification for such delay has been demonstrated. Gray has made a *prima facie* showing of prejudice. As the trial court correctly found, the record reveals at least three instances of prejudice:

. . . (i) the lapse of time has diminished the victim's memory; (2) witnesses thought to be material are now unavailable; and (3) the victim cannot specifically date the incident, thereby requiring Gray to account for his whereabouts and his conduct during a six-month period forty-two years past. *Id.*

The standard applied by the Tennessee court is similar to those used in other states for examining instances of preindictment delay. See *People v. Morris*, 46 Cal. 3d 1, 756 P.2d 843, 249 Cal. Rptr. 119 (1988); *State v. Chavez*, 111 Wash. 2d 548, 761 P.2d 607 (1988). How does the Tennessee standard differ from that applied in *Marion*? Under the *Marion* test, how would *Gray* be decided?

Marion held that prearrest/preindictment delay does not violate a defendant's Sixth Amendment right to a speedy trial. What if the delay is (a) after the defendant is indicted and (b) deliberately caused by the government in an effort to gain a tactical advantage? Consider this issue as you read *Barker v. Wingo.*

Barker v. Wingo, 407 U.S. 514, 92 S. Ct. 2182, 33 L. Ed. 2d 101 (1972)

Mr. Justice **Powell** delivered the opinion of the Court. . . .

I

On July 20, 1958, in Christian County, Kentucky, an elderly couple was beaten to death by intruders wielding an iron tire tool. Two suspects, Silas Manning and Willie Barker, the petitioner, were arrested shortly thereafter. The grand jury indicted them on September 15. Counsel was appointed on September 17, and Barker's trial was set for October 21. The Commonwealth had a stronger case against Manning, and it believed that Barker could not be convicted unless Manning testified against him. Manning was naturally unwilling to incriminate himself. Accordingly, on October 23, the day Silas Manning was brought to trial, the Commonwealth sought and obtained the first of what was to be a series of 16 continuances of Barker's trial. Barker made no objection. By first convicting Manning, the Commonwealth would remove possible problems of self-incrimination and would be able to assure his testimony against Barker.

The Commonwealth encountered more than a few difficulties in its prosecution of Manning. The first trial ended in a hung jury. A second trial resulted in a conviction, but the Kentucky Court of Appeals reversed because of the admission of evidence obtained by an illegal search. Manning v. Commonwealth, 328 SW2d 421 (Ky 1959). At his third trial, Manning was again convicted, and the Court of Appeals again reversed because the trial court had not granted a change of venue. Manning v. Commonwealth, 346 SW2d 755 (Ky 1961). A fourth trial resulted in a hung jury. Finally, after five trials, Manning was convicted, in March 1962, of murdering one victim, and after a sixth trial, in December 1962, he was convicted of murdering the other. . . .

[Barker's trial was continued 14 times while the State was securing its conviction of Manning. Subsequent to the final conviction of Manning, Barker's trial was continued several times due to illness of the chief investigating officer in the case. These continuances were made over Barker's objections. Barker's trial began on October 9, 1963. With Manning testifying as the chief prosecution witness, Barker was convicted and given a life sentence.]

II

The right to a speedy trial is generically different from any of the other rights enshrined in the Constitution for the protection of the accused. In addition to the general concern that all accused persons be treated according to decent and fair procedures, there is a societal interest in providing a speedy trial which exists separate from, and at times in opposition to, the interests of the accused. The inability of courts to provide a prompt trial has contributed to a large backlog of cases in urban courts which, among other things, enables defendants to negotiate more effectively for pleas of guilty to lesser offenses and otherwise manipulate the system. In addition, persons released on bond for lengthy periods awaiting trial have an opportunity to commit other crimes. Moreover, the longer an accused is free awaiting trial, the more tempting becomes his opportunity to jump bail and escape. Finally, delay between arrest and punishment may have a detrimental effect on rehabilitation.

If an accused cannot make bail, he is generally confined, as was Barker for 10 months, in a local jail. This contributes to the overcrowding and generally deplorable state of those institutions. Lengthy exposure to these conditions "has a destructive effect on human character and makes the rehabilitation of the individual offender much more difficult." At times the result may even be violent rioting. Finally, lengthy pretrial detention is costly. The cost of maintaining a prisoner in jail varies from $3 to $9 per day, and this amounts to millions across the Nation. In addition, society loses wages which might have been earned, and it must often support families of incarcerated breadwinners.

A second difference between the right to speedy trial and the accused's other constitutional rights is that deprivation of the right may work to the accused's advantage. Delay is not an uncommon defense tactic. As the time between the commission of the crime and trial lengthens, witnesses may become unavailable or their memories may fade. If the witnesses support the prosecution, its case will be weakened, sometimes seriously so. And it is the prosecution which carries the burden of proof. Thus, unlike the right to counsel or the right to be free from compelled self-incrimination, deprivation of the right to speedy trial does not per se prejudice the accused's ability to defend himself.

Finally, and perhaps most importantly, the right to speedy trial is a more vague concept than other procedural rights. It is, for example, impossible to determine with precision when the right has been denied. We cannot definitely say how long is too long in a system where justice is supposed to be swift but deliberate. As a consequence, there is no fixed point in the criminal process when the State can put the defendant to the choice of either exercising or waiving the right to a speedy trial. . . .

The amorphous quality of the right also leads to the unsatisfactorily severe remedy of dismissal of the indictment when the right has been deprived. This is indeed a serious consequence because it means that a defendant who may be guilty of a serious crime will go free, without having been tried. Such a remedy is more serious than an exclusionary rule or a reversal for a new trial, but it is the only possible remedy.

III

Perhaps because the speedy trial right is so slippery, two rigid approaches are urged upon us as ways of eliminating some of the uncertainty which courts experience in protecting the right. The first suggestion is that we hold that the Constitution requires a criminal defendant to be offered a trial within a specified time period. The result of such a ruling would have the virtue of clarifying when the right is infringed and of simplifying courts' application of it. . . .

But such a result would require this Court to engage in legislative or rulemaking activity, rather than in the adjudicative process to which we should confine our efforts. We do not establish procedural rules for the States, except when mandated by the Constitution. We find no constitutional basis for holding that the speedy trial right can be quantified into a specified number of days or months. The States, of course, are free to prescribe a reasonable period consistent with constitutional standards but our approach must be less precise.

The second suggested alternative would restrict consideration of the right to those cases in which the accused has demanded a speedy trial. The demand-waiver doctrine provides that a defendant waives any consideration of his right to speedy trial for any period prior to which he has not demanded a trial. Under this rigid approach, a prior demand is a necessary condition to the consideration of the speedy trial right. This essentially was the approach the Sixth Circuit took below.

Such an approach, by presuming waiver of a fundamental right from inaction, is inconsistent with this Court's pronouncements on waiver of constitutional rights. The Court has defined waiver as "an intentional relinquishment or abandonment of a known right or privilege." Johnson v. Zerbst, 304 US 458, 464, 58 S Ct 1019, 82 L Ed 1461 (1938). Courts should "indulge every reasonable presumption against waiver," Aetna Ins. Co. v. Kennedy, 301 US 389, 393, 57 S Ct 809, 81 L Ed 1177 (1937), and they should "not presume acquiescence in the loss of fundamental rights." Ohio Bell Tel. Co. v. Public Utilities

Comm'n, 301 US 292, 307, 57 S Ct 724, 81 L Ed 1093 (1937).

The nature of the speedy trial right does make it impossible to pinpoint a precise time in the process when the right must be asserted or waived, but that fact does not argue for placing the burden of protecting the right solely on defendants. A defendant has no duty to bring himself to trial; the State has that duty as well as the duty of insuring that the trial is consistent with due process. Moreover, for the reasons earlier expressed, society has a particular interest in bringing swift prosecutions, and society's representatives are the ones who should protect that interest.

It is also noteworthy that such a rigid view of the demand-waiver rule places defense counsel in an awkward position. Unless he demands a trial early and often, he is in danger of frustrating his client's right. If counsel is willing to tolerate some delay because he finds it reasonable and helpful in preparing his own case, he may be unable to obtain a speedy trial for his client at the end of that time. Since under the demand-waiver rule no time runs until the demand is made, the government will have whatever time is otherwise reasonable to bring the defendant to trial after a demand has been made. Thus, if the first demand is made three months after arrest in a jurisdiction which prescribes a six-month rule, the prosecution will have a total of nine months—which may be wholly unreasonable under the circumstances. The result in practice is likely to be either an automatic, pro forma demand made immediately after appointment of counsel or delays which, but for the demand-waiver rule, would not be tolerated. Such a result is not consistent with the interests of defendants, society, or the Constitution.

We reject, therefore, the rule that a defendant who fails to demand a speedy trial forever waives his right. We think the better rule is that the defendant's assertion of or failure to assert his right to a speedy trial is one of the factors to be considered in an inquiry into the deprivation of the right. Such a formulation avoids the rigidities of the demand-waiver rule and the resulting possible unfairness in its application. It allows the trial court to exercise a judicial discretion based on the circumstances, including due consideration of any applicable formal procedural rule. It would permit, for example, a court to attach a different weight to a situation in which the defendant knowingly fails to object from a situation in which his attorney acquiesces in long delay without adequately informing his client, or from a situation in which no counsel is appointed. It would also allow a court to weigh the frequency and force of the objections as opposed to attaching significant weight to a purely pro forma objection. . . .

We, therefore, reject both of the inflexible approaches—the fixed-time period because it goes further than the Constitution requires; the demand-waiver rule because it is insensitive to a right which we have deemed fundamental. The approach we accept is a balancing test, in which the conduct of both the prosecution and the defendant are weighed.

IV

A balancing test necessarily compels courts to approach speedy trial cases on an ad hoc basis. We can do little more than identify some of the factors which courts should assess in determining whether a particular defendant has been deprived of his right. Though some might express them in different ways, we identify four such factors: Length of delay, the reason for the delay, the defendant's assertion of his right, and prejudice to the defendant.

The length of the delay is to some extent a triggering mechanism. Until there is some delay which is presumptively prejudicial, there is no necessity for inquiry into the other factors that go into the balance. Nevertheless, because of the imprecision of the right to speedy trial, the length of delay that will provoke such an inquiry is necessarily dependent upon the peculiar circumstances of the case. To take but one example, the delay that can be tolerated for an ordinary street crime is considerably less than for a serious, complex conspiracy charge.

Closely related to length of delay is the reason the government assigns to justify the delay. Here, too, different weights should be assigned to different reasons. A deliberate attempt to delay the trial in order to hamper the defense should be weighed heavily against the government. A more neutral reason such as negligence or overcrowded courts should be weighed less heavily but nevertheless should be considered since the ultimate responsibility for such circumstances must rest with government rather than with the defendant. Finally, a valid reason, such as a missing witness, should serve to justify appropriate delay.

We have already discussed the third factor, the defendant's responsibility to assert his right. Whether and how a defendant asserts his right is closely related to the other factors we have mentioned. The strength of his efforts will be affected by the length of the delay, to some extent by the reason for the delay, and most particularly by the personal prejudice, which is not always readily identifiable, that he experiences. The more serious the deprivation, the more likely a defendant is to complain. The defendant's assertion of his speedy trial right, then, is entitled to strong evidentiary weight in determining whether the defendant is being deprived of the right. We emphasize that failure to assert the right will make it difficult for a defendant to prove that he was denied a speedy trial.

A fourth factor is prejudice to the defendant. Prejudice, of course, should be assessed in the light of the interests of defendants which the speedy trial right was designed to protect. This Court has identified three such interests: (i) to prevent oppressive pretrial incarceration; (ii) to minimize anxiety and concern of the accused; and (iii) to limit the possibility that the defense will be impaired. Of these, the most serious is the last, because the inability of a defendant adequately to prepare his case skews the fairness of the entire system. If witnesses die or disappear during a delay, the prejudice is obvious. There is also prejudice if defense witnesses are unable to recall accurately events of the distant past. Loss of memory, however, is not always reflected in the record because what has been forgotten can rarely be shown. . . .

We regard none of the four factors identified above as either a necessary or sufficient condition to the finding of a deprivation of the right of speedy trial. Rather, they are related factors and must be considered together with such other circumstances as may be relevant. In sum, these factors have no talismanic qualities; courts must still engage in a difficult and sensitive balancing process. But, because we are dealing with a fundamental right of the accused, this process must be carried out with full recognition that the accused's interest in a speedy trial is specifically affirmed in the Constitution.

V

The difficulty of the task of balancing these factors is illustrated by this case, which we consider to be close. It is clear that the length of delay between arrest and trial—well over five years—was extraordinary. Only seven months of that period can be attributed to a strong excuse, the illness of the ex-sheriff who was in charge of the investigation. Perhaps some delay would have been permissible under ordinary circumstances, so that Manning could be utilized as a witness in Barker's trial, but more than four years was too long a period, particularly since a good part of that period was attributable to the Commonwealth's failure or inability to try Manning under circumstances that comported with due process.

Two counterbalancing factors, however, outweigh these deficiencies. The first is that prejudice was minimal. Of course, Barker was prejudiced to some extent by living for over four years under a cloud of suspicion and anxiety. Moreover, although he was released on bond for most of the period, he did spend 10 months in jail before trial. But there is no claim that any of Barker's witnesses died or otherwise became unavailable owing to the delay. The trial transcript indicates only two very minor lapses of memory—one on the part of a prosecution witness—which were in no way significant to the outcome.

More important than the absence of serious prejudice, is the fact that Barker did not want a speedy trial. Counsel was appointed for Barker immediately after his indictment and represented him throughout the period. No question is raised as to the competency of such counsel. Despite the fact that counsel had notice of the motions for continuances, the record shows no action whatever taken between October 21, 1958, and February 12, 1962, that could be construed as the assertion of the speedy trial right. On the latter date, in response to another motion for continuance, Barker moved to dismiss the indictment. The record does not show on what ground this motion was based, although it is clear that no alternative motion was made for an immediate trial. Instead the record strongly suggests that while he hoped to take advantage of the delay in which he had acquiesced, and thereby obtain a dismissal of the charges, he definitely did not want to be tried. Counsel conceded as much at oral argument:

"Your honor, I would concede that Willie Mae Barker probably—I don't know this for a fact—probably did not want to be tried. I don't think any man wants to be tried. And I don't consider this a liability on his behalf. I don't blame him." Tr. of Oral Arg. 39.

The probable reason for Barker's attitude was that he was gambling on Manning's acquittal. The evidence was not very strong against Manning, as the reversals and hung juries suggest, and Barker undoubtedly thought that if Manning were acquitted, he would never be tried. Counsel also conceded this:

"Now, it's true that the reason for this delay was the Commonwealth of Kentucky's desire to secure the testimony of the accomplice, Silas Manning. And it's true that if Silas Manning were never convicted, Willie Mae Barker would never have been convicted. We concede this." Id., at 15.

That Barker was gambling on Manning's acquittal is also suggested by his failure, following the pro forma motion to dismiss filed in February 1962, to object to the Commonwealth's next two motions for continuances. Indeed, it was not until March 1963, after Manning's convictions were final, that Barker, having lost his gamble, began to object to further continuances. At that time, the Commonwealth's excuse was the illness of the ex-sheriff, which Barker has conceded justified the further delay.

We do not hold that there may never be a situation in which an indictment may be dismissed on speedy trial grounds where the defendant has failed to object to continuances. There may be a situation in which the defendant was represented by incompetent counsel, was severely prejudiced, or even cases in which the continuances were granted ex parte. But barring extraordinary circumstances, we would be reluctant indeed to rule that a defendant was denied this constitutional rule on a record that strongly indicates, as does this one, that the defendant did not want a speedy trial. We hold, therefore, that Barker was not deprived of his due process right to a speedy trial.

The judgment of the Court of Appeals is Affirmed.

Notes and Questions

1. How does the *Barker* test differ from the test used in *Marion*? Which test do you consider preferable?

2. What rights are at issue in *Barker*? How is *Marion* different?

3. Do the four factors considered in determining whether a speedy-trial violation occurred seem reasonable? Which factor, if any, do you think should be given the greatest weight?

4. If a defendant's right to a speedy trial is violated, what remedy should he or she have?

5. The *Barker* Court emphasized the lack of prejudice against the defendant caused by the delay. The Court went so far as to imply that Barker accepted and even wanted the delay in the hope that it would weaken the prosecution's case against him. What happens if a case involves (a) an inordinately long delay caused solely by the government and (b) no demonstrable prejudice against the defendant? Consider *Doggett v. United States*.

Doggett v. United States, 505 U.S. 647, 112 S. Ct. 2686, 120 L. Ed. 2d 520 (1992)

Justice **Souter** delivered the opinion of the Court. . . .

I

On February 22, 1980, petitioner Marc Doggett was indicted for conspiring with several others to import and distribute cocaine. . . . On March 18, 1980, two police officers set out . . . to arrest Doggett at his parents' house in Raleigh, North Carolina, only to find that he was not there. His mother told the officers that he had left for Colombia four days earlier.

To catch Doggett on his return to the United States, [the DEA investigator] sent word of his outstanding arrest warrant to all United States Customs stations and to a number of law enforcement organizations. He also placed Doggett's name in the Treasury Enforcement Communication System (TECS), a computer network that helps Customs agents screen people entering the country, and in the National Crime Information Center computer system, which serves similar ends. The TECS entry expired that September, however, and Doggett's name vanished from the system.

In September 1981, [the DEA] found out that Doggett was under arrest on drug charges in Panama and, thinking that a formal extradition request would be futile, simply asked Panama to "expel" Doggett to the United States. Although the Panamanian authorities promised to comply when their own proceedings had run their course, they freed Doggett the following July and let him go to Colombia, where he stayed with an aunt for several months. On September 25, 1982, he passed unhindered through Customs in New York City and settled down in Virginia. Since his return to the United States, he has married, earned a college degree, found a steady job as a computer operations manager, lived openly under his own name, and stayed within the law. . . .

Doggett remained lost to the American criminal justice system until September 1988, when the Marshal's Service ran a simple credit check on several thousand people subject to outstanding arrest warrants and, within minutes, found out where Doggett lived and worked. On September 5, 1988, nearly 6 years after his return to the United States and 8½ years after his indictment, Doggett was arrested.

He naturally moved to dismiss the indictment, arguing that the Government's failure to prosecute him earlier violated his Sixth Amendment right to a speedy trial. The Federal Magistrate hearing his motion applied the criteria for assessing speedy trial claims set out in *Barker v. Wingo*, 407 U.S. 514, 92 S. Ct. 2182, 33 L. Ed. 2d 101 (1972): "[l]ength of delay, the reason for the delay, the defendant's assertion of his right, and prejudice to the defendant." Id., at 530 (footnote omitted). The Magistrate found that the delay between Doggett's indictment and arrest was long enough to be "presumptively prejudi-

cial," Magistrate's Report, reprinted at App to Pet for Cert 27-28, that the delay "clearly [was] attributable to the negligence of the government," id., at 39, and that Doggett could not be faulted for any delay in asserting his right to a speedy trial, there being no evidence that he had known of the charges against him until his arrest, id., at 42-44. The Magistrate also found, however, that Doggett had made no affirmative showing that the delay had impaired his ability to mount a successful defense or had otherwise prejudiced him. In his recommendation to the District Court, the Magistrate contended that this failure to demonstrate particular prejudice sufficed to defeat Doggett's speedy trial claim.

The District Court took the recommendation and denied Doggett's motion. Doggett then entered a conditional guilty plea under Federal Rule of Criminal Procedure 11(a)(2), expressly reserving the right to appeal his ensuing conviction on the speedy trial claim. . . .

[The 11th Circuit Court of Appeals affirmed.]

II

The Sixth Amendment guarantees that, "[i]n all criminal prosecutions, the accused shall enjoy the right to a speedy . . . trial. . . ." On its face, the Speedy Trial Clause is written with such breadth that, taken literally, it would forbid the government to delay the trial of an "accused" for any reason at all. Our cases, however, have qualified the literal sweep of the provision by specifically recognizing the relevance of four separate enquiries: whether delay before trial was uncommonly long, whether the government or the criminal defendant is more to blame for that delay, whether, in due course, the defendant asserted his right to a speedy trial, and whether he suffered prejudice as the delay's result. See Barker, supra, at 530.

The first of these is actually a double enquiry. Simply to trigger a speedy trial analysis, an accused must allege that the interval between accusation and trial has crossed the threshold dividing ordinary from "presumptively prejudicial" delay, since, by definition, he cannot complain that the government has denied him a "speedy" trial if it has, in fact, prosecuted his case with customary promptness. If the accused makes this showing, the court must then consider, as one factor among several, the extent to which the delay stretches beyond the bare minimum needed to trigger judicial examination of the claim. This latter enquiry is significant to the speedy trial analysis because, as we discuss below, the presumption that pretrial delay has prejudiced the accused intensifies over time. In this case, the extraordinary 8½ year lag between Doggett's indictment and arrest clearly suffices to trigger the speedy trial enquiry;[1] its further significance within that enquiry will be dealt with later.

As for Barker's second criterion, the Government claims to have sought Doggett with diligence. The findings of the courts below are to the contrary, however, and we review trial court determinations of negligence with considerable deference. . . . For six years, the Government's investigators made no serious effort to test their progressively more questionable assumption that Doggett was living abroad, and, had they done so, they could have found him within minutes. While the Government's lethargy may have reflected no more than Doggett's relative unimportance in the world of drug trafficking, it was still findable negligence, and the finding stands.

The Government goes against the record again in suggesting that Doggett knew of his indictment years before he was arrested. Were this true, Barker's third factor, concerning invocation of the right to a speedy trial, would be weighed heavily against him. But here again, the Government is trying to revisit the facts. At the hearing on Doggett's speedy trial motion, it introduced no evidence challenging the testimony of Doggett's wife, who said that she did not know of the charges until his arrest, and of his mother,

---

1. Depending on the nature of the charges, the lower courts have generally found postaccusation delay "presumptively prejudicial" at least as it approaches one year. See 2 W. LaFave & J. Israel, Criminal Procedure § 18.2, p 405 (1984); Joseph, Speedy Trial Rights in Application, 48 Fordham L Rev 611, 623, n 71 (1980) (citing cases). We note that, as the term is used in this threshold context, "presumptive prejudice" does not necessarily indicate a statistical probability of prejudice; it simply marks the point at which courts deem the delay unreasonable enough to trigger the Barker enquiry. Cf. Uviller, Barker v. Wingo: Speedy Trial Gets a Fast Shuffle, 72 Colum L Rev 1376, 1384-1485 (1972).

who claimed not to have told him or anyone else that the police had come looking for him. . . . [It was stipulated at the trial court that Doggett was completely ignorant of the indictment against him until his arrest. As such] . . . the trial and appellate courts were entitled to accept the defense's unrebutted and largely substantiated claim of Doggett's ignorance. Thus, Doggett is not to be taxed for invoking his speedy trial right only after his arrest.

III

The Government is left, then, with its principal contention: that Doggett fails to make out a successful speedy trial claim because he has not shown precisely how he was prejudiced by the delay between his indictment and trial.

A

We have observed in prior cases that unreasonable delay between formal accusation and trial threatens to produce more than one sort of harm, including "oppressive pretrial incarceration," "anxiety and concern of the accused," and "the possibility that the [accused's] defense will be impaired" by dimming memories and loss of exculpatory evidence. Of these forms of prejudice, "the most serious is the last, because the inability of a defendant adequately to prepare his case skews the fairness of the entire system." Doggett claims this kind of prejudice, and there is probably no other kind that he can claim, since he was subjected neither to pretrial detention nor, he has successfully contended, to awareness of unresolved charges against him. . . .

[T]he Government claims Doggett has failed to make any affirmative showing that the delay weakened his ability to raise specific defenses, elicit specific testimony, or produce specific items of evidence. Though Doggett did indeed come up short in this respect, the Government's argument takes it only so far: consideration of prejudice is not limited to the specifically demonstrable, and . . . affirmative proof of particularized prejudice is not essential to every speedy trial claim. Barker explicitly recognized that impairment of one's defense is the most difficult form of speedy trial prejudice to prove because time's erosion of exculpatory evidence and testimony "can rarely be shown." And though time can tilt the case against either side, one cannot generally be sure which of them it has prejudiced more severely. Thus, we generally have to recognize that excessive delay presumptively compromises the reliability of a trial in ways that neither party can prove or, for that matter, identify. While such presumptive prejudice cannot alone carry a Sixth Amendment claim without regard to the other Barker criteria, it is part of the mix of relevant facts, and its importance increases with the length of delay.

B

. . .

Our speedy trial standards recognize that pretrial delay is often both inevitable and wholly justifiable. The government may need time to collect witnesses against the accused, oppose his pretrial motions, or, if he goes into hiding, track him down. We attach great weight to such considerations when balancing them against the costs of going forward with a trial whose probative accuracy the passage of time has begun by degrees to throw into question. Thus, in this case, if the Government had pursued Doggett with reasonable diligence from his indictment to his arrest, his speedy trial claim would fail. Indeed, that conclusion would generally follow as a matter of course however great the delay, so long as Doggett could not show specific prejudice to his defense.

The Government concedes, on the other hand, that Doggett would prevail if he could show that the Government had intentionally held back in its prosecution of him to gain some impermissible advantage at trial. That we cannot doubt. Barker stressed that official bad faith in causing delay will be weighed heavily against the government, and a bad-faith delay the length of this negligent one would present an overwhelming case for dismissal.

Between diligent prosecution and bad-faith delay, official negligence in bringing an accused to trial occupies the middle ground. While not compelling relief in every case where bad-faith delay would make relief virtually automatic, neither is negligence automatically tolerable simply because the accused cannot demonstrate exactly how it has prejudiced him. It was on this point that the Court of Appeals erred, and on the facts before us, it was reversible error.

Barker made it clear that "different weights [are to be] assigned to different reasons" for delay. Although negligence is obviously to be weighed more lightly than a deliberate intent to harm the accused's defense, it still falls on the wrong side of the divide between acceptable and unacceptable reasons for delaying a criminal prosecution once it has begun. And such is the nature of the prejudice presumed that the weight we assign to official negligence compounds over time as the presumption of evidentiary prejudice grows. . . . Condoning prolonged and unjustifiable delays in prosecution would both penalize many defendants for the state's fault and simply encourage the government to gamble with the interests of criminal suspects assigned a low prosecutorial priority. The Government, indeed, can hardly complain too loudly, for persistent neglect in concluding a criminal prosecution indicates an uncommonly feeble interest in bringing an accused to justice; the more weight the Government attaches to securing a conviction, the harder it will try to get it.

To be sure, to warrant granting relief, negligence unaccompanied by particularized trial prejudice must have lasted longer than negligence demonstrably causing such prejudice. But even so, the Government's egregious persistence in failing to prosecute Doggett is clearly sufficient. The lag between Doggett's indictment and arrest was 8½ years, and he would have faced trial 6 years earlier than he did but for the Government's inexcusable oversights. The portion of the delay attributable to the Government's negligence far exceeds the threshold needed to state a speedy trial claim; indeed, we have called shorter delays "extraordinary." When the Government's negligence thus causes delay six times as long as that generally sufficient to trigger judicial review, see n 1, supra, and when the presumption of prejudice, albeit unspecified, is neither extenuated, as by the defendant's acquiescence, nor persuasively rebutted, the defendant is entitled to relief.

IV

We reverse the judgment of the Court of Appeals and remand the case for proceedings consistent with this opinion.

So ordered.

Justice **O'Connor**, dissenting. . . .

Although the delay between indictment and trial was lengthy, petitioner did not suffer any anxiety or restriction on his liberty. The only harm to petitioner from the lapse of time was potential prejudice to his ability to defend his case. We have not allowed such speculative harm to tip the scales. Instead, we have required a showing of actual prejudice to the defense before weighing it in the balance. As we stated in United States v. Loud Hawk, 474 US 302, 315, 106 S Ct 648, 88 L Ed 2d 640 (1986), the "possibility of prejudice is not sufficient to support respondents' position that their speedy trial rights were violated. In this case, moreover, delay is a two-edged sword. It is the Government that bears the burden of proving its case beyond a reasonable doubt. The passage of time may make it difficult or impossible for the Government to carry this burden." . . .

Justice **Thomas**, with whom The **Chief Justice** and Justice **Scalia** join, dissenting.

Just as "bad facts make bad law," so too odd facts make odd law. Doggett's 8½-year odyssey from youthful drug dealing in the tobacco country of North Carolina, through stints in a Panamanian jail and in Colombia, to life as a computer operations manager, homeowner, and registered voter in suburban Virginia, is extraordinary. But even more extraordinary is the Court's conclusion that the Government denied Doggett his Sixth Amendment right to a speedy trial despite the fact that he has suffered none of the harms that the right was designed to prevent. I respectfully dissent.

I

We have long identified the "major evils" against which the Speedy Trial Clause is directed as "undue and oppressive incarceration" and the "anxiety and concern accompanying public accusation." United States v. Marion, 404 US 307, 320, 92 S Ct 455, 30 L Ed 2d 468 (1971). The Court does not, and cannot, seriously dispute that those two concerns lie at the heart of the Clause, and that neither concern is implicated here. Doggett was neither in United States custody nor subject to bail during the entire 8½-year period at issue. Indeed, as this case comes to us, we must assume that he was blissfully unaware of his indictment all the while, and thus was not subject to the anxiety or humiliation that typically accompany a known criminal charge.

Thus, this unusual case presents the question whether, independent of these core concerns, the Speedy Trial Clause protects an accused from two additional harms: (1) prejudice to his ability to defend himself caused by the passage of time; and (2) disruption of his life years after the alleged commission of his crime. The Court today proclaims that the first of these additional harms is indeed an independent concern of the Clause, and on that basis compels reversal of Doggett's conviction and outright dismissal of the indictment against him. As to the second of these harms, the Court remains mum.

I disagree with the Court's analysis. In my view, the Sixth Amendment's speedy trial guarantee does not provide independent protection against either prejudice to an accused's defense or the disruption of his life. . . .

COMPETENCY TO STAND TRIAL

The due-process clause of the Fourteenth Amendment prohibits the trial of an individual if he or she is *incompetent*. A person is incompetent to stand trial if he or she lacks the capacity to (1) understand the nature and object of the proceedings against him or her, (2) consult with counsel, and (3) assist in preparing a defense.

Dusky v. United States, 362 U.S. 402, 402, 80 S. Ct. 788, 4 L. Ed. 2d 824 (1960) (per curiam).

As explained by Justice Blackmun in his dissent in *Medina v. California*, 505 U.S. 437, 457–458, 112 S. Ct. 2572, 2584, 120 L. Ed. 2d 353 (1992):

The right to be tried while competent is the foundational right for the effective exercise of a defendant's other rights in a criminal trial. . . . In the words of Professor Morris, one of the world's leading criminologists, incompetent persons "are not really present at trial; they may not be able properly to play the role of an accused person, to recall relevant events, to produce evidence and witnesses, to testify effectively on their own behalf, to help confront hostile witnesses, and to project to the trier of facts a sense of their innocence." N. Morris, Madness and the Criminal Law 37 (1982).

While it clearly is unconstitutional to try a person who is incompetent, the Supreme Court has struggled with how incompetency is to be proven. As you read the majority opinion in *Cooper v. Oklahoma*, consider what effect the premises that Justice Blackmun put forth in his *Medina* dissent may have had on the decision in *Cooper*.

Cooper v. Oklahoma, 517 U.S. 348, 116 S. Ct. 1373, 134 L. Ed. 2d 498 (1996)

Justice **Stevens** delivered the opinion of the Court.

In Oklahoma the defendant in a criminal prosecution is presumed to be competent to stand trial unless he proves his incompetence by clear and convincing evidence. Okla. Stat., Tit. 22, § 1175.4(B) (1991). Under that standard a defendant may be put to trial even though it is more likely than not that he is incompetent. The question we address in this case is whether the application of that standard to petitioner violated his right to due process under the Fourteenth Amendment.

I

In 1989 petitioner was charged with the brutal killing of an 86-year-old man in the course of a burglary. After an Oklahoma jury found him guilty of first-degree murder and recommended punishment by death, the trial court imposed the death penalty. The Oklahoma Court of Criminal Appeals affirmed the conviction and sentence.

Petitioner's competence was the focus of significant attention both before and during his trial. On five separate occasions a judge considered whether petitioner had the ability to understand the charges against him and to assist defense counsel. On the first occasion, a pretrial judge relied on the opinion of a clinical psychologist employed by the State to find petitioner incompetent. Based on that determination, he committed petitioner to a state mental health facility for treatment.

Upon petitioner's release from the hospital some three months later, the trial judge heard testimony concerning petitioner's competence from two state-employed psychologists. These experts expressed conflicting opinions regarding petitioner's ability to participate in his defense. The judge resolved the dispute against petitioner, ordering him to proceed to trial. . . .

Petitioner's competence was addressed a fourth time on the first day of trial, when petitioner's bizarre behavior prompted the court to conduct a further competency hearing at which the judge observed petitioner and heard testimony from several lay witnesses, a third psychologist, and petitioner himself.[1] The expert concluded that petitioner was presently incompetent and unable to communicate effectively with counsel, but that he could probably achieve competence within six weeks if treated aggressively. While stating that he did not dispute the psychologist's diagnosis, the trial judge ruled

---

1. During the hearing petitioner, who had refused to change out of prison overalls for the trial because the proffered clothes were "burning" him, talked to himself and to an imaginary "spirit" who petitioner claimed gave him counsel. On the witness stand petitioner expressed fear that the lead defense attorney wanted to kill him. . . .

against petitioner. In so holding, however, the court voiced uncertainty:

Well, I think I've used the expression . . . in the past that normal is like us. Anybody that's not like us is not normal, so I don't think normal is a proper definition that we are to use with incompetence. My shirt-sleeve opinion of Mr. Cooper is that he's not normal. Now, to say he's not competent is something else. . . .

But you know, all things considered, I suppose it's possible for a client to be in such a predicament that he can't help his defense and still not be incompetent. I suppose that's a possibility, too.

I think it's going to take smarter people than me to make a decision here. I'm going to say that I don't believe he has carried the burden by clear and convincing evidence of his incompetency and I'm going to say we're going to go to trial.

Incidents that occurred during the trial,[2] as well as the sordid history of petitioner's child-hood that was recounted during the sentencing phase of the proceeding, were consistent with the conclusions expressed by the expert. In a final effort to protect his client's interests, defense counsel moved for a mistrial or a renewed investigation into petitioner's compe-tence. After the court summarily denied these motions, petitioner was convicted and sen-tenced to death. . . .

II

No one questions the existence of the funda-mental right that petitioner invokes. We have repeatedly and consistently recognized that "the criminal trial of an incompetent defendant vio-lates due process." Medina v. California, 505 U.S. 437, 453, 112 S. Ct. 2572, 2581–2582, 120 L. Ed. 2d 353 (1992). Nor is the significance of

this right open to dispute. As Justice KENNEDY recently emphasized:

"Competence to stand trial is rudimentary, for upon it depends the main part of those rights deemed essential to a fair trial, including the right to effective assistance of counsel, the rights to summon, to confront, and to cross-examine witnesses, and the right to testify on one's own behalf or to remain silent without penalty for doing so." Riggins v. Nevada, 504 U.S. 127, 112 S. Ct. 1810, 118 L. Ed. 2d 479 (1992) (opinion concurring in the judgment).

The test for incompetence is also well-settled. A defendant may not be put to trial unless he "'has sufficient present ability to consult with his lawyer with a reasonable degree of rational understanding . . . [and] a rational as well as fac-tual understanding of the proceedings against him.'" Dusky v. United States, 362 U.S. 402, 402, 80 S.Ct. 788, 4 L.Ed.2d 824 (1960) (per curiam).

Our recent decision in Medina v. California establishes that a State may presume that the defendant is competent and require him to shoulder the burden of proving his incompe-tence by a preponderance of the evidence. In reaching that conclusion we held that the rele-vant inquiry was whether the presumption "'offends some principle of justice so rooted in the traditions and conscience of our people as to be ranked as fundamental.'" We contrasted the "deep roots in our common-law heritage" under-lying the prohibition against trying the incompe-tent with the absence of any settled tradition concerning the allocation of the burden of proof in a competency proceeding. Our conclusion that the presumption of competence offends no recognized principle of "fundamental fairness" rested in part on the fact that the procedural rule affects the outcome "only in a narrow class of cases where the evidence is in equipoise; that is, where the evidence that a defendant is com-petent is just as strong as the evidence that he is incompetent."

The question we address today is quite differ-ent from the question posed in Medina. Peti-tioner's claim requires us to consider whether a State may proceed with a criminal trial after the defendant has demonstrated that he is more likely than not incompetent. Oklahoma does not contend that it may require the defendant to

---

2. Petitioner did not communicate with or sit near defense counsel during the trial. Through much of the proceedings he remained in prison overalls, crouching in the fetal position and talking to himself.

prove incompetence beyond a reasonable doubt.

The State maintains, however, that the clear and convincing standard provides a reasonable accommodation of the opposing interests of the State and the defendant. We are persuaded, by both traditional and modern practice and the importance of the constitutional interest at stake, that the State's argument must be rejected.

III

"Historical practice is probative of whether a procedural rule can be characterized as fundamental," Medina. In this case, unlike in Medina, there is no indication that the rule Oklahoma seeks to defend has any roots in prior practice. Indeed, it appears that a rule significantly more favorable to the defendant has had a long and consistent application.

[The Court provided a detailed history of the legal history of England and the United States regarding competency to stand trial. The Court concluded that there was no historical basis for the clear and convincing evidence standard in the competency determination.] . . .

Contemporary practice demonstrates that the vast majority of jurisdictions remain persuaded that the heightened standard of proof imposed on the accused in Oklahoma is not necessary to vindicate the State's interest in prompt and orderly disposition of criminal cases. Only 4 of the 50 States presently require the criminal defendant to prove his incompetence by clear and convincing evidence. None of the remaining 46 jurisdictions imposes such a heavy burden on the defendant. Indeed, a number of States place no burden on the defendant at all, but rather require the prosecutor to prove the defendant's competence to stand trial once a question about competency has been credibly raised. The situation is no different in federal court. Congress has directed that the accused in a federal prosecution must prove incompetence by a preponderance of the evidence. 18 U.S.C. § 4241.

The near-uniform application of a standard that is more protective of the defendant's rights than Oklahoma's clear and convincing evidence rule supports our conclusion that the heightened standard offends a principle of justice that is deeply "rooted in the traditions and conscience of our people." Medina v. California. We turn next to a consideration of whether the rule exhibits "'fundamental fairness' in operation."

IV

Contemporary and historical procedures are fully consistent with our evaluation of the risks inherent in Oklahoma's practice of requiring the defendant to prove incompetence by clear and convincing evidence. In Addington v. Texas, we explained that:

"The function of a standard of proof, as that concept is embodied in the Due Process Clause and in the realm of fact finding, is 'to instruct the fact finder concerning the degree of confidence our society thinks he should have in the correctness of factual conclusions for a particular type of adjudication.'

"The 'more stringent the burden of proof a party must bear, the more that party bears the risk of an erroneous decision.' For that reason, we have held that due process places a heightened burden of proof on the State in civil proceedings in which the 'individual interests at stake . . . are both "particularly important" and 'more substantial than mere loss of money.'"

Far from "jealously guard[ing]," an incompetent criminal defendant's fundamental right not to stand trial, Oklahoma's practice of requiring the defendant to prove incompetence by clear and convincing evidence imposes a significant risk of an erroneous determination that the defendant is competent. In Medina we found no comparable risk because the presumption would affect only the narrow class of cases in which the evidence on either side was equally balanced. "Once a State provides a defendant access to procedures for making a competency evaluation," we stated, there is "no basis for holding that due process further requires the State to assume the burden of vindicating the defendant's constitutional right by persuading the trier of fact that the defendant is competent to stand trial." Unlike the presumption at issue in Medina, however, Oklahoma's clear and convincing evidence standard affects a class of cases in which the defendant has already demonstrated that he is more likely than not incompetent.

For the defendant, the consequences of an erroneous determination of competence are dire. Because he lacks the ability to communicate effectively with counsel, he may be unable to exercise other "rights deemed essential to a fair trial." Riggins v. Nevada, (Kennedy, J., concurring in judgment). After making the "profound" choice whether to plead guilty, Godinez v. Moran, 509 U.S. 389, 398, 113 S. Ct. 2680, 2686, 125 L. Ed. 2d 321 (1993), the defendant who proceeds to trial "will ordinarily have to decide whether to waive his 'privilege against compulsory self-incrimination,' Boykin v. Alabama, 395 U.S. 238, 243, 89 S. Ct. 1709, 1712, 23 L. Ed. 2d 274 (1969), by taking the witness stand; if the option is available, he may have to decide whether to waive his 'right to trial by jury,' and, in consultation with counsel, he may have to decide whether to waive his 'right to confront [his] accusers,' by declining to cross-examine witnesses for the prosecution."

With the assistance of counsel, the defendant also is called upon to make myriad smaller decisions concerning the course of his defense. The importance of these rights and decisions demonstrates that an erroneous determination of competence threatens a "fundamental component of our criminal justice system"—the basic fairness of the trial itself.

By comparison to the defendant's interest, the injury to the State of the opposite error—a conclusion that the defendant is incompetent when he is in fact malingering—is modest. To be sure, such an error imposes an expense on the state treasury and frustrates the State's interest in the prompt disposition of criminal charges. But the error is subject to correction in a subsequent proceeding and the State may detain the incompetent defendant for "the reasonable period of time necessary to determine whether there is a substantial probability that he will attain [competence] in the foreseeable future." Jackson v. Indiana, 406 U.S. 715, 738, 92 S. Ct. 1845, 1858, 32 L. Ed. 2d 435 (1972).[21] . . .

VI

For the foregoing reasons, the judgment is reversed and the case is remanded to the Oklahoma Court of Criminal Appeals for further proceedings not inconsistent with this opinion.

It is so ordered.

---

21. Under *Jackson*, if the defendant regains competence or is found to be malingering, the State may proceed to trial.

Notes and Questions

1. While the Constitution prohibits the government from prosecuting a person who is not competent to stand trial, an incompetent defendant is not necessarily entitled to simply get off scot-free. The State always has the right to dismiss charges against an individual. However, if the State chooses not to dismiss the case, a defendant who is found to be incompetent to stand trial may be held in a psychiatric facility for "a reasonable period of time necessary to determine whether there is a substantial probability that he will attain that capacity in the foreseeable future." *Jackson v. Indiana*, 406 U.S. 715, 738, 92 S. Ct. 1845, 1858, 32 L. Ed. 2d 435 (1972). Under *Jackson*, the State may hold a defendant until he or she has regained competency to stand trial or until it is determined that he or she will not be competent in the foreseeable future. While the Court in *Jackson* did not place time limits on the length of confinement, it did note that the 3½ years that Jackson had been confined was too long when there was no evidence that Jackson was making progress toward competency.

THE BURDEN OF PERSUASION

We have mentioned the well-known adage that a person is presumed innocent until proven guilty. In *Bell v. Wolfish*, 441 U.S. 520, 533, 99 S. Ct. 1861, 1870–1871, 60 L. Ed. 2d 447 (1979), the Court described the presumption of innocence in the following manner:

> The presumption of innocence is a doctrine that allocates the burden of proof in criminal trials; it also may serve as an admonishment to the jury to judge an accused's guilt or innocence solely on the evidence adduced at trial and not on the basis of suspicions that may arise from the fact of his arrest, indictment, or custody, or from other matters not introduced as proof at trial. . . . It is "an inaccurate, shorthand description of the right of the accused to 'remain inactive and secure, until the prosecution has taken its burden and produced evidence and effected persuasion; . . .' an 'assumption' that is indulged in the absence of contrary evidence." . . . Without question, the presumption of innocence plays an important role in our criminal justice system.

How firm must our conviction be that a person committed the crime with which he or she has been charged before we are confident in upsetting the presumption of innocence, declaring him or her guilty, and imposing punishment accordingly?

Cooper v. Oklahoma (p. 629) presented a burden-of-proof issue but involved a threshold stage of the proceedings. *Cooper* established that an accused may not be required to prove his or her incompetency to stand trial by "clear and convincing evidence." Let us now assume that an accused's competence is not at issue and that the question concerns the amount of proof required before it may be concluded that a defendant is guilty as charged.

Different standards of proof are commonly used to resolve disputed issues in the criminal justice process. Proof by *a preponderance of the evidence* simply means proof sufficient to establish that it is more likely than not that a contested fact or event occurred. *Clear and convincing evidence* requires more proof than the preponderance of the evidence standard but less than is required for proof beyond a reasonable doubt. The highest burden of proof is proof *beyond a reasonable doubt.* While this is well known as the standard that must be satisfied to convict a person of a criminal offense, prior to 1970 the Supreme Court had never explicitly so ruled. Ironically, the Court did not make this announcement in a criminal case but in a juvenile delinquency case involving a 12-year-old boy.

In re Winship, 397 U.S. 358, 90 S. Ct. 1068, 25 L. Ed. 2d 368 (1970)

Mr. Justice Brennan delivered the opinion of the Court. . . .

[Sam Winship, a 12-year-old boy, was adjudicated a juvenile delinquent and committed to a training school for not less than 18 months upon proof that he stole $112 from a woman's pocketbook. The act, if committed by an adult, would have constituted the crime of larceny. The New

York statute under which Winship was adjudicated a delinquent and ordered committed to a training school required the State to prove the essential facts at issue by "a preponderance of the evidence." The lawyer for Winship objected to the use of this standard of proof, in the following colloquy with the juvenile court judge:

Counsel: "Your Honor is making a finding by a preponderance of the evidence."
Court: "Well, it convinces me."
Counsel: "It's not beyond a reasonable doubt, your Honor."
Court: "That is true. . . . Our statute says a preponderance and a preponderance it is."]

This case presents the single, narrow question whether proof beyond a reasonable doubt is among the "essentials of due process and fair treatment" required during the adjudicatory stage when a juvenile is charged with an act which would constitute a crime if committed by an adult. . . .

I

The requirement that guilt of a criminal charge be established by proof beyond a reasonable doubt dates at least from our early years as a Nation. The "demand for a higher degree of persuasion in criminal cases was recurrently expressed from ancient times, [though] its crystallization into the formula 'beyond a reasonable doubt' seems to have occurred as late as 1798. It is now accepted in common law jurisdictions as the measure of persuasion by which the prosecution must convince the trier of all the essential elements of guilt." C. McCormick, Evidence § 321, pp. 681–682 (1954); see also 9 J. Wigmore, Evidence § 2497 (3d ed. 1940). Although virtually unanimous adherence to the reasonable-doubt standard in common-law jurisdictions may not conclusively establish it as a requirement of due process, such adherence does "reflect a profound judgment about the way in which law should be enforced and justice administered." Duncan v. Louisiana, 391 US 145, 155, (1968). Expressions in many opinions of this Court indicate that it has long been assumed that proof of a criminal charge beyond a reasonable doubt is constitutionally required. . . .

The reasonable doubt standard plays a vital role in the American scheme of criminal procedure. It is a prime instrument for reducing the risk of convictions resting on factual error. The standard provides concrete substance for the presumption of innocence—that bedrock "axiomatic and elementary" principle whose "enforcement lies at the foundation of the administration of our criminal law."

As the dissenters in the New York Court of Appeals observed, and we agree, "a person accused of a crime . . . would be at a severe disadvantage, a disadvantage amounting to a lack of fundamental fairness, if he could be adjudged guilty and imprisoned for years on the strength of the same evidence as would suffice in a civil case." 24 NY2d, at 205, 247 NE2d, at 259.

The requirement of proof beyond a reasonable doubt has this vital role in our criminal procedure for cogent reasons. The accused during a criminal prosecution has at stake interests of immense importance, both because of the possibility that he may lose his liberty upon conviction and because of the certainty that he would be stigmatized by the conviction. Accordingly, a society that values the good name and freedom of every individual should not condemn a man for commission of a crime when there is reasonable doubt about his guilt. As we said in Speiser v. Randall, [357 U.S. 513,] 525–526 [(1958)]: "There is always in litigation a margin of error, representing error in factfinding, which both parties must take into account. Where one party has at stake an interest of transcending value—as a criminal defendant his liberty—this margin of error is reduced as to him by the process of placing on the other party the burden of . . . persuading the factfinder at the conclusion of the trial of his guilt beyond a reasonable doubt. Due process commands that no man shall lose his liberty unless the Government has borne the burden of . . . convincing the factfinder of his guilt." To this end, the reasonable-doubt standard is indispensable, for it "impresses on the trier of fact the necessity of reaching a subjective state of certitude on the facts in issue." Dorsen & Reznick, In re Gault and the Future of Juvenile Law, 1 Family Law Quarterly, No. 4, pp. 1, 26 (1967).

Moreover, use of the reasonable-doubt standard is indispensable to command the respect and confidence of the community in applications of the criminal law. It is critical that the moral force of the criminal law not be diluted by a standard of proof that leaves people in doubt whether innocent men are being condemned. It is also important in our free society that every individual going about his ordinary affairs have confidence that his government cannot adjudge him guilty of a criminal offense without convincing a proper factfinder of his guilt with utmost certainty.

Lest there remain any doubt about the constitutional stature of the reasonable-doubt standard, we explicitly hold that the Due Process Clause protects the accused against conviction except upon proof beyond a reasonable doubt of every fact necessary to constitute the crime with which he is charged.

II

We turn to the question whether juveniles, like adults, are constitutionally entitled to proof beyond a reasonable doubt when they are charged with violation of a criminal law. The same considerations that demand extreme caution in factfinding to protect the innocent adult apply as well as to the innocent child. . . .

Finally, we reject the . . . suggestion that there is, in any event, only a "tenuous difference" between the reasonable-doubt and preponderance standards. The suggestion is singularly unpersuasive. In this very case, the trial judge's ability to distinguish between the two standards enabled him to make a finding of guilt that he conceded he might not have made under the standard of proof beyond a reasonable doubt. Indeed, the trial judge's action evidences the accuracy of the observation of commentators that "the preponderance test is susceptible to the misinterpretation that it calls on the trier of fact merely to perform an abstract weighing of the evidence in order to determine which side has produced the greater quantum, without regard to its effect in convincing his mind to the truth of the proposition asserted." Dorsen & Reznek, supra, at 26–27.

III

. . . We therefore hold, in agreement with Chief Judge Fuld in dissent in the Court of Appeals, "that, where a 12-year-old child is charged with an act of stealing which renders him liable to confinement for as long as six years, then, as a matter of due process . . . the case against him must be proved beyond a reasonable doubt." 24 NY2d, at 207, 247 NE2d, at 260.

Reversed.

Mr. Justice **Harlan**, concurring.

. . .

I

Professor Wigmore, in discussing the various attempts by courts to define how convinced one must be to be convinced beyond a reasonable doubt, wryly observed: "The truth is that no one has yet invented or discovered a mode of measurement for the intensity of human belief. Hence there can be yet no successful method of communicating intelligibly . . . a sound method of self-analysis for one's belief," 9 J. Wigmore, Evidence 325 (3d ed. 1940).

Notwithstanding Professor Wigmore's skepticism, we have before us a case where the choice of the standard of proof has made a difference: the juvenile court judge below forthrightly acknowledged that he believed by a preponderance of the evidence, but was not convinced beyond a reasonable doubt, that appellant stole $112 from the complainant's pocketbook. Moreover, even though the labels used for alternative standards of proof are vague and not a very sure guide to decisionmaking, the choice of the standard for a particular variety of adjudication does, I think, reflect a very fundamental assessment of the comparative social costs of erroneous factual determinations.

To explain why I think this so, I begin by stating two propositions, neither of which I believe can be fairly disputed. First, in a judicial proceeding in which there is a dispute about the facts of some earlier event, the factfinder cannot acquire unassailably accurate knowledge of what happened. Instead, all the factfinder can acquire is a belief of what *probably* happened. The intensity of this belief—the degree to which a factfinder is convinced that a given act actually occurred—can, of course, vary. In this regard, a standard of proof represents an attempt to instruct the factfinder concerning the degree of confidence our society thinks he should have in the correctness of factual conclusions for a particular type of adjudication. Although the phrases "preponderance of the evidence" and "proof beyond a reasonable doubt" are quantitatively imprecise, they do communicate to the finder of fact different notions concerning the degree of confidence he is expected to have in the correctness of his factual conclusions.

A second proposition, which is really nothing more than a corollary of the first, is that the trier of fact will sometimes, despite his best efforts, be wrong in his factual conclusions. In a lawsuit between two parties, a factual error can make a difference in one of two ways. First, it can result in a judgment in favor of the plaintiff when the true facts warrant a judgment for the defendant. The analogue in a criminal case would be the conviction of an innocent man. On the other hand, an erroneous factual determination can result in a judgment for the defendant when the true facts justify a judgment in plaintiff's favor. The criminal analogue would be the acquittal of a guilty man.

The standard of proof influences the relative frequency of these two types of erroneous outcomes. If, for example, the standard of proof for a criminal trial were a preponderance of the evidence rather than proof beyond a reasonable doubt, there would be a smaller risk of factual errors that result in freeing guilty persons, but a far greater risk of factual errors that result in convicting the innocent. Because the standard of proof affects the comparative frequency of these two types of erroneous outcomes, the choice of the standard to be applied in a particular kind of litigation should, in a rational world, reflect an assessment of the comparative social disutility of each.

When one makes such an assessment, the reason for different standards of proof in civil as opposed to criminal litigation becomes apparent. In a civil suit between two private parties for money damages, for example, we view it as no more serious in general for there to be an erroneous verdict in the defendant's favor than for there to be an erroneous verdict in the plaintiff's favor. A preponderance of the evidence standard therefore seems peculiarly appropriate for, as explained most sensibly, it simply requires the trier of fact "to believe that the existence of a fact is more probable than its nonexistence before [he] may find in favor of the party who has the burden to persuade the [judge] of the fact's existence."

In a criminal case, on the other hand, we do not view the social disutility of convicting an innocent man as equivalent to the disutility of acquitting someone who is guilty. As Mr. Justice Brennan wrote for the Court in Speiser v. Randall, 357 US 513, 525–526 (1958):

"There is always in litigation a margin of error, representing error in fact finding, which both parties must take into account. Where one party has at stake an interest of transcending value—as a criminal defendant his liberty—this margin of error is reduced as to him by the process of placing on the other party the burden . . . of persuading the fact finder at the conclusion of the trial of his guilt beyond a reasonable doubt."

In this context, I view the requirement of proof beyond a reasonable doubt in a criminal case as bottomed on a fundamental value determination of our society that it is far worse to convict an innocent man than to let a guilty man go free. It is only because of the nearly complete and long-standing acceptance of the reasonable-doubt standard by the States in criminal trials that the Court has not before today had to hold explicitly that due process, as an expression of fundamental procedural fairness, requires a more stringent standard for criminal trials than for ordinary civil litigation. . . .

Notes and Questions

1. In *Victor v. Nebraska*, 511 U.S. 1, 114 S. Ct. 1239, 127 L. Ed. 2d 583 (1994), the Court held that a trial court is not required to define "reasonable doubt." As long as the court instructs the jury that it must find that the prosecution proved each element of the offense beyond a reasonable doubt, the defendant's due-process rights are protected.

2. The following jury instruction provides a typical definition of proof beyond a reasonable doubt: "A reasonable doubt is a doubt based upon reason and common sense, and may arise from a careful and impartial consideration of all of the evidence, or from lack of evidence. Proof beyond a reasonable doubt is proof that leaves a person firmly convinced that the defendant is guilty." *Manual of Model Criminal Jury Instructions for the Ninth Circuit*, No. 3.02 (1992).

3. Figure 10–2 illustrates the three common levels of proof used in the adjudication process. Notice that if a juror believes only that it is more likely than not that a defendant is guilty, or even that the defendant "probably" is guilty, then he or she is duty bound to return a verdict of not guilty, since guilt has not been proven beyond a reasonable doubt. Under the Oklahoma statute at issue in *Cooper*, if the trial judge thought the defendant was more likely than not incompetent but there was not clear and convincing evidence to prove it, the judge would find the defendant competent. Conversely, the New York statute challenged in *Winship* authorized the judge to confine a child as a juvenile delinquent under the preponderance-of-the-evidence standard, even if "reasonable doubt" existed about the child's guilt.

TRIAL BY JURY

As we have already seen, both Article III, Section 2, of the U.S. Constitution and the Sixth Amendment unequivocally seem to guarantee an individual charged with a crime the right to be tried by a jury. However, this language is not to be taken at face value. Prior to the 1968 case of *Duncan v. Louisiana*, the Sixth Amendment right to a trial by jury in criminal cases did not apply to the states (see Chapter 2). Of course, this does not mean that jury trials were not pro-vided in state criminal cases before 1968; they clearly were, but they could be limited according to peculiar rules of state law. In *Duncan*, the Court provided guidance concerning when a criminal defendant in a state case is entitled to a jury trial under the federal Constitution. As you read *Duncan* and consider its holding, contemplate what the Court actually said and, just as importantly, what the Court did not say concerning the scope of the Sixth Amendment's right to trial by jury in state criminal cases.

Level of Proof	Proceeding	Defendant	Prosecution
Beyond a reasonable doubt	Guilt phase of criminal trial; juvenile delinquency adjudication hearing where child risks deprivation of liberty. *In re Winship*		
Clear and convincing evidence	Burden imposed on criminal defendant to establish incompetency for trial under Oklahoma statute; Supreme Court declared unconstitutional. *Cooper v. Oklahoma*		
Preponderance of the evidence	Constitutionally acceptable burden imposed on criminal defendants to establish incompetency for trial. *Medina v. California*		

Figure 10–2 The Three Levels of Proof

Duncan v. Louisiana, 391 U.S. 145, 88 S. Ct. 1444, 20 L. Ed. 2d 491 (1968)

Mr. Justice WHITE delivered the opinion of the Court.

Appellant, Gary Duncan, was convicted of simple battery in the Twenty-fifth Judicial District Court of Louisiana. Under Louisiana law simple battery is a misdemeanor, punishable by a maximum of two years' imprisonment and a $300 fine. Appellant sought trial by jury, but because the Louisiana Constitution grants jury trials only in cases in which capital punishment or imprisonment at hard labor may be imposed, the trial judge denied the request. Appellant was convicted and sentenced to serve 60 days in the parish prison and pay a fine of $150. Appellant sought review in the Supreme Court of Louisiana, asserting that the denial of jury trial violated rights guaranteed to him by the United States Constitution. The Supreme Court, finding "[n]o error of law in the ruling complained of," denied appellant a writ of certiorari. Pursuant to 28 U.S.C. § 1257(2) appellant sought review in this Court, alleging that the Sixth and Fourteenth Amendments to the United States Constitution secure the right to jury trial in state criminal prosecutions where a sentence as long as two years may be imposed. . . .

Appellant was 19 years of age when tried. While driving on Highway 23 in Plaquemines Parish on October 18, 1966, he saw two younger cousins engaged in a conversation by the side of the road with four white boys. Knowing his cousins, Negroes who had recently transferred to a formerly all-white high school, had reported the occurrence of racial incidents at the school, Duncan stopped the car, got out, and approached the six boys. At trial the white boys and a white onlooker testified, as did appellant and his cousins. The testimony was in dispute on many points, but the witnesses agreed that appellant and the white boys spoke to each other, that appellant encouraged his cousins to break off the encounter and enter his car, and that appellant was about to enter the car himself for the purpose of driving away with his cousins. The whites testified that just before getting in the car appellant slapped Herman Landry, one of the white boys, on the elbow. The Negroes testified that appellant had not slapped Landry, but had merely touched him. The trial judge concluded that the State had proved beyond a reasonable doubt that Duncan had committed simple battery, and found him guilty.

I.

The Fourteenth Amendment denies the States the power to "deprive any person of life, liberty, or property, without due process of law." In resolving conflicting claims concerning the meaning of this spacious language, the Court has looked increasingly to the Bill of Rights for guidance; many of the rights guaranteed by the first eight Amendments to the Constitution have been held to be protected against state action by the Due Process Clause of the Fourteenth Amendment. That clause now protects the right to compensation for property taken by the State; the rights of speech, press, and religion covered by the First Amendment; the Fourth Amendment rights to be free from unreasonable searches and seizures and to have excluded from criminal trials any evidence illegally seized; the right guaranteed by the Fifth Amendment to be free of compelled self-incrimination; and the Sixth Amendment rights to counsel, to a speedy and public trial, to confrontation of opposing witnesses, and to compulsory process for obtaining witnesses.

The test for determining whether a right extended by the Fifth and Sixth Amendments with respect to federal criminal proceedings is also protected against state action by the Fourteenth Amendment has been phrased in a variety of ways in the opinions of this Court. The question has been asked whether a right is among those "'fundamental principles of liberty and justice which lie at the base of all our civil and political institutions,'" Powell v. State of Alabama, 287 U.S. 45, 67, 53 S. Ct. 55, 63, 77 L. Ed. 158 (1932); whether it is "basic in our system of jurisprudence"; and whether it is "a fundamental right, essential to a fair trial," Gideon v.

Wainwright, 372 U.S. 335, 343–344, 83 S. Ct. 792, 796, 9 L.Ed.2d 799 (1963). The claim before us is that the right to trial by jury guaranteed by the Sixth Amendment meets these tests. The position of Louisiana, on the other hand, is that the Constitution imposes upon the States no duty to give a jury trial in any criminal case, regardless of the seriousness of the crime or the size of the punishment which may be imposed. Because we believe that trial by jury in criminal cases is fundamental to the American scheme of justice, we hold that the Fourteenth Amendment guarantees a right of jury trial in all criminal cases which—were they to be tried in a federal court—would come within the Sixth Amendment's guarantee. Since we consider the appeal before us to be such a case, we hold that the Constitution was violated when appellant's demand for jury trial was refused. . . .

Jury trial came to America with English colonists, and received strong support from them. Royal interference with the jury trial was deeply resented. Among the resolutions adopted by the First Congress of the American Colonies (the Stamp Act Congress) on October 19, 1765—resolutions deemed by their authors to state "the most essential rights and liberties of the colonists"—was the declaration:

"That trial by jury is the inherent and invaluable right of every British subject in these colonies.". . .

The Declaration of Independence stated solemn objections to the King's making "judges dependent on his will alone, for the tenure of their offices, and the amount and payment of their salaries," to his "depriving us in many cases, of the benefits of Trial by Jury," and to his "transporting us beyond Seas to be tried for pretended offenses." The Constitution itself, in Art. III, § 2 commanded:

"The Trial of all Crimes, except in Cases of Impeachment, shall be by Jury; and such Trial shall be held in the State where the said Crimes shall have been committed."

Objections to the Constitution because of the absence of a bill of rights were met by the immediate submission and adoption of the Bill of Rights. Included was the Sixth Amendment which, among other things, provided:

"In all criminal prosecutions, the accused shall enjoy the right to a speedy and public trial, by an impartial jury of the State and district wherein the crime shall have been committed."

The constitutions adopted by the original States guaranteed jury trial. Also, the constitution of every State entering the Union thereafter in one form or another protected the right to jury trial in criminal cases. . . .

The guarantees of jury trial in the Federal and State Constitutions reflect a profound judgment about the way in which law should be enforced and justice administered. A right to jury trial is granted to criminal defendants in order to prevent oppression by the Government. Those who wrote our constitutions knew from history and experience that it was necessary to protect against unfounded criminal charges brought to eliminate enemies and against judges too responsive to the voice of higher authority. The framers of the constitutions strove to create an independent judiciary but insisted upon further protection against arbitrary action. Providing an accused with the right to be tried by a jury of his peers gave him an inestimable safeguard against the corrupt or overzealous prosecutor and against the compliant, biased, or eccentric judge. If the defendant preferred the common-sense judgment of a jury to the more tutored but perhaps less sympathetic reaction of the single judge, he was to have it. Beyond this, the jury trial provisions in the Federal and State Constitutions reflect a fundamental decision about the exercise of official power—a reluctance to entrust plenary powers over the life and liberty of the citizen to one judge or to a group of judges. Fear of unchecked power, so typical of our State and Federal Governments in other respects, found expression in the criminal law in this insistence upon community participation in the determination of guilt or innocence. The deep commitment of the Nation to the right of jury trial in serious criminal cases as a defense against arbitrary law enforcement qualifies for protection under the Due Process Clause of the Fourteenth Amendment, and must therefore be respected by the States.

Of course jury trial has "its weaknesses and the potential for misuse," Singer v. United States, 380 U.S. 24, 35, 85 S. Ct. 783, 790, 13 L. Ed. 2d 630 (1965). We are aware of the long debate, especially in this century, among those who write about the administration of justice, as to the wisdom of permitting untrained laymen to determine the facts in civil and criminal proceedings. Although the debate has been intense, with powerful voices on either side, most of the controversy has centered on the jury in civil cases. Indeed, some of the severest critics of civil juries acknowledge that the arguments for criminal juries are much stronger. In addition, at the heart of the dispute have been express or implicit assertions that juries are incapable of adequately understanding evidence or determining issues of fact, and that they are unpredictable, quixotic, and little better than a roll of dice. Yet, the most recent and exhaustive study of the jury in criminal cases concluded that juries do understand the evidence and come to sound conclusions in most of the cases presented to them and that when juries differ with the result at which the judge would have arrived, it is usually because they are serving some of the very purposes for which they were created and for which they are now employed.

The State of Louisiana urges that holding that the Fourteenth Amendment assures a right to jury trial will cast doubt on the integrity of every trial conducted without a jury. Plainly, this is not the import of our holding. Our conclusion is that in the American States, as in the federal judicial system, a general grant of jury trial for serious offenses is a fundamental right, essential for preventing miscarriages of justice and for assuring that fair trials are provided for all defendants. We would not assert, however, that every criminal trial—or any particular trial—held before a judge alone is unfair or that a defendant may never be as fairly treated by a judge as he would be by a jury. Thus we hold no constitutional doubts about the practices, common in both federal and state courts, of accepting waivers of jury trial and prosecuting petty crimes without extending a right to jury trial. However, the fact is that in most places more trials for serious crimes are to juries than to a court alone; a great many defendants prefer the judgment of a jury to that of a court. Even where defendants are satisfied with bench trials, the right to a jury trial very likely serves its intended purpose of making judicial or prosecutorial unfairness less likely.

Louisiana's final contention is that even if it must grant jury trials in serious criminal cases, the conviction before us is valid and constitu-

tional because here the petitioner was tried for simple battery and was sentenced to only 60 days in the parish prison. We are not persuaded. It is doubtless true that there is a category of petty crimes or offenses which is not subject to the Sixth Amendment jury trial provision and should not be subject to the Fourteenth Amendment jury trial requirement here applied to the States. Crimes carrying possible penalties up to six months do not require a jury trial if they otherwise qualify as petty offenses. But the penalty authorized for a particular crime is of major relevance in determining whether it is serious or not and may in itself, if severe enough, subject the trial to the mandates of the Sixth Amendment. The penalty authorized by the law of the locality may be taken "as a gauge of its social and ethical judgments" of the crime in question. . . . In the case before us the Legislature of Louisiana has made simple battery a criminal offense punishable by imprisonment for up to two years and a fine. The question, then, is whether a crime carrying such a penalty is an offense which Louisiana may insist on trying without a jury.

We think not. So-called petty offenses were tried without juries both in England and in the Colonies and have always been held to be exempt from the otherwise comprehensive language of the Sixth Amendment's jury trial provisions. There is no substantial evidence that the Framers intended to depart from this established common-law practice, and the possible consequences to defendants from convictions for petty offenses have been thought insufficient to outweigh the benefits to efficient law enforcement and simplified judicial administration resulting from the availability of speedy and inexpensive nonjury adjudications. These same considerations compel the same result under the Fourteenth Amendment. Of course the boundaries of the petty offense category have always been ill-defined, if not ambulatory. In the absence of an explicit constitutional provision, the definitional task necessarily falls on the courts, which must either pass upon the validity of legislative attempts to identify those petty offenses which are exempt from jury trial or, where the legislature has not addressed itself to the problem, themselves face the question in the first instance. In either case it is necessary to draw a line in the spectrum of crime, separating petty from serious infractions. This process, although essential, cannot be wholly satisfactory, for it requires attaching different consequences to events which, when they lie near the line, actually differ very little.

In determining whether the length of the authorized prison term or the seriousness of other punishment is enough in itself to require a jury trial, we are counseled by District of Columbia v. Clawans [300 U.S. 617, 57 S. Ct. 660 81 L. Ed. 843 (1937)], to refer to objective criteria, chiefly the existing laws and practices in the Nation. In the federal system, petty offenses are defined as those punishable by no more than six months in prison and a $500 fine. In 49 of the 50 States crimes subject to trial without a jury, which occasionally include simple battery, are punishable by no more than one year in jail. Moreover, in the late 18th century in America crimes triable without a jury were for the most part punishable by no more than a six-month prison term, although there appear to have been exceptions to this rule. We need not, however, settle in this case the exact location of the line between petty offenses and serious crimes. It is sufficient for our purposes to hold that a crime punishable by two years in prison is, based on past and contemporary standards in this country, a serious crime and not a petty offense. Consequently, appellant was entitled to a jury trial and it was error to deny it.

The judgment below is reversed and the case is remanded for proceedings not inconsistent with this opinion.

Reversed and remanded.

Mr. Justice HARLAN, whom Mr. Justice STEWART joins, dissenting.

Every American jurisdiction provides for trial by jury in criminal cases. The question before us is not whether jury trial is an ancient institution, which it is; nor whether it plays a significant role in the administration of criminal justice, which it does; nor whether it will endure, which it shall. The question in this case is whether the State of Louisiana, which provides trial by jury for all felonies, is prohibited by the Constitution from trying charges of simple battery to the court alone. In my view, the answer to that question, mandated alike by our constitutional history and by the longer history of trial by jury, is clearly "no.". . .

Since, as I see it, the Court has not even come to grips with the issues in this case, it is necessary to start from the beginning. When a criminal defendant contends that his state conviction lacked "due process of law," the question before this Court, in my view, is whether he was denied any element of fundamental procedural fairness. . . .

The argument that jury trial is not a requisite of due process is quite simple. The central proposition of *Palko* [v. Connecticut, 302 U.S. 319, 58 S. Ct. 149, 82 L. Ed. 288 (1937)], a proposition to which I would adhere, is that "due process of law" requires only that criminal trials be fundamentally fair. As stated above, apart from the theory that it was historically intended as a mere shorthand for the Bill of Rights, I do not see what else "due process of law" can intelligibly be thought to mean. If due process of law requires only fundamental fairness, then the inquiry in each case must be whether a state trial process was a fair one. The Court has held, properly I think, that in an adversary process it is a requisite of fairness, for which there is no adequate substitute, that a criminal defendant be afforded a right to counsel and to cross-examine opposing witnesses. But it simply has not been demonstrated, nor, I think, can it be demonstrated, that trial by jury is the only fair means of resolving issues of fact.

The jury is of course not without virtues. It affords ordinary citizens a valuable opportunity to participate in a process of government, an experience fostering, one hopes, a respect for law. It eases the burden on judges by enabling them to share a part of their sometimes awesome responsibility. A jury may, at times, afford a higher justice by refusing to enforce harsh laws (although it necessarily does so haphazardly, raising the questions whether arbitrary enforcement of harsh laws is better than total enforcement, and whether the jury system is to be defended on the ground that jurors sometimes disobey their oaths). And the jury may, or may not, contribute desirably to the willingness of the general public to accept criminal judgments as just. . . .

The jury system can also be said to have some inherent defects, which are multiplied by the emergence of the criminal law from the relative simplicity that existed when the jury system was devised. It is a cumbersome process, not only imposing great cost in time and money on both the State and the jurors themselves, but also contributing to delay in the machinery of justice. Untrained jurors are presumably less adept at reaching accurate conclusions of fact than judges, particularly if the issues are many or complex. And it is argued by some that trial by jury, far from increasing public respect for law, impairs it: the average man, it is said, reacts favorably neither to the notion that matters he knows to be complex are being decided by other average men, nor to the way the jury system distorts the process of adjudication.

That trial by jury is not the only fair way of adjudicating criminal guilt is well attested by the fact that it is not the prevailing way, either in England or in this country. For England, one expert makes the following estimates. Parliament generally provides that new statutory offenses, unless they are of "considerable gravity" shall be tried to judges; consequently, summary offenses now outnumber offenses for which jury trial is afforded by more than six to one. Then, within the latter category, 84% of all cases are in fact tried to the court. Over all, "the ratio of defendants actually tried by jury becomes in some years little more than 1 per cent."

In the United States, where it has not been as generally assumed that jury waiver is permissible, the statistics are only slightly less revealing. Two experts have estimated that, of all prosecutions for crimes triable to a jury, 75% are settled by guilty plea and 40% of the remainder are tried to the court. In one State, Maryland, which has always provided for waiver, the rate of court trial appears in some years to have reached 90%. The Court recognizes the force of these statistics in stating,

> "We would not assert, however, that every criminal trial—or any particular trial—held before a judge alone is unfair or that a defendant may never be as fairly treated by a judge as he would be by a jury."

I agree. I therefore see no reason why this Court should reverse the conviction of appellant, absent any suggestion that his particular trial was in fact unfair, or compel the State of Louisiana to afford jury trial in an as yet unbounded category of cases that can, without unfairness, be tried to a court.

Indeed, even if I were persuaded that trial by jury is a fundamental right in some criminal cases, I could see nothing fundamental in the rule, not yet formulated by the Court, that places the prosecution of appellant for simple battery within the category of "jury crimes" rather than "petty crimes." . . .

The point is not that many offenses that English-speaking communities have, at one time or another, regarded as triable without a jury are more serious, and carry more serious penalties, than the one involved here. The point is rather that until today few people would have thought the exact location of the line mattered very much. There is no obvious reason why a jury trial is a requisite of fundamental fairness when the charge is robbery, and not a requisite of fairness when the same defendant, for the same actions, is charged with assault and petty theft. The reason for the historic exception for relatively minor crimes is the obvious one: the burden of jury trial was thought to outweigh its marginal advantages. Exactly why the States should not be allowed to make continuing adjustments, based on the state of their criminal dockets and the difficulty of summoning jurors, simply escapes me.

In sum, there is a wide range of views on the desirability of trial by jury, and on the ways to make it most effective when it is used; there is also considerable variation from State to State in local conditions such as the size of the criminal caseload, the ease or difficulty of summoning jurors, and other trial conditions bearing on fairness. We have before us, therefore, an almost perfect example of a situation in which the celebrated dictum of Mr. Justice Brandeis should be invoked. It is, he said,

> "one of the happy incidents of the federal system that a single courageous state may, if its citizens choose, serve as a laboratory * * *." New State Ice Co. v. Liebmann, 285 U.S. 262, 280, 311, 52 S. Ct. 371, 386, 76 L. Ed. 747 [(1932)] (dissenting opinion).

This Court, other courts, and the political process are available to correct any experiments in criminal procedure that prove fundamentally unfair to defendants. That is not what is being done today: instead, and quite without reason, the Court has chosen to impose upon every State one means of trying criminal cases; it is a good means, but it is not the only fair means, and it is not demonstrably better than the alternatives States might devise.

I would affirm the judgment of the Supreme Court of Louisiana.

Notes and Questions

1. Do the same circumstances and reasons that gave rise to the inclusion of a right to jury trial in the Constitution in the 18th century seem persuasive or valid today?

2. The *Duncan* Court states, "If the defendant preferred the common-sense judgment of a jury to the more tutored but perhaps less sympathetic reaction of a single judge, he was to have it." Does this language mean that a defendant is guaranteed the right to trial by jury because the jury might find him or her sympathetic and show him or her mercy? Is this fair?

3. *Duncan* tells us that a defendant who is charged with a serious crime is entitled to a jury trial and that one who is charged with a petty crime is not. The *Duncan* Court, however, did not define when a crime is serious, petty, or somewhere in between. The Court addressed this issue two years later in *Baldwin v. New York*.

Baldwin v. New York, 399 U.S. 117, 90 S. Ct. 1914, 26 L. Ed. 2d 437 (1970)

Mr. Justice White announced the judgment of the Court and delivered an opinion in which Mr. Justice Brennan and Mr. Justice Marshall join.

Appellant was arrested and charged with "jostling"—a Class A misdemeanor in New York, punishable by a maximum term of imprisonment of one year. He was brought to trial in the New York City Criminal Court. Section 40 of the New York City Criminal Court Act declares that all trials in that court shall be without a jury. Appellant's pretrial motion for jury trial was accordingly denied. He was convicted and sentenced to imprisonment for the maximum term. The New York Court of Appeals affirmed the conviction, rejecting appellant's argument that § 40 was unconstitutional insofar as it denied him an opportunity for jury trial. We noted probable jurisdiction. We reverse.

In Duncan v. Louisiana, 391 US 145, 88 S Ct 1444, 20 L Ed 2d 491 (1968), we held that the Sixth Amendment, as applied to the States through the Fourteenth, requires that defendants accused of serious crimes be afforded the right to trial by jury. We also reaffirmed the long-established view that so-called "petty offenses" may be tried without a jury. Thus the task before us in this case is the essential if not wholly satisfactory one, of determining the line between "petty" and "serious" for purposes of the Sixth Amendment right to jury trial.

Prior cases in this Court narrow our inquiry and furnish us with the standard to be used in resolving this issue. In deciding whether an offense is "petty," we have sought objective criteria reflecting the seriousness with which society regards the offense, and we have found the most relevant such criteria in the severity of the maximum authorized penalty. Applying these guidelines, we have held that a possible six-month penalty is short enough to permit classification of the offense as "petty," but that a two-year maximum is sufficiently "serious" to require an opportunity for jury trial. The question in this case is whether the possibility of a one-year sentence is enough in itself to require the opportunity for a jury trial. We hold that it is. More specifically, we have concluded that no offense can be deemed "petty" for purposes of the right to trial by jury where imprisonment for more than six months is authorized.

New York has urged us to draw the line between "petty" and "serious" to coincide with the line between misdemeanor and felony. As in most States, the maximum sentence of imprisonment for a misdemeanor in New York is one year, for a felony considerably longer. It is also true that the collateral consequences attaching to a felony conviction are more severe than those attaching to a conviction for a misdemeanor. And, like other States, New York distinguishes between misdemeanors and felonies in determining such things as whether confinement shall be in county or regional jails, rather than state prison, and whether prosecution may proceed by information or complaint, rather than by grand jury indictment. But while these considerations reflect what may readily be admitted—that a felony conviction is more serious than a misdemeanor conviction—they in no way detract from appellant's contention that some misdemeanors are also "serious" offenses. Indeed we long ago declared that the Sixth Amendment right to jury trial "is not to be construed as relating only to felonies, or offences punishable by confinement in the penitentiary. It embraces as well some classes of misdemeanors, the punishment of which involves or may involve the deprivation of the liberty of the citizen." Callan v. Wilson, 127 US 540, 549, 8 S Ct 1301, 32 L Ed 223 (1888).

A better guide "[i]n determining whether the length of the authorized prison term or the seriousness of other punishment is enough in itself to require a jury trial" is disclosed by "the existing laws and practices in the Nation." In the federal system, as we noted in Duncan, petty offenses have been defined as those punishable by no more than six months in prison and a $500 fine. And, with a few exceptions, crimes triable without a jury in the American States since the late 18th century were also generally punishable by no more than a six-month prison term. Indeed, when Duncan was decided two Terms ago, we could discover only three instances in which a State denied jury trial for a crime punishable by imprisonment for longer than six months: the Louisiana scheme at issue in Duncan, a New Jersey statute punishing disorderly conduct, and the New York City statute at issue in this case. These three instances have since been reduced to one. In response to the decision in Duncan, Louisiana has lowered the penalty for certain misdemeanors to six months, and has provided for a jury trial where the penalty still exceeds six months. New Jersey has amended its disorderly persons statute by reducing the maximum penalty to six months' imprisonment and a $500 fine. Even New York State would have provided appellant with a six-man jury trial for this offense if he had been tried outside the City of New York. In the entire Nation, New York City alone denies an accused the right to interpose between himself and a possible prison term of over six months, the commonsense judgment of a jury of his peers. This near-uniform judgment of the Nation furnishes us with the only objective criterion by which a line could ever be drawn—on the basis of the possible penalty alone—between offenses that are and that are not regarded as "serious" for purposes of trial by jury.

Of necessity, the task of drawing a line "requires attaching different consequences to events which, when they lie near the line, actually differ very little." One who is threatened with the possibility of imprisonment for six months may find little difference between the potential consequences that face him, and the consequences that faced appellant here. Indeed, the prospect of imprisonment for however short a time will seldom be viewed by the accused as a trivial or "petty" matter and may well result in quite serious repercussions affecting his career and his reputation. Where the accused cannot possibly face more than six months' imprisonment, we have held that these disadvantages, onerous though they may be, may be outweighed by the benefits that result from speedy and inexpensive nonjury adjudications. We cannot, however, conclude that these administrative conveniences, in light of the practices that now exist in every one of the 50 States as well as in the federal courts, can similarly justify denying an accused the important right to trial by jury where the possible penalty exceeds six months' imprisonment. The conviction is Reversed.

Notes and Questions

1. The length of the maximum possible term of imprisonment for a crime is not the sole factor for determining whether the offense is "petty" or "serious." In *Blanton v. City of North Las Vegas*, 489 U.S. 538, 544, 109 S. Ct. 1289, 103 L. Ed. 2d 550 (1989), the Court stated, "A defendant is entitled to a jury trial . . . if he can demonstrate that any additional statutory penalties, viewed in conjunction with the maximum authorized period of incarceration, are so severe that they clearly reflect a legislative determination that the offense in question is a 'serious' one." The *Blanton* Court went on to hold that automatic driver's license suspension, coupled with a maximum period of incarceration of six months for a first-time DUI conviction, is not sufficiently severe to make the crime "serious."

2. Does a defendant have a right to a jury trial if he is being prosecuted in a single proceeding for multiple petty offenses whose aggregate maximum period of incarceration exceeds six months? In *Lewis v. United States*, 518 U.S. 322, 116 S. Ct. 2163, 135 L. Ed. 2d 590 (1996), the Supreme Court held that a defendant in such a situation does not have a Sixth Amendment right to a jury trial. The Court held that the right to a jury trial applies only to serious offenses and that the cumulation of two or more petty offenses does not entitle the accused to a trial by jury.

3. If a person has a right to a jury trial for a crime punishable by over six months in jail, does she have the corollary right to decline to have a jury hear his or her case and instead to opt for a trial before a judge, sitting without a jury? In *Singer v. United States*, 380 U.S. 24, 85 S. Ct. 783, 13 L. Ed. 2d 630 (1965), the Supreme Court unanimously held that a defendant did not have a right to have his or her case tried before a judge alone. On the other hand, several states provide that a defendant may waive his or her right to a jury trial without the consent of the prosecution so long as the waiver is approved by the trial judge. *Cf.* NY Const. Art. 1, § 22, Ore. Const. Art. 1, § 2. Do you think a defendant should be allowed to be tried without a jury over the objections of the prosecution? What factors affect your decision?

4. Many states, through state constitutions and judicial interpretation, guarantee a criminal defendant the right to a jury trial under circumstances where a jury trial is not mandated by the U.S. Constitution.[2] A few states require that all criminal defendants be provided with trial by jury. *Cf. State v. Becker*, 130 Vt. 153, 287 A.2d 580 (1972). Several state constitutions require that a defendant be given a jury trial whenever there is the possibility of imprisonment. *Cf.* Opinion of the Justices, 135 N.H. 538, 608 A.2d 202 (1992); NH Const. Part 1 Art 15. Still other states provide the right to a jury trial in cases where a jail sentence is actually imposed. *Cf. City of Ferment v. Schumaker*, 180 W. Va. 153, 375 S.E.2d 785 (1988).

The Right to an Impartial Jury: Pretrial Publicity

One of the most difficult yet important tasks that courts are called upon to perform is to resolve cases where two or more constitutional rights are in conflict. Conflicts of this nature may arise in notorious cases that have received a great deal of pretrial publicity. On the one hand, the defendant (and also the government) has a right to an impartial jury. Also, under the Sixth Amendment, the defendant has a right to a trial in the jurisdiction where the alleged crime took place. A conflict arises when pretrial publicity—generated as the media exercise their First Amendment rights to report on newsworthy events—is so extensive in the locale where the crime occurred that it is difficult, if not impossible, to find jurors who have not been exposed to potentially prejudicial information about the defendant or the alleged crime. If the defendant wants to have the trial relocated in an effort to find an impartial jury, yet the prosecution insists on keeping the trial in the jurisdiction where the crime occurred, a court must resolve the conflicting interests. In *Murphy v. Florida*, the Supreme Court addressed the need to preserve the accused's right to an impartial jury in a highly publicized case involving a defendant known as "Murph the Surf."

Murphy v. Florida, 421 U.S. 794, 95 S. Ct. 2031, 44 L. Ed. 2d 589 (1975)

Mr. Justice **Marshall** delivered the opinion of the Court.

The question presented by this case is whether the petitioner was denied a fair trial because members of the jury had learned from news accounts about a prior felony conviction or certain facts about the crime with which he was charged. Under the circumstances of this case, we find that petitioner has not been denied due process, and we therefore affirm the judgment below.

I

Petitioner was convicted in the Dade County, Fla., Criminal Court in 1970 of breaking and entering a home, while armed, with intent to commit robbery, and of assault with intent to commit robbery. The charges stemmed from the January 1968 robbery of a Miami Beach home and petitioner's apprehension, with three others, while fleeing from the scene.

The robbery and petitioner's arrest received extensive press coverage because petitioner had been much in the news before. He had first made himself notorious for his part in the 1964 theft of the Star of India sapphire from a museum in New York. His flamboyant lifestyle made him a continuing subject of press interest; he was generally referred to—at least in the media—as "Murph the Surf."

Before the date set for petitioner's trial on the instant charges, he was indicted on two counts of murder in Broward County, Fla. Thereafter the Dade County court declared petitioner mentally incompetent to stand trial; he was committed to a hospital and the prosecutor nolle prossed the robbery indictment. In August 1968 he was indicted by a federal grand jury for conspiring to transport stolen securities in interstate commerce. After petitioner was adjudged competent for trial, he was convicted on one count of murder in Broward County (March 1969) and pleaded guilty to one count of the federal indictment involving stolen securities (December 1969). The indictment for robbery was refiled in August 1969 and came to trial one year later.

The events of 1968 and 1969 drew extensive press coverage. Each new case against petitioner was considered newsworthy, not only in Dade County, but elsewhere as well. . . .

Jury selection in the present case began in August 1970. Seventy-eight jurors were questioned. Of these, 30 were excused for miscellaneous personal reasons; 20 were excused peremptorily by the defense or prosecution; 20 were excused by the court as having prejudged petitioner; and the remaining eight served as the jury and two alternates. Petitioner's motions to dismiss the chosen jurors, on the ground that they were aware that he had previously been convicted of either the 1964 Star of India theft or the Broward County murder, were denied, as was his renewed motion for a change of venue based on allegedly prejudicial pretrial publicity. . . .

II . . .

Petitioner relies principally upon Irvin v. Dowd, 366 US 717, 81 S Ct 1639, 6 L Ed 2d 751 (1961), Rideau v. Louisiana, 373 US 723, 83 S Ct 1417, 10 L Ed 2d 663 (1963), Estes v. Texas, 381 US 532, 85 S Ct 1628, 14 L Ed 2d 543 (1965), and Sheppard v. Maxwell, 384 US 333, 86 S Ct 1507, 16 L Ed 2d 600 (1966). In each of these cases, this Court overturned a state court conviction obtained in a trial atmosphere that had been utterly corrupted by press coverage.

In Irvin v. Dowd the rural community in which the trial was held had been subjected to a barrage of inflammatory publicity immediately prior to trial, including information on the defendant's prior convictions, his confession to 24 burglaries and six murders including the one for which he was tried, and his unaccepted offer to plead guilty in order to avoid the death sentence. As a result, eight of the 12 jurors had formed an opinion that the defendant was guilty before the trial began; some went "so far as to say that it would take evidence to overcome their belief" in his guilt. In these circumstances, the Court readily found actual prejudice against the petitioner to a degree that rendered a fair trial impossible.

Prejudice was presumed in the circumstances under which the trials in Rideau, Estes, and Sheppard were held. In those cases the influence of the news media, either in the community at large or in the courtroom itself, pervaded the proceedings. In Rideau the defendant had "confessed" under police interrogation to the murder of which he stood convicted. A 20-minute film of his confession was broadcast three times by a television station in the community where the crime and the trial took place. In reversing, the Court did not examine the voir dire for evidence of actual prejudice because it considered the trial under review "but a hollow formality"—the real trial had occurred when tens of thousands of people, in a community of 150,000, had seen and heard the defendant admit his guilt before the cameras.

The trial in Estes had been conducted in a circus atmosphere, due in large part to the intrusions of the press, which was allowed to sit within the bar of the court and to overrun it with television equipment. Similarly, Sheppard arose from a trial infected not only by a background of extremely inflammatory publicity but also by a courthouse given over to accommodate the public appetite for carnival. The proceedings in these cases were entirely lacking in the solemnity and sobriety to which a defendant is entitled in a system that subscribes to any notion of fairness and rejects the verdict of a mob. They cannot be made to stand for the proposition that juror exposure to information about a state defendant's prior convictions or to news accounts of the crime with which he is charged alone presumptively deprives the defendant of due process. To resolve this case, we must turn, therefore, to any indications in the totality of circumstances that petitioner's trial was not fundamentally fair.

III

The constitutional standard of fairness requires that a defendant have "a panel of impartial, 'indifferent' jurors." Irvin v. Dowd, 366 US, at 722, 81 S Ct 1639, 6 L Ed 2d 751. Qualified jurors need not, however, be totally ignorant of the facts and issues involved.

"To hold that the mere existence of any preconceived notion as to the guilt or innocence of an accused, without more, is sufficient to rebut the presumption of a prospective juror's impartiality would be to establish an impossible standard. It is sufficient if the juror can lay aside his impression or opinion and render a verdict based on the evidence presented in court." Id., at 723, 81 S Ct 1639, 6 L Ed 2d 751.

At the same time, the juror's assurances that he is equal to this task cannot be dispositive of the accused's rights, and it remains open to the defendant to demonstrate "the actual existence of such an opinion in the mind of the juror as will raise the presumption of partiality."

The voir dire in this case indicates no such hostility to petitioner by the jurors who served in his trial as to suggest a partiality that could not be laid aside. Some of the jurors had a vague recollection of the robbery with which petitioner was charged and each had some knowledge of petitioner's past crimes, but none betrayed any belief in the relevance of petitioner's past to the present case. Indeed, four of the six jurors volunteered their views of its irrelevance, and one suggested that people who have been in trouble before are too often singled out for suspicion of each new crime—a predisposition that could only operate in petitioner's favor. . . .

Even these indicia of impartiality might be disregarded in a case where the general atmosphere in the community or courtroom is sufficiently inflammatory, but the circumstances surrounding petitioner's trial are not at all of that variety. Petitioner attempts to portray them as inflammatory by reference to the publicity to which the community was exposed. The District Court found, however, that the news articles concerning petitioner had appeared almost entirely during the period between December 1967 and January 1969, the latter date being seven months before the jury in this case was selected. . . .

The length to which the trial court must go in order to select jurors who appear to be impartial is another factor relevant in evaluating those jurors' assurances of impartiality. In a community where most veniremen will admit to a disqualifying prejudice, the reliability of the others' protestations may be drawn into question; for it is then more probable that they are part of a community deeply hostile to the accused, and more likely that they may unwittingly have been influenced by it. In Irvin v Dowd, for example, the Court noted that 90% of those examined on the point were inclined to believe in the accused's guilt, and the court had excused for this cause 268 of the 430 veniremen. In the present case, by contrast, 20 of the 78 persons questioned were excused because they indicated an opinion as to petitioner's guilt. This may indeed be 20 more than would occur in the trial of a totally obscure person, but it by no means suggests a community with sentiment so poisoned against petitioner as to impeach the indifference of jurors who displayed no animus of their own.

In sum, we are unable to conclude, in the circumstances presented in this case, that petitioner did not receive a fair trial. Petitioner has failed to show that the setting of the trial was inherently prejudicial or that the jury selection process of which he complains permits an inference of actual prejudice. The judgment of the Court of Appeals must therefore be Affirmed.

Mr. Justice **Brennan**, dissenting.

I dissent. Irvin v. Dowd requires reversal of this conviction. As in that case, petitioner here was denied a fair trial. The risk that taint of widespread publicity regarding his criminal background, known to all members of the jury, infected the jury's deliberations is apparent, the trial court made no attempt to prevent discussion of the case or petitioner's previous criminal exploits among the prospective jurors, and one juror freely admitted that he was predisposed to convict petitioner.

During voir dire, petitioner's counsel had the following colloquy with that juror:

"Q. Now, when you go into that jury room and you decide upon Murphy's guilt or innocence, you are going to take into account that fact that he is a convicted murderer; aren't you?

"A. Not if we are listening to the case, I wouldn't.

"Q. But you know about it?

"A. How can you not know about it?

"Q. Fine, thank you.

"When you go into the jury room, the fact that he is a convicted murderer, that is going to influence your verdict; is it not?

"A. We are not trying him for murder.

"Q. The fact that he is a convicted murderer and jewel thief, that would influence your verdict?

"A. I didn't know he was a convicted jewel thief.

"Q. Oh, I see.

"I am sorry I put words in your mouth.

"Now, sir, after two or three weeks of being locked up in a downtown hotel, as the Court determines, and after hearing the State's case, and after hearing no case on behalf of Murphy, and hearing no testimony from Murphy saying, 'I am innocent, Mr. [Juror]'—when you go into the jury room, sir, all these facts are going to influence your verdict?

"A. I imagine it would be.

"Q. And in fact, you are saying if Murphy didn't testify, and if he doesn't offer evidence, 'My experience of him is such that right now I would find him guilty.'

"A. I believe so."

I cannot agree with the Court that the obvious bias of this juror may be overlooked simply because the juror's response was occasioned by a "leading and hypothetical question." Indeed, the hypothetical became reality when petitioner chose not to take the stand and offered no evidence. Thus petitioner was tried by a juror predisposed, because of his knowledge of petitioner's previous crimes, to find him guilty of this one.

Others who ultimately served as jurors revealed similar prejudice toward petitioner on voir dire. One juror conceded that it would be difficult, during deliberations, to put out of his mind that petitioner was a convicted criminal. He also admitted that he did not "hold a convicted felon in the same regard as another person who has never been convicted of a felony," and admitted further that he had termed petitioner a "menace."

A third juror testified that she knew from several sources that petitioner was a convicted murderer, and was aware that the community regarded petitioner as a criminal who "should be put away." She disclaimed having a fixed opinion about the result she would reach, but acknowledged that the fact that petitioner was a convicted criminal would probably influence her verdict:

> "Q. Now, if you go into that jury room and deliberate with your fellow jurors, in your deliberations, will you consider the fact that Murphy is a convicted murderer and jewel thief?
> "A. Well, he has been convicted of murder. So, I guess that is what I would—
> "Q. You would consider that in your verdict, right?
> "A. Right.
> "Q. And that would influence your verdict; would it not?
> "A. If that is what you say, I guess it would."
> "Q. I am not concerned about what I say, because if I said it, they wouldn't print it. It would influence your verdict?
> "A. It probably would.
> "Q. When you go into that jury room, you cannot forget the fact that it is Murph the Surf; that he is a convicted murderer, and a jewel thief—you can't put that out of your

mind, no matter what they tell you; can you, ma'am?
> "A. Probably not.
> "Q. And it would influence your verdict; right?
> "A. Probably."

Still another juror testified that the comments of venire members in discussing the case had made him "sick to [his] stomach." He testified that one venireman had said that petitioner was "thoroughly rotten," and that another had said: "Hang him, he's guilty."

Moreover, the Court ignores the crucial significance of the fact that at no time before or during this daily buildup of prejudice against Murphy did the trial judge instruct the prospective jurors not to discuss the case among themselves. Indeed the trial judge took no steps to insulate the jurors from media coverage of the case or from the many news articles that discussed petitioner's last criminal exploits.

It is of no moment that several jurors ultimately testified that they would try to exclude from their deliberations their knowledge of petitioner's past misdeeds and of his community reputation. Irvin held in like circumstances that little weight could be attached to such self-serving protestations:

> "No doubt each juror was sincere when he said that he would be fair and impartial to petitioner, but the psychological impact requiring such a declaration before one's fellows is often its father. Where so many, so many times, admitted prejudice, such a statement of impartiality can be given little weight. As one of the jurors put it, 'You can't forget what you hear and see.'" 366 US, at 728, 81 S Ct 1639, 6 L Ed 2d 751.

On the record of this voir dire, therefore, the conclusion is to me inescapable that the attitude of the entire venire toward Murphy reflected the "then current community pattern of thought as indicated by the popular news media," and was infected with the taint of the view that he was a "criminal" guilty of notorious offenses, including that for which he was on trial. It is a plain case, from a review of the entire voir dire, where "the extent and nature of the publicity has caused such a build up of prejudice that excluding the preconception of guilt from the deliberations would be too difficult for the jury to be honestly found impartial." United States ex rel. Bloeth v. Denno, 313 F2d 364, 372 (CA2 1963). In my view, the denial of a change of venue was therefore prejudicial error, and I would reverse the conviction.

Notes and Questions

1. Note that complete ignorance on the part of jurors is not necessary. Would such ignorance be desirable? If so, should we strive for it? Some cases are so notorious that the chances are very slim of finding people, either inside or outside of the jurisdiction where the crime occurred, who have not heard anything about them. The following joke that circulated during jury selection for the O.J. Simpson murder trial illustrates the absurdity of such a goal.

Judge Ito (to juror):	Knock knock.
Juror:	Who's there?
Judge Ito:	O.J.
Juror:	O.J. who?
Judge Ito:	Okay, you can be on the jury.

Obviously, this is not the way jurors should be selected. The example illustrates the ramifications of requiring jurors to be totally ignorant about a case or a defendant. Accordingly, people may serve on a jury if they can put the knowledge they have gained about the case from other sources out of their minds, and reach a verdict based solely on the evidence presented to them in the courtroom. Do you think that people, try as they might, actually can perform such mental gymnastics? In light of the alternative, is the law justified in holding prospective jurors to this exception?

2. The Sixth Amendment provides for a "*public* trial, by an impartial jury." Since trials are open to the public, the press also has access to courtrooms, so it can be difficult to find jurors who have not been influenced by media reports of the crime or pretrial proceedings. As a result of this tension, courts have resorted to several methods to protect the defendant's right to a fair trial by an impartial jury and also to respect the press's and public's right to be present at and report on the proceedings.

If the trial court believes that the defendant cannot receive a fair trial in the jurisdiction where the crime was committed, it may order a change of venue: that is, it may remove the trial to another location where potential jurors have been exposed to less extensive pretrial publicity. The judge can also postpone the trial for a period of time until the furor over the case dies down. Under appropriate circumstances, the judge can issue a *gag order* that bars the participants in the trial from speaking about the case publicly or with members of the media.

While actions such as these sometimes are taken, in practice they are reserved for exceptional cases. Moreover, trial judges' decisions about scheduling trials are given a great deal of latitude by appellate courts. Absent at least a reasonable likelihood of prejudice to the defendant resulting from pretrial publicity, appellate courts will not disturb a trial court's refusal to take the steps listed above.

In *Sheppard v. Maxwell*, 384 U.S. 333, 86 S. Ct. 1507, 16 L. Ed. 2d 600 (1966), the Supreme Court considered how a trial court should handle a situation in which the publicity surrounding a case endangers the defendant's ability to receive a fair trial. Dr. Sam Sheppard was accused of murdering his wife in 1954. Prior to trial, the case received extensive media attention. It was the subject of countless newspaper articles and editorials, as well as extensive coverage by television and radio stations. As the trial of Dr. Sheppard began, the media coverage only intensified.

Sheppard v. Maxwell, 384 U.S. 333, 86 S. Ct. 1507, 16 L. Ed. 2d 600 (1966)

Mr. Justice **Clark** delivered the opinion of the Court.

This federal habeas corpus application involves the question whether Sheppard was deprived of a fair trial in his state conviction for the second-degree murder of his wife because of the trial judge's failure to protect Sheppard sufficiently from the massive, pervasive and prejudicial publicity that attended his prosecution. The United States District Court held that he was not afforded a fair trial and granted the writ subject to the State's right to put Sheppard to trial again, 231 F Supp 37 (DCSD Ohio 1964). The Court of Appeals for the Sixth Circuit reversed by a divided vote, 346 F2d 707 (1965). We granted certiorari, 382 US 916, 86 S Ct 289, 15 L Ed 2d 231 (1965). We have concluded that Sheppard did not receive a fair trial consistent with the Due Process Clause of the Fourteenth Amendment and, therefore, reversed the judgment.

I.

Marilyn Sheppard, petitioner's pregnant wife, was bludgeoned to death in the upstairs bedroom of their lakeshore home in Bay Village, Ohio, a suburb of Cleveland. . . .

[The Court proceeded to give details about the extensive media coverage surrounding the case.]

II.

With this background the case came on for trial two weeks before the November general election at which the chief prosecutor was a candidate for common pleas judge and the trial judge, Judge Blythin, was a candidate to succeed himself. Twenty-five days before the case was set, 75 veniremen were called as prospective jurors. All three Cleveland newspapers published the names and addresses of the veniremen. As a consequence, anonymous letters and telephone calls, as well as calls from friends, regarding the impending prosecution were received by all of the prospective jurors. The selection of the jury began on October 18, 1954.

The courtroom in which the trial was held measured 26 by 48 feet. A long temporary table was set up inside the bar, in back of the single counsel table. It ran the width of the courtroom, parallel to the bar railing, with one end less than three feet from the jury box. Approximately 20 representatives of newspapers and wire services were assigned seats at this table by the court. Behind the bar railing there were four rows of benches. These seats were likewise assigned by the court for the entire trial. The first row was occupied by representatives of television and radio stations, and the second and third rows by reporters from out-of-town newspapers and magazines. . . .

Representatives of the news media also used all the rooms on the courtroom floor, including the room where cases were ordinarily called and assigned for trial. Private telephone lines and telegraphic equipment were installed in these rooms so that reports from the trial court could be speeded to the papers. Station WSRS was permitted to set up broadcasting facilities on the third floor of the courthouse next door to the jury room, where the jury rested during recesses in the trial and deliberated. Newscasts were made from this room throughout the trial, and while the jury reached its verdict.

On the sidewalk and steps in front of the courthouse, television and newsreel cameras were occasionally used to take motion pictures of the participants in the trial, including the jury and the judge. Indeed, one television broadcast carried a staged interview of the judge as he entered the courthouse. In the corridors outside the courtroom there was a host of photographers and television personnel with flash cameras, portable lights and motion picture cameras. This group photographed the prospective jurors during selection of the jury. After the trial opened, the witnesses, counsel, and jurors were photographed and televised whenever they entered or left the courtroom. Sheppard was brought to the courtroom about 10 minutes before each session began; he was surrounded by reporters and extensively photographed for the newspapers and television. . . .

All of these arrangements with the news media and their massive coverage of the trial continued during the entire nine weeks of the trial. The courtroom remained crowded to capacity with representatives of news media. Their movement in and out of the courtroom often caused so much confusion that, despite the loud-speaker system installed in the courtroom, it was difficult for the witnesses and counsel to be heard. Furthermore, the reporters clustered within the bar of the small courtroom made confidential talk among Sheppard and his counsel almost impossible during the proceedings. They frequently had to leave the courtroom to obtain privacy. And many times when counsel wished to raise a point with the judge out of the hearing of the jury it was necessary to move to the judge's chambers. Even then, news media representatives so packed the judge's anteroom that counsel could hardly return from the chambers to the courtroom. The reporters vied with each other to find out what counsel and the judge had discussed, and often these matters later appeared in newspapers accessible to the jury. . . .

The jurors themselves were constantly exposed to the news media. Every juror, except one, testified at voir dire to reading about the case in the Cleveland papers or to having heard broadcasts about it. Seven of the 12 jurors who rendered the verdict had one or more Cleveland papers delivered in their home; the remaining jurors were not interrogated on the point. Nor were there questions as to radios or television sets in the jurors' homes, but we must assume that most of them owned such conveniences. As the selection of the jury progressed, individual pictures of prospective members appeared daily. During the trial, pictures of the jury appeared over 40 times in the Cleveland papers alone. The court permitted photographers to take pictures of the jury in the box, and individual pictures of the members in the jury room. One newspaper ran pictures of the jurors at the Sheppard home when they went there to view the scene of the murder. Another paper featured the home life of an alternate juror. The day

before the verdict was rendered—while the jurors were at lunch and sequestered by two bailiffs—the jury was separated into two groups to pose for photographs which appeared in the newspapers.

III.

We now reach the conduct of the trial. While the intense publicity continued unabated, it is sufficient to relate only the more flagrant episodes: . . .

2. On the second day of voir dire examination a debate was staged and broadcast live over WHK radio. The participants, newspaper reporters, accused Sheppard's counsel of throwing roadblocks in the way of the prosecution and asserted that Sheppard conceded his guilt by hiring a prominent criminal lawyer. Sheppard's counsel objected to this broadcast and requested a continuance, but the judge denied the motion. When counsel asked the court to give some protection from such events, the judge replied that "WHK doesn't have much coverage," and that "[a]fter all, we are not trying this case by radio or in newspapers or any other means. We confine ourselves seriously to it in this courtroom and do the very best we can."

3. While the jury was being selected, a two-inch headline asked: "But Who Will Speak for Marilyn?" . . . The author—through quotes from Detective Chief James McArthur—assured readers that the prosecution's exhibits would speak for Marilyn. "Her story," McArthur stated, "will come into this courtroom through our witnesses." The article ends:

"Then you realize how what and who is missing from the perfect setting will be supplied.

"How in the Big Case justice will be done.

"Justice to Sam Sheppard."

"And to Marilyn Sheppard.". . .

5. On November 19, a Cleveland police officer gave testimony that tended to contradict details in the written statement Sheppard made to the Cleveland police. Two days later, in a broadcast heard over Station WHK in Cleveland, Robert Considine likened Sheppard to a perjurer and compared the episode to Alger Hiss' confrontation with Whittaker Chambers. Though defense counsel asked the judge to question the jury to ascertain how many heard the broadcast, the

court refused to do so. The judge also overruled the motion for continuance based on the same ground, saying:

"Well, I don't know, we can't stop people, in any event, listening to it. It is a matter of free speech, and the court can't control everybody. . . . We are not going to harass the jury every morning. . . . It is getting to the point where if we do it every morning, we are suspecting the jury. I have confidence in this jury. . . ."

6. On November 24, a story appeared under an eight-column headline: "Sam Called A 'Jekyll-Hyde' By Marilyn, Cousin To Testify." It related that Marilyn had recently told friends that Sheppard was a "Dr. Jekyll and Mr. Hyde" character. No such testimony was ever produced at the trial. The story went on to announce: "The prosecution has a 'bombshell witness' on tap who will testify to Dr. Sam's display of fiery temper—countering the defense claim that the defendant is a gentle physician with an even disposition." Defense counsel made motions for change of venue, continuance and mistrial, but they were denied. No action was taken by the court.

7. When the trial was in its seventh week, Walter Winchell broadcast over WXEL television and WJW radio that Carole Beasley, who was under arrest in New York City for robbery, had stated that, as Sheppard's mistress, she had borne him a child. The defense asked that the jury be queried on the broadcast. Two jurors admitted in open court that they had heard it. The judge asked each: "Would that have any effect upon your judgment?" Both replied, "No." This was accepted by the judge as sufficient; he merely asked the jury to "pay no attention whatever to that type of scavenging. . . . Let's confine ourselves to this courtroom, if you please." In answer to the motion for mistrial, the judge said:

"Well, even, so, Mr. Corrigan, how are you ever going to prevent those things, in any event? I don't justify them at all. I think it is outrageous, but in a sense, it is outrageous even if there were no trial here. The trial has nothing to do with it in the Court's mind, as far as its outrage is concerned, but—

"Mr. Corrigan: "I don't know what effect it had on the mind of any of these jurors, and I can't find out unless inquiry is made.

"The Court: How would you ever, in any jury, avoid that kind of a thing?". . .

IV.

The principle that justice cannot survive behind walls of silence has long been reflected in the "Anglo-American distrust for secret trials." In re Oliver, 333 US 257, 268, 68 S Ct 499, 92 L Ed 682, 691 (1948). A responsible press has always been regarded as the handmaiden of effective judicial administration, especially in the criminal field. Its function in this regard is documented by an impressive record of service over several centuries. The press does not simply publish information about trials but guards against the miscarriage of justice by subjecting the police, prosecutors, and judicial processes to extensive public scrutiny and criticism. This Court has, therefore, been unwilling to place any direct limitations on the freedom traditionally exercised by the news media for "[w]hat transpires in the court room is public property." Craig v. Harney, 331 US 367, 374, 67 S Ct 1249, 91 L Ed 1546, 1551 (1947). The "unqualified prohibitions laid down by the framers were intended to give to liberty of the press . . . the broadest scope that could be countenanced in an orderly society." Bridges v. California, 314 US 252, 265, 62 S Ct 190, 86 L Ed 192, 204 (1941). And where there was "no threat or menace to the integrity of the trial," Craig v. Harney, supra, 331 US at 377, we have consistently required that the press have a free hand, even though we sometimes deplored its sensationalism.

But the Court has also pointed out that "[l]egal trials are not like elections, to be won through the use of the meeting-hall, the radio, and the newspaper." Bridges v. California, supra. And the Court has insisted that no one be punished for a crime without "a charge fairly made and fairly tried in a public tribunal free of prejudice, passion, excitement, and tyrannical power." Chambers v. Florida, 309 US 227, 236–237, 60 S Ct 472, 84 L Ed 716, 722 (1940). "Freedom of discussion should be given the widest range compatible with the essential requirement of the fair and orderly administration of justice." Pennekamp v. Florida, 328 US 331, 347, 66 S Ct 1029, 90 L Ed 1295, 1303 (1946). But it must not be allowed to divert the trial from the "very purpose of a court system . . . to adjudicate controversies, both criminal and civil, in the calmness and solemnity of the courtroom according to legal procedures." Cox v. Louisiana, 379 US 559, 583, 13 L Ed 2d 487, 503, 85 S Ct 476 (1965) (Black, J., dissenting). Among these "legal procedures" is the requirement that the jury's verdict be based on evidence received in open court, not from outside sources. Thus, in Marshall v. United States, 360 US 310, 79 S Ct 1171, 3 L Ed 2d 1250 (1959), we set aside a federal conviction where the jurors were exposed "through news accounts" to information that was not admitted at trial. We held that the prejudice from such material "may indeed be greater" than when it is part of the prosecution's evidence "for it is then not tempered by protective procedures." At the same time, we did not consider dispositive the statement of each juror "that he would not be influenced by the news articles, that he could decide the case only on the evidence of record, and that he felt no prejudice against petitioner as a result of the articles." Likewise, in Irvin v. Dowd, 366 US 717, 81 S Ct 1639, 6 L Ed 2d 751 (1961), even though each juror indicated that he could render an impartial verdict despite exposure to prejudicial newspaper articles, we set aside the conviction holding:

"With his life at stake, it is not requiring too much that petitioner be tried in an atmosphere undisturbed by so huge a wave of public passion. . . ."

The undeviating rule of this Court was expressed by Mr. Justice Holmes over half a century ago in Patterson v. Colorado, 205 US 454, 462, 27 S Ct 556, 51 L Ed 879, 881 (1907):

"The theory of our system is that the conclusions to be reached in a case will be induced only by evidence and argument in open court, and not by any outside influence, whether of private talk or public print."

Moreover, "the burden of showing essential unfairness . . . as a demonstrable reality," Adams v. United States ex rel. McCann, 317 US 269, 281, 63 S Ct 236, 87 L Ed 268, 276 (1942), need not be undertaken when television has exposed the community "repeatedly and in depth to the spectacle of [the accused] personally confessing in detail to the crimes with which he was later to be charged. . . ."

V.

It is clear that the totality of circumstances in this case also warrants such an approach. . . . Sheppard was not granted a change of venue to a locale away from where the publicity originated; nor was his jury sequestered. . . . [T]he Sheppard jurors were subjected to newspaper, radio and television coverage of the trial while not taking part in the proceedings. They were allowed to go their separate ways outside of the courtroom, without adequate directions not to read or listen to anything concerning the case. The judge's "admonitions" at the beginning of the trial are representative:

"I would suggest to you and caution you that you do not read any newspapers during the progress of this trial, that you do not listen to radio comments nor watch or listen to television comments, insofar as this case is concerned. You will feel very much better as the trial proceeds . . . I am sure that we shall all feel very much better if we do not indulge in any newspaper reading or listening to any comments whatever about the matter while the case is in progress. After it is all over, you can read it all to your heart's content . . . ."

At intervals during the trial, the judge simply repeated his "suggestions" and "requests" that the jurors not expose themselves to comment upon the case. Moreover, the jurors were thrust into the role of celebrities by the judge's failure to insulate them from reporters and photographers.

The numerous pictures of the jurors, with their addresses, which appeared in the newspapers before and during the trial itself exposed them to expressions of opinion from both cranks and friends. The fact that anonymous letters had been received by prospective jurors should have made the judge aware that this publicity seriously threatened the jurors' privacy. . . .

Sheppard stood indicted for the murder of his wife; the State was demanding the death penalty. For months the virulent publicity about Sheppard and the murder had made the case notorious. Charges and countercharges were aired in the news media besides those for which Sheppard was called to trial. In addition, only three months before trial, Sheppard was examined for more than five hours without counsel during a three-day inquest which ended in a public brawl. The inquest was televised live from a high school gymnasium seating hundreds of people. Furthermore, the trial began two weeks before a hotly contested election at which both Chief Prosecutor Mahon and Judge Blythin were candidates for judgeships.[9]

While we cannot say that Sheppard was denied due process by the judge's refusal to take precautions against the influence of pretrial publicity alone, the court's later rulings must be considered against the setting in which the trial was held. In light of this background, we believe that the arrangements made by the judge with the news media caused Sheppard to be deprived of that "judicial serenity and calm to which [he] was entitled." Estes v. Texas, supra. The fact is that bedlam reigned at the courthouse during the trial and newsmen took over practically the entire courtroom, hounding most of the participants in the trial, especially Sheppard. At a temporary table within a few feet of the jury box and counsel table sat some 20 reporters staring at Sheppard and taking notes. The erection of a press table for reporters inside the bar is unprecedented. The bar of the court is reserved for counsel, providing them a safe place in which to keep papers and exhibits, and to confer privately with client and co-counsel. It is designed to protect the witness and the jury

---

9. At the commencement of trial, defense counsel made motions for continuance and change of venue. The judge postponed ruling on these motions until he determined whether an impartial jury could be impaneled. Voir dire examination showed that with one exception all members selected for jury service had read something about the case in the newspapers. Since, however, all of the jurors stated that they would not be influenced by what they had read or seen, the judge overruled both of the motions. Without regard to whether the judge's actions in this respect reach dimensions that would justify issuance of the habeas writ, it should be noted that a short continuance would have alleviated any problem with regard to the judicial elections. The court in Delaney v. United States, 199 F2d 107, 115 (CA 1st Cir 1952), recognized such a duty under similar circumstances, holding that "if assurance of a fair trial would necessitate that the trial of the case be postponed until after the election, then we think the law required no less than that."

from any distractions, intrusions or influences and to permit bench discussions of the judge's rulings away from the hearing of the public and the jury. Having assigned almost all of the available seats in the courtroom to the news media, the judge lost his ability to supervise the environment. . . .

Moreover, the judge gave the throng of newsmen gathered in the corridors of the courthouse absolute free rein. Participants in the trial, including the jury, were forced to run a gantlet of reporters and photographers each time they entered or left the courtroom. The total lack of consideration for the privacy of the jury was demonstrated by the assignment to a broadcasting station of space next to the jury room on the floor above the courtroom, as well as the fact that jurors were allowed to make telephone calls during their five-day deliberation.

VI.

. . . Much of the material printed or broadcast during the trial was never heard from the witness stand, such as the charges that Sheppard had purposely impeded the murder investigation and must be guilty since he had hired a prominent criminal lawyer; that Sheppard was a perjurer; that he had sexual relations with numerous women; that his slain wife had characterized him as a "Jekyll-Hyde"; that he was "a bare-faced liar" because of his testimony as to police treatment; and, finally, that a woman convict claimed Sheppard to be the father of her illegitimate child. As the trial progressed, the newspapers summarized and interpreted the evidence, devoting particular attention to the material that incriminated Sheppard, and often drew unwarranted inferences from testimony. At one point, a front-page picture of Mrs. Sheppard's bloodstained pillow was published after being "doctored" to show more clearly an alleged imprint of a surgical instrument.

Nor is there doubt that this deluge of publicity reached at least some of the jury. On the only occasion that the jury was queried, two jurors admitted in open court to hearing the highly inflammatory charge that a prison inmate claimed Sheppard as the father of her illegitimate child. Despite the extent and nature of the publicity to which the jury was exposed during trial, the judge refused defense counsel's other requests that the jurors be asked whether they had read or heard specific prejudicial comment about the case, including the incidents we have previously summarized. In these circumstances, we can assume that some of this material reached members of the jury.

VII.

The court's fundamental error is compounded by the holding that it lacked power to control the publicity about the trial. From the very inception of the proceedings the judge announced that neither he nor anyone else could restrict prejudicial news accounts. And he reiterated this view on numerous occasions. Since he viewed the news media as his target, the judge never considered other means that are often utilized to reduce the appearance of prejudicial material and to protect the jury from outside influence. We conclude that these procedures would have been sufficient to guarantee Sheppard a fair trial and so do not consider what sanctions might be available against a recalcitrant press nor the charges of bias now made against the state trial judge.

The carnival atmosphere at trial could easily have been avoided since the courtroom and courthouse premises are subject to the control of the court. As we stressed in Estes, the presence of the press at judicial proceedings must be limited when it is apparent that the accused might otherwise be prejudiced or disadvantaged. Bearing in mind the massive pretrial publicity, the judge should have adopted stricter rules governing the use of the courtroom by newsmen, as Sheppard's counsel requested. . . .

Secondly, the court should have insulated the witnesses. All of the newspapers and radio stations apparently interviewed prospective witnesses at will, and in many instances disclosed their testimony. . . .

Thirdly, the court should have made some effort to control the release of leads, information, and gossip to the press by police officers, witnesses, and the counsel for both sides. Much of the information thus disclosed was inaccurate, leading to groundless rumors and confusion. . . .

Defense counsel immediately brought to the court's attention the tremendous amount of publicity in the Cleveland press that "misrepresented entirely the testimony" in the case. Under such circumstances, the judge should have at least warned the newspapers to check the accuracy of their accounts. And it is obvious that the judge should have further sought to alleviate this problem by imposing control over the statements made to the news media by counsel, witnesses, and especially the Coroner and police officers. The prosecution repeatedly made evidence available to the news media which was never offered in the trial. Much of the "evidence" disseminated in this fashion was clearly inadmissible. The exclusion of such evidence in court is rendered meaningless when news media make it available to the public. . . .

The fact that many of the prejudicial news items can be traced to the prosecution, as well as the defense, aggravates the judge's failure to take any action. Effective control of these sources—concededly within the court's power—might well have prevented the divulgence of inaccurate information, rumors, and accusations that made up much of the inflammatory publicity, at least after Sheppard's indictment. . . .

Due process requires that the accused receive a trial by an impartial jury free from outside influences. Given the pervasiveness of modern communications and the difficulty of effacing prejudicial publicity from the minds of the jurors, the trial courts must take strong measures to ensure that the balance is never weighed against the accused. And appellate tribunals have the duty to make an independent evaluation of the circumstances. Of course, there is nothing that proscribes the press from reporting events that transpire in the courtroom. But where there is a reasonable likelihood that prejudicial news prior to trial will prevent a fair trial, the judge should continue the case until the threat abates, or transfer it to another county not so permeated with publicity. In addition, sequestration of the jury was something the judge should have raised sua sponte with counsel. If publicity during the proceedings threatens the fairness of the trial, a new trial should be ordered. But we must remember that reversals are but palliatives; the cure lies in those remedial measures that will prevent the prejudice at its inception. The courts must take such steps by rule and regulation that will protect their processes from prejudicial outside interferences.

Neither prosecutors, counsel for defense, the accused, witnesses, court staff nor enforcement officers coming under the jurisdiction of the court should be permitted to frustrate its function. Collaboration between counsel and the press as to information affecting the fairness of a criminal trial is not only subject to regulation, but is highly censurable and worthy of disciplinary measures.

Since the state trial judge did not fulfill his duty to protect Sheppard from the inherently prejudicial publicity which saturated the community and to control disruptive influences in the courtroom, we must reverse the denial of the habeas petition. The case is remanded to the District Court with instructions to issue the writ and order that Sheppard be released from custody unless the State puts him to its charges again within a reasonable time.

It is so ordered.

Notes and Questions

1. State trial judges are elected in many jurisdictions, including in Ohio when Dr. Sheppard was tried. Does this practice put undue pressure on judges who must be concerned with reelection? See *Harris v. Alabama*, 513 U.S. 504, 115 S. Ct. 1031, 1038–1039, 130 L. Ed. 2d 1004 (1995) (Stevens, J., dissenting).

2. For an excellent depiction of the Sheppard case see C.L. Cooper and S.R. Sheppard, *Mockery of Justice: The True Story of the Sheppard Murder Case*, Boston: Northeastern University Press, 1995, which was coauthored by Dr. Sheppard's son.

3. What parallels do you draw between *Sheppard* and the trial of O.J. Simpson? Assume for a moment that Mr. Simpson asked the trial court to transfer his trial out of Los Angeles County. Under the Supreme Court's rulings in *Murphy* and *Sheppard*, if Mr. Simpson had been convicted of murder, how do you suppose an appellate court would have ruled on a claim that he was denied the right to a fair trial because of pretrial publicity? In reality, Mr. Simpson would have waived his right to raise this matter on appeal given the fact that he did not request a change of venue. He was in fact pleased to have his trial held in central Los Angeles.

4. In 1991, four Los Angeles police officers were charged with assault and other related charges arising from their conduct during the apprehension of Rodney King. The incident, which was recorded on videotape, entailed a group of white police officers using physical force against Rodney King, a black man, following a lengthy high-speed chase. Several of the officers were indicted in Los Angeles County. The officers filed a motion for a change of venue due to the notoriety the case received in Los Angeles. The trial court denied the motion, but the California Court of Appeals reversed, holding that the defendants could not receive a fair trial in Los Angeles County. *Powell v. Superior Court*, 232 Cal. App. 3d 785 (1991). The trial was subsequently transferred to the affluent suburb of Simi Valley. At trial, the four police officers were acquitted on all counts by an all-white jury. Following the acquittals, Los Angeles erupted in riot.

Jury Selection

It is often said and widely believed that a jury trial can be won or lost during jury selection. Consequently, actions and rules that affect the composition of juries have been highly litigated. The litigation has focused on actions taken during two stages of the adjudication process: calling potential jurors to court from the general population and excluding potential jurors who appear in court from serving on juries as a result of selection procedures.

Names of potential jurors who might be called to court can be chosen from several different sources. Some jurisdictions identify potential jurors solely from voter registration lists and/or property tax registries. Others also get names from driver's license records, public assistance lists, and other sources. Which sources seem most likely to include the greatest number of names of persons eligible for jury service? Are there any drawbacks to using less inclusive lists? Do any of the lists exclude a recognizable class of individuals?

Whatever the source, and however the lists used to identify potential jurors are compiled, the selection system used must pass constitutional muster. Specifically, it must not discriminate against a discrete or "cognizable" class of individuals, and it must represent a fair cross-section of the community. Of course, invidious discrimination would be easy to detect if a jurisdiction had laws or court rules prohibiting a class of people from serving as jurors. *Strauder v. West Virginia*, 100 U.S. 303, 25 L. Ed. 664 (1880). However, what if instead of explicitly precluding certain members of society from jury service, a state permitted members of a group to be jurors, but only if they individually petitioned to serve? Such was the system the Supreme Court considered in *Taylor v. Louisiana*.

Taylor v. Louisiana, 419 U.S. 522, 95 S. Ct. 692, 42 L. Ed. 2d 690 (1975)

Mr. Justice **White** delivered the opinion of the Court.

When this case was tried, Art VII, § 41, of the Louisiana Constitution, and Art 402 of the Louisiana Code of Criminal Procedure provided that a woman should not be selected for jury service unless she had previously filed a written declaration of her desire to be subject to jury service. The constitutionality of these provisions is the issue in this case.

I

Appellant, Billy J. Taylor, was indicted by the grand jury of St. Tammany Parish, in the Twenty-second Judicial District of Louisiana, for aggravated kidnapping. On April 12, 1972, appellant moved the trial court to quash the petit jury venire drawn for the special criminal term beginning with his trial the following day. Appellant alleged that women were systematically excluded from the venire and that he would therefore be deprived of what he claimed to be his federal constitutional right to "a fair trial by jury of a representative segment of the community. . . ."

The Twenty-second Judicial District is comprised of the parishes of St. Tammany and Washington. The appellee has stipulated that 53% of the persons eligible for jury service in these parishes were female, and that no more than 10% of the persons on the jury wheel in St. Tammany Parish were women. During the period from December 8, 1971, to November 3, 1972, 12 females were among the 1,800 persons drawn to fill petit jury venires in St. Tammany Parish. It was also stipulated that the discrepancy between females eligible for jury service and those actually included in the venire was the result of the operation of La Const, Art VII, § 41, and La Code Crim Proc, Art 402. In the present case, a venire totaling 175 persons was drawn for jury service beginning April 13, 1972. There were no females on the venire.

Appellant's motion to quash the venire was denied that same day. After being tried, Appellant was convicted. . . .

II

The Louisiana jury selection system does not disqualify women from jury service, but in operation its conceded systematic impact is that only a very few women, grossly disproportionate to the number of eligible women in the community, are called for jury service. In this case, no women were on the venire from which the petit jury was drawn. The issue we have, therefore, is whether a jury-selection system which operates to exclude from jury service an identifiable class of citizens constituting 53% of eligible jurors in the community comports with the Sixth and Fourteenth Amendments.

The State first insists that Taylor, a male, has no standing to object to the exclusion of women from his jury. But Taylor's claim is that he was constitutionally entitled to a jury drawn from a venire constituting a fair cross section of the community and that the jury that tried him was not such a jury by reason of the exclusion of women. Taylor was not a member of the excluded class; but there is no rule that claims such as Taylor presents may be made only by those defendants who are members of the group excluded from jury service. . . .

Taylor, in the case before us, was . . . entitled to tender and have adjudicated the claim that the exclusion of women from jury service deprived him of the kind of factfinder to which he was constitutionally entitled.

III

The background against which this case must be decided includes our holding in Duncan v. Louisiana, 391 US 145, 88 S Ct 1444, 20 L Ed 2d 491 (1968), that the Sixth Amendment's provision for jury trial is made binding on the States by virtue of the Fourteenth Amendment. Our inquiry is whether the presence of a fair cross section of the community on venires, panels, or lists from which petit juries are drawn is essential to the fulfillment of the Sixth Amendment's guarantee of an impartial jury trial in criminal prosecutions.

The Court's prior cases are instructive. Both in the course of exercising its supervisory powers over trials in federal courts and in the constitutional context, the Court has unambiguously declared that the American concept of the jury trial contemplates a jury drawn from a fair cross section of the community. A unanimous Court stated in Smith v. Texas, 311 US 128, 130, 61 S

Ct 164, 85 L Ed 84 (1940), that "[i]t is part of the established tradition in the use of juries as instruments of public justice that the jury be a body truly representative of the community." To exclude racial groups from jury service was said to be "at war with our basic concepts of a democratic society and a representative government." . . .

A federal conviction by a jury from which women had been excluded, although eligible for service under state law, was reviewed in Ballard v. United States, 329 US 187, 67 S Ct 261, 91 L Ed 181 (1946). Noting the federal statutory "design to make the jury 'a cross-section of the community'" and the fact that women had been excluded, the Court exercised its supervisory powers over the federal courts and reversed the conviction. . . .

The unmistakable import of this Court's opinions, at least since 1940, and not repudiated by intervening decisions, is that the selection of a petit jury from a representative cross section of the community is an essential component of the Sixth Amendment right to a jury trial. Recent federal legislation governing jury selection within the federal court system has a similar thrust. Shortly prior to this Court's decision in Duncan v. Louisiana, the Federal Jury Selection and Service Act of 1968 was enacted. In that Act, Congress stated "the policy of the United States that all litigants in Federal courts entitled to trial by jury shall have the right to grand and petit juries selected at random from a fair cross section of the community in the district or division wherein the court convenes." In that Act, Congress also established the machinery by which the stated policy was to be implemented. In passing this legislation, the Committee Reports of both the House and the Senate recognized that the jury plays a political function in the administration of the law and that the requirement of a jury's being chosen from a fair cross section of the community is fundamental to the American system of justice. Debate on the floors of the House and Senate on the Act invoked the Sixth Amendment, the Constitution generally, and prior decisions of this Court in support of the Act.

We accept the fair-cross-section requirement as fundamental to the jury trial guaranteed by the Sixth Amendment and are convinced that the requirement has solid foundation. The purpose of a jury is to guard against the exercise of arbitrary power—to make available the common-sense judgment of the community as a hedge against the overzealous or mistaken prosecutor and in preference to the professional or perhaps overconditioned or biased response of a judge. Duncan v. Louisiana, 391 US, at 155–156, 88 S Ct 1444, 20 L Ed 2d 491. This prophylactic vehicle is not provided if the jury pool is made up of only special segments of the populace or if large, distinctive groups are excluded from the pool. Community participation in the administration of the criminal law, moreover, is not only consistent with our democratic heritage but is also critical to public confidence in the fairness of the criminal justice system. Restricting jury service to only special groups or excluding identifiable segments playing major roles in the community cannot be squared with the constitutional concept of jury trial. "Trial by jury presupposes a jury drawn from a pool broadly representative of the community as well as impartial in a specific case. . . . [T]he broad representative character of the jury should be maintained, partly as assurance of a diffused impartiality and partly because sharing in the administration of justice is a phase of civic responsibility." Thiel v. Southern Pacific Co. 328 US 217, 227, 66 S Ct 984, 90 L Ed 1181 (1946) (Frankfurter, J., dissenting).

IV

We are also persuaded that the fair-cross-section requirement is violated by the systematic exclusion of women, who in the judicial district involved here amounted to 53% of the citizens eligible for jury service. This conclusion necessarily entails the judgment that women are sufficiently numerous and distinct from men and that if they are systematically eliminated from jury panels, the Sixth Amendment's fair-cross-section requirement cannot be satisfied. This very matter was debated in Ballard v. United States. Positing the fair-cross-section rule—there said to be a statutory one—the Court concluded that the systematic exclusion of women was unacceptable. The dissenting view that an all-male panel drawn from various groups in the community would be as truly representative as if women were included, was firmly rejected:

The thought is that the factors which tend to influence the action of women are the same as those which influence the action of men—personality, background, economic status—and not sex. Yet it is not enough to say that women when sitting as jurors neither act nor tend to act as a class. Men likewise do not act as a class. But, if the shoe were on the other foot, who would claim that a jury was truly representative of the community if all men were intentionally and systematically excluded from the panel? The truth is that the two sexes are not fungible; a community made up exclusively of one is different from a community composed of both; the subtle interplay of influence one on the other is among the imponderables. To insulate the courtroom from either may not in a given case make an iota of difference. Yet a flavor, a distinct quality is lost if either sex is excluded. The exclusion of one may indeed make the jury less representative of the community than would be true if an economic or racial group were excluded. 329 US, at 193–194, 91 L Ed 181.

In this respect, we agree with the Court in Ballard: If the fair-cross-section rule is to govern the selection of juries, as we have concluded it must, women cannot be systematically excluded from jury panels from which petit juries are drawn. This conclusion is consistent with the current judgment of the country, now evidenced by legislative or constitutional provisions in every State and at the federal level qualifying women for jury service.

V

There remains the argument that women as a class serve a distinctive role in society and that jury service would so substantially interfere with that function that the State has ample justification for excluding women from service unless they volunteer, even though the result is that almost all jurors are men. . . .

The States are free to grant exemptions from jury service to individuals in cases of special hardship or incapacity and to those engaged in particular occupations the uninterrupted performance of which is critical to the community's welfare. Rawlins v Georgia, 201 US 638, 26 S Ct 560, 50 L Ed 899 (1906). It would not appear that such exemptions would pose substantial threats that the remaining pool of jurors would not be representative of the community. A system excluding all women, however, is a wholly different matter. It is untenable to suggest these days that it would be a special hardship for each and every woman to perform jury service or that society cannot spare *any* women from their present duties. This may be the case with many, and it may be burdensome to sort out those who should be exempted from those who should serve. But that task is performed in the case of men, and the administrative convenience in dealing with women as a class is insufficient justification for diluting the quality of community judgment represented by the jury in criminal trials. . . .

VII

Our holding does not augur or authorize the fashioning of detailed jury-selection codes by federal courts. The fair-cross-section principle must have much leeway in application. The States remain free to prescribe relevant qualifications for their jurors and to provide reasonable exemptions so long as it may be fairly said that the jury lists or panels are representative of the community. Carter v. Jury Comm'n, as did Brown v. Allen, Rawlins v. Georgia, and other cases, recognized broad discretion in the States in this respect. We do not depart from the principles enunciated in Carter. But, as we have said, Louisiana's special exemption for women operates to exclude them from petit juries, which in our view is contrary to the command of the Sixth and Fourteenth Amendments.

It should also be emphasized that in holding that petit juries must be drawn from a source fairly representative of the community we impose no requirement that petit juries actually chosen must mirror the community and reflect the various distinctive groups in the population. Defendants are not entitled to a jury of any particular composition, but the jury wheels, pools of names, panels, or venires from which juries are drawn must not systematically exclude distinctive groups in the community and thereby fail to be reasonably representative thereof.

The judgment of the Louisiana Supreme Court is reversed and the case remanded to that court for further proceedings not inconsistent with this opinion.

So ordered.

Notes and Questions

1. If Louisiana used the same petitioning procedure for jury service for all people, would such a system be constitutional?

2. In your opinion, what would be a fair, practical, and constitutional method of calling people to court for jury duty? Is it possible to have a completely nondiscriminatory selection method?

Once people are identified as potential jurors, they receive a summons to report to the courthouse for jury duty at a specific time. Potential jurors typically assemble for preliminary instructions and then are assigned to different courtrooms where trials will be taking place. The group of individuals assigned to report to a given courtroom is called the *venire*, or jury panel. A venire may range anywhere from 25 people or fewer to 250 or more, depending on the notoriety of the case, the offense charged, and how many jurors must be seated. The trial jury is selected from this group of people.

Challenges "for Cause"

The members of the jury panel are given an oath binding them to give honest answers to questions asked during the jury selection process. The venire members are then asked questions, either individually or collectively, by the judge and/or the lawyers in the case. This questioning process, known as the *voir dire*, is designed to determine whether an individual is suitable to serve as a juror in the case. The primary goal of voir dire is to ascertain whether a potential juror can fairly and impartially view the evidence presented at trial and apply the law to that evidence. The process seeks to uncover any biases or prejudices that would make a juror favor one side or the other. Questions usually deal with such issues as whether the potential jury member has ever been the victim of a crime, whether he knows any attorneys or witnesses involved in the case, and whether there is anything about the crime(s) alleged to have occurred that would make it difficult for the person to be a juror in the case. For example, a person who was molested as a child may find it difficult to serve as a juror in a case involving child molestation, or a person whose son was killed by a drunk driver might find it difficult to maintain objectivity in a driving-while-intoxicated trial. If it appears that a person cannot be fair and impartial, the judge may remove the person *for cause*: that is, there is a legally recognized cause that excludes the person from jury service by operation of law. Removal of a potential juror for cause can be accomplished upon the motion of one of the lawyers, or by the judge on his own initiative.

Voir dire is a critical part of any jury trial. If a person is picked for the jury who is biased or prejudiced against one of the parties, the disfavored party faces an uphill challenge that he may not be able to overcome. Accordingly, it is important to obtain as much information as possible about potential bias during the jury selection process. On the basis of this premise, does the Constitution guarantee a criminal defendant the right to limitless voir dire? As you might suspect, the Supreme Court has held that it does not. However, how much questioning designed to uncover grounds for a challenge for cause is enough?

Ristiano v. Ross, 424 U.S. 589, 96 S. Ct. 1017, 47 L. Ed. 2d 258 (1976)

Mr. Justice POWELL delivered the opinion of the Court.

Respondent is a Negro convicted in a state court of violent crimes against a white security guard. The trial judge denied respondent's motion that a question specifically directed to racial prejudice be asked during voir dire in addition to customary questions directed to general bias or prejudice. The narrow issue is whether, under our recent decision in *Ham v. South Carolina*, 409 U.S. 524, 93 S.Ct. 848, 35 L.Ed.2d 46 (1973), respondent was constitutionally entitled to require the asking of a question specifically directed to racial prejudice. The broader issue presented is whether Ham announced a requirement applicable whenever there may be a confrontation in a criminal trial between persons of different races or different ethnic origins. We answer both of these questions in the negative.

I

Respondent, James Ross, Jr., was tried in a Massachusetts court with two other Negroes for armed robbery, assault and battery by means of a dangerous weapon, and assault and battery with intent to murder. The victim of the alleged crimes was a white man employed by Boston University as a uniformed security guard. The Voir dire of prospective jurors was to be conducted by the court. . . . Each defendant, represented by separate counsel, made a written motion that the prospective jurors also be questioned specifically about racial prejudice.[1] . . . [The court denied this request.] . . .

The Voir dire of five panels of prospective jurors then commenced. The trial judge briefly familiarized each panel with the facts of the case, omitting any reference to racial matters. He then explained to the panel that the clerk would ask a general question about impartiality. . . .[3] Panelists answering a question affirmatively were questioned individually at the bench by the judge, in the presence of counsel. This . . . led to the excusing of 18 veniremen for cause on grounds of prejudice, including one panelist who admitted a racial bias.

The jury eventually impaneled convicted each defendant of all counts. . . .

II

The Constitution does not always entitle a defendant to have questions posed during Voir dire specifically directed to matters that conceivably might prejudice veniremen against him. Voir dire "is conducted under the supervision of the court, and a great deal must, of necessity, be left to its sound discretion." This is so because the "determination of impartiality, in which demeanor plays such an important part, is particularly within the province of the trial judge." Thus, the State's obligation to the defendant to impanel an impartial jury generally can be satisfied by less than an inquiry into a specific prejudice feared by the defendant.

In *Ham*, however, we recognized that some cases may present circumstances in which an impermissible threat to the fair trial guaranteed

---

1. The question proposed by Ross, who did not adopt as his own various other questions proposed by his codefendants, was: "5. Are there any of you who believe that a white person is more likely to be telling the truth than a black person?"

3. The questions were, in substance, the following:

"If any of you are related to the defendants or to the victim, or if any of you have any interest in this case, or have formed an opinion or is sensible of any bias or prejudice, you should make it known to the court at this time.". . .

[This] question was required by Mass. Gen. Laws Ann., c. 234, § 28 (1959).

by due process is posed by a trial court's refusal to question prospective jurors specifically about racial prejudice during Voir dire. *Ham* involved a Negro tried in South Carolina courts for possession of marihuana. He was well known in the locale of his trial as a civil rights activist, and his defense was that law enforcement officials had framed him on the narcotics charge to "get him" for those activities. Despite the circumstances, the trial judge denied Ham's request that the court-conducted Voir dire include questions specifically directed to racial prejudice. We reversed the judgment of conviction because "the essential fairness required by the Due Process Clause of the Fourteenth Amendment requires that under the facts shown by this record the (defendant) be permitted to have the jurors interrogated (during voir dire) on the issue of racial bias."

By its terms *Ham* did not announce a requirement of universal applicability. Rather, it reflected an assessment of whether under all of the circumstances presented there was a constitutionally significant likelihood that, absent questioning about racial prejudice, the jurors would not be as "indifferent as (they stand) unsworn." Coke on Littleton 155b (19th ed. 1832).

In this approach *Ham* was consistent with other determinations by this Court that a State had denied a defendant due process by failing to impanel an impartial jury.

The circumstances in *Ham* strongly suggested the need for Voir dire to include specific questioning about racial prejudice. Ham's defense was that he had been framed because of his civil rights activities. His prominence in the community as a civil rights activist, if not already known to veniremen, inevitably would have been revealed to the members of the jury in the course of his presentation of that defense. Racial issues therefore were inextricably bound up with the conduct of the trial. Further, Ham's reputation as a civil rights activist and the defense he interposed were likely to intensify any prejudice that individual members of the jury might harbor. In such circumstances we deemed a Voir dire that included questioning specifically directed to racial prejudice, when sought by Ham, necessary to meet the constitutional requirement that an impartial jury be impaneled.

We do not . . . [believe] that the need to question veniremen specifically about racial prejudice also rose to constitutional dimensions in this case.[9] The mere fact that the victim of the crimes alleged was a white man and the defen-

_____

9. Although we hold that Voir dire questioning directed to racial prejudice was not constitutionally required, the wiser course generally is to propound appropriate questions designed to identify racial prejudice if requested by the defendant. Under our supervisory power we would have required as much of a federal court faced with the circumstances here. The States also are free to allow or require questions not demanded by the Constitution. . . .

dants were Negroes was less likely to distort the trial than were the special factors involved in *Ham*. . . . The circumstances thus did not suggest a significant likelihood that racial prejudice might infect Ross' trial. This was made clear to the trial judge when Ross was unable to support his motion concerning Voir dire by pointing to racial factors such as existed in *Ham* or others of comparable significance. In these circumstances, the trial judge acted within the Constitution in determining that the demands of due process could be satisfied by his more generalized but thorough inquiry into the impartiality of the veniremen. Accordingly, the judgment is Reversed.

Notes and Questions

1. What evidence would have supported a claim that racial prejudice might infect Ross's trial? Would the trial of two African Americans charged with robbery and assaulting a white security guard with the intent to murder necessarily be tainted by racial prejudice?

2. *Ross* emphasized that the Court in *Ham* limited its holding to the specific facts of that case. By using the limiting language quoted in *Ristiano*, the *Ham* Court sent a signal to courts hearing similar issues that its holding should not be widely applied. Accordingly, the Court in *Ristiano* felt free to distinguish the case it was considering from *Ham* on a factual basis, thereby making the *Ham* rule inapplicable.

A Note on Death Qualification

The primary function of the jury selection process is to prevent individuals who could not be fair and impartial in a particular case from serving on the jury for that case. Biases based on race or gender prejudices may be grounds to have a juror excused for cause, but they are not the only areas of concern to the parties and the court. A potential juror's strong convictions about issues relevant to a case may reflect his or her ability to be fair and impartial. For example, a person who firmly believes that smoking marijuana should be legal may not be able to fairly judge a defendant charged with unlaw-

fully possessing marijuana. Similarly, a victim of an alcohol-related accident may not be able to be impartial in a trial where a defendant is charged with driving while intoxicated (DWI).

It is important to remember that only an individual's ability to be fair and impartial should lead to her removal for cause, and not her abstract beliefs and attitudes. Thus, the president of Mothers Against Drunk Drivers (MADD) would not automatically be disqualified from serving as a juror in a DWI trial. She could be removed for cause only if she could not put aside her beliefs regarding DWI and judge the case on the basis of the evidence and law in a fair and impartial manner.

The ability of jurors to set aside their personal views and judge a case on its own merits has been a key issue in death penalty cases. The issue first gained prominence with the Supreme Court's decision in *Witherspoon v. Illinois*, 391 U.S. 510, 88 S. Ct. 1770, 20 L. Ed. 2d 776 (1968). *Witherspoon* held that individuals cannot be excluded from a jury "simply because they voiced general objections to the death penalty or expressed conscientious or religious scruples against its infliction." *Id.* at 522. In an adjacent footnote, the Court stated, "[T]he most that can be demanded of a venireman in this regard is that he be willing to *consider* all of the penalties provided by state law, and that he not be irrevocably committed, before the trial has begun, to vote against the penalty of death regardless of the facts and circumstances that might emerge in the course of the proceedings. . . ." *Id.* Note 21. In the same footnote, the Court stated that it would be acceptable for a state to exclude for cause veniremen "who make unmistakably clear (1) that they would *automatically* vote against the imposition of capital punishment without regard to any evidence that might be developed at the trial of the case before them, or (2) that their attitude toward the death penalty would prevent them from making an impartial decision as to the defendant's *guilt*." *Id.*

This standard for "death qualification" was designed to ensure that the fate of defendants charged with capital crimes was not determined by juries stacked with people strongly in favor of capital punishment and lacking people who were against it. Under the Illinois scheme in place during Witherspoon's trial, nearly half of the venire were excused for cause because they expressed "conscientious scruples" against capital punishment. The standard expressed by the Supreme Court in *Witherspoon* was designed to alleviate this problem while still allowing members of the venire to be removed for cause if they could not be fair and impartial in considering the death penalty.

The Supreme Court modified Witherspoon's death qualification standard several years later in *Wainwright v. Witt*, 469 U.S. 412, 420, 105 S. Ct. 844, 83 L. Ed. 2d 841 (1985). The Court held that the proper standard for "death-qualifying" a potential juror is whether the person's views about the death penalty "would prevent or substantially impair the performance of his duties as a juror in accordance with his instructions and his oath." Under *Witherspoon*, a juror could not be removed for cause unless he automatically would vote against the imposition of the death penalty regardless of evidence that might justify that sanction. Under *Wainwright v. Witt*, the trial judge only has to determine that the juror's attitude toward the death penalty would *substantially impair* his ability to deliberate and render a verdict based on the law and evidence. This standard is not as demanding as the test announced in *Witherspoon* and thus allows potential jurors to be disqualified for cause more easily in capital cases.

The Use of Peremptory Challenges

If venire members are not disqualified for cause, they may still be excluded from serving on the jury on other grounds. After challenges for cause have been resolved and voir dire has been completed, the attorneys are given a limited number of *peremptory challenges*. Traditionally, prosecutors and defense lawyers were allowed to use peremptory challenges to remove prospective jurors without a stated cause or reason. Often based on an attorney's hunches or intuition, peremptory challenges are used by both sides to excuse venire members who have been sized up as making less-than-ideal jurors. Until recently, attorneys enjoyed virtually unlimited discretion in exercising their peremptory challenges. This license came abruptly to a halt when the Supreme Court recognized other values, reflected in the equal protection of the law, that came into conflict with the lawyers' quest to exclude potential jurors from participating in trials by exercising peremptory challenges.

Batson v. Kentucky, 476 U.S. 79, 106 S. Ct. 1712, 90 L. Ed. 2d 69 (1986)

Justice **Powell** delivered the opinion of the Court.

This case requires us to reexamine that portion of Swain v. Alabama, 380 US 202, 85 S Ct 824, 13 L Ed 2d 759 (1965), concerning the evidentiary burden placed on a criminal defendant who claims that he has been denied equal protection through the State's use of peremptory challenges to exclude members of his race from the petit jury.

I

Petitioner, a black man, was indicted in Kentucky on charges of second-degree burglary and receipt of stolen goods. On the first day of trial in Jefferson Circuit Court, the judge conducted voir dire examination of the venire, excused certain jurors for cause, and permitted the parties to exercise peremptory challenges. The prosecutor used his peremptory challenges to strike all four black persons on the venire, and a jury composed only of white persons was selected. Defense counsel moved to discharge the jury before it was sworn on the ground that the prosecutor's removal of the black veniremen violated petitioner's rights under the Sixth and Fourteenth Amendments to a jury drawn from a cross section of the community, and under the Fourteenth Amendment to equal protection of the laws. Counsel requested a hearing on his motion. Without expressly ruling on the request for a hearing, the trial judge observed that the parties were entitled to use their peremptory challenges to "strike anybody they want to." The judge then denied petitioner's motion, reasoning that the cross-section requirement applies only to selection of the venire and not to selection of the petit jury itself. . . .

II

In Swain v. Alabama, this Court recognized that a "State's purposeful or deliberate denial to Negroes on account of race of participation as jurors in the administration of justice violates the Equal Protection Clause." 380 US, at 203-204, 85 S Ct 824, 13 L Ed 2d 759. This principle has been "consistently and repeatedly" reaffirmed, in numerous decisions of this Court both preceding and following Swain. We reaffirm the principle today.

A

More than a century ago, the Court decided that the State denies a black defendant equal protection of the laws when it puts him on trial before a jury from which members of his race have been purposefully excluded. Strauder v. West Virginia, 100 US 303, 25 L Ed 664 (1880). That decision laid the foundation for the Court's unceasing efforts to eradicate racial discrimination in the procedures used to select the venire from which individual jurors are drawn. In Strauder, the Court explained that the central concern of the recently ratified Fourteenth Amendment was to put an end to governmental discrimination on account of race. Exclusion of black citizens from service as jurors constitutes a primary example of the evil the Fourteenth Amendment was designed to cure.

In holding that racial discrimination in jury selection offends the Equal Protection Clause, the Court in Strauder recognized, however, that a defendant has no right to a "petit jury composed in whole or in part of persons of his own race." "The number of our races and nationalities stands in the way of evolution of such a conception" of the demand of equal protection. But the defendant does have the right to be tried by a jury whose members are selected pursuant to nondiscriminatory criteria. The Equal Protection Clause guarantees the defendant that the State will not exclude members of his race from the jury venire on account of race, Strauder, supra, at 305, 25 L Ed 664, or on the false assumption that members of his race as a group are not qualified to serve as jurors.

Purposeful racial discrimination in selection of the venire violates a defendant's right to equal protection because it denies him the protection that a trial by jury is intended to secure. "The very idea of a jury is a body . . . composed of the peers or equals of the person whose rights it is selected or summoned to determine; that is, of his neighbors, fellows, associates, persons having the same legal status in society as that which he holds." The petit jury has occupied a central position in our system of justice by safeguarding a person accused of crime against the arbitrary exercise of power by prosecutor or judge. Duncan v. Louisiana, 391 US 145, 156, 88 S Ct 1444, 20 L Ed 2d 491 (1968). Those on the venire must be "indifferently chosen," to secure the defendant's right under the Fourteenth Amendment to "protection of life and liberty against race or color prejudice."

B

In Strauder, the Court invalidated a state statute that provided that only white men could serve as jurors. We can be confident that no State now has such a law. The Constitution requires, however, that we look beyond the face of the statute defining juror qualifications and also consider challenged selection practices to afford "protection against action of the State through its administrative officers in effecting the prohibited discrimination." . . .

While decisions of this Court have been concerned largely with discrimination during selection of the venire, the principles announced there also forbid discrimination on account of race in selection of the petit jury. Since the Fourteenth Amendment protects an accused throughout the proceedings bringing him to justice, the State may not draw up its jury lists pursuant to neutral procedures but then resort to discrimination at "other stages in the selection process." . . .

As long ago as Strauder, . . . the Court recognized that by denying a person participation in jury service on account of his race, the State unconstitutionally discriminated against the excluded juror.

The harm from discriminatory jury selection extends beyond that inflicted on the defendant and the excluded juror to touch the entire community. Selection procedures that purposefully exclude black persons from juries undermine public confidence in the fairness of our system of justice. . . .

Accordingly, the component of the jury selection process at issue here, the State's privilege to strike individual jurors through peremptory challenges, is subject to the commands of the Equal Protection Clause. Although a prosecutor ordinarily is entitled to exercise permitted peremptory challenges "for any reason at all, as long as that reason is related to his view concerning the outcome" of the case to be tried, the Equal Protection Clause forbids the prosecutor to challenge potential jurors solely on account of their race or on the assumption that black jurors as a group will be unable impartially to consider the State's case against a black defendant.

III

. . .

A

Swain required the Court to decide, among other issues, whether a black defendant was denied equal protection by the State's exercise of peremptory challenges to exclude members of his race from the petit jury. The record in Swain showed that the prosecutor had used the State's peremptory challenges to strike the six black persons included on the petit jury venire. While rejecting the defendant's claim for failure to prove purposeful discrimination, the Court nonetheless indicated that the Equal Protection Clause placed some limits on the State's exercise of peremptory challenges.

The Court sought to accommodate the prosecutor's historical privilege of peremptory challenge free of judicial control, and the constitutional prohibition on exclusion of persons from jury service on account of race, id., at 222–224, 85 S Ct 824, 13 L Ed 2d 759. While the Constitution does not confer a right to peremptory challenges, those challenges traditionally have been viewed as one means of assuring the selection of a qualified and unbiased jury. To preserve the peremptory nature of the prosecutor's challenge, the Court in Swain declined to scrutinize his actions in a particular case by relying on a presumption that he properly exercised the State's challenges.

The Court went on to observe, however, that a state may not exercise its challenges in contravention of the Equal Protection Clause. It was impermissible for a prosecutor to use his challenges to exclude blacks from the jury "for reasons wholly unrelated to the outcome of the particular case on trial" or to deny blacks "the same right and opportunity to participate in the administration of justice enjoyed by the white population." Accordingly, a black defendant could make out a prima facie case of purposeful discrimination on proof that the peremptory challenge system was "being perverted" in that manner. For example, an inference of purposeful discrimination would be raised on evidence that a prosecutor, "in case after case, whatever the circumstances, whatever the crime and whoever the defendant or the victim may be, is responsible for the removal of Negroes who have been selected as qualified jurors by the jury commissioners and who have survived challenges for cause, with the result that no Negroes ever serve on petit juries." Evidence offered by the defendant in Swain did not meet that standard. While the defendant showed that prosecutors in the jurisdiction had exercised their strikes to exclude blacks from the jury, he offered no proof of the circumstances under which prosecutors were responsible for striking black jurors beyond the facts of his own case.

A number of lower courts following the teaching of Swain reasoned that proof of repeated striking of blacks over a number of cases was necessary to establish a violation of the Equal Protection Clause. Since this interpretation of Swain has placed on defendants a crippling burden of proof, prosecutors' peremptory challenges are now largely immune from constitutional scrutiny. For reasons that follow, we reject this evidentiary formulation as inconsistent with standards that have been developed since Swain for assessing a prima facie case under the Equal Protection Clause.

B

. . . As in any equal protection case, the "burden is, of course," on the defendant who alleges discriminatory selection of the venire "to prove the existence of purposeful discrimination." Whitus v. Georgia, 385 US, at 550, 87 S Ct 643, 17 L Ed 2d 599 (citing Tarrance v. Florida, 188 US 519, 23 S Ct 402, 47 L Ed 572 (1903)). In deciding if the defendant has carried his burden of persuasion, a court must undertake "a sensitive inquiry into such circumstantial and direct evidence of intent as may be available."

Circumstantial evidence of invidious intent may include proof of disproportionate impact. Washington v. Davis, 426 US, at 242, 96 S Ct 2040, 48 L Ed 2d 597. We have observed that under some circumstances proof of discriminatory impact "may for all practical purposes demonstrate unconstitutionality because in various circumstances the discrimination is very difficult to explain on nonracial grounds." Ibid. For example, "total or seriously disproportionate exclusion of Negroes from jury venires," ibid., "is itself such an 'unequal application of the law . . . as to show intentional discrimination,'" id., at 241, 96 S Ct 2040, 48 L Ed 2d 597 (quoting Akins v. Texas, 325 US, at 404, 65 S Ct 1276, 89 L Ed 1692).

Moreover, since Swain, we have recognized that a black defendant alleging that members of his race have been impermissibly excluded from the venire may make out a prima facie case of purposeful discrimination by showing that the totality of the relevant facts gives rise to an inference of discriminatory purpose. Once the defendant makes the requisite showing, the burden shifts to the State to explain adequately the racial exclusion. The State cannot meet this burden on mere general assertions that its officials did not discriminate or that they properly performed their official duties. Rather, the State must demonstrate that "permissible racially neutral selection criteria and procedures have produced the monochromatic result."

The showing necessary to establish a prima facie case of purposeful discrimination in selection of the venire may be discerned in this Court's decisions. The defendant initially must show that he is a member of a racial group capable of being singled out for differential treatment. In combination with the evidence, a defendant may then make a prima facie case by proving that in the particular jurisdiction members of his race have not been summoned for jury service over an extended period of time. Proof of systematic exclusion from the venire raises an inference of purposeful discrimination because the "result bespeaks discrimination."

Since the ultimate issue is whether the State has discriminated in selecting the defendant's venire, however, the defendant may establish a prima facie case "in other ways than by evidence of long-continued unexplained absence" of members of his race "from many panels." Cassell v. Texas, 339 US 282, 290, 70 S Ct 629, 94 L Ed 839 (1950) (plurality opinion). In cases involving the venire, this Court has found a prima facie case on proof that members of the defendant's race were substantially underrepresented on the venire from which his jury was drawn, and that the venire was selected under a practice providing "the opportunity for discrimination." This combination of factors raises the necessary inference of purposeful discrimination because the Court has declined to attribute to chance the absence of black citizens on a particular jury array where the selection mechanism is subject to abuse. When circumstances suggest the need, the trial court must undertake a "factual inquiry" that "takes into account all possible explanatory factors" in the particular case.

Thus, since the decision in Swain, this Court has recognized that a defendant may make a prima facie showing of purposeful racial discrimination in selection of the venire by relying solely on the facts concerning its selection *in his case*. These decisions are in accordance with the proposition, articulated in Arlington Heights v. Metropolitan Housing Development Corp., that "a consistent pattern of official racial discrimination" is not "a necessary predicate to a violation of the Equal Protection Clause. A single invidiously discriminatory governmental act" is not "immunized by the absence of such discrimination in the making of other comparable decisions." For evidentiary requirements to dictate that "several must suffer discrimination" before one could object, would be inconsistent with the promise of equal protection to all.

C

The standards for assessing a prima facie case in the context of discriminatory selection of the venire have been fully articulated since Swain. These principles support our conclusion that a defendant may establish a prima facie

case of purposeful discrimination in selection of the petit jury solely on evidence concerning the prosecutor's exercise of peremptory challenges at the defendant's trial. To establish such a case, the defendant first must show that he is a member of a cognizable racial group, and that the prosecutor has exercised peremptory challenges to remove from the venire members of the defendant's race. Second, the defendant is entitled to rely on the fact, as to which there can be no dispute, that peremptory challenges constitute a jury selection practice that permits "those to discriminate who are of a mind to discriminate." Finally, the defendant must show that these facts and any other relevant circumstances raise an inference that the prosecutor used that practice to exclude the veniremen from the petit jury on account of their race. This combination of factors in the empaneling of the petit jury, as in the selection of the venire, raises the necessary inference of purposeful discrimination.

In deciding whether the defendant has made the requisite showing, the trial court should consider all relevant circumstances. For example, a "pattern" of strikes against black jurors included in the particular venire might give rise to an inference of discrimination. Similarly, the prosecutor's questions and statements during voir dire examination and in exercising his challenges may support or refute an inference of discriminatory purpose. These examples are merely illustrative. We have confidence that trial judges, experienced in supervising voir dire, will be able to decide if the circumstances concerning the prosecutor's use of peremptory challenges creates a prima facie case of discrimination against black jurors.

Once the defendant makes a prima facie showing, the burden shifts to the State to come forward with a neutral explanation for challenging black jurors. Though this requirement imposes a limitation in some cases on the full peremptory character of the historic challenge, we emphasize that the prosecutor's explanation need not rise to the level justifying exercise of a challenge for cause. But the prosecutor may not rebut the defendant's prima facie case of discrimination by stating merely that he challenged jurors of the defendant's race on the assumption—or his intuitive judgment—that they would be partial to the defendant because of their shared race.

Just as the Equal Protection Clause forbids the States to exclude black persons from the venire on the assumption that blacks as a group are unqualified to serve as jurors, so it forbids the States to strike black veniremen on the assumption that they will be biased in a particular case simply because the defendant is black. The core guarantee of equal protection, ensuring citizens that their State will not discriminate on account of race, would be meaningless were we to approve the exclusion of jurors on the basis of such assumptions, which arise solely from the jurors' race. Nor may the prosecutor rebut the defendant's case merely by denying that he had a discriminatory motive or "affirm[ing] [his] good faith in making individual selections." If these general assertions were accepted as rebutting a defendant's prima facie case, the Equal Protection Clause "would be but a vain and illusory requirement." The prosecutor therefore must articulate a neutral explanation related to the particular case to be tried. The trial court then will have the duty to determine if the defendant has established purposeful discrimination.

IV

The State contends that our holding will eviscerate the fair trial values served by the peremptory challenge. Conceding that the Constitution does not guarantee a right to peremptory challenges and that Swain did state that their use ultimately is subject to the strictures of equal protection, the State argues that the privilege of unfettered exercise of the challenge is of vital importance to the criminal justice system.

While we recognize, of course, that the peremptory challenge occupies an important position in our trial procedures, we do not agree that our decision today will undermine the contribution the challenge generally makes to the administration of justice. The reality of practice, amply reflected in many state and federal court opinions, shows that the challenge may be, and unfortunately at times has been, used to discriminate against black jurors. By requiring trial courts to be sensitive to the racially discriminatory use of peremptory challenges, our decision enforces the mandate of equal protection and furthers the ends of justice. In view of the heterogeneous population of our Nation, public respect for our criminal justice system and the rule of law will be strengthened if we ensure that no citizen is disqualified from jury service because of his race. . . .

V

In this case, petitioner made a timely objection to the prosecutor's removal of all black persons on the venire. Because the trial court flatly rejected the objection without requiring the prosecutor to give an explanation for his action, we remand this case for further proceedings. If the trial court decides that the facts establish, prima facie, purposeful discrimination and the prosecutor does not come forward with a neutral explanation for his action, our precedents require that petitioner's conviction be reversed.

It is so ordered. . . .

Justice **Marshall**, concurring. . . .

I applaud the Court's holding that the racially discriminatory use of peremptory challenges violates the Equal Protection Clause, and I join the Court's opinion. However, only by banning peremptories entirely can such discrimination be ended.

Notes and Questions

1. Must a prosecutor always explain his or her reason for using a peremptory challenge against an African American venire member? What do you understand a "prima facie" case of race discrimination to be? How can it be demonstrated?

2. Which of the following would be race-neutral reasons upon which a lawyer could base peremptory challenges? (a) The juror was not paying attention. (b) The juror smiled at the defendant. (c) The juror glared at the prosecutor. Can any of these reasons be proven or disproven? How does this affect the use of the *Batson* test? If you were a judge, and the prosecutor explained that she excused a potential juror because he smiled at the defendant, would you accept this as a race-neutral reason under the *Batson* rules?

In *People v. Richie*, 635 N.Y.S.2d 263 (N.Y. App. Div. 1995), the court presented a list of factors that the trial court should consider in determining whether an explanation for the use of a peremptory challenge is pretextual or simply designed to mask an impermissible reason. The factors listed by the court included whether the explanation relates to the facts of the case, the extent to which the party exercising the peremptory challenge questioned the challenged juror, whether the offered reason was applied to a particular group of jurors, and whether the reason was based on "hard data" or was solely intuitive. *Id.* at 266–267. Do you think these factors are relevant to evaluate the propriety of a peremptory challenge? Can you think of any other factors that might help in this evaluation?

3. Note that the defendant in *Batson*, like the excluded jurors, was African American. Should a white defendant be able to raise a *Batson* objection to a prosecutor striking black jurors? In *Powers v. Ohio*, 499 U.S. 400, 111 S. Ct. 1364, 113 L. Ed. 2d 411 (1991), the Supreme Court answered this question affirmatively. The Court explained that "the Equal Protection Clause prohibits a prosecutor from using the State's peremptory challenges to exclude otherwise qualified and unbiased persons from the petit jury solely by reason of their race, a practice that forecloses a significant opportunity to participate in civic life. An individual juror does not have a right to sit in on any particular petit jury, but he or she does possess the right not to be excluded from one on account of race." The Court held that since the excused juror does not have a means of redressing the improper exclusion, the defendant has the right to object to an improper exercise of a peremptory challenge.

4. *Batson* and *Powers* held that the prosecution cannot exclude potential jurors because of their race. Should the defendant face the same restrictions? In *Georgia v. McCollum*, 505 U.S. 42, 112 S. Ct. 2348, 120 L. Ed. 2d 33 (1992), the Court said yes. For the same reasons stated in *Batson* and *Powers*, the Court held that the

prosecution has the right to object to defense counsel's peremptory challenges that violate the *Batson* rule.

5. Can a party use peremptory challenges to remove potential jurors because they are men, or because they are women? In *J.E.B. v. Alabama*, 511 U.S. 127, 114 S. Ct. 1419, 128 L. Ed. 2d 89 (1994), the Supreme Court said no. *J.E.B.* involved a trial to determine paternity and child support. During jury selection, the State, on behalf of the mother of the child, used 9 of its 10 peremptory challenges to strike male jurors. As a result, an all-female jury was seated. J.E.B., the alleged father, objected and argued that the State had unconstitutionally struck male jurors solely because of their gender. The trial court overruled the objection, and the jury found J.E.B. to be the father of the child. The Supreme Court held that it is unconstitutional to use peremptory challenges to remove potential jurors from the panel based solely on gender. The Court stated that it is improper to assume that a person would be biased in a particular case solely because of gender stereotypes and ruled that J.E.B.'s equal-protection rights had been violated.

6. What other groups may be affected by *Batson* and *J.E.B.*? Can lawyers exercise their peremptory challenges to remove prospective jurors because they are "young" or "old"? Because of their religious affiliation? Because they are Republicans, or Democrats? Because they are college students? What are the appropriate limits of the *Batson* rule?

Since *Batson* was decided, state and lower federal courts have been grappling with questions such as these. In *People v. McCoy*, 47 Cal. Rptr. 2d 599, 40 Cal. App. 4th 778 (Ct. App. 1st Dist. 1995), the court held that individuals 70 years of age and older do not constitute a distinctive or cognizable class of people to give rise to a *Batson* objection.

It is widely held that peremptory challenges may be used to remove individuals on the basis of their religious affiliation. The reason for this is that a person's religious persuasion reflects on his or her beliefs and attitudes, as opposed to race or gender, which are merely anatomical and physiological characteristics of a person. See *Casarez v. State*, 913 S.W.2d 468 (TX Ct. Cr. App. En Banc 1994). Do you agree with this distinction?

Size of the Trial Jury

Duncan and *Baldwin* held that a person charged with a nonpetty offense is entitled to a jury trial. They did not, however, say what constitutes a jury. Do three people make a jury? How about six, or eight? Under the common law, and when the Sixth Amendment was adopted, juries comprised 12 people. Does this historical fact mean that contemporary criminal trial juries must continue to have 12 members? The Supreme Court confronted this question in *Williams v. Florida*, which was decided the same day as *Baldwin*, when it was asked to give its stamp of approval to six-person juries.

Williams v. Florida, 399 U.S. 78, 90 S. Ct. 1893, 26 L. Ed. 2d 446 (1970)

Mr. Justice **White** delivered the opinion of the Court.

Prior to his trial for robbery in the State of Florida, petitioner filed a . . . motion to impanel a 12-man jury instead of the six-man jury provided by Florida law in all but capital cases. That motion was denied. Petitioner was convicted as charged and was sentenced to life imprisonment. . . .

II

In Duncan v. Louisiana, 391 US 145, 88 S Ct 1444, 20 L Ed 2d 491 (1968), we held that the Fourteenth Amendment guarantees a right to trial by jury in all criminal cases that—were they to be tried in a federal court—would come within the Sixth Amendment's guarantee. Petitioner's trial for robbery on July 3, 1968, clearly falls within the scope of that holding.

The question in this case then is whether the constitutional guarantee of a trial by "jury" necessarily requires trial by exactly 12 persons, rather than some lesser number—in this case six. We hold that the 12-man panel is not a necessary ingredient of "trial by jury," and that respondent's refusal to impanel more than the six members provided for by Florida law did not violate petitioner's Sixth Amendment rights as applied to the States through the Fourteenth.

We had occasion in Duncan v. Louisiana, supra, to review briefly the oft-told history of the development of trial by jury in criminal cases. That history revealed a long tradition attaching great importance to the concept of relying on a body of one's peers to determine guilt or innocence as a safeguard against arbitrary law enforcement. That same history, however, affords little insight into the considerations that gradually led the size of that body to be generally fixed at 12. Some have suggested that the number 12 was fixed upon simply because that was the number of the presentment jury from the hundred, from which the petit jury developed.

Other, less circular but more fanciful reasons for the number 12 have been given, "but they were all brought forward after the number was fixed," and rest on little more than mystical or superstitious insights into the significance of "12." Lord Coke's explanation that the "*number of twelve* is much respected *in holy writ*, as 12 *apostles*, 12 *stones*, 12 *tribes, etc.*" is typical. In short, while sometime in the 14th century the size of the jury at common law came to be fixed generally at 12, that particular feature of the jury system appears to have been a historical accident, unrelated to the great purposes which gave rise to the jury in the first place. The question before us is whether this accidental feature of the jury has been immutably codified into our Constitution. . . .

The purpose of the jury trial, as we noted in Duncan, is to prevent oppression by the Government. "Providing an accused with the right to be tried by a jury of his peers gave him an inestimable safeguard against the corrupt or overzealous prosecutor and against the compliant, biased, or eccentric judge." Given this purpose, the essential feature of a jury obviously lies in the interposition between the accused and his accuser of the commonsense judgment of a group of laymen, and in the community participation and shared responsibility that results from that group's determination of guilt or innocence. The performance of this role is not a function of the particular number of the body that makes up the jury. To be sure, the number should probably be large enough to promote group deliberation, free from outside attempts at intimidation, and to provide a fair possibility for obtaining a representative cross-section of the community. But we find little reason to think that these goals are in any meaningful sense less likely to be achieved when the jury numbers six, than when it numbers 12—particularly if the requirement of unanimity is retained. And, certainly the reliability of the jury as a factfinder hardly seems likely to be a function of its size.

It might be suggested that the 12-man jury gives a defendant a greater advantage since he has more "chances" of finding a juror who will insist on acquittal and thus prevent conviction. But the advantage might just as easily belong to the State, which also needs only one juror out of twelve insisting on guilt to prevent acquittal. What few experiments have occurred—usually in the civil area—indicate that there is no discernible difference between the results reached by the two different-sized juries. In short, neither currently available evidence nor theory suggests that the 12-man jury is necessarily more advantageous to the defendant than a jury composed of fewer members.

Similarly, while in theory the number of viewpoints represented on a randomly selected jury ought to increase as the size of the jury increases, in practice the difference between the 12-man and the six-man jury in terms of the cross-section of the community represented seems likely to be negligible. Even the 12-man jury cannot insure representation of every distinct voice in the community, particularly given the use of the peremptory challenge. As long as arbitrary exclusions of a particular class from the jury rolls are forbidden, see, e.g., Carter v. Jury Commission, 396 US 320, 329–330, 90 S Ct 518, 24 L Ed 2d 549, 557 (1970), the concern that the cross-section will be significantly diminished if the jury is decreased in size from 12 to six seems an unrealistic one.

We conclude, in short, as we began: the fact that the jury at common law was composed of precisely 12 is a historical accident, unnecessary to effect the purposes of the jury system and wholly without significance "except to mystics." Duncan v. Louisiana, supra, at 182, 20 L Ed 2d at 514 (Harlan, J., dissenting). To read the Sixth Amendment as forever codifying a feature so incidental to the real purpose of the Amendment is to ascribe a blind formalism to the Framers which would require considerably more evidence than we have been able to discover in the history and language of the Constitution or in the reasoning of our past decisions. . . .

Legislatures may well have their own views about the relative value of the larger and smaller juries, and may conclude that, wholly apart from the jury's primary function, it is desirable to spread the collective responsibility for the determination of guilt among the larger group. In capital cases, for example, it appears that no State provides for less than 12 jurors—a fact that suggests implicit recognition of the value of the larger body as a means of legitimating society's decision to impose the death penalty. Our holding does no more than leave these considerations to Congress and the States, unrestrained by an interpretation of the Sixth Amendment that would forever dictate the precise number that can constitute a jury. Consistent with this holding, we conclude that petitioner's Sixth Amendment rights, as applied to the States through the Fourteenth Amendment, were not violated by Florida's decision to provide a six-man rather than a 12-man jury. The judgment of the Florida District Court of Appeal is Affirmed.

Notes and Questions

1. Eight years after *Williams* was decided, the Court ruled that criminal trial juries cannot shrink below six members. In *Ballew v. Georgia*, 435 U.S. 223, 98 S. Ct. 1029, 55 L. Ed. 2d 234 (1978), the justices invalidated Georgia's use of five-person juries in misdemeanor trials. The Court found that juries of fewer than six members are less likely to recall evidence, to conduct effective deliberations, and to reflect a representative cross-section of the community. The Court went so far as to say that the use of such juries "calls into doubt the results achieved." Justice Blackmun's lead opinion in *Ballew*, which was joined by only one other justice, relied heavily on social science evidence about jury decision making. Not surprisingly, most of the studies concerning the consequences of reducing the size of juries from 12 members to six members found that the larger size jury conducts "higher quality" deliberations than the smaller jury. Nevertheless, the Court in *Ballew* expressly reaffirmed *Williams*'s holding that six-person juries are constitutionally permissible.

2. If you were being tried for a crime, would you prefer to have your fate determined by a jury made up of 12 or six citizens? What are the state's interests in impaneling a jury of only six members?

3. While *Williams* and *Ballew* define the lower limit under the U.S. Constitution for the number of jurors required in a criminal trial, many states provide that juries of more than six persons are required for some, if not all, criminal trials.

As explained by the Arkansas Supreme Court in *Byrd v. State*, 317 Ark. 609, 879 S.W.2d 435, 436–438 (1994):

In the wake of Williams v. Florida, several state courts followed suit and adopted the rationale of that case with respect to statutes authorizing fewer than twelve jurors in certain trials. See, e.g., State v. Ritchie, 114 Idaho 528, 757 P.2d 1247 (Ct.App. 1988); Carter v. State, 702 S.W.2d 774 (Tex.Ct.App. 1986); State v. Thrall, 39 Conn.Sup. 347, 464 A.2d 854 (1983); City of Seattle v. Hesler, 98 Wash.2d 73, 653 P.2d 631 (1982); O'Brien v. State, 422

N.E.2d 1266 (Ind. Ct. App. 1981); State ex rel City of Columbus v. Boyland, 58 Ohio St.2d 490, 391 N.E.2d 324 (1979).

We decline the temptation to accept the Williams v. Florida rationale that the jury number can be changed by legislative act and are more persuaded by the reasoning of the Minnesota Supreme Court in State v. Hamm, 423 N.W.2d 379 (Minn. 1988) (plurality decision). In Hamm, the defendant asked for a twelve-person jury for his DWI charge but was limited to a jury of six under a state statute. . . . The Minnesota Constitution, similar to Arkansas's, provided that the right to a jury trial was "inviolate" but did not state the number of jurors. The lead opinion by Justice Yetka looked to an 1869 Minnesota case interpreting the term "jury" as a "body of twelve persons." Justice Yetka underscored the fact that the right to a trial before an impartial jury was fundamental and one of the "keystones to which other rights are anchored. . . ." 423 N.W.2d at 385. He concluded that the early case law defining juries as consisting of twelve persons was persuasive and that there was no good reason to overrule it. . . .

We agree and are reluctant to erode the fundamental right of trial by jury under our system of state government without a vote of the people, particularly in light of Amendment 16 which installed nine-juror verdicts in civil cases and was a clear recognition by the people of this State that twelve-member juries are the standard. Nor are we persuaded by arguments that the number twelve is merely mystical and unnecessary and unimportant as suggested by Williams v. Florida, supra. The utilization of that number for jury composition for at least seven hundred years belies that. A panel of six jurors for misdemeanor trials may seem economical and, therefore, desirable at first blush because less serious offenses are involved. However, many misdemeanors including the DWI offense at hand are serious and carry with them maximum jail terms of one year and substantial fines.

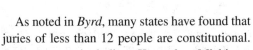

As noted in *Byrd*, many states have found that juries of less than 12 people are constitutional. Some states, including Kentucky, Michigan, Idaho, and Louisiana, permit six-person juries only for misdemeanor trials. On the other hand, Arizona mandates 12-person juries only for the trial of cases in which a sentence of over 30 years or execution is authorized, and Connecticut mandates 12-person juries only for capital crimes.

Is a Unanimous Verdict Required?

A key reason for having juries decide the outcome of criminal trials is that a group representative of the community can be expected to have different life experiences and thus to bring different perspectives to the evidence they hear when they are asked to make judgments about it. During the process of deliberations, these differing perspectives presumably will be evident in the jurors' discussions and will help the jury to determine more accurately the truth about what happened in the case. This collective decision-making process is designed to protect the prosecution and the defendant from the idiosyncrasies of any one or a small number of decision makers.

If the jury is to deliberate and reach a verdict collectively, must their verdict be unanimous? Not necessarily. In *Apodaca v. Oregon*, 406 U.S. 404, 92 S. Ct. 1628, 32 L. Ed. 2d 184 (1972), the Supreme Court held that jury verdicts decided by votes of 10–2 and 11–1 were constitutionally valid in state criminal trials. The Court said that there were no significant differences between "juries required to act unanimously and those permitted to convict or acquit by votes of 10 to two or 11 to one. Requiring unanimity would obviously produce hung juries in some situations where nonunanimous juries will convict or acquit. But in either case, the interest of the defendant in having the judgment of his peers interposed between himself and the officers of the state who prosecute and judge him is equally well served." *Id.* at 411, 92 S. Ct. at 1633 (footnote omitted).

Are you persuaded? Will the views of jurors who do not share the majority's perspectives be given the same consideration when a jury is allowed to return a verdict without the unanimous agreement of its members? Is there a risk that minority viewpoints will be ignored altogether? Do nonunanimous verdicts seem consistent with the values that underlie the principle that jury venires should reflect a representative cross-section of the community? What are the state's interests in wanting a system that allows nonunanimous jury verdicts?

In *Johnson v. Louisiana*, 406 U.S. 356, 92 S. Ct. 1620, 32 L. Ed. 2d 152 (1972), decided the same day as *Apodaca*, the Supreme Court held that jury verdicts based on a 9–3 vote are also constitutional in state criminal trials. The Court stated that three jurors dissenting from the majority did not demonstrate reasonable doubt about the defendant's guilt in light of the fact that nine jurors—or a "substantial majority" of the jury—were convinced of guilt. If the concurrence of a "substantial majority" of a jury is all that is required, what are the implications for nonunanimous verdicts in six- or eight-person juries? If a 9–3 majority verdict (75%) is constitutionally permissible as a substantial majority of a 12-person jury, is a 5–1 (83%) verdict permissible from a six-member jury? The Court considered this question in *Burch v. Louisiana*.

Burch v. Louisiana, 441 U.S. 130, 99 S. Ct. 1623, 60 L. Ed. 2d 96 (1979)

Mr. Justice **Rehnquist** delivered the opinion of the Court.

The Louisiana Constitution and Code of Criminal Procedure provide that criminal cases in which the punishment imposed may be confinement for a period in excess of six months "shall be tried before a jury of six persons, five of whom must concur to render a verdict." We granted certiorari to decide whether conviction by a nonunanimous six-person jury in a state criminal trial for a nonpetty offense as contemplated by these provisions of Louisiana law violates the rights of an accused to trial by jury guaranteed by the Sixth and Fourteenth Amendments.

Petitioners, an individual and a Louisiana corporation, were jointly charged in two counts with the exhibition of two obscene motion pictures. Pursuant to Louisiana law, they were tried before a six-person jury, which found both petitioners guilty as charged. A poll of the jury after verdict indicated that the jury had voted unanimously to convict petitioner Wrestle, Inc., and had voted 5-1 to convict petitioner Burch. Burch was sentenced to two consecutive 7-month prison terms, which were suspended, and fined $1,000. . . .

Petitioners appealed their convictions to the Supreme Court of Louisiana, where they argued that the provisions of Louisiana law permitting conviction by a nonunanimous six-member jury violated the rights of persons accused of nonpetty criminal offenses to trial by jury guaranteed by the Sixth and Fourteenth Amendments. Though acknowledging that the issue was "close," the court held that conviction by a nonunanimous six-person jury did not offend the Constitution. The court concluded that none of this Court's decisions precluded use of a nonunanimous six-person jury. "'If 75 percent concurrence (9/12) was enough for a verdict as determined in Johnson v. Louisiana, 406 US 356, 92 S Ct 1620, 32 L Ed 2d 152 . . . (1972), then requiring 83 percent concurrence (5/6) ought to be within the permissible limits of Johnson.'" . . .

We agree with the Louisiana Supreme Court that the question presented is a "close" one.

Nonetheless, we believe that conviction by a nonunanimous six-member jury in a state criminal trial for a nonpetty offense deprives an accused of his constitutional right to trial by jury.

Only in relatively recent years has this Court had to consider the practices of the several States relating to jury size and unanimity. Duncan v. Louisiana, 391 US 145, 88 S Ct 1444, 20 L Ed 2d 491 (1968), marked the beginning of our involvement with such questions. The Court in Duncan held that because trial by jury in "serious" criminal cases is "fundamental to the American scheme of justice" and essential to due process of law, the Fourteenth Amendment guarantees a state criminal defendant the right to a jury trial in any case which, if tried in a federal court, would require a jury under the Sixth Amendment.

Two Terms later in Williams v. Florida, 399 US 78, 86, 90 S Ct 1893, 26 L Ed 2d 446 (1970), the Court held that this constitutional guarantee of trial by jury did not require a State to provide an accused with a jury of 12 members and that Florida did not violate the jury trial rights of criminal defendants charged with nonpetty offenses by affording them jury panels comprised of only six persons. After canvassing the common-law development of the jury and the constitutional history of the jury trial right, the Court concluded that the 12-person requirement was "a historical accident" and that there was no indication that the Framers intended to preserve in the Constitution the features of the jury system as it existed at common law. Thus freed from strictly historical considerations, the Court turned to examine the function that this particular feature performs and its relation to the purposes of jury trial. The purpose of trial by jury, as noted in Duncan, is to prevent government oppression by providing a "safeguard against the corrupt or overzealous prosecutor and against the compliant, biased, or eccentric judge." Given this purpose, the Williams Court observed that the jury's essential feature lies in the "interposition between the accused and his accuser of the commonsense judgment of a group of laymen, and in the community participation and shared responsibility that results from that group's determination of guilt or innocence." These purposes could be fulfilled, the Court believed, so long as the jury was of a sufficient size to promote group deliberation, free from outside intimidation, and to provide a fair possibility that a cross-section of the community would be represented on it. The Court concluded, however, that there is "little reason to think that these goals are in any meaningful sense less likely to be achieved when the jury numbers six, than when it numbers 12 —*particularly if the requirement of unanimity is retained.*"

A similar analysis led us to conclude in 1972 that a jury's verdict need not be unanimous to satisfy constitutional requirements, even though unanimity had been the rule at common law. Thus, in Apodaca v. Oregon, 406 US 404, 92 S Ct 1628, 32 L Ed 2d 184 (1972), we upheld a state statute providing that only 10 members of a 12-person jury need concur to render a verdict in certain noncapital cases. In terms of the role of the jury as a safeguard against oppression, the plurality opinion perceived no difference between those juries required to act unanimously and those permitted to act by votes of 10 to two. Nor was unanimity viewed by the plurality as contributing materially to the exercise of the jury's commonsense judgment or as a necessary precondition to effective application of the requirement that jury panels represent a fair cross section of the community.

Last Term, in Ballew v. Georgia, 435 US 223, 98 S Ct 1029, 55 L Ed 2d 234 (1978), we considered whether a jury of less than six members passes constitutional scrutiny, a question that was explicitly reserved in Williams v. Florida. The Court, in separate opinions, held that conviction by a unanimous five-person jury in a trial for a nonpetty offense deprives an accused of his right to trial by jury. While readily admitting that the line between six members and five was not altogether easy to justify, at least five Members of the Court believed that reducing a jury to five persons in nonpetty cases raised sufficiently substantial doubts as to the fairness of the proceeding and proper functioning of the jury to warrant drawing the line at six.

We thus have held that the Constitution permits juries of less than 12 members, but that it requires at least six. Ballew v. Georgia, supra; Williams v. Florida, supra. And we have approved the use of certain nonunanimous verdicts in cases involving 12-person juries. Apodaca v. Oregon, supra (10-2); Johnson v. Louisiana, 406 US 356, 92 S Ct 1620, 32 L Ed 2d 152 (1972) (9-3). These principles are not questioned here. Rather, this case lies at the intersection of our decisions concerning jury size and unanimity. As in Ballew, we do not pretend the ability to discern a priori a bright line below which the number of jurors participating in the trial or in the verdict would not permit the jury to function in the manner required by our prior cases. But having already departed from the strictly historical requirements of jury trial, it is inevitable that lines must be drawn somewhere if the substance of the jury trial right is to be preserved. . . .

This line drawing process, "although essential, cannot be wholly satisfactory, for it requires attaching different consequences to events which, when they lie near the line, actually differ very little." However, much the same reasons that led us in Ballew to decide that use of a five-member jury threatened the fairness of the proceeding and the proper role of the jury, lead us to conclude now that conviction for a nonpetty offense by only five members of a six-person jury presents a similar threat to preservation of the substance of the jury trial guarantee and justifies our requiring verdicts rendered by six-person juries to be unanimous. We are buttressed in this view by the current jury practices of the several States. It appears that of those States that utilize six-member juries in trials of nonpetty offenses, only two, including Louisiana, also allow nonunanimous verdicts. We think that this near-uniform judgment of the Nation provides a useful guide in delimiting the line between those jury practices that are constitutionally permissible and those that are not.

The State seeks to justify its use of nonunanimous six-person juries on the basis of the "considerable time" savings that it claims results from trying cases in this manner. It asserts that under its system, juror deliberation time is shortened and the number of hung juries is reduced. Undoubtedly, the State has a substantial interest in reducing the time and expense associated with the administration of its system of criminal justice. But that interest cannot prevail here. First, on this record, any benefits that might accrue by allowing five members of a six-person jury to render a verdict, as compared with requiring unanimity of a six-member jury, are speculative, at best. More importantly, we think that when a State has reduced the size of its juries to the minimum number of jurors permitted by the Constitution, the additional authorization of non-unanimous verdicts by such juries sufficiently threatens the constitutional principles that led to the establishment of the size threshold that any countervailing interest of the State should yield.

The judgment of the Louisiana Supreme Court affirming the conviction of petitioner Burch is, therefore, reversed, and its judgment affirming the conviction of petitioner Wrestle, Inc., is affirmed. The case is remanded to the Louisiana Supreme Court for proceedings not inconsistent with this opinion.

It is so ordered.

Notes and Questions

1. If you were a criminal defendant, would you want your case to be heard by (1) a 12-person jury with a 9–3 (75%) rule, (2) an eight-person jury with a 7–1 (87.5%) rule, (3) a six-person jury where unanimity is required, or (4) a 12-person jury where unanimity is required? If you were prosecuting a case, which system would you prefer? What weight do you assign to the respective interests of the defendant and the state in choosing between these systems? Which system is preferable from a policy perspective? From a constitutional perspective?

2. While the Supreme Court has held that the U.S. Constitution does not require verdicts in criminal cases be unanimous, several state constitutions explicitly mandate unanimous verdicts in criminal trials. See Latzer, *supra*, at 8–42.

TESTIMONIAL RIGHTS OF THE DEFENDANT

The Right To Refrain from Testifying

The Fifth Amendment provides that "no person . . . shall be compelled in any criminal case to be a witness against himself." Despite this right, might there not be an appearance or inference of guilt if a defendant does not testify in his or her own defense in order to refute the allegations made against him or her? For example, if you were a juror in a case in which a defendant was accused of committing a brutal murder, what would you think if he did not take the witness stand and maintain his innocence? Is it at least possible that a defendant who does not testify cannot refute the charge because he is in fact guilty of the crime? If that is one possible inference, should a prosecutor or the trial judge be allowed to explain to the jury that they might draw this conclusion from the defendant's failure to testify? This issue is considered in *Griffin v. California*.

Griffin v. California, 380 U.S. 609, 85 S. Ct. 1229, 14 L. Ed. 2d 106 (1965)

Mr. Justice DOUGLAS delivered the opinion of the Court.

Petitioner was convicted of murder in the first degree after a jury trial in a California court. He did not testify at the trial on the issue of guilt, though he did testify at the separate trial on the issue of penalty. The trial court instructed the jury on the issue of guilt, stating that a defendant has a constitutional right not to testify. But it told the jury:[2]

As to any evidence or facts against him which the defendant can reasonably be expected to deny or explain because of facts within his knowledge, if he does not testify or if, though he does testify, he fails to deny or explain such evidence, the jury may take that failure into consideration as tending to indicate the truth of such evidence and as indicating that among the inferences that may be reasonably drawn therefrom those unfavorable to the defendant are the more probable.

It added, however, that no such inference could be drawn as to evidence respecting which he had no knowledge. It stated that failure of a defendant to deny or explain the evidence of which he had knowledge does not create a presumption of guilt nor by itself warrant an inference of guilt nor relieve the prosecution of any of its burden of proof.

Petitioner had been seen with the deceased the evening of her death, the evidence placing him with her in the alley where her body was found. The prosecutor made much of the failure of petitioner to testify:

The defendant certainly knows whether Essie Mae had this beat up appearance at the time he left her apartment and went down the alley with her. What kind of man is it that would want to have sex with a woman that beat up if she was beat up at the time he left?

He would know that. He would know how she got down the alley. He would know how the blood got on the bottom of the concrete steps. He would know how long he was with her in that box. He would know how her wig got off. He would know whether he beat her or mistreated her. He would know whether he walked away from that place cool as a cucumber when he saw Mr. Villasenor because he was conscious of his own guilt and wanted to get away from that damaged or injured woman.

These things he has not seen fit to take the stand and deny or explain. And in the whole world, if anybody would know, this defendant would know. Essie Mae is dead, she can't tell you her side of the story. The defendant won't.

The death penalty was imposed and the California Supreme Court affirmed. . . . The case is here on a writ of certiorari. . . . [3] If this were a federal trial, reversible error would have been committed. Wilson v. United States, 149 U.S. 60, 13 S. Ct. 765, 37 L. Ed. 650, so holds. It is said, however, that the Wilson decision rested not on the Fifth Amendment, but on an Act of Congress, now 18 U.S.C. § 3481. That indeed is the fact, as the opinion of the Court in the Wilson case states. . . . But that is the beginning, not the end, of our inquiry. The question remains whether, statute or not, the comment rule, approved by California, violates the Fifth Amendment.

We think it does. It is in substance a rule of evidence that allows the State the privilege of tendering to the jury for its consideration the fail-

_____

2. Article I, § 13, of the California Constitution provides in part: "In any criminal case, whether the defendant testifies or not, his failure to explain or to deny by his testimony any evidence or facts in the case against him may be commented upon by the court and by counsel, and may be considered by the court or the jury."

_____

3. . . . The overwhelming consensus of the States, however, is opposed to allowing comment on the defendant's failure to testify. The legislatures or courts of 44 States have recognized that such comment is, in light of the privilege against self-incrimination, "an unwarrantable line of argument." State v. Howard, 35 S.C. 197, 203, 14 S.E. 481, 483. See 8 Wigmore, Evidence § 2272, n. 2 (McNaughton rev. ed. 1961 and 1964 Supp.). Of the six States which permit comment, two, California and Ohio, give this permission by means of an explicit constitutional qualification of the privilege against self-incrimination. Cal. Const. Art. I, § 13; Ohio Const. Art. I, § 10. . . .

ure of the accused to testify. No formal offer of proof is made as in other situations; but the prosecutor's comment and the court's acquiescence are the equivalent of an offer of evidence and its acceptance. The Court in the Wilson case stated:

> The act was framed with a due regard also to those who might prefer to rely upon the presumption of innocence which the law gives to every one, and not wish to be witnesses. It is not every one who can safely venture on the witness stand, though entirely innocent of the charge against him. Excessive timidity, nervousness when facing others and attempting to explain transactions of a suspicious character, and offenses charged against him, will often confuse and embarrass him to such a degree as to increase rather than remove prejudices against him. It is not every one, however, honest, who would therefore willingly be placed on the witness stand. The statute, in tenderness to the weakness of those who from the causes mentioned might refuse to ask to be witnesses, particularly when they may have been in some degree compromised by their association with others, declares that the failure of a defendant in a criminal action to request to be a witness shall not create any presumption against him. 149 U.S., p. 66, 13 S. Ct. p. 766. . . .

[C]omment on the refusal to testify is a remnant of the "inquisitorial system of criminal justice," which the Fifth Amendment outlaws. It is a penalty imposed by courts for exercising a constitutional privilege. It cuts down on the privilege by making its assertion costly. It is said, the Federal Bill of Rights, and I am prepared to agree that . . . the inference of guilt for failure to testify as to facts peculiarly within the accused's knowledge is in any event natural and irresistible, and that comment on the failure does not magnify that inference into a penalty for asserting a constitutional privilege. What the jury may infer, given no help from the court, is one thing. What it may infer when the court solemnizes the silence of the accused into evidence against him is quite another. That the inference of guilt is not always so natural or irresistible is brought out in the [People v.] Modesto opinion itself.

> Defendant contends that the reason a defendant refuses to testify is that his prior convictions will be introduced in evidence to impeach him and not that he is unable to deny the accusations. It is true that the defendant might fear that his prior convictions will prejudice the jury, and therefore another possible inference can be drawn from his refusal to take the stand.

We said in Malloy v. Hogan, that "the same standards must determine whether an accused's silence in either a federal or state proceeding is justified." We take that in its literal sense and hold that the Fifth Amendment, in its direct application to the Federal Government and in its bearing on the States by reason of the Fourteenth Amendment, forbids either comment by the prosecution on the accused's silence or instructions by the court that such silence is evidence of guilt.

Reversed.

Notes and Questions

1. If you were on a jury, what, if anything, would you infer if a defendant did not testify?

2. Would a judge's instruction informing you not to consider the defendant's silence make a difference in how you decided the case? Do you think such an instruction would be beneficial to a defendant? In *Carter v. Kentucky*, 450 U.S. 288, 101 S. Ct. 1112, 67 L. Ed. 2d 241 (1981), the Court held that to protect a defendant from unjustified speculation by a jury concerning his failure to testify, a judge must give such an instruction at the defendant's request. However, some defendants may not want a judge to deliver such an instruction, fearing that it may "red-flag" their failure to testify. In *Lakeside v. Oregon*, 435 U.S. 333, 98 S. Ct. 1091, 55 L. Ed.

2d 319 (1978), the Court held that it was constitutionally permissible for a judge to give a protective instruction despite the defendant's objection to it. What would explain why an instruction designed to protect the defendant can be given in the face of an objection made by the very person who presumably benefits from the instruction but does not want its "protection"?

3. What if a prosecutor did not come right out and say that the defendant did not testify but rather told the jury in closing argument that the state's evidence was "unrefuted" and "uncontradicted"? Would such an argument constitute improper comment on the defendant's failure to testify? Would it make a difference if defense counsel earlier had alluded to the fact that the defendant would testify on his or her own behalf? See *Lockett v. Ohio*, 438 U.S. 586, 98 S. Ct. 2954, 57 L. Ed. 2d 973 (1978).

In *United States v. Robinson*, 485 U.S. 25, 108 S. Ct. 864, 99 L. Ed. 2d 23 (1988), the defense attorney maintained during closing argument that the government had not allowed the defendant to testify and tell his side of the story. In rebuttal, the prosecutor argued that the defendant could have "taken the stand and explained it to you." The Court found no *Griffin* violation because the defense attorney's argument had "opened the door" for the prosecutor's remarks, which were "a fair response to a claim made by" defense counsel.

4. A person's right to remain silent is not absolute. The Fifth Amendment protects an individual from compelled self-incrimination. If the government wishes, it may grant a witness *immunity.* A grant of "use immunity" guarantees a witness that any testimony she gives will not be used against her. "Transactional immunity" ensures that the witness will not be prosecuted at all for crimes that are the subject of her testimony. A witness conferred immunity may not refuse to testify on the basis of the privilege against self-incrimination, since she no longer risks incrimination as a result of her testimony. See *Kastigar v. United States*, 406 U.S. 441, 92 S. Ct. 1653, 32 L. Ed. 2d 212 (1972). When the government grants a witness "use immunity" and later seeks to prosecute the witness, it must prove that it obtained all of its evidence from a source that is wholly independent of the compelled testimony. *Id.* While use immunity has

been held to be sufficient to remove the bar of "self-incrimination" in federal matters, *Kastigar v. United States, supra*, several states have held, on state constitutional grounds, that only a grant of transactional immunity is sufficient to compel a witness's testimony.

In *State v. Miyasaki*, 62 Haw. 269, 614 P.2d 915 (1980), the Hawaii Supreme Court considered whether a statute authorizing the compulsion of testimony following a grant of use immunity, instead of transactional immunity, was consistent with the state constitution. Initially, the Hawaii Supreme Court quoted Justice Goldberg's opinion in *Murphy v. Waterfront Commission*, 378 U.S. 52, 84 S. Ct. 1594, 12 L. Ed. 2d 678 (1964), to illustrate the importance and sanctity of the right not to be forced to incriminate oneself:

> The privilege against self-incrimination "registers an important advance in the development of our liberty—'one of the great landmarks in man's struggle to make himself civilized.'" Ullmann v. United States, 350 U.S. 422, 426, 76 S. Ct. 497, 100 L. Ed. 511. It reflects many of our fundamental values and most noble aspirations: our unwillingness to subject those suspected of crime to the cruel trilemma of self-accusation, perjury or contempt; our preference for an accusatorial rather than an inquisitorial system of criminal justice; our fear that self-incriminating statements will be elicited by inhumane treatment and abuses; our sense of fair play which dictates "a fair state-individual balance by requiring the government to leave the individual alone until good cause is shown for disturbing him and by requiring the government in its contest with the individual to shoulder the entire load," 8 Wigmore, Evidence (McNaughton rev., 1961), 317; our respect for the inviolability of the human personality and of the right of each individual "to a private enclave where he may lead a private life," United States v. Grunewald, 2 Cir., 233 F.2d 556, 581–582 (Frank, J., dissenting), rev'd 353 U.S. 391, 77 S. Ct. 963, 1 L. Ed. 2d 931; our distrust of self-deprecatory statements; and our realization that the privilege, while sometimes "a shelter to the guilty," is often "a pro-

tection to the innocent." Quinn v. United States, 349 U.S. 155, 162, (75 S. Ct. 668, 99 L. Ed. 964). Id. at 55, 84 S. Ct. 1594, 1597 (footnotes omitted). . . .

After reviewing the historical basis for its decision, the court proceeded to explain why the "use immunity" statute violated the Hawaii state constitution:

> The statute gives the government access to otherwise unavailable information by nullifying a constitutional privilege. Compulsion sanctioned by law is applied to elicit information on a promise that it will not be used in any way to prosecute the witness and the government receives something it would not be entitled to but for the statute. The witness, on the other hand, receives nothing he does not already have, for Article I, Section 10 already guarantees that he need not incriminate himself. Hence, he is not in the same position he was before he gave evidence—he may now have incriminated himself and he will also have been deprived of his privilege with respect to the transactions that are the subject of inquiry. While the statute precludes the use of the information, the witness remains subject to prosecution. If the investigation produces allegedly "independent" evidence in sufficient quantity to prosecute him, he may then face a task at trial of establishing possible links between the government's case and his appearance before the investigatory body in the face of prosecutorial assertions to the contrary. The essential difficulty of determining whether a prosecution derives in some way from compelled evidence in the single jurisdiction situation involved here was captured by Justice Brennan when he said:

> > In dealing with a single jurisdiction, we ought to recognize the enormous difficulty in attempting to ascertain whether a subsequent prosecution of an individual, who has previously been compelled to incriminate himself in regard to the offense in question, derives from the compelled testimony or from an "independent source." For one thing, all the relevant evidence will obviously be in the hands of the government—the government whose investigation included compelling the individual involved to incriminate himself. Moreover, this argument does not depend upon assumptions of misconduct or collusion among government officers. It assumes only the normal margin of human fallibility. Men working in the same office or department exchange information without recording carefully how they obtained certain information; it is often impossible to remember in retrospect how or when or from whom information was obtained. By hypothesis, the situation involves one jurisdiction with presumably adequate exchange of information among its various law enforcement officers. Moreover, the possibility of subtle inferences drawn from action or non-action on the part of fellow law enforcement personnel would be difficult if not impossible to prove or disprove. Piccirillo v. New York, 400 U.S. 548, 568, 91 S. Ct. 520, 530–531, 27 L. Ed. 2d 596 (1971) (dissenting opinion).

> A prosecution would bring further problems that may not be resolved without prejudice to the witness, problems related to a decision to testify and a possible use in cross-examination of information gained from his appearance before the investigatory body. If he should testify at trial, he would, of course, be subject to cross-examination. The prosecutor may then be able to chart the cross-examination on the defendant's prior testimony and it is improbable he would be able to demonstrate that such questioning involved the direct or indirect use of immunized testimony. He may well be influenced to forego a right to testify.

Note the balancing done by the courts between a person's right to remain silent and society's need to secure evidence in order to arrest and prosecute criminals.

The Right To Testify

We have seen that the Fifth Amendment guarantees criminal defendants the right not to testify. Do defendants also have a constitutional right to testify in their own defense if they so desire? The Supreme Court considered this issue at some length in *Rock v. Arkansas.*

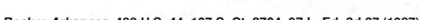

Rock v. Arkansas, 483 U.S. 44, 107 S. Ct. 2704, 97 L. Ed. 2d 37 (1987)

Justice BLACKMUN delivered the opinion of the Court. . . .

I

Petitioner Vickie Lorene Rock was charged with manslaughter in the death of her husband, Frank Rock, on July 2, 1983. . . . That night a fight erupted when Frank refused to let petitioner eat some pizza and prevented her from leaving the apartment to get something else to eat. When police arrived on the scene they found Frank on the floor with a bullet wound in his chest. Petitioner urged the officers to help her husband, and cried to a sergeant . . . "Please save him" and "Don't let him die." . . .

Because petitioner could not remember the precise details of the shooting, her attorney suggested that she submit to hypnosis in order to refresh her memory. Petitioner was hypnotized twice by Doctor Bettye Back, a licensed neuropsychologist with training in the field of hypnosis. Doctor Back interviewed petitioner for an hour prior to the first hypnosis session, taking notes on petitioner's general history and her recollections of the shooting. Both hypnosis sessions were recorded on tape. Petitioner did not relate any new information during either of the sessions, but, after the hypnosis, she was able to remember that at the time of the incident she had her thumb on the hammer of the gun, but had not held her finger on the trigger. She also recalled that the gun had discharged when her husband grabbed her arm during the scuffle. As a result of the details that petitioner was able to remember about the shooting, her counsel

arranged for a gun expert to examine the handgun, a single-action Hawes .22 Deputy Marshal. That inspection revealed that the gun was defective and prone to fire, when hit or dropped, without the trigger's being pulled.

When the prosecutor learned of the hypnosis sessions, he filed a motion to exclude petitioner's testimony. The trial judge held a pretrial hearing on the motion and concluded that no hypnotically refreshed testimony would be admitted. The court issued an order limiting petitioner's testimony to "matters remembered and stated to the examiner prior to being placed under hypnosis." At trial, petitioner introduced testimony by the gun expert, but the court limited petitioner's own description of the events on the day of the shooting to a reiteration of the sketchy information in Doctor Back's notes. The jury convicted petitioner on the manslaughter charge and she was sentenced to 10 years' imprisonment and a $10,000 fine. . . .

On appeal, the Supreme Court of Arkansas rejected petitioner's claim that the limitations on her testimony violated her right to present her defense. The court concluded that "the dangers of admitting this kind of testimony outweigh whatever probative value it may have," and decided to follow the approach of States that have held hypnotically refreshed testimony of witnesses inadmissible per se. 288 Ark. 566, 573, 708 S.W.2d 78, 81 (1986). Although the court acknowledged that "a defendant's right to testify is fundamental," id., at 578, 708 S.W.2d, at 84, it ruled that the exclusion of petitioner's testimony did not violate her constitutional rights. Any "prejudice or deprivation" she suffered "was minimal and resulted from her own actions and not by any erroneous ruling of the court." Id., at 580, 708 S.W.2d, at 86. . . .

II

The right to testify on one's own behalf at a criminal trial has sources in several provisions of the Constitution. It is one of the rights that "are essential to due process of law in a fair adversary process." Faretta v. California, 422 U.S. 806, 819, n. 15, 95 S. Ct. 2525, 2533 n. 15, 45 L. Ed. 2d 562 (1975). The necessary ingredients of the Fourteenth Amendment's guarantee that no one shall be deprived of liberty without due process of law include a right to be heard and to offer testimony: "A person's right to reasonable notice of a charge against him, and an opportunity to be heard in his defense— a right to his day in court—are basic in our system of jurisprudence; and these rights include, as a minimum, a right to examine the witnesses against him, to offer testimony, and to be represented by counsel." In re Oliver, 333 U.S. 257, 273, 68 S. Ct. 499, 507, 92 L. Ed. 682 (1948). . . .

The right to testify is also found in the Compulsory Process Clause of the Sixth Amendment, which grants a defendant the right to call "witnesses in his favor," a right that is guaranteed in the criminal courts of the States by the Fourteenth Amendment. Logically included in the accused's right to call witnesses whose testimony is "material and favorable to his defense," is a right to testify himself, should he decide it is in his favor to do so. In fact, the most important witness for the defense in many criminal cases is the defendant himself. There is no justification today for a rule that denies an accused the opportunity to offer his own testimony. Like the truthfulness of other witnesses, the defendant's veracity, which was the concern behind the original common-law rule, can be tested adequately by cross-examination.

Moreover, in Faretta v. California, 422 U.S., at 819, 95 S. Ct., at 2533, the Court recognized that the Sixth Amendment "grants to the accused personally the right to make his defense. It is the accused, not counsel, who must be 'informed of the nature and cause of the accusa-tion,' who must be 'confronted with the witnesses against him,' and who must be accorded 'compulsory process for obtaining witnesses in his favor.'"

Even more fundamental to a personal defense than the right of self-representation, which was found to be "necessarily implied by the structure of the Amendment," ibid., is an accused's right to present his own version of events in his own words. A defendant's opportunity to conduct his own defense by calling witnesses is incomplete if he may not present himself as a witness.

The opportunity to testify is also a necessary corollary to the Fifth Amendment's guarantee against compelled testimony. In Harris v. New York, 401 U.S. 222, 230, 91 S. Ct. 643, 648, 28 L. Ed. 2d 1 (1971), the Court stated: "Every criminal defendant is privileged to testify in his own defense, or to refuse to do so." Id., at 225, 91 S. Ct., at 645. . . .

III

The question now before the Court is whether a criminal defendant's right to testify may be restricted by a state rule that excludes her posthypnosis testimony. . . .

Of course, the right to present relevant testimony is not without limitation. The right "may, in appropriate cases, bow to accommodate other legitimate interests in the criminal trial process." But restrictions of a defendant's right to testify may not be arbitrary or disproportionate to the purposes they are designed to serve. In applying its evidentiary rules a State must evaluate whether the interests served by a rule justify the limitation imposed on the defendant's constitutional right to testify.

IV

The Arkansas rule enunciated by the state courts does not allow a trial court to consider whether posthypnosis testimony may be admissible in a particular case; it is a per se rule prohibiting the admission at trial of any defendant's hypnotically refreshed testimony on the ground that such testimony is always unreliable.[12] Thus, in Arkansas an accused's testimony is limited to matters that he or she can prove were remembered before hypnosis. This rule operates to the detriment of any defendant who undergoes hypnosis, without regard to the reasons for it, the circumstances under which it took place, or any independent verification of the information it produced.

In this case, the application of that rule had a significant adverse effect on petitioner's ability to testify. It virtually prevented her from describing any of the events that occurred on the day of the shooting, despite corroboration of many of those events by other witnesses. Even more importantly, under the court's rule petitioner was not permitted to describe the actual shooting except in the words contained in Doctor Back's notes. The expert's description of the gun's tendency to misfire would have taken on greater significance if the jury had heard petitioner testify that she did not have her finger on the trigger and that the gun went off when her husband hit her arm.

In establishing its per se rule, the Arkansas Supreme Court simply followed the approach taken by a number of States that have decided that hypnotically enhanced testimony should be excluded at trial on the ground that it tends to be unreliable. Other States that have adopted an exclusionary rule, however, have done so for the testimony of witnesses, not for the testimony of a defendant. The Arkansas Supreme Court failed to perform the constitutional analysis that is necessary when a defendant's right to testify is at stake.

Although the Arkansas court concluded that any testimony that cannot be proved to be the product of prehypnosis memory is unreliable, many courts have eschewed a per se rule and permit the admission of hypnotically refreshed testimony. Hypnosis by trained physicians or psychologists has been recognized as a valid therapeutic technique since 1958, although there is no generally accepted theory to explain the phenomenon, or even a consensus on a single definition of hypnosis. . . .

––––––––
12. The rule leaves a trial judge no discretion to admit this testimony, even if the judge is persuaded of its reliability by testimony at a pretrial hearing.

The more traditional means of assessing accuracy of testimony also remain applicable in the case of a previously hypnotized defendant. Certain information recalled as a result of hypnosis may be verified as highly accurate by corroborating evidence. Cross-examination, even in the face of a confident defendant, is an effective tool for revealing inconsistencies. Moreover, a jury can be educated to the risks of hypnosis through expert testimony and cautionary instructions. Indeed, it is probably to a defendant's advantage to establish carefully the extent of his memory prior to hypnosis, in order to minimize the decrease in credibility the procedure might introduce.

We are not now prepared to endorse without qualifications the use of hypnosis as an investigative tool; scientific understanding of the phenomenon and of the means to control the effects of hypnosis is still in its infancy. Arkansas, however, has not justified the exclusion of all of a defendant's testimony that the defendant is unable to prove to be the product of prehypnosis memory. A State's legitimate interest in barring unreliable evidence does not extend to per se exclusions that may be reliable in an individual case. Wholesale inadmissibility of a defendant's testimony is an arbitrary restriction on the right to testify in the absence of clear evidence by the State repudiating the validity of all posthypnosis recollections. The State would be well within its powers if it established guidelines to aid trial courts in the evaluation of posthypnosis testimony and it may be able to show that testimony in a particular case is so unreliable that exclusion is justified. But it has not shown that hypnotically enhanced testimony is always so untrustworthy and so immune to the traditional means of evaluating credibility that it should disable a defendant from presenting her version of the events for which she is on trial.

In this case, the defective condition of the gun corroborated the details petitioner remembered about the shooting. The tape recordings provided some means to evaluate the hypnosis and the trial judge concluded that Doctor Back did not suggest responses with leading questions. Those circumstances present an argument for admissibility of petitioner's testimony in this particular case, an argument that must be considered by the trial court. Arkansas' per se rule excluding all posthypnosis testimony infringes impermissibly on the right of the defendant to testify on his own behalf.

The judgment of the Supreme Court of Arkansas is vacated, and the case is remanded to that court for further proceedings not inconsistent with this opinion.

Notes and Questions

1. Notice that a defendant's right to testify is not unlimited. A criminal defendant's testimony is generally governed by the same rules of evidence that apply to the testimony of other witnesses. Does this seem fair?

2. The Court in *Rock* objected to the absolute nature of the Arkansas statute. How could the Arkansas legislature reformulate the rule to have a similar yet constitutional effect?

CONFRONTATION AND CROSS-EXAMINATION

The Sixth Amendment provides that a defendant has a right "to be confronted with the witnesses against him." The confrontation clause provides the basis for several rights realized by a criminal defendant. It generally requires that the witnesses who will provide testimony against the defendant appear at trial and confront the defendant face to face. As with many other rules, there are exceptions to this policy.

"Face-to-Face" Confrontation

In *Coy v. Iowa*, 487 U.S. 1012, 108 S. Ct. 2798, 101 L. Ed. 2d 857 (1988), the Court was asked to recognize an exception to the "face-to-face" testimony contemplated by the confronta-

tion clause in a case involving an Iowa statute that required that children who were the alleged victims of sexual abuse be allowed to testify in criminal trials from behind a screen. Under this arrangement, the defendant would be in the same room as the witness and could hear the witness, but the defendant and the witness could not see each other. The Supreme Court held that the statutory procedure, which applied in all cases of child abuse without regard to the peculiar circumstances of the alleged offense or the particularities of a child witness, violated the defendant's right to a "face-to-face" confrontation with accusing witnesses. While the Court declared the Iowa statute unconstitutional, it stated in *dicta* that the right to face-to-face confrontation "may give way to other important interests." Two years later, in *Maryland v. Craig*, the Court picked up where it left off in *Coy*.

Maryland v. Craig, 497 U.S. 836, 110 S. Ct. 3157, 111 L. Ed. 2d 666 (1990)

Justice O'CONNOR delivered the opinion of the Court. . . .

I

In October 1986, a Howard County grand jury charged respondent, Sandra Ann Craig, with child abuse, first and second degree sexual

offenses, perverted sexual practice, assault, and battery. The named victim in each count was a 6-year-old girl who, from August 1984 to June 1986, had attended a kindergarten and prekindergarten center owned and operated by Craig.

In March 1987, before the case went to trial, the State sought to invoke a Maryland statutory procedure that permits a judge to receive, by one-way closed circuit television, the testimony of a child witness who is alleged to be a victim of child abuse. To invoke the procedure, the trial judge must first "determin[e] that testimony by the child victim in the courtroom will result in the child suffering serious emotional distress such that the child cannot reasonably communicate." Md.Cts. & Jud.Proc.Code Ann. § 9-102(a)(1)(ii) (1989). Once the procedure is invoked, the child witness, prosecutor, and defense counsel withdraw to a separate room; the judge, jury, and defendant remain in the courtroom. The child witness is then examined and cross-examined in the separate room, while a video monitor records and displays the witness's testimony to those in the courtroom. During this time the witness cannot see the defendant. The defendant remains in electronic communication with defense counsel, and objections may be made and ruled on as if the witness were testifying in the courtroom.

In support of its motion invoking the one-way closed circuit television procedure, the State presented expert testimony that the named victim, as well as a number of other children who were alleged to have been sexually abused by Craig, would suffer "serious emotional distress such that [they could not] reasonably communicate," § 9-102(a)(1)(ii), if required to testify in the courtroom. . . .

Craig objected to the use of the procedure on Confrontation Clause grounds, but the trial court rejected that contention, concluding that although the statute "take[s] away the right of the defendant to be face to face with his or her accuser," the defendant retains the "essence of the right of confrontation," including the right to observe, cross-examine, and have the jury view the demeanor of the witness. The trial court further found that, "based upon the evidence presented . . . the testimony of each of these children in a courtroom will result in each child suffering serious emotional distress . . . such that each of these children cannot reasonably communicate." The trial court then found the named victim and three other children competent to testify and accordingly permitted them to testify against Craig via the one-way closed circuit television procedure. The jury convicted Craig on all counts, and the Maryland Court of Special Appeals affirmed the convictions, 76 Md. App. 250, 544 A.2d 784 (1988).

The Court of Appeals of Maryland reversed and remanded for a new trial. 316 Md. 551, 560 A.2d 1120 (1989). . . .

We granted certiorari to resolve the important Confrontation Clause issues raised by this case. 493 U.S. 1041, 110 S. Ct. 834, 107 L. Ed. 2d 830 (1990).

II

The Confrontation Clause of the Sixth Amendment, made applicable to the States through the Fourteenth Amendment, provides: "In all criminal prosecutions, the accused shall enjoy the right . . . to be confronted with the witnesses against him."

We observed in Coy v. Iowa that "the Confrontation Clause guarantees the defendant a face-to-face meeting with witnesses appearing before the trier of fact." 487 U.S., at 1016, 108 S. Ct., at 2801 (citing Kentucky v. Stincer, 482 U.S. 730, 748–750, 107 S. Ct. 2658, 2669, 2670, 96 L. Ed. 2d 631 (1987) (MARSHALL, J., dissenting)). . . .

We have never held, however, that the Confrontation Clause guarantees criminal defendants the absolute right to a face-to-face meeting with witnesses against them at trial. Indeed, in Coy v. Iowa, we expressly "le[ft] for another day . . . the question whether any exceptions exist" to the "irreducible literal meaning of the Clause: 'a right to meet face to face all those who appear and give evidence at trial.'" 487 U.S., at 1021, 108 S.Ct., at 2803 (quoting Green, supra, 399 U.S., at 175, 90 S.Ct., at 1943 (Harlan, J., concurring)). The procedure challenged in Coy involved the placement of a screen that prevented two child witnesses in a child abuse case from seeing the defendant as they testified against him at trial. In holding that the use of this procedure violated the defendant's right to confront witnesses against him, we suggested that any exception to the right "would surely be allowed only when necessary to further an important public policy"—i.e., only upon a showing of something more than the generalized, "legislatively imposed presumption of trauma" underlying the statute at issue in that case. Id., at 1021, 108 S. Ct., at 2803. We concluded that "[s]ince there ha[d] not been an individualized findings that these particular witnesses needed special protection, the judgment [in the case before us] could not be sustained by any conceivable exception." Id., at 1021. Because the trial court in this case made individualized findings that each of the child witnesses needed special protection, this case requires us to decide the question reserved in Coy.

The central concern of the Confrontation Clause is to ensure the reliability of the evidence against a criminal defendant by subjecting it to rigorous testing in the context of an adversary proceeding before the trier of fact. The word "confront," after all, also means a clashing of forces or ideas, thus carrying with it the notion of adversariness. . . .

[T]he right guaranteed by the Confrontation Clause includes not only a "personal examination," 156 U.S., at 242, 15 S. Ct., at 339, but also "(1) insures that the witness will give his statements under oath—thus impressing him with the seriousness of the matter and guarding against the lie by the possibility of a penalty for perjury; (2) forces the witness to submit to cross-examination, the 'greatest legal engine ever invented for the discovery of truth'; [and] (3) permits the jury that is to decide the defendant's fate to observe the demeanor of the witness in making his statement, thus aiding the jury in assessing his credibility." Green, supra, 399 U.S., at 158, 90 S. Ct., at 1935.

The combined effect of these elements of confrontation—physical presence, oath, cross-examination, and observation of demeanor by the trier of fact—serves the purposes of the Confrontation Clause by ensuring that evidence admitted against an accused is reliable and subject to the rigorous adversarial testing that is the norm of Anglo-American criminal proceedings. . . .

For this reason, we have never insisted on an actual face-to-face encounter at trial in every instance in which testimony is admitted against a defendant. Instead, we have repeatedly held that the Clause permits, where necessary, the admission of certain hearsay statements against a defendant despite the defendant's inability to confront the declarant at trial. . . . In Mattox, for example, we held that the testimony of a Government witness at a former trial against the defendant, where the witness was fully cross-examined but had died after the first trial, was admissible in evidence against the defendant at his second trial. We explained:

> There is doubtless reason for saying that . . . if notes of [the witness's] testimony are permitted to be read, [the defendant] is deprived of the advantage of that personal presence of the witness before the jury which the law has designed for his protection. But general rules of law of this kind, however beneficent in their operation and valuable to the accused, must occasionally give way to considerations of public policy and the necessities of the case. . . . Id., at 243, 15 S. Ct., at 339–340.

We have accordingly stated that a literal reading of the Confrontation Clause would "abrogate virtually every hearsay exception, a result long rejected as unintended and too extreme." Roberts, 448 U.S., at 63, 100 S. Ct., at 2537. Thus, in certain narrow circumstances, "competing interests, if 'closely examined,' may warrant dispensing with confrontation at trial." Id., at 64, 100 S. Ct., at 2538 (quoting Chambers v. Mississippi, 410 U.S. 284, 295, 93 S. Ct. 1038, 35 L. Ed. 2d 297 (1973), and citing Mattox, supra). . . .

In sum, our precedents establish that "the Confrontation Clause reflects a preference for face-to-face confrontation at trial," Roberts, supra, 448 U.S., at 63, 100 S. Ct., at 2537, a preference that "must occasionally give way to considerations of public policy and the necessities of the case," Mattox, supra, 156 U.S., at 243, 15 S. Ct., at 339–340. "[W]e have attempted to harmonize the goal of the Clause—placing limits on the kind of evidence that may be received against a defendant—with a societal interest in accurate fact finding, which may require consideration of out-of-court statements." We have accordingly interpreted the Confrontation Clause in a manner sensitive to its purposes and sensitive to the necessities of trial and the adversary process. . . . Thus, though we reaffirm the importance of face-to-face confrontation with witnesses appearing at trial, we cannot say that such confrontation is an indispensable element of the Sixth Amendment's guarantee of the right to confront one's accusers. Indeed, one commentator has noted that "[i]t is all but universally assumed that there are circumstances that excuse compliance with the right of confrontation." Graham, The Right of Confrontation and the Hearsay Rule: Sir Walter Raleigh Loses Another One, 8 Crim. L. Bull. 99, 107–108 (1972).

This interpretation of the Confrontation Clause is consistent with our cases holding that other Sixth Amendment rights must also be interpreted in the context of the necessities of trial and the adversary process. . . . We see no reason to treat the face-to-face component of the confrontation right any differently, and indeed we think it would be anomalous to do so.

That the face-to-face confrontation requirement is not absolute does not, of course, mean that it may easily be dispensed with. As we suggested in Coy, our precedents confirm that a defendant's right to confront accusatory witnesses may be satisfied absent a physical, face-to-face confrontation at trial only where denial of such confrontation is necessary to further an important public policy and only where the reliability of the testimony is otherwise assured.

III

Maryland's statutory procedure, when invoked, prevents a child witness from seeing the defendant as he or she testifies against the defendant at trial. We find it significant, however, that Maryland's procedure preserves all of the other elements of the confrontation right: The child witness must be competent to testify and must testify under oath; the defendant retains full opportunity for contemporaneous cross-examination; and the judge, jury, and defendant are able to view (albeit by video monitor) the demeanor (and body) of the witness as he or she testifies. Although we are mindful of the many subtle effects face-to-face confrontation may have on an adversary criminal proceeding, the presence of these other elements of confrontation—oath, cross-examination, and observation of the witness's demeanor—adequately ensures that the testimony is both reliable and subject to rigorous adversarial testing in a manner functionally equivalent to that accorded live, in-person testimony. These safeguards of reliability and adversariness render the use of such a procedure a far cry from the undisputed prohi-

bition of the Confrontation Clause: trial by ex parte affidavit or inquisition, see Mattox, 156 U.S., at 242, 15 S.Ct., at 389; see also Green, 399 U.S., at 179, 90 S.Ct., at 1946 (Harlan, J., concurring) ("[T]he Confrontation Clause was meant to constitutionalize a barrier against flagrant abuses, trials by anonymous accusers, and absentee witnesses"). Rather, we think these elements of effective confrontation not only permit a defendant to "confound and undo the false accuser, or reveal the child coached by a malevolent adult," Coy, supra, 487 U.S., at 1020, 108 S.Ct., at 2802, but may well aid a defendant in eliciting favorable testimony from the child witness. Indeed, to the extent the child witness's testimony may be said to be technically given out of court (though we do not so hold), these assurances of reliability and adversariness are far greater than those required for admission of hearsay testimony under the Confrontation Clause. We are therefore confident that use of the one-way closed circuit television procedure, where necessary to further an important state interest, does not impinge upon the truth-seeking or symbolic purposes of the Confrontation Clause.

The critical inquiry in this case, therefore, is whether use of the procedure is necessary to further an important state interest. The State contends that it has a substantial interest in protecting children who are allegedly victims of child abuse from the trauma of testifying against the alleged perpetrator and that its statutory procedure for receiving testimony from such witnesses is necessary to further that interest.

We have of course recognized that a State's interest in "the protection of minor victims of sex crimes from further trauma and embarrassment" is a "compelling" one.

We . . . conclude today that a State's interest in the physical and psychological well-being of child abuse victims may be sufficiently important to outweigh, at least in some cases, a defendant's right to face his or her accusers in court. That a significant majority of States have enacted statutes to protect child witnesses from the trauma of giving testimony in child abuse cases attests to the widespread belief in the importance of such a public policy. . . .

Given the State's traditional and "'transcendent interest in protecting the welfare of children,'" and buttressed by the growing body of academic literature documenting the psychological trauma suffered by child abuse victims who must testify in court, we will not second-guess the considered judgment of the Maryland Legislature regarding the importance of its interest in protecting child abuse victims from the emotional trauma of testifying. Accordingly, we hold that, if the State makes an adequate showing of necessity, the state interest in protecting child witnesses from the trauma of testifying in a child abuse case is sufficiently important to justify the use of a special procedure that permits a child witness in such cases to testify at trial against a defendant in the absence of face-to-face confrontation with the defendant.

The requisite finding of necessity must of course be a case-specific one: The trial court must hear evidence and determine whether use of the one-way closed circuit television procedure is necessary to protect the welfare of the particular child witness who seeks to testify. The trial court must also find that the child witness would be traumatized, not by the courtroom generally, but by the presence of the defendant. Denial of face-to-face confrontation is not needed to further the state interest in protecting the child witness from trauma unless it is the presence of the defendant that causes the trauma. In other words, if the state interest were merely the interest in protecting child witnesses from courtroom trauma generally, denial of face-to-face confrontation would be unnecessary because the child could be permitted to testify in less intimidating surroundings, albeit with the defendant present. Finally, the trial court must find that the emotional distress suffered by the child witness in the presence of the defendant is more than de minimis, i.e., more than "mere nervousness or excitement or some reluctance to testify." We need not decide the minimum showing of emotional trauma required for use of the special procedure, however, because the Maryland statute, which requires a determination that the child witness will suffer "serious emotional distress such that the child cannot reasonably communicate," clearly suffices to meet constitutional standards.

To be sure, face-to-face confrontations may be said to cause trauma for the very purpose of eliciting truth, but we think that the use of Maryland's special procedure, where necessary to further the important state interest in preventing trauma to child witnesses in child abuse cases, adequately ensures the accuracy of the testimony and preserves the adversary nature of the trial. Indeed, where face-to-face confrontation causes significant emotional distress in a child witness, there is evidence that such confrontation would in fact disserve the Confrontation Clause's truth-seeking goal.

In sum, we conclude that where necessary to protect a child witness from trauma that would be caused by testifying in the physical presence of the defendant, at least where such trauma would impair the child's ability to communicate, the Confrontation Clause does not prohibit use of a procedure that, despite the absence of face-to-face confrontation, ensures the reliability of the evidence by subjecting it to rigorous adversarial testing and thereby preserves the essence of effective confrontation. Because there is no dispute that the child witnesses in this case testified under oath, were subject to full cross-examination, and were able to be observed by the judge, jury, and defendant as they testified, we conclude that, to the extent that a proper finding of necessity has been made, the admission of such testimony would be consonant with the Confrontation Clause.

IV

The Maryland Court of Appeals held, as we do today, that although face-to-face confrontation is not an absolute constitutional requirement, it may be abridged only where there is a "'case-specific finding of necessity.'" 316 Md., at 564, 560, A.2d, at 1126 (quoting Coy, 487 U.S., at 1025, 108 S. Ct., at 2805) (O'Connor, J., concurring)). . . . Given this latter requirement, the Court of Appeals reasoned that "[t]he question of whether a child is unavailable to testify . . . should not be asked in terms of inability to testify in the ordinary courtroom setting, but in the much narrower terms of the witness's inability to testify in the presence of the accused." 316 Md., at 564, 560 A.2d., at 1126 (footnote omitted). "[T]he determinative inquiry required to preclude face-to-face confrontation is the effect of the presence of the defendant on the witness or the witness's testimony." Id., at 565, 560 A.2d, at

1127. The Court of Appeals accordingly concluded that, as a prerequisite to use of the § 9-102 procedure, the Confrontation Clause requires the trial court to make a specific finding that testimony by the child in the courtroom in the presence of the defendant would result in the child suffering serious emotional distress such that the child could not reasonably communicate. Id., at 566, 560 A.2d, at 1127. This conclusion, of course, is consistent with our holding today.

In addition, however, the Court of Appeals interpreted our decision in Coy to impose two subsidiary requirements. First, the court held that "§ 9-102 ordinarily cannot be invoked unless the child witness initially is questioned (either in or outside the courtroom) in the defendant's presence." Id., at 566, 560 A.2d, at 1127. Second, the court asserted that, before using the one-way television procedure, a trial judge must determine whether a child would suffer "severe emotional distress" if he or she were to testify by two-way closed circuit television. 316 Md., at 567, 560 A.2d, at 1128.

Reviewing the evidence presented to the trial court in support of the finding required under § 9-102(a)(1)(ii), the Court of Appeals determined that "the finding of necessity required to limit the defendant's right of confrontation through invocation of § 9-102 . . . was not made here." Id., at 570–571, 560 A. 2d, at 1229. The Court of Appeals noted that the trial judge "had the benefit only of expert testimony on the ability of the children to communicate; he did not question any of the children himself, nor did he observe any child's behavior on the witness stand before making his ruling. He did not explore any alternatives to the use of one-way closed-circuit television. Id., at 568, 560 A.2d, at 1128 (footnote omitted). The Court of Appeals also observed that "the testimony in this case was not sharply focused on the effect of the defendant's presence on the child witnesses." Id., at 569, 560 A.2d, at 1129. . . .

The Court of Appeals appears to have rested its conclusion at least in part on the trial court's failure to observe the children's behavior in the defendant's presence and its failure to explore less restrictive alternatives to the use of the one-way closed circuit television procedure. Although we think such evidentiary requirements could strengthen the grounds for use of protective measures, we decline to establish, as a matter of federal constitutional law, any such categorical evidentiary prerequisites for the use of the one-way television procedure. The trial court in this case, for example, could well have found, on the basis of the expert testimony before it, that testimony by the child witnesses in the courtroom in the defendant's presence "will result in [each] child suffering serious emotional distress such that the child cannot reasonably communicate." So long as a trial court makes such a case-specific finding of necessity, the Confrontation Clause does not prohibit a State from using a one-way closed circuit television procedure for the receipt of testimony by a child witness in a child abuse case. Because the Court of Appeals held that the trial court had not made the requisite finding of necessity under its interpretation of "the high threshold required by [Coy] before § 9-102 may be invoked," 316 Md., at 554–555, 560 A.2d, at 1121 (footnote omitted), we cannot be certain whether the Court of Appeals could reach the same conclusion in light of the legal standard we establish today. We therefore vacate the judgment of the Court of Appeals of Maryland and remand the case for further proceedings not inconsistent with this opinion.

Justice SCALIA, with whom Justice BRENNAN, Justice MARSHALL, and Justice STEVENS join, dissenting.

Seldom has this Court failed so conspicuously to sustain a categorical guarantee of the Constitution against the tide of prevailing current opinion. The Sixth Amendment provides, with unmistakable clarity, that "[i]n all criminal prosecutions, the accused shall enjoy the right . . . to be confronted with the witnesses against him." The purpose of enshrining this protection in the Constitution was to assure that none of the many policy interests from time to time pursued by statutory law could overcome a defendant's right to face his or her accusers in court. . . .

I

According to the Court, "We cannot say that [face-to-face] confrontation [with witnesses appearing at trial] is an indispensable element of the Sixth Amendment's guarantee of the right to confront one's accusers." That is rather like saying, "We cannot say that being tried before a jury is an indispensable element of the Sixth Amendment's guarantee of the right to jury trial." The Court makes the impossible plausible by recharacterizing the Confrontation Clause, so that confrontation (redesignated "face-to-face confrontation") becomes only one of many "elements of confrontation."

The reasoning is as follows: The Confrontation Clause guarantees not only what it explicitly provides for—"face-to-face" confrontation—but also implied and collateral rights such as cross-examination, oath, and observation of demeanor (TRUE); the purpose of this entire cluster of rights is to ensure the reliability of evidence (TRUE); the Maryland procedure preserves the implied and collateral rights (TRUE), which adequately ensure the reliability of evidence (perhaps TRUE); therefore the Confrontation Clause is not violated by denying what it explicitly pro-

vides for—"face-to-face" confrontation (unquestionably FALSE). This reasoning abstracts from the right to its purposes, and then eliminates the right. It is wrong because the Confrontation Clause does not guarantee reliable evidence; it guarantees specific trial procedures that were thought to assure reliable evidence, undeniably among which was "face-to-face" confrontation. Whatever else it may mean in addition, the defendant's constitutional right "to be confronted with the witnesses against him" means, always and everywhere, at least what it explicitly says: the "'right to meet face to face all those who appear and give evidence at trial.'" Coy v. Iowa, 487 U.S. 1012, 1016, 108 S.Ct. 2798, 2800, 101 L.Ed.2d 857 (1988), quoting California v. Green, 399 U.S. 149, 175, 90 S.Ct. 1930, 1943–44, 26 L.Ed.2d 489 (1970) (Harlan, J., concurring). . . .

Notes and Questions

1. What kind of signal about the defendant's guilt or innocence do you think the jury is given by having the child testify in another room while the defendant stays in the courtroom? Do you think such an arrangement adds credibility to the child's claims?

2. Could the Maryland procedure used in *Craig* be applied to other proceedings? Would such a procedure make it easier and less traumatic for adult rape victims to testify? Should the Maryland procedure be limited to child witnesses, or should a court consider each witness on a case-by-case basis?

3. What if a defendant charged with child abuse in Maryland wants to act as his own attorney? Should he be allowed to conduct face-to-face cross-examination of the child victims despite evidence that such a confrontation would be detrimental to the children? See *Fields v. Murray*, 49 F.3d 1024 (4th Cir. 1995), *cert. denied*, 516 U.S. 884 (1995).

4. Several state supreme courts have held that procedures similar to the one employed in *Craig* violate their state constitutional guarantees of face-to-face confrontation. *See* Latzer (1995), *supra* at § 6:7. Illustrative of these decisions is the Pennsylvania Supreme Court's opin-

ion in the case of *Commonwealth v. Ludwig*, 527 Pa. 472, 594 A.2d 281 (1991). Ludwig involved the trial of a man who was charged with molesting his five-year-old daughter. At Ludwig's trial, the judge permitted the child to testify via closed-circuit television from a separate room in the courthouse. Ludwig was convicted of the charged offense. The Pennsylvania Supreme Court reversed the conviction on the basis of its interpretation of the confrontation clause of the Pennsylvania state constitution:

* * * *

Article I, § 9 of our state constitution guarantees an accused the right to meet his accusers:

In all criminal prosecutions the accused hath a right to be heard by himself and his counsel, to demand the nature and cause of the accusations against him, to meet the witnesses face to face . . .

This language is unlike its federal counterpart, the Sixth Amendment, which provides that a defendant in a criminal case "shall enjoy the right . . . to be confronted with the witnesses against him." . . .

Unlike the Sixth Amendment to the United States Constitution, Article 1, Section 9 of the Pennsylvania Constitution specifically provides for a "face to face" confrontation. . . .

Unlike its federal counterpart, Article 1, Section 9, of the Pennsylvania Constitution does not reflect a "preference" but clearly, emphatically and unambiguously requires a "face to face" confrontation. This distinction alone would require that we decline to adopt the United States Supreme Court's analysis and reasoning in Maryland v. Craig. However, in addition, we have our own case law which mandates a "face to face" confrontation.

In Commonwealth v. Russo, 388 Pa. 462, 470–471, 131 A.2d 83, 88 (1957) we addressed the "face to face" requirement of Article I, § 9 of our Constitution, stating:

> Many people possess the trait of being loose tongued or willing to say something behind a person's back that they dare not or cannot truthfully say to his face or under oath in a courtroom. It is probably for this reason, as well as to give the accused the right to cross-examine his accusers and thereby enable the jury to better determine the credibility of the Commonwealth's witnesses and the strength and truth of its case, that this important added protection was given to every person accused of crime. We have no right to disregard or (unintentionally) erode or distort any provision of the constitution, especially where, as here, its plain and simple language make its meaning unmistakably clear; indeed, because of the times in which we live we have a higher duty than ever before to zealously protect and safeguard the constitution.

Although we were quite emphatic about the importance of this right, no right is absolute. Indeed, the right to confront an accuser is not without exception. In Commonwealth v. Rodgers, 472 Pa. 435, 372 A.2d 771 (1977), we permitted the prosecution to use preliminary hearing testimony of a witness at trial when that witness was unavailable. In Commonwealth v. Stasko, 471 Pa. 373, 370 A.2d 350 (1977), the prosecutor was permitted to use a videotape deposition of a witness unavailable for trial. In both instances, the original testimony was given in the presence of the defendant with the defendant having the opportunity to face and cross-examine his accuser. However, in each instance, the witnesses' subjective reaction to testifying in the presence of the accused were not a consideration.

Although we have recognized exceptions to the right to confront a witness, the policy reasons underlying those decisions are absent in this case. The witness in this case was neither unavailable nor subjected to cross-examination during prior testimony given in the presence of the accused. In fact, the trial judge instructed the jury that the victim was totally unaware of the existence of the trial itself. "We want her [the child] to be as relaxed and casual and normal as possible and she doesn't really know that you are here in this setting, she doesn't really understand that this is all actually a trial, it probably has little significance to her."

Having diluted the significance of her testimony to that extent, it is questionable whether the victim would be testifying under the proper aura. . . .

We are cognizant of society's interest in protecting victims of sexual abuse. However, that interest cannot be preeminent over the accused's constitutional right to confront the witnesses against him face to face. The record in this case does not disclose any conduct by the appellant during the proceedings that would give rise to the need to isolate the witness. The subjective fears of the witness, without more, are insufficient to restrict this important constitutional right. Since the trial court relied exclusively upon these fears, its actions cannot be affirmed. The appellant is entitled to face his accusers and the failure to protect that right was error. The appellant is therefore entitled to a new trial during which time the victim must testify in the courtroom before the judge, jury and appellant.

* * * *

Cross-Examination as a Means of Confrontation

The primary and unquestionably most important purpose behind the confrontation clause is protecting the defendant's right to cross-examine adverse witnesses. The scope of this right was at issue in *Davis v. Alaska*.

Davis v. Alaska, 415 U.S. 308, 94 S. Ct. 1105, 39 L. Ed. 2d 347 (1974)

Mr. Chief Justice BURGER delivered the opinion of the Court. . . .

(1)

When the Polar Bar in Anchorage closed in the early morning hours of February 16, 1970, well over a thousand dollars in cash and checks was in the bar's Mosler safe. About midday, February 16, it was discovered that the bar had been broken into and the safe, about two feet square and weighing several hundred pounds, had been removed from the premises.

Later that afternoon the Alaska State Troopers received word that a safe had been discovered about 26 miles outside Anchorage near the home of Jess Straight and his family. . . . Richard Green, Jess Straight's stepson, told investigating troopers on the scene that at about noon on February 16 he had seen and spoken with two Negro men standing alongside a late-model metallic blue Chevrolet sedan near where the safe was later discovered. The next day Anchorage police investigators brought him to the police station where Green was given six photographs of adult Negro males. After examining the photographs for 30 seconds to a minute, Green identified the photograph of petitioner as that of one of the men he had encountered the day before and described to the police. Petitioner was arrested the next day, February 18. On February 19, Green picked petitioner out of a lineup of seven Negro males. . . .

Richard Green was a crucial witness for the prosecution. He testified at trial that while on an errand for his mother he confronted two men standing beside a late-model metallic blue Chevrolet, parked on a road near his family's house. . . . On his return from the errand Green again passed the two men and he saw the man with whom he had had the conversation standing at the rear of the car with "something like a crowbar" in his hands. Green identified petitioner at the trial as the man with the "crowbar." The safe was discovered later that afternoon at the point, according to Green, where the Chevrolet had been parked.

Before testimony was taken at the trial of petitioner, the prosecutor moved for a protective order to prevent any reference to Green's juvenile record by the defense in the course of cross-examination. At the time of the trial and at the time of the events Green testified to, Green was on probation by order of a juvenile court after having been adjudicated a delinquent for burglarizing two cabins. Green was 16 years of age at the time of the Polar Bar burglary but had turned 17 prior to trial.

In opposing the protective order, petitioner's counsel made it clear that he would not introduce Green's juvenile adjudication as a general impeachment of Green's character as a truthful person but, rather, to show specifically that at the same time Green was assisting the police in identifying petitioner he was on probation for burglary. From this petitioner would seek to show—or at least argue—that Green acted out of fear of concern of possible jeopardy to his probation. Not only might Green have made a hasty and faulty identification of petitioner to shift suspicion away from himself as one who robbed the Polar Bar, but Green might have been subject to undue pressure from the police and made his identifications under fear of possible probation revocation. Green's record would be revealed only as necessary to probe Green for bias and prejudice and not generally to call Green's good character into question.

The trial court granted the motion for a protective order, relying on Alaska Rule of Children's Procedure 23,[1] and Alaska Stat. § 47.10.080(g) (1971).[2]

Although prevented from revealing that Green had been on probation for the juvenile delinquency adjudication for burglary at the same time that he originally identified petitioner, counsel for petitioner did his best to expose Green's state of mind at the time Green discovered that a stolen safe had been discovered near his home. Green denied that he was upset or uncomfortable about the discovery of the safe. He claimed not to have been worried about any suspicions the police might have been expected to harbor against him, though Green did admit that it crossed his mind that the police might have thought he had something to do with the crime.

Defense counsel cross-examined Green in part as follows: . . .

Q. Did that thought ever enter your mind that you—that the police might think that you were somehow connected with this?

A. No, it didn't really bother me, no.

Q. Well, but . . .

A. I mean, you know, it didn't—it didn't come into my mind as worrying me, you know.

Q. That really wasn't—wasn't my question, Mr. Green. Did you think that—not

whether it worried you so much or not, but did you feel that there was a possibility that the police might somehow think that you had something?

A. That came across my mind, yes sir.

Q. That did cross your mind?

A. Yes.

Q. So as I understand it you went down to the—you drove in with the police in—in their car from mile 25, Glenn Highway down to the city police station?

A. Yes, sir.

Q. And then went into the investigators' room with Investigator Gray and Investigator Weaver?

A. Yeah.

Q. And they started asking your questions about—about the incident, is that correct?

A. Yeah.

Q. Had you ever been questioned like that before by any law enforcement officers?

A. No.

MR. RIPLEY: I'm going to object to this, Your Honor, it's a carry-on with rehash of the same thing. He's attempting to raise in the jury's mind. . . .

THE COURT: I'll sustain the objection.

Since defense counsel was prohibited from making inquiry as to the witness's being on probation under a juvenile court adjudication, Green's protestations of unconcern over possible police suspicion that he might have had a part in the Polar Bar burglary and his categorical denial of ever having been the subject of any similar law-enforcement interrogation went unchallenged. The tension between the right of confrontation and the State's policy of protecting the witness with a juvenile record is particularly evident in the final answer given by the witness. Since it is probable that Green underwent some questioning by police when he was arrested for the burglaries on which his juvenile adjudication of delinquency rested, the answer can be regarded as highly suspect at the very least. The witness was in effect asserting, under protection of the trial court's ruling, a right to give a questionably truthful answer to a cross-examiner pur-

---

1. Rule 23 provides:

No adjudication, order, or disposition of a juvenile case shall be admissible in a court not acting in the exercise of juvenile jurisdiction except for use in a presentencing procedure in a criminal case where the superior court, in its discretion, determines that such use is appropriate.

2. Section 47.10.080(g) provides in pertinent part: "The commitment and placement of a child and evidence given in the court are not admissible as evidence against the minor in a subsequent case or proceedings in any other court."

suing a relevant line of inquiry; it is doubtful whether the bold "No" answer would have been given by Green absent a belief that he was shielded from traditional cross-examination. It would be difficult to conceive of a situation more clearly illustrating the need for cross-examination. . . .

The Alaska Supreme Court affirmed petitioner's conviction, concluding that . . . since "our reading of the trial transcript convinces us that counsel for the defendant was able adequately to question the youth in considerable detail concerning the possibility of bias or motive." 499 P.2d 1025, 1036 (1972). Although the court admitted that Green's denials of any sense of anxiety or apprehension upon the safe's being found close to his home were possibly self-serving, "The suggestion was nonetheless brought to the attention of the jury, and that body was afforded the opportunity to observe the demeanor of the youth and pass on his credibility." Ibid. The court concluded that, in light of the indirect references permitted, there was no error.

(2)

The Sixth Amendment to the Constitution guarantees the right of an accused in a criminal prosecution "to be confronted with the witnesses against him." This right is secured for defendants in state as well as federal criminal proceedings under Pointer v. Texas, 380 U.S. 400, 85 S. Ct. 1065, 13 L. Ed. 2d 923 (1965). Confrontation means more than being allowed to confront the witness physically. "Our cases construing the (confrontation) clause hold that a primary interest secured by it is the right of cross-examination." Douglas v. Alabama, 380 U.S. 415, 418, 85 S. Ct. 1074, 1076, 13 L. Ed. 2d 934 (1965). Professor Wigmore stated:

The main and essential purpose of confrontation is to secure for the opponent the opportunity of cross-examination. The opponent demands confrontation, not for the idle purpose of gazing upon the witness, or of being gazed upon by him, but for the purpose of cross-examination, which cannot be had except by the direct and personal putting of questions and obtaining

immediate answers. 5 J. Wigmore, Evidence § 1395, p. 123 (3d ed 1940).

Cross-examination is the principal means by which the believability of a witness and the truth of his testimony are tested. Subject always to the broad discretion of a trial judge to preclude repetitive and unduly harassing interrogation, the cross-examiner is not only permitted to delve into the witness's story to test the witness's perceptions and memory, but the cross-examiner has traditionally been allowed to impeach, i.e., discredit, the witness. . . . The partiality of a witness is subject to exploration at trial, and is "always relevant as discrediting the witness and affecting the weight of his testimony." 3A J. Wigmore, Evidence § 940, p. 775 (Chadbourn rev. 1970). . . .

In the instant case, defense counsel sought to show the existence of possible bias and prejudice of Green, causing him to make a faulty initial identification of petitioner, which in turn could have affected his later in-court identification of petitioner.

We cannot speculate as to whether the jury, as sole judge of the credibility of a witness, would have accepted this line of reasoning had counsel been permitted to fully present it. But we do conclude that the jurors were entitled to have the benefit of the defense theory before them so that they could make an informed judgment as to the weight to place on Green's testimony which provided "a crucial link in the proof . . . of petitioner's act." Douglas v. Alabama, 380 U.S., at 419, 85 S.Ct., at 1077. The accuracy and truthfulness of Green's testimony were key elements in the State's case against petitioner. The claim of bias which the defense sought to develop was admissible to afford a basis for an inference of undue pressure because of Green's vulnerable status as a probationer, as well as of Green's possible concern that he might be a suspect in the investigation.

We cannot accept the Alaska Supreme Court's conclusion that the cross-examination that was permitted defense counsel was adequate to develop the issue of bias properly to the jury. While counsel was permitted to ask Green whether he was biased, counsel was unable to make a record from which to argue why Green might have been biased or otherwise lacked that degree of impartiality expected of a witness at trial. On the basis of the limited cross-examination that was permitted, the jury might well have thought that defense counsel was engaged in a speculative and baseless line of attack on the credibility of an apparently blameless witness or, as the prosecutor's objection put it, a "rehash" of prior cross-examination. On these facts it seems clear to us that to make any such inquiry effective, defense counsel should have been permitted to expose to the jury the facts from which jurors, as the sole triers of fact and credibility, could appropriately draw inferences relating to the reliability of the witness. Petitioner was thus denied the right of effective cross-examination which "would be constitutional error of the first magnitude and no amount of showing of want of prejudice would cure it."

(3)

The claim is made that the State has an important interest in protecting the anonymity of juvenile offenders and that this interest outweighs any competing interest this petitioner might have in cross-examining Green about his being on probation. . . .

We do not and need not challenge the State's interest as a matter of its own policy in the administration of criminal justice to seek to preserve the anonymity of a juvenile offender. Here, however, petitioner sought to introduce evidence of Green's probation for the purpose of suggesting that Green was biased and, therefore, that

his testimony was either not to be believed in his identification of petitioner or at least very carefully considered in that light. Serious damage to the strength of the State's case would have been a real possibility had petitioner been allowed to pursue this line of inquiry. In this setting we conclude that the right of confrontation is paramount to the State's policy of protecting a juvenile offender. Whatever temporary embarrassment might result to Green or his family by disclosure of his juvenile record—if the prosecution insisted on using him to make its case—is outweighed by petitioner's right to probe into the influence of possible bias in the testimony of a crucial identification witness. . . .

The State's policy interest in protecting the confidentiality of a juvenile offender's record cannot require yielding of so vital a constitutional right as the effective cross-examination for bias of an adverse witness. The State could have protected Green from exposure of his juvenile adjudication in these circumstances by refraining from using him to make out its case; the State cannot, consistent with the right of confrontation, require the petitioner to bear the full burden of vindicating the State's interest in the secrecy of juvenile criminal records. The judgment affirming petitioner's convictions of burglary and grand larceny is reversed and the case is remanded for further proceedings not inconsistent with this opinion. . . .

Reversed and remanded.

Notes and Questions

1. Cross-examination is a key aspect of the right to confront witnesses. In part, the right to cross-examine helps distinguish the American criminal justice system from many others. An adversarial system assumes that the best way to test a witness's veracity and accuracy of recollection is through effective cross-examination. Since this right is designed to help promote the truth-seeking process, attorneys generally are given great latitude in cross-examining witnesses.

2. What if a witness to a crime who has given a statement to the police is not alive at the time of the trial? Can this statement, which is hearsay (an out-of-court statement being introduced to prove the matter asserted), be admitted at trial against the defendant? The general rule is that hearsay is not admissible in a criminal trial. If hearsay evidence is admitted against a defendant, the defendant has no opportunity to cross-examine the witness who made the statement. Nor, in most cases, will the hearsay statement have been made under oath. Furthermore, because the witness does not appear in court, the jury has no opportunity to observe the witness's demeanor, or the "cut of his jib," and make corresponding judgments about his credibility.

The prosecution, however, is not forbidden in all cases from using hearsay statements against a defendant. Numerous exceptions exist to the "hearsay rule." In *Ohio v. Roberts*, 448 U.S. 56, 100 S. Ct. 2531, 65 L. Ed. 2d 597 (1980), the Supreme Court adopted the "rule of necessity" for the introduction of hearsay statements against a criminal defendant who challenged the admission of out-of-court statements on Sixth Amendment grounds.

In sum, when a hearsay declarant is not present for cross-examination at trial, the Confrontation Clause normally requires a showing that he is unavailable.[3] Even then, his statement is admissible only if it bears adequate "indicia of reliability." Reliability can be inferred without more in a case where the evidence falls within a firmly rooted hearsay exception.[4] In other cases, the evidence must be excluded, at least absent a showing of particularized guarantees of trustworthiness. *Id.* at 66 (footnote omitted).

Does such a rule seem fair to the prosecution and the defense? If not, which party do you believe is impaired by the rule of necessity?

The Defendant's Right To Be Present during the Trial

The Confrontation Clause of the Sixth Amendment implicitly guarantees a defendant's right to be present at his or her trial. As with most constitutional rights, the right to be present at trial is not absolute. If it were, a defendant could not be placed on trial if she refused to go to court or disrupted the proceedings to such a degree that they could not go forward. An Illinois trial court faced such a situation during William Allen's trial for armed robbery.

Illinois v. Allen, 397 U.S. 337, 90 S. Ct. 1057, 25 L. Ed. 2d 353 (1970)

Mr. Justice BLACK delivered the opinion of the Court.

The Confrontation Clause of the Sixth Amendment to the United States Constitution provides that: "In all criminal prosecutions, the accused shall enjoy the right to be confronted with the witnesses against him." . . . One of the most basic of the rights guaranteed by the Confrontation Clause is the accused's right to be present in the courtroom at every stage of his trial. The question presented in this case is whether an accused can claim the benefit of this constitutional right to remain in the courtroom while at the same time he engages in speech and conduct which is so noisy, disorderly, and disruptive

that it is exceedingly difficult or wholly impossible to carry on the trial. . . .

[Allen was charged with and convicted of armed robbery. At his trial, he insisted on acting as his own attorney. During the jury selection process, Allen repeatedly disrupted the proceedings, doing such things as threatening the judge, refusing to follow the court's instructions, and tearing his advisory counsel's file apart and throwing its remains across the courtroom. The judge had Allen removed from the courtroom until such time as he could behave properly.

[After the lunch break, the judge allowed Allen to reappear in court. As before, Allen was very disruptive. He repeatedly yelled, "There is going to be no proceeding." Allen was once again removed from the courtroom.

[After this second removal, Allen remained out of the courtroom during the presentation of the State's case-in-chief, except that he was brought in on several occasions for purposes of identification. During one of these latter appearances, Allen responded to one of the judge's questions with vile and abusive language. After the prosecution's case had been presented, the trial judge reiterated his promise to Allen that he could return to the courtroom whenever he agreed to conduct himself properly. Allen gave some assurances of proper conduct and was permitted to be present through the remainder of the trial, principally his defense, which was conducted by his appointed counsel.

[Allen was convicted and sentenced to serve 10 to 30 years in prison. His conviction was affirmed by the Supreme Court of Illinois. Upon considering the denial of Allen's Petition for Habeas Corpus, the 7th Circuit Court of Appeals reversed, holding that a defendant has an absolute right to be present at his trial.]

The Court of Appeals [held] that the Supreme Court of Illinois was wrong in ruling that Allen had by his conduct relinquished his constitutional right to be present, declaring that:

No conditions may be imposed on the absolute right of a criminal defendant to be present at all stages of the proceeding. The insistence of a defendant that he exercise this right under unreasonable conditions does not amount to a waiver. Such conditions, if insisted upon, should and must be dealt with in a manner that does not compel the relinquishment of his right. . . .

The Court of Appeals felt that the defendant's Sixth Amendment right to be present at his own trial was so "absolute" that, no matter how unruly or disruptive the defendant's conduct might be, he could never be held to have lost that right so long as he continued to insist upon it, as Allen clearly did. Therefore the Court of Appeals concluded that a trial judge could never expel a defendant from his own trial and that the judge's ultimate remedy when faced with an obstreperous defendant like Allen who determines to make his trial impossible is to bind and gag him.

We cannot agree that the Sixth Amendment, the cases upon which the Court of Appeals relied, or any other cases of this Court so handicap a trial judge in conducting a criminal trial. . . . We accept instead the statement of Mr. Justice Cardozo who, speaking for the Court in Snyder v. Massachusetts, 291 U.S. 97, 106, 54 S. Ct. 330, 332, 78 L. Ed. 674 (1934), said: "No doubt the privilege (of personally confronting witnesses) may be lost by consent or at times even by misconduct." Although mindful that courts must indulge every reasonable presumption against the loss of constitutional rights, Johnson v. Zerbst, 304 U.S. 458, 464, 58 S. Ct. 1019, 1023, 82 L. Ed. 1461 (1938), we explicitly hold today that a defendant can lose his right to be present at trial if, after he has been warned by the judge that he will be removed if he continues his disruptive behavior, he nevertheless insists on conducting himself in a manner so disorderly, disruptive, and disrespectful of the court that his trial cannot be carried on with him in the courtroom. Once lost, the right to be present can, of course, be reclaimed as soon as the defendant is willing to conduct himself consistently with the decorum and respect inherent in the concept of courts and judicial proceedings.

It is essential to the proper administration of criminal justice that dignity, order, and decorum be the hallmarks of all court proceedings in our country. The flagrant disregard in the courtroom of elementary standards of proper conduct should not and cannot be tolerated. We believe trial judges confronted with disruptive, contumacious, stubbornly defiant defendants must be given sufficient discretion to meet the circumstances of each case. No one formula for maintaining the appropriate courtroom atmosphere will be best in all situations. We think there are at least three constitutionally permissible ways for a trial judge to handle an obstreperous defendant like Allen: (1) bind and gag him, thereby keeping him present; (2) cite him for contempt; (3) take him out of the courtroom until he promises to conduct himself properly.

I

Trying a defendant for a crime while he sits bound and gagged before the judge and jury would to an extent comply with that part of the

Sixth Amendment's purposes that accords the defendant an opportunity to confront the witnesses at the trial. But even to contemplate such a technique, much less see it, arouses a feeling that no person should be tried while shackled and gagged except as a last resort. Not only is it possible that the sight of shackles and gags might have a significant effect on the jury's feelings about the defendant, but the use of this technique is itself something of an affront to the very dignity and decorum of judicial proceedings that the judge is seeking to uphold. Moreover, one of the defendant's primary advantages of being present at the trial, his ability to communicate with his counsel, is greatly reduced when the defendant is in a condition of total physical restraint. It is in part because of these inherent disadvantages and limitations in this method of dealing with disorderly defendants that we decline to hold with the Court of Appeals that a defendant cannot under any possible circumstances be deprived of his right to be present at trial. However, in some situations which we need not attempt to foresee, binding and gagging might possibly be the fairest and most reasonable way to handle a defendant who acts as Allen did here.

II

In a footnote the Court of Appeals suggested the possible availability of contempt of court as a remedy to make Allen behave in his robbery trial, and it is true that citing or threatening to cite a contumacious defendant for criminal contempt might in itself be sufficient to make a defendant stop interrupting a trial. If so, the problem would be solved easily, and the defendant could remain in the courtroom. Of course, if the defendant is determined to prevent any trial, then a court in attempting to try the defendant for contempt is still confronted with the identical dilemma that the Illinois court faced in this case. And criminal contempt has obvious limitations as a sanction when the defendant is charged with a crime so serious that a very severe sentence such as death or life imprisonment is likely to be imposed. In such a case the defendant might not be affected by a mere contempt sentence when he ultimately faces a far more serious sanction. Nevertheless, the contempt

remedy should be borne in mind by a judge in the circumstances of this case.

Another aspect of the contempt remedy is the judge's power, when exercised consistently with state and federal law, to imprison an unruly defendant such as Allen for civil contempt and discontinue the trial until such time as the defendant promises to behave himself. . . . It must be recognized, however, that a defendant might conceivably, as a matter of calculated strategy, elect to spend a prolonged period in confinement for contempt in the hope that adverse witnesses might be unavailable after a lapse of time. . . .

III

The trial court in this case decided under the circumstances to remove the defendant from the courtroom and to continue his trial in his absence until and unless he promised to conduct himself in a manner befitting an American courtroom. As we said earlier, we find nothing unconstitutional about this procedure. Allen's behavior was clearly of such an extreme and aggravated nature as to justify either his removal from the courtroom or his total physical restraint. Prior to his removal he was repeatedly warned by the trial judge that he would be removed from the courtroom if he persisted in his unruly conduct, and, as Judge Hastings observed in his dissenting opinion, the record demonstrates that Allen would not have been at all dissuaded by the trial judge's use of his criminal contempt powers. Allen was constantly informed that he could return to the trial when he would agree to conduct himself in an orderly manner. Under these circumstances we hold that Allen lost his right guaranteed by the Sixth and Fourteenth Amendments to be present throughout his trial.

IV. . .

[O]ur courts, palladiums of liberty as they are, cannot be treated disrespectfully with impunity. Nor can the accused be permitted by his disruptive conduct indefinitely to avoid being tried on the charges brought against him. It would degrade our country and our judicial system to permit our courts to be bullied, insulted, and humiliated and their orderly progress thwarted and obstructed by defendants brought before them charged with crimes. . . . [I]f our courts are to remain what the Founders intended, the citadels of justice, their proceedings cannot and must not be infected with the sort of scurrilous, abusive language and conduct paraded before the Illinois trial judge in this case. The record shows that the Illinois judge at all times conducted himself with that dignity, decorum, and patience that befit a judge. . . . We do not hold that removing this defendant from his own trial was the only way the Illinois judge could have constitutionally solved the problem he had. We do hold, however, that there is nothing whatever in this record to show that the judge did not act completely within his discretion. Deplorable as it is to remove a man from his own trial, even for a short time, we hold that the judge did not commit legal error in doing what he did.

The judgment of the Court of Appeals is reversed.

Notes and Questions

1. If a defendant is so disruptive that he must be removed from the courtroom, does the state have an obligation to provide him with access to the proceedings via closed-circuit television? Must he be given a telephone to speak with his attorney from outside the courtroom? In other words, how far must the state go to protect a defendant's right to be present at trial when the accused will not behave well enough to remain in the courtroom?

2. In a situation like *Allen*, would it make a difference if the defendant were behaving improperly as a result of a mental illness beyond his control?

3. Does the confrontation clause guarantee a defendant the right to be at all proceedings connected with his trial? *Kentucky v. Stincer*, 482 U.S. 730, 107 S. Ct. 2658, 96 L. Ed. 2d 631 (1987), involved the prosecution of a man charged with molesting three young children. Shortly after his trial began, the judge conducted an examination in his chambers of two of the children, ages eight and seven, to determine whether they were competent to testify. No substantive issues were dealt with during the examination, but only matters relating to the children's ability to distinguish the truth from lying and to recall and describe the facts of the case. Stincer was not permitted to attend this examination. The judge subsequently found the children competent to testify, and Stincer was convicted on the strength of their testimony and other evidence. Stincer appealed his conviction, asserting a Sixth Amendment right to be present in the judge's chambers during the competency hearing. The Supreme Court held that the Confrontation Clause does not guarantee a criminal defendant the right to be present at such a proceeding. The justices ruled that since defense counsel was present and was given the opportunity to cross-examine the children, Stincer's right to confrontation was not violated.

DOUBLE JEOPARDY

The Fifth Amendment to the Constitution provides, "No person shall . . . be subject for the same offence to be twice put in jeopardy of life or limb." The double-jeopardy clause "represents a constitutional policy of finality for the defendant's benefit in criminal proceedings." *Oregon v. Kennedy*, 456 U.S. 667, 682, 102 S. Ct. 2083, 2092, 72 L. Ed. 2d 416 (1982) (Stevens, J., concurring, footnote omitted). In common with the Sixth Amendment's speedy-trial provision, the double-jeopardy clause is designed to help provide closure to criminal proceedings.

The double-jeopardy clause protects an individual from (a) being prosecuted twice for the same offense and (b) being punished twice for the same offense. While these protections may seem straightforward, they can be somewhat complex in practice.

Multiple Prosecutions for the Same Offense

As noted above, the Fifth Amendment prohibits the prosecution of an individual twice for the "same offence." In *Blockburger v. United States*, 284 U.S. 299, 52 S. Ct. 180, 76 L. Ed. 306 (1932), the Supreme Court announced a test for determining whether a second prosecution is barred by a previous one involving the *same offense*. The *Blockburger* or "same-offense" test hinges on whether each offense contains an element (legal part of the crime that must be proved by the prosecution) not included in the other. If the elements of the ostensibly different crimes completely overlap, the crimes are considered the *same offense*, and the accused may not be prosecuted (or punished) as if the crimes were different. For example, assault (offensively touching an individual) and aggravated assault (offensively touching an individual causing serious physical injury) would be considered the same offense under the *Blockburger* test in that all of the elements of assault are present in an aggravated assault. As such, a prosecution for assault, after the defendant had been acquitted of aggravated assault involving the same conduct, would be barred.

While the *Blockburger* test is straightforward, the U.S. Supreme Court has struggled in formulating its double-jeopardy jurisprudence. *United States v. Dixon* typifies the difficulty the Court has had in maintaining consistency in its double-jeopardy jurisprudence.

United States v. Dixon, 509 U.S. 688, 113 S. Ct. 2849, 125 L. Ed. 2d 556 (1993)

Justice **Scalia** announced the judgment of the Court and delivered the opinion of the Court with respect to Parts I, II, and IV, and an opinion with respect to Parts III and V, in which Justice **Kennedy** joins.

In both of these cases, respondents were tried for criminal contempt of court for violating court orders that prohibited them from engaging in conduct that was later the subject of a criminal prosecution. We consider whether the subsequent criminal prosecutions are barred by the Double Jeopardy Clause.

I

Respondent Alvin Dixon was arrested for second-degree murder and was released on bond. Consistent with the District of Columbia's bail law authorizing the judicial officer to impose any condition that "will reasonably assure the appearance of the person for trial or the safety of any other person or the community," DC Code Ann § 23-1321(a) (1989), Dixon's release form specified that he was not to commit "any criminal offense," and warned that any violation of the conditions of release would subject him "to revocation of release, an order of detention, and prosecution for contempt of court."

While awaiting trial, Dixon was arrested and indicted for possession of cocaine with intent to distribute, in violation of DC Code Ann § 33-541(a)(1) (1988). The court issued an order requiring Dixon to show cause why he should not be held in contempt or have the terms of his pretrial release modified. At the show-cause hearing, four police officers testified to facts surrounding the alleged drug offense; Dixon's counsel cross-examined these witnesses and introduced other evidence. The court concluded that the Government had established "'beyond a reasonable doubt that [Dixon] was in possession of drugs and that those drugs were possessed with the intent to distribute.'" 598 A2d 724, 728 (DC 1991). The court therefore found Dixon guilty of criminal contempt under § 23-1329(c), which allows contempt sanctions after expedited proceedings without a jury and "in accordance with principles applicable to proceedings for criminal contempt." For his contempt, Dixon was sentenced to 180 days in jail. DC Code § 23-1329(c) (maximum penalty of six months' imprisonment and $1000 fine). He later moved to dismiss the cocaine indictment on double jeopardy grounds; the trial court granted the motion.

Respondent Michael Foster's route to this Court is similar. Based on Foster's alleged physical attacks upon her in the past, Foster's estranged wife Ana obtained a civil protection order (CPO) in Superior Court of the District of Columbia. The order, to which Foster consented, required that he not "'molest, assault, or in any manner threaten or physically abuse'" Ana Foster.

Over the course of eight months, Ana Foster filed three separate motions to have her husband held in contempt for numerous violations of the CPO. Of the 16 alleged episodes, the only charges relevant here are three separate instances of threats (on November 12, 1987, and March 26 and May 17, 1988) and two assaults (on November 6, 1987, and May 21, 1988), in the most serious of which Foster "threw [his wife] down basement stairs, kicking her body[,] . . . pushed her head into the floor causing head injuries, [and Ana Foster] lost consciousness." 598 A2d, at 726.

After issuing a notice of hearing and ordering Foster to appear, the court held a 3-day bench trial. Counsel for Ana Foster and her mother prosecuted the action; the United States was not represented at trial, although the United States Attorney was apparently aware of the action, as was the court aware of a separate grand jury proceeding on some of the alleged criminal conduct. As to the assault charges, the court stated that Ana Foster would have "to prove as an element, first that there was a Civil Protection Order, and then [that] . . . the assault as defined by the criminal code, in fact occurred." At the close of the plaintiffs' case, the court granted Foster's motion for acquittal on various counts, including the alleged threats on November 12 and May 17. Foster then took the stand and generally denied the allegations. The court found Foster guilty beyond a reasonable doubt of four counts of criminal contempt (three violations of

Ana Foster's CPO, and one violation of the CPO obtained by her mother), including the November 6, 1987 and May 21, 1988 assaults, but acquitted him on other counts, including the March 26 alleged threats. He was sentenced to an aggregate 600 days' imprisonment. See § 16-1005(f) (authorizing contempt punishment); Sup Ct of DC Intrafamily Rules 7(c), 12(e) (maximum punishment of six months' imprisonment and $300 fine).

The United States Attorney's Office later obtained an indictment charging Foster with simple assault on or about November 6, 1987 (Count I, violation of § 22-504); threatening to injure another on or about November 12, 1987, and March 26 and May 17, 1988 (Counts II-IV, violation of § 22-2307); and assault with intent to kill on or about May 21, 1988 (Count V, violation of § 22-501). Ana Foster was the complainant in all counts; the first and last counts were based on the events for which Foster had been held in contempt, and the other three were based on the alleged events for which Foster was acquitted of contempt. Like Dixon, Foster filed a motion to dismiss, claiming a double jeopardy bar to all counts, and also collateral estoppel as to Counts II-IV. The trial court denied the double-jeopardy claim and did not rule on the collateral-estoppel assertion.

The Government appealed the double jeopardy ruling in Dixon, and Foster appealed the trial court's denial of his motion. The District of Columbia Court of Appeals consolidated the two cases, reheard them en banc, and, relying on our recent decision in Grady v. Corbin, 495 US 508, 110 S Ct 2084, 109 L Ed 2d 548 (1990), ruled that both subsequent prosecutions were barred by the Double Jeopardy Clause. 598 A2d, at 725. In its petition for certiorari, the Government presented the sole question "[w]hether the Double Jeopardy Clause bars prosecution of a defendant on substantive criminal charges based upon the same conduct for which he previously has been held in criminal contempt of court." Pet for Cert I. We granted certiorari, 503 US 1004, 112 S Ct 1759, 118 L Ed 2d 422 (1992).

II . . .

The Double Jeopardy Clause provides that no person shall "be subject for the same offence to be twice put in jeopardy of life or limb." US Const, Amdt 5. This protection applies both to successive punishments and to successive prosecutions for the same criminal offense. It is well established that criminal contempt, at least the sort enforced through nonsummary proceedings, is "a crime in the ordinary sense." . . .

In both the multiple punishment and multiple prosecution contexts, this Court has concluded that where the two offenses for which the defendant is punished or tried cannot survive the "same-elements" test, the double jeopardy bar applies. See, e.g., Brown v. Ohio, 432 US 161, 168–169, 97 S Ct 2221, 53 L Ed 2d 187 (1977); Blockburger v. United States, 284 US 299, 304, 52 S Ct 180, 76 L Ed 306 (1932) (multiple punishment); Gavieres v. United States, 220 US 338, 342, 31 S Ct 421, 55 L Ed 489 (1911) (successive prosecutions). The same-elements test, sometimes referred to as the "Blockburger" test, inquires whether each offense contains an element not contained in the other; if not, they are the "same offence" and double jeopardy bars additional punishment and successive prosecution. In a case such as Yancy, for example, in which the contempt prosecution was for disruption of judicial business, the same-elements test would not bar subsequent prosecution for the criminal assault that was part of the disruption, because the contempt offense did not require the element of criminal conduct, and the criminal offense did not require the element of disrupting judicial business.

We recently held in Grady that in addition to passing the Blockburger test, a subsequent prosecution must satisfy a "same-conduct" test to avoid the double jeopardy bar. The Grady test provides that, "if, to establish an essential element of an offense charged in that prosecution, the government will prove conduct that constitutes an offense for which the defendant has already been prosecuted," a second prosecution may not be had. 495 US, at 510, 110 S Ct 2084, 109 L Ed 2d 548.

III

A

The first question before us today is whether Blockburger analysis permits subsequent prosecution in this new criminal contempt context, where judicial order has prohibited criminal act. If it does, we must then proceed to consider whether Grady also permits it.

We begin with Dixon. The statute applicable in Dixon's contempt prosecution provides that "[a] person who has been conditionally released . . . and who has violated a condition of release shall be subject to . . . prosecution for contempt of court." § 23-1329(a). Obviously, Dixon could not commit an "offence" under this provision until an order setting out conditions was issued. The statute by itself imposes no legal obligation on anyone. Dixon's cocaine possession, although an offense under DC Code Ann § 33-541(a) (1988 and Supp 1992), was not an offense under § 23-1329 until a judge incorporated the statutory drug offense into his release order.

In this situation, in which the contempt sanction is imposed for violating the order through commission of the incorporated drug offense, the later attempt to prosecute Dixon for the drug offense resembles the situation that produced our judgment of double jeopardy in Harris v. Oklahoma, 433 US 682, 53 L Ed 2d 1054, 97 S Ct 2912 (1977) (per curiam). There we held that a subsequent prosecution for robbery with a firearm was barred by the Double Jeopardy Clause, because the defendant had already been tried for felony-murder based on the same underlying felony. We have described our terse per curiam in Harris as standing for the proposition that, for double jeopardy purposes, "the crime generally described as felony murder" is not "a separate offense distinct from its various elements." Illinois v. Vitale, 447 US 410, 420–421, 100 S Ct 2260, 65 L Ed 2d 228 (1980). Accord, Whalen v. United States, 445 US 684, 694, 100 S Ct 1432, 63 L Ed 2d 715 (1980). So too here, the "crime" of violating a condition of release cannot be abstracted from the "element" of the violated condition. The Dixon court order incorporated the entire governing criminal code in the same manner as the Harris felony-murder statute incorporated the several enumerated felonies. Here, as in Harris, the underlying substantive criminal offense is "a species of lesser-included offense." Vitale, supra, at 420, 100 S Ct 2260, 65 L Ed 2d 228. . . .

Both the Government, and Justice Blackmun contend, that the legal obligation in Dixon's case may serve "interests . . . fundamentally different" from the substantive criminal law, because it derives in part from the determination of a court rather than a determination of the legislature. That distinction seems questionable, since the court's power to establish conditions of release, and to punish their violation, was conferred by statute; the legislature was the ultimate source of both the criminal and the contempt prohibition. More importantly, however, the distinction is of no moment for purposes of the Double Jeopardy Clause, the text of which looks to whether the *offenses* are the same, not the interests that the offenses violate. This Court stated long ago that criminal contempt, at least in its nonsummary form, "is a crime in every fundamental respect." Because Dixon's drug offense did not include any element not contained in his previous contempt offense, his subsequent prosecution violates the Double Jeopardy Clause.

The foregoing analysis obviously applies as well to Count I of the indictment against Foster, charging assault in violation of § 22-504, based on the same event that was the subject of his prior contempt conviction for violating the provision of the CPO forbidding him to commit simple assault under § 22-504. The subsequent prosecution for assault fails the Blockburger test, and is barred.

B

The remaining four counts in Foster, assault with intent to kill (Count V; § 22-501) and threats to injure or kidnap (Counts II-IV; § 22-2307), are not barred under Blockburger. As to Count V: Foster's conduct on May 21, 1988 was found to violate the Family Division's order that he not "molest, assault, or in any manner threaten or physically abuse" his wife. At the contempt hearing, the court stated that Ana Foster's attorney, who prosecuted the contempt, would have to prove first, knowledge of a CPO, and second, a willful violation of one of its conditions, here simple assault as defined by the criminal code.

On the basis of the same episode, Foster was then indicted for violation of § 22-501, which proscribes assault with intent to kill. Under governing law, that offense requires proof of specific intent to kill; simple assault does not. Similarly, the contempt offense required proof of knowledge of the CPO, which assault with intent to kill does not. Applying the Blockburger elements test, the result is clear: These crimes were different offenses and the subsequent prosecution did not violate the Double Jeopardy Clause.

Counts II, III, and IV of Foster's indictment are likewise not barred. These charged Foster under § 22-2307 (forbidding anyone to threate[n] . . . to kidnap any person or to injure the person of another or physically damage the property of any person") for his alleged threats on three separate dates. Foster's contempt prosecution included charges that, on the same dates, he violated the CPO provision ordering that he not "in any manner threaten" Ana Foster. Conviction of the contempt required willful violation of the CPO—which conviction under § 22-2307 did not; and conviction under § 22-2307 required that the threat be a threat to kidnap, or inflict bodily injury, or to damage property—which conviction of the contempt (for violating the CPO provision that Foster not "in any manner threaten") did not. Each offense therefore contained a separate element, and the Blockburger test for double jeopardy was not met.

IV

Having found that at least some of the counts at issue here are not barred by the Blockburger test, we must consider whether they are barred by the new, additional double jeopardy test we announced three Terms ago in Grady v. Corbin. They undoubtedly are, since Grady prohibits "a subsequent prosecution if, to establish an essential element of an offense charged in that prosecution [here, assault as an element of assault with intent to kill, or threatening as an element of threatening bodily injury], the government will prove conduct that constitutes an offense for which the defendant has already been prosecuted [here, the assault and the threatening, which conduct constituted the offense of violating the CPO]." 495 US, at 510, 110 S Ct 2084, 109 L Ed 2d 548.

We have concluded, however, that Grady must be overruled. Unlike Blockburger analysis, whose definition of what prevents two crimes from being the "same offence," US Const, Amdt

5, has deep historical roots and has been accepted in numerous precedents of this Court, Grady lacks constitutional roots. The "same-conduct" rule it announced is wholly inconsistent with earlier Supreme Court precedent and with the clear common-law understanding of double jeopardy. . . .

But Grady was not only wrong in principle; it has already proved unstable in application. Less than two years after it came down, in United States v. Felix, 503 US 378, 112 S Ct 1377, 118 L Ed 2d 25 (1992), we were forced to recognize a large exception to it. There we concluded that a subsequent prosecution for conspiracy to manufacture, possess, and distribute methamphetamine was not barred by a previous conviction for attempt to manufacture the same substance. We offered as a justification for avoiding a "literal" (i.e., faithful) reading of Grady "longstanding authority" to the effect that prosecution for conspiracy is not precluded by prior prosecution for the substantive offense. Felix, supra, at 388–391, 112 S Ct 1377, 118 L Ed 2d 25. Of course the very existence of such a large and longstanding "exception" to the Grady rule gave cause for concern that the rule was not an accurate expression of the law. This "past practice" excuse is not available to support the ignoring of Grady in the present case, since there is no Supreme Court precedent even discussing this fairly new breed of successive prosecution (criminal contempt for violation of a court order prohibiting a crime, followed by prosecution for the crime itself). . . .

Having encountered today yet another situation in which the pre-Grady understanding of the Double Jeopardy Clause allows a second trial, though the "same-conduct" test would not, we think it time to acknowledge what is now, three years after Grady, compellingly clear: the case was a mistake. We do not lightly reconsider a precedent, but, because Grady contradicted an "unbroken line of decisions," contained "less than accurate" historical analysis, and has produced "confusion," we do so here. Solorio v. United States, 483 US 435, 439, 442, 450, 97 L Ed 2d 364, 107 S Ct 2924 (1987). Although stare decisis is the "preferred course" in constitutional adjudication, "when governing decisions are unworkable or are badly reasoned, 'this Court has never felt constrained to follow precedent.'" Payne v. Tennessee, 501 US 808, 827, 111 S Ct 2597, 115 L Ed 2d 720 (1991). We would mock stare decisis and only add chaos to our double jeopardy jurisprudence by pretending that Grady survives when it does not. We therefore accept the Government's invitation to overrule Grady, and Counts II, III, IV, and V of Foster's subsequent prosecution are not barred.

V

Dixon's subsequent prosecution, as well as Count I of Foster's subsequent prosecution, violate the Double Jeopardy Clause. For the reasons set forth in Part IV, the other Counts of Foster's subsequent prosecution do not violate the Double Jeopardy Clause. . . .

Notes and Questions

1. In *Dixon*, the Court took the relatively unusual step of explicitly overruling a prior decision. *Grady v. Corbin* was decided by a 5–4 vote. Just three years later, the *Dixon* Court held that *Grady* was a mistake. Does the Supreme Court create instability in the criminal justice system by overruling precedent? Should it matter that the overruled case was decided by a 5–4 vote or other close division? See *Payne v. Ten-*

nessee, 501 U.S. 808, 111 S. Ct. 2597, 115 L. Ed. 2d 720 (1991) (Marshall, J., dissenting).

2. If you were doing a research project or writing a paper on double jeopardy, it would obviously be important for you to know that *Dixon* had overruled *Grady v. Corbin*. Although you could use *Shepard's* to check if *Grady* had been overruled, there are several other tools available on WESTLAW that are easier to use and more up to date and that can help you determine the continued validity of *Grady* or any other published opinion.

WESTLAW provides four "citator" services. These are *Shepard's, Shepard's Preview*, Insta-Cite, and QuickCite. *Shepard's* on WESTLAW provides the same information as is contained in the printed version. To *Shepardize* a case on WESTLAW, you need only type "sh" while viewing a case. An alternative method, which is very convenient when you have numerous cases to *Shepardize*, is to type "sh," followed by the case's citation. For example, to *Shepardize Grady v. Corbin* on WESTLAW, you could type "sh 495 US 508" (or use the "sh" command with one of the case's parallel cites).

While *Shepard's* on WESTLAW is very convenient, updates routinely lag several weeks behind the publication of an opinion. WESTLAW thus provides several other, more up-to-date services. *Shepard's Preview* provides similar information to *Shepard's* but is updated much more frequently. *Shepard's Preview* is used similarly to *Shepard's*, except that instead of the command "sh," you type "sp." WESTLAW also offers a service called QuickCite that provides continuous updates to its *Shepard's* and *Shepard's Preview* databases. QuickCite gives citation information on all published opinions as well as on the unpublished opinions that are provided on WESTLAW. To check a case on QuickCite, simply type "qc" and the case citation. The fourth service offered on WESTLAW is Insta-Cite. Insta-Cite provides the complete procedural history of a case, as well as any indirect negative history on a case. For example, if you look up *Grady* on Insta-Cite, you will find citations to the opinions and docket numbers of the trial court and lower appellate court, along with the information that the Supreme Court's decision in *Grady* was overruled by *Dixon*. Insta-Cite is updated every 24 to 36 hours and can be accessed by typing "ic" and the case citation.

3. *Grady* prohibited a "subsequent prosecution if, to establish an essential element of an offense charged in that prosecution, the government will prove conduct that constitutes an offense for which the defendant has already been prosecuted." 495 U.S. at 510. This analy-

sis, known as the "same-conduct" test, proved extremely difficult to apply and caused confusion throughout the criminal justice system. The defendant in *Grady* had been involved in a vehicular homicide. He originally was charged with driving while intoxicated, a misdemeanor, along with other traffic infractions. Following his guilty plea and convictions to these charges, Grady was indicted for manslaughter and aggravated assault. He argued that the new indictment was barred by the double-jeopardy clause since his conviction on the traffic charges had arisen out of the same conduct. As discussed in *Dixon*, the *Grady* Court accepted this argument.

4. In *State v. Lessary*, 75 Haw. 446, 865 P.2d 150 (1994), the Hawaii Supreme Court held that the test applied in *Dixon* violated the double-jeopardy clause of the Hawaii state constitution:

> James Easter Lessary was charged with committing the offenses of Abuse of a Family or Household Member (Abuse), Unlawful Imprisonment in the First Degree (Unlawful Imprisonment) . . . , and Terroristic Threatening in the First Degree (Terroristic Threatening) [arising out of a single incident with his estranged wife]. After Lessary was found guilty of the Abuse charge in family court, the circuit court dismissed the Unlawful Imprisonment and Terroristic Threatening charges on double jeopardy grounds. . . . [The State appealed.] . . .
>
> Because of its focus on the statutory definitions of offenses, however, the [Blockburger] "same elements" test does not prevent the government from initiating multiple prosecutions against an individual based on a single act as long as the subsequent prosecutions are for offenses with "different" elements. In Grady v. Corbin, the United States Supreme Court recognized the dangers inherent in allowing the government to pursue multiple prosecutions against an individual. The Court described the dangers as follows:
>
>> Successive prosecutions, however, whether following acquittals or convictions, raise concerns that extend beyond merely the possibility of an

enhanced sentence[.] The underlying idea, one that is deeply ingrained in at least the Anglo-American system of jurisprudence, is that the State with all its resources and power should not be allowed to make repeated attempts to convict an individual for an alleged offense, thereby subjecting him to embarrassment, expense and ordeal and compelling him to live in a continuing state of anxiety and insecurity[.] Multiple prosecutions also give the State an opportunity to rehearse its presentation of proof, thus increasing the risk of an erroneous conviction for one or more of the offenses charged. Even when a State can bring multiple charges against an individual under Blockburger, a tremendous additional burden is placed on that defendant if he must face each of the charges in a separate proceeding. Grady, 495 U.S. at 518–19, 110 S. Ct. at 2091–92.

Although Dixon overruled Grady and reestablished the "same elements" test as the sole protection against double jeopardy, four justices continued to believe that the Blockburger test alone does not provide adequate protection. The State urges us to follow Dixon and argues that any test more restrictive than the "same elements" test would contravene the public policy of having different courts handle different offenses (e.g., traffic court for traffic violations, juvenile court for offenses committed by minors, and family court for intra-family offenses committed by adults). In "instances of successive prosecutions," however, "the interests of the *defendant* are of paramount concern." Dixon, 509 U.S. at 724, 113 S. Ct at 2870–71 (White, J., concurring in part and dissenting in part) (emphasis in original). We do not believe that the State's interest in prosecuting different offenses in different courts outweighs a defendant's "paramount" interest in being free from vexatious multiple prosecutions. Moreover, the State should not be allowed to circumvent the constitutional prohibition against double jeopardy by creating a variety of courts, each having limited jurisdiction, in which to bring successive prosecutions that could not otherwise be pursued.

Thus, we are not persuaded by the State's argument and agree with the majority in Grady and the "dissenters" in Dixon that individuals should be protected against multiple prosecutions even when multiple punishments are permissible under the "same elements" test. Therefore, we conclude that the interpretation given to the double jeopardy clause by the United States Supreme Court in Dixon does not adequately protect individuals from being "subject for the same offense to be twice put in jeopardy." Having concluded that the protections afforded under the United States Constitution are inadequate, we must determine what further protections are required by the Hawaii Constitution. The protections must ensure that individuals are not subjected to multiple prosecutions for a single act. The "same conduct" test set forth by the United States Supreme Court in Grady attempted to provide those protections. The Court there held that the Double Jeopardy Clause bars any subsequent prosecution in which the government, to establish an essential element of an offense charged in that prosecution, will prove conduct that constitutes an offense for which the defendant has already been prosecuted. Grady, 495 U.S. at 521, 110 S. Ct. at 2093 (footnote omitted). . . .

The "same conduct" test as set forth in Grady . . . protects individuals from multiple prosecutions for the same act without unnecessarily restricting the ability of the State to prosecute individuals who perform separate acts that independently constitute separate offenses. In addition, the "same conduct" test was applied in criminal prosecutions in Hawaii for the three years that Grady was the applicable law under the United States Constitution. We believe that the application of the Grady rule is necessary to afford adequate double jeopardy protection, and, therefore, we adopt the "same conduct" test under the Hawaii Constitution. . . .

Reprosecution after Mistrial

Jeopardy attaches at a criminal trial once the jury has been empaneled and sworn in. The prosecution ordinarily is barred from aborting a trial, and later beginning a new prosecution for the same crime, after jeopardy has attached. The Court has recognized that a defendant has a "valued right to have his trial completed before a particular tribunal." *United States v. Perez*, 9 Wheat. 579, 6 L. Ed. 165 (1824). This rule also protects a defendant from facing continued "harassing exposure to the harrowing experiences of a criminal trial. . . ." *Crist v. Bretz*, 437 U.S. 28, 98 S. Ct. 2156, 57 L. Ed. 2d 24 (1978).

The most common way in which a trial ends prior to a verdict is the judge's declaring a mistrial. Mistrials can occur when a mistake or error committed during the trial makes it inappropriate to continue.[5] Examples include improper testimony or argument being presented that would prejudice the jury and interfere with the jurors' ability to reach a just verdict. The judge may declare a mistrial under such circumstances, either on his or her own or at the request of one or both of the parties. After a mistrial is declared, the prosecution may seek to retry the defendant before a different jury. The defendant, on the other hand, may claim that a second trial is barred on double-jeopardy grounds.

Oregon v. Kennedy, 456 U.S. 667, 102 S. Ct. 2083, 72 L. Ed. 2d 416 (1982)

Justice REHNQUIST delivered the opinion of the Court. . . .

I

Respondent was charged with the theft of an oriental rug. During his first trial, the State called an expert witness on the subject of Middle Eastern rugs to testify as to the value and the identity of the rug in question. On cross-examination, respondent's attorney apparently attempted to establish bias on the part of the expert witness by asking him whether he had filed a criminal complaint against respondent. The witness eventually acknowledged this fact, but explained that no action had been taken on his complaint. On redirect examination, the prosecutor sought to elicit the reasons why the witness has filed a complaint against respondent, but the trial court sustained a series of objections to this line of inquiry. The following colloquy then ensued:

> Prosecutor: Have you ever done business with the Kennedys?

Witness: No, I have not.
Prosecutor: Is that because he is a crook?

The trial court then granted respondent's motion for a mistrial.

When the State later sought to retry respondent, he moved to dismiss the charges because of double jeopardy. After a hearing at which the prosecutor testified, the trial court[2] found as a fact that "it was not the intention of the prosecutor in this case to cause a mistrial." On the basis of this finding, the trial court held that double jeopardy principles did not bar retrial, and respondent was then tried and convicted.

Respondent then successfully appealed to the Oregon Court of Appeals, which sustained his double jeopardy. The court set out what it con-

---

2. These proceedings were not conducted by the same trial judge who presided over respondent's initial trial.

sidered to be the governing principles in this kind of case:

> The general rule is said to be that the double jeopardy clause does not bar reprosecution, "where circumstances develop not attributable to prosecutorial or judicial overreaching, . . . even if defendant's motion is necessitated by a prosecutorial error." United States v. Jorn, 400 U.S. 470, 485 [91 S.Ct. 547, 557, 27 L. Ed. 2d 543 (1971). However, retrial is barred where the error that prompted the mistrial is intended to provoke a mistrial or is "motivated by bad faith or undertaken to harass or prejudice" the defendant.

The Court of Appeals accepted the trial court's finding that it was not the intent of the prosecutor to cause a mistrial. Nevertheless, the court held that the retrial was barred because the prosecutor's conduct in this case constituted what it viewed as "overreaching." Although the prosecutor intended to rehabilitate the witness, the Court of Appeals expressed the view that the question was in fact "a direct personal attack on the general character of the defendant." This personal attack left respondent with a "Hobson's choice—either to accept a necessarily prejudiced jury, or to move for a mistrial and face the process of being retried at a later time." . . .

II

The Double Jeopardy Clause of the Fifth Amendment protects a criminal defendant from repeated prosecutions for the same offense. As a part of this protection against multiple prosecutions, the Double Jeopardy Clause affords a criminal defendant a "valued right to have his trial completed by a particular tribunal." Wade v. Hunter, 336 U.S. 684, 689, 69 S. Ct. 834, 837, 93 L. Ed. 974 (1949). . . .

Where the trial is terminated over the objection of the defendant, the classical test for lifting the double jeopardy bar to a second trial is the "manifest necessity" standard first enunciated in Justice Story's opinion for the Court in United States v. Perez, 9 Wheat. 579, 580, 6 L.Ed. 165 (1824). Perez dealt with the most common form of "manifest necessity": a mistrial declared by the judge following the jury's declaration that it was unable to reach a verdict. . . . The "manifest necessity" standard provides sufficient protection to the defendant's interests in having his case finally decided by the jury first selected while at the same time maintaining "the public's interest in fair trials designed to end in just judgments."

But in the case of a mistrial declared at the behest of the defendant, quite different principles come into play. Here the defendant himself has elected to terminate the proceedings against him, and the "manifest necessity" standard has no place in the application of the Double Jeopardy Clause. . . .

Our cases, however, have indicated that even where the defendant moves for a mistrial, there is a narrow exception to the rule that the Double Jeopardy Clause is no bar to retrial. The circumstances under which respondent's first trial was terminated require us to delineate the bounds of that exception more fully than we have in previous cases.

Since one of the principal threads making up the protection embodied in the Double Jeopardy Clause is the right of the defendant to have his trial completed before the first jury empaneled to try him, it may be wondered as a matter of original inquiry why the defendant's election to terminate the first trial by his own motion should not be deemed a renunciation of that right for all purposes. We have recognized, however, that there would be great difficulty in applying such a rule where the prosecutor's actions giving rise to the motion for mistrial were done "in order to goad the [defendant] into requesting a mistrial." United States v. Dinitz, supra, 424 U.S. at 611, 96 S. Ct., at 1081. In such a case, the defendant's valued right to complete his trial before the first jury would be a hollow shell if the inevitable motion for mistrial were held to prevent a later invocation of the bar of double jeopardy in all circumstances. But the precise phrasing of the circumstances which will allow a defendant to interpose the defense of double jeopardy to a second prosecution where the first has terminated on his own motion for a mistrial have been stated with less than crystal clarity in our cases which deal with this area of the law. In United States v. Dinitz, 424 U.S., at 611, 96 S. Ct., at 1081, we said: "The Double Jeopardy Clause does protect a defendant against governmental actions intended to provoke mistrial requests and thereby to subject defendants to the substantial burdens imposed by multiple prosecutions."

This language would seem to follow the rule of United States v. Tateo, supra, 377 U.S. at 468, n. 3, 84 S. Ct., at 1590 n. 3, in limiting the exception to cases of governmental actions intended to provoke mistrial requests. But immediately following the quoted language we went on to say: "[The Double Jeopardy Clause] bars retrials where 'bad-faith conduct by judge or prosecutor,' threatens the '[h]arassment of an accused by successive prosecutions or declaration of a mistrial so as to afford the prosecution a more favorable opportunity to convict' the defendant." United States v. Dinitz, 424 U.S., at 611, 96 S. Ct., at 1081 (citation omitted).

The language just quoted would seem to broaden the test from one of intent to provoke a motion for a mistrial to a more generalized standard of "bad faith conduct" or "harassment" on the part of the judge or prosecutor. It was upon this language that the Oregon Court of Appeals apparently relied in concluding that the prosecutor's colloquy with the expert witness in this case amount to "overreaching."

The difficulty with the more general standards which would permit a broader exception than one merely based on intent is that they offer virtually no standards for their application. Every act on the part of a rational prosecutor during a trial is designed to "prejudice" the defendant by placing before the judge or jury evidence leading to a finding of his guilt. Given the complexity of the rules of evidence, it will be a rare trial of any complexity in which some proffered evidence by the prosecutor or by the defendant's attorney will not be found objectionable by the trial court. . . .

More serious infractions on the part of the prosecutor may provoke a motion for mistrial on the part of the defendant, and may in the view of the trial court warrant the granting of such a motion. The "overreaching" standard applied by the court below and urged today by Justice STEVENS, however, would add another classification of prosecutorial error, one requiring dismissal of the indictment, but without supplying any standard by which to assess that error.

By contrast, a standard that examines the intent of the prosecutor, though certainly not entirely free from practical difficulties, is a manageable standard to apply. It merely calls for the court to make a finding of fact. Inferring the existence or nonexistence of intent from objective facts and circumstances is a familiar process in our criminal justice system. When it is remembered that resolution of double jeopardy questions by state trial courts are reviewable not only within the state court system, but in the federal court system on habeas corpus as well, the desirability of an easily applied principle is apparent.

Prosecutorial conduct that might be viewed as harassment or overreaching, even if sufficient to justify a mistrial on defendant's motion, therefore, does not bar retrial absent intent on the part of the prosecutor to subvert the protections afforded by the Double Jeopardy Clause. A defendant's motion for a mistrial constitutes "a deliberate election on his part to forgo his valued right to have his guilt or innocence determined before the first trier of fact." United States v. Scott, 437 U.S. 82, 93, 98 S. Ct. 2187, 2195, 57 L. Ed. 2d 65 (1978). Where prosecutorial error even of a degree sufficient to warrant a mistrial has occurred, "[t]he important consideration, for purposes of the Double Jeopardy Clause, is that the defendant retain primary control over the course to be followed in the event of such error." United States v. Dinitz, supra, 424 U.S., at 609, 96 S. Ct., at 1080. Only where the governmental conduct in question is intended to "goad" the defendant into moving for a mistrial may a defendant raise the bar of double jeopardy to a second trial after having succeeded in aborting the first on his own motion. . . .[6]

We do not by this opinion lay down a flat rule that where a defendant in a criminal trial successfully moves for a mistrial, he may not thereafter invoke the bar of double jeopardy against a

---

6. This Court has consistently held that the Double Jeopardy Clause imposes no limitation upon the power of the government to retry a defendant who has succeeded in persuading a court to set his conviction aside, unless the conviction has been reversed because of the insufficiency of the evidence. See, e.g., United States v. DiFrancesco, 449 U.S. 117, 130–131, 101 S. Ct. 426, 433, 66 L. Ed. 2d 328 (1980).

second trial. But we do hold that the circumstances under which such defendant may invoke the bar of double jeopardy in a second effort to try him are limited to those cases in which the conduct giving rise to the successful motion for a mistrial was intended to provoke the defendant into moving for a mistrial.

Since the Oregon trial court found, and the Oregon Court of Appeals accepted, that the prosecutorial conduct culminating in the termination of the first trial in this case was not so intended by the prosecutor, that is the end of the matter for purposes of the Double Jeopardy Clause of the Fifth Amendment to the United States Constitution. The judgement of the Ore-

gon Court of Appeals is reversed, and the cause is remanded for further proceedings not inconsistent with this opinion.

Justice BRENNAN, with whom Justice MARSHALL joins, concurring in the judgment.

I concur in the judgment and join in the opinion of Justice STEVENS. However, it should be noted that nothing in the holding of the Court today prevents the state courts, on remand, from concluding that respondent's retrial would violate the provision of the Oregon Constitution that prohibits double jeopardy, Ore. Const., Art. I, § 12, as that provision has been interpreted by the state courts, State v. Rathbun, 287 Or. 421, 600 P.2d 392 (1979).

Notes and Questions

1. On remand, the Oregon Supreme Court followed Justice Brennan's suggestion and held that a second trial of Kennedy would violate the Oregon Constitution. *State v. Kennedy*, 295 Or. 260, 666 P.2d 1316 (1983). The reasoning behind this state constitutional interpretation, and similar rulings by other state supreme courts, was eloquently articulated by the Arizona Supreme Court in *Pool v. Superior Court*, 139 Ariz. 98, 677 P.2d 261 (1987):

> The issue is narrow. When does double jeopardy attach if mistrial is granted on motion of defendant or court because of prosecutorial misconduct and overreaching? Is it only when the prosecutor's intent in pursuing an improper course of conduct was to cause a mistrial? The plurality of the United States Supreme Court adopted that position. Four members of that court disagreed. The Oregon Supreme Court also disagreed and held that the Oregon constitutional prohibition against double jeopardy was violated:

>> When improper official conduct is so prejudicial to the defendant that it cannot be cured by means short of a mistrial, and if the official knows that the conduct is improper and prejudicial and either intends or is indifferent to the [danger of] resulting mistrial or rever-

sal. When this occurs, it is clear that the burden of a second trial is not attributable to the defendant's preference for a new trial over completing the trial infected by error. Rather, it results from the state's readiness, though perhaps not calculated intent, to force the defendant to such a choice. State v. Kennedy, 295 Or. at 276, 666 P.2d at 1326.

> The question has never been clearly presented to this court. . . . We acknowledge, with respect, that decisions of the United States Supreme Court have great weight in interpreting those provisions of the state constitution which correspond to the federal provisions. We acknowledge that uniformity is desirable. However, the concept of federalism assumes the power, and duty, of independence in interpreting our own organic law. With all deference, therefore, we cannot and should not follow federal precedent blindly.

> We cannot agree with the fundamental premise of the plurality in Oregon v. Kennedy, that a test broader than intent to provoke a mistrial, "would offer virtually no standards." Oregon v. Kennedy, 456 U.S. at 674, 102 S. Ct. at 2089. We agree with the opinion of Justice Stevens for the four-member minority that so specific an intent must

necessarily involve a subjective inquiry and is too difficult to determine. Also, we believe that the Court's decision fails to give effect to its own pronouncements regarding the purpose of the double jeopardy clause. The Court acknowledges that the clause gives the defendant an interest in having the prosecution completed by the tribunal before which the trial is commenced. This "interest" expresses a policy against multiple trials. The fundamental principle is that:

> [T]he State with all its resources and power should not be allowed to make repeated attempts to convict an individual for an alleged offense, thereby subjecting him to embarrassment, expense and ordeal and compelling him to live in a continuing state of anxiety and insecurity, as well as enhancing the possibility that even though innocent he may be found guilty. Green v. United States, 355 U.S. 184, 187–88, 78 S.Ct. 221, 223, 2 L.Ed.2d 199 (1957). . . .

In our view, therefore, the resolution of the question of when jeopardy attaches should turn upon the concept of enforcing the constitutional guarantee against double jeopardy when the right to be free from multiple trials, which that clause was meant to guarantee, would be impaired by the prosecutor's intentional, improper conduct. We do not agree that standards cannot be formulated to accomplish the objectives of the clause in situations such as this. We hold, therefore, that jeopardy attaches under art. 2, § 10 of the Arizona Constitution when a mistrial is granted on motion of defendant or

declared by the court under the following conditions:

1. Mistrial is granted because of improper conduct or actions by the prosecutor; and
2. such conduct is not merely the result of legal error, negligence, mistake, or insignificant impropriety, but, taken as a whole, amounts to intentional conduct which the prosecutor knows to be improper and prejudicial, and which he pursues for any improper purpose with indifference to a significant resulting danger of mistrial or reversal; and
3. the conduct causes prejudice to the defendant which cannot be cured by means short of a mistrial.

We agree with the Oregon Supreme Court that when such conduct occurs the burden of another trial cannot be attributed to defendant's preference to start anew rather than "completing the trial infected by error" and is, rather, attributable to the "state's readiness, though perhaps not calculated intent, to force the defendant to such a choice." State v. Kennedy, 295 Or. at 276, 666 P.2d at 1326. In such a situation, the State has intentionally exposed the defendant to multiple trials for the same crime and has destroyed his expectation of completing the proceeding before the original tribunal. This is exactly what the double jeopardy provision was intended to prevent.

2. Do you find the Arizona Supreme Court's analysis and reasoning more persuasive than the U.S. Supreme Court's justification of the federal rule?

Reprosecution after Acquittal

The chief evil that the double-jeopardy clause was designed to prevent was giving the government repeated opportunities to prosecute a person for the same crime. As such, one would

expect reprosecution of a person to be barred following an acquittal. In *United States v. Scott*, the Supreme Court discussed whether reprosecution is barred when a trial judge grants a motion to dismiss a case during a trial (after jeopardy has attached).

United States v. Scott, 437 U.S. 82, 98 S. Ct. 2187, 57 L. Ed. 2d 65 (1978)

Mr. Justice **Rehnquist** delivered the opinion of the Court.

On March 5, 1975, respondent, a member of the police force in Muskegon, Mich., was charged in a three-count indictment with distribution of various narcotics. Both before his trial in the United States District Court for the Western District of Michigan, and twice during the trial, respondent moved to dismiss the two counts of the indictment which concerned transactions that took place during the preceding September, on the ground that his defense had been prejudiced by preindictment delay. At the close of all the evidence, the court granted respondent's motion. Although the court did not explain its reasons for dismissing the second count, it explicitly concluded that respondent had "presented sufficient proof of prejudice with respect to Count I." The court submitted the third count to the jury, which returned a verdict of not guilty.

The Government sought to appeal the dismissals of the first two counts to the United States Court of Appeals for the Sixth Circuit. That court, relying on our opinion in United States v. Jenkins, 420 US 358, 95 S Ct 1006, 43 L Ed 2d 250 (1975), concluded that any further prosecution of respondent was barred by the Double Jeopardy Clause of the Fifth Amendment, and therefore dismissed the appeal. 544 F2d 903 (1976). The Government has sought review in this Court only with regard to the dismissal of the first count. We granted certiorari to give further consideration to the applicability of the Double Jeopardy Clause to Government appeals from orders granting defense motions to terminate a trial before verdict. We now reverse.

I . . .

In 1971, Congress adopted the current language of the [Criminal Appeals] Act, permitting Government appeals from any decision dismissing an indictment, "except that no appeal shall lie where the double jeopardy clause of the United States Constitution prohibits further prosecution." 18 USC § 3731 (1976 ed). . . .

In our first encounter with the new statute, we concluded that "Congress intended to remove all statutory barriers to Government appeals and to allow appeals whenever the Constitution would permit." United States v. Wilson, 420 US 332, 337, 95 S Ct 1013, 43 L Ed 2d 232 (1975). Since up to that point Government appeals had been subject to statutory restrictions independent of the Double Jeopardy Clause, our previous cases construing the statute proved to be of little assistance in determining when the Double Jeopardy Clause of the Fifth Amendment would prohibit further prosecution. A detailed canvass of the history of the double jeopardy principles in English and American law led us to conclude that the Double Jeopardy Clause was primarily "directed at the threat of multiple prosecutions," and posed no bar to Government appeals "where those appeals would not require a new trial." Id., at 342, 95 S Ct 1013, 43 L Ed 2d 232. We accordingly held in Jenkins, supra, at 370, 43 L Ed 2d 250, 95 S Ct 1006, that, whether or not a dismissal of an indictment after jeopardy had attached amounted to an acquittal on the merits, the Government had no right to appeal, because "further proceedings of some sort, devoted to the resolution of factual issues going to the elements of the offense charged, would have been required upon reversal and remand."

If Jenkins is a correct statement of the law, the judgment of the Court of Appeals relying on that decision, as it was bound to do, would in all likelihood have to be affirmed. Yet, though our assessment of the history and meaning of the Double Jeopardy Clause in Wilson, Jenkins, and Serfass v. United States, 420 US 377, 95 S Ct 1055, 43 L Ed 2d 265, (1975), occurred only three Terms ago, our vastly increased exposure to the various facets of the Double Jeopardy Clause has now convinced us that Jenkins was wrongly decided. It placed an unwarrantedly great emphasis on the defendant's right to have his guilt decided by the first jury empaneled to try him so as to include those cases where the defendant himself seeks to terminate the trial before verdict on grounds unrelated to factual guilt or innocence. We have therefore decided to overrule Jenkins, and thus to reverse the judgment of the Court of Appeals in this case.

II

The origin and history of the Double Jeopardy Clause are hardly a matter of dispute. The constitutional provision had its origin in the three common-law pleas of autrefois acquit, autrefois convict, and pardon. These three pleas prevented the retrial of a person who had previously been acquitted, convicted, or pardoned for the same offense. As this Court has described the purpose underlying the prohibition against double jeopardy:

"The underlying idea, one that is deeply ingrained in at least the Anglo-American system of jurisprudence, is that the State with all its resources and power should not be allowed to make repeated attempts to convict an individual for an alleged offense, thereby subjecting him to embarrassment, expense and ordeal and compelling him to live in a continuing state of anxiety and insecurity, as well as enhancing the possibility that even though innocent he may be found guilty." Green, supra, at 187–188, 78 S Ct 221, 2 L Ed 2d 199, 77 Ohio L Abs 202, 61 ALR2d 1119.

These historical purposes are necessarily general in nature, and their application has come to abound in often subtle distinctions which cannot by any means all be traced to the original three common-law pleas referred to above.

Part of the difficulty arises from the development of other protections for criminal defendants in the years since the adoption of the Bill of Rights. At the time the Fifth Amendment was adopted, its principles were easily applied, since most criminal prosecutions proceeded to final judgment, and neither the United States nor the defendant had any right to appeal an adverse verdict. . . .

It was not until 1889 that Congress permitted criminal defendants to seek a writ of error in this Court, and then only in capital cases. Act of Feb. 6, 1889, ch 113, § 6, 25 Stat 656. Only then did it become necessary for this Court to deal with the issues presented by the challenge of verdicts on appeal.

And, in the very first case presenting the issues, United States v. Ball, 163 US 662, 16 S Ct 1192, 41 L Ed 300 (1896), the Court established principles that have been adhered to ever since. Three persons had been tried together for murder; two were convicted, the other acquitted. This court reversed the convictions, finding the indictment fatally defective, whereupon all three defendants were tried again. This time all three were convicted and they again sought review here. This Court held that the Double Jeopardy Clause precluded further prosecution of the defendant who had been *acquitted* at the original trial but that it posed no such bar to the prosecution of those defendants who had been *convicted* in the earlier proceeding. The Court disposed of their objection almost peremptorily:

"Their plea of former conviction cannot be sustained, because upon a writ of error sued out by themselves the judgment and sentence against them were reversed, and the indictment ordered to be dismissed. . . . [I]t is quite clear that a defendant, who procures a judgment against him upon an indictment to be set aside, may be tried anew upon the same indictment, or upon another indictment, for the same offence of which he had been convicted." 163 US, at 671–672, 16 S Ct 1192, 41 L Ed 300. . . .

III

Although the primary purpose of the Double Jeopardy Clause was to protect the integrity of a final judgment, this Court has also developed a body of law guarding the separate but related interest of a defendant in avoiding multiple prosecutions even where no final determination of guilt or innocence has been made. Such interests may be involved in two different situations: the first, in which the trial judge declares a mistrial; the second, in which the trial judge terminates the proceedings favorably to the defendant on a basis not related to factual guilt or innocence. . . .

B

We turn now to the relationship between the Double Jeopardy Clause and reprosecution of a defendant who has successfully obtained not a mistrial but a termination of the trial in his favor before any determination of factual guilt or innocence. Unlike the typical mistrial, the granting of a motion such as this obviously contemplates that the proceedings will terminate then and there in favor of the defendant. The prosecution, if it wishes to reinstate the proceedings in the face of such a ruling, ordinarily must seek reversal of the decision of the trial court.

The Criminal Appeals Act, 18 USC § 3731 (1976 ed), as previously noted, makes appealability of a ruling favorable to the defendant depend upon whether further proceedings upon reversal would be barred by the Double Jeopardy Clause. Jenkins, 420 US, at 370, 95 S Ct 1006, 43 L Ed 2d 250, held that, regardless of the character of the midtrial termination, appeal was barred if "further proceedings of some sort, devoted to the resolution of factual issues going to the elements of the offense charged, would have been required upon reversal and remand." However, only last Term, in Lee, supra, the Government was permitted to institute a second prosecution after a midtrial dismissal of an indictment. The Court found the circumstances presented by that case "functionally indistinguishable from a declaration of mistrial." 432 US, at 31, 97 S Ct 2141, 53 L Ed 2d 80. Thus, Lee demonstrated that, at least in some cases, the dismissal of an indictment may be treated on the same basis as the declaration of a mistrial.

In the present case, the District Court's dismissal of the first count of the indictment was based upon a claim of preindictment delay and not on the court's conclusion that the Government had not produced sufficient evidence to establish the guilt of the defendant. Respondent Scott points out quite correctly that he had moved to dismiss the indictment on this ground prior to trial, and that had the District Court chosen to grant it at that time the Government could have appealed the ruling under our holding in Serfass v. United States 420 US 377, 43 L Ed 2d 265, 95 S Ct 1055 (1975). He also quite correctly points out that jeopardy had undeniably "attached" at the time the District Court terminated the trial in his favor; since a successful Government appeal would require further proceedings in the District Court leading to a factual resolution of the issue of guilt or innocence, Jenkins bars the Government's appeal. However, our growing experience with Government appeals convinces us that we must re-examine the rationale of Jenkins in light of Lee, Martin Linen, and other recent expositions of the Double Jeopardy Clause.

IV

Our decision in Jenkins was based upon our perceptions of the underlying purposes of the Double Jeopardy Clause, see supra, at 87, 57 L Ed 2d, at 71–72:

> "The underlying idea, one that is deeply ingrained in at least the Anglo-American system of jurisprudence, is that the State with all its resources and power should not be allowed to make repeated attempts to convict an individual for an alleged offense, thereby subjecting him to embarrassment, expense and ordeal and compelling him to live in a continuing state of anxiety and insecurity. . . .'" Jenkins, supra, at 370, 95 S Ct 1006, 43 L Ed 2d 250 quoting Green, 355 US, at 187, 78 S Ct 221, 2 L Ed 2d 199.

Upon fuller consideration, we are now of the view that this language from Green, while entirely appropriate in the circumstances of that opinion, is not a principle which can be expanded to include situations in which the defendant is responsible for the second prosecution. It is quite true that the Government with all its resources and power should not be allowed to make repeated attempts to convict an individual for an alleged offense. This truth is expressed in the three common-law pleas of autrefois acquit, autrefois convict, and pardon, which lie at the core of the area protected by the Double Jeopardy Clause. As we have recognized in cases from United States v. Ball, 163 US 662, 16 S Ct 1192, 41 L Ed 300 (1896), to Sanabria v. United States, ante p 54, 57 L Ed 2d 43, 98 S Ct 2170, a defendant once acquitted may not be again subjected to trial without violating the Double Jeopardy Clause.

But that situation is obviously a far cry from the present case, where the Government was quite willing to continue with its production of evidence to show the defendant guilty before the jury first empaneled to try him, but the defendant elected to seek termination of the trial on grounds unrelated to guilt or innocence. This is scarcely a picture of an all-powerful state relentlessly pursuing a defendant who had either been found not guilty or who had at least insisted on having the issue of guilt submitted to the first trier of fact. It is instead a picture of a defendant who chooses to avoid conviction and imprisonment, not because of his assertion that the Government has failed to make out a case against him, but because of a legal claim that the Government's case against him must fail even though it might satisfy the trier of fact that he was guilty beyond a reasonable doubt.

We have previously noted that "the trial judge's characterization of his own action cannot control the classification of the action." . . . .

[A] defendant is acquitted only when "the ruling of the judge, whatever its label, actually represents a resolution [in the defendant's favor], correct or not, of some or all of the factual elements of the offense charged." Martin Linen, supra, at 571, 97 S Ct 1349, 51 L Ed 2d 642. Where the court, before the jury returns a verdict, enters a judgment of acquittal pursuant to Fed Rule Crim Proc 29, appeal will be barred only when "it is plain that the District Court . . . evaluated the Government's evidence and determined that it was legally insufficient to sustain a conviction." 430 US, at 572, 97 S Ct 1349, 52 L Ed 2d 642. . . .

By contrast, the dismissal of an indictment for preindictment delay represents a legal judgment that a defendant, although criminally culpable, may not be punished because of a supposed constitutional violation.

We think that in a case such as this the defendant, by deliberately choosing to seek termination of the proceedings against him on a basis unrelated to factual guilt or innocence of the offense of which he is accused, suffers no injury cognizable under the Double Jeopardy Clause if the Government is permitted to appeal from such a ruling of the trial court in favor of the defendant. We do not thereby adopt the doctrine of "waiver" of double jeopardy rejected in Green. Rather, we conclude that the Double Jeopardy Clause, which guards against Government oppression, does not relieve a defendant from the consequences of his voluntary choice. In Green the question of the defendant's factual guilt or innocence of murder in the first degree was actually submitted to the jury as a trier of fact; in the present case, respondent successfully avoided such a submission of the first count of the indictment by persuading the trial court to dismiss it on a basis which did not depend on guilt or innocence. He was thus neither acquitted nor convicted, because he himself successfully undertook to persuade the trial court not to submit the issue of guilt or innocence to the jury which had been empaneled to try him. . . .

It is obvious from what we have said that we believe we pressed too far in Jenkins the concept of the "defendant's valued right to have his trial completed by a particular tribunal." We now conclude that where the defendant himself seeks to have the trial terminated without any submission to either judge or jury as to his guilt or innocence, an appeal by the Government from his successful effort to do so is not barred by 18 USC § 3731 (1976 ed) [18 USCS § 3731].

We recognize the force of the doctrine of stare decisis, but we are conscious as well of the admonition of Mr. Justice Brandeis:

"[I]n cases involving the Federal Constitution, where correction through legislative action is practically impossible, this Court has often overruled its earlier decisions. The Court bows to the lessons of experience and the force of better reasoning, recognizing that the process of trial and error, so fruitful in the physical sciences, is appropriate also in the judicial function." Burnet v Coronado Oil & Gas Co. 285 US 393, 406–408, 52 S Ct 443, 76 L Ed 815 (1932) (dissenting opinion).

Here, "the lessons of experience" indicate that Government appeals from midtrial dismissals requested by the defendant would significantly advance the public interest in assuring that each defendant shall be subject to a just judgment on the merits of his case, without "enhancing the possibility that even though innocent he may be found guilty." Green, 355 US, at 188, 2 L Ed 2d 199, 78 S Ct 221, 77 Ohio L Abs 202, 61 ALR2d 1119. Accordingly, the contrary holding of United States v. Jenkins is overruled.

The judgment of the Court of Appeals is therefore reversed, and the cause is remanded for further proceedings.

Notes and Questions

1. Can you distinguish between an outright judgment of acquittal and a dismissal based on a legal motion? Is this distinction a fair one for deciding whether an accused's double-jeopardy rights have been violated?

Multiple Punishments for a Single Offense

As noted above, the double-jeopardy clause bars punishing a person twice for the same criminal act. *Hudson v. United States* is a not-so-atypical case in which a person is prosecuted by the government in the criminal courts and is also sued by the government in the civil court system on the basis of the same conduct. In *Hudson*, the Court discusses when a civil sanction becomes "punishment" and transforms the civil action into a "criminal prosecution," which would make a subsequent criminal prosecution double jeopardy and consequently barred.

Hudson v. United States, ___ U.S. ___, 118 S. Ct. 488, 139 L. Ed. 2d 450 (1997)

Chief Justice REHNQUIST delivered the opinion of the Court. . . .

During the early and mid-1980's, petitioner John Hudson was the chairman and controlling shareholder of the First National Bank of Tipton (Tipton) and the First National Bank of Hammon (Hammon). During the same period, petitioner Jack Rackley was president of Tipton and a member of the board of directors of Hammon, and petitioner Larry Baresel was a member of the board of directors of both Tipton and Hammon.

An examination of Tipton and Hammon led the Office of the Comptroller of the Currency (OCC) to conclude that petitioners had used their bank positions to arrange a series of loans to third parties, in violation of various federal banking statutes and regulations. According to the OCC, those loans, while nominally made to third parties, were in reality made to Hudson in order to enable him to redeem bank stock that he had pledged as collateral on defaulted loans.

On February 13, 1989, OCC issued a "Notice of Assessment of Civil Money Penalty." The notice alleged that petitioners had violated 12 U.S.C. §§ 84(a)(1) and 375b and 12 CFR §§ 31.2(b) and 215.4(b) by causing the banks with which they were associated to make loans to nominee borrowers in a manner that unlawfully allowed Hudson to receive the benefit of the loans. The notice also alleged that the illegal loans resulted in losses to Tipton and Hammon of almost $900,000 and contributed to the failure of those banks. However, the notice contained no allegation of any harm to the Government as a result of petitioners' conduct. . . .

In October 1989, petitioners resolved the OCC proceedings against them by each entering into a "Stipulation and Consent Order." These consent orders provided that Hudson, Baresel, and Rackley would pay assessments of $16,500, $15,000, and $12,500 respectively. In addition, each petitioner agreed not to "participate in any manner" in the affairs of any banking institution without the written authorization of the OCC and all other relevant regulatory agencies.

In August 1992, petitioners were indicted in the Western District of Oklahoma in a 22-count indictment on charges of conspiracy, misapplication of bank funds, and making false bank entries. The violations charged in the indictment rested on the same lending transactions that formed the basis for the prior administrative actions brought by OCC. Petitioners moved to dismiss the indictment on double jeopardy grounds, but the District Court denied the motions. The Court of Appeals affirmed the District Court's holding on the nonparticipation sanction issue, but vacated and remanded to the District Court on the money sanction issue. The District Court on remand granted petitioners' motion to dismiss the indictments. This time the Government appealed, and the Court of Appeals reversed. That court held, following United States v. Halper [, 490 U.S. 435, 109 S.Ct. 1892, 104 L. Ed. 2d 487 (1989)], that the actual fines imposed by the Government were not so grossly disproportional to the proven damages to the Government as to render the sanctions "punishment" for double jeopardy purposes. We granted certiorari, because of concerns about the wide variety of novel double jeopardy claims spawned in the wake of Halper. We now affirm, but for different reasons.

The Double Jeopardy Clause provides that no "person [shall] be subject for the same offence to be twice put in jeopardy of life or limb." We have long recognized that the Double Jeopardy Clause does not prohibit the imposition of any additional sanction that could, "'in common parlance,'" be described as punishment. The Clause protects only against the imposition of multiple criminal punishments for the same offense.

Whether a particular punishment is criminal or civil is, at least initially, a matter of statutory construction. A court must first ask whether the legislature, "in establishing the penalizing mechanism, indicated either expressly or impliedly a preference for one label or the other." United States v. Ward, 448 U.S., at 248, 100 S.Ct., at 2641. Even in those cases where the legislature "has indicated an intention to establish a civil penalty, we have inquired further whether the statutory scheme was so punitive either in purpose or effect," as to "transfor[m] what was clearly intended as a civil remedy into a criminal penalty."

In making this latter determination, the factors listed in Kennedy v. Mendoza-Martinez, 372 U.S. 144, 83 S.Ct. 554, 9 L.Ed.2d 644 (1963), provide useful guideposts, including: (1) "[w]hether the sanction involves an affirmative disability or restraint"; (2) "whether it has historically been regarded as a punishment"; (3) "whether it comes into play only on a finding of scienter"; (4) "whether its operation will promote the traditional aims of punishment—retribution and deterrence"; (5) "whether the behavior to which it applies is already a crime"; (6) "whether an alternative purpose to which it may rationally be connected is assignable for it"; and (7) "whether it appears excessive in relation to the alternative purpose assigned." It is important to note, however, that "these factors must be considered in relation to the statute on its face," and "only the clearest proof" will suffice to override legislative intent and transform what has been denominated a civil remedy into a criminal penalty, Ward, supra, at 249, 100 S.Ct., at 2641–2642.

Our opinion in United States v. Halper marked the first time we applied the Double Jeopardy Clause to a sanction without first determining that it was criminal in nature. In that case, Irwin Halper was convicted of, inter alia, violating the criminal false claims statute, based on his submission of 65 inflated Medicare claims each of which overcharged the Government by $9. He was sentenced to two years' imprisonment and fined $5,000. The Government then brought an action against Halper under the civil False Claims Act. The remedial provisions of the False Claims Act provided that a violation of the Act rendered one "liable to the United States Government for a civil penalty of $2,000, an amount equal to 2 times the amount of damages the Government sustains because of the act of that person, and costs of the civil action." Given Halper's 65 separate violations of the Act, he appeared to be liable for a penalty of $130,000, despite the fact he actually defrauded the Government of less than $600. However, the District Court concluded that a penalty of this magnitude would violate the Double Jeopardy Clause in light of Halper's previous criminal conviction. While explicitly recognizing that the statutory damages provision of the Act "was not itself a criminal punishment," the District Court nonetheless concluded that application of the full penalty to Halper would constitute a second "punishment" in violation of the Double Jeopardy Clause.

On direct appeal, this Court affirmed. As the Halper Court saw it, the imposition of "punishment" of any kind was subject to double jeopardy constraints, and whether a sanction constituted "punishment" depended primarily on whether it served the traditional "goals of punishment," namely "retribution and deterrence." Any sanction that was so "overwhelmingly disproportionate" to the injury caused that it could not "fairly be said solely to serve [the] remedial purpose" of compensating the government for its loss, was thought to be explainable only as "serving either retributive or deterrent purposes."

The analysis applied by the Halper Court deviated from our traditional double jeopardy doctrine in two key respects. First, the Halper Court bypassed the threshold question: whether the successive punishment at issue is a "criminal" punishment. Instead, it focused on whether the sanction, regardless of whether it was civil or criminal, was so grossly disproportionate to the harm caused as to constitute "punishment." In so doing, the Court elevated a single Kennedy factor—whether the sanction appeared excessive in relation to its nonpunitive purposes—to dispositive status. But as we emphasized in Kennedy itself, no one factor should be considered controlling as they "may often point in differing directions." The second significant departure in Halper was the Court's decision to "asses[s] the character of the actual sanctions imposed," rather than, as Kennedy demanded, evaluating the "statute on its face" to determine whether it provided for what amounted to a criminal sanction.

We believe that Halper's deviation from long-standing double jeopardy principles was ill considered. As subsequent cases have demonstrated, Halper's test for determining whether a particular sanction is "punitive," and thus subject to the strictures of the Double Jeopardy Clause, has proved unworkable. We have since recognized that all civil penalties have some deterrent effect. If a sanction must be "solely" remedial (i.e., entirely nondeterrent) to avoid implicating the Double Jeopardy Clause, then no civil penalties are beyond the scope of the Clause. Under Halper's method of analysis, a court must also look at the "sanction actually imposed" to determine whether the Double Jeopardy Clause is implicated. Thus, it will not be possible to determine whether the Double Jeopardy Clause is violated until a defendant has proceeded through a trial to judgment. But in those cases where the civil proceeding follows the criminal proceeding, this approach flies in the face of the notion that the Double Jeopardy Clause forbids the government from even "attempting a second time to punish criminally." . . .

Applying traditional double jeopardy principles to the facts of this case, it is clear that the criminal prosecution of these petitioners would not violate the Double Jeopardy Clause. It is evident that Congress intended the OCC money penalties and debarment sanctions imposed for violations of 12 U.S.C. SS 84 and 375b to be civil in nature. As for the money penalties, both 12 U.S.C. SS 93(b)(1) and 504(a), which authorize the imposition of monetary penalties for violations of SS 84 and 375b respectively, expressly provide that such penalties are "civil." . . .

Turning to the second stage of the Ward test, we find that there is little evidence, much less the clearest proof that we require, suggesting that either OCC money penalties or debarment sanctions are "so punitive in form and effect as to render them criminal despite Congress' intent to the contrary." First, neither money penalties nor debarment have historically been viewed as punishment. We have long recognized that "revocation of a privilege voluntarily granted," such as a debarment, "is characteristically free of the punitive criminal element." Similarly, "the payment of fixed or variable sums of money [is a] sanction which ha[s] been recognized as enforceable by civil proceedings since the original revenue law of 1789."

Second, the sanctions imposed do not involve an "affirmative disability or restraint," as that term is normally understood. While petitioners have been prohibited from further participating in the banking industry, this is "certainly nothing approaching the 'infamous punishment' of imprisonment." Third, neither sanction comes into play "only" on a finding of scienter. The provisions under which the money penalties were imposed, allow for the assessment of a penalty against any person "who violates" any of the underlying banking statutes, without regard to the violator's state of mind.

Finally, we recognize that the imposition of both money penalties and debarment sanctions will deter others from emulating petitioners' conduct, a traditional goal of criminal punishment. But the mere presence of this purpose is insufficient to render a sanction criminal, as deterrence "may serve civil as well as criminal goals." For example, the sanctions at issue here, while intended to deter future wrongdoing, also serve to promote the stability of the banking industry. To hold that the mere presence of a deterrent purpose renders such sanctions "criminal" for double jeopardy purposes would severely undermine the Government's ability to engage in effective regulation of institutions such as banks.

In sum, there simply is very little showing, to say nothing of the "clearest proof" required by Ward, that OCC money penalties and debarment sanctions are criminal. The Double Jeopardy Clause is therefore no obstacle to their trial on the pending indictments, and it may proceed.

The judgment of the Court of Appeals for the Tenth Circuit is accordingly Affirmed.

The Dual-Sovereignty Doctrine

Each of the 50 states in this country has its own government, constitution, laws, and courts. Moreover, each state has the right, if not duty, to prosecute individuals who violate the law within its territory. Under our federal system of government, the United States has a national government, with a federal constitution, laws, and courts. As with the individual states, the federal government has the right to prosecute individuals who violate federal laws in the United States. What happens if a person commits a crime that violates the laws of both a state and the federal government? Can the person be prosecuted separately by both governments? What if a person commits a single crime that takes place in two states? Do both states get the chance to prosecute the criminal?

Heath v. Alabama, 474 U.S. 82, 106 S. Ct. 433, 88 L. Ed. 2d 387 (1985)

Justice O'CONNOR delivered the opinion of the Court.

The question before the Court is whether the Double Jeopardy Clause of the Fifth Amendment bars Alabama from trying petitioner for the capital offense of murder during a kidnapping after Georgia has convicted him of murder based on the same homicide. In particular, this case presents the issue of the applicability of the dual sovereignty doctrine to successive prosecutions by two States.

I

In August 1981, petitioner, Larry Gene Heath, hired Charles Owens and Gregory Lumpkin to kill his wife, Rebecca Heath, who was then nine months pregnant, for a sum of $2,000. On the morning of August 31, 1981, petitioner left the Heath residence in Russell County, Alabama, to meet with Owens and Lumpkin in Georgia, just over the Alabama border from the Heath home. Petitioner led them back to the Heath residence, gave them the keys to the Heaths' car and house, and left the premises in his girlfriend's truck. Owens and Lumpkin then kidnapped Rebecca Heath from her home. The Heath car, with Rebecca Heath's body inside, was later found on the side of a road in Troup County, Georgia. The cause of death was a gunshot wound in the head. The estimated time of death and the distance from the Heath residence to the spot where Rebecca Heath's body was found are consistent with the theory that the murder took place in Georgia, and respondent does not contend otherwise.

Georgia and Alabama authorities pursued dual investigations in which they cooperated to some extent. On September 4, 1981, petitioner was arrested by Georgia authorities. Petitioner waived his Miranda rights and gave a full confession admitting that he had arranged his wife's kidnapping and murder. In November 1981, the grand jury of Troup County, Georgia, indicted petitioner for the offense of "malice" murder under Ga. Code Ann. § 16-5-1 (1984). Georgia then served petitioner with notice of its intention to seek the death penalty, citing as the aggravating circumstance the fact that the murder was "caused and directed" by petitioner. On February 10, 1982, petitioner pleaded guilty to the Georgia murder charge in exchange for a sentence of life imprisonment, which he understood could involve his serving as few as seven years in prison.

On May 5, 1982, the grand jury of Russell County, Alabama, returned an indictment against petitioner for the capital offense of murder during a kidnapping. Before trial on this indictment, petitioner entered pleas of autrefois convict and former jeopardy under the Alabama and United States Constitutions, arguing that his conviction and sentence in Georgia barred his prosecution in Alabama for the same conduct. Petitioner also entered a plea contesting the jurisdiction of the Alabama court on the ground that the crime had occurred in Georgia.

After a hearing, the trial court rejected petitioner's double jeopardy claims. It assumed, arguendo, that the two prosecutions could not have been brought in succession by one State but held that double jeopardy did not bar successive prosecutions by two different States for the same act. The court postponed a ruling on petitioner's plea to jurisdiction until the close of the State's case in chief. . . .

On January 12, 1983, the Alabama jury convicted petitioner of murder during a kidnapping in the first degree. After a sentencing hearing, the jury recommended the death penalty. Pursuant to Alabama law, a second sentencing hearing was held before the trial judge. The judge accepted the jury's recommendation. . . .

Petitioner sought a writ of certiorari from this Court, raising double jeopardy claims and claims based on Alabama's exercise of jurisdiction. . . .

II

Successive prosecutions are barred by the Fifth Amendment only if the two offenses for which the defendant is prosecuted are the "same" for double jeopardy purposes. . . .

The . . . question upon which we granted certiorari is whether the dual sovereignty doctrine permits successive prosecutions under the laws of different States which otherwise would be held to "subject [the defendant] for the same offence to be twice put in jeopardy." U.S. Const., Amdt. 5. Although we have not previously so held, we believe the answer to this query is inescapable. The dual sovereignty doctrine, as originally articulated and consistently applied by this Court, compels the conclusion that successive prosecutions by two States for the same conduct are not barred by the Double Jeopardy Clause.

The dual sovereignty doctrine is founded on the common-law conception of crime as an offense against the sovereignty of the government. When a defendant in a single act violates the "peace and dignity" of two sovereigns by breaking the laws of each, he has committed two distinct "offenses." United States v. Lanza, 260 U.S. 377, 382, 43 S.Ct. 141, 67 L.Ed. 314 (1922). As the Court explained in Moore v. Illinois, 14 How. 13, 19, 14 L.Ed. 306 (1852), "[a]n offence, in its legal signification, means the transgression of a law." Consequently, when the same act transgresses the law of two sovereigns, "it cannot be truly averred that the offender has been twice punished for the same offence; but only that by one act he has committed two offences, for each of which he is justly punishable." Id., at 20.

In applying the dual sovereignty doctrine, then, the crucial determination is whether the two entities that seek successively to prosecute a defendant for the same course of conduct can be termed separate sovereigns. This determination turns on whether the two entities draw their authority to punish the offender from distinct sources of power. Thus, the Court has uniformly held that the States are separate sovereigns with respect to the Federal Government because each State's power to prosecute is derived from its own "inherent sovereignty," not from the Federal Government. Wheeler, supra, at 320, n. 14, 98 S. Ct., at 1084, n. 14. As stated in Lanza, supra, 260 U.S., at 382, 43 S. Ct., at 142:

> [E]ach government in determining what shall be an offense against its peace and dignity is exercising its own sovereignty, not that of the other. It follows that an act denounced as a crime by both national and state sovereignties is an offense against the peace and dignity of both and may be punished by each. . . .

The States are no less sovereign with respect to each other than they are with respect to the Federal Government. Their powers to undertake criminal prosecution derive from separate and independent sources of power and authority originally belonging to them before admission to the Union and preserved to them by the Tenth Amendment. The States are equal to each other "in power, dignity and authority, each competent to exert that residuum of sovereignty not delegated to the United States by the Constitution itself." Thus, "[e]ach has the power, inherent in any sovereign, independently to determine what

shall be an offense against its authority and to punish such offenses, and in doing so each 'is exercising its own sovereignty, not that of the other.'" Wheeler, supra, 435 U.S., at 320, 98 S.Ct., at 1084 (quoting Lanza, supra, 260 U.S., at 382, 43 S.Ct., at 142). . . .

In those instances where the Court has found the dual sovereignty doctrine inapplicable, it has done so because the two prosecuting entities did not derive their powers to prosecute from independent sources of authority. Thus, the Court has held that successive prosecutions by federal and territorial courts are barred because such courts are "creations emanating from the same sovereignty." Similarly, municipalities that derive their power to try a defendant from the same organic law that empowers the State to prosecute are not separate sovereigns with respect to the State. These cases confirm that it is the presence of independent sovereign authority to prosecute, not the relation between States and the Federal Government in our federalist system, that constitutes the basis for the dual sovereignty doctrine. . . .

III . . .

A State's interest in vindicating its sovereign authority through enforcement of its laws by definition can never be satisfied by another State's enforcement of its own laws. Just as the Federal Government has the right to decide that a state prosecution has not vindicated a violation of the "peace and dignity" of the Federal Government, a State must be entitled to decide that a prosecution by another State has not satisfied its legitimate sovereign interests. In recognition of this fact, the Court consistently has endorsed the principle that a single act constitutes an "offence" against each sovereign whose laws are violated by that act. The Court has always understood the words of the Double Jeopardy Clause to reflect this fundamental principle, and we see no reason why we should reconsider that understanding today.

The judgment of the Supreme Court of Alabama is affirmed. . . .

Notes and Questions

1. *Heath* reflects a very permissive attitude about dual prosecutions of individuals by different sovereigns. This view has been rejected by several states. For example, the Michigan Supreme Court, in *People v. Cooper*, 398 Mich. 450, 247 N.W.2d 866 (1976), limited the ability of the state to prosecute individuals for state crimes following an acquittal at a federal trial on a charge involving the same conduct. The court held that the Michigan Constitution prohibits a state prosecution following an acquittal in a second jurisdiction involving the same criminal act unless the interests of the State of Michigan and the second jurisdiction are "substantially different." The court in *Cooper* suggested three guidelines to determine whether the interests of the different jurisdictions are "substantially different."

Such factors, for prosecutions arising out of the same criminal act, may include whether the maximum penalties of the statutes involved are greatly disparate, whether some reason exists why one jurisdiction cannot be entrusted to vindicate fully another jurisdiction's interests in securing a conviction, and whether the differences in the statutes are merely jurisdictional or are more substantive. *Id.* at 871.

In 1980, the Michigan Supreme Court explained and extended its decision in *Cooper:*

[In *Cooper*] we found that emerging Federal trends in recent years and the dictates of our own Constitution required us to impose limits on what dual sovereignty would permit. We held that where a criminal act involves the legitimate interests of both the state and Federal governments and the Federal criminal prosecution cannot adequately represent the state's independent interests, then the state in those rare instances is justified in protecting its interest by prosecuting the defendant, even after

conviction or acquittal in Federal court. Dual prosecution of these differing interests violates neither the Federal nor Michigan Constitution.

On the other hand, this Court also recognized the fundamental need to safeguard defendants' constitutional rights. We therefore prohibited dual prosecution where the interests of the state are not "substantially different." Distinct risks and penalties arise for defendants from the very fact of multiple prosecution, among which are, (1) continued embarrassment, expense and ordeal; (2) being compelled to live in a continuing state of anxiety and insecurity; and (3) the possibility that even though innocent they may be found guilty through repeated prosecutions.

When weighed against the interest of the state in dual prosecutions, we concluded that the defendant's right not to be twice tried and convicted prevailed and that second prosecutions were prohibited unless the record demonstrated substantially different state interests.

Cooper represents a strong and uncompromising statement by this Court that a defendant's right not to be twice tried in Federal and State court for the same criminal act will be jealously guarded except in extreme cases where Federal laws are framed to protect substantially different social interests. Cooper makes clear that as a firm rule dual prosecution ordinarily will not be tolerated in Michigan. It is only in the rare instance where the social interests of the state are not addressed in substance by the Federal statute that a second prosecution will be allowed. *People v. Gay*, 407 Mich. 681, 693–695, 289 N.W.2d 651, 654–55 (1980) (citations omitted).

2. How would *Heath* have been decided if the second prosecution had occurred in Michigan?

CONCLUSION

The trial is a central component to the criminal justice system. It is the stage in the process where a defendant is judged to be guilty or not guilty. Due to the ramifications of such a determination, numerous procedural safeguards are built into the process to protect the rights of individuals charged with crimes.

Defendants have a right to be brought to trial within a reasonable period of time. At this trial, the government must prove the defendant guilty beyond a reasonable doubt. Additionally, individuals charged with serious crimes have the right to be tried by a jury. Concomitant with this right is the right to have the jury drawn from a fair cross-section of the community. While the jury does not necessarily have to reach a unanimous verdict, it must consist of at least six individuals.

One of the key elements of a trial is that it gives the defendant an opportunity to confront witnesses against him. To effectuate this, defendants have a right to cross-examine witnesses. At the same time, the defendant has the right to remain silent and refrain from testifying as well as the right to testify if he or she so chooses.

ENDNOTES

1. We use the term *innocence* loosely here. The two verdict options in a criminal trial are "guilty" and "not guilty." A verdict of not guilty means that the prosecution has not succeeded in proving the charges made against the defendant. There can be a significant difference between a declaration that the prosecution's proof was insufficient and a statement that an accused is innocent of committing a crime. In some countries, three verdict options are available in a criminal trial: guilty, not proven, and innocent.

2. For references to state constitutional mandates regarding a defendant's right to a jury trial, see Latzer (1995), *State Constitutional Criminal Law*, Deerfield, Illinois: Clark, Boardman, Callaghan.

3. A person is considered "unavailable" if he or she is dead, incompetent to testify, or permanently located outside of the United States.

4. There are 27 enumerated hearsay exceptions in the Federal Rules of Evidence. Additionally, there are two "catch-all" provisions that permit a court to consider admitting hearsay statements into evidence despite the fact that they do not fall into one of the enumerated exceptions. See Rules 803 and 804, Federal Rules of Evidence, 28 U.S.C. Individual state rules of evidence contain similar exceptions.

5. A mistrial may also be declared when a jury is unable to reach a verdict. In such an event, a retrial is not barred by double jeopardy.

APPENDIX A

Legal Research Guide

The law, and even a subfield of law such as criminal procedure, is far too varied, expansive, and rapidly changing for anyone to completely master. Consequently, if students (as well as practicing attorneys, judges, and professors) are to be able to answer questions of law and keep pace with constantly developing legal rules and doctrine, it is imperative that they know how to locate and make use of primary and secondary legal authorities and the finding tools that provide researchers access to these references. As essential as legal research techniques are, they are not particularly difficult to acquire. Legal reference materials are logically organized and are interconnected by several helpful indexing systems. They are available in traditional printed form and are accessible through computers.

In this appendix, we identify several primary and secondary authorities necessary for basic legal research. We illustrate how those authorities can be used to help answer questions and analyze issues that may arise as you read cases and related materials. Although we briefly describe legal references and research techniques in these pages, we emphasize that there is no substitute for going to a library, directly consulting the law books or a computer terminal, and practicing these skills.

THE TOOLS OF THE TRADE: PRIMARY AND SECONDARY LEGAL AUTHORITIES AND FINDING TOOLS

Primary legal authorities are "the law." They are legally binding rules that are enforceable in the courts. The four kinds of primary legal authorities are *administrative regulations, statutes, constitutions,* and *judicial decisions* (case law). Because judicial decisions interpret and apply administrative regulations, statutes, and constitutional provisions and often make new law in their own right, legal research typically is not complete until relevant case law is produced.

In contrast, *secondary legal authorities* are not legally binding or enforceable in the courts. Nevertheless, these authorities can be highly informative and useful. They typically (1) describe what the law is, (2) explain or critically analyze different aspects of the law, and/or (3) assist us in locating primary and other secondary legal authorities. We review several secondary legal authorities, including *law dictionaries, Words and Phrases, legal encyclopedias, legal treatises, American Law Reports,* and *law reviews.*

Finding tools help us locate primary and secondary legal authorities. They serve as connecting links between different authorities. Some of these reference aids can be used to confirm that the authorities on which we seek to rely remain current and valid. Finding tools are not a form of legal authority and should not be used or cited as such. They include *indexes, digests,* and *Shepard's citators.*

In addition to printed legal reference materials, two outstanding computerized legal research systems also exist: *WESTLAW* and *LEXIS*. Computer-assisted legal research can have several advantages over using traditional, printed sources, including convenience, timeliness, and making available helpful alternative search strategies. For most students, WESTLAW and LEXIS will not be as readily accessible as the printed legal reference materials. Using these programs can be expensive. For students whose libraries make WESTLAW or LEXIS available, we recommend that the instructional programs accompanying these systems be studied. In the following pages, we focus on how to use printed legal reference materials, such as books and periodicals, and we briefly mention analogous legal research strategies made available through WESTLAW and LEXIS.

Secondary Legal Authorities

Secondary legal authorities commonly are consulted first in the course of legal research. Researchers are especially likely to begin with secondary authorities when they are relatively unfamiliar with the subject or issue they are investigating. We first discuss secondary legal authorities that provide the most basic and primarily descriptive information. We continue with a description of other secondary authorities that become increasingly refined and analytical.

Law Dictionaries

When unfamiliar legal terms are encountered in cases, statutes, articles, and other writings, a law dictionary may be consulted for a definition. Several law dictionaries are available, and some are published in both unabridged and abridged editions. Two widely used sources are *Black's Law Dictionary* (West Publishing Co.) and *Ballantine's Law Dictionary* (Lawyers Cooperative Publishing Co.). Law dictionaries are arranged and used just like a *Webster's Dictionary*. They differ only in that they define legal terms and often cite judicial decisions as the source of their definitions.

Words and Phrases

The multivolume *Words and Phrases* (West Publishing Co.) extracts definitions of legal terms and phrases from judicial decisions and reprints those definitions and the accompanying case citations. Several pages of definitions may be devoted to each word (e.g., *search, indigent*) or phrase (e.g., *probable cause, statutory rape*). Because *Words and Phrases* relies on and cites case law for the definitions it provides, this source has the added benefit of directing researchers to judicial decisions relevant to an issue. Like many other legal authorities and finding tools, *Words and Phrases* is kept up to date by annual paper supplements inserted in a special pocket in the rear of the hard-bound volume. It is essential to check for "pocket supplements" in all legal reference materials. If you neglect to do so, you run the risk of relying on outdated, obsolete, or invalid statements of law.

Legal Encyclopedias

Two legal encyclopedias of national scope exist: *Corpus Jurus Secundum* (*C.J.S.*) (West Publishing Co.) and *American Jurisprudence 2d* (*Am. Jur. 2d*) (Lawyers Cooperative Publishing Co.). Several other legal encyclopedias focus on the law of individual states. Much like a *World Book Encyclopedia* or another, similar set, legal encyclopedias contain descriptive articles about a wide range of topics. The topics, of course, are law related, and the articles are extensively footnoted and refer the reader to related judicial decisions and other legal authorities.

Topics are presented alphabetically, but in legal encyclopedias, unlike regular encyclopedias, a researcher must first consult a general subject index to be referred to relevant articles. The indexes are conveniently arranged, and they direct the researcher to specific sections within articles for information about a variety of topics. *C.J.S.* and *Am. Jur. 2d* are used similarly and provide similar information. Each makes use of pocket part supplements to keep articles current and to provide the most recent supporting authority.

Legal Treatises

Books providing systematic coverage of select legal topics are available in many libraries and bookstores. For example, we have frequently cited Barry Latzer, *State Constitutional Criminal Law* (Clark Boardman, Callaghan 1995), which is an excellent source describing criminal procedure issues resolved pursuant to state constitutional analysis. A good treatise covering federal criminal procedure law is Charles H. Whitebread and Christopher Slobogin, *Criminal Procedure: An Analysis of Cases and Concepts* (3d ed., Foundation Press 1993). A detailed examination of search and seizure law is presented in Wayne R. LaFave, *Search and Seizure: A Treatise on the Fourth Amendment* (3d ed., West Publishing Co. 1996). Many other legal treatises addressing criminal procedure issues are available. These books describe and often critically analyze case law and other relevant legal authorities. They can provide helpful summaries of cases, explain obscure points of law, and refer readers to other related authorities.

American Law Reports

American Law Reports (A.L.R.) (Lawyers Cooperative Publishing Co.) provide a detailed account of judicial decisions relevant to particular issues of law. These volumes can be enormously useful. The researcher who finds an *A.L.R.* "annotation" on point with his or her topic is spared the major task of assembling the body of case law from scratch and instead can begin with the information already compiled in the annotation (and its pocket supplement).

*A.L.R.*s comprise *A.L.R. 1st* through *A.L.R. 5th, A.L.R. Federal*, and annotations of Supreme Court decisions that are included in the *United States Supreme Court Reports, Lawyers' Edition*. In general, information about state court decisions is presented in *A.L.R. 3d* through *A.L.R. 5th,* federal court cases are described in *A.L.R. Federal*, and Supreme Court decisions are summarized and discussed in the annotations found in the *United States Supreme Court Reports, Lawyers' Edition*. The older volumes in the *A.L.R.* series, especially *A.L.R. 1st* and *A.L.R. 2d*, contain a mixture of state and federal case law.

A.L.R. annotations are useful because they exhaustively summarize state or federal judicial decisions that relate to a point of law. For example, an *A.L.R.* annotation on the "good-faith exception" to the exclusionary rule could be expected to provide a detailed description of case holdings on issues important to that topic. Access to *A.L.R.* annotations is gained through a descriptive word index: the *A.L.R. Index, ALR 2d-3d-4th-5th, Federal, LEd2d.* The researcher simply investigates this alphabetically arranged index for subjects relevant to his or her topic and, with luck, will be referred to specific volumes and pages in the *A.L.R.* series that contain relevant annotations.

Law Reviews

Published individually by the nation's law schools, law reviews include articles written by law professors, judges, attorneys, and law students. These articles typically are replete with footnotes, making them an especially useful source for other authorities relevant to the topic being researched. Unlike many other secondary legal authorities, law review articles typically are not limited to providing a description of the law. Instead, they normally offer an analysis and critique of legal issues and thus may alert the researcher to nuances of a topic that were not previously considered.

Law review articles can be located through a set of printed indexes, recently renamed the *Index to Legal Periodicals and Books* (formerly the *Index to Legal Periodicals*). This index is arranged according to subject and author. It also contains a table of cases and a table of statutes that are the subject of articles. A list of hundreds of subject headings appears in the first few pages of the index. This list can be consulted if the researcher is stymied about what topics in the index relate to his or her subject. Each volume of the *Index to Legal Periodicals and Books* includes the authors, titles, and citations of law review articles published within the time period covered by the particular volume. Several consecutive volumes of this index must be consulted to complete a comprehensive search for potentially useful articles.

An alternative index for law review articles is *LegalTrac*, which is available on a CD-ROM. Because it is stored on a computer disk, *LegalTrac* can be updated cumulatively. Thus, the *LegalTrac* index begins with materials published in 1980 and compiles and logically organizes more recently published articles under appropriate subject, author, case, or statutory headings. In this respect, it is more convenient to use than the several printed volumes of the *Index to Legal Periodicals and Books*.

Primary Legal Authorities

Administrative Regulations

Much of the business of federal, state, and local government agencies is conducted pursuant to published rules and regulations. Departments of corrections, parole, probation, and a host of other law enforcement agencies are likely to be governed by administrative regulations. Owing to the tremendous variation among states and localities, we focus our discussion on federal regulations.

The operating rules of federal administrative agencies first appear in the *Federal Register*, which is published daily, Monday through Friday, except for national holidays. These same regulations are organized according to subject in the *Code of Federal Regulations (C.F.R.)*, which is updated annually. To find regulations that may be of interest—for example, those pertaining to the business of the Federal Bureau of Prisons—it is necessary to consult the *C.F.R. Index*, which is arranged alphabetically by subject matter. The *Index*, in turn, refers the researcher to the appropriate "title" and sections of the *Code of Federal Regulations*, where the agency rules are published.

Statutes

Each state has a unique set of statutes, including legislation relevant to criminal procedure. Federal statutes, passed by Congress, exist in addition to state laws. Both state and federal statutes are published in *annotated* form. That is, they have handy reference aids that will direct the researcher to information about when and why a law was passed (the "legislative history"), and they cite and briefly describe judicial decisions that have interpreted and applied the legislation.

Relevant statutes can be located with the assistance of the subject index that accompanies the statutory volumes. You must first locate the statutes for the jurisdiction of interest—for example, a specific state, or the federal government—and consult the General Index applying to that jurisdiction's laws. The index will direct you to the specific title, chapter, and/or sections of the statute relevant to the issue you are investigating. After you locate the particular statute, you will find citations documenting its legislative history, in the form of committee hearings and reports, and you will find information about when the law was adopted and/or amended. You should also expect to find a section providing "Notes of Decisions," which consists of an index of topics addressed by judicial decisions, and brief descriptions of case holdings relevant to the statute. If you peruse the *United States Code Annotated* (*U.S.C.A.*), which includes federal legislation, or an analogous set of annotated state statutes, you will quickly learn how to use these valuable research tools.

Constitutions

Constitutional provisions are used for legal research purposes just like annotated statutes. First, decide whether you are interested in the U.S. Constitution or a state constitution, and refer to the appropriate volumes. Constitutions are published in the same set of books that include a jurisdiction's statutes. Use the index to the constitution for assistance in locating the specific provision applicable to the issue you are investigating. After you find the particular provision, refer to the "legislative history" features to learn about its origins. The "Notes of Decisions" summarize judicial decisions that have interpreted and applied the constitutional provision in different contexts.

Judicial Decisions

In Chapter 2, we discussed the structure of the state and federal court systems. We also described how judicial decisions are published in case reporters and identified the reporters in the West Publishing Company system. We illustrated standard case citation format during this process. This background information is essential to an understanding of the legal research techniques used to find case law. Remember that you frequently can (and should) rely on secondary legal authorities and other primary legal authorities, such as annotated statutes and constitutions, to locate case authority. Here, we consider how to find relevant judicial decisions by using descriptive word indexes, case digests, and West Publishing Company's "key number system."

When the editors at West prepare a case for publication in one of their reporters (e.g., the *Supreme Court Reporter, F.3d, F. Supp.*, or one of the state regional reporters such as *A.2d* or *N.E.2d*), they analyze and subdivide the decision according to the different legal principles discussed in the majority opinion. Each legal principle is assigned to one of over 400 preex-

isting topics, such as "Constitutional Law," "Criminal Law," or "Searches and Seizures." Then a unique "key number" is assigned to each of the hundreds or thousands of individual subtopics covered within each general topic. For example, cases discussing the "good-faith exception" to the exclusionary rule might be classified under the topic "Search and Seizure" and the key number 394.4, or "Search and Seizure ☞ 394.4." Each and every case, from all federal and state jurisdictions, that discusses the same principle of law will be categorized under the same topic and key number.

Thus, to make use of West's key number legal research system, it is necessary to be able to link the principle of law in which you are interested to the applicable topic and key number. One way of discovering the useful topic and key number is to use one of West's *descriptive word indexes*. These indexes accompany the *case digests* that West compiles for different case reporters. For example, a *United States Supreme Court Digest* applies exclusively to U.S. Supreme Court decisions; a *Federal Practice Digest* covers all levels of federal court decisions (U.S. district court, U.S. court of appeals, and U.S. Supreme Court); and other digests correspond to the state regional reporters and/or individual state court decisions. West's *Decennial Digests*, and the accompanying *General Digests*, cover *all* federal and state court decisions. Digests include very brief descriptions of case holdings and the related principles of law that are used as a basis for those holdings. These case descriptions commonly are called "squibs" or "blurbs." The squibs of judicial decisions include the accompanying case citations. Case digests are arranged according to subject topics and key numbers.

To gain entry to the case digests and make use of the key number system, it is helpful to make a comprehensive list of words or terms that relate to the issue you are investigating. Then look for these terms in the *Descriptive Word Index* that accompanies the case digest you have selected. It does not matter which words you look up first; *Descriptive Word*

Indexes are exhaustively cross-referenced to point you to a common destination. With any luck, you will be directed to one or more topics and key numbers that correspond to the issue you are researching. Then, simply consult the case squibs included under the topic and key number in the digest. You should find references to cases that are on point. Never rely on the squib presented in the digest as case authority. The squib is no more than a brief summary of a principle of law extracted from a case. You should consult the case reporter that reproduces the decision and read the case in its entirety.

In West's case reporters, you will find that judicial decisions are reprinted with several handy editorial embellishments. West's editors do not alter a single word of judges' opinions, but they do supplement them to facilitate legal research efforts. Among these editorial aids are the "headnotes" inserted before the start of an opinion. These headnotes correspond precisely to the squibs found in West's case digests and are identified by the same topics and key numbers used in the digests. They summarize the principles of law discussed in the case's majority opinion and direct the reader to the portion of the opinion from which those principles have been gleaned.

It is impossible to overstate the usefulness of West's interlocking key number system. Once you find even one case relating to the issue you are investigating—and thus identify the topic and key number associated with the relevant legal issues—you can use the digests to find all cases, decided in all court systems, that address that same point of law. The most comprehensive digests are the *Decennial Digests*, which are kept current through supplementary *General Digest* volumes. On the other hand, if you are interested only in Supreme Court cases, or only in New York cases, you can limit your search by referring to the separate digests that include those specific jurisdictions.

Shepardizing

Even after one or more cases are located that appear to answer the question being investi-

gated, the researcher's work is not finished. The law changes over time. Principles of law sometimes are refined or modified substantially. Lower court cases may be reversed by higher courts, and courts occasionally overrule their own precedent. You can ascertain whether a case you have found is still "good law" by *Shepardizing* the decision.

A *Shepard's* case citator additionally points you to judicial decisions that have cited the case being *Shepardized*. These cases may be of interest as you attempt to ensure that you have uncovered the latest and most relevant decisions that have addressed an issue. *Shepard's* frequently will include a notation about why the case being *Shepardized* was cited (e.g., the holding was "followed" in the decision citing it, or the holding was "criticized" or "questioned"). And finally, a *Shepard's* provides both the official and unofficial citations of case decisions. For example, if you know only the official (*United States Reports*) citation to a Supreme Court decision but would like to look up the decision in West's *Supreme Court Reporter* to take advantage of the key number system and other editorial aids, you can quickly find the missing information by *Shepardizing* the citation that you know.

Different sets of *Shepard's* case citators correspond to the decisions of different courts. Thus, separate *Shepard's* exist for U.S. Supreme Court cases, and for federal court of appeals, district court, and individual state court decisions, as well as for West's regional reporters (*A.2d, N.E.2d*, etc.). To *Shepardize* a case you must consult the appropriate set of *Shepard's* and then gather all volumes that cover the case in which you are interested. Depending on how old the case is, you may have to collect one or more hard-bound *Shepard's* volumes and one or more paper supplements. The covers of the *Shepard's* volumes report the range of case citations that is included.

You *Shepardize* a case by looking for its citation in the books you have assembled. First, find the volume of the case reporter in which it has been published, and then locate the page at which the opinion begins. The *Shepard's* will report the parallel citations for the opinion (i.e., where it appears in the official or unofficial case reporter), it will trace the judicial history of the case (as the case progressed through the lower courts, and relevant developments following a remand), and finally it will identify other court decisions citing the case you are *Shepardizing*, with information about the treatment the case received (e.g., whether it was overruled, affirmed, or criticized). *Shepard's* frequently will identify the headnote number associated with the principle of law for which the case was cited. This is an especially helpful feature for cases that have been cited many times because it can help the researcher focus more quickly on cases that may be of special relevance. A *Shepard's* reports the specific page or pages from an opinion in which the case being *Shepardized* is cited.

Other types of primary and secondary legal authorities can be *Shepardized* by using analogous techniques in appropriate volumes of *Shepard's*. For example, statutes can be *Shepardized* in order to locate court decisions citing specific legislation. Constitutional provisions likewise can be *Shepardized*, as can law review articles and various other authorities. We reiterate that it is imperative to *Shepardize* court decisions to ensure their continuing validity and to keep abreast of significant judicial developments that may have occurred following the decision of cases you have uncovered through other legal research techniques.

AN EXAMPLE

We provide a hypothetical case example to help illustrate the legal research techniques just described. Assume that you are a judge presiding over a criminal trial in the State of Texas. The defendant, Sally Protest, has been accused of obstructing a woman's access to a medical clinic in which abortions are performed. Assume that Sally's conduct allegedly was in violation of a hypothetical Texas statute mod-

eled after 18 U.S.C.A. § 248(1)(a), which subjects to criminal penalties any person who "by force or threat of force or by physical obstruction, intentionally injures, intimidates or interferes with or attempts to injure, intimidate or interfere with any person . . . from, obtaining . . . reproductive health services."

Assuming that Catholics might be sympathetic to Sally in the trial of this charge, the county prosecutor asked prospective jurors about their religious faiths during the voir dire and then used peremptory challenges to excuse three Catholics from service. The defense lawyer objected, arguing that it was unconstitutional for the prosecutor to use peremptory challenges based on the religion of the excused potential jurors. What is the appropriate resolution of this issue?

In Chapter 10, we studied the law governing the exercise of peremptory challenges, and we learned that a state prosecutor (or a defense lawyer) who uses the race or sex of prospective jurors as a basis for those challenges violates the equal-protection clause of the Fourteenth Amendment. *See Batson v. Kentucky*, 476 U.S. 79, 106 S. Ct. 1712, 90 L. Ed. 2d 69 (1986) (race); *J.E.B. v. Alabama*, 511 U.S. 127, 114 S. Ct. 1419, 128 L. Ed. 2d 89 (1994) (sex). We now must investigate whether similar principles prohibit lawyers from relying on religious affiliation when exercising peremptory challenges. We will consult the various secondary and primary legal authorities we have just reviewed, beginning with the most rudimentary sources and progressing through increasingly helpful reference materials.

It generally makes sense to begin a legal research project by consulting secondary legal authorities, since those authorities describe the law, often analyze the involved legal principles, and point the researcher to relevant primary authorities. The most basic form of secondary legal authority is a law dictionary. If we did not understand the meaning of the term *peremptory challenge*, we could look it up in a law dictionary. Here, we consult *Black's Law Dictionary*, which defines *peremptory challenge* and cites a related federal rule of criminal procedure and a federal statute in the process. (See Exhibit A–1.)

Words and Phrases can be expected to provide fuller and more varied definitions of terms, and the definitions provided are drawn from judicial decisions. Because the cases that are the sources of the definitions are cited, *Words and Phrases* also serves as a case-finding tool. We locate the phrase *peremptory challenge* in this alphabetically arranged set by consulting volume 32 (which covers "Pep to Petit"). This volume was published in 1956, so it obviously is dated. We thus make use of the pocket supplement inserted in the back of the book, which is current through 1997. (See Exhibit A–2.)

We can consult either of the national legal encyclopedias, *Corpus Jurus Secundum* (*C.J.S.*) or *American Jurisprudence, 2d* (*Am. Jur. 2d*), to read a descriptive article about peremptory challenges and make note of accompanying case citations. For this exercise, we have selected *C.J.S.* We can consult *C.J.S.*'s General Index under "Juries" (see Exhibit A–3), "Peremptory Challenges" (see Exhibit A–4), or other relevant terms to find an appropriate article. Note that we are referred to promising sections in at least two different articles. Peremptory challenges appear to receive extended discussion in "Juries § 445." (See Exhibit A–3.) The topic "Religious affiliation, use to exclude person on basis of," is addressed in "Constitutional Law § 525." (See Exhibit A–4.) We of course would want to read each of these articles, but for purposes of this exercise we consult the former.

To locate this article, we use volume 50A of *C.J.S.*, which includes the topics "Judicial Sales" through "Juries." When we turn to section 445 of the "Juries" article, we receive a helpful narrative addressing prohibited acts of discrimination associated with peremptory challenges, including brief treatment of discrimination based on religion. Note that the encyclopedia article very helpfully cites cases in support of its textual discussion. (See Exhibit A–5.) As with other legal reference sources, we would be sure to check the pocket supplement

Exhibit A–1
Entry in *Black's Law Dictionary* defining *Peremptory Challenge*

Peremptory /pərém(p)təriy/. Imperative; final; decisive; absolute; conclusive; positive; not admitting of question, delay, reconsideration or of any alternative. Self-determined; arbitrary; not requiring any cause to be shown. Wolfe v. State, 147 Tex.Cr.R. 62, 178 S.W.2d 274, 279.

As to *peremptory* Defense; Jury instructions; Mandamus; Nonsuit; Plea; and Writ, see those titles.

Peremptory challenge. The right to challenge a juror without assigning, or being required to assign, a reason for the challenge. In most jurisdictions each party to an action, both civil and criminal, has a specified number of such challenges and after using all his peremptory challenges he is required to furnish a reason for subsequent challenges. Fed.R.Crim.P. 24, 28 U.S.C.A. § 1870 (civil cases). *See also* Challenge; Jury challenge.

Source: Reprinted with permission from *Black's Law Dictionary*, 6th Edition, p. 1136, © 1990, West Group.

for updated text and more recently decided cases.

In our discussion of state constitutional issues throughout this book, we have made frequent use of an excellent treatise, Barry Latzer's *State Constitutional Criminal Law*. Because the issue we are now researching hypothetically arose in a state court in Texas, the Latzer treatise may help alert us to relevant state constitutional case holdings. We locate this treatise just as we would other books, by making use of the library's computerized referencing index. When we look in the book's index, we note that section 8:21 addresses "Discrimination in jury selection— voir dire." (See Exhibit A–6.) Although the text does not specifically mention peremptory challenges based on religion, it does provide a helpful general discussion of related issues. (See Exhibit A–7.)

Exhibit A–2
Portion of Pocket Supplement of *Words and Phrases*
Defining *Peremptory Challenge*

Peremptory Challenge

See, also, Exercise of Peremptory Challenge.

"Challenge for cause" permits rejection of jurors on narrowly specified, provable, and legally cognizable basis of partiality, but "peremptory challenge" permits rejection for real or imagined partiality that is less easily designated or demonstrable. People v. Munson, 662 N.E.2d 1265, 1273, 215 Ill.Dec. 125, 133, 171 Ill.2d 158.

"Peremptory challenges" allowed each party are challenges which may be made or omitted according to judgment, will, or caprice of party entitled thereto, without assigning any reason therefor, or without being required to assign reason. Allen v. State, Ala.Cr.App., 414 So.2d 163, 167.

"Peremptory challenges" allowed each party are challenges which may be made or omitted according to the judgment, will, or caprice of the party entitled thereto, without assigning any reason therefor, or without being required to assign a reason. State v. Smith, 231 S.E.2d 663, 676, 291 N.C. 505.

"Peremptory challenge" is one exercised without reason stated, without inquiry, and without being subject to court's control; no party is required to explain its reasons for exercise of such challenge. Phillips v. State, Ind., 496 N.E.2d 87, 88.

"Peremptory challenge" is a right to challenge a certain number of jurors without showing any cause or reason, or inquiry into motives. People v. Thornhill, 333 N.E.2d 8, 14, 31 Ill.App.3d 779.

"Peremptory challenges" are challenges that may be made according to the judgment of the party entitled thereto without being required to assign the reason therefor. State v. Wetmore, 215 S.E.2d 51, 55, 287 N.C. 344.

A "peremptory challenge" in criminal practice is a species of challenge which the prosecution or the prisoner is allowed to have against a certain number of jurors without assigning cause. Plummer v. State, 194 S.E.2d 419, 421, 229 Ga. 749.

"Peremptory challenge" is a challenge of a proposed juror without assigning cause. State v. Anderson, 229 So.2d 329, 337, 254 La. 1107.

In criminal cases, there is allowed to the prisoner an arbitrary and capricious species of challenge to a certain number of jurors, without showing any cause at all, which is called "peremptory challenge." Spencer v. State, 314 A.2d 727, 730, 20 Md.App. 201.

Source: Reprinted with permission from 32 *Words and Phrases*, p. 6 (1997 Supp.), © 1997, West Group.

Exhibit A–3
Portion of *C.J.S.*'s General Index
dealing with Peremptory Challenges under Heading of "Juries"

JURIES

JURIES—Continued
Challenges—Continued
  New trial,
    Denial of challenge of juror for cause, as
      ground, New Tr § 22
    Failure to challenge juror as waiver of disqual-
      ification or incompetency, New Tr § 23
  Panel.
    Generally, Juries § 359
    Grounds, Juries §§ 360, 361
  Peremptory challenges,

    Age-based, Juries § 445
      Generally, Juries § 354
    Batson standard applicable, Juries § 445
    Exclude jurors on basis of race, Juries § 445
    Gender, basis for, Juries § 445
    Persons with physical disabilities, Juries § 445
    Race-based, prohibition, Juries § 445
   Time, waiver, Juries § 357
   Waiver, procedure, Juries § 410
  Change of Venue, this index
  Charge to. Instructions to Jury, generally, this index
  Circumstantial Evidence, this index
  Citizens, this index

Source: Reprinted with permission from *Corpus Jurus Secundum*, 1997 *General Index*, (E to M) p. 868, © 1997, West Group.

Exhibit A–4
Entries in *C.J.S.*'s General Index under Heading
"Peremptory Challenges"

PEREMPTORY CHALLENGES

Appeal and Review, generally, this index
Batson inquiry, prosecution's failure to object,
  Juries § 445
Discrimination, equal protection clause
  prohibits, Juries § 445
Federal courts, joint trial, preservation of rights,
  Fed Civ Pro § 916
Grand juries, Gr Jur § 61

Minority groups, use of to exclude, accused's bur-
  den to prove denial of constitutional rights.
  Juries §§ 354, 424, 428
Prejudice, replacement of juror. Juries § 434 et
  seq.
Religious affiliation, use to exclude person on
  basis of Const L § 525
Trial court, objection to, Juries § 280
Withdrawal, Juries § 441

Source: Reprinted with permission from *Corpus Jurus Secundum*, 1997 *General Index* (N to Z), p. 192, © 1997, West Group.

Exhibit A–5

Portion of *C.J.S.* dealing with Peremptory Challenges under the subject "Juries"

§ 445. Groups Covered

The prohibition on discrimination in the use of peremptory challenges applies to discrimination on the basis of race, ethnicity, or gender.

Library References

Jury ⚷ 33(1.2–1.25, 5.15).

The prohibition on discrimination in the use of peremptory challenges applies to discrimination on the basis of race.[28] Race is an unconstitutional proxy for juror competence and impartiality.[29] A challenge may not be based on either the race of the juror[30] or the racial stereotypes held by the challenging party.[31] The prosecution may not challenge jurors solely on account of their race[32] or on the assumption that black jurors as a group will be unable impartially to consider the prosecution's case against a black defendant.[33]

28. U.S.—Powers v. Ohio, Ohio, 111 S.Ct. 1364, 499 U.S. 400, 113 L.Ed.2d 411, appeal after remand 635 N.E.2d 1298, 92 Ohio App.3d 409 dismissed, jurisdictional motion overruled 632 N.E.2d 910, 690 Ohio St.3d 1442, certiorari denied 115 S.Ct. 366, 139 L.Ed.2d 319—Batson v. Kentucky, Ky., 106 S.Ct. 1712, 476 U.S. 79, 90 L.Ed.2d 69.

How group defined

"Racial" groups can be defined by variety of factors such as national origin, ethnicity, appearance, habits, and ideas.

U.S.—Pemberthy v. Beyer, D.N.J., 800 F.Supp. 144, reversed 19 F.3d 857, rehearing and suggestion for rehearing en banc denied, certiorari denied 115 S.Ct. 439, 130 L.Ed.2d 350.

29. U.S.—J.E.B. v. Alabama ex rel. T.B., Ala., 114 S.Ct. 1419, 511 U.S. 127, 128 L.Ed.2d 89, on remand 641 So.2d 821.
30. U.S.—Georgia v. McCollum, Ga., 112 S.Ct. 2348, 505 U.S. 42, 120 L.Ed.2d 33, on remand 422 S.E.2d 866, 262 Ga. 554.
31. U.S.—Georgia v. McCollum, Ga., 112 S.Ct. 2348, 505 U.S. 42, 120 L.Ed.2d 33, on remand 422 S.E.2d 866, 262 Ga. 554.
32. U.S.—Batson v. Kentucky, Ky., 106 S.Ct. 1712, 476 U.S. 79, 90 L.Ed.2d 69.
33. Batson v. Kentucky, Ky., 106 S.Ct. 1712, 476 U.S. 79, 90 L.Ed.2d 69.

* * * *

While it has been held that the prohibition applies to discrimination on the basis of religion,[43] there is authority to the contrary.[44]

43. Cal.—People v. Fudge, 31 Cal.Rptr.2d 321, 875 P.2d 36, 7 C.4th 1075, rehearing denied, certiorari denied Fudge v. California, 115 S.Ct. 1367, 131 L.Ed.2d 223, rehearing denied 115 S.Ct. 1993, 131 L.Ed.2d 879.
Colo.—Fields v. People, 732 P.2d 1145.
Mass.—Commonwealth v. Carleton, 629 N.E.2d 321, 36 Mass.App.Ct. 137, affirmed 641 N.E.2d 1057, 418 Mass. 773.
44. Minn.—State v. Davis, 504 N.W.2d 767, certiorari denied 114 S.Ct. 2120, 128 L.Ed.2d 679, denial of post-conviction relief affirmed 1996 WL 679682.

Source: Reprinted with permission from *50A Corpus Jurus Secundum,* "Juries," pp. 480–481, © 1997, West Group.

Exhibit A–6

Portion of Index of Latzer's *State Constitutional Criminal Law* dealing with "Discrimination in Jury Selection—Voir Dire"

Source: Reprinted with permission from B. Latzer, *State Constitutional Criminal Law,* Index (Juries and Jury Trial), © 1995, Clark, Boardman, Callaghan.

Exhibit A–7

Portion of Latzer's *State Constitutional Criminal Law* Discussing Discrimination at Voir Dire

§ 8:21

§ 8:21. Discrimination at Voir Dire

Generally, after the venire has been selected, the prosecution and defense may conduct a *voir dire*, or inquiry into the competency of potential jurors. During *voir dire*, biased venire members may be challenged for cause. A statutorily limited number of would-be jurors believed to be less than partial, but for whom cause could not be shown, may be excused peremptorily, i.e., without explanation.[61]

61. There is no federal constitutional right to peremptory challenge. Ross v Oklahoma (1988) 487 US 81, 101 L Ed 2d 80, 108 S Ct 2273, reh den 487 US 1250, 101 L Ed 2d 962, 109 S Ct 11, post-conviction proceeding (Okla Crim) 872 P2d 940, cert den (US) 130 L Ed 2d 352, 115 S Ct 441; Gray v Mississippi (1987) 481 US 648, 95 L Ed 2d 622, 107 S Ct 2045, appeal after remand (Miss) 605 So 2d 791, reh den (Miss) 1992 Miss LEXIS 652 Accord: People v Gordon (1990) 50 Cal 3d 1223, 270 Cal Rptr 451, 792 P2d 251, 265, reh den (Cal) 1990 Cal LEXIS 3936 and cert den 499 US 913, 113 L Ed 2d 231, 111 S Ct 1123 n. 4 (construing state and federal constitutions).

A few state constitutions provide an express right to make peremptory challenges. E.g., Conn Const Art First, § 19: "In all civil and criminal actions tried by a jury, the parties shall have the right to challenge jurors peremptorily, the number of such challenges to be established by law. The right to question each juror individually by counsel shall be inviolate." See State v Hill (1985) 196 Conn 667, 495 A2d 699 (there is no right to ask an unlimited number of questions on race prejudice, to pose questions in a particular form, or to make irrelevant or vexatious inquiries).

La Const Art 1 § 17: "The accused shall have the right to full *voir dire* examination of prospective jurors and to challenge jurors peremptorily."

It has also been held that there is no state or federal constitutional right to peremptory challenges. State v Sutphin (1988) 107 NM 126, 753 P2d 1314 (defendant may be granted fewer peremptory challenges when tried jointly than when tried singly).

* * * *

Although the United States Supreme Court recently extended Batson to women,[86] several state courts had already afforded state constitutional protection to other-than-racial groups. As indicated above, Massachusetts approached the issue by reference to the state Equal Rights Amendment, which lists sex, race, color, creed and national origin.[87] Hawaii[88] and New Mexico[89] did the same.

continues

Exhibit A–7 continued

Practice Tip: Counsel in a potential *Batson*-type case should determine whether or not the prosecuting state has an equal rights or civil rights provision in the state constitution, because such a provision may serve as the predicate for challenging the peremptory excusals of members of the protected classes—classes which may not be protected under federal constitutional law.

86. J. E. B. v Alabama ex rel. T. B. (1994, US) 128 L Ed 2d 89, 114 S Ct 1419, 94 CDOS 2680, 94 Daily Journal DAR 5174, 64 CCH EPD ¶ 42967, 8 FLW Fed S 42, on remand, remanded sub nom J.E.B. v State ex rel. T.B. (Ala App) 641 So 2d 821.

87. Soares, 387 NE2d at 516 (Article I of the Declaration of Rights, as amended by Article 106). California extended the *Wheeler* rule to Hispanics, People v Trevino (1985) 39 Cal 3d 667, 217 Cal Rptr 652, 704 P2d 719, and held that black women are a "cognizable subgroup." People v Motton (1985) 39 Cal 3d 596, 605–606, 217 Cal Rptr 416, 704 P2d 176.

88. Levinson, 71 Hawaii 492, 795 P2d 845 (purposeful exclusion of woman held to violate Article 1 Section 5 of state constitution, barring discrimination in the enjoyment of civil rights "because of race, religion, sex or ancestry.").

89. State v Gonzales (1991, App) 111 NM 590, 808 P2d 40, cert den 111 NM 416, 806 P2d 65 (discrimination on the basis of gender in the use of peremptory challenges violates NM Const Art 2, § 18, which says: "Equality of rights under law shall not be denied on account of the sex of any person.")

Source: Reprinted with permission from B. Latzer, *State Constitutional Criminal Law,* pp. 8–54, 8–59, © 1995, Clark, Boardman, Callaghan.

Next, we will try to find an *American Law Reports (A.L.R.)* annotation pertaining to our issue. We begin by examining the *A.L.R. Index, 2d-3d-4th-5th-Federal-L.Ed.2d* for annotations that may be helpful. We look in this index for terms that logically are suggested by our issue, for example, *peremptory challenges, jury,* and *religion.* Through this process, we find some promising citations to annotations, including "State criminal cases, use of peremptory challenges to exclude ethnic and racial groups, other than black Americans, from criminal jury—post-*Batson* state cases, 20 ALR5th 398" (see Exhibit A–8) and "Voir dire, affiliation, or prejudice of prospective juror as proper subject of inquiry or ground for challenge on voir dire, 95 ALR3d 172" (see Exhibit A–9).

For illustrative purposes, we locate the former annotation, at 20 *A.L.R. 5th* 398, and reproduce portions of its initial pages. (See Exhibit A–10.) We also reprint part of the pocket supplement, which reveals that a new section 6.5 has been added to the annotation. This section discusses a case from Florida involving the use of peremptory challenges to excuse Jewish prospective jurors. (See Exhibit A–11.)

Exhibit A–8
Entries of *A.L.R. Index* under heading "Peremptory Challenges"

ALR INDEX

Peremptory Challenges

Caucasians, use of peremptory challenges to exclude Caucasian persons, as a racial group, from criminal jury—post-Batson state cases, **47 ALR5th 259**

Discrimination

caucasians, use of peremptory challenges to exclude Caucasian persons, as a racial group, from criminal jury—post-Batson state cases, **47 ALR5th 259**

sex discrimination in jury selection—Supreme Court cases, **128 L Ed 2d 919**

state criminal cases, use of peremptory challenges to exclude ethnic and racial groups, other than black Americans, from criminal jury—post-Batson state cases, **20 ALR5th 398**

use of peremptory challenges to exclude persons from jury on basis of race or color—Supreme Court cases, **131 L Ed 2d 1123**

Source: Reprinted with permission from *ALR Index, ALR 2d-3d-4th-5th, Federal,* LEd2d (O-S), p. 16, (1998 Pocket Supp.). Further reproduction of any kind is strictly prohibited. For additional information, please contact West Group Customer Services representative at 1-800-328-4880.

Exhibit A–9
Entries of *A.L.R. Index* on Peremptory Challenges under heading
"Religion and Religious Societies"

ALR INDEX

RELIGION AND RELIGIOUS SOCIETIES—Cont'd

Jehovah's Witnesses (this index)

Jews (this index)

Jury and jury trial

—exemption, religious belief as ground for exemption or excuse from jury service, 2 ALR3d 1392

—voir dire, affiliation, or prejudice of prospective juror as proper subject of inquiry or ground for challenge on voir dire, 95 ALR3d 172

Kosher food, validity and construction of regulations dealing with misrepresentation in the sale of kosher food, 52 ALR3d

Source: Reprinted with permission from *ALR Index, ALR 2d-3d-4th-5th, Federal*, LEd2d (O-S) p. 737 (1993). Further reproduction of any kind is strictly prohibited. For additional information, please contact West Group Customer Services representative at 1-800-328-4880.

Exhibit A–10
Portion of A.L.R. Annotation dealing with Peremptory Challenges

---

20 ALR5th 398

USE OF PEREMPTORY CHALLENGES TO EXCLUDE ETHNIC AND RACIAL GROUPS, OTHER THAN BLACK AMERICANS, FROM CRIMINAL JURY—POST-BATSON STATE CASES

by
Jay M. Zitter, J.D.

The Supreme Court in Batson v Kentucky (1986) 476 US 79, 90 L Ed 2d 69, 106 S Ct 1712, posited a number of rules regarding whether strikes of ethnic or racial minority members from petit jury panels are discriminatory. Numerous cases have applied such factors and, although the Batson Case involved African American defendants and jurors, many cases deal with members of other groups. For example, in State v Alen (1993, Fla) 616 So 2d 452, 20 ALR5th 961, the court ruled that although there are certain differences among subgroups, Hispanics were a cognizable group, so that discriminatory use of peremptory challenges against Hispanics constituted a violation of equal protection principles.

* * * *

Table of Contents

Research References
Index
Jurisdictional Table of Cited Statutes and Cases

ARTICLE OUTLINE

continues

Exhibit A–10 continued

§ 7. Where one minority juror challenged—no similar minorities left on panel, generally
    [a] Prima facie case found
    [b] Prima facie case not found
§ 8. —Other minorities left on panel
§ 9. More than one minority juror challenged—no similar minority left on panel, generally
§ 10. —Other similar minorities left on panel
    [a] Prima facie case found
    [b] Prima facie case not found
      III. ALLEGATIONS OF NONDISCRIMINA-TORY, RACE-NEUTRAL REASONS FOR CHALLENGING MINORITIES
        A. IN GENERAL
§ 11. View that subjective and trivial reasons may suffice

* * * *

RESEARCH SOURCES

The following are the research sources that were found to be helpful in compiling this annotation:

Texts

3 Cook, Constitutional Rights of the Accused 2d § 17:14
1 Wharton's Criminal Procedure 14th ed § 188

Encyclopedias

47 Am Jur 2d, Jury § 235
50 CJS, Juries §§ 124–127

Law Reviews

Raphael, Discriminatory Jury Selection: Lower Court Implementation of Batson v Kentucky, 25 Willamette LR 293 (1989)

Electronic Search Query

(peremptory w/1 challenge or strike) w/15 eliminate or select! or challenge or exercise! w/15 juror w/15 race or racial! or ethnic! or descent or heritage or group bias and date aft 1985 and not black w/5 juror

West Digest Key Numbers

Jury 33(1.10, 1.15, 5.15), 119, 120, 121

INDEX

Age of defendant, § 62
Age of juror, §§ 12[b], 34, 35, 36[b], 53[b]
Age of witnesses, §§ 34[b], 56
Aggravated assault or battery, §§ 10[b], 24
Aggravated robbery, §§ 34[b], 37
Alcohol tests, juror's views, § 48
All peremptory challenges not used, § 10
Antagonism toward prosecutor, §§ 25, 30
Anti-law enforcement or anti-prosecution, juror as, §§ 16, 33
Appearance of juror, §§ 24, 34[b], 40, 41
Apprehensiveness of juror, § 25
Armed robbery, § 60
Arrest of juror, previous, § 20
Arrogance, § 28
Asian-American jurors, §§ 4, 8, 35, 42[a], 43, 44, 46, 47, 52[a], 53[a]
Assault and battery, §§ 7[a], 10[b], 20, 24, 34[b], 40, 53[b], 56
Attempted murder, §§ 12[a], 34[a]
Attentiveness or interest in proceedings, §§ 29, 52[a]
Attorney-client relationship, defense attorneys and jurors, § 14
Attorneys, parties, or case, juror's or relative's connection with, §§ 13–19
Attractiveness of juror, § 41
Attractiveness of youthful defendant, § 62
Bad feeling about juror, § 30
Bar fight, §§ 21, 24, 40, 53[b], 55
Bias, juror's admission of, § 9
Blue collar workers, § 53[b]

Exhibit A–11
Portion of *A.L.R.* Pocket Supplement dealing with Peremptory Challenges

20 ALR5th 398–498

New sections and subsections added:

§ 6.5. Other groups
§ 10.5. Other inferences
§ 24.5. Other connections with criminal justice system
§ 33.5. Other expressions of demeanor and attitude
§ 42.5. Other personal and physical characteristics, manifestations, and abilities
§ 48.5. Reluctance to deal with other cases on penalties
(§ 53) [e] Other professions or jobs
§ 55.5. Other employment related reasons
§ 65. Other reasons
§ 66. Juror spoke language to be translated at trial

---

§ 2. Summary and comment
[b] Practice pointers
Defendant has standing to challenge racially discriminatory use of peremptory strikes against members of other races. People v Mendoza (1994, Colo App) 876 P2d 98, reh den (May 12, 1994).

§ 3. Hispanics
Also recognizing that Hispanics are cognizable group for purposes of alleged improper use of peremptory strikes:
US—United States v Perez 1994. CA1 Mass 35 F3d 632.

* * * *

§ 6.5. [New] Other groups
Jewish persons constituted cognizable class where Jewish population of county was approximately 10 percent and group had sufficient cohesiveness of beliefs and experiences to constitute ethnic group; therefore, striking of Jewish venire person for that reason alone was unconstitutional. Joseph v State (1994 Fla App D3) 636 So 2d 777, 19 FLW D 861.

In prosecution for criminal contempt, commonwealth improperly exercised its peremptory challenges to excuse all jurors with arguably Irish-sounding surnames. Commonwealth v Carleton (1994) 418 Mass 773, 641 NE2d 1057.

The last secondary authority we consult, which often is the most helpful kind, is the legal periodical literature, or law reviews. We begin by using the printed *Index to Legal Periodicals and Books* (Sept. 1996-Aug. 1997). We alternatively could have chosen the *LegalTrac* database, which is stored on a computer disk. We turn to "Peremptory Challenges" in the Subject Index of the *Index to Legal Periodicals and Books*, and quickly spot an article with a promising title: "The equal protection clause, the free exercise clause and religion-based peremptory challenges." The article is published in 63 *University of Chicago Law Review* 1639–1672 (Fall 1996). (See Exhibit A–12.)

After we locate this article in volume 63 of the *University of Chicago Law Review*, we are reminded why law review articles can be so helpful for legal research. A good article describes and analyzes legal issues and provides hundreds of supporting authorities in its copious footnotes. Note that the article discusses a Texas case, *Casarez v. State*, 913 S.W.2d 468 (Tex. Crim. App. 1995) [sic—the *Casarez* case actually was decided in 1994], that should be of special interest since our problem has arisen in a hypothetical Texas prosecution. (See Exhibit A–13.)

Exhibit A–12
Heading "Peremptory Challenges" from Subject Index of the
Index to Legal Periodicals and Books

Index to Legal Periodicals & Books

Peremptory challenges

Arbitrary rationality, G. N. Maghocca, student author. 106 *Yale L.J.* 1959-64 Ap '97

Controversy over the peremptory challenge: should Batson [Batson v Kentucky, 106 S. Ct. 1712 (1986)] be expanded? D. C. Smith, student author, R. Dennehy, student author. 10 *St. Johns J. Legal Comment*, 453–73 Spr '95

Equal protection and peremptory challenges: reconciling the irreconcilable. M. M. Albright, student author. 25 *Cap. U. L. Rev* 425–52 '96

The equal protection clause, the free exercise clause and religion-based peremptory challenges. A. B. Gendleman, student author. 63 *U. Chi. L. Rev.* 1639–72 Fall '96

The future of the post-Batson [Batson v. Kentucky, 106 S. Ct. 1712 (1996)] peremptory challenge: voir dire by questionnaire and the "blind" peremptory. J. Montoya. 29 *U. Mich. J.L. Ref.* 981–1037 Summ '96

J.E.B. v. Alabama ex rel. T.B. [114 S. Ct. 1419 (1994)]: peremptory challenges in private litigation—an endangered species. D. Obritsch, student author. 21 *J. Contemp. L.* 341–63 '95

Source: Reprinted with permission from 36 *Index to Legal Periodicals and Books*, p. 714, (September 1996–August 1997), © 1997, H.W. Wilson Company.

Exhibit A–13
Portion of *University of Chicago Law Review* Article on
Religion-Based Peremptory Challenges

The Equal Protection Clause, the Free Exercise Clause and Religion-Based Peremptory Challenges

Amy B. Gendleman

* * * *

D. Religion-Based Peremptory Challenges in the Lower Courts

Lower courts have both upheld and rejected the extension of *Batson* to religion-based peremptory challenges,[62] but only the Texas Court of Criminal Appeals, in *Casarez v State*,[63] has considered this issue in light of *J.E.B.* and its suggestion that all peremptories against groups that receive heightened scrutiny may be unconstitutional.[64] The *Casarez* court, however, held that all religion-

based peremptory challenges were constitutional.[65] The court reasoned that excluding a potential juror on the basis of his religious affiliation was reasonable because a religion is based upon a system of beliefs shared by all its members. To hold that a venireman could not be excluded on account of his religious preference was tantamount, the court thought, to holding that he could not be struck on account of his beliefs, an idea that the court believed to be beyond the scope of *Batson*.[66]

The dissent was "astounded" by the lack of authority for the majority's holding and disputed the majority's assumption that the beliefs of a religion are held by all of its members.[67] The dissent then argued that religion-based peremptory challenges did not advance a compelling state interest and, therefore, should be eliminated.[68]

continues

Exhibit A–13 continued

The *Casarez* dissent accurately pointed out the crucial problem with the majority opinion: the absence of empirical data to support the majority's tenuous conclusion that religion is an accurate predictor of a juror's individually held beliefs and his vote.[69] One cannot just assume that, for example, the millions of Catholics in this country are all opposed to birth control without some data to support this conclusion.[70] But because the *Casarez* court based its opinion on these debatable assumptions about the . . .

62. See, for example, *United States v Greer*, 939 F2d 1076, 1085 (5th Cir 1991) (holding that the defendants accused of vandalizing a temple could not constitutionally strike Jewish veniremen from the panel). But see *Davis*, 504 NW2d at 771 (upholding the exclusion of a prospective juror based on religious affiliation); *Casarez*, 913 SW2d at 495–96 (same).

Courts have also held that some state constitutions forbid religion-based peremptory challenges as well. See, for example, *Joseph v State*, 636 S2d 777, 781 (Fla Dist Ct App 1994) (peremptory strike of a potential juror executed solely because the juror was Jewish violated the Florida constitution's guarantee of an impartial jury); *State v Eason*, 336 NC 730, 445 SE2d 917, 921–23 (1994), cert denied, 115 S Ct 764 (1995) (holding that North Carolina constitution specifically prohibits exclusion from jury service on account of religion, but that prohibition does not apply to exclusion on the basis of religious opposition

to capital punishment); *State v Levinson*, 71 Hawaii 492, 795 P2d 845, 849–50 (1990) (same for the Hawaii constitution); *Commonwealth v Carleton*, 36 Mass App 137, 629 NE2d 321, 325 (1994) (holding that religion-based peremptory challenges violate clause of the Massachusetts Declaration of Rights guaranteeing defendants a jury of their peers); *People v Fudge*, 7 Cal 4th 1075, 31 Cal Rptr 2d 321, 332 (1994), cert denied, 115 S Ct 1367 (1995) (same for California constitution's guarantee of a jury drawn from a representative cross-section of the community). For more detailed analyses of the various constitutional prohibitions on religion-based peremptory challenges, see Angela J. Mason. *Discrimination Based on Religious Affiliation: Another Nail in the Peremptory Challenge's Coffin?*, 29 Ga L Rev 493 (1995); Keith A. Ward, *"The Only Thing in the Middle of the Road is a Dead Skunk and a Yellow Stripe": Peremptory Challenges—Take 'em or Leave 'em*, 26 Tex Tech L Rev 1361 (1995).

63. 913 SW2d 468 (Tex Crim App 1995).

64. *J.E.B.*, 114 S Ct at 1424–28. Consequently, pre-*J.E.B.* decisions such as *Davis* are not that helpful in assessing the constitutionality of religion-based peremptories. The Minnesota Supreme Court in *Davis* held that *Batson* did not extend to religion since race-based classifications were sufficiently distinguishable. *Davis*, 504 NW2d at 771. *J.E.B.* puts *Davis* in severe doubt.

65. *Casarez*, 913 SW2d at 495–96.

66. Id at 495.

67. Id at 501–02, 506 n 18 (Baird dissenting).

68. Id at 506.

69. Id at 501–02.

70. See text accompanying notes 121–23.

Source: Reprinted with permission from A.B. Gendleman, *The Equal Protection Clause, the Free Exercise Clause and Religion-Based Peremptory Challenges*, 63 *University of Chicago Law Review*, pp. 1639 and 1650–1651, © 1996, University of Chicago Law School.

We have covered much ground by relying on secondary legal authorities to begin researching the question confronting us. We now turn to primary legal authorities. The issue we are investigating—the constitutionality of a prosecutor's exercising peremptory challenges based on the religion of prospective jurors—is not likely to be governed by state or federal administrative regulation. We take a brief diversion here to illustrate how federal regulations can be located, by constructing a different issue.

Suppose that we are interested in whether the Federal Bureau of Prisons has adopted regulations designed to accommodate prisoners' religious beliefs and practices. We would consult the *Code of Federal Regulations (CFR) Index* under "Prisons," or perhaps "Religion." We find the heading "Religious discrimination" in the *C.F.R.*

Index, with "Prisons Bureau" listed as a subtopic. We are referred to title 28 of the *C.F.R.*, at parts 551 and 548. (See Exhibit A–14.) We locate title 28, turn to the relevant parts, and now are in a position to learn more about the relevant Bureau of Prisons' regulations. (See Exhibit A–15.)

We next investigate Texas statutes that might govern the exercise of peremptory challenges. When we look up "peremptory challenges" in the *General Index* accompanying *Vernon's Texas Statutes and Codes Annotated*, we are directed to "Jury, this index." Pursuing this lead, we turn to "Jury" in the *General Index* and find the subtopic "Peremptory challenges" and a reference to "CCrP 35.13 et seq., 35.14, 35.25" (see Exhibit A–16). Accordingly, we must find those statutory sections in Texas's Code of Criminal Procedure.

Exhibit A–14
Entries on Prisons Bureau Regulations regarding Religious Discrimination in *C.F.R. Index*

CFR Index

Religious discrimination

    Equal credit opportunity (Regulation B), 12 CFR 202

    Farm Credit Administration, 12 CFR 613

* * * *

Prisons Bureau

    Nondiscrimination toward inmates, 28 CFR 551

    Prisoners, religious programs, 28 CFR 548

Source: Reprinted from *CFR Index* pp. 540, 544.

Exhibit A–15
Portion of *C.F.R.* entry on Prisons Bureau Regulations regarding
Religious Beliefs and Practices

Part 548—Religious Programs

Subpart A [Reserved]

Subpart B—Religious Beliefs and Practices of Committed Offenders

Sec.

548.10 Purpose and scope.

548.11 Definition.

548.12 Chaplains.

548.13 Schedules and facility

548.14 Community involvement with contractors.

548.15 Equity.

548.16 Inmate religious property.

548.17 Work assignments.

548.18 Observance of religious holy days.

548.19 Pastoral visits.

548.20 Dietary practices.

AUTHORITY: 5 U.S.C. 301; 18 U.S.C. 3621, 3622, 3624, 4001, 4042, 4081, 4082 (Repealed in part as to offenses committed on or after November 1, 1987), 5006–5024 (Repealed October 12, 1984 as to offenses committed after that date) 5039; 28 U.S.C. 509, 510; 42 U.S.C. 1996; 28 CFR 0.95-0.99.

SOURCE: 44 FR 38251, June 29, 1979, unless otherwise noted.

Source: Reprinted from 28 *CFR*, Ch. V (7-1-97 Edition), p. 522.

Subpart A [Reserved]

Subpart B—Religious Beliefs and Practices of Committed Offenders

AUTHORITY: 5 U.S.C. 301; 18 U.S.C. 4001, 4042, 4081, 4082, 5006–5024, 5039; 28 U.S.C. 509, 510; 12 U.S.C. 1996; 28 CFR 0.95–0.99.

SOURCE: 60 FR 46486, Sept. 6, 1995, unless otherwise noted.

§ 548.10 Purpose and scope.

(a) The Bureau of Prisons provides inmates of all faith groups with reasonable and equitable opportunities to pursue religious beliefs and practices, within the constraints of budgetary limitations and consistent with the security and orderly running of the institution and the Bureau of Prisons.

(b) When considered necessary for the security or good order of the institution, the Warden may limit attendance at or discontinue a religious activity. Opportunities for religious activities are open to the entire inmate population, without regard to race, color, nationality, or ordinarily, creed. The Warden, after consulting with the institution chaplain, may limit participation in a particular religious activity or practice to the members of that religious group. Ordinarily, when the nature of the activity or practice (e.g., religious fasts, wearing of headwear, work proscription, ceremonial meals) indicates a need for such a limitation, only those inmates whose files reflect the pertinent religious preference will be included. . . .

Exhibit A–16
Portions of General Index to *Vernon's*
Texas Statutes and Code Annotated
regarding Peremptory Challenges

JURY—Cont'd
Minorities, peremptory challenges, racial discrimination, CCrP 35.261
Misconduct, venue, CCrP 31.08
Mistrial, generally. Trial, this index
Municipal Courts, this index

* * * *

Peremptory challenges, CCrP 35.13 et seq., 35.14, 35.25; Gov 62.020
   Justices of the peace, CCrP 45.28
   Racial discrimination, CCrP 35.261
Perjury, exclusion, Const. Art. 16, § 2
Personal waiver of right, CCrP 1.13

Source: Reprinted with permission from *Vernon's Texas Statutes & Codes 1998 General Index (A to K)* p. 1675, © 1998, West Group.

We find that article 35.14 of the Texas Code of Criminal Procedure contains just a brief explanation of a peremptory challenge and provides little help with our specific issue. However, we have consulted an *annotated* statute, which includes an outline of topics addressed in court decisions that have interpreted or applied the statute ("Notes of Decisions"), as well as accompanying squibs summarizing those court decisions. (See Exhibit A–17.) We observe in the pocket supplement to the statute that the Notes of Decisions include the topic "Religious beliefs 9.4." When we consult that note, we are rewarded with a brief description of a case that appears to be directly on point with our issue. (See Exhibit A–18.) This case, *Casarez v. State*, 913 S.W.2d 468 (Tex. Crim. App. 1994), also was cited and discussed in the *University of Chicago Law Review* article that we uncovered previously.

We can consult both the U.S. Constitution and the Texas Constitution for further leads to solving our research problem. Although the right to trial by jury and even religious freedoms might be implicated, we know from *Batson v. Kentucky* (and from the research we have completed thus far) that the courts typically have resolved peremptory challenge issues by applying equal-protection principles. We begin our constitutional research accordingly.

If we did not know that the federal Constitution's equal-protection clause was in the Fourteenth Amendment, we could readily ascertain that fact by consulting the General Index of the *United States Code Annotated*. The Fourteenth Amendment is reprinted in the constitutional volumes that are a part of the *U.S.C.A.* We there encounter the same types of research aids that accompany annotated statutes. Specifically, after we read the equal-protection clause of the Fourteenth Amendment (see Exhibit A–19), we would scan the "Notes of Decisions" for subtopics pertaining to jury selection. The reference to "Jury Trial" looks promising. (See Exhibit A–20.) We turn to the detailed outline accompanying "Jury Trial" and also check the pocket supplement that updates the main volume. In that supplement, we find that the subject "Religious affiliation, peremptory challenges," is assigned a unique number, 959e. (See Exhibit A–21.) The squibs of judicial decisions reported in connection with note 959e may prove to be of interest. (See Exhibit A–22.)

Exhibit A–17
Annotated Statute on Peremptory Challenges from
Vernon's Texas Statutes and Code Annotated

Art. 35.14. [614] [690] [671] A peremptory challenge

A peremptory challenge is made to a juror without assigning any reason therefor.

Acts 1965, 59th Leg., p. 317, ch. 722, § 1, eff. Jan. 1, 1966.

Historical Note

Prior Law:
Vernon's Ann.C.C.P.1925, art. 614.
O.C. 571.

Cross References

Civil actions, challenge to jurors, see Vernon's Ann. Rules Civ.Proc., rule 227.

Peremptory challenges based on race, see art. 35.261.

Law Review Commentaries

Unlawful discrimination in jury selection. 21 Baylor L.Rev. 73 (1969).

Library References

Jury ☞ 135.
WESTLAW Topic No. 230.

United States Supreme Court

Prohibition from exercising peremptory challenges to remove racial minorities from venire, see Batson v. Kentucky, 1986, 106 S.Ct. 1712, 476 U.S. 79, 90 L.Ed.2d 69.

Specific questions to veniremen as to racial prejudice, necessity in criminal proceedings, see Ristaino v. Ross, 1976, 96 S.Ct. 1017, 424 U.S. 589, 47 L.Ed.2d 258.

Notes of Decisions

Accepted jurors   15
Bias or prejudice   2
Burden of proof, race discrimination   9
Examination of prospective jurors, procedure   11
Exhaustion of challenges   13
Harmless error   17
Mistake   16
Nature of peremptory challenge   1
Objection to racial composition, race
   discrimination   8
Opportunity to strike   12
Procedure   10, 11
   In general   10
   Examination of prospective jurors   11
Punishment   3
Purposeful discrimination, race discrimination   6
Race discrimination   4–9
   In general   4
   Burden of proof   9
   Objection to racial composition   8
   Purposeful discrimination   6
   Race-neutral explanation   7
   Systematic exclusion   5

Exhibit A–18
Notes of Decisions on Religious Beliefs and Peremptory Challenges in
Vernon's Texas Statutes and Code Annotated

Art. 35.14. [614] [690] [671] A peremptory challenge

Library References

Motion for additional preemptory [sic] challenges, see McCormick et al., 7A Texas Practice § 65.25 (10th ed.).

Peremptory challenges, in general, see Dix & Dawson, 42 Texas Practice § 35.91.

United States Supreme Court

Jury selection, peremptory challenges, sex discrimination, see J.E.B. v. Alabama ex rel. T.B., 1994, 114 S.Ct. 1419, 511 U.S. 127, 128 L.Ed.2d 89, on remand 641 So.2d 821.

Peremptory challenges, racial discrimination, retroactivity of prima facie showing requirements, see Teague v. Lane, U.S.Ill.1989, 109 S.Ct. 1060, 489 U.S. 288, 103 L.Ed.2d 334, rehearing denied 109 S.Ct. 1771, 490 U.S. 1031, 104 L.Ed.2d 206.

Notes of Decisions

In general   ½

Additional challenges   13.5
Appearance and demeanor   3.7
Criminal background   3.8
Death penalty views   3.1
Gender   3.5
Gender, purposeful discrimination, race discrimination   6.4
Intelligence   15.6
Juveniles   3.6
Neutral challenges   15.8
Race discrimination   4–9
Gender, purposeful discrimination   6.4
Religious beliefs   9.4

* * * *

9.4. Religious beliefs

Litigants may use peremptory challenges to exclude persons from service on juries in individual cases on basis of their religious affiliation. Casarez v. State (Cr.App. 1994) 913 S.W.2d 468, on rehearing.

Source: Reprinted with permission from *2A Vernon's Texas Statutes Annotated, Code of Criminal Procedure*, pp. 82, 83, 95, © 1989, West Group.

Exhibit A–19
Equal Protection Clause of the Fourteenth Amendment to the U.S. Constitution, in
United States Code Annotated

AMENDMENT XIV—CITIZENSHIP; PRIVILEGES AND IMMUNITIES; DUE PROCESS; EQUAL PROTECTION; APPORTIONMENT OF REPRESENTATION; DISQUALIFICATION OF OFFICERS; PUBLIC DEBT; ENFORCEMENT

Materials for the Equal Protection Clause of Section 1 and Sections 2 to 5 are set out in this volume. See the preceding three volumes for materials pertaining to the Citizenship, Privileges and Immunities, and Due Process Clauses of Section 1.

Section 1. All persons born or naturalized in the United States, and subject to the jurisdiction thereof, are citizens of the United States and of the State wherein they reside. No State shall make or enforce any law which shall abridge the privileges or immunities of citizens of the United States; nor shall any State deprive any person of life, liberty, or property, without due process of law; nor deny to any person within its jurisdiction the equal protection of the laws.

Source: Reprinted with permission from *United States Code Annotated Constitution*, Amend. 14 to End, p. 6, © 1987, West Group.

Exhibit A–20
Partial List of Notes of Decisions on Equal Protection in *United States Code Annotated*,
Fourteenth Amendment to U.S. Constitution.

Notes of Decisions

I.	GENERALLY 1–50	XIX.	PROBATION 1141–1170
II.	STANDARDS OR TESTS— GENERALLY 51–110	XX.	APPEAL OR REVIEW 1171–1240
III.	RATIONAL RELATIONSHIP OF CLASSIFICATION TO PURPOSE OR OBJECTIVE 111–160	XXI.	PRISONS AND PRISONERS— GENERALLY 1241–1330
		XXII.	PAROLE 1331–1380
IV.	STRICT SCRUTINY 161–210	XXIII.	CONTEMPT PROCEEDINGS 1381–1410
V.	STATE ACTION— GENERALLY 211–240	XXIV.	JUVENILE PROCEEDINGS 1411–1480
VI.	PERSONS OR ENTITIES ACT- ING AS STATE 241–290	XXV.	COMMITMENT OF MENTALLY ILL OR RETARDED
VII.	ACTIVITIES CONSTITUTING STATE ACTION 291–390		PERSONS 1481–1540
		XXVI.	ABORTIONS 1541–1590
VIII.	METHODS OF DEPRIVATION— GENERALLY 391–430	XXVII.	ALCOHOLIC BEVERAGES— GENERALLY 1591–1640
IX.	SELECTIVE PROSECUTION OR ENFORCEMENT 431—500	XXVIII.	LICENSES TO SELL 1641–1700
X.	ADMINISTRATIVE PROCEDURE GENERALLY 501–520	XXIX.	ANIMALS; HUNTING AND FISHING 1701–1760
XI.	CIVIL PROCEDURE— GENERALLY 521–610	XXX.	ARMED FORCES AND SELEC- TIVE SERVICE 1761–1810
XII.	STATUTES OF LIMITATIONS 611–660	XXXI.	BANKS AND BANKING 1811–1860
		XXXII.	BUSINESS AND TRADE 1861–2050
XIII.	REMEDIES OR RELIEF 661–730	XXXIII.	CONDEMNATION AND EMINENT DOMAIN 2051–2090
XIV.	CRIMINAL PROCEDURE— GENERALLY 731–830	XXXIV.	CORPORATIONS 2091–2130
		XXXV.	CRIMES 2131–2230
XV.	POLICE MISCONDUCT 831–870	XXXVI.	DOMESTIC RELATIONS 2231–2310
		XXXVII.	DRUGS 2311–2350
XVI.	GRAND JURY 871–920	XXXVIII.	EDUCATION, SCHOOLS, AND STUDENTS—
XVII.	JURY TRIAL 921–980		GENERALLY 2351–2460
XVIII.	SENTENCE AND PUNISHMENT 981–1140	XXXIX.	DESEGREGATION 2461–2530
		XL.	HIGH SCHOOLS 2531–2580

Exhibit A–21
Portion of Outline of Notes of Decisions on Jury Trials dealing with Peremptory Challenges, *United States Code Annotated*, Fourteenth Amendment to the U.S. Constitution, Pocket Supplement

Peremptory challenges
    Adversarial hearing   955a
    Age   956c
    Credibility of counsel   955b
    Death penalty opponents   959d
    Employment status   959c
    Family   959g
    Foreign languages   955c
    Friends   959h
    Gender   956a
    Good faith   959i
    Homosexuals   956b
    Religious affiliation   959e
    Remedies for violation   959j
    Sex disqualification   959b
    Statistical proof   959a
    Victimization status   959f
    Waiver   959k

Source: Reprinted with permission from *United States Code Annotated Constitution,* Amend. 14 to End, 1997 (Supp.), p. 114, © 1997, West Group.

Exhibit A–22
Notes of Decisions on Peremptory Challenges and Religious Affiliation, *United States Code Annotated,* Fourteenth Amendment to the U.S. Constitution, Pocket Supplement

959e. —Religious affiliation

Prosecution's peremptory challenge of black prospective juror, because of her membership in Pentecostal church, was pretextual: prosecution had made no inquiry into depth of her religious convictions and whether they would impair her ability to follow law. People v. Woods, Ill.App. 1 Dist. 1994, 643 N.E.2d 1331, 205 Ill.Dec. 724, rehearing denied, rehearing pending.

Conviction would not be reversed due to entry on jury questionnaire asking prospect to list membership in church; there was no indication that defendant was required to use peremptory challenge to strike a prospective juror on basis of religion, and there was nothing unconstitutional about inquiring into whether a prospective juror was a church member. Alexander v. State, Tex.App.-Fort Worth 1995, 903 S.W.2d 881, rehearing overruled.

Source: Reprinted with permission from *United States Code Annotated Constitution*, Amend. 14 to End, 1997 (Supp.), p. 173, © 1997, West Group.

Because our hypothetical case arises in Texas, we will want to replicate these search procedures using the Texas Constitution. After using the *Index* to *Vernon's Texas Constitution Annotated* to locate the state constitution's "equal-rights" provision in Article 1, section 3, we find that one of the Notes of Decisions corresponds to "peremptory challenges, generally." On consulting the squibs accompanying that note, we are referred to some state cases that may be worth checking, including a case we have encountered before, *Casarez v. State*, 913 S.W.2d 468 (Tex. Crim. App. 1994). (See Exhibit A–23.)

Finally, we are ready to tackle case law. We already have been referred by a number of secondary and primary authorities to judicial decisions that appear to be relevant to our issue. Remember that there are several ways to locate cases. You should not hesitate to make use of these multiple research avenues. We now discuss how to find case law "from scratch" by using *Descriptive Word Indexes* and *Case Digests*.

Because we are interested primarily in Texas law for the hypothetical issue we are investigating, we first refer to the *Descriptive Word Index* for the *Texas Digest 2d*. Of the several terms that could make logical starting places for our problem, we have chosen to look up *peremptory challenges*. The *Descriptive Word Index* instructs us to see the topic "Challenges." (See Exhibit A–24.) When we take that step, we find nothing that deals specifically with peremptory challenges and religion, but the subtopic "Discriminatory practices" looks worth pursuing. We will find case squibs corresponding to this general subject in the *Digest* under the topic "Jury," key number 33 (5.1). (See Exhibit A–25.)

We first consult the general outline for the subissues covered under the topic "Jury." We learn that key number 33 (5.15) corresponds to peremptory challenges under the broader heading of the "Constitution and selection of jury."

(See Exhibit A–26.) We should expect to find case squibs that are somewhat removed from the specific issue we are investigating, but this subtopic also seems as if it might include cases of more direct interest. Turning next to the squibs in the *Digest*, we note, among others, one that is associated with *Casarez v. State*: "Litigants may use peremptory challenges to exclude persons from service on juries in individual cases on basis of their religious affiliation." (See Exhibit A–27.)

Exhibit A–23
Notes of Decisions on Peremptory
Challenges in *Vernon's Texas Constitution Annotated*, Article 1 § 3

28. —Peremptory challenges, generally, jury selection

Jury selection system applicable to capital cases, which requires defendants to exercise peremptory challenges following examination of each individual juror, as compared to noncapital cases in which defendants exercise peremptory challenges after all prospective jurors have been examined, did not constitute violation of state or federal due process or equal protection [Const.Art. 1, §§ 3, 19; U.S.C.A. Const.Amend. 14]; capital defendants were given certain advantages over noncapital defendants such as five additional peremptory challenges and ability to examine each prospective juror individually and in isolation. Janecka v. State (Cr.App. 1987) 739 S.W.2d 813.

System according to which jurors are selected for service in courts by allowing litigants to exercise peremptory challenges against individual veniremembers is a government practice subject to equal protection rules. Casarez v. State (Cr.App. 1994) 913 S.W.2d 468, on rehearing.

Preserving right to system of peremptory challenges is a legitimate interest of government; accordingly, most peremptory challenges are not constitutionally exceptionable. Casarez v. State (Cr.App. 1994) 913 S.W.2d 468, on rehearing.

Government's interest in system of peremptory challenges is generally not great enough to support exclusion of persons from jury service on basis of classification which is subject to strict or heightened scrutiny under equal protection clause. Casarez v. State (Cr.App. 1994) 913 S.W.2d 468, on rehearing.

Source: Reprinted with permission from *1 Vernon's Texas Constitution Annotated*, p. 349, © 1997, West Group.

Exhibit A–24
Entry in Descriptive Word Index of *Texas Digest 2d* for "Peremptory Challenges"

55 Tex D2d–537

References are to Digest Topics and Key Numbers

PERCENTAGE CONTRACTS
COMPENSATION under contract, Contracts 229(2)
COST—PLUS contracts, see, generally, this index Cost-Plus
    Contracts
RENT, see this index RENT

PERCOLATING OIL
STATE ownership as part of mineral estate in land
    leased. Mines 5
PERCOLATING WATERS
See this index Subterranean and Percolating
    Waters
PEREMPTORY CHALLENGES
See this index Challenges

Source: Reprinted with permission from *55 West's Texas Digest*, 2nd Edition, Descriptive Word Index, (J–Q) p. 537, © 1984, West
Group.

Exhibit A–25
Portions of Descriptive Word Index of *Texas Digest 2d* dealing with Peremptory Challenges

References are to Digest Topics and Key Numbers

CHALLENGES—Cont'd
PETIT jurors—Cont'd

* * * *

Order of—
    Challenges on different grounds   Jury 112
    Parties in making challenges   Jury 113
Passing juror as waiver of challenge   Jury
    110(11)
Peremptory challenges   Jury 134–140
    Assignment of errors preserving for appellate
        review.   App & E 302(1)
    Civil actions and proceedings   Jury 136(7.4)

Co-defendants   Jury 136(6)
Criminal prosecution, number   Jury 136(4.8)
    Counts of indictment as affecting
        number   Jury 136(8)
Denial of right to jury trial, see this index Jury
Disabling of jurors pending trial affecting
    number.   Jury 136(9)
Discretion of court as to—
    Order and exhaustion   Jury 138(1)
    Time for exercising   Jury 137(2)
Discriminatory effect   Jury 33(5.1)
Discriminatory practices   Jury 33(5.1)
District Court of United States   Fed Civ Proc
    2098
Exceptions to rulings   Jury 142

Source: Reprinted with permission from *53 West's Texas Digest*, 2nd Edition, Descriptive Word Index, (A-C) p. 439, © 1984, West
Group.

Exhibit A–26
Portion of Outline for Subissues of Topic "Jury" dealing with
Peremptory Challenges, *Texas Digest 2d*

JURY

II. RIGHT TO TRIAL BY JURY.—Continued.

🗝 33. —Constitution and selection of jury.—Continued.
    (1.15). —Race.
    (1.20). —Age.
    (1.25). —Sex.
    (2). Competence for trial of cause.
    (2.10). —In general.
    (2.15). —View of capital punishment.
    (3). Selection from vicinage.

    (4). Summoning and impaneling; voir dire.
    (5). Challenges and objections.
    (5.10). —In general.
    (5.15). —Peremptory challenges.
    (5.20). —Standing and waiver.
34. —Restriction or invasion of functions of jury.
    (1). In general.
    (2). Weight and sufficiency of evidence.
    (3). Taking case or question from jury.
    (4). Requiring special verdict.

Source: Reprinted with permission from *34 West's Texas Digest*, 2nd Edition, p. 6, © 1997, West Group.

Exhibit A–27
Squibs on Peremptory Challenges in *Texas Digest 2d*

🗝 **33(5.15). —Peremptory challenges.**

    C.A.5 (Tex.) 1997. Pursuant to *Batson* rule, prosecutor violates equal protection clause when potential jurors are challenged solely on basis of their race. U.S.C.A. Const.Amend. 14.
    U.S. v. Perkins, 105 F.3d 976.

* * * *

    Tex.Cr.App. 1994. Preserving right to system of peremptory challenges is a legitimate interest of government; accordingly, most peremptory challenges are not constitutionally exceptionable.
    Casarez v. State, 913 S.W.2d 468, on rehearing.

    Government's interest in system of peremptory challenges is generally not great enough to support exclusion of persons from jury service on basis of classification which is subject to strict or heightened scrutiny under equal protection clause. U.S.C.A. Const.Amend 14.
    Casarez v. State, 913 S.W.2d 468, on rehearing.

    Litigants may use peremptory challenges to exclude persons from service on juries in individual cases on basis of their religious affiliation. U.S.C.A. Const.Amends. 1, 14.
    Casarez v. State, 913 S.W.2d 468, on rehearing.

Source: Reprinted with permission from *34 West's Digest*, 2nd Edition, pp. 156, 165, © 1997, West Group.

With this reassurance that we have located a topic and key number that will help point us to relevant cases, we can expand our search to cover other jurisdictions by consulting other sets of West's *Case Digests*. The broadest array of jurisdictions is included in the *Decennial Digests* and the companion *General Digests* that keep the former volumes current. Thus, for example, we look in a recently published volume (14) of *West's General Digest, Ninth Series*, under "Jury 🗝 33(5.15)," and note that a Massachusetts case, *Commonwealth v. Burns*, also appears to involve peremptory challenges being exercised on account of a prospective juror's religion. (See Exhibit A–28.) We would continue our search for cases by consulting other *Case Digests*.

By now, we would be interested in reading the case to which we have been referred so frequently, *Casarez v. State*, 913 S.W.2d 468 (Tex. Crim. App. 1994). We look up this opinion in volume 913 of the *South Western Reporter, 2d*, at page 468. At the start of the opinion, we find the headnotes and key numbers inserted by the editors at West Publishing Co. Necessarily, one or more of those headnotes will be linked to "Jury ☞ 33(5.15)." The opinion confirms that the case squibs have not misled us. The Texas Court of Criminal Appeals squarely ruled that neither the federal nor the state constitution prohibits the use of peremptory challenges on the basis of religion. (See Exhibit A–29.)

Now we must ascertain whether *Casarez v. State* has been reversed or overruled and whether subsequently decided cases have modified its holding or reasoning. We also will be interested in learning whether this case has been cited in other decisions, and perhaps by courts in other jurisdictions. We take these steps by *Shepardizing* the *Casarez* decision. We first locate *Shepard's South Western Reporter Citations* and consult all volumes in which cases from volume 913 of the *South Western Reporter, 2d* are included. We should expect to find one or more hard-bound volumes and one or more paper issues of *Shepard's*. We reprint a portion of a recently published *Shepard's* that includes *Casarez* (913 S.W.2d 468). (See Exhibit A–30.) We observe that *Casarez* has been cited twice, once at page 849 of a case reported in 946 S.W.2d and once at page 247 of a case reported in 953 S.W.2d. We would learn by consulting the "Abbreviations-Analysis" legend at the beginning of the *Shepard's* volume that the letter "j" assigned to these case citations indicates that *Casarez* was cited in dissenting opinions. (See Exhibit A–31.) By checking this and other volumes of *Shepard's*, we would learn that *Casarez* remains good law.

It does not appear that the U.S. Supreme Court has definitively resolved whether it is constitutionally permissible for attorneys to exercise peremptory challenges based on the religion of prospective jurors. Even though our research efforts have produced a Texas case, *Casarez v. State*, that upholds such a practice, we would want to continue our search for other authorities. You now should be prepared to meet this challenge and to pursue other legal research issues.

Exhibit A–28
Squibs on Peremptory Challenges in
West's General Digest, Ninth Series, **Jury** 33(5.15)

33(5.15) JURY

.... persons without determining genuineness of reasons.—Id.

Feeling about prospective juror is not valid, neutral reason to exercise peremptory strike, absent support in record.—Id.

Since there was no evidence of Hispanic venireperson's bias for defense counsel in record, it was erroneous for trial court to accept as race neutral prosecutor's stated reason for exercising peremptory strike, namely amicable relation between venireperson and defense counsel.—Id.

Pretext may exist when juror is struck from jury panel based on reason equally applicable to unchallenged juror.—Id.

State's explanation that it was exercising peremptory strike against Hispanic venireperson because her specific response concerning defendant's right to remain silent was passing judgment on quality of his testimony without any knowledge of facts was pretextual, where venireperson's response was shared by another juror who was not challenged by state.—Id.

Ga.App. 1997. Prosecutor's concern about youth and lack of experience of potential African-American juror was legitimate race-neutral explanation for striking potential juror, even though 19-year old was empaneled, where stricken juror was in her teens and had graduated from high school only two weeks before and 19-year-old juror had been out of school for two years. U.S.C.A. Const.Amend. 14.—Robert v. State, 488 S.E.2d 105, 227 Ga.App. 26.

Age, under some circumstances, can be race-neutral reason for striking juror. U.S.C.A. Const.Amend. 14.—Id.

Work experience and education may be legitimate nondiscriminatory reasons for striking potential juror. U.S.C.A. Const.Amend. 14.—Id.

Mass.App.Ct. 1997. Defendant alleging that Commonwealth impermissibly exercised peremptory challenges to exclude jurors because of their religious affiliation or national origin failed to satisfy initial burden of showing impropriety.—Com. v. Burns, 683 N.E.2d 284, 43 Mass.App.Ct. 263.

Minn.App. 1997. To establish prima facie case of purposeful racial discrimination in jury selection in violation of *Batson*, criminal defendant must show (1) that defendant is member of cognizable racial group and that prosecution used peremptory challenges to remove members of that racial group from jury, and (2) that this and other relevant circumstances raise inference that prosecution is discriminating on basis of race. U.S.C.A. Const.Amend. 14.—Tsipouras v. State, 567 N.W.2d 271, review denied.

Source: Reprinted with permission from *14 West's General Digest*, Ninth Series, p. 862, © 1997, West Group.

Exhibit A–29
Relevant portions of *Casarez v. State* in *South Western Reporter, 2d*

George Toby CASAREZ, Appellant,

v.

The STATE of Texas, Appellee.

No. 1114–93.

Court of Criminal Appeals of Texas,

En Banc.

Dec. 14, 1994.

Opinion Granting Rehearing

Dec. 13, 1995.

Defendant was convicted in the 371st District Court, Tarrant County, Bill Burdock, J., of aggravated sexual assault, and he appealed. The Fort Worth Court of Appeals affirmed, 857 S.W.2d 779, and defendant petitioned for discretionary review. The Court of Criminal Appeals initially reversed, but on rehearing, per Meyers, J., held that litigants may use peremptory challenges to exclude persons from service on juries in individual cases on basis of their religious affiliation.

Affirmed.

McCormick, P.J., concurred with note.

Mansfield, J., concurred and filed opinion.

Clinton, Overstreet, and Maloney, JJ., dissented.

Baird, J., dissented and filed opinion.

1. Constitutional Law ☜ 213.1(2)

In general, government has broad discretion in performance of its functions, and it may usually structure its laws in any way bearing some rational relationship to its legitimate purposes, even though advantage or disadvantage may thereby inure to members of certain class; however, when government classifies individuals on basis historically used to enforce illegal or irrational group preferences or in such a way as to inhibit exercise of basic constitutional rights, its discretion is more limited and its classifications require a more particularized and convincing justification. U.S.C.A. Const.Amend. 14.

2. Constitutional Law ☜ 215

Official classification based on race is strictly scrutinized and considered to be incompatible with equal protection principles unless there is a compelling reason for it. U.S.C.A. Const.Amend. 14.

3. Constitutional Law ☜ 224(1)

Discriminatory practices based on sex are viewed with more than the usual level of suspicion and are prohibited unless substantially related to accomplishment of an important government purpose. U.S.C.A. Const. Amend. 14.

4. Constitutional Law ☜ 250.2(4)

System according to which jurors are selected for service in courts by allowing litigants to exercise peremptory challenges against individual veniremembers is a government practice subject to equal protection rules. U.S.C.A. Const.Amend. 14.

5. Jury ☜ 33(5.10)

No party may exclude prospective juror from service if basis for exclusion is offensive to Federal Constitution.

6. Jury ☜ 33(5.15)

Preserving right to system of peremptory challenges is a legitimate interest of government; accordingly, most peremptory challenges are not constitutionally exceptionable.

7. Jury ☜ 33(5.15)

Government's interest in system of peremptory challenges is generally not great enough to support exclusion of persons from jury service on basis of classification which is subject to strict or heightened scrutiny under equal protection clause. U.S.C.A. Const.Amend 14.

8. Constitutional Law ☜ 84.1, 211(2)

Constitutional analysis applicable to religious classification by government is the same whether raised as equal protection claim or as freedom of religion complaint. U.S.C.A. Const.Amends. 1, 14.

continues

Exhibit A–29 continued

9. Constitutional Law ☞ 84.5(1)

Jury ☞ 33(5.15)

Litigants may use peremptory challenges to exclude persons from service on juries in individual cases on basis of their religious affiliation. U.S.C.A. Const.Amends. 1, 14.

* * * *

IV.

RELIGIOUS DISCRIMINATION

Today, we are asked to determine whether the Equal Protection Clause of the Fourteenth Amendment prohibits the use of peremptory challenges on the basis of religion.[11] To resolve this issue, we must first determine whether discriminatory classifications based

11. The Minnesota Supreme Court rejected an attempt to extend the Equal Protection Clause to peremptory challenges based on religion. *State v. Davis*, 504 N.W.2d 767, 771–72 (Minn. 1993). Notably, *Davis* was decided prior to *J.E.B.* when the Supreme Court had seemingly limited *Batson* to race. *Id.* However, *J.E.B.* undermined the Minnesota Court's rationale.

Despite the Minnesota Court's faulty belief that *Batson* was limited to race, the United States Supreme Court denied certiorari. *Davis v. Minnesota*, __ U.S. __, __, 114 S.Ct. 2120, 2120–22, 128 L.Ed.2d 679 (1994). Although the denial of a writ of certiorari imports no expression of opinion upon the merits of the case, and opinions accompanying the denial of certiorari do not have the same effect as decisions on the merits, *Teague v. Lane*, 489 U.S. 288, 296, 109 S.Ct. 1060, 1067–1068, 103 L.Ed.2d 334 (1989), it should be noted that Justices Scalia and Thomas dissented to the denial of certiorari, arguing (1) the Minnesota Court's holding should be vacated because it was based on the traditional restriction of *Batson* to racial discrimination and, (2) *J.E.B.'s* reliance on "heightened equal protection scrutiny" opened the door to a broader application of equal protection than race and gender discrimination. *Davis.* —U.S. at —, 114 S.Ct. at 2121–2122.

Several other jurisdictions have extended *Batson* protection to ethnicity and religion. *See, State v. Alen*, 616 So.2d 452 (Fla. 1993); *People v. Snow*, 44 Cal.3d 216, 242 Cal.Rptr. 477, 746 P.2d 452 (1987); *and, State v. Gilmore*, 103 N.J. 508, 511 A.2d 1150, 1159 n. 3. (1986).

Source: Reprinted with permission from *913 South Western Reporter*, 2nd Edition, pp. 468, 469, 475, © 1994, West Group.

Exhibit A–30
Portion of a Recently Published *Shepard's* for *Southwestern Reporter 2d*
That Includes Citations to *Casarez*

SOUTHWESTERN REPORTER, 2d SERIES

Vol. 913	952SW[15]246	944SW[1]786	952SW[9]656	945SW[4]88	951SW[1]297
—7—	Ill	—208—	952SW[10]656	—382—	—468—
948SW[2]720	679NE[2]454	949SW[1]373	—293—	954SW[p]492	j 946SW[2]849
948SW[7]721	NJ	949SW498	947SW382	—384—	j 953SW247
Colo	j 696A2d708	953SW511	—306—	945SW[1]579	—511—
942P2d1372	Ore	954SW103	j 946SW[2]195	945SW[4]579	953SW[3]272
—16—	936P2d1016	—242—	—330—	—388—	—523—
949SW[14]162	—101—	a 945SW[2]115	Cir. 6	Case 2	953SW[3]771
950SW[13]321	945SW[10]481	s 118SC236	f 964FS[1]234	948SW[5]637	953SW[9]771
950SW[15]321	—106—	949SW[10]515	—341—	—393—	953SW[10]771
—28—	s 950SW621	—255—	943SW[3]17	950SW[6]5	—542—
944SW[5]338	—108—	944SW[1]828	943SW[6]17	—399—	944SW[33]649
—38—	s 948SW706	953SW889	943SW[11]17	945SW[2]472	948SW[11]24
cc 947SW[3]424	—114—	—257—	—344—	945SW[25]583	949SW[24]382
945SW[3]549	Case 2	947SW[5]791	Case 2	949SW[4]631	950SW[20]401
945SW[4]549	944SW[4]263	—259—	945SW[5]660	949SW[24]941	f 953SW[45]274
952SW778	—137—	952SW[3]137	—362—	949SW[26]942	f 953SW[46]274
Cir. 8	Case 2	—264—	952SW385	950SW[23]340	953SW457
966FS911	945SW[1]617	944SW[12]90	—366—	951SW[10]730	ND
—73—	—150—	953SW[12]36	Case 2	953SW[25]91	561NW612
943SW[5]278	952SW[1]833	953SW[12]897	944SW[1]268	—416—	—564—
943SW[4]774	—163—	64USLW4259	—373—	s 945SW10	j 943SW890
947SW[5]124	945SW[14]747	—283—	945SW[2]30	—425—	950SW[5]162
954SW[p]446	—175—	Cir. 8	949SW[2]234	945SW[4]639	950SW[1]163
—92—	947SW[7]858	112F3d[2]309	f 949SW235	945SW[10]640	950SW[6]163
	—207—	—288—	—376—	—467—	

Source: 91 Shepard's Southwestern Reporter Citations, p. 177 (No. 1, January, 1998). Reproduced by permission of Shepard's. Further reproduction of any kind is strictly prohibited.

Exhibit A–31
"Abbreviations Analysis" Legend in *Shepard's*

ABBREVIATIONS—ANALYSIS

History of Case

a	(affirmed)	Same case affirmed on appeal.
cc	(connected case)	Different case from case cited but arising out of same subject matter or intimately connected therewith.
D	(dismissed)	Appeal from same case dismissed.
m	(modified)	Same case modified on appeal.
r	(reversed)	Same case reversed on appeal.
s	(same case)	Same case as case cited.
S	(superseded)	Substitution for former opinion.
v	(vacated)	Same case vacated.
US	cert den	Certiorari denied by U.S. Supreme Court.
US	cert dis	Certiorari dismissed by U.S. Supreme Court.
US	reh den	Rehearing denied by U.S. Supreme Court.
US	reh dis	Rehearing dismissed by U.S. Supreme Court.
(writ of error)		Writ of error adjudicated.

Treatment of Case

c	(criticised)	Soundness of decision or reasoning in cited case criticised for reasons given.
d	(distinguished)	Case at bar different either in law or fact from case cited for reasons given.
e	(explained)	Statement of import of decision in cited case. Not merely a restatement of the facts.
f	(followed)	Cited as controlling.
h	(harmonized)	Apparent inconsistency explained and shown not to exist.
j	(dissenting opinion)	Citation in dissenting opinion.
L	(limited)	Refusal to extend decision of cited case beyond precise issues involved.
o	(overruled)	Ruling in cited case expressly overruled.
p	(parallel)	Citing case substantially alike or on all fours with cited case in its law or facts.
q	(questioned)	Soundness of decision or reasoning in cited case questioned.

Source: 91 Shepard's Southwestern Reporter Citations, p.xii (Abbreviations-Analysis) (No. 1, January, 1998). Reproduced by permission of Shepard's. Further reproduction of any kind is strictly prohibited.

COMPUTER-ASSISTED LEGAL RESEARCH

We will not go into detail about how to use the computerized legal research databases WESTLAW and LEXIS. Remember that these computerized systems exist and that they can be tremendously useful legal research tools. If we wanted to continue investigating the research issue that we just illustrated, we could do so by using WESTLAW or LEXIS.

For example, WESTLAW offers a "Natural Language" search strategy. To find relevant case decisions by using this straightforward system, we first would select the jurisdiction or jurisdictions from which we seek judicial authority. We could confine our search to Texas cases, or search more broadly for cases decided by all state courts, or all federal courts, or choose other options. Then, we simply would type in a description of the research issue—for example, "Does exercising peremptory challenges based on religion violate equal protection of the law?" The computer would produce cases in which the interrelated terms from our research issue are discussed. Similarly, we could produce relevant law review articles by using this same search strategy in WESTLAW's journal and law review database. *Shepardizing* cases can be performed on WESTLAW and LEXIS through a single command.WESTLAW and LEXIS have many capabilities, and learning to conduct computer-assisted legal research can both enhance your efficiency and save much time. Nevertheless, it is important to be familiar with the printed reference materials and to know how to complete legal research the "old-fashioned" way. Computer-assisted legal research techniques generally presume knowledge of the former references and skills and to a large extent build on them. You should consult the training manuals and programs that provide instruction in computer-assisted legal research to learn more about these valuable tools.

For further information about how to use both printed references and WESTLAW and LEXIS for legal research, we recommend that you consult James R. Acker and Richard Irving, *Basic Legal Research for Criminal Justice and the Social Sciences* (Aspen Publishers, Inc. 1998).

Select Provisions of the U.S. Constitution

ARTICLE I

. . .

Section 9.

. . .

[2] The Privilege of the Writ of Habeas Corpus shall not be suspended, unless when in Cases of Rebellion or Invasion the public Safety may require it.

[3] No Bill of Attainder or ex post facto Law shall be passed.

. . .

ARTICLE III

Section 1. The judicial Power of the United States, shall be vested in one supreme Court, and in such inferior Courts as the Congress may from time to time ordain and establish. The Judges, both of the supreme and inferior Courts, shall hold their Offices during good Behaviour, and shall, at stated Times, receive for their Services a Compensation, which shall not be diminished during their Continuance in Office.

Section 2. [1] The judicial Power shall extend to all Cases, in Law and Equity, arising under this Constitution, the Laws of the United States, and Treaties made, or which shall be made, under their Authority;—to all Cases affecting Ambassadors, other public Ministers and Consuls;—to all Cases of admiralty and maritime Jurisdiction;—to controversies to which the United States shall be a Party;—to Controversies between two or more States;—between a State and Citizens of another State;—between Citizens of different States;—between Citizens of the same State claiming Lands under the Grants of different States, and between a State, or the Citizens thereof, and foreign States, Citizens or Subjects.

[2] In all Cases affecting Ambassadors, other public Ministers and Consuls, and those in which a State shall be a Party, the supreme Court shall have original Jurisdiction. In all the other Cases before mentioned, the supreme Court shall have appellate Jurisdiction, both as to Law and Fact, with such Exceptions, and under such Regulations as the Congress shall make.

[3] The trial of all Crimes, except in Cases of Impeachment, shall be by Jury; and such Trial shall be held in the State where the said Crimes shall have been committed; but when not com-

mitted within any State, the Trial shall be at such Place or Places as the Congress may by Law have directed.

Section 3. [1] Treason against the United States, shall consist only in levying War against them, or, in adhering to their Enemies, giving them Aid and Comfort. No Person shall be convicted of Treason unless on the Testimony of two Witnesses to the same overt Act, or on Confession in open Court.

[2] The Congress shall have Power to declare the Punishment of Treason, but no Attainder of Treason shall work Corruption of Blood, or Forfeiture except during the Life of the Person attained.

. . .

AMENDMENT I [1791]

Congress shall make no law respecting an establishment of religion, or prohibiting the free exercise thereof; or abridging the freedom of speech, or of the press; or the right of the people peaceably to assemble, and to petition the Government for a redress of grievances.

AMENDMENT II [1791]

A well regulated Militia, being necessary to the security of a free State, the right of the people to keep and bear Arms, shall not be infringed.

AMENDMENT III [1791]

No Soldier shall, in time of peace be quartered in any house, without the consent of the Owner, nor in time of war, but in a manner to be prescribed by law.

AMENDMENT IV [1791]

The right of the people to be secure in their persons, houses, papers, and effects, against unreasonable searches and seizures, shall not be violated, and no Warrants shall issue, but upon probable cause, supported by Oath or affirmation, and particularly describing the place to be searched, and the persons or things to be seized.

AMENDMENT V [1791]

No person shall be held to answer for a capital, or otherwise infamous crime, unless on a presentment or indictment of a Grand Jury, except in cases arising in the land or naval forces, or in the Militia, when in actual service in time of War or public danger; nor shall any person be subject for the same offence to be twice put in jeopardy of life or limb; nor shall be compelled in any criminal case to be a witness against himself, nor be deprived of life, liberty, or property, without due process of law; nor shall private property be taken for public use, without just compensation.

AMENDMENT VI [1791]

In all criminal prosecutions, the accused shall enjoy the right to a speedy and public trial, by an impartial jury of the State and district wherein the crime shall have been committed, which district shall have been previously ascertained by law, and to be informed of the nature and cause of the accusation; to be confronted with the witnesses against him; to have compulsory process for obtaining witnesses in his favor, and to have the Assistance of Counsel for his defence.

AMENDMENT VII [1791]

In Suits at common law, where the value in controversy shall exceed twenty dollars, the right of trial by jury shall be preserved, and no fact tried by jury, shall be otherwise re-examined in any Court of the United States, than according to the rules of the common law.

AMENDMENT VIII [1791]

Excessive bail shall not be required, nor excessive fines imposed, nor cruel and unusual punishments inflicted.

AMENDMENT IX [1791]

The enumeration in the Constitution, of certain rights, shall not be construed to deny or disparage others retained by the people.

AMENDMENT X [1791]

The powers not delegated to the United States by the Constitution, nor prohibited by it to the States, are reserved to the States respectively, or to the people.

. . .

AMENDMENT XIV [1868]

Section 1. All persons born or naturalized in the United States, and subject to the jurisdiction thereof, are citizens of the United States and of the State wherein they reside. No State shall make or enforce any law which shall abridge the privileges or immunities of citizens of the United States; nor shall any State deprive any person of life, liberty, or property, without due process of law; nor deny to any person within its jurisdiction the equal protection of the laws.

. . .

Section 5. The Congress shall have power to enforce, by appropriate legislation, the provisions of this article.

. . .

Index

Page numbers in *italics* denote figures and exhibits.

Z